D0849797

Handbook of Multimethod Measurement in Psychology

Handbook of **Multimethod Measurement in Psychology**

Edited by
Michael Eid and Ed Diener

American Psychological Association • Washington, DC

Published by
American Psychological Association
750 First Street, NE
Washington, DC 20002
www.apa.org

To order
APA Order Department
P.O. Box 92984
Washington, DC 20090-2984
Tel: (800) 374-2721; Direct: (202) 336-5510
Fax: (202) 336-5502; TDD/TTY: (202) 336-6123
Online: www.apa.org/books/
E-mail: order@apa.org

In the U.K., Europe, Africa, and the Middle East, copies may be ordered from
American Psychological Association
3 Henrietta Street
Covent Garden, London
WC2E 8LU England

Typeset in Berkeley by NOVA Graphic Services, Jamison, PA, and World Composition Services, Sterling, VA

Printer: United Book Press, Inc., Baltimore, MD
Cover Designer: Naylor Design, Washington, DC
Project Manager: NOVA Graphic Services, Jamison, PA

The opinions and statements published are the responsibility of the authors, and such opinions and statements do not necessarily represent the policies of the American Psychological Association.

Library of Congress Cataloging-in-Publication Data

Handbook of multimethod measurement in psychology / [edited by] Michael Eid and Ed Diener.— 1st ed.
   p. cm.
 Includes bibliographical references and index.
 ISBN 1-59147-318-7
 1. Psychometrics. 2. Psychology—Research—Methodology. I. Eid, Michael. II. Diener, Ed.

 BF39.H2644 2005
 150'.28'7—dc22

2005015922

British Library Cataloguing-in-Publication Data
A CIP record is available from the British Library.

Printed in the United States of America
First Edition

Dedicated to

Donald T. Campbell (1916–1996) and Donald W. Fiske (1917–2003),
who have strongly influenced our way of thinking about psychological measurement.

Contents

Contributors

Brendan M. Baird, Michigan State University, East Lansing

Roger Bakeman, Georgia State University, Atlanta

Aaron S. Benjamin, University of Illinois at Urbana–Champaign

Gary G. Berntson, Ohio State University, Columbus

G. Leonard Burns, Washington State University, Pullman

John T. Cacioppo, University of Chicago, Chicago, IL

Siang Chee Chuah, University of Illinois at Urbana–Champaign

Clayton Curtis, New York University, New York, NY

Ed Diener, University of Illinois at Urbana–Champaign

Fritz Drasgow, University of Illinois at Urbana–Champaign

Michael Eid, University of Geneva, Switzerland

Nancy Eisenberg, Arizona State University, Tempe

Edgar Erdfelder, University of Mannheim, Germany

Immo Fritsche, Friedrich-Schiller-Universität, Jena, Germany

Augusto Gnisci, Seconda Università degli Studi di Napoli, Italy

Peter Harms, University of Illinois at Urbana–Champaign

Monica J. Harris, University of Kentucky, Lexington

Kit-Tai Hau, The Chinese University of Hong Kong

Stephen N. Haynes, University of Hawaii, Manoa

Joop Hox, Utrecht University, the Netherlands

Charles L. Hulin, University of Illinois at Urbana–Champaign

Siek-Toon Khoo, Australian Council for Educational Research, Victoria

Rupert Klein, McGill University, Montreal, Canada

Bärbel Knäuper, McGill University, Montreal, Canada

Oi-Man Kwok, Texas A & M University, College Station

Randy J. Larsen, Washington University in St. Louis, MO

Volker Linneweber, Otto-von-Guericke-Universität, Magdeburg, Germany

Tanja Lischetzke, University of Geneva, Switzerland

Leighann Litcher-Kelly, Stony Brook University, Stony Brook, NY

David Lubinski, Vanderbilt University, Nashville, TN

Richard E. Lucas, Michigan State University, East Lansing

Cora Maas, Utrecht University, the Netherlands

Herbert W. Marsh, University of Western Sydney, Australia

Andrew J. Martin, University of Western Sydney, Australia

Andrew G. Miner, University of Minnesota, Minneapolis
Matthias R. Mehl, University of Arizona, Tempe
Amanda Sheffield Morris, University of New Orleans, New Orleans, LA
Jochen Musch, University of Mannheim, Germany
Clayton Neighbors, University of Washington, Seattle
Franz J. Neyer, Humboldt-Universität zu Berlin, Germany
Fridtjof W. Nussbeck, University of Geneva, Switzerland
Zvjezdana Prizmic-Larsen, Washington University in St. Louis, MO
Ulf-Dietrich Reips, University of Zürich, Switzerland
Lara R. Robinson, University of New Orleans, New Orleans, LA
Michael D. Robinson, North Dakota State University, Fargo
Brent W. Roberts, University of Illinois at Urbana–Champaign
Jürgen Rost, Institute for Science Education, Kiel, Germany
Manfred Schmitt, University of Koblenz-Landau, Germany
Jennifer L. Smith, University of Illinois at Urbana–Champaign
Richard H. Smith, University of Kentucky, Lexington
Arthur A. Stone, Stony Brook University, Stony Brook, NY
Oliver Walter, Institute for Science Education, Kiel, Germany
Michelle Webb, University of Illinois at Urbana–Champaign
Stephen G. West, Arizona State University, Tempe
Dustin Wood, University of Illinois at Urbana–Champaign
Wei Wu, Arizona State University, Tempe
David H. Zald, Vanderbilt University, Nashville, TN

Preface

More than 2,000 citations in 40 years clearly demonstrate the important role that Campbell and Fiske's (1959) multitrait–multimethod framework plays in scientific psychology (Sternberg, 1992). The basic ideas of multitrait–multimethod analysis and multimethod research strategies in general have strongly influenced the way in which validity has been tested, and they have gained much importance in practically all areas of psychological research.

Although the advantages and importance of multimethod strategies are generally accepted in scientific psychology and applied assessment, integrative textbooks and handbooks of multimethod assessment that assimilate all phases of a multimethod assessment process and that are written in comprehensible language are still missing. The various methods that can be applied in psychology are often described in different theoretical contexts (e.g., brain imaging in neurosciences, peer ratings in personality and social psychology) and are usually not accessible to a broader audience. Students and researchers who want to read a comprehensible overview of the meaning of different methods, and their advantages as well as limitations, often do not know where to find a comprehensive introduction, in particular, when either more up-to-date methods or recently developed methods such as brain imaging, the assessment of hormone levels in saliva, or ambulatory assessment methods are of interest. Moreover, new and sophisticated methods for analyzing multimethod data such as multitrait–multimethod methods of structural equation modeling, item response theory, or multilevel modeling are often published in sophisticated methodological journals that are not directed to the broad audience of researchers in the social sciences. Generally, the most sophisticated and appropriate methods of data analysis are not applied. Another shortcoming is that there are not widely available discussions in the literature of what multimethods mean conceptually and how to think about whether methods and concepts are the same or different. Finally, students and researchers who desire to conduct a multimethod study in their area of research or who want to understand a published study often do not know where to look for an overview explaining the meaning of the various methods as well as listing the advantages and problems of multimethod strategies in different research areas.

This book offers answers to questions such as, "What issues must be considered when conducting a multimethod study in ecologically valid nonexperimental field studies? How strong is the convergent validity and method-specificity in different areas of research? What methods should be selected for proving validity in a particular research context?" In other words, this book should fill a large gap in the psychological handbook landscape because it provides researchers and students alike with an up-to-date instructive introduction and comprehensive overview of the theoretical, methodological, and applied aspects of multimethod assessment.

Given the great diversity of the fields considered, the aims of the handbook could only be reached by including the contributions of many authors with expertise in different areas of multimethod assessment. The book brings together a multitude of authors from three continents who worked together on their chapters over a period of many months. We are very grateful to all the authors who contributed with excellent scholarship to this handbook. Moreover, we are very thankful to Lisa Trierweiler for her very thorough proofreading and correcting of the chapters written by the authors who are nonnative English speakers. Delphine Gross formatted the chapters and created the reference list. Fridtjof W. Nussbeck and Walter Schreiber contributed to the management of the review process via an Internet platform. Kris Eaton assisted us in organizing the review process. They all assisted us greatly, and we are very grateful for their support.

During the genesis of this book Donald W. Fiske (1917–2003) died. He strongly influenced more than one generation of researchers in our thinking about psychological measurement. Together with Donald T. Campbell (1916–1996) he wrote one of the most important articles of psychological research. "Convergent and Discriminant Validation by the Multitrait–Multimethod Matrix" has become one of the great classics of psychology and has been cited more than 4,000 times. It has not lost its relevance up to the present day. In appreciation of their historic work, we dedicate this handbook of multimethod measurement to Donald T. Campbell and Donald W. Fiske.

PART I

THEORETICAL CONCEPTS

CHAPTER 1

INTRODUCTION: THE NEED FOR MULTIMETHOD MEASUREMENT IN PSYCHOLOGY

Michael Eid and Ed Diener
We must measure what can be measured, and make measurable what cannot be measured.
—Galileo Galilei (1610)

The history of empirical psychology is one of making measurable what most laypeople think cannot be measured—emotions, cognitions, motivations, personality traits, and so forth. As in all other empirical and natural sciences, the progress of psychology is closely and inextricably linked to the development of new and more refined methods for measuring psychological concepts. New technical developments (e.g., modern methods of brain imaging or biochemical analyses) allow deeper insights into psychological processes than ever expected at the end of the 19th century when psychology began establishing itself as an empirical science. Modern computer technology enables traditional psychological methods (e.g., ability testing, behavior observation, text analysis, and reaction time measures) to come into full flower and makes it possible to realize old dreams like measuring individuals in their everyday lives far away from the anonymity and artificiality of the psychological laboratory. Modern communication tools like the Internet make it possible to conduct experiments around the world across borders closed to researchers.

Besides the rapid progress that technological revolutions cause throughout the sciences, each science has its classical standard measures that withstand the tide of technological progress, almost unchanged. Just as a medical doctor does not abandon listening to lung sounds with instruments that have not fundamentally changed over the years, virtually no psychologist discards the treasure chests of self- and informant-reports, even though the way he or she uses them also remains virtually unchanged.

And there are previously popular methods (e.g., unobtrusive and nonreactive measures), which must be preserved and revived as valuable measurement tools that offer insights not otherwise obtained.

Although each epoch has its own scientific paradigms and methods that fit better than other methods, it would be unwise to stake scientific insight on just one. A multimethod approach offers insights into scientific phenomena and can contribute to confirming psychological theories in a way a single-method approach cannot (Schmitt, this volume, chap. 2). There are at least two reasons why psychology research and applied work make a multimethod research necessary: the multicomponential structure of psychological phenomena and the validity of a research program.

MULTICOMPONENTIAL AND MULTILEVEL STRUCTURE OF PSYCHOLOGICAL PHENOMENA

Psychological phenomena usually consist of many facets. Emotions, for example, refer not only to the conscious representation of the feeling itself ("I am happy") but also to many other changes in the individual (Davidson, Goldsmith, & Scherer, 2003; Kahneman, Diener, & Schwarz, 1999; Larsen & Prizmic-Larsen, this volume, chap. 23). An individual feeling happiness might jump up, feel an inner ease, and even embrace and kiss passersby. Moreover, muscle changes in the face might accompany this feeling, the brain might produce endorphins, and the individual may likely entertain positive

thoughts. This simple example shows that a psychological phenomenon has many facets. To understand these emotional reactions it is necessary to have various, appropriate research methods to analyze the diverse facets. A method that measures muscle movements in the face is not appropriate to assess endorphin levels in the brain. Moreover, a method for determining the endorphin level is probably not useful for assessing subjective feelings. A thorough understanding of an emotional reaction requires a set of appropriate multimethod tools to measure the different facets of the phenomena.

Multilevel analyses are a related example of multimethod research programs. Berntson and Cacioppo (this volume, chap. 12) define multilevel analyses as a subset of multimethod approaches where the measures, constructs, and theories extend across levels of organization—from the psychological to the physiological to the cellular and ultimately to the gene and beyond.[1] To assess the different levels, different methods are needed. Hence, the first aim of using multimethod approaches is the precise *description* of the multicomponent and multilevel phenomena that are the focus of the behavioral sciences.

A second aim of multimethod research is providing information for detecting *general* associations between different components and levels of a phenomenon. For example, to analyze the reasons why happy individuals might be healthier, research must show a link between the feeling component and relevant physiological measures that explain individual differences in health. Insight into these processes can be obtained by multimethod research programs. However, general relations between the different components form only one side of the coin. Beyond general associations *individual differences* must be considered because not all individuals behave in the same way. If an emotional reaction were patterned in a uniform way, measuring one component would suffice when predicting other components. However, strong individual differences often exist when exploring different components.

For example, while two individuals may feel pride after receiving a compliment, one might jump for joy, while the other quietly sits down. Analyzing individual differences in the associations between the components might reveal that the first person grew up in a culture in which pride is a highly appreciated emotion (e.g., the United States), whereas the other was raised in a culture in which pride is undesirable and should not be expressed, for example in East Asian cultures (e.g., Eid & Diener, 2001). Hence, combining multimethod approaches for analyzing individual differences in the covariation of different components of a multicomponent phenomenon may help us understand individual and social regulation processes.

These simple examples show that a multimethod research program is necessary for a thorough description of multicomponent phenomena, as well as for analyzing the different components of phenomena to detect general and individual rules of behavior. A classic example of multimethod research strategies is Murray's (1938) famous *Explorations in Personality*, where he used such diverse methods as aptitude tests, projective tests, questionnaires, interviews, and so forth to learn more about the different components of the personality of the participants of his study.

VALIDITY

Validity, one of the key issues of research, concerns the question whether the inferences drawn from the results of a study are true or not (Shadish, Cook, & Campbell, 2002). In particular, with respect to measurement methods, validity represents the degree to which the adequacy and appropriateness of inferences and actions based on the results of a measurement device are supported by empirical evidence and theoretical rationales (Messick, 1989). Multimethod research plays a key role in the validation process. In their groundbreaking article, "Convergent and discriminant validation by the multitrait–multimethod matrix," Campbell and

---

[1] In this handbook the term *multilevel analyses* will also be used for statistical methods for analyzing nested data (e.g., students nested within classes, measurement occasions nested within individuals, etc). There are strong differences between multilevel analyses as a research program for measuring different determinants of behavior and multilevel analysis as statistical method. However, the appropriate meaning will be clearly determined by the context.

Fiske (1959) described the cornerstones of a multi-trait–multimethod research program regarding the validation process. The basic promises of the multi-trait–multimethod approach have strongly influenced the process of exploring validity. First, Campbell and Fiske pointed out that several methods are needed to appropriately analyze validity, and these different methods should converge in the measurement of the same trait. The convergence of different independent methods indicates *convergent validity*. Second, they convincingly argued that *discriminant validity* must be shown before introducing a new construct into science. Third, Campbell and Fiske clarified that a score on a psychological variable not only reflects the psychological construct under consideration, but also reflects systematic method-specific influences. Fourth, they demonstrated the necessity of including at least two different methods in psychological studies to separate trait from method influences. Hence, for a complete understanding of psychological processes it is necessary to apply a multimethod research strategy. Therefore, the multitrait–multimethod analysis has become an essential strategy for proving the construct validity of psychological measures.

Convergent validity is a core aspect of validity, and validation research programs have been focused for a long time on seeking high convergent validity coefficients. Although high validity coefficients are desirable many reasons explain why convergent validity coefficients are often lower than hoped. For example, if one compares physiological measures with other measures one must contend with individual response-uniqueness (e.g., Berntson & Cacioppo, 2004). Not all individuals react to stimulus in the same way, and this response specificity can lower convergence when measured with a correlation coefficient. Moreover, if one wants to compare a self-rating with a peer-rating, one often uncovers medium-sized correlation coefficients. In comparing self- and other-ratings one must recognize rater biases (Hoyt, 2000). Raters may not only interpret scale items differently but might also have opportunities to observe different behavior, they might use different indicators of behavior, and they might link the indicators to the response scale in a different way (Hoyt, 2000; Kenny, 1991). Moreover, leniency

or severity errors and halo effects can affect peer ratings, and peer- as well as self-rating might also be distorted by social desirability effects (Neyer, this volume, chap. 4). All these forms of bias and distortion can cause small convergent validity coefficients. Therefore, Westen and Rosenthal (2003) recommend quantifying construct validity by comparing the observed patterns of correlations with the theoretically expected patterns of correlations. They contend that if a good theoretical reason for expecting lower correlations between multiple measures exists, and this pattern of correlations can be empirically confirmed, modest degrees of convergence can confirm construct validity.

High convergent validity is not always the goal of research. Take, for example, a questionnaire measuring different facets of marital satisfaction. Spouses rate their own satisfaction and also their perception of the satisfaction of their spouse. If the aim of the test construction process was to develop a questionnaire that detects deficiencies in intraspouse perception and communication processes, the items with the lowest convergences might be the most interesting. In other words, method influences are not inevitably unwanted random disturbances (e.g., measurement error) but they can indicate valid and valuable information. A deeper understanding of method influences can enlarge our knowledge of the construct under consideration, and this knowledge, in turn, can help explain method effects, correct for method effects, and plan and conduct studies in which method effects are minimized or—depending on the aim of the study considered—maximized. Beyond the traditional search for maximum convergent validity, a thorough analysis of method influences might tell a more interesting story of the construct under consideration. Hence, a multimethod study should always have two facets: first, the proof of convergent validity on the basis of theoretical expectations, and second, the analysis of the nature of method-specific influences. Whereas multimethod studies intend to meet the first goal, the second goal is often not considered when planning the study's design. A careful analysis of method effects requires the inclusion of variables that may explain method influences, and that might suppress

method-specific effects to enhance convergent validity. This makes a thorough knowledge of measurement methods necessary for all researchers.

AIMS OF THIS HANDBOOK AND OVERVIEW

Because multimethod research and assessment strategies are superior to monomethod approaches, this handbook aims to provide the reader with the necessary knowledge to plan and conduct multi-method studies and to analyze multimethod data. We present the most important measurement methods and show their applications (Part II). Furthermore, we present the most up-to-date methods for analyzing multimethod data (Part III). Finally, several chapters discuss applications of multimethod research programs in different areas of psychology (Part IV). These chapters show how multimethod research programs can be successfully applied and discuss problems related to the implementation of multimethod strategies. Although these chapters focus on single subdisciplines of psychology, they also discuss issues relevant to other fields. Because the ways multimethod strategies are implemented differ between subdisciplines, we strongly recommend consulting applications chapters in domains different from those in which one is primarily interested. Examining methods in other subdisciplines gives readers new ideas about how to improve their own research and how to develop new and innovative research programs.

Part I: Theoretical Concepts

The first part of the handbook introduces the importance of multimethod assessment in psychology, the philosophical and historical aspects of multimethod research strategies, and the different concepts of consistency and method specificity.

Part II: Assessment Methods

The second part presents the current state of the art—the most important measurement methods in modern psychology, which comprise traditional methods like self-report as well as the most recent developments in brain imaging and Web-based methods. Not all methods applied in psychology can be presented, and selections had to be made.

This selection was guided by the goal of presenting methods at the basic level, which can be combined to understand more complex assessment strategies. For example, you will not find a chapter on interviewing, as an interview situation combines many more basic methods (e.g., self-report, observational methods, informant assessment, and text-analysis of the transcript of the interview). The handbook focuses more on assessment methods than on research methods in general. It follows the tradition of Campbell and Fiske's (1959) multimethod approach; therefore, we present methods that can be used to measure human behavior, attitudes, and feeling. We do not present research methods to test theories without assessing humans (e.g., animal studies and computer simulation techniques). These methods may hold importance for multi-method research in general, but they are less significant for assessment purposes. We use the term *multimethod*, in most cases, in the sense of applying different methods for measuring human beings although some chapters also refer to multimethod research programs in the sense of applying different research strategies (e.g., experimental vs. nonexperimental research).

Moreover, we focus on widely applied and established methods, including more recent developments (like brain imaging). Some new methods may have a high potential for psychological assessment and measurement but are less established, with a status more comparable to research methods. Some of these methods include virtual environment technology (Blascovich et al., 2002) and molecular genetic analysis (e.g., Caspi et al., 2003) and are not considered in this volume.

The handbook covers the most basic assessment methods that are relevant for a thorough understanding of human behavior, attitudes, and feelings. These include self-report (Lucas & Baird, this volume, chap. 3), informant assessment (Neyer, this volume, chap. 4), ability tests (Lubinski, this volume, chap. 8), implicit methods (Robinson & Neighbors, this volume, chap. 9), observational methods (Bakeman & Gnisci, this volume, chap. 10), physiological and biochemical methods (Berntson & Cacioppo, this volume, chap. 12), functional neuroimaging (Zald & Curtis, this vol-

ume, chap. 13), nonreactive methods (Fritsche & Linneweber, this volume, chap. 14), and assessment methods of experimental psychology (Erdfelder & Musch, this volume, chap. 15).

The revolution taking place in the area of computer technologies has also strongly influenced psychological assessment methods and the development of new assessment strategies like computerized ambulatory assessment methods (Stone & Litcher-Kelly, this volume, chap. 5), Web-based methods (Reips, this volume, chap. 6), computerized testing (Drasgow & Chuah, this volume, chap. 7), and computerized forms of text analysis (Mehl, this volume, chap. 11), which are also described.

Multimethod research is also necessary to analyze the generalizability of results across research settings. Although experiments in the laboratory remain indispensable in psychology, they have severe limitations. The high guarantee of internal validity possible in randomized laboratory experiments does not guarantee external validity (Shadish et al., 2002). The artificial uncorrelatedness of independent variables in experimental studies might not represent the naturally occurring covariation of these causal variables in real life (Brunswik, 1956). Processes that might explain behavior, attitudes, and feelings in a laboratory might not explain everyday behavior in the real world. The analysis of the generalizability of results, which is labeled *external validity*, requires a research plan that comprises several research settings. Besides experimental research contexts (Erdfelder & Musch, this volume, chap. 15), psychological research has concentrated on the development of methodological research strategies that focus on individual behavior in natural environments such as experience sampling methods (Stone & Litcher-Kelly, this volume, chap. 5) and nonreactive methods (Fritsche & Linneweber, this volume, chap. 14). Moreover, cross-sectional studies that focus on analyzing interindividual differences need to be complemented by longitudinal studies (Khoo, West, Wu, & Kwok, this volume, chap. 21) to verify if the results can be generalized to explaining intraindividual processes. An intelligent combination of laboratory and field-assessment strategies, as well as of cross-sectional and longitudinal approaches, estab-

lishes a much more powerful research design, which permits an in-depth analysis of issues of external validity; the pursuit of one single research paradigm will not provide such results. Hence, this handbook also focuses on different research strategies and situations, particularly on research contexts outside the laboratory (e.g., experience sampling and nonreactive methods).

Part III: Methods of Data Analysis

The implementation of multimethod research strategies requires the knowledge of statistical approaches that consider the characteristics of the data inherent in multimethod strategies. These models must contend with the fact that an observed variable not only reflects the construct under consideration but also method-specific influences. Consequently, each measured value can be decomposed into a component that reflects the construct and is shared with other methods, as well as a component not shared with other methods. This method-specific component includes not only systematic method-specific influences, but also unsystematic measurement error. To separate true measurement error from systematic method-specific influences, appropriate methodological approaches are needed. Only by separating unsystematic measurement error from method-specific effects may one evaluate the degree to which the unique part of a measure reflects unsystematic measurement error versus systematic method-specific influences. Hence, data analytic procedures can be classified into methods that allow a separation of method-specific and error-specific influences and those that do not. Moreover, some data analytic approaches focus on the multimethod analysis of one construct, whereas other, more elaborated approaches, consider several methods measuring several constructs. Only the latter approach allows a systematic analysis of the generalizability of method effects across constructs (e.g., whether the bias of a rater is the same for all constructs being considered or whether a rater-bias is construct-specific). Hence, data-analytic procedures can be classified into approaches that allow analyzing the generalizability of method effects across traits and those that do not. Finally, data-analytic approaches can be classified according to

the nature of the data being analyzed. Methodological approaches developed for metrical variables are usually not appropriate for categorical variables and vice versa.

This handbook gives an overview of advanced statistical approaches for analyzing multimethod data. Models for categorical data include classical approaches like Cohen's (Bakeman & Gnisci, this volume, chap. 10; Nussbeck, this volume, chap. 17) as well as more advanced methods like log-linear models (Nussbeck, this volume, chap. 17) and models of item response theory (Rost & Walter, this volume, chap. 18). Modern methodological approaches for metrical variables include multilevel models (Hox & Maas, this volume, chap. 19) and models of structural equation modeling (Eid, Lischetzke, & Nussbeck, this volume, chap. 20).

Part IV: Applied Multimethod Research

The need for multimethod research is accepted in most areas of psychological research. Results of applied multimethod research in different areas of psychology prove the importance of multimethod research strategies. Moreover, successful applications of multimethod research strategies show how multimethod research programs can be reasonably implemented. However, in spite of the many applications of multimethod research programs, multimethod strategies could be more widely implemented and shortcomings of previously conducted multimethod research should be surmounted. The last goal of this handbook aims at presenting the state of the art, the problems, and the issues of multimethod research in different areas of psychology: personality psychology (Roberts, Harms, Smith, Wood, & Webb, this volume, chap. 22), emotion and motivation (Larsen & Prizmic-Larsen, this volume, chap. 23), cognition (Benjamin, this volume, chap. 24), developmental psychology (Morris, Robinson, & Eisenberg, this volume, chap. 25), social psychology (Smith & Harris, this volume, chap. 26), clinical psychology (Burns & Haynes, this volume, chap. 27), health psychology (Knäuper & Klein, this volume, chap. 28), organizational psychology (Miner & Hulin, this volume, chap. 29), and educational psychology (Marsh, Martin, & Hau, this volume, chap. 30).

We hope readers will learn from these applied chapters how a successful multimethod research program can be implemented in their own research. Although multimethod research usually requires more time and effort than research relying on single methods, we believe that in the long run breakthroughs and firm findings will result from using multiple methods and measures in systematic programs of research.

USE OF THIS HANDBOOK

For readers planning a new multimethod study we recommend a three-step approach:

1. Go through the chapters of the first and second part presenting the different multimethod strategies and measurement methods. Decide for each method if its inclusion in your research programs would enhance the quality of your study and if it could lead to new and innovative insights.
2. Read the application chapters in Part IV. Examine how other research groups have set multimethod research programs into action. Get inspired by the successful implementation of multimethod strategies in different domains of psychology.
3. Consult the chapters in Part III (Methods of Data Analysis) to decide which data-analytic method fits the study you are planning. Select the method before planning the study in detail and particularly before collecting data. Think about whether or not you need to change your research plan to apply your chosen data-analytic method. Adapt your research plan to allow an optimal application of those methods chosen for analyzing your data.

Sometimes readers will decide that the multimethod research program cannot be realized without the assistance of other research groups that have the needed competence in applying one specific method. In this case, we would strongly encourage readers to establish multimethod research networks. We hope this handbook will not only contribute to the development of multimethod research and assessment programs, but also to the establishment of new and innovative multimethod networks of scientists.

CHAPTER 2

CONCEPTUAL, THEORETICAL, AND HISTORICAL FOUNDATIONS OF MULTIMETHOD ASSESSMENT

Manfred Schmitt

BASIC CONCEPTS AND FUNDAMENTAL PSYCHOLOGICAL PRINCIPLES

Lay and scientific epistemics have much in common (Kruglanski, 1989a). Ordinary people and scientists share a desire for knowledge, use similar methods for acquiring knowledge, need knowledge for similar purposes, collect similar data, and use similar criteria for judging the usefulness of data. Lay and academic psychologists alike want to describe individuals and social situations in psychological terms. Both construct theories for the explanation of behavior and rules for its prediction. Both try to maximize the accuracy and simplicity of theories and predictive rules. Both compromise between accuracy and simplicity because of the inverse relation of those two qualities. Both are more sensitive to variability than to constancy. Both use the principle of replication to ascertain lawfulness and reliability. All of these commonalities are fundamental for understanding the psychological and conceptual foundations of the multimethod approach.

This chapter explains how these epistemic strategies of laypersons and scientists can be transformed into research designs and methods of data analysis. Simple everyday examples are used for illustrating the most important concepts and principles on which all multimethod approaches rest. The chapter begins with an introduction of these concepts and principles. The second part of the chapter provides a historical review of the most important milestones of multimethod thinking. The last part

contains a discussion of some unresolved challenges, emerging issues, and directions in which multimethod work must proceed.

Variability and Discrimination

Discrimination is a core ability of living beings and adaptive for survival. Evolution has made our information processing systems sensitive to differences and changes to the point of our ability to contrast objects actively. At the same time, our sensory systems adapt to, ignore, and actively inhibit invariant input. By ignoring invariant input, we maximize our capacity for more informative input (Lindsay & Norman, 1972).

Attending to variation and ignoring invariance are pervasive phenomena in lay personality assessment and self-concept formation. Social comparison is crucial for the acquisition of knowledge about ourselves and about others (Festinger, 1954). Observing individual differences makes us aware of potentially relevant information for social interaction. The lexical approach assumes that human language has created names for personality differences, which allow for the prediction of behavior and thus provide the basis for effective social interaction (John, Angleitner, & Ostendorf, 1988).

Measurement in scientific psychology follows the same basic logic. Measurement is about discrimination, and discrimination is a basis of knowledge. Scientific psychology strives for precise and parsimonious discrimination. Parsimony is desirable because it eases scientific communication and the

application of knowledge. Precision is a sine qua non criterion of scientific quality. Without precise measurement instruments, scientific psychology loses a crucial tool for the advancement of knowledge.

Absolute Stability and Absolute Consistency

Social comparisons are not the only sources of psychological knowledge. *Temporal* comparisons can also provide important information about self and others (Albert, 1977). Consider this example: Suppose I had asked my neighbor many times to water my plants while I was out of town. If my neighbor had always agreed to help, it seems reasonable to predict on the basis of his *absolutely stable* behavior that he will continue to water my plants in the future.

Comparisons across *situations* can provide psychological insight as well. My neighbor's helpfulness might depend on whether I was out of town for a short conference or a long sabbatical. It might matter whether or not my dog stayed in the house while I was gone. It might matter whether or not I offered to return my neighbor's favor. If my neighbor watered my plants irrespective of these variations, he displays *absolute transsituational consistency*. I might conclude from such a pattern that he will water my plants in any situation.

Making comparisons across *types of behavior* can also provide information. I might learn more about my neighbor if I asked him not only to water my plants, but also to check my mail, to mow my lawn, to put my garbage out, or to walk my dog. If my neighbor complies with all these requests, I might conclude from his *absolute consistency across types of behavior* that he will do me any kind of favor.

Modes of behavior can also be compared. Assuming that helping is intrinsically rewarding (Weiss, Buchanan, Altstatt, & Lombardo, 1971), I might assess my neighbor's emotions in addition to his behavior. I could explore whether he feels good or bad while watering my plants. Assuming that helping originates from normative beliefs (Schwartz, 1977), I could inquire into whether my neighbor considers helping a moral mandate. If my neighbor waters my plants, feels good when doing so, and agrees that helping is a moral obligation, he displays *absolute transmodal consistency* (i.e., behavior, emotion, cognition).

Last and most important, I could compare results obtained with different *assessment methods*. To assess my neighbor's plant watering, I could ask him if he watered my plants; I could pretend to be out of town but in truth watch secretly whether he waters my plants; I could check after returning whether the soil of my plants is wet; and I could ask my neighbor's wife about her husband's behavior. If every method yields the same result, I might infer from this *absolute consistency across methods* that I could obtain the same result with any method.

Note that at this point the comparisons introduced so far require a common standard. Concluding absolute consistency from comparing behavior across individuals, time, situations, modes, and other dimensions is meaningful only when using the same metric for all observations. Comparability becomes possible in our example if the result of each observation were projected on a binary scale, discriminating help versus no help. Comparing observations of helpfulness is not as easy to achieve if we want to discriminate degrees of helpfulness. Although this issue of scaling cannot be elaborated in this chapter, it is important to remember that the concepts of variability and consistency are meaningful only when using a well-defined standard of comparison (Stevens, 1946).

Each facet of comparison introduced so far (i.e., individuals, occasions, situations, types of behavior, modes of behavior, methods) can be considered dimensions of a data matrix. Comparing objects on a single dimension creates a vector. Crossing dimensions creates a matrix. Three dimensions make a box. There is no theoretical limit on the number of facets (e.g., each of the facets introduced so far could be crossed with an attribute facet). Persons have attributes and so do situations and stimuli. In line with Cattell (1966) and Ozer (1986), I will use the data box concept in a figurative sense and not limit its meaning to a three-dimensional matrix.

Covariation and Relative Consistency

Absolute stability and absolute consistency imply predictability. However, absolute consistency cannot satisfy our need for *causal* knowledge—a need that ordinary people and scientists share (Kelley, 1973). Knowing that my neighbor is absolutely stable and

consistent does not tell me why this is the case. I could conceive many causes. Perhaps my neighbor has a strong helping norm (Schwartz, 1977), a strong sense of social responsibility (Berkowitz & Daniels, 1964), a strong need for approval (Crowne & Marlowe, 1964), or an excessive need for consistency (Lecky, 1945). He might also water my plants because he wants to stay away from his overbearing wife. Invariant behavior cannot teach me which explanation is correct or how much each factor contributes to my neighbor's behavior.

Insights into causality require variation. Without variation, the laws that generate data cannot be identified. Variation on one dimension is insufficient for causal analyses (Kenny, 1979). If my neighbor helped more in some situations than in others, I could not possibly explain his inconsistency unless I had identified at least one other dimension on which the situations also differ beside the amount of help I received. Using value theory (Tolman, 1932), I might speculate that gains and losses cause variation across situations. Helping takes more effort and provides less rewards in some situations than in others. I might conduct a cost–benefit analysis and compute a net outcome for each situation. I could then explore whether this net outcome *covaries* with helping, which is often the case (Piliavin, Dovidio, Gaertner, & Clark, 1981).

Such a covariation indicates *relative consistency*. This means that my neighbor's behavior although not absolutely consistent, did not differ in an arbitrary fashion between situations. Rather, the variation was *systematic* and *lawful*. It was relatively consistent because more help was provided when the net value of helping was high than when the net value of helping was low.

Relative consistency is a general concept. Its specific meaning depends on which facets of the data box are combined in search of lawfulness (Ozer, 1986). Relative consistency can occur across time (= *relative stability*), situations, types of behavior, modes of behavior, methods, and across other dimensions. Relative consistency across methods, often called convergence, is crucial in the context of this handbook. Convergence among methods is an essential criterion for their quality (Brunswik, 1934; Campbell & Fiske, 1959). Ideally, different methods

for measuring the same property of objects will be perfectly consistent. In this case, the methods measure the same property—whatever it is. Given their equivalence, the method used holds little significance. More important, each measure could be trusted, especially if methods were heterogeneous (Houts, Cook, & Shadish, 1986). If my neighbor said that he had watered my plants and if I could feel that the soil of my plants was wet, I would feel confident that both methods are trustworthy.

Intraindividual and Interindividual Consistency

In the neighbor example, relative consistency refers to systematic behavioral consistencies or differences within a single person. This type of relative *intraindividual consistency* has been termed *coherence* or *congruence*. The substantive examples to follow illustrate its significance. Most psychologists assume that behavior depends on the subjective interpretation of the situation in which behavior occurs. Empirical support for this idea was provided by Magnusson and Ekehammar (1978) and Krahé (1986) who determined the intraindividual congruence between situation perception and reactions. Searching for lawfulness as intraindividual coherence is appropriate whenever it is impossible or meaningless to include several individuals in the same study. In clinical psychology, it is sometimes impossible to compare clients because of their unique symptoms (Blampied, 2000). Luborsky (1953) defined lawfulness of change due to intervention in such cases as relative intraindividual stability in symptoms across time. As a third example, scholars have distinguished between general traits and individual traits (Allport, 1937). General traits are useful for describing everybody whereas individual traits are restricted in usefulness to a specific individual. When identifying individual traits one must rely on coherence analyses (Cattell, Cattell, & Rhymer, 1947).

Although single case studies are indispensable, the more typical approach to the discovery of lawfulness relies on comparing individuals. Ozer (1986) defines relative *interindividual consistency* as the degree of covariation of at least two dimensions on which individuals differ. Returning to the

neighbor example, I could assess the helpfulness of several neighbors at two different times or in two situations. I could also compare two types of behavior or two modes of behavior. Last but not least, I could measure helpfulness with two methods. The data I obtain from these studies enables me to determine the amount of relative interindividual consistency across time, situations, types, modes, and methods.

Replication, Lawfulness, and Reliability

Absolute consistency is displayed when repeated observations yield identical results on a single dimension of comparison. *Several* methods could be used for measuring one mode of one type of helpfulness of one individual in one situation at one point in time. One obtains absolute consistency if all methods yield identical results. As was explained earlier, all methods must use the same metric. Otherwise results cannot be compared.

Relative consistency occurs when repeated observations yield corresponding results, with correspondence meaning, for instance, that the difference between two individuals on two dimensions of comparison is equal. *Several* methods could be used for measuring one mode of one type of helpfulness of *several* individuals in one situation at one point in time. In such a design, helpfulness could be compared on the dimension of individuals (Neighbors A, B, and C) and on the dimension of methods (Methods 1, 2, and 3). There is perfect relative consistency in this example when the differences between the helpfulness scores of A, B, and C are identical for all three methods. Again, this definition of consistency holds meaning only if all of the methods use the same metric or if the different metrics are transformed into a common metric (e.g., via z-standardization).

Absolute and relative consistency imply *lawfulness* and *reliability*. Both lay judgment and scientific analysis define reliability as *replicability* (Willoughby, 1935). If a result can be replicated, we conclude that it was generated by a lawful process and that the method we used for obtaining the result was reliable. A single observation is insufficient to determine whether a result was generated by a systematic or a random process. Furthermore,

it is impossible to know on the basis of a single observation whether or not the assessment method was reliable.

In the neighbor example, perfect relative consistency suggests that the behavioral differences between Neighbors A, B, and C are lawful and that the methods that revealed these differences are reliable. The consistent differences between the neighbors might result from differences in their altruistic personality. If this interpretation is correct, the methods then reliably assess altruistic personality. However, the interpretation may be wrong. Possibly, the neighbors do not differ in altruistic personality, but rather, in their need for praise. If this is true, the methods measure need for approval rather than altruistic personality.

Multidetermination

Both interpretations hold validity to some extent. Individuals differ in altruistic personality (Bierhoff, Klein, & Kramp, 1991) and in their need for approval (Crowne & Marlowe, 1964). Because helping is a social norm, it is likely that individual differences in helping reflect individual differences in both personality characteristics. Furthermore, altruistic personality and need for approval may not be the only determinants of helping (Montada & Bierhoff, 1990). Most psychological phenomena studied in the history of psychology were found to be multidetermined. Helping is not an exception to this rule.

The multidetermination of human behavior has extremely important implications for research designs in general (Shadish, Cook, & Campbell, 2002) and for multimethod assessment in particular (Wiggins, 1973). This is true because the explanations of behavior and its measurement are two sides of the same coin. Our example again serves to illustrate this important fact. Consider the three methods for assessing help previously suggested: I could obtain self-reports from my neighbors (Method 1), I could observe their behavior secretly (Method 2), and I could interview their wives (Method 3). The result of each method will be multidetermined. To keep things simple, consider two causes for each method. Individual differences in helping behavior according to Method 1 might be caused by individ-

ual differences in altruistic personality and by individual differences in need for approval. Individual differences obtained with Method 2 might be caused by individual differences in altruistic personality and by my sympathy for the neighbors. Liking versus disliking may create a perceptual bias, leading me to overestimate or underestimate the help. Individual differences obtained with Method 3 might be caused by individual differences in altruistic personality and by individual differences in marital satisfaction. In a happy relationship, a neighbor's spouse might overestimate her husband's help, whereas in an unhappy relationship, she might underestimate that help.

Several important conclusions can be drawn from this analysis: First, a method usually measures more than one cause or factor. Second, the results obtained with different methods will converge to the extent that they share causes or factors. In our example, the common factor was altruistic personality. In addition to this common factor, each method measured a unique or specific factor. The unique factors of Methods 1, 2, and 3 were needed for approval, sympathy, and marital satisfaction, respectively. Third, the extent of convergence among different methods depends on the relative weight of their common and unique factors. If altruistic personality has strong effects on behavior in comparison to need for approval, sympathy, and marital satisfaction, consistency across methods is increased. By contrast, if the specific factors had large effects on behavior compared to altruistic personality, convergence among the methods is decreased. Fourth, the example shows choice of methods as a matter of *theory*. The more we know about the causes of behavior, the better can we measure behavior and the more likely we can develop methods that measure predominantly what we want to measure. Regarding our example, if we wanted to measure altruistic personality, we would select, on the basis of theory, methods that were affected as much as possible by altruistic personality and as little as possible by diagnostically irrelevant factors.

Construct Validity

A measure is construct-valid to the extent that it measures the attribute (construct, factor) it is supposed to measure (Cronbach & Meehl, 1955). Construct validity implies reliability but reliability does not guarantee construct validity (Thurstone, 1937). Reliability means that a measure reflects a systematic factor, whereas construct validity means that it reflects *the* systematic factor we want to assess. Construct validity is thus directly related to multidetermination. If several causes affect the results obtained with a method, the method measures each cause but none with perfect validity. The methods in our example were not perfectly valid measures of altruistic personality because individual differences depended on other causes as well. As a consequence of multidetermination, *methods have several validities* (e.g., achievement tests measure ability with a certain validity but also achievement motivation with a certain validity). If the test was made for measuring ability, its (primary) validity as an ability measure should be much higher than its (secondary) validity as an achievement motivation measure.

Depending on the measurement purpose, the same factor can either be diagnostically relevant or irrelevant. In our helping example, the approval motive is diagnostically irrelevant and reduces the construct validity of self-reported help as a measure of helpfulness. By contrast, the approval motive is diagnostically relevant if we want to use self-reported help as a social desirability measure. In this case, helpfulness becomes diagnostically irrelevant and reduces the construct validity of our social desirability measure. Assuming that helpfulness is a stronger factor of self-reported help than is the approval motive, the example shows that the primary validity of a method is sometimes lower than its secondary validity.

Diagnostically irrelevant factors of assessment methods can be method-specific (nonshared) or common (shared). Although both types of factors reduce the construct validity of an assessment method, they have different implications for convergence. Whereas method-specific factors reduce convergence among methods, common method factors increase convergence (Hoyt, 2000). Consider our helpfulness example. If I asked my neighbor and his wife whether my plants had been watered, both answers will probably measure true helpfulness. In addition, however, both answers might

reflect social desirability as a second common factor. My neighbor might exaggerate his help as a result of his approval motive as well as his wife. She may hope that my approval and gratefulness will be directed not only to her husband but also to her. Both factors, helpfulness and social desirability, are common factors here and contribute to convergence. However, social desirability as a diagnostically irrelevant common factor reduces the construct validity of both measures. The example demonstrates that convergence among methods is an insufficient criterion of construct validity (Campbell & Fiske, 1959). Convergence across methods reflects their construct validity only if they are heterogeneous in the sense that they only share the diagnostically relevant factor (Houts et al., 1986). Defining heterogeneity in practice is a challenge, however, because separating the diagnostically relevant sources of variance from the irrelevant sources requires what we seek: valid measures. This explains why choice of method is a matter of theory (Fiske, 1987b).

Generalizability and Specificity

Although the implications of multidetermination were discussed with regard to methods, they apply to all facets of a data box. The degree of relative consistency across time, situations, and other facets always depends on the relative weights of common and unique factors. Again, this has important consequences for psychological measurement (e.g., if helping in different situations depends only on altruistic personality, individual differences in helping remain nonspecific across situations). Every single act is then a perfect measure of altruistic personality. In contrast, if helping was caused by different specific factors in different situations with altruistic personality being the only common source of individual differences, the *generalizability* of individual differences across situations is then limited. Accordingly, the construct validity of each act as a measure of altruistic personality is also limited.

The reasoning also applies when differences on facets other than the person facet are of interest (Shadish et al., 2002; Wittmann, 1988). In general psychology, we want to discriminate among situations and replicate situation differences across other facets. In educational psychology and intervention research, we want to discriminate among time points and obtain consistent changes across other facets. Sometimes we are even interested in generalized differences between methods. We might want to know, for instance, whether better grades are given in oral versus written exams or whether grades differ systematically among teachers. Although method differences of this kind are undesirable in many research contexts because they limit the comparability of results, exploring systematic differences between methods can be important for making them comparable (Hoyt, 2000).

Aggregation

The consistency of differences and thus the reliability and validity of assessment methods can be increased by aggregation (Epstein, 1986; Steyer & Schmitt, 1990). The principle of aggregation is an integral part of lay epistemics and used intuitively in many life domains for neutralizing sources of inconsistency that are deemed *irrelevant*. Aggregation is used in sports, education, professional evaluation, and democratic elections of political leaders. The logic of aggregation follows directly from multidetermination. If different behaviors are caused partly by a common factor and partly by unique factors, each behavior is a poor measure of the common factor. Averaging behaviors reduces the impact of the unique factors, whereas the impact of the common factor remains the same. The average behavior therefore reflects the common factor more than it reflects any of the unique factors. As a consequence, the average behavior measures the common factor better than it measures the unique factors. This principle is an integral part of Classical Test Theory and the reason why the reliability of tests depends on their length (Brown, 1910; Lord & Novick, 1968; Spearman, 1910).

Choosing appropriate facets of aggregation is a matter of substantive interest. In personality research, we hope to measure individual differences. We want to discriminate on the person facet, whereas differences on other facets are of less substantive interest. Consequently, aggregation across time, situations, types, modes, and methods is appropriate (Epstein, 1986). In general psychology,

we want to identify generalized differences between situations. Differences on other facets are irrelevant. Accordingly, aggregation across individuals and other facets is appropriate. The same rationale applies to all other facets of the data box including the methods facet.

Note, however, that the irrelevant facets across which aggregation occurs must not be correlated (confounded) with the facet on which we want to discriminate. Consider the person and the situation facet of our helpfulness example. If we observe neighbor A only in situations where help is easy and neighbor B only in situations where help is effortful, we would overestimate A's helpfulness and underestimate B's. Just like confounded factors in experimental and quasi-experimental designs damage their internal validity, confounding diagnostically relevant facets with irrelevant facets damages the construct validity of measures (Messick, 1989; Shadish et al., 2002).

Interaction, Method Bias, and the Bandwidth-Fidelity-Dilemma

Inappropriate aggregation cannot only damage the construct validity of a measure but also disguise systematic patterns in the data and lead to misleading substantive conclusions. Aggregation can be inappropriate and can potentially disguise important information whenever facets of the data box interact (i.e., when *differences* between objects on one dimension differ *systematically* on another dimension). Consider differences in grades on three facets, the person (student) facet and two method facets: the teacher facet and the type of exam facet (oral versus written). Assume that every student received a better grade from Teacher A in an oral exam than in a written exam, whereas Teacher B gave a better grade to every student in a written exam than in an oral exam. Assume further that grades differed consistently among students across all four methods. Figure 2.1 schematically depicts the entire data pattern. Aggregation across students is appropriate because grade differences are perfectly generalized across the other two facets. However, aggregation across the two method facets masks two sources of *method bias*. Aggregation across teachers suggests that exam type does not matter. Aggregation across exam types suggests that teachers make no difference. Although these conclusions are technically correct on the level of grade averages, they preclude a deeper understanding of the methods by ignoring an *interaction* between the teacher and exam type facets. Aggregation thus results in a loss of information that might be of theoretical interest and great practical importance for avoiding method bias. Method bias occurs in this example when only written or only oral exams are administered and if some of the students are tested by Teacher A, whereas the rest are tested by Teacher B. For a comprehensive treatise of the method bias issue, see Hoyt (2000).

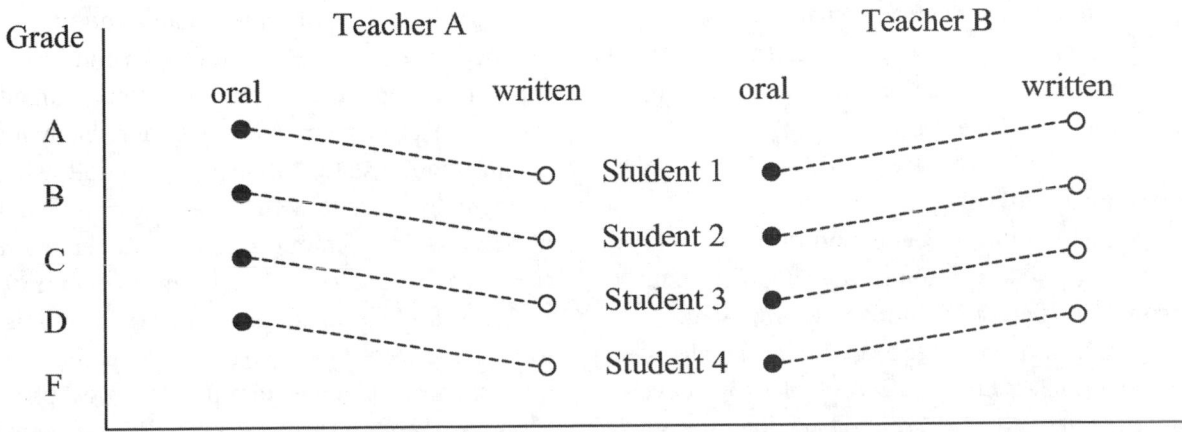

FIGURE 2.1. Lack of generalizability of individual differences in grades across the teacher and type of exam facet.

Lack of relative consistency always results from interactions among two or more facets of the data box. However, in the research world interactions are rarely as clear cut as our example. Usually, interactions are less systematic and smaller in size. Therefore, it is often difficult to measure the importance of an interaction. Ignoring an interaction increases parsimony but decreases precision. Taking interactions into account increases precision and decreases parsimony. This conflict between parsimony and precision remains a general dilemma in lay epistemics, the sciences, and technology (Gigerenzer & Selten, 2001). Shannon and Weaver (1949) called it the bandwidth-fidelity-dilemma. Cronbach (1960) and Wiggins (1973) discussed its implications for psychological assessment and prediction. Several rules have suggested how to deal with this dilemma. One of these rules states that as long as differences between objects on one dimension vary only in size but not in sign across another dimension (ordinal interaction), aggregation is appropriate. According to this rule, aggregation is inappropriate whenever the sign of differences on one facet changes across another facet—as was the case in our example (disordinal interaction). However, this is only a rule of thumb. Whether or not aggregation is appropriate must be carefully considered and depends on research goals and practical purposes. In basic research, precision often presides over parsimony, whereas the opposite is true in applied contexts (Schmitt & Borkenau, 1992). Intelligence and achievement serve as typical examples. In applied contexts, a general IQ score or a grade point average may be sufficient for discriminating individuals (e.g., job applicants). In basic research, it is more useful to break down intelligence and achievement into specific components.

Traits and States

The interaction of the person and the time facet is of utmost relevance in human development and personality. Theories of human development explain normative change and differential change (Baltes, Reese, & Lipsitt, 1980). Normative development is defined as age differences that generalize across individuals. The time facet and the person facet do not interact. By contrast, differential change reflects interindividual differences in intraindividual change and thus an interaction of the time and the person facets. As a consequence, later individual differences cannot be well predicted, if at all, from earlier individual differences (Bloom, 1964).

Trait models neglect person × time interactions by assuming that individual differences remain relatively constant across age (Carr & Kingsbury, 1938). Although longitudinal studies have supported this notion in the domain of personality (Costa & McCrae, 1980), ability (Deary, Whalley, Lemmon, Crawford, & Starr, 2000), and attitude (Alwin, Cohen, & Newcomb, 1991), person × time interactions are relevant for two related reasons.

First, traits are not the only meaningful attributes for describing the personalities of individuals. Unstable personality differences, called states, are no less important than traits for understanding and predicting behavior (Nesselroade & Bartch, 1977; Steyer, Ferring, & Schmitt, 1992). The state-trait distinction is common in lay personality theory and represented in language (Chaplin, John, & Goldberg, 1988). It dates back to, at least, Cicero (Eysenck, 1983).

Secondly, and more directly related to the focus of this handbook, person × time interactions are important because assessment methods differ in their sensitivity to intraindividual change. Consequently, *person × time × method interactions* can be expected. Some assessment methods measure stable individual differences whereas others measure, in the same psychological domain, individual differences that change with time. Small changes in instructions may be sufficient for generating a person × time × method interaction. Asking individuals how they feel at the moment will more likely measure an emotion state than an emotion trait, whereas asking individuals how they feel in general will more likely measure an emotion trait than an emotion state (Eid, Notz, Steyer, & Schwenkmezger, 1993).

These findings again demonstrate the crucial role of theory in the construction of methods. If intraindividual changes in a psychological phenomenon like emotion can be expected *on the basis of theory*, methods for assessing this phenomenon must be sensitive to intraindividual change. Using a

measure for enduring individual differences instead results in an underestimation of change. Exploring person × time × method interactions is therefore crucial for both the advancement of theory and the improvement of methods.

Method

Thus far, I have not defined the crucial concept of this book—the concept of method. What is a psychological assessment method? It is a set containing a variety of instruments and procedures that uncover psychological attributes of objects and transform these attributes into symbols that can be processed. "Psychological attribute," "object," "symbol," and "processing" are themselves sets that contain a variety of elements. Typical attributes are personality attributes, typical objects are individuals, typical symbols are numbers, and computing a mean is a typical way of processing symbols. This book gives an overview of the large variety of assessment methods constructed in the history of scientific psychology.

Good assessment methods are objective, reliable, and valid (Anastasi, 1988; Cronbach, 1960; Wiggins, 1973). Objectivity means that results do not depend on who administered or scored the instrument. Reliability means that results can be replicated under the same conditions. Validity means that the method measures what it is supposed to measure. Regarding each criteria, the quality of an assessment method can be defined as a special type of consistency or convergence. Objectivity can be defined as the amount of convergence across researchers or practitioners who use the method. Reliability can be defined as the amount of convergence across repeated applications of the method for the same objects under the same conditions. Construct validity can be defined as the amount of convergence of the measured (manifest) attribute with the true (latent) attribute or construct (Shadish et al., 2002). Because constructs are hypothetical and cannot be observed directly, they must be substituted either by another measure or some criterion (Cronbach & Meehl, 1955). Although broader and more complex definitions of construct validity have been offered and although multifold procedures for establishing construct validity have

been proposed (Messick, 1989), all conceptualizations of construct validity eventually result in the notion of convergence between the measured attribute and the "true" attribute as it appears in theoretical statements about the phenomenon to be described and explained.

Convergent and Discriminant Validity

Given the lack of knowledge about the "true" attributes of objects, convergence across *different methods* for the *same attribute* is often the best alternative. This type of validity has been called *convergent validity* (Campbell & Fiske, 1959). Demonstrating convergent validity is not sufficient, however, because convergence alone does not yet guarantee that the methods measure what they should measure. It only shows that the methods measure the same factors. As previously outlined, some or even all of the common factors two methods share may be diagnostically irrelevant. Therefore, additional validation strategies and validity criteria are important (Cronbach & Meehl, 1955; Messick, 1989). In the present context, *discriminant* validity is a criterion of special interest (Campbell & Fiske, 1959). If a method predominantly measures what it should, it will not converge with measures for attributes *unrelated* to the attribute of interest, whereas highly consistent individual differences across several intelligence tests indicate convergent validity, equally consistent individual differences between an intelligence test and a creativity test indicate a lack of discriminant validity for either one or both tests.

The above example shows that demonstrating discriminant validity is more difficult than demonstrating convergent validity. This is true because the divergence of two methods indicates their validity only to the extent that the attributes they measure are truly unrelated (e.g., we can expect divergence between an intelligence test and a creativity test only to the extent that intelligence and creativity are unrelated). Yet how can we know the true relation without valid measures? This problem again points to the importance of theory. If a theory states that intelligent individuals are also more creative (Lubart, 2003), some convergence of intelligence tests and creativity tests must occur and total divergence may raise concerns about the validity of either one or both tests.

Semantic and Formal Commonalities Among the Concepts

Relative consistency, relative stability, generalizability, reliability, convergence, and convergent validity are closely related concepts, introduced separately because they have been used in the literature for denoting different substantive applications and interpretations of the same general principle—the principle of covariation. The concepts of specificity, interaction, divergence, and discriminant validity are also closely related to each other and commonly denote a lack of covariation.

The relation among the concepts of consistency and specificity becomes evident from the use of these concepts in statistical analyses of the data box. All concepts can be and have been defined mathematically, and these definitions are either identical or closely related. Most mathematical definitions of consistency and specificity stem from two well-known statistical coefficients: the coefficient of *variance* and the coefficient of *covariance*. This is true for the Pearson correlation coefficient, the multiple correlation coefficient, coefficients of determination, intraclass correlation coefficients, as well as for other coefficients of relative consistency and convergence proposed in generalizability theory (Cronbach, Gleser, Nanda, & Rajaratnam, 1972) and multivariate reliability theory (Wittmann, 1988).

The general linear model is another mathematical construct that unifies on a formal level many of the substantive principles discussed in this section. The general linear model makes the principle of multidetermination concrete in the language of algebra. It serves as a common formal denominator of many statistical procedures developed for the analysis of consistency and specificity (e.g., analysis of variance, factor analysis, and the more recent and more sophisticated methods of modeling covariance structures among facets of the data box (Eid, 2000; Jöreskog, 1969; Kenny & Kashy, 1992; Kenny & Zautra, 2001; Marsh, 1989; Steyer et al., 1992; Steyer, Schmitt, & Eid, 1999; Widaman, 1985). Several chapters of this volume will provide a detailed analysis of the formal and mathematical commonalities among the concepts of consistency, specificity, and multidetermination introduced here on a conceptual level.

LOOKING BACK: HISTORICAL MILESTONES IN MULTIMETHOD ASSESSMENT

The history of multimethod thinking in psychological assessment and construct validation can be described metaphorically as an avenue from an (unknown) starting point to an (unknown) end point from which many roads stem. Some of them turn back to the main route, whereas others become dead end streets. These pathways cannot and do not need a detailed description here. Rather, I concentrate on important milestones along the developmental route of the general multimethod approach. As I see it, the most important milestones are Brunswik's (1934) work on probabilistic functionalism in human perception, Campbell and Fiske's (1959) multitrait–multimethod (MTMM) matrix, covariance structure modeling based on Jöreskog's (1969) confirmatory factor analysis (CFA), Generalizability Theory (Cronbach et al., 1972), and Critical Multiplism (Cook, 1985).

Brunswik

Brunswik's work on probabilistic functionalism in human perception (1934, 1956) is fundamental for multimethod assessment for at least five related reasons. First, recognizing the *multidetermination* of behavior as a general principle, Brunswik reconceptualized perception, impression formation, and clinical judgment from a *multivariate perspective*. Whereas traditional psychophysics was mainly concerned with the effects of *physical* stimulus properties, Brunswik expanded the causal scope for the explanation of optical illusions, perceptual constancy, and physiognomic trait impressions by including *psychological* codeterminants (e.g., intelligence, perceptual attitude, practice, and attributes of the task and its context). The multivariate nature of Brunswik's research became important for multimethod thinking because its results suggested that measurement methods relying on human perception and judgment can hardly ever be perfectly valid. Second, Brunswik described the many ways in which relative consistencies can be defined in the multivariate space. He discussed several types of correlations and defined validity as convergence among

tests. Third, Brunswik claimed that the multivariate approach was not only essential for the description of individuals but also for the classification of other psychological entities like stimuli and situations.

> Each situation is a 'variate package,' that is, a more or less incidental combination of specific values along a large, and indeed unknown, number of dimensions. Ecologies, and the situations that constitute them, are in many ways like persons, which also are variate packages. Ecologies or situations exhibit consistencies and 'habits' all of their own, although perhaps less strikingly than do individuals; we may 'know' them and like or dislike them as we do our fellow men. It is by virtue of these relative consistencies that variate packages as a whole, and not their isolated dimensions, should be taken to define a universe. (Brunswik, 1956, p. 139)

The quest for *representative design* and *representative sampling* was a fourth important contribution. Brunswik, concerned about the generalizability of experimental results, warned that their *ecological validity* will be limited if experimental designs and samples are nonrepresentative. Designs are nonrepresentative when they ignore correlations among dimensions of the data box in the real world. Individuals select situations, types, and modes of behavior are confounded, and situations and time cannot be combined at will. Brunswik illustrated this issue with reference to his own research on the validity of physiognomic trait impressions for personality and ability judgment. In his early studies, Brunswik used schematized drawings and fully crossed facial properties (e.g., eye separation and forehead height) for creating "Gestalten" (holistic impressions). Later, he recognized that such an orthogonal design violates the natural correlation among facial facets and continued his research with photographs of real people. He argued that untying correlated facets of the data box via orthogonal designs violates the principle of *representative covariation*. This issue is important for multimethod assessment. Methods cannot be crossed at will with

properties of psychological objects. Abilities cannot be measured with the same methods as emotions, and implicit attitudes cannot be measured with the same methods as explicit attitudes. Constructs and assessment methods are units that cannot be untied easily. Brunswik was also concerned about the double standards for sampling the person facet versus sampling other facets of the data box. He desired to improve ecological validity in multivariate research via *representative sampling on all dimensions*. It is difficult to know what this means for the method dimension, because the universe of methods can be less well-defined than the universe of persons. Despite this difficulty, researchers should be sensitive to the issue and careful when generalizing results across methods without considering the range of methods that could be conceived.

Finally, Brunswik's lens model provides a flexible tool for conceptualizing multimethod designs and the effects of multidetermination on convergence (Wittmann, 1988). Figure 2.2 schematically depicts the lens model as a path diagram. The corpus of the lens contains three traits (TA, TB, TC). The foci of the lens represent two methods (M1, M2). The loadings of the traits are symbolized as arrows. The curved lines in the corpus indicate correlations among the traits. The curved line between the methods represents their correlation. Its size depends on the correlation among the traits and the factor loadings. Perfect convergence of the methods occurs, for instance, if each method measures only one trait and if this trait was the same for both methods. Perfect divergence also occurs if both methods had no trait-factor in common and if the traits were independent.

Campbell and Fiske

Multimethod thinking in psychological assessment was influenced most strongly by the seminal paper of Campbell and Fiske (1959). No other publication so importantly shaped researchers' awareness of the crucial role multimethod designs play in the construction and validation of measurement instruments (Shrout & Fiske, 1995). Although Campbell and Fiske (1959) did not make reference to Brunswik's work, their proposals were guided by similar insights and ideas. Campbell and Fiske

(1959) introduced the multitrait–multimethod matrix, a flexible, conceptual and methodological framework for the examination of convergent and discriminant validity. The MTMM matrix is a matrix of correlations among tests. Tests are trait–method units. An MTMM matrix is usually derived from a three-dimensional raw data box consisting of a person facet, a facet of attributes (traits), and a method facet. Although not commonly done, the general MTMM idea could be applied to any other combination of three dimensions of the data box. Instead of measuring traits of persons, properties of stimuli could be measured with different methods and submitted to an MTMM analysis.

For obtaining the most common type of an MTMM matrix, two or more traits (of several individuals) must be measured with two or more methods. The matrix contains four kinds of correlations (see Table 2.1). The elements in the main diagonal are called monotrait–monomethod (mTmM) correlations. They compose the reliabilities of the tests (trait–method units). Correlations among different traits measured with the same method are heterotrait–monomethod (hTmM) correlations. Correlations among different methods for the same trait are termed monotrait–heteromethod (mThM) correlations. Finally, correlations among different traits that were measured with different methods are named heterotrait–heteromethod (hThM) correlations.

Correlations among different methods for the same trait (mThM) display *convergent validity*. These correlations should be high. Correlations among different methods for different traits (hThM) are usually the lowest correlations in an MTMM matrix because these tests have neither traits nor methods in common. However, hThM correlations differ from zero if traits or methods are correlated. A self-report measure (Method 1) of Trait A may be correlated with a peer-rating measure (Method 2) of Trait B because A and B are correlated. In addition, both measures may share method variance. Common method variance may be caused by individual differences in self-presentational concerns. If both traits are socially desirable, individuals will differ regarding how favorably they present themselves in the self-report measure of Trait A. Individuals may also differ regarding how

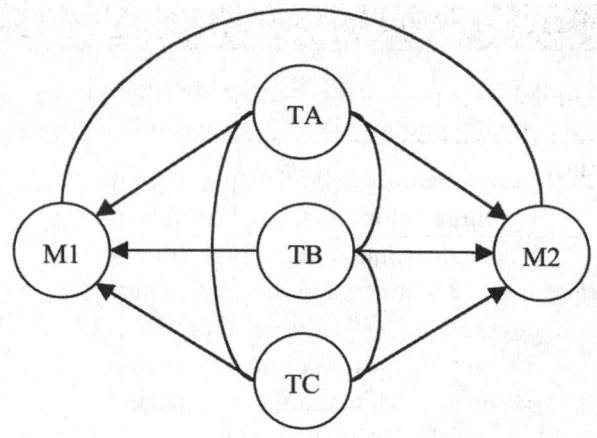

FIGURE 2.2. A Brunswik lens model for three traits and two methods.

favorably they present themselves to peers. As a consequence, peer-ratings of Trait B will also be affected by self-presentational concerns, and both measures will correlate even if A and B are independent traits. Evidently, correlations among tests are only inflated if the correlations among the traits and the methods have the same sign. If correlations among traits differ in sign from correlations among methods, they may cancel each other out, resulting in low or zero hThM correlations, even if the traits are correlated.

Correlations among different traits measured with the same method (hTmM) ideally should not exceed correlations among different traits measured with different methods (hThM). Such an ideal pattern suggests that using the same method for different traits does not inflate the correlations among the tests because of the use of the same method. For the same reason, correlations among different methods for the same trait (mThM; convergent validity) should ideally not be lower than the reliabilities of the tests (mTmM). Again, such an ideal pattern suggests that the reliabilities of the tests are only because of trait variance but not to shared method variance. The last two comparisons (hTmM versus hThM; mThM versus mTmM) provide estimates for the *discriminant validity* of tests. Tests display discriminant validity if they do not measure traits they should not. In an MTMM analysis, discriminant validity is achieved when the reliability of a test was not inflated compared to its convergent validity and

---

TABLE 2.1

General Structure of the Multitrait–Multimethod Matrix According to Campbell and Fiske (1959)

Method	Trait	Method 1			Method 2			Method 3		
		A	B	C	A	B	C	A	B	C
Method 1	A	*mTmM*								
	B	hTmM	*mTmM*							
	C	hTmM	hTmM	*mTmM*						
Method 2	A	**mThM**	hThM	hThM	*mTmM*					
	B	hThM	**mThM**	hThM	hTmM	*mTmM*				
	C	hThM	hThM	**mThM**	hTmM	hTmM	*mTmM*			
Method 3	A	**mThM**	hThM	hThM	**mThM**	hThM	hThM	*mTmM*		
	B	hThM	**mThM**	hThM	hThM	**mThM**	hThM	hTmM	*mTmM*	
	C	hThM	hThM	**mThM**	hThM	hThM	**mThM**	hTmM	hTmM	*mTmM*

Note. mTmM = monotrait–monomethod; hTmM = heterotrait–monomethod; mThM = monotrait–heteromethod; hThM = heterotrait–heteromethod.

when the correlations among tests for different traits are not inflated by use of the same method.

Covariance Structure Modeling

Despite its vast impact on multimethod thinking in psychological assessment, the Campbell and Fiske (1959) strategy of comparing correlations suffers from a number of shortcomings of which Campbell and Fiske had been aware without offering satisfactory solutions. First, no statistical test exists for evaluating the pattern of differences among the correlations of the MTMM matrix *simultaneously*. Second, no straightforward decomposition of test variance into trait variance and method variance can be obtained from the comparisons among correlations suggested by Campbell and Fiske. Third, the comparison of correlations does not consider differences in test reliability and other factors affecting the magnitude of correlations.

Jöreskog (1969) presented the most elegant solution to these problems with his general CFA approach to confirmatory factor analysis. Since Jöreskog's seminal contribution, MTMM research has shifted from the mere description of correlations to modeling the covariance structure among trait–method units. This methodology has several advantages over the descriptive comparison among

correlations. First, by modeling traits and methods as latent variables, reliability differences between tests can be handled. Second, models can be tested and different models can be tested against each other if they are nested (Widaman, 1985). Third, the variance of tests can be decomposed into proportions due to trait factors, method factors, and measurement error. Fourth, if the time facet is included in addition to the person, construct, and method facets, latent state–trait method analyses can be performed, and the variances of tests can be decomposed into proportions due to traits, occasion-specific effects of the situation, methods, and random measurement error (Kenny & Zautra, 2001; Schmitt & Steyer, 1993). Given these advantages of confirmatory factor analyses, it is not surprising that Marsh (1989) counted twenty different CFA-MTMM models 20 years after Jöreskog's paper.

Widaman (1985) proposed a taxonomy for many of these models by cross-classifying four trait structures with four method structures. Both structures differ in the number of common factors and whether these factors are orthogonal or oblique. The taxonomy generates a family of 16 hierarchically nested models with the null model (no trait factor, no method factor) being the most restrictive model and the correlated-traits-correlated-methods

model (CTCM) being the least restrictive model. Widaman's (1985) taxonomy holds value because it is more systematic than any earlier proposal, provides a heuristic for conceptualizing alternative trait and method structures, and serves as a guideline for testing models sequentially.

Although the general CFA approach has advanced MTMM research tremendously, it has limits. Improper solutions are a common problem with the popular CTCM model. Iterative procedures for estimating parameters of this model often fail to converge or lead to estimates outside the permissible range with a negative variance of one of the method factors being the most frequent problem. Solutions for overcoming this and other problems (e.g., Eid, 2000; Kenny & Kashy, 1992; Marsh, 1989) will be discussed in chapter 20.

Generalizability Theory (GT)

Generalizability Theory (Cronbach, Rajaratnam, & Gleser, 1963; Cronbach et al., 1972; Gleser, Cronbach, & Rajaratnam, 1965; Shavelson & Webb, 1991) combines Brunswik's request for representative multifacet designs with the true-score model of Classical Test Theory (CTT; Lord & Novick, 1968; Spearman, 1910). Like CTT, GT assumes that each person (or other object of measurement) has a true score on the measured attribute. In GT, this score is called the *universe score*. Whereas CTT treats the difference between the true score and the observed score as measurement error that lacks substantive significance, GT proposes to decompose the difference between the universe score and the observed score into psychologically meaningful sources of variance. These sources of variance must be specified on the basis of theoretical and practical considerations as facets of a factorial measurement design. For example, if leniency differences between teachers are assumed to cause grade differences, the design must include a teacher facet. If grades were used to make absolute decisions (only A students get a stipend), the *main effect* of the teacher facet reduces the *absolute* generalizability of grades across teachers. If grades were used to make relative decisions (upper 10% of students get a stipend), an *interaction* between the student facet and the teacher

facet then limits the *relative* generalizability of grades across teachers.

Assuming the use of equivalent interval scales, the universe score of an object of measurement is defined as its expected value on the attribute scale (i.e., the mean of all admissible observations). Relative generalizability is defined as the squared correlation between the observed score variable and the universe score variable (i.e., the ratio of universe score variance to observed score variance). This definition of relative generalizability corresponds directly to the definition of reliability in CTT. Because the universe score is unknown, relative generalizability must be estimated from several observed score variables. The intraclass correlation among conditions provides this estimate. It is an overall index of relative consistency and reflects the degree of interaction between persons (or other measurement objects) and the facets. Coefficients of absolute generalizability are sometimes defined as variance ratios. Their denominator includes variance components attributable to facet main effects and interaction effects. Shavelson, Webb, and Rowley (1989) illustrated the difference between absolute and relative generalizability with simple substantive examples. Marcoulides (1996) showed how variance components can be estimated with structural equation modeling. Hoyt (2000) provides a comprehensive treatment of absolute and relative bias (lack of generalizability) in univariate and multivariate applications of GT.

The first proposal of GT was limited to the one facet case (Cronbach et al., 1963). Gleser et al. (1965) extended GT to the multifacet case and defined generalizability coefficients for several types of two facet designs. Cronbach et al. (1972) offered the most comprehensive version of GT. They introduced additional designs and, more important, multivariate GT. Multivariate GT focuses on the generalizability of *attribute profiles* (i.e., the *joint generalizability* of measures for two or more attributes). Whereas univariate GT decomposes the *variance* of one observed variable into components due to facet main effects, facet interaction effects and person × facet interactions, multivariate GT also decomposes the *covariance* of two or more observed variables (Hoyt, 2000; Wittmann, 1988).

The models and methods of GT are useful for understanding the psycho-logic and methodo-logic of multimethod approaches. (a) Compared to CTT, GT provides a more comprehensive, differentiated, and flexible conceptualization of reliability. (b) GT contributes to understanding and defining the concepts of convergent and discriminant validity. Convergent validity corresponds to the generalizability of *inter*individual differences in the measured attribute across the method facet. Discriminant validity corresponds to a *lack of generalizability* of *intra*individual differences between two or more theoretically unrelated attributes across the method facet. (c) By combining generalizability studies with decision studies, GT links basic research on the properties of measurement instruments with the usefulness of diagnostic information in applied psychology. (d) Last but not least, measurement designs including nested facets inspired hierarchical linear modeling of multilevel data, a methodological framework that has greatly enriched multimethod research during recent years (Hox & Maas, this volume, chap. 19; Raudenbush & Bryk, 2002).

Before we turn to the last milestone, note that the ideas that were advanced in covariance structure models of multitrait multimethod data and in generalizability theory are also dealt with in multicomponent item response models (Rost & Walter, this volume, chap. 18).

Critical Multiplism

Critical Multiplism (CM) is closely related in its premises and goals with all previously presented milestones. In comparison to these, CM is more general (compared with the MTMM framework), broader in substantive scope (compared with Brunswik), and less technical (compared with covariance structure modeling and Generalizability Theory). Critical Multiplism is a way of thinking, a philosophy of science (Cook, 1985; Houts et al., 1986; Shadish, 1995). It starts from the premise that no perfect route to scientific knowledge exists and that all scientific options have their own strengths and weaknesses. Scientific options include theories, research designs, sampling strategies, measurement instruments, assessment procedures, rules for weighing and combining information, statistical models for analyzing data, guidelines for interpreting results, and principles for transforming scientific evidence into decisions and actions (e.g., intervention programs). Assuming that alternative research strategies always differ in their advantages and disadvantages, CM requires that research programs never rely on a single strategy but always combine several strategies. It is critical from the CM view that strategies are not chosen and combined at random but instead selected according to the principles of best quality and maximum heterogeneity. Heterogeneous strategies are preferable compared to homogeneous strategies because the convergence of results across highly dissimilar strategies is more convincing and increases the trustworthiness of evidence more than convergence among highly similar strategies. A specific application of this rule was outlined earlier: Combining heterogeneous assessment methods means that they share only the diagnostically relevant factors. The quality criterion is more difficult to operationalize. According to CM, high quality research requires that researchers make their implicit assumptions explicit, justify each component of their work (theory, design, sampling strategies, measurement methods, etc.), and invite members of the scientific community to challenge these justifications. Diversity in theory and method is considered in CM as the best safeguard against systematic error. Just like discrimination is a fundamental principle of knowledge, diversity is a fundamental prerequisite to determine convergence of evidence. Not surprisingly, CM supports multimethod assessment on the basis of quality and heterogeneity.

LOOKING AHEAD: SOME EMERGING ISSUES AND CHALLENGES

In what direction should multimethod work progress? All of this handbook's contributors likely have their own view regarding where progress is necessary and possible. Below, I address two important yet unresolved issues.

Methods Are Hypothetical Constructs

The language in which methods are often treated in the literature suggests that they are something

technical, nonpsychological, or different than substantive variables. But "method" is a summary concept for a multitude of ways in which we obtain psychological information. The result of a method has psychological significance as does the method itself. Returning to the neighbor example, self-report, other-report, and observation were introduced as methods because the different procedures collected the method's provided data. Yet the data are psychological data and the status of these data is the same for each method. They are indicators of assumed causes (altruistic personality, need for approval, marital satisfaction, sympathy). Methods are sets of causes and different sets (methods) contain different elements (causes). Causes as components of a method do not differ from causes that appear in psychological theories. Both the causes of substantive models and the causal components of methods are *hypothetical constructs*. Therefore, methods (self-report) can be imbedded in psychological theories like substantive causes (altruistic personality). Moreover, methods not only *can* be imbedded in psychological theories, they *must* be imbedded in psychological theories. It follows from this claim that methods must be submitted to construct validation (Cronbach & Meehl, 1955) just like what Campbell and Fiske (1959) termed trait–method units (tests). This view has several important consequences, not seriously treated in the literature thus far. To hint at only two of these consequences: First, designing new methods and improving methods is as much a matter of theory as a matter of craftsmanship. Furthermore, selecting methods for multitrait–multimethod research must rely on assumptions about the causal components of methods. Methods are not the same because they capture the same type of data. Two self-report questionnaires are the same method only to the extent that they share diagnostically irrelevant causal components. In some cases, two self-report questionnaires may share fewer diagnostically irrelevant causal components than a self-report and an other-report questionnaire. If so, the two self-report questionnaires are not the same methods. In fact, they are less similar as methods than the self- and other-report questionnaires.

Methods Are Traits and States

The terminology introduced by Campbell and Fiske (1959) may be (mis)interpreted that methods are not traits. However, if methods are composites of the causes we want to measure and causes we consider irrelevant, they can be stable dispositions. Both in a substantive sense and on a formal level, no qualitative difference exists between traits and methods. The only difference is that, ideally, traits are single causes (altruistic personality) and methods are composites of causes (altruistic personality + need for approval).

It follows from this view that methods cannot only be "traits" in the formal sense of stable behavioral dispositions; they can also be "states" in the formal sense of systematic individual differences in intraindividual change across time because of the systematic but occasion-specific effects of the measurement situation. In other words, individual differences that stem from shared method variance may not be stable. Self-presentational concerns as a causal component of self-report measures, for instance, may vary systematically across time and situations. At some occasions of measurement, like during a job interview or a date, self-presentational concerns may be stronger than at other occasions. This possibility holds important implications for modeling methods as latent factors in longitudinal multitrait-multimethod designs. It may be appropriate and even necessary in some applications to model latent method factors both as latent states and latent traits. This could be easily done by extending the general latent state–trait framework (Steyer et al., 1992: Steyer, Schmitt, & Eid, 1999) to the domain of methods. Leaving aside issues of model identification, Figure 2.3 depicts the general structure of such a model for two constructs, two occasions of measurement, and two methods with Y_{ijk}, ST_i, SS_{ij}, $LSSR_{ij}$, MT_k, MS_{jk}, $LMSR_{jk}$, and e_{ijk} denoting manifest variables, substantive traits, substantive states, latent substantive state residuals, method trait, method states, latent method state residuals, and measurement error and with i, j, and k denoting the construct, the occasion of measurement, and the method, respectively.

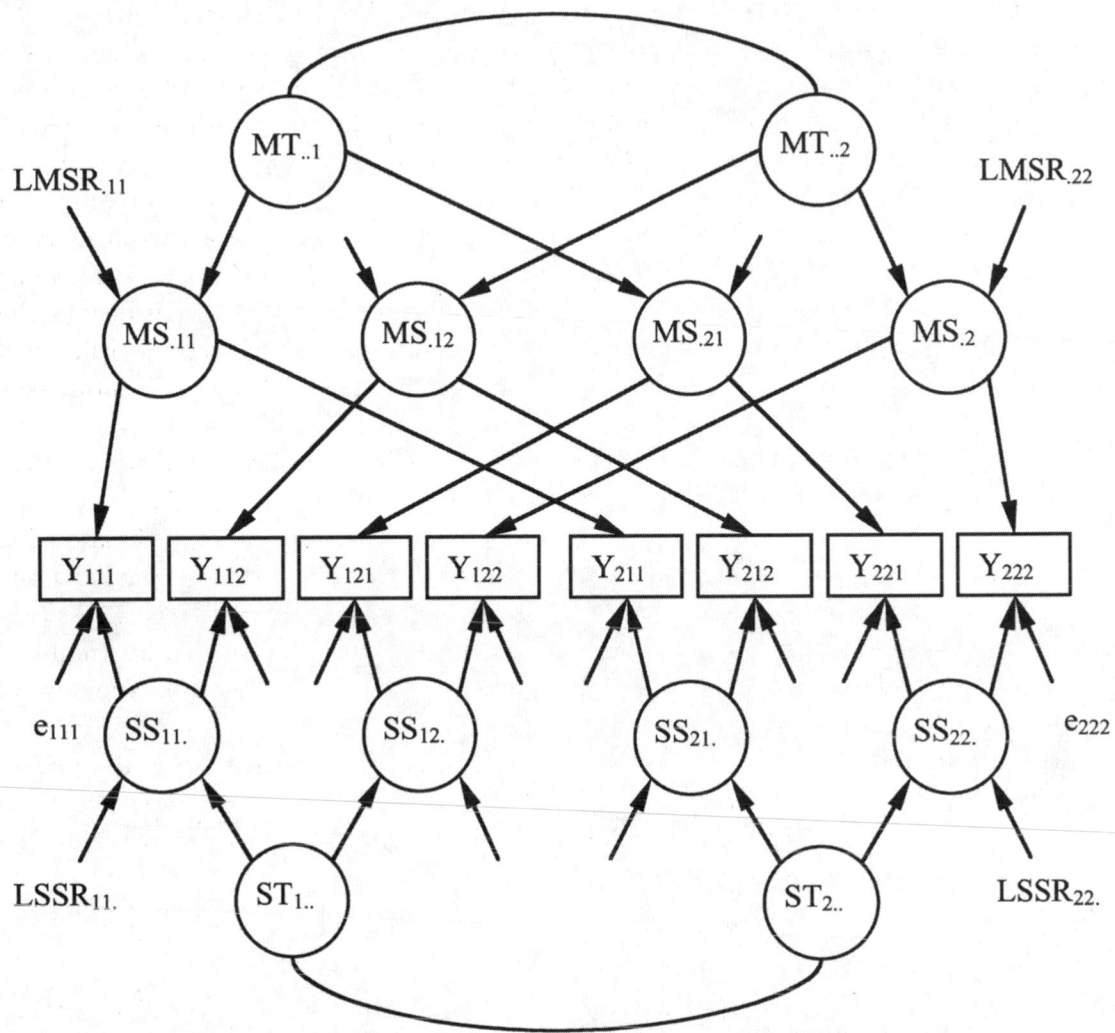

FIGURE 2.3. Latent substantive state–trait and method state–trait model for two constructs (first index), two occasions of measurement (second index), and two methods (third index). MT = Method Trait; MS = Method State; SS = Substantive State; ST = Substantive Trait.

The model shows that methods do not differ in a formal sense from substantive constructs. In fact, this is true for all other facets of the data box. Instead of containing methods, the model in Figure 2.3 could contain modes of behavior. Some modes or types of behavior may be more trait-like than others although both are indicators of the same substantive construct. Therefore, the model in Figure 2.3 could be extended and include latent states and traits for modes of behavior and types of behavior, as well as any other theoretically meaningful facet of the data box.

PART II

ASSESSMENT METHODS

CHAPTER 3

GLOBAL SELF-ASSESSMENT

Richard E. Lucas and Brendan M. Baird

Global self-assessment is a broad category of measurement techniques that includes many variations on a seemingly simple process—participants are asked to provide information about events, behaviors, attitudes, feelings, emotions, symptoms, or some other objective or subjective state of affairs. Simplicity and ease of administration have made self-report methodology one of the most popular methods of psychological inquiry; yet the fallibility of human memory and judgment has made this methodology the subject of much scrutiny and criticism. The skepticism about self-report methods is exacerbated by the fact that self-reports are often used when no readily available objective alternative exists that could be used as a criterion for validation (Critchfield, Tucker, & Vuchinich, 1998).

Careful investigation of the self-report method reveals that what appears to be a simple process is actually the end result of a series of more complicated steps. A number of cognitive models of self-report assessment have been proposed to clarify these steps (e.g., Schwarz, 1999; Strack & Martin, 1987; Tourangeau, Rips, & Rasinski, 2000). These models and their supporting evidence show that when answering a self-report question, respondents must first understand and interpret the question, search their memory for relevant information, construct an answer, translate that answer into a meaningful response, and then edit that response for the particular audience. These processes can be affected in undesirable ways by such factors as question wording, question order, and available response options. In turn, each process has the potential to

influence the final self-reported judgment. Numerous studies have demonstrated the problems that emerge when researchers who use self-report assessment ignore the complex and sometimes surprising ways that these factors can influence the responses to self-report measures.

Yet despite the potential limitations, self-report techniques can provide useful and valid measures of many constructs. In this chapter, we discuss the reasons why one might choose to use self-reports, the various forms of self-reports that exist, the processes that underlie self-reports, and the advantages and disadvantages of this technique. We focus on steps that researchers can take to evaluate and improve the quality of their global self-assessments.

ADVANTAGES AND DISADVANTAGES OF SELF-REPORT METHODS

Self-report methods offer clear advantages over other assessment techniques. These methods are simple, quick, inexpensive, flexible, and often provide information that would be difficult or impossible to obtain any other way. Yet each advantage corresponds to specific disadvantages that may go unnoticed by researchers. For example, the ubiquity of self-report techniques results from the fact that they are so easy to administer. However, this ease of use may result in an overreliance on self-reports even when more appropriate but more difficult-to-obtain methods are available. Similarly, the simplicity of self-reports may belie the complex processes that underlie self-reported judgments. Researchers

may take self-reports at face value and ignore the subtle ways that unwanted method variance sneaks into these reports. Self-reports are also very flexible. Researchers can choose open-ended questions or closed-ended response scales; they can vary the time frame of the question, the specific response options used, and the precise wording of the questions. The drawback of this flexibility is that these seemingly unimportant decisions can have serious consequences for the results of the self-report assessment.

As this volume makes clear, conducting multimethod investigations of validity can increase confidence in any single method of assessment. However, in situations where multimethod assessment cannot be used, the choice of a specific method must be guided by an explicit consideration of the advantages and disadvantages of that approach. There are a number of types of self-reports, and there are different advantages and disadvantages depending on the purpose of the assessment.

One major distinction is between self-reports of objectively verifiable phenomena like behaviors and events and self-reports of psychological constructs (e.g., beliefs, intentions, and attitudes; Schwarz, Groves, & Schuman, 1998). Different processes likely operate when constructing these two types of judgments, and thus, different concerns may arise depending on how the measure is being used. Presumably, when participants are asked to report on behaviors, an objective criterion exists and the validity of the self-report can be assessed by determining the extent to which the self-report matches the criterion. For example, a researcher may be interested in the number of alcoholic beverages a person consumes over the course of a week. Rather than following that individual over time and recording these instances, the researcher may simply ask the person to retrospectively report on this behavior. The validity of this report can be assessed by comparing it to an objective measure.

Self-reports of attitudes, intentions, and other psychological variables are somewhat more complicated. In this case, there is no objective criterion to verify the self-reports, and errors in self-reports are difficult to detect. As Schwarz et al. (1998) have noted in the context of attitude research, "If we

want to talk of 'errors' in attitude measurement at all, we can only do so relative to what we were trying to measure in the questionnaire, not relative to any objective standard that reflects respondents' 'true' attitudes" (p. 158). Thus, a flawed self-report is one that is not logical or one shown to be influenced by some feature or stimulus that is theoretically unrelated to the attitude in question. A number of experimental studies have shown that such errors do occur. Participants often respond in illogical ways or they may respond differently depending on irrelevant contextual factors.

Finally, a self-report can be used as a form of behavior, in and of itself (Critchfield et al., 1998). When researchers use self-reports in this way, they are not interested in the extent to which the report is "correct." Instead, they are solely interested in the ways that variations in responses correlate with relevant predictor or outcome variables. In fact, much of the research investigating the cognitive processes underlying self-report methodology uses self-report methodology in this way. Researchers in these studies are not interested in the content of the responses per se, but in the ways that those responses are affected by various experimental factors. For example, in their famous study examining the way mood affects life satisfaction judgments, Schwarz and Clore (1983) found that individuals reported higher life satisfaction on a warm, sunny day than on a cold, rainy one. Schwarz and Clore were not interested in life satisfaction (i.e., they were not interested in getting a true measure of an individual's standing on this construct). Instead, they were interested in the cognitive processes that individuals used to construct satisfaction judgments, and the satisfaction reports themselves were a form of behavior that indicated the underlying process.

The distinctions among the various types of self-report methodology matter because the factors that influence the validity of self-reports and the ways in which we validate self-report measures often vary depending on how the measure is being used. For example, a personality researcher interested in assessing extraversion may ask participants to respond to an item like, "I enjoy going to parties." The researcher may have one of three expectations about responses to this item. First, he or she may

expect responses on this item to be similar to self-reports of behavior. If so, responses to the item should strongly correlate with the frequency with which a person goes to parties. If the response does not correlate with the behavior, this suggests that the item is not valid.

Alternatively, the item could be thought of as a self-report of an attitude toward parties. In this case, responses to the item are not necessarily expected to correlate strongly with the number of times that a person goes to parties, but should predict the enjoyment a person experiences when he or she does go to parties. Validation of the global self-report could be accomplished by comparing responses on this item to online assessment of enjoyment actually experienced during a party.

Finally, responses to the item "I enjoy going to parties" may be seen as a form of behavior that can predict some other criterion, even if the item is not a valid measure of the behavior or attitude it appears to tap. For example, a respondent may consider himself or herself to be an extravert and recognize that the item "I enjoy going to parties" is an extraversion item. This respondent may then respond positively to the item, even if he or she does not particularly enjoy parties. Alternatively, the respondent may try to answer the question accurately but because of flawed memory or judgment processes he or she may make a mistake. In either case, if responses to the item predict relevant outcomes like the number of sensation seeking behaviors in which people engage or the number of friends that individuals have, then the item holds some degree of validity. This is the principle behind empirical criterion keying, in which items are selected based on the extent to which they can predict some meaningful criterion (Anastasi, 1988; Meehl, 1945). Thus, even if we can show flaws in the processes that lead to self-reported judgments, these flaws do not necessarily invalidate the self-report measure. To assert that a measure lacks validity, researchers must also show that the measure fails to predict relevant criteria. Often, studies that purport to demonstrate the invalidity of self-report measures do so by showing that participants use irrelevant sources of information when constructing judgments. However, the measures themselves may

still be valid, even if judgments are constructed in a nonintuitive or flawed manner.

Much of the research on the fallibility of self-reports comes from survey research, and the goals of survey research often differ from the goals of other forms of psychological measurement. In survey research, researchers often focus on mean levels or frequencies within a specific population. For instance, researchers may wish to assess the likelihood of a certain population voting for a particular political candidate. If some feature of the questionnaire leads to an overestimation of support for a candidate, then the self-reported survey response is invalid. But in much psychological research, the absolute level of a characteristic is not meaningful, and researchers use scores on a self-report inventory as correlates or predictors of other outcomes. As Schwarz et al. (1998) have noted, many of the response effects identified in the survey literature have a larger effect on mean levels and other characteristics of item distributions than on correlational results. Thus, when possible, we will distinguish between these two types of effects.

THE PROCESS OF SELF-REPORT JUDGMENTS

Researchers have proposed a number of theories that outline processes thought to occur when a participant responds to a self-report measure. These theories are described elsewhere in great detail (e.g., Schwarz, 1999; Schwarz et al., 1998; Schwarz & Sudman, 1996; Strack & Martin, 1987; Sudman, Bradburn, & Schwarz, 1996; Tourangeau et al., 2000), and a comprehensive review of these theories is beyond the scope of this chapter. Instead, we provide an overview of some of the major processes that underlie self-reports, focusing on ways that these processes can influence self-reports. In addition, we examine the evidence that exists about the extent to which artifacts and unwanted method effects can influence the validity of self-reports of various constructs.

Understanding the Question
When an individual responds to a self-report measure, he or she must first make sense of the question being asked (Schwarz, 1999; Tourangeau et al.,

2000). To do this, the respondent must understand the literal meaning of the question, and anything that impedes this understanding (e.g., vague or unfamiliar words, complicated sentence structure) will undermine the quality of the self-report measure. Psychological assessment and survey methodology textbooks suggest that to avoid misunderstandings, question writers should keep items simple and avoid potentially unfamiliar words (see Tourangeau et al., 2000, and Schmitt, this volume, chap. 2, for more detailed recommendations). Careful pretesting of items can prevent misunderstandings from occurring (see Schwarz & Sudman, 1996, for discussions of these pretesting techniques).

Yet understanding the words themselves gets the respondent only so far. Respondents must then discern the pragmatic meaning of a question. Often, a question that is clear in a literal sense can be interpreted in many different ways. When interpreting questions, respondents may try to infer what the experimenter had in mind. As Schwarz (1996) and others (e.g., Clark & Shober, 1992; Tourangeau et al., 2000) have noted, these inferences are often based on norms regarding how a conversation should progress (see Grice, 1975, 1989, for a detailed discussion of these principles). For instance, conversation participants implicitly expect that their counterparts will not provide nor expect redundant information. Thus, respondents who come across two similar questions in the same questionnaire may assume that the experimenter meant something different with each question unless there is some plausible explanation for the repetition.

Strack, Schwarz, and Wänke (1991) demonstrated that this nonredundancy norm affects how individuals respond to questionnaire items. In their study, experimenters asked participants two questions about their subjective well-being. First, the experimenters asked participants how "happy" they were and then how "satisfied" they were. Strack et al. also varied the manner in which these questions were presented. In one condition, the happiness and satisfaction questions were presented as two questions within the same questionnaire. In a second condition, experimenters presented the two questions as the last question of one questionnaire

and the first question of a separate, unrelated questionnaire. Responses to the two questions were less strongly correlated when presented as part of the same questionnaire than when the two questions were presented as the last question on one questionnaire and as the first question on a separate questionnaire. Presumably, respondents who were asked the two questions within the same questionnaire assumed that the experimenter believed that happiness and satisfaction formulated two distinct constructs, and therefore these respondents exaggerated the subtle difference in meaning when responding to the question.

Strack et al.'s (1991) study provides important insight into the processes that occur when respondents interpret and answer survey questions. Yet it is unclear whether these processes are likely to affect the validity of most self-report items—the same conversational norms that guide respondents' interpretation of questions may also guide questionnaire construction. It may seem unlikely that researchers would put two questions with nearly identical content side by side in a questionnaire unless the experimenter was actually interested in the subtle distinctions among similar items. However, there are a number of reasons why Strack et al.'s findings are important for researchers interested in self-report methods. First, researchers may include very similar questions in different parts of a questionnaire to check for careless responding, and the same conversational norms may still apply when the questions are not presented side by side.

But more important, Schwarz, Strack, and colleagues have demonstrated that these principles also apply in more subtle situations. For example, Schwarz, Strack, and Mai (1991) found similar effects with a more realistic example of questions that might be asked in a questionnaire. Specifically, they asked respondents two different questions about their life satisfaction, again varying the presentation of the questions. In one condition, respondents were first asked about their satisfaction with their marriage and then asked about their satisfaction with life. In a second condition, these two questions were preceded by a joint lead-in that informed participants that they would be asked two questions about their subjective well-being. With-

out the joint lead-in, responses to the two questions correlated .67; with the lead-in, responses correlated .18. Presumably, the joint lead-in activated the norm of nonredundancy and participants interpreted the life satisfaction question in such a way that they excluded satisfaction with marriage from the overall life satisfaction judgment. Conclusions about the role of marital satisfaction in life satisfaction will vary depending on this subtle difference in question presentation.

Respondents use a variety of contextual features to interpret the meaning of questions (see Schwarz, 1996, for a more comprehensive review). For instance, Winkielman, Knäuper, and Schwarz (1998) manipulated the time frame of a survey question about the experience of anger. They found that people interpreted the question differently depending on the time frame that was used. Specifically, Winkielman et al. found that when respondents were asked about episodes in which they were angry "during the past week," they described less severe anger episodes than when the question asked about episodes occurring "during the past year."

Schwarz, Knäuper, Hippler, Noelle-Neumann, and Clark (1991) also showed that the response options provided with a scale could influence interpretation of the question. In their studies, Schwarz et al. asked participants to rate how successful they have been in life. Some participants were presented with a response scale that ranged from 0 ("not at all successful") to 10 ("extremely successful") whereas other participants were presented with a response scale that ranged from –5 to +5, and which used the same response anchors. Although the anchors were identical, fewer participants responded with values between –5 and 0 on the –5 to +5 scale than with values between 0 and 5 on the 0 to 10 scale. Although researchers might treat these two scales as being identical (because both use 11 points), the specific numbers on the scale may influence the interpretation of the item.

Schimmack, Böckenholt, and Reisenzein (2002) demonstrated a similar phenomenon using affect ratings. However, in their study, Schimmack et al. showed that response scales do not just affect the number of participants who choose a particular response option, but also that these subtle differences can affect correlations with other variables. Specifically, Schimmack et al. sought to determine whether positive affect (which consists of positive emotions, e.g., joy, happiness, and excitement) and negative affect (which consists of negative emotions and moods, e.g., unhappiness, fear, and depression) formed a single bipolar dimension or two unipolar dimensions. The researchers investigated the correlations between positive affect and negative affect when various response options were used (e.g., "strongly disagree" to "strongly agree," "does not describe me at all" to "describes me perfectly," and "not at all" to "with maximum intensity"). In addition, they asked participants to indicate where on the response scale a person scores if they were in a neutral mood.

In accordance with their hypotheses, Schimmack et al. (2002) found that when respondents were asked whether they experienced a particular emotion (e.g., cheerful) using a scale that ranged from "strongly disagree" to "strongly agree," most participants indicated that the neutral point was in the middle of the scale at the point labeled "neither agree nor disagree." When participants were asked to indicate where the neutral point was on an intensity scale that ranged from "not" to "maximum intensity," a large minority indicated that the lowest score on the scale should reflect a neutral response. Schimmack et al. argued that when given an agree/disagree response scale, respondents infer that the experimenter is asking about a bipolar dimension that ranges from extremely happy to extremely unhappy. When given an intensity scale, on the other hand, respondents are more likely to infer that the experimenter is asking about a unipolar dimension that ranges from extremely happy to neutral. In accordance with this interpretation, positive and negative affect items correlated more strongly when an agree/disagree response scale was used than when an intensity scale was used. The Schimmack et al. study is important because it demonstrates that differences in conclusions about bipolarity that have been found across studies may be due to the subtle contextual information that respondents use to understand the content of self-report items.

The research reviewed above demonstrates that contextual factors play an important role in

question comprehension. Subtle changes in question wording, question order, question presentation, and response options can influence the responses that respondents give. In discussing the effects of contextual variables in the context of self-reports of well-being, Schwarz and Strack (1999) argued that after seeing this evidence most people would conclude, "there is little to be learned from global self-reports of well-being" (p. 80). They went on to argue that "although these reports do reflect subjectively meaningful assessments, what is being assessed, and how, seems too context dependent to provide reliable information about a population's well-being" (p. 81). Although it is clear that in carefully controlled experimental settings, respondents' answers to self-report questions can be affected, very little research has examined how pervasive these effects are. It is possible that these subtle manipulations may add only a small amount of unwanted variance relative to the amount of true variance that these scales capture. For instance, when conducting multimethod research, researchers may find that contextual factors do not substantially change the correlation between self-reports and other indicators (e.g., informant reports). Contextual factors may influence self-reported assessments, but more work is needed in this area to determine the impact these factors have on existing self-report methods.

Formulating a Response

Once respondents understand a self-report question, they must formulate an answer. The processes involved in constructing an answer vary depending on the type of self-report being made. When reporting on the frequency of a specific behavior, for instance, respondents might be able to search their memory, count the number of occasions on which the behavior occurred, and report the counted value. When reporting an attitude, on the other hand, respondents must search their memory for relevant information about the object, compare the attitude object to some relevant standard of comparison, and then make a judgment about their feelings toward that object (Schwarz, 1999). In this section, we distinguish between self-reports of behaviors and events that have occurred in the past,

and self-reports of ongoing psychological phenomena (e.g., attitudes, beliefs, and intentions). We acknowledge, however, that this is not the only way to categorize self-report judgments, and that many self-reports do not fit neatly into either category.

Retrospective self-reports on events and behaviors. Many self-report questions ask participants to retrospectively evaluate the frequency, intensity, or some other characteristic of an event, a behavior, or a psychological phenomenon that was experienced in the past. This type of report can include self-reports of specific behaviors (e.g., "Did you vote in the last election?" or "During the past month, how many times have you been to the hospital?"), self-reports of events (e.g., "Have you ever been laid off from a job?"), and even self-reports of psychological phenomena (e.g., "How much pain did you feel over the course of the past hour?" or "How often have you felt unhappy over the past month?"). To answer this type of self-report question, respondents should simply be able to search their memory and compute a response. Unfortunately, although this idealized process might occur in a few rare occasions, limitations of memory are likely to complicate the recall of relevant information. Specifically, when the behavior or event is fairly frequent, people may forget about certain instances and underreport. Alternatively, if the phenomenon is somewhat rare, participants may be likely to over-report or to telescope—to remember it as having occurred within a particular reference period although it happened at some point before or after (Loftus, Smith, Klinger, & Fiedler, 1992; Sudman & Bradburn, 1973).

To deal with these problems, researchers can use a number of different strategies. First, researchers can limit their questions to behaviors and events that are likely to be recalled. For example, accuracy of recall usually decreases as the length of time since the event increases, and therefore recent events will be remembered better than more distant events (Bradburn, Rips, & Shevell, 1987). Similarly, accuracy tends to decrease as the length of the reference period increases, and therefore, accuracy can be maintained by focusing on relatively short reference periods. Unfortunately, there are disadvantages of these

approaches. For example, Schwarz et al. (1998) noted that when assessing rare behaviors, short reference periods might lead to frequent zero responses. In addition, it may not always be possible to ask people about events soon after they have occurred. Thus, there may be certain research questions that require longer time periods or longer delays.

When researchers cannot limit the focus of their investigation to easily remembered phenomena, they can use alternative strategies that have been shown to improve recall. For example, providing meaningful temporal boundaries for reference periods (e.g., important life events), allowing respondents adequate time to recall events, providing recall cues, and breaking the reference period down into smaller periods (a technique called decomposition) may all improve accuracy (see Tourangeau et al., 2000, and Schmitt, this volume, chap. 2, for a review). Even variations in the order in which people are asked to remember events may affect recall. Loftus et al. (1992), for example, showed that having people remember events in a chronological order was more successful than having people remember events in a reverse chronological order.

Yet even with these techniques, recall is likely to be inaccurate in many situations. People are unlikely to have specific memories of each and every occurrence of a behavior, and reports of past experiences may reflect estimation processes rather than direct memory processes (Strube, 1987). Thus, a third strategy is to develop a better understanding of the estimation processes that respondents use when searching their memory and when responding to retrospective questions. By doing so, researchers may be better able to understand the ways that these answers are flawed and better able to interpret patterns of responses that may not reflect a direct memory of the underlying event (Pearson, Ross, & Dawes, 1992).

For instance, Tourangeau et al. (2000) outlined four broad strategies that individuals can use when reporting on the frequency of behaviors or events (also see Blair & Burton, 1987). In some cases, individuals may be able to remember specific episodic information and then extrapolate from those instances to determine an overall frequency. In other cases, individuals may not search episodic

memory at all. Instead, they may rely on general ideas about the behaviors they exhibit. For example, when asked to report on specific foods that they ate over the past week, respondents may rely on general knowledge about what they typically eat rather than searching memory for specific instances from the past week. Respondents may also use what Tourangeau et al. call a "general impression" approach in which very little information is actually accessed from memory. Instead, respondents form a general impression and translate that impression into a meaningful response. Strategies within this approach range from pure guessing to translating a vague notion to a specific answer based on contextual information (e.g., the available response options; Schwarz, Hippler, Deutsch, & Strack, 1985). Finally, for certain types of frequency judgments, people may have a stored tally that they can report with little effort. For example, graduate students who are on the job market may be able to quickly access a stored report of how many journal articles they have published in their career.

A variety of factors may influence the strategies people use. These different strategies may, in turn, affect the judgment at which people arrive. For instance, characteristics of the individuals themselves may influence judgments. Ross (1989) posited that implicit theories of personal stability and change influence the way people construct retrospective judgments of behaviors, traits, and attitudes. Specifically, he argued that recall of personal experiences and attributes involves a two-step process in which people first judge their present status and then determine whether this is different from where they were in the past. People's implicit theories about whether they are the same or different may then influence the information recalled (Pearson et al., 1992).

In addition to characteristics of the respondent, aspects of the question itself can influence frequency estimates. Schwarz et al. (1985) demonstrated this in an experiment designed to assess the impact that available response options have on people's answers. In their study, participants were asked to estimate how much television they watch on a daily basis. In one condition, participants responded on a scale that ranged from "up to a half

hour" to "more than two and a half hours"; in a second condition, participants responded on a scale that ranged from "up to two and a half hours" to "more than four and a half hours." Participants in the former condition reported watching television for a shorter period of time than did participants in the latter condition. This pattern of findings is consistent with a "general impression" approach to answering self-report questions. Some respondents may quickly formulate a general idea about how much television they watch and then translate that general notion into a meaningful response based on contextual information. For instance, a respondent may believe that he or she watches a lot of television compared to other individuals. He or she may then simply mark the highest category regardless of what the anchor for that category is.

More general features of the task may also influence recall. Blair and Burton (1987) identified five features of the self-report task that may influence which strategy individuals will use in responding to a particular question. Specifically, they argued that the effort required to complete a task, the motivation of the respondent to expend the necessary effort, the accessibility of the events or behaviors to be remembered, the availability of additional estimation processes besides searching episodic memory, and other task features "that encourage or require particular cognitive processes" (p. 282) are all likely to affect recall. Thus, even when respondents are asked to respond to similar questions, various task features may make it more or less likely that they will engage in a systematic search of their memory. These processes may result in different self-reported judgments for very similar questions.

Robinson and Clore (2002a) recently proposed a model of emotional self-report that builds on these ideas (also see Robinson & Neighbors, this volume, chap. 9). Specifically, they argued that different characteristics of the emotion judgment lead to different types of processing. Individuals who are asked to describe an ongoing emotional experience can access and report this experiential information quite easily. In addition, when asked to report on recent emotions experienced over relatively short periods of time, individuals can search their mem-

ory and retrospectively reconstruct their emotional experience. However, beyond periods of a few hours, this task gets very difficult, and participants are more likely to rely on semantic knowledge including beliefs about how they should feel in such a situation. Thus, respondents may give very different information when asked to report how they are feeling right now than if they were asked to remember their current feelings at some later point. The latter judgments may be more likely to be influenced by beliefs and stereotypes.

To test this idea, Robinson, Johnson, and Shields (1998) induced emotion in a group of participants and then randomly assigned participants to report on their emotion immediately (the online condition) or after a week-long delay (the retrospective condition). In accordance with their predictions, sex differences in reports of emotion were only found in the retrospective condition. Robinson et al. also asked a third group of participants to imagine how they would feel in this situation, and participants in this hypothetical condition showed sex differences in emotional reports that were similar to the sex differences in the retrospective condition.

Studies that examine retrospective reports of emotion should also alert readers to an additional complicating factor in global self-assessment. Certain reports may require participants to go beyond simply counting the number of occurrences. For instance, researchers may be interested in determining how much pain a person has felt over the course of a week. Presumably, the researcher would want to know the number of occasions during which a respondent felt pain in addition to the duration and intensity of those episodes. An overall judgment of pain would require the integration of the frequency, duration, and intensity information. Unfortunately, this type of integration is difficult to do, and judgments that require such computations are very difficult to make (Kahneman, 1999).

For instance, Kahneman and his colleagues have shown that respondents often neglect the duration of an episode when making an overall evaluation (although see Ariely, Kahneman, & Loewenstein, 2000, for a discussion of some unresolved issues regarding this effect). In one study that demonstrated

this effect, Redelmeier and Kahneman (1996) examined the amount of pain patients experienced during a colonoscopy. Participants reported their pain every minute during the procedure, and then at the end of the procedure they provided an overall evaluation of the amount of pain they experienced. Redelmeier and Kahneman showed that the duration of the painful experience was relatively unimportant in determining the overall evaluation of the procedure. Instead, two factors—the peak intensity and the end intensity—were strongly predictive of the overall evaluation. Participants seemed to focus on the worst pain they experienced during the procedure and the pain they experienced at the end of the procedure when computing an overall evaluation.

Redelmeier, Katz, and Kahneman (2003) took advantage of this "peak/end" phenomenon to improve patients' evaluation of a colonoscopy procedure. In their study, two groups of participants went through similar colonoscopies, with pain that varied from mild to fairly extreme over the course of the procedure. For one group of participants, the procedure was then unnecessarily extended with a period of mild pain. The group who experienced the extended procedure reported a more positive global evaluation than the group that experienced the shorter procedure. This study and others like it (e.g., Fredrickson & Kahneman, 1993; Kahneman, Fredrickson, Schreiber, & Redelmeier, 1993; Varey & Kahneman, 1992) demonstrate that global judgments that require computations beyond simple counting often involve heuristic processes that lead to judgments that are not necessarily logical.

Self-reports of ongoing psychological phenomena. Reporting the frequency and intensity of past experiences is clearly a complicated process. But additional processes come into play when people are asked to report on psychological constructs like attitudes, intentions, and beliefs. For instance, when reporting on an attitude, respondents must first develop an understanding of the object to be evaluated, search their memory for relevant information about the object, and then determine how they feel about it (Schwarz, 1999). Similar processes must occur when reporting on beliefs and intentions, although there may not be any evaluative component with these latter reports.

Initially, researchers interested in this type of self-report judgment relied on what is known as a "file-drawer" model of psychological judgment (Tourangeau et al., 2000, for a review of these early theories). According to the file-drawer model, when researchers ask people to respond to a self-report item (e.g., an attitude question or a personality item), individuals should have ready-made responses that they can simply access and report. Subsequent research has shown that self-reports of psychological phenomena are rarely made in this way. Instead, people often construct judgments on the spot using information available to them at the time (Schwarz, 1999). Some of this information—chronically accessible information—may be used very consistently from one judgment occasion to the next. Other temporarily accessible information may be used inconsistently across occasions. Judgments based on chronically accessible information should be stable across situations, whereas judgments based on temporarily accessible information will likely be unstable over time (Schimmack, Diener, & Oishi, 2002).

To demonstrate that respondents do use temporarily accessible information to construct attitude judgments on the spot, Schwarz and Clore (1983) examined the situational factors that influenced judgments about satisfaction with life. In their study, experimenters called participants and asked them about their life satisfaction either on a warm, sunny day or on a cold, rainy day. Presumably, people should feel better on the sunny day than on the rainy day. If people construct satisfaction judgments on the spot, then judgments may be influenced by current mood. In accordance with this prediction, satisfaction judgments were higher on the sunny day than on the rainy day.

Interestingly, Schwarz and Clore (1983) were able to demonstrate how the temporarily accessible mood information was used in constructing global satisfaction judgments. Mood effects have repeatedly been shown to influence judgments, but there has been debate about the process that underlies this effect (see Schwarz & Clore, 1996, for a

review). Some researchers argue that mood affects judgment by increasing the likelihood that mood-congruent information will be accessible at the time of judgment (e.g., Bower, 1981; Isen, Shalker, Clark, & Karp, 1978). A person in a good mood who is asked to make a satisfaction judgment may be able to remember more positive aspects of his or her life than would someone in a bad mood, and this increased recall of positive information would lead to higher satisfaction judgments. Schwarz and Strack (1999), on the other hand, argued that people's current mood serves as "a parsimonious indicator of their well-being in general" (p. 75). In other words, rather than thinking carefully about the conditions in their lives, people may simply consider how they feel at that moment and use that as a proxy for a more carefully constructed judgment. To demonstrate that this process is likely occurring, Schwarz and Clore manipulated situational factors in such a way as to have participants discount the informational value of their current mood. Specifically, in one condition, the caller first asked participants how the weather was at their location. Presumably, this manipulation alerted the participant to the fact that their mood might be due to the weather. In this condition, there were no differences between people who were asked about their satisfaction on sunny days versus those who were asked on rainy days.

Research shows that many different types of information can be used in self-reported judgments. For instance, when judging one's satisfaction with life, a person presumably reviews the conditions in his or her life and uses that information to make a judgment. Unless the search is always exhaustive, anything that makes relevant information more salient at the time of judgment will increase the likelihood that that information will be used. Thus, simply asking people to think about relevant information before making a judgment will increase the probability that that information will be used. Schwarz et al. (1991; also see Strack, Martin, & Schwarz, 1988), for example, showed that asking people about their satisfaction with life immediately after they were asked about their satisfaction with their relationship increased the correlation between responses to the two questions (as long as non-

redundancy norms were not activated). Presumably, by making the relationship salient at the time of judgment, the experimenters increased the likelihood that the respondent would use that information when making the life satisfaction judgment.

In addition, making an evaluative judgment of some object often requires comparing that judgment to some additional standard (Schwarz, 1999). Thus, any situational factors that influence the comparison standards that participants use will influence their evaluation. For instance, Strack, Schwarz, and Gschneidinger (1985) asked participants to report on three positive or negative life events that happened to them in the recent or distant past. Then, participants were asked to rate their current life satisfaction. Presumably, participants who reported on recent events would exhibit assimilation effects in which the recent positive events made their current life seem better and recent negative events made their current life seem worse. Participants who reported on more distant events, on the other hand, should exhibit contrast effects in which the positive and negative events were part of a previous state of affairs against which his or her current life could be compared. Not surprisingly, the participants who reported recent positive events reported higher life satisfaction than participants who reported recent negative life events. However, participants who reported three distant positive events actually reported lower satisfaction than participants who reported distant negative events. This study shows that salient information about comparison standards may also affect evaluative judgments of an object itself.

A complete review of all the sources of information that could influence self-reported judgments is beyond the scope of this chapter, but it is important to note that respondents often use information that is not always obvious. For instance, Schwarz and Clore (1996) reviewed evidence that people use feelings as information, even if those feelings have very little to do with the judgment itself. Schwarz, Bless, Strack, Klumpp, Rittenauer-Schatka, and Simons (1991) demonstrated this in a study that investigated whether people use the perceived difficulty of recalling trait-relevant behaviors when making personality judgments. Specifically, they

asked one group of participants to report 6 examples of assertive behaviors in which they engaged, and they asked a second group of participants to report 12 examples of assertive behaviors. The former task should be accomplished more easily than the second task, and participants may use feelings of difficulty in retrieval as information about their standing on a trait. In accordance with their hypotheses, Schwarz et al. found that participants in the 12-behavior condition rated themselves as being lower in assertiveness than did participants in the 6-behavior condition although participants in the 12-behavior condition remembered and reported more assertive behaviors. Studies like this one show that a broad array of informational factors can influence subjective judgments.

The major question for researchers who use self-reports is the extent to which global self-assessments are driven by irrelevant and temporarily accessible information versus relevant and chronically accessible information. Although numerous experimental studies show that temporarily accessible information does affect judgments, other correlational research shows that chronically accessible information may outweigh these irrelevant factors. To address this question, Schimmack, Diener, and Oishi (2002) explicitly asked participants to report on the information that they used to compute well-being judgments. They found that people reported using chronically accessible information when making judgments, and the factors that respondents said they used did, in fact, correlate with their satisfaction judgments. In addition, those individuals who reported using different sources of information at different times had less stability in their well-being scores. Similarly, Eid and Diener (2004) showed that factors like current mood do not play a large role in subjective reports of well-being. Instead, well-being reports are relatively stable, even in the face of changing mood across situations.

Reporting a Response

The final step in making a self-reported judgment is to communicate that judgment to the investigator. Anything that impedes the accuracy of this communication will affect the validity of the report. For instance, when reporting on illegal or other socially undesirable behaviors, participants may simply decide not to tell the truth. Alternatively, when asked to respond using a Likert response scale, respondents may attempt to provide an accurate response, but different respondents may use the scale differently, resulting in unwanted method variance. As with all the other steps in the process of constructing a self-reported judgment, we must first ask what can go wrong when communicating a response. We can then go on to investigate the evidence that such errors do occur and the impact that these errors have on the validity of self-report measures.

Perhaps the most widely studied issue in the communication of self-reported judgments is the extent to which socially desirable responding distorts the validity of self-report measures. At its simplest, socially desirable responding can be defined as the tendency to endorse items that others would consider to be positive. Early work in the area focused on social desirability both as a property of items or scales and as an individual difference variable (Edwards, 1957; Messick, 1960; Wiggins, 1964). Edwards (1953, 1957), for instance, demonstrated that the probability that respondents would endorse an item could be predicted by the degree to which the trait or characteristic in the item was socially desirable. Researchers used this finding to argue that participants were not responding to the content of the items, but rather to the desirability of the items (see Hogan & Nicholson, 1988; Nicholson & Hogan, 1990, for a discussion). An alternative possibility, of course, is that desirable characteristics are, in fact, more common than undesirable ones (Edwards, 1953).

What is more troublesome for researchers interested in self-report methodology is that the tendency to endorse socially desirable responses varies across individuals, and this individual difference tends to correlate moderately to strongly with measures of adjustment. Messick (1960), for instance, showed that the tendency to respond in a socially desirable manner was reliably correlated with several clinical and personality scales. Such findings have led to the question of whether individual differences in personality and adjustment scales reflect individual differences in socially desirable responding to a greater

extent than they reflect the content the scale developers intended to measure.

Attempts to understand and control for social desirability are complicated by the fact that most modern researchers believe that social desirability is not a single, unidimensional construct. Instead, most current models focus on a two-factor structure that may underlie the various measures of social desirability (Paulhus, 1984). The first of these factors reflects an intentional attempt to present oneself in a favorable light. Paulhus labeled this individual difference as impression management. He contrasted individual differences in this conscious process with individual differences in self-deception. According to Paulhus, self-deception was a more unconscious process that reflects respondents' belief that they are better than objective information would suggest.

Several theorists have offered suggestions on how to deal with the unwanted variance that socially desirable responding adds to scale scores (Block, 1965; Edwards, 1957; Nederhof, 1985; Paulhus, 1981). These suggestions vary depending on which aspect of social desirability one wants to control. For instance, some researchers have noted that socially desirable responding seems to be more pronounced in face-to-face interviews than in mail surveys or other more anonymous formats (e.g., Richman, Kiesler, Weisband, & Drasgow, 1999; Strack, Schwarz, Chassein, Kern, & Wagner, 1990). If so, the impact of social desirability may be reduced by ensuring anonymity. However, this strategy may work better for the more conscious process of impression management than for the more unconscious process of self-deception.

In addition, there are various statistical techniques and questionnaire construction techniques that researchers can use to limit the effect of social desirability. Paulhus (1981) organized these methods into three categories: rational, covariate, and factor-analytic techniques. Rational techniques focus on developing scales in which it is difficult to determine which items or responses are socially desirable or in which all items are matched for desirability (e.g., forced choice items in which respondents are asked to choose between two

equally desirable responses can lessen the impact of social desirability).

The second strategy for dealing with social desirability is the use of covariation techniques (Paulhus, 1981). These methods require the administration of some measure of socially desirable responding in addition to the content scales of interest. If social desirability adds unwanted variance to a measure, then it should act as a suppressor variable. Thus, by first controlling for the effects of social desirability, the correlation between a self-report and an outcome or criterion variable should increase (Paulhus, 1981). However, the usefulness of this technique may vary depending on which aspect of social desirability one is measuring. A number of researchers have argued that the self-deception aspect of social desirability is related to measures of adjustment, and controlling for individual differences in self-deception may remove valid variance (McCrae & Costa, 1983; Paulhus, 1984).

To test this possibility, McCrae and Costa (1983) compared corrected and uncorrected self-reports of personality with the external criterion of spouse reports. If social desirability distorts test scores, then the corrected self-reports should correlate more strongly with the spouse reports than the uncorrected self-reports. However, their results indicated that correcting for social desirability failed to improve the validity of self-reported personality. Instead, McCrae and Costa sometimes found lower correlations between corrected self-reports and the criterion variables. This pattern of findings suggests that controlling for social desirability may remove meaningful variance from test scores.

The third approach to dealing with social desirability is useful when extracting factors from an item (or scale) correlation matrix (Paulhus, 1981). Early research on social desirability focused on the extent to which the factors that emerged when a broad array of personality and adjustment scales were factor analyzed represented content factors versus social desirability (e.g., Block, 1965; Messick, 1991). Paulhus (1981) argued that because socially desirable responding will affect most items, the first unrotated factor that emerges from a factor analysis

will reflect social desirability (Paulhus gives strategies for verifying this). If so, the first factor could be dropped, the item communalities adjusted, and the remaining factors rotated in any way that the researcher feels is appropriate. Presumably, this would result in factors that are free from influence of socially desirable responding.

There are two major types of effects that researchers examine when looking at the role of social desirability in self-reported assessment: the effect of social desirability on the criterion validity of a measure and the effect of social desirability on the underlying factor structure. Researchers have debated the pervasiveness and importance of these effects for decades (see, e.g., Block, 1965; McCrae & Costa, 1983; Messick, 1991; Rorer, 1965; Smith & Ellingson, 2002). However, in a recent series of studies within the organizational literature, Ellingson and her colleagues provided evidence that neither of these two types of effects tends to be large. Ellingson, Sackett, and Hough (1999) asked participants to complete personality inventories under two separate instructions, an honest condition and a "fake-good" condition. Ellingson et al. then corrected the faked scores for social desirability and compared corrected reports with the honest reports. They found that the corrected mean scores on the personality scales were closer in value to the honest scores, but that validity of the scales (as indicated by the correlation between the corrected and honest scores) was not improved after correction. In addition, when examining the implications for selection procedures in an organizational context, they concluded that "applying a correction made little difference in the proportion of correct selection decisions across various selection scenarios" (p. 163). Ellingson, Smith, and Sackett (2001) also examined the effects of social desirability on the factor structure of personality scales by using multigroup confirmatory factor analysis across groups of high and low socially desirable responders. Social desirability had very little effect on the factor structure of the measures (although other studies have found such effects; see Ellingson et al., 2001, for a review).

Social desirability is not the only process that can affect the communication of self-reported judg-ments. Researchers have also focused on such response styles and response sets as acquiescence (the tendency to answer "true" or "yes"), deviance (the tendency to give strange or unusual responses), or extreme responding (the tendency to use extreme numbers). Anastasi (1988) noted that like research on social desirability, debate about these response sets and styles has focused on the extent to which these individual differences reflect irrelevant versus meaningful trait variance. Although debate about the pervasiveness of these response processes continues, researchers should be aware that these effects may influence the communication of self-reports and take steps to avoid them or measure their impact. Of course, as the other chapters in this volume make clear, multimethod research is one of the best ways to overcome the problems associated with communicating self-reported judgments.

ACCURACY OF SELF-REPORTS

Given that many problems can emerge when respondents construct a self-reported judgment, the final issue that we will address concerns the accuracy and validity of the self-report method. Although errors surely do occur, they often do not severely limit the validity of the measures. For instance, self-reports often agree with non-self-report measures of the same construct. Within the well-being domain, for instance, researchers have shown that self-reports of happiness and life satisfaction correlate moderately to strongly with such diverse methods as observer ratings, online assessments, and cognitive measures including the number of positive and negative memories that can be recalled in a short period of time (Lucas, Diener, & Suh, 1996; Pavot, Diener, Colvin, & Sandvik, 1991). Similarly, personality researchers have shown that although the accuracy of self-reports varies across individuals, contexts, and the specific trait or behavior being rated, self-reports are often very good predictors of alternative measures of the same construct (Gosling, John, Craik, & Robins, 1998; John & Robins, 1993; Spain, Eaton, & Funder, 2000).

Furthermore, even when self-reports disagree with non-self-report methods, there is often evidence that the disagreement is not due to mistakes on the part of the respondent. For instance, Nelson et al. (1983) examined the discrepancies between self-reported and doctor-rated health. When Nelson et al. asked doctors about the discrepancies, they found that in 44% of the cases, the doctors reported that the discrepancy was due to their own error. An additional 12% of discrepancies stemmed from a lack of knowledge of the patient. Other studies show that even when self-reports of health differ from non-self-report methods, the self-reports often predict important outcomes including mortality (e.g., Ganz, Lee, & Siau, 1991; McClellan, Anson, Birkeli, & Tuttle, 1991; Mossey & Shapiro, 1982; Rumsfeld et al., 1999). Thus, although errors in self-reported judgments surely occur, self-reports often demonstrate impressive accuracy, predictability, and utility in important research settings.

SUMMARY

The research reviewed in this chapter demonstrates that some degree of skepticism about global self-assessment is warranted. The processes involved in constructing responses to self-report questions are complicated, and these processes do not always occur in a logical and consistent manner. Respondents may fail to think carefully about their judgments, they may use idiosyncratic processes when making a response, and they may rely on inconsistent and temporarily accessible information rather than conducting an exhaustive search of their memory. Furthermore, in many situations it is difficult to tell whether respondents are accurately communicating their true response to the researcher. Some respondents may wish to present themselves in a favorable light, whereas others may simply use response scales in idiosyncratic and unpredictable ways.

Yet in spite of these limitations, self-reports have many benefits. These methods are very flexible and efficient; and perhaps most important, they provide access to information that would be very difficult to

obtain in any other way. Thus, the key question for researchers interested in using self-report is whether the errors and the sources of unwanted variance described in this chapter strongly affect the validity of self-report measures. Simply demonstrating that these effects can occur in experimental studies does not prove that they severely limit the validity of self-reports used in other contexts. In some cases, effects that have been demonstrated in experimental settings have been shown to have only a minimal impact on the validity of self-report measures (e.g., Eid & Diener, 2004). In addition, research in a number of domains shows that self-reports can be accurate, valid, and predictive of important outcomes.

Self-reports, like any measurement technique, have distinct strengths and weaknesses. Respondents may have unique access to information about the construct of interest, but they may be unable or unwilling to accurately report on this construct. However, errors that result from respondents' inability to remember past behaviors or their unwillingness to accurately report their feelings are unlikely to be shared across different measurement techniques. For instance, experience sampling measures of online experiences can be used to counteract memory problems (Stone & Litcher-Kelly, this volume, chap. 5); informant reports can be used to overcome respondents' unwillingness to respond honestly (Neyer, this volume, chap. 4). In addition, new developments in implicit and other cognitive measures (Robinson & Neighbors, this volume, chap. 9), as well as advances in psychophysiological measurement (Berntson & Cacioppo, this volume, chap. 12) offer new alternatives to self-report in domains like emotion and attitude assessment. Each technique has its own set of problems, and any single strategy will likely be most useful when used in combination with additional techniques. Thus, self-reports, like all assessments, are most effective when used as part of a comprehensive multimethod battery. Researchers who use multimethod assessment in this way can reap the benefits of self-report while avoiding many of the problems associated with this useful technique.

CHAPTER 4

INFORMANT ASSESSMENT

Franz J. Neyer

Knowledgeable informants are frequently employed as data-gathering instruments in all domains of research in psychology. Informant assessments correspond with one of the basic data types known in psychology, which has been called *L-data* (i.e., life data recorded by observers) by Cattell (1957), *O-data* (i.e., data generated by observers) by Block (1977), or *I-data* (i.e., data derived from informants) by Funder (2004). Informants are people who usually share some brief history with a studied target. In addition to close relationship partners (e.g., spouses, peers, parents, siblings), other people with a lesser degree of acquaintance can also serve as informants (e.g., experts, teachers, workmates, etc.). Even so-called zero-acquaintances, who only observe episodes of a target's behavior within short interactions or from brief exposure, can also be informative. A variety of formats are used in informant assessment, including frequency estimates of specific behavior, ratings on global personality scales, Q-sort ratings of trait or behavioral profiles, and rank orders of individuals in groups. From a multitrait–multimethod perspective, informant assessment is a highly desirable tool to establish convergent validity. A strong convergent validation of a trait or behavioral construct is verified by strong *heteromethod* correlations of informant-rated measures with self-ratings, behavioral measures, or other operational criteria (Campbell & Fiske, 1959; Hoyt, 2000; Moskowitz, 1986; Ozer & Reise, 1994).

The problem of informant assessment equates to the problem of accuracy in interpersonal judgment, which Allport (1937) considered as a central topic

of personality psychology. The veridicality of informant assessment usually depends on the knowledge of informants, the observability of assessed traits, the aggregation level of informant ratings, and judgmental biases (Epstein, 1983; Rushton, Brainerd, & Pressley, 1983). Despite these problems, informant assessment is successfully used in many fields of psychological research. In personality and social psychology, informant ratings are frequently used to validate self-ratings of personality traits (e.g., Costa & McCrae, 1988; McCrae, 1994; Moskowitz & Schwarz, 1982; Roberts, Harms, Smith, Wood, & Webb, this volume, chap. 22; Smith & Harris, this volume, chap. 26). Sometimes self-ratings are contrasted with informant ratings (i.e., to study the extent and the effects of self-enhancement—e.g., Asendorpf & Ostendorf, 1998; Colvin, Block, & Funder, 1995). In developmental psychology, knowledgeable informants (e.g., parents, teachers, or peers) can be asked about the personality and behavior of children (e.g., Achenbach, McConaughy, & Howell, 1987; Coie, Cillessen, Dodge, Hubbard, Schwartz, Lemerise, & Bateman, 1999; Kremen & Block, 1998; Morris, Robinson, & Eisenberg, this volume, chap. 25). In clinical psychology, informants can provide important knowledge on adults' and children's psychopathology like symptomatic or personality disorders (e.g., Bagby, Rector, Bindseil, Dickens, Levitan, & Kennedy, 1998; Ball, Rounsaville, Tennen, & Kranzler, 2001; Burns & Haynes, this volume, chap. 27; Stanger & Lewis, 1993; Zucker, Morris, Ingram, Morris, & Bakeman, 2002).

This chapter gives an overview of the conceptual and methodological basics of informant assessment. Starting with a brief outline of Brunswik's lens model approach, the problem of accurate informant assessment is discussed. After a historical sketch of the role of informant assessment in accuracy research, three basic theoretical models of person perception are presented and discussed regarding their usefulness for informant assessment. The chapter then focuses on the validity of informant assessment and how it can be improved by considering important moderator variables. Finally, some guidelines for practice with respect to research design and statistical issues are presented.

BRUNSWIK'S LENS MODEL OF PERCEPTION

The veridicality of informant assessment is best conceptualized in terms of Brunswik's (1956) lens model, which serves as a common base for contemporary approaches to person perception (see Schmitt, this volume, chap. 2, Figure 2.2). The left side of the model is the target, or sender, who encodes cues, some of which are veridical indicators of underlying traits or behavioral dispositions (i.e., M1). On the right side is the informant, or perceiver, who decodes the behavioral cues that serve as a kind of lens through which a perceiver infers the underlying trait of a given target (i.e., M2). Overt cues, for instance, "seeks direct eye contact" and "initiates conversation" may serve as indirect cues leading the informant to infer a target's high level of extraversion. In Brunswik's model, *cue utilization* refers to the link between the observable cues and an informant's judgment. The link between the observable cue and the target's actual standing on the trait is referred to as *cue validity*. If both these links are veridical, then the informant's judgment should converge with the underlying trait and will result in *functional achievement*, which is equivalent to accurate informant assessment and is the third link.

How can the three links in Brunswik's lens model be operationalized? Cue utilization refers to the informant's decoding of behavioral cues and results when the informant's trait ratings of the target correlate with observable behavioral cues. Cue validity, in contrast, refers to a target's encoding of behavioral cues and results when the target's underlying trait correlates with the observed behavioral cues. Functional achievement represents the accuracy of the informant, which is a probabilistic association or in other words the correlation of the informant's trait rating with a given criterion. In general, decoding (i.e., cue utilization) is found to be stronger than encoding (i.e., cue validity), suggesting that the empirical association between informant ratings and observable cues is stronger than the association between the underlying traits and observable cues, especially when reliable assessments are obtained by using multiple informants (e.g., Borkenau & Liebler, 1992, 1993; Funder & Sneed, 1993; Gifford, 1991, 1994; Gosling, Ko, Mannarelli, & Morris, 2002; Scherer, 1978).

THE CRITERION PROBLEM OF ACCURATE INFORMANT ASSESSMENT

In terms of Brunswik's lens model, accurate perception is characterized by the convergence of cue validity and cue utilization. When researchers examine the accuracy of informant assessment, they inevitably face the criterion problem. Kruglanski (1989b) discussed three distinct notions of accuracy criteria used throughout the literature (i.e., the correspondence between a judgment and one or more independent indicators of the psychological construct, interpersonal consensus, and pragmatic utility). The first two meanings of accuracy appear most commonly, although they still leave researchers with the difficult challenge to convincingly justify their choice of criterion. Kenny (1994) proposed a general taxonomy of such correspondence-based criterion measures, which are either implicitly or explicitly used in informant assessment: (a) self-reports, (b) consensus, (c) expert ratings, (d) behavioral observations, and (e) operational criteria.

Self-reports can focus on personality traits, preferences, internal states, and cognitions, etc. Researchers frequently validate self-ratings and informant-ratings against each other and use the convergence of self-ratings and informant ratings

(i.e., *self–other agreement*) as one indicator of accuracy (e.g., Borkenau & Liebler, 1992; Funder, 1995), whereas others warn against using self-ratings as accuracy criteria, because self-reports may be invalid for several reasons (Kenny, 1994). First, self-reports may be biased because of social desirability and self-enhancement tendencies. Second, in some instances informants may have more privileged access to information than the self, or vice versa. Third, when the informant and the target are acquainted, the target may influence the informant with his or her standing on the trait. Nevertheless, self-ratings may be a valid criterion of informant accuracy if informant assessment is used to determine the subjective self-concept of one's personality.

Consensus refers to the agreement between two or multiple informants and is frequently observed to reach considerable levels (e.g., Ambady & Rosenthal, 1992; Borkenau, Mauer, Rieman, Spinath, & Angleitner, 2004; Borkenau, Riemann, Angleitner, & Spinath, 2001; Kenrick & Stringfield, 1980; Malloy & Albright, 1990; Paunonen & Jackson, 1987). In a general sense, accuracy implies consensus, and some researchers view consensus as a prerequisite of accuracy, rather than accuracy as a prerequisite of consensus. According to Funder (1995), consensus may be a necessary condition of accuracy, if accuracy is conceptualized in realistic terms. If parents, siblings, and teachers agree on an adolescent's level of introversion, for instance, the mean impression of these informants may converge with how this adolescent really behaves with peers or strangers. Although informants may certainly agree on a target, informants may not reach consensus, even though each informant may be partially accurate (e.g., the adolescent may be judged as cool by his peers, whereas his parents see him as irritable and anxious). Although these views are inconsistent, both are accurate in the contexts in which they were observed. Therefore, according to Kenny (1991), consensus is neither a necessary nor a sufficient condition for accuracy.

Expert ratings, obtained by professionals (e.g., teachers, clinicians, superiors, subordinates, colleagues, etc.) are used when a professional person, by definition, is judged to know the true state or disposition of the target under study. However, experts are not necessarily more useful than knowledgeable informants, because expert judgments also need validation. Thus the issue of accuracy of experts is as unresolved as the issue of accuracy of knowledgeable informants; why in a strict sense, expert ratings provide a criterion of consensus rather than accuracy in terms of Brunswik's model. In addition, a single expert might not exist to serve as the perfect criterion, and some experts hold more "expertise" than others, especially when studying a highly domain-specific trait or behavior.

Behavioral observation is often considered as the king's road to estimate a target's true trait, because it relies more on concretely coded or categorized behaviors instead of on vague judgments. The disadvantage of behavior observation as a criterion of accuracy is, however, related to its high costs in terms of time and methodology and its poor retest-consistency (Kenny, 1994). Although behavior observations can be improved by establishing high interrater reliability and the employment of objectively defined rating scales, in the end, behavioral observations strongly depend on situational factors and may be therefore conceived as arbitrary. Nevertheless, some important studies have shown that personality judgments by knowledgeable informants could yield substantial behavioral prediction (e.g., Funder & Colvin, 1991; Moskowitz & Schwarz, 1982). The epistemic relationship between behavior observation and accuracy is different from the relationship between consensus and accuracy: Whereas accuracy generally (albeit not always) implies consensus but consensus does not imply accuracy, the relation is reversed in behavior observation. An informant judgment can certainly hold accuracy regarding a particular observed behavior, but as noticed by Funder (1999, p. 106), a judgment that does not predict a particular behavior may still show accuracy toward predicting other behaviors.

Operational criteria can be useful if the criterion is known directly by definition (e.g., job performance or diagnostic criteria of psychological disorders). Such operational criteria can be also defined through experimental manipulation, as it is often used in lie detection and deception research (DePaulo, Lindsay, Malone, Muhlenbruck, Charlton,

& Cooper, 2003). According to Kenny (1994), operational criteria are less useful in determining the validity of personality ratings because it seems difficult to think of operational criteria. Nevertheless, some progress has been made, for instance, by the act frequency approach of personality, which maintains that personality crystallizes in the frequency of behavioral acts in the past (Buss & Craik, 1983). Extraversion ratings, for instance, could be validated by the number of sociable acts, whereas agreeableness could be reflected in the frequency of conflict at the workplace.

In general, self–other agreement and consensus are the most frequently used strategies of measuring the accuracy of informant assessment. Informant accuracy certainly requires self–other agreement and consensus. In a very strict sense, however, consensus and self–other agreement refer to the consistency of ratings and thus pertain to the issue of reliability that can be increased by the use of multiple informants, which in turn may increase validity in terms of behavior prediction (McCrae, 1994; Moskowitz & Schwarz, 1982). Although there are similarities between consensus and self–other agreement, there are also empirical and theoretical differences (e.g., John & Robins, 1993; Kenny, 1994; Kenrick & Stringfield, 1980). Informant ratings can also be aggregated across multiple informants, which obviously is impossible with self-ratings, and informant ratings are sometimes found to be more predictive of actual behavior than self-ratings (e.g., Kolar, Funder, & Colvin, 1996). It could therefore be argued that—contrary to a naïve appreciation of self-ratings as being more valid than other ratings—informants' ratings were generally as, or even more, valid in terms of behavior prediction. Only very few studies have addressed this question and asserted that informant ratings are sometimes more predictive of actual behavior than self-ratings (e.g., John & Robins, 1993; Levesque & Kenny, 1993). Although the evidence is not very strong, informant ratings are slightly more valid if highly evaluative traits are assessed (e.g., physical attractiveness or charm, which are traits that can only be known via impression on others). In contrast, self-ratings may be more predictive regarding inner emotional states, which are only made known to others if the self

shares them or accidentally gives a clue about his or her emotion.

THEORETICAL MODELS OF PERSON PERCEPTION

The history of using informant assessment is closely linked to the history of research in accuracy of person perception. Two waves of accuracy research can be distinguished. During the first half of the 20th century, when research on the accuracy of personality judgment was flourishing (e.g., Taft, 1955; Vernon, 1933), researchers commonly questioned how well members of a group agreed in their judgments of each other. The typical accuracy criterion of the informant judgments was self–other agreement or consensus. One of the first critiques of judgmental accuracy research argued that judges did nothing other than project their own personality characteristics on their target. The most damaging critique was proposed by Cronbach (1955) and Gage and Cronbach (1955), who argued that measures of accuracy used in studies of self–other agreement and consensus (e.g., discrepancy or profile-similarity scores) were hopelessly contaminated by artifactual components, which were often independent of an informant's ability to assess a target's personality or behavior.

According to Cronbach's critique, accuracy measures consist of four components (see Figure 4.1). The first component, *elevation*, reflects the correspondence between the informant's mean judgment across targets and traits and the overall mean across targets and traits. Elevation occurs if judges and targets use the same response sets. As a result, self–other agreement and consensus would be high for artificial reasons. The second component, *stereotype*, pertains to the correspondence between an informant's mean rating over all targets and targets' average criterion ratings on that trait in question. Stereotype ratings result when an informant's ratings reflect the "average" personality, although the rating could be accurate to the extent to which the target resembles the average person. The third component, *differential elevation*, refers to the correspondence between an informant's trait ratings averaged for one target and the target's averaged criterion ratings,

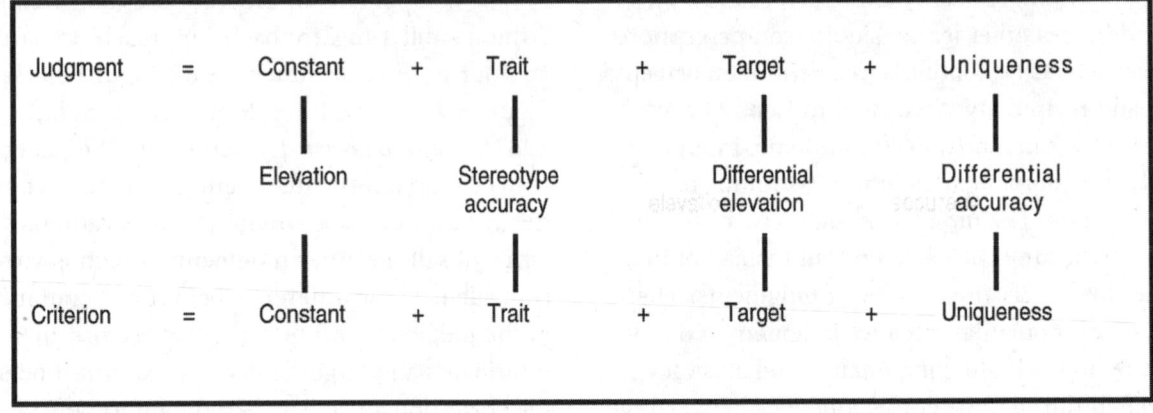

FIGURE 4.1. Cronbach's four components of accuracy. Adapted from "Accuracy in Interpersonal Perception: A Social Relations Analysis," by D. A. Kenny and L. Albright, 1987, *Psychological Bulletin, 102,* p. 391. Copyright 1987 by the American Psychological Association.

which is the general view the informant has of a specific target. The final component of informant judgments is *differential accuracy*, which refers to what is left when all the other components are controlled for: the correspondence between the judge's rating of each trait for each target and the criterion scores of each trait for each target. *Projection*, or assumed similarity, another possible component of judgments, results when an informant uses his or her self-concept as a proxy for the target rating. According to Cronbach, only two of these components reflect meaningful accuracy: differential elevation and differential accuracy. Elevation and stereotype accuracy, in contrast, result from the match between the judge's response set and the criteria, whereas projection is viewed as an error of interpersonal perception.

Cronbach's criticism has led to many misunderstandings. It did not call into question the possibility of self–other agreement or consensus and not even the existence of accuracy per se, rather it was concerned with how the accuracy of informant ratings was calculated. Cronbach's critique had tremendous consequences for research in personality and social psychology and directed psychological science to other supposedly less complicated topics like the study of error and cognitive processes in person perception (Funder, 1995, 1999). No one wanted to open a Pandora's box of methodological problems, components, and artifacts, although "a few brave souls continued to work on the topic" (Kenny, 1994, p. 124).

The second wave of accuracy research, beginning in the 1980s, started out on the Brunswikean premise that accurate judgment of real people is possible in real settings. According to Funder (1995, 1999), three approaches to accuracy can be currently distinguished. First, the pragmatic approach views person perception as accurate if it is useful and improves social functioning (Swann, 1984). Second, the constructivist approach as discussed by Kruglanksi (1989) assumes that personality and behavior can never be known for certain, and the best researchers can do is to look for where observers reach consensus. Third, the realistic approach by Funder (1995) relies on critical realism, which maintains that psychological reality does exist, although there may be multiple accesses to it. The following review presents three models of interpersonal perception. David Kenny's two models, the social relations model and the weighted average model, are best characterized as constructivist, whereas David Funder's realistic accuracy model is guided by the realistic approach. Although these models are general approaches to interpersonal perception, this review examines specific implications for informant assessment.

The Social Relations Model (SRM)

The social relations model (SRM) can be viewed as an application of the generalizability theory to data obtained from interpersonal, reciprocal designs. The SRM explicitly accounts for several of the accuracy

components suggested by Cronbach (1955), but it also addresses other features of person perception like consensus, self–other agreement, metaperception, and reciprocity. According to Kenny (1994), accuracy research must be nomothetic, interpersonal, and componential—the SRM fulfills these requirements: The model is nomothetic in that it measures accuracy for a given trait instead of individual differences in accuracy of judgments. The SRM is componential, because judgment and criterion are divided into components, and accuracy is estimated through the correspondence between the sets of components. Finally, the SRM is interpersonal and explicitly acknowledges the two-sided nature and reciprocity of interpersonal perception, where people are both judges and targets at the same time. Consistent with Cronbach's suggestions, the SRM examines the accuracy among informants' ratings of single personality traits instead of measuring accuracy across profiles of traits. Unlike Cronbach's approach, however, the SRM does not consider the accuracy of a single informant, but rather focuses on accuracy for a given trait across a set of informants and targets. The employment of the SRM, therefore, requires a "round-robin" design, in which all informants rate all targets. Alternatively, one may also apply a "block" design, in which participants are divided in two groups, and each participant rates all members of the other group.

The components of accuracy are estimated in a fashion similar to Cronbach's approach. In particular, four types of accuracy are distinguished (see Figure 4.2; Kenny, 1994; Kenny & Albright, 1987). *Elevation accuracy* pertains to the match between the informants' average response set and the average response on the criterion rating in terms of self- or other judgments, which is virtually equivalent to the difference between overall means of the judgment and the criterion (across all informants and targets). *Perceiver accuracy* refers to the correspondence between the informant's average response and the average score of targets. *Generalized accuracy* reflects how a person is generally viewed by others (i.e., specifically, the correlation between how one is generally predicted to behave and how he or she actually behaves). According to Kenny (1994), this kind of accuracy probably corresponds most closely to a naïve understanding of accuracy. The final component, *dyadic accuracy*, concerns an informant's unique prediction of a target's behavior, over and above the prediction of other informants. Consider a group of job applicants rating each other's cooperativeness in an assessment center task. Whereas elevation accuracy simply reflects the extent to which the mean evaluation of cooperativeness across perceivers and targets meets the mean criterion level of cooperation, the perceiver accuracy shows how a perceiver's

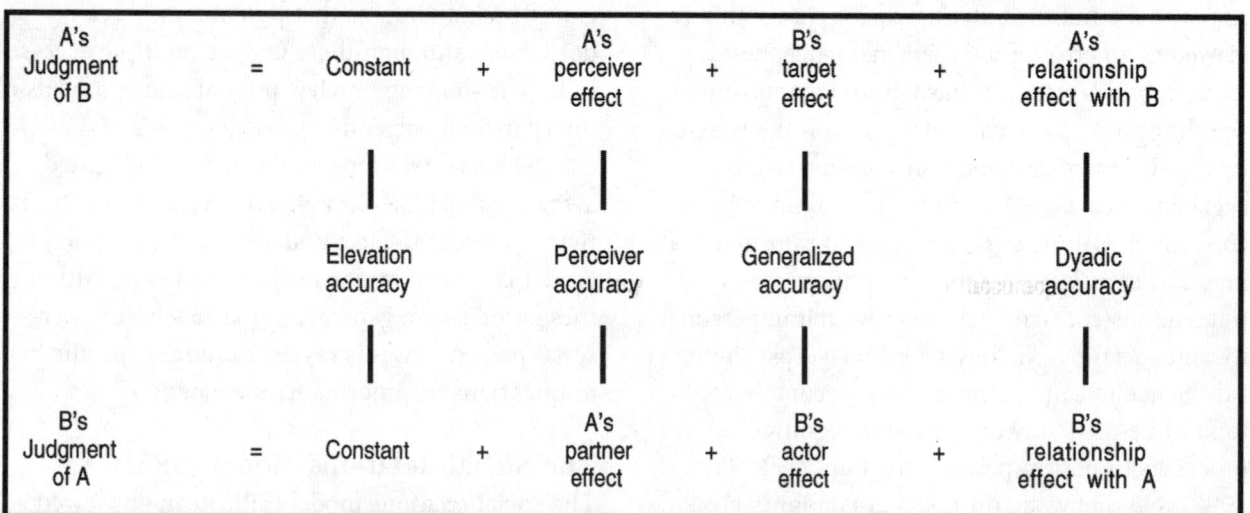

FIGURE 4.2. Four types of nomothetic accuracy. Adapted from "Accuracy in Interpersonal Perception: A Social Relations Analysis," by D. A. Kenny and L. Albright, 1987, *Psychological Bulletin, 102*, p. 396. Copyright 1987 by the American Psychological Association.

average rating corresponds with the average cooperativeness of others toward him and thus may eventually work like a self-fulfilling prophecy. Generalized accuracy, in contrast, reflects whether the cooperative behavior of a group member corresponds with how it is perceived and judged by all others, whereas the dyadic accuracy of a perceiver predicts exactly how much a group member will cooperate with him or her.

The SRM's definitions of accuracy are not identical with Cronbach's. Although generalized accuracy resembles Cronbach's differential accuracy, and dyadic accuracy corresponds with Cronbach's differential accuracy, there are fundamental differences between both approaches. Whereas the SRM considers accuracy for a trait across a set of judges and targets, Cronbach examined the accuracy of a judge across a set of targets and traits. Research involving the SRM has provided some important insights into interpersonal perception. In ratings of contact frequency in groups, for instance, the generalized accuracy and dyadic accuracy seem both stronger than perceiver accuracy (Kenny, 1994). In another study, zero-acquaintance ratings of extraversion appeared highly accurate in terms of behavior prediction, with generalized accuracy being again much stronger than dyadic and perceiver accuracy (Levesque & Kenny, 1993). Moreover, regarding consensus, judges tend to view targets as being similar to each other. At the same time different judges of the same target person show substantial agreement, even after only a brief acquaintance (Albright, Kenny, & Malloy, 1988). Perhaps the most important finding pertains to the fact that self–other agreement is substantial because the self and the judge base their impression on the same information (i.e., the target's behavior), rather than the self merely incorporating an impression of others, as suggested by symbolic interactionism (Kenny, 1994).

The SRM also has some complications (see Funder, 1999). First, employing a round-robin design can be time consuming and expensive, especially when groups of close relationships like families are of interest. In these cases, it may be difficult to bring each family member to the round-robin design. Second, the results of the SRM can most clearly be interpreted when each informant (or target, respectively) has comparable amounts of contact with everyone else. This situation could be established under experimental conditions, although such contexts are artificial in comparison to situations where informant assessment is typically used (e.g., classrooms, groups, families, etc.). Third, the interpretation of results is sometimes complicated because the SRM does not provide measures of consensus or accuracy in terms of correlation coefficients, but rather compares the relative proportions of variance accounted for by the different components of informant ratings (although these proportions can be converted into correlation coefficients; see Kenny, 1994).

The Weighted Average Model (WAM)

Whereas the SRM is a statistical model designed for the decomposition of the components of interpersonal perception, the WAM is a general theoretical model of perception sometimes applied to informant assessment to predict its qualities (e.g., consensus and self–other agreement). The WAM predicts that the qualities of informants' ratings are a weighted function of nine components:

1. *acquaintance* (i.e., amount of information informants have about the target),
2. *overlap* (i.e., the number of target behaviors to which informants simultaneously have access),
3. *consistency* (i.e., the cross-situational consistency of the target's behavior),
4. *similar meaning systems* (i.e., the extent to which informants consensually interpret a target's behavior),
5. *physical appearance stereotypes* (i.e., stereotypes related to age, sex, ethnicity, etc. that influence first impressions),
6. *agreement about stereotypes* (i.e., culturally driven stereotypes shared by informants),
7. *validity of stereotypes* (i.e., the "kernel" of truth in stereotypes),
8. *unique impression* (i.e., the informants' unique knowledge of the target), and
9. *communication* (i.e., degree to which informants communicate information about the target) (Kenny, 1991, 1994).

The nine components of the WAM can each be related to sources of variances in informant ratings (i.e., perceiver effects, target effects, and relationship effects). *Perceiver effects* are largely represented by unique impressions and physical appearance stereotypes, which are unique to perceivers across a set of targets (e.g., perceiver effects comprise the unique knowledge and valid stereotypes on age, sex, ethnicity, etc.). *Target effects*, in contrast, refer to effects shared between informants across a set of targets and result from overlap, similar meaning systems, agreement about stereotypes, consistency, and communication. Finally, *relationship effects* refer to the specific dyadic relationship of an informant with the target and are largely attributable to unique impressions, lack of similar meaning systems, and nonoverlap.

Similar to Brunswik's lens model of perception, the WAM assumes that informants differentially weigh the cues they perceive in such a manner that they assign scale values to each of the target's behaviors. The level of consensus, for instance, can then be predicted by a weighted function of all the nine factors. The WAM has a number of implications for consensus in informant assessment. One important prediction of the WAM is that general consensus does not always increase with greater acquaintance, but that accuracy does increase with greater acquaintance. This is because overlap and similar meaning systems drive consensus. If overlap is high (i.e., if informants observe the same target behavior), informants can achieve high consensus even if acquaintance (i.e., the number of observed acts) is low to moderate. Also, assuming no communication among informants, the similarity of informants' meaning systems places an upper limit on consensus. Thus, the most important sources of disagreement between informants seem to be a lack of overlap, dissimilar meaning systems, and the contribution of unique impressions (Kenny, 1991, 1994).

In general it is hypothesized, and supported empirically, that informant consensus is stronger than self–other agreement. At least three different explanations may account for this finding. First, self-ratings are inflated because of self-enhancement effects, which is why self–other agreement cannot be high. Second, informants may interact more with each other than with the targets. Third, informants may use different cues than the targets use, because other judgments are based more on observable reality and the targets' current behavior, whereas self-judgments are based more on implicit self-theories and inner states.

The Realistic Accuracy Model (RAM)

The realistic accuracy model (RAM) by Funder (1995) begins with the premise that personality traits are real and observable. As a consequence, the RAM assumes that informants reach consensus not because they share similar meaning systems or because of overlap, but rather because their judgments about a target's personality are at least partly accurate. According to the RAM, the path between a target's personality and the accurate informant judgment can be described in four steps, each associated with diverse moderators that may influence the achievement of accuracy (see Figure 4.3). These four steps include the *relevance* and *availability* of cues from the target person and the *detection* and *utilization* of these cues by the informant. To achieve accuracy within informant ratings, each step must be successfully completed. First, the target must display behavioral cues relevant to the underlying trait (e.g., extraversion). Second, the cues must be presented in a way that makes it available to the informant (e.g., either visibly or audibly). Third, the informant must detect the relevant cues (e.g., discern or register them). Finally, the informant must accurately use the previously detected, available, and relevant information. The central assumptions of the RAM can be represented by a formula, where its four elements are linked in a multiplicative manner implying that if any term in such a formula is zero, there will be no accuracy of informant ratings. Another implication of the model is that accuracy remains a probabilistic matter: Only if all four links in the process of judgment are strong will the resulting level of informant accuracy be substantial and meaningful. Moreover, the RAM suggests that accuracy is achieved via multiple cues and multiple traits because there never seems to be just one cue for one trait, and research has only recently begun to address the interactions among the cues that may be diagnostic for the same or different traits (e.g., Borkenau & Liebler, 1992, 1993; Funder & Sneed, 1993; Gifford, 1994; Gosling et al., 2002).

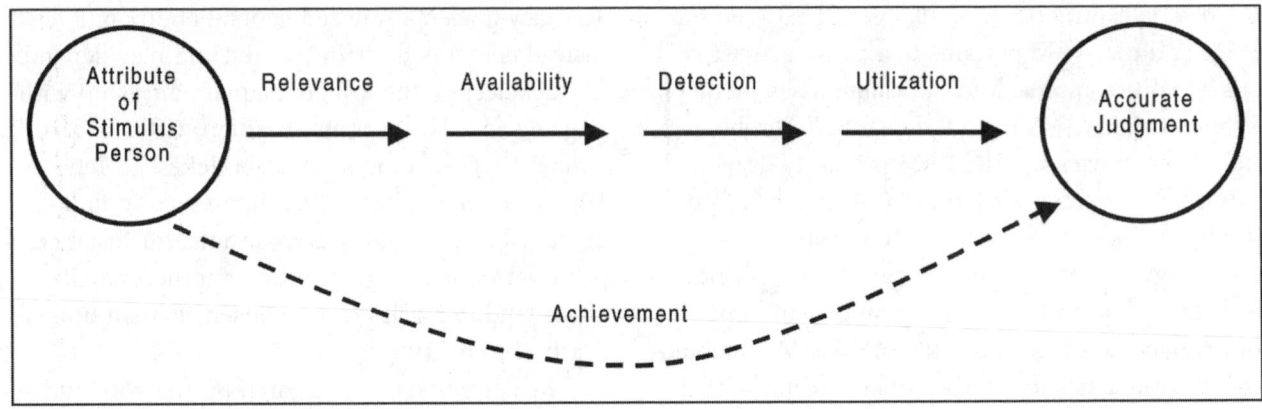

FIGURE 4.3. The realistic accuracy model. Adapted from "On the Accuracy of Personality Judgment: A Realistic Approach," by D. C. Funder, 1995, *Psychological Review, 112*, p. 659. Copyright 1995 by the American Psychological Association.

The RAM has several implications for informant assessment. First, it provides a relatively simple process model that organizes the different variables that affect accurate person perception. Second, a suggestion can be derived from the RAM for the improvement of informant assessment by interventions that affect one or more of the four steps of person perception. Third, the RAM implies that informant accuracy is influenced by characteristics of the target (i.e., through the display of relevant and available cues) and by characteristics of the perceiver (i.e., through his or her detecting and utilizing cues), with both implications pointing toward a set of important moderator variables of informant accuracy. Finally, the RAM suggests that self–other agreement is best measured when the self and informants are asked to describe what the target is really like. When researchers are interested in the convergent validity of different ratings of a target, this strategy seems most reasonable instead of asking informants about the target's self-perception or asking targets about the other informants' perception, which merely constructs a matter of metaperception (Funder, 1999; Funder & Colvin, 1988; Funder & Dobroth, 1987; Park & Judd, 1989).

How Are the SRM, the WAM, and the RAM Different?

The described models, the SRM, the WAM, and the RAM, sometimes complement and sometimes compete with each other. The models are more or less based on Brunswik's approach and share the assumption that interpersonal perception should be observed in real settings. Each of them has contributed to the revival of interpersonal perception research and has yielded important, potentially useful insights when using informant assessment in research. The SRM is a statistical model that enables data to be analyzed from round-robin designs (or mixed block designs) and allows the decomposition of the variance of judgments into components often related to the target, the trait, and the informant. The SRM answers a wide range of questions concerning interpersonal perception, only some of which address accuracy, consensus, and self–other agreement. In contrast, the WAM focuses on theoretical and psychological rather than methodological and statistical issues. Moreover, the WAM makes predictions about the sources of variance in perceiver, target, and relationship effects, which in turn can be analyzed using the SRM, but also with other, more traditional methods.

The RAM and the SRM differ in three ways (Funder, 1995). First, the central concern of the RAM is informant accuracy, whereas the SRM studies accuracy as only one among other issues in interpersonal perception. Second, the RAM does not necessarily require the use of round-robin designs, which indeed pose inconveniences. Third, and most important, it is difficult with the SRM to study moderator effects in interpersonal perception, whereas moderators are a central concern of the

RAM. The central point of divergence between the RAM and the WAM pertains to a constructivist versus a realistic approach to informant assessment: Whereas the WAM's central dependent variable is informant consensus, the RAM primarily deals with informant accuracy. As Funder (1995, p. 666) put it, "In the WAM, accuracy is one variable that affects agreement. In the RAM, agreement is one indicator of accuracy." Another more central point of divergence is that both SRM and WAM are nomothetic approaches to interpersonal perception that do not address the question of individual differences in informant accuracy, whereas the RAM provides information about these individual differences.

MODERATORS OF ACCURATE INFORMANT ASSESSMENT

The accuracy of informant assessment depends on properties of the informant, properties of the target, properties of the trait, and the kind of information on which the judgment is based (Funder, 1995, 1999; Kenny, 1993). The following review considers accuracy in its various meanings (e.g., self–other agreement, consensus, or behavioral prediction). Moreover, I will explicitly acknowledge the cases in which the different kinds of accuracy are differentially affected by moderator variables (e.g., informant-based, target-based, trait-based, and information-based moderators).

The Good Informant

One of the oldest questions in research on interpersonal perception pertains to the characteristics of the good informant and is concerned with whether consistent individual differences can be found in the ability to accurately judge the traits and behaviors of others (Colvin & Bundick, 2001). In an early empirical review, Taft (1955) arrived at the somewhat unsurprising conclusion that the good judge tends to be intelligent, socially skilled, and psychologically well-adjusted. In general, however, the ability to accurately judge others seems well developed in humans, which is why individual differences across judges are not supposed to be very large (Funder, 1999). It is also likely that informant

accuracy does not reflect a general ability but instead is highly domain-specific and may depend, for instance, on the level of acquaintanceship with targets and kinds of traits (Bernieri, Gillis, Davis, & Grahe, 1996; Marangoni, Garcia, Ickes, & Teng, 1995). Moreover, individual differences in judgmental ability may vary across traits, for instance, perceivers who are apt at rating another's intelligence tend to reach greater consensus than others (Park & Judd, 1989).

The current state of research on the good judge is still tentative and has led to fairly inconsistent results. A recent meta-analysis by Davis and Kraus (1997), for instance, included very different kinds of accuracy (e.g., trait accuracy, empathic accuracy, nonverbal decoding, and lie detection), each of which taps different underlying constructs. The results indicated that judgmental accuracy is positively (albeit weakly) related to intellectual functioning—cognitive style characterized by cognitive complexity and field independence, social sensitivity, and interpersonal orientation. Thus the good judge certainly appears to have the average psychologically well-adjusted personality. This does not necessarily imply, however, that people are generally accurate about their own ability to judge others, because self-assessments of judgmental ability are mostly uncorrelated with actual levels of achieved accuracy (Ickes, 1993; Marangoni et al., 1995). Because of the inconsistent state of research, theoretical assumptions on the nature of individual differences therefore remain vague. Whereas the WAM and the SRM conceive individual differences in accuracy as negligible (Kenny, 1994), the RAM suggests that at least three variables influence individual differences in informants' accuracy (i.e., knowledge, ability, and motivation, Funder, 1999).

The informant's *knowledge* may be either explicit or implicit. Explicit knowledge refers to the use of cues that are deemed as valid for inferring underlying personality traits. It is not likely, however, that this kind of knowledge is teachable because personality judgments are fast, complex, and intuitive. It is nearly impossible, for instance, to teach people to accurately detect lies in others. Still, it seems possible to improve the knowledge by feedback and practice (Hammond, 1996; Marangoni et al., 1995). *Percep-*

tual and *cognitive abilities* may also increase informants' accuracy. In general, individual differences in cognitive abilities are more pronounced than individual differences in social perceptiveness, which is why it seems reasonable to expect that IQ, as well as more specific cognitive abilities, are positively associated with accuracy (Funder, 1999). *Motivational factors* that may affect accuracy are related to the personality and the situation. John and Robins (1994), for instance, showed that a narcissistic view of oneself is associated with low accuracy, whereas Ambady, Hallahan, and Rosenthal (1995) speculated that psychologically vulnerable individuals, low in expressiveness, sociability, and self-esteem, might be better judges than others. Researchers have also shown a relationship between basic personality traits of informants (e.g., conscientiousness and agreeableness) and rating leniency (Bernardin, Cooke, & Villanova, 2000). Finally, motivational factors may interfere with accuracy when the informant–target relationship is very close. Thus romantic and marital relationships may be interactions where accuracy is not always easy to achieve. In fact, Simpson, Ickes, and Blackstone (1995) observed that dating couples in insecure relationships could be motivated to avoid accurately perceiving their partner's attraction to another person.

Three general characteristics may help paint a portrait of the good informant, using mixed empirical evidence on individual differences in accuracy. First, the good informant needs a strong sensitivity to what is happening in his or her social environment. Second, the good informant can make a connection between the observed behaviors and the personality traits underlying them. Finally, the good informant needs to be objective, rational, and unconcerned with the opinions of others when making judgments. The three characteristics of the good informant may be improved by informants' training and adequate instructions.

The Good Target

Informant accuracy also depends on characteristics of the target, and the RAM predicts that individual differences in the tendency to be judged accurately are a result of cue relevance and availability (Funder, 1995, 1999). Both cue relevance and availability are influenced by situational pressures (i.e., is the observed situation strong or weak enough to elicit behavioral cues?), the target's tendency to deceive (i.e., how much is the target inclined to suppress cues?), and by incoherence (i.e., how consistent are the target's personality and behavioral cues?). The concept of individual consistency is closely related to the concept of *scalability,* which refers to the degree to which the behavior of a person is patterned like ordinary trait constructs. The notion of scalability, which originally stems from item response theory of the psychometric field, has also been used in personality assessment. Reise and Waller (1993), for instance, showed that individuals differed to the extent to which they were scalable on certain traits, and it can be expected that individuals low in scalability are more difficult to judge. In addition, certain traits may be easily judged in certain targets. Funder (1995) coined the term *palpability,* referring to the relative obviousness and detectability of certain traits in certain individuals.

The elaborated concept of *judgability* was proposed by Colvin (1993a, 1993b). According to Colvin, judgability refers to a manifestation of personality coherence and is reflected by the fact that consistent people are more likely to be judged consensually by informants as compared with less consistent people. In fact, judgability appears to be a stable personality trait over young adulthood and seems closely associated with ego resiliency, a general trait reflecting psychological health and adjustment. Judgability also seems to be a function of personality stability, which is why it is plausible to expect some kind of temporary nonjudgability in childhood and adolescence, where personality and behavior is usually less consistent as compared to adults. Nevertheless, some adults may still appear nonjudgable, because their personality is less consistent and associated with less adaptive reactions to stress and less self-control (Reise & Waller, 1993), or a result of personality disorders (e.g., narcissism; John & Robins, 1994). Thus, all in all, judgability seems to be a healthy personality trait related to socially desirable levels of extraversion, agreeableness, conscientiousness, and emotional stability, and care should be taken when knowledgeable informants are used to assess less psychologically adjusted

targets, who may be judged less accurately than more psychologically adjusted targets.

The Good Trait

Some traits may be more difficult to judge than others. Some traits such as extraversion, for instance, are easy to judge, whereas others require more specific information and longer acquaintanceship (e.g., Colvin & Funder, 1991; Park & Judd, 1989; Paunonen, 1989). According to the RAM, differences between the judgability of traits may stem from their visibility, their availability and relevance, evaluative properties, and adaptive importance.

A large body of research has consistently demonstrated the effect of *trait visibility*, or trait observability, on trait perception. It is well established that trait visibility is highly correlated with self–other agreement and consensus (e.g., Bernieri, Zuckerman, Koestner, & Rosenthal, 1994; Borkenau & Liebler, 1992; Funder & Colvin, 1988; Funder & Dobroth, 1987; Kenny, Albright, Malloy, & Kashy, 1994; Kenrick & Stringfield, 1980; Kurtz & Sherker, 2003; Levesque & Kenny, 1993; Watson, Hubbard, & Wiese, 2000). The WAM and the RAM have different views on the trait visibility effects. Whereas the WAM assumes that visibility results from the match of similar meaning systems between the self and others (Kenny, 1991, 1994), the RAM supposes that trait visibility results in higher self–other agreement or consensus because it is based more on direct behavioral observation than on arbitrary social construction (Funder, 1995, 1999). However, the established effect of trait visibility has clear implications for research practice. According to the RAM, *availability* and *relevance* are different aspects of a trait's visibility. One specific behavior may be relevant to a trait, whereas it may not be available for informants. Behavioral cues, for instance, relevant for conscientiousness may be inferred from viewing peoples' bedrooms and offices, but these cues are not available in restaurants or gyms (Gosling et al., 2002).

The observability of traits is also related to their *evaluative properties*. Some traits may be more desirable than others, which is why social desirability of a trait may affect consensus or self–other agreement. John and Robins (1993), for instance, found that

extremely desirable or undesirable traits yielded lower self–other agreement as compared with more neutral traits. Judgments of evaluatively loaded traits may be more likely to become biased by self-protective and self-enhancing motivational effects. John and Robins found that targets judged by others as high on evaluatively extreme traits (i.e., "saints") rate themselves modestly, whereas people negatively rated by others (i.e., "jerks") generally present themselves in the best light. In this vein, it may be concluded that self–peer agreement is lower on ambiguous traits (Asendorpf & Ostendorf, 1998; Hayes & Dunning, 1997). Finally, few personality traits are completely evaluatively neutral, which is why trait evaluativeness should be considered when utilizing informant assessment (Borkenau, 1990).

From an evolutionary perspective, traits have differential *adaptive importance*. A person's environment primarily consists of other individuals, which is why Buss (1999) argued that individual differences between one's social partners represent important vectors of the human adaptive landscape. It may follow from this line of reasoning that accuracy may be more adaptive for some traits, while at the same time inaccuracy may be even more adaptive for other traits. A trait adaptive to both detection and to display might be sociosexuality, and it was indeed shown that judgmental accuracy of others' sociosexuality was greater than accuracy of traits with less evolutionary significance (e.g., social potency and closeness), although accuracy of sociosexuality also varied as a function of both the judge's and the target's sex (Gangestad, Simpson, DiGeronimo, & Biek, 1992).

Good Information

According to Funder (1999), good information has two facets—quantity and quality. One feature of the *quantity of information* a judge can use pertains to his or her level of acquaintanceship with the target. However, even so-called "zero-acquaintance" studies usually yield substantial informants' consensus regarding basic personality traits (Borkenau & Liebler, 1992; Chaplin, Phillips, Brown, Clanton, & Stein, 2000; Kenny et al., 1994). There is also evidence that personality ratings by strangers resulting from enough "thin slices" of (sometimes video-

based) behavior can reach high consensus and substantial accuracy, which can be additionally increased if ratings of multiple informants are combined (e.g., Ambady & Rosenthal, 1992; Borkenau et al., 2001, 2004; Borkenau & Liebler, 1993; Kenny, 1994; Levesque & Kenny, 1993; Watson, 1989).

The level of acquaintanceship, however, is difficult to quantify because it is related to time and contexts in which informants and targets have been together. In general, the validity of informant assessment benefits from the acquaintanceship effect. A simple explanation for this effect is that increased length of acquaintance is probably accompanied by more information (e.g., Bernieri et al., 1994; Blackman & Funder, 1998; Colvin & Funder, 1991; Funder & Colvin, 1988; Funder, Kolar, & Blackman, 1995; Kurtz & Sherker, 2003; Paulhus & Bruce, 1992; Paunonen, 1989; Stinson & Ickes, 1992; Watson & Clark, 1991; Watson et al., 2000). One question about the acquaintanceship effect is, however, concerned with the possibility of assumed similarity, reflecting that well-acquainted judges resemble their targets and achieve accuracy by simply projecting their self-concept on them. Some studies have tried to rule out assumed similarity (e.g., Funder et al., 1995; Watson et al., 2000), whereas others have asserted that where informants and targets are really similar, the use of projection constitutes a successful and reasonable heuristic, instead of just an artifact, to achieve accurate judgments (Kenny & Acitelli, 2001; Neyer, Banse, & Asendorpf, 1999).

Self–other agreement and consensus may be quite differently affected by the acquaintanceship effect. From the WAM perspective, Kenny (1994) anticipated that consensus would be established very early when judges share stereotypes. Over time, however, these stereotypic judgments would be replaced by judgments deduced from actual behavioral observation leading to a change in the content of consensus rather than its level, although at the same time, accuracy in terms of behavior prediction would be improved. This exact process was observed in an experimental study by Blackman and Funder (1998). However, even when accuracy increases, accuracy cannot exceed consensus for the

same basic psychometric reasons that validity cannot exceed the square root of the reliability.

Finally, the acquaintanceship effect may also be context specific (Branje, van Aken, van Lieshout, & Mathijssen, 2003; Kurtz & Sherker, 2003). Informants may know the targets from different contexts (e.g., school, workplace, marriage, family, etc.). Achenbach et al. (1987) reported high agreement between the mother and father's ratings and between teachers' ratings of behavioral problems of schoolchildren, but a much lower agreement was found between the parental and teacher ratings. Although the parental and teacher judgments were not independent, because they may have talked to each other about the children, they certainly based their judgments on different contexts. Thus, although informants may have varying opportunities to observe the target in different situations, they may be equally accurate in predicting how the target will behave in other situations. Funder (1999) argued that this could be explained by the ability of the human judge to generalize his or her judgments from one context to a vastly different context.

Whereas the acquaintanceship effect pertains to the sheer amount of information that informants share about targets, the quality of information is also important. The issue of *information quality* is related to the question of where it is best to look for certain traits. Almost two decades ago, Anderson (1984) showed that listening to people talk about their thoughts and feelings results in a more accurate personality judgment than listening to people talk about their hobbies and leisure activities. More recently, some studies have addressed this question more profoundly. A study on handshaking and first impressions, Chaplin et al. (2000), showed that firm handshakes were related to extraversion, emotional stability, and openness to experience (the latter was only true for women). Gosling et al. (2002) showed in a study that personality judgments when viewing offices and bedrooms were consensual between independent observers and could predict self-rated personality traits (e.g., conscientiousness and openness to experience). Moreover, Gosling et al. found that both environmentally based consensus and accuracy were comparable and sometimes even stronger than the levels in zero-acquaintance

and long-term acquaintance studies, as was summarized by Kenny (1994). It therefore seems that personal environments contain richer information for informant assessment than zero-acquaintance contexts, and sometimes even more than long-term acquaintance contexts.

GUIDELINES FOR RESEARCH PRACTICE

Several practical guidelines on informant assessment can be derived from this review of theoretical approaches to person perception and the empirical findings on the validity of self- versus other ratings. Above all, informant assessment results from the assumption that knowledgeable informants may have had the opportunity to observe the target on many different occasions (or at least brief interactions) and may, therefore, have begun to collect data much earlier than data recorded by the researchers. This general confidence in the veridicality of informant knowledge rests on two conditions: First, there must be considerable consensus between informants, and second, informant ratings must be accurate in terms of convergence with external criteria (Wiggins, 1973; Woodruffe, 1984). Both conditions require care when forming research designs and data analyses.

Design Issues

Informant errors may provide a serious threat to the validity of assessment. Potential errors include response sets, reactivity, social desirability, halo effect, implicit personality theory, and so forth. There are procedures that may help to reduce these errors, some of which are related to item construction and treatment of informants, whereas others pertain to the effect of data aggregation. The selection of certain formats (e.g., Q-sorts or forced choice), decreases the effect of individual response sets and the social desirability of items. Another approach is simply to vary the rating format. Guilford (1954) advises the use of blanks instead of numbers. Another way to minimize response sets is to let the informants rate one target at a time on all the items, as opposed to allowing the informants to rate all targets on each item before moving on to the next item (Kenny, 1994). Moreover, training of informants may increase the reliability

and validity of assessment (Thornton & Zorich, 1980). Finally, researchers should be aware of motivational and tiring effects and use only a limited number of rating scales.

The calculation of aggregated ratings resulting from the use of multiple informants may also reduce rating errors. When two self-report measures are correlated, for instance, content and method are confounded. But when a self-report measure is correlated with an informant rating, shared method effects are unlikely—which is the obvious benefit of aggregation. The error minimizing effect of aggregation depends not only on the number of informants, but also on the level of consensus and the difference between anticipated and true correlations between the rated items. According to the Spearman–Brown formula, the reliability (and certainly, validity) of informant ratings can be increased by including additional informants whose rater biases are uncorrelated. Sometimes the aggregation across informants is much stronger than aggregation across occasions or test items. Although there may be negligible consensus between single informants, there may be nearly perfect consensus between large samples of informants (Epstein, 1983). Cheek (1982) demonstrated that the correlation between self-rating and informant rating could be considerably increased by aggregating the ratings of three informants instead of using single informants. In another influential study, Moskowitz and Schwarz (1982) showed that the correlation between global informant ratings and behavior could be markedly increased if the behavior is observed for a sufficient length of time, and the ratings are aggregated across multiple knowledgeable informants. The number of knowledgeable informants is limited, but when it is possible to use more than one informant, aggregation across ratings will decrease rating errors. The number of informants necessary to achieve valid composite ratings will depend on the ambiguity of the trait or behavioral construct, the base rates and the variability of the relevant behaviors, and the moderators of informant accuracy discussed above (Funder, 1999; Hayes & Dunning, 1997; Kenny, 1994; Moskowitz, 1986).

In contrast with self-assessments stemming from single self-reports, informant assessments

may achieve higher reliability (and perhaps higher validity), because it is possible to obtain them from multiple informants (e.g., peers and family members). It could be argued that self-ratings of personality could be outnumbered and outperformed by the average other rating (i.e., the averaged informant rating; Hofstee, 1994). The aggregation effect possibly results for two reasons: the reduction in error variance and multiple informants having more information to provide than single informants. Taking both into account, Kolar et al. (1996) concluded on the basis of their study that the superiority of multiple informants does not guarantee the validity of single informant ratings, given that single informants usually achieve only slightly better predictive validity than single self-ratings. The most reliable source of information of a target's personality is thus neither to be found in his or her self-ratings, nor is it guaranteed by single informant ratings; rather, it is found in the consensus of the judgments from the community of the target's knowledgeable informants.

Aggregation across multiple informants should nevertheless be conducted with caution. Informants may use very different standards to make their judgments or they may know targets from very different contexts. Because informant judgments are not homogenous in such cases, the effect of aggregation will be small or negligible, revealing that—at least under such circumstances—single informant ratings could be more valid than aggregated ratings. However, in other cases, aggregated informant ratings could simply be more valid because they are more reliable, and appropriate psychometric corrections must be made to take data aggregation into account (Kenny, 1994). Researchers should therefore distinguish between the average correlation or the intraclass correlation between informants (reflecting the reliability of one average informant) and the internal consistency across informants such as coefficient alpha (reflecting the reliability of the average judgment). Some researchers prefer to report the average correlation because it does not depend on the number of informants (Kenny, 1993; Lucas & Baird, this volume, chap. 3).

Data Analytic Issues

Statistical issues primarily deal with the calculation of accuracy in terms of self–other agreement or consensus. The potential artifacts identified by Cronbach can be estimated easily when multiple informant ratings are replicated across multiple targets. The social relations model provides unique methods that allow separating the very different components of informant ratings, (i.e., genuine elevation, differential elevation, stereotype accuracy, and differential accuracy; see Figure 4.1). The SRM is only applicable when using a round-robin or mixed block design. With designs in which each group member is an informant and a target at the same time (e.g., in families or peer groups), the SRM is certainly the method of choice. In most cases, however, researchers use a set of informants who rate a set of targets for one or more items or traits, respectively. In these cases, the components cannot be isolated, although they might be controlled. Confounds caused by general response set effects, for instance, can be avoided by using correlational measures of consensus or self–other agreement, whereas artifacts caused by differential stereotype ratings are more difficult to control. As a general rule, intraclass correlations should be used instead of Pearson correlations, especially when informant pairs are interchangeable (Shrout & Fleiss, 1979). All correlational measures of consensus, self–other agreement, and accuracy can be derived from generalizability theory (Cronbach, Gleser, Nanda, & Rajaratnam, 1972). Two general correlational methods can be distinguished, item-level and profile correlations.

Item-level correlations. Item-level correlations are computed separately for each rating item, across all informant-target (self–other agreement) or target–target pairs (consensus). The item-level correlation has an advantage in that it removes genuine elevation and stereotype accuracy, although individual differences in response tendencies (e.g., differential elevation) may still lead to complications. Differential elevation can be controlled for by standardizing the data within ratings or by using Q-sort procedures (Bernieri et al., 1994). In addition, there are at least three more complications with item-level correlations. First, item correlations describe con-

sensus or self–other agreement across either a set of informants or targets rather than the accuracy for individual targets or informants. Therefore, it is difficult to study differences between pairs of informants or differences between self-informant pairs, although moderator effects can be analyzed by moderated multiple regression (see Bernieri et al., 1994), and correlations can be decomposed into individual consistencies (where the correlation can be interpreted as the mean of individual consistencies, i.e., differences between squared z-scores of raters; see Asendorpf, 1991). Second, with nested designs where each target has a unique "nested" set of informants, the effect of differential stereotype accuracy arises if differential stereotypes of informants are systematically correlated with characteristics of particular targets (Funder, 1999). Also, elevation cannot be removed in nested designs, because the elevation components may vary across groups (Kenny, 1993). Third, assumed similarity, or alternatively, projection, may also lead to artifactual accuracy if informants and targets are similar for genetic or acquaintanceship reasons, which in turn leads informants to judge themselves instead of the targets. Whereas there is no doubt on the emergence of assumed similarity effects, its effects on accuracy measures as either artifactual or valid are still controversially debated (e.g., Funder, 1999; Funder et al., 1995; Neyer et al., 1999; Stinson & Ickes, 1992; Watson et al., 2000).

Profile correlations. The profile correlation assesses the similarity between the complete set of judgments made by one informant and another informant or the self, respectively. This procedure is mostly used with Q-sort data, and typically yields as many correlations (or partial correlations) as informant pairs or informant-target pairs are included in the study. When using profile correlations, however, researchers should be aware of reflection and stereotypes (Kenny, 1993). Reflection can lead to inflated correlations and occurs when researchers fail to reverse negatively poled items within a profile of positive ones. If the rating profiles of neuroticism items are correlated, for instance, each item should be scored consistently (Kraemer, 1984). Whereas genuine or differential

elevation effects are negligible with profile correlations, stereotypes may inflate the correlations because the means of the traits are likely to vary. Thus, the correlations between trait profiles become greater to the degree that a particular target has a typical personality profile and the informant is accurately using this prototypical profile.

It is possible to partial out the stereotype profile from the criterion or from the informant rating (e.g., by subtracting the mean across judges from each trait rating, which also corrects the bias that results from failure to reverse items), or by partialling out the mean profiles from each of the informant's rating profiles (Funder, 1999; Kenny & Acitelli, 1994). However, there are several points that need to be considered with partial or semipartial correlations. First, because average self-ratings and average informant ratings are likely to be correlated, the issue of partial versus semipartial correlation is usually of little interest. Second, partial correlations stemming from residual scores are less reliable than nonadjusted correlations. Third, partial correlations may remove true information along with error, because stereotypes may at least in part contain valid information. Especially the corrected ratings of targets, whose true scores resemble what one may call the average person, will receive less significant levels of accurate judgments. Therefore, a blind trust in partial correlations is not advisable.

CONCLUDING REMARKS

The validity coefficients of informant ratings in terms of consensus and self–other agreement rarely exceed moderate levels (e.g., Bernieri et al., 1994; Borkenau & Liebler, 1992, 1993; Borkenau et al., 2001; Funder, 1999; Harkness, Tellegen, & Waller, 1995; Kenny, 1994). Researchers should be careful in attributing less than perfect validity as solely a result of method variance. The reason for this is simply that personality or behavior ratings are not only influenced by the methods by which they are obtained, but also by traits and behaviors themselves. A rating score, whether it is derived from one or more knowledgeable informants or from the target, should be psychologically understood and evaluated through the consideration of both the

method and the trait. Ozer (1989) reminded researchers not to be too demanding of hetero-method correlations: "Expecting convergence of measurement results across methods should be a theoretical prediction when warranted, not an unvarying methodological imperative" (p. 230; see also Eid & Diener, this volume, chap. 1).

CHAPTER 5

MOMENTARY CAPTURE OF REAL-WORLD DATA

Arthur A. Stone and Leighann Litcher-Kelly

There are many complexities and difficulties inherent in reliably and validly measuring psychological and behavioral constructs. This chapter discusses a collection of techniques for capturing peoples' self-reports, including private, subjective states; behaviors emitted by an individual; and qualities of the environment. It addresses the measurement of these data in individuals' normal environments and at the moment that the reported construct has occurred to achieve ecological validity and to avoid biases associated with recall.

The vast majority of data collected by behavioral scientists stem from self-reports (Stone, Turkkan, Bachrach, Jobe, Kurtzman, & Cain, 2000). There are two important reasons for this. First, certain kinds of information are only accessible by asking individuals for it; examples include pain, fatigue, malaise, depression, affect, and various symptoms. Although there are other manifestations of these states that are observable to others (e.g., facial expressions associated with pain or depression), it is commonly accepted that self-reports represent the gold standard for these phenomena. Second, there is a pragmatic reason for using self-reports even when valid alternatives exist, with respect to the additional expense of obtaining nonself-reported data. While it is relatively easy to ask an individual about significant major life events, it is time consuming and expensive to collect the same data by examining archival records or by conducting interviews with others familiar with the individual. Thus, self-reports remain the convenient way to gather a wide variety of information about people and their environments, both past and present.

This chapter reviews potential problems for collecting self-reports with commonly used questionnaire and interview techniques. We briefly cover the most salient threats to the validity of self-reports, especially reports that involve significant recall. We then introduce the concept of diary and momentary approaches to the collection of self-report data. Details of the primary methodological features of momentary designs are discussed, and methods for developing such protocols are presented. We also discuss recent developments on the use of paper versus electronic diaries, new data on the acceptability and validity of the methodology, standards for reporting momentary studies, challenges in the analysis of momentary data, and clinical and research applications of this methodology.

HISTORY

A primary reason for the development of momentary methods was the scientific evidence and clinical anecdotes suggesting the inaccuracies in people's recalled reports of events (this topic will be covered in detail below). A second reason was the importance of moving out of the laboratory and into the real world, termed ecological validity (Brunswik, 1949). This concept grew from the notion that individuals may act differently in artificial situations than in the circumstances they typically inhabit. A related issue is that reports about past behaviors or feelings are likely to be influenced by immediate circumstances. Therefore, it is important that the

local environment is as representative of the individual's usual environment as possible.

Descriptive time budgeting studies also encouraged the movement to momentary studies (Chappel, 1970; Monroe & Monroe, 1971; Szalai, 1966). These investigations examined how individuals allocated their time to various activities, and the investigations ultimately moved to national and cross-cultural studies. Similarly, other behavioral researchers made detailed observations of children throughout the day (Barker, 1978). Research on circadian rhythms also supported the notion that intensive study of within-day phenomena could yield valuable insights in human and animal behavior (Kleitman, 1963). Finally, the development of devices that allowed ambulatory measurement of physiological variables (e.g., blood pressure and heart rate) demonstrated the advances that could be achieved by using a more detailed approach to measurement in the field (vanEgeren & Madarasmi, 1992).

Diaries completed at the end of a day (EOD) provided a solution to the issues raised above. This is an adequate strategy for collecting self-report data as long as the variable studied is not likely to be biased by recall that occurred over the 12- to 18-hour period. Many behaviors may fall into this category; it is hard to imagine that an individual would have difficulty remembering a major argument with a spouse or would distort the occurrence of a severe asthma attack. Notice, however, that these examples include an adjective that enhances the saliency of the occurrence ("major," "severe"), and reassures the reader that recall of the event was manageable. However, when mundane events are considered (e.g., number micturitions, if teeth were brushed, number of interactions with coworkers), the accuracy of daily recall becomes more suspect. Moving to less tangible occurrences, like changes in affect or stress, occurrence of particular thoughts, or evaluations of various events (e.g., how good was it?), however, raises concerns about recall even over a day. It is easy to imagine that mood at the time of recall could affect the recall of mood earlier that morning or could affect the evaluation of an event early in the afternoon (Stone, Hedges, Neale, & Satin, 1985). The detailed study of cycles through the day is also quite difficult with an EOD

diary protocol given the demands on memory to generate such a continuous record of many hours.

A large variety of phenomena have been investigated with momentary data capture techniques, and a few examples provide a "flavor" of these topics. Pain is an experience quite variable, and clinicians and researchers recognized this phenomenon long ago. Therefore, diary techniques have been extensively used in this area, including within-day diaries (Affleck, Tennen, Urrows, & Higgins, 1991; Jamison et al., 2002; Peters et al., 2000). Stress and coping processes were initially studied with trait-like and recall-based questionnaires, but to appreciate the dynamic interplay among these variables, diary methods have been extensively used (Affleck, Tennen, Urrows, & Higgins, 1992; Baba, Ozawa, Nakamoto, Ueshima, & Omae, 1990; Bolger, DeLongis, Kessler, & Schilling, 1989; Bolger & Eckenrode, 1987; Marco & Suls, 1993; Suls, Wan, & Blanchard, 1994). Diary methods also have a long history in medical research where they are used to measure symptom levels and patterns over time (Lehrer, Isenberg, & Hochron, 1993; Rand, Hoon, Massey, & Johnson, 1990; Roghmann & Haggerty, 1973). Finally, real-time data collection methods have been used in association with biological measurements, like blood pressure (Gerber, Schwartz, & Pickering, 1998), cortisol (Nicolson, 1991; Smyth et al., 1997), and immune function (Stone, 1987). These are only a small sample of the topics that have been studied with diaries.

RECALL BIASES IN SELF-REPORT DATA

A major theme in the development of diary and momentary capture of self-report data is the possibility that biases contaminate recall. As it turns out, at least three fields of scientific study have contributed to our knowledge of these biases: survey research, autobiographical memory research, and cognitive science. Many excellent reviews of factors exist that can influence self-reports (e.g., Bradburn, Rips, & Shevell, 1987; Gorin & Stone, 2001; Schwarz, Wanke, & Bless, 1994; Schwarz, 1999), and we describe several of the major factors below.

Figure 5.1 shows a graphical depiction of biasing factors. The figure shows how these factors influence

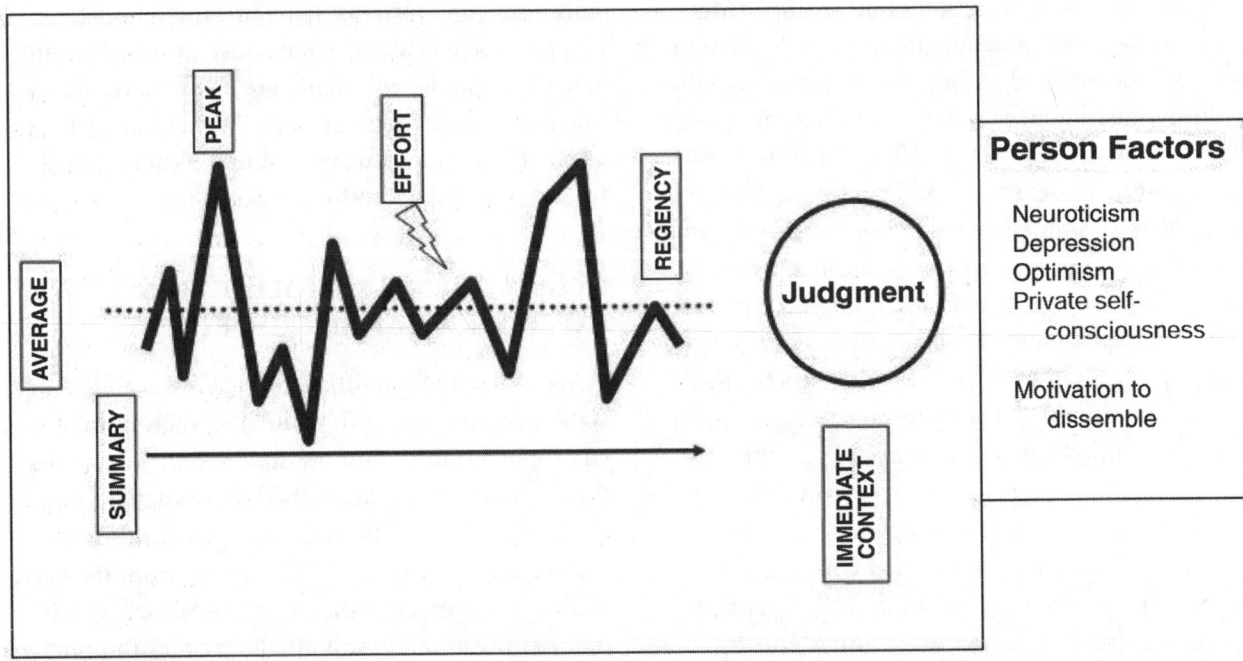

FIGURE 5.1. Schematic of factors that can influence a recall judgment.

the recall rating, which is represented by the circle labeled "Judgment." We have chosen this term because the process of recalling information is best viewed as making a judgment, implying a dynamic process comprised of the differential weighting of information. To the left of the circle is a jagged line indicating the level of the variable to be recalled (for ease of presentation, we will use pain) studied over the period of time (e.g., a week). It is depicted as having considerable variation around its average level (the dotted line). Each of the rectangles signifies a potential recall biasing effect. The box labeled "Recency" means that making a judgment of pain for the entire time period is overly influenced by recent pain levels: if recent pain was high, the judgment of weekly pain would be higher. Similarly, the box labeled "Peak" indicates that peak experiences, in this case a pain exacerbation, will also overly influence the judgment of weekly pain. Both peak and recency effects have been elegantly demonstrated by Redelmeier and Kahneman (1996; Kahneman, Fredrickson, Schreiber, & Redelmeier, 1993).

"Effort" is shorthand for the term effort-after-meaning, which refers to a process wherein the recall of experiences that occur early on in the period is influenced by events occurring later in the period (Brown & Harris, 1978). An argument with one's boss, for instance, might be deemed very upsetting at the time. However, if reconciliation with the boss occurs a day later, then subsequent recall of the original level of upset could be affected by the reconciliation, diminishing the recalled stressfulness of the event. In other words, the memory of past events can be colored by later events. "Summary" refers to the process of taking whatever information one has about the experience from a particular period and creating a single rating from this information. In fact, we know that only a small subset of all experiences is encoded into memory, which means that all information is not even available for summarizing. We also know that the process of retrieving this stored information is an active process, influenced by a number of factors. Finally, it is unclear how people mathematically combine the retrieved information into a meaningful index. This is an area in need of research.

The box labeled "Immediate Context" is a very influential and well-researched factor. We know that a number of cognitive heuristics come into play during the moment of judgment. The degree to which the process is influenced is itself affected by

the nature of the information to be recalled (Menon & Yorkston, 2000); one quality of the information especially salient at this stage is the degree to which the individual has access to the information requested by the researcher. When asked for a rating of how sad one is feeling, for instance, a person usually has an immediate response stemming from their current experience. However, when asked about how their life is currently going (life satisfaction), there is not an immediate experience, but rather a process of evaluation that occurs. In the latter case, when the answer to the query is not apparent, immediate circumstances (e.g., the person's mood) have a greater influence on the response. So, a person in a happy mood is more likely to say that they are satisfied with life than a person who is currently sad, even if they actually have quite similar lives. Schwarz and Menon, among others, have detailed the cognitions underlying many of these processes (Menon & Yorkston, 2000; Schwarz, 1999). Surprisingly, even seemingly trivial manipulations of circumstances surrounding judgments can have a major impact on the judgments.

The large box labeled "Person Factors" on the right side of Figure 5.1 shows a number of personality traits and concepts shown to influence judgments of past experiences. Several of these variables, among many, have been listed.

Other research on the types of memory that are used in the recall process have provided an additional line of evidence on recall bias. Episodic knowledge has been described by cognitive scientists as representing the autobiographical experiences that are linked to specific events; its form is loosely represented in memory, and it is susceptible to forgetting. Semantic memory may be considered a symbolic form of memory that is conceptual in form; it is more tightly linked to individuals' beliefs about the world than to specific occurrences. In recent work on the remembrance of emotions, Robinson and Clore (2002a, 2002b) have demonstrated evidence of a shift from episodic memory to semantic memory as the interval to be remembered is increased (in particular, latencies to recall information increased and then decreased as the interval for recall increased). This may show a tendency to

shift from summarizing specific experiences to reporting beliefs about what those experiences are generally like, when people are asked to recall information over long periods. We expect that advances in the cognitive and brain sciences will inform our understanding of recall bias.

MOMENTARY DATA COLLECTION: EXPERIENCE SAMPLING METHOD

To minimize the potential for recall bias and understand people within the context of their normal environment, more intense momentary data collection protocols were developed. In particular, Experience Sampling Method (ESM; Csikszenmihalyi & Larson, 1987; DeVries, 1992) sprang from the early studies of Csikszentmihalyi on the "flow," which intensely examined individuals in order to understand the interactions between experiences during their daily life (Csikszentmihalyi, 1994). The methodological advance (over the use of end-of-day diaries) was the collection of information about how the individual was feeling at the moment preceding an electronically administered auditory signal. The technology used in these studies involved having study participants carry electronic pagers activated by a central station; the investigators provided the central station with a list of times throughout the day when pagers should be activated. When signaled, individuals were to record information on a pocket-size diary, where one or two pages of the multipage diary would be used for each beep. A typical study might be comprised of 7 "beeps" per day for a 1-week period.

DEVELOPMENT OF ECOLOGICAL MOMENTARY ASSESSMENT

Ecological Momentary Assessment (EMA) was formally defined in 1994 (Stone et al., 1994; Stone, Shiffman, & DeVries, 1998) to expand momentary sampling methods from experiences (as per the name) to experiences, behaviors, and physiological measurements. All EMA studies contain three qualities. The first is that measurements are made in the environments that people typically inhabit to ensure ecological validity. This is a characteristic of

many of the above-mentioned methods (e.g., ambulatory monitoring of cardiovascular function, the ESM, and circadian rhythm work).

The second characteristic is the measurement of momentary phenomena to eliminate or at least greatly reduce biases associated with recall. Thus, participants are asked to report about their experiences, behaviors, and environment, or to take physiological measures (e.g., activate a blood pressure monitor, although this can also be accomplished automatically via programming those devices) at the moment of the signal. In fact, however, many investigators have made informed decisions about the period of recall considered acceptable for their research goals and have thus asked participants to report about a period prior to the signal (e.g., 5 minutes, 30 minutes, etc.). Care must be taken when extending the assessment for the moment, given the possibility that recall bias may contaminate even seemingly brief recall periods.

The third EMA quality is that many momentary reports are taken from each participant, yielding a within-person design. Multiple observations are important in three ways:

1. They can be averaged to yield a measure that represents the level of experience (or behavior, environment, etc.) for an individual. Given the large number of observations contributing to an average, this should be a relatively stable estimate. Researchers can also estimate the measures' variability by computing a dispersion statistic like a standard deviation, which may be useful for assessing individual differences.
2. Multiple observations allow a detailed examination of the variable over time, so that, for instance, cyclicity of the variable (within-day, over days) can be examined.
3. Many observations of the variable of interest may be associated with other momentary variables yielding knowledge about within-person associations (also known as time-varying covariates). One might, for instance, be interested in the level of negative affect according to whether or not the individual was with other people (and who those people were). However, thoughtful selection of the sampling strategy used to collect

momentary data is essential to address study hypotheses, because the study conclusions depend on the sampling schemes.

Many review chapters have been published on diary methods and real-time data capture, which the reader may consult to appreciate the versatility and broad scope of the application of EMA and related methods (Affleck, Zautra, Tennen, & Armeli, 1999; Bolger, Davis, & Rafaeli, 2003; Delespaul, 1995; DeVries, 1992; Eckenrode & Bolger, 1995; Reis & Gable, 2000; Stone, Kessler, & Haythornthwaite, 1991; Stone, Shiffman, & Atienza, in press; Tennen & Affleck, 2002). Special issues of major journals (e.g., *Health Psychology, Journal of Nervous and Mental Disorders, Annals of Behavioral Medicine*) have published special sections or issues on the topic.

Sampling Schedules

EMA rely on sampling moments from peoples' daily lives with a sampling protocol chosen according to the purpose(s) of the study (Delespaul, 1995; Wheeler & Reis, 1991). A few examples demonstrate this point. If the goal of a study was to measure the level of a person's fatigue, then many reports of momentary fatigue would likely be averaged to provide a single measure of fatigue. However, for this measure to represent all possible moments that a person could have been sampled, the sampling should be done randomly throughout the day. If this was not done and reports were taken primarily in the morning hours, then it is easy to see how an average taken from that sampling scheme is likely to be biased (toward whatever level of fatigue was typical for mornings). Thus, *random sampling* (and high levels of compliance) is crucial for providing unbiased estimates of typical experiences. A second, entirely different sampling protocol is necessary if an investigator was concerned with understanding the antecedents of an event (e.g., smoking a cigarette). In this case, it is important that a report be made just before the onset of smoking. This is called *event-driven* sampling and is predicated on having participants monitor their thoughts or actions and initiate a report whenever an event occurs or a threshold on a subjective variable (e.g., craving) is met. The third sampling

scheme is based entirely on time (either time-of-day or time intervals) and is called *interval-contingent* sampling. An example of this protocol is to signal individuals every hour or every 20 minutes to make a recording. Actually, many ambulatory blood pressure monitors operate on exactly this scheme, and the investigator can adjust the interval between blood pressure readings. One issue with this sampling scheme considered important for self-reported data is that participants may come to expect signals given their predictability and alter their behavior so that they are able to make a report.

Although these three schemes represent the main classes used to date, a couple of comments are in order. First, one might wonder about the need for any sampling scheme whatsoever (i.e., why not have participants make recordings throughout the day when convenient?). In fact, some versions of pain diaries do just that or specify broad blocks of time (e.g., afternoon) for making recordings. The objection to this form of sampling is that participants will pick and choose the times in nonrandom ways that may be correlated with predictions or outcomes. For instance, in sampling pain levels in patients with chronic pain, patients may select times when they are in greater than average pain, believing that the investigator is interested in such times. Alternatively, periods of extreme pain might not be selected for reports, because the individual is so incapacitated that participating in research is the furthest activity from his or her mind. Either of these forms of self-selection have the capacity to distort our understanding of pain. Second, it is not unusual for research studies to incorporate two or more sampling schemes to meet study goals. Such hybrid protocols may not only be desirable, but in many instances are also conceptually necessary.

To return to the example of the antecedents of cigarette smoking (Shiffman et al., 2002), the information (e.g., examination of momentary stress levels to address the hypothesis that increased stress leads to smoking) collected from event-driven sampling indicates that stress was at a particular level prior to smoking. But with what stress levels should the data be compared to test the hypothesis? Some might argue that stress levels taken at random points throughout the day (random sampling)

might be the appropriate comparison, because the investigator could then conclude, compared to other times of the day, that stress was higher just before smoking. One could strengthen this result by determining the social and setting characteristics of the smoking episodes and then select episodes with those qualities from the random sampling. This eliminates the argument that it wasn't high stress that was associated with smoking, but certain situations or settings. Clearly, the strategy of using more than one type of sampling could prove useful for refining hypothesis testing.

Mode of Data Collection: Paper Versus Electronic

Early versions of the ESM used pagers to signal participants to make a diary recording. Later versions used digital watches with auditory alarms and the capability of storing many (e.g., 100) preprogrammed dates and times for alarms. Some of the watches were linkable to personal computers so that stored alarm schedules could be easily downloaded.

Both the pager and watch methods have inherent limitations. First, because alarm schedules are preprogrammed based on "usual" awakening and bedtimes, participants who alter their wake–sleep schedules or who naturally have unusual schedules may be beeped when they are asleep and not beeped when awake. This can result in chunks of the participant's waking day not being included in the sampling scheme, which is a threat to the validity of the method. Some investigators have individualized sampling protocols by obtaining individuals' typical waking hours and have scheduled the sampling so that it falls within those hours. This helps resolve the validity threat, but does not allow for variability in daily wakening hours (e.g., weekday vs. weekend). Second, preprogrammed devices are limited in their flexibility. They do not have the capacity to alter the manner in which questions are presented to participants (context-specific shifts like program branching when a response indicates, e.g., that some questions are not relevant). They also do not have the capability to alter their sampling routine in accordance with the participants' behavior (e.g., alter the time to the next random beep based on the occurrence

of event-driven beeps to prevent beeps from being too close to one another).

Technological developments in palmtop computers in the 1980s culminated in the current crop of Personal Digital Assistants (PDAs), which was a boon to the EMA field. These compact, fully functional computer devices allow the programming of sophisticated sampling schemes that can present questions to participants directly on the PDA screen (see Figure 5.2). Most of the screens are touch-sensitive, so responses as well as the questions themselves can be presented. This eliminates the need for paper diaries and a signaling device and replaces them with a single, compact unit, which stores the electronic diary (ED) data until the information is uploaded to a personal computer. Of course, this also eliminates the process of transcribing paper questionnaire responses to electronic form, a time-consuming and error-producing process.

Researchers have used EDs in many ways, but only some of them realized the full capacity of these

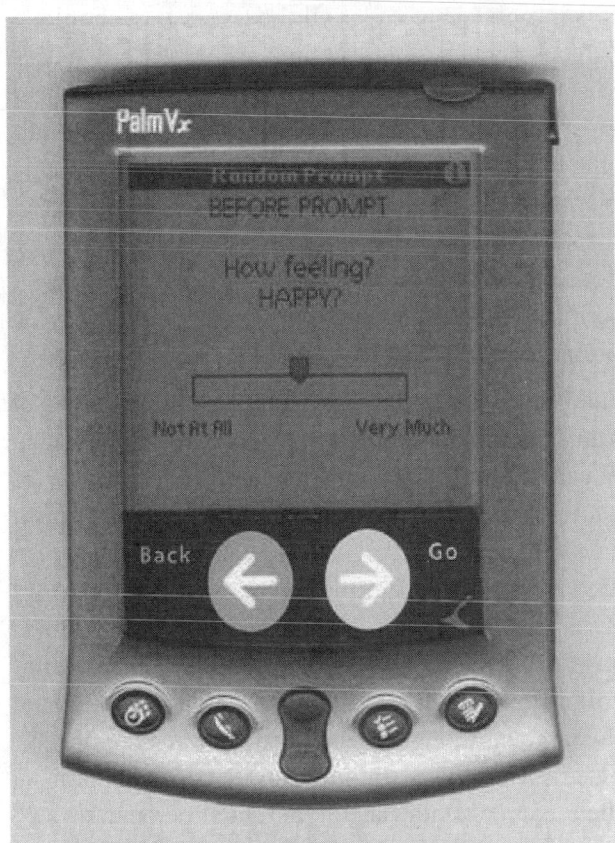

FIGURE 5.2. An electronic diary displaying a visual analog scale.

devices. Some implementations of EDs have mimicked the method of uploading preprogrammed alarms described above with watches; however, this method does not solve the sampling exposure problem. Other programs have been developed that generate prompts in real time and that result in the ability to adapt to participants' schedules. Some of the most sophisticated programs randomly implement a sampling strategy according to a set of parameters. For instance, if a random schedule was desired, the investigator would input both the average and minimum intervals between signals and the program would prompt the individual using these parameters. Thus, an individual who was awake for a 20-hour period would obviously receive a greater number of prompts compared with one who had a shorter number of hours awake, but both people could provide information during the entire time period they were awake.

One of the most compelling reasons for using EDs concerns the issue of participant compliance with sampling protocols, or the proportion of prompts completed according to the protocol. Although low levels of noncompliance probably do not unduly impact the validity of data, very high levels of noncompliance are detrimental to data quality. Data collected with paper diaries do not provide investigators with direct information about compliance; instead, compliance is inferred by examining the times and dates that participants record on the paper diaries. Inferred compliance rates have actually been quite high, at least at the 90% level (Hufford, Stone, Shiffman, Schwartz, & Broderick, 2002). However, researchers have been concerned about this apparently high level of compliance for paper diaries for a couple of reasons. First, experiences with instrumented medication delivery devices, where an unobtrusive computer monitors the use of the device (e.g., a steroid inhaler or a pill dispenser), have shown poor levels of compliance with medication protocols (Simmons, Nides, Rand, Wise, & Tashkin, 2000; Straka, Fish, Benson, & Suh, 1997). Second, many anecdotes from investigators running clinical trials with paper diaries suggest that diaries are often hoarded and completed at one time, sometimes right before a visit to the research site (known as "parking lot" compliance).

A recent study (Stone, Shiffman, Schwartz, Broderick, & Hufford, 2002; Stone et al., 2003) examined compliance with a sampling protocol wherein chronic pain patients were to make diary entries about their pain thrice daily (10 a.m., 4 p.m., and 8 p.m.), over a 3-week period. The study used an instrumented binder that held paper diary sheets and recorded the openings and closings of the binder. By defining periods of time around each of the targeted recording hours (e.g., ± 15 m or ±45 m) and examining the times when the diary binder was actually open, we could determine actual compliance rates. In summary, compliance rates computed by examining subjects' self-reported entry times and dates were consistent with past reports (about 90%). However, when actual compliance was computed based on the openings, compliance dropped dramatically to 11% (30 m window) and 19% (90 m window). More detailed examination of individual records produced evidence of back-filling of paper diaries and, surprisingly, of completion of diaries in advance (forward-filling). Altering the protocol to include an auditory reminder alarm just before the targeted completion times increased compliance only by about 10% (Broderick, Schwartz, Shiffman, Hufford, & Stone, 2003). For us, the data suggest the importance of actually confirming protocol compliance, which EDs are easily able to do. (A comparison group using EDs was also incorporated into this study using the same protocol; EDs that included auditory signals and other compliance enhancing features yielded an actual compliance rate of 94%.)

Application. EMA data collection protocols (using both paper and electronic diaries) have been applied to a variety of situations, including (but not limited to) pain assessment, symptom reports in clinical trials, smoking and alcohol cessation or cravings, food consumption, mood and stress assessments, and psychiatric and physiological symptoms (Hufford & Shields, 2002; Stone et al., 1998). In fact, it has been reported that about 25% of Phase 2 to Phase 4 clinical trials use some type of diary to monitor patients' responses (Hufford et al., 2002). These studies have examined both healthy volunteers as well as various disease populations.

Furthermore, studies have not been limited to adults; adolescents and children have also participated in studies using EDs (Henker, Whalen, & Jamner, 2002; Walker & Sorrells, 2002).

As technology has advanced, both clinicians and researchers have increasingly implemented electronic diaries with EMA designs. Hufford and Shields (Hufford & Shields, 2002) identified 76 empirical articles that used electronic diaries published in peer-reviewed, English language journals from 1990 to 2001. Since then, an additional 24 have been published (identified by replicating Hufford's original searches).

The ease of use of the devices and depth of information obtained using the various sampling strategies explain the shift to studies utilizing EMA and EDs. In addition, the ability to address within-person hypotheses that are clinically relevant (Stone et al., 2003) make this ideal for the interdisciplinary research conducted in behavioral medicine.

Implementation

It is impossible to cover all the issues that should be considered when designing an EMA study within this chapter, but we will briefly cover many of the most important considerations (more detail is available in Delespaul, 1998). In 2002, Stone and Shiffman published a paper on "reporting guidelines" for momentary studies that suggest which study design information should be reported in manuscripts. We use their outline as a convenient way of presenting design issues.

Sampling. We have already discussed basic types of sampling schemes used in EMA and the importance of careful planning about the data needed to address a study's hypotheses. Sampling density indicates the number of signals participants receive per day; with random and time interval prompting, this is decided in advance. Determining sampling density a priori with event-driven sampling can be difficult unless one has considerable information about the targeted thought or behavior's frequency of occurrence. This is an important consideration if the target behavior has the potential of occurring quite frequently. Some researchers have implemented ingenious schemes for sampling event-driven behaviors with electronic diaries to

overcome this problem. Shiffman and colleagues studied antecedents of cigarette smoking, but felt that full momentary assessments of every cigarette smoked might prove too burdensome for participants. They therefore asked participants to indicate all instances of smoking, but randomly selected a portion of these for comprehensive assessment (Shiffman et al., 1997). When choosing a sampling strategy one must ensure that the proper time periods are sampled throughout the day. This maximizes validity of the results and minimizes bias.

Momentary procedures. Researchers face many decisions pertaining to the actual protocols used to collect momentary data, especially with EDs, given the great flexibility afforded by the programming (e.g., Delespaul, 1995; Hufford & Shields, 2002). A few examples show issues that need consideration. In the case of event-driven recording, participants need a very clear understanding of the "rules" for making a diary entry. To use a medically oriented example, researchers studying bowel movements would need to accentuate to participants exactly when they should make the recording (e.g. during, immediately after, within an hour) and if a recording should be made for each event. For discrete events and actions like this, the criteria for initiating a recording may be straightforward. However, when individuals must initiate a recording on the basis of having a certain intensity of a feeling or having a particular thought, then potential bias issues arise. Are individuals capable of detecting the threshold sought by the investigator (e.g., "moderately stressed"), and how can the reliability of these reports be verified? Extensive piloting with well-trained, extensively debriefed participants may help determine the success of such event-driven prompting schemes.

Another example of these reporting issues concerns how an investigator handles a missed prompt in a random or interval-contingent sampling study. Has a period of time after (or before) the targeted time been designated in advance as an acceptable period for completing a prompt? Does the ED administer another prompt a few minutes after a missed prompt? How many times? Thus, the development of a sampling protocol, which can impact the quality and validity of the data collected, is a complex process. In all cases, the electronic protocol needs extensive field testing prior to implementation in the trial—research staff must use the ED for several days, essentially exposing themselves to all kinds of circumstances that participants may encounter.

Data acquisition interface. The type and size of the data acquisition interface is another consideration for users of electronic diaries (Hufford & Shields, 2002). Most EDs have a small display screen, about 6 cm × 6 cm, making it a challenge to devise ways of presenting moderate length questions and responses in a legible, efficient manner. When transferring standardized questionnaires to ED platforms, it is typical to rewrite the questions to fit the display. Questions must retain their original meaning, however, and pretesting of significant rewrites may be necessary to ensure accuracy. Similarly, response options in questionnaires can take many forms ranging from "Yes/No" options to checklists of items to 5-point and visual analog scales (VAS). The "Yes/No" response option is usually not a problem given its brevity; however, lists of items can be problematic. One solution is to allow participants to scroll through a list of options where some of the options are not shown until the scrolling reaches them. In this way, many response options can be made available. Likewise, VAS scales in questionnaires are usually 10 cm in length, which is beyond the available presentation real estate of most PDA displays. Some have raised questions about whether or not a shorter VAS scale yields the same information as 10 cm scales; so far, the evidence is that they are equivalent ($r = 0.97$; Jamison et al., 2002).

Compliance. Compliance issues were discussed above and here we simply stress the importance of reporting the *actual* protocol compliance.

Training of participants. An important, yet often overlooked, feature of an EMA study is the procedures used to train participants in the use of the diaries and procedures to monitor and enhance compliance (Hufford & Shields, 2002). Participants need a thorough understanding of the study proto-

col and the data collection device prior to the onset of field recording. In many laboratories, participants are first trained in small groups about the purpose of the study and the procedures for making diary entries, and they can then practice completing the diary in the presence of the investigators. This ED training is especially important given the unfamiliarity that some individuals have with PDAs and the complexity of the implementation. Many features of sophisticated EDs (e.g., sleep, nap, and delay) are perfectly understandable once fully explained, although not self-explanatory. Therefore, we strongly urge investigators using EDs to have participants practice with them during the training session. We find that 30 to 60 minutes is usually adequate for training a small group.

Apart from excellent training, obtaining good protocol compliance is really an ongoing process wherein participants are provided with performance feedback. Follow-up phone calls may be made after the training session. During this phone call the researcher can make sure the device is working properly in the field and ensure that the participant is comfortable using the ED for the study's duration. This troubleshoots problems during the early stages of data collection and sees that the participant is using the ED correctly. Another type of ongoing feedback involves providing participants with information about compliance or the quality of their data (e.g., missing entries) at regular intervals throughout a study. This sort of feedback may be especially important early in the study, when participants are still learning the protocol requirements; corrective feedback at this stage can largely impact data quality and compliance for the remainder of the study. Some implementations of EDs have on-screen compliance feedback, such that, when prompts are missed, information is provided about the missed prompt—perhaps with an encouraging word about the importance of timely diary completion. These and other clever ways of enhancing compliance are critical to achieving the goals of a momentary study.

Data management. These are rather technical, nevertheless important, issues for the overall success of a momentary study. However, we will not detail these issues here. Some things to remember when undertaking a study of this kind are (a) to have trained staff who are able to troubleshoot problems with the hardware and software of the device and (b) to have an adequate database program that can handle the amount of data generated from such a study.

Analytic issues. Momentary data present investigators with many challenges. The volume of data is often immense given the substantial number of recordings made by each participant. Most challenging, though, is the multilevel structure and repeated nature of the data. Unlike between-person studies where the individual is usually the smallest unit of analysis, in EMA research the moment is nested within persons, and this demands techniques specifically designed for this data structure. Multilevel analyses, hierarchical linear models, and random regression are all analysis techniques that can be used for analyzing momentary data. Several review papers including Schwartz and Stone (Schwartz & Stone, 1998, in press) and Tennen and Affleck (2002) discuss the pitfalls of using traditional analysis of variance procedures with momentary data and provide overviews and technical references for the other techniques. All novice researchers who are considering conducting a momentary study should familiarize themselves with these models or obtain expert consultation, as there are many subtleties to successfully conducting analyses of momentary data. Within the next year or so a book on conventional and alternative statistical approaches to real-time data, edited by Ted Walls, should be available.

Reactivity and Participant Burden

A concern that users of EMA have expressed is the possibility of reactive arrangements. This is the potential for the use of diaries to affect the experience of the phenomenon being studied. Certainly, this is a reasonable concern given the additional and unusual attention that will be paid to whatever is being recorded in the diary. Nevertheless, several studies suggest that a moderate density of momentary reporting does not have a major impact on reporting, at least over a 2- to

3-week period (Cruise, Porter, Broderick, Kaell, & Stone, 1996). Recently, Stone and colleagues (Stone et al., 2003) examined the possibility that the use of an ED affects the level of pain being reported over a 2-week period, using random sampling schedules with densities of 3, 6, or 12 times per day. Consistent with prior studies, Stone et al. observed little evidence of a shift in pain over time or according to sampling density. This study also examined the possibility that momentary reporting alters the recall of weekly pain reports that stem from reactive arrangements, and this was tested with both between-person and within-person analyses. The study showed no evidence that momentary recording procedures altered recall of pain.

Clearly, EMA protocol can be quite burdensome and possibly annoying for participants unless considerable care is taken. Although there are no "rules" about what is too much, several factors need consideration, including the following:

1. the length of the diary interview (from under a minute to many minutes),
2. the daily sampling density (from once a day to 25 or more per day),
3. the duration of study (from a single day to many weeks), and
4. the characteristics of the participant sample (from healthy adolescents to chronically ill patients).

If the burden is too great or the annoyance too high, then attrition will likely increase and compliance with the recording will decrease, both serious threats to the internal validity of a study.

The reactivity study mentioned above (Stone et al., 2003) used a 2-minute diary on pain over a 14-day period with chronically ill pain patients and examined three sampling densities. Protocol compliance was extremely good (94%) and did not differ by sampling density group. At the end of the study, participants rated how they felt about being in the study. In brief, although there were some expected effects in perceived burden according to sampling density, even the 12-day group rated the burden as just above "slightly burdensome" and the same for the degree of interference with daily activi-

ties. Importantly, all groups said they were at least "moderately" sure that if offered, they would participate in another study like the one they had just completed. Although this was only a single study addressing the issue, it seems reasonable that EMA protocols can be well tolerated by patients.

Other Forms of Momentary Data Capture

In addition to the paper and electronic diary methods described above, other methods are available for capturing momentary data in the real world, and we briefly mention them here. One method is interactive voice recording or IVR where a dedicated computer is programmed to present questions and response options to participants via telephone. This well-developed technology can be used in several ways, and one common approach is to have participants call the computer at designated times (e.g., the end of the day). Using either the telephone's digital keypad or their own voice, users are instructed to identify themselves and then are taken through a series of verbal questions and, again, with either keypad or voice, are able to provide responses. The system records the time and date of the responses and is capable of the same complex branching of questions as described for high level EDs. The ubiquity of cell phone usage increases the probability of convenient access to the IVR system. In another version of this system, the computer calls participants at designated times for the data collection.

A rapidly growing methodology stemmed from the popularity of the Internet. With this system, researchers develop a questionnaire and program a Web site to present the information to participants. For their part, participants simply access the site and complete the questionnaire, which is time and date stamped. Although serious questions remain regarding the security of such systems for collecting sensitive information, we imagine that such problems will be resolved in the future.

Finally, investigators have developed means of sampling the auditory environment of individuals as they go about their normal activities, including conversations with others as well as ambient sounds (Mehl & Pennebaker, 2003). From these short recordings, made by a specially modified

voice-activated tape recorder, the developers purport to be able to derive many indices of the psychological state of the targeted person, the nature of their interactions, and the characteristics of their social environment. Creative uses of technology like this one are exciting.

SUMMARY

In sum, the collection of self-report data has undergone an interesting evolution. From studies involving interviews to those using electronic diaries to collect momentary data, the techniques for understanding peoples' experiences have become more refined, comprehensive, and have moved from the office to the field. Some of the challenges that researchers using EMA (in particular, with EDs) must address are analytical issues (handling and interpreting the large amount of data generated) and cost issues incurred from using state-of-the-art technology (both hardware and software). However, the benefits include having a large amount of data for each individual (making clinically relevant, within-person analyses possible), being able to monitor compliance (thus, being confident that compliance is not being "faked"), assessing people in their normal environment (to increase ecological validity), and making decisions a priori about the time frame to assess each construct (to reduce recall bias). Depending on the research hypothesis being studied, these benefits may outweigh the challenges. Thus, EMA is the next step for self-report research to attain the goal of measuring real-world data.

CHAPTER 6

WEB-BASED METHODS

Ulf-Dietrich Reips

What can be gained from applying Web-based methods to psychological assessment? In the last decade it has become possible to collect data from participants who are tested via the Internet rather than in the laboratory. Although this type of assessment has inherent limitations stemming from lack of control and observation of conditions, it also has a number of advantages over laboratory research (Birnbaum, 2004; Krantz & Dalal, 2000; Reips, 1995, 1997, 2000, 2002c; Schmidt, 1997). Some of the main advantages are that (a) one can test large numbers of participants very quickly; (b) one can recruit large heterogeneous samples and people with rare characteristics; and (c) the method is more cost-effective in time, space, and labor in comparison with laboratory research.

This chapter comprises seven sections. In the first section, Web-Based Methods in Psychology, I briefly look at the short history of Web-based methods in psychological research, describe their characteristics, and present a systematic overview of different types of methods. The second section, Advantages of Web-Based Methods, illustrates that Web-based methods promise a great number of benefits to psychological assessment, several of which have been empirically supported or are confined to specific conditions. The third section, Common Concerns Regarding Internet-Based Studies, presents some typical concerns regarding Web-based research, along with findings and reasons that convincingly soften most concerns.

However, the theoretical and empirical work conducted by pioneers in research on Web-based methods has also identified some basic problems and some typical errors. The fourth section, Techniques, demonstrates several techniques to avoid, solve, or alleviate these issues. The fifth section, Three Web-Based Assessment Methods, explains several specific methods, including log file analysis, using the randomized response technique (RRT) on the Web, and game scenarios as covers for Web experiments. The sixth section, Using Web-Based Methods: An Example, gives the reader the opportunity to become active and experience Web-based methods by creating and conducting a Web-based experiment and, subsequently, a log file analysis in a step-by-step fashion. The example used is from Internet-based psychological research on framing effects. It shows how the use of Web-based tools can create a whole new type of research experience in psychology when Web-based methods of assessment are integrated with new communication and presentation modes. The concluding section looks at potential future trends and the continuing evolution of Web-based methods and their use in psychological assessment. The rapid development of Web technology and the spread of knowledge among psychologists regarding its characteristics creates the expectation that Web-based methods will inevitably impact the way psychological assessment is conducted in the future.

Thanks to Michael Birnbaum for his helpful comments.

WEB-BASED METHODS IN PSYCHOLOGY

Since the beginning (i.e., when the interactive Web became available with the advent of forms in HTML standard 2.0), this technology has been used in psychological research. The first psychological questionnaires appeared in 1994. Krantz, Ballard, and Scher (1997) and Reips (1997) conducted the first Internet-based experiments in the summer of 1995, and Reips opened the first virtual laboratory in September 1995 (Web Experimental Psychology Lab: http://www.psychologie.unizh.ch/sowi/Ulf/Lab/WebExpPsyLab.html[1]). Studies conducted via the World Wide Web (WWW) have grown exponentially since 1995, when researchers began to take advantage of the new standard for HTML, which allowed for convenient data collection (Musch & Reips, 2000).

To get an overall impression of the kinds of psychological studies currently in progress on the Web, the reader may visit studies linked at the Web Experimental Psychology Lab or at the following Web sites:

> Web experiment list (Reips & Lengler, 2005):
>   http://genpsylab-wexlist.unizh.ch/
> Web survey list:
>   http://genpsylab-wexlist.unizh.ch/
>   browse.cfm?action=browse&modus=survey
> Psychological Research on the Net by Krantz:
>   http://psych.hanover.edu/research/
>   exponnet.html
> International Personality Item Pool by Goldberg:
>   http://ipip.ori.org/ipip/
> Online Social Psychology Studies by Plous:
>   http://www.socialpsychology.org/expts.htm
> Decision Research Center by Birnbaum:
>   http://psych.fullerton.edu/mbirnbaum/
>   decisions/thanks.htm

Types of Web-Based Methods
Web-based studies can be categorized as *nonreactive Web-based methods, Web surveys, Web-based tests,* and *Web experiments.*

Nonreactive Web-based methods refer to the use and analysis of existing databases and text collec-

tions on the Internet (e.g., server log files or newsgroup contributions). The Internet provides an ocean of opportunities for nonreactive data collection. The sheer size of Internet corpora multiplies the specific strengths of this class of methods: Nonmanipulable events can be studied *in natura,* facilitating the examination of rare behavioral patterns. An early example of the use of nonreactive data is the study of communicative behavior among members of several mailing lists, conducted in 1996 and 1997 (at a time when SPAM was a rare phenomenon) by Stegbauer and Rausch (2002). These authors were interested in the so-called "lurking behavior" (i.e., passive membership in mailing lists, newsgroups, and other forums). By analyzing the number and time of postings and the interaction frequencies pertaining to e-mail headers in contributions, Stegbauer and Rausch empirically clarified several questions regarding the lurking phenomenon. For instance, about 70% of subscribers to mailing lists could be classified as lurkers, and ". . . among the majority of users, lurking is not a transitional phenomenon but a fixed behavior pattern [within the same social space]" (p. 267). On the other hand, the analysis of individuals' contributions to different mailing lists showed a sizeable proportion of people may lurk in one forum but are active in another. With this result, Stegbauer and Rausch empirically supported the notion of so-called weak ties as a basis for the transfer of knowledge between social spaces.

The fifth section, Three Web-Based Assessment Methods, describes log file analysis as an (important) example of a nonreactive Web-based method. For more examples refer to Nonreactive Methods in Psychological Research (Fritsche & Linneweber, this volume, chap. 14).

Web surveys: The most commonly used Web-based assessment method is the Web survey. The frequent use of surveys on the Internet can be explained by the apparent ease with which Web surveys can be constructed, conducted, and evaluated. However, this impression is somewhat fallacious. Work by Dillman and his group (Dillman

---

[1]Because Web addresses (URLs) may change, the reader is advised to use a search engine like Google (http://www.google.com/) to access the Web pages mentioned in this chapter. In the present case, typing "Web Experimental Psychology Lab" into the search field will return the link to the laboratory as the first listed result. The Web Experimental Psychology Lab can also be accessed using the short URL http://tinyurl.com/dwcpx

& Bowker, 2001; Dillman, Tortora, & Bowker, 1998) has shown that many Web surveys are plagued by problems of usability, display, sampling, or technology. Joinson and Reips (in press) have shown through experiments that the degree of personalization and the power attributable to the sender of an invitation to participate in the survey can impact survey response rates. Data quality can be influenced by degree of anonymity, and this factor as well as information about incentives also influences the frequency of dropout (Frick, Bächtiger, & Reips, 2001). Design factors like the decision whether a "one screen, one question" procedure is applied or not may trigger context effects that turn results upside down (Reips, 2002a). Despite these findings, converging evidence shows that Web-based survey methods result in qualitatively comparable results to traditional surveys, even in longitudinal studies (Hiskey & Troop, 2002).

Web-based psychological testing constitutes one specific subtype of Web surveying (unless an experimental component is part of the design, see Erdfelder & Musch, this volume, chap. 15). Buchanan and Smith (1999), Buchanan (2001), Preckel and Thiemann (2003), and Wilhelm and McKnight (2002), among others, have shown that Web-based testing is possible if the particularities of the Internet situation are considered (e.g., computer anxiety may keep certain people from responding to a Web-based questionnaire). Buchanan and Smith found that an Internet-based self-monitoring test not only showed similar psychometric properties to its conventional equivalent but compared favorably as a measure of self-monitoring. Their results support the notion that Web-based personality assessment is possible. Similarly, Buchanan, Johnson, and Goldberg (2005) showed that a modified International Personality Item Pool (IPIP) inventory they evaluated appears to have satisfactory psychometric properties as a brief online measure of the domain constructs of the Five-Factor Model. Across two studies using different recruiting techniques, they observed acceptable levels of internal reliability and significant correlations with relevant criterion variables. However, the issue of psychometric equivalence of paper-and-pencil versions of questionnaires with their Web-based counterparts is not a simple "all equal." For instance, Buchanan et al. (in press) could only recover two of four factor-analytically derived subscales of the Prospective Memory Questionnaire with a sample of $N = 763$ tested via the Internet. The other two subscales were essentially meaningless. Buchanan and Reips (2001) showed that technical aspects of how the Web-based test is implemented may interact with demography or personality and, consequently, introduce a sampling bias. In their study they showed that the average education level was higher in Web-based assessment if no JavaScript was used, and that Mac users scored significantly higher on Openness than PC users.

Web experiments show a certain categorical distinctiveness from experiments conducted in the laboratory or in the field (Reips, 1995, 2000). However, the underlying logical criteria are the same as those in the other experimental methods. Hence, the definition of "experiment" used here requires manipulation of the independent variable(s), repeatability, and random assignment to conditions. Likewise, a quasi-Web experiment would involve nonrandom assignment of subjects to conditions (see Campbell & Stanley, 1963; Kirk, 1995).

Web experiments offer a chance to validate findings that were acquired using laboratory experiments and field experiments. The number of participants is notoriously small in many traditional studies because researchers set the Type I error probability to a conventional level (and therefore the power of these studies is low; Erdfelder, Faul, & Buchner, 1996). One of the greatest advantages in Web research is the ease with which large numbers of participants can be reached. The Web Experimental Psychology Lab, for instance, is visited by about 4,000 people per month (Reips, 2001). On the Internet the participants may leave at any time, and the experimental situation is usually free of the social pressure often inherent in experiments conducted for course credit with students. Because Web experiments are often visible on the Internet and remain there as a documentation of the research method and material, overall transparency of the research process is increased.

ADVANTAGES OF WEB-BASED METHODS

One of the principal reasons why Web-based methods are so popular is the *fundamental asymmetry of accessibility*: What is programmed to be accessible from any Internet-connected place in the world will surely also be accessible in a university laboratory, but what is programmed to work locally may most likely not be accessible anywhere else. A laboratory experiment, for instance, cannot simply be turned into a Web experiment by connecting the host computer to the Internet. But any Web experiment can also be used in the laboratory. Consequently, it is a good strategy to design a Web-based study, if possible. As demonstrated later in this chapter, however, the ease with which laboratory studies can be connected to the Web when developed with Internet software carries the danger of overlooking the specific methodological requirements of using Web-based methods. The requirements and associated techniques are outlined in the next section of this chapter; however, some primary advantages of Internet-based assessment must first be stressed.

Web-based methods offer various benefits to the researcher (for summaries, see Birnbaum, 2004; Reips, 1995, 2000, 2002c). Main advantages are that (a) one can test large numbers of participants quickly; (b) one can recruit large heterogeneous samples and people with rare characteristics (Schmidt, 1997); and (c) Web-based methods are more cost-effective in time, space, administration, and labor in comparison with laboratory research. Of course, all advantages of computerized assessment methods (see Drasgow & Chuah, this volume, chap. 7) apply to Web-based assessment methods as well. Methodological analyses and studies reveal that Web-based methods are usually valid (e.g., Krantz, Ballard, & Scher, 1997; Krantz & Dalal, 2000) and sometimes even generate higher quality data than laboratory studies (Birnbaum, 2001; Buchanan & Smith, 1999; Reips, 2000) and facilitate research in previously inaccessible areas (e.g., Bordia, 1996; Coomber, 1997; Rodgers et al., 2001).

Other benefits of Web-based methods are (d) the ease of access for participants (bringing the experiment to the participant instead of the opposite); (e) the ease of access to participants from different cultures—for instance, Bohner, Danner, Siebler, and Samson (2002) conducted a study in three languages with 440 women from more than nine countries (but see the discussion about the physical and educational *digital divide* in access to Web technology); (f) truly voluntary participation (unless participants are required to visit the Web site); (g) detectability of confounding with motivational aspects of study participation; (h) the better generalizability of findings to the general population (e.g., Brenner, 2002; Horswill & Coster, 2001); (i) the generalizability of findings to more settings and situations because of high external validity—Laugwitz (2001), for instance, was able to show that a color perception effect in software ergonomics persisted despite the large variance of conditions of lighting, monitor calibration, and so forth in participants' settings; (j) the avoidance of time constraints; (k) the *simultaneous* participation of very large numbers of participants is possible; (l) the reduction of experimenter effects (even in automated computer-based assessments there is often some kind of personal contact, not so in most Web-based assessments); (m) the reduction of demand characteristics (see Orne, 1962); (n) greater visibility of the research process (Web-based studies can be visited by others, and their links can be published in articles resulting from the research); (o) the access to the number of people who see the announcement link to the study, but decide not to participate; (p) the ease of cross-method comparison—comparing results with results from a sample tested in the laboratory; (q) greater external validity through greater technical variance; and (r) the heightened public control of ethical standards.

These are the reasons why 70% of those who have conducted a Web experiment intend to *certainly* use this method again (with the other 30% who are keeping this option open). "Large number of participants" and "high statistical power" were rated by surveyed researchers who had made the decision to conduct a Web experiment as the two most important benefits (Musch & Reips, 2000).

COMMON CONCERNS REGARDING INTERNET-BASED STUDIES

Many routinely raised concerns involve the lack of proper sampling and the lack of control in Internet-based studies. There are also issues of coverage, measurement, and nonresponse (Dillman, 2001). According to D. Dillman (personal communication, April 1, 2004) the situation gets worse, partly because of the ever increasing variety of media and differences in access to and knowledge about media. Along with other researchers (e.g., Brenner, 2002; Dillman, 2000), I have continuing concerns about potential problems in both Internet-based and laboratory studies. Many unresolved issues remain in traditional studies, including contaminated student samples, experimenter effects, demand characteristics, motivational confounding, low power, and generalizability (for an extensive discussion see Reips, 2000), and these issues can be alleviated or even resolved with Web-based methods. Experience has shown initial concerns regarding Web-based methods, like the frequency and detectability of multiple submissions, nonrepresentativeness of Internet users, dishonest or malicious behavior (false responses and "hacking"), are not as problematic as previously considered (Birnbaum, 2004; Birnbaum & Reips, 2005), and the real issues tend to be overlooked (Reips, 2002b, 2002c).

When designing a study one must find a balance between methodological advantages and disadvantages. From a multimethod perspective, the opportunity to validate findings with a new set of methods in a new setting is an exciting one: Design the study for the Web, and for comparison, run a subsample in the traditional way.

Response Time Measurement

One of the more technical concerns about Web-based methods deals with response or even reaction time measurement. How can these times be accurate if the computer equipment is not standardized and calibrated, and if the response is transferred over a fragile net connection? The simple answer is: The noise is small enough to detect relative differences in a proper design, even with the weaker techniques of Internet-based response time measurement, like JavaScript. Reips, Morger, and Meier (2001) demonstrated in an experiment on the previously established *list context effect* with a Web and a lab condition that an effect is detectable on the Web using JavaScript time measurement. However, for the same number of participants, the power to detect effects is lower on the Web. Fortunately, as mentioned earlier, it is also much easier to recruit many participants on the Web.

One of the ways to measure response times is via JavaScript. Because JavaScript is a "client-side" language (it does not run on the server, but on the participants' computers), depending on the exact JavaScript methods used in the scripts, OS, browser type, browser version, and other software running on the client, there is a probability for variance in timing and technical problems with JavaScript. Accumulating technical interactions with JavaScript can even lead to crashes of browsers and computers (for an experiment showing that using JavaScript in a Web experiment will lead to a 13% higher overall dropout rate compared to the same Web experiment without JavaScript, see Schwarz & Reips, 2001). The likelihood for problems seems to decrease, though, with newer browsers and newer OS versions that obviously adapt well to the problems.

A second crude way of measuring response times is to calculate the time differences of when materials are accessed on the Web server. Scientific LogAnalyzer (Reips & Stieger, 2004; see Using Web-Based Methods: An Example, this chapter) includes a routine to calculate these times from servers' log files.

So, is there any way to accurately measure reaction times via the Internet? There is: Eichstaedt (2001) developed a Java-based method for very accurate response time measurements. A clever combination of applets ensures continuous synchronization and calibration of timing between server and client, which minimizes timing inaccuracies produced by the Internet.

TECHNIQUES

Two types of techniques were developed in Internet-based research. One type guards against common errors and problems, the other one increases

the usefulness of Web-based assessment methods. Also, techniques can be grouped, along the stages of the research process, according to their applications: techniques for design and procedure, techniques for recruitment, techniques for data analysis. Many of the techniques have been implemented in those Web services or software that allow the creation of Web-based assessments.

Techniques Against Common Errors and Problems

Every coin has two sides, and so the great advantage of revealing assessment materials to a large worldwide audience via the Internet also means that the collected information may be accessible for many people. There is evidence that confidential data is often openly accessible (an estimate runs at 25%–33%, and this is a cause for concern) because of configuration errors on the part of the researcher that can be easily made in certain operating systems (Reips, 2002b). Several measures help delete this problem: (a) choosing the right (secure) combination of operating system and Web server, (b) using a pretested system to develop and run the Web-based assessment, and (c) having people with good Internet knowledge test the Web-based assessment for security weaknesses.

In dealing with *multiple submissions* that may become a problem in highly motivating study scenarios (see the description of game-based Web experiments in Three Web-Based Assessment Methods, this chapter), one can use techniques for *avoiding* and techniques for *controlling* the respondents' behavior (Reips, 2002c). Avoidance of multiple submissions, for instance, can be achieved by limiting participation to members of a group known to the researcher, like a class, an *online participant pool,* or *online panel* (Göritz, Reinhold, & Batinic, 2002) and working with a *password scheme* (Schmidt, 1997). A technique that helps control multiple submissions is the *sub-sampling technique* (Reips, 2000, 2002b): For a limited random sample from all data sets, every possible measure is taken to verify the participants' identity, resulting in an estimate for the total percentage of multiple submissions. This technique can help estimate the number of wrong answers by checking verifiable responses (e.g., age,

sex, occupation). Applications for Web-based assessment may include routines that check for internal consistency and search for answering patterns (Gockenbach, Bosnjak, & Göritz, 2004). Overall, it has repeatedly been shown that multiple submissions are rare in Internet-based research (Reips, 1997; Voracek, Stieger, & Gindl, 2001), and that data quality may vary with a number of factors (e.g., whether personal information is requested at the beginning or end of a study, Frick et al., 2001; information about the person who issues the invitation to the study, Joinson & Reips, in press; or whether scripts are used that do not allow participants to leave any items unanswered and, therefore, cause psychological reactance, Reips, 2002c).

Techniques to Increase the Usefulness of Web-Based Assessment

One major asset available in Web-based assessment methods is the information gained from different types of nonresponse behavior (Bosnjak, 2001), particularly dropout (attrition). Dropout is always present in Web-based assessment methods because subjectively the participant is in a much more voluntary setting than in a laboratory situation. Although one may consider dropout a serious problem in any type of study, dropout can also be put to use and turned into a detection device for motivational confounding, i.e. the confounding of the motivation to continue participating in the study with any other difference caused by differing influences between conditions (Reips, 1997, 2000, 2002b; Reips, Morger, & Meier, 2001). If desired, dropout can also be reduced by implementing a number of measures, like promising immediate feedback, giving financial incentives, and by personalization (Frick et al., 2001). Or, the *warm-up technique* for dropout control can be implemented (Reips, 2000, 2002b): the actual study begins several pages deep into the material, so a high compliance is already established.

Only a selection of the available techniques can be explained in this chapter, but the reader is referred to Birnbaum (2001), Birnbaum and Reips (2005), and Reips (2000, 2002b, 2002c, 2002d) for more detailed explanations of these and other techniques of Web-based assessment.

THREE WEB-BASED ASSESSMENT METHODS

In this section, three specific Web-based methods are presented: log file analysis as an example of a nonreactive method, using the randomized response technique in surveys conducted on the Web, and games as a cover format for Internet-based experiments.

Log file analysis is at the core of many nonreactive methods of behavioral research on the Web. Navigation behavior in Web sites can be captured as so-called *click streams*, both on an individual and on a group level. Scientific applications for Web log analysis can be used to extract information about behaviors from log files, calculate response times and nonresponse behavior, and find relevant differences between users' navigation behaviors. The tool STRATDYN (Berendt, 2002; Berendt & Brenstein, 2001), for instance, provides classification and visualization of movement sequences in Web navigation and tests differences between navigation patterns in hypertexts. Scientific LogAnalyzer (Reips & Stieger, 2004) is geared toward analyzing data provided on forms and was developed for the analysis of data from most types of Internet-based experimenting (see Using Web-Based Methods: An Example, this chapter, for a description of how to use Scientific LogAnalyzer). LOGPAT (Richter, Naumann, & Noller, 2003) is useful in analyzing sequential measures, (i.e., counting the frequency of specific paths or path types in a log file). Like Scientific LogAnalyzer, LOGPAT was developed as a platform-independent, Web-based tool. In addition to these scientific applications, a large number of commercial and free log file analysis programs are available that primarily focus on helping the user maintain a Web site. This type of software can help identify access errors, points of entry, and user paths through a Web site. Many of the applications are user friendly and create visually appealing graphical output. Example programs are Analog (http://www.analog.cx/), FunnelWeb (http://www.quest.com/funnel_web/analyzer/), TrafficReport (http://www.seacloak.com/), and Summary (http://www.summary.net/).

Testing large numbers of participants very quickly via the Web is particularly important for the success of research projects that depend on the availability of a large sample. Therefore, a Web-based format is always a good choice if the *randomized response technique* (RRT; Warner, 1965) is to be used. Researchers have demonstrated the feasibility of the RRT in a large number of studies (e.g., Antonak & Livneh, 1995; for an explanation of the method see Erdfelder & Musch, this volume, chap. 15).

One of the better versions of the RRT, the cheater detection model by Clark and Desharnais (1998), which operates with an experimental between-subjects manipulation, has been repeatedly used on the Web (Musch, Bröder, & Klauer, 2001; Reips & Musch, 1999). Figure 6.1 shows a screen capture taken from the Web-based RRT study by Reips and Musch on the feasibility and trustworthiness of a computerized random generator. The participant is asked to click on the random wheel on the left side of the window. A click results in one of two events: If the left portion of the window turns blue then a true answer to the question is requested. If the window turns red, then the participant is asked to answer with "Yes," independently of the true answer. This condition is compared with one in which a different "random" device independent of computers and the Internet is used: the participant's month of birth. From various other conditions the behavior's incidence rate and the proportion of "cheaters" (sic!) in the sample can be calculated, as well as the influence of the computerized "random wheel." The enhanced anonymity often associated with Web-based questioning has provided additional advantages when conducting RRT surveys on the Internet.

Web experiments designed in game style are likely to attract a very large number of participants who will participate with high motivation (e.g., Reips & Mürner, 2004; Ruppertsberg, Givaty, Van Veen, & Bülthoff, 2001). Ruppertsberg et al. (2001) used games written in Java as research tools for visual perception over the Internet. They concluded that presenting games ". . . on the Internet resulted in large quantities of useful data, and allowed us to draw conclusions about mechanisms in face recognition in a broader, less selected participant population" (p. 157).

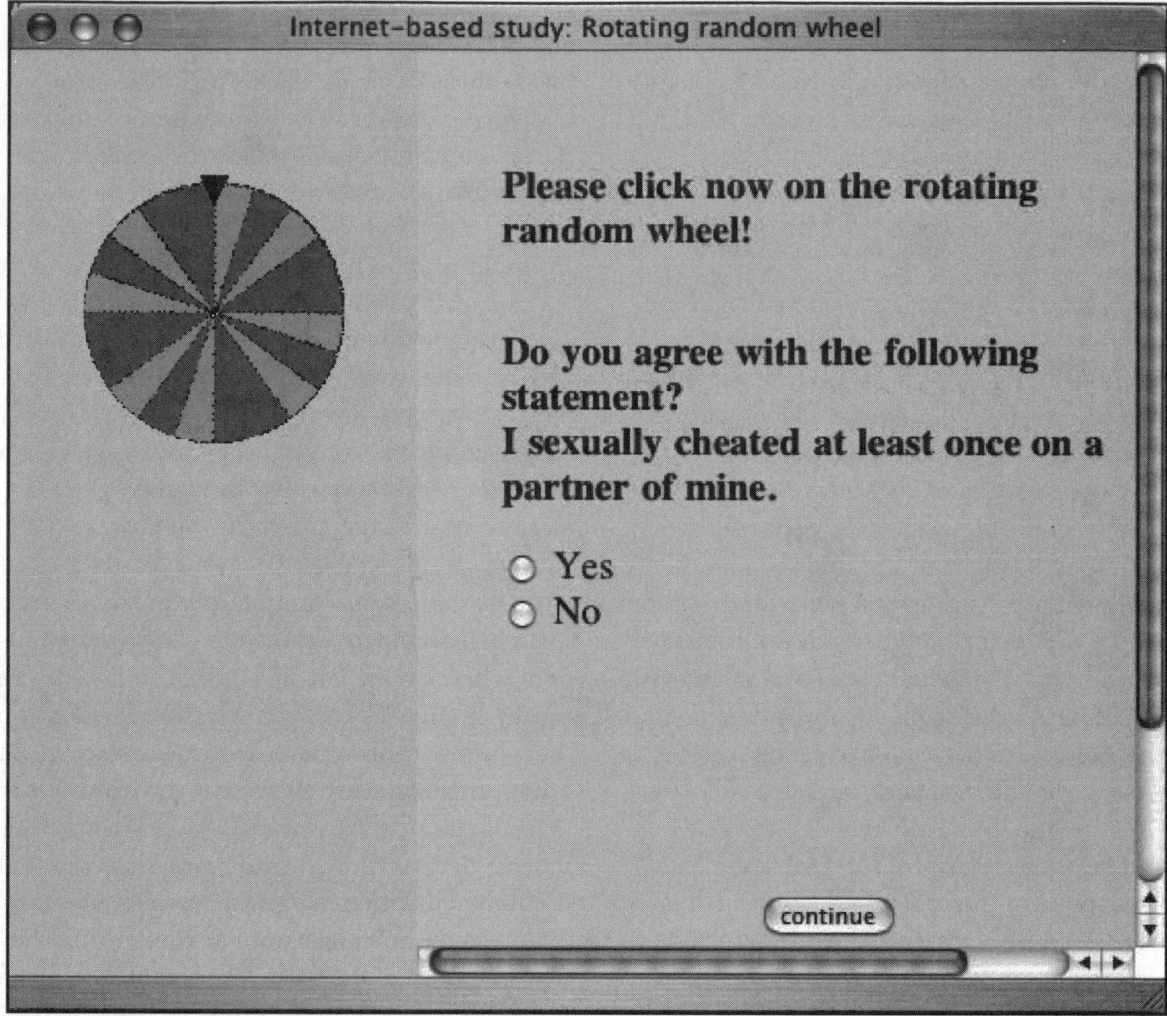

FIGURE 6.1. A Web-based survey using the randomized response technique (RRT) in a study on the trustworthiness of computerized random generators.

Reips and Mürner (2005) recently developed a Web site that allows researchers and students to develop their own Web-based Stroop experiments in an arcade game style. This Web site is available at http://www.psychologie.unizh.ch/sowi/reips/stroop/. The researcher can configure many aspects of the Stroop paradigm, like colors and names of objects, rules for events, rates for the different event types, speed, and the overall style in which the game is presented (i.e., "skins"). Access to the created Web experiment can be restricted using a login and password. The Web experiment is immediately available online, and the resulting data can be downloaded as tab-delimited text file in a format optimized for analysis in Scientific LogAnalyzer. Figure 6.2 shows the game pad page of "Stroop Invaders."

Using Web-Based Methods: An Example

Reading about an assessment method can be useful. However, to gain insights on a deeper level and to take concrete steps in acquiring knowledge about the method, it may be even more useful to experience it. Therefore, this section provides the opportunity to create and conduct a Web experiment, in a step-by-step fashion. Along the way, several useful tools for Web-based methods are presented, that is, *WEXTOR* (Reips & Neuhaus, 2002), the *web experiment list* (Reips & Lengler, 2005), the *Web Experimental Psychology Lab* (Reips, 2001), and *Scientific LogAnalyzer* (Reips & Stieger, 2004). A portion of McKenzie and Nelson's (2003) "cup experiment" is recreated for replication on the Web. This study deals with the information implic-

FIGURE 6.2. "Stroop Invaders": A Web site that allows researchers, teachers, and students to design and conduct Web-based Stroop experiments.

itly conveyed by the speaker's choice of a frame—for instance, describing a cup as being "half full" or "half empty."

WEXTOR

First, we use WEXTOR (Reips & Neuhaus, 2002), a Web service, to create, store, and visualize experimental designs and procedures for experiments on the Web and in the laboratory. WEXTOR dynamically creates the customized Web pages needed for the experimental procedure. It supports complete and incomplete factorial designs with between-subjects, within-subjects, and quasi-experimental (natural) factors, as well as mixed designs. It implements client-side, response time measurement and contains a content wizard for creating materials and dependent measures (button scales, graphical scales, multiple-choice items, etc.) on the experiment pages.

Several of the techniques presented earlier in this chapter are built into WEXTOR, (e.g., the warm-up and high hurdle techniques), and it automatically avoids several methodological pitfalls in Internet-based research. WEXTOR uses nonobvious file naming, automatic avoidance of page number confounding, JavaScript test redirect functionality to minimize dropout, and randomized distribution of participants to experimental conditions. It also provides for optional assignment to levels of quasi-experimental factors, optional client-side response time measurement, optional implementation of the high hurdle technique for dropout management, and randomly generated continuous user IDs for enhanced multiple submission control, and it automatically implements meta tags that keep the materials hidden from search engine scripts and prevents the caching of outdated versions at proxy servers.

The English version of WEXTOR is available at http://psych-wextor.unizh.ch/wextor/en/index.php. WEXTOR is currently available in version 2.2. After going through a sign-up procedure, WEXTOR can be used to design and manage experiments from anywhere on the Internet using a login/password combination. For the purpose of guiding the reader through the process, I created an account in WEXTOR that already contains a complete version of the cup experiment. Readers of this chapter may log in using the login/password combination "APA/handbook." Also, a step-by-step explanation of how to create a Web-based replication of the cup experiment (Reips, 2003) is at http://www.psychologie.unizh.ch/sowi/reips/SPUDM_03/index.html. Figure 6.3 shows WEXTOR's entry page.

The process of creating an experimental design and procedure for an experiment with WEXTOR involves ten steps. The first steps are decisions that an experimenter would make whether using WEXTOR or any other device for generating the experiment, like listing the factors and levels of within- and between-subjects factors, deciding what quasi-experimental factors (if any) to use, and specifying how assignment to conditions will function. WEXTOR adapts to the user input and produces an organized, pictorial representation of the experimental design and the Web pages required to implement that design. Figure 6.4 shows the visualization of

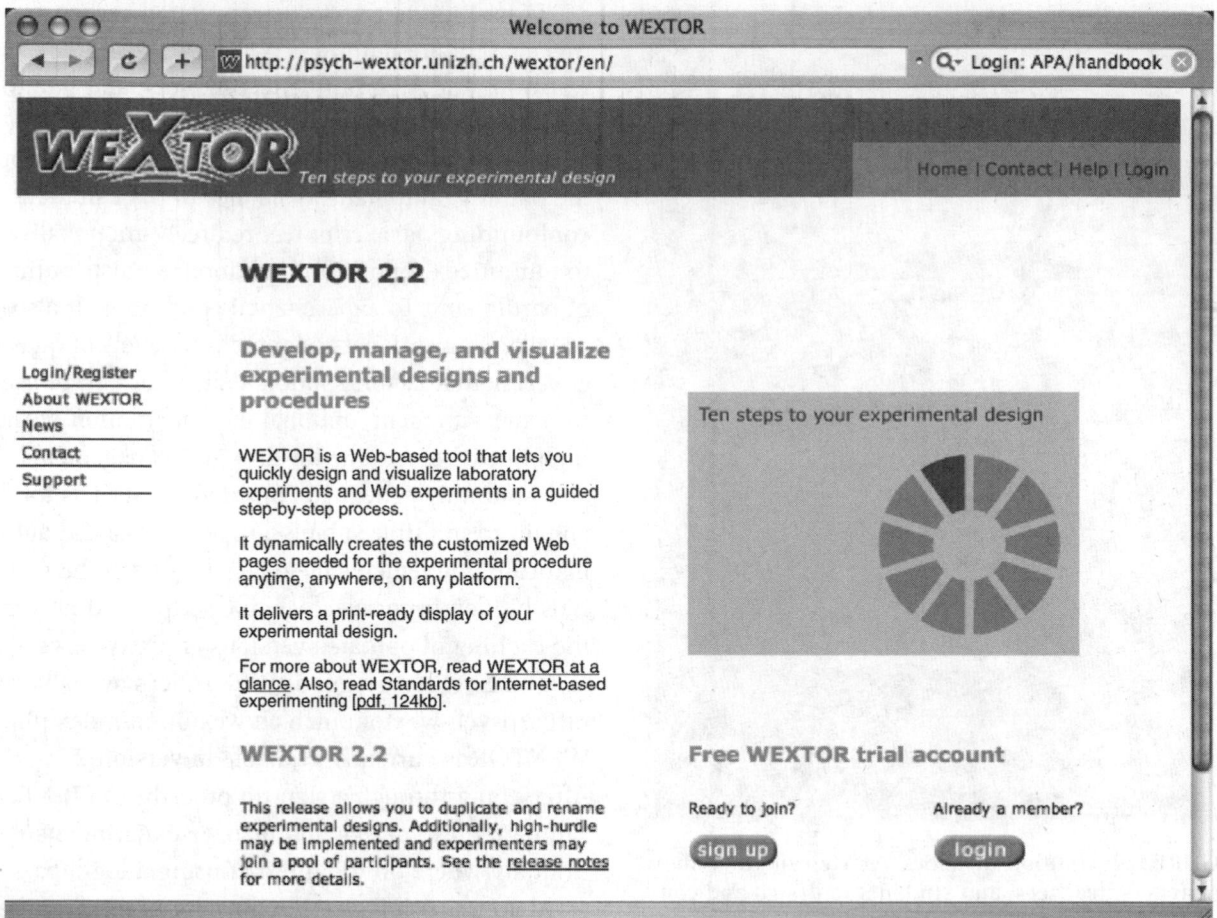

FIGURE 6.3. WEXTOR's entry page.

the design and procedure for the experiment by McKenzie and Nelson. It is a 2 × 2 between-subjects factorial design, resulting in four experimental conditions. Each condition is represented by one folder containing the Web pages the participants will see in that condition. Every Web page holds the dynamically created scripts that translate into the study procedure and response time measurement. After creating the experimental materials in WEXTOR they can be downloaded in one compressed archive that contains all folders (directories), scripts, and Web pages. WEXTOR contains a description of how to give these pages the "editing finish" and how to configure a Web server to post the pages on the Web (also see Birnbaum & Reips, 2005).

Recruitment

Once the materials for a Web-based study have been assembled and are available on the Web, the recruitment phase begins. Following traditional recruitment methods, participants can be recruited offline, of course. In addition, there are now many Internet methods (e.g., recruitment via Web site, e-mail [including mailing lists], online panel, newsgroup, listings, and banner ads). Recruitment for Web-based studies can be much more effective with one or several of the techniques described by Birnbaum (2001), Birnbaum and Reips (2005), and Reips (2000, 2002b, 2002c, 2002d).

Some of the best places for recruitment are institutionalized Web sites for Internet-based assessment, like those mentioned at the beginning of this chapter. In the case of Web experiments (e.g., the cup example), the study can be announced on the web experiment list and in the Web Experimental Psychology Lab. Figure 6.5 shows the entry form that an experimenter must fill out to put a Web experiment on the Web experiment list.

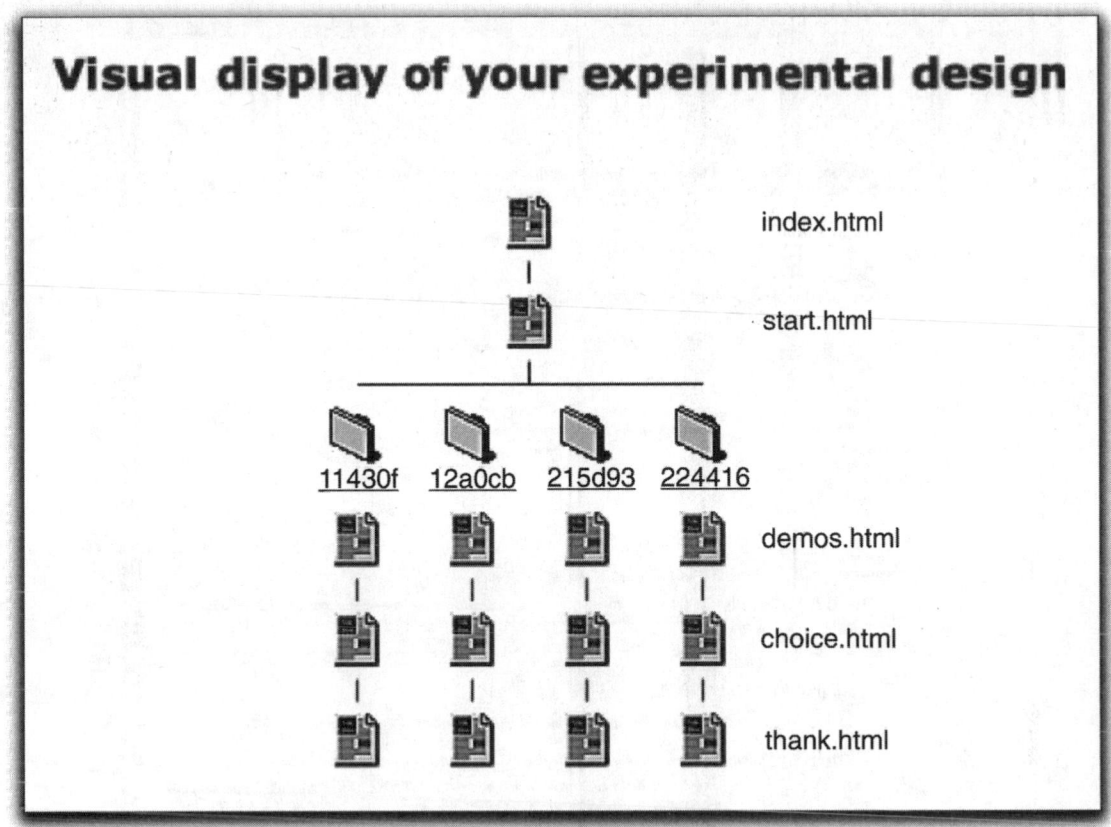

FIGURE 6.4. A visual display of the design and materials in the cup Web experiment, showing the four experimental conditions to which participants are randomly distributed as well as the folders and Web pages used in the Web experiment. The display is created in Step 9 in WEXTOR.

Data Analysis

Because of the large numbers of possible participants recruited on the Internet within a short period of time, data analysis can often follow briefly after the recruitment process. In the case of the replication of the cup experiment, I collected 162 data sets within 8 hours (Reips, 2003). Log files contain information in a format of one line per accessed piece of material. However, for a useful statistical analysis, most often a "one row per participant" format is needed. A Web-based service to do this transformation is Scientific LogAnalyzer. Several methodological features specifically needed for the analyses of data collected using Web-based assessment methods were implemented in Scientific LogAnalyzer (e.g., the detection and handling of multiple sessions, computation of response times, and a module for analyzing and visualizing dropout). Figure 6.6 shows an example of the dropout tree generated by Scientific LogAnalyzer.

Each node can be expanded or collapsed, and absolute and relative frequencies of choices of paths are calculated and displayed. After a speedy analysis of even large log files (Reips & Stieger, 2004), Scientific LogAnalyzer creates output in HTML or a tab-delimited form suited for import into statistics software. A more detailed example of a log file analysis is available from Scientific LogAnalyzer's online help.

This section presented a description of how to create, conduct, and analyze data from a Web-based study with those tools my colleagues and I developed in our group. Of course there are alternative approaches. (For the design of simple, one-page Web surveys, use SurveyWiz; Birnbaum, 2000.) FactorWiz, also by Birnbaum (2000), is a tool for one-page within-subjects factorial experiments. Yule and Cooper (2003) recently published Express, a program for large-scale simulations also used for Internet-based experimenting. Web-based

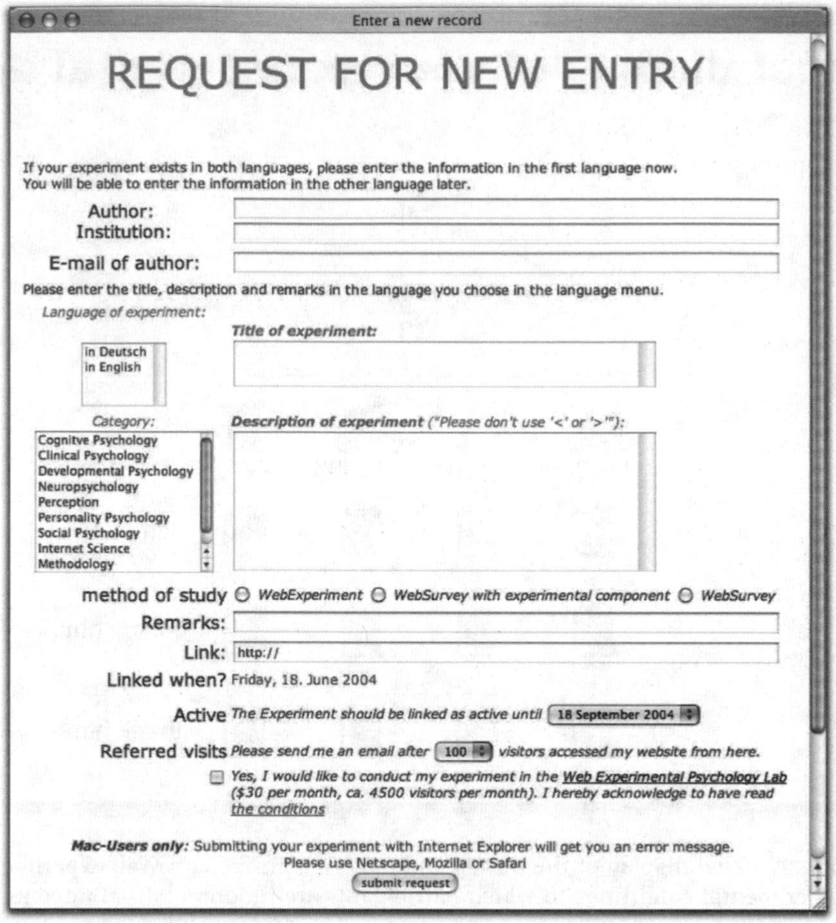

FIGURE 6.5. The form to be used to submit a Web experiment to be linked on the Web experiment list.

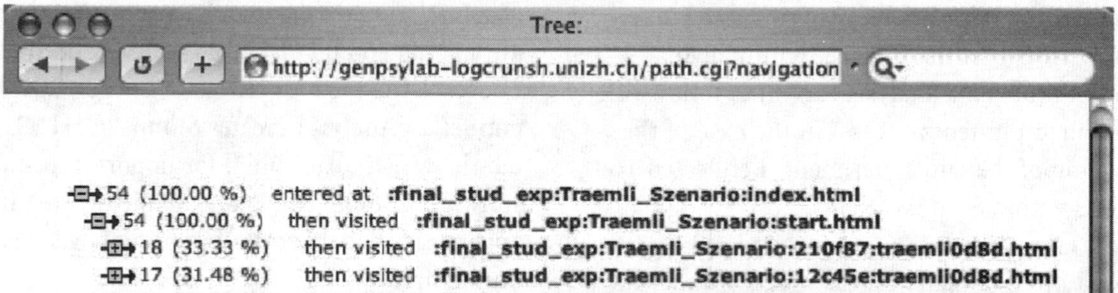

FIGURE 6.6. An example for the dropout tree that can be generated with Scientific LogAnalyzer. Each node can be expanded or collapsed, and absolute and relative frequencies of choices of paths are calculated and displayed.

assessments can also be created with proprietary software. One example is Authorware (McGraw, Tew, & Williams, 2000), which can be used to create functional and attractive study materials. The downside of this approach is a steep learning curve, certain timing issues (Schmidt, 2001), and the fact that it is difficult to get participants to download and install the required plug-in.

FUTURE DEVELOPMENTS OF WEB-BASED ASSESSMENT METHODS

The previous sections of this chapter illustrated that Web-based methods offer a number of advantages to psychological assessment. The field has evolved enough to develop techniques and applications that allow for a smooth flow of the Web-based assessment process and secure the researcher with a good quality of data. Therefore, Web-based methods are inevitably being used in psychological research with much frequency during recent years. The Web experiment list, for instance, now provides more

than 300 Web studies (Reips & Lengler, 2005). With continued spread of knowledge of these methods and their integration into curricula, we will see a further increase in their professional use.

Apart from an increase in use and professionalism, a future trend of Web-based methods may be the development of more specialized Web-based methods in psychological assessment. Because many traditional methodological paradigms can somehow be transformed into a Web-based version, and the advantages are so appealing, we will likely see many more of these special applications.

The rapid development of Web technology and the spread of knowledge regarding its characteristics among psychologists ensures that Web-based methods will strongly impact the way psychological assessment will be conducted in the future. The unending possibilities offered by this branch of media will perhaps be the beginning of a new era for psychological assessment and research.

Chapter 7

COMPUTER-BASED TESTING

Fritz Drasgow and Siang Chee Chuah

The history of human advancement has shown few innovations with the wide-ranging impact of the computer. The ENIAC, or Electronic Numerical Integrator and Computer, was the first general-purpose electronic computer (Rojas, 2001). Perhaps the greatest asset of the ENIAC and successive generations of multifunction computers is their adaptability to various tasks. As described in this chapter, the computer's flexibility has provided a great advantage for psychological measurement.

Significant improvements have been made to the computer since the days of the ENIAC. In 1965, Gordon Moore predicted that computer processor speed would double every 18 months. This prediction has proved remarkably accurate: Processor speed has indeed doubled at this rate and shows no signs of slowing down. Computers have advanced from paper tapes and punch cards to sophisticated graphic user interfaces (GUIs) and from teletypes and line printers to virtual environments. Computers no longer cost millions of dollars and fill large rooms. Testing programs can now afford computers that fit conveniently on desktops and easily transported laptops that allow in situ assessment. It is no surprise, therefore, that computer usage has grown exponentially.

Computers have been used in many ways for psychological measurement. Perhaps most straightforward is the computerization of tests previously developed for paper-and-pencil administration. Such tests offer little in terms of improved psychometric properties but can have important administrative advantages.

More sophisticated are tests that adapt their difficulty level to match the ability of the examinee. Computer adaptive sequential tests (CASTs; Luecht & Nungester, 1998), computerized adaptive tests (CATs; Sands, Waters, & McBride, 1997), and shadow tests (van der Linden, 2000) provide examples. These tests generally use traditional multiple-choice questions, but use the computer to strategically select items of appropriate difficulty for each individual examinee. By omitting items that are too easy or too hard for a particular individual, test length can be substantially reduced with no loss of measurement accuracy.

Computerization also allows more radical innovation in assessment. Consider that in many situations, tests are designed to predict future behavior. For example, academic admissions tests are intended to predict performance in college, employment tests are used to predict job performance, and licensing and credentialing tests seek to assess whether candidates have the requisite skills to practice their profession without harming the public. Campbell's (1990) model suggests that performance is a function of declarative knowledge, procedural knowledge, and motivation. Declarative knowledge consists of an individual's repertoire of facts, rules, and principles; procedural knowledge involves knowing how to perform a task; and motivation concerns the amplitude, direction, and persistence of one's efforts. Based on their success in predicting performance (Kuncel, Hezlett, & Ones, 2001; Schmidt & Hunter, 1998), it appears that traditional multiple-choice items do a good job of

assessing declarative knowledge. However, there is a growing consensus that multiple-choice items are inadequate for assessing procedural knowledge.

Computer-based testing provides an opportunity to improve the assessment of an individual's ability to perform by simulating tasks that are important in the workplace or classroom (Computerization Implementation Committee, 2001). For example, consider the job of a certified public accountant (CPA). Multiple-choice items can accurately assess an individual's repertoire of accounting facts, rules, and principles. However, the American Institute of Certified Public Accountants added simulations of client encounters to their licensing exam in 2004 because declarative knowledge appears necessary, but not sufficient, to ensure competence as a practicing accountant. More specifically, the exam now attempts to assess whether a CPA candidate can successfully solve the vague and ill-defined problems posed by clients. A computer simulation of a client encounter can simultaneously test knowledge of accounting facts, rules, and principles as well as the application of that knowledge to the problems presented by clients (Computerization Implementation Committee, 2001). In this way, computer-based testing provides an opportunity for more comprehensive assessment.

Computerized assessment can also broaden the domain of assessment by incorporating multimedia stimuli. Vispoel (1999), for example, used the computer's ability to present sound clips to assess musical aptitude, Olson-Buchanan et al. (1998) incorporated video clips in their computerized assessment of conflict resolution skills, and Ackerman, Evans, Park, Tamassia, and Turner (1999) displayed images on a high-resolution color monitor to assess medical students' ability to diagnose dermatological skin disorders.

In sum, there has been a proliferation of research designed to explore and exploit opportunities provided by computer-based assessment. This chapter provides an overview of the diverse efforts by researchers in this area. It begins by describing how paper-and-pencil tests can be adapted for administration by computers. Computerization provides the important advantage that items can be selected so they are of appropriate difficulty for

each examinee. Some of the psychometric theory needed for computerized adaptive testing is reviewed. Then research on innovative computerized assessments is summarized. These assessments go beyond multiple-choice items by using formats made possible by computerization. Then some hardware and software issues are described, and finally, directions for future work are outlined.

ADAPTING PAPER-AND-PENCIL TESTS FOR COMPUTERIZED ADMINISTRATION

To take advantage of computers as a platform, it is natural for test developers to convert their existing paper-and-pencil tests and administer them via this medium. Much of the early work on computer-based testing was focused on converting paper-and-pencil tests such as the California Psychological Inventory (CPI; Scissons, 1976), Sixteen Personality Factor (16PF; Harrell & Lombardo, 1985), and Job Descriptive Inventory (JDI; Donovan, Drasgow, & Probst, 2000) to computer versions.

Converting tests to a computer-based administration has several advantages. Once a test has been developed for computer administration, the cost of administration can be relatively small. There is no longer a need to print and transport paper forms, the computer can administer the test and consequently a proctor may be unnecessary for some types of assessments, and tests can be scored quickly and accurately. Moreover, some problems such as missing responses can be prevented by the test software, and administration errors by fallible proctors can be minimized. Examinees' response times for each item can be tracked and used to identify some types of testing problems. Additionally, with computer-based scoring, it is possible to provide instant feedback regarding an individual's performance on a test.

However, converting a test from a paper-and-pencil format to a computer format is not without difficulties. Green, Bock, Humphreys, Linn, and Reckase (1984) noted that computerized tests cannot be automatically assumed to yield scores that are comparable to their paper-and-pencil counterparts: "The two tests are equally valid only if they have been demonstrated to yield equivalent meas-

ures" (p. 357). Such equivalence is important when a test or scale was validated using paper-and-pencil administration samples: If the computer version does not produce scores that are equivalent, it must be revalidated for this administrative medium.

Many studies have examined the equivalence of computerized tests and their paper-and-pencil counterparts. From these studies we know that the nature of the test and the features of the administration format can threaten measurement equivalence. In a meta-analysis of cognitive ability tests, Mead and Dragsow (1993) showed that computer-based *speeded* tests were not equivalent to their paper-and-pencil counterparts, but carefully developed *power* tests were equivalent. Similarly, Richman, Kiesler, Weisband, and Dragsow's (1999) meta-analysis suggests that test format and test environment affect responses to noncognitive tests. For example, when there is a lack of anonymity, an inability to revise responses, and the assessment is administered in a group setting, respondents to the computer version have a greater tendency to distort their responses in a socially desirable direction. These results suggest that the more similar a computer-based test is to its paper-and-pencil counterpart, the more likely that scores are equivalent across media.

Some individuals may be disadvantaged by the use of computers as an administration medium. Anxiety has been shown to be related to a broad range of performance criteria. Certain respondents may experience greater anxiety during a computer-administered test (Llabre et al., 1987), and individuals who are not familiar with computers may also experience greater anxiety (Rosen & Maguire, 1990). However, research has been inconclusive as to whether computer anxiety affects performance on computer-based tests (Dimock & Cormier, 1991; Shermis & Lombard, 1998). With the increasing prevalence of computers in society, the lack of computer familiarity may become a nonissue.

TESTS THAT ADAPT TO THE TEST TAKER

Although adapting conventional tests for computerized administration has many procedural advantages, the psychometric properties of the tests are not improved. Specifically, highly capable examinees answer easy items correctly with high probability, and weak examinees answer difficult items at near chance levels. As described in this section, the computer's dynamic capabilities can be used to selectively administer items to examinees so that the items are of appropriate difficulty for each individual and thereby provide useful information about the respondent's ability level.

In its simplest form, a computerized adaptive test (CAT) begins by administering an item of moderate difficulty. If the examinee answers correctly, the computer branches to an item of greater difficulty; if the examinee answers incorrectly, the computer branches to an easier item. After the second item is answered, the computer again branches to a more difficult or easier item, depending on whether the answer was correct or incorrect. This process continues, and ordinarily the computer rapidly homes in on the examinee's ability level.

By targeting items to examinees' ability levels, it is possible for a test to provide more precise assessment with fewer items: A reduction in test length of approximately 50% might be expected. However, testing time is not usually reduced by this amount because examinees tend to take longer answering items of appropriate difficulty than items that are too easy or difficult. Nonetheless, substantial reductions in test length and moderate reductions in testing time can be achieved with no loss of measurement precision.

Adapting item difficulty has a derivative benefit for testing programs with important consequences for examinees (i.e., "high-stakes" tests). Ordinarily, high-stakes tests are administered only a few times per year. For example, the conventional CPA licensing exam was administered only twice per year (in May and November). Such tests are offered infrequently because a new form must be created for each administration to eliminate any opportunity for cheating. Obviously, developing a new form for every administration requires a great deal of time, effort, and expense. By using the computer to adapt item difficulty, each examinee receives a unique test form. Consequently, with item exposure controls in place (see following), test security is maintained, and continuous test administration is possible.

Thus, examinees can go to a testing program's Web site and schedule their exam at a time convenient for them. For example, the CPA licensing exam allows candidates to schedule their test at any time during a 2-month window within every quarter of the year. Obviously, this convenience is greatly appreciated by examinees. In sum, using the computer to adapt test difficulty allows tests to be shorter in length, take less time, and can be scheduled at times that are convenient to examinees, yet maintain test security.

Challenges

Item selection. Adapting test difficulty creates challenges for the test developers. First, items must be selected according to the test specification plan. The specifications detail the content of the test, including the knowledge and skills to be assessed, and how many items should be included in each area assessed. For paper-and-pencil tests, test developers thoroughly inspect a test form to ensure that it satisfies the test specifications and avoids item cluing (i.e., one item provides information that can be used to answer another item).

To satisfy content requirements on adaptive tests, subject matter experts must code each item for its content. In addition, an "enemy list" must be developed that enumerates sets of items from which only one item can be selected. For example, suppose items 13, 72, and 547 are enemies because they have highly similar content or provide cluing; if any one of these items is selected, the others become ineligible for inclusion in the CAT. Stocking and Swanson's (1993) weighted deviation model and van der Linden's (2000) shadow test provide sophisticated methods for accomplishing these goals; a simpler approach introduced by Kingsbury and Zara (1991) is described in the following section.

Scoring. With paper-and-pencil tests, the most common approach to scoring is the number of correct answers given by an examinee. The number correct score is usually transformed to a score scale that is used for reporting the results of the exam, but scaled scores are generally based on the number of correct answers. With a CAT, number correct scoring is not appropriate because two examinees may have answered the same number of items correctly, but the difficulty of the items may be dramatically different. Thus, a more sophisticated approach to scoring, based on item response theory (IRT), is necessary. Reise and Waller (2002) provide a lucid introduction to IRT; a more detailed treatment of IRT and computerized testing is given by van der Linden and Glas (2000).

IRT models the probability of a positive response as a function of an individual's standing on the latent trait. In cognitive ability testing, the most commonly used model is the three-parameter logistic model. Here, the probability of a positive response, $P_i(\theta)$, is

$$P_i(\theta) = c_i + \frac{1 - c_i}{1 + \exp[-Da_i(\theta - b_i)]},$$

where θ is an individual's standing on the trait assessed by the test, D is a constant set equal to 1.702 for historical reasons, a_i is a parameter that describes the extent to which the item discriminates between individuals with higher and lower θs, b_i is a parameter that indexes item difficulty, and c_i is called the guessing parameter because it reflects the chance that very low ability examinees will answer correctly. θ is usually scaled to have a mean of 0 and a standard deviation of 1.

The two-parameter logistic model sets $c_i = 0$ for all items, so that

$$P_i(\theta) = \frac{1}{1 + \exp[-Da_i(\theta - b_i)]}.$$

This model is often used for personality assessment (Reise & Waller, 1990; see also Chernyshenko, Stark, Chan, Drasgow, & Williams, 2001). The one-parameter logistic or Rasch model makes the additional restriction that $a_i = 1$:

$$P_i(\theta) = \frac{1}{1 + \exp[-D(\theta - b_i)]}.$$

This model is widely used in Europe and in licensing and certification testing programs in the United States.

Figure 7.1 shows a plot of $P_i(\theta)$, which is usually called an item characteristic curve, for an item with $a_i = 1.1$, $b_i = 0.4$, and $c_i = 0.15$. Note that the curve is nearly flat at low and high θ levels. Consequently, the item provides little discrimination between individuals with, say, θ of −3.0 versus −2.0 or 2.0 versus 3.0. In the psychometric argot, the item provides little information in these ranges of θ. Alternatively, note the difference in the probability of a positive response between individuals with θ = 0.0 versus 1.0: .42 versus .80. Here the lower θ individuals have clearly lower chances of responding positively than higher θ, and so the item provides substantial information in this range of θ values.

The item characteristic curves for Rasch model items are particularly convenient. With $a_i = 1$ and $c_i = 0$ for all items, the only item parameter that varies is item difficulty, b_i. The restricted form of Rasch model item characteristic curves leads to many desirable statistical properties. However, it is an empirical question whether $a_i = 1$ for all items; this condition should be carefully examined before applying the Rasch model.

Scoring an individual's responses in IRT refers to locating the value along the θ continuum that best represents the individual's standing on the latent trait. Maximum likelihood estimation can be used for this purpose; the principle of maximum likelihood estimation states that the estimate of $\hat{\theta}$ of θ should be the value that makes the individual's responses appear most probable. If the responses are coded $u_i = 1$ for a correct or positive response and $u_i = 0$ for an incorrect or negative response, then the likelihood of a positive response is just $P_i(\theta)$, and the likelihood of a negative response is $[1 - P_i(\theta)]$. Mathematically, this can be expressed compactly as

$$[P_i(\theta)]^{u_i}[1 - P_i(\theta)]^{1-u_i}.$$

Provided that the test or scale is unidimensional (i.e., all the items measure a single latent trait), the likelihood of all the responses is

$$L = \prod_{i=1}^{n}[P_i(\theta)]^{u_i}[1 - P_i(\theta)]^{1-u_i},$$

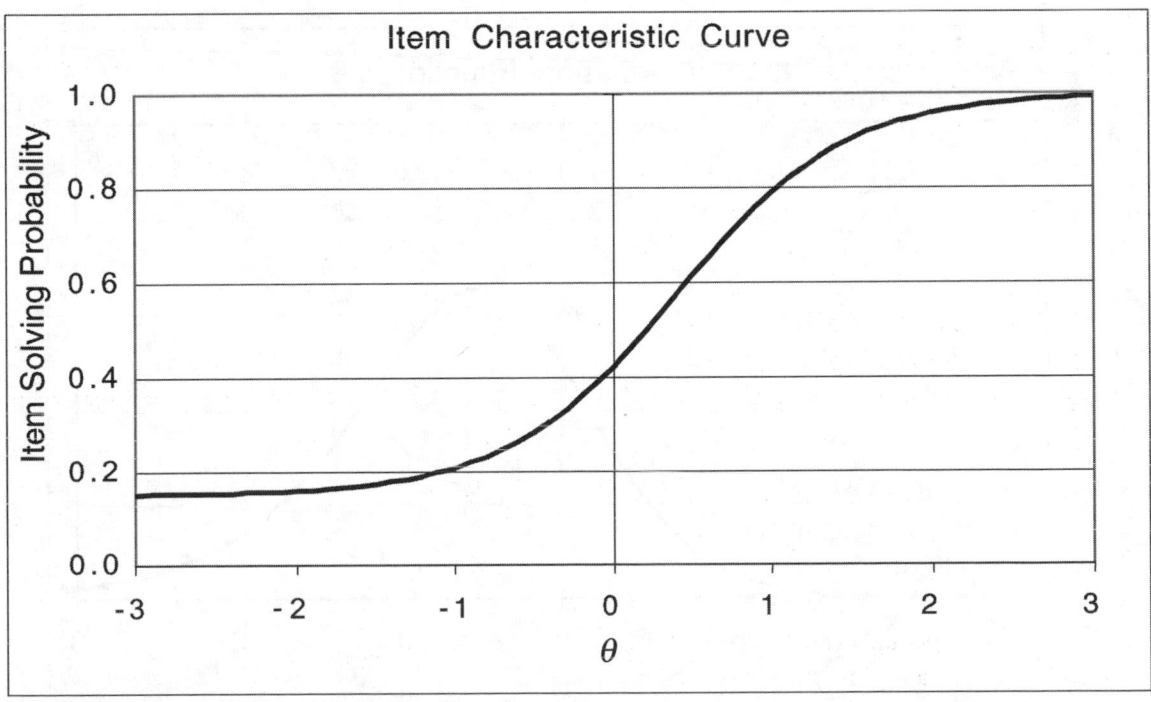

FIGURE 7.1. **Item characteristic curve.**

and the maximum likelihood ability estimate $\hat{\theta}$ is the value along the θ continuum that maximizes L. This value is obtained by iterative numerical methods that would be very difficult to compute by hand but can be determined by the computer nearly instantly.

After the estimate $\hat{\theta}$ is obtained, it is usually transformed to a score scale that is used to report scores to examinees. Let $X = \sum_{i=1}^{n} u_i$ denote the number right score on a conventional test; the process of transforming $\hat{\theta}$ to the reporting scale is analogous to the process of transforming X. The simplest transformation is linear (e.g., $k_1\hat{\theta}+k_2$ or $k_1 X + k_2$). More complicated transformations are sometimes used; see Kolen and Brennan (1995) for details.

Adapting item difficulty to a person's ability level. A critical element in adaptive testing is selecting items that are most informative about an individual's standing on the trait assessed by the test or scale. Going beyond the simple notion of branching to a more difficult item following a correct answer and an easier item following an incorrect answer, it is possible to determine the item in the item pool that is most informative about an examinee's ability. Statisticians have developed the notion of information to refer to the reduction of uncertainty about a parameter being estimated (θ in the present context). For IRT and psychological measurement, Lord (1980a) showed that the information an item provides at ability level θ is

$$I_i(\theta) = \frac{[P_i(\theta)']^2}{P_i(\theta)[1-P_i(\theta)]},$$

where $P_i(\theta)'$ is the slope (i.e., derivative) of the item characteristic curve at ability θ.

$I_i(\theta)$ is called the item information function, and it shows the range of θ where an item is discriminating—that is, has a large value of $I_i(\theta)$—and where the item is not discriminating. Figure 7.2 shows the item information function for the item with $a_i = 1.1$, $b_i = 0.4$, and $c_i = 0.15$ described previously. Note that this item provides substantial information near its item difficulty (for θ values near 0.4), but little information for θ levels below −1.0 or above 2.0.

Thus, a simple approach to determining which item to administer next, given that a respondent's

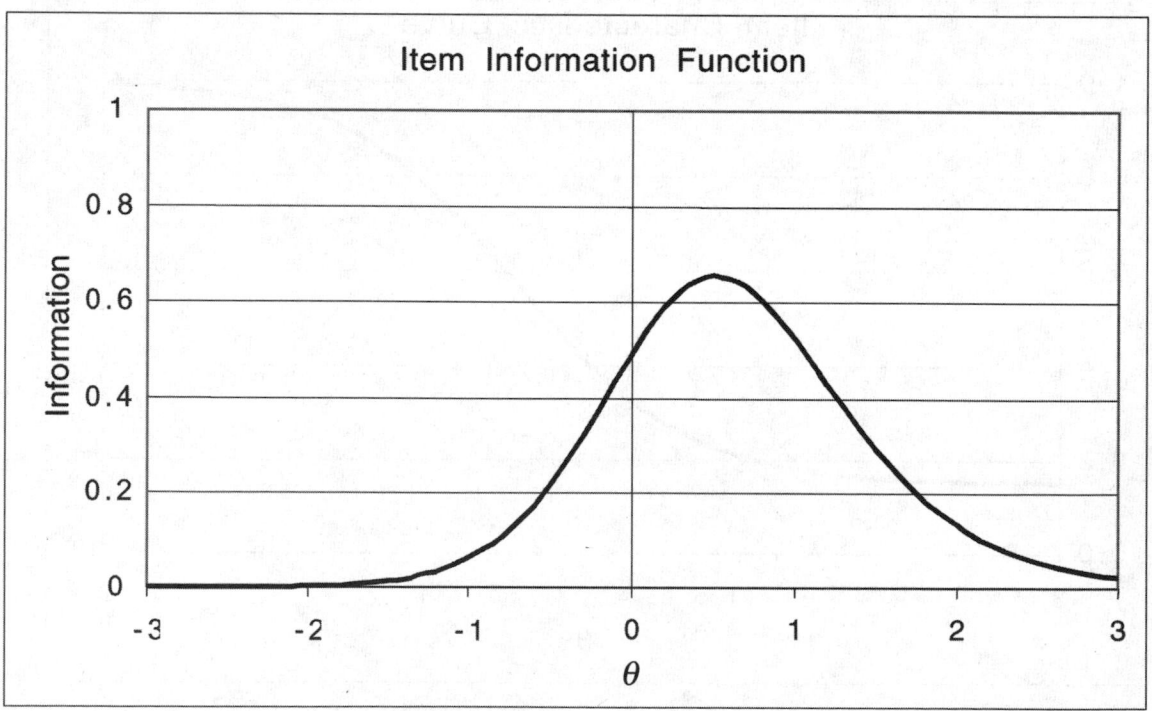

FIGURE 7.2. Item information function.

current ability estimate is $\hat{\theta}$, is to compute $I_i(\hat{\theta})$ for all the items in the item pool and select the item with the largest item information. This approach, called *maximum information item selection*, must be modified in high-stakes testing programs because items must be selected to satisfy content specifications, avoid violating enemy lists, and satisfy item exposure controls. Kingsbury and Zara's (1991) method provides a straightforward means of accomplishing these goals. It involves forming subsets of items according to the content specifications, selecting the number of items from each subset as dictated by the content specifications, and using maximum information item selection to determine which items within a subset would be the best choices for administration. To avoid overexposure, Kingsbury and Zara suggested picking items at random from among the items in each subset with the greatest information.

Precision of estimation. The total amount of information at ability θ given n items have been administered is defined as

$$I(\theta) = \sum_{i=1}^{n} I_i(\theta).$$

Lord (1980) showed that the conditional standard error of measurement is

$$SEM_{\hat{\theta}|\theta} = 1 / \sqrt{I(\theta)}$$

for the maximum likelihood ability estimate $\hat{\theta}$ of θ. Consequently, after an adaptive test is completed, $I(\hat{\theta}) = \sum I_i(\hat{\theta})$ can be estimated, and the standard error of $\hat{\theta}$ can be determined.

Test security. Computerized testing has allowed many exams to go to "walk-in testing," where examinees schedule tests at testing centers at times that are convenient to them. To minimize cheating, however, testing programs must take care to prevent overexposure of some items.

First, note that if a CAT begins by initializing $\hat{\theta}$ = 0 (i.e., by assuming that an examinee is average before any items have been administered) and then selects the item with the greatest information at that ability level, all examinees will receive the same first item. Moreover, all examinees who answer correctly will be branched to the same second item. Such item selection algorithms are said to be deterministic because individuals with the same sequence of right and wrong answers will receive the same set of items.

There are two interrelated problems with deterministic item selection algorithms. First, many items in the item pool will never be administered. In a simulation of a CAT with an item pool of 260 items, Hulin, Drasgow, and Parsons (1983) found that 141 items were never chosen by the item selection algorithm just described. Thus, functionally, the Hulin et al. item pool consisted of just 119 items. It is widely believed that CATs with smaller item pools are more easily compromised than CATs with larger items pools, so using just 119 of the 260 items would be a source of concern for a high-stakes testing program.

The second problem with deterministic item selection arises when coaching schools or other conspiracies attempt to "crack the test" by having a series of individuals take the test and memorize items. The first person to take the test would memorize the first item and report it to the coaching school or post it on a Web site. The correct answer would then be quickly determined. The second conspirator to take the exam would see the same first item, answer it correctly, and then be branched upward to a second item, which the conspirator would memorize and report. The third conspirator would be able to answer the first two items correctly and be branched upward to a third item, which that person would memorize. As the Educational Testing Service learned with the Graduate Record Exam, it is possible for a relatively small number of conspirators to compromise a CAT.

To minimize the chance of cheating, it is critical to control how often each item is administered. *Item exposure control algorithms* (see Stocking & Lewis, 2000, for a review) use randomization for this purpose. For example, the exam may begin by randomly selecting one of the 20 items with the largest information at $\hat{\theta} = 0$.

The Sympson-Hetter (1985) method has frequently been used to control item exposure. Here every item in the item pool has an exposure control

parameter, which is a number between zero and one. If an item is tentatively selected for administration, a random uniform number between zero and one is drawn. If the random number is less than the exposure control parameter, the item is administered; otherwise, the item is rejected and another item is tentatively selected and the process repeated. The exposure control parameters are chosen so that no item is administered to more than a prespecified percentage (say, 15%) of examinees.

Experience with high-stakes CATs clearly indicates that item pools must be quite large to maintain test security (Mills, 1999). If computer simulations show that a CAT has satisfactory psychometric properties with an item pool of 250 items, a high-stakes CAT may need a pool of perhaps 2,500 items to resist compromise.

Alternative Approaches to Adaptive Testing

Several alternative approaches to CATs have been suggested. Two are briefly described next.

Testlets. Wainer and Kiely (1987) suggested the use of what they termed "testlets" as an improvement on adaptive testing as described earlier. Testlets are "the coagulation of items into coherent groups that can be scored as a whole" (Wainer, Bradlow, & Du, 2000, p. 246). Perhaps the most common version of a testlet consists of a reading passage followed by four to six questions. Wainer, Bradlow, and Du noted several reasons for using testlets. First, and perhaps most important, is that the traditional multiple-choice test composed of many short questions has been criticized as producing a form of assessment constituted by "decontextualized items" that are "abstracted too far from the domain of inference" (Wainer et al., 2000, p. 245). Because a testlet consists of a stem and several interrelated questions, a meaningful context is created. A more pragmatic advantage of testlets is that reading a passage or studying a spreadsheet takes time; asking several questions improves the information yield per unit of time.

Testlets (or avoiding Wainer & Kiely's [1987] jargon, sets of items that refer to the same stem) violate a central assumption of IRT in that items within a testlet are ordinarily more highly corre-

lated than expected based on the assumption that items measure a single latent trait θ. That is, from the perspective of psychological measurement, five independent items provide more information about an individual's θ than five dependent items referring to a common stem. Thus, analyzing tests consisting of testlets via a standard IRT model such as the three-parameter logistic may produce misleadingly optimistic results about the accuracy of measurement. Wainer et al. (2000) provided an appropriate psychometric model for tests composed of testlets and conducted a simulation study that demonstrated its effectiveness.

CAST. Computer-adaptive sequential testing (CAST; Luecht & Nungester, 1998) also uses sets of items as the fundamental building block for a test. These sets of items are called *modules,* and the collection of modules constituting a test is called a *panel.* Figure 7.3 illustrates a 1-3-3 panel. All examinees would be administered Module 1M, which might contain 15 to 20 items and be moderately difficult. Examinees with high, moderate, and low scores would be branched to Modules 2H, 2M, and 2E, respectively; ordinarily about one third of the examinees would be branched to each stage 2 module. In stage 3, examinees who completed Module 2M would be routed to Module 3E, 3M, or 3H, depending on whether their scores were low, moderate, or high. Cut scores for routing would be set

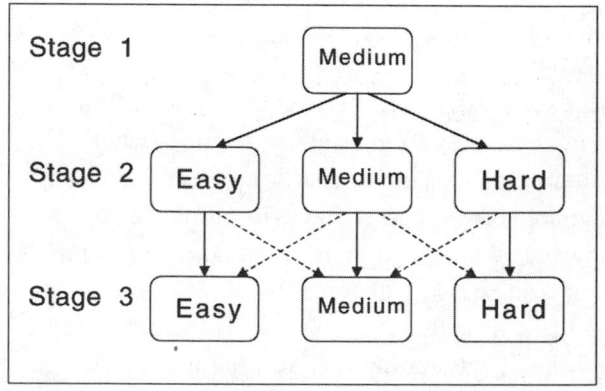

FIGURE 7.3. **Computer-adaptive sequential test (CAST) panel.**

so that approximately one third of the examinees are administered Modules 3E, 3M, and 3H.

CAST represents a compromise between CATs, which are created on the fly and consequently cannot be reviewed by test developers prior to administration, and conventional tests, which are not adaptive but can be carefully studied by test developers to ensure that they satisfy content requirements. A CAST is not as psychometrically efficient as a maximum information item selection CAT, but many testing programs constrain item selection to satisfy content specification and therefore become less than optimal. Martha Stocking (2000, personal communication), a leading psychometrician at the Educational Testing Service, has described the Graduate Record Examination CAT as a BAT—a barely adaptive test—because there are so many constraints on item selection that its adaptivity is greatly reduced.

Reactions to CATs

In the 1990s, a significant body of research accumulated on job candidates' reactions to employment selection procedures. Candidates' reactions have been found to be related to their satisfaction with the hiring organization, intentions to accept a job offer, job performance, and intentions to remain with the organization after being hired (Gilliland, 1994; Smither, Reilly, Millsap, Pearlman, & Stoffey, 1993). Principles of justice—distributive and procedural—explain many of these reactions.

Tonidandel and Quinones (2000) explored the applicability of justice principles to CAT test-takers. They noted important differences between paper-and-pencil tests and CATs: CAT test-takers must answer all items in the order presented (they can't skip items), they cannot review previously answered items and perhaps change their answers, different examinees answer different items, and test scores are not directly based on the number of correctly answered items. Although early research found that examinees like CATs that are shorter than their paper-and-pencil counterparts, Tonidandel and Quinones found that individuals preferred CATs that were more similar to conventional tests (e.g., all examinees answer the same items, examinees are allowed to skip questions and return later).

INNOVATIVE COMPUTERIZED TESTS

The previous sections in this chapter have shown great advances in testing and assessment due to the introduction of computer-based tests. However, a legacy of paper-and-pencil testing—the multiple-choice question—seems to have constrained the way test developers think about assessment: This item type has continued as the predominate format. But there are many skills and abilities that do not lend themselves to assessment with multiple-choice items. For instance, how should a physician's ability to diagnose patients be assessed? One would hope that diagnostic skill would not be assessed by knowledge of static information derived from textbooks. A physician should be able to differentiate disorders with highly similar symptoms by a problem-solving *process*. Computer-based assessment offers the flexibility to simulate the task of diagnosing disorders and circumvent a critical limitation of paper-and-pencil tests.

Research on innovative item types administered via computer has examined changes designed to improve measurement. Zenisky and Sireci (2002) provide a comprehensive review of innovative item types (e.g., moving objects to create a tree structure, inserting text, editing text, highlighting text, and many other formats).

Dimensions of Innovation

Parshall, Spray, Kalohn, and Davey (2002) described five dimensions that characterize innovative computer item types. In the following paragraphs, each dimension of innovation is briefly described.

Item format refers to the different types of response to a question, for example, multiple-choice items (i.e., selected response) and essays (i.e., constructed response). An innovative item format might require a constructed response such as creating the design for a bridge from its engineering specifications on an architectural examination.

Response action deals with how the respondent answers the question. Most test-takers are familiar with using a pencil to fill an answer bubble on an optical scan sheet. Clicking a mouse on a button to endorse an answer would constitute the computer

equivalent. Advances in response action include drag-and-drop and voice recognition of oral responses.

Media inclusion refers to all non–text-based test media. Examples include the use of high-resolution color images on a test of dermatological skin disorders (Ackerman et al., 1999), sound clips on a computerized test of musical aptitude (Vispoel, 1999), and full-motion video to assess conflict resolution skills (Olson-Buchanan et al., 1998).

Degree of interactivity pertains to the degree to which a test reacts in response to the test-taker. The degree of interactivity can range from a total lack of interactivity, much akin to static paper-and-pencil tests, to highly fluid computer simulations that are much like today's video games.

Scoring method is closely tied to item format and response action. Scoring constructed responses is challenging because there may be more than one suitable answer or answers may vary in their degree of correctness or incorrectness (e.g., essays and architectural designs). Consequently, there has been much interest in the development of scoring algorithms for innovative item types (e.g., Bennett, Steffen, Singley, Morley, & Jacquemin, 1997).

Why Innovate?

The purpose of innovation is to improve a test and not innovate for the sake of innovation. Jodoin (2003) compared innovative item types and traditional multiple-choice items and found that although innovative item types returned more information per item than multiple-choice items, the amount of time spent by respondents was disproportionately higher than the return. Thus, innovative item types were less efficient in terms of information yield per unit of time than multiple-choice items. So, what does innovation add to a test? Research by Bennett, Morley, and Quardt (2000) suggests that innovative item types broaden the construct measured by the test. They compared a test form consisting of their innovative item type with a test consisting of traditional items; they found that the disattenuated correlation between them was $r \approx .70$. This suggests some, but not complete, overlap between the latent traits assessed by the item types.

A further consideration is the extent to which a test authentically represents real-world skills required of the respondent. With the use of graphics, sound, and full-motion video, we can emulate many important real-world situations. Candidate performance on such realistic simulations is assumed to tap the same skills required by real-world situations and, therefore, constitutes a valid measure of an individual's performance in real-world situations. Therefore, innovative item types using new formats and video, graphics, or sound clearly broaden the skills assessed and improve the substantive richness of tests.

These innovative items can have very high face validity/authenticity. For example, some situational judgment tests used in preemployment testing use written passages that describe social situations. However, in the real world we are dependent on interpersonal cues such as verbal tone and facial expression for information regarding the situation. Full-motion video simulations are able to capture such subtle nuances and convey a more natural experience of the situation. On the other hand, written passages must rely on explicit description of otherwise subtle nuances to convey the situation. This may compromise validity because directing the attention of the respondent to particular cues makes it impossible to assess the candidate's ability to notice those nuances.

Examples

To give an indication of the range of possibilities, this section provides descriptions of some innovative assessments. Of course, space limits the number of examples that can be given. Nonetheless, the variety in these examples demonstrates the ability of computerized assessment to evaluate a wide range of human attributes.

Interpersonal skills. Assessing interpersonal skills has proved to be difficult and at times fruitless. Thorndike and Stein (1937) criticized early efforts because they did not provide measures with sufficient reliability. More recent evaluations (e.g., Davies, Stankov, & Roberts, 1998) have found that some measures are adequately reliable, but are confounded with intelligence or personality. Underly-

ing this problem is that most of these assessments have relied on text-based items. Interpersonal interactions involve more than is conveyed in a terse written description of the context and events. Because people often communicate nonverbally, a transcript of dialogue omits much that is important. Nonverbal communication has been shown to be important in a variety of circumstances (e.g., Motowidlo & Burnett, 1995; Rinella, Ferguson, & Sager, 1970). Moreover, by including descriptions of emotion or attitude, we are calling attention to those cues, rather than relying on the respondent's interpersonal skill to take notice. Furthermore, text-based items prime respondents to rely on intellectual processing, rather than their interpersonal skills: Chan and Schmitt (1997) found that a paper-and-pencil test of work habits and interpersonal skills correlated $r = .45$ with reading comprehension, but a parallel assessment based on video clips correlated only $r = .05$.

Olson-Buchanan et al. (1998) developed a computer-administered test of conflict resolution skills in the workplace. The assessment uses video clips to present typical workplace conflicts; the expressions and verbal tone of the actors are salient in each scene. At a critical point in each conflict, the respondent is presented with several potential responses to the problem and asked to pick the best option. With samples from multiple organizations in a variety of industries, Olson-Buchanan assessed the criterion-related validity of the assessment in comparison to tests of verbal and quantitative abilities. They found that the conflict resolution skills assessment correlated significantly with independent ratings of the assessees' performance in resolving conflict in the workplace, whereas the cognitive ability measures were unrelated. This suggests that a video-based simulation of an important interpersonal skill has criterion-related validity that is separate and distinct from intelligence. Subsequent research has found little relation of a similar video-based assessment with personality (Bergman, Donovan, & Drasgow, 2001).

National Board of Medical Examiners case simulation. Candidates for the medical licensing examination for the National Board of Medical Examiners

(NBME) take a computer-based case simulation (Clyman, Melnick, & Clauser, 1999). In this exam, the candidate physician diagnoses and treats a series of virtual patients. Candidates can request the patient's history, order a physical exam, order one or more tests, provide a treatment, or request a consultation, all of which are typically available to a physician. The condition and symptoms of the virtual patient change in response to the actions of the candidate. For example, if the candidate physician orders a test that requires 30 minutes to perform, he or she must move the clock forward 30 minutes to receive the results. Concomitantly, the virtual patient's condition progresses for 30 minutes with the symptoms changing accordingly.

The computer-based simulation is designed to accurately assess a physician's patient care strategy. In real-world situations, diagnosing and treating patients often requires more than a single straightforward decision. A problem-solving process may be required in which possible causes are assessed in an interrelated series of tests. Multiple-choice questions may artificially isolate components of this process and therefore fail to provide an adequate evaluation of the candidate's patient care strategy. Clyman et al. (1999) found a disattenuated correlation of only about .5 between scores on the multiple-choice section of the NBME examination and the case simulation. At the very least, this suggests that the case simulation is assessing an aspect of patient care not covered by the multiple-choice questions. Moreover, from the perspective of the patient, diagnosis and treatment is arguably the most critical aspect of a candidate physician's skill.

Uniform Certified Public Accountant Examination. The Uniform Certified Public Accountant (UCPA) examination moved to a computer-based format in 2004. In addition to a multiple-choice section, the exam incorporates simulations of typical accounting tasks for entry-level certified public accountants (CPAs). The simulations require examinees to enter values into spreadsheets, conduct research, evaluate risk, and justify conclusions. This last component is particularly interesting: Candidates must examine a searchable version of the authoritative accounting standards to find the regulation that justifies their

decision and then copy and paste it into a text box. In other words, rather than simply testing rote memory, the assessment evaluates whether a candidate knows where to look for answers and how to apply them to accounting problems.

Architect Registration Exam (ARE). At first glance, computerized scoring of architectural design would appear to be impossible. After all, beauty is in the eye of the beholder, and it seems improbable that a computer algorithm would be able to capture the most human of abilities, creativity. Consequently, the ARE answers were previously scored holistically by human graders. Nonetheless, the ARE has switched to a computerized format scored via computer.

Rather than trying to emulate human graders, the ARE scoring algorithms were built to produce consistent scores that reflect key features of designs. Here, a single design receives the same score when rescored, and the scoring criteria remain consistent across answers (Bejar & Braun, 1999). To achieve such consistency, the designs are scored based on a microlevel analysis rather than holistically. To allow this type of scoring, design tasks must be constructed according to a detailed set of specifications, which imposed a rigor during item development.

Developing new scoring algorithms for each new design problem would be a huge burden. The ARE research team developed a number of standard design tasks, which they called vignettes. Each vignette has a specific scoring algorithm, which was time consuming and labor intensive to create. However, to develop new tasks, the features of the vignette were changed, although the basic design problem remained the same. These "isomorphs," or clones of a specific vignette, are scored with the same scoring algorithm.

Musical Aptitude. Assessing musical aptitude has been challenging because reproducing acoustic tones accurately has traditionally been dependent on audiocassette players. The poor quality of the cassettes and the degradation of sound quality over time made accurate reproduction unreliable. In cases where the audio clips are played for a group, various factors such as the examinee's seating position relative to the speakers, sneezing or coughing by another examinee, and the acoustic qualities of the examination room can all influence the performance of the examinee.

Multimedia computers are particularly suitable for assessing musical aptitude. They can play audio clips, present text and graphical images that ask about the audio clips, and then record the examinee's responses. Additionally, because digital recordings do not degenerate over time, the sound quality remains constant. Further benefits with computerized assessment include examinees proceeding at their own pace and using headphones that minimize the effects of other noises.

Walter Vispoel has pioneered the development of musical aptitude testing since the early days of personal computers (Vispoel, 1987, 1999). One recent version of Vispoel's (1999) musical aptitude test has the computer play a short musical melody and then repeat the melody. The examinee's task is to determine which note, if any, was changed in the second melody. The assessment is a CAT that uses IRT to determine the next item (i.e., melody) to administer and requires far fewer items than a conventional test to obtain the same measurement precision.

SOFTWARE AND HARDWARE

In terms of the actual hardware, most new computers are powerful enough to run computer-based tests. However, to maintain uniform administration of a test, certain basic features of the computer should be standardized. For example, for a musical aptitude test, the quality of the headphones may affect the sound quality. Candidates who receive poor-quality headphones may be disadvantaged relative to those who receive higher quality headphones.

Deciding the best deployment solution for a test depends on a number of issues, including security, platform or computer hardware accessibility, and expected number of examinees. From a software perspective, there are two basic design options. The program can either be a stand-alone system or a system integrated with the scheduling, administration, scoring, and item authoring applications. A stand-alone system is clearly simpler to design and build. Such a system is appropriate if the test developer does not expect to widely deploy the program,

and the response data do not need to be collected at a central location.

A stand-alone system may be more at risk for compromise because the scoring key must be deployed along with the test to compute and report test scores. When maintaining testing facilities at various physical locations, each location is a potential avenue for test compromise. In such cases, encryption may be a necessary precaution against persistent hackers.

For large-scale testing programs such as the GRE or ASVAB, it becomes important to integrate the various development, administration, and scoring systems. For example, to maintain a continuous testing program, item pools must be rotated to avoid overexposure. New items must also be written and pretested to maintain the quality of the item pool. Integrating the item development tools into the administration software is needed, because pretesting new items is usually done with the operational test and actual examinees.

Of course, there are many intermediate solutions between a stand-alone and a fully integrated system. If the security of the scoring key is a concern, a stand-alone system may be connected over the Internet to the central server that scores the test. In this fashion, the scoring key never leaves the secure facilities of the test developer. A variant of the stand-alone and network configurations is the application service provider (ASP) solution. The ASP solution is essentially a network solution, except that the applications and computer servers are rented from the service provider. It is not an Internet assessment in the truest sense because the user is not able to freely access the test at any computer; the Internet is merely used as a means to distribute the applications.

CONCLUSIONS

Computerized assessment has progressed greatly in the past few decades. Dumb terminals connected to a mainframe computer have been replaced by multimedia personal computers with tremendous computational power, high-resolution color monitors, stereo sound, and full-motion video. These capabilities allow test developers to assess individual differences in ways that were impossible just a few years ago. The innovative assessments described in this chapter provide an indication of the variety of new tests. Certainly, the years ahead will see a proliferation of innovations.

Olson-Buchanan et al.'s (1998) Conflict Resolution Skills assessment provides an example of how computerized assessment has progressed. Their initial version of the test, created in the early 1990s, required a laser disk player and IBM's M-Motion Video Adaptor board, both of which cost more than $1,000 and were awkward to use. A skilled programmer spent months writing a Pascal program to play the video clips. The second version of the assessment replaced the laser disks with CDs, which had become standard by the mid 1990s. A critical issue, however, was whether a computer's video adapter card was fast enough to play full-motion video; some were, some were not. Software was developed using specialized computer-based training software, which took months to learn and proved to be very unstable. The third and current version is a Microsoft Access application; the program was written in a few days. Access is a very stable program; the frequent crashes of the previous version have been replaced by a program that runs reliably. Moreover, virtually all currently available computers have CD drives and video adaptor cards that play video smoothly.

There are many directions for future work in computerized assessment. Many new computerized tests will be developed to assess individual differences difficult to measure with paper-and-pencil multiple-choice items. As software tools improve, assessments using virtual reality may become widespread. Limitations on assessments may lie in the imaginations of test developers, rather than in computer hardware and software.

Concomitantly, work on scoring computerized assessments will be critical. Interestingly, researchers investigating computerized scoring of essays (Powers, Burstein, Chodorow, Fowles, & Kukich, 2002) recently challenged skeptics to beat their algorithm. A professor of computational linguistics provided the most successful entry; his bogus essay fooled the software into giving a spuriously high score. In general, however, the computer

software was surprisingly effective in producing scores similar to those of human raters.

In sum, computerized assessment has made great strides during the past four decades. Computer hardware and software can now implement the creative visions of test developers. Many new advances seem likely in the near future.

CHAPTER 8

ABILITY TESTS

David Lubinski

Annually, literally millions of military personnel, students, and workers are evaluated with the aid of ability tests for educational opportunities, differential training, and promotion. Yet, the attributes assessed by these instruments and the extent to which they are distinguished from other assessments (e.g., achievement tests and measures of more circumscribed competencies) have been a source of confusion and contention ever since the advent of ability testing (Campbell, 1996; Cleary, Humphreys, Kendrick, & Wesman, 1975; Cronbach, 1975; Thorndike & Lohman, 1990). In addition, there are literally hundreds of measures purporting to assess human abilities, and although the magnitude of redundancy in this area has been acknowledged for over 75 years (Kelley, 1927) and continues to receive attention (Lubinski, 2004), each distinct measure typically has a unique name and often is welcomed as bringing a fresh approach to ability testing. Most recently, new formulations of emotional, multiple, and practical intelligence have added complexity to this state of affairs. Happily, however, modern methods and findings can bring considerable clarity and parsimony to ability, achievement, and competency testing. This serves as the topic for this chapter.

This chapter is parsed into four sections: (a) the organization of cognitive abilities and measures thereof, (b) evaluating the constructs assessed by ability tests, (c) approaches to validation, and (d) augmenting the construct validation process through similar and different modalities. Across these sections, convergent and discriminant validity is stressed for isolating common and distinct constructs. In addition, two complementary albeit underappreciated concepts are also underscored: *extrinsic convergent validity* (Fiske, 1971) and *incremental validity* (Sechrest, 1963). The former is especially useful for ascertaining when two measures are conceptually equivalent and empirically interchangeable (reducing scale redundancy), whereas the latter is particularly helpful for evaluating when innovative measures capture unaccounted for criterion variance (constituting a genuine scientific advance).

THE ORGANIZATION OF COGNITIVE ABILITIES

There are literally hundreds of ability tests (Carroll, 1993; Cattell, 1971; Jensen, 1980, 1998; Sternberg, 1994),[1] and a framework is needed to organize them. Over the years, proposals have been made to

Support for this article was provided by a Templeton Award for Positive Psychology, a NICHD Grant P30HD15052 to the John F. Kennedy Center at Vanderbilt University, and a Cattell Sabbatical Award. Earlier versions of this manuscript profited from many excellent suggestions by Camilla P. Benbow.

[1]Given the scope of phenomena surrounding ability tests, there are several topics that interested readers may wish to pursue that space limitations preclude. Following the publication of Herrnstein and Murray's (1993), *The Bell Curve*, for example, misinformation on all sides of the debate motivated the American Psychological Association (APA) to assemble a task force (and issue a report): "Intelligence: Knowns and Unknowns" (Neisser et al., 1996). In addition, *Intelligence* published a special issue entitled, "Intelligence and Social Policy" (Gottfredson, 1997). Two special issues of *Psychology, Public Policy, and Law* also appeared (Ceci, 1996; Williams, 2000). In addition, Sternberg's (1994) *Encyclopedia of Intelligence* is an excellent resource on tests, the history of testing, and creators of major advances; Thorndike and Lohman (1990) provide an excellent treatment of the

organize cognitive abilities within 120 categories (Guilford, 1967), seven primary dimensions (Thurstone, 1938), and one dominant dimension (Spearman, 1904). The former two abstract multiple abilities at uniform levels of molarity. However, as Snow (1986) has pointed out, as empirical evidence accrued, a clear but different picture emerged: The dimensionality and organization of human cognitive abilities is neither unitary (Anderson, 1983; Spearman, 1904, 1927) nor consisting of specific modules (Fodor, 1983; Gardner, 1983, 1993; Guilford, 1967). Rather, cognitive abilities are organized hierarchically, and tests designed to measure individual differences in cognitive abilities—when applied to a wide range of talent—have replicated this idea repeatedly (Carroll, 1993; Gustafsson, 2002; Snow & Lohman, 1989). With respect to the psychological import of dimensions within this hierarchy, dimensions at the highest level of generalization have the most *referent generality* (Coan, 1964)—or breadth and depth of their external relationships—whereas more molecular dimensions are relevant to fewer psychological phenomena (Brody, 1992; Cronbach & Snow, 1977; Gustafsson, 2002; Jensen, 1980, 1998).

The most definitive treatment of the hierarchical organization of cognitive abilities is Carroll's (1993), wherein he reviews (and reanalyzes) over 460 factor-analytic data sets collected over most of the past century. Carroll's (1993) hierarchical (three-stratum) model contains about 60 first-order stratum I factors, eight stratum II group factors, and one general factor or general intelligence ("g") at its vertex, stratum III (see Carroll, 1993, Figure 15.1, p. 626). Snow (Gustafsson & Snow, 1997; Marshalek, Lohman, & Snow, 1983; Snow & Lohman, 1989) and his students have corroborated this hierarchical structure through a more parsimonious radex scaling model (see Figure 8.1a). A complexity dimension (general intelligence, "g," or intellectual sophistication) is found at the core, and three content domains (or more specific abilities)—quantitative/numerical, spatial/mechanical, and verbal/linguistic—surround this general dimension. In Snow's radex model, two bits of information are required to conceptualize and locate a test in two-dimensional space, *complexity* and *content*. Content and complexity are inextricably intertwined in all cognitive tests.

Figure 8.1a illustrates three different types of tests (viz., "A," "B," and "C"), and the subscripts of each letter denote tests of varying degrees of complexity (larger numbers are associated with more complex tests). Figure 8.1b illustrates the parallel between the radex and hierarchical factor-analytic solutions quantitatively, whereas Figure 8.1c illustrates these parallels structurally. This model is useful for conceptualizing and organizing the overwhelming number of ability tests, because it helps explain why tests covary or are psychologically close—because they share content or complexity. The letters in Figure 8.1a denote similarity in content, whereas subscripts denote degree of complexity.

To the extent that tests are highly correlated, they are found in close proximity in this two-dimensional space (Figure 8.1a); the distance between any two tests in this space indicates the magnitude of their correlation. Complex tests are found near the center (or centroid of the radex), whereas less-complex tests occupy the periphery. Geometrically, the radex is formed by a series of circumplexes and simplexes: Tests located on or near lines running from the origin of the radex to its periphery form *simplexes* (tests having similar content but differing in complexity form arrays on which correlations between tests decrease as they become farther apart). Second, circular bands formed by radii extending from the centroid at uniform distances define tests of comparable complexity, but that vary in content; these circular bands form *circumplexes* (circles on which tests may be arrayed and on which correlations between tests decrease as they become farther apart). Hence, knowing the complexity and content (quantitative, spatial, verbal) locates specific tests within the radex.

Figure 8.2 is an empirical example of a radex scaling of a number of ability tests and composites formed by various aggregations of ability tests (Marshalek et al., 1983); well-known clusters of fluid abilities (G_F), crystallized abilities (G_C), and spatial visualization (G_V) are readily identified in

Parallelism Between the Radex and the Hierarchical Factor Model

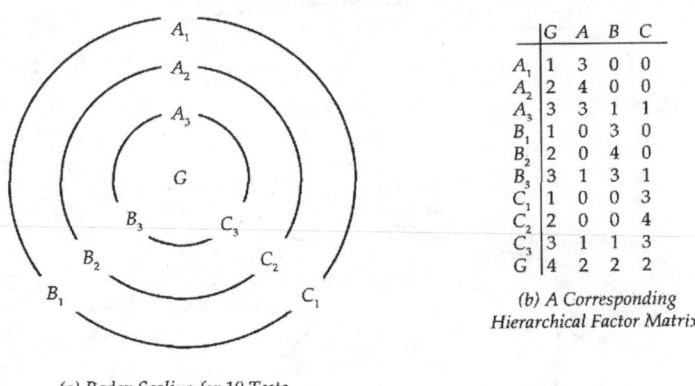

	G	A	B	C
A_1	1	3	0	0
A_2	2	4	0	0
A_3	3	3	1	1
B_1	1	0	3	0
B_2	2	0	4	0
B_3	3	1	3	1
C_1	1	0	0	3
C_2	2	0	0	4
C_3	3	1	1	3
G	4	2	2	2

(b) A Corresponding
Hierarchical Factor Matrix

(a) Radex Scaling for 10 Tests

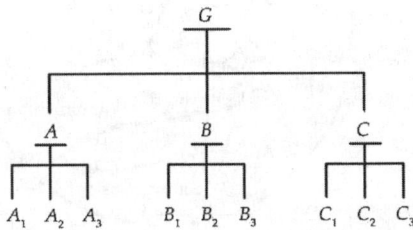

(c) The Associated Hierarchical Factor Diagram

FIGURE 8.1. This is a hypothetical example illustrating the degree of overlap between the radex and hierarchical factor model. From "The Topography of Ability and Learning Correlations" (p. 61), by R. E. Snow, P. L. Kyllonen, and B. Marchalek in *Advances in the Psychology of Human Intelligence* (Vol. 2), R. J. Sternberg, Ed., 1984, New Jersey: Erlbaum. Copyright 1984. Reprinted with permission.

this space. Complex, abstract, and content free tests are familiar tests of fluid abilities (G_F), whereas more crystallized (G_C) and visualization (G_V) tests are more content focused and a bit less complex. Other more content-focused tests are in this space as well.[2] As the next section illustrates, other competency tests may be found in this space (i.e., the space defined by conventional ability tests), which

highlights the ever present need for establishing convergent, discriminant, and incremental validity.[3]

Evaluating the Constructs Underlying Ability, Achievement, and Other Tests of Cognitive Competencies

It is important to appreciate that the vertex of the hierarchical model (derived factor analytically) and

---

[2]To be sure, other frameworks have been proposed, involving emotional, moral, multiple, and practical intelligence; but these have yet to generate meaningful empirical advances beyond what conventional cognitive ability assessments afford (cf. Brody, 2003; Gottfredson, 2003b; Hunt, 1999; Lubinski & Benbow, 1995). Messick (1992) in particular has skillfully demonstrated that many of these proposed innovations are found in earlier frameworks.

[3]Attracting considerable attention nowadays is "stereotypic threat," a hypothesis purporting that the validity of psychometric assessments is markedly attenuated for certain underrepresented groups. For multiple reasons, assessment specialists question the tenability of this idea; interested readers will find the following five pages both informative and intriguing (Jensen, 1998, pp. 513–515; Sackett, Schmidt, et al., 2001, pp. 309–310). (Also see, Cullen, Hardison, & Sackett, 2004; Sackett, Hardison, & Cullen, 2004; Stricker & Bejar, 2004; Stricker & Ward, 2004.) Finally, the National Science Foundations has published several validation reports on psychological tests in school and work settings (e.g., Hartigan & Wigdor, 1989; Wigdor & Garner, 1982; Wigdor & Green, 1991).

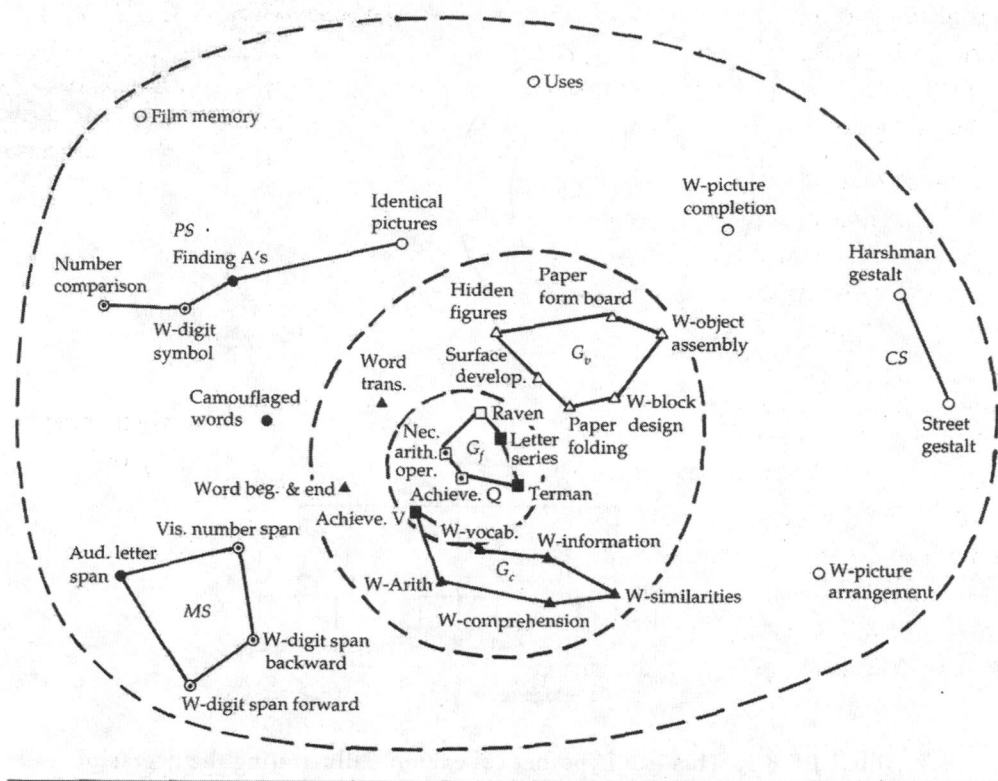

FIGURE 8.2. Each point in the diagram represents a test. These tests are organized by content and by complexity. Complex, intermediate, and simple tests are indicated by squares, triangles, and circles, respectively. Distinct forms of content are represented as black (verbal), dotted (numerical), and white (figural-spatial). Clusters of abilities that define well-known factors are indicated by a G. G_f = fluid ability, G_c = crystallized ability, G_v = spatial visualization. Tests having the greatest complexity are located near the center of the centroid of the radex. Reprinted from *Intelligence*, 7, B. Marshalek, D. F. Lohman, and R. E. Snow, "The Complexity Continuum in the Radex and Hierarchical Models of Intelligence," p. 122. Copyright 1983, with permission from Elsevier.

the centroid of the radex model (uncovered through multidimensional scaling) constitute psychologically equivalent factors. This dimension accounts for approximately 50% of the common variance running through heterogeneous collections of cognitive tests in a wide range of talent. It is also a source of variance traveling through more assessment vehicles than many psychologists realize, and it accounts for the preponderance of criterion variance that cognitive abilities are capable of predicting. There are certainly other cognitive abilities beyond the general

factor that are useful in predicting real-world criteria (Humphreys, Lubinski, & Yao, 1993; Shea, Lubinski, & Benbow, 2001), and a subsequent section will provide examples. However, to evaluate the unique psychological import of specific abilities, it is necessary to establish their discriminant validity from the general factor, as well as their incremental validity, relative to it, in the prediction of meaningful psychological criteria. This latter point needs to be particularly stressed, as all too often, innovative instruments are correlated with general intelligence

and manifest modest correlations. Then, high reliability coefficients are used to argue that the new indicator is distinctive because the majority of its reliable variance is unique to general intelligence. This line of reasoning says nothing about the measure's psychological importance.

Reliable variance that is psychologically uninteresting. The measurement literature is replete with examples of components of variance that are reliable but not necessarily psychologically important: method variance (Campbell & Fiske, 1959), constant error (Loevinger, 1954), systematic bias (Humphreys, 1990), systematic ambient noise (Lykken, 1968), and crud (Meehl, 1990). These terms denote reliable sources of variance that are *construct irrelevant* (Cook & Campbell, 1979), which saturate all psychological measuring devices. The point is that discriminant validity is only one step in the process of evaluating the psychological significance of measuring tools. Incremental validity is also needed (Sechrest, 1963). Moreover, given that general intelligence accounts for the preponderance of variance that cognitive abilities account for in predicting performance criteria in educational, employment, and training settings (Brody, 1992; Jensen, 1980, 1998; Schmidt & Hunter, 1998; Viswesvaran & Ones, 2002), unless there are compelling reasons to do otherwise, parsimony suggests that innovative tools be evaluated for their incremental validity relative to this standard (cf. Lubinski, 2000; Lubinski & Dawis, 1992). After all, general intelligence is the ability construct with the most referent generality, which is why Humphreys (1976) refers to this dimension as, "*the* primary mental ability." Earlier treatments of this idea are well worth reading (Humphreys, 1962, 1976; McNemar, 1964), as are the words of Messick (1992, p. 379): "Because IQ is merely a way of scaling measures of general intelligence ["g"], the burden of proof in claiming to move beyond IQ is to demonstrate empirically that . . . test scores tap something more than or different from general intelligence. . . ."

Reliable variance that is psychologically interesting. Technically, of course, all ability tests carry multiple constructs. That this is true of all assessments of individual differences is partly what motivated Campbell and Fiske (1959) to develop the MTMM matrix and the idea of convergent validity. (Actually, method variance itself can be construed as a construct.) However, some ability tests carry large components of variance relevant to psychologically important general (complexity) and specific (more content focused) constructs, whereas others carry variance primarily restricted to the former. For multifaceted indicators, containing appreciable components of multiple constructs (e.g., those illustrated in Figure 8.3 [viz., X_1, X_2, and X_3]), it is important to ascertain whether *general* ("*g*") or *specific constructs* (viz., S_1, S_2, or S_3) are at work when they manifest validity by forecasting important external criteria: Are the scale's external relationships due to common variance (g, shared with all cognitive measures) or specific variance (S, more indicative of the scale's manifest content)? Answering this question speaks to Messick's (1992) requirement for going beyond IQ.

Given the preceding, several considerations need to be entertained before launching causal inferences about constructs underlying test performance (Gustaffson, 2002; Lubinski, 2004). Consider, for example, mathematical, spatial, and verbal abilities. Content-focused measures within intermediate tiers of the hierarchical organization of cognitive abilities typically carry appreciable components of general and specific variance. So, in studies of the external validity of specific ability instruments (e.g., the constituents in Figure 8.3, viz., X_1, X_2, or X_3), these investigations need to incorporate indicators involving predominantly general factor variance (e.g., the composite in Figure 8.3, viz., $X_1 + X_2 + X_3$), if the underlying constructs are to be appraised. Doing so enables evaluations of the extent to which general or specific constructs or both are operating (and to what degree). When measures consisting of predominantly specific variance add incremental validity to the prediction of relevant criteria, after a composite that consists largely of the general factor has been entered in a multiple regression equation, evidence is gleaned for the psychological significance of an important cognitive ability distinct from

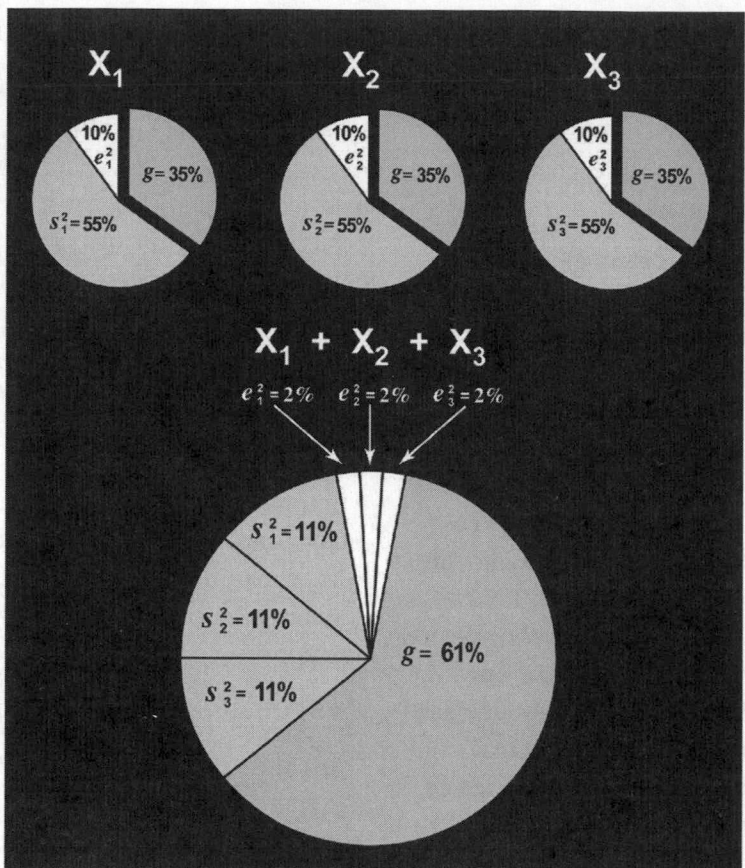

FIGURE 8.3. Three scales each composed of 35% common variance, 55% specific variance, and 10% error variance (top). When these three scales are aggregated (bottom), the resulting composite consists mostly of the variance they share (61% common variance). Modified and reproduced by special permission of the Publisher CPP, Inc. Mountain View, CA 94043, from "Aptitudes, skills, and proficiencies" by D. Lubinski & R. V. Dawis, in *Handbook of Industrial and Organizational Psychology* (2nd ed., Vol. 3), by M. D. Dunnette & L. M. Hough (Eds.). Copyright 1992 by CPP, Inc. All rights reserved. Future reproduction is prohibited without the Publisher's written consent.

general intelligence.[4] This is also true for innovative tests developed to measure innovative constructs.

Other tests of cognitive competencies. A large literature has emerged (independent of the psychometric assessment of human abilities) to suggest that investigators from other disciplines have built measures of general intelligence without knowing it. This is why it is important to distinguish between the complexity and the content of a test and, subsequently, conducting incremental validity appraisals (Sanders, Lubinski, & Benbow, 1995).

---

[4]When general factor variance is operating predominantly, as Cronbach and Snow (1977) have revealed for many educational treatments, and Schmidt and Hunter (1998) have revealed for multiple performance criteria in the world of work, content-focused specific ability tests will typically achieve significant results as well, if used in isolation. However, the general variance is probably what is doing the work. The construct operating involves the complexity of the test (or its general factor variance) rather than the content of the test (or its specific factor variance). Venturing causal inferences about the operative construct from specific ability measures used in isolation is hazardous. For the same reasons, venturing causal inferences about the operative construct underlying innovative measures without considering their overlap with powerful preexisting measures within the hierarchy of cognitive abilities is hazardous as well. All too often, what is purported to be a major advance turns out to be a manifestation of the Jangle fallacy (Kelley, 1927) or a "psychological factor of no importance" (Kelley, 1939). For further and more detailed reading on these ideas, see Gustaffson (2002) and Lubinski (2004; Lubinski & Dawis, 1992).

Complexity travels through multiple content domains and frequently carries most, sometimes all, of the predictable criterion variance.

Three independent lines of work on "functional literacy" (i.e., health literacy [National Work Group on Literacy and Health, 1998], adult literacy [Kirsch, Jungeblut, Jenkins, & Kolstad, 1993], and worker literacy [Sticht, 1975]) have generated distinct measures designed to assess, respectively: knowledge critical for healthy behavior (taking medication properly), everyday skills (interpreting a bus schedule accurately), and employability (skills related to individual differences in employability). Each team built assessment tools with content saturated with effective functioning for good health, life in general, or the world of work (see Gottfredson, 2002, for a detailed analysis of these three lines of research). These instruments, however, all appear to converge on the same underlying construct, a dominant dimension involving individual differences in processing complex information (the vertex of Carroll's hierarchy, or the centroid of Snow's radex). In the information age, it is the processing of complex information that is critical for adaptive performance in multiple arenas. Indeed, the authors of the U.S. Department of Education's National Literacy Survey (NALS) began their scale construction procedures aiming to assess three kinds of literacy: prose, documents, and quantitative. They found, however, that despite an effort to create relatively distinctive measures, their three scales correlate over .90. Thus, "major [NALS] survey results are nearly identical for each of the three scales . . . with findings appearing to be reported essentially in triplicate, as it were" (Reder, 1998, pp. 39, 44).

Just like inventors of the initial specific ability measures were aiming for a parsimonious set of relatively independent dimensions, primarily defined by different content and a theory of group factors (Kelley, 1928; Thurstone, 1938), modern investigators seeking to evaluate individual differences pertaining to health knowledge, reading comprehension, and work competency underappreciated the amount of psychological similarity running through these various cognitive tasks—content domains—that people encounter in everyday life.

Higher levels of general intelligence facilitate the acquisition of many different kinds of knowledge, relative to lower levels.

The preceding findings demonstrate the scope of general intelligence. This construct travels through many different kinds of assessment vehicles, because it travels through many different aspects of life. Individual differences in this attribute reflect differential capabilities for assimilating cultural content. Therefore, general intelligence seems closely aligned with Woodrow's (1921) initial characterization; namely, intelligence is "the capacity to develop capacity."

In the preceding example, the instruments that were developed all measure general intelligence to a remarkable degree. It would be interesting to ascertain whether they manifest any incremental validity beyond general intelligence in the life domains that they were designed for. Moreover, reading, per se, is not the source of overlap, because these findings replicate when questions are given orally (Kirsch et al., 1993; Sticht, 1975). Assimilating, comprehending, and processing information are the individual differences assessed by these measures. Moreover, as reading researchers discovered long ago, there is much more to reading comprehension than simply decoding words. These orally administered assessments constitute an important line of convergent validity (Campbell & Fiske, 1959) because they use a distinctly different medium (viz., oral as opposed to written instructions or listening as opposed to reading). For native speakers, reading ability is *comprehension* (Jensen, 1980, pp. 325–326); spoken language and written language are just different vehicles—different methods—for conveying information (cf. Carroll, 1997).

Therefore, social scientists interested in the study of health, life competencies, and work competencies can draw on a broad nomological network afforded from decades of psychometric research on ability tests. Traditional ability tests assess individual differences relevant to the phenomena that they are interested in. They generalize to many important life domains outside the educational, occupational, and training settings used for their initial development (cf. Gordon, 1997; Gottfredson, 2002, 2004).

Distinguishing ability and achievement tests. The forgoing discussion about the generality of contrasting "literacies," or tests initially designed to measure more circumscribed competencies, is in many ways not surprising. Because again, the general factor accounts for the majority of the variance that cognitive abilities are capable of predicting. Therefore, it might be expected that when measures are developed without taking into consideration what conventional tests afford, some reinventing of the wheel will occur. Back in the 1920s, Kelley (1927) knew that tiny slivers of general intelligence run through all achievement items. Therefore, when achievement items are sampled broadly and aggregated to form composites, functionally equivalent measures of general intelligence are formed (cf. Roznowski, 1987). Indeed, when Kelley (1927) bemoaned the amount of redundancy across multiple psychological tests and introduced his well-known *jangle fallacy* to bring this problem to light, he used ability and achievement tests to exemplify the problem.

> Equally contaminating to clear thinking is the use of two separate words or expressions covering in fact the same basic situation, but sounding different, as though they were in truth different. The doing of this . . . the writer would call the "jangle" fallacy. "Achievement" and "intelligence" . . . We can mentally conceive of individuals differing in these two traits, and we can occasionally actually find such by using the best of our instruments of mental measurement, but to classify all members of a single school grade upon the basis of their difference in these two traits is sheer absurdity. (Kelley, 1927, p. 64)

Cronbach (1976) reinforced this idea 50 years later: When heterogeneous collections of routine achievement measures are combined to form a total score, an excellent measure of general intelligence is formed. Just prior to this, an APA task force concluded that different "achievement" and "aptitude or ability" tests can be reduced to four dimensions

(Cleary et al., 1975): (a) breadth of item sampling, (b) the extent to which items are tied to a specific educational program, (c) recency of learning assessed, and (d) the purpose of assessment (viz., current status, *concurrent* validity, or potential for growth, *predictive* validity). Ability and achievement tests do not differ qualitatively; they differ quantitatively along these four dimensions. Indeed, the same kinds of items (frequently identical items) are routinely found on both "kinds" of tests.

When large numbers of items are broadly sampled from different kinds of information and problem-solving content, not necessarily tied to an educational curriculum, which may involve recent as well as old learning (acquired formally or informally), their aggregation forms a composite that accurately assesses general intelligence. This idea, of course, is Spearman's (1927) *indifference of the indicator*. However, if familiar achievement or information items are to be used—rather than relatively content free reasoning problems (e.g., Raven matrices)—it is important to stress that sampling should be broad to assess the general factor (cf. Roznowski, 1987). The reason "achievement" items are not used more routinely in assessing broad cognitive abilities is because they contain less construct relevant variance than conventional "ability" items (which are more abstract, complex, and content free). Hence, to assess abilities with high referent generality, many more achievement (knowledge) items, relative to ability (reasoning) items are required (Brody, 1994)—but this is a technical matter, not a conceptual or psychological issue.

Although pools formed by heterogeneous collections of information items may appear unsystematic, or a "hotchpotch" (Spearman, 1927), the communality they distill generates functionally equivalent correlates (Hulin & Humphreys, 1980). To be clear, for individual items, a large component of construct irrelevant uniqueness is associated with each. Indeed, at the item level, over 95% construct irrelevant variance is typical (Green, 1978). However, aggregation attenuates these contaminants and reduces their overall influence in the composite; the small communality associated with each item piles

up as more items are added. The composite reflects mostly *construct relevant* variance (signal), even though each item consists mostly of *construct irrelevant* variance (noise).

Evaluating the interchangeability of tests. The foregoing discussion highlights why general intelligence variance needs to be controlled before specific ability and innovative cognitive competency measures can be adequately appraised. It also illustrates how similar constructs may travel through instruments that differ widely in content. However, although Cronbach (1970; Cronbach & Snow, 1977) has stressed the importance of a general cognitive ability dimension, he also has expressed concern about capturing this dimension precisely. His concern is germane to other dimensions of cognitive abilities as well.

Reflecting on "construct validity after 30 years," Cronbach (1989) noted that localizing the general dimension running through all cognitive abilities is problematic: Because the center of the radex (Snow & Lohman, 1989), or the vertex of a hierarchical organization (Carroll, 1993), always varies somewhat from sample to sample, and as a function of the diversity of the tests used, how is one ever to know whether the "true" center or summit has been found? Clearly, a method is needed to ascertain when experimentally distinct indicators measure the same construct in the same way.

To determine if two experimentally distinct assessment vehicles are indeed measuring the same construct to the same degree, Fiske (1971) developed *extrinsic convergent validity*. The idea is this: Two measures may be considered conceptually equivalent and empirically interchangeable if they display corresponding correlational profiles across a heterogeneous collection of external criteria. Examples of the integrative power of this idea can be found in the psychological literature (Judge, Erez, Bono, & Thoresen, 2002; Lubinski, Tellegen, & Butcher, 1983; Schmidt, Lubinski, & Benbow, 1998), but it is surprising that it is not more routinely used, given the amount of concern about redundancy in psychological measuring instruments (cf. Block, 2002; Dawis, 1992; Tellegen,

1993). Another attractive feature of this method is that when multiple measures generate the same pattern of correlations across a heterogeneous collection of external criteria (Judge et al., 2002; Lubinski et al., 1983; Schmidt et al., 1998), ostensibly distinct bodies of literature may be combined under one unifying construct. Consider Table 8.1, which reinforces the earlier discussion of a general cognitive ability running through all specific ability measures as well as all achievement tests.

Table 8.1 contains three experimentally independent measures with verbal content: literary information, reading comprehension, and vocabulary. They have intercorrelations of around .75, so they share approximately half of their variance. And their uniform reliabilities (high .80s) afford each appreciable nonerror uniqueness. Yet, examine the correspondence across their external correlational profiles, which include criteria ranging from other specific abilities to vocational interests. All three correlational profiles are essentially functionally equivalent. All three measures assess the same underlying construct, even though each possesses a large component of nonerror uniqueness or room for divergence. Essentially all the information they afford about individual differences is located in their overlap (or communality). To refer to these three measures as assessing distinct constructs just because they have different labels and manifest content would constitute the jangle fallacy. For many research purposes, these three measures may be used interchangeably.

Notice also in Table 8.1 how these verbal measures covary with other cognitive *abilities* (quantitative and spatial *reasoning*) and tests of *achievement* (music and social studies *knowledge*), but are only lightly associated with educational–vocational interest measures, if at all. This convergent–discriminant pattern reflects the construct of general intelligence. When measures of quantitative, spatial, and verbal ability are systematically aggregated, an excellent measure of general intelligence is formed (Figure 8.3). The question now becomes, Is the external validity evinced by the three measures in Table 8.1 a function of their verbal content, or the general factor ("g") that runs through them? This is important to ascertain because, again, only after incremental

TABLE 8.1

Extrinsic Convergent Validation Profiles Across Three Measures Having Verbal Content

	Literature	Vocabulary	Reading comprehension
Aptitude Tests			
Mechanical reasoning	.43	.52	.54
2-D visualization	.25	.32	.35
3-D visualization	.35	.43	.47
Abstract reasoning	.45	.53	.61
Arithmetic reasoning	.54	.63	.63
High-school math	.57	.59	.57
Advanced math	.42	.43	.39
Information or "Achievement" Tests			
Music	.67	.68	.62
Social studies	.74	.74	.71
Mathematics	.62	.63	.57
Physical science	.64	.67	.60
Biological science	.57	.61	.56
Interest Questionnaires			
Physical sciences	.24	.25	.22
Biological sciences	.26	.25	.22
Public service	.16	.12	.12
Literary–linguistic	.37	.32	.32
Social service	.07	.06	.07
Art	.32	.30	.29
Music	.23	.20	.20
Sports	.12	.12	.13
Office work	−.35	−.29	−.27
Labor	−.08	−.06	−.06

Note. These correlations were based only on female subjects (male profiles are parallel). N = 39,695. Intercorrelations for the three measures were the following: literature/vocabulary = .74, literature/reading comprehension = .71, and vocabulary/reading comprehension = .77. Correlations across the three profiles were all > .90, whereas congruence coefficients across the three profiles were all > .95. Modified and reproduced by special permission of the Publisher CPP, Inc. Mountain View, CA 94043, from "Aptitudes, skills, and proficiencies" by D. Lubinski & R. V. Dawis, in *Handbook of Industrial and Organizational Psychology* (2nd ed., Vol. 3), by M. D. Dunnette & L. M. Hough (Eds.). Copyright 1992 by CPP, Inc. All rights reserved. Future reproduction is prohibited without the Publisher's written consent.

validity analyses are preformed, which used both general and specific measures, can it be determined whether general or specific variance is operating (cf. Figure 8.3)—or whether both are. This is critical for making valid inferences about the operative construct(s). This is also useful for stopping the superfluous proliferation of tests purporting to measure "new" constructs, but which in reality measure familiar things that we already have excellent measures of (the jangle fallacy).

APPROACHES TO VALIDATION

What can ability tests do for psychological science? What do they predict to and how longitudinally robust are they? Huge amounts of data have been

compiled over the years on general and specific abilities. That general ability is related to learning, training, and work performance is widely acknowledged (Corno, Cronbach, et al., 2002; Cronbach & Snow, 1977; Gottfredson, 1997, 2003a; Jensen, 1980, 1998; Schmidt & Hunter, 1998), although, when predicting performance, specific abilities can add incremental validity (Lubinski & Dawis, 1992). This literature does not need to be reviewed here. Rather, this section will be restricted to two points: niche selection and predicting group membership.

It is important to keep in mind that different criteria are needed to answer different psychological questions. Predicting individual differences in learning, training, and work performance is important for validating ability tests, but performance it is not always the optimal criterion variable (cf. Humphreys et al., 1993; Lubinski, Webb, Morelock, & Benbow, 2001; Murray, 1998; Wilk, Desmarais, & Sackett, 1995; Wilk & Sackett, 1996). There are other criteria that matter. For example, students and workers do not select educational tracks and occupational paths randomly. They do so in part based on the level and pattern of their general and specific abilities. General ability level has more to do with educational or occupation level or prestige (e.g., uniform levels of high prestige cut across doctor, lawyer, and professor), whereas specific abilities differentially predispose development toward learning about and working with different media (e.g., working with ideas, working with people, working with things). Because making choices is different than performance after choice, the criteria needed for validating the role that abilities play in making choices are different. For answering these questions, the prediction of group membership is more optimal. Investigations along these lines are more associated with names like Truman Kelley, Phillip Rulon, and Maurice Tatsuoka. These validation designs involve multivariate discriminant function analyses aimed at classification and selection, rather than multiple regression analyses predicting individual differences in learning and work performance (see Humphreys et al., 1993, for a review).

For example, the four panels of Figure 8.4 track a group of intellectually precocious participants at three time points over a 20-year interval. At age 13,

participants were in the top 1% of their age mates in general intellectual ability; at this time, they were also assessed on quantitative, spatial, and verbal reasoning measures (Shea et al., 2001). At ages 18, 23, and 33, individual differences in their mathematical, spatial, and verbal abilities assessed in early adolescence were related in distinct ways to subsequent preferences for contrasting disciplines and ultimate educational and occupational group membership. Specifically, panels A and B, respectively, show whether participants' favorite and least favorite high school course was in math/science or the humanities/social sciences. Panels C and D, respectively, reflect college major at age 23 and occupation at age 33.

All four panels represent a three-dimensional view of how mathematical (X), verbal (Y), and spatial (Z) ability factor into educational–vocational preferences and choice. For all four panels, all three abilities are standardized in z-score units (A and B are within sex, C and D are combined across sex). For each labeled group within each panel, the direction of the arrows represents whether spatial ability (Z-axis) was above (*right*) or below (*left*) the grand mean for spatial ability. These arrows were scaled in the same units of measurement as the SAT (math and verbal) scores. Thus, one can envision how far apart these groups are in three-dimensional space in standard deviation units as a function of these three abilities. Across these developmentally sequenced panels, exceptional verbal ability, relative to mathematical and spatial ability, is characteristic of group membership in the social sciences and humanities, whereas higher levels of math and spatial abilities, relative to verbal abilities, characterize group membership in engineering and math/computer science. For example, engineering is relatively high space, high math, and relatively low verbal. Other sciences appeared to require appreciable amounts of all three abilities. These findings were highly consistent for other outcome criteria as well (e.g., graduate field of study; Shea et al., 2001). Across all time points, all three abilities achieved incremental validity relative to the other two in predicting group membership. This amount of differentiation could not have been achieved with one dimension, or what these measures have in

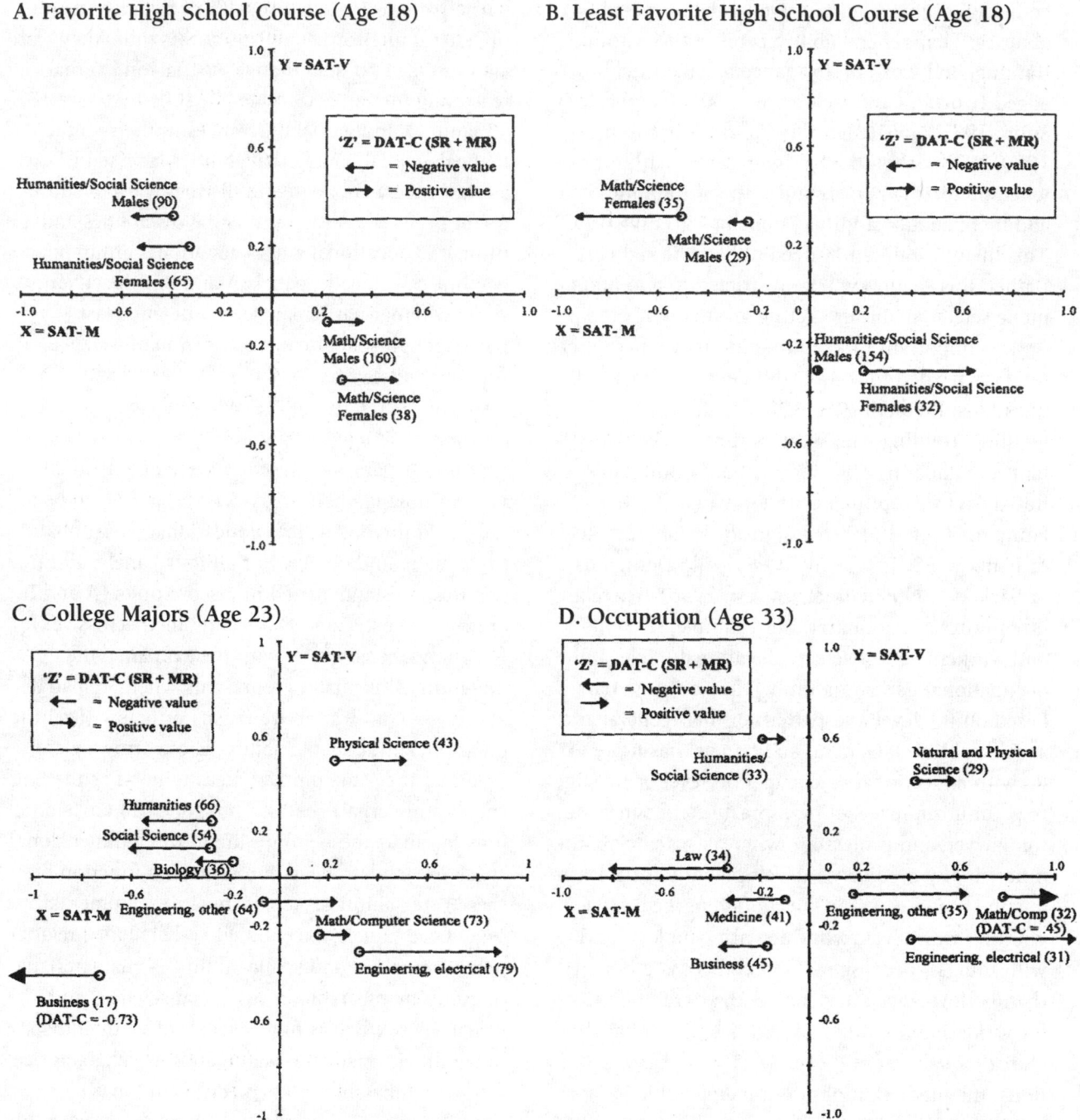

FIGURE 8.4. Trivariate means for (A) favorite high school class and (B) least favorite class at age 18, (C) conferred bachelor's degree at age 23, and (D) occupation at age 33. Group *ns* are in parentheses. SAT-V = Verbal subtest of the Scholastic Assessment Test; SAT-M = Mathematical subtest of the Scholastic Assessment Test; and DAT-C = Composite of two subtests of the Differential Aptitude Test (space relations, SR + mechanical reasoning, MR). Panels A and B are standardized within sexes, panels C and D between sexes. The large arrowhead in panel C indicates that this group's relative weakness in spatial ability is actually twice as great as that indicated by the displayed length. From "Importance of Assessing Spatial Ability in Intellectually Talented Young Adolescents: A Longitudinal Study," by D. L. Shea, D. Lubinski, and C. P. Benbow, 2001, *Journal of Educational Psychology, 93,* pp. 607–610. Copyright 2001 by the American Psychological Association.

common; rather, their specific variance (illustrated in Figure 8.3) is responsible for distinguishing these groups psychologically.

Assessing Similar Constructs Through Different Modalities

Except for the example of orally administered health and worker literacy tests, the discussion thus far has focused on ability measures involving the same source. In this final section, a genuinely distinct method will be reviewed, the chronometric assessment of elementary cognitive processes (ECTs): memory, inspection time, and reaction time.

An intriguing history is associated with ECTs and the relationship between chronometric assessments thereof and intelligence. Although early on people like E. G. Boring recognized the potential significance of ECTs and intellectual appraisals (Peak & Boring, 1926), work in the area came to an abrupt halt following the publication of two dissertations, one supervised by James McKeen Cattell at Columbia (Wissler, 1901), the other supervised by E. B. Titchener at Cornell (Sharp, 1898–1899). This fascinating history is detailed in Deary (2000, pp. 70–81). In a nutshell, both of these investigations argued against the hypothesized relationship between ECTs and familiar indicators of intelligence. The two publications were widely cited as falsifying the idea that human intellectual behavior was associated with chronometric assessments of ECT (Deary, 2000). Yet, the studies were methodologically frail. Sharp's (1899) study, for example, used only seven postgraduate students. Wissler's (1901) study was more elaborate, but still only used high-ability subjects, and the simple reaction time measurements were based on only three to five trials. Furthermore, Wissler (1901) computed less than 10% of the possible correlations from his procedures and did not take errors of measurement into account. Thus, these two studies were not the strong "debunkers" most people have come to believe.

Modern experimentation has cast a different light on this modality as well. Over the past 20 years, experimentalists have come to appreciate that ECTs aggregate like psychometric items (Green, 1978). Aggregates of different kinds of basic cognitive processes have been constructed to form gen-

eral measures of conventional experimental phenomena (e.g., working memory, speed of cognitive processing), and these indicators have, in turn, been combined to reveal that their communality covaries highly with conventional measures of psychometric g. To be sure, there are experimental details to be worked out, because chronometric assessments of ECTs vary as a function of time of day, blood sugar level, medication, age, and a variety of individual differences variables (e.g., hormonal fluctuations). The work also requires vigilance of multiple experimental controls. Nonetheless, chronometric procedures are here to stay (Deary, 2000; Jensen, 2005; Lohman, 2000), because they appear to add incremental validity to conventional psychometric assessments (Luo et al., 2003, 2005). To say the least, they marshal an intriguing source of convergent validity on conventional psychometric assessments. Perhaps some day they will even effectively handle those annoying experiential contaminants associated with culture, learning, and opportunity that have always troubled appraisers of intellectual capabilities.

SUMMARY

Tests of human cognitive abilities assess arguably the most scientifically significant individual differences uncovered by psychological science. Tests of general intelligence were the focus of this chapter because the dominant dimension that runs through them accounts for 50% of the variance in heterogeneous tests (across a wide range of talent) and the majority of criterion variance that cognitive abilities can predict in school, training, and work settings. This latter generalization pertains to other real-world criteria (Gottfredson, 2002). Cronbach's (1970) earlier appraisal of general mental ability tests, namely, "[t]he general mental test stands today as the most important technical contribution psychology has made to the practical guidance of human affairs" (Cronbach, 1970, p. 197), is likely still valid.

Across many psychological niches, well beyond educational and occupational settings, powerful empirical evidence reveals that social scientists would markedly advance their scientific capabilities

by more routinely incorporating ability tests into their research programs (cf. Benbow & Stanley, 1996; Gordon, 1997; Gottfredson, 2002, 2003a, 2004; Lubinski, 2004; Lubinski & Humphreys, 1997; Schmidt & Hunter, 1998). Given the array of important behaviors and outcomes that cognitive abilities predict across longitudinally impressive time frames, neglecting ability constructs and measures in several social science arenas virtually guarantees incomplete theoretical formulations and underdetermined causal modeling.

CHAPTER 9

CATCHING THE MIND IN ACTION: IMPLICIT METHODS IN PERSONALITY RESEARCH AND ASSESSMENT

Michael D. Robinson and Clayton Neighbors

Key to implicit methods is the assumption that many of a person's most important tendencies are revealed only through performance. An intelligent person, for example, is not someone who claims to be intelligent, as such self-ratings may or may not correlate with performance measures (for a pessimistic view, see Brown & Dutton, 1995). Rather, an intelligent person is someone who can process information efficiently and reliably, even with concurrent mental load or distraction. Performance measures need not be limited to examining intelligence, however, as important contributions to social (e.g., Higgins, 1996), personality (e.g., McClelland, 1987), and clinical (e.g., Mathews & MacLeod, 1994) psychology have similarly been based on performance rather than on self-reports of performance.

Implicit methods are based on performance (e.g., reaction times) and therefore do not require self-insight; explicit methods (e.g., trait measures) are based on self-report and therefore require self-insight. The history of research on introspection has taught us that self-reports of mental processes cannot be trusted (MacLeod, 1993). This is why cognitive psychologists measure reaction time, memory accuracy, and perception within tightly controlled experimental paradigms (MacLeod, 1993). Thus, a focus on implicit methods should, ideally, foster a greater integration of personality psychology with cognitive psychology, a cross-fertilization that should enrich both areas.

Before commencing, it is important to note that, given page limitations, this chapter can neither be exhaustive of implicit methods nor sufficiently detailed to permit immediate use in research. The reader will be referred to appropriate sources for further reading; see also Table 9.1 in this regard. In the chapter, we will first make some general comments on the contrasting assumptions of mind represented by implicit and explicit methods. Second, we will present an overview on four classes of implicit measures, namely those related to (a) attention, (b) depressogenic thought, (c) category accessibility, and (d) associations in memory. Within the context of the last heading, we will describe the Implicit Association Test (IAT), which has generated considerable interest recently. Third, we will discuss the reliability and validity of implicit measures. And fourth and finally, we will present some closing thoughts on the importance of implicit methods to the science of personality and assessment.

LIMITATIONS TO THE TRAIT APPROACH

Personality traits are stable, cross-situational consistencies in behavior, thought, or experience. Although personality traits could in principle be based on multiple types of data, there has been an overwhelming reliance on self-report. On trait scales, participants are asked to characterize themselves "in general," that is, without regard to time frame or situational contingencies. Trait scores are reliable and valid and

Preparation of this chapter was assisted by funding from NSF (9817649) and NIMH (MH068241).

TABLE 9.1

Discussed Implicit Tests and References for Further Reading

Implicit test	Targeted process	Reference for further reading
Attitude Latencies	Attitude accessibility	Fazio (1995)
Emotional Stroop	Selective attention	Williams et al. (1996)
Spatial Probe Task	Selective attention	Mogg & Bradley (1998)
Various Priming Tasks	Negative self-schema	Segal & Ingram (1994)
Categorization	Construct accessibility	Robinson, Solberg, et al. (2003)
Implicit Association Task	Associations in memory	Greenwald et al. (1998)
Thematic Apperception	motivation	McClelland (1987)

do predict trait-relevant behavior and experiences, although perhaps not as robustly as one might hope (Pervin, 1994). Nonetheless, a number of critics point to the limitations of the trait approach (e.g., Cervone & Shoda, 1999).

To understand what self-reported traits are, it is useful to consider how trait judgments are made. When people decide whether they are introverted or extraverted, they do so without recalling any trait-relevant behaviors or experiences. This point has been convincingly made by Stanley Klein and colleagues, who have shown that (a) making a trait judgment does not facilitate recall for trait-relevant behaviors and (b) recalling trait-relevant behaviors does not facilitate making a trait judgment (e.g., Schell, Klein, & Babey, 1996). More dramatically, Klein, Loftus, and Kihlstrom (1996) found that an amnesic could make trait judgments about herself, despite the inability to recall a single relevant behavior from the recent past.

As suggested by Robinson and colleagues (Robinson & Clore, 2002a, 2002b; Robinson, Vargas, & Crawford, 2003), such results have important implications for the validity of self-reported traits. If trait judgments are made on the basis of different information than are reports of everyday behavior and experience, then they, in some very real sense, do not capture everyday behavior and experience. Along these lines, Robinson and Clore (2002a) reviewed evidence for the idea that many reports of emotion, particularly retrospective ones, are vulnerable to reconstruction in a belief-consistent direction. For example, the retrospective

reports of people high in self-esteem are systematically distorted such that those high in self-esteem remember more positive self-feelings than was actually the case in daily experience (Christensen, Wood, & Barrett, 2003).

Another major issue with trait self-reports is social desirability. Regardless of whether one considers social desirability to be a valid or invalid source of variance, there remains the serious issue that self-reports seem to be based, to a large extent, on social desirability considerations. That is, people tend to endorse trait items if they reflect beneficially on the self and reject trait items if they reflect poorly on the self, regardless of their actual standing on the trait dimension (Paulhus & John, 1998).

Social desirability can sometimes detract from the validity of self-report. For example, in an investigation by Shedler, Mayman, and Manis (1993), the authors found that clinician-based reports of distress were useful in distinguishing two categories of people. One group, who scored low in both self-reported and clinical distress, exhibited little behavioral and physiological reactivity within a laboratory stressor paradigm. The other group, who scored low in self-reported distress, but high in clinician ratings of distress, exhibited the most extreme behavioral and physiological reactivity to the laboratory stressor paradigm (for a recent review, see Norem, 1998). From this investigation, we can conclude that not all people who score mentally healthy on a self-report questionnaire are in fact mentally healthy.

Another concern is that self-reported traits provide little in the way of *explaining* why traits are associated with behaviors or experiences. This problem was somewhat forcefully stated by Ozer and Reise (1994): "In the absence of theory, measured traits are static variables, good for describing what someone is like . . . but poor at providing a rich and deep understanding of personality dynamics" (p. 367). Pervin (1994) similarly expressed disappointment with the status of trait-based explanations. Mechanisms linking traits to behavior or experience could be offered; however, our impression is that investigators often link traits to behavior or experience without providing empirical support for a mediating mechanism (Robinson, Vargas, et al., 2003).

There is a potentially more serious problem in linking self-reported traits to behavior and experience. Cervone and Shoda (1999) call this the "tautology" problem. If neuroticism is defined as a tendency to experience negative affect, then neuroticism cannot *explain* negative affect. Rather, the relation is definitional. Zelli and Dodge (1999) likened trait-based explanation to the following tautology: "The desert climate keeps it from raining" (p. 99). What is the definition of a desert climate? A lack of much rain. What does a lack of rain imply about the local climate? It is a desert. In sum, traits, if they are defined in terms of specific behaviors and experiences, have to predict those behaviors and experiences. Only an alternate universe, without logic or identity, could predict anything different. Traits, in sum, may label regularities in behavior and experience rather than explain them.

TRAITS AND IMPLICIT PROCESSING TENDENCIES

Researchers interested in individual differences may wish to capture processes that are more dynamic than those measured by traits (Pervin, 1994). If self-reported traits were somehow exhaustive of personality functioning, we would expect implicit processing measures to correlate with self-reported traits. However, they often do not. Theoretical reasons for such dissociations are discussed next.

As in many other areas of psychology, William James (1890) made significant contributions to the psychology of mind and consciousness. In a chapter on habit, he contrasted procedural knowledge, automated with repeated use, with volition. Once habits become a matter of procedural knowledge, the person has little insight into their operation. In a chapter on the stream of thought, he bemoaned the "baleful" failures of attempting to discern why or how one thought triggers another thought. In a chapter on the self, James contrasted the "I," which perceives and interprets, from the "me," which can be reflected upon. Other chapters, like those related to attention, memory, and will, similarly contrast operative processes with awareness concerning those processes.

Dissociations between knowledge use and awareness of knowledge use are not confined to James (1890). Indeed, modern statements on procedural knowledge (e.g., Anderson, 1982) make the case that knowledge is often used without awareness of knowledge use. That is, people attend to, perceive, categorize, and choose behaviors without awareness of what their minds are doing. One useful contribution in this regard was provided by Jacoby and Kelley (1987), who suggested that it is critical to distinguish "memory as an object" (i.e., explicit memory) from "memory as a tool" (i.e., implicit memory). When memory is an object, participants are asked to recall or recognize events that they were exposed to in the past. When memory is a tool, by contrast, no memory instructions are provided. Rather, the investigator is interested in the question of whether a prior exposure to a word or object speeds subsequent recognition. The short answer is that it does even when there is no conscious awareness of the prior event (Kihlstrom, 1987).

Somewhat parallel to Jacoby and Kelley's (1987) distinction between implicit and explicit memory is Bassili's (1996) distinction between operative and meta-attitudinal measures of attitude strength. A meta-attitudinal judgment asks the person to rate the importance of the attitude, their certainty about their attitude, its centrality to the self-concept, or some other judgment that presumably taps the likelihood that the attitude guides their behavior in

everyday life. Operative measures of attitude strength do not require such insight. Rather, operative measures seek to tap what is happening in the mind when the person is confronted by the object. Among some people, the mere presence of an attitude object (e.g., a Snickers bar) is enough to trigger an evaluation from memory (e.g., yum) without extensive deliberation or thought. Among others, this is not the case.

The accessibility of attitudes can be measured by asking people to, as quickly as possible, evaluate attitude objects (Fazio, 1989, 1995). People who make such judgments quickly have more accessible attitudes, a quality that should, and does, predict relevant behavioral outcomes (Fazio, 1989, 1995). For example, independent of the extremity of attitudes, Fazio and Williams (1986) found that they could predict biased perceptions of the Reagan–Mondale debates as well as voting behavior better among those with more accessible attitudes toward Reagan. Accessible attitudes are also more stable over time (Fazio, 1989, 1995). Finally, consistent with the dissociation theme, attitude accessibility is empirically distinct from self-reported measures of attitude strength such as importance and certainty (Bassili, 1996).

The purpose of this section has been to establish three points. One, implicit methods capture the mind in action rather than as an object of self-reflection. Two, mental events take time and therefore can be measured chronometrically. And three, assessments based on the mind in action should not, in principle, be seen as tapping the same constructs as those tapped by self-report. In the following sections, we review four types of cognitive processing tasks and their contributions to an implicit science of personality.

TRAITS, STATES, AND SELECTIVE ATTENTION

It is common to think that, because self-reported traits are the dominant approach to personality, they must capture people's tendencies related to attention, encoding, and retrieval. However, this assumption appears to be a mistake. Considering attention first, there is some consensus that normal variations in self-reported traits play a relatively small role in selective attention. In the emotional Stroop task, a person is asked to name the color of words. Of interest is whether the semantic nature of the ignored word interferes with attention to the primary color-naming task. For example, one might expect trait anxious participants to exhibit slower color-naming latencies for words like *criticism* because such words capture attention among anxious individuals. However, a substantial literature review (Williams, Mathews, & MacLeod, 1996) has concluded that subclinical variations in anxiety do not seem to be robust predictors of performance. That is, subclinically anxious participants do not, by and large, exhibit selective attention for threatening words. This conclusion is reinforced by work with the spatial probe paradigm. In this paradigm, several words are simultaneously presented, and attention toward a threatening word is inferred from fast latencies to respond to spatial probes presented in the area of the threatening word. Based on numerous studies, Mogg et al. (2000) concluded that the links between anxiety and selective attention for threat, although relatively robust in the clinical literature (Mogg & Bradley, 1998), are not particularly robust concerning trait anxiety.

Because most work on selective attention has involved threatening information, we (Tamir & Robinson, 2004) recently sought to investigate the correlates of attention to rewarding words (e.g., *love, success*). Based on theorizing linking extraversion to reward sensitivity, one might expect a correlation between extraversion and selective attention to reward (Robinson, Vargas, et al., 2003). However, in none of our studies did we find correlations between extraversion and attention to reward. Does this mean that attention to reward is affectively irrelevant? No. In the same studies, we showed that mood states, but not extraversion or neuroticism, predicted attention performance. In Study 2, for example, we showed that aggregated measures of high activation positive affect (based on an experience-sampling protocol) predicted selective attention. Specifically, those who had been experiencing lots of excitement and joy in their daily lives exhibited a significant tendency to selectively attend to rewarding words in a spatial probe paradigm. In

Studies 3 and 4, we showed that manipulated mood states predicted selective attention such that the induction of excited mood states biased attention toward rewarding words. Somewhat related to these findings, Mogg and colleagues (Mogg & Bradley, 1998) have suggested that state anxiety, but not trait anxiety, is more predictive of attention to threat.

If selective attention covaries with emotional states, but not traits, then attention to threat might be expected to disappear with successful therapy. Indeed, this is the case (MacLeod, 1999). Furthermore, the degree to which the therapy is successful predicts the degree to which the attention bias is reduced (MacLeod, 1999). Going further in this direction, MacLeod and Hagan (1992) suggested that attention performance might serve as a diathesis in predicting vulnerability to anxiety. In this study, they measured attention to threat using a subliminal version of the emotional Stroop test. At a later time, some of the women in the study were given a positive diagnosis for possible cervical cancer. The dependent measure in the study pertained to dysphoric reactions to the diagnosis. As predicted, there was a high correlation ($r > .5$) between the information processing measure of attention to threat on the one hand and dysphoric reactions to the diagnosis on the other. The finding has been conceptually replicated (MacLeod, 1999).

If attention to threat correlates with anxiety, improves with therapy, and acts as a diathesis in predicting stress in everyday life (MacLeod, 1999), then attention to threat may actually *cause* anxiety. Indeed, this appears to be the case. In an important study, MacLeod, Rutherford, Campbell, Ebsworthy, and Holker (2002) chose to examine the causal hypothesis by manipulating attention to threat in a modified spatial probe task. They randomly assigned some subjects to an avoidance condition in which attention was systematically drawn away from threat. By contrast, the other condition was sensitized toward threat. They trained attention by manipulating the spatial probes (requiring a manual response) such that they either replaced the nonthreatening word of the word pair (avoid condition) or the threatening word of the word pair (sensitize condition). Over the course of the 576 training trials, such a procedure was hypothesized to train or

alter patterns of selective attention either toward or away from threatening information. Reaction time performance confirmed this hypothesis. More important, the authors showed that those trained toward threatening information reacted with more anxiety and depression to a laboratory stressor task (unsolvable anagrams). That is, training altered reactivity to stressors. Related results have been reported by MacLeod (1999).

The results reported in this section offer a productive model for implicit personality research. Those who are clinically anxious display selective attention to threatening information in the environment (Mathews & MacLeod, 1994). This initial result set the stage for assessing attentional performance as an indicator of successful therapy (MacLeod, 1999) and a risk factor in developing future anxiety (MacLeod & Hagan, 1992). Finally, such results set the stage for treatments for anxiety based on altering patterns of selective attention (MacLeod, 1999). Implicit personality measures, these results suggest, are more malleable than self-reported personality traits. Thus, an implicit science of personality both (a) captures tendencies not revealed by self-reported traits and (b) offers mechanisms that can be changed, thereby altering behavior and experience.

IN SEARCH OF DEPRESSOGENIC THOUGHT PROCESSES

A variety of studies using a variety of cognitive methods have sought to discover the depressogenic thought processes responsible for depression (for reviews, see MacLeod & Mathews, 1994; Segal, 1988; Segal & Ingram, 1994). However, one problematic result emerges from this research. Specifically, it is extremely difficult to distinguish formerly depressed participants from never depressed participants on measures of cognitive bias (e.g., Segal & Ingram, 1994). That is, depressive biases in cognition seem to be more statelike than traitlike. The reader will note that such findings are parallel to those involving anxiety disorders and attentional threat bias, in that successful psychotherapy eliminates the attentional threat bias (MacLeod, 1999).

There has been a rather extensive search for a "latent" (as opposed to state-dependent) processing bias that might underlie depression (Segal, 1988; Segal & Ingram, 1994). What we can say from this research is that there may not be one. Rather, depressogenic thought is only revealed when the person is self-focused or in a sad mood at the time of testing (Segal & Ingram, 1994). From the perspective of an implicit science of personality, we believe that these results are important. They suggest that depression is nothing like a trait. Rather, it is a phenomenon that co-occurs with negative mood states and certain dispositional vulnerabilities. Thus, it may come as little surprise that self-reported traits play a relatively minimal role in understanding clinical depression (Segal & Ingram, 1994).

One further direction for progress in this area relates to Segal's (1988) observations about the role of the negative self-schema in depression. Such a schema would not be revealed by self-report or even by implicit processing biases per se (Segal, 1988). Rather, evidence for such a schema must come from priming methodologies in which one negative self-related piece of information primes another negative self-related piece of information.

Our lab has been pursuing relevant procedures for a couple of years now (e.g., Robinson & Clore, 2002b). Participants are asked to judge the extent to which they generally feel various positive and negative emotions. Because stimuli are presented in a random order, any particular trial might involve a negative (N) or positive (P) emotion and in turn be succeeded by a positive or negative emotion. Speed to make a judgment can then be examined as a function of the valence of the "target" emotion as well as the valence of the "prime" emotion (i.e., the valence of the emotion on the preceding trial). This produces four means of interest: PP, NP, PN, and NN. A negative self-schema is revealed by the following contrast: PN minus NN. Because the target emotions in this difference score are both negative, any differential speed must be due to priming. Thus far, we have found evidence for (a) robust valence-specific priming (PP and NN faster than PN and NP), (b) more pronounced priming for positive emotions (NP–PP) than for negative emotions (PN–NN), and (c) moderation by traits. As an example of the latter effect, those high in life satisfaction had much higher priming scores for positive emotions (~200 ms) than those low in life satisfaction did (~100 ms). This suggests that life satisfaction relates to the strength or interconnectivity of positive knowledge about the self (Robinson & Kirkeby, in press). It seems likely that similar priming procedures could be used to understand the role of the self-schema in depression (Segal, 1988).

TRAITS, STATES, AND ACCESSIBLE CONSTRUCTS

Modern work on chronic accessibility traces its lineage back to a paper by Jerome Bruner (1957). Bruner was one of the main protagonists behind the New Look, which emphasized motivational and dispositional influences on perception. In the 1957 paper, Bruner argued that perception is not a passive process, but rather that the person is prepared to see events that match accessible concepts. An accessible concept is one that is activated and ready for use given the right stimulus input conditions.

At least three factors influence the accessibility of a concept (Higgins, 1996). First, a concept is activated to the extent that it matches the current stimulus conditions. Being around furniture activates thoughts about furniture and being around fish activates thoughts about fish. Second, however, a concept can be primed or activated by recent exposure or use. So, for example, exposure to media violence activates or primes aggressive thoughts (Anderson & Bushman, 2002). This temporary activation persists for some time, resulting in an increased likelihood of subsequent aggression (Anderson & Bushman, 2002).

In addition to the situational factors mentioned, a third influence on accessibility relates to chronic accessibility (Higgins, 1996). A chronically accessible concept is one that is habitually activated in the person. For example, one approach to individual differences in aggression might be to propose that certain individuals typically have a higher level of activation for antisocial thoughts. As a result, they

are more likely, on average, to select aggressive actions in dealing with social conflicts (Zelli & Dodge, 1999). Chronically accessible concepts are of obvious relevance to personality psychology.

Although Bruner (1957) did not say much about chronically accessible concepts, Kelly (1963) did. Kelly's theory was based on "personal constructs," which are habitual dimensions used to interpret events. A construct is somewhat similar to a concept, except that it explicitly endorses a bipolar structure (Robinson, Solberg, Vargas, & Tamir, 2003). Kelly, like Bruner, believed that accessible concepts have a tremendous influence on interpretation, emotional experience, and behavior. In fact, Kelly (1963) offered accessible constructs as a comprehensive theory of personality; he did not say much if anything about self-reported traits.

How can one determine what a person's accessible constructs are? According to Bruner (1957), accessibility is marked by the speed or ease with which a person can place an object (e.g., a knife) in a relevant category (e.g., a weapon). Therefore, a straightforward operationalization of accessibility would involve a choice reaction time task in which people are told to, as quickly and accurately as possible, decide whether each word belongs to one category (e.g., a weapon) or another (e.g., not a weapon). Habitual use of the construct would make it likely that the person would find the task fairly easy (and be fast); by contrast, inaccessible constructs would produce marked difficulties with the task. Thus, speed to categorize objects can be taken as an indication of the accessibility of the construct of interest (Robinson, 2004).

In several investigations, we have adopted this straightforward approach to construct accessibility. In addition to asking participants to make the relevant categorizations, we also asked them to perform a neutral categorization task (such as judging whether a word represents an animal or not). By use of a regression equation and the computation of residual scores, we were then able to statistically remove "baseline" individual differences in categorization speed. What results is a set of scores that are correlated with the block of interest, but uncorrelated with the nontarget categorization block (see Robinson, Solberg, et al., 2003, for further details).

The investigations have been remarkably consistent in suggesting that accessible constructs are uncorrelated with self-reported traits. This is true even when the categorization task is designed, in some sense, to match or be relevant to the trait in question. For example, trait femininity does not correlate with speed to categorize words as feminine (Robinson, Vargas, et al., 2003), extraversion does not correlate with speed to categorize words as positive (Robinson, Solberg, et al., 2003), neuroticism does not correlate with speed to categorize words as threatening (Robinson, Vargas, et al., 2003), and agreeableness does not correlate with speed to categorize words as blameworthy (Meier & Robinson, 2004).

Our interest, however, related to emotional states rather than emotional traits. In these studies, participants have been asked to complete daily reports of life satisfaction (Robinson, Solberg, et al., 2003), palmtop computer reports concerning pleasant and unpleasant emotions (Robinson, Vargas, Tamir, & Solberg, 2004), and laboratory reports of anger following an anger induction (Meier & Robinson, 2004). At least four patterns of findings have emerged from these studies. First, we have found that accessible negative constructs predispose people to negative emotions and somatic symptoms in everyday life, even after extraversion and neuroticism are controlled (Robinson et al., 2004). Second, we have found that extraversion predicts subjective well-being, particularly for those slow to distinguish neutral and positive words in a categorization task (Robinson, Solberg, et al., 2003). Third, we have found that anger is a joint (interactive) product of accessible blame and low agreeableness (Meier & Robinson, 2004). And fourth, we have found evidence for the idea that people are happier when their categorization abilities are well matched to their traits (Robinson, in press; Robinson, Vargas, et al., 2003). As an example of the latter interaction, those high in trait femininity are happier when they are fast (versus slow) to categorize feminine words, whereas those low in trait femininity

are happier when they are slow (versus fast) to categorize feminine words.

In summarizing this recent program of research, three points seem especially evident. One, accessible concepts cannot be viewed in any way as synonymous with self-reported traits. In fact, in no study have we found a consistent relation between self-reported traits on the one hand and categorization performance on the other. Two, there are dispositional influences on our emotional states that are quite distinct from emotional traits. For example, being fast to categorize objects as negative predisposes people to negative affect, precisely because such negative categorization tendencies are also used in interpreting daily events and outcomes (Robinson et al., 2004). The first two points suggest that one might be able to develop a science of personality without reference to traits (Cervone & Shoda, 1999). However, our results, in many cases, suggest otherwise. Specifically, we have found many cases in which categorization tendencies interacted with self-reported traits, so much so that our understanding of the findings critically depended on knowing a person's traits. For example, in one investigation, accessible blame predicted anger and aggression only among those low in agreeableness (Meier & Robinson, 2004). Findings such as these highlight the importance of traits in moderating the influence of implicit processes (Robinson, 2004).

IMPLICIT ATTITUDES

Following an initial paper by Greenwald and Banaji (1995), there has been somewhat of an explosion of research on implicit measures of attitudes and the self-concept. The case Greenwald and Banaji made was that there are important implicit aspects of attitudes and the self-concept that are introspectively unidentifiable, but nevertheless influence behavior. Drawing to some extent on Fazio's (1989) idea that an attitude could be represented as an association between an object and an evaluation (Banaji, 2001), Greenwald and colleagues (Greenwald, McGhee, & Schwartz, 1998) devised the Implicit Association Test (IAT) to be a flexible method of examining associations in memory. In the initial investigation, the authors showed, among other things, that people

implicitly like flowers (versus insects), that Korean and Japanese Americans have an implicit in-group preference, and that Caucasian Americans are prejudiced against Black Americans, at least at the implicit level. Two other results from this investigation are noteworthy. One, the extent of one's preference (for flowers, own-race members, or Caucasians) was remarkably strong at the implicit level. And two, correlations between implicit and self-reported attitudes were weak, hovering around the $r = .2$ mark.

Following the initial investigation by Greenwald et al. (1998), there have been numerous studies using the IAT in the context of social cognition. The IAT continues to be impressive on several counts. One, the size of the normative effects is often large ($d > .7$). For example, Caucasian participants in Study 3 of the initial investigation (Greenwald et al., 1998) exhibited an implicit preference for White (over Black) Americans at the $d = 1.13$ level. Two, demographic variables often substantially affect IAT scores. For example, men score masculine, whereas women score feminine, on an IAT designed to measure femininity versus masculinity (Greenwald et al., 2002). And three, IAT-based measures of attitudes are quite stable, at least for implicit measures. Greenwald et al. (2002) reported several studies exhibiting test–retest correlations in the neighborhood of $r = .6$. Thus, whatever the IAT is measuring, it is somewhat stable.

Despite considerable enthusiasm for this research, we should at least voice some potential concerns. The IAT seems to tap universal attitudes most prominently. For example, most participants favor flowers and White people at the implicit level. However, evidence for the correlational validity of IAT-based measures is comparatively lacking. For example, Bosson, Swann, and Pennebaker (2000) conducted a study examining the reliability and validity of various measures of implicit self-esteem. They found that the IAT-based measure was relatively unique in having high test–retest stability. However, this test, like the other implicit measures, did not predict their criterion measures (e.g., observer ratings of self-esteem) very well. By contrast, a self-report measure of self-esteem did. Thus, we feel that further evidence related to criterion validity, using criteria other than trait self-report, would be useful for furthering the

successes of IAT-based measures (see Banaji, 2001, for further discussion).

STRENGTHS AND LIMITATIONS OF IMPLICIT MEASURES

Having presented considerable evidence for the validity of implicit measures of personality, we are now in a position to consider some of the unique strengths and limitations of implicit measures (see also McClelland, 1987).

Internal Consistency

When assessing the reliability of a self-report measure of personality, it is common practice to compute internal consistency coefficients. A test that is reliable should exhibit high correlations across items; a test that is unreliable should not. How do implicit measures fare concerning this criterion? By and large, we do not know. Word fragment completions are believed to have low internal consistency, at least as a measure of memory (Buchner & Wippich, 2000). Similarly, our impression of projective measures of accessible constructs (Higgins, 1996) and motives (McClelland, 1987) is that such measures rarely approach the internal consistency of self-report tests. Concerning latency-based measures, Buchner and Wippich (2000) offered the opinion that such measures should exhibit reasonably high internal consistency coefficients, specifically because responses are quite constrained in comparison to more projective tests of memory. However, computing the internal consistency of "speed" is somewhat irrelevant. Participants who are fast on one item will be fast on another. So trials in a reaction time test are quite different than items on a self-report test, in that it is crucial to remove speed from the former. When this is done, internal consistency coefficients can sometimes be low.

Test–Retest Stability

Although IAT-based measures of association display somewhat impressive test–retest correlations, the same cannot be said for other implicit measures. For example, Bosson et al. (2000) obtained low test–retest correlations for implicit self-esteem measures based on (a) preference for the letters of one's own name, (b) priming facilitation, and (c) an emotional Stroop task constructed to tap self-esteem. Our categorization tendency measures have 1-month test–retest correlations in the $r = .5$ range (Meier & Robinson, 2004; Robinson, Solberg, et al., 2003). TAT-based measures of motives have test–retest correlations in the $r = .2–.4$ range (McClelland, 1987). Finally, Kindt and Brosschot (1998) have reported that test–retest correlations for attention to threat are so low as to be nonsignificant.

In summarizing the data on test–retest stability, it is useful to make two points. One, the test–retest correlations for self-reported traits (which are quite impressive; McCrae & Costa, 1994) may be inflated by the fact that people form certain beliefs about themselves that are relatively permanent (Robinson & Clore, 2002a). Two, in contrast to self-reported traits, implicit processes are inherently unstable. One can train patterns of selective attention (MacLeod et al., 2002), alter the accessibility of constructs (Higgins, 1996), or implicit associations (Greenwald et al., 2002), by relatively trivial situational manipulations. In the opinion of the authors, these results do not necessarily detract from the validity of implicit measures of cognition. Cognitive associations in memory are plausibly altered by every single event affecting the individual (Anderson, 1982). Thus, it is not surprising that contextual factors alter implicit measures, just as it is not surprising that many implicit measures have low test–retest stability coefficients. Despite these thoughts, we believe there is an onus on investigators of implicit cognition to confront the issue of test–retest stability as directly as possible.

Convergent Validity

Alternate measures of a construct would ideally be correlated with each other (Campbell & Fiske, 1959). However, data based on implicit tests rarely meet this criterion (for a discussion, see Cunningham, Preacher, & Banaji, 2001). For example, different measures of attention to threat do not tend to correlate (Kindt & Brosschot, 1998; Mogg et al., 2000). Similarly, latency-based measures of implicit prejudice do not tend to correlate very highly, at

least without considering measurement error (Cunningham et al., 2001; De Houwer, 2003).

In this context, it is worth mentioning that implicit measures may be relatively heterogeneous. For example, De Houwer (2003) presents convincing arguments that the extent to which two implicit attitude measures will be correlated depends on the extent to which the measures are tapping similar processes. Based on prior work related to a taxonomy of reaction time processes, De Houwer suggested that measures based on Fazio's work (e.g., Fazio, 1995) tap stimulus compatibility mechanisms. By contrast, measures based on Greenwald's work (e.g., Greenwald et al., 1998) tap response compatibility mechanisms. Therefore, it comes as little surprise to De Houwer that priming- and IAT-based measures of implicit prejudice do not correlate very highly. De Houwer's analysis offers a necessary corrective to the assumption that scores based on implicit methods are tapping the same thing; additionally, however, De Houwer's work raises additional questions about what is being tapped by different implicit measures (see also Fazio & Olson, 2003).

Criterion Validity

Robinson, Solberg, et al. (2003) suggested that criterion-related correlations for implicit tests are often surprisingly high given reliability concerns; by contrast, those for explicit tests are often fairly disappointing given their internal consistency. This conclusion was based on prior knowledge concerning the validity of implicit and self-report tests (Bornstein, 1999), as well as findings from the investigation at hand (Robinson, Solberg, et al., 2003). Bornstein (1999), for example, has concluded that projective measures of dependency motivation predict behavioral outcomes somewhat (although nonsignificantly) better than self-report measures of dependency do. Similarly, Spangler (1992) has concluded that projective measures of achievement motivation predict behavioral outcomes somewhat (although nonsignificantly) better that self-report measures of achievement motivation do. Nevertheless, considering that there are legitimate concerns about the reliability and convergent validity of implicit tests, we must regard the evidence for the criterion validity of implicit tests as quite impressive. Implicit tests, these results suggest, are very real predictors of construct-relevant outcomes (Robinson, 2004).

Assessment

Many applied investigators are interested in personality tests (and other measurement devices) because of their worth in assessing individuals. For example, personnel psychologists might be interested in implicit measures because they improve the validity of predictions about job performance. In a related vein, clinicians might be interested in implicit measures because they increase the accuracy of diagnoses. Can we offer advice to such researchers and clinicians concerning the validity of implicit tests? By and large, we are reluctant to do so. At the present, concerns about the reliability and validity of implicit tests are sufficient to discourage people from relying upon them within assessment contexts. Perhaps this situation will be changed in the future. In this connection, it is worth mentioning that reaction time-based measures of personality are just now receiving systematic treatment (Robinson, Vargas, et al., 2003). More basic research will be necessary before we are willing to advise practitioners to incorporate implicit tests into their assessment batteries (see also Banaji, 2001).

TOWARD A PROCESS-ORIENTED VIEW OF PERSONALITY

For quite a long time, psychologists have realized that self-reports of personality represent only one approach; lurking beneath the surface of self-report are implicit tendencies related to selective attention, accessibility, categorization, and information retrieval. To the extent that one can measure these patterns, one unlocks important clues to what makes us different in our daily transactions with the environment.

Self-reported traits, we believe, are not exhaustive of personality. Although people are able to encode and represent certain facts about themselves, there are also major blind spots. One source of blind spots relates to inaccessibility. People do not, by and large, know how they process informa-

tion. For example, imagine asking people the following questions: "Just how activated was that thought?"; "To what extent did that thought trigger another related thought?"; "Do you engage in an attention allocation pattern that favors threatening information when multiple objects are present?"; or "To what extent did that thought activate your left hemisphere?" As we hope these questions suggest, there are many workings of the mind that are inaccessible to introspective awareness (MacLeod, 1993). Such inaccessibility is not necessarily motivated (Kihlstrom, 1987). Indeed, the fundamental fact of information processing may be that it is invisible to introspective analysis (Dixon, 1981).

A second major source of blind spots is that self-reported traits *are* significantly influenced by social desirability motives (Paulhus & John, 1998). People have overwhelmingly favorable views of themselves, views that are at odds with the actual circumstances of their lives. A way to reconcile this discrepancy (i.e., perception versus reality) is to propose that some, if not most, people engage in a motivated pattern of distortion such that they see themselves more positively that the circumstances warrant (Paulhus & John, 1998; Shedler et al., 1993). Such a view of self-report certainly leaves room for implicit measures of personality. Implicit measures cannot be "faked" in any obvious way, rendering them an appropriate check on conscious patterns of self-endorsement.

Finally, we would be remiss if we didn't highlight one final point. We have made the case that self-reported traits and implicit processes often do not correlate, precisely because they tap different aspects of the person. An important implication of this dissociation is that a study examining only self-reported traits and patterns of information process-

ing is likely to be a failure (i.e., there may be no correlation). Does this mean that information processing mechanisms are irrelevant to daily experience and behavior? No, not at all. To determine the role that information processing plays in behavior and experience, we are generally calling for a *third variable* approach. In particular, experience-sampling protocols can be used to determine the regularities, in emotion and behavior, of people's lives. In many cases, we have found that implicit measures predict daily experiences just as strongly as self-reported traits do, despite being uncorrelated with traits (e.g., Robinson et al., 2004). In other cases, we have found that self-reported traits and implicit measures interact in predicting daily experience and behavior (e.g., Robinson, Solberg, et al., 2003). The point is that one must measure daily experience and behavior to understand how implicit tendencies contribute to personality functioning.

SUMMARY

In this chapter, we have presented evidence related to the validity of implicit measures of personality. Existing results lead us to believe that implicit measures can reveal new facts about the individual not available on the basis of self-reported traits. Of considerable importance, implicit processes are modifiable. This renders it likely that implicit measures of personality will set the stage for successful cognitive interventions to reduce psychological distress. Self-reported traits, although capturing important continuities in the individual, are relatively insensitive to the moment-to-moment variations in information processing that determine concurrent behavior and experience. A focus on implicit measures can fill this gap.

CHAPTER 10

SEQUENTIAL OBSERVATIONAL METHODS

Roger Bakeman and Augusto Gnisci

Observational methods are about measurement. Like most of the assessment methods described in other chapters in this section, they provide ways to extract scores from behavior. Thus observational methods, in common with assessment methods generally, are defined by procedures that when applied to events produce scores. Such scores are usually refined and reduced and then, often in combination with scores from other sources (thus becoming multimethod), are subjected to the sorts of statistical analyses described in the next section of this volume.

This volume urges readers to take a multimethod perspective. This chapter is much narrower. Here, a particular approach to measurement is presented, systematic observation of behavior, with a particular emphasis on capturing sequential aspects of the observed behavior. This is hardly the only approach to measurement, nor do the methods we emphasize here even exhaust the domain of observational methods understood broadly. Our intent in writing this chapter was to describe a particular approach, revealing its promises and pitfalls with sufficient specificity so that investigators could judge when it might prove useful. Thus we hope to contribute to a multimethod perspective, not so much directly, but indirectly. We think that sequential observational methods often capture aspects of behavior that other approaches do not and thus have much to contribute when used in combination with other approaches as investigators develop their own unique multimethod strategies.

If observational refers to methods for measuring behavior, what distinguishes them from other measurement approaches such as self-assessment questionnaires, peer ratings, standardized tests, physiological recording, and the like? For what kinds of circumstances and what sorts of research questions are they recommended? What kinds of researchers have found them useful? In an attempt to address these questions, we consider five topics in turn. First, we discuss defining characteristics of observational methods generally along with their advantages and disadvantages; second, ways of recording observational data; third, methods of representing observational data for computer analysis; fourth, the reliability of observational data; and finally, data reduction and analytic approaches that let us answer the questions that motivated our research in the first place. Throughout, concrete examples are used to illustrate specific points.

CHARACTERISTICS OF SEQUENTIAL OBSERVATIONAL METHODS

As we define matters here, coding schemes are a central defining characteristic of sequential observational methods. Sometimes it useful to use the phrase *systematic observation* to distinguish the sorts of methods we are talking about from simply looking at behavior or producing narrative, journalistic reports. Then a brief definition of systematic observation might be the application of predefined coding schemes to sequences of live or recorded

behavior (or transcripts of behavior) based on rules and with attention to observer reliability.

It is also important to define what observation is not. In the definition of observational methods just given, no mention was made of the context in which observation occurs. It could be either a field or a laboratory setting and, in either setting, experimental manipulation might or might not be used (although usually experimental manipulations are far more frequent in laboratory settings). Thus systematic observation, which is often thought of as a naturalistic technique, is inherently neither correlational nor causal; it depends on context. Second, no element of psychological theory is present in the definition, and in fact, observation can serve many different theories providing specific contents to categories. However, if the definition of observation is context- and content-free, it is not free of epistemological assumptions: As you might deduce from the definition itself, it is based on Stevens' (1951) theory of measurement and on the belief that human behavior can be quantified and formalized in models.

Coding schemes can be thought of as measuring instruments, something like rulers or thermometers. However, unlike rulers and thermometers, which measure length and temperature on interval scales, coding schemes usually make categorical or nominal (or at most ordinal) distinctions. They consist of sets of predefined behavioral categories representing the distinctions that an investigator finds conceptually meaningful, often explicitly theory based, to check important psychological hypotheses or to answer important research questions. One classic example is Parten's (1932) coding scheme for preschool children's play. She defined six categories—unoccupied, onlooker, solitary, parallel, associative, and cooperative—and then asked coders to observe children for 1 minute each on many different days and to assign the most appropriate code to each minute.

Examples of other coding schemes can be found in Bakeman and Gottman (1997), but most share this in common: Like Parten's scheme, they consist of a single set of mutually exclusive and exhaustive codes (there is a code for each event, but in each instance only one applies), or of several such sets, each set coding a different dimension of interest.

For example, when interacting with her mother, an infant's gaze (to mother, to object, to other), vocalization (neutral/pleasure, fuss/cry, none), and body movement (active, still) might be coded, using three sets of mutually exclusive and exhaustive (ME&E) codes. In the simplest case, a set could consist of just two codes, presence or absence of a particular behavior; thus if observers were asked to note occurrences of five different behaviors, any of which could co-occur, this could be regarded as five sets with each set containing two codes, yes or no. As a general rule, it is useful to structure codes into ME&E sets; it eases exposition, aids recording, and facilitates subsequent analysis.

The objection is sometimes raised that coding schemes are too restrictive and that predefined codes may allow potentially interesting behavior to escape unremarked. Sometimes a more open stance is recommended, similar to that of a participant observer or a qualitative researcher. We assume that such qualitative, unfettered observation occurs while coding schemes are being developed and will influence the final coding schemes. However, once defined, coding schemes have the merits of replicability and greater objectivity that they share with other quantitative methods. Even so, coders should remain open to the unexpected and make qualitative notes as circumstances suggest. Further refinement of even well-developed coding schemes is a possibility to which investigators should always remain open. We could go even further and claim that a qualitative stance is important in other phases of observational research, not just when developing coding schemes, because such a stance often provides deeper insight into phenomena, which is useful when generating and defining hypotheses and when interpreting results in natural contexts.

Coding schemes are presented to behavioral observers, not participants. Participants may be aware that an observer is present or that a video image is being recorded, but they don't interact with the measuring device itself in the way they do, for example, with a questionnaire that they fill out, nor is their behavior constrained as with a structured interview. They are free to simply behave, sometimes restricted only by the instructions the researcher provides them, the structure of the

experimental session, or the features of the environment (i.e., novelty, artificiality). True, their behavior may be altered by the presence of an observer, although most investigators report that participants rapidly habituate, whether observers are recording live or using video. As a result, the behavior captured by observational methods often seems more natural and less constrained than it is with other methods. Although not absolute, in general we think that the ability to capture relatively naturally occurring behavior is perhaps one of the major advantages of observational methods.

A second advantage is the ability to capture nonverbal behavior. Again, the coding scheme resides with the observer; there is no presumption that participants need to be verbal (or able to read), as is the case with many other methods. Thus it is not surprising that, historically, observational methods have been developed primarily by investigators studying animals (e.g., S. Altmann, 1965) and nonverbal humans, that is, infants (e.g., Tronick, Als, Adamson, Wise, & Brazelton, 1978). Of course, verbal behavior can be captured explicitly by observational methods, for example, when coding transcripts of couples' conversation (e.g., Gottman, 1979).

A third, and perhaps major, advantage is the way observational methods can be used to study process. Although Parten coded 1-minute samples from different days, this is the exception. More typically observational methods are used to capture a more or less continuous record of behavior as it unfolds sequentially in time. Thus the book that Bakeman wrote with Gottman (1997), titled *Observing Interaction*, has as its subtitle, *An Introduction to Sequential Analysis*, understanding that sequential analysis can be a general approach that takes into account both sequences and co-occurrences of events ordered in time. For example, Bakeman and Brownlee (1980), using codes similar to Parten's (their codes were unoccupied, solitary, together, parallel, and group play), recorded sequences of children's *play states*, which allowed them to discover that parallel play acted as a bridge to group play (because solitary often preceded parallel play, and parallel often preceded group play, but solitary rarely preceded group play).

Not all investigators who use observational methods to capture records of behavior in time are interested in sequential (or concurrent) associations among behaviors. Some may be interested primarily in time-budget information, that is, in what proportion of time an animal foraged or slept, or what proportion of time, on average, 3-year-old children spent in parallel play. Still, investigators interested in one, the other, or both of these uses of observational data will experience what may be the primary disadvantage of these methods, which is the voluminous amounts of data that can be generated. Thus issues of data management, and especially data reduction, although not unique to observational methods, often demand considerable attention when observational methods are used.

We began this section with the statement that coding schemes are a defining characteristic of sequential observational methods. Although this chapter follows this definition, the definition itself is arguably somewhat narrow. Other, very useful possibilities exist and are worth mentioning. One is the use of rating scales. Although the terms *coding* and *rating* are sometimes used interchangeably, it seems clearer to maintain that *coding* relies on categorical scales and *rating* on at least ordinal scales. Ratings could be applied sequentially. For example, raters might be asked to rate successive 10-second intervals for emotional intensity (e.g., 1 = very negative, 2 = somewhat negative, 3 = neutral, 4 = somewhat positive, 5 = very positive). More typically, raters might be asked, for example, to rate an entire 5-minute mother–infant interaction session for maternal warmth, maternal responsiveness, infant responsiveness, and so forth. The two strategies can also be combined. For example, coders could code mother and infant behaviors throughout the session and then rate various characteristics at the end.

In a number of ways, problems, techniques, statistics, and other matters are different for coding compared to rating. Coding is usually more labor intensive and time consuming, but it provides a level of concrete detail and exploration of process (e.g., moment-by-moment changes and effects) that rating typically does not. Moreover, reliability approaches can be quite different (see Hox & Mass, chap. 19, this volume, for the intraclass correlation,

which is used with ratings). In this chapter we have chosen to focus on coding and its particular problems and techniques because we believe that the more, different approaches investigators know about, the more likely multimethod approaches become. There are many reasons to choose between, for example, detailed moment-by-moment coding and summary ratings, but lack of knowledge about a particular approach should not be one of them.

RECORDING OBSERVATIONAL DATA

Once the hard work of developing coding schemes is past, trained observers are expected to categorize (i.e., code) quickly and efficiently various aspects of the behavior passing before their eyes, audible by their ears, or both. The behavior may be live, an audio or video recording (in either analog or digital form), or a previously prepared transcript, but one basic question concerns the *coding unit*: To what entity is a code assigned? Is it a neatly bounded time interval such as the single minute used by Parten? Or is it successive *n*-second intervals as is often encountered, especially in older literature? Or is it an event of some sort? For example, observers might be asked to identify episodes of struggles over objects between preschoolers and then code various dimensions of those struggles (Bakeman & Brownlee, 1982). Or—and this is the approach we generally favor— are observers asked to record onset and offset times of events, or to segment the stream of behavior into sequences of ME&E states, coding the type of the event and its onset times.

When onset and offset times of events are not recorded, the coding unit is usually straightforward. It could be a turn-of-talk in a transcript, a specified time interval, or a specified event. The practice of coding successive time intervals, which is often called zero-one or partial-interval or simply time sampling (Altmann, 1974), requires further comment. Given today's technology, interval recording has less to recommend it than formerly. As usually practiced, rows on a paper recording form represented successive intervals (often quite short, e.g., 15 seconds), columns represented particular behaviors, and observers noted with a tick mark when a behavior occurred within, or predominately characterized, each interval. The intent of the method was to provide approximate estimates of both frequency and duration of behaviors in an era before readily available recording devices automatically preserved time; it was a compromise between accuracy and ease that reflected the technology of the time.

Given today's technology, almost always the time over which events occur can be preserved quite easily, and so no compromise is required. When coding live, for example, whenever a key representing a code is pressed on a laptop computer or similar device, not just the code but also the time can be automatically recorded. Or video recordings may display time as part of the picture, allowing observers to note the onset times of codable events. Or computers may display video recordings that contain electronic time codes as part of the recording, which automates entry of time codes into data files. With video recording and appropriate technology, the coder's task is reduced to viewing the image (and re-viewing, which is an advantage of working with a video recording), and pressing keys corresponding to onsets of codable events. When codes are organized into sets of ME&E codes, as recommended earlier, only onset times need be recorded because each onset implies the offset of an earlier code from the same set.

When this approach is used—when onset and explicit or implied offset times are recorded—what is the coding unit? It does not make sense to say it is the event, which would imply a single decision, made once. The task is more complex. The coder is continuously alert, coding moment by moment, trying to decide if in this moment a particular code still applies. However, a *moment* is too imprecise to serve as a coding unit. As a practical matter, we need to quantify moment, and although arbitrary, probably the best choice is to let precision define the unit. Thus if we record times to the nearest second, as is common and reflects human reaction time, it is useful to think of the second as our coding unit, the entity to which a code is assigned. This is a fiction, of course, but a very useful one with implications for representing data and determining their reliability, as we discuss subsequently.

Two comments seem in order, one dealing with smaller, one with larger time units: First, half-second or tenth of a second intervals could be used, but without specialized equipment, hundredths of a second intervals make little sense. Even though time in seconds may be displayed with two digits after the decimal point, only 30 or 25 frames per second of video are recorded (in the American NTSC or National Television Systems Committee, or the European PAL or Phase Alteration Line system, respectively), so the precision is illusory. Second, thinking of codes being assigned to successive 1-second intervals is no different logically than assigning codes to other intervals (e.g., 10- or 15-second ones), with one key difference: 1-second intervals reflect plausible precision in a way that larger intervals do not.

REPRESENTING OBSERVATIONAL DATA

With many measurement approaches, the question, How should one represent one's data? does not arise. The standard rectangular data matrix suffices. Rows represent sampling units (participants, dyads, etc.), columns represent variables, and columns are filled in with the relatively few scores generated by the measurement approach. That is all the standard statistical packages need or expect, and even a preliminary step like scoring the items of a self-esteem scale, for example, is relatively straightforward. Such data matrices (e.g., the Data Editor window in SPSS) are useful for observational studies as well, but usually the columns are filled with scores that result from data reduction, not initial data collection.

More so than with many other measurement approaches (physiological recording is one important exception), observational methods produce diverse and voluminous data, so how data are represented (literally, re-presented) for the inevitable subsequent computer processing becomes an important consideration. We are convinced that if data are structured well initially, they may not analyze themselves exactly, but their analysis may well be facilitated. To this end, Bakeman and Quera have defined standard conventions for formatting sequential data (SDIS or Sequential Data Interchange Standard; Bakeman & Quera, 1995). Such

data files can then be analyzed with GSEQ, a program for sequential observational data that has considerable capability and flexibility (Generalized Sequential Querier; for current information see http://www.gsu.edu/~psyrab/sg.htm or http://www.ub.es/comporta/sg.htm). In particular, GSEQ effects the kinds of data reduction we have mentioned earlier and demonstrate subsequently.

Taking into account different possible coding units and different approaches, Bakeman and Quera (1995) defined five data types. The first three are used when onset and offset times are not recorded, whereas the last two assume such recording of time:

1. *Event sequences* consist of a single stream of coded events without time information; a code from a single ME&E set is assigned to each event.
2. *Multievent sequences* consist of a single stream of cross-classified events (i.e., codes from different ME&E sets are assigned to each event).
3. *Interval sequences* consist of a stream of timed intervals, each of which may contain one or more codes.
4. *State sequences* consist of single stream of coded states (onset time of each is recorded) or several such streams, each representing a ME&E set.
5. *Timed-event sequences* consist of a record of onsets and offsets of events that may, or may not, be organized into ME&E sets.

Conventions for expressing data as one or the other of these five types are designed to be easy to use and easy to read. To illustrate, segments from an event sequential, a state sequential, and a timed event sequential data file are given in Figure 10.1. Our intent is that these five types reflect what investigators do and how they think about their data, but there are other possibilities. For example, coding with the assistance of various computerized systems typically produces files of codes along with their associated onset times. In such cases, we have found it easy to write programs that reformat such data into SDIS format (e.g., Bakeman & Quera, 2000).

In a number of ways, the five SDIS data types are quite similar. In fact, once observational data have been represented according to SDIS conventions, producing what we call SDS files, these SDS data

```
Event (un lo tog par grp);
   <Jenny> ,10:30 un lo un tog lo tog par tog par grp
      lo 10:33/


State (un lo tog par grp);
<Alex> un,0:00 lo,0:32 un,0:48 tog,1:02 lo,1:08 tog,1:22
   par,1:41 tog,1:53 par,2:05 grp,2:31 lo,2:41 ,3:00/


Timed (MRV MOV)(IRV IOV);
   <Dyad AK> ,0  MRV,8-12  MRV,32-38  MOV,53-57 … &
      IOV 18-21  IRV,33-35  IOV,43-46 … ,60 /
```

FIGURE 10.1. Examples of event, state, and timed-event sequential data formatted per SDIS conventions. The data type and, in these examples, a set or sets of ME&E codes in parentheses are declared before the semicolon. Codes for the event and state sequence are un = unoccupied, lo = onlooking, tog = together, par = parallel, and grp = group. Codes for the timed sequence are MRV = mother rhythmic vocalization, MOV = mother other vocalization, IRV = infant rhythmic vocalization, IOV = infant other vocalization. For the event sequence, the observation began at 10:30 and ended at 10:33; such information is needed only if rates are computed. For the state sequence, the observation began at 0:00 and ended at 3:00; in this case units were seconds, and the onset time for each code was given. For the timed event sequence, units were integer seconds; it began at second 0 and ended at second 60. The end of the observation is indicated with a forward slash. For the timed sequence, an ampersand separates mother and infant streams.

files are then compiled by the GSEQ program, which produces an MDS or modified SDS file. Whereas SDS files are easy to read, MDS files are formatted to facilitate analysis. Moreover, no matter the initial data type, the format for MDS files is common. Logically, one can think of an MDS file as a matrix. Each row represents a different code, and each column represents a coding unit (event, interval, or time unit). Then cells are checked for presence or absence of that code within that unit. If we think of this matrix as a scroll, clearly quite lengthy scrolls can result. Especially when a unit of time such as a second serves as the coding unit, we can imagine a scroll unfurling into the far future, and we can imagine this matrix of binary numbers as being quite sparse (in practice, however, actual computer files are compressed).

This common underlying format for sequential observational data is both extremely simple and powerfully general. A wealth of new codes can be created from those initially collected, which is perhaps the greatest advantage of representing sequential data this way. For example, especially useful for interval, state, and timed sequences, where co-occurrences are often of concern, are the standard logical commands of And, Or, and Not (see Figure 10.2). A single superordinate code can be formed from several subordinate codes using the Or command; for example, a single positive behavior code could be defined, which would be coded as occurring anytime any of a number of different positive codes had been coded. Also, a single code that occurs only when other codes co-occur can be formed using the And command; for example, a new code might characterize those times when an infant was gazing at the mother while the mother was concurrently vocalizing (or gazing) to her infant. Then co-occurrences of this new joint code with other codes could be examined.

The Window command is an additional, powerful data modification available in the GSEQ program (again, see Figure 10.2). With it, new codes can be formed that are tied to onset or offsets of existing codes. For example, if mother and infant rhythmic vocalization were coded (MRV and IRV), new codes could be defined for just the second that the infant (or mother) begins rhythmic vocalization (i.e., the onset second), and another new code could be defined for the onset second of IRV and the fours seconds thereafter, thus defining a 5-second window.

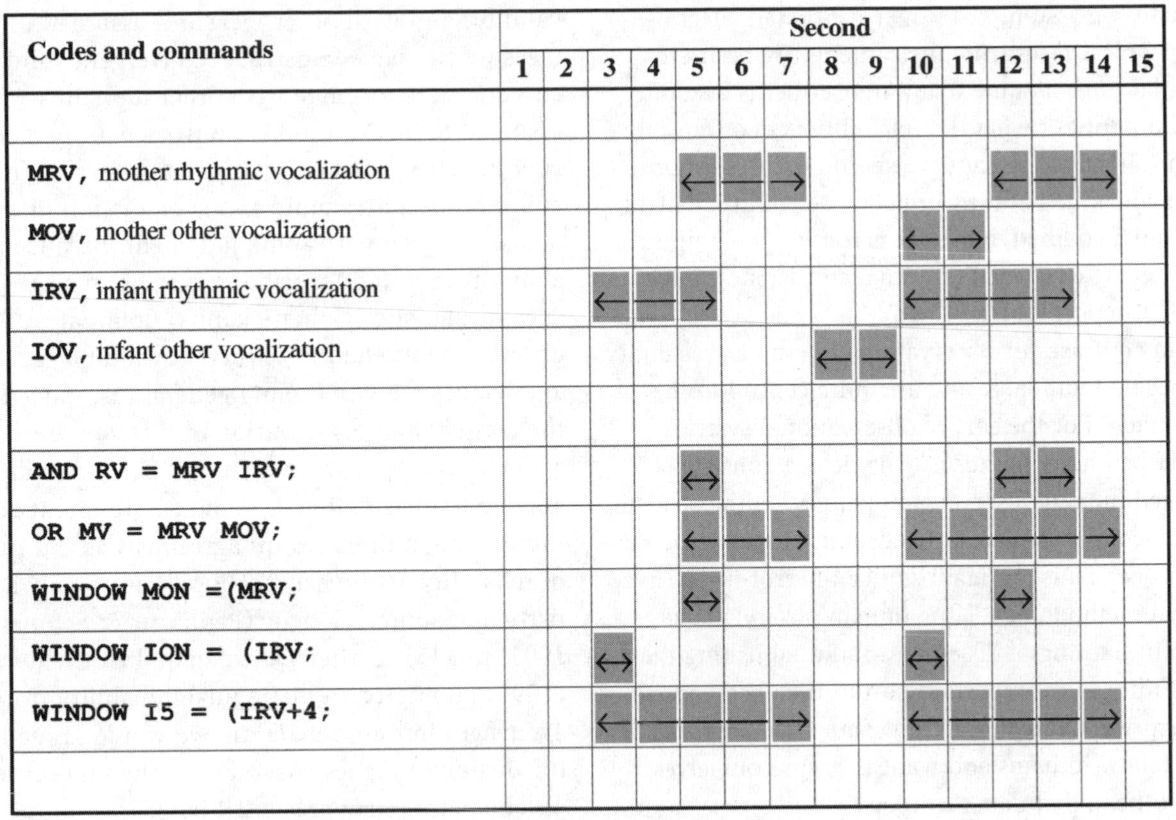

Codes and commands	Second														
	1	2	3	4	5	6	7	8	9	10	11	12	13	14	15
MRV, mother rhythmic vocalization					←	—	→					←	—	→	
MOV, mother other vocalization										←	→				
IRV, infant rhythmic vocalization			←	—	→					←	—	—	→		
IOV, infant other vocalization								←	→						
AND RV = MRV IRV;					↔							←	→		
OR MV = MRV MOV;					←	—	→			←	—	—	—	→	
WINDOW MON =(MRV;					↔							↔			
WINDOW ION = (IRV;			↔							↔					
WINDOW I5 = (IRV+4;			←	—	—	—	→			←	—	—	—	→	

FIGURE 10.2. Examples of And, Or, and Window commands; used primarily to modify multiple-stream state and timed sequential data. Double-headed arrows represent time units (here a second) during which the initial code or new code occurs. A left parenthesis before a code represents the onset second.

This would allow investigators to ask, for example, whether mothers were likely to begin a rhythmic vocalization within 5 seconds of their infants beginning one than at other times, thereby demonstrating reciprocity or matching.

Other modifications are possible. For example, Becker, Buder, Bakeman, Price, and Ward (2003) coded vocalizations of bush baby mothers with their infants (*Otolemur garnettii*, a small primate). A new code—a short growl bout—was defined that characterized stretches of time when mothers' brief growls occurred with 7 seconds or less between individual maternal growls. This permitted Becker et al. to ask whether infants responded specifically to growl bouts or equally to isolated growls (it was primarily to bouts). We hope that this example, along with the examples in the previous paragraphs, has demonstrated that data modification is both flexible and useful (see also Bakeman, Deckner, & Querea, 2004). Appropriate creation of new codes from existing data can give users more direct and compelling answers to the research questions that led them to collect their data in the first place. Such modification usually matters much more for observational than for other kinds of data, but first data must be represented in a way that facilitates modification, which is why we have emphasized matters of data representation here.

RELIABILITY OF OBSERVATIONAL DATA

The standard psychometric concerns of reliability and validity are in no way unique to observational methods. The precision and accuracy of any measuring device needs to be established before weight can be given to the data collected with it. Such considerations apply no matter whether observational methods or other measuring approaches are used. Nonetheless, for some measuring approaches, reliability issues do not loom large. For example,

usually we assume that, once calibrated, electro-mechanical measuring instruments are accurate. Similarly, we assume that a transcriber is accurate and do not ask what the reliability is of a transcription (although perhaps we should). Furthermore, for some kinds of measurement, reliability matters are quite codified, and so it is routine to compute and report Cronbach's internal consistency alpha for self-report scales.

In contrast, for observational methods, reliability issues do loom large and are quite central to the approach. For the sort of observational systems described here, the measuring device consists of trained human observers applying a coding scheme or schemes to streams of behavior, often video recorded. Thus the main source of error in observational methodology is the human observer. The careful training of observers, and establishing their reliability, is an important part of the observational enterprise. Quite correctly, we are a bit skeptical of our fellow humans and want to assure ourselves, and others, that data recorded by one observer are not idiosyncratic, unique to that observer's way of viewing the world.

Thus the first concern is for reliability. Validity is more complex, and evidence for it accumulates slowly, as we will discuss subsequently. As is standard (e.g., Nunnally & Bernstein, 1994; Pedhazur & Schmelkin, 1991), by reliability we understand agreement and replicability. Whatever is being measured is being measured consistently. When two observers agree with each other, or agree with themselves over time, we have evidence for reliability. It is possible, of course, that two observers might share a deviant worldview, in which case they would be reliable but not valid. Validity implies accuracy, that we are indeed measuring what we intend. As is widely appreciated, measures may be reliable without being valid, but they cannot be valid without being reliable.

Reliability can be established using fairly narrow statistical means (e.g., Cronbach's alpha for internal consistency of self-report scales), whereas validity involves demonstrating that a measure correlates in sensible ways with different measures allegedly associated with it in the present (concurrent validity) or in the future (predictive validity) and with other measures assumed to measure the same construct (convergent validity), and does not correlate with other measures assumed to measure other constructs (divergent validity). It is not necessarily demonstrated in one study, but requires more an accumulation of evidence, coupled with some judgment. Because reliability is required for validity, and because a specific statistic (Cohen's kappa) dominates observational reliability, whereas validity approaches are much more general (as, indeed, the content and organization of this volume attests), in this chapter we emphasize reliability as applied to observational methods. We might add that not all authors regard agreement as "an index of reliability at all" because it addresses only a particular source of error (Pedhazur & Schmelkin, 1991, p. 145). Earlier Bakeman and Gottman (1997) attempted to distinguish reliability from agreement but, on reflection, we would argue that the distinction is less useful than the more firmly psychometric view presented here.

As previously noted, usually observers are asked to make categorical distinctions, thus the most common statistic used to establish interobserver reliability in the context of observational studies is Cohen's kappa, a coefficient of agreement for categorical scales (Cohen, 1960; also see Nussbeck, chap. 17, this volume). Cohen's kappa corrects for chance agreement and thus is much preferred to the percentage agreement statistics sometimes encountered, especially in older literature. Moreover, the agreement matrix (also called a confusion matrix), required for its computation, is helpful when training observers due to the graphic way it portrays specific sources of disagreement. In the following paragraphs, we demonstrate the use of kappa using an example based on research in the development of joint attention in infants and toddlers by Adamson and colleagues. This example is useful because it allows us to integrate material introduced earlier in this chapter concerning coding schemes and the representation of observational data with reliability in a way that demonstrates what has been a theme throughout, the usefulness of conceptualizing observational data as a sequence of coded time units.

First, the coding schemes: Adamson, Bakeman, and Deckner (2004) have examined how language (or symbolic means generally) becomes infused into and transforms joint attention with toddlers. To this end, and based on earlier work (Bakeman & Adamson, 1984), they defined seven engagement states for toddlers playing with their mothers. Four, listed first, are of primary theoretic interest, whereas three more complete the ME&E set:

1. *Supported Joint Engagement* (**sj**), infant and mother actively involved with same object, but the infant does not overtly acknowledge the mother's participation; symbols (primarily language) not involved.
2. *Coordinated Joint Engagement* (**cj**), infant and mother actively involved with same object or event, and the infant acknowledges the mother's participation; symbols not involved.
3. *Symbol-Infused Supported Joint Engagement* (**Ss**), toddler and mother involved with same object, the toddler is attending to symbols, but the toddler does not overtly acknowledge mother's participation.
4. *Symbol-Infused Coordinated Joint Engagement* (**Cs**), toddler and mother involved with same object, the toddler is attending to symbols, and the toddler actively acknowledges mother's participation.
5. *Unengaged, Onlooking,* or *Person* (**ulp**). Initially these three were coded separately but the distinctions were not of primary interest, so we combined them into a single code (using GSEQ's OR command).
6. *Object,* infant engaged with objects alone (**ob**).
7. *Symbol-Only, Object-Symbol, Person-Symbol* (**Yop**). These three were defined to complete logical possibilities but, as expected, were very infrequent, and not of primary interest, so we combined them into a single code.

Once codes are defined, a focus on issues of reliability serves several purposes, ranging from training of coders to final publication of research reports. Three important questions investigators face are as follows: First, given that we are asking coders to identify times when behaviors (in this case, engagement states) occur, how do we provide them feedback concerning their reliability? Second,

how do we assure ourselves that they are reliable? And third, how do we convince colleagues, including editors and reviewers, that they are reliable? When the timing of events is recorded, these questions become tractable once we identify a time unit as the coding unit and represent the data as a sequence of coded time units, as discussed earlier. Assume a time unit of a second, as is common. Then the seconds of the observation become the thing tallied. Rows and columns of a matrix are labeled with the codes in a ME&E set. Rows represent one observer and columns a second observer. Then, each second of the observation is cross classified. Tallies in the cells on the upper-left to lower-right diagonal represent agreement, whereas tallies in off-diagonal cells represent disagreement.

Such an agreement matrix provides coders a graphic display of the coders' agreement and disagreement. It pinpoints codes on which they disagree; for example, for the agreement matrix in Figure 10.3 the most common disagreement was between object and supported joint engagement (31 seconds). Moreover when codes are ordered from simpler to more complex (as they are in Figure 10.3), tallies disproportionately above the diagonal, for example, would suggest that the second observer consistently had lower thresholds (was more sensitive) than the first. Thus patterns of disagreement suggest areas for further training, whereas patterns of agreement assure investigators that coders are faithfully executing the coding.

Moreover, the extent of agreement can be quantified using Cohen's kappa (1960; Robinson & Bakeman, 1998), which is used in published reports to assure others of the reliability with which the coding scheme was applied. Kappa is an index that summarizes agreement between two coders when assigning things (here seconds) to the codes of an ME&E set. Thus kappa is an index of the reliability with which two coders use a categorical scale (i.e., a set of ME&E codes), derived from the agreement matrix. Let x_{ij} indicate a cell of the matrix and a plus sign indicate summation, then x_{i+} indicates the total for the ith row and x_{++} indicates the total number of tallies in the matrix, where k is the number of codes in the set. Then

```
kappa =  .84, %agree =  87%, window = +|- 2
Rows: 1255A, columns: 1255B
        ulp   ob  Ypo   sj   cj   Ss   Cs  Totals
------------------------------------------------------
ulp     10    0    0    0   10    0    0     20
 ob      3  251    4    4   16    0    4    282
Ypo      0    1   93    0    0    0    1     95
 sj      0   31    0  109    5    4    0    149
 cj      0    3    0    0  165    2   10    180
 Ss      0   22    5   27    0  291    2    347
 Cs      8    2    0    0    0    0  172    182
------------------------------------------------------
Totals  21  310  102  140  196  297  189   1255
         u    o    Y    s    c    S    C
```

FIGURE 10.3. An agreement matrix, as displayed by GSEQ, for which kappa is .84; an agreement was tallied if coders agreed within ± 2 seconds. A total of 1255 seconds were coded. Code ulp combines unoccupied, onlooking, and person; ob = object; Yop combines symbol-only, object-symbol, and person-symbol; sj = supported joint and cj = coordinated joint engagement; Ss = symbol-infused supported and Cs = symbol-infused coordinated joint engagement.

$$P_{obs} = \frac{\sum_{i=1}^{k} x_{ii}}{x_{++}}$$

represents the proportion of agreement actually observed (.87 for the tallies in Figure 10.3),

$$P_{exp} = \frac{\sum_{i=1}^{k} x_{+i} x_{i+}}{x_{++}^2}$$

represents the proportion of agreement expected due to chance (.18 for the tallies in Figure 10.3), and

$$K = \frac{P_{obs} - P_{exp}}{1 - P_{exp}}$$

indicates how kappa is computed (.84 in this case). Agreement expected due just to chance is subtracted from both numerator and denominator, thus kappa gives the proportion of agreement corrected for chance.

Exact second-by-second agreement may be too stringent. Given human reaction time and other considerations, investigators may be willing to permit their coders some tolerance, which the GSEQ program allows. For the tallies in Figure 10.3, a 2-second tolerance was specified, thus agreements were tallied as long as the second observer agreed with the first within 2 seconds. Figure 10.4 shows how this works in practice. Displayed is a 40-second segment of a time plot from a reliability session of the sort GSEQ produces. The first coder's second-by-second record is shown on the first line, the second coder's on the second line, and disagreements on the third line. Seconds underlined with periods were disagreements but were not counted as such because the second coder agreed with the first coder within 2 seconds. For example, coder 1 assigned cj at 54:23 and 54:24 whereas coder 2 assigned Ss. However coder 2 assigned cj at 54:21 and 54:22, which was within the tolerance specified. In contrast, seconds underlined with hyphens did count as disagreements. For example, coder 1 assigned Ss at 54:35; because coder 2 did not assign Ss within 2 seconds (i.e., from 54:33-54:37), this counted as a disagreement.

The procedure of cross classifying time units to assess observer reliability raises a couple of potential concerns. First, because the time unit is arbitrary (recall the minute vs. moment discussion earlier), what would happen if half-seconds or tenths of a second were used instead, thereby dou-

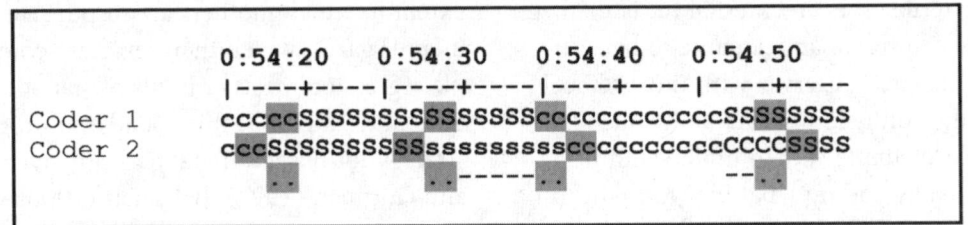

FIGURE 10.4. A segment from a plot, as displayed by GSEQ, of 40 seconds coded by two observers, with a tolerance of 2 seconds. Here, s = supported, c = coordinated, S = symbol-infused supported, and C = symbol-infused coordinated joint engagement. Seconds underlined with dashes are counted as disagreements. Seconds underlined with periods were not counted as disagreements because there was agreement within ± 2 seconds, but they would be counted as disagreement if 0 tolerance was specified. Seconds not underlined represent exact agreement.

bling or increasing the number of tallies by an order of magnitude? Other things being equal, the value of kappa would not be affected; it is a magnitude of effect statistic, unchanged by the number of tallies (unlike, e.g., chi-square). True, its standard error would decrease with more tallies, but whether or not a kappa is statistically significantly different from zero is almost never of concern; significant kappas could still indicate unacceptable agreement. Quite rightly, investigators are concerned with the size of kappa, not its statistical significance. For example, Fleiss (1981) characterized values over .75 as excellent, between .60 and .75 as good, and between .40 and .60 as fair; nonetheless, Bakeman and Gottman (1997) recommended viewing values of kappa less than .70 with some concern.

Which coder is designated first and which second is also arbitrary. When no tolerance is specified, values of kappa are identical, no matter which coder is considered first. However, and this is the second concern, when a tolerance is specified slightly different values of kappa are generated depending on which coder is first (because the algorithm considers each time unit for the first coder in turn and tallies an agreement if a match is found for the second coder within the tolerance specified). In practice, any difference in the values of the two kappas is usually quite small. Nonetheless, such indeterminacy makes most of us a bit uncomfortable, and so we recommend computing both values and then reporting the lower of the two, which seems a conservative strategy.

Cohen's kappa has many advantages with respect to the traditional percentage of agreement. By eliminating the portion of nonreliable agreement due to chance from the total agreement, the index becomes an index of reliability in a classical measurement theory sense that assumes a ratio between true variance and total variance; it can be weighted when the variable is ordinal so that more versus less serious confusions about codes between observers can be taken into account (for details see Bakeman & Gottman, 1997). Kappa can be calculated both for the general category system and even for each single category (by extracting a series of 2 × 2 tables from the agreement matrix); thus, along with the help of the agreement matrix, different kappas for different codes within the same set can be compared to detect particularly unreliable codes.

In sum, when using observational methods, reliability is a central concern, from training of coders to publication of research reports. Validity is a concern too, but one that applies to all our studies, all the time, no matter what measurement approach is used, and that usually is integrated with data analysis. Still, it is worth noting that one common approach to training observers combines both validity and reliability concerns. This approach involved preparation of standard protocols that are assumed accurate and against which observers are tested. The standard protocol is regarded as a "gold standard," one that the researcher prepares with the consultation of experts and that is regarded as representing "the true state of affairs;" that is, in

psychometric terms, it is an external measure that the researcher can reasonably assume to be accurate. Comparing each observer with this protocol by means of the confusion matrix and Cohen's kappa provides a simple way to understand if observers are really coding what the researcher wants them to code. This procedure has at least two advantages: It identifies coders' errors while eliminating the possibility that the coders share a common but nonetheless deviant worldview, and it permits all future coders to be trained to a common criterion of known (presumed) validity.

When observational methods are used, and the timing of events is recorded (i.e., onset times and implicit or explicit offset times)—a circumstance that current technology makes easy, routine, and increasingly common—assessing reliability of coders is facilitated when data are represented as successive coded time units (e.g., seconds). An alternative strategy, sometimes encountered in older literature, is to attempt to align two protocols and somehow, attempting to take commissions and omissions into account, identify similar stretches of time assigned the same code as a single agreement, and then report a percentage of agreement statistic. This is both imprecise and does not give coders credit for the moment-by-moment nature of their decisions. It also does not give them credit for not coding an event, even when that may be the correct decision. The time-based approach to reliability presented here seems preferable. In the next section we demonstrate how representing data as successive coded time units can facilitate data analysis as well.

REDUCING AND ANALYZING OBSERVATIONAL DATA

In contrast with both self-report or questionnaire methods, and more similar with automatic collection of physiological data, observational methods often result in voluminous data. Thus data reduction is often a necessary prelude to analysis. A useful strategy is to collect slightly more detailed data than one intends to examine, thus initial data reduction may consist of combining some codes. Other data reduction may involve computation of conceptually targeted indices (e.g., an index of the extent to which mothers are responsive to their infants' gaze), which then serve as scores for multiple regression or other kinds of statistical analyses. Several examples of this useful and productive strategy for observational data are given in Bakeman and Gottman (1997); Bakeman (2000); and Bakeman, Deckner, and Quera (2004), and a specific example is presented in the following paragraphs.

Earlier we noted that sequences of events might be coded without recording their onset or offset time. Such *event sequences* are amenable to Sackett's (1979) lag-sequential analysis. However, when events are coded along with their onset and offset times—and current technology makes timing information ever easier to record—such *timed sequences* afford analytic options not available with event sequences (Bakeman & Quera, 1995). Timed sequences can consist of any number of mutually exclusive or co-occurring behaviors, and the time unit, not the event, can be used as the tallying unit when constructing contingency tables. This can be very useful. Often we want to know whether one behavior occurred within a specified time relative to another, and we are not particularly concerned with its lag position (i.e., with whether or not other behaviors intervened).

For example, Deckner, Adamson, and Bakeman (2003) wanted to know whether mothers and their toddlers matched each other's rhythmic vocalizations and so coded onset and offset times for mothers' and toddlers' rhythmic vocalizations. Their time unit was a second, and Figure 10.5 shows results for one dyad. For the rows, each second of the observed interaction was classified as within (or not within) a 5-second time window; the window began the second the mother began a rhythmic vocalization and extended for the next 4 seconds. For the columns, seconds were classified as a second the toddler began a rhythmic vocalization, or not. A useful way to summarize this 2 × 2 table is to note that the odds the toddler began a rhythmic vocalization within 5 seconds of her mother beginning one were 0.0582 to 1 (i.e., 11 ÷ 189), whereas the corresponding odds otherwise were 0.0299 to 1 (i.e., 29 ÷ 971). Thus the odds ratio—a statistic probably more used in epidemiology than in other social science fields—is 1.95 (i.e., 0.0582 ÷ 0.0299).

Within 5s of mother's onset	Toddler onset Yes	No	Totals
Yes	11	189	200
No	29	971	1000
Totals	40	1160	1200

FIGURE 10.5. This mother–toddler dyad was observed for 1200 seconds or 20 minutes; the tallying unit is the second. For these data the odds ratio is 1.95 (11/189 divided by 29/971) indicating that a toddler was almost twice as likely to begin a rhythmic vocalization within 5 seconds of the mother beginning a rhythmic vocalization than at other times.

If the cells of a 2 × 2 table are labeled x_{ij}, where the first subscript represents the row and the second the column, then the

$$\text{odds ratio } = \frac{x_{11} \div x_{12}}{x_{21} \div x_{22}} = \frac{x_{11} x_{22}}{x_{12} x_{21}}$$

The odds ratio deserves to be better known and used more by psychologists and other behavioral researchers. It is useful on two counts: First, it is useful descriptively to say how much greater the odds are that a behavior will occur in the presence as opposed to the absence of another behavior (here, that the toddler will start a rhythmic vocalization more often shortly after the mother does as opposed to other times). Second, the natural logarithm of the odds ratio, which varies from minus to plus infinity with zero indicting no effect, is an excellent score for standard statistical analyses (the odds ratio itself, which varies from zero to plus infinity with 1 representing no effect, is not; see Wickens, 1993). Thus Deckner et al. (2003) could report that 24-month-old female children were more likely to match their mother's rhythmic vocalization than 24-month-old male children or either male or female 18-month-old toddlers, using a standard mixed-design analysis of variance (sex was the between-subjects variables and age the within-subjects variable), where the log of the natural logarithm of the odds ratio served as the score analyzed.

In sum, Deckner et al. provide an excellent example of how analysis of observational data can proceed with timed sequences. Onset and offset times for events are recoded, then a computer program (GSEQ; Bakeman & Querea, 1995) tallies seconds and computes indices of sequential process (here, an odds ratio) for individual cases, and finally a standard statistical technique (here, mixed model analysis of variance) is applied to the sequential scores (here, the natural logarithm of the odds ratio). Deckner et al. were interested specifically in whether mothers and toddlers matched each other's rhythmic vocalizations but the same technique could apply to a variety of behaviors and to other sets of partners or to behaviors within an individual. It is very general.

SUMMARY

Historically, sequential observational methods have proved useful when process aspects of behavior are more important than behavioral products or for studying any behavior that unfolds over time. They have been widely used for studying nonverbal organisms (e.g., infants) and nonverbal behavior generally, especially social behavior. The study of social interaction generally and interactional synchrony in particular (here exemplified with the matching of toddler–mother rhythmic behavior) are two areas in which observational methods have been widely used. Observational methods seem to have a kind of naturalness not always shared with

other measurement strategies. Observers are not always passive or hidden, and situations may be contrived, and yet the behavior captured by observational methods seems freer to unfold, reflecting more the target's volition than seems the case with, for example, self-report questionnaires. Self-reflection is not captured, but aspects of behavior outside immediate articulate awareness often are.

With recent advances in technology, observational methods have become dramatically easier. Handheld devices can capture digital images and sound, computers permit playback and coding while automating clerical functions, and computer programs permit flexible data reduction and analysis. Whether or not future investigators select observational methods will come to depend more on whether the method fits at least some aspect of the behavior under study and far less on some of the technical obstacles of the past. All this makes it more likely that the data analyzed at the end of the day will, in the spirit of this volume, represent multiple methods and permit a genuinely multimethod perspective on the behavior that brought us to research in the first place.

CHAPTER 11

QUANTITATIVE TEXT ANALYSIS

Matthias R. Mehl

Text analysis has been receiving increasing attention within the social sciences. This surge of interest is reflected in several recent books (Neuendorf, 2002; Popping, 2000; Smith, 1992; Weber, 1990; West, 2001), chapters (e.g., Smith, 2000), and review articles (e.g., Lee & Peterson, 1997; Pennebaker, Mehl, & Niederhoffer, 2003) on the topic. This chapter seeks to demonstrate that quantitative text analysis is a powerful, efficient, and easy-to-use scientific method with a wide spectrum of applications in psychology. It is organized into four major sections. At the beginning, an example of text analysis from social psychology is presented. This is followed by a brief historical overview of text analysis and an introduction to the conceptual foundation of text analysis. The third section reviews nine influential text analysis approaches in psychology. The final part discusses potentials and problems of quantitative text analysis.

A TEXT ANALYSIS EXAMPLE FROM SOCIAL PSYCHOLOGY

How do people respond to physical symptoms, and what makes them decide whether or not to seek treatment? The methodological toolbox in psychology is large, and there are a number of potential ways to address this question. Yet the default strategy has been to rely on just one tool—the questionnaire. In this case, for example, a researcher might create a health-decision questionnaire consisting of a number of Likert-scaled items, such as "How serious do your symptoms have to be before you see a doctor?" and "When you experience symptoms, how long do you wait before you see a doctor?" An alternative approach is simply to ask people what they normally do when they experience some rather common physical symptoms.

In a recent introductory psychology class, students wrote brief essays on how they would react if they woke up sweating, feeling terrible with a 102°F fever, and having a rash on their chest. Consider the following three responses[1]:

Participant A: My initial impressions would be panic, going through heightened anxiety. Health is probably my highest priority here at the university, and any slight deviation from feeling decent would send off warning signals to get help ASAP. Initially, I would go to my primary source of 24/7 counseling: calling home. They wouldn't mind at all. Calling them would give me a good idea of what I might be coming

Preparation of this chapter was aided by a grant from the National Institutes of Health (MH52391) to James W. Pennebaker. I am grateful to Sherlock Campbell, Michael Eid, Samuel Gosling, James Pennebaker, Lisa Trierweiler, and an anonymous reviewer for their comments on previous drafts of this chapter.

[1] I thank Carla Groom and James Pennebaker for providing the essays.

down with. I have my own physician's number at hand, and if the symptoms persisted throughout the rest of the morning, I wouldn't be hesitant as to calling him.

Participant B: I would first call my mother and tell her about my situation. I would see what she would suggest, which would most likely be to go see a doctor. I would call the University Health Center and make an appointment to see a doctor that day. Because I am covered by my mother's health insurance, the co-pay for me visiting the doctor would be twenty dollars. If the doctor knows what is wrong with me and gives me a prescription, the twenty dollars would be well spent.

Participant C: First thing I would do is try and remember if I had ever experienced similar symptoms so I could try to figure out on my own what was wrong with me. I would then probably call my mother to see if she had any idea what could be causing my symptoms and if she thought I should see a doctor. Knowing me, I would worry myself into a panic attack if I let the symptoms persist since I do not like not knowing what is wrong with me. I have gotten sick so often during the past few years that I have given up on trying to just cope with any sort of illness by myself.

What is striking about these answers is that, on the surface, all three participants reacted quite similarly. They all say they would go to see a doctor on the first day. For all three participants, one of the first things they thought about was calling their family. They probably also didn't differ much in terms of how serious they considered their symptoms to be. Thus, their responses to a multiple-choice questionnaire would most likely be comparable. However, a quick read of their responses conveys impressions of psychological reactions that are quite distinct.

For example, Participant B adopted a rather cool and rational attitude, compared to Participants A and C, who reacted rather emotionally. The free responses also tell us that health is clearly an important—almost dramatic—factor in Participant A's life, whereas economic considerations prevail in Participant B's thinking. Finally, there is a sense that Participant C is somewhat self-preoccupied and slightly socially isolated. It is likely that these differences—although not having an immediate impact on whether or not to see a doctor—ultimately translate into behavior relevant to the researcher's question (e.g., in terms of their expectations of the doctor or compliance with a prescribed treatment).

Of course, ad hoc impressions always run the risk of being subjective. A text analysis program such as *Linguistic Inquiry and Word Count* (LIWC; Pennebaker, Francis, & Booth, 2001) can paint a more objective picture. LIWC calculates the percentage of words that falls into a number of grammatical (e.g., pronouns, articles, prepositions) and psychological (e.g., words indicating emotional, cognitive, or social processes) categories. As shown in Table 11.1, LIWC analyses of the three essays generally support our intuitions: Participant C indeed used fewer emotion words than Participants A and B, and the considerably lower rate of social words and the frequent use of first-person-singular self-references (I, me, my) support our hunch that Participant C is less socially integrated and more self-absorbed than the other two students.

The LIWC analyses, however, reveal more than meets the eye: Participant A has a tendency to use long words (a marker of cognitive complexity); Participant B uses articles at a high rate (a marker of a concrete thinking); Participant C's writings contained a large number of cognitive words (a marker of mental processing). The three also differ in other important ways, such as their orientations to time (Participant A, B, and C: future, present, and past tense, respectively). Thus, a simple word count analysis provides insights into the participants' psychological worlds that go far beyond what multiple-choice questionnaires typically capture.

TABLE 11.1

Linguistic Inquiry and Word Count (LIWC) Analysis of Three Participants' Answers to the Question, "How Would You React If You Woke Up with a Series of Physical Symptoms?"

LIWC Variable	Participant A	Participant B	Participant C
Total word count	100.0	89.0	116.0
Words of more than six letters	25.0	12.4	10.3
First-person-singular pronouns	9.0	11.2	15.5
Articles	5.0	10.1	3.5
Prepositions	15.0	7.9	16.4
Emotion words	5.0	1.1	3.5
Positive emotion words	2.0	0.0	0.0
Negative emotion words	3.0	1.1	3.5
Cognitive mechanisms	10.0	16.9	21.2
Social processes	9.0	10.1	4.3
Past-tense words	0.0	1.1	5.2
Present-tense words	6.0	14.6	10.3
Future-tense words	4.0	3.4	0.9
School-related words	2.0	1.1	0.0
Money-related words	0.0	4.5	0.0

Note. All LIWC variables except total word count are expressed in percentages of total words.

TEXT ANALYSIS AS A SCIENTIFIC METHOD: HISTORICAL OVERVIEW AND CONCEPTUAL FOUNDATION

As a scientific method, text analysis is still young. It experienced its first surge during World War II, when Allied governments launched a series of large-scale projects to analyze the content of Nazi propaganda (Krippendorff, 1980). Stimulated by Murray's (1938) work on the Thematic Apperception Test (TAT), the first postwar decade in psychology was characterized by an avalanche of studies on the assessment of implicit motives via thematic content analysis (Smith, 1992). The advent of mainframe computers in the early 1960s revolutionized the field. Stone and his colleagues at Harvard University developed the first computerized text analysis program: the General Inquirer (Stone, Dunphy, Smith, & Ogilvie, 1966).

Since the 1970s, scientific text analysis has been shaped by two other technological advancements: the diffusion of personal computers with exponentially growing processor speeds and the rapidly increasing digitalization of data—through the Internet and progress in optical character and voice recognition (West, 2001). Computers have become increasingly sophisticated word search engines and, most recently, have been used for extracting semantic and grammatical relationships among words (Foltz, Kintsch, & Landauer, 1998; Roberts, 1997).

Defining Text Analysis

Not surprisingly, there has been disagreement on how to define text analysis. Shapiro and Markoff (1997) suggest the following minimal definition: Text analysis is "any systematic reduction of a flow of text (or other symbols) to a standard set of statistically manipulable symbols representing the presence, the intensity, or the frequency of some characteristics relevant to social science" (p. 14). This definition includes both qualitative (Riessman, 1993; Shiffrin, 1994) and quantitative approaches. In accord with the notion of measurement in this handbook, this chapter focuses exclusively on quantitative text analysis applications.

Classification of Quantitative Text Analysis Approaches

Quantitative text analysis approaches vary along a variety of different dimensions (Popping, 2000; Robins, 1997; Smith, 1992). The following section introduces four conceptual distinctions that provide a framework for organizing the existing approaches in psychology.

Aim: representational versus instrumental. On the broadest level, text analysis methods differ with regard to whether they are representational or instrumental in aim (Popping, 2000; Roberts, 1997). The role of the receiver in normal communication is to decode as accurately as possible the intended meaning of a message. This is what representational text analysis seeks to achieve. Its goal is to develop a representation of the sender's original intention of a message. In doing so, representational analysis is interested in the manifest content of a text.

Instrumental analyses focus mainly on latent content. Independent of the author's intention, a message is analyzed for occurrences of a set of themes (e.g., hostility, anxiety, need for power). The linguistic analysis at the beginning of the chapter, for instance, was instrumental because—rather than representing what the students intended to say—it focused on selected psychological aspects of language use (e.g., words hinting at emotional and social functioning).

So far, most existing text analysis applications in psychology have been instrumental. Compared to other sciences, psychology is highly deductive in its research. Instrumental analyses allow the specification of linguistic variables as the operationalizations of theoretical constructs and thus facilitate hypothesis testing. Also, psychology has a history of going beyond manifest content by reading between the lines to unravel the "unspoken" yet psychologically existing meaning—a task that only instrumental analyses accomplish. Finally, instrumental analyses can be performed on any desktop computer; a representational analysis' mimicking of natural syntax is computationally intensive and generally requires specialized machines (as well as users).

Approach: thematic versus semantic. The second conceptual distinction concerns the extent to which text analysis exclusively identifies themes or also models the relationships among them (Popping, 2000; Roberts, 1997). Until the 1980s, virtually all text analysis was thematic in nature. Thematic text analysis maps the occurrence of a set of concepts in a text and thus can technically be solved by counting the frequency of particular target words or phrases.

Semantic text analysis seeks to extract information on the conversational meaning of a theme. For example, it can be crucial to know not only that the theme "killing" is mentioned in a text but also whether it occurred in the context of "self" or "other people." Semantic text analysis solves this problem by specifying the concrete nature of relations among themes. Hence, the level of analysis in the semantic approach is typically the clause. Semantic text analysis first specifies a semantic grammar, a subject–verb–object (S-V-O) template, in which the concepts of interest are arranged like pull-down menus (e.g., [I/we] or [he/she/they] or [an object]; [S]–killed [V]–the dog [O]). It then determines the frequency with which certain concept constellations occur. In the example at the beginning of the chapter, semantic analysis could, for example, determine how often students call their mother and go to the doctor on her recommendation—as compared to the mother calling the student or the student calling the mother after returning from the doctor.

Recently, a new development in the field, latent semantic analysis (LSA), has received an increasing amount of attention (Folz et al., 1998; Landauer & Dumais, 1997). Compared to traditional semantic approaches where an investigator defines the context in a "top-down" manner, LSA constitutes a "bottom-up" approach, where information about the semantic similarity of words is extracted by analyzing their usage across a large body of texts. Because of its flexibility, computational power, and conceptual similarity to human cognition, it is a tool with great potential for the area of psychology (Campbell & Pennebaker, 2003).

In allowing the identification of themes *and* the relations that exist among them, semantic text analysis provides an additional degree of freedom. For evaluating its overall effectiveness, however, it is important to keep in mind that the meaning of a sentence is rarely revealed in its surface grammar. A powerful semantic analysis thus would need to identify the underlying deep structure—a task that is yet impossible to delegate entirely to a computer. Consequently, most semantic text analysis relies on human coders to parse large amounts of texts (Popping, 2000).

Bandwidth: broad versus specific. Text analysis approaches also differ in their bandwidth (Pennebaker et al., 2003). Some approaches focus on less than a handful of specific linguistic variables. Mergenthaler (1996), for example, analyzes therapy protocols exclusively for a client's use of emotion words and cognitive words and ignores other potentially relevant information, such as the content of the therapy session or a client's linguistic style. Other approaches intend to provide a broad linguistic profile of a text. LIWC, the text analysis program from our initial example, for instance, measures up to 82 grammatical and psychological language parameters.

Although specific approaches tend to have a stronger theoretical background, broad approaches usually are more inductive and phenomenon oriented. Researchers who find a text analysis program that captures exactly what they are interested in might prefer it to an "all-rounder" type of software because of its supposed better power. However, in those cases where a compromise needs to be made between what one is interested in and what is "out there," applications with broader bandwidth offer more flexibility.

Focus: content versus style. The fourth distinction concerns the "what" versus "how" in text analysis (Groom & Pennebaker, 2002). Conceptually, it dates back to Allport's (1961) distinction between adaptive and stylistic aspects of behavior. Whereas the adaptive components of a behavior are intended and purposeful in a given context (e.g., initiating a conversation), its stylistic aspects are mostly unintended, automatic, and serve expressive rather than instrumental functions (e.g., nervous gestures while initiating the conversation). Applied to verbal behavior, this distinction captures the difference between *why* a person is saying something, that is, the content of a statement (e.g., "When does the next number 5 bus pass by?"), and *how* the person is saying it (e.g., "Excuse me, would you possibly know when the next number 5 bus is supposed to pass by here, please?"). Looking "behind" a message for verbal mannerisms (Weintraub, 1981) or linguistic styles (Pennebaker & King, 1999) reveals more subtle aspects of a communication.

Historically, both strategies have been successful in psychology (Pennebaker et al., 2003; Smith, 1992). What makes stylistic language analyses particularly intriguing is that humans naturally attend to what people are saying or writing. It is cognitively quite demanding to tune out the meaning of a message for the sake of attending to particularities in word choice (cf. Hart, 2001). Consequently, for human judges linguistic styles are hard to detect and thus constitute the perfect target for computerized word count programs that are blind to meaning.

Summary. Conceptually, text analysis applications can be organized according to whether they are representational or instrumental in their aim, thematic or semantic in their approach, broad or specific in bandwidth, and focused on language content or style. Although these distinctions may not always be clear in practice, they offer a heuristic framework for deciding which text analysis strategy to use for a certain kind of research question. The following section provides a more concrete picture of how text analysis has been applied in psychology.

QUANTITATIVE TEXT ANALYSIS APPROACHES IN PSYCHOLOGICAL RESEARCH

This section reviews nine quantitative text analysis approaches that have been highly influential in psychology. The approaches were selected to be reasonably representative of the spectrum of existing text

analysis strategies. More comprehensive reviews can be found in Popping (2000), Roberts (1997), Smith (1992), and Pennebaker et al. (2003). For each method, the historical and theoretical background is provided along with a description of how text samples are analyzed. Finally, each approach is located within the four-dimensional conceptual framework introduced in the previous section. Table 11.2 provides an overview of the depicted approaches. The approaches are presented roughly in order of historical development.

Thematic Content Analysis

Thematic content analysis is used here as a summary label for a number of approaches that have been developed in the context of motivational psychology (Smith, 1992). Generally, these approaches have human judges identify critical thematic references in a text. Ratings are made either each time a theme occurs or as global ratings reflecting the prevalence of a theme across an entire text. In either case, the analyses are based on standardized coding systems that define a psychological construct by specifying rules for when a certain theme is and is not considered indicative of the construct. Judges undergo extensive training until a predefined degree of agreement is obtained. Smith's (1992) *Motivation and Personality: Handbook of Thematic Content Analysis* contains detailed descriptions of 14 different coding systems. The following section highlights three conceptually distinct approaches that have been extensively applied in psychology.

Scoring motive imagery from TAT protocols. Murray's (1938) work on the TAT has had a profound effect on researchers interested in implicit aspects of human motivation. In a typical study, participants write brief stories about ambiguous black-and-white pictures. The essays are then scored for the presence of motive-relevant themes in participants' imagery. Whereas the original work by McClelland and Atkinson (1948) focused on how an aroused hunger motive surfaces in TAT fantasies, the main body of research has evolved around a small number of social motives. Various scoring systems are available for the need for achievement, the need for power, the need for affiliation, and the need for intimacy (for details, see Smith, 1992).

Recently, Winter (1994) integrated the different existing scoring systems into a unified manual that allows the simultaneous coding of achievement, power, and affiliation/intimacy imagery. According to this system, themes including improvement concerns such as "she wanted to find a better solution" are considered achievement imagery, whereas attempts to influence others (e.g., "he tried to convince him of the importance of this project") or references to status (e.g., "he impressed his friends with his new sports car") are interpreted as expressions of a need for power. Affiliation and intimacy themes are merged into one category and include both statements about friendships ("the two college friends were glad to see each other again") and intimate relationships ("they were young and in love"). A motive score is calculated by adding imagery scores across all stories and correcting for verbal productivity. More than 50 years after its development, TAT-based need assessment has recently experienced a surge in scientific attention (Schultheiss & Brunstein, 2001; Tuerlinckx, De Boeck, & Lens, 2002; Winter, John, Stewart, Klohnen, & Duncan, 1998).

Content Analysis of Verbatim Explanations. Peterson and Seligman developed Content Analysis of Verbatim Explanations (CAVE; Peterson, 1992) as a text analysis technique to complement questionnaire-based assessments of causal attributions. CAVE allows the scoring of any text document for the author's explanatory style.

The CAVE procedure involves two steps. First, all causal explanations in a text are identified. Trained scorers then rate each explanation on three dimensions (internality, stability, globality). Whereas "I can't go to the wedding because I have to go to a conference" is rated as not at all stable, "I didn't get the job because I am a woman" reflects a highly stable attribution. Similarly, "I did well on the paper because the assignment was easy" is considered highly external, whereas "I didn't get the job because I am too young" refers to a highly internal

TABLE 11.2

Overview of Nine Influential Quantitative Text Analysis Approaches in Psychology

Name	Reference	Linguistic parameters	Coding	Conceptual Classification			Focus
				Aim	Approach	Bandwidth	
Thematic Content Analysis	Smith (1992)	Need for power, need for achievement, need for affiliation, explanatory style, integrative complexity	judges	instrumental	thematic	specific	content/style
General Inquirer	Stone et al. (1966)	Harvard III Psychosociological Dictionary, Stanford Political Dictionary, Need-Achievement Dictionary	computer	instrumental	thematic	broad/specific	content/style
Gottschalk–Gleser Method	Gottschalk et al. (1969)	Clinical phenomena (e.g., anxiety, hostility, social alienation, depression, cognitive impairment)	judges/computer	instrumental	semantic	specific	content
Regressive Imagery Dictionary	Martindale (1990)	29 categories of primary process cognition (e.g., oral, sex, Icarian imagery), 7 categories of secondary process cognition (e.g., abstraction, social behavior), 7 categories of emotions (e.g., positive affect, anxiety)	computer	instrumental	thematic	broad	content
Analysis of Verbal Behavior	Weintraub (1981)	15 dimensions including pronouns (I, we, me), negatives (e.g., not, no, never), qualifiers (e.g., kind of), expressions of feelings (e.g., love), and adverbial intensifiers (e.g., really, so)	judges	instrumental	thematic	broad	style
TAS/C	Mergenthaler (1996)	Emotional tone, abstraction, referential activity	computer	instrumental	thematic	specific	style
DICTION	Hart (1984)	5 master variables (certainty, optimism, activity, realism, commonality) with a total of 35 linguistic subdimensions	computer	instrumental	thematic	broad	style
LIWC	Pennebaker et al. (2001)	82 variables; standard linguistic dimensions (e.g., pronouns, articles), psychological processes (e.g., emotion words, causation words), relativity (past tense, inclusive words), personal concerns (e.g., school, religion, sexuality)	computer	instrumental	thematic	broad	content/style
LSA	Landauer et al. (1998)	n/a; 2 strategies with focus either on low (content approach) or high (style approach) frequency words	computer	representational	semantic	n/a	content/style

cause (Peterson, Schulman, Castellon, & Seligman, 1992). Intensive coding training is offered.

The CAVE technique has been applied to a wide variety of text sources, including therapy protocols, newspaper articles, presidential addresses, personal letters, and TAT protocols. People's explanatory styles have been successfully linked to optimism, depression, and health behaviors (Peterson, 1992). The strength of the CAVE analysis lies in its theoretical foundation, its broad applicability, and its real-world relevance (Peterson, 1992).

Content analysis of conceptual/integrative complexity. Suedfeld, Tetlock, and their colleagues have developed a text analysis system to assess a person's information processing and decision making. Conceptual/integrative complexity (IC) measures the degree of differentiation and integration achieved in describing a phenomenon (Suedfeld, Tetlock, & Streufert, 1992).

Originally the Sentence/Paragraph Completion Test (S/PCT) was used as a source for assessing IC. In the S/PCT participants write open-ended answers to a series of sentence stems, such as "When I am criticized . . .," "When I don't know what to do . . .," or "When a friend acts differently. . . ." Each answer is then rated on a 7-point scale ranging from 1 (*no evidence of either differentiation or integration*) to 7 (*high differentiation and high integration*). In general, a high degree of differentiation is achieved when a phenomenon is acknowledged as having multiple causes and dimensions. Integration is obtained when interconnections are made between the acknowledged dimensions (Baker-Brown et al., 1992). IC scores are positively correlated with the total number of words in a text, the average sentence length, and the number of words with more than three syllables (Coren & Suedfeld, 1990).

Because the rating process involves subtle semantic inferences about the author's intention, intensive coder training is required (Suedfeld et al., 1992). More recently, IC analysis has been extended to the study of archival material. IC has been linked to a variety of social psychological topics such as attitude change, attribution, problem solving, and interpersonal communication (Suedfeld et al., 1992).

Summary and evaluation. Three influential thematic content analysis approaches have been reviewed. Several other coding systems are available but could not be included here (e.g., personal causation, deCharms, 1968; uncertainty orientation, Sorrentino, Roney, & Hanna, 1992; object relatedness, Rosenberg, Blatt, Oxman, McHugo, & Ford, 1994; for a more exhaustive review, see Smith, 1992). With regard to the four-dimensional conceptual framework, thematic content analysis is instrumental in its aim and thematic in its approach. It focuses either on verbal content (e.g., IC) or style (e.g., CAVE) and typically is specific in bandwidth. The fact that thematic content analysis involves human judges who make inferences about the meaning of a statement is typically considered a threat to its reliability. Generally, however, when quality standards such as appropriate test administration, careful judge training, and duplicate scoring of materials are met, good reliabilities are achieved (Schultheiss & Brunstein, 2001; Smith, 1992).

The main weakness of thematic content analysis lies in the time that judges spend coding verbal material. It has become increasingly attractive to replace moderately reliable and expensive human judges by perfectly reliable and cost-effective computer coders (cf. Hogenraad, 2003). Shapiro (1997) pointed to a weakness in this argument: Computer-based systems typically consist of two components, a processing device with the text analysis routine (e.g., the word count algorithm) and a dictionary with the linguistic information (e.g., lists of emotion- or achievement-related words). Whereas the processing device is 100% reliable, the deeper problem lies in the fact that coding ambiguity is shifted from the coding procedure to the construction of a comprehensive dictionary. Still, beyond their incomparable efficiency, computer codings also have the advantage of facilitating cross-study and cross-laboratory comparisons of findings.

The General Inquirer

In the early 1960s, Stone and his colleagues developed the "mother" of computerized text analysis, the General Inquirer (Stone et al., 1966). The General Inquirer is a compilation of a set of word count routines. It was designed as a multipurpose text analysis

tool strongly influenced by both need-based and psychoanalytic traditions. Historically, three dictionaries, the Harvard III Psychosociological Dictionary, the Stanford Political Dictionary, and the Need-Achievement Dictionary have been applied the most with the General Inquirer. The Need-Achievement Dictionary was created to automate the judge-based scoring of TAT achievement imagery.

More important, the General Inquirer goes beyond counting words. In a two-step process, it first identifies so-called homographs (ambiguous words that have context-dependent meaning). It then applies a series of preprogrammed disambiguation rules aimed at clarifying their meanings in the text. For example, human judges score the statement "He is determined to win" as achievement imagery. The General Inquirer identifies the word *determined* as an ambiguous NEED word and *win* as an ambiguous COMPETE word (because they both can have nonachievement-related meaning) and codes a statement as achievement imagery only if both aspects are present and occur in the NEED–COMPETE order.

The General Inquirer is unique in its flexibility. It can be used to study virtually any topic of interest by creating user-defined dictionaries (e.g., Semin & Fiedler, 1988, 1991). Its most critical advantage, the power to perform context-dependent word counts, is also its most serious pragmatic drawback. The construction of a custom dictionary with the specification of disambiguation rules is time consuming and, in many cases, not well suited to the many ambiguous ways words are used. Nevertheless, the General Inquirer continues to shape the field of computerized text analysis. A third-generation version is now available for desktop computers as well as Internet usage. As shown in Table 11.2, the General Inquirer is instrumental in its aim and thematic in its approach. Its bandwidth and focus depend on the actual dictionary in use; the Need-Achievement dictionary, for example, is specific and content focused.

Gottschalk–Gleser Method of Content Analysis

Also in the 1960s, Gottschalk and his colleagues started developing what became known as the Gottschalk–Gleser Method of content analysis (Gottschalk, 1995). The Gottschalk–Gleser Method involves participants giving a 5-minute speech on a personal life experience. The verbatim transcripts are then submitted to a content analysis.

Several scales tapping into what Gottschalk calls "psychobiological dimensions" have been developed and validated. Most of the scales are derived from a psychoanalytic framework and are designed to diagnose clinical phenomena (Gottschalk, Stein, & Shapiro, 1997). Schizophrenic tendencies, for example, are meant to be revealed by the Social Alienation and Personal Disorganization Scale. Other scales diagnose depression, hostility, and cognitive impairment. Each scale consists of a number of subcategories that list the themes to be scored along with the respective scoring weights. The Anxiety Scale, for example, comprises death anxiety, castration anxiety, separation anxiety, guilt anxiety, and shame anxiety. Whenever one of these themes is mentioned, a weight is assigned according to the degree of (psychodynamic) association with the self (e.g., self: "I was scared I could die," +3 vs. other people: "He was scared he could die," +2 vs. objects: "The dog was scared it could die," +1).

The Gottschalk–Gleser Method relied originally on human judges. Recently, however, Gottschalk and Bechtel (1989, 1995) have introduced a computerized version. The computerized method is one of the few existing semantic text analysis tools in psychology (Popping, 2000). It uses a semantic grammar consisting of S-V-O templates to identify the action of the sentence (e.g., "to die") as well as the agent (e.g., "I" vs. "he") and—if applicable—the object. The Gottschalk–Gleser approach is specific in that it concentrates on selected clinical phenomena and focuses on the content of a person's statement.

Analysis of Artistic Change: Martindale's Regressive Imagery Dictionary

To identify regularities underlying changes in artistic work over time, Martindale (1990) developed a word count program that is based on the Regressive Imagery Dictionary. Martindale's (1990) theorizing starts from the observation that artistic work shows a steady increase in complexity over time. He explains this increase by drawing on two funda-

mental psychological processes: humans' preference for medium levels of arousal (and hence moderately complex sensory input) and the physiological mechanism of stimulus habituation (leading to changes in what is considered moderately complex). Grounded in psychodynamic thinking, he plotted how two major linguistic dimensions in literature, primordial (i.e., primary process) and conceptual (i.e., secondary process) cognition, have changed over the decades.

Martindale's Regressive Imagery Dictionary has been translated into several languages (e.g., French, German, and Portuguese). The English version is composed of about 3,200 words and word stems that fall into 29 categories of primary process cognition (e.g., regressive cognition, Icarian imagery), 7 categories of secondary process cognition (e.g., abstraction, social behavior), and 7 emotion categories (e.g., positive affect, anxiety).

Over the last 30 years, Martindale (1990) has accumulated an impressive body of studies that identify linguistic indicators of an aesthetic evolution. Unfortunately, his work has not enjoyed widespread attention in mainstream psychology (cf. Bestgen, 1994; Hogenraad, McKenzie, Morval, & Ducharme, 1995). As depicted in Table 11.2, Martindale's text analysis approach is instrumental in aim, thematic in approach, and broad in bandwidth. It focuses on the content of literature from a psychodynamic perspective.

Weintraub's Analysis of Verbal Behavior

Weintraub's (1981, 1989) work on verbal mannerisms was inspired by the clinical observation that individuals speaking under stress often reveal important information about their psychological adjustment. Drawing on his medical training and practice, Weintraub argued that psychological defense mechanisms manifest themselves in speech patterns obtained under mildly stressful conditions. He assessed these defense mechanisms from the language that participants spontaneously use when they talk for 10 minutes about a personal topic (Weintraub, 1981).

Unlike most other word count approaches, Weintraub's linguistic analysis is performed by naïve judges who "can score . . . [the transcripts] without extensive knowledge of lexical meaning"

(Weintraub, 1989, p. 11). The linguistic parameters that he is interested in are largely intuitively derived and drawn from his clinical experiences. Weintraub's most recent work has focused on 15 linguistic dimensions, including three pronoun categories (I, we, me), negatives (e.g., not, no, never), qualifiers (kind of, what you might call), expressions of feelings (e.g., I love, we were disgusted), and adverbial intensifiers (really, so).

Weintraub has explored verbal behavior in multiple ways. In addition to his main interest, the language of psychopathology, he also analyzed the Watergate transcripts, characterized speaking styles of post–World War II U.S. presidents, identified linguistic correlates of intimacy, and related language use to personality. Weintraub's analyses are instrumental in aim, are thematic in approach, capture a broad spectrum of language use, and are stylistic in focus (see Table 11.2).

Analyzing Emotion–Abstraction Patterns: TAS/C

Mergenthaler and his research group use text analysis to characterize key moments in psychotherapy sessions. They developed a computer program called TAS/C that focuses on two language dimensions—emotional tone and abstraction. According to Mergenthaler's theory, emotion–abstraction patterns occur periodically in psychotherapy sessions with insight processes (abstraction) following emotional events (emotion) with a time lag (Mergenthaler, 1996).

For the analysis of emotional tone, defined as the density (rather than the valence) of emotion words, a dictionary with more than 2,000 entries was developed. The final list of emotion words comprises three dimensions (pleasure, approval, and attachment) and captures roughly 5% of the words of a text (Mergenthaler, 1996). Abstraction is defined as the number of abstract nouns in a text. Abstract nouns are identified via suffixes such as -ity, -ness, -ment, -ing, or -ion. The abstraction dictionary includes 3,900 entries and captures about 4% of the words of a text.

TAS/C analysis of emotion–abstraction patterns has been applied to verbatim therapy protocols (Mergenthaler, 1996) and attachment interviews

(Buchheim & Mergenthaler, 2000). More recently, TAS/C has been extended to include a measure of referential activity. Referential activity refers to the ability to verbalize nonverbal experiences and is characterized in speech by concreteness, specificity, clarity, and imagery (Mergenthaler & Bucci, 1999). The TAS/C approach is instrumental in its aim, is thematic in its approach, and concentrates on two specific stylistic aspects of language use in psychotherapeutic settings.

Analyzing Verbal Tone With DICTION

Hart (1984, 2000) is interested in word choice in political communication. Over the last two decades he has developed a computerized word count program called DICTION (Hart, 2001). DICTION is designed to reveal the verbal tone of political statements by characterizing text on five statistically independent master variables: activity, optimism, certainty, realism, and commonality. The rationale behind these master variables is that "if only five questions could be asked of a given passage, these five would provide the most robust understanding" (Hart, 2001, p. 45). The five master variables are composed of 35 linguistic subfeatures (e.g., optimism is composed of the subfeatures praise, satisfaction, inspiration, blame, hardship, denial).

DICTION relies on 10,000 search words that are assigned to the categories without overlap. The output is either a profile of absolute values or norm scores that is based on 20,000 samples of verbal discourse. Special features of DICTION are the ability to learn, that is, to update its database with every processed text, and a statistical weighting procedure for homographs. DICTION has been used to analyze presidential and campaign speeches, political advertising, public debates, and media coverage. It is instrumental in aim, is thematic in the approach, captures language at a broad level, and focuses on stylistic aspects of texts.

Linguistic Inquiry and Word Count

Linguistic Inquiry and Word Count (LIWC; Pennebaker et al., 2001) was originally developed in the context of Pennebaker's work on emotional writing. It was designed to reveal aspects of writing about negative life experiences that predict subsequent health improvements (Pennebaker & Francis, 1996; Pennebaker, Mayne, & Francis, 1997). More recently LIWC has been used to analyze language use in a wide variety of text sources including literature, personal narratives, press conferences, and transcripts of everyday conversations (Pennebaker et al., 2003).

LIWC searches for over 2,300 words or word stems within any given text file. Independent judges previously categorized the search words into 82 language dimensions. These dimensions include standard linguistic categories (e.g., articles, prepositions, pronouns), psychological processes (e.g., positive and negative emotion words, words referring to cognitive or social processes), relativity-related words (e.g., time, motion, space), and traditional content dimensions (e.g., sex, death, job). Most LIWC dimensions are hierarchically organized; for example, the word *cried* falls into the four categories of sadness, negative emotion, overall affect, and past-tense verb. The program also offers the option to create user-defined categories.

Although some LIWC dimensions are based on specific psychological theories (e.g., inhibition words, discrepancy words), most categories extract information at a basic grammatical (e.g., pronouns, articles, prepositions) and psychological level (e.g., emotion words). LIWC is instrumental in its aim and thematic in its approach. It captures broad aspects of language use. Currently, LIWC has been found to be most effective in tracking stylistic aspects of language use. However, with its traditional content categories, it also allows for a basic analysis of text content (e.g., achievement, religion, sexuality). Recently, Spanish, German, and Italian versions of the LIWC dictionary have been developed and tested for equivalence to the original English version. LIWC has been applied to a wide spectrum of research questions in social, personality, and clinical psychology, including coping with trauma, depression, suicidality, gender differences, personality expression, and aging (Groom & Pennebaker, 2002; Pennebaker et al., 2003).

Extracting Word Patterns: Latent Semantic Analysis

Latent Semantic Analysis (LSA; Foltz et al., 1998; Landauer & Dumais, 1997; Landauer, Foltz, &

Laham, 1998) is a semantic text analysis strategy and concerned with the use of words in their context. Compared to most existing semantic text analysis programs, however, LSA does not adopt the top-down strategy of specifying a semantic grammar and looking at the occurrence of S-V-O constellations. Instead—in a bottom-up manner—it distills information about the semantic similarity of words by analyzing their usage across a large body of text.

Applying singular value decomposition, a mathematical data reduction technique akin to factor analysis, LSA creates a multidimensional semantic space that allows one to calculate the similarity between any two words used in a given body of text by comparing their coordinates in the semantic space. If, for example, the words *patient* and *physician* consistently co-occur in a sentence across a large amount of text, LSA assigns them similar factor weights. Ignoring syntactical information, LSA infers similarity in meaning from patterns of word co-occurrences. LSA was initially developed as a search engine with a focus on words that carry content (i.e., nouns, verbs, adjectives). This has lead to its application as a tool to measure textual coherence (e.g., Foltz et al., 1998) and to provide computerized tutoring (e.g., Graesser et al., 1999).

More recently, LSA has been adapted to analyze textual style. For this, LSA ignores low-frequency content words and focuses on high-frequency words that have minimal semantic function (i.e., pronouns, articles, prepositions). In a reanalysis of three studies on the salutary effects of emotional writing, Campbell and Pennebaker (2003) linked an LSA measure of similarity in people's essays across 3 days of writing to their subsequent health. They found that similarity in the use of common words, especially personal pronouns, was negatively related to health benefits. This study underscores that LSA is not an esoteric tool for cognitive scientists, but can offer a fresh perspective on persistent problems in social psychology.

Clearly, LSA's word pattern analysis has limitations (Perfetti, 1998). Its inability to consider syntactic structure or to make use of acquired word knowledge certainly distinguishes it from human coders. However, Landauer et al. (1998) argued that "one might consider LSA's maximal knowledge of the world to be analogous to a well-read nun's knowledge of sex, a level of knowledge often deemed a sufficient basis for advising the young" (p. 261). LSA is representational in its aim and semantic in the approach. As explained earlier, it can focus on low-frequency words that carry content or on high-frequency words that convey linguistic style.

Summary and Evaluation

This section reviewed nine influential text analysis strategies in psychology. The selected approaches span a broad spectrum of methodological and theoretical orientations. How should a researcher decide which one to use? The most immediate question is whether the options are restricted to computerized solutions or whether the burden of manual coding appears tolerable (Smith, 1992; Weintraub, 1981). Another question concerns what kind of analysis a researcher is interested in. The four-dimensional framework was introduced to help with this question.

Over and beyond this, however, other characteristics of the programs also help determine the most appropriate solution for a given research project. Several of the reviewed approaches emerge from psychodynamic theorizing. For researchers whose interest lies in this area, the solutions offered by Gottschalk (1995), Martindale (1990), Weintraub (1981), or Mergenthaler (1996) are good choices—with the Gottschalk–Gleser Method having the strongest clinical focus, Martindale's Regressive Imagery Dictionary being particularly useful for the analysis of literature, and Mergenthaler's TAS/C being the ideal tool for the analysis of therapy protocols. DICTION (Hart, 1984) assesses psychological variables at a comparatively abstract level and—because of its background in communication research—seems most useful for the study of political communication and persuasion. For researchers interested in basic grammatical text features (e.g., pronouns, articles, prepositions) or low-level psychological constructs (e.g., emotional, cognitive, or social processes), LIWC (Pennebaker et al., 2001) offers an extensively validated solution. The General Inquirer (Stone et al., 1966) also captures a wide variety of psychological parameters and, in its

most recent version, includes an operationalization of Semin and Fiedler's (1988, 1991) Linguistic Category Model. Finally, LSA (Landauer et al., 1998) is a powerful text analysis tool that is not word count based and has applications in modeling cognitive processes such as knowledge representation, coherence, and perspective taking.

QUANTITATIVE TEXT ANALYSIS: A METHOD REFLECTION

The final section of this chapter steps back and reflects more broadly on the potentials and pitfalls of text analysis as a scientific method. The discussion revolves around three major questions: The first question asks what makes text analysis an attractive method for psychology. The second question looks at text analysis from a measurement perspective and asks to what extent is verbal data psychometrically good data. The third question is fueled by the apparent paradox that on the one hand, the vast majority of existing text analysis programs are word count based but that, on the other hand, simple word count solutions often appear overly simplistic and fraught with problems. How far can we go with simply counting words?

What Makes Text Analysis an Attractive Method for Psychology?

From the time we get up in the morning—listening to the radio or reading the newspaper—until we go to bed—watching TV or reading a book—we are surrounded by words. Every day we have dozens of conversations, make numerous phone calls, write and receive an increasing number of e-mails, surf the Internet, and chat in chat rooms. As teachers we assign writing assignments and grade essays. As researchers we use language to communicate with our participants; we collect responses to open-ended questionnaires, conduct interviews, videotape discussions, and record conversations. It is overwhelming how our daily lives are saturated with words. Thus, it is surprising how little psychologists have used language as a source of data.

With the advent of the Internet, various new opportunities for studying linguistic phenomena have opened up. Without running a single partici-

pant, researchers can now collect large amounts of text from personal Web pages, chat room conversations, message board entries, and e-mails (e.g., Cohn, Mehl, & Pennebaker, in press). Also, all major newspapers, magazines, periodicals, and journals are now available online and maintain comprehensive electronic archives. Important statements of public figures such as presidential addresses or press conferences are usually available soon after they occur—often already in transcribed form. Virtually any song's lyrics and even entire movie scripts can be downloaded from the Web. In short, text analysis researchers never experience a data shortage.

However, there is more to text analysis than the opportunity to draw on easily available data. As a method for analyzing archival data it offers another critical advantage (Lee & Peterson, 1997; Simonton, 2003; Winter, 1992). The data collection is less constrained than in most other methods. Survey studies yield scaled answers on a limited set of items—selected by the investigator on conceptual grounds prior to the onset of the study. Questionnaires work by a "what you ask is what you get" principle. No further information can be obtained once the data are collected. Open-ended questions, essays, or other verbal productions are different; they allow researchers to go back to the data and explore aspects that one had not originally considered.

Going back to our initial example about students' motivation to seek out a doctor, for instance, one might later become interested in whether self-focused attention operationalized as the use of first-person singular ("I") could predict who goes to the doctor. The data is also available for unrelated research questions such as sex differences in language use (Groom, Stone, Newman, & Pennebaker, 2004). It is even possible for other researchers now or in the future to analyze the data using their own text analysis approach and interpretative framework. The analysis of verbal material provides a flexibility that is hard to obtain with other methods.

So far, the vast majority of text analysis researchers have relied on a single type of text source. From a multimethod perspective, for a more elaborate understanding of how people use

language it is necessary to start comparing language effects across text sources, genres, or contexts. For example, are there systematic differences in the way humans express themselves in written as compared to spoken language (Biber, 1988; Mehl & Pennebaker, 2003; Weintraub, 1981)? Or is language use in e-mails more similar to how people actually talk or write letters (Baron, 1998)? Identifying the degree of linguistic convergence and uniqueness across different language sources is an important area for future research (Pennebaker et al., 2003).

Is Verbal Data Psychometrically Good Data?

There might be many good reasons to use text data for psychological research. From a measurement perspective, one of the most important questions concerns the extent to which verbal data is psychometrically good data. Unfortunately, it is common for text analysis researchers, after developing a new method, to proceed to its application without establishing its psychometric properties. Thorough construct validation in the area of text analysis is yet rare. However, at least two notable exemptions to this rule deserve to be mentioned. A large body of research has established the validity of TAT-based motive measures. From this it has become clear that implicit motives (a) can be reliably assessed with the TAT (Lundy, 1988; Smith, 1992; Tuerlinckx et al., 2002; Winter & Stewart, 1977), (b) are distinct from self-reported motives and traits (King, 1995; Schultheiss & Brunstein, 2001), and (c) uniquely predict types of behavior (McClelland, Koestner, & Weinberger, 1989; Winter et al., 1998).

The basic psychometric properties are also comparatively well understood for word count–based measures. Across a series of studies, the words that people use in their spoken and written language have emerged as stable over time and across context (Gleser, Gottschalk, & Watkins, 1959; Mehl & Pennebaker, 2003; Pennebaker & King, 1999; Schnurr, Rosenberg, & Oxman, 1986). Also, spontaneous word choice shows reliable and theoretically meaningful associations with demographic variables (Groom et al., 2004; Pennebaker & Stone, 2003) and traditional personality measures (Pennebaker et al., 2003), but also predicts, for example, real-life

health behaviors over and beyond the Big Five dimensions (Pennebaker & King, 1999).

To summarize, the question to what extent text analysis yields good data from a measurement perspective is important and needs to be answered for each method separately. So far, at least for TAT-assessed motives and word count–based measures, the existing evidence suggests good psychometric properties. Thorough construct validation that, for example, establishes aspects of convergent validity between different text analysis methods (e.g., emotion words across different programs) and between text analysis methods and other psychological methods (e.g., self-reported, observed, and linguistic measures of emotions) are needed.

How Far Can We Go With Counting Words?

Given that word count–based measures possess rather good psychometric properties, how far can we go with counting words? Frequently researchers voice their scientific disdain for text analysis programs that are unable to distinguish between sentences as simple as "the dog bit the man" and "the man bit the dog" (Hart, 2001, p. 53). Its blindness to context makes word-count approaches sometimes appear painfully dumb. Not only are they unable to pick up irony or sarcasm (e.g., "Thanks a lot," accompanied by a roll of the eyes) and metaphoric language use (e.g., "He had the key to her heart"), but they also confuse words that have different meanings in different contexts (e.g., "What he did made me *mad*" vs. "I'm *mad* about the cute person in my class"). In a discussion of the shortcomings of a program such as the General Inquirer, Zeldow and McAdams (1993) went as far as to entirely question the value of lower-level word counts.

Over the last five decades, however, word-count approaches have repeatedly demonstrated their potentials in virtually all domains of psychology (e.g., Gottschalk, 1995; Hart, 1984; Martindale, 1990; Pennebaker et al., 2003; Stone et al., 1966; Weintraub, 1981). Often, to test psychological hypotheses, it is not necessary to specify grammatical relationships between themes; instead, it is sufficient to know *that* certain themes (co-)occur in a text. In fact, Hart (2001) even construed thematic text analysis' blindness toward context as its biggest

advantage. Because humans so readily understand the communicative meaning of words, having a computer that counts themes under full neglect of their semantic surroundings provides researchers with information that is largely inaccessible to self-report or observational methods.

If one accepts that the study of words can be psychologically meaningful, which words should researchers focus on? It is interesting that virtually every text analysis approach has started from the assumption that emotional states can be detected by studying the use of emotion words (cf. Bestgen, 1994). The reality is that in daily speech, emotional writing, and even affect-laden poetry, less than 5% of the words can be classified as emotional (Mehl & Pennebaker, 2003; Pennebaker & King, 1999). From an evolutionary perspective, it is unlikely that language has evolved as a vehicle to express emotion. Instead, humans use intonation, facial expression, or other nonverbal cues to convey feelings. Emotional tone is also expressed through metaphor and other means not related to emotion words. Taken together, embarking on emotion words to study human emotions has not emerged as a particularly promising strategy (Pennebaker et al., 2003).

Content-based dictionaries are generally comprised of word categories that the researcher created based on more or less empirically supported intuitions of what words are indicative of certain themes (e.g., the word *football* is indicative of the theme *sport*). Hence, content dictionaries always have a subjective and culture-bound component (Shapiro, 1997). Markers of linguistic style, however, are generally associated with relatively common "content-free" words, such as pronouns, articles, prepositions, conjunctives, and auxiliary words—also referred to as particles (Miller, 1995). Particles are easier to handle because their meaning is less ambiguous, less context bound, and more determined by grammatical rules. In the English language, there are fewer than 200 commonly used particles, yet they account for over half the words we use.

From a psychological perspective, not all particles are equal; personal pronouns have emerged as particularly revealing (Pennebaker et al., 2003). Although the use of the first-person singular ("I"), for example, indicates an explicit distinction that speakers make between themselves and their social world, the use of the first-person plural ("we") suggests speakers experience themselves as part of a larger social unit. Empirically, the use of the first-person singular is associated with age, sex, neuroticism, depression, illness, and more broadly, attention focused on the self (Pennebaker et al., 2003). The use of second-person ("you") and third-person ("he," "she") pronouns, by definition, show that the speaker is socially engaged or aware. So, it becomes clear that in the conversational context, pronouns have important social implications. The empirical evidence to date underlines this by pointing to their role as powerful markers of psychological processes and predictors of mental and physical health (Pennebaker et al., 2003).

SUMMARY

One purpose of this chapter was to demonstrate that quantitative text analysis is a powerful, efficient, and easy-to-use tool for psychological research. The review of nine different text analysis strategies showed that the spectrum of existing applications is wide—although some methods continue to rely on human judges, the majority use computers to count isolated words, and a few harness more sophisticated techniques to assess the semantic relationships.

Where will the field go from here? Extrapolating from current progress in artificial intelligence, there is no doubt that in the years to come, text analysis applications will become increasingly complex (West, 2001). Will simple word count programs soon be declared scientific history? Considering that they are currently the only solutions in which complete automation has been achieved (Shapiro, 1997), this scenario seems unlikely. With their ability to process large amounts of texts in a matter of seconds without any preformatting, word-count programs have a tremendous pragmatic advantage over more sophisticated tools that require a human labor force for extensive data preparation and text parsing.

Hence, researchers who are interested in text analysis are encouraged to be aware of the "bigger is better" fallacy. Tempting as it might seem, the assumption that more technically advanced pro-

grams will necessarily be more appropriate for addressing a researcher's question does not always hold up. Simple word-count approaches—crude, fuzzy, and error prone as they are—can often go a long way. After all, by only using a simple home-made telescope and not high-resolution satellite pictures, Galileo was able to detect the four moons of Jupiter.

CHAPTER 12

MULTILEVEL ANALYSIS: PHYSIOLOGICAL AND BIOCHEMICAL MEASURES

Gary G. Berntson and John T. Cacioppo

The National Institute on Aging commissioned the National Academies of Science to organize scientific discussion that culminated in a workshop volume whose title queried, *"Cells and surveys: Should biological measures be included in social science research?"* (Committee on Population, 2001). The short answer to that question was *yes*.

Although psychologists have long appreciated the value of converging operations using multimethod approaches, the NAS report found that psychologists are increasingly engaged in research entailing multilevel analyses that extend well beyond the traditional disciplinary boundaries. Multilevel analyses represent a subset of multimethod approaches in which the measures, constructs, and theories extend across levels of organization—from the psychological to the physiological to the cellular and ultimately to the gene and beyond. Efforts to integrate information across levels of analyses are especially challenging, but this is precisely what is necessary for the ultimate interdisciplinary convergence on mind–body issues.

Multilevel analyses can be problematic, as the terms, constructs, and measures are often diverse, and the concepts and theories at different levels of analyses may develop largely independently of those of another level. This fosters what has been termed the category error, wherein seemingly parallel concepts from different levels of analysis may reflect only partially overlapping domains, rather than representing a one-to-one isomorphism. The ultimate goal of multilevel analysis is to mutually calibrate concepts, relate measures, and integrate information across levels, so as to inform processes and constrain theories at multiple levels of analysis.

More important, this process entails *reductionism*, but not in the pernicious sense of *substitutionism*. Although it may be conceivable to explicate a motivational state in terms of the interactions of atomic elements, there are several important limitations to this approach. The first is the matter of efficiency and scale. The atomic underpinnings of motivational states are so extraordinarily complex that the language and constructs pertaining to atoms may not be the most efficient or feasible way to conceptualize motivation.

A second problem is the likelihood of a category error. Even if we could identify a set of atomic events that correspond to the motivational state, this does not imply an isomorphism. Motivation is a construct that has developed to account for variations in behavior of organisms; in the absence of behavior there would be no need for such a concept. Not only would there not be an agent to conjure up such a notion, but there would be no applicability at the atomic level. Although motivation certainly has causal relations to processes at the atomic level of analysis, there is not an identity across these vast levels, and it is patently silly to apply motivational constructs to atoms. Motivation applies to functional properties of more complex living organisms.

Preparation of this manuscript was supported in part by a grant from the National Heart, Lung, and Blood Institute (HL54428).

One might argue that motivational phenomena may be explicable ultimately in terms of the properties of atomic particles, and that the problem is simply one of the intricacy of mapping across such distal levels. This is a specious perspective, however. The third and most important limitation to substitutionism is that it *begs the question*[1] if the properties imputed to lower level elements to account for higher level phenomena are knowable only by observations from the higher level of organization. This is a logical fallacy (begging the question or circular reasoning) because the "explanatory" properties are derived from the phenomena to be explained. These properties cannot be said to be proper to the elements, but only derivable from a higher level of analysis that studies the elements in relation to others. Some properties of atoms may be knowable by the study of individual atoms, but others (e.g., atomic behavior in crystals) may become known only in interactions with other atoms. Similarly, although atomic or subatomic events ultimately underlie all our thoughts, feelings, and actions, the latter phenomena could not be said to be proper characteristics of the atomic elements. If they were, then all principles and properties would be assigned to quantum particles, which would be patently senseless because these properties and principles would *not* be of the particles, but of their configurations into aggregates, which may be meaningfully explained by constructs at different levels of organization.

Multilevel analysis is not about *substitutionism*, but about the ability of information derived from distinct levels of analysis to mutually inform others. *Reductionism* refers to the ability of events at lower levels of analysis to inform or explicate events at higher levels of analysis. Multilevel analysis is a two-way process, however, as higher level analyses can also elucidate or inform lower level processes (*extensionism*). Important in this effort is the development and refinement of meaningful *theories* of the relations between levels. Also central to this reductionism–extensionism process is the mutual tuning and calibration of concepts to enhance cross-level mappings and minimize category errors. This is especially important because of the intricacies and multiple mappings across distinct levels and the associated need for model constraints. This chapter highlights some features of multilevel analysis, provides a reductionism–extensionism framework for conceptualizing and implementing such analyses, and offers illustrative examples. A major theme is the mutual benefit that multilevel analyses offers for both the higher (e.g., psychological) and lower (e.g., physiological) levels of analysis.

PRINCIPLES OF MULTILEVEL ANALYSIS

Some principles pertaining to multilevel analysis have been articulated by Cacioppo and Berntson (1992; see also Cacioppo, Berntson, et al., 2000), which serve to frame issues and organize research perspectives. They are enumerated following.

The principle of *multiple determinism* stipulates that a target event at one level of organization, especially at more molar levels, will have multiple antecedents within and across levels of analysis. Parenting, for example, has both social and genetic determinants (Meaney, 2001). Because of the multiple antecedents across even proximal levels, the mappings across more divergent levels of analysis become increasingly complex. This is captured by an important corollary to the principle of multiple determinism. Although the ultimate goal of multilevel analysis is to bridge distal levels, the *corollary of proximity* suggests that this effort may be more straightforward for more proximal levels. As bridges are built among adjacent levels, those integrations will facilitate the superordinate mappings across progressively more disparate levels. This is not to say that bridging across broader levels of analysis is not possible or desirable. There are examples of programmatic research efforts that span multiple levels, such as the collaborative effort of Michael Meaney to map from the gene to maternal behavior and back again (Meaney, 2001). This was accomplished, however, through a systematic series of interdisciplinary collaborative efforts, which individually cut across a more limited span of levels.

---

[1]Originally *petitio principii* from Aristotle (350 B.C.) Posterior Analytics, translated by G. R. G. Mure, MIT Internet Classics Archive: http://classics.mit.edu/Aristotle/posterior.mb.txt.

The principle of *reciprocal determinism* asserts that there may be mutual, reciprocal influences among levels of organization—that is, the direction of causation is not one way. To continue with our example of gene–maternal interaction, there is a clear genetic bias in the pattern of maternal behavior in rats, but the pattern of maternal behavior has also been shown to impact specific gene expression in the offspring (Meaney, 2001). Moreover, this experience-dependent influence on gene regulation can extend beyond the subsequent generation, through nongenomic inheritance (Meaney, 2001). The principle of reciprocal determinism also has a guiding research corollary. Because causal influences among levels can be bi-directional, the *corollary of interdependence* states that a single level of analysis cannot yield a comprehensive account of multilevel phenomena, and that no single, preferred level of analysis applies uniformly. This is not to say that researchers should not do single-level research, as important phenomena for multilevel analyses derive from research and theory within a single level of analysis. Moreover, the selection of the most optimal level of analysis for single-level research depends on the experimental question and the theoretical interest (e.g., genetic vs. maternal determinants). The corollary indicates, however, that a comprehensive understanding of multilevel phenomena will require multilevel analysis.

Finally, the principle of *nonadditive determinism* reflects the fact that the properties of the whole cannot always be predicted by knowledge of properties of the parts. The sources of variance from higher level processes are often broader than those for lower levels of organization, so higher level systems tend to be more complex. Following the preceding example, the mere knowledge of a genotype may be uninformative as to phenotype, which in critical ways depends on multiple interactions with the social/maternal context (Meaney, 2001). Consequently, understanding genetics would not be complete if the study were restricted to the cellular domain. This principle reflects the increase in relational complexity with higher levels of organization and introduces the final corollary. The *corollary of asymmetry* states that the definition of a phenomena of interest should include observations at the highest level of organization at which it manifests, as it may not be understood by appeal exclusively to lower levels of analysis. That is, higher level analyses can identify and characterize phenomena that may be explicated in part by lower level organizations, but these phenomena may never be known from analyses limited to the lower level processes. This corollary would not preclude strictly lower level (e.g., molecular) analyses, but would apply at the point those molecular analyses were invoked to account for higher level phenomena (e.g., behavior).

The principles and corollaries just outlined are conceptual guidelines rather than prescriptions. Moreover, we wish to emphasize that merely mapping concepts from one level to another, although informative, does not in itself constitute an explanation of those relations. The latter will require well-developed theories that can foster predictions, allow experimental control, and permit hypothesis testing and theoretical refinements.

APPLICATIONS TO MULTILEVEL ANALYSES

Psychophysiological measures offer a unique vantage for multilevel analysis as they index physiological processes and events that may intervene between psychological processes and health or behavioral outcomes. Because they represent the operations of integrated physiological systems rather than isolated molecular events, these measures are more proximal to psychological processes than are molecular events. This is in keeping with the *corollary of proximity*, and the intermediate level of psychophysiological processes may provide important bridges between psychological and more molecular levels of organization.

Heart Rate Measures of Psychological States and Processes: Multiple Determinism

There is now an extensive history of theory and research on the potential links between psychological states, autonomic regulation, and disease processes. A common measure in this literature has been heart rate. The electrical signature of the heart beat is readily recorded as the electrocardiogram (EKG) by noninvasive surface electrodes, and heart rate has been known for centuries to be sensitive to

psychological states. It is theorized, for example, that decreases in heart rate are triggered by an external direction of attention, a decrease in arousal, passive coping, or an orienting response; whereas increases in heart rate have been said to reflect inwardly directed attention, an increase in arousal, effort, active coping, or a startle or defensive response (Graham, 1984; Lacey & Lacey, 1980; Obrist, 1981). A potential advantage of heart rate is the fact that it may reflect implicit psychological states in the absence of verbal or other behavioral actions and thus may provide a metric of psychological processes that may otherwise not be apparent.

The principle of multiple determinism, however, cautions against an overly simplistic interpretation of heart rate and heart rate change. Not only is there a wide range of psychological states or processes that influence heart rate, physical (e.g., temperature, posture) and physiological (e.g., activity, blood pressure) variables also impact heart rate. Hence, the utility of heart rate as an index of psychological processes is dependent on the rigor of the experimental design and the interpretive logic to be applied. This is underscored by the high error rates (both hits and misses) in the misapplication of physiological measures to the detection of deception (see Committee report, 2003; Lykken, 1998).

Part of the difficulty in this area relates to the multiple mappings across levels of organization and analysis. Although a fear stimulus may alter heart rate, there are many translations in this cascade: from the stimulus to percept, from percept to emotion, and from emotion to autonomic outflows. There is one further translation involved as the heart is not an autonomic organ, per se, but is merely regulated by the autonomic nervous system. As each translation likely entails multiple mappings from one stage of processing to the next, the overall intricacy in psychophysiological relations can be staggering. The *corollary of proximity* emphasizes the advantages of bridging across more proximal levels. A major goal of multilevel research is to progressively elucidate the mapping between disparate levels by building a series of local bridges among more adjacent levels.

The measurement model: heart versus autonomic outflow. The heart is dually innervated by the sympathetic and parasympathetic divisions of the autonomic nervous system, with the sympathetic system exerting a positive chronotropic effect (increasing heart rate) and the parasympathetic system exerting a negative chronotropic influence (decreasing heart rate). Changes in heart rate represent at best an indirect reflection of autonomic control. One legacy from the Walter Cannon era is that the autonomic branches are subject to reciprocal central control, with increases in activity of one branch associated with decreases in the activity of the other (see Berntson & Cacioppo, 2000; Berntson, Cacioppo, & Quigley, 1991). Within this conceptual framework, heart rate should reflect the state of sympathetic–parasympathetic balance, and this appears to hold for many autonomic reflexes that are organized at lower levels of the brain stem. Higher neurobehavioral substrates, however, can inhibit, modulate, or bypass lower reflex substrates and thereby exert broader and more flexible control over the autonomic branches (Berntson & Cacioppo, 2000; Berntson et al., 1991).

In behavioral contexts, one can see not only the classical reciprocal mode of control, but also independent changes of the autonomic branches, or even the concurrent coactivation or coinhibition of both branches. This clearly necessitates an expansion of the theoretical model, and hence the measurement model, from the classical bipolar continuum from sympathetic to parasympathetic dominance, to a bivariate autonomic space that more appropriately characterizes the multiple modes of control. As illustrated in Figure 12.1, the bivariate model subsumes the bipolar model for a reciprocal mode of control, but also expands this model to capture independent or coactive changes that cannot be represented in the bipolar model. This in turn raises serious questions about the utility of heart rate measures as an index of autonomic outflow, as increases in heart rate, for example, could result from an independent increase in sympathetic control, an independent decrease in parasympathetic control, a sympathetically domi-

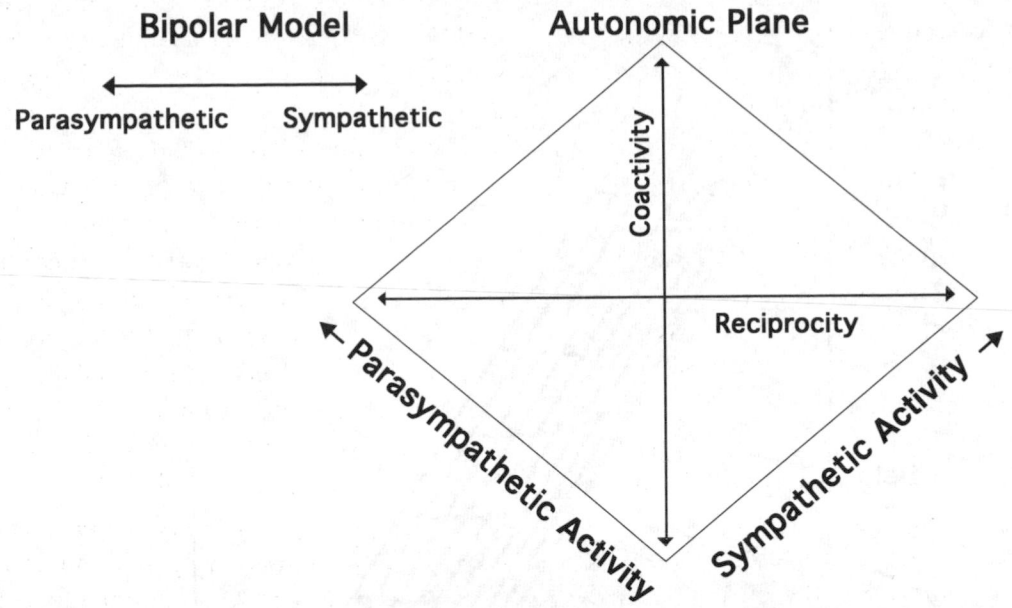

FIGURE 12.1. Conceptual models of autonomic control. Left: Bipolar model of reciprocal sympathetic/parasympathetic control. Right: Bivariate model of sympathetic and parasympathetic control that allows independent and coactive as well as reciprocal modes of autonomic response.

nated coactivation, or a parasympathetically dominated coinhibition. This ambiguity is illustrated by the isofunctional contour lines in the three-dimensional map of Figure 12.2, which illustrates the chronotropic state of the heart as a function of location within the autonomic plane.[2] These contour lines illustrate loci within the autonomic plane (i.e., different combinations of sympathetic and parasympathetic activities) that translate into equivalent chronotropic states. Consequently, the chronotropic state of the heart does not map simply on patterns of autonomic outflow, as a given chronotropic state is ambiguous with regard to its autonomic origins. Because neurobehavioral substrates control autonomic outflows, not the heart directly, measures of the chronotropic state of the heart necessarily entail a loss of fidelity in psychophysiological mappings.

Metrics of autonomic space. Differences in the modes of cardiac control for physiological reflexes

and psychological contexts are illustrated by a human study of autonomic responses to an orthostatic stressor (assumption of an upright posture) and to psychological stressors (mental arithmetic, speech stressor, and speeded reaction time task). Before considering those results, however, a measurement issue must be addressed. The change in measurement model from a bipolar to a bivariate representation has obvious implications for experimental dependent measures. If heart rate or heart period are not adequate, how does one measure autonomic outflows? That is, what constitutes a valid measure of sympathetic and parasympathetic activities? In anesthetized animal studies, direct recordings have been made of neural firing in sympathetic and parasympathetic cardiac nerves. This is not feasible in human subjects, however, and has limited applicability even in animals as the requirement for anesthesia precludes meaningful psychophysiological investigations. Microneurography (using a fine microelectrode) has been applied to

---

[2]From here on, the chronotropic state of the heart will be designated in the metric of heart period, or the reciprocal of heart rate. The former has advantages as heart period is more linearly related to neural activity within the autonomic branches.

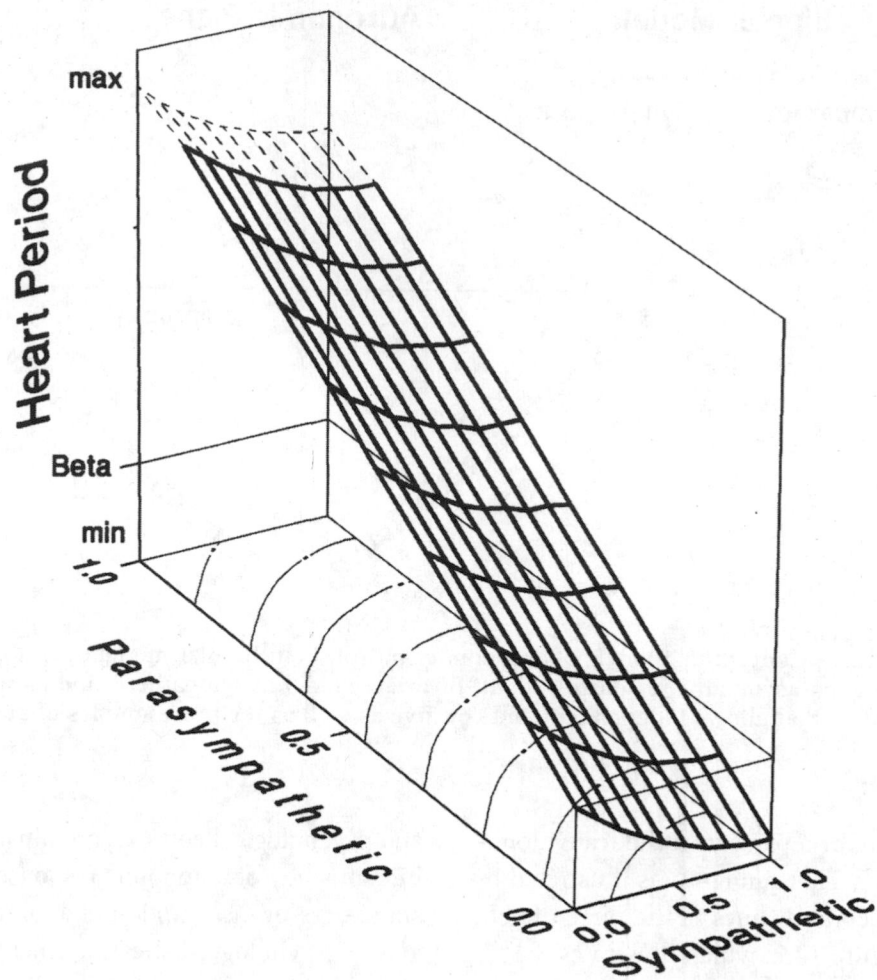

FIGURE 12.2. Three-dimensional autonomic space representation of chronotropic control of the heart. The effector surface depicts the heart period level for all possible loci within the autonomic plane. Parasympathetic and sympathetic axes are scaled in proportion to the extent of their functional range of control, and the curvature in the surface reflects nonlinearities in these controls. Beta (on the abscissa) illustrates the heart period in the absence of autonomic control. The curved lines on the autonomic plane are isofunctional contour lines, which represent varying combinations of sympathetic and parasympathetic control that yield comparable heart period effects. Reprinted from *Behavioral Brain Research, 94*, Berntson, Sarter, and Cacioppo "Anxiety and Cardiovascular Reactivity: The Basal Forebrain Cholinergic Link," 225–248. Copyright (1998), Elsevier.

measure autonomic neural activity in conscious humans, but this technique is only applicable for rather superficial autonomic nerves (e.g., Macefield, Elam, & Wallin, 2002).

Another approach to measuring the separate contributions of the autonomic branches to cardiac control entails pharmacological blockade of the branches. Blockade of the parasympathetic branch, for example, will prevent the action of that branch and reveal the isolated contribution of the sympathetic branch, and vice versa. This has been problematic, however, as blocking one branch may indirectly alter the other (e.g., by reflex adjustments). Moreover, although drugs may be highly specific to a receptor type and can thus differentiate sympathetic and parasympathetic effector synapses, they are not specific as to the target organ and may exert actions at some remote site, including the

brain. Such remote actions could alter the psychological states of interest or otherwise bias reactivity. The complications with pharmacological blockades have been sufficiently serious as to question their validity and limit their application. A new measurement methodology was clearly needed.

A more extensive pharmacological protocol and a more comprehensive analytical approach provided that methodology (Berntson, Cacioppo, & Quigley, 1994). Consider the observed heart period response ($\emptyset$) to some evocative stimulus occurring at the vertical line in Figure 12.3. As depicted, blockade of the parasympathetic branch would reveal the isolated sympathetic response $\emptyset Pblk$, which provides an estimate of the sympathetic contribution (termed the residual estimate or s'). At the same time, the response decrement from the unblocked condition ($\emptyset - \emptyset Pblk$) offers an estimate of the normal contribution of the parasympathetic branch (termed the subtractive estimate, or p'). Conversely, blockade of the sympathetic branch ($\emptyset Sblk$) provides a residual index of the isolated parasympathetic response (p') and the response decrement from the unblocked

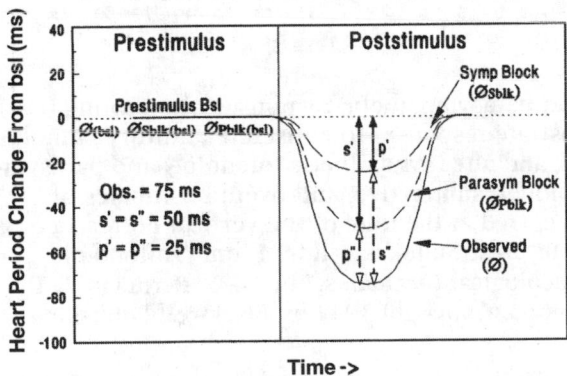

Figure 12.3. Illustration of heart period response in pharmacological blockade analyses. Solid line illustrates the observed response in the absence of blockade (under saline control conditions). Dashed lines illustrate the response under selective sympathetic and parasympathetic blockades. Arrows illustrate the residual (s' and p') and subtractive (s'' and p'') estimates of sympathetic and parasympathetic control. From "Autonomic Cardiac Control. I. Estimation and Validation from Pharmacological Blockades," by G. G. Bertson, J. T. Cacioppo, and K. S. Quigley, 1994, *Psychophysiology, 31,* 572–585. Copyright 1994 by Blackwell Publishing, Ltd. Reprinted with permission.

condition ($\emptyset - \emptyset Sblk$) offers an estimate of the normal contribution of the sympathetic branch (s'').

The preceding analyses provide two estimates of the functional contributions of each autonomic branch, and an overall estimate can be derived as the means:

Estimate of sympathetic response (at time t) =

$$\Delta S_t = (\Delta s_t' + \Delta s_t'')/2$$

Estimate of parasympathetic response (at time t) =

$$\Delta P_t = (\Delta p_t' + \Delta p_t'')/2$$

More important, because the residual and subtractive estimates are derived from distinct pharmacological blockers (muscarinic cholinergic antagonists for the parasympathetic branch and β_1 adrenergic antagonists for the sympathetic branch), their side effects and remote actions would be different. If the estimates agree, despite these differences, one would have increased confidence in the estimates of autonomic control. Moreover, any discrepancy in the independent estimates could be indexed by an error term (εblk), which is the difference between the two estimates at a given point in time. This value can be formally shown to be equivalent for the two branches. Thus

$$\Delta \varepsilon blk_t = (\Delta s_t' - \Delta Ps_t'') = (\Delta p_t' + \Delta p_t'')$$

As the discrepancy between the two estimates becomes larger, εblk_t increases, and one would have lower confidence in the estimate. This is formalized in a validity coefficient:

$$v_\delta = (|\text{effect size}|/ |\text{effect size}| + \varepsilon blk)$$

The validity coefficient can range from 0 when the error is very large relative to the estimated response, to 1.0 when the error term is negligible. An example of this analysis is shown in Figure 12.4 for orienting responses of rats to auditory stimuli. The top panel illustrates the observed responses under the control condition and after sympathetic (atenolol) and parasympathetic (scopolamine) blockade. The lower panels illustrate the overall as well as the residual and subtractive estimates of the contributions of the branches to the observed

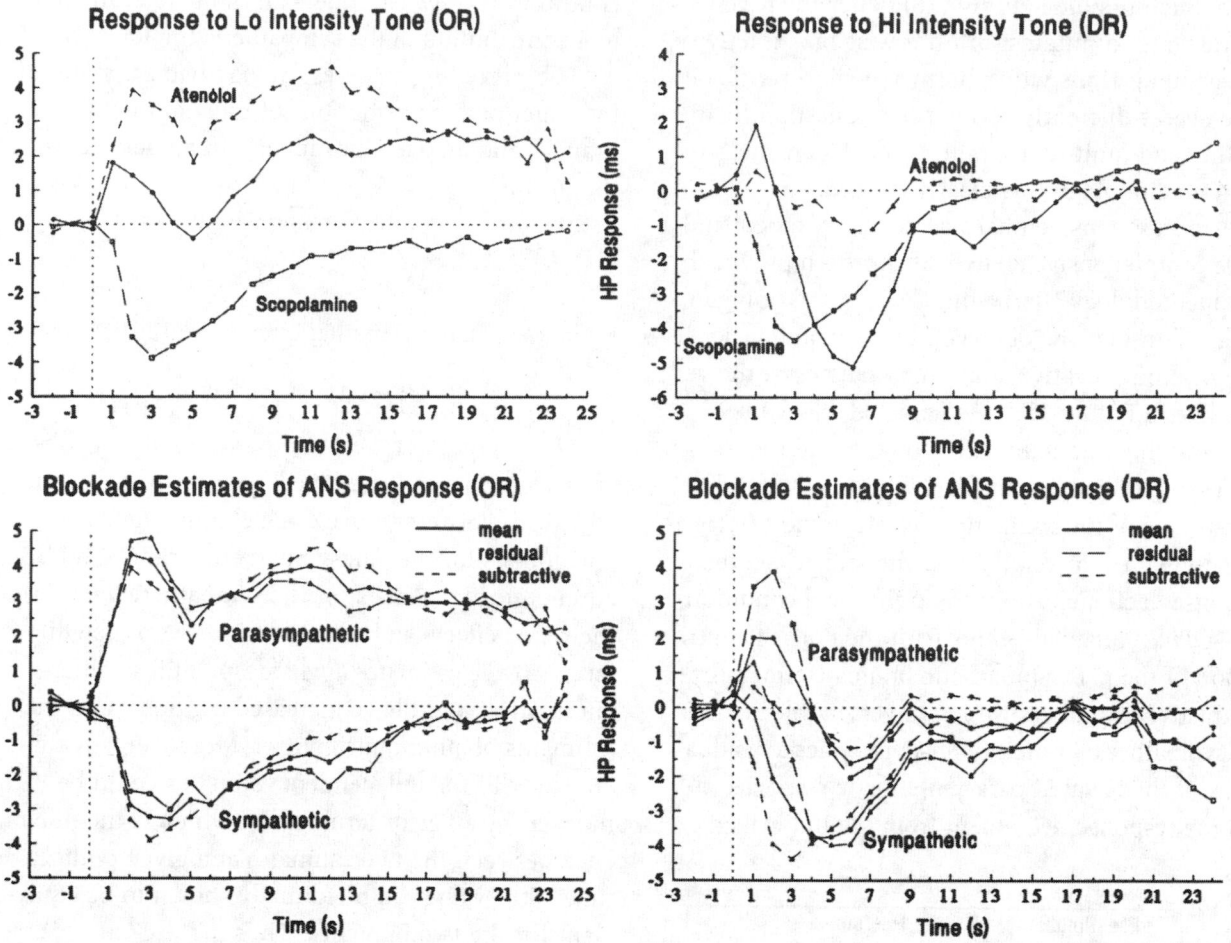

FIGURE 12.4. Pharmacological analysis of sympathetic and parasympathetic responses of orienting (OR) and defensive (DR) responses in the rat. Upper panels illustrate responses to a discrete auditory stimulus of low or high intensity under the saline control condition, and after sympathetic (atenolol) and parasympathetic (scopolamine) blockades. Bottom panels show residual, subtractive, and overall estimates of sympathetic and parasympathetic response. The stimuli occurred at the time of the vertical dotted line in each panel, and responses are expressed as a change from prestimulus baseline. From "Autonomic Cardiac Control. I. Estimation and Validation from Pharmacological Blockades," by G. G. Berntson, J. T. Cacioppo, and K. S. Quigley, 1994, *Psychophysiology, 31,* 572–585. Copyright 1994 by Blackwell Publishing, Ltd. Reprinted with permission.

response. As can be seen, there was relatively good agreement between the residual and subtractive estimates, yielding a small error term and a high validity coefficient. The response to the orienting stimulus revealed autonomic coactivation, as the increased heart period due to parasympathetic control indicates parasympathetic activation, and the decrease in heart period under sympathetic control similarly revealed sympathetic activation. Because activation of the two branches tends to oppose one another, the observed response in the unblocked

condition was smaller than under either blockade condition.

With the refined measurement method outlined, we now return to the human study of physical and psychological stress. Nine human subjects were tested for the autonomic response to the orthostatic stressor and the psychological stressors after intravenous infusions of saline, Metoprolol (a sympathetic β_1 blocker), and atropine (a parasympathetic blocker). Estimates were derived as outlined, and response vectors were derived on the autonomic plane, based on

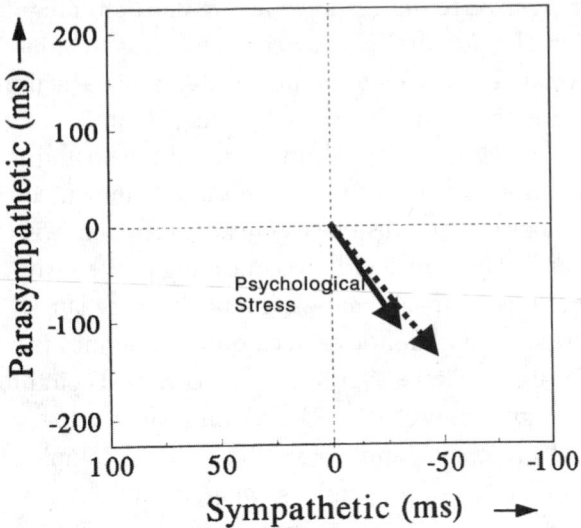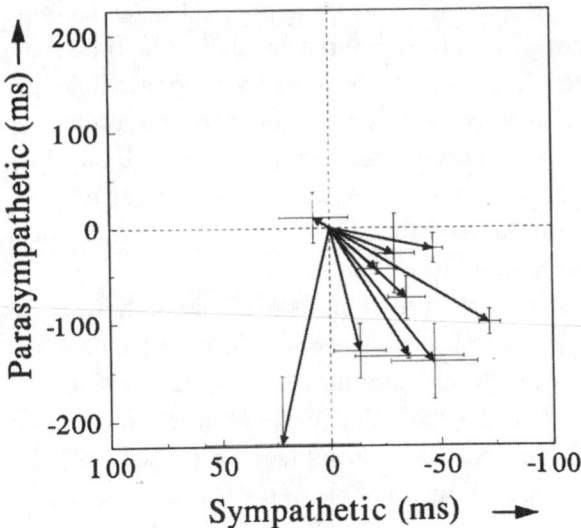

FIGURE 12.5. Orthostatic versus psychological stress. Left: Group mean responses to orthostatic and psychological stressors depicted as response vectors on the autonomic plane, from prestress baseline (intersection of horizontal and vertical dotted lines) to the stress conditions (arrowheads). Axes depict *ms* of heart period change related to sympathetic and parasympathetic control. Right: Individual response vectors (*N* = 9) to the psychological stressors revealing individual differences in the direction of response. Individual differences were stable, as evidenced by standard deviation bars at the arrowheads, reflecting deviations across the three psychological stressors (mental arithmetic, speech stress, and reaction time). Note that responses for a given individual were generally consistent across stressors. From "Autonomic Cardiac Control. III. Psychological Stress and Cardiac Response in Autonomic Space as Revealed by Pharmacological Blockades," by G. G. Berntson, J. T. Cacioppo, and K. S. Quigley, 1994, *Psychophysiology, 31,* 599–608. Copyright 1994 by Blackwell Publishing, Ltd. Reprinted with permission.

the change score along the sympathetic and parasympathetic axes. Results are illustrated in Figure 12.5, which displays response vectors from baseline (intersecting dotted lines). Both classes of stressors yielded an overall reciprocal pattern of sympathetic activation and parasympathetic withdrawal.

This similarity at the group level, however, belies a fundamental difference between the two classes of stressors. In accord with the reciprocal pattern of control in many autonomic reflexes, there was a significant negative correlation between the responses of the autonomic branches across subjects with the orthostatic stressor. Greater increases in sympathetic control were associated with larger decreases in parasympathetic control. All subjects showed similar response vectors, differing only in magnitude. In contrast, there was no correlation between the autonomic branches to the psychological stressors. Rather, as illustrated in Figure 12.5 (*right*), there were notable individual dif-

ferences in responses to psychological stress. Some subjects showed primarily parasympathetic withdrawal, others reciprocal sympathetic activation and parasympathetic withdrawal, and still others primarily sympathetic activation. This was not attributable simply to an increase in error variance to psychological stress, as individual response vectors were stable across the psychological stressors. This can be seen in the error bars at the arrowheads of Figure 12.5 (*right*), which depict the standard errors for the response vectors under the different psychological stressors.

Why does it matter? Without independent measures of sympathetic and parasympathetic control, lawful differences between orthostatic and psychological stressors would not have been apparent, and individual differences in the response to psychological stress would not have been discerned. In accord with the corollary of proximity, psychophysiological

mapping in this case was improved by the deployment of a more appropriate analytical method that assessed autonomic control at a more proximal level than could be derived from the end organ response. This is important not only for basic studies of psychophysiological relations, but also because different modes of autonomic control may have distinct health implications.

There have been reports of a relation between cardiac reactivity to stressors and negative health status, including diminished immune functions, although the predictive power of heart rate is small and not always significant (see Cacioppo, 1994). This is likely attributable to the use of heart rate measures, as Cacioppo (1994) found no relation between overall heart rate reactivity and the immune response to vaccine, but did find a significant relation between immune status and the sympathetically mediated component of heart rate reactivity. Multilevel analysis, capitalizing on more proximal mappings, revealed order in psychosomatic relations where none was apparent with more distal mappings.

Glucocorticoids and Behavioral States: Reciprocal Determinism

Glucocorticoids (cortisol in humans, corticosterone in rats) are steroid hormones of the adrenal cortex that have potent effects on glucose metabolism and immune function, as well as on psychological processes (Gore & Roberts, 2003; Lovallo & Thomas, 2000; Schimmer & Parker, 1996). Glucocorticoids are classic stress hormones and have been commonly used as biochemical markers of stress reactions (McEwen, 2000). As illustrated in Figure 12.6, the secretion of glucocorticoids is regulated by the anterior pituitary hormone adrenocorticotropic hormone (ACTH), which in turn is controlled by the hypothalamic peptide corticotropin releasing hormone (CRH). CRH is released in a pulsatile fashion (see Veldhuis et al., 2001), regulated by pituitary, hypothalamic, and hippocampal circuits that bear glucocorticoid receptors and are sensitive to glucocorticoid levels. These circuits exert a feedback inhibitory influence on CRH release. The hypothalamic and pituitary negative feedback mechanisms represent the traditionally

recognized routes responsible for short-term regulation of glucocorticoid secretion, whereas the hippocampus appears to be involved in stress reactions and longer term glucocorticoid regulation.

In addition to the short-term pulsatile patterns of release, the hypothalamic-pituitary-adrenal-cortical axis (HPAC) displays a circadian rhythm, with plasma glucocorticoid levels peaking in the early morning hours and showing a nadir in the late afternoon and minor peaks around mealtimes (see Lovallo & Thomas, 2000). Glucocorticoids bind to both glucocorticoid (GR) and mineralocorticoid (MR) receptors, and the steroid/receptor complex is translocated to the nucleus, where it can serve as a transcription factor to regulate gene expression (Gore & Roberts, 2003). More rapid actions may be exerted by glucocorticoid binding to membrane bound receptors (see Lupien & McEwen, 1997).

Measurement issues: reliability and validity. The pulsatile nature of ACTH and cortisol release poses a problem of reliability, as the level of hormone in plasma will vary depending on the time relation of the sampling to the pulsatile pattern of release. One approach to improving reliability has been to take multiple samples (e.g., Veldhuis et al., 2001) and then aggregating over samples if the interest is in tonic levels or preserve the temporal samples if the interest is in time-varying patterns of secretion. An additional measurement complication is the notable circadian rhythm in cortisol release. The measurement of the diurnal rhythm, by repeated cortisol measurements across the day, has been used to assess the status of the HPAC. If a more limited sample of cortisol is desired (e.g., as a stress marker), the diurnal rhythm not only imposes the restriction that samples be taken at the same time of the day, but also raises a question concerning the optimal time for sampling.

Measures derived late in the day or at night generally are not optimal for studies of chronic stress, because of the low levels of secretion and sensitivity limits. Consequently, for measures of chronic stress, samples are commonly taken during peak levels in the morning. The change in cortisol over 30 minutes (or so) from waking, for example, has been suggested to be a sensitive measure of adreno-

HPAC System and Hormonal Secretion

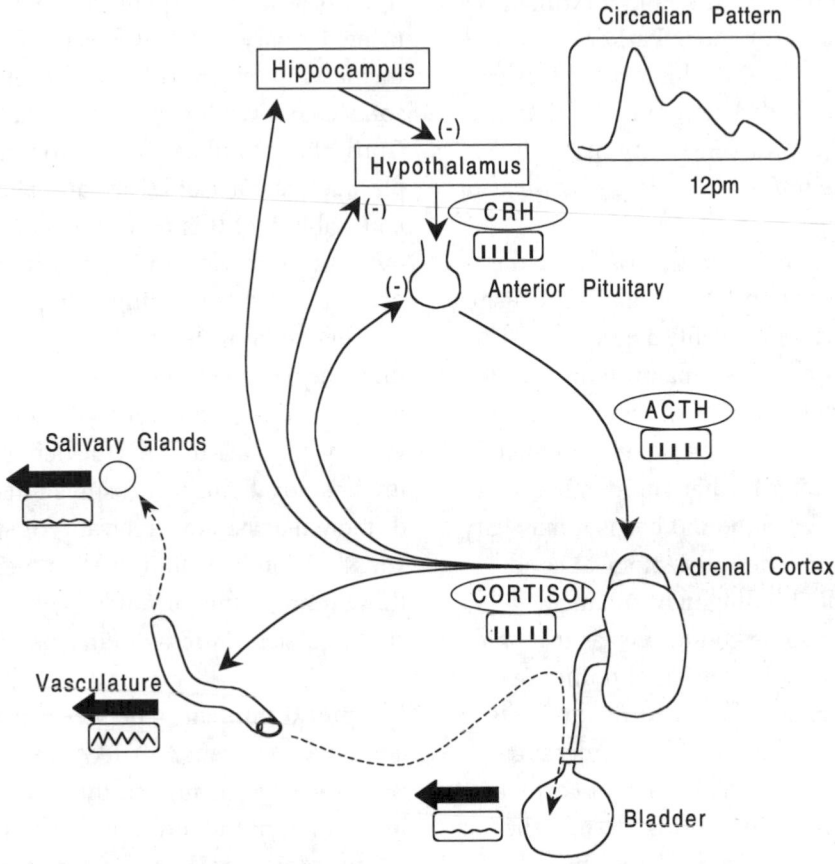

Figure 12.6. Structures and secretions of the glucocorticoid system. Hormones are listed in oval text boxes, and the rectangular inserts illustrate time-varying patterns of secretion or local concentrations, from pulsatile to more steady state, and over the circadian cycle. Solid arrows illustrate sample methods, salivary, vascular, and urinary. As illustrated, plasma cortisol levels are the highest and most variable and include both bound and unbound hormones, whereas salivary and urinary are more time stable and are considerably lower, as they represent unbound hormones.

cortical reactivity (Schmidt-Reinwald et al., 1999). Conversely, phasic reactivity to stress may be more appropriately assessed in the afternoon, when basal levels are lower and more stable. Some conditions such as chronic stress or depression may be associated with blunted negative feedback regulation and hence a diminished circadian pattern. This pattern may be more readily identified by evening measures or by indices of circadian fluctuations. Circadian fluctuations are often thought to arise in large part from changes in feedback regulation, but other factors could also impact these rhythms, including

altered or disrupted sleep/waking cycles, and should be considered when interpreting differences in circadian fluctuations (Spath-Schwalbe et al., 1993).

A more direct test of feedback control, having high construct validity, is the dexamethasone-suppression test. This procedure entails the administration of a standardized dose of the synthetic steroid dexamethasone, along with pre- and postadministration measurements of ACTH or cortisol. Secretion of these endogenous hormones will be suppressed in proportion to the potency of

steroid feedback inhibition. A subset of depressed patients (50%–60%) show elevated cortisol levels, an attenuated circadian rhythm, and a blunted response to dexamethasone (see Parker, Schatzberg, & Lyons, 2003). This may reflect conditions within brain feedback circuits or changes in glucocorticoid receptor sensitivity. We will return to these possibilities later, in the context of stress effects.

Additional measurement issues arise over the fact that typically less than 10% of plasma cortisol is in a free, unbound, biologically active state. The rest is reversibly bound to plasma proteins (corticosteroid-binding globulin, CBG), which decrease bioavailability and metabolic clearance (Breuner & Orchinik, 2002). Adding further complexity is the fact that the proportion of bound cortisol may vary with cortisol levels or other physiological conditions, Moreover, CBG binding may enhance bioavailability under some conditions, as it represents a releasable cortisol reservoir (Breuner & Orchinik, 2002). Because plasma cortisol reflects both the free and bound fractions, this measure may not provide the most valid index of cortisol tissue bioactivity under all conditions, despite the fact that plasma levels are often considered the gold standard of cortisol measures.

As illustrated by the solid arrows in Figure 12.6, plasma cortisol represents only one metric of HPAC activity. With regard to the issue of bound vs. unbound cortisol, salivary cortisol levels offer the advantage of indexing only the unbound fraction. This is because CBG and other proteins do not readily diffuse across cellular membranes. Consequently, protein-bound cortisol does not readily enter the salivary glands, and salivary cortisol levels reflect primarily the unbound fraction of plasma cortisol. Salivary cortisol levels are also noninvasive and can be obtained under a wider range of experimental conditions, including ambulatory studies. Although the time constant of cortisol diffusion into salivary glands tends to dampen pulsatile patterns somewhat, salivary cortisol can still show short-term pulse-related fluctuations. Time required to acquire an assayable saliva sample also tends to blunt, but does not eliminate, short-term fluctuations. Consequently, the time sampling issues raised

earlier for plasma cortisol levels also apply to salivary cortisol measures.

A measure of cortisol can be derived also from urine. Urinary cortisol reflects the free, unbound fraction of plasma cortisol, as protein-bound cortisol does not readily enter the renal tubular system. Cortisol accumulates in the urine in proportion to plasma free-cortisol levels, and because of the general stability of this molecule, collection of urinary output can provide an integral index of cortisol over extended (including daily) periods.

There is considerable debate as to what constitutes the best measure of HPAC activity, and there may be no single answer to this question. Rather, the validity of a measure may be defined by the problem under study. Urinary measures integrated over a day or more may be most relevant for studies of chronic stress. In contrast, shorter term measures such as those from plasma or saliva may be more useful for studies of acute stress or circadian rhythms.

Reciprocal influences between neurobehavioral and HPAC systems. In accord with the principle of Reciprocal Determinism, the HPAC system offers an illustration of the multiple interactions between neuroendocrine systems, neurobehavioral substrates, and psychological processes. Although physical stressors are known activators of the HPAC system (Selye, 1956), psychological stressors are among the most potent (Mason, 1968, 1975; McEwen, 2000). It is also clear that HPAC activity can impact both cognitive and emotional processes (e.g., Lupien & McEwen, 1997; Parker et al., 2003). Psychological states can alter HPAC activity, and HPAC activity can modulate the psychological states that gave rise to this activity. These reciprocal actions can be dose and context dependent. Glucocorticoid administration can either enhance or impair cognitive processes, as a function of dose, context, and the specific receptor populations activated (Lupien & McEwen, 1997).

Some of the complexity of these effects relate to the multiple reciprocal interactions within the HPAC system (e.g., CRH and cortisol feedback) and between the HPAC and psychological processes (e.g., stress and cortisol). Reciprocally interacting systems are difficult to study and characterize in isolation, as

their functional outputs represent a close interplay across levels of organization. Consequently, manipulations at one point may have diverse effects throughout these circuits. The central CRH system, in addition to its regulation of pituitary ACTH release, is considered to be a general orchestrator of the cognitive, affective, behavioral, autonomic, and neuroendocrine aspects of stress. Local intracerebroventricular infusions of CRH in primates results in an activation of stress-related brain circuits, induces anxiety- and depressive-like reactions, and decreases social interactions (Strome et al., 2002). Because glucocorticoid administration alters central CRH activity, it is not immediately apparent whether the effects of this manipulation reveal the direct actions of glucocorticoids or indirect effects on CRH systems. Dissecting reciprocally interacting systems requires multiple experimental approaches and converging data that can provide a more comprehensive perspective than a more restricted analyses. Because interactions may never be known by studying hormonal systems in isolation, the *corollary of interdependence* asserts that the most meaningful studies will entail manipulations and observations of both CRH and cortisol, involving a combination of methods.

Social psychological influences and the corollary of interdependence. Relations across levels are particularly difficult to conceptualize when the reciprocally interacting nodes extend across broad spans of organization or analysis, as the complexity of mappings tends to increase across more distal levels. A recent line of research in psychoneuroimmunology illustrates this. It has long been recognized that psychological stressors are potent activators of the HPAC system (Mason, 1968, 1975; McEwen, 2000). In contrast to the general adaptation model of Selye (1956), it further appears that there may be fundamental differences in kind among physical and social–psychological stressors. Social reorganization stress in mice (rotation of alpha males among housing colonies) can lead to reactivation of herpes simplex Type 1 virus (HSV1), similar to the stress-related HSV1 reactivation that causes cold sores in humans (Padgett et al., 1998). In contrast, physical stressors (e.g., restraint-stress or shock) are ineffective despite producing comparable glucocor-

ticoid levels. Subsequent work has revealed further unique characteristics of social stressors, highlighting the need for multilevel research and mandating expansion and refinements in the concept of stress and the nature of stressors.

Subsequent studies revealed that social stressors in mice are associated with an exaggerated and often lethal inflammatory response to influenza virus, compared to restraint stress (Sheridan, Stark, Avitsur, & Padgett, 2000). The difference between the social and the physical stressors could not be accounted for by differences in secretion of anti-inflammatory glucocorticoids, because both classes of stressors again yielded comparable glucocorticoid levels. Rather, it appears that social stress induced a state of glucocorticoid resistance or receptor insensitivity attributable to an impairment in nuclear translocation of the glucocorticoid/receptor complex in specific macrophages of socially stressed animals (Quan et al., 2003). As a result, glucocorticoids failed to suppress the actions of a transcription factor (NF-kappaB), which promotes the production of pro-inflammatory cytokines (interleukin 1 and tumor-necrotizing factor alpha). In this research, a bridge was established between social processes and gene expression in the health effects of stress.

These examples illustrate the principle of Reciprocal Determinism and its Corollary of Interdependence. Multilevel studies can elucidate influences across levels of organization and clarify relations that could not be known by studies limited to a single level of analysis.

Loneliness and Health: Nonadditive Determinism

The utility of multilevel analysis to understanding psychological processes and psychosomatic relations is illustrated by our recent work on loneliness. Social isolation and loneliness are potent but little understood risk factors for broad-based morbidity and mortality (Seeman, 2000). Although loneliness has a heritable component, differences in social cognition provide a better explanation for the physiological characteristics of lonely versus nonlonely individuals than does a model based on invariant traits or genetic determinism. Lonely individuals tend to construe their world, including the behavior

of others, as punitive or potentially punitive. Consequently, lonely individuals are more likely to be socially anxious and to adopt a prevention focus rather than a promotion focus in their social interactions (Ernst & Cacioppo, 1999). Lonely individuals are more likely to appraise stressors as threats rather than challenges and to cope in a passive, isolative fashion rather than an active fashion that includes seeking the help and support of others. These differences in social cognition predictably result in an increased likelihood of lonely individuals acting in self-protective and, paradoxically, self-defeating ways (Cacioppo, Berntson, et al., 2000).

From the dual clues that isolation and loneliness are associated with broad-based mortality and with a higher death rate across the adult life span, one can surmise that the underlying mechanism operates on a wide range of bodily systems, or that there is more than one mechanism through which loneliness influences health. In the absence of lower level analyses, however, the relations between loneliness and health remain mere empirical associations. Recent evidence suggests that different transduction pathways account for acute effects of loneliness on morbidity and mortality (e.g., suicide) and chronic effects (e.g., heart diseases, cancers). Two of the neurobehavioral mechanisms that contribute to the association between loneliness and chronic disease are (a) catabolic processes—lonely individuals perceive more hassles and stressors in daily life and are characterized by higher tonic levels of peripheral resistance in the cardiovascular system, which over time may have damaging effects on body organs and systems; and (b) anabolic processes—lonely individuals show physiological repair and maintenance processes (e.g., wound healing, sleep) that are less efficient than nonlonely individuals (Cacioppo, Hawkley, & Berntson, 2003).

A variety of autonomic differences have been found to distinguish lonely and nonlonely individuals. The bivariate model of autonomic control outlined previously represents a significant advance in our understanding of higher neural influences on autonomic substrates, considerably clarifies psychophysiological relations, and increases the fidelity of mappings from psychological processes to autonomic cardiac control.

Characterization of response modes. As discussed earlier, pharmacological blockade analyses represent a gold standard for the quantification of patterns of sympathetic and parasympathetic control of end organs such as the heart. Blockade analyses are not always possible, however, so noninvasive measures are desirable. Noninvasive measures of parasympathetic and sympathetic control have now been validated, at least for the heart.

Respiratory sinus arrhythmia (RSA) is a fluctuation in heart rate in phase with respiration, inspiration being associated with an increase in heart rate and expiration with a decrease. RSA arises from pulmonary and thoracic stretch receptor afferents to brain stem reflex substrates that trigger inhibition of vagal outflow and excitation of sympathetic outflow (Berntson, Cacioppo, & Quigley, 1993). Both of these changes synergistically act to increase heart rate, but there are differences in the time constants of the sympathetic and parasympathetic synapses at the cardiac sinoatrial node pacemaker (see Berntson et al., 1997). The consequence of these temporal dynamics is that respiratory rhythms in the parasympathetic cardiac innervation is translated into rhythmical fluctuations in heart rate, whereas the sympathetic synapses are sufficiently slow that respiratory fluctuations are filtered out. Respiratory rhythms in heart rate thus reflect vagal cardiac control, with larger fluctuations associated with higher vagal tone (Berntson et al., 1993). RSA has been repeatedly validated as an index of vagal control of the heart, with some caveats (see Berntson et al., 1997; Berntson, Cacioppo, Binkley, et al., 1994; Cacioppo et al., 1994).

An additional noninvasive measure, pre-ejection period (PEP) is available to index sympathetic control of the heart. Pre-ejection period is the time between the electrical invasion of the ventricular myocardium (Q wave of the EKG) to the opening of the aortic valve and the onset of ventricular ejection. The pre-ejection period is a standard marker of ventricular myocardial contractility, as more forceful myocardial contractions result in the more rapid rise of intraventricular pressure and hence earlier ventricular ejection. A decrease in PEP thus indicates an increase in contractility. The sympathetic innervation enhances myocardial contractil-

ity, whereas the parasympathetic system plays only a minor role. Consequently, variations in sympathetic control yield corresponding changes in contractility and inverse changes in PEP. With appropriate controls and caveats, PEP has been validated as an index of sympathetic cardiac control (Berntson, Cacioppo, Binkley, et al., 1994b; Cacioppo et al., 1994).

Through a combination of measurements and calculations, additional parameters of cardiodynamic and hemodynamic processes can be derived noninvasively. Heart rate (HR) and stroke volume (SV) each has sympathetic and parasympathetic contributions, and together these parameters determine cardiac output (CO) or the amount of blood expelled by the heart into the vascular system each minute (i.e., CO = HR*SV). Blood pressure, which must be maintained within relatively narrow ranges to maintain adequate circulation, is a function of the cardiac output and total peripheral resistance (TPR; the resistance to blood flow through the circulatory system). Systolic and diastolic blood pressure (SBP and DBP, respectively) can be measured noninvasively, and mean arterial pressure (MAP) can be calculated from these measures (e.g., MAP = .33*SBP + .67*DBP). TPR, therefore, can be calculated from MAP and CO (i.e., TPR = BP/CO).

Psychophysiological patterns in loneliness. In the pursuit of psychophysiological mappings across levels of organization and analysis, the corollary of proximity specifies that the complexity of mapping generally increases across more disparate levels. Consequently, simple isomorphic relations between events or processes are less likely to hold across more disparate levels of organization. Rather, relations across levels may need to consider patterns of multivector mappings to achieve more isomorphic mappings. Work on loneliness highlights this issue.

The cardiovascular autonomic features of lonely individuals do not organize simply on a single sympathetic–parasympathetic dimension. Lonely and nonlonely *young* adults have comparable blood pressure, but the underlying physiology differs between these groups: lonely individuals have been found to be characterized by higher total peripheral resistance and lower cardiac output than nonlonely individuals.

This difference is equally apparent at rest (baseline) as when performing orthostatic or psychological stressors (Cacioppo, Hawkley, Crawford, et al., 2002), and ambulatory recordings further revealed that this difference is evident not only in the laboratory but also during a typical day in their lives (Hawkley, Burleson, Berntson, & Cacioppo, 2003). These physiological differences and their links to health would go unrecognized with measures of blood pressure alone, which highlights the importance of theoretical systems that aid in the selection of appropriate measures to effectively bridge across levels.

Chronic elevations in total peripheral resistance not only mean that the heart muscle must work harder to distribute the same amount of blood through the circulatory system, but the reduced diameter of the blood vessels may also increase turbulence in and potential damage to the vasculature. Both central (e.g., baroreceptor reflex) and peripheral (e.g., vascular elasticity) mechanisms may degrade over time, further diminishing the ability to maintain normotensive pressure even during rest. Consistently elevated levels of vascular resistance, coupled with age-related decreases in vascular compliance, may set the stage for the development of hypertension. A study of older adults in a south Chicago apartment development confirmed this hypothesis. Because the sample size was relatively small, participants were categorized into low or high lonely groups by a median split on their scores on the UCLA loneliness scale. Results indicated that age was positively and significantly correlated with systolic blood pressure among lonely individuals, whereas there were no age-related increases in systolic blood pressure among nonlonely individuals.

Corollary of asymmetry. The patterns of neuroendocrine and autonomic control in lonely individuals are not intuitively obvious, but may have substantial basic and health significance. Further studies will be necessary to elucidate the neurophysiological and neurobehavioral origins of these patterns, and their health implications. Both of these efforts will require multilevel analyses, through which information at multiple levels can provide converging perspectives and insights. There is no single level of analysis that would permit meaningful pur-

suit of these questions. Moreover, there is no single level that can be universally assumed to be preeminent in multilevel analyses. On the other hand, the levels of organization and analysis cannot be viewed as "equivalent," and conceptualizations of the relationships among levels are not simply a matter of preference. Rather, there is a fundamental asymmetry across levels in multilevel research.

The most optimal approach may be to conceptually guide research by the data and constructs deriving from the level that confers the greatest organization on the problem. For the question of how social stress impacts glucocorticoid resistance, for example, the most useful organizing level of organization and analysis may revolve around neuroimmune systems. In contrast, for the question as to physiological features of loneliness, the more salient level of analysis may be the psychosocial. Indeed, the organization in the literature is apparent only by parsing populations on the dimension of loneliness. In the absence of that, the lawful variance associated with loneliness would be relegated to the error term, and there would be no way of identifying this source of variance based on physiological studies alone.

This discussion is not intended to foster largely meaningless debates as to the "ultimate" level of analysis, nor is it intended to deny reductionism or support substitutionism. Rather, the organizing level of analysis is that which serves most effectively to structure knowledge and guide research and theory. In the case of loneliness, there is a natural asymmetry, with preeminence of the social psychological level that defines the primary conceptual dimension. This does not imply that the research and findings of this level of analysis are any more important that those of other levels, as all are required. Moreover, the optimal level of analysis may change over time, as constructs at the social-psychological level come to be implemented or integrated at lower levels, whereby the focus of research may shift to a lower level.

The corollary of asymmetry asserts that the optimal level of analysis for guiding research and theory may be that at which the major conceptual dimensions are implemented or realized. Studies of the relations between physical stress and disease may not necessarily need to appeal to the social-psychological level of organization, at least not initially. Social-psychological processes are likely important modulators of such relations, however, as social relations have been shown to be important moderator variables in stress-immune relations. This is an illustration of where a shift in focus toward higher levels of organization and analysis may be as informative as a reductionistic shift toward lower levels.

SUMMARY

Cross-disciplinary, multilevel research is an increasingly salient feature of contemporary science in general and of psychology in particular. It is a trend that will undoubtedly continue. Realization of the full potential of the explosive developments within neurosciences, genetics, and molecular biology will require the integration of this information within the broader knowledge base concerning higher level behavioral, cognitive, and social psychological domains. It may appear to be a rather daunting task to integrate, for example, cellular biology with social psychology, but it is a task that must be accomplished. The principles of multiple determinism, reciprocal determinism, and nonadditive determinism, together with their corollaries, offer some strategic guidelines to organize such efforts. The ultimate goal of this enterprise is not to obliterate social sciences in a puff of *substitutionism*, but rather to promote meaningful *reductionism* and *extensionism* so that knowledge and constructs at multiple levels of organization and analysis can mutually inform, elucidate, and constrain theory and research at other levels. This goal may never be finalized, but it is already apparent that keen insights and important scientific developments can be derived from multilevel research approaches and interdisciplinary theoretical systems that can integrates information across levels of organization and analysis.

CHAPTER 13

BRAIN IMAGING AND RELATED METHODS

David H. Zald and Clayton Curtis

Modern neuroimaging techniques enable researchers to noninvasively assess brain structure and function in humans. The knowledge gained from these techniques has led to a revolution in our understanding of brain–behavior relationships and has dramatically altered the psychological sciences. Several brain imaging techniques are currently in wide use, including computerized tomography (CT), magnetic resonance imaging (MRI), positron emission tomography (PET), single photon emission computed tomography (SPECT), magnetoencephalography (MEG), and near infrared optical imaging. In this chapter we focus on functional MRI (fMRI) and PET techniques because of their enormous impact on the psychological sciences. Although they are most often used in isolation, both PET and fMRI are adaptable to a multitrait–multimethod (MTMM) approach toward assessment. Indeed, it may be argued that these techniques require integration within a broad multimethod framework if they are to reach their full scientific potential. This chapter provides a brief primer on fMRI and PET imaging, followed by a discussion of the benefits of placing neuroimaging data within a MTMM approach.

Depending on the specific technique used, PET and MRI scanners can assess a number of different statewise and traitwise characteristics of the brain. These include measurement of brain structure (MRI), neurotransmitter functioning (PET and magnetic resonance spectroscopy [MRS]), glucose metabolism (PET), blood oxygenation (PET and fMRI), and blood flow (PET and fMRI). Because

changes in neural activity are accompanied by changes in metabolism, blood oxygenation, and blood flow (Raichle, 1988), PET and fMRI measurements of these physiological variables allow researchers to index changes in brain functioning in relationship to specific perceptual, cognitive, and behavioral tasks. However, PET and fMRI take very different approaches to these measurements. It therefore is useful to first discuss how these measurements are made in each technique.

fMRI PHYSICS AND PHYSIOLOGY

When biological tissue is placed within a strong externally applied magnetic field, denoted B_0, the axis of individual nuclei, like hydrogen, tend to align with the field. Nuclei line up with the field because this results in the lowest energy state of the system. Outside the magnetic field, the alignment of all nuclei tends to be randomly oriented and produce no net magnetic field. However, when placed in a strong magnetic field, the nuclei align in the same direction as the field. This alignment produces a net magnetization, referred to as M, which represents the sum of all of the magnetic moments of the individual hydrogen nuclei (see Haake, Brown, Thompson, & Venkatesan, 1999, for a full review of MRI physics).

Hydrogen nuclei consist of a single positively charged particle, the proton, which spins around its axis. An individual proton not only spins around its axis, but also precesses (revolves) about the external magnetic field, much like a top both

spins around its axis and precesses about the direction of gravity's magnetic field. Importantly, each type of atomic nuclei precesses at a characteristic frequency, the resonance or *Larmor frequency*, which is directly proportional to the strength of the applied magnetic field. This proportional dependence of the resonance frequency on the applied magnetic field forms the basis for MRI. Specifically, by spatially manipulating the field strength and measuring resonance frequencies, it becomes possible to resolve the source and location of signals from the brain.

When all the nuclei in a sample are at the resting equilibrium state, the net magnetization of the nuclei are aligned with the field, and no MR signal can be detected because each of the nuclei precesses at the same rate, but out of phase with one another. Magnetic resonance occurs when a radiofrequency (RF) pulse is transmitted to the sample at the Larmor frequency of a specific type of nuclei. For instance, hydrogen (H) precesses at a frequency of 64 MHz in a 1.5 Tesla (T) magnetic field (standard clinical scanners possess a 1.5 T field strength, whereas research dedicated scanners often use higher field strengths, such as 3 T, 4 T, or even 7 T). When an RF pulse is applied at the Larmor frequency of H, energy is selectively absorbed by H nuclei, exciting their spins from their lower resting state to an unstable higher energy state. The RF pulse also deflects the net magnetization of the nuclei away from the direction of the external magnetic field and causes each precessing nuclei to precess in phase with one another (i.e., they become phase coherent). At the point in time when the RF field is extinguished, the nuclei are in an excited, high-energy state because the axes of their small magnetic fields are not oriented with that of the strong external field. This unstable state decays quickly as the nuclei begin to realign with the external field. The precessing nuclei radiate the energy that they absorbed from the RF pulse as the phase coherence exponentially decays and the net magnetization of the nuclei realign with the external magnetic field. The energy that is emitted during this brief process induces a detectable current (known as the free induction decay or FID) and is detectable

by an RF coil placed around the stimulated sample (i.e., the subject's head). This is the MR signal and forms the basis of all MRI techniques.

When the application of the RF energy is terminated, the system reapproaches equilibrium, a process known as *relaxation*. Different types of tissue have different rates of relaxation, which is why we can obtain MR images that can distinguish between gray and white matter, bone, cerebrospinal fluid, and vasculature. For most functional MRI studies, the critical source of contrast derives from changes in the oxygen content of cerebral vasculature, typically referred to as *Blood Oxygen Level Dependent* (BOLD) signal (Bandettini, Wong, Hinks, Tikofsky, & Hyde, 1992; Kwong et al., 1992; Ogawa, Lee, Kay, & Tank, 1990; Ogawa et al., 1992).

The BOLD Signal

The fMRI signal is a function of the metabolic demands of local neural activity. However, the coupling between the measured BOLD signal and the underlying neural activity is neither direct nor straightforward (Heeger & Ress, 2002; Logothetis, Pauls, Augath, Trinath, & Oeltermann, 2001). As neural activity increases, there are changes in both the amount of blood flow to the region and a change in the concentration of oxygenated and deoxygenated forms of hemoglobin. The oxy- and deoxyhemoglobin have different magnetic properties (diamagnetic vs. paramagnetic) and because of this behave differently within a magnetic field. The paramagnetic properties of deoxyhemoglobin lead it to have a greater interaction with the magnetic field than oxyhemoglobin such that shifts in the concentration of oxy- and deoxyhemoglobin cause changes in the MR signal. Specifically, as the concentration of oxyhemoglobin increases in response to neural metabolic demands, the BOLD signal increases. Importantly, the BOLD signal does not convey an *absolute* value—it is only a *relative* measure. Therefore, one rarely sees attempts to compare the BOLD signal between individuals. Instead, research focuses on the location and magnitude of relative changes in BOLD during different task conditions.

There are three characteristic phases of the hemodynamic response to a neural event (Figure 13.1a).

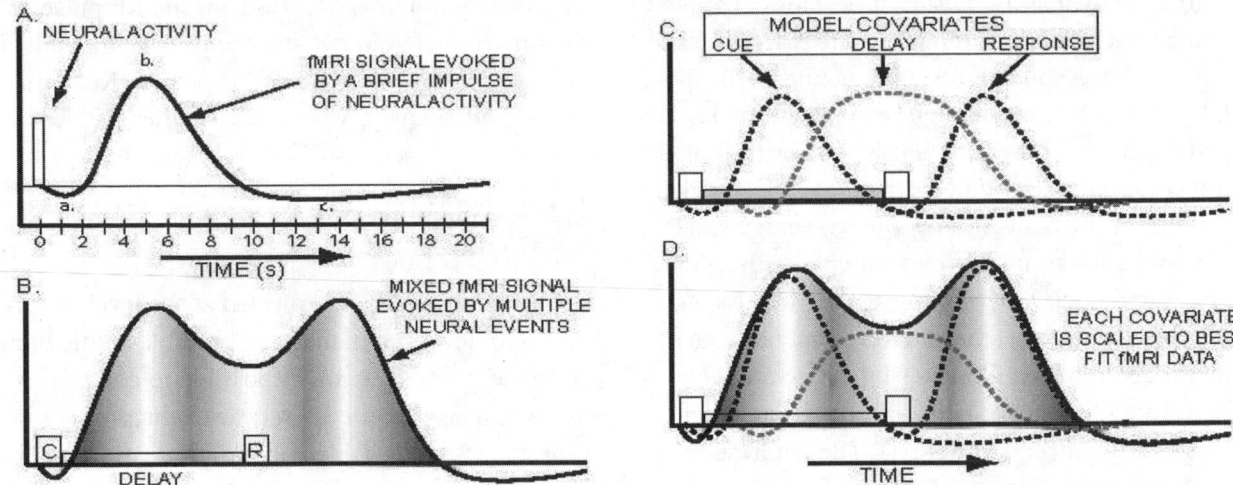

FIGURE 13.1. Modeling fMRI signals. A. In response to a single brief impulse of neural activity, the fMRI BOLD response lags the neural activity by about 5 seconds and is characterized by 3 epochs: a) the initial dip, b) the positive hemodynamic response, and c) the postresponse undershoot. B. Hypothetical neural activity during a delayed-response task, where C is a cue to be remembered, and R is the response occurring after an imposed delay. The evoked fMRI BOLD response involves a mixture of signals emanating from more than one time and more than one trial component. The gradient under the curve schematically represents the mixing or temporal overlap of the various signal components. Whiter regions reflect purer (less colinear) BOLD signal, and darker regions reflect highly colinear signal. For example, the white region at the peak of the first hump is almost exclusively evoked from neural processing during the cue phase of the task. However, just a few seconds later, in the darker portion just to the right, the signal is a mixture of processing at the cue phase and the beginning of the delay period. C. To resolve the individual components of the mixed fMRI signal, ideal hemodynamic response functions (which take into account the lag and spread of the BOLD response) are used to model within-trial components. In this case, a separate covariate is used to model the cue, delay, and response phase of the trial. D. The covariates are entered into the modified GLM of the fMRI time-series data, and a least-squares procedure is used to derive parameter estimates (i.e., beta values) that scale with the degree to which a given covariate accounts for the variance in the observed data. For example, the height of the delay covariate can be used as an index of the amount of delay-period activity.

First, in response to transient increases in neuronal oxygen consumption, the BOLD signal decreases because the ratio of oxy-/deoxyhemoglobin in blood decreases. This transient decrease has been termed the *initial dip* and is currently under increased scrutiny because it may provide greater spatial localization than subsequent responses (Ugurbil et al., 1999; Yacoub & Hu, 2001). Second, a large increase in signal above baseline is observed beginning approximately 2 seconds and peaking 4 to 6 seconds after the onset of a brief impulse of neural activity (the precise latency and time course of the response can vary depending on the individual, the brain region, or the length of the neural activation; Aguirre, Zarahn, & D'Esposito, 1998; Buckner,

1998). This increase is caused by a local increase in blow flow that actually overcompensates for the amount of oxygen consumed. Thus, the ratio of oxy-/deoxyhemoglobin increases in the vasculature near the site of neural activity. Most fMRI studies primarily focus on this positive phase. Finally, there is a decrease in signal that most often falls below baseline and can require tens of seconds to return to baseline.

Echo Planar Imaging

In a completely uniform magnetic field, the spatial location of the measured MR signal cannot be determined. However, by temporarily imposing a separate magnetic field that varies linearly across a

volume, known as a *gradient*, it becomes possible to temporarily alter the strength of the external magnetic field in a spatially specific manner. This *spatial encoding* is achieved by the application of gradient fields in three dimensions at critical times in relation to the RF pulse. Gradients affect which portions of the brain receive the RF energy (*slice selection gradient, z-direction*), the phase in which the excited nuclei are precessing (*phase encoding gradient, y-direction*), and the frequency in which the excited nuclei are precessing at the time that the emitted RF energy is reradiated (*frequency or "read-out" gradient, x-direction*). The application of these gradients allows for the transformation of an acquired free induction decay signal into an image in Cartesian space, where the matrix size of the volume is a function of the number of steps in the three gradients. For example, if an image was created using 20 *z*, 128 *y*, and 128 *x* encoding steps, it would result in a volume of 20 slices containing 128 × 128 pixels or voxels on each slice (a pixel refers to a distinguishable square of information within a two-dimensional image, whereas a voxel corresponds to a box of information in a three-dimensional image).

The type of information that is obtained by an MRI scan depends on how and when magnetic gradients and RF pulses are applied (commonly referred to as the pulse sequence). Fast echo planar imaging (EPI) is by far the most dominant pulse sequence technique used for fMRI (Buxton, 2002; Jezzard, Matthews, & Smith, 2001; Moonen & Bandettini, 1999). EPI differs from other standard imaging methods in that it acquires multislice volumes of MR images very rapidly. It does this by applying a rapid cycling phase encoding gradient where all the phase encoding steps are done in a single *repetition time* (TR) after a single RF pulse. In contrast, more traditional structural MRI techniques apply a single phase encoding gradient step per TR. Depending on the slice thickness and matrix size, fMRI studies using EPI may obtain whole brain coverage every 1 to 3 seconds, (TR = 1–3 s). A number of alternative pulse sequences, such as spin echo or spiral sequences, can be used to detect changes in BOLD signal (Haacke et al., 1999; Noll, Cohen, Meyer, & Schneider, 1995). These techniques vary in terms of aspects of the RF pulse or the ordering of gradient steps and have both advantages and disadvantages relative to EPI (Kennan, 1999; Noll, Stenger, Vazquez, & Peltier, 1999).

FMRI EXPERIMENTAL DESIGN AND ANALYSIS

Because images can be collected at the level of seconds (TR for a single slice can be < 1 s, whole brain coverage < 3 s), it becomes possible to collect hundreds of images consecutively, with the primary limiting factors being subject to fatigue or movement over time, or hardware processing constraints. This allows a wide range of study designs. The prototypical fMRI experimental design involves a "boxcar" in which two behavioral tasks alternate over the course of a scanning session, and the fMRI signal between the two tasks or between a task and a resting condition is compared. In the most typical application of this *block* design, subjects will perform multiple trials of the stimulation (i.e., experimental) task (say for 20 seconds) and then multiple trials of the control task (say for the next 20 seconds), and these conditions will repeatedly alternate over time. The primary analysis essentially involves a subtraction in which one condition is subtracted from the other.

Event-related designs provide the primary alternative to the block design (Buckner et al., 1996; D'Esposito, Zarahn, & Aguirre, 1999). In these studies, individual trials are treated as discrete events, rather than being grouped together as a block of trial. The trials can either be performed in a temporally discrete manner, such that the hemodynamic response is allowed to return to baseline between each trial, or trials can be performed in a manner in which the hemodynamic responses temporally overlap, but are separated enough that the responses can be modeled in relation to a reference function. If responses have significant temporal overlap, as is the case with rapid event-related designs, successful estimation of the evoked hemodynamic responses rely on random presentation of stimuli (i.e., trial Type A is followed by Type B as often as B is followed by A) and highly jittered intertrial-interval durations (Buckner et al., 1996).

Block designs have an advantage over event-related designs in that they provide strong signal detection characteristics over relatively brief times (a single functional scan on the level of 4–7 minutes is often sufficient to detect a substantial BOLD change) (Liu, Frank, Wong, & Buxton, 2001). However, the interpretational power of this design is limited because it cannot disambiguate differential contributions of events occurring within a block or trial (see Figure 13.1b). As described following, event-related designs provide a far more powerful tool in separating the different components of a task.

Consider a spatial delayed response task. The task has three main epochs; a cue period where stimuli to be remembered are presented (say the location of a briefly appearing dot), an unfilled retention period where the location of the dot must be retained in memory, and finally a response period where a memory-guided response is required (say a saccade to the remembered location). In a typical block design, a control condition (not requiring maintenance but attempting to control for other sensory and motor features) is subtracted from the delayed response condition. Because the requirements of the experimental and control tasks have similar visual and motor attributes, but differ in the attribute of interest (i.e., maintenance of the location), subtracting these two blocks is reasoned to yield areas active during memory maintenance. The inferential framework of *cognitive subtraction* attributes differences in neural activity between the two tasks to the specific cognitive process (i.e., maintenance; Friston et al., 1996; Posner, Petersen, Fox, & Raichle, 1988). However, the assumptions required for this method may not always hold (Zarahn, Aguirre, & D'Esposito, 1999) and could produce erroneous interpretation of functional neuroimaging data. Cognitive subtraction relies on the assumption of *pure insertion*—that a cognitive process can be added to a preexisting set of cognitive processes without altering the other processes. If pure insertion fails as an assumption, then a difference in the BOLD signal between the two tasks might be observed, not because a specific cognitive process was engaged in one block and not the other, but because the added cognitive process and the preexisting cognitive processes interact.

Continuing with our delayed-response example, the insertion of a maintenance requirement may directly impact the other encoding and retrieval/response processes (e.g., visual encoding; why encode the cue if it will not be used to guide the response made after the delay?). The result is a failure to meet the assumption of cognitive subtraction. Thus, inferences drawn from the results of such blocked experiments may fail to specifically isolate maintenance-related activity.

Event-related designs allow researchers to statistically disambiguate the hemodynamic signals specifically related to encoding the cue stimulus and generating memory-guided responses from the maintenance-related activity present in the retention interval (Aguirre & D'Esposito, 1999). Event-related designs model each component of the trial independently (e.g., cue, delay, and response; see Figures 13.1c and 13.1d). Task designs are often complicated due to the sluggish hemodynamic response, but are feasible as long as different components of the task are temporally varied in relation to each other so that separate aspects of the task can be modeled. Such designs allow separate identification of brain regions involved in encoding spatial locations, maintaining that information across the retention interval, and making the memory-guided response. The ability to model maintenance separately from other task components thus makes it possible to avoid assumptions of pure insertion.

Image Preprocessing

Analysis of fMRI data (or PET data) is almost never performed without first preprocessing the raw data. These preprocessing steps variably include *temporal filtering* to remove signal jitter across adjacent scans, removal of linear trends in signal intensity, *spatial filtering* (also called spatial smoothing), filtering to remove sources of periodic signal fluctuation related to vascular pulsation or breathing, *intrasubject spatial alignment* to remove movement across scans, and *coregistration* of BOLD data to the subject's structural MRI to allow visualization of the images. Finally, *intersubject alignment* and *warping* (resizing) to a common stereotactic space are frequently performed. This final stage allows group statistical analyses on a voxelwise basis, but comes

at the cost of spatial resolution and an understanding of individual variability (Brett, Johnsrude, & Owen, 2002).

Statistical Analysis

A wide range of techniques has been applied to look at changes in brain activity (Lange, 1999), with most using some variant of the *general linear model* (GLM; Friston et al., 1994). The change in BOLD signal intensity over time represents the dependent variable in fMRI studies. Typically, a reference time series is created that denotes what type of event and when it happened during a scanning session. This time series is then convolved with a standard or empirically derived hemodynamic response function (which incorporates the sluggish nature of the hemodynamic response) yielding a suitable estimate or model of the predicted BOLD signal. Each of the independent variables (e.g., different types of task events) is represented by a set of covariates that are shaped like hemodynamic responses and are shifted in time to account for the lag. These can be either categorical variables (such as presence or absence of a task demand) or quantitative variables (such as number of stimuli presented at a time). The covariates are entered into the modified GLM with the fMRI time-series data, and a least-squares procedure is used to derive parameter estimates (i.e., beta values) that scale with the degree to which a given covariate accounts for the variance in the observed data. Similar to traditional statistical methods, these parameter estimates, when normalized by estimates of noise, are used to compute inferential statistics such as *t* values or F-statistics. These inferential statistics are calculated on a voxel-by-voxel (voxelwise) basis to create statistical parametric brain maps.

Some researchers alternatively perform analyses based on structurally defined regions of interests. This can have advantages when investigators have a specific hypothesis about a specific brain region. However, most investigators prefer a voxelwise approach because it is not constrained by preconceived ideas regarding the volume or location of expected activations. The primary drawback with the voxelwise approach involves the large number of voxels in the brain, causing a high risk of Type I statistical error. Thus one needs to perform an adjustment for the number of independent comparisons in each analysis. Because neighboring voxels are correlated and there exists temporal autocorrelation over time, it is overconservative to apply a simple Bonferroni correction to these data sets. Instead, investigators typically apply corrections based on an estimate of the number of independent resolution elements (RESELs) or adjust the degrees of freedom to account for the nonuniformity in the noise. For instance, an estimate may be made for the number of independent spatial resolution elements by correcting the total size of the volume of interest by the Full-Width at Half-Maximum estimate of spatial resolution (Worsley et al., 1996).

In addition to looking at individual activations, increased attention is being paid to the functional relationships between different brain regions (Mesulam, 1990). Because most psychological phenomena are not mediated by single brain regions, but instead involve networks of brain regions, it becomes essential to understand how these brain regions interact, when their activity is functionally coupled or uncoupled, and the extent to which these changes in functional connectivity are related to experimental variables of interest. Toward this end, researchers have used a number of strategies, ranging from correlation analysis to principle components analysis and structural equation modeling (McIntosh, 1999).

PET PHYSICS AND PHYSIOLOGY

Functional neuroimaging with PET predates the development of fMRI. PET imaging takes advantage of the fact that unstable elements (such as ^{15}O, ^{11}C, or ^{18}F, which possess too few neutrons relative to protons) go through a rapid process of decay involving the release of a positron (positively charged electron) from the nucleus. Once released, the positron collides with an electron, which causes the annihilation of both the electron and the positron and the production of two high-energy (511 keV) photons that travel at 180° from each other (see Figure 13.2). PET cameras consist of rings of crystals that produce light scintillation

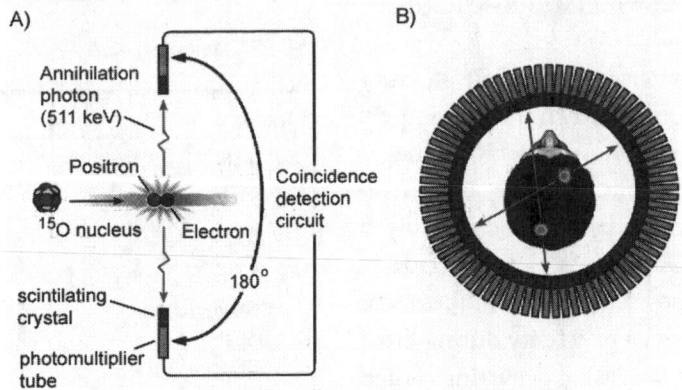

FIGURE 13.2. Measurement of positron emissions. A) An unstable ^{15}0 nucleus emits a positron that collides with an electron, releasing a pair of high-energy 511 keV photons at a 180° angle. The photons are detected by an annihilation photon detector, which is comprised of crystals that scintillate when struck by a photon and photomultiplier tubes that transform the light emitted by the crystals into an electrical impulse. When two detectors 180° apart are activated, the coincidence is registered and sent on for signal processing and image reconstruction. B) Rings of annihilation photon detectors are arrayed around a subject's head. PET scanners have multiple rings arrayed in parallel, allowing multislice data collection. Detection of coincident scintillations at 180° angles within a ring (in 2-D imaging) or across rings (in 3-D imaging) allows identification of the approximate location from which the positron emitting radiotracer is located. Figure from pages 62 and 63 of *Images of Mind* by Michael I. Posner and Marcus E. Raichle. Copyright 1994, 1997 by Scientific American Library. Reprinted by permission of Henry Holt and Company, LLC.

when penetrated by photons (Raichle, 1983). This scintillation is then converted to electrical impulses that can be amplified and analyzed. Within the crystals' range of sensitivity, there exists a direct relationship between the concentration of radiotracer present in a brain region and the level of photon detections arising from that region.

PET allows assessment of multiple aspects of brain functioning depending on the radiotracer used. Importantly, PET can be used to measure regional cerebral blood flow (rCBF). Recall that when neurons in a brain region become active, they increase their oxygen consumption, which is compensated for by a substantial increase in rCBF (Figure 13.1a). This increase in blood flow exceeds the oxygen consumption demanded by the neurons,

making rCBF a particularly robust index of regional neural activity (Fox & Raichle, 1986; Fox, Raichle, Mintun, & Dence, 1988). When unstable ^{15}0 is attached to H_2, it can be injected directly into the bloodstream. Once in the bloodstream, $H_2{}^{15}0$ will travel wherever the blood travels, such that areas with the highest levels of rCBF will emit the most positrons (Herscovitch, Markham, & Raichle, 1983). Thus, by measuring ^{15}0 positron emissions, we can index neural activity. Indeed, the measurement of rCBF with ^{15}O PET represents a far more simple and direct index of neural activity than the BOLD response, which is influenced by several different features of the hemodynamic response (i.e., blood volume, flow rate, and oxyhemoglobin–deoxyhemoglobin ratios). The directness of the

relationship also makes PET less sensitive to some of the artifacts associated with fMRI discussed at greater length later.

The temporal window measured in PET studies is directly linked to the speed at which the radiotracer decays. To get adequate signal-to-noise ratios, the detected positron annihilations are aggregated over time. With ^{15}O, which decays rapidly, one typically scans for 30 seconds to 90 seconds to achieve adequate signal-to-noise ratios. The data from these scans thus represents the aggregate of activity during this window, with the largest weighting occurring earlier in the scan when positron emissions are highest (Silbersweig et al., 1993). Therefore, the minimum temporal resolution of ^{15}O PET is on the level of about 30 seconds. In cognitive studies, this dictates that tasks need to Engage Brain regions for a substantial portion of a 30-second to 90-second scan window if they are to produce robust changes in rCBF measurements.

In addition to measuring rCBF, PET can also be used to measure glucose metabolism in the brain, which provides an even more direct index of neural activity. Glucose metabolism is assessed by labeling a deoxygenated form of glucose with ^{18}F. ^{18}F-deoxyglucose (FDG) is injected into the bloodstream, and the FDG is taken up by brain regions in direct proportion to their metabolic demands (Raichle, 1988). In contrast to ^{15}O, the slower decay of ^{18}F requires imaging over substantially longer temporal windows, requiring tasks to be carried on for 20 minutes or longer. Because of this, ^{15}O provides the primary tool for studying brain activations, whereas FDG is more frequently used to make baseline (resting) comparisons between different subject populations.

Radiotracers can also be created by tagging ligands or precursors for various neurotransmitter systems with ^{18}F or ^{11}C (Fowler, Ding, & Volkow, 2003). These radiotracers allow for the assessment of many of the major neurotransmitters systems, providing the ability to detect individual or group differences in neuroreceptor density, transporter density, and even neurotransmitter synthesis (see Table 13.1). This has proved highly useful both for research and, in some cases, clinical diagnosis such

TABLE 13.1

PET Tracers

Tracer	System measured
^{15}O (half life = 2.1 min.)	
H$_2$^{15}O	Blood flow/oxygen extraction fraction
^{15}O–CO$_2$	Blood flow
^{18}F (half life = 109 min.)	
deoxyglucose	Glucose metabolism
Dopa	Dopamine synthesis
Fallypride	Extrastriatal D2 receptors
FLB 457	Extrastriatal D2 receptors
CFT	Dopamine transporter
spiperone	5HT2a receptors
altanserin	5HT2a receptors
setoperone	5HT2a receptors
^{11}C (half life = 20.4 min.)	
raclopride	Striatal D2 receptors
N-methylspiperone	Striatal D2 receptors
cocaine	Dopamine transporter
altropane	Dopamine transporter
SCH23390	Striatal D1 receptors
carfentanil	Mu Opioid receptors
diprenorphine	Opioid receptors
flumazenil	Benzodiazipine receptors
WAY100635	5HT1a receptors
spiperone	5HT2a receptors
MDL100907	5HT2a receptors
McN 5652	Serotonin transporter
ketamine	NMDA receptors

as assessment of the dopaminergic system in patients with Parkinson's disease (Kaasinen & Rinne, 2002).

The binding potential (level at which ligands bind) is affected by factors such as synaptic competition, receptor internalization, and changes in affinity states of receptors following stimulation (Laruelle & Huang, 2001). This allows PET imaging to assess the effects of medications on the functioning of different neurotransmitter systems and has provided insights into the occupancy levels necessary to achieve therapeutic effects (Fowler et al., 1999). Moreover, in some cases it has become possible to examine the degree to which behavioral tasks cause endogenous release of neurotransmitters (Koepp et al., 1998; Zald et al., 2004; Zubieta et al., 2001).

PET EXPERIMENTAL DESIGN AND DATA ANALYSIS

The range of experimental design strategies for PET is limited by the physical constraints associated with delivering and measuring radioisotopes. At a minimum, ^{15}O studies involve an aggregation of activity occurring over 30 seconds or more, and for metabolism and neurotransmitter studies the aggregation covers 20 to 60 minutes. This temporal resolution precludes event-related types of designs and makes it difficult to dissociate the different processes involved in a task. The total number of radiotracer injections (and hence scans) is limited by radiation exposure and the need to allow previously administered radiotracers to decay substantially before starting the next scan (this takes hours for ^{11}C and ^{18}F and about 8 to 10 minutes for ^{15}O). With ^{15}O, one is typically limited to about 12 scans in a 2-hour scanning session, and with ^{18}F and ^{11}C, one is typically limited to 2 to 4 scans (usually scheduled on different days because the subjects would need to spend hours waiting for the isotope to decay between scans). However, because the data in each scan is an aggregate of activity over time, a single contrast between two PET scans can be informative, whereas a contrast between two individual BOLD images (one phase each) has little value.

The most common PET analysis involves a simple subtraction paradigm. As with block designs in fMRI, these analyses are efficient and straightforward, but often depend on the problematic assumption of pure insertion. Parametric designs, where a variable is quantitatively manipulated across different conditions, and factorial designs are also frequently implemented. All of the preceding designs can be analyzed within the framework of the general linear model (Friston et al., 1995). Studies examining the covariance of activity across regions and application of techniques to assess functional connectivity are also possible, although the statistical power to apply such techniques is often restricted by the limited number of scans (Friston, Frith, Liddle, & Frackowiak, 1993; Zald, Dondelinger, & Pardo, 1998).

CONVERGENCE ANALYSIS TO DEAL WITH METHOD VARIANCE WITHIN NEUROIMAGING STUDIES

Although rarely attributed to Campbell and Fiske's pioneering descriptions of the MTMM approach, the core ideas inherent in the MTMM concept can be seen in the convergence approaches that are used in many neuroimaging studies. Convergence approaches have become increasingly popular in functional neuroimaging in response to one of the core problems in the field. Specifically, a multitude of stimulation tasks or procedures exist that can be used to engage a particular psychological construct or brain region, with each variation possessing slightly different properties. In other words, each stimulation paradigm comes with its own method variance, and not surprisingly, substantial inconsistencies emerge in the literature. To deal with this, many neuroimaging researchers have begun to use procedures to look at the convergence of responses across procedures. In its simplest form, this is accomplished with a simple logistic analysis in which each effect is transformed voxel by voxel into a binary representation of whether the voxel was activated above a certain threshold. These binary representations are then summed or multiplied across contrasts to produce a spatial map of areas activated in more than one condition.

A convergence approach also helps deal with the problem of pure insertion. As noted earlier, in a simple subtraction design it is impossible to determine if a change in brain activity relates to the inserted cognitive component or to changes in other components that arise as a consequence of the inserted component. However, by using multiple stimulation–control contrasts it becomes possible to more clearly parse the component in question from its effects on other task components. Imagine, for instance, a judgment task in a given sensory modality that is contrasted with a passive task in which the stimulus is presented but no judgment is made. It is difficult to know if changes in brain activity are related to the judgment itself or if the act of making the judgment caused modality-

specific changes in sensory processing because of increased attention to the stimulus rather than the act of making the judgment. Now, if we run similar experiments in other sensory modalities, we can analyze them to determine common vs. modality-specific activations. The areas that are active in all tasks can be considered modality independent processes and cannot be attributed to factors such as increased attention to a specific stimulus category. Thus, even if the assumption of pure insertion fails in a given task, it becomes possible to separate activations related to the component of interest (the judgment) from changes in other processes (modality-specific attention) that arise as a consequence of the task insertion. Of course, a delineation of the common activations may fail to detect sensory-specific processes that are directly related to the component in question. Nevertheless, the remaining modality insensitive, common regions of activation will be more clearly attributable to the component of interest.

Price and Friston (1997) referred to this approach of examining the commonalities between activations arising in different contrasts as "cognitive conjunction analysis." It is worth noting that when applied in neuroimaging, particularly among researchers using the popular SPM program (Department of Cognitive Neurology, London, UK), the conjunction refers to the presence of a main effect in the absence of differences in simple effects at a given voxel. The analysis is performed by taking the sum of all activations [(stimulation$_1$ – control$_1$) + (stimulation$_2$ – control$_2$) . . .] and eliminating voxels where there exist significant differences among the individual contrasts [(stimulation$_1$ – control$_1$) – (stimulation$_2$ – control$_2$) . . .].

Convergence and Divergence Across Brain Regions

Because neuroimaging experiments provide data on multiple brain regions simultaneously, neuroimaging data need not be limited to a single entry in an MTMM matrix. Rather, different brain regions can be sampled to examine the extent to which activity converges or diverges across brain regions. For instance, in considering a measure related to attention, it may be useful to know that task performance correlates with activity within the frontal eye field, parietal cortex, and anterior cingulate (all areas involved in attention), but not with activity in the temporal lobe or Broca's area (which is not a component of the system). In this situation, the different brain regions can be equated with different traits in the MTMM matrix. The question becomes, Do anatomically connected or functionally related brain regions (i.e., related traits) show convergence, whereas functionally or anatomically unconnected (i.e., unrelated traits) show divergence? Applying a network approach, one can treat functional couplings (covariance) between regions as separate traits. We can then ask whether different tasks produce convergent or divergent effects on the functional connectivity between regions.

Considered in this framework, neuroimaging is highly compatible with the MTMM approach, allowing the assessment of convergence and divergence across stimulation methods and the brain regions activated by those methods. However, this approach is rarely formally applied in the neuroimaging field. This in part reflects the difficulty in ascribing brain activations in a given region to a specific function. For instance, although the dorsolateral prefrontal cortex frequently activates during working memory tasks, it also activates during tasks that are not specifically related to working memory (D'Esposito, Ballard, Aguirre, & Zarahn, 1998). Indeed, the multitude of functions proposed for the prefrontal cortex makes it unlikely that a single discrete process can explain all the varied tasks that lead to increased activity in the region (Duncan & Owen, 2000). Thus, it would be unwise to assume that activation of the dorsolateral prefrontal cortex (or other brain regions involved in working memory tasks) necessarily indicate the involvement of working memory in a given task. On the other hand, if we have three areas, each of which are engaged by multiple cognitive tasks, but that only show simultaneous activation during working memory, then the multiregion approach could prove highly useful.

Integrating Neuroimaging Data With Other Data in a Multitrait–Multimethod Framework

Assessment of psychological constructs has traditionally focused on behaviors that are either directly

observable by a researcher or can be reported by the examinee. Neuroimaging can supplement these methods of assessment by providing information at a neural level. Although, one might be tempted to view this at a causal level (i.e., the brain activity causes the behavior, or the behavior causes the brain activity), it need not be viewed as such. Rather, neuroimaging data can be viewed as just another indicator or correlate of a psychological process or trait. However, neuroimaging data are qualitatively different from most other types of measures in psychological research in that the brain's response can be measured without requiring the subject to make a behavioral response or use introspection. Thus response may be measured uncontaminated by requirements to self-monitor or control a motor act (both of which may add method variance in psychological studies).

Imagine, for instance, the assessment of a personality trait. A number of investigators have found neural correlates of personality either in terms of resting data or the degree of activation during stimulation (see Canli, Sivers, Whitfield, Gotlib, & Gabrieli, 2002; Gusnard et al., 2003; Zald et al., 2004). By combining neuroimaging data with other self-report, observer rating, or experimental performance measures, we may increase accuracy in assessment. In such a paradigm, levels of regional brain activity would be predicted to converge with self-report and objective ratings of the trait of interest, but not other traits.

The MTMM approach can similarly be applied to the assessment of a psychological process. Imagine you are testing subliminal processing of visual stimuli using a tachistoscopic method. The presence of subliminal processing is traditionally tested by having subjects "guess" about stimulus features in the absence of an explicit awareness of having seen the stimulus. Performance significantly above chance provides evidence for subliminal processing. Now, if we simultaneously scan subjects with fMRI and see BOLD responses that are temporally linked to the presentation of the stimuli, we could use the fMRI data as a second source of evidence that subliminal processing occurred. Because neither measure is likely to be 100% sensitive or selective, the combination of the two types of data may dramatically increase predictive power.

A critical problem must be resolved before including functional imaging data in a MTMM matrix. Specifically, the precise relationship between activations and behavioral performance cannot always be predicted in advance. In some cases, higher activations may reflect greater performance or ability level. However, in some cases, subjects with lower ability may have to activate a region more to perform a task at an equivalent level to a more skilled person. This issue has been particularly salient in the psychiatric imaging literature, where researchers attempt to draw conclusions about the relationship between functional activations and the neural substrates of psychiatric conditions. This is essentially an empirical question. Once we understand the nature of performance-activation relationships, it becomes reasonable to consider the neuroimaging data in a MTMM matrix.

Unfortunately, because of the expense of collecting neuroimaging data, it seems unlikely that neuroimaging data will be routinely used as a component in MTMM matrices. However, its utility may be appraised in terms of a cost–benefit analysis. In situations where the neuroimaging data has significantly greater sensitivity or selectivity than other forms of data, then the benefit of its inclusion may outweigh the costs. Plus, with the advent of data sharing through the fMRI data center (http://www.fmridc.org), which is a public repository of peer-reviewed published fMRI data, researchers can potentially pool data from dozens of studies that fit key cells in MTMM matrices.

Simultaneous Measurement of Other Variables to Enhance Understanding of Neuroimaging Data

Although the preceding discussions have focused on the ability of neuroimaging data to provide information on psychological constructs, a multimethod approach can also prove extremely useful in directing the interpretation of neuroimaging data. Group statistical analyses often proceed on the assumption that all subjects performed a cognitive task in a similar manner or responded similarly to procedures aimed at inducing a specific psychological state.

Unfortunately, verification of this assumption is often difficult. For instance, if we wish to study fear, it is important that we verify that we indeed induced fear and not disgust or other negative emotions. If we lack certainty that the intended state was provoked, then we cannot confidently assume that the brain responses occurred in relationship to the cognitive process or psychological state in question. The solution to this problem is to triangulate on the desired response using multiple methods, including, for example, measurement of task performance, self-report, and psychophysiological recording. As convergent evidence verifies the induction of the intended process or state (and not an unintended state), confidence in interpreting brain responses increases. This triangulation strategy is an example of the multilevel analytic approach described in the preceding chapter by Berntson and Cacioppo, in which information from different levels is used to mutually tune and calibrate data or concepts across different levels of analysis.

Unfortunately, a problem arises in trying to integrate fMRI data with simultaneous collection of other types of data. Specifically, fMRI is both sensitive to artifacts caused by psychophysiological recording devices and causes interference in those same devices. Nevertheless, it is possible to implement psychophysiological recordings such as galvanic skin response, heart rate, blood pressure, and eye tracking within the fMRI environment (Savoy, Ravicz, & Gollub, 1999). These measures are all easily implemented in the PET environment as well. Similarly, measures of hormonal responses such as cortisol can be collected in the scanner environment. The large differences in time scales of these various measures can cause interpretational issues when moving across levels. Nevertheless, the benefit of collecting such measures should be increasingly apparent.

METHOD VARIANCE AND NEUROIMAGING

Neuroimaging researchers have often highlighted sources of method variance associated with specific technical steps in neuroimaging, such as the effects of using different techniques for spatial normalization, movement correction, or modeling the hemo-

dynamic response. In contrast, because neuroimaging data has usually been collected in relative isolation, much less attention has been paid to overall sources of method variance when attempting to include neuroimaging data as part of a larger multimethod approach. In such a context, attention to the temporal, spatial, and other methodological limitations of PET and fMRI become paramount. Because these limitations substantially influence both the level of noise in the data and the ability to detect relevant activations, they will directly influence the utility of including neuroimaging in a MTMM matrix. The following section describes six important sources of method variance in neuroimaging studies: (a) temporal resolution, (b) the nature and source of the signal change, (c) spatial resolution, (d) anatomical variability, (e) imaging artifacts, and (f) influences on functional activations unrelated to brain processes.

Temporal Resolution

Because of the nature of both radioisotope decay and the slow time course of the hemodynamic response, the temporal resolution of neuroimaging is inherently limited. The sluggish nature of the hemodynamic response prohibits the detection of numerous events that occur on a millisecond time scale and may be conceptualized as a low-pass filter that prevents detection of higher frequency information. The temporal resolution is particularly poor for PET, which is largely insensitive to transient responses unless they are sustained or of large magnitude. The different temporal limitations of PET and fMRI almost certainly lead to situations in which the results of the two techniques disagree with each other, leading to nontrivial differences in conclusions (Zald, 2003). Similarly, both techniques may fail to converge with data from techniques such as single-cell recordings, event-related potentials, and near infrared optical imaging, which are sensitive to changes at the millisecond level.

The Nature and Source of the Signal Change

Neuroimaging studies measure changes in signal magnitude. However, many processes in the brain

may be characterized by changes in firing patterns or synchronization among neurons, rather than changes in overall firing rates (Lestienne, 2001; Neuenschwander, Castelo-Branco, Baron, & Singer, 2002). Neuroimaging studies will often be insensitive to such changes.

Equally important is a consideration of the source of rCBF/BOLD changes, which in addition to the neuronal output signals are also significantly associated with input to a region and local processing within the activated region (Logothetis, 2002). Thus, when an area shows increased rCBF or BOLD signal, the finding may not directly inform us about the region's output. This differs from many electrophysiological techniques that solely examine a brain region's output.

Spatial Resolution

The inherent resolution of high-quality, commercially available PET scanners is around 4 to 7 mm (full-width half-maximum; DeGrado et al., 1994; Spinks et al., 2000). This is high enough to measure activity in most cortical and subcortical regions, but limits the ability to look at subnuclei and often leads to difficulties in determining the exact origin of foci that occur near the boundaries between regions. By comparison, fMRI is capable of higher spatial resolution. However, many fMRI studies are performed with parameters that provide no higher spatial resolution than that produced by high-quality PET cameras. Moreover, draining vein effects often lead to mislocalization of the source of fMRI signals (Lai et al., 1993), thus lowering the effective resolution for localizing responses. Both fMRI and PET images are usually filtered to a lower spatial resolution after the data is collected. This filtering serves several purposes. First, it reduces noise and hence improves signal to noise characteristics. Second, it lowers the number of resolution elements and hence reduces correction factors for multiple comparisons. Third, it improves the detectability of large-volume activations (Poline & Mazoyer, 1994). However, this comes at the cost of restricting the ability to detect more discrete focal activations and therefore biases the methods toward detections of large-volume activations. This bias is at its most

extreme in older PET studies, but remains a bias in the fMRI literature as well.

Anatomic Variability

Imaging data is also smoothed to remove minor differences in anatomical variability across subjects. Anatomical variability is a constant issue faced in neuroimaging. Different warping algorithms and landmark systems have been proposed to optimize coregistration in different regions of the brain. It is clear, though, that humans show variability in both the structural and functional topography of the brain that cannot be overcome by coregistration. Most researchers naturally focus on group analyses to report common areas of activation. However, this approach fails to capture more idiosyncratic activations. Moreover, in regions of high structural variability and in tasks that localize to variable locations, the group analysis may fail to detect relevant activations. For instance, portions of the fusiform gyrus are responsive to faces, but the precise location varies across subjects (Kanwisher, McDermott, & Chun, 1997). In such a situation, group analyses could easily fail to detect the presence of this region.

Imaging Artifacts

All neuroimaging techniques are sensitive to artifacts associated with data collection that can appear as either false positives (signal change unrelated to brain activity) or false negatives (failure to detect real changes in brain activity). With PET, the most significant artifacts are associated with subject movement and variability in the timing or amount of radiotracer delivery. Many of these can be measured and adjusted for, but they may nevertheless impact the quality of PET results.

Functional MRI is more prone than PET to artifacts, with even small movements producing large changes in signal within individual voxels. Signal changes caused by periodic motion from breathing or cardiac pulsation can similarly hinder detection of changes in brain activation (Hu, Le, Parrish, & Erhard, 1995). Indeed, in many cases artifactual changes in MRI signals are substantially larger than the changes in BOLD signal associated with neural activation. Moreover, certain areas of the brain are

extremely difficult to measure with fMRI because of signal dropout caused by boundaries between brain tissue and air (Farzaneh, Riederer, & Pelc, 1990). Because of this signal dropout, PET can detect changes in certain brain regions where many fMRI studies will produce false-negative results (particularly in ventromedial frontal and anteriormedial temporal regions). Many techniques exist to address these problems, but the quality of the data must be considered on a case-specific basis, especially when considering negative findings.

Influences on Functional Activations Unrelated to Brain Processes

When we see individual or group differences in the magnitude of activations in brain-imaging studies, we frequently assume that these differences arise from differences in the level of brain activity in a given region. However, this assumption can be problematic. For instance, in fMRI, the magnitude of the BOLD response to visual stimulation is associated with levels of hematocrit in the blood (Levin et al., 2001). Because individuals differ in hematocrit levels, and men have higher overall hematocrit levels than women, these differences can easily confound interpretation of differences in BOLD magnitude. Attention to such variables becomes especially important if functional activations are going to be used as an assessment measure.

PSYCHOMETRIC PROPERTIES OF NEUROIMAGING DATA

The selectivity, sensitivity, criterion validity, and test–retest reliability can be calculated for both PET and MRI studies. Establishing the test–retest reliability of most baseline PET measures is relatively straightforward (Ball, Fox, Herscovitch, & Raichle, 1988; Nyberg, Farde, & Halldin, 1996; Schmidt et al., 1996), although this literature remains surprisingly small considering the increasing use of these measures in clinical diagnosis. Establishing the test–retest reliability of activations caused by stimulation paradigms is a trickier issue. Reliability in these paradigms will always be task and region specific, making it impossible to make generalizable statements about reliability. Nevertheless, there are increasing attempts

to define the test–retest reliability of the activations associated with specific cognitive and motor tasks (Fernandez et al., 2003; Kiehl & Liddle, 2003; Maitra, Roys, & Gullapalli, 2002; Specht, Willmes, Shah, & Jancke, 2003). This issue has proved particularly important when fMRI is used as part of presurgical planning for intractable epilepsy. Obviously, a neurosurgeon needs to know which measures (neuropsychological data, WADA procedure, etc.) provide the most valid and reliable information about functional localization of cognitive tasks (particularly language tasks) before choosing to remove part of a patient's cortex. However, determination of the psychometric properties of neuroimaging data is complicated by the fact that the data sets include information on magnitude of change (or the degree of temporal correlation) and location of activation. For instance, imagine performing a receptive language study on a patient on two occasions. In both cases the subject demonstrates activation in the left superior temporal gyrus, but the emerging foci, although within 5 mm of each other, do not overlap. Depending on one's criteria, this could be viewed as a replication or a failure to replicate. When viewed loosely (for instance, in terms of hemispheric asymmetries within the temporal or frontal lobe), such tasks have typically shown good reliability (Fernandez et al., 2003; Rutten, Ramsey, van Rijen, & van Veelen, 2002). In contrast, when viewed on a voxelwise basis, the overlap between activations across sessions tends to be much lower (Fernandez et al., 2003).

Attempts to use functional neuroimaging for diagnoses have also provided information regarding the sensitivity and selectivity of this information. This has received particularly strong attention in the diagnosis of early Alzheimer's disease (Petrella, Coleman, & Doraiswamy, 2003). Research along similar lines will clearly need to be performed if functional neuroimaging is to reach its full potential as an assessment tool, regardless of whether it is used in isolation or as part of a MTMM matrix.

IMPLICATIONS BEYOND THE FORMAL MTMM APPROACH

The examples given in earlier sections of this chapter have described how neuroimaging data can be

used within a formal application of the MTMM approach. However, the general approach toward looking for convergence and discrepancies across methods and traits can be applied as an evaluative strategy, even in situations where it is not possible to use the same methods in the same subjects. In such a situation one cannot produce a covariance matrix across methods, but one can nevertheless use an emphasis on convergence and divergence for evaluating hypotheses.

Sarter, Cacioppo, Berntson, and colleagues (Cacioppo et al., 2003; Sarter, Berntson, & Cacioppo, 1996) have articulated the importance of understanding the type of information that functional neuroimaging studies provide relative to other types of neuroscientific data. Specifically, most neuroimaging studies provide information on the probability that a given brain area activates as a function of a cognitive process (i.e., the experimenter performs a task aimed at inducing a specific cognitive process and determines whether the task leads to activity in a specific brain region). In contrast, such studies do not typically provide information on the probability that a given cognitive process arises as a function of activation of a specific brain region (although researchers frequently make the erroneous interpretation that the results provide this information). Such a conclusion would only be true if there is a one-to-one correspondence between the brain region's activity and the cognitive process, and we rarely possess evidence for such a one-to-one correspondence. Sarter et al. argue that to fully understand the bidirectional relationship between brain activity and cognitive processes, one needs to integrate other types of paradigms (such as lesion or electrical stimulation data) that allow direct manipulation of brain regions and thus provide information on the probability of a cognitive process given activity (or lack of activity) within a specific brain region.

The preceding analysis parallels a classic distinction in the neurobehavioral field between brain areas that are activated in a task and brain areas that are necessary for performance of the task. Taken alone, neuroimaging typically only addresses the question of what is activated and fails to address whether that activation is necessary. In contrast, neuropsychological studies of patients address what is necessary, but not what is activated. Thus, to answer the question of what is both engaged and necessary in a task, one needs to use both methods. The greatest clarity arises when both methods converge to show that an area is both necessary for and engaged by a task involving a given psychological process, but is not necessary or engaged by tasks that do not require that psychological process.

Considered in this light, it also becomes necessary to expand the MTMM approach to include data from other species. Specifically, most techniques that allow us to look at the causative effects of manipulating brain regions can only ethically be carried out in nonhuman populations. These animal studies typically proceed on the assumption that (a) there are "homologous" brain regions across species, (b) these regions perform the same tasks, and (c) the regions perform the tasks in the same way. However, despite many features that are conserved across species, even a cursory study of neuroanatomy reveals substantial interspecies differences. Given these potential cross-species differences, we need evidence of convergence and divergence across methods used in different species. It thus may prove useful to take a multitrait–multimethod–multispecies approach to evaluating brain–behavior relationships. In summary, the core logic articulated by Campbell and Fiske provides an extremely useful overall strategy for placing neuroimaging research within the larger field of psychology and neuroscience, even in situations where formal MTMM analyses are not feasible.

CHAPTER 14

NONREACTIVE METHODS IN PSYCHOLOGICAL RESEARCH

Immo Fritsche and Volker Linneweber

Participants in social science research usually think. That is, they interpret the actions of a researcher and relate it to their own beliefs, emotions, and intentions. Accordingly, the behavior they exhibit during investigations is controlled by what they think is appropriate, depending on their interpretation of the study situation and their motivation to comply with these assumed requirements. Hence, what is often measured is not a "natural state" but the participant's intentional presentation. Imagine inviting people to participate in a study on helping behavior in which you are interested in the individual inclination to help others in need. You ask the subjects to indicate whether they would be willing to donate blood for a charitable organization. In many cases, however, the answer you receive might not say a lot about the participant's actual behavior or corresponding intentions, but rather about the participant's proper understanding of the study's *demand characteristics* (Orne, 1962) or about the relevant social desirability norms.

However, even if we adopt the more optimistic view that research participants do *not* think (even not unconsciously), the validity of the data obtained in investigations specifically designed to record some variable of interest might still be doubtful. That is because we can at least expect thinking on the part of the researcher. More specifically, we may assume that the researcher arranges the research setting in such a way to allow the practical and convenient measurement of the construct of interest. Unfortunately, even the nonthinking participant's willingness to donate blood does not necessarily say a lot about his daily conduct. We can suppose that throughout the course of his daily life, your subject will never be confronted with appeals for help like the one you were kind enough to present in your investigation.

Participant behavior under the influence of thinking by both the participant and the researcher can be called "reactive" if it is a subject's reaction to a specific situation, intentionally created for research by a researcher. Here, bias occurs not only by fault of the participants (subject bias) but also due to the influence of the researcher (experimenter or observer bias[1]) as well. Reactive measurement restricts what Brunswik (1947) called the data's "ecological validity." Although not yet ultimately defined in the psychological science, high ecological validity indicates that the results from an investigation may predict the item's behavior in its ordinary context.

Psychologists have tried to cope with the shortcomings of reactive methods by introducing various measures aimed at preventing subject and experimenter biases. Probably the most radical approach has been the proposal of "nonreactive" or "unobtrusive" measures, first stated in the groundbreaking work of Webb, Campbell, Schwartz, and Sechrest (1966). They systematically start discussing what has been previously known as "reactive effect of measurement" and "reactive arrangement bias"

[1]For the dynamics of experimenter effects, see also research on what has been called the "Rosenthal effect" in psychological experimentation (Rosenthal, 1976) and the "Pygmalion effect" in education (McNatt, 2000).

(p. 13). The table of contents reflects what was of interest when psychology started discussing alternatives to traditional measurement. Nonreactive measures suggested by Webb et al. (1966) include an examination of physical traces such as natural erosion and accretion and archives such as those found in various public and private records. Finally, they elaborated on the potential utility of simple and contrived observation methods for unobtrusive measures. Even though these unobtrusive measures refer explicitly to overt behavior and its products, it is often a goal of researchers to measure not only the behavior in a nonreactive manner, but internal variables such as attitudes, emotions, and abilities as well. More than 10 years later, in a reader edited by Lee Sechrest (1979), Bochner (1979) added some considerations concerning unobtrusive field experiments in social psychology, thus demonstrating that further developments occurred, particularly with respect to the issue of social desirability and in applied research in general.

APPROXIMATION TOWARD NONREACTIVITY

Now that the phenomenon of reactivity has been introduced and the development of nonreactive techniques has been briefly outlined, we will elaborate in more detail on the nature of nonreactive measurement. First, we give an overview of classical as well as recently developed techniques followed by a sketch of the boundaries of nonreactive measurement, consisting of validity threats and ethical considerations.

Nonreactive Measures as Distinct Techniques

In the literature, the term *nonreactive measurement* is used in at least two senses, in a dichotomous as well as a continuous sense. Textbooks often think of nonreactive measures as representing a distinct set of procedures sharply different from reactive methods. Actually, there is a comparatively stable core of measures that are commonly subsumed under this heading. In social psychology, for instance, one of the most cited and consequently most prototypical nonreactive method is the so-called lost letter technique (Milgram, Mann, & Harter, 1965), which is used as an indirect measure of attitudes. To implement this technique, stamped letters are distributed in specified residential areas, appearing to the chance observer to be lost by someone. They are addressed to different organizations, representing the attitude objects. For example, if researchers are interested in the relative approval of religious groups like Christian and Muslim, not biased by social desirability concerns, they could "lose" those letters addressed to either a church or a mosque. In actuality, the letters are addressed to the researcher via a post office box. The number of letters the researchers receive is taken as an indicator of the prevailing attitude toward the respective group (i.e., Christian or Muslim) in a specified area (for a test of the technique's convergent validity, see Cherulnik, 1975; for an advanced version, see also the lost e-mail technique by Castelli, Zogmaister, & Arcuri, 2001; also applied in Vaes, Paladino, Castelli, Leyens, & Giovanazzi, 2002). Although the interpretation of this method might be flawed by some problems (see following text), the technique guarantees nonreactive measurement insofar as the participants are not aware of their participation in an attitude test. This nonawareness is the most important criterion of nonreactivity that was identified by Webb et al. (1966) in their classic work on *unobtrusive measures*. This term is applied to those measures in which the studied individual "is not aware of being tested and there is little danger that the act of measurement will itself serve as a force for change or elicit role-playing that confounds the data" (p. 175). Unobtrusiveness and nonreactivity are often used synonymously. However, the term *nonreactivity* should be differentiated from unobtrusiveness in two ways. First, nonreactive measurement should be defined in a more comprehensive way than has been done for unobtrusive techniques (cf. Folger & Belew, 1985), not only focusing on whether and how research subjects perceive the act of measurement but also keeping in mind the researcher and her potential contribution to instrument reactivity (experimenter or observer effects; e.g., Rosenthal, 1976). Ideally, not only the subject but also the researcher should not be aware of the measurement

when it occurs. As the second aspect of definition, it should be made clear that nonreactivity refers to the ultimate outcome of measurement and not to the means by which this end is achieved (i.e., that the subjects are not aware of being tested). Hence, we define nonreactive measures simply as those measures in that *participant's behavior that are not influenced by social interaction with the researcher*, because both directions of this interaction are perceived as potential sources of distortion. However, although measures like the lost letter technique are commonly perceived as nonreactive, in many of these measures an interaction between researcher and research subject occurs that might influence the participant's behavior in an indirect fashion. With regard to our example, the letters are not really lost but are placed in precise locations by researchers. Time and place of the letter distribution as well as the choice of addressee follow intentional action by the researcher that might subtly influence the participant's behavior in the sense of "cuing" (Folger & Belew, 1985). One might be able to counteract these potential distortions by balancing time, place, and research assistant according to the variables assumed to be confounding like the economic background of the sample, social status, or political attitudes of the assistants, and so on. Although these additional steps would be likely to reduce reactivity, they are not a unique part of the technique itself. Furthermore, the additional techniques that reduce a measurement's reactivity are incorporated into most psychological methods of data acquisition. Therefore, instead of thinking of reactive and nonreactive measures in a dichotomous way, a continuous definition of nonreactivity might actually be more suitable.

Nonreactivity as a Continuous Concept

A continuous conception of nonreactivity assumes it to be an ideal state rather than a feature inherent in certain techniques of measurement. Here, measures are assumed to vary in the extent to which they come close to this ideal. According to this notion, the reactivity of a measure increases with the extent to which both the research subject and the researcher are involved in the act of measurement. We will now introduce six types of measures (see Table 14.1) that vary in the extent to which nonreactivity is realized, starting with the Type 5 measures that exhibit the highest degree of nonreactivity.

Type 5. This type of data is generated without any initial intention of measurement on the part of the researcher and, consequently, is also collected without any awareness of such an intention on part of the participant, thus representing the most nonreactive and unobtrusive method that can be thought of (Table 14.1, Type 5). Examples of such measures are the various natural accretion and erosion measures (Webb et al., 1966) referring to material and settings not placed or designed for research purposes. These measures use physical "traces" of behavior that, for example, might manifest themselves as remnants like garbage that can be interpreted as an indicator of certain lifestyles, or they can be found in erosion phenomena such as in the paths pedestrians make in the snow showing their preferred routes. Another example of a Type 5 measure (Table 14.1) is the content analysis (see Lubinski, this volume, chap. 8) of archival material. This may be considered a nonreactive measure if there is a guarantee that the records represent natural behavior or if, at the very least, the researchers are aware of the conditions and original aims of potentially reactive data generation in the past. They have to make sure that those specific circumstances of data generation have not distorted measurement in a way that could influence the results of their present investigations. Accordingly, as a database for the measurement of an individual's health status, for instance, using archival self-report data on individual absenteeism should be less reliable than analyzing the individual costs statistics from a health insurance company. Although such analyses are not immune to the researchers' interpretational bias, the mere generation of the data is indeed free of researcher bias.

Type 4. Table 14.1 specifies additional types of measurement that represent differing lesser degrees of nonreactivity. Type 4 measures do not make use of naturally occurring records, but rather measure behavior in a deliberately selected setting or even create opportunities for subjects to behave in a certain way. This behavior is a top-down operationalization of the variables the researcher is interested

---

TABLE 14.1

Continuum of Nonreactivity in Measurement

| | Level of nonreactivity | | | | | |
| | Low | | | | | High |
	Type 0	Type 1	Type 2	Type 3	Type 4	Type 5
Setting initially designed or selected for research	yes	yes	yes	yes	yes	no
Participants are aware of the research setting	likely	likely	likely	likely	no	no
Participants are aware of the research question	likely	likely	likely	no	no	no
Participants are aware of the research hypothesis	likely	likely	no	no	no	no
Participants are aware of the measures' manipulability	likely	no	no	no	no	no
Examples	*Participative expert interviews*	*Bogus pipeline technique*	*Personality questionnaires*	*Cover story experiments*	*Lost letter technique*	*Analysis of archival data*

in and has hypotheses about. However, in this type of measure, subjects are not aware of being the object of measurement. Examples of Type 4 techniques include hidden observation, many of the controlled accretion and erosion measures (Webb et al., 1966; see also later in this chapter), as well as the lost letter technique mentioned earlier. In the latter method, for example, a behavior is recorded that would not have occurred naturally and without the intervention of the researchers, simply because the letter addressed to the mosque would not have been found lying in front of a mailbox. We have previously discussed possible experimenter effects in applying the lost letter technique that might be transmitted by the active design of the situation. Of course, Type 4 measures also have important advantages over the use of already existing records. If, for example, researchers are interested in inferences of causal relationships between predefined variables, they must be able to manipulate specific features of the subject's environment to ascribe differences in the dependent measure to the work of specific experimental conditions (see also Erfelder &

Musch, this volume, chap. 15). Take, for instance, the director of an arts museum who assumes that children are more attracted to colored pictures than adults and that adults, as opposed to children, are more interested in looking at pictures of high unconventionality. To test both hypotheses in a 2 (picture in color vs. black and white) × 2 (picture of high vs. low unconventionality) × 2 (adults vs. children) factorial design, the director could first equip one exhibition room with pictures representing combinations of the respective conditions (color and high unconventionality, color and low unconventionality, black/white and high unconventionality, black/white and low unconventionality). In a second step, the director would measure the amount of attention paid to each picture and whether children or adults are paying the attention. Following Webb et al. (1966), measuring carpet erosion in front of each picture would also provide an estimate of relative attractiveness. Because of the need to differentiate between adult and children visitors, the underlying material should be sensitive enough to depict the size of shoes. Hence, the

director decides that a high and soft flooring is necessary. The director instructs an assistant to vacuum the room every 30 minutes and to count the differently sized footprints before vacuuming. This example provides an obvious demonstration of how Type 4 measures can offer additional opportunities for a more purposeful and controlled measurement than simply using preexisting records. This method is often more efficient and sometimes even the only way that a specific research question can be answered in a nearly nonreactive manner.

Type 3. In measures of Type 3, not only is the research setting prepared by the researcher, but the research context is also not intended to be unobtrusive to the participants. Thus, they are very likely to be aware of participating in a purposeful study. However, it is important to note that the participants' general knowledge about the research context does not necessarily imply their knowledge about the research *aims*. In fact, Type 3 participants are not informed about or are even actively hindered from elaborating their own assumptions about the research question. As people are usually very interested in knowing about the aim of the research they are participating in, withholding initial information about hypotheses is a necessary feature of most Type 3 methods. Social psychological experiments, for example, often involve active deception of research participants to avoid distortions that can often be traced back to social desirability concerns (for an overview of different methods, see Aronson, Ellsworth, Carlsmith, & Gonzales, 1990). For instance, in an experimental study on the impact of justifications and excuses on the violation of proenvironmental norms, Fritsche's (2003) aim was to manipulate the accessibility of valid accounts prior to the measurement of the norm violating behavior. Because it could be expected that people who are informed about the research topic are both willing and able to influence the dependent measure in the direction of (or contrary to) their own hypotheses (in this case on the relationship between account-giving and socially appropriate behavior), to prevent the generation of

participants' own hypotheses, this study was introduced as an investigation of communication over the Internet. The instructions and procedures made this plausible because participants were asked to interview an anonymous partner in a chat room about apparently randomized pairs of topics including "environmental protection" and "guilty conscience." Shielded by this cover story, the confederate chat partner was able to present standardized justifications and excuses in the course of "natural communication" without revealing the actual research question. The experimenter told the participants that they could order a drink, which they would receive later during the experiment. After the manipulation of a specific account's accessibility (i.e., its mere introduction by the confederate) and validity (i.e., its evaluation as situationally appropriate by the confederate) the drinks (in aluminum cans!) were brought in. A previous study with a comparable sample had shown that drinking from cans was perceived as harmful to the environment. Whereas nearly all (92%) of the participants who disposed of valid accounts for drinking from a can actually took the can, only 64% of the participants without compelling justifications or excuses did so. When asked to indicate the "true" research question, none of the participants could specify the topic correctly.[2] In addition to the technique of designing a plausible cover story, dependent variables of Type 3 measures are often assessed on an implicit or even physiological level. These measures are assumed to be immune against intentional distortion by the participant. In this textbook, implicit and physiological measures are discussed in separate chapters (see chapter 9 for the former and chapters 12 and 13 for the latter set of methods).

Type 2. In Type 2 measures, participants are informed about the general topic of an investigation, but particular hypotheses are hidden. These kinds of techniques might underlie the measurement most often used in psychology. Examples can be found in most questionnaire techniques measuring state or trait personality, situated cognitions, or emotions. Even though people most often know

---

[2]A more thorough discussion of ethical considerations concerning deception studies is presented later in this chapter.

and are aware of the fact that they are actually being asked about their environmental attitudes, the degree of their introversion, or actual self-esteem in such studies, as a rule they do not know the specific hypotheses such as the item assignment to different scale dimensions or assumptions about relationships between variables or the expected results. However, in a narrower sense, not only the participants should be blind to specific hypotheses: To minimize possible experimenter effects beyond those associated with the mere research setting, assistants of the experimenter should not be informed about the hypotheses (Type 2) or even about the research question as a whole (Type 3). In a way, those research assistants who are involved in *double-blind studies* are de facto participants in the wider sense because they are (ideally) not the principal investigator. Being blind to particular hypotheses implies that it is not possible for participants to systematically counteract the primary research goal. Nevertheless, participants who know about the field of research they are contributing to might be motivated to extend their contribution to the researcher. They often generate their own hypotheses that they want to prove immediately by responding in a respective manner. Hence, Type 2 measurement might be flawed with increased unsystematic measurement error.

Type 1. In some studies it cannot be avoided that the participants are aware of a researcher's hypotheses. Yet there are also investigations where the hypotheses are deliberately disclosed to the participants. This might be done for ethical as well as for feasibility reasons. Even though revealing hypotheses is generally assumed to open the door to systematic distortion, this tendency can be counteracted by either decreasing or preventing altogether the participants' awareness of a measure's manipulability. This is the goal of Type 1 nonreactive measures. Although different strategies can be incorporated that might reduce the perceived manipulability (e.g., simply informing participants about a measure's nonmanipulability, using highly complex materials), the most prominent example of a Type 1 measure is the bogus pipeline technique (Jones &

Sigall, 1971). In studies using this technique, participants are led to believe that it is possible to pump their psyche directly using an apparatus that apparently records physiological signals. This technique has been found to considerably reduce reactivity in attitude assessment that is rooted in the social desirability concerns of the participants (for a review, see Roese & Jamieson, 1993).

Type 0. Until now we have expounded on the different types of measurement techniques that approximate nonreactivity to different degrees. To present a complete picture, Table 14.1 also includes Type 0 techniques, that is, measures that definitely do not fulfill the criterion of nonreactivity. In Type 0 measures, the interaction of researcher and participants is designed and perceived as serving the investigation of particular hypotheses, and the participant is fully aware of being able to manipulate the results. One might assume that an atmosphere of cooperation between researcher and participant, fueled by the full disclosure of all research hypotheses, could minimize a participant's possible tendency to sabotage the results or might even motivate participants to give their best. For some purposes this effect might have some benefits, for example, when the research is very dependent on the information provided by single participants as, for example, in the case of witnesses recounting rare events. However, the negative implications of fully informed participants for measurement quality prevail over the possible benefits. Research on the demand characteristics of psychological studies (e.g., Orne, 1962) has often described the tendency of cooperatively motivated subjects to distort their behavior or statements toward the assumed hypothesis. This fundamental danger (as well as the further pitfalls of reactivity) can be found in all forms of collaborative and consensual research techniques (for a discussion see, Page, 2000).

In the following sections, we will describe and discuss important nonreactive measures in more detail. After reviewing a few classical measures, a description will be given of the recent trends and techniques in nonreactive measurement that have

in part developed because of sociotechnological changes of human behavior.

CLASSICAL MEASURES AND TECHNIQUES

Looking back on several decades of concern about reactivity in psychological research as well as related fields (e.g., school education) allows us to now talk of classical methods for avoiding or reducing reactivity. In various contributions we find classifications closely related to the one originally presented by Webb et al. (1966). Shaughnessy and Zechmeister (1990) as well as Schweigert (1998) basically differentiated between physical traces (use traces and products) and archival data (analyses of communication and trends and assessing the effects of natural treatments). Bloom and Fischer (1982) differentiated the latter in public versus private and consider simple observations as an additional category. In the following section, we will briefly describe the classical methods discussed in the literature. As previously mentioned and in accordance with Bungard and Lück's (1997) position, we generally consider methods to be more or less (non)reactive instead of differentiating between reactive versus nonreactive.

Physical Traces

Our physical environment provides various sources for us to recognize behavior without observing it directly and, therefore, without being in danger of influencing what is under investigation (Kazdin, 1979). According to Webb et al. (1966, p. 36), the measurement of these natural traces might be separated into *erosion* and *accretion measures*. Erosion refers to "the degree of selective wear on some material," whereas accretion measures record the "deposit of materials." Natural traces may be used to determine preferences and to interpret them in various situations: for studying the impact of situational variables on the viewing of erotic material (Kirschner, 1976), for example, magazines available for reading in a doctor's waiting room indicate the relative rate of being read after some time. The degree of abrasion of museum floors indicates the number of visitors attracted to a particular exhibit

(Gillespie & Perry, 1973; Webb et al., 1966; see earlier discussion). In environmental psychology, Bechtel's (1967) "hodometer research" has become quite famous: Bechtel studied the movement of visitors in art galleries by placing invisible electronic counting devices in the floor (Willems & Raush, 1969). Even temporary traces like fingerprints on glass doors may indicate the age of people using the door because they vary in height. Traces on manipulated material may also be interpreted for research purposes: Friedmann and Wilson (1975) affixed tiny glue seals between pages in textbooks to study their usage unobtrusively.

Analyses of traces are particularly interesting for environmental design and other fields concerned with the interface between people and their physical surroundings (Baxter, 1970; Kates & Adams, 1982; Rubenstein, Paradis, & Munro, 1993). Traces may be analyzed to recognize suboptimal relationships between behavior, needs, and arrangements conceptualized to meet these. Barker (1968) called this "synomorphy," a term that indicates a kind of relationship between persons (i.e., their regularly occurring behavior) and settings. Traces may indicate actions to enhance synomorphy. For example, in offices and other workplaces where possible, people rearrange the furniture and other items to work more effectively or comfortably (Davis, 1984; Schaible-Rapp & Kugelmann, 1982). Traces may also show us environmental design errors. In restrooms on German trains, for instance, the traces left by passengers pressing their fingers on signs indicate that the signs have been confused with the actual switches for initiating the toilet flush mechanism, sink, and electronic hand dryer. For remodeling, traces were correctly understood and the restrooms remodeled.

Nature is even more indicative of human activities. In public parks, for example, paths indicate where people regularly walk or drive. Because more solid surfaces are less likely to show signs of wear, the natural emergence of traces on lawns or topsoil may be used to determine the position of the paths, but only after the park has been used for some length of time. This unobtrusive method allows the variation of not only the route but also the width of

trails. Because user needs analyses (Linneweber, 1993; Sommer, 1983) became an applied field for psychology increasingly, it is important to improve environmental design in method and theory based on these experiences. The role of psychologists in user needs analysis is to read and—even more demanding—interpret the traces and, finally, to advise environmental designers.

The nonreactive research on litter and littering behavior is well documented. As traces of consumption, packaging material, cans, empty bottles, and other types of garbage can be examined to indicate what the people who threw the items away use or prefer (see the extensive research by Rathje, 1984). Because rummaging through other people's garbage as well as applying other measures of trace analysis might appear to some readers as being just a cute technique of creative people calling themselves scientists, one cannot highlight enough the scientific importance that trace measures like the littering technique can have when investigating certain research questions. Litter analysis is the method of choice when social desirability distortions or the inaccessibility of a certain population might prevent reliable measurement of consumption patterns or attitudes. Reilly (1984), for example, described the great importance of these measures for market research. Consider a household being asked to indicate the relative amount of fast or canned food consumed per week. Because it may be (socially) desirable to underestimate this amount in favor of fresh products, an analysis of waste is much more representative (Nay, 1979; Schweigert, 1998). Cialdini and Baumann (1981) demonstrated the applicability of litter analysis as a nonreactive attitude measure. At a parking lot they placed campaign flyers of presidential candidates on car windshields and observed whether the drivers threw them away or kept them. Littering significantly correlated with the driver's previously assessed voting preference. In a second study the authors compared attitudes on topics either high or low in social desirability, measured by both a standard interview and the littering technique. Both measures provided comparable results for those attitude objects low on social desirability. However, in line with the notion of nonreactivity, both meas-

urement techniques lead to different attitude values when objects of high social desirability had been assessed. Here, relative to the littering results, interview data was significantly distorted into the socially desired direction.

Archival Data

Whereas traces may be considered indications for behavior that are "simply there," archives and other types of records are arranged intentionally. This may be related to research questions, for example, in observation studies (Shaughnessy & Zechmeister, 1990). Here we are primarily interested in archives that exist independent of specific scientific investigations. Data files in administration as well as sales records may be subsumed under this category. Moreover, as archival data, material written by persons who are the target of research may also be investigated. Not only are descriptions of accidents and complaints about nuisances interesting from a psychological aspect, but so are private materials like letters and other forms of written communications (Laucken, Mees, & Chassein, 1988). Basically, when the generation of the material is not affected by the research process, the method is considered highly nonreactive and likely represents the techniques of Type 5.

We must bear in mind, however, that archival data may be generated under circumstances that can be considered highly reactive. Actors may very well know that important data are being documented, and they may be motivated to influence this data. With respect to the considerations on nonreactive methods, we can offer two solutions concerning this problem. First, the process and the result of a participant's intentionally influencing archival data may be the target of research. This is possible when different perspectives are available such as in records of conflict in which, for example, mutual accusations directed at the involved actors or third parties are of interest. Second, if biases occurring during the creation of archival data are identified by the investigation, we may cope with the effect particularly when interpreting archival data.

Compared with physical traces, archival data may be more suitable and effective for research purposes, but they are more susceptible to undesirable

effects at the same time. Traces may be less simple to read and to interpret, but they are usually less susceptible to those effects we intend to minimize.

Simple Observations

Observations for scientific purposes (see also Bakeman & Gnisci, chap. 10, this volume) may significantly vary with respect to their obtrusiveness and hence (non)reactivity. When the social sciences started developing its arsenal of methods, alternatives of—at least at that time—highly obtrusive procedures had been discussed. In the beginning of the debate, "participatory observation" was—and still is—called a type of research with fuzzy definitions of the relations between investigators and targets (Couto, 1987). The investigators are not unobtrusive at all because they act in the field under investigation. Their specific impact on the processes to be observed, however, is considered low because their positions as researchers are masked by their activity in the field. For targets under investigation, the researchers' position is less extraordinary—and hence probably less salient to the subjects—than the position of a scientific observer in a laboratory. Presently, the concept is of some importance in culture-specific contexts or some areas of clinical and family research.

"Simple observations" are considered as potentially nonreactive. Bloom and Fischer (1982) discussed four types:

- The observation of physical and bodily signs (jewelry, changes in hairstyle, clothing, and makeup) that are potential indicators of attitudes or behaviors. This is also addressed by studies on symbolic self-completion (Wicklund & Gollwitzer, 1981).
- The analysis of expressive movements (smiles, frowns, gestures) as indicators of attitudes and feelings.
- Physical location analysis that can indicate certain attitudes (e.g., seating patterns as an index of interracial relations).
- The analysis of language behavior (which is tape-recorded for various research goals).

The process of observation may not be unobtrusive in its literal sense because either people or equipment or both are present. However, as long as "the observer has no control over the behavior or sign in question, and plays an unobserved, passive and unobtrusive role in the research situation" (Webb et al., 1966, p. 112), reactivity should be reduced considerably.

NEW APPROACHES

The existing social and technological conditions often determine the development of psychological assessment methods in two ways. On the one hand, the content of research is often oriented toward questions relevant to current society and its sociotechnological conditions, and suitable methods of assessment must be developed or adapted. For instance, the necessity for researching driver aggression in traffic made it essential to find valid measures of driver behavior (e.g., Boyce & Geller, 2002). On the other hand, the research instrument itself depends heavily on the tools or other forms of aid that are available in the particular sociotechnological context. For instance, the ever increasing technological possibilities of monitoring brain activity have led not only to increased and sometimes inflationary use of imaging methods but also to the differentiation of several techniques for applying and interpreting these methods (Zald & Curtis, chap. 13, this volume). In the following we would like to demonstrate how Types 4 and 5 nonreactive measures have developed with the changing sociotechnological conditions. As a reminder, Types 4 and 5 measures (Table 14.1) are those that build on data that is not originally recorded or data that is not perceived as being recorded for research purposes. To do this, we focus exemplarily on nonreactive online research in the Internet.

Nonreactive Research Using the Internet

The rapid development of computer-mediated communication in global network structures has led to an increased interest in research on "online behavior." At the same time, the Internet is emerging as a powerful research tool that can be efficiently used for the collection of real-world data (see Reips, chap. 6, this volume). Besides the interesting opportunities for Web-based surveys as well as experimental studies (e.g., Reips & Bosnjak,

2001), the technological properties of the Internet environment provide benefits for Types 4 and 5 nonreactive measurement in particular.

Analyzing written material on the Internet. One kind of nonreactive Internet data is the written material that people produce on the Internet, for instance, on their personal home pages (e.g., Schütz & Machilek, 2003), virtual discussion groups, or e-mail lists. These texts are usually written for a potentially unrestricted public, and the researcher has the opportunity to save and analyze such data. (For an overview of the methods of text analysis, see Mehl, chap. 11, this volume). Interestingly, communication on the Internet is often two-sided at least, making it possible to analyze the interaction between individuals and also higher social aggregates. Bordia (1996), for example, described the use of online discussion group archives in rumor transmission research. Here it is possible to take a process-oriented perspective on occasions of naturally occurring rumor transmission that can be found in the Internet comparatively easily. Bordia analyzed relevant episodes by quantitative content analysis, using statement categories such as "interrogatory statements" or "prudent statements" referring to an individual's tentativeness or hesitancy in discussing a rumor. The quantity of these statements could not only be compared throughout the entire discourse but also over time. From the latter perspective, Bordia (1996) found that although the analyzed discussions progressed, the frequency of prudent statements related to the rumor decreased. The author highlighted the finding that although this phenomenon has been mentioned in the literature before, this was the first time it could be shown in a natural context. Another illustrative example of research on written material located on the Internet can be found in Stone and Pennebaker (2002), who analyzed collective trauma coping in Internet chat room conversations following the death of Princess Diana. The authors were able to detect significant changes of language and content over a period of 4 weeks. Whereas during the first days after Diana's death, personal and emotional responses were common, after 1 week, expressions of compassion changed into hostile comments, and

the dominance of collective language during the first period changed into more individual language, indicating the disappearance of collective shared grief. Here, it is valid to question whether communication on the Internet can legitimately be called "natural." However, even though several differences between computer-mediated communication and face-to-face interaction have been identified (e.g., Kiesler, Siegel, & McGuire, 1984), widespread accessibility and increasing competence in using the technological environment has made online communication an integral part of behavior in industrialized countries. Hence, the *specific* nature of Internet behavior does not make it *less* natural.

Log file analysis. Analyzing the texts available on the Internet represents the classical method of archival data analysis, although the interactional, dynamic, and mostly well-documented structure of Internet content increases the potency of such analyses. Yet there is also another, possibly even more important, way in which online research might enhance the capacities of nonreactive measurement. This is embedded in the fact that Internet behavior is continuously and automatically recorded without the explicit awareness of its users. Interestingly, these records can be assigned to the behavior of single individuals or at least to single machines. A highly nonreactive technique not yet frequently used in psychological research is the analysis of the log files generated on Internet server machines and optionally on client computers as well. This type of log file analysis would make the hidden protocols accessible for other broad and complex research activities. A simple form of log file analysis has been applied in advertising contexts, for example, by indicating the attractiveness of certain Web pages and the success of particular advertising links by following users' navigation through the net (e.g., Wiedmann & Buxel, 2001). In a similar fashion, log file analysis can also be used in descriptive research. Berker (2002), for example, reported a nonreactive study on Internet behavior that examined the Internet usage of people with an account at the Internet server of a large German university. Analyzing the proxy log files for a 2-week period in 1998 revealed an interesting

preference order of the Web pages viewed by the users. Twenty-four percent of the hits were to pornographic sites, followed by multipurpose sites such as probably preset Internet providers (22%) and to Web sites offering technical support and search engines (both 9%). Using log file information such as time and duration of access led to additional results concerning content-specific user habits. A more controlled and theory-driven Type 4 approach was suggested by Kulikowich and Young (2001), who recommended assessing the problem-solving behavior of individuals by using log file data from an online learning tool. Here, the different problem-solving activities of the participants should be represented by examining their retrieval of particular Web pages. Analyzing the sequential order and duration of access might allow conclusions about both the individuals' learning behavior as well as the appropriateness of specific learning environments.

As in conventional accretion measures, the traces of individual behavior can be followed throughout the Internet or in specific online environments. Further development of this method might also include analyzing navigation behavior more directly and should not only be restricted to behavior that is only relevant in the virtual environment. In the context of environmental planning, for instance, it might be a useful strategy to present 3-D versions of various architectural alternatives and then analyze how long the respective models are visited, which alternatives are entered, and which perspectives are selected for further viewing. This may become a new type of "social design" (Sommer, 1983). For a thorough and controversial discussion of the merits and boundaries of using virtual environments for psychological research, we recommend the debate by Blascovich, Loomis, Beall, Swinth, Hoyt, and Bailenson (2002) in *Psychological Inquiry*.

For conducting log file analysis, a variety of software tools have been developed. Interested readers may retrieve one of various free software offers from the Internet (e.g., Analog, 2003; Richter, Naumann, & Noller, 2003). For a compilation of log file analysis tools, see Janetzko (2003). Two major problems in conducting log file analysis are that accessing an

Internet page is not always recorded in the same way at the same place and that not every access to a particular page is actually documented by a log file. Reducing the first problem might be aided by a standardization of the content and location log file protocols for research purposes (Type 4 measurement). The latter problem comes up when pages are retrieved from cache memories without accessing a server machine or when proxy servers are involved that do not always inform the original server machine about access to one of its pages. Conversely, if records are analyzed that are located on the user machine, this method might suffer from the nonacceptance of so-called cookies that are set by many users. To deal with these problems, particularly in the commercial sector, efforts have been made to standardize the feedback of proxy servers (Werner, 2002). Furthermore, potential self-selection of the sample in a log file analysis should be kept in mind that depends on the activation of proxies, cookies, and cache use on the user's computer. Ideally, possible confounding with variables relevant to the research subject should be ruled out in a prestudy comparing, for instance, those users who have activated proxies in the preferences menu of their Web browser with those who have not. Concerning patterns of Internet use, results by Berker (2002) indicate only small differences between both user groups.

Another problem of nonreactive Internet research might be the identification of single-person behavior. Although log files usually identify single accessing computers, it is both not clear whether multiple individuals use this particular computer at one time and whether the pages are accessed automatically without the intent or even the awareness of the user. To reduce these interpretational weaknesses, it is sometimes advisable to set a duration of inactivity that, if exceeded, marks the beginning of another session by a different user (e.g., exceeding the average time of inactivity by 1.5 standard deviations as suggested by Catledge & Pitkow, 1995). Furthermore, depending on the research question, one should exclude those Web addresses that are usually contacted automatically from analysis (e.g., home pages of browser software, Berker, 2002). As individual behavior can be identified with satisfac-

tory reliability without the knowledge or agreement of subjects, anonymity of analysis is an important requirement. Berker (2002), for example, eliminated all information from the log files that could have facilitated identification of individual computers prior to his analysis.

This brief overview of different pitfalls of nonreactive online research points to the important roles that the technological properties of the medium and the recording of information play in the use and interpretation of behavioral traces. Thus, researchers have to be well acquainted with the technological details of data generation to prevent ethically inappropriate behavior or interpretational errors.

Sociotechnological Changes—Chance and Risk for Nonreactive Measurement

One reason why we have chosen to describe nonreactive online research in more detail is because this field has recently expanded very quickly and will soon lead to a multitude of new nonreactive research strategies that offer analyses of incomparable potency with regard to the availability of information and the efficiency of analysis. The other reason can be found in the exemplary character this type of research has on the influence that technological developments may exert on the development of nonreactive measurement. However, access to information has also increased due to societal rather than technological developments. In Wim Wender's 1991 science fiction movie *Until the End of the World*, the protagonist can only be found by his pursuers on his voyage around the world because of their access to his bank card data. Now, 15 years later, the inhabitants of industrialized societies are accustomed to a broad variety of relatively new technological equipment including satellite navigation for private cars, health insurance data cards, or globally operational mobile phones, all producing additional traces of behavior that can be gathered and analyzed fairly well by "researchers" of different affiliations. Beyond technological developments, a strong need for security in many industrialized societies seems to further increase the recording of individual data (e.g., security cameras at public places). Although systematic access to this kind of data is often restricted, it can be both a valuable

source for nonreactive research (e.g., Brizer, Crowner, Convit, & Volavka, 1988) as well as a serious danger for individual freedom by data abuse. A related question is whether an awareness of increased data recording or even surveillance will change the public and semipublic behavior of individuals. Although people will not become chronically self-presenting inhabitants of a reality TV show, they might behave in a more self-focused (Carver & Scheier, 1981) and socially desirable way when they enter settings where surveillance is salient or even feared, for example in an airport's departure area or in a nonsmoking subway station.

THE LIMITATIONS OF NONREACTIVE MEASUREMENT

In the introduction, we verified that participants in social scientific research have the attributes that are also present in most situations occurring naturally: awareness and capacities for information processing. However, in a reader edited more than 20 years ago (Bungard, 1980), various authors ironically discussed why "good subjects" don't think in social psychology. What is the origin for this discrepancy? We learned that occasionally hiding goals or the process of data collection may be desirable for social scientific research to not "spoil" what is under investigation (i.e., behavior). In other words, we want our subjects to behave in research settings as they would do in natural contexts.

Validity

In the research literature on nonreactive or unobtrusive methods, questions of validity are frequently addressed implicitly but are only occasionally addressed explicitly (Campbell, 1957). Because of the fact that highly nonreactive research—particularly that of Types 4 and 5—is certainly more unconventional, sometimes considered primarily as "cute," spectacular, and (therefore?) less serious and influential, defensive argumentations by scientists favoring these methods are met. Part of the arguments that doubt nonreactive measures' validity refer to the fact that a substantial amount of Types 4 and 5 nonreactive research occurs in field settings with less control than in the laboratory. Compared with stud-

ies, for instance, on "(male) undergraduates in partial fulfillment of course requirements," *representativeness* at a first glance may be more likely given in the field. Because we as researchers are more adapted to the laboratory, however, field research is more under investigation concerning validity criteria. Maybe that because in laboratory research we are sure of *not* fulfilling criteria such as representativeness of participant and setting sample, we are in more danger of attesting this feature to field research. Visitors in an art gallery are simply gone after having been "under investigation." Were they representative? If yes (or no)—for which entity? Furthermore, because we are only occasionally interested in studying psychological variables specific for settings under investigation, we have to consider the questions of ecological validity (Brunswik, 1956) both inside and outside the laboratory. Nonreactive field research is not ecologically valid per se: Are we, for example, able to enhance our knowledge about human aggression by observing interactions in traffic, a football stadium, a school yard, a court proceeding, or an experiment with a highly efficient cover story? Where are the opportunities for and limitations of generalizability? Or is it more appropriate to select groups of situations in which behavioral variance may be explained instead of looking for broad generalizability? In the laboratory our awareness of external validity is directed toward the acceptability of withdrawing the context and reducing the naturally occurring complexity. This may be independent of the fact of whether the respective method is unobtrusive or not (see, e.g., Type 3 studies). In field research, more frequently met when highly unobtrusive methods are applied, the format of the question differs: May we transfer the results of research in complex, naturally occurring situations to other contexts, or do we ignore the specifics of situations when interpreting the findings? At this point the methodological interrelations, but at the same time independence between field versus laboratory setting and reactive versus nonreactive research, are evident.

Even though they try to avoid effects violating validity resulting from reactivity, nonreactive methods are not at all immune to threats. Do worn carpets, garbage, or archival data on absenteeism

indeed indicate what researchers attribute to them (Schweigert, 1998)? It is easy to imagine the effect of change in the recording procedure on a time series of data. Imagine, for example, a change of criteria when recording norm violating behavior. At first glance, the occurrence of specific behavior may have changed whereas in fact only the categorization has been modified, for instance, resulting from an administrative act (for an example, see following text). The type of research discussed here must be particularly aware of these threats to validity. Occasionally, true predictors of variance are highly unobtrusive themselves: In analyzing time series on statutory rape, Linneweber (2000) identified a significant decline in violence in one region he investigated. At the same time, in other areas, the number of complaints decreased, however, only moderately. What made this region become less violent all of a sudden? A closer investigation revealed a simple cause: Because the opening hours of the police station had been reduced, the police were less able to respond as quickly to complaints from the victims of violent crime, and it is known that the willingness to engage declines with temporal distance to critical events such as observing violence.

In cross-cultural research, the danger of misinterpreting differences (or similarities) has been discussed extensively (Doucette-Gates, Brooks-Gunn, & Chase-Lansdale, 1998). Nonreactive researchers would be well advised to learn lessons from this area. Basically, the advantage of reducing objectionable effects resulting from reactivity is paid for by reduced controllability. With respect to validity, the respective trade-off must be calculated.

To estimate the risk of misinterpretation, it might be advisable to carefully assess the convergent and discriminant validity of each specific nonreactive measure one considers using. An example for such an assessment is the study mentioned earlier by Cialdini and Baumann (1981) that compared the results of a nonreactive measurement technique with a standard interview procedure. They found that the results corresponded considerably. Most interestingly, this correspondence was qualified by the finding that "when the responses were laden with social desirability, attitudes measured by the

interview technique were skewed in the socially desirable direction relative to those measured by the littering technique" (p. 254).

Ethical Limits

In highly nonreactive research, the subjects or participants are not aware of being the objects of research. They are not aware of person(s) or installations recording data related to themselves. They may not be aware that others in their proximity or those who are able to observe them by using technical equipment or reading the traces of behavior are in the positions of scientist, experimenter, or confederate. Consequently, they are unable to refuse their participation. This fact has been discussed with respect to ethical considerations, and we will discuss these referring to the ethical principles of psychologists and the code of conduct of the APA (American Psychological Association; APA, 2002). In other national scientific associations we find more or less similar formulations. Because the APA's standards were recently revised, we will concentrate on these in this chapter.

At a first glance, nonreactive research contradicts principle 3.10 "Informed Consent," which states: "When psychologists conduct research [. . .] they obtain the informed consent of the individual or individuals [. . .]." (p. 1065). Also principle 4.03 "Recording" seems to be violated: "Before recording the voices or images of individuals to whom they provide services, psychologists obtain permission [. . .]". However, principle 3.10 continues "except when conducting such activities without consent is mandated by law or governmental regulation or as otherwise provided in this Ethics Code." Referring to formulations in Part 8 (Research and Publication of the ethical principles), the term *otherwise* hence legitimizes research activities without consent.

Because formulations 8.03, 8.05, 8.07, and 8.08 are of particular interest with respect to nonreactive research, they are cited nearly in full length:

> *8.03 Informed Consent for Recording Voices and Images in Research.* Psychologists obtain informed consent from research participants prior to recording their voices or images for data collec-

tion unless (1) the research consists solely of naturalistic observations in public places, and it is not anticipated that the recording will be used in a manner that could cause personal identification or harm, or (2) the research design includes deception, and consent for the use of the recording is obtained during debriefing.

> *8.05 Dispensing With Informed Consent for Research.* Psychologists may dispense with informed consent only (1) where research would not reasonably be assumed to create distress or harm and involves . . . (b) only anonymous questionnaires, naturalistic observations, or archival research for which disclosure of responses would not place participants at risk of criminal or civil liability or damage their financial standing, employability, or reputation, and confidentiality is protected. . . .

> *8.07 Deception in Research.* (a) Psychologists do not conduct a study involving deception unless they have determined that the use of deceptive techniques is justified by the study's significant prospective scientific, educational, or applied value and that effective nondeceptive alternative procedures are not feasible. . . . (c) Psychologists explain any deception that is an integral feature of the design and conduct of an experiment to participants as early as is feasible, preferably at the conclusion of their participation, but no later than at the conclusion of the data collection, and permit participants to withdraw their data.

> *8.08 Debriefing.* (a) Psychologists provide a prompt opportunity for participants to obtain appropriate information about the nature, results, and conclusions of the research, and they take reasonable steps to correct any misconceptions that participants may have of which the psychologists are

aware. (b) If scientific or humane values justify delaying or withholding this information, psychologists take reasonable measures to reduce the risk of harm. (c) When psychologists become aware that research procedures have harmed a participant, they take reasonable steps to minimize the harm.

(pp. 1069–1070)

As we can see, the formulations are rather comprehensive. We find an explicit reference to *naturalistic observations* that is not yet the case in the ethical standards of other national psychological associations. The principles allow nonreactive research of Types 4 and 5 even without debriefing (8.08) where some criteria are met, for example, preventing personal identification or harm (8.03:1) and the risk of criminal or civil liability or damaging the participants' financial standing, employability, or reputation, and confidentiality (8.05:b). *Deception*, which might be included in nonreactive methods from Types 1 to 4, is only accepted as an exception when explicitly justified (8.07:a) and when consent for the use of the recording is obtained during debriefing (8.03:2 and 8.07:c).

With respect to our discussion of various nonreactive measures, we realize that the scientific community has developed principles for highly responsible conduct in observations, in laboratory settings, and in field experiments. This includes reporting to ethic commissions as well as consulting peers. Ethical standards are continuously reviewed. As researchers facing the continued development of nonreactive methods in particular, the necessity to continue this effort is evident.

CONCLUSION

Summarizing our view on nonreactive measurement, we suggested a continuous conception of nonreactivity by identifying five types of nonreactive research (from less to more nonreactive) rather than by defining nonreactive methods in a dichotomous way. Measures of high nonreactivity are usu-

ally marked by a large degree of unobtrusiveness with regard to the subject's actual or perceived participation in a research study. Specifically those kinds of nonreactive measures (Types 4 and 5) may profit or at least change with the current and future sociotechnological developments, thus enabling us to apply new techniques and media explicitly relevant for highly nonreactive measures. In the meantime, the phrase "traces of behavior" appears in new light because the electronic means for collecting, saving, and processing data have significantly improved over the last decade. At least two areas are still rapidly developing: consumer behavior in various fields and individual behavior in "intelligent" technological environments.

Yes, our credit card companies are aware of any unusual expenditures we might make on the basis of our previous charging behavior. Of course this is "only"—or at least primarily—to protect us from misuse of our card. Our cell phones "know" where we are. Our cars determine the interval between service inspections on the basis of our driving behavior. Vehicles soon will start communicating so that they can form clusters with other vehicles for defined parts of routes (by "knowing" our destination and computing the optimal routes) enabling us to do things more important than steering—of course these activities will be recorded for later use for improving our own comfort. In household technology, the revolution is still to come: When approaching our home, the TV will switch to our favorite station, the room temperature and lighting will be regulated based on analyses of our preferences, and our refrigerators will order items based on the continuous monitoring of our consumption patterns.

Basically, for new forms of psychological research, the database for highly nonreactive research seems to be exploding. Presently, we can be fairly certain of one development: The responsibility of researchers when collecting new and processing available data will become a highly important topic for basic as well as applied research. This is particularly true for information that can be accessed or collected in nonreactive ways.

CHAPTER 15

EXPERIMENTAL METHODS OF PSYCHOLOGICAL ASSESSMENT

Edgar Erdfelder and Jochen Musch

What can be gained from applying methods of experimental psychology to problems of psychological assessment? Experimental psychology and psychological assessment, although both being important branches of psychology, are clearly distinct scientific disciplines with unique histories, characterized by discipline-specific theories, paradigms, and research methods (see Bringmann, Lück, Miller, & Early, 1997). Consequently, there has been little overlap between research in experimental psychology and research in psychological assessment. Despite some influential attempts at bringing the disciplines more closely together (e.g., Cronbach, 1957), little has been said about how the two disciplines could profit from each other. In this chapter, we aim at closing this gap by describing and illustrating benefits that can be gained from applying experimental methods to problems of psychological assessment.

Our chapter comprises seven sections. In the first section, we look at the origins of the experimental method in psychological research, describe its characteristics, and present a definition of the term *psychological experiment*. We then show in section two that if the term *experimental* has been used in the context of psychological assessment, it typically has been associated with meanings different from that in experimental psychology. We argue that it is both possible and useful to redefine experimental assessment methods in a way that is consistent with the notion of a psychological experiment

in experimental psychology. In sections three and four, major benefits and potential problems of the experimental approach to psychological assessment are discussed.

Sections five and six are devoted to illustrating the benefits of experimental assessment methods and ways to overcome the problems associated with this approach. In section five, we describe experimental methods of assessing the truth in cases in which people are motivated to conceal this truth. Four methods will be critically discussed: the randomized response technique (RRT), the unmatched count technique (UCT), the control question technique (CQT), and the guilty knowledge test (GKT). Consistent with the multimethod approach to psychological measurement, these techniques adhere to decidedly different rationales to overcome response bias in sensitive areas. The RRT and the UCT are techniques to ensure the anonymity of respondents in surveys. They aim at encouraging more honest responding on a voluntary basis and use an experimental between-subject manipulation of question content. The CQT and the GKT are the most frequently used methods of polygraph lie detection and coercively try to determine the guilt or innocence of suspects who deny liability for a crime. Both the CQT and the GKT are based on a within-subject manipulation of question content. It will soon become clear why we classify these four approaches as truly experimental, whereas related methods of assessing the truth that are often given

The work on this chapter has been supported in part by grants from the TransCoop Program of the Alexander von Humboldt Foundation and the Otto Selz Institute, University of Mannheim, Germany.

the label "experimental" as well (e.g., the bogus pipeline procedure; Jones & Sigall, 1971) do not qualify as experimental assessment methods in the sense defined here and, consequently, will not be discussed further in the present chapter.

In survey research, the true answer to a question is often better conceived of as lying on a continuous rather than a dichotomous scale. Section six addresses the problem of systematic errors in rating-scale or multiple-choice assessments induced, for example, by the order in which questions are arranged or by the range of response options offered to the respondent. We summarize how to cope with these problems using methods of experimental psychology. The concluding seventh section presents guidelines on how problems of psychological measurement can be solved effectively using experimental methods. Moreover, we present a list of criteria that should be met whenever experimental assessment methods are to be applied in practice.

THE EXPERIMENTAL METHOD IN PSYCHOLOGY

From the very beginning, the experimental method has been closely tied to hypothesis testing and theory evaluation in psychological research (see Boring, 1950; Bredenkamp, 2001; Calfee, 1985; Cook & Campbell, 1979; Davis, 1995; Shadish, Cook, & Campbell, 2002). During the past 50 to 60 years in particular, experiments have been used fairly routinely for testing hypotheses from different branches of psychology. Typical examples include "frustration causes aggression" (Berkowitz, 1989, p. 61), "elaborate semantic processing of information improves later recall memory" (Craik & Tulving, 1975, p. 270), and "client-centered short-term psychotherapy is more effective than conflict-centered therapy" (Meyer, Stuhr, Wirth, & Ruester, 1988, p. 196). Common to all applications of the experimental method is the comparison of at least two conditions, treatments, or groups of participants with respect to the mean or some other aspect of the distribution of a so-called dependent variable. The experimental conditions define the levels of the so-called independent variable, and the causal effect of

the independent variable on the dependent variables is the target of the research. For instance, in the three examples just presented, amount of frustration experienced (strong vs. no frustration), type of information processing during encoding (semantic vs. phonetic processing), and type of psychotherapy received (client-centered vs. conflict-centered), respectively, might be the independent variables, each manipulated in two levels preselected by the experimenter. In the same three experiments, amount of aggressive acts shown by the participants, proportion of items recalled 1 week later, and ratings of subjective well-being after psychotherapy, respectively, could serve as dependent variables. Different group means of the dependent variables are typically taken as evidence in favor of causal effects of the independent variable, as specified by the psychological hypothesis under investigation.

Of course, not every observed mean difference establishes a true causal effect, and not every comparison of two or more conditions meets the criteria of a psychological experiment. A defining feature of the experimental method is that the experimental conditions need to be comparable, that is, they should differ only with respect to the independent variable under scrutiny and not with respect to other variables, so-called confounding variables, that might also affect the dependent variable. Important candidates for confounding variables are person attributes such as aggressiveness, intelligence, or gender and features of the experimental situation such as presence versus absence of other people, background noise, or hour of the day. Ideally, all potential confounding variables should be kept constant to prevent possible nuisance effects by *fixation*. An example would be the elimination of background noise by using soundproof experimental booths. Typically, however, not all confounding variables can be controlled by fixation. *Counterbalancing* experimental conditions is often a good remedy in such situations. For example, in a within-subject experiment, each participant is observed under two or more treatment conditions. Thus, a potential confounding variable is the order in which treatments are applied. Nuisance effects can be controlled by assigning an equal number of

participants to each of the possible treatment order permutations. This method guarantees that the treatments do not differ with respect to the average position of a treatment in the treatment sequence.

The control techniques of fixation and counterbalancing can only be applied to confounding variables known in advance. Effects of unknown variables have to be controlled by *randomization*, that is, by the method of random assignment of experimental units to experimental conditions. Randomization is the most powerful experimental control technique because it makes sure that the distribution of all confounding variables associated with the experimental units, including even the unknown ones, does not differ between experimental conditions. This minimizes the possibility that a treatment effect observed in a randomized experiment is "spurious," that is, artificially caused by one or more confounding variables rather than by the experimental independent variable itself (Shadish et al., 2002; Steyer, Gabler, & Rucai, 1996). It is for this reason that many researchers prefer to tie the definition of the psychological experiment to the method of randomization. Bredenkamp's (2001) definition is a typical example: "An experiment can be defined by the following criteria: The experimenter creates the conditions, systematically varies them, and applies the principle of randomization" (pp. 8226–8227).

WHAT IS AN EXPERIMENTAL ASSESSMENT METHOD?

Compared to its important role in the context of psychological hypothesis testing, the experimental method has been largely neglected or even ignored in the field of psychological assessment and psychological testing. Indeed, if the term *experimental* has been used in this context, it typically has been associated with meanings different from that defined earlier. Historically, it has been used to refer to (a) new assessment instruments still in the phase of construction (e.g., Goldman & Saunders, 1974, p. xi; Graves, 1991); (b) measurement techniques based on technical equipment such as tachistoscopes, millisecond timers, or response counters

(e.g., Kretschmer, 1928); or (c) assessment methods using paradigms, tasks, and measures typically used in experimental cognitive psychology (e.g., Trepagnier, 2002).

In contrast to these historical meanings, we advocate a definition that is consistent with the notion of a psychological experiment discussed in the last section. We propose to call assessment methods "experimental" if and only if the following two conditions are met:

a. Predefined aspects of human behavior are observed under at least two experimental conditions manipulated by the experimenter.
b. A measurement model or law specifies how the to-be-measured psychological construct is related to the behavior observed in the different experimental conditions.

As a possible example, consider Shepard and Metzler's mental rotation task. This task can be converted into a truly experimental assessment method by making use of the linear law of mental rotation proposed by Shepard and Metzler (1971). To illustrate this law, recall that each single mental rotation task consists of pictures of two abstract three-dimensional geometric figures that are either identical or not. If they are identical, then one of the figures can be rotated in three-dimensional space until it coincides with the other. Participants are asked to judge as quickly as possible whether the two figures can be brought to congruence or not. Typically, half the figure pairs to be judged consist of identical figures, whereas the other half consists of figures with identical features but different three-dimensional structures so that they cannot be rotated into each other.

If α denotes the angle of rotation for identical figures, the linear law of mental rotation states that $E(T_i \mid \alpha)$, and the conditional expectation of the response time T of participant i for identical figures separated by an angle of α, is given by

$$E(T_i \mid \alpha) = a_i + b_i^{*}\alpha. \qquad (1)$$

In other words, for a given angle α, the average response time of any participant i is a linear combi-

nation of a sensorimotor component, the simple reaction time a_i, and a cognitive processing component, namely, the time required per degree of mental rotation b_i. Let us assume now that one is interested in assessing the mental rotation speed $v_i = 1/b_i$ selectively, uncontaminated by the sensorimotor speed component. Obviously, a simple way of achieving this goal would be to observe the response times under two experimental conditions that differ only in the angles of rotation α_1 and α_2, such that $\alpha_2 > \alpha_1$. According to the linear law of mental rotation, the average difference in response times in these two conditions is

$$E(T_i \mid \alpha_2) - E(T_i \mid \alpha_1) = b_i(\alpha_2 - \alpha_1). \quad (2)$$

Hence a pure measure of the mental rotation speed v_i of participant i can be derived by simple algebraic manipulation from the participant's mean response times observed under two experimental conditions:

$$v_i = 1/b_i = (\alpha_2 - \alpha_1)/(E(T_i \mid \alpha_2) - E(T_i \mid \alpha_1)). \quad (3)$$

To preclude misunderstandings, it should be noted that the experimental approach to psychological assessment we advocate here does not necessarily require quantitative laws relating two or more physical variables such as the Shepard-Metzler law. Experimental assessment techniques can be applied to dichotomous categorical data (see Birnbaum, 1992, for examples in the context of utility measurement) and quite simple measurement models, too. For example, the speed of accessing letter meaning can be measured using a very simple additive measurement model in combination with an experimental paradigm suggested by Posner, Boies, Eichelman, and Taylor (1969). The response time of a "same" judgment to physically different letters with the same name (i.e., "Aa"), minus the response time for a "same" judgment to physically identical letters (i.e., "AA"), is generally regarded as a valid measure of the time needed for accessing the name of a letter (Petrill & Brody, 2002, p. 585). In addition, multinomial models for categorical data (Batchelder & Riefer, 1999) provide a very general framework for developing and testing psychologically motivated measurement models that are tai-

lored to specific experimental designs. This class of models is likely to be very useful for solving problems of experimental assessment, at least at the group level (Batchelder, 1998).

These examples may suffice to illustrate that it is not important what particular type of law or model applies to the experimental task. Mandatory for experimental assessment techniques, as we understand them, is that there *has* to be at least some model or a law that precisely specifies how the to-be-assessed attribute or construct is related to the behavior observed under different experimental conditions.

Benefits of Experimental Assessment

What are the benefits of the experimental approach to psychological assessment? First, and perhaps most important, the experimental method provides sound solutions to what we have called decomposition problems elsewhere (e.g., Buchner, Erdfelder, & Vaterrodt-Plünnecke, 1995; Erdfelder & Buchner, 1998a, 1998b). Decomposition problems arise because empirical psychological variables (such as test scores, response times, etc.) are almost always affected by more than a single psychological state or trait. In general, therefore, the observed scores cannot be regarded as "trait-pure" or "state-pure" measures of specific psychological constructs. Rather, the empirical measures are better conceived of as composites of different psychological constructs, each contributing to the observed scores in an uncontrollable manner. For example, as we have seen earlier, the number X_i of Shepard-Metzler problems that can be solved in a prespecified time frame (e.g., 3 minutes) is a composite of a sensorimotor component a_i and a mental rotation speed component b_i.

A decomposition problem can be defined as the problem of finding a method that provides pure measures of the psychological constructs of interest, uncontaminated by other psychological traits or states that are involved in the task. In other words, decomposition problems are problems of maximizing the validity of psychological assessment by decomposing the observed test scores into pure measures of the to-be-assessed constructs. A decomposition problem can be

solved if an identifiable measurement model is available that essentially defines a one-to-one mapping of parameters characterizing the to-be-assessed psychological constructs ("latent variables") on parameters characterizing the distribution of the empirical variables observed in the test situation ("manifest variables"). Data obtained under single testing conditions are usually insufficient for defining measurement models that are both psychologically plausible and identifiable. As we have illustrated using the Shepard-Metzler task, experimental methods can often help in such situations by enriching the empirical domain of the assessment paradigm. We will further illustrate this point in the next section by showing how responses in interviews can be decomposed, roughly speaking, into true responses and a social desirability component.

A second benefit of experimental assessment methods is closely related to the first. When psychologists assess individual or group characteristics in applied settings, they often aim to *explain* a particular state of affairs, for example, failure at school, phobia symptoms, or memory problems (e.g., Westmeyer, 1972). What does it mean to explain human behavior scientifically? Since the pioneering work of Hempel and Oppenheim (1948), scientific explanations are generally conceived of as logically correct answers to "why" questions such as "Why does my son fail at school?" or "Why does my daughter suffer from a spider phobia?" The description of the to-be-explained state of affairs is called the "explanandum," and the sentences from which it is logically deduced are called the "explanans." According to Hempel and Oppenheim (1948), the explanans always consists of at least one empirically well-established general law and at least one empirically verifiable antecedent condition that together imply the explanandum. For example, if E denotes the explanandum, then a permissible explanation of E might be an argument of the following modus ponens structure:

If (A1 and A2) then E   (general law)
            A1   (antecedent condition 1)
            A2   (antecedent condition 2)
Therefore: E   (explanandum)

The goal of experimental psychology is to develop and to test general laws that can be used for scientific explanation (e.g., Bredenkamp, 2001). In contrast, psychological assessments aim to show that the antecedent conditions necessary for deducing the explanandum from the general laws are in fact met. To stick with the preceding example, assessments investigate whether A1 and A2 are indeed true for a particular individual or group to which the explanandum refers (Westmeyer, 1972). Unfortunately, however, the constructs measured by standard clinical or educational tests very often do not match any of the psychological constructs or processes involved in the laws of experimental psychology. Therefore, the classical Hempel-Oppenheim schema of scientific explanation, although accepted by many psychologists, is useless unless a solution is found to this "correspondence problem" between theories of experimental psychology on the one hand and psychological assessment methodology on the other hand. Obviously, by directly referring to particular laws and models of human behavior, experimental assessment methods show a way to address this problem. Thus, experimental measures provide a means of explaining behavior in the strict sense defined by Hempel and Oppenheim (1948).

A third benefit is more measurement–theoretic in nature. Psychological assessment methodology is often plagued by the problem of meaningfulness (e.g., Suppes & Zinnes, 1963). In representational measurement theory, a proposition about measurement results is called "meaningful" if a permissible rescaling of the measures never changes the truth value of the proposition. For example, the sentence "the measures X and Y correlate by $r = .80$" is meaningful if only if X and Y are interval scales with respect to the underlying constructs they supposedly measure. If this assumption is true, then the measures are unique up to linear increasing transformations, leaving Pearson correlations unaffected. However, if they are actually ordinal rather than interval scales, then the scale values may be subjected to any monotonically increasing transformation, and this can affect Pearson correlations more or less drastically. Obviously, any interpretation of Pearson correlations presumes, either implicitly (e.g., in most validity studies) or explic-

itly (e.g., in structural equation modeling), that the measures involved are interval scales with respect to the underlying constructs.

The key problem with assumptions on measurement scales is that there is often neither a way of testing them directly nor a way of proving their truth mathematically (Aiken, 1999, p. 40). Again, experimental assessment offers a way to address this problem. Because the measures derived from these methods are, by definition, components of psychological laws or measurement models, their scale properties can often be analyzed mathematically by investigating the structure of the laws that define these measures.

To illustrate, let us again consider the linear law of mental rotation. It relates two physical quantities, the angle of rotation (in degrees) and the response time (in milliseconds), both of which are ratio scales with respect to the physical dimensions of rotation angle and response time, respectively. We could thus arbitrarily decide to use other units of measurement for both scales. If c' denotes the multiplicative scale factor implied by changing the units of measurement for the rotation angle, and if c'' represents the corresponding scale factor for time, Equation (3) would change as follows:

$$v_i' = 1/b_i' = c' \, (\alpha_2 - \alpha_1)/(c'' \, (E(T_i \mid \alpha_2) \\ - E(T_i \mid \alpha_1))) = (c'/c'') \, v_i. \quad (4)$$

Thus, a permissible scale transformation of the physical variables induces a linear transformation of the type $v_i' = (c' / c'') \, v_i$ on the psychological scale values measuring mental rotation speed. We may conclude that v_i measures the mental rotation speed on a ratio scale, provided that the linear law of mental rotation is indeed valid.

Problems of Experimental Assessment Methods

Methods providing benefits often do not come without costs. This principle also holds for experimental assessment methods. First, because these methods require measurement models or laws accounting for behavior in several experimental conditions, applications of these methods are limited to those fields in which appropriate laws or models have already been developed. Hence, progress in theory development must always precede progress in experimental assessment methodology.

Second, if we want to rely on models or laws for purposes of psychological assessment, we have to make sure that these models and laws are actually valid. Measuring mental rotation speed using Equation (3) makes sense only if the law used to derive this equation holds for each person. Evidence from experimental psychology often only shows that laws of behavior hold at the aggregate level, however. If we use a law for the purpose of individual assessments, we need to make sure that this law also holds for single individuals.

Third, because experimental assessment methods require observations obtained under at least two different conditions, control techniques must be used that minimize effects of confounding variables. The choice among possible control techniques should depend on whether the unit of psychological assessment is (a) an individual or (b) a group of persons. If groups are the unit of assessment, experimental assessments typically require *between-subjects designs*. To control for nuisance effects of person attributes while comparing *groups*, randomization, the most important control technique in experimental psychology, should routinely be applied to keep unknown confounding influences constant across conditions.

If *individuals* are the units of assessment, a more frequent case in psychological assessment, *within-subject designs* are required in which each to-be-assessed individual is observed under each of the conditions of the design. In this situation, nuisance effects, particularly those associated with the order in which the experimental conditions are arranged, are most threatening. We can distinguish *retest effects* and *carryover effects* (Davis, 1995). Retest effects refer to systematic differences between early and late tests in a test sequence, irrespective of the type of treatment that precedes the other. Training and fatigue effects are examples of positive and negative retest effects, respectively: Training effects help the participants to perform better the longer the experiment lasts, and fatigue effects do just the opposite. Carryover effects, in contrast, are not simply additive effects of the treatment position in a

treatment sequence. They refer to treatment-sequence interactions, that is, to the phenomenon that the effect of a treatment is modified by the treatment that precedes it. For example, carryover effects can take the form of positive or negative transfer effects: Practicing one task A trains skills that either facilitate or interfere with the performance in a subsequent task B. Another type of carryover effect refers to task comprehension: The way a specific task is understood depends on the experimental conditions experienced previously.

Whether randomization of the conditions is appropriate in within-subject assessment designs primarily depends on how often each individual is observed under each condition. Obviously, randomization would not make much sense if each individual is observed only once per condition. For example, if we are interested in assessing the mental rotation speed of an individual i by applying Equation (3) to just two response times measured under two different angles of rotation, we must assume that the order in which the two rotation conditions are arranged does not affect the response times systematically. If this assumption would be false, then the estimate of v_i based on Equation (3) would be biased irrespective of whether the condition order was determined randomly or not. However, the situation would be different if we could observe each individual many times under each of the two angles of rotation. By randomizing the order of the two rotation conditions and applying Equation (3) to the average response times registered for each rotation angle, unbiased estimates of v_i could be obtained. More precisely, if each additional observation causes an additive, treatment-independent increment or decrement to the response times (e.g., representing fatigue effects or training effects), then this effect could be eliminated by repeating the treatments several times and by arranging them in a random order. Of course, the efficiency of randomization depends on the number of repetitions. For just a few repetitions, randomization does not necessarily eliminate nuisance effects in the sample.

Next to randomization, single-case experimental designs with a fixed, predefined order of the conditions (e.g., the A-B-B-A design) can be applied to

control for additive retest effects. By counterbalancing the order of the conditions across replications, these designs can effectively eliminate additive retest effects even for few repetitions. In addition, retest effects can be reduced by practicing the relevant tasks prior to the experimental session so that further training effects are unlikely.

Unfortunately, however, all these techniques are not really helpful for controlling carryover effects. The only possible remedy against carryover effects is to select the order of the conditions and the breaks between them carefully. Carryover effects may be strong for one treatment order AB and weak or absent for the reverse order BA. For example, assume that A is a yes–no recognition test for a set of words learned previously, whereas B is a free recall test for the same words. Obviously, the recognition test A would have a very strong impact on the subsequent free recall performance B, especially in the case of a short time lag between both tests. Reversing the order of conditions (recall-then-recognition procedure) might be a better idea, although it is not without problems either (Batchelder & Riefer, 1999).

We recommend a two-step strategy to cope with these problems. First, the experimenter should carefully select (a) the order of conditions and (b) the breaks between conditions so that the likelihood of order effects, especially carryover effects, is minimized. Second, the experimenter should perform a pilot experiment comparing the treatment sequence defined in the first step to several control groups lacking the first treatment(s) of the sequence. If the data patterns do not depend on whether other treatments had been undergone before, this provides evidence that carryover effects do not pose a major problem. Retest effects can be examined in a similar way, using several permutations of the original treatment sequence in the control groups.

Finally, next to the validity of the assessment procedure we also need to consider its reliability. Other things being equal, measures derived from experimental assessment procedures are likely to be less reliable than measures derived from single conditions because they typically combine several random influences. For example, using Equation (3)

for measuring the mental rotation speed involves the estimation of the difference between two mean response times. Because the variance of the difference between two independent random variables, $V(X - Y)$, equals the sum of the single variances, $V(X) + V(Y)$, the standard error of the difference between two independent sample means will always be larger than the standard error of a single mean. As a consequence, the measure of v_i derived from Equation (3) will be less reliable than the mean response times from which it is derived.

Depending on the measurement model involved, there may be several ways to address the reliability problem. In general, increasing the number of observations is an effective remedy. One way of increasing the number of observations would be to keep the number of experimental conditions constant and increase m, the number of observations per condition. Another way would be to add more experimental conditions to the design. In case of the Shepard-Metzler law, for example, one could make use of a third or a fourth rotation angle and then estimate v_i by inverting the slope b_i of the regression line fitted through the response times for the three or four rotation angles.

EXPERIMENTAL ASSESSMENT OF TRUTH

Survey research has proved to be extremely useful for measuring opinions, attitudes, and behaviors across a broad spectrum of interest, including the most highly sensitive and controversial topics. But can a researcher really expect to get honest answers when asking for sensitive, socially disapproved, or incriminating attitudes and behaviors? In this section, we discuss four instructive examples of experimental assessment methods, all of which are concerned with the assessment of truth in sensitive areas. The first two of these methods, the randomized response technique (RRT) and the unmatched count technique (UCT), are examples for assessments at the group level, whereas the control question technique (CQT) and the guilty knowledge test (GKT) provide assessments at the level of single individuals. The RRT and the UCT are used in surveys to ask sensitive questions respondents might be willing to answer in principle, given that they are

assured complete anonymity in a credible manner. In a more coercive way, the CQT and the GKT are used in polygraph tests to uncover the truth in cases in which guilty respondents are by no means willing to tell the truth because they have to fear serious consequences on disclosure of their misdoings.

The randomized response technique (RRT) was first suggested by Warner (1965). He based his technique on the notion that arguably the most promising method to encourage honest responding in surveys is to collect data anonymously. To credibly ensure respondents' anonymity, Warner directed the respondents to answer to one of two logical opposites, depending on the outcome of a randomizing device that selects the question to be answered with probability p and $(1 - p)$, respectively. For example, a randomized response survey may consist of the following set of questions pertaining to a stigmatized Group A (which may consist, e.g., of tax evaders or marijuana consumers):

Question 1: Is it true that you are a member of A?
Question 2: Is it true that you are not a member of A?

The respondent is asked to answer "yes" or "no" to one of these questions. Importantly, a randomizing device (e.g., dice) is used to determine the question to which the respondent is asked to answer. With probability p, the respondent is asked to answer Question 1; with probability $(1 - p)$, the respondent is asked to answer Question 2. Even though the researcher does not need nor want to know the outcome of the dice throw and, consequently, the question that is actually being answered, he does know the probability p that is determined by the nature of the randomizing device and can, therefore, use elementary probability theory to determine the percentage of respondents' affirmative responses at the aggregate level:

$$P(\text{yes}) = p \, \pi + (1 - p) \, (1 - \pi), \qquad (5)$$

where π denotes the proportion of the total population belonging to the stigmatized group A. Equation (5) defines the measurement model of the RRT; it relates the to-be-measured latent parameter π to the overall proportion of "yes" responses, $P(\text{yes})$, that

can be estimated directly from the data. Note that because the outcome of the randomizing device is unknown to the interviewer, the respondent's anonymity is guaranteed; nobody can know whether a given "yes" answer indicates that a respondent belongs to the sensitive group. However, solving for π in the preceding model equation, an estimate of the proportion of respondents being a member of the stigmatized Group A can be obtained from the proportion of "yes" responses in the sample and p, the probability determined by the randomization device (Warner, 1965):

$$\pi = (P(\text{yes}) - (1 - p))/(2p - 1). \qquad (6)$$

Warner's original formulation of the RRT was followed by many improvements aimed at enhancing the validity of the approach. For example, to address the problem that the efficiency of the model is less than optimal, the sensitive question may be paired with an unrelated question. The following questions may then be presented to the two groups to which each respondent is assigned with probability p and $1 - p$, respectively:

Question 1: Have you ever used heroin?
Question 2: Do you subscribe to *Newsweek*?

The prevalence of "yes" responses to the neutral question has to be known in the randomized response estimation procedure. If it is not known a priori, additional empirical evidence is required. Alternatively, the directed-answer variant of the RRT may be used in which the respondents are either asked to report truthfully to the sensitive question or to ignore the question altogether and to just say "yes," thereby also protecting those who give a "yes" answer to the sensitive question (Fox & Tracy, 1986; Greenberg, Abdul-Ela, Simmons, & Horvitz, 1969). In each case, the prevalence of the sensitive attribute in the population may be estimated from the individual responses, while the anonymity of each individual respondent is upheld.

The feasibility of the RRT has been demonstrated in a large number of studies. The questions at issue concerned drug abuse, exam cheating, illegal abortions, Social Security fraud, child abuse, tax evasion, and a host of other sensitive topics. In most validation studies, the randomized response approach produced considerably higher estimates of π than did the "yes" responses of direct questioning, thus providing evidence for the usefulness and validity of the approach. Detailed summaries of this research can be found in Antonak and Livneh (1995), Chaudhuri and Mukerjee (1988), Fox and Tracy (1986), and Scheers (1992).

For more than 30 years, all randomized response models tried to divide the population into two distinct and exhaustive classes: those respondents who engaged in the critical behavior and those respondents who did not. The respective sizes of these classes were represented by the population parameters p and b, respectively. Because these two parameters add up to 1, only one parameter had to be estimated. This could easily be done based on the one data category available in most RRT models, namely, the overall proportion of "yes" responses. However, despite their many successful applications, traditional RRT approaches can be criticized as being susceptible to cheaters, that is, respondents who do not answer as directed by the randomizing device. There is indeed evidence that cheating does occur (Locander, Sudman, & Bradburn, 1976). Clark and Desharnais (1998) therefore proposed an extension to the traditional RRT technique that no longer assumes that all respondents necessarily conform to the rules of the RRT. In their cheater detection model, Clark and Desharnais (1998) took into account that some respondents may answer "no," regardless of the outcome of the randomizing device. Their model, therefore, endeavors to divide the population into the following three classes: p (the proportion of compliant and honest "yes" respondents, i.e., respondents who honestly admit the critical behavior); b (the proportion of compliant and honest "no" respondents, i.e., respondents who truthfully deny the critical behavior); and g ($1-p-b$, the proportion of noncompliant respondents who do not conform to the rules of the RRT and answer "no" to the sensitive question, regardless of the outcome of the randomization process). Obviously, there are two independent parameters in this model (because the three proportions add up to 1), and two parameters cannot be estimated on the

basis of only one proportion of "yes" responses provided by traditional RRT methods. The problem of parameter estimation for this model can, however, be solved by an experimental between-subject manipulation of the probability with which participants are forced by the randomizing device to simply say "yes." Thus, the experimental approach to psychological assessment again leads to a considerable improvement in the assessment quality. By assigning participants randomly to two groups for which the probability of being forced to say "yes" by the randomizing device is different, the null hypothesis that no cheating occurs (g = 0) can be tested.

Another interesting and appealing alternative to the traditional randomized response method was developed by Miller (1984). In what has been called the unmatched count or randomized list technique (RLT/UCT), much of the complexity and distrust sometimes associated with the use of randomizing devices and the seemingly bizarre instructions used in the RRT are avoided. In the UCT, respondents are simply given a list of behaviors including the sensitive behavior of interest as well as a number of innocuous additional items. The respondent is then asked to report *in total* how many of the activities in the list he or she has engaged in. The assumption is that the respondent will feel comfortable reporting this total count because it does not reveal any particular activities he or she has been involved in. In an experimental between-subjects manipulation, a second sample of respondents is given a similar list that, however, does not contain the sensitive question. Let μ denote the mean number of activities people engage in without the critical activity. If π again represents the proportion of the total population engaging in the critical activity, the model equations of the UCT describing the mean counts μ_1 and μ_2 in experimental Conditions 1 and 2, respectively, as a function of μ and π can be written as follows:

$$\mu_1 = (1 - \pi)\, \mu + \pi\, (\mu + 1) = \mu + \pi \qquad (7)$$

$$\mu_2 = \mu \qquad (8)$$

Thus, by subtracting the mean counts in the two samples, an estimate of π, the prevalence of the sensitive behavior, may be obtained as illustrated in Table 15.1.

Despite its apparent simplicity, some caution must be exercised when using this technique. For example, if the nonsensitive items are uncommon, any total count greater than zero will rouse suspicion. On the other hand, if the nonsensitive items are common, the total count can reach its theoretical maximum, no longer offering protection to the respondents. Fox and Tracy (1986) therefore recommended the use of (a) as many items as feasible and (b) items ranging midway between a 0 and 100% prevalence, making extreme total counts unlikely. Applied appropriately, the randomized list technique has been shown to lead to higher estimates for sensitive behaviors than could be obtained using direct questioning (LaBrie & Earleywine, 2000; Wimbush & Dalton, 1997).

What is common to both the randomized response and the unmatched count technique is that because of their between-subjects design, they can only be used to determine the prevalence of the target behavior at an aggregate level. The status of a single individual can never be determined without undermining the honest promise of anonymity on which these methods are based. However, there are situations—most often in the course of police investigations and legal proceedings—in which the

TABLE 15.1

The Randomized List/Unmatched Count Technique (RLT/UCT)

Sample 1	Sample 2
own a computer.	I own a computer.
I've been to France.	I've been to France.
—	I tried heroin.
I was born in August.	I was born in August.
Total count 1	**Total count 2**

true status of an *individual*, for example with regard to his or her guilt in a criminal case, has to be determined. Cooperation cannot be expected under such circumstances because of the severe negative consequences a suspect often has to face in the case of a conviction. There are, however, experimental methods of psychological assessment that can be used to obtain sensitive information even under such adverse conditions. Unlike the RRT and the UCT, these techniques rely on within-subject experimental manipulations and are commonly referred to as the polygraph method.

Polygraphic measurement is certainly among the most controversial experimental methods of psychological assessment. This is perhaps not surprising, given that few psychological assessments have more profound consequences for those who take them. In the United States, the Employee Polygraph Protection Act of 1988 eliminated most private-sector uses of polygraph tests, but there still is a widespread reliance on polygraph testing by state and local police departments and national security and law enforcement agencies in the United States. Polygraph testing is also regularly used by the police forces in Canada, Israel, and Japan. In child custody and child abuse cases, they are also often used in Germany.

The most frequently used procedures in polygraph testing are the CQT (control question technique) and the GKT (guilty knowledge test). Both rely on a within-subjects experimental manipulation: Suspects are presented with different questions, and their reactions to these questions are used to either judge their guilt (in the case of the CQT) or to demonstrate their knowledge of details of the crime (in the case of the GKT). We will discuss the theoretical rationale of these two different approaches in turn.

The CQT is based on the assumption that guilty people will be more concerned about questions pertaining to their misdeed ("Did you rob the bank?") than to control questions also designed to elicit emotional reactions ("Have you ever taken something from someone who trusted you?"). Accordingly, their nervous system is expected to react more strongly to the relevant than to the control questions. On the other hand, innocent people are assumed to be less concerned about their responses to crime-relevant questions. Instead they are expected to respond more strongly to the control questions because they are led to believe that lying to these questions is also cause for failing the test. Thus the model equations underlying the CQT assume that autonomic responses to critical questions differ by a certain additive increment or decrement from the corresponding responses to control questions, depending on whether a person is actually guilty or not guilty, respectively. The most frequently used measures of autonomic reaction to the test questions are electrodermal responsivity (skin resistance or conductance), respiration, and blood pressure.

The standard scoring method for the CQT considers control and relevant questions in pairs. For each physiological channel, a decision is made whether the control or the relevant questions elicit the larger response. Scores are assigned for each channel depending on how much larger or smaller the response to the control questions is as compared to the response to the relevant questions. By summing the scores across all question pairs and the different psychophysiological channels, a total score is obtained that is interpreted as indicating either truthfulness or deception. Middle scores are usually considered inconclusive.

A major criticism of the CQT, forcefully advanced by Lykken (1974), is that it is biased against innocent people. To the extent that innocent individuals are more disturbed by the threatening accusations contained in the crime-related relevant questions than by the comparatively innocuous control questions, false positives will occur. Skeptics have even argued that the CQT hardly has much more than chance accuracy with innocent subjects. Contrary to these claims, CQT advocates have argued—often based on different studies using different criteria, but sometimes even on the same studies interpreted differently—that existing research supports the conclusion that CQT accuracy with innocent persons (i.e., its specificity) exceeds 90%. (For a more-detailed treatment of this controversy, see Iacono, 2000.) With regard to guilty suspects, proponents argue that the sensitivity of the

CQT exceeds 95% and that it is very difficult for guilty individuals to learn how to appear nondeceptive by using appropriate countermeasures to defeat the test. In contrast, skeptics argue that the accuracy with guilty subjects is probably closer to 75% when no countermeasures are used and significantly less if countermeasures are used, such as biting the tongue or performing mental arithmetic during the presentation of the control questions. Skeptics also argue that information on how best to use countermeasures is easily accessible nowadays, and that it would be unrealistic to assume that a defendant would undergo polygraph testing in an important issue without trying to use appropriate countermeasures. Unfortunately, it is possible and indeed quite easy to train guilty examinees to "pass" a CQT examination (Ben-Shakhar & Dolev, 1996).

With regard to the objectivity of polygraph testing, interscorer agreement has been shown to be uniformly high across a wide variety of studies. For example, Honts (1996) reported the reliability of blind chart evaluation of numerically scored charts to be over 0.90. When blindly rescoring polygraph examinations conducted by Canada's national police force, however, Patrick and Iacono (1991) found that examiners often relied on information not contained in the original polygraph charts. In 93% of the cases in which they contradicted their own numerical scoring, they favored the truthfulness of the suspect in their report. This finding seems to suggest that examiners were at some level aware of the inherent bias of the CQT against innocent people and tried to counteract this bias by overriding the physiological data if it did not agree with extrapolygraphic information.

Almost nothing is known about polygraph test–retest reliability. This is unfortunate given the lack of standardization of applied polygraph tests and the extent to which subjective factors may influence the outcome. Research on possible differences in outcome between "adversarial" tests administered by law enforcement officials and "friendly" tests arranged by the suspect's attorney is also completely missing, a serious shortcoming, given that it is the results of friendly tests that are most often presented in court (Iacono, 2000).

To assess the validity of polygraph testing, two types of studies have typically been used. Laboratory studies required volunteers to act out a mock crime and then to lie about it on a polygraph test, whereas field studies used criminal suspects who had already taken a test and whose true status could reliably be determined on the basis of independent evidence. Both types of validation studies have serious limitations regarding their generalizability to real-life circumstances, however (Ben-Shakhar & Furedy, 1990; Iacono & Patrick, 1999). Although one might reasonably assume that the embarrassing nature of the control questions is similar in the laboratory and in real-life situations, innocent laboratory subjects are likely to be relatively more responsive to control than to relevant questions because to them, the relevant questions have less emotional impact than in real-life investigations. Laboratory studies are therefore likely to overestimate the accuracy of polygraph tests for innocent individuals. Accordingly, permitting participants in a mock crime study to choose whether they wanted to be "innocent" or "guilty" (to win more money if they passed the CQT) has been shown to reduce CQT accuracy in laboratory tests, presumably due to the participants' increased sense of personal involvement in the mock crime (Forman & McCauley, 1986). Another factor potentially contributing to an overestimation of the validity of polygraph testing is that laboratory tests are usually carried out as part of a standardized experimental procedure, whereas field tests are likely to vary substantially across examiners and suspects.

Criminal investigations in which the suspect is later proved to be deceptive have been used as an alternative way of assessing the validity of polygraph testing. However, it is difficult to collect a sufficiently large number of cases in which the guilt or innocence of a suspect can be determined by a method that is independent of the outcome of the polygraph test. Patrick and Iacono (1991) found independent evidence for only 1 of 402 presumably guilty individuals. More important, the fact that failing the test leads to confessions in a substantial fraction of test administrations is no evidence for their validity. If a person passes a polygraph test, he

or she will usually not be asked to confess, and the polygrapher will most likely never know if he just produced a false-negative outcome. The kind of feedback the polygrapher is most likely to receive—a confession of a suspect believing in the validity of the polygraph test he just failed or the conviction by a judge who himself is influenced by the outcome of the polygraph interrogation—constitutes a biased sample and will almost always confirm the test outcome (Fiedler, Schmid, & Stahl, 2002). However, the most severe criticism of the CQT certainly is the lack of convincing evidence for its core assumption that the occurrence of stronger reactions to crime-related than to control questions will always be limited to guilty suspects.

A serious and arguably superior competitor to the CQT that avoids this problematic assumption is the GKT (guilty knowledge test) developed by David Lykken (1959, 1960). Even though the GKT also uses a within-subjects manipulation of question content, it has been argued to have a sounder theoretical rationale and scientific foundation (MacLaren, 2001). The GKT consists of a series of multiple-choice questions, all dealing with facts only the true delinquent can be familiar with. Each question contains one critical crime-related item presented among homogeneous control items unrelated to the crime. If, for example, the amount of money that was stolen in a robbery is not known by the public and only the police and the robber know that the amount stolen was $10,000, the suspect could be asked, "What was the amount stolen . . . $5,000 . . . $10,000 . . . $15,000?" A suspect is incriminated if his or her physiological responses to the crime-related alternatives consistently differ in some way from those evoked by the unrelated control alternatives. In the preceding example, a guilty person's autonomic reaction can expected to be highest at $10,000, thus revealing his or her knowledge and likely involvement in the crime. Unlike the CQT, the GKT does not have to rely on the questionable assumption that only the guilty react more strongly to critical crime-related questions than to emotionally laden control questions. Rather, the very construction of the GKT ensures that "for the guilty subject only, the 'correct' alternative will

have a special significance, an added 'signal value' which will tend to produce a stronger orienting reflex than that subject will show to other alternatives" (Lykken, 1974, p. 728). The special significance of the critical item in the GKT is mediated through simple recognition and need not be attributed to deception, motivation, or fear of punishment. The GKT has, therefore, been called the cognitive approach to psychophysiological detection (Ben-Shakhar & Furedy, 1990).

The power of the GKT to detect the guilty increases in a predictable manner with the number of items asked. Simultaneously, the probability of a false positive decreases with an increasing number of items. A particular strength of the GKT is that when it is competently performed and based on a sufficient number of questions, an innocent person very rarely fails. Therefore, it is not surprising that the GKT's specificity (proportion of innocent classified as innocent) has been reported to average from 94% (Ben-Shakhar & Furedy, 1990) to 98% (Elaad, 1990; Elaad, Ginton, & Jungman, 1992). The sensitivity of the GKT (proportion of guilty classified as guilty) was found to be 76% in a recent meta-analysis by MacLaren (2001). The most frequently cited disadvantage of the GKT, however, is that factual evidence must be available that can be developed into GKT items. Some crimes do not easily lend themselves to the GKT format because GKT items should best be based on information that is known to the police and the perpetrator, but not to innocent suspects. However, details of the crime that are already known by the public will also likely be known by innocent suspects. Accordingly, in a review of FBI case files, Podlesny (1993) concluded that only a minority of the case files could be used to develop GKT items. Moreover, several of the criticisms raised against the CQT also apply to the GKT. Most important, the GKT is also susceptible to countermeasures of suspects who are actually guilty based on the voluntary augmentation of reactions to the control items (Honts, Devitt, Winbush, & Kircher, 1996).

For several decades, an often-heated controversy surrounded the use of polygraph testing (e.g., Faigman, Kaye, Saks, & Sanders, 1997). Today, virtually

all professional polygraphers believe that the existing evidence, despite its limitations, supports the use of polygraph testing as a forensic tool. Social scientists rather tend to stress the need for more compelling evidence of validity before techniques are adopted that severely affect the judicial system and the civil liberties of those tested. Given the commitment of the large number of professional polygraphers in many countries and the often-fundamental criticism raised against their methodology by basic research scientists, polygraphic measurement will likely continue to be the most controversial experimental method of psychological assessment.

EXPERIMENTAL METHODS IN SURVEY RESEARCH

All the methods discussed previously largely assume that truth is known to the respondents and that it is a dichotomous variable. There are, however, situations in which there is no absolute truth and in which the "real" answer may not be an unequivocal true or false. For example, a common assumption in cognitively oriented survey research is that people construct judgments of attitudes or behavior on the spot on demand, using the information that is accessible from their memories at the time of judgment (e.g., Schwarz & Bless, 1992; Strack & Martin, 1987). Some of this information may be chronically accessible and brought to mind whenever an issue is being referred to, resulting in judgments that are relatively stable over time. Other information, however, may be less accessible, and the context is an important determinant of whether it will be activated. Such information may inadvertently be made accessible to respondents via features of a self-report instrument as, for example, the presentation order of questions or the range of numerical response scales. This temporarily accessible information is capable of influencing the respondent during any of the stages of the response process, including question interpretation, retrieval of information from memory, judgment, and the generation of a response. In the worst case, the effects of such temporarily accessible information may lead to systematic measurement error. Experi-

mental methods of controlling the effects of contextual features on response processes can help to address this problem.

For example, according to the *inclusion–exclusion* model (Schwarz & Bless, 1992), assimilation occurs when information retrieved for answering a preceding question comes to mind and is used to form a temporary representation of the target of the current question. On the other hand, contrast effects occur when the information retrieved for an earlier question is excluded from the respondent's temporary representation of the target. The experimental variation of question order makes such context effects visible and also provides a means of controlling them.

Along a similar vein, several studies have shown that the range of frequencies in response options also affects the response process of survey respondents (e.g., Schwarz, Hippler, Deutsch, & Strack, 1985). For example, in an experimental investigation of response option ranges, respondents who were presented with a high-frequency range of responses (from "4 or less" to "9 or more") indicated to have been more often emotionally depressed during the past month than respondents presented with a lower range of response options (from "0" to "5 or more"; Harrison & McLaughlin, 1996). Again, only an experimental variation of different response options allows detecting and addressing such effects. Additional variables affecting the likelihood and direction of item order effects, as well as ways of addressing them, are summarized in Schwarz (1999); Sudman, Bradburn, and Schwarz (1996); Tourangeau (1999); and Tourangeau, Singer, and Presser (2003).

GUIDELINES FOR USING EXPERIMENTAL ASSESSMENT METHODS

The previous sections of this chapter have shown how experimental methods can help address problems of psychological assessment for which alternative solutions based on more traditional methods still appear to be lacking. Therefore, it should not come as a surprise that experimental assessment methods have become more and more frequent in psychological research during the past two decades.

In the area of memory assessment, for example, both the process dissociation procedure of measuring controlled ("explicit") and automatic ("implicit") memory processes (e.g., Jacoby, 1991, 1998) and the source monitoring paradigm (e.g., Johnson, Hashtroudi, & Lindsay, 1993) designed to assess simultaneously item memory (i.e., memory for a piece of information) and source memory (i.e., memory for the source or the context of a piece of information) have become frequently used tools. Most of the measurement models developed for these and other cognitive paradigms belong to a very general class called multinomial processing tree models (Batchelder & Riefer, 1999; Riefer, Knapp, Batchelder, Bamber, & Manifold, 2002).

As another example from the field of biopsychology, consider the subtraction method routinely used in neuroimaging studies to detect brain regions that are associated with specific cognitive processes. The difference method also belongs to the class of experimental assessment techniques because it is based on the within-subjects comparison of brain activities under two experimental conditions that presumably differ only in the cognitive activity that is performed in response to the demands of a task. Still another example is the Implicit Association Test (IAT) recently introduced by Greenwald, McGhee, and Schwartz (1998) to assess "implicit" or unconscious attitudes in social psychological and personality research. Like some of the techniques considered previously, the IAT is based on the within-subjects comparison of response times registered under two experimental conditions, a congruent condition that favors fast responding and an incongruent condition that hinders fast responding to the extent that there is an implicit association between two concepts of interest. These examples may suffice to illustrate that the list of possible applications of experimental assessment techniques is indeed long and includes all branches of psychology.

As we have seen, however, experimental assessments, like more traditional assessment methods, are not without problems. First, the validity of an experimental assessment method depends on the validity of the measurement model or law on which it is based. Therefore, these techniques should not be applied in practice unless strong evidence supporting the underlying model or law has been accumulated. This necessary process of model validation may even lead to better measurement models than the one the validation process has started with. In the area of memory assessment, this has happened quite frequently, for example, in the case of measurement models developed for the process dissociation procedure (e.g., Buchner, Erdfelder, Steffens, & Martensen, 1997; Buchner et al., 1995; Erdfelder & Buchner, 1998b; Steffens, Buchner, Martensen, & Erdfelder, 2000; Yonelinas & Jacoby, 1996; Yu & Bellezza, 2000) or source monitoring tasks (Batchelder & Riefer, 1990; Bayen, Murnane, & Erdfelder, 1996; Dodson, Holland, & Shimamura, 1998; Klauer & Wegener, 1998; Meiser & Bröder, 2002; Riefer, Hu, & Batchelder, 1994). The randomized response and polygraph lie detection techniques have taken similar routes (see earlier discussion, this chapter).

In testing measurement models or laws for purposes of psychological assessment, three aspects should be kept in mind. First, one should try to avoid saturated models that can fit any empirical data structure simply because the number of estimated parameters equals the number of data points to which the model is being fitted. To provide for testable models, it is much better to ensure that the number of independent data points exceeds the number of parameters estimated from these data. Second, in testing nonsaturated measurement models, one should refer to the empirical level that is implied by the assessment technique. If the assessment technique refers to aggregates, then the empirical tests should refer to the same aggregates. In contrast, if the assessment method refers to individuals, then the empirical model tests should also pertain to individuals. Model validity on one level does not imply validity on the other level. Third, model validation requires more than just establishing acceptable goodness-of-fit indices. Systematic validation studies have to establish the construct validity of the model parameters by showing that they differ between certain populations or treatment conditions in a way that is consistent with their psychological interpretation (see Bayen et al., 1996; Buchner et al., 1995; Erdfelder & Buchner, 1998a; Klauer & Wegener, 1998; Meiser & Bröder, 2002).

If a model has passed all these validation hurdles, reliability of parameter estimates is a final issue. The standard way of enhancing reliability by increasing the number of data points is not always applicable because it can be costly, time consuming, or even interfere with the validity of the assessment method. In such a situation it is useful to study how the confidence intervals of the to-be-assessed parameters depend on the values of other model parameters that are of minor importance in the assessment context. In Clark and Desharnais' (1998) cheater detection RRT model, for example, the test administrator may choose any pair of probabilities p_1 and p_2 underlying the two random devices required for this method. Although the values p_1 and p_2 might be less relevant psychologically, they do affect the error of the estimate of the target parameter π and thus the reliability of the assessment method in total. By carefully selecting both the context of the test and the values of background parameters such as p_1 and p_2 in the model of Clark and Desharnais (1998), test administrators often can maximize the reliability of experimental assessment at no additional cost.

PART III

METHODS OF DATA ANALYSIS

CHAPTER 16

METHODOLOGICAL APPROACHES FOR ANALYZING MULTIMETHOD DATA

Michael Eid

Multimethod research programs require diverse methods of data analysis that take the multimethod character into account. Methods analyzing the convergence of different methods that are supposed to measure the same latent construct have a long tradition in psychometrics. They can be traced back to Spearman's (1904) claim of a *correlational psychology* that should detect common structures underlying fallible measures that are distorted by several error influences. The history of psychometrics can be considered the refinement of methodological approaches explaining multivariate associations in a more appropriate way. Because of the great importance of multimethod research strategies, a host of methodological approaches for the analysis of multimethod structures have been developed (Dumenci, 2000; Schmitt & Stults, 1986). However, not all of them can be considered in this handbook, and some reasons why we selected certain methodological approaches to be discussed in more detail in the following chapters will given in the current chapter. The aim of this chapter is threefold. First, five conceptual distinctions will be discussed that influence the choice of data-analytic approaches for analyzing multimethod data. Second, an overview of several statistical approaches for multimethod data that are dealt with in more detail in the following chapters will be given to highlight their essentials and to provide reasons why these approaches have been chosen. Third, more traditional approaches such as correlation analysis, which is not discussed in more detail in the following chapters, will be considered here to provide the reader with in-depth knowledge of multimethod approaches.

MAJOR DISTINCTIONS OF METHODOLOGICAL APPROACHES FOR ANALYZING MULTIMETHOD DATA

It is important to understand the distinctions among methods before choosing an approach to any research question under consideration. To this end, I will discuss five general distinctions among methodological approaches: single versus multiple trait methods, single-indicator versus multiple-indicator methods, interchangeable versus structurally different methods, temporal versus nontemporal methods, and metrical versus categorical data methods.

Methods for Measuring Single Versus Multiple Traits

An important first distinction concerns the question of whether methods are appropriate for analyzing one construct or several constructs. To be in line with the terminology of multitrait–multimethod analysis, all constructs will be called "traits" in this chapter. Data-analytic methods for a single trait can be applied to separate a common trait-specific source of variance from systematic method-specific influences and unsystematic measurement error. Consequently, convergent validity as well as method specificity can be estimated. Data-analytic methods

for multiple traits additionally allow the analysis of the generalizability of method effects across traits. If one considers different raters to be different methods in one's research, one could analyze, for example, whether a rater bias generalizes across the traits (i.e., whether a rater over- or underestimates all traits of an individual in the same way) or whether there is an interaction between the rater and the trait indicating that the method effect depends on a trait. For example, a rater might overestimate an individual's neuroticism but not his or her extraversion. Only multitrait analyses can detect the generalizability versus trait specificity of method influences. If the method effect generalizes perfectly across traits, measurement error can be separated from systematic method-specific effects. In this case, the different methods serve as different indicators for one trait, and the different traits measured by the same method serve as different indicators for the method effect. However, if a method effect does not generalize perfectly across traits and there is only one indicator for a trait–method unit, measurement error and method-specific effects cannot be sufficiently separated (Eid, Lischetzke, Nussbeck, & Trierweiler, 2003). However, this separation is possible if there are multiple indicators for each trait-method unit.

Single-Indicator Versus Multiple-Indicator Methods

A second distinction separates models into those with single indicators and those with multiple indicators for each trait–method unit. In single-indicator approaches like the traditional multitrait–multimethod (MTMM) matrix of Campbell and Fiske (1959), there is only one indicator for a trait–method unit (e.g., one self-report item measuring extraversion). Multiple-indicator approaches require at least two indicators for each trait–method unit (e.g., several self-report items measuring extraversion). Multiple-indicator approaches have the advantage that unsystematic measurement error can be more appropriately separated from systematic method-specific effects, and that the generalizability of method effects can be

more adequately analyzed (Eid et al., 2003; Marsh & Hocevar, 1988).

Interchangeable Versus Structurally Different Methods

A third important distinction concerns the type of method considered. Generally, one can distinguish between interchangeable methods and methods that are structurally different (Kenny, 1995). Interchangeable methods cannot be distinguished with respect to psychological criteria. An example could be students who are randomly chosen from the classes of different teachers to provide a rating of the teaching quality. In this case, there is no structural difference between the students. All students have more or less the same access to the teacher's behavior, and it does not really matter who rates the teacher. Interchangeable and randomly selected raters are typically used if one is interested in (a) measuring a trait (e.g., teaching ability) and (b) estimating the precision with which this trait can be measured on the basis of multiple ratings (convergent validity).

The situation is quite different if one asks, for example, the teacher him- or herself, a student, and the principal of the school to rate the teaching quality of the teacher. In this case, the three raters are structurally different because they are not randomly chosen from the same set of possible raters. Whereas in the case of multiple student ratings it is reasonable to assume that the different students have the same access to the teacher's behavior, this is quite different with the teacher, the principal, and the student rating. Because the raters have different perspectives, it might be more interesting to contrast the ratings and to explain the differences between them. For example, it would be interesting to find out why the ratings of the principal and the student might differ from the self-report. Whereas the mean value of randomly chosen students is a reasonable measure of the teacher's quality of teaching (as the average opinion of the students), this is not necessarily the case for structurally different raters if one does not know why the ratings differ. If the principal has never visited the teacher while

he or she was teaching, one might hesitate to define the teaching quality as the mean of the three ratings. Nevertheless, it would be interesting to analyze why the principal's view differs from the teacher's and the student's view to learn more about principals' subjective theory of teacher qualities. Along a similar vein, it would be interesting to examine the differences in the views of the teacher and the student and not to just simply aggregate the two ratings to diminish method specificity.

The distinction between randomly selected (interchangeable) and structurally different raters is quite similar to the distinction between random and fixed factors in the analysis of variance (e.g., Hays, 1994). In the case of random factors, the different groups (methods) of a factor are considered as randomly chosen from a population, and the researcher aims to estimate the variation of the factor. In the fixed effect model of analysis of variance, the aim is to analyze the effect of different groups and to contrast them. Hence, the concept of interchangeable versus structurally different methods has consequences for the choice of a methodological approach.

Temporal Versus Nontemporal Methods

Temporal methods use the same measure to analyze the same individuals repeatedly (Kenny, 1995), meaning that the measurement occasions can be considered different methods. For example, the mood of an individual can be repeatedly assessed in different situational contexts to estimate his or her tonic mood level. In longitudinal studies, the methods (i.e., situations, occasions) have a temporal order, and methods for longitudinal data analysis must take this into consideration. As a consequence, methods of data analysis that are appropriate for multimethod research in general have to be adapted for temporal analysis by taking the temporal order into account (Khoo, West, Wu, & Kwok, chap. 21, this volume).

Methods for Metrical Versus Categorical Data

In choosing one method of data analysis it is also necessary to take the nature of the data into consideration. Methods that are appropriate for metrical variables are usually not appropriate for categorical data and vice versa.

OVERVIEW OF METHODOLOGICAL APPROACHES FOR MULTIMETHOD RESEARCH

The five distinctions presented so far influence the selection of the methodological approach most appropriate for examining a research question under consideration. Three classes of approaches will be dealt with in more detail in this handbook. They are either widely used traditional approaches or they provide a flexible modeling framework that can be used to model multimethod data with respect to the conceptual distinctions: (a) correlation and association methods, (b) latent variable models, and (c) models of analysis of variance, generalizability theory, and multilevel models.

Correlation and Association Models

The convergence of methods can be assessed by correlating the methods that are supposed to measure the same trait. Campbell and Fiske (1959) have extended this idea by defining an MTMM correlation matrix. In this matrix there is one indicator for each trait-method unit, and this matrix allows a thorough analysis of convergent and discriminant validity by comparing several correlation coefficients (e.g., the correlations between different methods measuring the same trait versus those between different methods measuring different traits). Schmitt (chap. 2, this volume) describes this approach in more detail. Campbell and Fiske's criteria for evaluating an MTMM matrix offer researchers a valuable and widely used approach to multimethod research. The interpretation of the MTMM correlations, however, is difficult when there are differences in the reliabilities of the measures because the reliabilities limit the sizes of the correlations (Millsap, 1995b). Therefore, analyzing and interpreting latent MTMM correlations that can be estimated by latent variable models is recom-

mended (Eid, Lischetzke, & Nussbeck, chap. 20, this volume; Rost & Walter, chap. 18, this volume).

The MTMM matrix was the basis for the refinement of correlation models testing specific hypotheses about the way trait and method influences are connected. It is based on Campbell and O'Connell's (1967) idea that the size of the correlations between traits depends on the similarity of methods used to measure the different traits, Swain (1975) developed a *direct product model* in which the correlations of an MTMM matrix are supposed to be a product of two correlations indicating convergent (correlation between methods) and discriminant (correlation between traits) validity. According to this model, the correlation $Cor(Y_{ik}, Y_{jl})$ between an observed variable Y_{ik} measuring the trait i with method k and an observed variable Y_{jl} measuring the trait j with the method l can be decomposed in the following way: $Cor(Y_{ik}, Y_{jl}) = Cor(T_i, T_j) \times Cor(M_k, M_l)$. The correlation $Cor(T_i, T_j)$ represents the association between two traits (discriminant validity); the correlation $Cor(M_k, M_l)$ denotes the correlation between the two methods (convergent validity). Moreover, the correlation between two observed variables measuring two different traits depends not only on the correlation of traits but also on the correlation of methods. If the same methods are used to measure the two different traits, the correlations of the observed variables equal the correlations of the two traits. If the same two traits are measured by two different methods, the correlation of the traits is attenuated by the correlation of the methods. Thus the smaller the correlations between the methods, the smaller are the expected correlations of the observed variables measuring the traits by these methods.

The Campbell and Fiske (1959) criteria can be evaluated by comparing different correlations of the direct product model (Browne, 1984; Cudeck, 1988; Marsh & Grayson, 1995). When considering the simplest example with two traits and two methods, these criteria can be evaluated as follows: (a) The correlations between two methods, for example, $Cor(M_1, M_2)$, should be large indicating convergent validity. (b) The monotrait–heteromethod correlations [e.g., $Cor(Y_{11}, Y_{12})$] should be higher than the heterotrait-heteromethod correlations [e.g., $Cor(Y_{11},$ $Y_{22})$]. Expressed in terms of the direct product model: $Cor(T_1, T_1) \times Cor(M_1, M_2) > Cor(T_1, T_2) \times Cor(M_1, M_2)$. Because $Cor(T_1, T_1) = 1$, this criterion is fulfilled whenever the correlation between traits is smaller than 1. (c) The monotrait–heteromethod correlations [e.g., $Cor(Y_{11}, Y_{12})$] should be higher than the heterotrait–monomethod correlations [e.g., $Cor(Y_{11}, Y_{21})$], for example: $Cor(T_1, T_1) \times Cor(M_1, M_2) > Cor(T_1, T_2) \times Cor(M_1, M_1)$. Because $Cor(T_1, T_1) = Cor(M_1, M_1) = 1$, this requirement is fulfilled when $Cor(M_1, M_2) > Cor(T_1, T_2)$, and—more generally—when the between method-correlations are larger than the between-trait correlations. (d) The pattern of trait interrelationships should be the same considering the submatrices of the MTMM matrix (see Schmitt, chap. 2, this volume) comparing all possible method combinations. This requirement is always fulfilled when the direct product model is appropriate for the data because in a heteromethod block, all trait correlations are weighted by the same method correlation, for example, $Cor(M_1, M_2)$, ensuring that the ratio of two trait correlations is the same for all different mono- and heteromethod blocks taken into consideration.

Browne (1984) extended the direct product model to the *composite direct product model*, which also considers measurement error influences. Wothke and Browne (1990) have shown how this model can be formalized as a model of confirmatory factor analysis (see also Dumenci, 2000). The direct product models are attractive models because their parameters are closely linked to Campbell and Fiske's (1959) criteria. Their application is most useful when the expected MTMM correlations follow the proposed structure. They are, however, also limited. For example, they do not imply a partition of the variance in separate trait and method portions (Millsap, 1995b). Moreover, the models assume that the correlations between traits are the same for all monomethod blocks. This means, for instance, that the correlations between traits measured by self-report must equal the correlations between traits that are all assessed by peer report. This is a limitation of the model. Moreover, these models are based on single indicators for each trait-method unit, making the appropriate determination of reliability difficult.

Correlation methods are most appropriate for metrical variables as the convergence between two methods is represented by one value. For categorical (nominal, ordinal) variables, other coefficients are needed that take the categorical nature of the data into account because the convergence between methods could be different for the single categories of a variable. Consider two ratings for example: There might be high agreement for one category (i.e., whenever one rater chooses this category, the other rater chooses the same category) but low agreement for other categories. Because researchers are often less familiar with association models for categorical data than with classical correlation analysis, these methods will be explained in more detail in Fridtjof Nussbeck's chapter (chap. 17, this volume). He shows how association coefficients for categorical data can be defined and how loglinear modeling can be used to test specific hypotheses about the association and agreement with respect to categorical data.

Latent Variable Models

The correlation and association methods described so far are correlations between observed variables that are usually affected by measurement error. Latent variable models are statistical approaches designed to separate measurement error from "true" individual differences. Moreover, latent variable models allow the definition of latent variables that represent different sources of influence on the observed variables. The advantage here is that one can model complex structures that link latent trait-specific and latent method-specific variables to other latent variables. Concepts of criterion-related validity can, therefore, easily be linked to concepts of convergent and discriminant validity.

Latent variable models can be classified into four groups depending on whether the observed variables and the latent variables are categorical or metrical (Bartholomew, 1987). Models with categorical observed variables and metrical latent variables are *models of item response theory* (IRT) and models of *factor analysis for categorical response variables*. Models with categorical observed and categorical latent variables are models of *latent class analysis*. Models with metrical observed and metrical latent variables are models of *factor analysis* (for metrical

observed variables) and, more generally, *structural equation models* (SEM), whereas models for metrical observed and categorical latent variables are *latent profile models*.

SEM and IRT are approaches for metrical latent variables. SEM is the methodological approach that has been most often applied to analyze multitrait–multimethod data. It offers a very flexible modeling framework for defining models for quite different purposes. SEM are very general models implying other approaches such as the composite direct model, covariance component models (Wothke, 1995), and models of analysis of variance as special cases. They allow easy extensions of existing models, for example, to consider multiple indicators of a trait–method unit. Eid et al. (chap. 22, this volume) provide an introduction to these models and present some models for analyzing MTMM data. Recent developments in IRT offer a similarly flexible modeling framework for categorical response variables. Rost and Walter (chap. 18, this volume) show how multicomponent IRT models can be applied to multimethod data structures.

SEM and multicomponent IRT models are very flexible methodological approaches. Several models for analyzing MTMM data have been developed in these frameworks. However, sometimes it might be necessary to adapt these models or to formulate new models for analyzing a research question. Therefore, the aim of the following chapters in this handbook is not to give a sufficient overview of all possible models that can be considered when conducting research, but to introduce the basic ideas of these approaches and to illustrate their advantages and limitations by referring to some important models and applications.

IRT models are models for categorical observed variables. SEM have been developed for metrical observed variables. However, there are also approaches for modeling dichotomous and ordinal variables with SEM. The development of new methods for estimating and testing SEM for ordinal variables (Muthén, 2002) makes it possible to analyze ordinal variables with structural equation modeling as well. In fact, Takane and de Leeuw (1987) have shown that SEM of ordinal variables are equivalent to special models of IRT. What are the differences

between IRT models and SEM for ordinal variables with respect to the analysis of MTMM data?

SEM for ordinal variables are closely linked to the traditional way of structural equation modeling, which means they aim to explain a bivariate association structure (in this case the polychoric correlation matrix) by a set of latent variables. The great advantage of SEM for ordinal variables is that this association structure can be modeled by different latent variables representing trait- and method-specific influences as first- or higher-order factors. SEM for ordinal variables is variable-centered as trait- and method-specific influences are analyzed on the level of individual differences. The covariances between latent trait–method units are usually the starting point for SEM, and these covariances can be modeled in a very flexible way considering several latent variables.

The covariances of latent trait–method units are almost the end point of Rost and Walter's (chap. 18, this volume) presentation of multicomponent IRT models for multimethod data. The IRT models that they discuss are more restrictive with respect to the homogeneity of the items considered because differences in the discrimination parameters are not allowed (which are represented by different factor loadings in SEM). Moreover, these models are less variable centered because the modeling of the associations of the latent trait-method unit is not at the center of their focus. IRT models for multimethod data focus more strongly on a decomposition of item parameters and person parameters to detect general and item- and person-specific method influences. A strong advantage of IRT models is the many possibilities to decompose the item parameters (which is not the focus of SEM), the extension of these models to mixture distribution models to detect structurally different subgroups, and the estimation of individual person parameters (which is less intended by SEM). Moreover, the measurement theoretical basis of the multicomponent IRT models and their implications for the estimation of the model parameters is impressive. Hence, both types of models stress different kinds of multimethod influences, and an interesting domain of future psychometric research would be a closer integration of both traditions.

Latent class and *latent profile analysis* are approaches for categorical latent variables. There is good reason to assign latent class models to the family of IRT models, and therefore, Rost and Walter (chap. 18, this volume) also introduce latent class models and show how they can be combined with other IRT models to analyze MTMM data. Several other approaches have applied the latent class modeling framework for analyzing interrater agreement, and Nussbeck (chap. 17, this volume) refers to these approaches. Latent class models have been extended to log-linear models with latent variables (Hagenaars, 1993). Log-linear models with latent variables are comparable to SEM in their flexibility to model latent structures. Eid and Langeheine (1999, 2003) have shown how latent state–trait models (see Khoo et al., chap. 21, this volume) can be formulated for categorical latent variables using this framework. This type of model can also be adapted for MTMM research, but there are currently very few applications to MTMM data (Eid, Lischetzke, Nussbeck, & Geiser, 2004).

Latent profile models are latent class models for metrical observed variables. However, a systematic application of this approach to multimethod data is, to our knowledge, still missing. Rather, new and versatile computer programs such as Mplus (Muthén & Muthén, 2004) will certainly contribute to a broader application of these models for MTMM research.

In sum, latent variable approaches for multimethod data have typically been applied to situations with metrical latent variables (IRT, SEM), and these approaches will be described in more detail in the current handbook. However, modeling approaches for latent categorical variables (latent class analysis, latent profile analysis) offer manifold and versatile new ways of analyzing the convergent and discriminant validity of typological structures that are of great importance for different areas of psychology (e.g., clinical psychology). This will certainly be one of the major future domains of psychometric research concerning multimethod measurement.

Analysis of Variance, Generalizability Theory, and Multilevel Modeling

Analysis of variance. The application of analysis of variance (ANOVA) models has a long tradition in multimethod research. To analyze the conver-

gence of several methods measuring the same trait, ANOVA models are routinely applied (Millsap, 1995b; Tinsley & Weiss, 2000). In general, two types of factors can be considered in ANOVA models: random and fixed factors. Random factors are considered when the levels of a factor are a random sample from a population and the research goal is to generalize to the population. For example, if different raters are randomly selected to rate the trait of different individuals, ANOVA with random factors can be applied to test convergent validity. In this case, variance components and intraclass correlation coefficients can be estimated to indicate the convergence of the different methods (Shrout & Fleiss, 1979; Tinsley & Weiss, 2000). In the case of structurally different methods, the factor can be considered fixed, and differences between the methods can, for example, be analyzed by planned contrasts. ANOVA designs can easily be adapted for MTMM studies if one considers the three factors *person*, *trait*, and *method*. Millsap (1995b) discussed the advantages and limitations of ANOVA models for MTMM research. He concluded that ANOVA designs are most appropriate when method influences generalize across traits but that ANOVA models have problems detecting method influences that are trait specific, that restrict variances (such as the central tendency response bias), and that are related to rater halo effects.

Generalizability theory. The classical ANOVA framework has been a starting point for many theoretical and methodological extensions from which generalizability theory has become very influential. Cronbach, Gleser, Nanda, and Rajaratnam (1972) developed *generalizability theory* based on the ANOVA methodology as a theoretical framework for analyzing the dependability of psychological measurements on different sources of influences (e.g., methods). Several coefficients for evaluating the generalizability of the results of a study can be estimated (Hox & Maas, chap. 19, this volume). Moreover, generalizability theory builds a fruitful theoretical framework for the conceptualization and the analysis of multimethod studies because it allows the considera-

tion of different types of methods (random, fixed) and different types of method structures. For example, the same raters can rate all individuals (crossed design) or raters can be specific for one individual, for example, friends (nested design). Multivariate generalizability models also allow multiple indicators for a trait-method unit, for example, by considering indicators as a further facet or by referring to multivariate models of generalizability theory (Jarjoura & Brennan, 1983). Hox and Maas (chap. 19, this volume) give an introduction to generalizability theory.

Multilevel modeling. In recent years, multilevel analysis, which represents another extension of linear models such as ANOVA and regression analysis, has become very popular in psychological research (Bryk & Raudenbush, 1992; Goldstein, 1995; Hox, 2002). Multilevel models have been developed to analyze data that are hierarchically ordered. For example, if an individual is rated by several friends who are chosen from his or her group of friends, this is a typical nested design with raters nested within targets. Multilevel models are particularly appropriate for these data structures, as they allow a very flexible modeling of method effects for these designs. For example, the number of friends chosen could be different for different target individuals. Multilevel models particularly allow a very flexible analysis of interchangeable methods, such as randomly selected raters, although other types of methods can also be considered.

The Coalescence of Statistical Models

Several statistical models have been described so far as distinct families of approaches that makes the flexible modeling of multimethod data possible. Although the distinctness helps us understand the peculiarities of each method, it conceals the close relationships between the methods. For example, IRT models can also be formulated as multilevel models for categorical variables (Rijmen, Tuerlincks, de Boeck, & Kuppens, 2003). Moreover, an increasing endeavor by psychometric researchers has been observed to integrate the advantages of several methodological approaches. For example,

Rost and Walter (chap. 18, this volume) show how Rasch models can be integrated with latent class models to detect population heterogeneity. Most recently, SEM have also been combined with latent class models to achieve structural equation mixture modeling (Bauer & Curran, 2004; Jedidi, Jagpal, & de Sarbo, 1997). Latent class models have been extended to multilevel models (Vermunt, 2003), and this is also true for SEM (Muthén, 1994) and models of IRT (Adams, Wilson, & Wu, 1997). These extended models offer enormous possibilities for formulating multimethod models. However, not everything that is possible is theoretically meaningful. Both the choice and the formulation of an appropriate model have to be guided by theoretical assumptions about the measurement process and the type of methods considered.

The following chapters demonstrate how the modeling frameworks of loglinear modeling (Nuss-beck, chap. 17, this volume), IRT (Rost & Walter, chap. 18, this volume), generalizability theory and multilevel modeling (Hox & Maas, chap. 19, this volume), and SEM (Eid et al., chap. 20, this volume) can be applied to define models for different purposes of multimethod research. Finally, Khoo et al. (chap. 21, this volume) show how different approaches such as SEM and multilevel modeling can be used for analyzing longitudinal data.

As previously mentioned, the aim of these chapters is not to present a complete list of multimethod models that have been discussed in these domains. Rather, it is intention of this handbook to provide a comprehensible introduction to the possibilities of these approaches to multimethod research, thus enabling readers to find or create the model that is most appropriate for their research question.

CHAPTER 17

ASSESSING MULTIMETHOD ASSOCIATION WITH CATEGORICAL VARIABLES

Fridtjof W. Nussbeck

This chapter provides an introduction to methods for analyzing the associations between categorical variables. The focus is on the analysis of nonordered categorical data, also referred to as *nominal data* or *nominal variables* (for the analysis of ordered categorical data, see Rost & Walter, chap. 18, this volume). First, general association indices such as the proportion (or percentage) agreement index, the occurrence (nonoccurrence) agreement index, the chi-square value, and coefficient kappa are presented. Their advantages and disadvantages are discussed. The second section shows how loglinear modeling can be used to analyze associations between categorical variables.

Nominal variables are variables whose values only serve to identify categories without any quantitative meaning. Clinical disorders, for example, are often assessed using nominal variables. The assignment of "1" to "paranoid schizophrenia disorder" and "2" to "major depressive disorder" is equally admissible as the reverse. The assignment of numbers to the categories has no impact on the further analysis of the data, because nominal variables are not ordered in a specific manner. Nominal variables can be obtained using a wide array of measurement methods such as self-ratings, peer ratings, and medical and psychological diagnoses (see Neyer, chap. 4, this volume; Bakeman & Gnisci, chap. 10, this volume). It is important to note that every subject has to be categorized and that he or she can only be classified into one category. In other words, the categories must be exhaustive and mutually exclusive. In most cases,

however, categories are not defined very accurately, and not all the information needed for a perfect diagnosis is available. Therefore, multimethod assessment can be used to verify the correct categorization by raters.

To analyze the convergence of different methods, nominal variables are usually presented in cross tables, in which the rows and columns represent the different categories of the manifest variables measured by the different methods. Two cross-classified variables are shown in Table 17.1a. This table demonstrates the simplest case consisting of two variables with two categories, where the variables are the ratings of two educational psychologists who assessed hyperactivity in a total of 500 pupils. Associations between both raters (Educational Psychologists A and B) are apparently evident. In the data set, for example, both tend to judge most pupils as "not hyperactive" and only a few (55 by A, 60 by B) as "hyperactive." Moreover, both raters agree in their ratings of the same 40 pupils as "hyperactive" and 425 pupils as "not hyperactive." They disagree in 35 cases. Both ratings converge in the majority of cases. The last column presents the marginal distribution for A, and the last row presents the marginal distribution for B.

When subjects are simultaneously rated by two or more observers, the ratings are associated when some combinations of categories are chosen more often than expected, given their marginal distributions—on the other hand, agreement only occurs when both observers assign the same categories to

TABLE 17.1

Cross-Classification of Hyperactivity Ratings by Two Educational Psychologists (Artificial Data)

(a) Data Set 1

		Educational Psychologist B		Marginal distribution of A
		hyperactive	Normal	n_{i+}
Educational Psychologist A	Hyperactive	40	15	55
	Normal	20	425	445
Marginal distribution of B	n_{+j}	60	440	500

(b) Data Set 2

		Educational Psychologist B		Marginal distribution of A
		Hyperactive	Normal	n_{i+}
Educational Psychologist A	Hyperactive	0	55	55
	Normal	0	445	445
Marginal distribution of B	n_{+j}	0	500	500

Note. n_{i+} represents the number of times Educational Psychologist A chooses "hyperactive" or "normal," respectively. The corresponding frequencies for Educational Psychologist B are denoted by n_{+j}. These marginals are obtained by adding the cell counts of the corresponding row (or column, respectively).

an individual. For example, the two ratings are associated if A assigns "hyperactive" to some of the pupils while B rates the same pupils as "normal," although there is no agreement (which only occurs when, e.g., both simultaneously rate "hyperactive" or "normal," respectively). Thus rater agreement can be seen as a special variant of association. In this chapter, the focus is on rater agreement, which plays an important role in the analysis of diagnostic accuracy. A high level of agreement between raters does not guarantee an individually correct diagnosis, but disagreement between raters often indicates a lack of diagnostic accuracy (Uebersax & Grove, 1990).

The association between variables and the extent to which methods or raters agree depend on two major criteria. First, it is important that both raters can distinguish well between any pair of categories. *Distinguishability* between two categories increases if the ratio of concordant ratings to discordant ratings of different observers increases. The second criterion is the lack of *bias* (Agresti, 1992). According to Agresti's definition, the amount of bias

depends on the comparison of the marginal distributions: If raters use the response categories with the same frequency, their marginal distributions are homogeneous, indicating that none of the raters prefers a particular category compared to the other raters. However, homogeneous marginal distributions do not imply that all raters judge the subjects correctly compared to the subjects' true status, but they show that they use the response categories in a similar way. If all raters distinguish between categories in the same way and their marginal distributions are similar, subjects are more congruently assigned to the categories of a variable, thus providing hints that observers define the categories in a similar way.

GENERAL ASSOCIATION INDICES

To quantify the association between categorical data a wide array of indices has been proposed (see Agresti, 1990, 1992; Fleiss, 1975; Suen & Ary, 1989; Suen, Ary, & Ary, 1986). In this chapter only

the most common indices will be introduced. A brief summary of more special indices will be given at the end of this section.

Proportion Agreement Index/Percentage Agreement Index

The proportion agreement index (p_O), which indicates how often two observers' ratings concur, is an intuitive and useful first measure of observer agreement. It is computed by dividing the number of times raters agree by the number of objects rated:

$$p_O = \frac{\sum_{i=1}^{I}(n_{ii})}{\sum_{i=1}^{I}\sum_{j=1}^{J}(n_{ij})},$$

n_{ij} denotes the number of cases in the cell ij of the cross-classified table, and n_{ii} represents the cells on the main diagonal (where $i = j$), which indicate concordant ratings. The same information is provided by the percentage agreement index ($p\%$), which is the p_O index multiplied by 100 to obtain the actual percentages (see Suen & Ary, 1989).

In Table 17.1a this index is $p_O = .93$. Sometimes p_O and $p\%$ are referred to as percent agreement (Hartmann, 1977), interval-by-interval agreement (Hawkins & Dotson, 1975), exact agreement (Repp, Deitz, Boles, Deitz, & Repp, 1976), overall reliability (Hopkins & Hermann, 1977), total agreement (House, House, & Campbell, 1981), or point-by-point reliability (Kelly, 1977).

Unfortunately, as Suen and Ary (1989) have shown, the proportion agreement index is inflated by chance agreement and suffers from its dependency on the marginal distributions. This can best be illustrated by the data in Table 17.1b. Assume, for example, that 55 pupils actually are hyperactive and 445 are not. Both raters agreed 445 times in their diagnoses of pupils as "not hyperactive," whereas in the other 55 times, Rater A correctly judged "hyperactive" while B assessed the same pupils as "not hyperactive." The proportion agreement index yields a value of $p_O = .89$, which is quite similar to the value obtained by the data presented in Table 17.1a. However, both raters did not agree in even one critical case, whereas in the first data set both raters agreed in 40 critical cases. The high agree-

ment stems only from the low prevalence of hyperactivity, which is correctly reflected by the marginal distribution of Psychologist A's judgments and the agreement between both raters for "normal" cases. Because A correctly identified hyperactive pupils, the high proportion agreement index may lead to the improper conclusion that B did as well—but B did not even detect one critical case. Hence, both the percentage agreement index and the proportion agreement index suffer severely from their insensitivity to critical cases and their dependency on the criterion's distribution (i.e., its prevalence). As the actual prevalence of behavior occurrence approaches unity or zero, there is a greater possibility that the proportion agreement index is inflated (Costello, 1973; Hartmann, 1977; Hopkins & Herman, 1977; Johnson & Bolstad, 1973; Mitchell, 1979). The closer the prevalence is to .50, the less likely the proportion agreement index is inflated (Suen & Ary, 1989).

If, for example, both raters assume a prevalence of .50 and if both raters are only guessing, their ratings could be based on the toss of a coin yielding probabilities of .25 for each cell of the cross-table. That is, given independent ratings (coin tosses), a base agreement of .25 would be expected in each cell (see Table 17.2a), and, therefore, $p_O = .50$. Assuming a prevalence of .90, these base agreements are not equally distributed but strongly skewed (see Table 17.2b), and the p_O is much higher ($p_O = .82$). Base agreement is most often referred to as agreement by chance (albeit this term is a bit misleading). Agreement by chance corresponds to the expected cell frequencies under the assumption of independence.

Because the magnitude of percentage agreement can be inflated by agreement by chance—which itself depends on the prevalence of behavior—it is impossible to provide a reasonable threshold for acceptable and unacceptable interobserver agreement. Additionally, the magnitudes of interobserver agreement cannot be directly compared between studies with different rates of prevalence. Thus, many authors have argued that the proportion agreement index should no longer be used (Hartmann, 1977; Hartmann & Wood, 1982; Hawkins & Dotson, 1975; Kratochwill & Wetzel, 1977; Suen &

TABLE 17.2

Agreement by Chance

(a) Agreement by chance with a prevalence rate of .50

		B		Marginal distribution of A
		1	**2**	p_{i+}
A	1	.25	.25	.50
	2	.25	.25	.50
Marginal distribution of B	p_{+j}	.50	.50	

(b) Agreement by chance with a prevalence rate of .90

		B		Marginal distribution of A
		1	**2**	p_{i+}
A	1	.01	.09	.10
	2	.09	.81	.90
Marginal distribution of B	$p+j$	.10	.90	

Note. p_{i+} and p_{+j} represent the marginal proportions of Raters A and B. Agreement by chance is computed by the product of the row and column marginals.

Lee, 1985), whereas others have supported its use because it is an intuitive, very simple, and easy-to-calculate concept (Baer, 1977). As demonstrated by Suen and Lee (1985), applied behavior analyses often include extreme prevalence rates that lead to considerably inflated agreement rates. Consequently, the proportion agreement index seems to be inflated by chance in most applications.

To overcome this problem, Birkimer and Brown (1979) suggested three methods to test the significance of an observed proportion agreement index against the possible percentage agreement by chance. These methods are approximations of the conventional chi-square (χ^2) test (Hartmann & Gardner, 1979). This index will be presented later in this chapter. Kelly (1977) suggested another method for avoiding the problem of inflation by chance. He postulated that the prevalence of the critical symptom should exceed .20 and should be less than .80 to compute the proportion agreement index. In addition, the computed proportion agreement value should be .90 or higher to indicate an acceptable

agreement. Unfortunately, there commonly is no prior knowledge about prevalence rates that would enable a theoretically founded application of the proportion agreement index. Nevertheless, it differs significantly from agreement by chance if (a) both conditions mentioned by Kelly are met and (b) there are more than 15 observations (Ary & Suen, 1985).

Hence, the proportion agreement index should only be used if these two conditions stated previously are met, but it is strongly recommended to test its significance by using the χ^2 test. Nevertheless, the fact that the proportion agreement index cannot be easily compared between studies remains an unsolved problem. For example, agreement of $p_O = .70$ with a prevalence of about .50 reflects much better interobserver agreement than agreement of $p_O = .90$ with a prevalence of .85.

Occurrence and Nonoccurrence Agreement Indices

To remedy the shortcomings of the proportion agreement index when the prevalence of a critical obser-

vation is very low or high, the occurrence and nonoccurrence agreement indices can be used. The computation of both indices is quite similar to the proportion agreement index, whereby the occurrence (or nonoccurrence, respectively) agreement index only reflects the number of times both raters agree on the occurrence (nonoccurrence) of the *critical* category and the number of times both raters disagree in general (on occurrence *and* nonoccurrence). The occurrence index (p_{occ}) should be used when the prevalence rate falls below .20. When the prevalence rate is higher than .80, the nonoccurrence agreement index (p_{non}) should be used (Kelly, 1977). The occurrence index is defined as

$$p_{occ} = \frac{\text{occurrence agreements}}{\text{occurrence agreements} + \text{disagreements}}.$$

By substituting the occurrence agreements with nonoccurrence agreements, the nonoccurrence agreement index can be computed. Given the data in Table 17.1a, where the prevalence rate is .11, the occurrence agreement index should be used. The occurrence agreement index provides a value of

$$p_{occ} = \frac{40}{40 + (15 + 20)} = .53.$$ For the data in Table 17.1b, the occurrence agreement index yields a value of zero, indicating that both raters did not agree for at least one critical observation. Thus occurrence and nonoccurrence agreement indices correct for most of the inflation by chance, but they do not correct for the total inflation by chance (Suen & Ary, 1989). One limitation of the occurrence agreement index can be viewed in the fact that often no prior knowledge about the prevalence rates exists, that is, knowledge that would enable a theoretically founded application.

Chi-Square (χ^2) Value

The χ^2 value, as a measure of association, compares observed cell frequencies with expected cell frequencies in a contingency table. There are several ways to compute expected frequencies depending on the researcher's hypothesis. One hypothesis that might be of interest for most researchers is the independence of two ratings. The expected cell frequencies in the independence model are computed as the product of the row and column sums, divided by the total number of observations. If a researcher is interested in any kind of association between variables, one has to test the joint distribution of two variables against the assumption of independence. In addition to the independence model, other hypotheses can be tested by comparing the expected frequencies implied by a particular hypothesis with the observed frequencies. For instance, if the object of interest is the agreement of two novices' ratings compared to the agreement of two experts' ratings, it would be necessary to set the frequencies of the experts' ratings contingency table as expected values. In general, the χ^2 value can be computed by

$$\chi^2 = \sum_{i=1}^{I} \sum_{j=1}^{J} \frac{\left(n_{ij} - e_{ij}\right)^2}{e_{ij}},$$

with n_{ij} as observed cell frequencies, e_{ij} as expected cell frequencies, and I and J denoting the number of categories. For the independence model, for example, the expected cell frequencies are computed by $e_{ij} = \frac{n_{i+} n_{+j}}{N}$, whereby n_{i+} and n_{+j} represent the marginal of category i of the first rating and j of the second rating. The degrees of freedom of the χ^2 value can be computed by $df = (I - 1)^2$ for quadratic contingency tables.

The higher the χ^2 value, the less the observed cell frequencies match the expected cell frequencies. Under the assumption of independence, a significant χ^2 value indicates that there is an association between both variables, which goes beyond the association expected by chance. If the expected cell frequencies are those of experts' ratings, a nonsignificant χ^2 value means that the novices generated a pattern of ratings that is similar to the experts' pattern. In this case the novices provided ratings of comparable quality.

Under the assumption of independence, the data in Table 17.1a yield the following χ^2 value:

$$\chi^2 = \frac{\left[40 - \left(\frac{55 \times 60}{500}\right)\right]^2}{\frac{55 \times 60}{500}} + \frac{\left[15 - \left(\frac{55 \times 440}{500}\right)\right]^2}{\frac{55 \times 440}{500}} + \frac{\left[20 - \left(\frac{445 \times 60}{500}\right)\right]^2}{\frac{445 \times 60}{500}} + \frac{\left[425 - \left(\frac{445 \times 440}{500}\right)\right]^2}{\frac{445 \times 440}{500}} = 215.81$$

with $df = 1$ and $p < .001$. This means that the observed cell frequencies deviate greatly from the expected cell frequencies.

To apply the χ^2 test, three conditions have to be met to achieve an approximation of the sampling χ^2 distribution to the theoretical one (e.g., Kennedy, 1983). First, the observations have to be independent. Thus, all members of the population of interest must have the same probability of inclusion in the sample. In the ideal case, the sample represents a perfect representation of this population. Second, the classifications have to be independent, mutually exclusive, and exhaustive. Third, as a rule of thumb, the χ^2 test requires expected cell frequencies of at least five observations per cell (for a more detailed discussion, see Clogg & Eliason, 1987; Hagenaars, 1990; Read & Cressie, 1988). Hence, the χ^2 test cannot be applied to contingency tables with a large number of categories and only a few observations. On the other hand, large sample sizes increase the power of the χ^2 statistic. Contingency tables with identical cell proportions yield higher χ^2 values for those with larger samples, thus the same proportional deviations from the expected cell frequencies can lead to significant and nonsignificant χ^2 values, depending on the sample size.

The χ^2 value is not restricted to a special range of values. Its distribution is larger than zero but infinite. To standardize its values and to make it more comparable, the corrected contingency coefficient C_{corr} and Cramer's V can be computed (see Liebetrau, 1983). Both coefficients transform the empirical χ^2 value to obtain values ranging from zero to one. In these transformations the empirical χ^2 value is compared to a maximal χ^2 value. Unfortunately C_{corr} cannot reach 1 in nonquadratic contingency tables (where $I \neq J$), whereas V, on the other hand, does. Both coefficients are hard to interpret because there is no operational standard for judging their magnitudes (Reynolds, 1977a).

Bishop, Fienberg, and Holland (1975, p. 386) concluded that these coefficients should only be used for comparing several tables.

Researchers who are interested in general associations between methods can use the χ^2 value to detect these relations, and moreover, when they compare observed and expected frequencies, they can determine beforehand which categories are more or less associated than expected using the χ^2 components (see Haberman, 1978). The χ^2 value corrects for associations by chance and, hence, can best be used to test the significance of associations.

Kappa Coefficient

Another coefficient to measure rater agreement corrected for chance inflation is Cohen's kappa coefficient (κ; Cohen, 1960). κ is a flexible index that is applicable to dichotomous or polytomous variables involving two or more observers and is computed by

$$\kappa = \frac{P_o - P_e}{1 - P_e},$$

with $P_o = \sum_{i=1}^{I} p_{ii}$ as observed proportion of identical ratings and $P_e = \sum_{i=1}^{I} p_{i+} p_{+i}$ as expected proportion of agreement by arbitrary ratings, $p_{ij} = \frac{n_{ij}}{N}$ denotes the proportion of observations within each cell, whereas I denotes the number of categories. The proportion of observed agreement is computed by adding the number of times both raters agree. The proportion of expected chance agreement is computed by the sum of the product of the marginals for each cell of interest. In contrast to the χ^2 indices, κ depends only on the agreement and is

not affected by high nonagreement rates. For the data presented in Table 17.1a, κ is computed as

$$\kappa = \frac{P_o - P_e}{1 - P_e} = \frac{\dfrac{40+425}{500} - \left[\left(\dfrac{55}{500} \times \dfrac{60}{500} \right) + \left(\dfrac{445}{500} \times \dfrac{440}{500} \right) \right]}{1 - \left[\left(\dfrac{55}{500} \times \dfrac{60}{500} \right) + \left(\dfrac{445}{500} \times \dfrac{440}{500} \right) \right]}$$

$$= \frac{.93 - .80}{1 - .80} = \frac{.13}{.20} = .65.$$

The value of ranges from −1 to +1.00, whereby a positive κ indicates that the observers agree more frequently than expected by chance, zero indicates that both raters agree on the same level as expected by chance, and a negative value indicates that both raters agree less often than expected by chance. A negative κ provides a strong hint that raters do not use all categories in the appropriate way. As a rule of thumb, a κ of .60 can be regarded as the minimal acceptable level of agreement (Gelfland & Hartmann, 1975), whereas a κ of .80 is an indication of good reliability (Landis & Koch, 1977).

Comparisons of General Association Indices

In general, associations between variables or methods can be detected by the χ^2 test. Normally, this test is conducted on the basis of the null hypothesis that all variables are independent. The χ^2 value provides information on whether the data differ significantly from the expected cell frequencies. Information about the strength of association can be obtained by the corrected contingency coefficient and Cramer's V.

The special case of rater agreement, on the other hand, can be estimated by several methods. As pointed out, many of them are afflicted by specific problems. The most promising approach seems to be the κ coefficient, a method that is a chance-corrected version of proportion agreement. Suen, Ary, and Ary (1986) demonstrated the mathematical relationship between κ and proportion agreement and also provided conversion procedures from one index to the other. Unfortunately, most journal articles do not provide sufficient information for taking advantage of these direct comparisons (Suen & Ary, 1989). In early psychological literature, but increas-

ingly less frequently, research reports presented percentage agreement values containing no information about the amount of chance inflation in them. To overcome this dissatisfying situation, Berk (1979) suggested that researchers should also report the original statistics (cell frequencies and marginals).

Many authors suggest κ to be the most preferable agreement index because it corrects for chance agreement, is related to percentage (proportion) agreement, and is comparable between studies (see Suen & Ary, 1989), whereas others state it is not comparable between studies (Cicchetti & Feinstein, 1990; Feinstein & Cicchetti, 1990; Thompson & Walter, 1988a, 1988b; Uebersax, 1987). Indeed, κ can be used to test whether ratings agree to a greater extent than expected by chance. Yet there is still concern about using κ as a measure of agreement because it is only chance-corrected for the assumption of independent ratings, an assumption that is implicitly made but legitimated by no means. Uebersax (1987) impressively demonstrated how differences in the accuracy with which positive and negative cases can be detected (i.e., differences in the mathematical characteristics of the particular decision-making process) affect the value of κ. Moreover, this problem increases when there are different base rates. In general, if the sample consists of cases that belong to an easily identifiable category, a higher κ is obtained, although the diagnostic accuracy remains the same compared to a sample consisting of less easily identifiable cases. Diagnosability curves representing the degree to which diagnosticians are able to accurately judge subjects with respect to the subjects' true status may actually differ so much that κ values obtained for the same symptom (criterion) with similar base rates cannot be compared across studies. Unless there is an explicit model of rater decision making, it remains unclear how chance affects decisions of actual raters and how one might correct for it (Uebersax, 1987).

All agreement indices were introduced for the simplest case consisting of two variables comprising two categories each creating a contingency table of four (2 × 2) cells. If there are more than two categories for each of the variables, the application of

the associations indices presented here can be applied in a straightforward manner. However, when the number of observers increases, the application of the general agreement indices becomes more complicated. In this case, κ should be determined for each rater pair, and the median value should be taken as the overall value (Conger, 1980; Fleiss, 1971). Fleiss (1971) developed modifications of κ to determine rater agreement when objects are rated by the same number of nonidentical raters, to compute agreement with regard to a particular object, and to estimate agreement within a particular category.

Coefficient κ can also be computed if some categories have more in common than others. Assume that there are two child psychologists who want to categorize a child's behavior as "very active, easy to distract, impulsive, aggressive, or restless," which are all indicators of hyperactivity, or as "playful." The overlapping of the first five categories can be considered by use of the *weighted kappa* (Cohen, 1968). The weighted kappa allows for differential weights for individual observed cells and individual marginals. Disagreement between raters choosing "very active" versus "impulsive" can be regarded as less striking than between them choosing "playful" versus "impulsive." Thus, the latter combination must be weighted to a larger degree than the first. Coefficient weighted kappa can be computed by

$$\kappa_w = \frac{P_{o(w)} - P_{e(w)}}{1 - P_{e(w)}}, \text{ where}$$

$$P_{o(w)} = \sum_{i=1}^{I} \sum_{j=1}^{J} w_{ij} p_{ij} \text{ and } P_{e(w)} = \sum_{i=1}^{I} \sum_{j=1}^{J} w_{ij} p_{i+} p_{+j},$$

w_{ij} serves as the weight.

The weighted kappa coefficient is seldom used because the weights have to be theoretically and, if possible, empirically founded. Moreover, if the data are metrical, the weighted kappa equals the intraclass correlation if all subsequent weights are equidistant (see Berry & Mielke, 1988; Fleiss & Cohen, 1973). If all categories can be ordered on a single dimension representing different levels of this dimension, models of item response theory can be

used to ascertain convergent validity (see Rost & Walter, chap. 18, this volume). Weighted kappa can, thus, be used if categories cannot be ordered on a single dimension and if some categories have more in common than others (for a more detailed discussion, see Landis & Koch, 1975a, 1975b).

ASSOCIATION MODELS

All general agreement indices described so far fail to provide more detailed information about various types and sources of agreement and disagreement. This kind of information can be obtained by modeling association between variables using *loglinear* models. Moreover, for special cases of association, effect sizes can be estimated representing the degree of association between variables. Conditional probabilities of receiving a particular response by an observer given the responses of other observers can be computed. Finally, residuals can be determined that compare the frequencies with which certain types of agreement and disagreement occur compared to what would be expected with some predicted pattern (Agresti, 1990, 1992).

Since the 1970s, the analysis of categorical data by means of loglinear models has strengthened its position as more and more investigators successfully applied loglinear models in their research. Many extensions of the models in several directions have been developed as, for example, the ordinary loglinear model, the standard latent class model, and the loglinear model with latent variables (for an overview, see Agresti, 1990; Hagenaars, 1990, 1993).

Table 17.3 presents a typical situation for the analysis of multimethod data. Two educational psychologists rated the behavior of 153 pupils as hyperactive, dyslexic, or normal. A rated 25 pupils as hyperactive, 20 dyslexic, and 108 normal. B classified the pupils' behavior in a similar manner (26 hyperactive, 19 dyslexic, and 108 normal). Both raters agreed on 16 hyperactive diagnoses, 15 dyslexic diagnoses, and 99 normal diagnoses. In sum, they agreed on 130 ratings and disagreed on 23 ratings, whereas the majority of discordant ratings is found in the categories "normal" and "hyperactive."

TABLE 17.3

Artificial Data of Pupils' Diagnoses by Two Educational Psychologists

		Educational Psychologist B			
		Hyperactive	**Dyslexic**	**Normal**	n_{i+}
Educational	Hyperactive	16	3	6	25
Psychologist A	Dyslexic	2	15	3	20
	Normal	8	1	99	108
	n_{+j}	26	19	108	153

Loglinear Models

Loglinear models aim to capture sources of associations between different categorical variables, and these associations are mirrored by different effects in the loglinear model. To understand the special meanings of loglinear models for the analysis of rater agreement, the most general loglinear model—the saturated model—will be introduced first.

Loglinear models are implemented to reproduce the joint frequency distribution of empirical data situations. Thus, the expected frequencies (e_{ij}) implied by a model have to match the observed frequencies. Expected frequencies can be determined by the multiplicative form of the model:

$$e_{ij} = \eta \tau_i^A \tau_j^B \tau_{ij}^{AB}. \tag{1}$$

The expected cell frequency (e_{ij}; with $i = 1, \ldots I$ and $j = 1, \ldots, J$ denoting the categories) are computed by the product of the overall effect (η), two one-variable effects $\left(\tau_i^A, \tau_j^B\right)$, and the two-variable effect $\left(\tau_{ij}^{AB}\right)$. The overall effect ($\eta$) represents the geometric mean of all cell frequencies and is, thus, nothing other than a mere reflection of the sample size (Hagenaars, 1993). The one-variable effects $\left(\tau_i^A, \tau_j^B\right)$ reflect deviations of the geometric mean of all cells belonging to the *i*th (*j*th) category of a variable.

Finally, the two-variable effect $\left(\tau_{ij}^{AB}\right)$ depicts deviations of the expected frequency of a particular cell beyond the overall and one-variable effects. The parameters can be estimated for the example given in Table 17.3 as follows:

$$\eta = \sqrt[9]{16 \times 2 \times 8 \times 3 \times 15 \times 1 \times 6 \times 3 \times 99} = 6.49,$$

$$\tau_1^A = \frac{\sqrt[3]{16 \times 3 \times 6}}{\eta} = \frac{6.60}{6.49} = 1.02,$$

$$\tau_1^B = \frac{\sqrt[3]{16 \times 2 \times 8}}{6.49} = 0.98, \text{ and}$$

$$\tau_{11}^{AB} = \frac{e_{11}}{\eta \tau_1^A \tau_1^B} = \frac{16}{6.49 \times 1.02 \times .98} = 2.48.$$

In the multiplicative loglinear model the product of all parameters belonging to one effect (e.g., $\tau_1^A \tau_2^A \tau_3^A$) is 1. Thus, their values are situated around 1, with no upper bound and a lower bound of zero. A value of 3 represents the same deviation as a value of 0.33, albeit in the opposite direction. To facilitate the intuitive understanding of these values, the natural logarithm (*ln*) is usually applied to make the values more comparable. Working with the *ln* turns the product into an additive combination, which gives the model its name:

$$\ln\left(e_{ij}\right) = \mu + \lambda_i^A + \lambda_j^B + \lambda_{ij}^{AB}$$

with (2)

$$\mu = \ln\left(\eta\right), \lambda_i^A = \ln\left(\tau_i^A\right), \lambda_j^B = \ln\left(\tau_j^B\right), \text{ and } \lambda_{ij}^{AB} = \ln\left(\tau_{ij}^{AB}\right)$$

The parameters of the additive loglinear model are symmetrically situated around zero with no negative or positive limit value. Consequently, the equally strong multiplicative parameters of 3 and 0.33 become *ln* (3) = 1.10 and *ln* (0.33) = −1.10.

Products of multiplicative parameters correspond to sums of additive parameters, and ratios correspond to differences. The model in Equations (1) and (2) is called a saturated model because it implies no constraints on the data; its estimated parameters can be found in Table 17.4. Hence, the model-implied cell frequencies always equal the observed cell frequencies. To generally identify loglinear models the parameters have to be constrained. Usually, the product of the multiplicative parameters has to equal 1 for each effect and, consequently, the sum of parameters belonging to one effect of the additive parameterization has to equal zero.

As stated earlier, multiplicative parameters of one-variable effects indicate the ratio to which the geometric mean of the frequencies pertaining to the three cells of this category differs from the overall geometric mean. For example, the geometric mean of the second category of Rater A (dyslexic) is 0.69 times as large as the overall geometric mean; the geometric mean of the third category of Rater A (normal) is 1.42 times larger than the overall geometric mean. This means that A categorized fewer students as dyslexic than normal. Two-variable effects denote the ratio to which the expected frequency of a particular cell differs from the expectation on the basis of the lower-order effects. For

example, the frequency of the cell dyslexic by A and dyslexic by B is 6.11 times as large as expected on the basis of the one-variable effects. The parameters τ_{ii}^{AB} belonging to the same symptoms rated by different raters are all larger than $1 \left(\tau_{11}^{AB} = 2.48, \tau_{22}^{AB} = 6.11, \text{and } \tau_{33}^{AB} = 5.75 \right)$ showing that the ratings are related to each other and that both ratings converge to a certain degree.

Expected cell frequencies depend on the product of the overall effect, the one-variable effects, and the two-variable effect. For example, the expected cell frequency (e_{22}), which is the combination of the ratings dyslexic by A and dyslexic by B, can be computed as

$$e_{22} = \eta \tau_2^A \tau_2^B \tau_{22}^{AB} =$$

$$6.49 \times 0.69 \times 0.55 \times 6.11 = 6.49 \times 2.32 = 15.05.$$

The product of the one- and two-variable parameters indicates that the expected frequency of this particular cell is 2.32 times larger than the overall geometric mean. The expected cell frequency of 15.05 equals the observed cell frequency (15) except for rounding errors.

The τ parameters can additionally be used to compare expected frequencies. One-variable effects

TABLE 17.4

Parameters of the Saturated Loglinear Model for the Data in Table 17.3

| | | Educational Psychologist B | | | | | | Main effects A | |
| | | 1 (Hyperactive) | | 2 (Dyslexic) | | 3 (Normal) | | | |
		τ_{ij}^{AB}	λ_{ij}^{AB}	τ_{ij}^{AB}	λ_{ij}^{AB}	τ_{ij}^{AB}	λ_{ij}^{AB}	τ_i^A	λ_i^A
Educational	1 (Hyperactive)	2.48	0.91	0.83	−0.19	0.49	−0.72	1.02	0.02
Psychologist A	2 (Dyslexic)	0.46	−0.78	6.11	1.81	0.36	−1.03	0.69	−0.37
	3 (Normal)	0.88	−0.12	0.20	−1.62	5.75	1.75	1.42	0.35
	Main effects B	0.98	−0.02	0.55	−0.60	1.87	0.62	$\eta = 6.49$	$\mu = 1.87$

Note. τ represents the parameter of the multiplicative model; λ is the parameter of the additive model. The main effects (one-variable effects) are depicted in the last and last but one column for Rater A and in the last row for Rater B. The cells of the cross-table represent the two-variable effects (interaction effects) of both variables.

can be used to compare expected frequencies of marginal distributions. For example, A rates the pupils as hyperactive $\frac{\tau_1^A}{\tau_2^A} = \frac{1.02}{0.69} = 1.48$ times more often than dyslexic. Similarly, B rates the pupils as hyperactive $\frac{\tau_1^B}{\tau_2^B} = \frac{0.98}{0.55} = 1.78$ times more often than dyslexic. If one is interested in the ratio of being judged normal by B compared to being judged hyperactive or dyslexic by B, the ratio

$$\frac{\tau_3^B}{\sqrt{\tau_1^B \times \tau_2^B}} = \frac{1.87}{\sqrt{.098 \times 0.55}} = \frac{1.87}{.73} = 2.56 \text{ must}$$

be computed. In other words, B chooses "normal" 2.56 more times than any other category.

Comparisons of conditional expected cell frequencies can be conducted as well. For example, the conditional probability of receiving a dyslexic rather than normal rating by A given that B rates normal is

$$\frac{\tau_{23}^{AB}}{\tau_{33}^{AB}} = \frac{0.36}{5.75} = .06 \, .$$

These comparisons of probabilities are very similar to the analyses that can be carried out by odds and odds ratios (see Hagenaars, 1993). Exactly as the corresponding odds ratio, this ratio shows that it is much less probable (.06 times as probable) to be judged dyslexic than normal by A, if B rates normal. One advantage of multiplicative parameterization is that these (conditional) probabilities can be calculated just by means of the τ parameters. The value of a τ parameter does not depend on the sample size but is a mere reflection of the structure between the variables. A more detailed introduction to the meaning of the τ parameters and their relation to the concept of odds and odds ratios lies beyond the scope of this chapter but can be found in the contributions of Agresti (1990), Bishop et al. (1975), Christensen (1997), Fienberg (1980), Haberman (1978, 1979), Hagenaars (1990, 1993), Knoke and Burke (1980), Reynolds (1977b), Sobel (1995), and Wickens (1989).

Goodness of Fit

Modeling approaches in the social sciences are always implemented to give an appropriate but parsimonious representation of social phenomena or—more precisely—of the empirical data representing

these phenomena. Saturated loglinear models exactly reproduce these data and do not put restrictions on the data. They always fit the data perfectly. In contrast, nonsaturated loglinear models impose a priori restrictions on the data and, thus, contain testable consequences. These consequences can be tested by the Pearson χ^2 goodness of fit index or the log-likelihood ratio χ^2 statistic L^2 (see, e.g., Bishop et al., 1975; Hagenaars, 1990; Knoke & Burke, 1980). The number of degrees of freedom equals the number of independent a priori restrictions. Parameters of nonsaturated loglinear models cannot be easily computed. Among others, Hagenaars (1990), Knoke and Burke (1980), as well as Vermunt (1997a) represent the relevant formulas for their maximum likelihood estimates.

Independence Model

A useful first analysis of agreement can be done by testing the independence model. The independence model assumes that there is no association between both raters; thus, the additive two-variable effect $\left(\lambda_{ij}^{AB}\right)$ parameters are set to equal zero. The model equation for the independence model appears as

$$\ln\left(e_{ij}\right) = \mu + \lambda_i^A + \lambda_j^B.$$

In this model, only the one-variable effects are implemented, which means that the marginal distributions of both variables are reproduced. If these one-variable effects are similar to each other, both variables' marginal distributions are homogeneous. Homogeneous marginal distributions imply that both raters choose each category with almost the same frequency; accordingly, no rater prefers any category to a greater extent than the other, which means that no rating is biased (Agresti, 1992).

This type of model will only rarely fit empirical data because, in general, different measures of a construct are related to a certain degree, and this relatedness represents the convergent validity. Useful information provided by the independence model stems from the analysis of its adjusted cell residuals. Adjusted cell residuals compare observed with expected cell frequencies (see Agresti, 1992):

$$r_{ij} = \frac{n_{ij} - e_{ij}}{\sqrt{e_{ij}\left(1 - \frac{n_{i+}}{n_{++}}\right)\left(1 - \frac{n_{+j}}{n_{++}}\right)}}$$

Large values indicate a stronger association between methods than would be expected by chance, and the introduction of effects that capture this association $\left(\lambda_{ij}^{AB}\right)$ could improve the fit of the model.

Hence, the adjusted cell residuals of the independence model (as the test) can be used to detect agreement as well as general associations. As Table 17.5 shows, the expected cell frequencies of the independence model differ greatly from the observed cell frequencies, whereas the marginal distributions are perfectly reproduced. A first glance at the table reveals that cells on the main diagonal are chosen much more frequently than would be expected if both ratings were independent.

Quasi-Independence Model

A useful extension of the independence model is the *quasi-independence model*. In this model a new parameter is introduced that is only implemented for cells on the main diagonal, which represent agreement between methods:

$$\ln\left(e_{ij}\right) = \mu + \lambda_i^A + \lambda_j^B + \delta_i I\left(i = j\right), \text{with}$$

$$I\left(i = j\right) = \begin{cases} 1, & \text{if } i = j \\ 0, & \text{if } i \neq j \end{cases}.$$

This model fits the data in Table 17.3 ($\chi^2 = 1.38$, $df = 1$, $p = .24$) very well. In contrast to the independence model, this model allows higher cell frequencies for cells on the main diagonal, but no overrepresentation in any other cell. For cells indicating disagreement, the independence model holds (see Table 17.6a). As a result of the newly introduced parameter δ_i, the estimated cell frequencies on the main diagonal indicating agreement are exactly equal to the empirical cell frequencies. The newly introduced parameter δ_i can be used to compare the probability of receiving a particular response by one method, given the rating of the other method (see Agresti, 1992). The probability of receiving an answer in the first cell on the main diagonal is $\exp(\delta_i) = \exp(0.61) = 1.84$ times larger than expected by chance. Similarly, the probabilities of falling into the second and third cell on the main diagonal are 21.25 and 17.54 times greater than expected by chance. This indicates that the agreement between both raters is much higher for the categories "dyslexic" and "normal" than for "hyperactive."

TABLE 17.5

Expected Cell Frequencies, Observed Cell Frequencies, and Adjusted Residuals of the Independence Model for the Data Presented in Table 17.3 ($\chi^2 = 136.73$, $df = 4$, $p < .01$)

			Educational Psychologist B			
			Hyperactive	**Dyslexic**	**Normal**	n_{i+}
Educational Psychologist A	Hyperactive	observed	16	3	6	25
		expected	4.24	3.11	17.65	25.00
		adj. residual	6.85	−0.07	−5.59	
	Dyslexic	observed	2	15	3	20
		expected	3.40	2.48	14.12	20.00
		adj. residual	−0.89	9.11	−5.86	
	Normal	observed	8	1	99	108
		expected	18.35	13.41	76.24	108.00
		adj. residual	−4.89	−6.68	8.87	
	n_{+j}	observed	26	19	108	153
		expected	25.99	19.00	108.01	153.00

TABLE 17.6

Expected and Observed (in Parentheses) Cell Frequencies of the Quasi-Independence Models for the Data Presented in Table 17.3

(a) Quasi-Independence Model I ($\chi^2 = 1.38$, *df* = 1, *p* = .24)

		Educational Psychologist B			
		Hyperactive	**Dyslexic**	**Normal**	n_{+j}
Educational Psychologist A	Hyperactive	16.00 (16)	2.19 (3)	6.81 (6)	25.00 (25)
	Dyslexic	2.80 (2)	15.00 (15)	2.20 (3)	20.00 (20)
	Normal	7.20 (8)	1.81 (1)	98.99 (99)	108.00 (108)
	n_{i+}	26.00 (26)	19.00 (19)	108.00 (108)	153.00 (153)

(b) Quasi-Independence Model II ($\chi^2 = 5.96$, *df* = 3, *p* = .11)

		Educational Psychologist B			
		Hyperactive	**Dyslexic**	**Normal**	n_{+j}
Educational Psychologist A	Hyperactive	18.40 (16)	1.69 (3)	4.92 (6)	25.01 (25)
	Dyslexic	2.13 (2)	13.19 (15)	4.68 (3)	20.00 (20)
	Normal	5.47 (8)	4.12 (1)	98.41 (99)	108.00 (108)
	n_{i+}	26.00 (26)	19.00 (19)	108.01 (108)	153.01 (153)

Note. [a]Quasi-Independence Model I represents the quasi-independence model with exactly fitted cell frequencies on the main diagonal: $\delta_1 = 0.61$; $\delta_2 = 3.06$; $\delta_3 = 2.86$.
[b]Quasi-Independence Model II represents the quasi-independence model with the fitted sum of cell frequencies on the main diagonal: $\delta = 2.10$.

If all parameters are equal to each other, all expected cell frequencies on the main diagonal differ from chance agreement to the same degree. Hence, a simpler model holds, which assumes to be constant:

$$\ln\left(e_{ij}\right) = \mu + \lambda_i^A + \lambda_j^B + \delta I(i = j),$$

$$I\left(i = j\right) = \begin{cases} 1, & \text{if } i = j \\ 0, & \text{if } i \neq j \end{cases}.$$

The sum of the expected cell frequencies on the main diagonal is exactly equal to the sum of the observed frequencies, whereas single expected cell frequencies may differ from the observed (see Table 17.6b). This model also fits the data well ($\chi^2 = 5.96$, *df* = 3, *p* = .11). The expected cell frequencies on the main diagonal are $\exp(\delta_i) = \exp(2.10) = 8.17$ times larger than would be expected by independent ratings. The difference between both models is that in the latter, the degree of agreement between both

methods is the same for all categories, whereas in the first model, agreement may differ from category to category.

To decide which model fits better, the likelihood ratio difference test can be calculated (e.g., Hagenaars, 1990; Knoke & Burke, 1980). This test is only available for hierarchical models. Hierarchical (or nested) models are models from which the more restrictive model is obtained by imposing restrictions on parameters of the less-restricted model (such as equality constraints or the fixation on a special value). As the latter quasi-independence model constrains all parameters δ_i to be equal, it is the more restrictive model compared to the first one. The conditional likelihood ratio test yields a value of $\chi_{diff}^2 = 5.96 - 1.38 = 4.59 \left(df_{diff} = 3 - 1 = 2, p = .10\right)$.

This test indicates that the more restrictive model fits the data as well as the less restrictive and,

thus, should be preferred as the more parsimonious representation.

Quasi-Symmetry Model and Symmetry Model

Models of agreement can also satisfy the property of quasi-symmetry (Darroch & McCloud, 1986). Because there is no objectively precise definition of classification categories for most cases in the social sciences, the discrepancies between classifications by different methods are attributable to measurement error and to different perceptions or interpretations of what a category definition means. "The correct category for an object exists partially in the eye of the beholder" (Darroch & McCloud, 1986, p. 376). On the other hand, there are signals sent out by each object that partially conform to each of the categories to a certain degree. These signals are assumed to differ between objects. Thus, the classification of an object into a particular category depends on the signals sent out by the object and the rater-specific category definition. Agreement between methods is displayed in the joint distribution of the marginal distributions of objects:

$$\ln\left(e_{ij}\right) = \mu + \lambda_i^A + \lambda_j^B + \lambda_{ij}^{AB},$$

with $\lambda_{ij}^{AB} = \lambda_{ji}^{AB}$ for all i and j.

Hence, this model does not only address agreement between methods but additionally provides some information about bias (Agresti, 1992). Information about bias can be obtained by the comparison of the one-variable effects that represent the marginal distributions. If these effects differ between observers, the observers have different classification probabilities for a given object, which simply means that they do not use every category in the same manner. This model is called the quasi-symmetry model because the expected cell frequency to receive a particular response by the first rater (e.g., hyperactive) and a particular response by the second rater (e.g., normal) differs by the same ratio [exp (λ_{ij}^{AB})] from the expected cell frequency given only the one-variable effects as the contrary combination (normal by A and hyperactive by B). In other words, associations between both raters are "mirrored" around the main diagonal (see Table 17.7a). For example, expected frequencies of the

---

TABLE 17.7

Expected and Observed (in Parentheses) Cell Frequencies of the Quasi-Symmetry and Symmetry Model for the Data Presented in Table 17.3

(a) Quasi-Symmetry Model (χ_2 = 1.37, *df* = 1, *p* = .24)

		Educational Psychologist B			
		Hyperactive	**Dyslexic**	**Normal**	n_{+j}
Educational Psychologist A	Hyperactive	16.00 (16)	2.19 (3)	6.81 (6)	25.00 (25)
	Dyslexic	2.81 (2)	15.00 (15)	2.20 (3)	20.01 (20)
	Normal	7.19 (8)	1.81 (1)	99.00 (99)	108.00 (108)
	n_{i+}	26.00 (26)	19.00 (19)	108.01 (108)	153.01 (153)

(b) Symmetry Model (χ_2 = 1.49, *df* = 3, *p* = .69)

		Educational Psychologist B			
		Hyperactive	**Dyslexic**	**Normal**	n_{+j}
Educational Psychologist A	Hyperactive	16.00 (16)	2.50 (3)	7.00 (6)	25.50 (25)
	Dyslexic	2.50 (2)	15.00 (15)	2.00 (3)	19.50 (20)
	Normal	7.00 (8)	2.00 (1)	99.00 (99)	108.00 (108)
	n_{i+}	25.50 (26)	19.50 (19)	108.00 (108)	153.00 (153)

combination of ratings "hyperactive" and "normal" by both raters differ by the same amount from their observed frequencies ($e_{13} - n_{13} = 6.81 - 6 = 0.81$, and $e_{31} - n_{31} = 7.19 - 8 = -0.81$). The *quasi-symmetry* model fits the data very well ($\chi^2 = 1.37$, $df = 1$, $p = .24$).

If the one-variable effects do not differ between variables the more restrictive assumptions of the *symmetry model* hold. Formally, the symmetry model appears to be quite similar to the quasi-symmetry model:

$$\ln\left(e_{ij}\right) = \mu + \lambda_i^A + \lambda_j^B + \lambda_{ij}^{AB},$$

with $\lambda_{ij}^{AB} = \lambda_{ji}^{AB}$ for all i and j; $\lambda_i^A = \lambda_j^B$ for $i = j$

In contrast to the quasi-symmetry model, the one-variable effects are set to equal each other. Thus, the marginal distributions of both variables have to be equal, meaning that neither rating is biased (see Table 17.7b). Hence, the symmetry model is a special case of the quasi-symmetry model. In this model, even the expected cell frequency of contrary combinations of categories is the same. For example, the combination of "hyperactive" and "normal" yields the same expected frequencies for both combinations ($e_{13} = e_{31} = 7.00$). The expected cell frequencies are mirrored around the main diagonal. The symmetry model also fits the data very well ($\chi^2 = 1.49$, $df = 3$, $p = .69$). The likelihood ratio difference test between the quasi-symmetry and the symmetry model yields a value of 0.11 ($df = 2$, $p = .95$); the symmetry model represents the empirical data as well as the quasi-symmetry model. One may now conclude that both raters use the categories with the same frequencies (implied by the equality constraints on the one-variable effects) and that neither rating is biased compared to the other because all expected cell frequencies are the same for contrary combinations of categories. Therefore, both raters are interchangeable (Agresti, 1992).

Comparison of Nonhierarchical Loglinear Association Models

As has been shown, the most restrictive models that fit the data are the quasi-independence model with a constrained δ parameter and the symmetry model.

Because both models are not nested, the likelihood ratio difference test cannot be conducted (see Figure 17.1). To decide which model fits best, information criteria have to be considered. Information criteria such as the Akaike information criterion (AIC) and the Bayesian information criterion (BIC) are based on the χ^2 value, and they weigh the number of parameters of a model with a penalty function to identify the most parsimonious model (for more details, see Akaike, 1987; Bozdogan, 1987; Sclove, 1987). The smallest information criterion indicates the most parsimonious model. The symmetry model is the most parsimonious well-fitted model and should be considered as the model of choice (see Table 17.8).

Besides these statistical considerations there are also some theoretical considerations that may influence the choice of a model. Compared to the quasi-independence models, the quasi-symmetry as well as the symmetry model yields the benefit that observer differences *and* category distinguishability can be examined in detail (Darroch & McCloud, 1986) because both agreement *and* disagreement have to be modeled. If the quasi-symmetry model holds, we can presume that raters produce the same amount of under- or overrepresentation for given

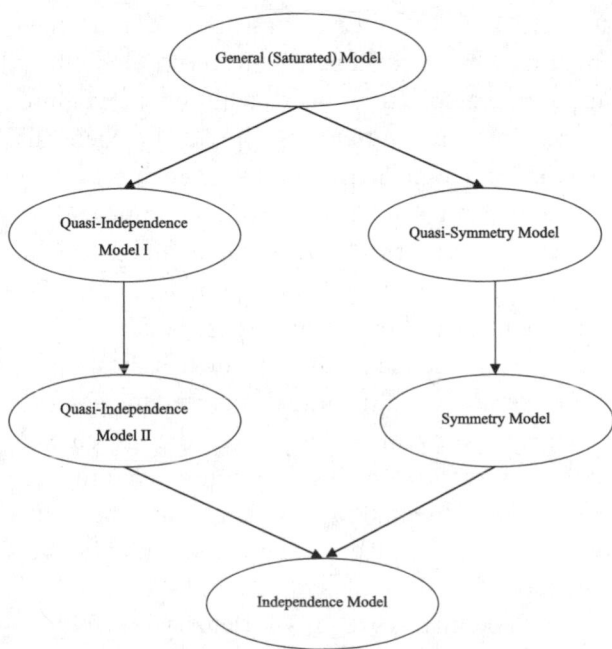

FIGURE 17.1. Nested structure of the loglinear association models.

TABLE 17.8

Comparison of the Information Criteria for the Quasi-Independence and Symmetry Model for the Data Presented in Table 17.3

Model	χ_2	df	p	BIC	AIC
Quasi-independence[a]	5.96	3	.11	420.69	405.53
Symmetry	1.49	3	.69	415.47	400.32

Note. [a]Quasi-independence model with constrained δ parameters on the main diagonal.

combinations of categories and are, thus, interchangeable to a certain degree. Moreover, if the symmetry model holds, both raters are completely interchangeable (Agresti, 1992). A better-fitting symmetry model compared to the quasi-symmetry model indicates a stronger association between ratings and greater interchangeability of raters

General Discussion of Association Methods for Categorical Data

As has been shown, there is no best way to measure agreement and disagreement by general agreement indices. However, some basic comparisons of association methods and models can be accomplished. In general, associations can be detected by the χ^2 test, and as a special case of association, rater agreement may be detected by coefficient κ. Model-based analysis of associations yields additional and more precise information than that provided by general association methods. In contrast to coefficient κ, agreement can also be analyzed in cases where the number of categories between raters differs. Loglinear models allow testing of the goodness of fit. They provide fitted cell probabilities and enable researchers to make predictions of classifications under certain conditions such as receiving a particular response by an observer given the responses of other observers, receiving a response given the true status of an observation or assessing the true status of an observation given ratings by several observers (Agresti, 1990, 1992; Bishop et al., 1975; Goodman, 1978; Haberman, 1978, 1979; Hagenaars, 1990). Thus, first analyses of rater agreement—as a special variant of convergence between multiple methods—

can be conducted by overall agreement indices, but more detailed information is only available by use of loglinear models.

Extensions and Special Variants of Methods for Rater Agreement

In this chapter, emphasis was placed on the analysis of rater agreement of two observers who rate each subject once. Extensions of this design have already been developed. Conger (1980) presented a generalization of coefficient kappa to assess agreement of multiple raters. Tanner and Young (1985) proposed loglinear models that determine interrater agreement when there are more than two observers; moreover, they developed a method to analyze agreement between several observers and a standard even if the nonstandard raters examine different subsamples of a larger sample. The model presented by Hui and Zhou (1998) examines the sensitivity and specificity of ratings when there is no "gold" standard.

Hagenaars (1993) introduced latent variables to the framework of loglinear modeling. Moreover, he showed that latent class analysis (LCA; Clogg, 1995; Lazarsfeld & Henry, 1968) is a special variant of loglinear modeling with latent variables. LCA has also been used to examine rater agreement (see Rost & Walter, chap. 18, this volume). For example, Dillon and Mullani (1984) developed a probabilistic latent class model for assessing interjudge reliability, and Agresti and Lang (1993) proposed symmetric latent class models to analyze rater agreement when there is more than one variable.

Much work has focused on solving the problems that arise during the analysis of contingency tables

by use of loglinear models (for an overview, see Clogg & Eliason, 1987). Some solutions for specific problems will be mentioned here. For example, many studies contain varying panels of diagnosticians and a varying number of ratings per case for which Uebersax and Grove (1990) provided a model to estimate diagnostic accuracy even under these conditions. Moreover, Becker and Agresti (1992) introduced the use of a jackknife procedure to solve sparse table problems that may arise when many observers are involved who only rate a few subjects. Hui and Zhou (1998) provided a model to estimate sensitivity and specificity of ratings when no golden standard is available. Rindskopf (1990) gave some valuable hints on how to deal with structurally missing data. His approach can even be used to detect homogeneous subgroups in multidimensional tables. Clogg (1982) as well as Becker and Clogg (1989) also developed mixture models to detect subgroups for which different models of agreement apply. Their extensions are based on the partitioning of χ^2 values.

Although there are various extensions of the loglinear modeling approach, much work is still necessary. For instance, we need additional information about the minimum sample size requirements for any given number of raters, number of categories, and number of observations to gain valid results. Moreover, the influence of chance on coefficient kappa, if the joint distribution is not assumed to follow the assumption of independence, is worth investigation. Because marginal distributions are not always independent from each other, individual decision-making processes have to be examined to detect the cases in which raters are guessing, in which they feel rather sure, or in which they feel absolutely sure. Only if we know more about the decision-making process can agreement by chance be solidly determined and rater agreement be accurately identified. These problems not only affect coefficient κ but loglinear models as well. As demonstrated by Schuster (2001), coefficient κ can be incorporated in the symmetry model yielding a new (equivalent) model equation. Hence, the process of decision making should be examined more deeply, and the findings should be incorporated into models of rater agreement.

Software Packages for the Analysis of Categorical Data Associations

Several software packages for the analysis of general agreement indices and association models are available. Only a few programs are mentioned here; an excellent overview can be found at the home page of J. Uebersax (2003). Outstanding programs are SAS (SAS, 2000) and LEM (Vermunt, 1997b). SAS is a powerful tool that allows the modeling of practically all possible loglinear models. LEM is a very flexible and easy-to-handle freeware program for the analysis of categorical data. All loglinear models presented in this chapter have been analyzed using LEM.

CHAPTER 18

MULTIMETHOD ITEM RESPONSE THEORY

Jürgen Rost and Oliver Walter

Item response theory (IRT) is a framework for an increasing number of statistical models that refer to the same kind of data structure. The data basis for applying IRT models is a matrix of responses of a (large) number of persons on a (small) number of questions, tasks, stimuli, or whatever, called the items. The item responses may be dichotomous (yes–no; correct–incorrect; true–false, etc.), ordinal (strongly disagree, disagree, agree, strongly agree), or nominal without a given order of the categories (for example, hair color: blond, brown, red, black, gray/white). In any case, they represent categorical data that makes IRT models different from most other statistical models that refer to metrical variables, for example, structural equation models (Eid, Lischetzke, & Nussbeck, chap. 20, this volume).

In contrast to the latter, which often are aimed at modeling the covariance structure of the observed variables, IRT models try to model the observed response patterns and their frequencies. For that purpose, some of the IRT models are modeling the distributions of one or more latent variables and, if there are more than one, also their (latent) correlations. But in general, correlations of observed or latent variables are not the primary concern of IRT models. Rather, the focus of IRT models is on the response patterns of the persons who filled out a test or a questionnaire. Moreover, it is the single-item response x_{vi} of a person v on an item i that is to be explained or predicted by an IRT model. Because almost all these models deal with the probabilities of these item responses, and not

with their occurrence or absence in a deterministic sense, the typical IRT model is a probabilistic model dealing with $p(x_{vi})$, that is, the probability of person v to give response x on item i.

Multimethod IRT models refer to an extended data structure. The item responses were gained or assessed with different methods. For example, Item 1 was assessed with Method A, Item 2 with Method B. Or all items of a test were administered once using Method A and another time using Method B. A classic example is a personality questionnaire that has been administered to three different persons: the subject being tested, the subject's (romantic) partner, and a good friend. The three modes of responding to the test items represent the three methods of self-report, partner rating, and good friend rating, so that the data matrix (persons × items) extends to a data cube (persons × items × methods). In general, the data structure of multimethod test data and related IRT models is seen in this chapter as a data cube with methods as the third dimension, in addition to persons and items in ordinary IRT. The aim of multimethod IRT models is to explain $p(x_{vij})$, that is, the probability that the score x on item i measured by method j is obtained for a particular person v.

Such a three-dimensional data structure (data cube) is not specific for multimethod IRT. A third dimension is also given in the situation of measurement of change, where "time" is the third dimension of the data structure (see Khoo, West, Wu, & Kwok, chap. 21, this volume). Time may be seen as

a special kind of "method" that is defined as the time point of test administration. If the test is applied at another time, the situation will also be different, and the repeated test application may be seen as a different "'method." It makes no sense to stress the differences between measurement of change and multimethod methodology. In fact, both can learn from each other, and as far as IRT is concerned, much can be learned from change or learning models that may be relevant for multimethod assessment.

In the first section, the basic models of all models described in this chapter, the Rasch model and latent class analysis, are presented. In the following sections these models are extended to the three-dimensional data structure. First, the Rasch model for multimethod data will be introduced and then generalized. Because there is no single way of generalizing to deal with the structure of a data cube, three different ways will be pursued. These three directions are the interaction between items and methods, the multidimensional extension, and the mixture distribution extension, which is a combination of the Rasch model and latent class analysis. Section 3 deals with more technical aspects like parameter estimation, missing data, measures of accuracy, and model fit. Section 4 presents the results of the application of the described models to the field test data of the German PISA 2003 science test. Section 5 summarizes the models that were applied and points out the directions of further development of IRT.

INTRODUCTION TO THE BASIC ITEM RESPONSE MODELS

Item response theory (IRT; see Baker, 1992; Hambleton & Swaminathan, 1989) usually is considered a class of statistical models for categorical data to which the Rasch model (RM) and the two-parameter logistic model belong, but not latent class analysis (LCA). However, there are at least two reasons why LCA can and should be seen as an IRT model. Whereas the Rasch model tries to measure a latent trait of the persons, LCA tries to identify latent classes of persons. Both measure a latent variable, which is a quantitative variable in the case of the RM and a categorical variable in the case of LCA. There are lots of good examples where test or questionnaire data have been analyzed using LCA. The second reason is that the RM can be generalized to a mixture distribution model, which is at the same time a generalized latent class model.

The Rasch Model

The Rasch model refers to a data matrix that is set up by the two factors persons and items (see Table 18.1).

The entries of such a data matrix are the responses x_{vi} of a set of persons on a set of items. In the simplest case, these item responses are dichotomous, meaning that they only distinguish a correct or "yes" response ($x_{vi} = 1$) from an incorrect or "no" response ($x_{vi} = 0$). To calculate the probability of an item response, each person is characterized by an

---

TABLE 18.1

The Data Structure of IRT Models

Factor: persons		Factor: items						
		1	2	3	...	*i*	*I*	Sum
	1							r_1
	2							r_2
	3							r_3
	4							r_4
Factor: persons	...							r
	v					x_{vi}		r_v
	N							r_N
	Sum	n_1	n_2	n_3	n	n_i	n_I	

"ability" parameter that is not necessarily an ability but any kind of latent trait, and each item is characterized by an item parameter. The Rasch model (Rasch, 1960, 1980) assumes only one parameter per item, that is, a difficulty parameter, whereas other IRT models have a second parameter that is defined as a discrimination parameter. The former can be formalized by the following equation.

$$p(x_{vi}) = \frac{\exp(x_{vi}(\theta_v - \sigma_i))}{1 + \exp(\theta_v - \sigma_i)}. \tag{1}$$

In this equation, the probability for person v to respond to item i is a logistic function of the person parameter θ_v and the item parameter σ_i. For one item this relationship is represented by the so-called item characteristic curve (ICC; see Figure 18.1), which is defined as the probability of an item response as a function of the person parameter value. The item parameter σ_i is defined as the x-coordinate of the turning point of the logistic function. Because the x-axis represents the *latent dimension*, the item parameter is defined on the same scale and has the same metric as the person parameters.

The reason why the present chapter only deals with Rasch-type models has to do with some advantageous statistical properties of this "simple" one-parameter logistic model (Rost, 2001). Rasch-type models are the only IRT models where the unweighted sum of correct item responses (the "number correct") is a sufficient statistic for the estimation of the trait parameters. Therefore, the Rasch model provides a formal framework for what is done anyway in naive analyses of test data: counting the number of items that were answered by a respondent in a certain direction. This property of Rasch models is called *sufficiency* and refers to the fact that the sum of correct responses ($x_{vi} = 1$) of a person contains all the information necessary to estimate the parameter of this person. The same is true for the item parameters: The sum of correct responses to an item contains all information necessary to estimate the item parameter (see following section).

The model Equation (1) shows that both types of parameters—person and item parameters—are combined additively, which is called the property of *latent additivity*. It can be seen from this equation that the item parameter is defined as a difficulty parameter because the item parameter is subtracted from the person parameter.

The Rasch model does not provide a second item parameter defining the discrimination of an item, which implies that all ICCs of a Rasch homogeneous test are parallel, so they do not intersect (see Figure 18.1). Parallel ICCs and constant item discriminations also mean that all items measure the same latent trait equally well (property of *item homogeneity*). Item homogeneity is a necessary condition for measuring the persons independently of the distribution of measures of the items (property of *specific objectivity*). Fischer (1995a) showed that the family of Rasch models is the only model type that fulfills this condition and that specific objectivity is related to the property of *latent additivity*: Whenever specific objectivity holds for a set of items and a set of persons, then a representation of the model exists where the person and the item parameter are connected by addition or subtraction as is the case for the Rasch model (Model 1).

Because of these properties, the likelihood of the data—the probability of the observed data given the assumed model—is just a function of the marginal sums of the data matrix n_i, the number of persons that solved item i, and r_v, the number of items that were solved by person v, that is, the *number correct scores*.

$$L(\mathbf{X}|\theta,\sigma) = f(r_v, n_i, \theta, \sigma). \tag{2}$$

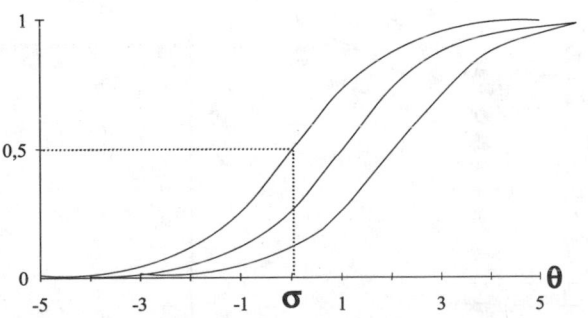

FIGURE 18.1. Nonintersecting item characteristic curves as assumed by the Rasch model.

Because the likelihood function L is used for estimating the parameters, it follows that the marginal sums are sufficient for estimating the parameters. The pattern of responses of a person does not contribute anything to the estimation of the person parameter that cannot be drawn from the simple sum score.

Parameter estimation procedures that are based on the preceding likelihood function are called *joint maximum likelihood* procedures because both types of parameters are *jointly* estimated. With Rasch models it is also possible to estimate the item parameters without estimating the person parameters simultaneously or knowing them beforehand. This is done by conditioning the likelihood on the sufficient statistics of the person parameters, that is, on the r_v scores. The consequence is a *conditional likelihood function* that does not contain the person parameters. Estimation procedures based on this likelihood are called *conditional maximum likelihood* methods (see following section).

LATENT CLASS ANALYSIS

Latent class analysis (LCA; Lazarsfeld & Henry, 1968; Rost, 2003) can be understood as an alternative explanatory approach to item response analyses. Whereas the Rasch model assumes a distribution of a quantitative person characteristic on a continuous latent dimension, LCA postulates that persons differ from each other with regard to their response pattern and, according to their pattern, belong to different latent classes. The classes are called latent because they are not observable, but constructed from the test data, just as the latent traits of the Rasch model.

The aim of LCA is the identification of groups of subjects who show different response patterns. Latent class models cannot be characterized by their ICCs because there is no latent dimension that the response probabilities could depend on. However, the response probabilities are specific for and constant within latent classes so that the meaning of a latent class is well represented by its item profile (see Figure 18.2). These profiles show the class-specific response probabilities. Because response probabilities are constant among the subjects within each class, the model parameters are simply defined as conditional response probabilities, given that person v belongs to class c.

$$p(X_{vi} = 1 | \theta_v = c) = \pi_{ic} \qquad (3)$$

Equation (3) defines the response probability $p(X_{vi} = 1)$ of a subject v that belongs to class c ($\theta_v = c$) to be a constant parameter π_{ic}. There is another type of parameter in LCA that represents the *unconditional* response probabilities, π_c. These parameters define the subject's probability to belong to class c and can be interpreted as class size parameters.

$$\pi_c = p(\theta_v = c) \qquad (4)$$

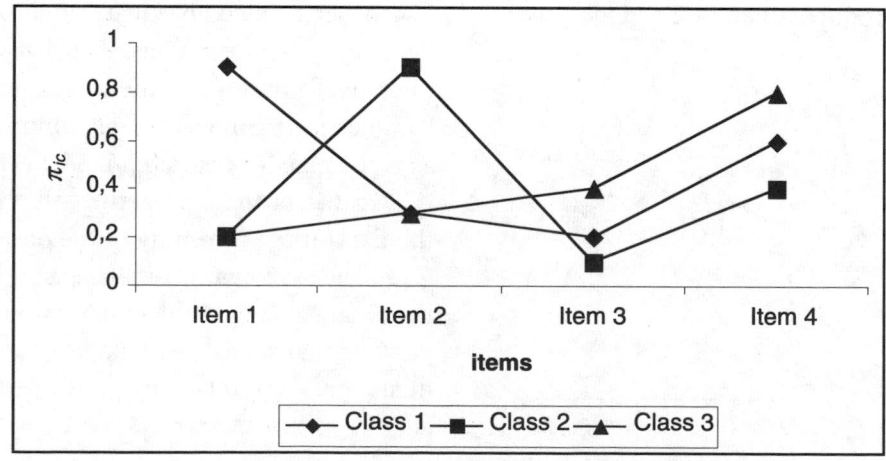

FIGURE 18.2. Item profiles of four items in three latent classes π_{ic}.

It is an important characteristic of LCA that subjects are not assigned to classes in a deterministic way, but rather are assigned with certain probabilities to any class. Therefore, incorrect assignments do not emerge, and it is not necessary to apply an error model to a classification made by LCA. But if subjects are assigned to classes according to their highest (modal) probability, a *manifest* classification of all subjects is obtained, and the probability of this assignment is a measure of the quality.

To illustrate, imagine that three latent classes were identified by LCA, and each subject is assigned to the class to which he/she has the highest probability of belonging, given his/her response pattern. Let the mean probability of all subjects assigned to the first *manifest* class be 0.91, for instance. The counterprobability for these subjects, that is, the probability of being assigned to Class 1 but actually belonging to *latent* Class 2 or 3, represents the measurement error. In this example the measurement error is $1 - 0.91 = 0.09$.

Similar to the Rasch model, the parameters are estimated using maximum likelihood procedures. In contrast to the Rasch model, however, the likelihood function of LCA cannot be simplified to a function of the marginal sums because only the pattern frequencies provide the sufficient information for parameter estimation.

ITEM RESPONSE THEORY MODELS FOR MULTIMETHOD DATA

In this section we will define the item response theory models more explicitly in relation to matrices used with multimethod data. First, we will discuss the Rasch model and then some generalized Rasch models. We will include discussion of interaction between items and methods and person and methods and will provide commentary on the Rasch model and latent class analysis with multimethod data.

The Rasch Model for Multimethod Data

A straightforward way to define a Rasch model for multimethod data, that is, a data cube consisting of persons × items × methods, would be to follow the principle of *latent additivity* and to define the probability of the response of person v on item i with method j as an additive logistic function of a person parameter θ_v, an item parameter σ_i, and a method parameter μ_j. Here the method parameter μ_j stands for the specific and item-independent contribution of method j (that is, its main effect) to the probability of solving an item:

$$p(X_{vij} = 1) = \frac{\exp(\theta_v - \sigma_i + \mu_j)}{d_{vij}}, \qquad (5)$$

where d_{vij} denotes 1 plus the exponential function of the numerator, in this case $d_{vij} = 1 + \exp(\theta_v - \sigma_i + \mu_j)$. This generalized Rasch model was described as early as 1970 by Micko (1970; in German) and has been discussed by Linacre (1989) as the *multifacets model*. Depending on the conceptualization of "methods," this model can be applied to different situations. For example, Rost and Spada (1983) and Spiel (1994) used it in the context of measurement of change as a model of global learning. Here, the method parameter represents the effect of learning over time, and each "method" j stands for a different point in time. Another example is revealed if the researcher also deems the raters to be "methods" to judge certain person characteristics. Then the model described can be used to identify the amount of rater bias, that is, the tendency of raters to rate generally higher or lower than other raters. Because the method parameter is independent of the item parameter, the application of this model is limited to the identification of main effects of biased ratings and cannot identify interactions between raters and items.

Applications of the model discussed in Europe, in particular by Gerhard Fischer and his students (Fischer, 1995b), used computer programs of the *linear logistic test model* (LLTM; Fischer, 1973). The LLTM is a general model structure for defining any kind of latent additive (but unidimensional) Rasch model. For this purpose, the item parameters are considered as a linear function of some basic parameters η_h:

$$\sigma_i = \sum_h q_{ih} \eta_h \qquad (6)$$

where the design matrix Q covers the weights q_{ih} of the item component h in item i. By means of an appropriate specification of the design matrix Q, the Rasch model for three-dimensional data structures can be defined as a LLTM model. Table 18.2 shows the Q matrix for four items and three methods. The Q matrix is built by taking account of the combination of method j and item i. For example, because the first item is an item-1-type item that has been administered according to Method 1, the first component (defining all item-1-type items) and the fifth component (defining all Method 1 items) were marked in the row of the "real" item 1. An empty cell in a Q matrix indicates a weight of 0.

Although there are certain advantages to specifying a model within the framework of a general model structure (e.g., for dealing with incomplete test designs and for model control and hypothesis testing), it may be more convenient to have a computer program for that particular model. Such a program is FACETS (Linacre, 1989), which provides many useful fit diagnostics for the *multifacets Rasch model*. A prototypical application of FACETS is given by Eckes (2004).

Generalized Rasch Models for Multimethod Data

The multimethod Rasch model introduced in the previous section can be considered to be a main effects model in the terminology of analysis of variance. Because there are three factors—persons, items, and methods—in this main effects model, three first-order interactions can be distinguished: interactions between methods and items, between persons and methods, and between items and persons. The last-mentioned interaction, however, would contradict the principle of Rasch models to separate the influence of persons and items on the response behavior. Such an interaction would mean that the item parameter differs among persons, that is, the difficulty of an item would be person specific. The mixed Rasch model (Rost, 1990, 1991), which is a combination of the Rasch model with latent class analysis, allows for a very restricted type of person–item interaction by assuming that different sets of item parameters hold for different groups of persons. Therefore, the approach of mixture dis-

TABLE 18.2

Design Matrix of the Main Effects Model (Model 5) as a Specification of the LLTM (Model 6)

Item i	Method j	Component h 1	2	3	4	5	6	7
1	1	1				1		
2	1		1			1		
3	1			1		1		
4	1				1	1		
1	2	1					1	
2	2		1				1	
3	2			1			1	
4	2				1		1	
1	3	1						1
2	3		1					1
3	3			1				1
4	3				1			1

tribution Rasch models will be considered as the third way of introducing an interaction into the main effects model.

Interaction between items and methods. The basic model (Model 5) is a rather restrictive assumption because the impact of different contexts or situations, of different response formats or representation modes, or whatever the methods of a test application may be on the response behavior may be different for different items. The interaction model is obtained by substituting the two single-indexed parameters σ_i and μ_j by a double-indexed parameter σ_{ij}, which parameterizes the difficulty of item i with method j:

$$p(X_{vij} = 1) = \frac{\exp(\theta_v + \sigma_{ij})}{d_{vij}}. \tag{7}$$

In case of a complete multimethod design, that is, if all items are administered using every method, the interaction model is equivalent to the ordinary Rasch model with as many items as there are item-by-method combinations. From this point of view, the original Rasch model is more general than the extension of the Rasch model by a third, latent additive method factor as is the case in the basic

model (Model 5). In fact, the LLTM (Model 6) itself is an ingenious *extension* of the Rasch model because it contains item components that the Rasch model does not take into consideration.

The advantage of treating the main effects model (Model 5) as a specification of the LLTM is that a large number of intermediate stages between the main effects model (Model 5) and the interaction model (Model 7) can be specified, and a very flexible way of dealing with incomplete multimethod test designs is given. Whereas in the latter case simply canceling the lines of the design matrix Q (see earlier) that relate to a missing item–method combination solves this situation, the specification of mixed interaction and conditional main effects requires a reorganization of the Q matrix. The following matrix (see Table 18.3) illustrates the assumption that the third method does interact with the items so that there is only a conditional main effect between Methods 1 and 2. An example for such a semi-interaction between item content and item method would be an achievement test in physics, where four different item contents are crossed by three kinds of response formats, that is, open verbal response, multiple choice, and numerical calculation. On one side, the difficulties of the four content areas, say electrical circuitry, optical lenses, gravity, and density, are combined additively with the (low) difficulty of giving a multiple-choice response or the (high) difficulty of giving a free response. On the other side, the third method in this hypothetical example, the numerical response format, interacts with the content area depending on which formula has to be applied and on the choice of the numbers. An easy numerical calculation makes the items easier, whereas the application of a complex formula and/or fractions can make the items rather difficult.

TABLE 18.3

Design Matrix of a Model With Main Effects and Interactions Between Items and Methods

		Components *h*									
Methods *j*	**Items *i***	**1**	**2**	**3**	**4**	**5**	**6**	**7**	**8**	**9**	**10**
1	1	1				1					
1	2		1			1					
1	3			1		1					
1	4				1	1					
2	1	1					1				
2	2		1				1				
2	3			1			1				
2	4				1		1				
3	1	1						1			
3	2		1						1		
3	3			1						1	
3	4				1						1

From this perspective, the main effects and the interaction model are not distinct types of models, but merely the extreme variants of a whole spectrum of models allowing for more or less interactions between the items and the methods. But even with the highest degree of interactions between items and methods, the interaction model is latent additive with respect to the person parameter θ_v; in other words, these models assume only one trait parameter for all items and methods, and hence, they remain *unidimensional*.

Interaction between persons and methods. When a test instrument has been administered by applying different methods, this may not only have implications for the item difficulties, but also for the latent traits used by the persons. Method A, for example, items with an open response format that require the respondents to verbalize the solution of a task, may address the respondents' verbal and creative abilities. The "same" items with a multiple-choice response format, in contrast, address the person's ability to make "good guesses" by some distracter elimination technique. Hence, methods may be associated to different traits or latent dimensions.

This is also a kind of interaction but an interaction between methods and persons. These models may be called *ability* models as compared to *difficulty* models. They can be formalized in the very same way as difficulty models, that is, by introducing double-indexed parameters θ_{vj} instead of latent additive (single-indexed) person and method parameters. The multidimensional multimethod model can be formalized as

$$p(X_{vij} = 1) = \frac{\exp(\theta_{vj} - \sigma_i)}{d_{vij}}, \tag{8}$$

where θ_{vj} is the trait parameter of person v if method j is used. The test items have the same difficulty irrespective of the method applied, but the persons respond by means of a different trait depending on which method has been used. This model belongs to the family of multidimensional Rasch models that has been described by Adams, Wilson, and Wang (1997; see also the computer program ConQuest; Wu, Adams, & Wilson, 1997) and Rost and Carstensen (2002; see also the computer program MULTIRA; Carstensen & Rost, 1998). Model 8 is a submodel of these generalized Rasch models, which is defined by the following properties.

- It is a *between-item multidimensionality* model, which means that the latent dimensions are specific for nonoverlapping subgroups of items, so that every item belongs to one and only one dimension.
- The item parameters σ_i remains the same for all methods.
- It is a kind of *facets model* that refers to a test design where each item is a specific combination of two facets, for example, a content facet and a process facet or, as in our case, the item content and the administration method. In contrast to the general case of facets models (Rost & Carstensen, 2002), Model 8 is not symmetric with respect to the two facets: The item content facet is assumed to have a main effect only on the item difficulty, whereas the method facet is assumed to interact with the trait.

As in the case of the LLTM and the simple main effects model, the model can be specified by means of design matrices and, hence, is embedded in a more general model structure. This general multidimensional model is the *multidimensional random coefficients multinomial logit model* (MRCMLM; Adams, Wilson, & Wang, 1997; see also the computer program ConQuest; Wu, Adams, & Wilson, 1997) in which two design matrices, **A** and **B**, are used for separately specifying the component structure of the item difficulties (as in the LLTM) and a (different) component structure defining the latent traits.

$$p(X_{vij}=1) = \frac{\exp(\sum_h \mathbf{A}_{mh}\theta_{vh} - \sum_g \mathbf{B}_{mg}\sigma_g)}{d_{vij}}, \quad (9)$$

where m is the index across all tasks (i.e., items × methods), h is the index of the components defining the traits, and g is the index of the components defining the difficulties. Both matrices, **A** and **B**, can be different and are different in our case. In fact they must be different to avoid identification problems.

This is illustrated for the example of four items and three methods, that is, 12 physical items, each four from three different methods in Table 18.4. The number of rows in both matrices must be identical because they refer to the same data, that is, to the same physical items. The columns, however, are different. There are three for the method-specific traits (Matrix A) and four for the method-free item contents.

One benefit of defining a multimethod model by means of design matrices is the flexibility of model specification. Again, incomplete test designs can be handled by the design matrices, and models can be specified that mix assumptions from different models.

As a multimethod model, Model 8 can be considered a model with weak assumptions for the traits (each method defining its own trait), but with strong assumptions regarding the items because they have the same difficulties under all methods.

TABLE 18.4

Two Different Design Matrices for the Ability and the Difficulty Structure

Methods j	Items i	A_{mh} Traits h			B_{mg} Item components g			
		1	2	3	1	2	3	4
1	1	1			1			
1	2	1				1		
1	3	1					1	
1	4	1						1
2	1		1		1			
2	2		1			1		
2	3		1				1	
2	4		1					1
3	1			1	1			
3	2			1		1		
3	3			1			1	
3	4			1				1

The latter type of assumption is not necessary because a multidimensional model can also be formalized without a decomposition of the difficulty parameters. The resulting model is a multidimensional Rasch model with as many dimensions as there are methods and a difficulty parameter for each item × method combination:

$$p(X_{vij} = 1) = \frac{\exp(\theta_{vj} - \sigma_{ij})}{d_{vij}}. \qquad (10)$$

This model allows for both kinds of interactions—person × method and item × method. Data analyses according to this model can be done using the computer programs MULTIRA and ConQuest.

Rasch model and latent class analysis: "Some interaction" between items and persons. From a formal point of view, the third kind of interaction, that is, between items and persons, could be treated quite similar to the interaction between methods and persons. A multidimensional model could be defined in which the traits are specific for each item:

$$p(X_{vij} = 1) = \frac{\exp(\theta_{vi} + \mu_j)}{d_{vij}}. \qquad (11)$$

Such a multidimensional approach to modeling the interaction of persons and items would again lead to the same family of models as discussed in the last section, with just items and methods exchanged. A "complete" interaction between items and persons in the sense that each item addresses its own latent trait certainly contradicts the basic idea of Rasch's theory of measurement to *separate* the influence of items and persons.

With the approach of mixture distribution Rasch models, a moderate way of introducing interactions between items and persons is provided. The *mixed Rasch model* is a combination of *latent class analysis* and the Rasch model. As described, LCA is used to identify groups of subjects, called classes, who respond to the test items in a qualitatively similar way. This is formalized by class-specific solving

probabilities for each item. But LCA does not take into account the quantitative differences between persons within each class. This extension is made by the mixed Rasch model (Rost 1990, 1991), which states that the Rasch model holds for each and every class, however, with its own set of parameters for each class. It assumes that both the item parameters and the person parameters are class specific, which means that the model assigns different item parameters to the same item and different person parameters to the same person depending on the latent class.

$$p(X_{vi} = 1) = \sum_c \pi_c \frac{\exp(\theta_{vc} - \sigma_{ic})}{d_{vic}}. \qquad (12)$$

The π_c-parameters are the *unconditional probabilities* of belonging to class c and are sometimes called the *class size parameters* or the *mixing proportions*. θ_{vc} symbolizes the class-specific person parameter, and σ_{ic} stands for the class-specific item parameter.

There are many different ways of generalizing the mixed Rasch approach to multimethod data. A straightforward way would be to separate the effects of items and methods within each class, namely, to assume the main effects model (Model 5) for each latent class c:

$$p(X_{vij} = 1) = \sum_c \pi_c \frac{\exp(\theta_{vc} - \sigma_{ic} + \mu_{jc})}{d_{vijc}}. \qquad (13)$$

A more general model structure would be obtained when a latent additive decomposition of the item-method parameters is introduced,

$$p(X_{vij} = 1) = \sum_c \pi_c \frac{\exp(\theta_{vc} - \sum_m q_{mh}\eta_h)}{d_{vijc}}, \qquad (14)$$

which would be the *mixture distribution LLTM* (Rost, 2001). The basic idea of this model is the assumption of different latent classes in which the LLTM holds. Obviously the mixture distribution

LLTM (Model 14) is a restricted case of the mixed Rasch model (Model 12).

Moreover, the possibility of defining so-called hybrid models (which are mixture models in which a different kind of model holds in each latent class) inflates the family of multimethod Rasch models to an intractable framework of thousands of models, and this situation would not really help us understand the psychometric issues of multimethod data.

Instead of searching for the model that is most general but not applicable to any data set (because no appropriate software would be available), we will restrict ourselves to the simple case of the mixed Rasch model. This model takes an interaction between items and methods into account and restricts the interaction with persons to a limited (small) number of latent classes:

$$p(X_{vij} = 1) = \sum_c \pi_c \frac{\exp(\theta_{vc} - \sigma_{ijc})}{d_{vijc}}. \qquad (15)$$

The σ_{ijc} parameters are combined item–method parameters and specific for each class c. The unidimensional θ_{vc} parameters refer to all tasks, so that (similar to interaction Model 7) there is no difference between items and methods in the formalization of the model. Both may contribute to the identification of subgroups of persons. Therefore, it is not a model that is specific for the multimethod situation. Rather, it provides us with an elegant heuristic tool to identify interactions between items and methods and the latent trait.

All models described in this section have been defined for dichotomous data. All these models can also be defined for ordinal response variables, for example, for rating scales as a response format or partial credit scoring in the case of achievement tests.

THE APPLICATION OF MULTIMETHOD MODELS TO INCOMPLETE DATA

Some of the generalized Rasch models for multimethod data presented in Section 2 require parameter estimation methods that do not belong to the standard repertoire of the ordinary Rasch model, particularly if the data stem from incomplete test designs or if a multimatrix design has been used for data collection. In both cases, the data cube is incomplete, that is, it has many submatrices or subcubes where no responses were observed. In this section, some methods of parameter estimation and measures of accuracy will be discussed.

The application of the Rasch model requires the estimation of both types of parameters, those for persons and for items. There are at least three possibilities for estimating the parameters in the Rasch model:

- *Joint maximum likelihood* (JML), that is, the maximization of the likelihood function, which contains both types of parameters.
- *Conditional maximum likelihood* (CML), that is, the likelihood function is maximized after the elimination of the person parameters by conditioning on the sum scores.
- *Marginal maximum likelihood* (MML), that is, the likelihood function is maximized while the distribution of person parameters is modelled by some type of distribution like the normal.

The best way to estimate the item parameters of the Rasch model is to use the CML approach because it leads to consistent item parameter estimates without making an assumption about the latent trait distribution. Such an assumption must be made for the MML approach. Usually a normal distribution is assumed, the parameters of which can be directly and consistently estimated together with the item parameters (Mislevy, 1984).

Considering the JML approach, the estimates of the item and person parameters are only consistent if the number of persons and the number of items increase to infinity (Molenaar, 1995). As a consequence, the JML method is not used for estimating the item parameters anymore. However, it is still applied for the estimation of person parameters.

Traditionally these parameters are estimated as maximum likelihood estimators (MLE) using the first partial derivatives of the JML function of all items i to which a person v has responded:

$$\frac{\partial \log p(\mathbf{x}|\theta,\sigma)}{\partial \theta} = 0. \qquad (16)$$

$p(\mathbf{x}\,|\,\theta,\sigma)$ represents the likelihood of the response vector $\mathbf{x}$ of a certain person with parameter θ under the condition of known or sufficiently well estimated item parameters. For the Rasch model this likelihood is

$$p(\mathbf{x}|\theta,\sigma) = \prod_i \frac{\exp(x_i(\theta - \sigma_i))}{1 + \exp(\theta - \sigma_i)}.$$

The MLE has several disadvantages. First, it is infinite for persons who either do not solve any or solve every item. Second, it has a considerable bias, that is, the expectation of $(\hat{\theta}_v - \theta_v)$ is not zero. To circumvent these disadvantages, Warm (1989) modified the MLE via Bayes' theorem

$$p(\theta|\mathbf{x},\sigma) \propto L \cdot f(\theta). \qquad (17)$$

In this equation, L stands for the likelihood function, and the latent trait distribution is denoted by $f(\theta)$. Warm (1989) used a *prior* distribution for $f(\theta)$, which is equal to the square root of the Fisher information function. Such a prior is called *noninformative* because it is a constant over the latent dimension and does not contain information about the latent distribution of person abilities. By means of Warm's method, an estimator for θ_v is obtained that has a finite value for persons who solve either none or every item. It also has a smaller bias than the MLE. The estimator is called the *weighted likelihood estimator* (WLE) or Warm's estimator.

Using an informative instead of a noninformative prior in combination with the likelihood function, an a posteriori distribution is obtained that contains all information about the θ_v parameters. The expectation of this distribution for a single person can be used as a point estimator of θ_v, called the *expected a posteriori estimator* (EAP; Bock & Aitkin, 1981). In contrast to the WLE, this estimator does not minimize the bias but the mean square error, $\frac{1}{N}\sum_v \left(\hat{\theta}_v - \theta_v\right)^2$.

Although WLE and EAP estimators are the best way to estimate each individual's latent trait value, in other words, they are the best point estimators, they do have one major drawback: The sample distributions of both point estimators do not converge to the latent trait distribution. Although the *mean* of the latent distribution can consistently be estimated by both point estimators, the *variance* cannot. The variance of the WLE exceeds the latent variance because the measurement error is part of it. In contrast, the EAP distribution is shrunken compared to the latent distribution because the EAPs (which are the *means* of each individual's posterior distribution) have smaller variances than the "true values."

Alternatively, it is possible to draw a number of values at random from each individual's posterior distribution and to use these values for the estimation of the latent distribution. Because these values are plausible estimators for the individuals' latent trait value, they are called *plausible values* (Mislevy, Beaton, Kaplan, & Sheehan, 1992). The variance of these plausible values is a consistent estimate of the variance of the latent distribution. Although plausible values reproduce the latent variance, they are poor point estimators as compared to the WLE or EAP.

The advantage of the MML method is not only the consistent estimation of the latent distribution, but also the possibility of applying it under missing data conditions. In this case, the property of estimating the latent distribution consistently depends on the condition that the missing data are *missing at random* (MAR). MAR means that the missing data are a random sample of the observed data (Schafer, 1997). If this assumption is true, then the estimation of the latent distribution only on the basis of the observed data will be consistent. The likelihood of the observed data contains all the necessary and sufficient information for this estimation. Missing data that are due to an incomplete test design usually fulfill the MAR condition so that consistent estimates are ensured.

A third advantage of the MML method is connected to its property of providing consistent estimates of the latent variance. The estimator of the latent variance can be used as a measure of the "true score" variance in the classical definition of reliability. In the definition of reliability as the ratio of true score variance and observed score variance, the true score variance is represented by the variance of the latent trait, and the observed score variance is given by the variance of the WLE estimates. Thus, reliability can be calculated as

$$\text{Re}\, l = \frac{est.Var\left(\theta\right)}{Var\left(\hat{\theta}\right)} \qquad (18)$$

where $est.Var(\theta)$ is the variance of the latent trait estimated by means of the MML method.

This measure of reliability has turned out to be much closer to classical measures. In particular, it is not distorted by the overestimation of error variance defined as the expected standard error of person parameter estimates (Andrich, 1988; Rost, 1996).

After the estimation of the model parameters and the calculation of a measure of accuracy, it is necessary to determine whether the considered model fits the data. This is a question of internal *validity*. In other words, a measure of a latent trait by means of multimethod data is said to be internally valid if the model used to estimate the trait fits the data. One possibility is to calculate the ratio of the likelihoods (LR) of the model being considered and a less-restrictive model (*likelihood ratio test*). Then the test statistic $-2\ln(LR)$ is approximately chi-square distributed, and the degrees of freedoms are equal to the difference of the numbers of parameters in both models. If the likelihood ratio test is significant, then the assumptions of the more restrictive model do not hold.

The likelihood ratio test requires—among other things—that the model under consideration be a submodel of the comparison model. If two or more nonnested models are to be compared, it is possible to use so-called information indices like *Akaike's information criterion* (AIC) or *Bayes information criterion* (BIC). These indices allow the comparison of models by combining the likelihood value and the number of model parameters. The rationale is that models that have more parameters can fit the data better than models with fewer parameters. Consequently, each model is penalized for its number of parameters. Additionally, the sample size is also considered in BIC estimates because the number of different response patterns usually increases with the number of subjects so that a model assuming many parameters is more likely when the sample size is large. Because this effect is considered by the BIC, this index is preferable to the AIC if the number of response patterns is high. Although it is possible to compare very different models by means of these two indices, a serious disadvantage is that it is not possible to make the difference between two values subject to a statistical significance test.

AN ANALYSIS OF THE GERMAN SCIENCE TEST IN OECD/PISA 2003 (FIELD TRIAL DATA)

In this section, the models presented earlier will be used to analyze the field trial data of the German science test of the OECD Program for International Student Assessment in 2003 (OECD/PISA 2003). OECD/PISA 2003 is the second of at least three cycles of an international large-scale study designed to assess and analyze the educational systems of more than 30 countries (of which almost all are members of the Organization for Economic Co-operation and Development, OECD). The target population consists of 15-year-old high school students whose skills and competencies are assessed in the domains of reading, mathematical, and scientific literacy in real-life settings.

In addition to the international part of the study, each participating country has the opportunity to examine special national research questions by administration of their own national test. In Germany, the scientific literacy component has been (and still is) the responsibility of the Leibniz Institute for Science Education. A national expert team consisting of biologists, chemists, physicists, educational researchers, and psychologists from this institute and several German universities constructed the national science test. Based on the experience with the national science test of PISA 2000, a complete two-facet design was created for the national science test of PISA 2003.

The first facet refers to the content areas of the test items, which can be assigned to the three science subjects of the German school system, biology, chemistry, and physics. The test covered four content areas from physics, four from biology, and two from chemistry, that is, a total of 10 different contents. The second facet refers to seven so-called cognitive components:

1. "Evaluating" comprises the ability to analyze a specific, complex, and problematic situation in which no simple solution exists but several possible options to act exist.
2. "Divergent thinking" is the ability to create a number of different but correct answers to a cognitive task for which there is not just one solution.
3. "Dealing with graphical representations" stands for the ability to solve a cognitive task by using the information that is provided by a graph, a diagram, or an illustration.
4. "Convergent thinking/reasoning" represents the ability to solve problems by means of an inferred or introduced rule.
5. "Using mental models": A mental model can be described as a spatial or geometrical concept that represents scientific facts and their relations. By means of this concept, the student should be able to predict and explain experimental results and empirical findings.
6. "Describing the phenomenon" is the ability of a person to correctly describe the pieces of information given in tables, diagrams, graphs, or illustrations.
7. "Dealing with numbers" stands for the ability to perform numerical calculations in the context of a scientific concept. For a correct calculation it is not only necessary to do the right arithmetical operations, but it is essential that the underlying scientific concept has been understood.

In the facet design of the 2003 German science test, each combination of a content and a cognitive component is represented by one item. In summary, the field trial test version was based on a two-facet design with 70 items addressing 10 content areas and 7 cognitive components. Because of limited testing time, not all 70 tasks could be administered to each of the 1,955 students assessed in the field trial. Therefore, sampling followed a multimatrix design in which 10 subgroups of students responded to the tasks of either one, three, or five content areas. As a result, the final data matrix included an average of 70% missing data that is due to the test design. In the analyses described following, only those cases were included that responded at least to 21 items (781 students).

For the purpose of illustrating the analysis of multimethod test data, we will consider the content areas as the "items" and the cognitive components as the "methods." In the case of the German PISA 2003 science field test, a biological content such as "predators and prey" is connected to each of the cognitive competencies, so students work on a task dealing with, for example, the different possibilities for increasing the lynx population ("predators and prey" in connection with "divergent thinking"). In the terminology of the multitrait–multimethod approach, the combination of content area, for instance, "predators and prey," and cognitive components, for instance, "divergent thinking," would be called "items," whereas the content area would be the "trait" and the cognitive component would be the "method."

But the chosen kind of analysis here is not the only possible way of looking at these data. For instance, the items of one cognitive component ("method") are rather different with respect to the particular pieces of knowledge included in the 10 tasks. There is more variation among the items of the same method than could be expected by simply taking into account the differences in the content areas. This implies, for example, that a model assuming constant item (content) difficulties under all methods has little chance to fit the data. However, this conclusion will be drawn from the results and need not be subject to speculation in advance. The analyses were conducted along the structure of the family of multimethod Rasch models described earlier. In particular, the LLTM, the Rasch model, and its generalizations to the multidimensional and mixed population case will be applied.

Table 18.5 gives an overview of the application of all models mentioned. The first four models have been calculated using the ConQuest program, and the mixed Rasch models were calculated by means of a not-yet-published program by Matthias von Davier. Note that the likelihood and the number of parameters increases from left to right in Table 18.5. For model selection, the Bayes information criterion (BIC) is preferable to Akaike's information criterion (AIC) because the German PISA science test consists of 70 items and was administered to 781 students, resulting in a large number of different

TABLE 18.5

Results of the Fit Statistics for the Multimethod Models

	LLTM	7D LLTM	Rasch model	7D RM	Mixed RM 2 classes	Mixed RM 3 classes
Log likelihood	−15,179	−14,138	−13,706	−12,129	−12,069	−11.976
Number of independent parameters	18	38	71	98	143	215
AIC	30,394.80	28,351.76	27,554.28	24,453.43	24,424.69	24,381.42
BIC	30,478.69	28,528.86	27,885.18	24,910.16	25,091.15	25,383.45

Note. 7D LLTM = seven-dimensional linear logistic test model, 7D RM = seven-dimensional Rasch model.

response patterns, a situation that must be taken into account in model fitting (see Section 3). If the model selection was based on the BIC, the decision would be to choose the seven-dimensional Rasch model because the BIC value is the smallest for this model. Yet before a decision is made, let us first have a closer look at the models and their estimates.

For the first four models, it is necessary to set the sum of the person or item parameters to zero to let the models be identified. For these analyses the constraint was on the *cases* (persons), that is, all latent means were set to zero. In the first model, that is, the main effects model (5), known here as the LLTM, the probability of a task response is a function of one person parameter θ_v, one item parameter σ_i, and one cognitive component (method), μ_j. It is the most restrictive model because it only has 18 independent parameters and a log likelihood of −15,179, which is the lowest value of all the tested models. The 18 parameters cover the mean (which is set to zero and not counted as a parameter) and variance of the latent trait, 10 parameters for the content areas, and 7 parameters for the methods.

Analyses reveal a tremendous increment to the log likelihood of the ordinary Rasch model in which no additive decomposition of the task difficulty into an item effect and a method effect is assumed. The log likelihood value increases to −13,706 for the Rasch model, which has 70 item–method parameters. Both models can be compared by means of their task difficulties. These are the item–method parameters of the Rasch model and the sums of the content and the method parame-

TABLE 18.6

The Content and Method Parameters of the Simple Main Effects Model (LLTM)

Parameter	Parameter value
Contents	
Respiration & photosynthesis (biology)	−0.02
Wheat germ (biology)	−0.21
Predator & prey (biology)	−0.16
Having babies (biology)	0.30
At the swimming pool (chemistry)	0.33
Waste incineration (chemistry)	0.12
Traffic (physics)	0.09
Warmth & cold (physics)	−0.50
Electricity (physics)	0.19
Energy (physics)	0.02
Methods	
Evaluating	0.36
Divergent thinking	0.06
Graphical representations	−0.01
Convergent thinking	0.64
Mental models	1.76
Describing the phenomenon	0.07
Dealing with numbers	0.33

ters of the LLTM. The latter can be found in Table 18.6. As an example, we can look at the task where the method "dealing with numbers" has to be applied to "energy." The task difficulty of the LLTM is obtained by adding the difficulty of the method "dealing with numbers" (0.33) to the value of the content difficulty of "energy" (0.02) resulting in a value of 0.35. The estimated task dif-

TABLE 18.7

Reliabilities of the Latent Traits Under the Different Multimethod Models

	LLTM	Rasch model
Unidimensional model	0.777	0.812
Seven-dimensional model		
Evaluating	0.533	0.530
Divergent thinking	0.688	0.612
Dealing with graphics	0.496	0.474
Convergent thinking	0.448	0.428
Mental model	0.274	0.620
Describing the phenomenon	0.802	0.776
Dealing with numbers	0.941	0.959

ficulty of the Rasch model is 0.36, so that the task difficulty is very much the same in both models. This does not have to be the case for all items. If the estimates from both models were approximately the same, they would be positioned on the diagonal in Figure 18.3. This would mean that no interactions between content and cognitive components exist.

In fact, Figure 18.3 shows that the congruence of the task difficulties from both models is not very

high. As expected from the difference of the log likelihoods, the item parameters of the Rasch model and those calculated from the item components of the LLTM differ from each other substantially. The hypothesis of a simple additive model of content and cognitive component does not hold for the German PISA science test.

However, the reliability of the tests of both (unidimensional) models does not reflect the lack of fit of the main effects model. The reliability, estimated as the ratio of latent and WLE variance, is .812 for the Rasch model and .777 for the LLTM. The superiority of the Rasch model is better reflected by its higher variance (1.09) than that of the LLTM (.81).

In Section 2, the distinction between difficulty and ability models was introduced. According to this distinction, both models considered so far (the LLTM and Rasch model) are difficulty models. With regard to the present data, the impact of the methods on the response probabilities certainly cannot be modeled by a difficulty model. Maybe an ability model based on the same distinction between content and cognitive components is more appropriate for this data. The assumption that the methods refer to own latent dimensions is rather plausible for the PISA science test example because what is called

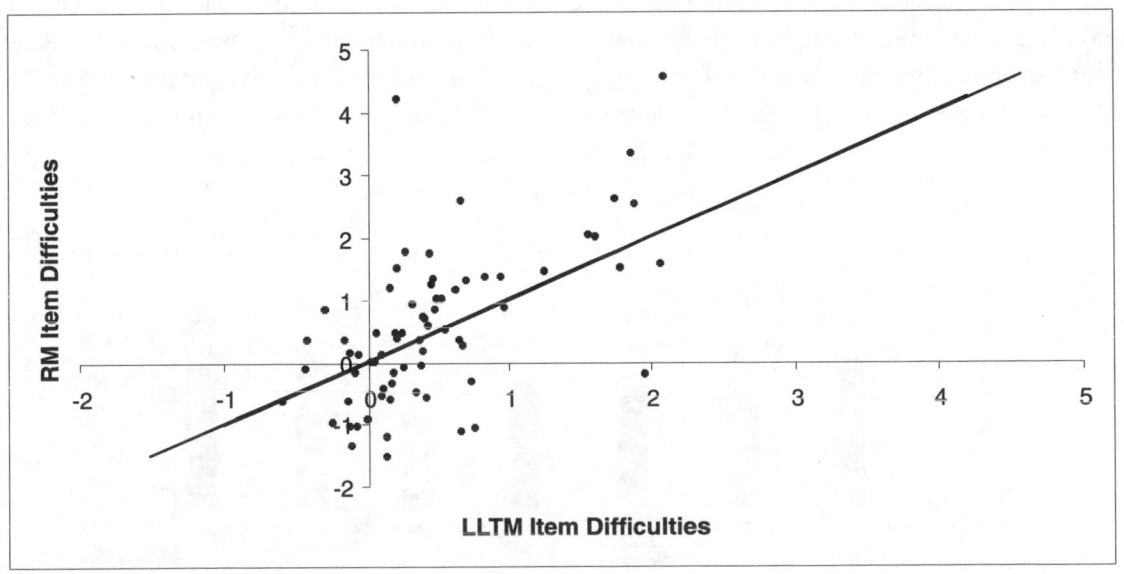

FIGURE 18.3. A graphical comparison of the task parameters in the main effects (LLTM) and the interaction model (unconstrained Rasch model).

cognitive components may also be considered as cognitive *competencies*, that is, as trait variables.

This leads us to the multidimensional multi-method Model (8), where latent variables are assumed for each method and difficulty parameters for each content. The model may be considered to be a multidimensional generalization of the LLTM, and it has a log likelihood of –14,138, which is notably better than the log likelihood of the ordinary LLTM. A total of 38 independent parameters have to be estimated: 10 content parameters, 7 latent variances, and 21 latent covariances.

The difficulty parameters of the items (content) are strongly related in both the unidimensional and the seven-dimensional models ($r = .98$). Figure 18.4 shows the latent variances and the WLE variances of Model (8), which were estimated along with the 7D LLTM. As can be seen, the latent variances range from a small value (0.235 for "mental model") to relatively large values for "describing the phenomenon" (1.239) and "dealing with numbers" (1.769). In contrast, the WLE variances do not have this broad range, but vary from 0.858 ("mental model") to 1.869 ("dealing with numbers"). As a consequence, the reliabilities of the seven competencies also vary considerably. Table 18.7 presents the reliability estimates, measured as the ratio of the latent variance to the WLE variance, for the first four models discussed in this chapter. At the top of the table the reliabilities of the unidimensional LLTM (second column) and of the Rasch model (third column) are presented. The lower portion of the table shows the reliabilities of the seven

cognitive competencies for the seven-dimensional LLTM (second column) and the seven-dimensional Rasch model (third column). Some of the reliabilities are very low (e.g., for "mental models," seven-dimensional LLTM), which may be due to a floor effect, that is, the mental model tasks only have a mean solution probability of 0.17. Nevertheless, for most of the competencies, the reliabilities are considerably high, which confirms that a multidimensional approach for analyzing the data is more appropriate than a unidimensional approach. Whether each trait requires its own parameter or whether a smaller number of dimensions would suffice to describe the data are questions that have not been subjected to model fit tests but have been answered by an exploratory principal components analysis. The first two principal components explain 88.6 percent of the variance. This is a strong indicator that two dimensions might suffice. The structure and interpretation of this two-factor space is very similar to that of the next model; therefore, a separate presentation of the results is not provided here.

The next step of analysis is motivated by the question of whether the superiority of the seven-dimensional LLTM can be increased even more if the assumption of the main effect of content on the task difficulty is omitted. The resulting model is the multidimensional Rasch model without a decomposition of the task parameters. The model has 70 item parameters (instead of 10) and, as the seven-dimensional LLTM, 7 latent variances and 21 covariances. Then the total number of independent

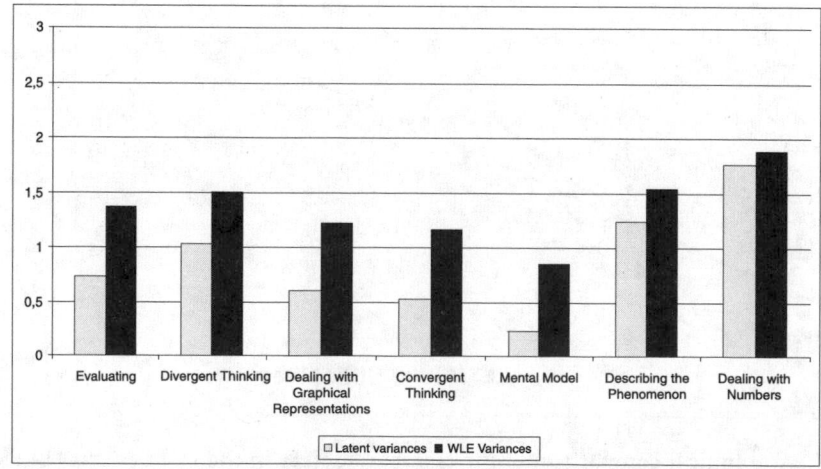

FIGURE 18.4. Latent and observed variances of the seven method traits according to Model 8.

parameters is 98. This seven-dimensional Rasch model has a log likelihood value of –12,129. Figure 18.5 shows the latent variances of the seven latent dimensions of this model. Compared to the variance estimates of the seven-dimensional LLTM, the estimates of the seven-dimensional Rasch model are generally higher. This is true for the latent as well as for the WLE variances. The latent variance estimates range from 0.725 for "convergent thinking" to 2.436 for "dealing with numbers," whereas the WLE variances vary from 1.285 for "mental model" to 2.540 for "dealing with numbers."

To interpret the 21 covariances of the 7 traits, a principal components analysis based on the latent correlations was calculated. Figure 18.6 shows the varimax rotation of the two-factor solution that explains 94.4% of the observed variance. With regard to the first two principal components, the cognitive competencies "dealing with graphical representations," "dealing with numbers," "employing mental models," and "convergent thinking" have

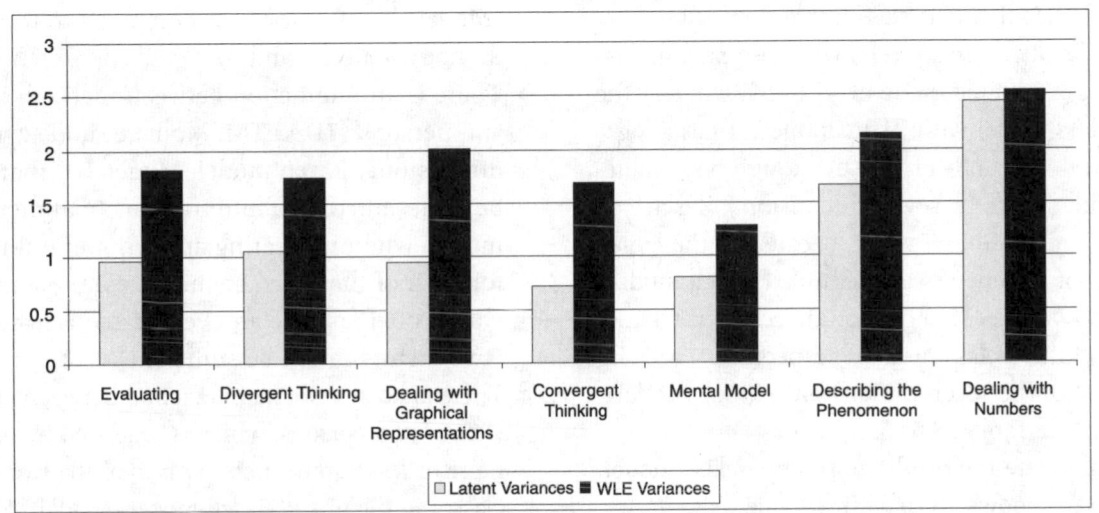

FIGURE 18.5. Latent and observed variances of the seven method traits according to Model 10.

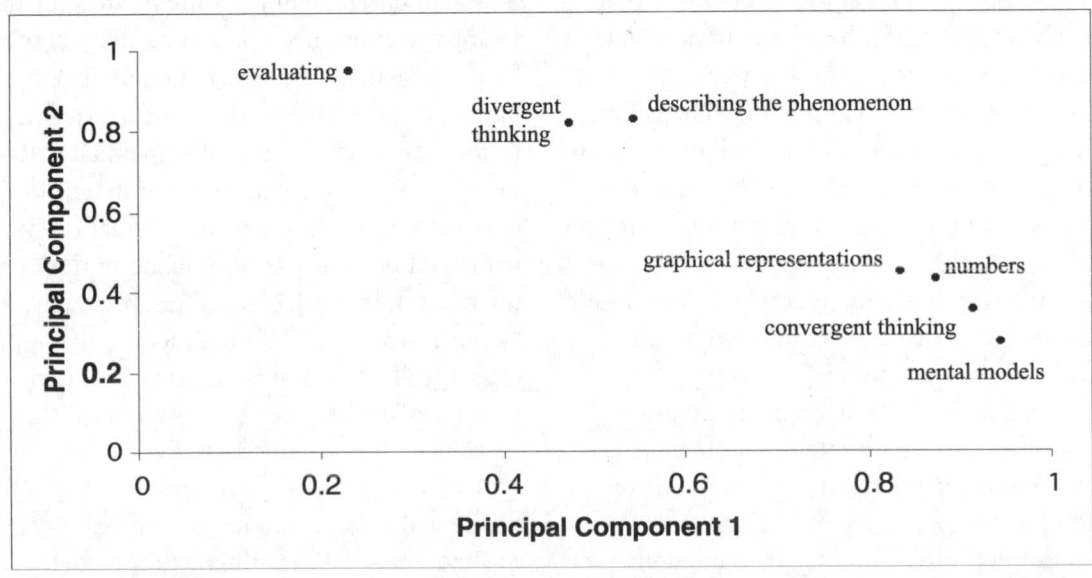

FIGURE 18.6. Loading plot of the first two principal components based on the latent correlations.

nearly the same loadings, that is, they form a kind of cluster in this two-dimensional space. The fact that 94% of the variance is explained by the first two components and the evident interpretation of the results provides support for the assumption that two latent dimensions would suffice to explain the data. With regard to the task difficulties, it makes no difference whether the unidimensional or multidimensional Rasch model is applied because the item difficulties of the unidimensional and the seven-dimensional model are approximately equal.

Finally, the results concerning the mixed Rasch model are to be discussed. Two different solutions were calculated: a two-class and a three-class model. The two-class model with 146 parameters has a log likelihood value of $-12,169$, whereas the three-class model with 219 parameters has a log likelihood value of $-11,976$. Although both values are smaller than the seven-dimensional Rasch model's log likelihood value, because of the large number of parameters of the mixed Rasch model, their BIC values (25,091 and 25,383 for the two-class and three-class models, respectively) are larger than that of the seven-dimensional Rasch model (24,910, see Table 18.5).

To illustrate the results of the two-class model, Figure 18.7 shows 10 diagrams—one diagram for each content area—that present the item parameters for each class of the two-class model. It turns out that the profiles of item parameters in both classes are, despite some deviations, more or less parallel. The irregularities, however, do not relate to one and only one of the cognitive components and, hence, are not specific to one method. The component "dealing with numbers," for example, seems to be the only item that makes a difference between the two classes in the content areas "respiration and photosynthesis" and "predator and prey." The use of mental models when solving a task is responsible for the existence of two classes (instead of one) in the areas "energy" and "waste."

An inspection of all 10 diagrams in Figure 18.7 provides no evidence that there is a systematic interaction among items (contents), methods (cognitive components), and persons. There is, however, a first-order interaction between methods (components) and contents (items) because the

profiles shown by the 10 diagrams are rather different. The distinction of two classes of persons is "only" needed for taking account of some content-specific method effects that seem to indicate some deficiencies in item construction rather than a systematic persons–methods interaction.

Summarizing the findings of all multimethod models considered so far, it can be concluded for the PISA 2003 field trial data that

- There is a strong interaction between the content and the method, which is indicated by the superiority of all models assuming such an interaction (Models 7, 10, and 15) as compared to those that do not (Models 5 and 8).
- There is an interaction between methods and persons (7D LLTM, Model 8, and seven-dimensional Rasch model, Model 10) that can be represented by a multidimensional methods model, whereas creating an own method factor for each of the seven cognitive components would obviously be an overparameterization (two factors might be sufficient).
- There is no systematic interaction between contents (items) and persons, which is indicated by the more or less parallel item profiles of the two latent classes in the mixed Rasch model (Model 15).

CONCLUSION

A system of five item response models for multimethod data has been presented that belongs to the family of generalized Rasch models. The basic model of this system is the most restrictive three-factor extension of the simple two-factor Rasch model. A kind of asymmetry is inherent in this system, because traditionally an interaction between items and persons has been taboo in item response theory and, in particular, in Rasch models. As a "weak" form of such an interaction, the approach of class-specific Rasch models (that is, the mixed Rasch model) has been proposed to fill this gap.

Hence, the system covers five models:

- The main effects model
- The items–methods interaction model
- The methods–persons interaction model

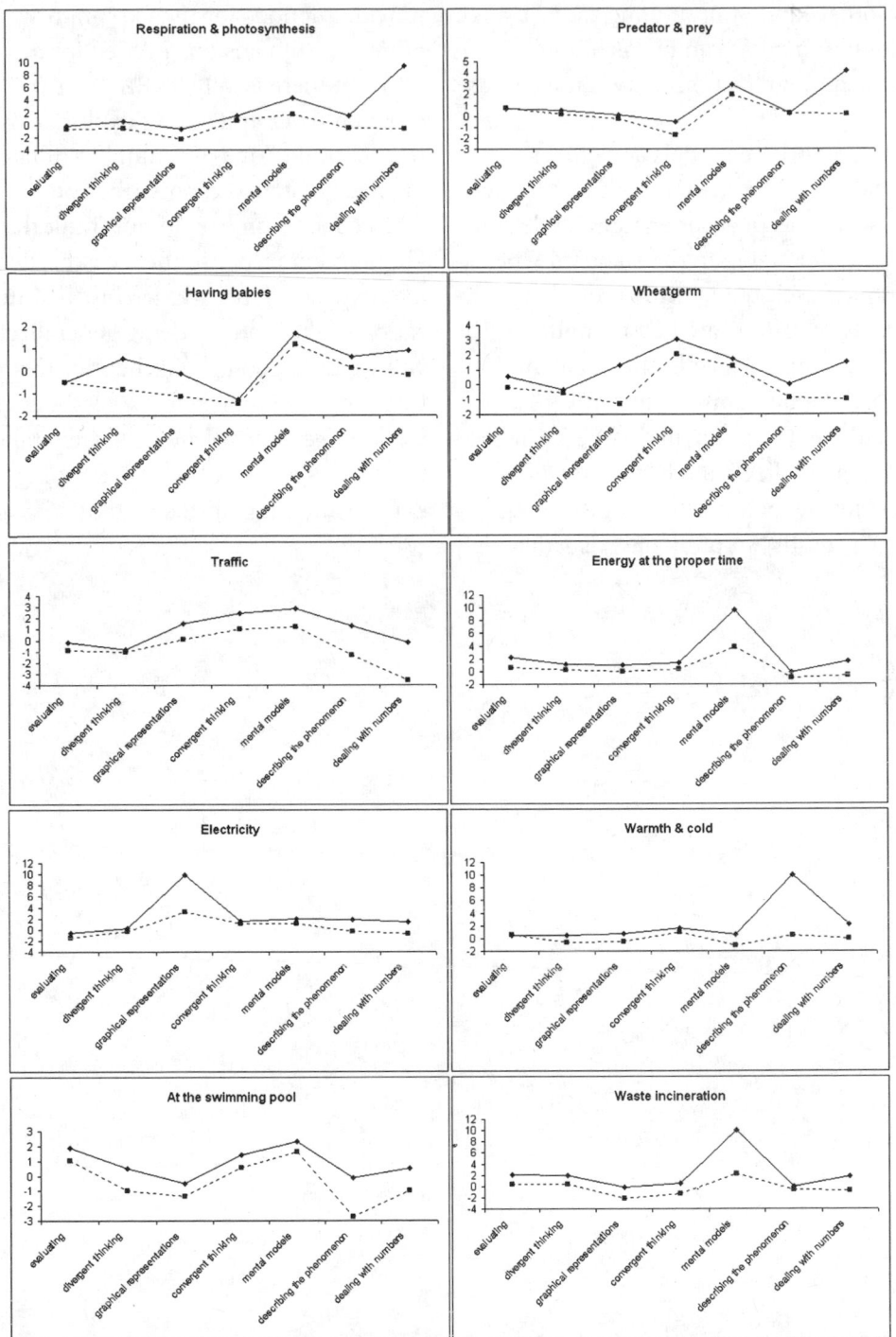

FIGURE 18.7. Item parameter values depending on the cognitive competence for each class of the two-class model.

- The methods–persons and items–methods interaction model
- The items–methods mixed Rasch model.

Methods–persons interaction simply means assuming method-specific dimensions, that is, mul-

tidimensionality. Items–methods interaction means assuming the ordinary Rasch model for as many items as there are items–methods interactions. In this case, it is the *absence* of an interaction (that is, the main effects model for methods and items) that leads to an extended model structure (linear logistic

models). As another kind of multidimensionality, mixture distribution models can be taken into account for modeling interactions between methods and persons.

The application of these models sometimes requires new and more flexible methods of parameter estimation, measures of accuracy, and model control than those belonging to the standard repertoire of the simple Rasch model. However, these methods do exist and can be applied to multimethod data. Other model specifications are only available in principle, but convenient software is lacking. For example, the program FACETS can be used to estimate main effects models or the program ConQuest for many kinds of multidimensional models. Currently, no program exists that provides options for the exploratory analysis of the number of dimensions needed for a given set of data. Yet there is WINMIRA (von Davier, 2001), a program that has a strong exploratory capacity with respect to the kind and number of latent classes involved in a mixture distribution.

In conclusion, we do not think that another kind of item response theory is needed for multimethod data. What we need is the intelligent application of the many existing generalized IRT models, and we need good, solid theories that guide us through the complex and sometimes confusing world of generalized models. General model structures that seem to explain everything do not really explain anything, if there is not an a priori theory.

CHAPTER 19

MULTILEVEL MODELS FOR MULTIMETHOD MEASUREMENTS

Joop Hox and Cora Maas

Theoretical constructs used in social and behavioral science are often complex, and they have an indirect relationship to the corresponding empirical observations. The distance between a theoretical construct and its observable phenomena can create problems for researchers, causing them to explicitly state how they plan to measure what they are theorizing about. To ensure construct validity, the methodological advice often given is to measure each construct in more than one way (e.g., Hoyle, Harris, & Judd, 2002; Kerlinger, 1973). Fiske (1971) advocated not only using multiple operationalizations of each construct, but also purposefully manipulating operationalizations to span different theoretical perspectives and modes of assessment. This raises questions about the convergence and discriminability of different constructs and measures, which underlies the development of the multitrait–multimethod method (Campbell & Fiske, 1959).

This chapter focuses on using multilevel modeling to combine information from different sources and on assessing the reliability and validity of the resulting estimates. It starts with a brief introduction to multilevel analysis. Following this introduction, three measurement approaches are discussed where multilevel modeling is a valuable and effective analysis tool: facet design, assessing contextual characteristics, and generalizability theory. These approaches were chosen because they all, each in their own fashion, aim to incorporate information from several distinct sources in one measurement instrument. Each approach is explained using an example including an analysis of a small data set. The role of multilevel analysis in all three approaches is to assess the contribution of different sources of variance (due both to different traits and to the specific measurement modes used) in designs where standard analysis methods encounter difficulties.

A BRIEF INTRODUCTION TO MULTILEVEL ANALYSIS

Multilevel models are needed for the analysis of data that have a hierarchical or clustered structure. Such data arise routinely in various fields, for instance, in educational research where pupils are nested within schools or in family studies with children nested within families. Clustered data may also arise as a result of the research design. For instance, repeated measures can be viewed as a series of measurements nested within individual subjects.

The models used in this chapter are multilevel regression models. The multilevel regression model assumes hierarchical data, with one response variable measured at the lowest level and explanatory variables at all existing levels. Conceptually the model is often viewed as a hierarchical system of regression equations. For example, assume we have data in J groups or contexts and a different number of individuals N_j in each group. On the individual (lowest) level, we have the dependent variable Y_{ij}

Unless stated otherwise, the data used in the examples are artificial data. Data sets used in the examples are available from the authors.

and the explanatory variable X_{ij}, and on the group level we have the explanatory variable Z_j. Thus, we have a separate regression equation in each group:

$$Y_{ij} = \beta_{0j} + \beta_{1j} X_{ij} + e_{ij}. \qquad (1)$$

The β_j are modeled by explanatory variables at the group level:

$$\beta_{0j} = \gamma_{00} + \gamma_{01} Z_j + u_{0j}, \qquad (2)$$

$$\beta_{1j} = \gamma_{10} + \gamma_{11} Z_j + u_{1j}. \qquad (3)$$

The substitution of (2) and (3) in (1) produces the single equation

$$Y_{ij} = \gamma_{00} + \gamma_{10} X_{ij} + \gamma_{01} Z_j + \gamma_{11} Z_j X_{ij} + u_{1j} X_{ij} + u_{0j} + e_{ij}. \qquad (4)$$

In general there will be more than one explanatory variable at the lowest level and also more than one explanatory variable at the highest level. The assumptions of the multilevel regression model are that the residual errors at the lowest level e_{ij} have a normal distribution with a mean of zero and a variance σ_j^2. It is usually assumed that the groups have a common variance σ^2. The second level residual errors u_{0j} and u_{1j} are assumed to be independent from the lowest level errors e_{ij} as well as to have a multivariate normal distribution with means of zero and variances $\sigma_{u_0}^2$ and $\sigma_{u_1}^2$. Other assumptions, identical to the common assumptions of multiple regression analysis, are fixed predictors and linear relationships. The estimators generally used in multilevel analysis are Maximum Likelihood (ML) estimators, with standard errors estimated from the inverse of the information matrix. These standard errors can be used to establish a confidence interval or to test for significance. This is, in general, not correct for the variance components because in this case the null hypothesis is on the boundary of the parameter space (variances cannot be negative). Therefore, variances are generally tested using a likelihood-ratio test or a chi-square test described by Raudenbush and Bryk (2002). Two different likelihood functions are commonly used in multilevel regression analysis: Full Maximum Likelihood (FML) and Restricted Maximum Likelihood (RML;

Raudenbush & Bryk, 2002; see also Goldstein, 1995). RML estimation is preferred when the interest is in estimating the variance components. For details on the statistical model and estimation techniques, we refer to the literature (e.g., Goldstein, 1995; Hox, 2002; Raudenbush & Bryk, 2002; Snijders & Bosker, 1999).

FACET DESIGN

A useful device for the systematic definition of a theoretical construct is Guttman's facet design (Guttman, 1954). Facet design defines a universe of observations by classifying them using a scheme of *facets* with elements subsumed within facets. Facets are different ways of classifying observations; the elements are distinct classes within each facet. The universe of observations is classified using three kinds of criteria: (a) the population facets that classify the population, (b) the content facets that classify the variables, and (c) the common range of response categories for the variables. The facet design approach can be expressed graphically as follows:

$$[\, X \,] \times [\, A \times B \times \ldots N \,] \rightarrow R$$

In this representation, [X] is the population of objects (respondents, research participants), [A], [B]... [N] are content facets, and R is the common response range. Roskam (1990) emphasized the importance of the response range because it defines the domain of observations. Thus, if the range is defined as "correct/wrong by an objective criterion," we are investigating intelligence behavior, and if the range is defined as "ordered as very positive/very negative toward that object," we are investigating attitude behavior (Roskam, 1990, p. 189).

For our present goal, we concentrate on the facet structure of the variables. The various content facets can be viewed as a cross-classification, analogous to an analysis of variance design that specifies the similarities and dissimilarities among questionnaire items. Each *facet* represents a particular conceptual classification scheme that consists of a set of elements that define possible observations. The content facets must be appropriate for the construct that they define. In selecting the most appropriate

facets and elements, the objective is to describe all important aspects of the content domain explicitly and unequivocally. For example, for many constructs, it may be useful to distinguish a behavior facet that defines the relevant behaviors and a situation facet that defines the situations in which the behaviors occur. An example of a facet design is Gough's (1985, p. 247) design for reasons for attending weight-reduction classes. Gough defined the person facet [X] as "married women attending slimming groups." There are two content facets: *source* and *motive*. The facet design can be summarized as: To what extent does the person [X] feel that *Source* [S] led her to believe that she would achieve *Motive* [M] if she lost weight, as rated using *Response* [R]. The source facet [S] has four elements: (a) own experience, (b) husband, (c) doctor, and (d) media. The motivation facet [M] has seven facets: (a) feel healthier, (b) feel fitter, (c) be more physically attractive, (d) have fewer clothing prob-

lems, (e) suffer less social stigma, (f) be less anxious in social situations, and (g) feel less depressed. The response range [R] is defined on a 7-point scale ranging from 1 (not really at all) to 7 (very much indeed). In facet design, the facet structure is often verbalized by a mapping sentence, which describes the observations in one or more ordinary sentences. Figure 19.1 presents a mapping sentence for the reasons for attending weight-reduction classes.

In this facet design the first facet (source) refers to the source of the belief, and the second facet (reason) refers to a specific consequence of losing weight. A facet design such as the one described can be used to generate questionnaire items. The [X] facet points to a specific target population of individuals. The source facet has four elements, the reason facet has seven, which defines $4 \times 7 = 28$ questions. For example, combining the first elements of the source and reason facets leads to the survey question, "Did your own experience lead

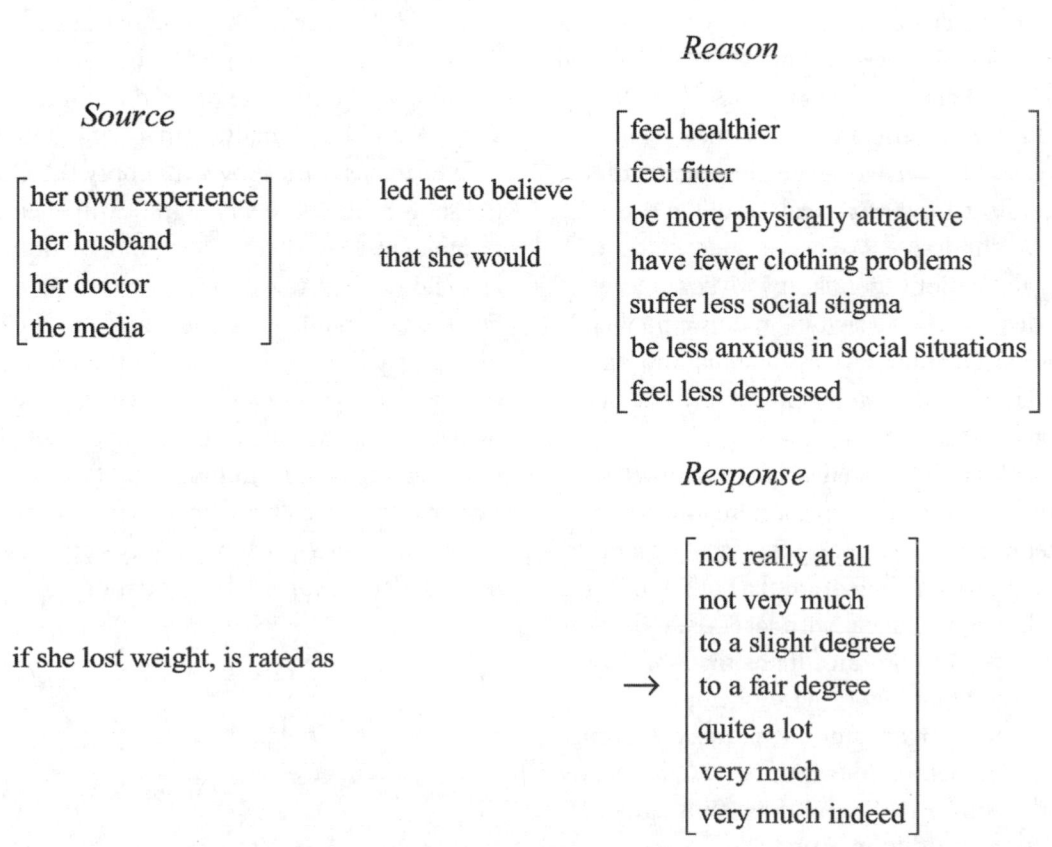

FIGURE 19.1. Mapping sentence for attending weight-loss classes.

you to believe that your health would improve if you lost weight?" (Gough, 1985, p. 257).

A facet design for a set of questions is a definition that should not be judged in terms of right or wrong, but whether it leads to productive research. Facet design contains no general guidelines to determine the need for specific facets; rather, it clearly assumes that we already have a good notion of the empirical domain under investigation.

ANALYSIS OF FACET DATA

Facet design is part of a more general approach called facet theory, which uses the facet structure to generate hypotheses about similarities between items. Facet theory relies almost exclusively on producing low-dimensional geometric representations of the data, which are then interpreted in terms of the properties of the defining facets (cf. Borg & Shye, 1995). Other approaches include confirmatory factor analysis (cf. Mellenbergh, Kelderman, Stijlen, & Zondag, 1979). A problem with both types of approaches is that the analysis focuses on similarities between items and attempts to relate characteristics of the facet design to these similarities. However, as Borg (1994) explained, the relationship between characteristics of the facet design and the geometric ordering of the ensuing items is weak at best. This can be illustrated with the idea of a confirmatory factor analysis of the reasons for losing weight design. We have a source facet with four levels and a motivation facet with seven levels. Do we predict 4 + 7 = 11 factors, or do we predict 4 × 7 = 28 factors? Or should we assume that the facet design merely ensures the content validity of a one-dimensional instrument?

A classical reliability analysis of a (simulated) data set for 50 respondents responding to the 28 items generated by Gough's (1985) facet design produces a reliability coefficient (alpha) of 0.93. This is very high, but not unusual with facet data, because facet designs tend to produce items that are very similar in content and wording. A factor analysis (principal factors, eigenvalue >1, promax rotation) produces seven factors: four factors that are mostly based on the source facet, and three subsequent factors that are not readily interpretable.

Multilevel modeling of facet data takes a different viewpoint. The responses on the common response range are viewed as observations of what occurs when a specific person encounters a specific item. The goal of the multilevel analysis is to determine which item and person characteristics (as defined by the facet design) predict the outcome of this encounter. If all respondents respond to all items, a facet design produces cross-classified data, which can be handled by standard analysis methods such as ANOVA. However, a large-facet design generates too many items to include them all in a single instrument. Older research (cf. Borg & Shye, 1995) typically solved this problem by taking a subsample from all possible items. However, modern computer-assisted data collection methods make it easy to present a different sample of questions to each respondent. In this case, the facet design produces multilevel data, with items nested within respondents, with the response as the outcome variable and person and item characteristics as predictors. The item characteristics are predictors at the lowest (item) level, and the person characteristics are predictors at the person level.

A multilevel analysis of the reasons for weight-loss design requires that both the categorical source and motives facets be expressed as dummy variables. A multilevel analysis involving only these item characteristics shows that only the effects of the source dummies vary significantly across respondents; the effects of the motive dummies have no random variation at the respondent level. For the final model it is convenient to include all four source dummy variables in the regression equation so we can model the (co)variances of all regression coefficients of the source facet. Therefore, the intercept is no longer part of the equation. The seven motive elements are still represented by the usual set of $7 - 1 = 6$ dummy variables. The final model is expressed in Equation (5):

$$Y_{ij} = \gamma_1 S_{1ij} + \gamma_2 S_{2ij} + \gamma_3 S_{3ij} + \gamma_4 S_{4ij} + \gamma_5 M_{1ij} + \gamma_6 M_{2ij}$$
$$+ \gamma_7 M_{3ij} + \gamma_8 M_{4ij} + \gamma_9 M_{5ij} + \gamma_{10} M_{6ij}$$
$$+ u_{1j} + u_{2j} + u_{3j} + u_{4j} + e_{ij}, \tag{5}$$

where S_1 to S_4 are dummy variables that indicate the four elements of the source facet, and M_1 to M_6 are dummy variables that represent the six elements of the motivation facet. The variances σ_{u1}^2 to σ_{u4}^2 of the person-level residual error terms u_1, u_2, u_3, and u_4 are significant (using a likelihood-ratio test; see Hox, 2002), which indicates that there is significant slope variation across persons for the source's (1) own experience, (2) husband, (3) doctor, and (4) media. The variances of the regression slopes for the motivation dummies are not in the model because they were not significant, which means that there is no individual variation in the impact of the motivation facet.

This multilevel analysis produces several interesting estimates. Table 19.1 presents the regression coefficients and the variances for this model. The regression slopes for the item characteristics express overall differences between the item means related to the item content. The (significant) variances of the regression slopes for the predictors belonging to

the source facet express differences between respondents in their sensitivity to item content coming from specific sources. The software HLM (Raudenbush, Bryk, Cheong, & Congdon, 2000) calculates reliability estimates for the random slopes (when using other software these must be hand calculated using formulas presented in Raudenbush & Bryk, 2002). The reliability estimates for the slope variation of s1, s2, s3, and s4 are 0.84, 0.83, 0.84, and 0.87, respectively. This means that variations in sensitivity to reasons originating from different sources can be measured with sufficient precision.

The slopes of doctor and media and of self and husband correlate strongly (0.93 and 0.89, respectively), but the other slopes are relatively independent (correlations lower than 0.61). If we need to use these measurements in a different context, we can estimate residuals or posterior means for the slopes. These are estimates of the slopes for the individual respondents. This is especially convenient if we want to use the slope estimates as predic-

---

TABLE 19.1

Multilevel Analysis of Reasons for Attending Weight-Reduction Classes

Model: Only item characteristics			Model: Item characteristics + age of respondent		
Regression slopes			*Regression slopes*		
Predictor	slope (s.e.)	p	slope (s.e.)	p	
Self	3.31 (.11)	.00	3.31 (.11)	.00	
Husband	3.42 (.10)	.00	3.42 (.10)	.00	
Doctor	3.30 (.11)	.00	3.30 (.10)	.00	
Media	2.91 (.12)	.00	2.91 (.11)	.00	
Health	0.96 (.07)	.00	0.96 (.07)	.00	
Fitness	1.38 (.07)	.00	1.38 (.07)	.00	
Attract.	1.76 (.07)	.00	1.76 (.07)	.00	
Clothing	0.70 (.07)	.00	0.70 (.07)	.00	
Stigma	0.24 (.07)	.00	0.24 (.07)	.00	
Anxious	0.35 (.07)	.00	0.35 (.07)	.00	
Age*Self	—		0.03 (.01)	.00	
Age*Husband	—		0.02 (.01)	.01	
Age*Doctor	—		−.02 (.01)	.01	
Age*Media	—		−.02 (.01)	.00	
Variances	χ^2 (df = 49)	p	χ^2 (df = 48)	p	
Self	0.39	303	.00	0.31	235	.00
Husband	0.36	281	.00	0.31	249	.00
Doctor	0.40	308	.00	0.36	278	.00
Media	0.51	381	.00	0.44	320	.00
σ_e^2	0.53	—		0.52		

tors of person characteristics in a different analysis. If we want to predict the slopes on the basis of person characteristics, a better strategy would be to include these as person-level predictors in the analysis. In addition to the item characteristics, we have the person-level variable "age." Because there are four slopes that vary across persons, we can use the respondents' age to predict these four slopes. Age is entered into the analysis centered on its grand mean; the model is presented in Equation (6):

$$
\begin{aligned}
Y_{ij} = {} & \gamma_1 S_{1ij} + \gamma_2 S_{2ij} + \gamma_3 S_{3ij} + \gamma_4 S_{4ij} + \gamma_5 M_{1ij} + \gamma_6 M_{2ij} \\
& + \gamma_7 M_{3ij} + \gamma_8 M_{4ij} + \gamma_9 M_{5ij} + \gamma_{10} M_{6ij} \\
& + \gamma_{11} S_{1ij} Age_j + \gamma_{21} S_{2ij} Age_j + \gamma_{31} S_{3ij} Age_j \\
& + \gamma_{41} S_{4ij} Age_j + u_{1j} + u_{2j} + u_{3j} + u_{4j} + e_{ij}.
\end{aligned} \tag{6}
$$

The estimates are presented in Table 19.1 next to the estimates of the previous model. The effects of age are not the same on all slopes. Sensitivity to reasons coming from the respondent herself and her husband increases with age, and sensitivity to reasons coming from the doctor or the media decreases with age.

In the example given, the facets are characteristics of the questions, which is how facet design is commonly used. However, the facet approach is very general and can be extended, for instance, by expanding the person facet, denoted by [X] in Figure 19.1, to include explicit definitions of important respondent characteristics. In addition, it is also possible to extend the response range by defining facets and elements for the responses. This is useful if there are multivariate outcomes or if the response range is assessed by multiple persons such as independent raters. Analyzing facet data with multiple responses requires a multilevel model for multivariate outcomes, which is set up using a separate level for the multiple 130 outcome variables (Hox, 2002). The multilevel model used is similar to the model used for contextual measurement, a subject taken up in the next section.

MEASURING CONTEXTUAL CHARACTERISTICS

The term *multilevel* refers to a hierarchical data structure that often consists of individuals nested within some social context, for example, individuals within families or in organizational contexts such as pupils in school classes. Individual outcome variables are viewed as influenced by both individual characteristics and characteristics of the higher-level units. In this perspective, measuring characteristics of these contexts is an important activity. Some of these characteristics may be measured directly at their natural level; for example, at the school level we can directly assess school size and school religious affiliation, and at the pupil level, intelligence and school success. In addition, we may move variables from one level to another, for instance, by aggregation. Aggregation means that the variables at a lower level are moved to a higher level, as is the case when the school mean of the pupils' intelligence scores are computed.

If the research interest is in the characteristics of the context, an approach often taken is to let subjects rate various characteristics of the context. In this case we are not necessarily interested in the subjects; they are just used as informants to judge the context. Such situations may arise in educational research where pupils may rate school characteristics such as school climate, or in health research where patients may be asked to express their satisfaction with their general practitioner, or community research where samples from different neighborhoods evaluate various aspects of the neighborhood in which they live. In these cases, we may use individual characteristics to control for possible measurement bias, but the main interest is in measuring some aspect of the higher-level unit (cf. Paterson, 1998; Raudenbush & Sampson, 1999; Sampson, Raudenbush, & Earls, 1997).

A simple example can be found in data from an educational research study by Krüger (1994) that was analyzed in more detail by Hox (2002). As part of the study, small samples of pupils from 96 schools rated their school principal on six items using 7-point rating scales to determine whether the principal had a people-oriented approach toward leadership. Ratings were available from 854 pupils in 96 schools; 48 of these schools had a male and 48 a female school principal. Cronbach's alpha for these six items is 0.80, a finding that is commonly considered sufficient (Nunnally & Bernstein, 1994).

However, this reliability estimate is difficult to interpret because it is based on a mixture of school-level and pupil-level variance. Because all judgments from the same school are ratings of the same school principal, within-school variance does not provide us with information about the school principal. From the measurement point of view, we want to concentrate only on the between-schools variance.

Reliability and Multilevel Measurement

Raudenbush, Rowan, and Kang (1991) discussed the issues involved in multilevel measurement. One convenient way to model data such as these is to use a three-level model, with separate levels for the items, the pupils, and the schools. Using a model with no explanatory variables except the intercept, the variance between items is decomposed into variance components at the item, pupil, and school level. This model can be presented as

$$Y_{hij} = \gamma_{000} + u_{0hij} + u_{0ij} + u_{0j}, \quad (7)$$

where γ_{000} is the intercept term, and the subscript h refers to items, i to pupils, and j to schools. The variance components of items, pupils, and schools are 0.845, 0.341 and 0.179, respectively. The variance component σ^2_{item} can be interpreted as an estimate of the variation that is due to item inconsistency, σ^2_{pupil} as an estimate of the variation of the mean item score between different pupils within the same school, and σ^2_{school} as an estimate of the variation of the mean item score between different schools. The item level exists only to produce an estimate of the variance that is due to item inconsistency. The error variance in the mean of p items equals $\sigma^2_e = \sigma^2_{item}/p$, which for the example data equals 0.141.

The pupil-level internal consistency is given by $\alpha_{pupil} = \sigma^2_{pupil}/(\sigma^2_{pupil} + \sigma^2_{item}/p)$. For our example, data α_{pupil} is 0.71 and reflects the consistency in the item scores from different pupils in the same schools. The internal consistency coefficient of 0.71 indicates that this variability is not random error, but that it is systematic. It could be systematic error, for instance, response bias such as a halo effect in the judgments made by the pupils, or it

could be based on different experiences of pupils with the same principal. This could be explored further by adding pupil characteristics to the model. The school-level internal consistency can be calculated by (Raudenbush et al., 1991, p. 312)

$$\alpha_{school} = \sigma^2_{school} \Big/ \Big(\sigma^2_{school} + \big(\sigma^2_{pupil} + \sigma^2_{item}/p \big) \Big/ n_j \Big). \quad (8)$$

In Equation (8), p is again the number of items in the scale, and n_j is the number of pupils in school j. Because the number of pupils varies across schools, the school-level variability also varies. An indication of the average reliability can be calculated by using Equation (8) with the mean number of pupils for n_j. In our example, on average 8.9 pupils per school provided judgments, and the school-level internal consistency is $\alpha_{school} = 0.77$. The school-level internal consistency coefficient indicates that the school principal's leadership style is measured with reasonable consistency.

The school-level internal consistency depends on four factors: the number of items in the scale, the mean correlation between the items on the school level, the number of pupils sampled in the schools, and the intraclass correlation at the school level. The school-level reliability as a function of these quantities can be determined by

$$\alpha_{school} = \frac{kn_j \rho_I \bar{r}}{kn_j \rho_I \bar{r} + \big[(k-1)\bar{r} + 1 \big] (1 - \rho_I)}, \quad (9)$$

where $\bar{r}$ is the mean item intercorrelation at the school level, which can be estimated using the variances in the intercept-only model by

$\bar{r} = \sigma^2_{pupil} \Big/ \big(\sigma^2_{pupil} + \sigma^2_{item} \big)$. The relationship between Equation (8) and Equation (9), based on the Spearman–Brown formula, is explained by Raudenbush et al. (1991).

Equation (9) shows that the internal consistency reliability can be improved not only by including more items in the scale, but also by sampling a larger number of pupils in each school. Raudenbush et al. (1991) demonstrated that increasing the number of pupils making judgments per school increases the school-level reliability faster than

increasing the number of items in the scale. Even with a low interitem correlation and a low intraclass correlation, increasing the number of pupils to infinity will in the end produce a reliability equal to one, whereas increasing the number of items to infinity generally will not.

If we want to predict the evaluation scores of the school principal using school-level variables (e.g., the experience or gender of the school principal or type of school), we can simply include these variables as explanatory variables in the multilevel model. We can also estimate the school principals' evaluation scores using the school-level residuals. We can add pupil-level explanatory variables to the model, which would lead to evaluation scores that are conditional on the pupil-level variables. This can be used to correct the evaluation scores for inequalities in the composition of the pupil population across schools.

Multivariate Multilevel Measurement

Raudenbush et al. (1991) extended the measurement model by combining items from several different scales in one analysis. The constant in the multilevel model is then replaced by a set of dummy variables that indicate to which scale each item belongs. This is similar to a confirmative factor analysis, but with the restriction that the loadings of all items that belong to the same scale are equal and that there is one common error variance. These are strong restrictions, and multilevel structural equation modeling (Hox, 2002) is both more flexible and less restrictive. However, multilevel structural equation modeling does not model raw scores; it is based on simultaneous analysis of a person-level and a group-level covariance matrix. Therefore, it does not produce estimated scores on the latent variables. Consider the following example of combining individual-level and group-level information. Assume we ask pupils in 100 classes to rate their teacher using the semantic differential method (Hoyle et al., 2002). In the semantic differential method, three factors—"evaluation," "activity", and "potency"—are assumed to underlie a set of bipolar rating scales. In our example, each teacher is rated by the students on

a set of three items each for evaluation, activity, and potency. In addition, the teachers rate themselves on the same set of nine items, using the same bipolar rating scale that runs from −4 to +4. This creates a multitrait–multimethod structure where the three semantic differential factors are the traits, and the teacher and students are the measurement methods. In addition, we have multiple raters for the student ratings with generally a different number of student raters for each teacher.

The resulting data can be viewed as a multilevel structure, with nine items varying on both the pupil level and the teacher level, and nine items varying only on the teacher level. One convenient way to model data such as these is to use a multivariate multilevel model with separate levels for the items, the pupils, and the schools. At the lowest level we have 18 items, which refer to three semantic differential scales for the pupils and three for the teachers. Thus, we create 6 dummy variables, d_{pij} (d_{1ij} to d_{6ij}) to indicate the 3 scales × 2 types of raters, exclude the regression coefficient for the intercept from the model, but keep the lowest level variance term to estimate the residual variance among the 18 items. Hence, at the lowest level we have

$$Y_{hij} = \pi_{1ij}d_{1ij} + \pi_{2ij}d_{2ij} + \ldots + \pi_{6ij}d_{6ij} + e_{hij}. \quad (10)$$

At the pupil level we have

$$\pi_{pij} = \beta_{pj} + u_{pij}, \quad (11)$$

and at the class/teacher level (the third level in the multivariate model), we have

$$\beta_{pj} = \gamma_p + u_{pj}. \quad (12)$$

By substitution, we obtain the single equation version

$$
\begin{aligned}
Y_{hij} = {} & \gamma_1 d_{1ij} + \gamma_2 d_{2ij} + \ldots + \gamma_6 d_{6ij} \\
& + u_{1ij}d_{1ij} + u_{2ij}d_{2ij} + \ldots + u_{6ij}d_{6ij} \\
& + u_{1j}d_{1ij} + u_{2j}d_{2ij} + \ldots + u_{6j}d_{6ij} + e_{hij}.
\end{aligned}
\quad (13)
$$

The model described by Equation (13) provides us with estimates of the six scale means and of their variances and covariances at the pupil and class level. Because we are mostly interested in the variances and covariances in this application, RML estimation is preferred to FML estimation. Table 19.2 presents the RML estimates of the covariances and the corresponding correlations at the pupil level and at the school level.

Table 19.2 shows that most of the variance is between classes. The variances and covariances at the class level are important for inspecting the convergent and discriminant validity of the measures. In fact, at the class level we have a multitrait–multimethod matrix that consists of three traits and two methods. The pairwise correlations between the three methods measured both through pupils and teachers is the validity diagonal. The correlations of

0.64–0.66 indicate a substantial convergent validity for these measures.

GENERALIZABILITY THEORY

The central issue in Generalizability (G) theory (Cronbach, Gleser, Nanda, & Rajaratnam, 1972) is the generalization from a sample of measurements to a universe of possible measurements. This universe is defined in terms of measurement conditions from which the observed measurements are a random sample. The question to be answered is how well measures taken in one condition can be generalized to other conditions. In other words, how well the observed scores correspond to the average scores acquired under all possible conditions. In the classical true score model, observed scores consist of two components, a systematic component called the true score and a random error component. The reliability is then defined as the correlation between the observed and the true scores and all possible observed scores on this particular test. In generalizability theory, the variance of the measurements is divided into several different variance components. The generalizability coefficient based on this partition is defined analogous to the reliability coefficient: the true variance divided by the expected observed-score variance (Shavelson & Webb, 1991). The variance partition in generalizability theory requires a clear description of all relevant measurement conditions. These conditions are called *facets* (the terminology is similar to facet theory, where the facets refer mostly to question formats, whereas in generalizability theory they refer mostly to measurement conditions). In the simplest case, there is only one facet. For instance, when students take a test consisting of 20 multiple-choice items at the end of a course, the examiner is not interested in the answers on these particular 20 items, but in the students' knowledge of the whole course content. From this perspective, the 20 items are a sample of all possible items. The *items* are the facet of the measurement. When all students answer the same 20 items, the design is *crossed*. This means that all students have the same conditions (items). When all students answer different

---

TABLE 19.2

Covariances and Correlations of the Semantic Differential Scales at the Pupil and Class Level (Simulated Data)[a]

Covariances and correlations at the pupil level

	1	2	3	4	5	6
1 Eval. pup.	.377	*.02*	*.04*	—	—	—
2 Act. pup.	.007	.372	*-.02*	—	—	—
3 Pot. pup.	−.013	−.006	.372	—	—	—
4 Eval tch.	—	—	—	—	—	—
5 Act. tch.	—	—	—	—	—	—
6 Pot. tch.	—	—	—	—	—	—

Covariances and correlations at the class level

	1	2	3	4	5	6
1 Eval. pup.	.269	*.29*	*.01*	*.66*	*.14*	*-.04*
2 Act. pup.	.069	.211	*.23*	*.22*	*.64*	*.06*
3 Pot. pup.	.004	.061	.339	*-.01*	*.20*	*.64*
4 Eval tch.	.441	.128	−.007	1.671	*.16*	*.10*
5 Act. tch.	.090	.378	.145	.269	1.633	*.10*
6 Pot. tch.	−.020	.028	.401	.134	.136	1.167

Note. In both the upper and lower halves of the table, the entries in boldface italics in the upper diagonals are the correlations. eval. = evaluation; pup. = pupil; act. = activity; pot. = potential; tch. = teacher.
[a]Item level variance is 0.921.

items, the design is *nested*. Then, all students have different conditions.

Assume that the 20 items of the foregoing example are not multiple-choice items, but behavioral observations. When these observations are coded by trained judges, the design becomes a two-facet design. The observations are the first facet and the judges the second facet. In this case we must generalize over both observations and judges to obtain an estimate of the true score we are interested in.

One-Facet Crossed Design

To illustrate a one-facet crossed design, we created an example that assesses eight persons' responses on four multiple-choice items, and the data are in Table 19.3.

The person scores on the items are decomposed into four parts:

$$X_{pi} = \mu + (\mu_p - \mu) + (\mu_i - \mu) + (X_{pi} - \mu_p - \mu_i + \mu), \tag{14}$$

where X_{pi} is the score of person p on item i; μ is the grand mean, the expectation over persons and items; $(\mu_p - \mu)$ is the person effect, the expectation of the persons' score over items; $(\mu_i - \mu)$ is the item effect, the expectation of the item difficulty over persons; and $(X_{pi} - \mu_p - \mu_i + \mu)$ is the residual, which includes both the interaction effect between items and persons and all error components. These two effects cannot be distinguished because we have only one observation for each person–item combination.

Each effect in Equation (14), except the grand mean, has a distribution with a mean of zero and a nonzero variance (Shavelson & Webb, 1991). Standard ANOVA estimates the mean squares as MS_{person} = 0.268, MS_{item} = 0.375, and $MS_{residual}$ = 0.232. The variance components are calculated from these mean squares (Shavelson & Webb, 1991):

$$\hat{\sigma}^2_{residual} = MS_{residual} \tag{15}$$

$$\hat{\sigma}^2_i = (MS_{item} - \hat{\sigma}^2_{residual}) / n_p \tag{16}$$

$$\hat{\sigma}^2_p = (MS_{person} - \hat{\sigma}^2_{residual}) / n_i \tag{17}$$

TABLE 19.3

Item Score Results of Eight People on Four Items

Person	Item			
	1	2	3	4
1	0	0	1	1
2	0	1	0	1
3	0	0	1	0
4	1	0	0	1
5	0	1	1	1
6	0	0	1	0
7	1	0	1	1
8	1	1	0	0

The variance components are $\hat{\sigma}^2_p = 0.009$, $\hat{\sigma}^2_i = 0.018$, and $\hat{\sigma}^2_{residual} = 0.232$, which account for 3%, 7%, and 90% of the variance, respectively.

The variance components themselves are unstandardized; therefore, the interpretation uses the percentages. Three percent of the variance is associated with persons, 7% with items, and the remainder with the interaction and error.

The generalizability coefficient (G coefficient) for the preceding example depends on the decisions one wants to make (Shavelson & Webb, 1991). For relative decisions, only the variance component of the interaction between persons and items contributes to the measurement error. When the variance component is large, this means that the relative position of persons is different for the different items. Because all persons answer the same items, the item variance doesn't influence the relative position. In contrast, for absolute decisions, both the item variance and the variance of the interaction are important. In our example, the formulas for the estimated error variances are

$$\hat{\sigma}^2_{Abs} = \frac{\sigma^2_i}{n_i} + \frac{\sigma^2_{residual}}{n_i} \tag{18}$$

$$\hat{\sigma}^2_{Rel} = \frac{\sigma^2_{residual}}{n_i}, \tag{19}$$

where n_i is the number of items. Calculating the error variances yield 0.06 for both the relative vari-

ance and the absolute variance (the estimates are equal due to rounding). The formula for the G coefficient for relative decisions is

$$G-coefficient = \frac{\sigma_p^2}{(\sigma_p^2 + \sigma_{Rel}^2)}. \qquad (20)$$

The calculated G coefficient is 0.134. The interpretation of this coefficient is analogous to the interpretation of the reliability coefficient in classical test theory. Because of the simple data set used, we refrain from further interpretation.

The reliability-like index of dependability for absolute decisions is formulated as

$$dependability = \frac{\sigma_p^2}{(\sigma_p^2 + \sigma_{Abs}^2)}. \qquad (21)$$

For this example the calculated index is 0.125. The interpretation of this coefficient is not exactly the same as the interpretation of the G coefficient, but broadly speaking it has the same function. In both cases, the generalizability coefficient indicates to what extent the measurements converge across specific method facets, including possible interaction effects. The decision across which method effects we need to generalize (which leads to different generalizability coefficients) remains, of course, with the researcher.

One-Facet Nested Design

To describe the one-facet nested design, we created sample data for the responses of eight people to 16 multiple-choice items. These data are shown in Table 19.4.

The person scores on the items are decomposed into three parts:

$$X_{pi} = \mu + (\mu_p - \mu) + (X_{pi} - \mu_p), \qquad (22)$$

where X_{pi} is the score of person p on item i; μ is the grand mean; $(\mu_p - \mu)$ is the person effect; and $(X_{pi} - \mu_p)$ is the residual. There is no separate term for the item effect. Because all students have answered different items, the item effect cannot be estimated, and the item effect becomes part of the residual.

Each effect in Equation (22), except the grand mean, has a distribution with a mean of zero and a variance. The ANOVA estimates (people are random, items not) are $MS_{person} = 0.348$ and $MS_{residual} = 0.188$, and the calculated variance components (see Equations [15] and [17]) are $\hat{\sigma}_p^2 = 0.080$ and $\hat{\sigma}_{residual}^2 = 0.188$. Thus, 30% of the variance is associated with the people, the remainder with the items, the interaction, and error.

Two-Facet Designs

An example of a two-facet design is a design in which students complete assignments that are

---

	TABLE 19.4

Item Score Results of Eight People on 16 Multiple-Choice Items

								Item								
Person	1	2	3	4	5	6	7	8	9	10	11	12	13	14	15	16
1	0	0														
2			0	1												
3					1	0			.							
4							0	0								
5									1	1						
6											1	1				
7													0	0		
8															1	0

each graded by a different judge. When all students complete all assignments, and each judge evaluates one of the assignments, we have a two-facet crossed design. If we want to assign a single grade to the students, this constitutes a design with one trait and multiple methods (i.e. the cross-classification of assignments and judges). In this design, the person scores are decomposed into seven parts: the grand mean, the effects from students, assignments, and judges, and all the two-way interaction terms. The three-way interaction and the error components cannot be distinguished. When all students complete different assignments evaluated by different judges, we have a two-facet nested design. In practice, many designs are partly nested. For instance, all students complete the same assignments evaluated by different judges, or each student completes his/her assignments, which are then evaluated by all judges, but the subset of assignments completed is different for each combination of students and judges. For an elaborated description, we refer to Shavelson and Webb (1991).

Multilevel Models for Generalizability Analysis

Generalizability theory can be viewed as a special case of multilevel analysis. In the one-facet nested design, the nesting structure is clear: The items are nested in the persons. In the one-facet crossed design, the nesting structure is arbitrary: Items can be seen as nested in persons or persons nested in items. Both specifications lead to the same results. Because of the analogy with the nested design, we will use the specification structure of items in persons. In a two-facet design, the structure is more complicated because of the large number of interaction effects. Although it can be specified as a cross-classified multilevel model (Goldstein, 1995), current software cannot analyze data of a realistic size and complexity.

The specification of a one-facet nested design is straightforward. An intercept-only model is specified with two levels. At the lowest level we obtain a direct estimate of the residual variance and at the second level, a direct estimate of the person-level variance. These estimates are exactly the same as the variance components estimated before.

The one-facet crossed design, where all people respond to all items, is specified as a three-level intercept-only model. Although the analysis is set up using three separate levels, it should be clear that conceptually we have two levels, items nested in persons. The lowest level is added to estimate the residual variance; the item and person levels are "dummy" levels with only one unit that covers the entire data set (cf. Hox, 2002). At the lowest level the items are represented by a full set of dummy variables. The fixed coefficients of these dummies are excluded from the model, but their slopes are allowed to vary at the second (item) "dummy" level. The covariances between these dummy variables are all constrained to zero, and their variances are all constrained to be equal. Thus, we estimate one variance component for the items. The specification of the third (the person) level is similar. At the lowest level we obtain a direct estimate of the residual variance, at the second level the item variance is estimated, and at the third level the person variance. The estimates are exactly the same as the variance components estimated with ANOVA. Because the software specification for the multilevel approach requires as many dummy variables as there are subjects in the data set, it is clear that data of a realistic size and complexity pose severe difficulties.

A special case of crossed facet designs is the situation in which people only partially respond to the same items (see Table 19.5, as a special case of Table 19.4). Analyzing these data as a crossed design with the ANOVA approach is not feasible because of the empty cells in the observed data set. Multilevel analysis of these data is straightforward. Following the same procedure as described for the one-facet crossed design, estimates for the variance components for the items, persons, and residual are obtained.

The variance components are estimated as $\hat{\sigma}_p^2 = 0.006$, $\hat{\sigma}_i^2 = 0.019$, and $\hat{\sigma}_{residual}^2 = 0.239$. Two percent of the variance is associated with persons, 7% with items, and the remainder with the interaction and error.

TABLE 19.5

Item Scores of Eight Respondents on Four Multiple-Choice Items With Incomplete Data

		Item		
Person	**1**	**2**	**3**	**4**
1		0	0	1
2	0	1	0	
3		0	0	1
4	1	0	0	
5		1	1	1
6		0	1	0
7		0	1	1
8		1	0	0

CONCLUSIONS

Multilevel models can be especially useful when measures are constructed according to a logic that confers specific characteristics to the measures. We discuss facet design as an example, but other systematic question construction approaches result in similar data. If the measures can be assigned values on specific variables, multilevel models can be used to analyze the effect of both person and question characteristics on the responses. For those question characteristics whose effects vary across persons, residuals or posterior means can be assigned to people as scores on these characteristics. A second area where multilevel models are useful for measurement is when contextual characteristics must be assessed. We discuss the example of pupils rating the school principal. Various multilevel models can be used to assess the reliability and validity of such ratings at specific levels of the hierarchy. Multilevel modeling is useful in generalizability theory only if the design results in mostly nested data sets; data sets with a large number of crossed facets lead to large cross-classified data sets that current multilevel software does not handle well.

The measurement procedures outlined earlier are based on classical test theory, which means that they assume continuous multivariate normal outcomes. Most test items are categorical. If the items are dichotomous, we can use logistic multilevel modeling. If there are two levels, the item level and the person level, multilevel logistic regression is equivalent to a Rasch model (Andrich, 1988; Kamata, 2001; Rost & Walter, chap. 18, this volume).

A nice feature of using multilevel models for measurement scales is that it automatically accommodates incomplete data. If some of the item scores for some of the pupils are missing, this is compensated for in the model. The model results and estimated residuals or posterior means are the correct ones under the assumption that the data are missing at random (MAR). This is a weaker assumption than the missing completely at random (MCAR) assumption required by simpler methods, such as using only complete cases or replacing missing items by the mean of the observed items. The MAR assumption requires that the missing data are missing completely at random, conditional on the available observed data. Because items typically correlate strongly, the assumption that, conditional on the available item scores, any missed items are missing completely at random is reasonable. An interesting application is to assign different subsets of items to different subsets of persons by design. In this case, the missing data can be defined as MCAR, and multilevel analysis provides a straightforward method to estimate the individuals' scores as the person-level residuals or posterior means for the intercept. The typical estimates in multilevel modeling are empirical Bayes estimates, shrunken toward the overall mean, which are equivalent to the true score in classical test theory (cf. Lord & Novick, 1968; Nunnally & Bernstein, 1994).

CHAPTER 20

STRUCTURAL EQUATION MODELS FOR MULTITRAIT–MULTIMETHOD DATA

Michael Eid, Tanja Lischetzke, and Fridtjof W. Nussbeck

Models of confirmatory factor analysis (CFA) or structural equation modeling (SEM) have generally become the most often applied methodological approaches besides Campbell and Fiske's traditional approach of inspecting correlation matrices (e.g., Eid, 2000; Eid, Lischetzke, Nussbeck, & Trierweiler, 2003; Kenny, 1976, 1979; Marsh, 1989; Marsh & Grayson, 1995; Saris & van Meurs, 1991; Widaman, 1985). This is mainly due to the fact that SEM is an approach that tries to explain the correlations and covariances of variables by a set of underlying latent variables (factors). Hence, the multitrait–multimethod (MTMM) matrix proposed by Campbell and Fiske (1959) can be taken as input for more complex analyses by SEM. In contrast to Campbell and Fiske's approach, SEM has several advantages. First, SEM makes it possible to separate unsystematic measurement error from systematic individual differences that are due to trait and method effects. Second, measurement models for trait as well as method factors can be defined. This makes it possible to relate the latent trait and method variables to other latent variables. This is particularly important if one wants to explain trait and method effects by other variables. Third, SEM allows an empirical testing of the assumptions on which a model is based. Consequently, many hypotheses about the structure of trait and method effects can be tested.

The aim of this chapter is to illustrate these advantages by presenting several MTMM models that have been defined in the framework of SEM. In the first part of the chapter, we will discuss models that have been developed to analyze an MTMM matrix with the typical structure described by Campbell and Fiske (1959) and Schmitt (chap. 2, this volume). An important characteristic of this first type of MTMM models is that there is only one indicator for each trait–method unit. The major limitation of these single-indicator MTMM models is that unsystematic measurement error and systematic method-specific influences can be separated only if strong assumptions are fulfilled. The second part of the chapter shows how this limitation can be circumvented by selecting several indicators for each trait–method unit (multiple-indicator models).

Over the last years, many structural equation models for MTMM data have been proposed. Widaman (1985), for example, developed a taxonomy of 16 models of CFA for analyzing MTMM data with t traits and m methods by crossing four different types of trait structures (no trait factor, general trait factor, t orthogonal trait factors, t oblique trait factors) with four different types of method structures (no method factor, general method factor, m orthogonal method factors, m oblique method factors). In addition to the models covered by Widaman, several other CFA-based approaches have been developed (Eid, 2000; Eid et al., 2003; Kenny & Kashy, 1992; Marsh, 1993b; Marsh & Hocevar, 1988). Moreover, models for analyzing MTMM data have been defined in the frameworks of other methodological traditions such as variance component models (e.g., Millsap, 1995b; Wothke, 1995, 1996) or multiplicative correlation models (Browne, 1984; Dudgeon, 1994;

Wothke & Browne, 1990), which imply special CFA models (Dumenci, 2000). In this chapter we will not present all MTMM models that have been developed in the CFA framework. We will concentrate on those models that are most often applied and discuss their strengths and weaknesses. Moreover, we assume that all variables are centered (deviations from the mean), which means that we focus on covariance structures and do not deal with mean structures.

SINGLE-INDICATOR MODELS

The starting point of single-indicator models is the classical MTMM matrix. However, because models of SEM are covariance structure models and the covariance matrix is more informative, SEM of MTMM data is based on the MTMM covariance matrix, not on the correlation matrix (for problems analyzing correlation matrices with SEM, see Cudeck, 1989). In single-indicator models there is one indicator (observed variable) Y_{jk} for each combination of a trait j and a method k. These observed variables are decomposed in different ways. We will describe five models that are built on different assumptions: (a) the correlated trait model, (b) the correlated trait/correlated uniqueness model, (c) the correlated trait/uncorrelated method model, (d) the correlated trait/correlated method model, and the (e) correlated trait/correlated method (M-1) model.

The Correlated Trait Model

The correlated trait (CT) model is the simplest model. It assumes that each observed variable Y_{jk} can be decomposed into a common trait variable T_j and a residual E_{jk}. This model is depicted in Figure 20.1a for three trait variables (fear, anger, and sadness) measured each by three methods (self, friend, and acquaintance). The latent trait variable is the common factor of all observed variables that are appropriate for measuring the trait. The correlations between the different trait variables indicate discriminant validity. The variance of an observed variable that is explained by the trait variable indicates convergent validity or consistency, which is the degree of variance that is due to the common

trait variable. The variance of the residual is the unexplained variance that is due to measurement error or method-specific influences. The consistency coefficient equals the reliability coefficient of classical test theory if there are no systematic method effects and only measurement error influences. If the residual variable also covers method effects, these method effects do not generalize across traits because the residual variables are assumed to be uncorrelated between traits. This assumption will be violated and the model will not be appropriate if there are systematic method effects, which is the case, for example, when the friend of one target person consistently overestimates the target's fear, anger, and sadness, whereas the friend of another target person consistently underestimates his or her standing on these traits. In this case one would expect a correlation of the residuals belonging to the method *friend report*. If method effects and error influences are present and the CT model fits the data, the consistency coefficient will be a lower bound for the reliability coefficient, and the unreliability coefficient (the degree of variance that is explained by the residuals) will be the upper bound for method-specific effects. However, it is important to note that even if the model fits the data perfectly, it cannot be determined whether there are method-specific effects in addition to measurement error because the two sources of variance are confounded. The CT model is a rather restrictive model for multimethod research because it assumes that method effects do not generalize across traits. Because correlated method effects can be expected in most applications in psychology, this model is usually too restrictive. The model might be appropriate, however, if only one trait is considered and the different methods are randomly chosen raters from a group of possible raters. For example, when conducting an evaluation of teachers based on the ratings of three students randomly selected from one class of each teacher, the CT model with one trait can be applied. In this case, a one-factor model explains the consistency in the students' ratings. With only one trait, systematic method effects across traits are not of interest.

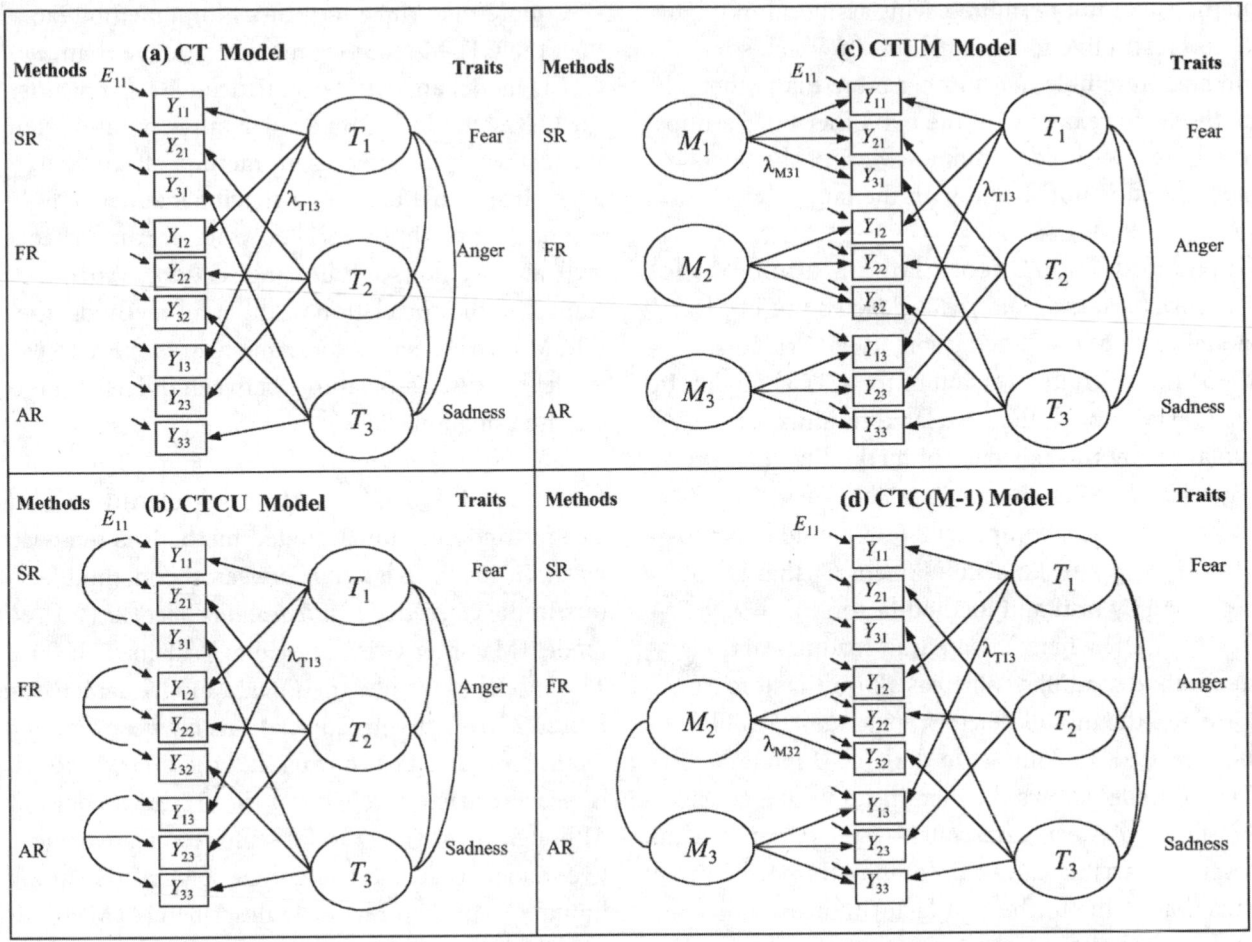

FIGURE 20.1. Single-indicator MTMM models. (a) CT model: correlated trait model; (b) CTCU model: correlated trait/correlated uniqueness model; (c) CTUM model: correlated trait/uncorrelated method model; and (d) CTC(M-1) model: correlated trait/correlated method model with one method factor less than methods considered. Y_{jk}: observed variable, j: trait, k: method; T_j: trait factor, M_k: method factor; E_{jk}: error variable; λ_{Mjk}, λ_{Tjk}: factor loadings. Factor loadings are only depicted for one path for each kind of factor, but they are estimated for all variables. SR = self-report; FR = friend report; AR = acquaintance report.

The Correlated Trait/Correlated Uniqueness Model

The *correlated trait/correlated uniqueness* (CTCU) model is an extension of the correlated trait model that allows generalization of methods effects across traits by correlated residual variables (Kenny, 1979; Marsh, 1989; Marsh & Grayson, 1995). The residual variables (uniqueness) are correlated in a method-specific manner (see Figure 20.1b). Whereas the basic decomposition is the same as in the CT model ($Y_{jk} = \lambda_{Tjk} T_j + E_{jk}$), all residuals E_{jk} with the same method index k can be correlated in the CTCU model. The CTCU model is a reasonable model for MTMM data and widely applied (e.g.,

Marsh, 1989; Marsh & Grayson, 1995). However, it is restricted in three ways (Bagozzi, 1993; Eid, 2000; Lance, Noble, & Scullen, 2002). First, as in the CT model, measurement error is confounded with method specificity because the residuals comprise both aspects. Hence, it is not possible to separate unreliability from method specificity. Consequently, the consistency coefficient is a lower bound of reliability, and the variance explained by the residuals is the upper bound of the method specificity. Second, "true" (error-free) method effects cannot be related to other external variables because pure method effects are not represented in the model. Third, correlations between different

methods are not permitted. This assumption might be too restrictive for applications in which some methods resemble one another more than other methods, for example, if the two other-rater groups in Figure 20.1 hold a common view of the target person that is not shared with the target's view.

Correlated Trait/Uncorrelated Method Model

The *correlated trait/uncorrelated method* (CTUM) model (e.g., Marsh & Grayson, 1995; Widaman, 1985) is a restricted version of the CTCU model. In the CTUM model, the correlated residuals are explained by the existence of method factors (see Figure 20.1c). An observed variable Y_{jk} is decomposed into a trait component T_j, a method component M_k, and a residual component E_{jk} that is not explained by trait and method factors: $Y_{jk} = \lambda_{Tjk} T_j + \lambda_{Mjk} M_k + E_{jk}$, where λ_{Tjk} are trait loadings and λ_{Mjk} are method loadings. Whereas all trait factors can correlate, the method factors are assumed to be uncorrelated. In contrast to the CTCU model, the CTUM model allows the identification of a consistent method effect. Consequently, the variance of an observed variable can be decomposed into the variance that is due to the trait factor (consistency or convergent validity), the variance that is due to the method factor (method specificity), and the variance that is due to the residual (influences due to measurement error and method-specific effects that are specific for a trait). Hence, this model is in a better position to separate true method-specific effects from measurement error. However, the residual might not only comprise measurement error but also trait-specific method effects. We will come back to this issue when we present multiple-indicator models. Because method factors are specified in the CTUM model, method-specific effects can be related to other criterion variables to explain method effects. Hence, the CTUM model solves the first two restrictions of the CTCU model by introducing method factors, however, not without costs. The CTUM model is a restrictive variant of the CTCU model because the introduction of method factors puts restrictions on the covariances of the residuals in the CTCU model—they have to follow the assumptions of a congeneric factor model. This means that in the case of more than three traits

(i.e., more than three indicators for a method factor), the CTUM model is more restrictive than the CTCU model and can be statistically tested against the CTCU model. From a substantive point of view, the method factors represent method effects that generalize across traits in a specific manner. This assumption might be violated when method effects are trait-specific (see following section). With respect to the correlation of different methods, the CTUM is restricted in the same way as the CTCU model because associations between different methods are not allowed.

Correlated Trait/Correlated Method Model

The restriction of uncorrelated methods is removed by admitting correlations between the method factors in the *correlated trait/correlated method* (CTCM) model (Marsh & Grayson, 1995; Widaman, 1985). This model looks like the CTUM model depicted in Figure 20.1c but with correlations between all method factors. That means that the CTUM model is also a restrictive version of the CTCM model. Although the CTCM model seems to be an attractive model because it overcomes some of the strong limitations of the previously described MTMM models, it is also afflicted by several problems that question its applicability. One of its major problems is that it is not globally identified (Grayson & Marsh, 1994). This means that there are data structures for which the parameters of the model cannot be estimated. These data structures, however, are not unusual, and they are often even desired. For example, in the case of perfectly homogeneous indicators (that all have the same loading parameters on the trait and method factors), the model is not identified and, therefore, not applicable. Hence, in addition to not being globally identifiable, another serious problem of the model is that it is not globally applicable. Moreover, applications of this model often reveal improper estimations such as negative variances. Beyond these more technical problems, there are also more substantive interpretation problems that exist when all of the method factors are correlated. In this case, the method factor correlations indicate a portion of the shared variance of all variables that might not be indicative of method-specific influences but are more likely to be indica-

tive of a general trait influence or associations between the traits (Marsh, 1989). Hence, it is unclear whether the correlations between the trait factors are valid estimators of discriminant validity because the different indicators are also related via the correlated method factors. Furthermore, the condition under which it is reasonable to assume that the trait and the method factors are uncorrelated is unclear because there is also a variant of the model that has correlated trait and method factors (Schmitt & Stults, 1986). The assumption of the uncorrelatedness of the trait and method factors is adhered to mainly to avoid technical problems and to make the decomposition of variances possible. Note that the question of whether trait and method factors should be uncorrelated or not is also relevant for the CTUM model.

Finally, the CTCM model, like the CTCU model, assumes that the method effect is due to one method that generalizes homogeneously across the different traits because the covariances of the indicators belonging to the same method are explained by one method factor. Consequently, the application of the CTCM model is restricted in strong ways.

Correlated Trait/Correlated Method (M-1) Model

As an alternative to the CTCM model, Eid (2000) proposed an MTMM model that is not affected by the identification problems of the CTCM model. Eid's model is a special variant of the CTCM model but differs from it in the number of method factors. It contains one method factor less than methods included and is, therefore, called the correlated trait/correlated method minus one [CTC(M-1)] model. The basic idea of the CTC(M-1) model is that one method has to be chosen as the comparison standard. All other methods are contrasted with this comparison standard. In this model (see Figure 20.1d), a latent trait factor is the true-score variable of the indicator that is measured by the comparison standard. A method factor is common to all variables measured by the same method. The method factor represents that part of the variance of an indicator that cannot be predicted by the trait factor (the standard method) and that is not due to random measurement error but to systematic method-specific influences. These method-specific influences are common to all indicators measured by the same method. Hence, a method factor comprises the systematic components a method does not share with the standard method. The model is defined by two basic equations, the equation for the standard method (denoted by $k = 1$): $Y_{j1} = \lambda_{Tj1} T_j + E_{j1}$, and the equation for all other methods ($k \neq 1$): $Y_{jk} = \lambda_{Tjk} T_j + \lambda_{Mjk} M_k + E_{jk}$.

According to this model, the identification and interpretation problems of the CTCM model might be due to an overfactorization. The CTC(M-1) model has several advantages. One property of the model is that the trait and method factors cannot be correlated with one another (see Eid, 2000, for a proof). Therefore, the decomposition of variance into trait-specific, method-specific, and error components can be achieved as in the CTUM and CTCM models. In contrast to the CTCM model, the correlations between the method factors cannot be confounded with a general trait effect because the indicators of the standard method are not related to a method factor. Compared with the CTCU and CTUM models, the CTC(M-1) model is less restricted because method factors can be correlated. The CTC(M-1) model, however, also has its limitations. An initial limitation is that one method has to be chosen as the comparison standard. Moreover, the model is not symmetrical, which means that the fit to the same data set can differ when different methods are chosen as the comparison standard. However, in the case of structurally different methods, this might not pose a problem because one method often stands out from the others. When self-ratings are compared with different informant ratings (see Neyer, chap. 4, this volume), for example, the self-ratings might be an interesting standard method because all method factors would indicate deviations from the scores expected by the self-report.

COMPARISON OF THE DIFFERENT MODELS

The models described so far have different advantages and limitations. Therefore, some guidelines for an appropriate choice of the models are necessary. One major difference between the models is whether they allow correlated methods or not.

Thus, one decision that has to be made is whether it is necessary to allow correlated methods or not. A second difference between the models is whether the researcher wants to define a trait as a common factor from which all methods deviate or whether he or she wants to contrast and compare methods.

One criterion for deciding whether method factors or residuals will be correlated or not is the type of methods considered (Eid, chap. 16, this volume): If methods are interchangeable, it is not likely that there will be correlated method factors or correlated residuals in the models considered. An example of interchangeable methods is the assessment of teacher behavior by randomly selected students. If, for example, three traits of a teacher are measured by three students that are randomly selected for each teacher (i.e., each teacher has different raters), there will be three methods (students). To apply the models, the students must be assigned to one of three groups (method groups). However, it does not make any difference whether a student belongs to Method 1, Method 2, or Method 3. The assignment of students to method groups is totally interchangeable. In this case, it is not reasonable to expect that method factors or residuals of different methods are correlated in the model because of the total interchangeability of the methods (students). Moreover, one would be interested in a trait measure that reflects a kind of common view of the teacher by his/her students. Because all students have more or less the same access to the teacher's behavior, the average of the ratings or the common factor score might be a good representation of the teacher's behavior. In this case, the CTCU or the CTUM model would be the most appropriate model because the trait factors are defined as common factors, and the models assume that the residuals and method factors are uncorrelated between the three rater groups.

The situation changes when the methods are not interchangeable but differ structurally. Consider, for example, the situation where the well-being of a teenager is assessed by the teenager him- or herself, his or her mother, and his or her father. In this case, the raters are not interchangeable. Moreover, one might assume that the parents have a common view of their child that is not shared with the child. The convergence between the parents' rating might

be higher than the convergence between the mother and the child and the father and the child, that is, the two methods *father* and *mother* might be more highly correlated. Hence, a model that can capture this stronger method correlation might be most appropriate, which leads us to the CTCM and CTC(M-1) model as the models of choice.

In a second step, one has to decide whether the idea of a trait as a common factor from which all methods deviate is meaningful or whether one assumes that it is preferable to contrast the methods. If one is interested in measuring a common factor, one should apply the CTCM model. However, in the case of structurally different methods, the trait loadings could be quite different, which makes it difficult to interpret the common factor. In the case of more than three structurally different methods, it is likely that the assumption of one common factor—which puts constraints on the covariances of the different indicators—might be violated and that the model might have to be rejected. If one would like to contrast the methods, the CTC(M-1) model should be chosen. In this case, the teenager report could serve as the comparison standard, so the trait factors would represent the latent teenager ratings. The method factor *mother* would represent the deviations of the mother rating from the rating that would have been expected on basis of the self-rating. The method factor values represent over- and underestimations made by the mother. The method factor *father* has an analogous meaning. A positive correlation of the method factors, for example, would indicate the degree to which mother and father over- vs. underestimate their children in the same direction. To explain parental over- and underestimation, the method factors can be related to other variables.

Applications

We will illustrate the five models by applying them to data from an MTMM study exploring the relations between self- and peer-rated frequency of negative emotions. The traits were *fear*, *anger*, and *sadness*. The three methods were *self-ratings*, *ratings by a good friend*, and *ratings by an acquaintance*. The sample consisted of 172 triples of self- and peer raters. This sample was a subgroup of individuals

from a larger MTMM study (see Eid et al., 2003; Trierweiler, Eid, & Lischetzke, 2002). While seated separately, all participants rated the frequency with which the target individual usually experienced different negative emotions using a four-category scale (from *not at all* to *very often*). Three scales, consisting of four emotion terms each, assessed fear, anger, and sadness. For the MTMM analyses, the scales were divided into two test halves comprising two items each. The applications of the single-indicator models were based on the first test halves for instructive reasons only. Both test halves will be analyzed conjointly in the next section. The covariance and correlation matrix is given in Table 20.1. The CT model had to be rejected (χ^2 = 94.56, *df* = 24, *p* < .01, CFI = .67, RMSEA = .13), demonstrating that there are systematic method-specific influences. The CTCU model and the CTUM model fitted the data equally well (χ^2 = 19.94, *df* = 15, *p* = .17, CFI = .98, RMSEA = .04) because they are data equivalent in the case of three traits (i.e., three loadings on each factor). However, in the CTUM model, one residual variance had a negative value. The estimation of the CTCM model did not converge. The CTC(M-1) model fitted the data well (χ^2 = 24.57, *df* = 17, *p* = .10, CFI = .96, RMSEA = .05). For the CTUM model and the CTC(M-1) model, the estimated loading parameters and variances of the factors are given in Figure 20.2. The CTCU model is

not depicted in this figure because the trait part of the CTUM model is identical to the trait part of the CTCU model in this application. The error variances and correlations (CTCU model) as well as the reliability, consistency, and method specificity coefficients are given in Table 20.2. The reliability coefficient is computed as the degree of variance of an observed variable that is explained by the factors of the model. The consistency coefficient is the degree of true variance of an observed variable that is explained by the respective trait factor; the method specificity coefficient indicates the degree of true variance of an observed variable that is due to the respective method factor. Consistency and specificity coefficients together add up to 1.

The trait parameters of the CTCU and the CTUM models (see Figure 20.2) showed that the three methods differed in their trait loadings. For the first trait the friend rating had the highest loading, for the second trait the self-rating had the highest loading, and for the third trait the acquaintance rating showed the highest loading. According to this result, the trait influences were not consistent across the different traits, and sometimes one method was "better" in terms of "explained variance by the common trait" than other methods. Moreover, the correlations of the residuals in the CTCU model (see Table 20.2) were rather different for one rater, indicating that method influences did

TABLE 20.1

Covariances, Variances, and Correlations of the Observed Variables for the Applications of the Single-Indicator MTMM Models

	SR-fear	SR-anger	SR-sadness	FR-fear	FR-anger	FR-sadness	AR-fear	AR-anger	AR-sadness
SR-fear	.35	.11	.12	.07	.04	.06	.05	.02	.08
SR-anger	*.31*	.36	.02	.03	.09	.03	.02	.08	.00
SR-sadness	*.33*	*.07*	.35	.05	.01	.08	−.01	.00	.05
FR-fear	**.22**	.09	.15	.29	.08	.14	.10	.02	.07
FR-anger	.12	**.24**	.04	*.25*	.35	.13	.06	.07	.02
FR-sadness	.19	.09	**.25**	*.47*	*.37*	.33	.05	.04	.08
AR-fear	**.16**	.06	−.04	**.35**	.18	.15	.29	.09	.11
AR-anger	.05	**.22**	−.01	.07	**.21**	.11	*.28*	.33	.08
AR-sadness	.26	.00	**.15**	.25	.07	**.26**	*.40*	*.27*	.27

Note. SR = self-report; FR = friend report; AR = acquaintance report. Covariances are depicted in the upper (right) triangular, variances appear in the main diagonal, and correlations are presented in the lower (left) triangular. Monotrait–heteromethod correlations appear in boldface type. Heterotrait–monomethod correlations are printed in italics.

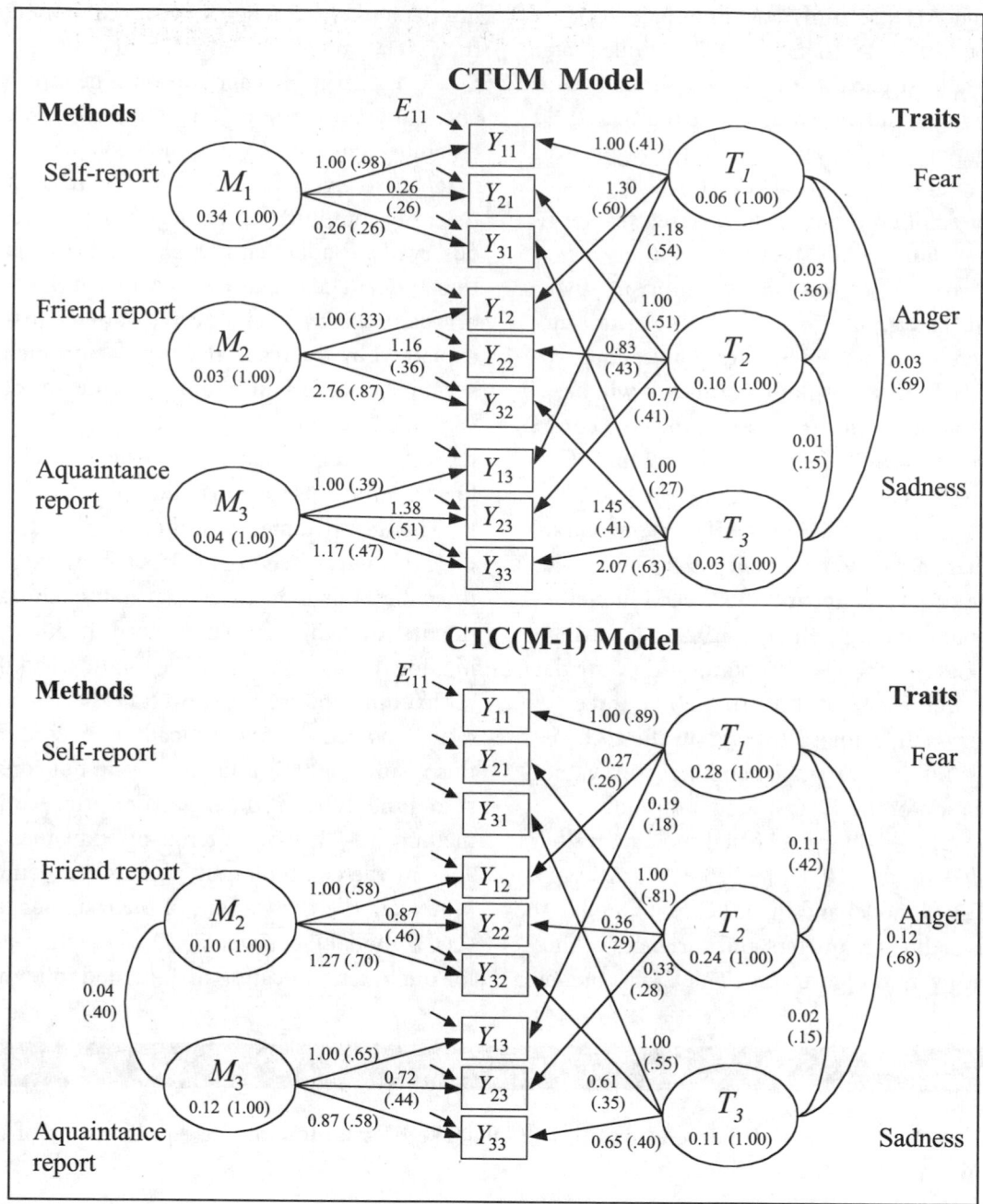

FIGURE 20.2. Parameter estimates for the single-indicator CTUM model and the CTC(M-1) model. CTUM model: correlated trait/uncorrelated method model; CTC(M-1) model: correlated trait/correlated method model with one method factor less than methods considered. Y_{jk}: observed variable, j: trait, k: method; T_j: trait factor; M_k: method factor; E_{jk}: error variable. Unstandardized parameter estimates and standardized parameter estimates (in parentheses) are depicted. Error variances and reliabilities can be found in Table 20.2.

not generalize strongly across traits. This was also revealed by the large differences between the loadings belonging to the same method factor in the CTUM model (standardized loadings between .26 and .98). The reliabilities were rather low, indicat-ing that the true reliabilities might have been underestimated in the two models. The higher relia-bilities found for the CTUM model are due to the fact that the method factors explain a certain amount of true variance. The consistency and

---

TABLE 20.2

Residual Variances, Reliabilities, Consistency Coefficients, and Method-Specificity Coefficients for the Single-Indicator MTMM Models Depicted in Figure 20.1

	Residual variance/reliability			Consistency		Method specificity	
	CTCU	**CTUM**	**CTC(M-1)**	**CTUM**	**CTC(M-1)**	**CTUM**	**CTC(M-1)**
Self-report							
Fear	.30 / .17	−.05 / undefined	.07 / .80	.15	1.00	.85	0
Anger	.26 / .26	.24 / .33	.12 / .66	.80	1.00	.20	0
Sadness	.32 / .07	.30 / .14	.24 / .31	.51	1.00	.49	0
Friend report							
Fear	.18 / .36	.15 / .47	.17 / .41	.76	.17	.24	.83
Anger	.28 / .19	.24 / .31	.25 / .30	.60	.29	.40	.71
Sadness	.27 / .17	.02 / .93	.13 / .61	.18	.20	.82	.80
Acquaintance report							
Fear	.21 / .29	.16 / .44	.16 / .45	.65	.08	.35	.92
Anger	.27 / .17	.19 / .43	.24 / .27	.60	.29	.40	.71
Sadness	.17 / .40	.11 / .61	.14 / .50	.64	.32	.36	.68

Residual correlations in the CTCU-model

	SR-fear	SR-anger		FR-fear	FR-anger		AR-fear	AR-anger
SR-anger	.32		FR-anger	.21		AR-anger	.22	
SR-sadness	.30	.08	FR-sadness	.40	.42	AR-sadness	.24	.34

Note. SR = self-report; FR = friend report; AR = acquaintance report.

method specificity coefficients of the CTUM model varied greatly even within the same method. This indicates that method effects might be trait specific. The consistency coefficients were generally high for *anger*. For *fear*, however, the consistency coefficient was very low for the self-report and comparably high for the peer reports. This might indicate that the peer raters have more in common than shared with the self-report. *Sadness* revealed a quite different pattern of a very low consistency coefficient for the friend rating and medium consistencies for the self- and acquaintance reports. In general, the parameter estimates and the coefficients of consistency and specificity were rather heterogeneous for the CTUM and the CTCU models and are, therefore, difficult to interpret.

The loading parameters and the coefficients of consistency and method specificity are more homogeneous for the CTC(M-1) model. The consistency coefficients show that between 8% and 32% of the variance of the (error-free) ratings of friends and acquaintances can be explained by the self-ratings and that between 68% and 92% are due to method

effects. Moreover, the correlation of the two method factors ($r = .40$) indicates that the friends and acquaintances share a common view of the target that is not shared by the target. This application shows that the parameters of the CTC(M-1) model have an easier interpretation than the parameters of the two other models in the case of structurally different raters.

General Limitations of Single-Indicator Models

The applications show that the single-indicator models can provide interesting insights into the MTMM structure. The major limitation of single-indicator models, however, is that measurement error can be separated from systematic trait-specific method effects only in models with method factors and only if method effects generalize across traits in a unidimensional way. This assumption, however, is very restrictive, and trait-specific method effects could be expected in several applications. For example, one peer rater might not consistently over- or underestimate different personality traits of

a target person. Trait-specific method effects might be especially likely when the traits differ in their proneness to response sets (e.g., social desirability and leniency effects). If trait-specific method effects exist, reliability will be underestimated in single-indicator models because the effects that are due to trait-specific method effects cannot be separated from the error variable (Eid, 2000; Marsh & Hocevar, 1988). These problems can only be dealt with appropriately in multiple-indicator models that are described in the next section. Hence, single-indicator models seem to be most appropriate when it is not possible to have multiple indicators for a trait–method unit.

MULTIPLE-INDICATOR MODELS

In contrast to single-indicator models, multiple-indicator models are able to separate measurement error from trait-specific method influences. Moreover, the hypothesis that method effects are trait specific and do not perfectly generalize across traits can be statistically tested. We will only describe three multiple-indicator extensions: a general model that is able to estimate the latent correlations between different trait–method units, a model that is related to the CTCU model, and a model that is an extension of the CTC(M-1) model. Furthermore, we will show how the ideas of the CTUM, the CTCM, and the CT models can be analyzed in the multiple-indicator context. To apply multiple-indicator models, it is necessary to have at least two indicators of each trait–method unit. Hence, an observed variable Y_{ijk} has three indices, the first pertaining to the item or test parcel, the second to the trait, and the third to the method.

MTMM Correlation Model

A multiple-indicator correlation model for our example of three emotional traits and three types of raters is depicted in Figure 20.3a. In this model, a latent variable is defined for the two indicators representing the same trait–method unit. This model allows the estimation of the latent correlations between the trait–method units and the construction of a latent MTMM correlation matrix. The correlations of this matrix represent an error-free

variant of the MTMM matrix and, therefore, circumvent one of the major criticisms of the MTMM correlation matrix. Because the MTMM matrix is based on observed correlations, their sizes depend on the reliability of the measures. When measures strongly differ in their reliabilities, the conclusions based on applying the Campbell and Fiske criteria to the MTMM matrix (see Schmitt, chap. 2, this volume) can be misleading (Wothke, 1995). The MTMM model is a very general model without restrictions on the latent correlations. All models depicted in Figure 20.1 for single indicators can be applied to the multiple-indicator case by replacing the observed variables in Figure 20.1 with the latent (trait and method) variables in Figure 20.3a. This means that a second-order factor structure would be defined for the first-order factors in Figure 20.3a, and the fit of these more restricted models could be tested against the fit of the general MTMM correlation model. The residuals of the first-order factors indicate systematic method influences that are specific for a trait–method unit. All other properties of the single-indicator models can be transferred to the multiple-indicator models with a second-order factor structure. In the following discussion, we will present a slightly different way to model these ideas by introducing trait and method factors as first-order factors. In our view, this approach is more flexible because it allows the testing of hypotheses about the structure of trait and method effects and allows a researcher to relate the latent variables representing method influences to other variables.

Multiple-Indicator CTCU Model

An extension of the CTCU model is depicted in Figure 20.3b. In this model there are two indicators for each trait–method unit. All indicators belonging to the same trait are indicators of a common trait factor T_j. Hence, there are three trait factors, one for each emotion considered in our application presented in the last section. Additionally, there is one method factor for each trait–method unit indicating the method influences that are specific (i.e., unique) for one trait. The correlations between the method factors belonging to the same method indicate the generalizability of method effects across traits. In this model, only correlations between

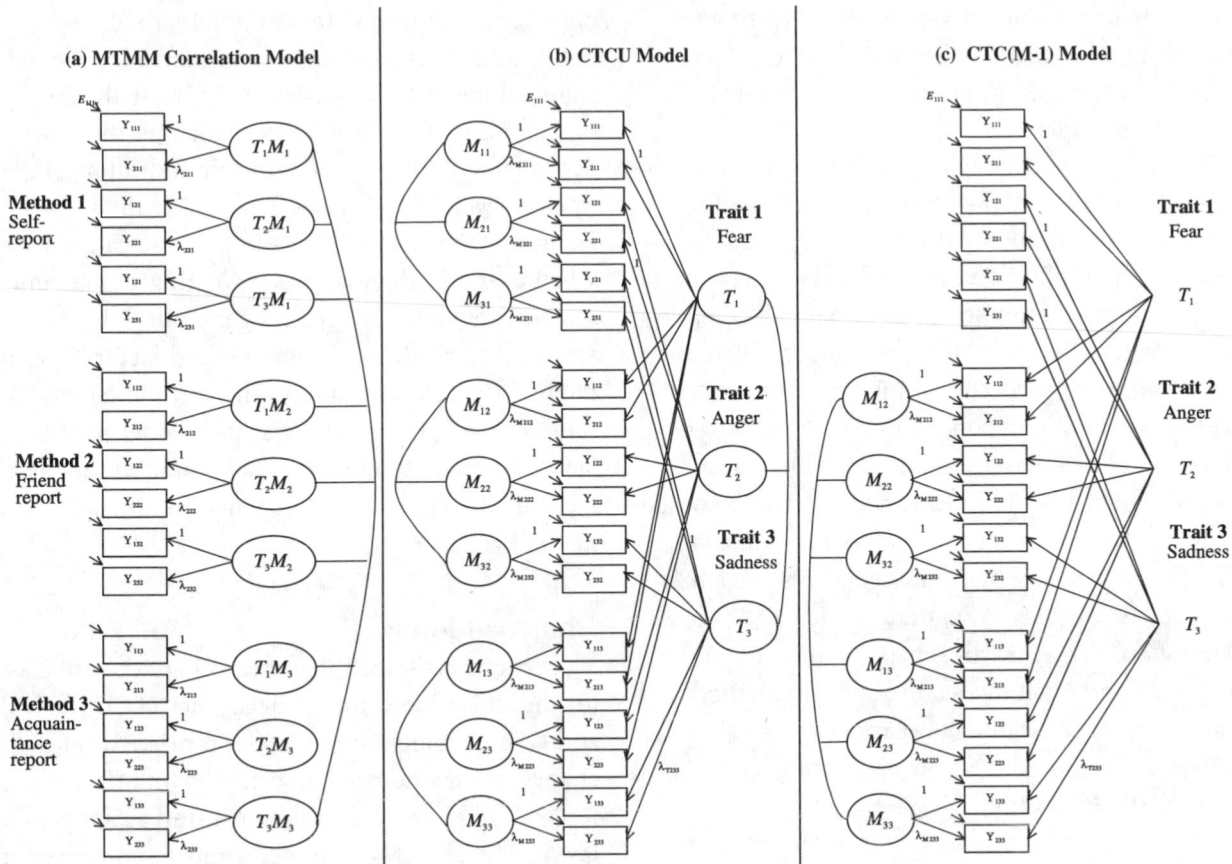

FIGURE 20.3. Multiple-indicator MTMM models. (a) MTMM correlation model; (b) CTCU model: correlated trait/uncorrelated uniqueness model; and (c) CTC(M-1) model: correlated trait/correlated method model with one method factor less than methods considered. Y_{ijk}: observed variable, i: indicator, j: trait, k: method; T_j: latent trait variable; M_{jk}: trait-specific method factor; E_{ijk}: Error variable; λ_{Mijk}, λ_{Tijk}: factor loadings. Factor loadings are only depicted for one path for each factor but they are estimated for all variables. The figure shows the general loading pattern. In the applications reported in the text, more-restricted versions are analyzed. In the general version of the CTC(M-1) model, correlations between a trait factor and the method factors that belong to another trait are allowed. However, they are not presented in this figure and are not admitted in the application reported in the text.

method factors belonging to the same method are allowed. Therefore, this model represents the idea of the CTCU model depicted in Figure 20.1b: There are trait-specific method influences (method factors) that are *unique* to one trait–method unit and that can be correlated across all traits but only if the method factors belong to the same method. In contrast to the model in Figure 20.1b, the model in Figure 20.3b separates measurement error from method-specific influences and represents method-specific influences by latent variables that can be related to other variables. If the three method factors belonging to the same method are identical, the model reduces to a CTUM model. If one allows the method factors of this CTUM model to be corre-

lated, the model becomes a CTCM model. The multiple-indicator CTUM and CTCM models are very strict variants of the CTCU model implying perfect unidimensionality of the method influences belonging to the same method. A somewhat less-restrictive variant would be to model a general method factor for each method as a second-order factor of all method factors belonging to the same methods. These general method factors can be assumed to be uncorrelated (less-restrictive CTUM model) or correlated (less-restrictive CTCM model). These second-order structures are less restrictive because residuals of the first-order method factors can capture the trait-specificity of a method influence. One would apply these second-order method models if

293

one wants to get a latent variable representing the general trait-unspecific effect of a method. Marsh and Hocevar (1988) have proposed a model that is related to this idea.

The CTCU model depicted in Figure 20.3b allows the decomposition of the variance of the observed indicators into components that represent trait influences, method influences, and influences that are due to measurement error. Because the method factors belonging to different methods are uncorrelated, the model is most appropriate for interchangeable methods (see earlier discussion). This model can also be conceived of as a multiple-trait extension of a so-called latent state–trait model and is related to special models of longitudinal confirmatory factor analysis (Eid, Schneider, & Schwenkmezger, 1999; Marsh & Grayson, 1994a; Steyer, Schmitt, & Eid, 1999; see Khoo, West, Wu, & Kwok, chap. 21, this volume). In this latent state–trait model, the different methods considered are the different occasions on which individuals are measured (e.g., Steyer, Ferring, & Schmitt, 1992; Steyer et al., 1999).

Multiple-Indicator CTC(M-1) Model

A multiple-indicator extension of the CTC(M-1) is depicted in Figure 20.3c. This model is described in detail by Eid et al. (2003). In this model there is a method factor for each combination of a trait and a nonstandard method. The method factors belonging to the same method can be correlated, thus representing the generalizability of method effects across traits. Also the method factors of different methods can be correlated, thus showing whether the nonstandard methods have more in common than can be explained by the standard method. The general version of this model, which is not depicted in Figure 20.3 but explained in detail by Eid et al. (2003), also allows correlations between the method factors belonging to one trait and the trait factors of the other traits. These correlations are heteromethod coefficients of discriminant validity, whereas the intercorrelations of the trait factors are discriminant validities with respect to the standard method. The CTC(M-1) model allows to estimate variance components that are due to trait, method, and error influences. The variance components that

are due to trait (consistency) and method (specificity) influences can only be estimated for the non-standard methods because they indicate the degree of variance that cannot be explained by the standard method. Like in the multiple-indicator CTCU model, several hypotheses concerning the method factors can be tested. For example, one can test whether the method factors belonging to the same method are identical (perfect generalizability) by specifying a model with one method factor for each method (instead of trait-specific method factors). Moreover, one can model a second-order method factor for all method factors belonging to the same method, if a measure of the general influence of one method is desired.

Choice of Model

The criteria for selecting a method are the same as for the single-indicator models. The CTCU, CTUM, and CTCM models are most appropriate if interchangeable methods are considered and the research interest is in modeling a trait as a common factor. The CTC(M-1) model is most appropriate in the case of structurally different methods and when the research interest is in contrasting methods.

Applications

To illustrate the multiple-indicator CTCU and CTC(M-1) models, we applied them to the same data set as the single-indicator models and included the second test halves of the scales as second indicators (see Table 20.3). In the multiple-indicator models, the first indicators were identical to the ones analyzed in the single-indicator models. This makes it possible to show the differences in the estimated parameters, particularly the reliabilities between the single-indicator and the multiple-indicator models. In the applications we assumed that the two indicators are homogeneous indicators of each trait–method unit. Thus, the loading parameters of the two indicators were set equal to each other. The fit of the two models was very good (CTCU: $\chi^2 = 127.32$, $df = 123$, $p = .38$, CFI = 1.00, RMSEA = .01; CTC(M-1): $\chi^2 = 123.08$, $df = 120$, $p = .41$, CFI = 1.00, RMSEA = .01). The fit of these models is in the same range as the fit of the MTMM

TABLE 20.3

Covariances, Variances, and Correlations of the Observed Variables of the Multiple-Indicator CTUM and CTC(M-1) Models Depicted in Figure 20.3

	SR-F1	SR-F2	SR-A1	SR-A2	SR-S1	SR-S2	FR-F1	FR-F2	FR-A1	FR-A2	FR-S1	FR-S2	AR-F1	AR-F2	AR-A1	AR-A2	AR-S1	AR-S2
SR-F1	.35	.28	.11	.10	.12	.15	.07	.05	.04	.04	.06	.06	.05	.04	.02	.02	.08	.07
SR-F2	.70	.45	.11	.12	.12	.19	.08	.06	.02	.02	.03	.05	.04	.00	-.01	.01	.06	.06
SR-A1	*.31*	*.27*	.36	.24	.02	.06	.03	.03	.09	.08	.03	.02	.02	-.01	.08	.07	.00	-.02
SR-A2	*.27*	*.29*	.64	.38	.02	.06	.04	.02	.06	.07	.05	.03	.02	-.01	.03	.05	-.02	-.03
SR-S1	*.33*	*.30*	*.07*	*.05*	.35	.23	.05	.05	.01	.05	.08	.09	-.01	.00	.00	-.02	.05	.03
SR-S2	*.45*	*.48*	*.19*	*.16*	.69	.34	.03	.03	.03	.05	.08	.07	.01	.01	-.01	.00	.06	.05
FR-F1	**.22**	**.23**	.09	.12	.15	.10	.29	.18	.08	.06	.14	.16	.10	.08	.02	.04	.07	.07
FR-F2	**.16**	**.16**	.10	.05	.15	.10	.61	.30	.07	.04	.11	.15	.06	.03	.05	.06	.05	.03
FR-A1	.12	.04	**.24**	**.16**	.04	.07	*.25*	*.21*	.35	.25	.13	.15	.06	.04	.07	.07	.02	.02
FR-A2	.11	.06	**.20**	**.18**	.15	.13	*.17*	*.13*	.68	.39	.10	.11	.02	.02	.06	.07	.03	.04
FR-S1	.19	.08	.09	.13	**.25**	**.24**	*.47*	*.37*	*.37*	*.29*	.33	.24	.05	.06	.04	.03	.08	.09
FR-S2	.18	.13	.07	.08	**.24**	**.19**	*.49*	*.47*	*.42*	*.30*	.70	.36	.06	.07	.04	.04	.07	.07
AR-F1	**.16**	**.11**	.06	.05	-.04	.02	**.35**	**.22**	.18	.05	.15	.20	.29	.19	.09	.06	.11	.13
AR-F2	**.12**	**.00**	-.02	-.02	-.01	.02	**.28**	**.12**	.13	.05	.20	.21	.66	.28	.06	.04	.12	.11
AR-A1	.05	-.02	**.22**	**.08**	-.01	-.02	.07	.17	**.21**	**.16**	.11	.11	*.28*	*.19*	.33	.26	.08	.08
AR-A2	.04	.03	**.19**	**.13**	-.05	.00	.11	.17	**.18**	**.17**	.07	.11	*.33*	*.11*	.70	.44	.09	.08
AR-S1	.26	.18	.00	-.06	**.15**	**.19**	.25	.16	.07	.08	**.26**	**.22**	*.40*	*.43*	*.27*	*.26*	.27	.23
AR-S2	.20	.15	-.06	-.08	**.07**	**.15**	.22	.11	.06	.10	**.27**	**.21**	*.40*	*.36*	*.25*	*.21*	.74	.34

Note. SR = self-report; FR = friend report; AR = acquaintance report; F = fear; A = anger; S = sadness; 1 = first indicator; 2 = second indicator. Covariances are depicted in the upper (right) triangular, variances appear in the main diagonal, and correlations are presented in the lower (left) triangular. Monotrait–heteromethod correlations appear in boldface type. Heterotrait–monomethod correlations are printed in italics.

correlation model (Figure 20.3a) with equal loadings ($\chi^2 = 109.99$, $df = 108$, $p = .43$, CFI = 1.00, RMSEA = .01). The parameters (loadings, latent correlations) of the MTMM correlation model are not presented because their interpretation is straightforward. The loading parameters as well as the coefficients of reliability, consistency, and method specificity of the CTCU and CTC(M-1) model are reported in Table 20.4. Table 20.5 and 20.6 show the correlations between the trait and method factors. First, the reliabilities (variance explained by the trait and method factors) were generally higher than the reliabilities in the single-indicator models. The reliabilities of the different indicators did not differ as much as in the single-indicator models. Moreover, the reliabilities were of reasonable sizes given that each indicator (test half)

consists of only two items. This shows that the reliabilities can be more appropriately estimated in multiple-indicator models. The consistency and method specificity coefficients are estimated as proportions of variance of the true variance (observed variance minus error variance). In the CTCU model, the consistency and method specificity coefficients differed greatly within and between the three methods. For two traits (fear, sadness), the friend ratings showed the highest consistency and lowest specificity coefficients. According to this criterion, the friend ratings were the "best" methods (highest correlations with the trait). For anger, however, the consistency coefficients of friend ratings were the lowest. These differences in the consistency coefficients indicated differences in the correlations of the three methods between the three

---

TABLE 20.4

Loading Parameters and Standardized Loading Parameters (in parentheses), Error Variances, Reliabilities, Consistency, and Method Specificity Coefficients of the Multiple-Indicator CTCU and CTC(M-1) Models Depicted in Figure 20.3

	CTCU Model						CTC(M-1) Model					
	Trait loading	Method loading	Error var.	CO	MS	Rel	Trait loading	Method loading	Error var.	CO	MS	Rel
						Self-report						
Fear 1	1.00 (.40)	1.00 (.78)	.09	.21	.79	.76	1.00 (.87)		.09	1.00	.00	.75
Fear 2	1.00 (.37)	1.00 (.71)	.16	.21	.79	.64	1.00 (.80)		.15	1.00	.00	.64
Anger 1	1.00 (.45)	1.00 (.70)	.11	.29	.71	.69	1.00 (.83)		.11	1.00	.00	.69
Anger 2	1.00 (.42)	1.00 (.66)	.15	.29	.71	.61	1.00 (.78)		.15	1.00	.00	.61
Sadness 1	1.00 (.33)	1.00 (.73)	.14	.17	.83	.64	1.00 (.80)		.14	1.00	.00	.63
Sadness 2	1.00 (.36)	1.00 (.79)	.08	.17	.83	.74	1.00 (.86)		.08	1.00	.00	.74
						Friend report						
Fear 1	1.25 (.59)	1.00 (.56)	.09	.52	.48	.66	.22 (.22)	1.00 (.79)	.09	.07	.93	.67
Fear 2	1.25 (.55)	1.00 (.52)	.14	.52	.48	.57	.22 (.21)	1.00 (.73)	.14	.07	.93	.57
Anger 1	.94 (.43)	1.00 (.75)	.09	.25	.75	.75	.27 (.23)	1.00 (.84)	.08	.07	.93	.75
Anger 2	.94 (.39)	1.00 (.68)	.15	.25	.75	.62	.27 (.21)	1.00 (.76)	.15	.07	.93	.62
Sadness 1	1.53 (.54)	1.00 (.64)	.10	.41	.59	.70	.30 (.25)	1.00 (.80)	.10	.09	.91	.70
Sadness 2	1.53 (.53)	1.00 (.63)	.11	.41	.59	.68	.30 (.25)	1.00 (.79)	.11	.09	.91	.68
						Acquaintance report						
Fear 1	.86 (.40)	1.00 (.71)	.09	.24	.76	.67	.08 (.08)	1.00 (.81)	.09	.01	.99	.67
Fear 2	.86 (.39)	1.00 (.70)	.10	.24	.76	.64	.08 (.08)	1.00 (.80)	.10	.01	.99	.65
Anger 1	.96 (.44)	1.00 (.78)	.06	.32	.68	.81	.26 (.22)	1.00 (.87)	.06	.06	.94	.81
Anger 2	.96 (.39)	1.00 (.68)	.17	.32	.68	.61	.26 (.19)	1.00 (.76)	.17	.06	.94	.61
Sadness 1	1.22 (.47)	1.00 (.77)	.05	.27	.73	.81	.26 (.24)	1.00 (.87)	.05	.07	.93	.82
Sadness 2	1.22 (.43)	1.00 (.70)	.11	.27	.73	.67	.26 (.22)	1.00 (.79)	.11	.07	.93	.67

Note. Error var. = error variance; CO = consistency; MS = method specificity; Rel = reliability.

TABLE 20.5

Factor Covariances, Variances, and Correlations in the Multiple-Indicator CTCU Model Depicted in Figure 20.3

	Fear	Anger	Sadness	SR-fear	SR-anger	SR-sadness	FR-fear	FR-anger	FR-sadness	AR-fear	AR-anger	AR-sadness
Fear	**.06**	.03	**.04**									
Anger	**.41**	**.07**	.02									
Sadness	**.74**	**.28**	**.04**									
SR-fear				**.22**	**.09**	**.11**						
SR-anger				**.46**	**.17**	.04						
SR-sadness				**.55**	.21	**.20**						
FR-fear							**.09**	.03	**.07**			
FR-anger							.21	**.19**	**.09**			
FR-sadness							**.65**	**.57**	**.14**			
AR-fear										**.14**	.05	**.08**
AR-anger										.27	**.20**	.07
AR-sadness										**.50**	**.39**	**.16**

Note. Fear, anger, sadness: Trait factors. Method factors are denoted by SR (self-report), FR (friend report), AR (acquaintance report). Covariances are depicted in the upper (right) triangular, variances appear in the main diagonal, and correlations are presented in the lower (left) triangular. Empty cells indicate nonadmissible covariances or correlations. Parameters that differ significantly from 0 ($\alpha = .05$) appear in boldface type.

TABLE 20.6

Factor Covariances, Variances, and Correlations of the Multiple-Indicator CTC(M-1) Model Depicted in Figure 20.3

	Fear	Anger	Sadness	FR-fear	FR-anger	FR-sadness	AR-fear	AR-anger	AR-sadness
Fear	**.27**	**.11**	**.15**						
Anger	**.41**	**.24**	**.05**						
Sadness	**.59**	**.20**	**.24**						
FR-fear				**.17**	**.06**	**.13**	**.07**	.03	**.04**
FR-anger				**.29**	**.23**	**.11**	.03	**.05**	.02
FR-sadness				**.69**	**.51**	**.21**	**.06**	.03	**.06**
AR-fear				**.39**	.17	**.29**	**.18**	**.07**	**.11**
AR-anger				.16	**.20**	.14	**.31**	**.25**	**.09**
AR-sadness				**.23**	.10	**.27**	**.57**	**.39**	**.21**

Note. Fear, anger, sadness: Trait factors. Method factors are denoted by SR (self-report), FR (friend report), AR (acquaintance report). Covariances are depicted in the upper (right) triangular, variances appear in the main diagonal, and correlations are presented in the lower right portion of the table. Empty cells indicate nonadmissible covariances or correlations. Parameters that differ significantly from 0 ($\alpha = .05$) appear in boldface type.

traits. These differences in correlations, however, were not visible in a simple manner but had to be inferred from the loading patterns.

The situation was quite different for the CTC(M-1) model. The consistency coefficients of the self-reports were perfect because the self-reports had been taken as the comparison standard. The consistency coefficients were rather low, and the method specificity coefficients were very high for the peer ratings. This finding means that both the friend and acquaintance ratings were rather weakly associated with the self-ratings. The standardized loading

parameters and the consistency coefficients were higher for the friend ratings than the acquaintance ratings, particularly for fear and sadness. However, the differences in the consistency and method specificity coefficients between the friend and acquaintance ratings were not very large and not significant. This was tested by comparing the model in Figure 20.3c with a model in which (a) the trait factor loadings of the friend ratings are set equal to the factor loadings of the acquaintance ratings, and (b) the variance of a trait-specific method factor for a friend rating was set equal to the variance of the corresponding method factor of the acquaintance rating. The method factor loadings were equal between the friend and acquaintances ratings because they had already been set to 1 for the assumption of homogeneous indicators. In this restricted model, the consistency and specificity coefficients have to be equal for the friend and acquaintance ratings. Although this model is more restrictive than the model in Figure 20.3c, it did not fit the data significantly worse than the unrestricted model ($\chi^2 = 125.95$, $df = 126$, $p = .48$, CFI = 1.00, RMSEA < .01), demonstrating that the friend ratings were not more closely linked to the self-ratings than the acquaintance ratings (χ^2–difference test: $\chi^2 = 2.87$, $df = 6$, $p = .82$).

Generalizability of method effects. In the CTCU and the CTC(M-1) models, the correlations of the method factors belonging to the same method indicated that method effects generalized across methods because the correlations were relatively large. However, the correlations were different from 1, indicating that the strong assumption of perfect generalizability of method effects across traits that is inherent in the single-indicator variants of these models had to be rejected. This was revealed by a statistical comparison of the models in Figure 20.3 with corresponding models in which there is only one method factor for each method. These models had to be rejected for both the CTUM and the CTC(M-1) model.

Correlations between methods. As in the single-indicator variant, the method factors are uncorrelated between methods in the multiple-indicator CTCU model. This, however, must not be misinterpreted in the sense that methods are not differentially related to each other. To a certain degree, differential associations between methods can be captured by the different trait factor loadings. In the CTC(M-1) model these differences are represented by the correlations between the method factors of the two other rater groups. The significant correlations between the method factors of the friend raters and the method factors of the acquaintance raters indicate that the peer raters share a common view of the person that is not shared with the person her- or himself.

MULTIPLE-INDICATOR MODELS WITH HETEROGENEOUS INDICATORS

The two multiple-indicator models assume that the indicators are homogeneous indicators of a trait-method unit. This means that they are indicators of the same trait and the same method factors without any unique component of the true score that is not shared with the other indicators of this trait-method unit. This assumption, however, is often too restrictive, particularly when the same indicator is repeatedly measured (e.g., by different raters or on different occasions of measurement). In this case, a unique indicator-specific component can be identified and its nonconsideration would result in the misfit of an MTMM model. There are several ways to consider indicator-specific components. The most prominent is to allow autocorrelations of residuals belonging to the repeatedly measured indicators. This means that all residuals belonging to the same indicator are correlated. Although autocorrelations are admissible representations of indicator-specific influences, they have the disadvantage that they indicate a valid source of variance that is not modeled by latent variables. Consequently, the reliabilities of the indicators will be underestimated. An alternative is to consider a multidimensional trait structure. In these extended models, each indicator measures a different indicator-specific trait factor but a common method factor. Hence, in our example there would be six (correlated) latent trait factors whereas the method factor structure of the model would not change. This way of considering

indicator specificity has been adopted in models of latent state–trait theory (e.g., Eid, 1996; Eid & Diener, 1999) and longitudinal confirmatory factor analysis (Marsh & Grayson, 1994a). A second way is to introduce an indicator-specific factor for one of the two indicators (see Eid et al., 1999). The repeated measures of the same indicator are assumed to have substantive loadings on the indicator-specific factor. This indicator-specific factor represents the uniqueness of an indicator that is not shared with the other indicator. Accordingly, there is one indicator-specific factor less than indicators. This approach is similar to the CTC(M-1) approach of modeling method factors. The basic idea of this type of modeling is that if we have two indicators, we need only one indicator-specific factor to contrast the differences between the two indicators. The two different approaches to modeling indicator-specific influences are strongly related and can be transferred to each other under specific conditions (see Eid et al., 1999).

SUMMARY

SEM is a very versatile tool for analyzing MTMM data because it allows the separation of measurement error from method-specific effects and trait influences. Moreover, these models enable researchers to test hypotheses concerning the structure of trait and method effects in a confirmatory way. The SEM approaches in this chapter refer to metrical observed variables, but SEM approaches for ordinal variables (e.g., Muthén, 2002) can be applied to analyze the same MTMM models (Nussbeck, Eid, & Lischetzke, in press). In the case of categorical variables, models of item response theory can be applied (Rost & Walter, chap. 18, this volume). Because of their considerable advantages, MTMM models of SEM have been widely and successfully applied in different areas of psychological research (e.g., Burns & Haynes, chap. 27, this volume; Marsh, Martin, & Hau, chap. 30, this volume).

CHAPTER 21

LONGITUDINAL METHODS

Siek-Toon Khoo, Stephen G. West, Wei Wu, and Oi-Man Kwok

The previous chapters in this volume have focused on the measurement of participants using multiple methods, multiple measures, and in multiple situations. In this chapter the focus shifts to the measurement of the same set of participants on multiple occasions, ideally using the same (or equivalent) measurement instruments. This focus on multiple occasions does not fundamentally alter the application of basic concepts and approaches presented in previous chapters (see Eid, chap. 16, this volume; Eid & Diener, chap. 1, this volume). What is new in this chapter is that longitudinal designs explicitly determine the temporal ordering of the observations. This temporal ordering of observations provides an enhanced ability to elucidate stability and change in individuals over time, to study time-related processes, and to establish the direction of hypothesized causal relationships (Dwyer, 1983; Singer & Willett, 2002).

Longitudinal studies are becoming increasingly prominent in several areas of psychology including clinical, community, developmental, personality, and health. For example, Biesanz, West, and Kwok (2003) found that 24% of the studies published in the 2000 and 2001 volumes of the *Journal of Personality: Personality Process and Individual Differences* section and the *Journal of Personality* included two or more waves of data collection. In the area of psychology most focused on issues of stability and change, we found that 32% of the articles in *Developmental Psychology* in 2002 met these minimum

criteria for a longitudinal study of two waves of data collection. This compares to only 15% of the articles published in 1990.

A more in-depth review focused on the longitudinal studies in the 2002 volume of *Developmental Psychology* provides a glimpse of current practice (see also Morris, Robinson, & Eisenberg, chap. 25, this volume). The duration of studies ranged from 12 weeks to 28 years. Approximately 25% of the studies collected only two waves of data, whereas approximately 25% of the studies reported 6 or more waves of data collection, with one study collecting more than 50 waves of data. Measures included standardized measures of ability and intelligence; self-, peer, parent, and teacher reports; ratings and counts of behaviors by trained observers; peer nominations; and physical measures such as weight and heart rate. Although most of the studies included a substantial core set of measures that were administered at each wave, some studies used different measures at each measurement wave, precluding the examination of change over time. The majority of articles reported traditional correlation/regression analyses or analysis of variance. Collins and Sayer (2001), McArdle and Nesselroade (2003), and Singer and Willett (2002) have highlighted the potential advantages of newer approaches to the analysis of longitudinal data, yet approaches such as structural equation modeling (approximately 10%) and growth modeling and

We thank Jeremy Biesanz, Patrick Curran, coeditor Michael Eid, Paras Mehta, Roger Millsap, Steven Reise, and an anonymous reviewer for their comments on an earlier version of this chapter.

examination of growth trajectories (approximately 15%) continue to represent a distinct minority of longitudinal studies.

This chapter considers a number of unique issues that arise when measurements are taken on multiple occasions. We begin with a consideration of some desiderata of measurement from cross-sectional research and consider how they may apply in longitudinal research. We then consider three different longitudinal models: (a) autoregressive models that focus on the stability of participants' relative standing on a construct over time; (b) latent trait–state models that partition the variance in measured constructs into relatively stable (trait) and measurement occasion specific (state) components; and (c) growth curve models that estimate individual growth trajectories. Finally, we consider these longitudinal models in light of measurement concerns and indicate some methods through which these concerns can be addressed.

SOME DESIDERATA FOR GOOD MEASUREMENT: LESSONS FROM CROSS-SECTIONAL RESEARCH

Sources on traditional and modern approaches to measurement (Crocker & Algina, 1986; Embretson & Reise, 2000; Lord & Novick, 1968; McDonald, 1999; West & Finch, 1997) have emphasized issues that arise in narrow windows of time that characterize cross-sectional and short-term (test–retest) studies. These approaches have developed several desiderata for good measurement; three are presented following. We also begin to consider how these desiderata may need to be extended for longitudinal studies. In this section we will use the framework of classical test theory and assume that measures have been collected on a numerical scale.

Reliability

In classical test theory the observed score on a measure (Y) can be partitioned into two parts: true score (T) and error (e). In symbols, this is expressed as $Y = T + e$. T can be defined as the mean of a very large number of independent measurements. e is assumed to be random and independent of the value of the true score. The

reliability coefficient represents the proportion of the variance in the observed Y scores (σ^2_Y) that is true score variance (σ^2_T),

$$\rho_{YY} = \frac{\sigma^2_T}{\sigma^2_Y}$$

Reliability is an index of the dependability of the measurement. Two measures of reliability are currently widely reported in the literature, coefficient alpha and the test–retest correlation.

Coefficient alpha. When the data are collected on a single measurement occasion, Cronbach's (1951) coefficient alpha (α) is typically reported. Conceptually, α can be thought of as the correlation between two equivalent scales of the same length given at the same time.

Coefficient alpha has several little-known properties that may limit its usefulness in application (Cortina, 1993; Feldt & Brennan, 1989; Schmitt, 1996). First, α assumes that all items are equally good measures of the underlying construct, a condition known as essential tau equivalence (see section on homogeneity for a fuller description). If some items should ideally be weighted more heavily in estimating the true score, then α will underestimate the reliability. Second, α is dependent on test length. For example, if a 10-item scale had an $\alpha = .70$ and another exactly parallel set of 10 items could be identified, then α for the 20-item scale would be .82. Third, α addresses sources of error that result from the sampling of equivalent items and potential variability *within* the measurement period (e.g., within-test variability in level of concentration). It does not address error resulting from sources that may vary over measurement occasions (e.g., $\rho_{y_i y_{i'}}$, daily changes in mood). Fourth, a high level of α does not indicate that a single dimension has been measured. For example, Cortina showed that if two *orthogonal* dimensions underlie a set of items, even if the intercorrelations between items within each dimension are modest (e.g., = .30), α will exceed .70 if the scale has more than 14 items. Even higher values of α will be achieved if the dimensions are correlated. Finally, α may differ for

measures collected during different periods of a longitudinal study. Both the variance in the true scores and the measured scores may change over time so that α can change dramatically. A measure of IQ collected on a group of children at age 4 will typically have a lower α than the same measure collected on the children at age 10. In later sections, we describe alternative approaches that address several of these issues as well as others that arise in longitudinal measurement contexts.

Test–retest correlations. A second method of estimating reliability is to calculate the correlation between the scores on the same set of items taken at two points in time. Test–retest approaches assume that (a) the participants' true scores do not change on the measure during the (short) interval between Time 1 and Time 2 and that (b) responding to the item at Time 1 has no effect on the response at Time 2 (e.g., no memory for prior responses on an ability test). Green (2003) has recently developed a test–retest version of α. Test–retest α eliminates sources of error that change across measurement occasions (e.g., daily mood changes), but otherwise shares the assumptions and properties of traditional α described earlier.

In longer-term studies, the interpretation of the test–retest correlation changes. It can no longer be assumed that there has been no change in the participants' true scores or that all participants change at the same rate. Children and adults change over time in their abilities, personality traits, and physical characteristics such as height and weight. In this case the test–retest correlation is an estimate of the stability of the measure—the extent to which the (rank) order of the participants at Time 1 is the same as the order of the participants at Time 2. Otherwise stated, the level of the measure (e.g., height) may change over time, but stability is shown to the degree that participants' amount of change is proportional to their initial level on the measure.

Homogeneity (Unidimensionality)

Interpretation of measures is greatly simplified if the measure assesses a single dimension (underlying factor). For example, imagine that a measure of

college aptitude were developed. Unbeknownst to the test developers the items reflect a major dimension of IQ and a secondary dimension of conscientiousness. These two dimensions have only a minimal correlation. Both dimensions may predict good performance in many classes. But the conscientiousness dimension may be a far better predictor of performance in a history course in which large amounts of material must be regularly learned. In contrast, IQ may be a far better predictor of performance in a calculus course. By separating the two dimensions, we can gain a far greater understanding of the influence of the two dimensions in performance in different college classes. Indeed, the interpretation of the body of research associated with several classic measures of personality has been difficult because of the existence of multiple dimensions underlying the personality scale (see Briggs & Cheek, 1986; Carver, 1989; Neuberg, Judice, & West, 1997 for discussions). Finch and West (1997) discussed testing of measures in cross-sectional studies that are hypothesized to have more complex, multidimensional structures.

In longitudinal research, these issues only become more difficult because dimensions within a scale may change at different rates. For example, Khoo, Butner, and Ialongo (2004) found that a preventive intervention led to a linear decrease on a dimension of general aggression, but no change on a secondary dimension of indirect aggression toward property during the elementary school years. Such findings make it necessary to consider a more complex measurement structure in assessing longitudinal effects on the aggression scale.

The most commonly used method of assessing the dimensionality of measures in cross-sectional studies is confirmatory factor analysis (see Eid, Lischetzke, & Nussbeck, chap. 20, this volume; Hattie, 1985 for a review). In this approach, the researcher hypothesizes that a specific measurement model consisting of one or more latent factors underlies a set of items. The measurement model is then tested against data with two aspects of the results of the test being of special interest. (a) The procedure provides an overall χ^2 test (likelihood ratio test) of whether the hypothesized model fits the observed covariances between the items. If the value of the

obtained χ^2 is *not* significant, then the hypothesized model fits the data. For large samples, the χ^2 test may reject even close-fitting models so that various fit indices such as the RMSEA and the CFI, which are less dependent on sample size, may be used to assess whether the model is adequate. (b) The strength of the relationship between the factor and each item (λ = factor loading) is estimated. In some models, the λs can be expressed in standardized form, in which case they represent the correlation between the latent factor and each item. Alternatively, one of the items may be treated as a reference variable (λ = 1). The strength of each of the other loadings is interpreted relative to the reference variable, values of λ >1 indicate a relatively larger change, and values of λ < 1 indicate a relatively smaller change in the measured variable corresponding to a one-unit change in the latent factor (see Steiger, 2002).

Confirmatory factor analysis can also be used to estimate coefficient alpha. We noted earlier that coefficient alpha assumes that all measures are equally good measures of the underlying construct. This assumption means that the factor loadings of all the items on the factor are equal, known as the assumption of essential tau equivalence. Comparing the fit of a model in which the λs are constrained to be equal, versus an alternative model in which the λs are freely estimated, tests essential tau equivalence. If the fit of the two models does not differ, then the assumption of essential tau equivalence is reasonable. McDonald (1999) and Raykov (1997) provide procedures for estimating α both when the assumption of essential tau equivalence is and is not met. Later in this chapter we will extend the idea of testing of assumptions about measurement structure to longitudinal data. To the extent measures have the same structure at two (or more) time points, the results of analyses using the measures become more interpretable.

Scaling

Stevens (1951) proposed an influential classification of measurement scales. Beginning with the lowest level in the hierarchy, nominal scales assign each participant to an unordered category (e.g., marital status: single, married, divorced, widowed). Ordinal

scales assign each participant to one of several ordered categories (e.g., clothing size: 1 = small, 2 = moderate, 3 = large). Interval scales assign participants a number such that a one-unit difference at any point on the scale represents an identical amount of change (e.g., a change from 3 to 4 degrees or from 30 to 31 degrees represents the same change in temperature on the Celsius scale). Finally, ratio scales share the same equal interval property as the interval scale, but in addition have a true 0 point where 0 represents absence of the measured quantity (e.g., height in centimeters).

Stevens originally argued that the level of measurement limits the type of statistical analysis that may be performed. This position is potentially disturbing because many measures in psychology may not greatly exceed an ordinal level of measurement. Indeed, Krosnick and Fabrigar (in press) have shown that labels used to represent points on Likert-type items often do not come close to approximating equal spacing on an underlying dimension. On the other hand, several authors (e.g., Cliff, 1993; McDonald, 1999) have noted that for *t*-tests and analysis of variance, whether the measurement scale is ordinal, interval, or ratio, makes only a modest difference in the conclusions about the existence of differences between groups, so long as the assumptions of the analysis (e.g., normality and equal variance of residuals) are met. Similarly, for linear regression analysis or structural equation modeling, the level of measurement also does not have a profound effect on tests of the significance of coefficients. These results occur because monotonic (order preserving) transformations typically maintain a high correlation between scores on the original and transformed scales. Often, ordinal measurement will be "good enough" to provide an adequate test of the existence of a relationship or group difference even with statistical tests originally designed for interval level data.

However, if we have hypotheses about the *form* of the relationship between one or more independent variables and the dependent variable, ordinal measurement is no longer "good enough." Longitudinal analyses testing trend over time require interval level measurement. The origin and units of the scale must be constant over time; otherwise, the test

of the form of the relationship will be confounded with possible effects of the measuring instrument. When standard statistical procedures designed for interval-level data are used with ordinal-level data, estimates of parameters of the growth model will be seriously biased. Special methods designed explicitly for ordinal-level data and large sample sizes are required (Mehta, Neale, & Flay, 2004).

Changes in the origin or units of the scale can happen because raters explicitly or implicitly make normative judgments relative to the participant's age and gender.[1] Consider the trait physically active. Informants may rate the second author as being very physically active—a rating of 8 on a 9-point scale ranging from "not at all" to "extremely" active at age 25 and then again at age 50. Yet, physical measures of activity (e.g., a pedometer) may show twice as much physical activity at age 25 as at 50. In effect, such ratings may be "rubber rulers" that correctly describe the standing of the individual *relative* to a same age comparison group. However, when changes occur in either the origin or the units of the scale, clear interpretation of the results of longitudinal analyses focused on the form of change is precluded. These problems do not characterize all longitudinal studies. Physical measures (e.g., height, blood pressure) and many cognitive measures provide invariant measurement at the interval level. Some rating scale measures may approximate interval-level measurement and be suitable for short-term longitudinal studies. But, few investigators consider this fundamental issue—the origin and units of the measure must be constant over time. Such invariance is fundamental in interpreting the results of longitudinal studies of change. We revisit this issue later in the chapter.

THREE LONGITUDINAL MODELS

At this point it would be beneficial to introduce several of the most common new longitudinal models for analyzing stability and change using continuous latent variables. These models include autoregressive models, trait–state models, and growth curve models.

Examining Stability: Autoregressive Models

Autoregressive models are used to examine the stability of the relative standing of individuals over time. Figure 21.1 illustrates an autoregressive model for a three-wave data set. In this data set (Biesanz, West, & Millevoi, 2004), 188 college students were assessed at weekly intervals on a measure of the personality trait of conscientiousness (Saucier & Ostendorf, 1999). According to Saucier and Ostendorf, conscientiousness is comprised of four closely related facets: orderliness, decisiveness, reliability, and industriousness. At each time period, we estimated the latent construct of conscientiousness. In the model presented in Figure 21.1, the factor loading of each facet was constrained to be equal over time so that the units of the latent construct would be the same at each measurement wave. Orderliness serves as the marker variable for the construct ($\lambda = 1$). λs for the other facets range from .62 to .67.

In the basic autoregressive model, the scores on the factor at Time t only affect the scores on the factor at Time $t +1$. If there is perfect stability in the rank order of the students on the factor from one time period to the next, then the correlation will be 1.0, whereas if there is no stability, then the correlation will be 0. In the present example, there is considerable stability in the conscientiousness factor: the unstandardized regression coefficients are .78 (correlation = .85) for Week 1 to Week 2 and .84 (correlation = .88) for Week 2 to Week 3. These stabilities greatly exceed the corresponding simple test–retest correlations of .63 and .65, respectively.

Multiindicator autoregressive models have two distinct advantages over simple test–retest correlations. First, the model partitions the variance associated with the four indicators (facets) at each time into variance associated with the factor of conscientiousness and residual variance so that the stability coefficients are not attenuated by measurement error. Second, part of the residual variance may be due to a systematic feature of the facet (uniqueness) that is not shared with the latent construct of conscientiousness. Correlating the uniquenesses over

---

[1]For example, Goldberg's (1992) measure of the Big Five personality traits explicitly instructs informants to rate the participant relative to others of the same age and gender.

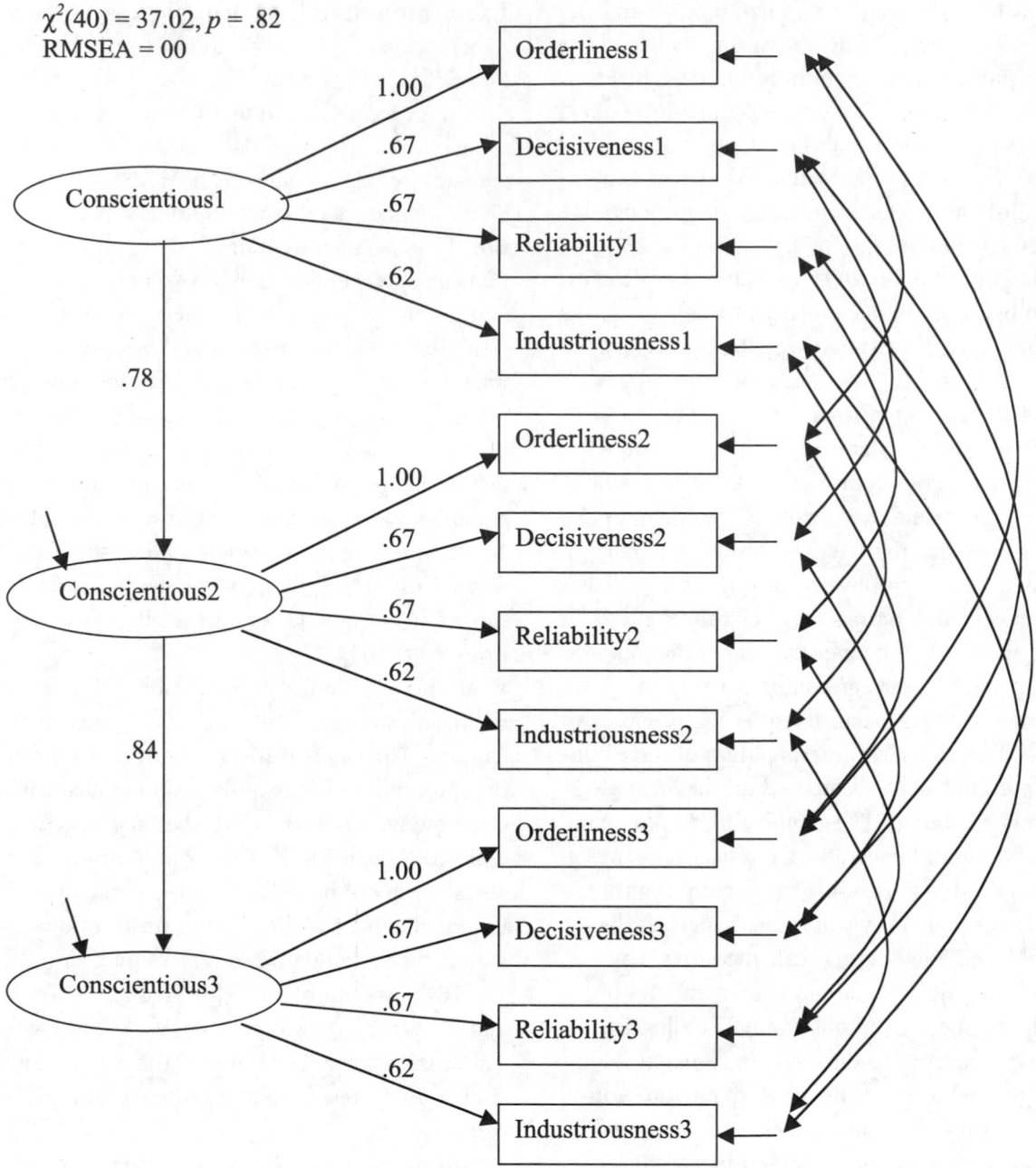

$\chi^2(40) = 37.02, p = .82$
RMSEA = 00

FIGURE 21.1. Autoregressive model.

each pair of time periods removes any influence of the stability of these systematic components of the residual. Otherwise, the estimate of the stability for the conscientiousness factor would be confounded by these unique components associated with each of the facets.

We estimated three alternative models to illustrate features of the model depicted in Figure 21.1. First, we investigated the effect of correlating the uniquenesses. Model (a), which included the correlated uniquenesses, showed a substantially better fit to the data, $\chi^2(40) = 35.1$, *ns*, RMSEA = .00, than Model (b), in which the correlations between the uniquenesses are deleted, $\chi^2(52) = 500.2, p < .0001$, RMSEA = .22). An RMSEA of .05 or less is typically taken as evidence of a close-fitting model. This result indicates that the correlated uniquenesses need to be

included in the model. Second, we investigated the effect of constraining the factor loadings to be constant over time. Model (c), which is portrayed in Figure 21.1, also resulted in an acceptable fit to the data, $\chi^2(46) = 37.0$, ns, RMSEA = .00. The difference in fit between Models (a) and (c) may be directly compared based on their respective χ^2 and *df* values using the likelihood ratio test (Bentler & Bonett, 1980), $\chi^2(6) = 1.9$, ns. Given that the fit of the two models to the data does not differ, Model (c) is preferred both because it has fewer parameters (parsimony) and more importantly, because it simplifies interpretation by guaranteeing that the conscientiousness construct has the same units at each measurement wave.

Cross-lagged autoregressive models may be used to investigate the ability of one longitudinal series to predict another series. For example, Aneshensel, Frerichs, and Huba (1984) measured several indicators of illness and several indicators of depression every 4 months. The two constructs were modeled as latent factors. Moderate stabilities were found for both the illness and depression constructs. The level of depression at Wave *t* consistently predicted the level of illness at Wave *t* + 1, over and above the level of illness at the Wave *t*. In a similar study, Finch (1998) found that social undermining consistently predicted negative affect 1 week later over and above the level of negative affect the previous week. Such lagged effects show both association and temporal precedence, providing support for hypothesized direction of the causal relationship between the two variables (e.g., depression → physical illness). Jöreskog (1979) and Dwyer (1983) presented several useful variants of the basic autoregressive model for longitudinal data. Of importance, clear interpretation of the findings of these models assumes there is *not* systematic change in the level of the series of measures (growth or decline) for each individual over time (Willett, 1988). Curran and Bollen (2001) and McArdle (2001) have proposed models that combine growth and autoregressive components to address this issue.

Trait–State Models

Many important psychological phenomena (e.g., moods) appear to be influenced both by an individual's chronic level (trait) as well as temporary fluctuations from that chronic level (state). Latent trait–state models (Steyer, Ferring, & Schmitt, 1992; Steyer, Schmitt, & Eid, 1999; see Figure 21.2) partition each measure collected at each measurement occasion into three components. First is a component that represents the trait construct measured at a specific time point (denoted Time 1, Time 2, and Time 3 in Figure 21.2). This component is further partitioned into (a) a latent trait factor that characterizes the person's stable general level on the construct of conscientiousness (denoted as Consci in Figure 21.2) and (b) a latent state residual that characterizes temporary (state) effects on the person associated with each measurement wave. Second, the method factor represents the stable influence of the specific measure (here, the measure of each facet of conscientiousness, denoted Order, Decis, Reliab, Indust, respectively). Third, as in previous models, another component reflects random measurement error.

The latent state–trait model shows a good fit to the conscientiousness data, $\chi^2(39) = 31.87$, *ns*, RMSEA = .00). The clear partitioning of the observed scores on the measure into trait, state, measure, and error variance components provides a strong basis for predicting external criteria. For example, the relatively pure measure of the trait of conscientiousness that is estimated can be used to predict conscientiousness-related behaviors such as class attendance or worker productivity. The latent trait–state model can also partition the total amount of variance in the observed scores into trait, state, measurement method, and error variance components (see Steyer et al., 1992). In the present example, 42% of the variance in the observed scores is associated with the stable latent trait factor for conscientiousness.[2] Or, if the researcher were interested in situational effects on conscientiousness (e.g., if midterm exams were given prior to the Week 2 measurement), the proportion of the total variance

---

[2]The instructions emphasized answering based only on the past week's behaviors.

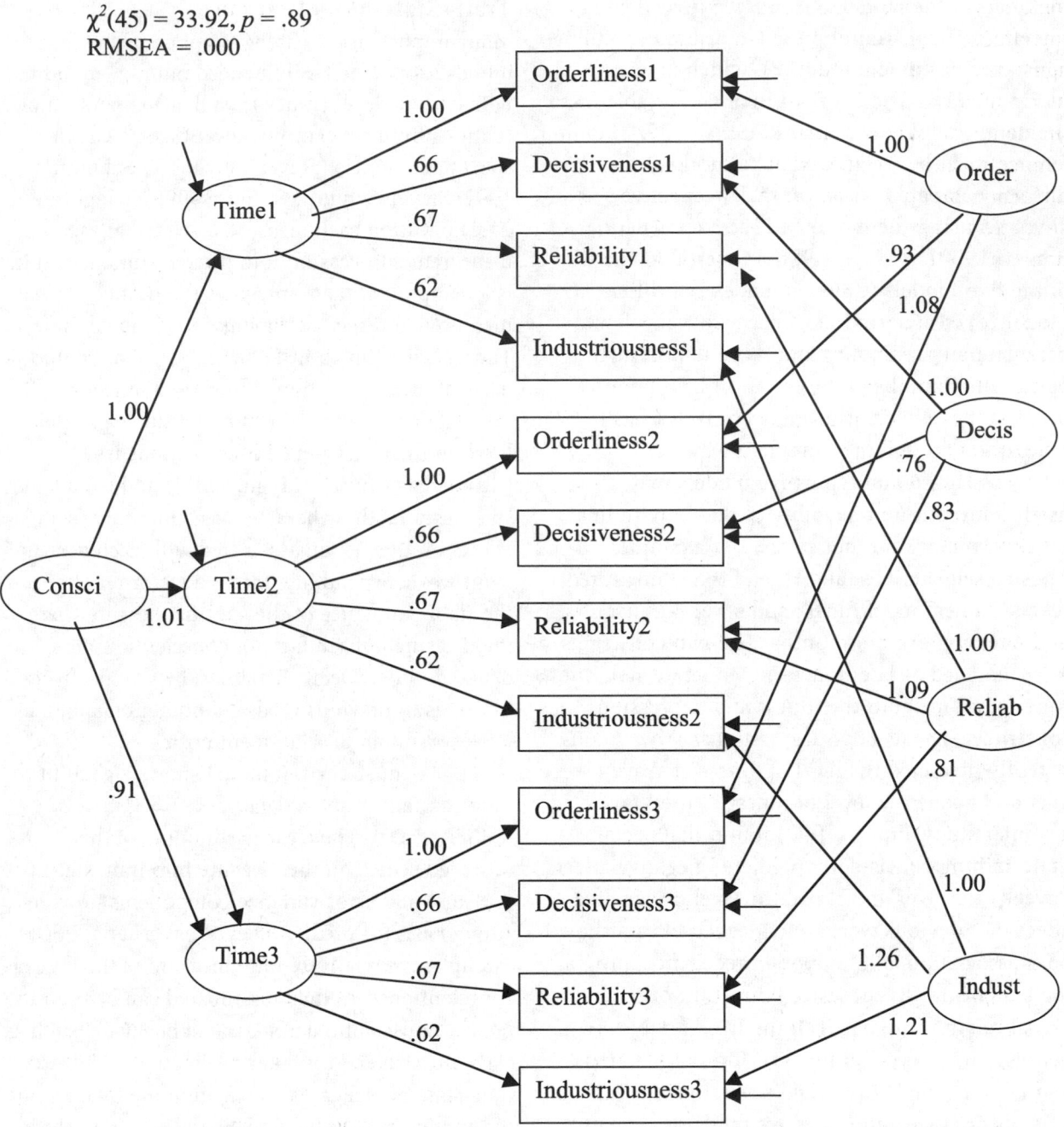

$\chi^2(45) = 33.92, p = .89$
RMSEA = .000

FIGURE 21.2. Latent state–trait model. Consci is the conscientiousness latent construct; Order, Decis (decisiveness), Reliab (reliability), Indust (industriousness) represent the four specific facets of conscientiousness.

in the observed scores associated with the latent state residuals could be computed. Steyer et al. (1992) discussed a variety of potential methods of partitioning the variance to produce estimates of several diverse forms of reliability and stability that may be useful in different research contexts. Steyer et al. (1992) and Kenny and Zautra (2001) compared several variants of the latent trait–state model.

Although the basic latent trait–state model has several important strengths, it also has three limita-

tions. First, like the autoregressive model, the basic state–trait model focuses only on the relative ordering of a set of individuals. Clear interpretation of findings requires there is *not* systematic growth or decline for each individual over time. Otherwise, more complex models that combine growth and trait–state components are required (Tisak & Tisak, 2002). Second, the temporal ordering of the observations is not represented in the analysis. Otherwise stated, the data from any two time periods (e.g., 2 and 3) can be exchanged without affecting the fit or any important features of the model. Third, like multitrait–multimethod models (Eid, 2000; Kenny & Kashy, 1992), latent trait–state models can be difficult to fit with many data sets. Data sets with small state components or small method components can lead to improper solutions. In general, adding more time periods, more measures, and more participants appears to improve estimation. Steyer et al. (1999) present approaches that may be used when there are problems in estimation.

Growth Curve Modeling

In longitudinal studies with three or more measurement waves, growth curve modeling can provide an understanding of individual change (Laird & Ware, 1982; McArdle & Nesselroade, 2003; Muthén & Khoo, 1998). Researchers may study individual growth trajectories and relate variations in the growth trajectories to covariates that vary between individuals. They may also get better estimates of true growth by studying the effects of covariates that vary over time within individuals. We use the hierarchical modeling framework here to describe the models.

Conceptually, growth curve modeling has two levels denoted as Level 1 (within individuals) and Level 2 (between individuals). At Level 1 we describe each individual's growth using a regression equation. We focus here on the simplest model, linear growth. With linear growth we express the measure Y_{ti} of an individual i at time t as the sum of the individual's linear growth plus a residual ε_{ti} that represents random error at occasion t,

$$Y_{ti} = \alpha_i + \beta_i x_{ti} + \varepsilon_{ti} \quad , t = 1, 2, ..., T \quad (1)$$

In Equation (1), x_{ti} is the time-related variable such as age, measurement wave, or the elapsed time following the occurrence of an event (e.g., surgery). Note that x_{ti} has two subscripts, t and i, indicating it varies both over measurement occasions and across individuals. The intercept α_i represents the predicted level of Individual i on the measure when $x_{ti} = 0$. When time is scaled so that the first measurement occasion equals 0, α_i may be interpreted as the individual "initial status" or level on Y at the beginning of the study. The slope β_i represents the individual growth rate, the change in Y per unit of time. The individual intercept α_i and the individual slope β_i form a pair of growth parameters that characterize the individual trajectory. Figure 21.3 shows hypothetical linear growth curves of three individuals on a variable Y over time. Note that the individuals start at different levels (different α_is) and grow at different rates (different β_is). Other time-varying covariates may be added as predictors to the Level 1 equation.

For example, suppose we collected daily measures of stressful events w_{ti} and well-being Y_{ti} in each patient for 10 days immediately following minor surgery. We can add the time-varying covariate w_{ti} to Equation (1). For patient i, we now have

$$Y_{ti} = \alpha_i + \beta_i x_{ti} + \pi_i w_{ti} + \varepsilon_{ti} \quad , t = 1, 2, ..., 10 \quad (2)$$

α_i is patient i's predicted well-being (initial status) at the completion of surgery; β_i is the rate of increase in well-being (slope). These parameters characterize each individual's growth function over and above the temporal disturbances accounted for by the time-varying covariate w_{ti}. π_i is the individually varying partial regression coefficient relating stress to well-being for Individual i, and ε_{ti} is the residual. Thus, Level 1 describes the change within individuals.

In the simplest Level 2 model, we assume that the set of α_is and the set of β_is are normally distributed. The means and variances of these growth parameters are estimated at Level 2. The means of the growth parameters allow us to obtain a mean trajectory for the whole group. To the extent that the variances of the growth parameters are greater than 0, there are differences between individuals in

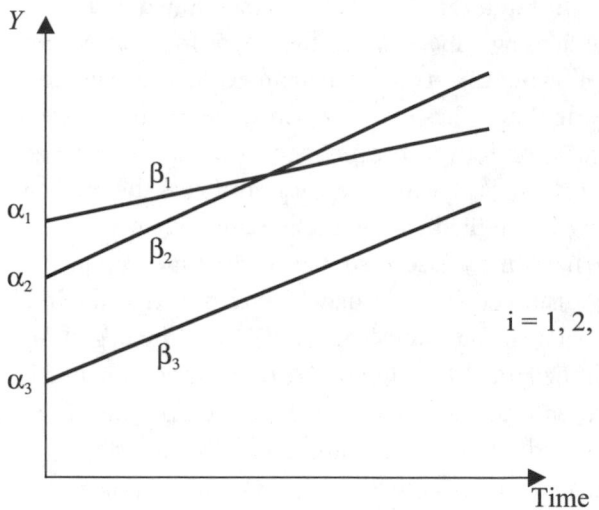

FIGURE 21.3. Growth trajectories for three individuals.

the growth patterns over time. With variation across individuals, the two individual growth parameters, α_i and β_i, can become outcome variables to be regressed on *time-invariant* individual background covariate variables. These background variables can be experimental treatment conditions (e.g., presurgical psychological intervention versus no intervention) or stable individual difference variables (e.g., neuroticism). The Level 2 equations for the intercepts and the slopes may be expressed as

$$
\begin{aligned}
\alpha_i &= \alpha_0 + \gamma_\alpha Z_i + \delta_{\alpha i} \\
\beta_i &= \beta_0 + \gamma_\beta Z_i + \delta_{\beta i}
\end{aligned}
\tag{3}
$$

where α_0 is the grand intercept (mean intercept across N individuals), β_0 is the grand slope (mean slope across N individuals), and Z_i is the time-invariant covariate (e.g., neuroticism) and $\delta_{\alpha i}$ and d_{bi} are the residuals associated with α_i and β_i respectively; and γ_α and γ_β are the regression coefficients. Besides the linear growth parameters, additional Level 2 equations may be written to account for variation in the Level 1 regression coefficients for the time-varying variables (e.g., daily stress) if these are included in the model. Thus, at Level 2, we model between individual differences in the values of the growth parameters (intercept and slope) and the regression coefficients for the time-varying variables.

Although we have focused on linear growth, more complex patterns including quadratic growth, growth to an asymptote, and other nonlinear forms of growth may be modeled as the number of measurement waves increases (Cudeck, 1996; Singer & Willett, 2002). In addition, different time-related metrics may be of focal interest such as age or elapsed time since an event (e.g., surgery) or the beginning of a developmental period (see Biesanz et al., 2003).

Standard growth curve models can also be estimated using structural equation modeling (Muthén & Khoo, 1998; Willett & Sayer, 1994). Mehta and West (2000) noted that the two approaches can both typically be used and produce the same results, but that some applications may be more amenable to one of the approaches. The hierarchical modeling approach discussed in this section may be more flexible in representing some nonlinear forms of growth. In contrast, the structural equation modeling approach often has more flexibility in modeling the measurement structure using multiple indicators of a construct at each time point and in modeling complex relationships between multiple series. Within the structural equation approach, features of autoregressive models (Curran & Bollen, 2001; McArdle, 2001) and features of latent trait–state models (Tisak & Tisak, 2002) can be combined with growth models.

The modeling of change using growth curve modeling described earlier calls for several very strong assumptions regarding the measurement scale. First, the repeated measurements must be made on at least an interval-level scale. Otherwise, the form of growth will be confounded by changes in the size of the measurement unit at each point in the scale. Second, there must be measurement invariance over time—the relationship between the observed measures and the underlying construct must remain constant with the passage of time. For example, items such as pushing and biting might measure physical aggression at age 4. However, at age 16 these items will no longer adequately reflect aggression, precluding meaningful study of change over time. On the other hand, if we measure aggression at age 16 with items like "threaten with gun or knife" and "hit with objects," then the meaning of

the construct has changed. (See Patterson, 1995, on developmental change in constructs.) In such cases in which the items on instruments do change over the course of the study (e.g., different items on a measure of math ability in first and fourth grades), there is a need to ensure that the meaning of the construct remains the same. Educational researchers have been successful to some extent in the area of assessing skills and knowledge using vertical equating of overlapping test forms of increasing difficulty levels (see section on vertical equating). Similar techniques are not as well developed for longitudinal studies of psychological and affective constructs.

Other Longitudinal Models

Our emphasis has been on several of the more common new longitudinal models for stability and change using continuous latent variables. New models for other forms of data have also been developed. Space considerations did not permit us to consider longitudinal modeling of discrete latent classes (Langeheine, 1994; Lanza, Flaherty, & Collins, 2003), combinations of continuous and discrete latent variables (Muthén, in press), longitudinal models for single subjects (Browne & Zhang, in press; West & Hepworth, 1991), or the linear logistic model with relaxed assumptions for measuring change (Fischer & Formann, 1982).

MEASUREMENT OF CHANGE

For researchers who are interested in quantitative change over time rather than (rank order) stability, the measurements need to be made on a common scale that achieves at least an interval level of measurement over time. This property characterizes many physical measurements such as height, blood pressure, or counts of behaviors. However, this property often does not characterize psychological measures of attitudes and traits. Attempts to measure abilities, attitudes, or traits usually rely on the collective strength of responses to individual items within instruments. In the measurement of psychological traits, the response to each item is typically assessed by either using a dichotomous response (e.g., "I enjoy parties"—true or false) or a Likert-type response scale that is essentially ordinal (e.g., "How much do you like parties?" rated on a 5-point scale from "not at all" to "very much"). In current research practice the same instrument is administered at each measurement wave, and the total scale score at each wave is used to model change. However, this practice involves several important untested assumptions: (a) the scale is unidimensional, (b) the total scores yields interval level measurements, (c) the same total score would indicate the same construct level over time, and (d) there is measurement invariance over time. These assumptions are seldom checked or addressed.

If the measurements are not made on an interval scale, equal differences in scores over time at different levels of the construct may *not* mean the same amount of change in the construct. The measurement unit stretches or shrinks as a function of the level that is measured—the rubber ruler problem. Desirable interval scale properties can usually be achieved through careful scale construction and through successfully applying measurement models.

External Scale Construction: Rasch and Item Response Theory Modeling

Several methods exist for developing strong measurement scales separately from the longitudinal model of stability or change (see Rost & Walter, chap. 18, this volume). These methods can be applied to dichotomous or ordinal data. The scales can be developed using the same or a different data set from that used to test the longitudinal model. The Rasch model (1-parameter; Rasch, 1960; Wright & Masters, 1982; Wright & Stone, 1979) provides interval-level measurement, and the 2-parameter logistic Item Response Theory model (IRT; see Embretson & Reise, 2000) provides a good approximation to interval-level measurement when the data are consistent with the model. These are probabilistic measurement models. For dichotomous items, equal changes in the underlying latent construct correspond to equal changes in the log of the odds of endorsing an item, for any level of the latent trait.

For items with multiple ordered response categories (1 = "not at all," 2, 3, 4, 5 = "very much) that typify Likert-type scales, there are extensions of both the Rasch and the 2-parameter IRT models.

A variety of polytomous models for multiple-ordered response categories have been developed. The Rasch extensions include the partial credit model (Masters, 1982) and the rating scale model (Andrich, 1978). The 2-parameter IRT extensions include the graded response model (Samejima, 1969) and the modified graded response model (Muraki, 1990). The basics of the Rasch model and its extensions are described and illustrated by Rost and Walter (chap. 18, this volume). Drasgow and Chuah (chap. 7, this volume) explain and illustrate the 2- and 3-parameter models in detail. In each of these models, there are multiple probability curves for each item, one for each response category. These probabilities provide information on how each category functions relative to other categories within an item. These models produce good approximations of interval level score estimates of the underlying construct while treating the response categories as ordinal. The interval level score estimates produced can be used to model longitudinal change.

Simultaneous Longitudinal and Measurement Modeling

Structural equation modeling permits simultaneous modeling of the measurement structure and the longitudinal model of stability or change. In the measurement portion of the model, each latent construct is hypothesized to be error free and normally distributed on an interval scale. The structural part represents the relationships between the latent constructs. This modeling approach can also be extended to two or more ordered categories (Muthén, 1984). This approach assumes that each dichotomous or ordered categorical measured variable is characterized by an underlying normally distributed continuous variable. For each measured variable, $c-1$ thresholds are estimated that separate each of the c categories (e.g., one threshold for a dichotomous variable). If the assumptions are met, then Muthén's approach will provide estimates of the underlying factors that approximate an interval-level scale of measurement. Indeed, Takane and de Leeuw (1987) have shown that 2-parameter IRT models and confirmatory factor models are identical for dichotomous items under certain conditions. Unfortunately, large sample sizes (e.g., 500–1,000

or more cases) are often required for the appropriate use of structural equation modeling approach to categorical data. Newer estimation methods may offer promise of adequate estimation with smaller sample sizes (Muthén & Muthén, 2004). However, separate scale development using external methods such as Rasch or IRT modeling will often be more efficient.

MEASUREMENT INVARIANCE ACROSS TIME

In cross-sectional research, a major concern is addressing the issue of measurement invariance across groups. Does a set of items measure cognitive ability equally well in African-American and Caucasian populations? Does a standard measure of extroversion or depression capture the same underlying construct in the United States and China? Similar issues can arise in longitudinal research when measures are collected over extended periods of time. Does a standard measure of childhood extroversion assess the same construct at age 12 and age 18? If change over time is to be studied, the same construct must be measured at each time point. Measurement invariance may be established within either (a) the Rasch/IRT or (b) the confirmatory factor analysis approaches.

Measurement invariance implies that the score on the instrument is independent of any variables other than the person's value on the theoretical construct of interest. To illustrate how measurement invariance might fail, consider a test of mathematics ability for intermediate school students. Suppose that the following item were devised: "A baseball player has 333 at bats and 111 hits. What is his batting average?" Although this item clearly reflects mathematical ability, it also reflects knowledge about baseball—knowledge that is more likely to be found in male than female students with the same level of mathematics ability. Such items that exhibit a systematic relationship with group characteristics after controlling for the construct level are said to be functioning differentially across groups. Differential item functioning (DIF) thus contributes to measurement *non*-invariance across groups. Similarly, if measurement invariance holds across time, then the probability of a set of observed scores

occurring is conditional only on the level of the latent construct and is independent of any variable related to time:

$$P(\mathbf{Y} \mid \theta, \mathbf{X}_t) = P(\mathbf{Y} \mid \theta),$$

where Y is the set of observed scores, θ is the level of latent construct and X_t is the set of time-related variables such as age and testing occasion. For example, an item such as, "Did you make your bed this morning?" might be a good measure of the orderliness facet of conscientiousness for college students at the beginning of the semester, but not during exam weeks. Only when measurement invariance over time is established can we conclude that the measurement scale for the underlying construct remains the same. Of importance, measurement invariance allows us to conclude that changes in scores are the result of changes over time on the construct of interest rather than on other characteristics of the instrument or the participants.

Rasch and IRT Approaches

For unidimensional constructs with dichotomous or ordered categorical items, the Rasch model and the 2-parameter logistic IRT model are commonly used (see Embretson & Reise, 2000). The Rasch model has one parameter (b_j) for each item representing its difficulty (level), whereas the two-parameter IRT model has both a difficulty parameter (b_j) and a discrimination (slope) parameter (a_j) for each item. Assessment of measurement invariance across time involves checking that the item parameters a_j and b_j have not changed over time. If the data fit the Rasch model, $a_j = 1$ for each item so only the set of b_js will be checked. For measures with multiple ordered categories, the item parameters corresponding to each possible response category will need to be checked for each item. These procedures work very well for unidimensional scales that are often developed for the assessment of abilities. Unfortunately, current measures of many psychological constructs (e.g., many attitudes; traits) are very often multidimensional, consisting of several underlying factors or a major factor and several minor factors. The use of Rasch and IRT procedures for the assessment of measurement invariance is not as well studied for multidimensional psychological scales.

Confirmatory Factor Analysis Approaches

When data are continuous and there are one or more underlying factors, confirmatory factor analysis procedures may be used to test measurement invariance. Meredith (1993) considered the issue of measurement invariance across groups, and he developed a sequence of model comparisons that provide a close parallel to the IRT approach. Widaman and Reise (1997) presented a clear description of these procedures, and Meredith and Horn (2001) have recently extended this approach to testing measurement invariance over time. In brief, a hierarchical set of models with increasingly strict constraints are compared. First, a baseline model is estimated. In this model, the value of the factor loadings of each measured variable on an underlying construct may differ over time. For example, consider the model of conscientiousness (Figure 21.1) discussed in the prior section on "examining stability: autoregressive models." Suppose we had allowed the factor loadings to vary over time (Model 1) and this model fit the data. Such a model, known as a configural model, would suggest that similar constructs were measured at each measurement wave. In contrast, imagine that although the single factor of conscientiousness fit the data adequately at Wave 1, over the course of a longer-term study the conscientiousness factor split into two separate factors—one factor representing orderliness and reliability and a second factor representing decisiveness and industriousness. Such a result would indicate the fundamental nature of the conscientiousness factor had changed over time (failure of configural invariance), making difficult any interpretation of stability or change in conscientiousness.

When the configural model fits the data (as in our earlier example), we can investigate questions related to the rank-order stability of the general construct. Note, however, that the conscientiousness latent construct (factor) at each measurement wave would not necessarily be characterized by a scale with the same units. To establish that the units are identical over time, we need to show that the factor loadings are equal across time. As we saw in the model represented in Figure 21.1, the imposition of equal factor loadings did not significantly affect the fit of the model in our example. Thus, our study of stability was improved by

our ability to correlate constructs measured using the same units at each measurement wave.

Finally, suppose that we wish to establish that the scale of the construct has both the same units and the same origin over time (i.e., interval level of measurement). Recall that this condition must be met for proper growth modeling. To illustrate differences in the origin, consider that the Celsius and Kelvin temperature scales have identical units (1 degree difference is identical on both scales). However, the origin (0 degrees) of the Celsius scale is the freezing point of water, whereas the origin of the Kelvin scale is absolute 0 (where molecular motion stops). To establish that the origins are identical, we need to consider the level of each measured variable (mean structure) in addition to the covariance structure. If the origin of the scale does not change over time, then the intercept (the predicted value on each measured variable when the level of the underlying construct $\theta = 0$) also must not change over time. If the fit of a model in which the intercepts for each measured variable are allowed to vary over time does not significantly differ from that of a more restricted model in which the each variable's intercept is constrained to be equal over time, this condition is established.[3] If this condition can be met, then the level of measurement invariance over time necessary for proper growth curve modeling has been established. Widaman and Reise (1997) discussed still more restrictive forms of measurement invariance that can be useful in some specialized applications. Muthén (1996), Mehta et al. (2004), and Millsap and Tein (in press) present extensions of the confirmatory factor analysis approach that can be used to establish measurement invariance for multidimensional constructs measured by dichotomous or ordered categorical measures.

VERTICAL EQUATING: ADDRESSING AGE-RELATED CHANGES IN ITEM CONTENT

The items required to measure a latent construct can change as participants age. In educational research children are expected to acquire knowledge and learn appropriate skills. For example, in a test of mathematical proficiency, items related to multiplication may be needed in third grade, whereas items related to fractions may be needed in sixth grade. The test forms for each grade level must be equated onto a single common metric to measure educational progress. Vertical equating must be achieved externally prior to any longitudinal modeling of the data.

Vertical equating uses Rasch models or the 2-parameter IRT models to calibrate tests onto a single common "long" interval scale. This "long" scale covers the full range of proficiency as assessed using easier tests in the lower grade levels and more difficult tests in the higher grade levels. The equating of test forms is made possible by embedding common item sets in the test forms. The common item sets serve as "anchor" or "link" items for the equating. Any change in the probability of getting each item correct should only occur if there is a change in the individual's level on the underlying construct; otherwise, the item is showing DIF as a function of grade level. For example, an item that is assessing problem-solving skills at Grade 2 but is just assessing routine skills at Grade 4 may very likely show DIF. Even though the wording of the item is identical, this item functions differently across the two different grades and will not make a good link item. Thus, for unidimensional constructs vertical equating combines testing for DIF and establishing measurement invariance of link items and linking scales (see Embretson & Reise, 2000). Applications of these equating procedures permit the development of computerized adaptive tests (see Drasgow & Chuah, chap. 7, this volume) that select the set of items that most precisely assess each participant's level on the underlying latent construct θ. Unfortunately, vertical equating of multidimensional constructs is difficult to achieve because the rate or form of growth may vary across dimensions so that common item set(s) that adequately represent each of the dimensions cannot always be constructed.

[3]The full confirmatory factor analysis model including mean structure can be expressed as $Y = v + \Lambda\eta + \varepsilon$. Y is the p x 1 vector of observed scores, v is p x 1 vector of intercepts, η is the m x 1 vector of latent variables, Λ is the p x m matrix of the loadings of the observed scores on the latent variables η, and ε is the p x 1 vector of residuals. For modeling longitudinal measurement, a model in which both Λ and v are constrained to be equal over time must fit the data.

In contrast to research on measures of educational progress and abilities, far less attention has been given to equating psychological constructs like traits and attitudes across age. Typically, the same instrument is used at each measurement wave to assess individuals on a construct of interest. This practice is often appropriate when the time spanning the study is relatively short and the study does not cross different periods of development. If the reading level and the response format are appropriate for the participants over the duration of the study, serious age-related problems with the instrument are unlikely to occur. However, when a measure crosses developmental periods, for example, in a study that follows subjects from adolescence to young adulthood, the instrument may not capture the same construct adequately as subjects mature. Some items may need to be phased out over time while other items are being phased in. What results are instruments that are not identical, but that have overlapping items for different developmental periods. For example, the Achenbach Youth Self-Report externalizing scale (YSRE) was developed for youth up to age 18 (Achenbach & Edelbrock, 1987), and the Young Adult Self-Report externalizing scale (YASRE) was developed for young adults over age 18. Each measure has approximately 30 items, yet only 19 of these items are in common across the two forms. If participants were administered the two forms of the YSRE during a longitudinal study that crossed these developmental periods, the two forms would need to be equated onto a common scale if growth is to be studied. Such vertical equating of psychological measures is rare.

Many of the standard measures used in psychology were designed for cross-sectional studies to examine differences between individuals; they were not developed for the study of change within an individual across time. As an illustration, many traditional instruments used for research in developmental psychological are normed for the different ages. Norm-referenced metrics do *not* comprise an interval scale and are often not suitable for capturing change. One example of a norm-referenced metric is the grade-equivalent scale (e.g., reading at a fifth-grade level) used in measuring reading achievement. Seltzer, Frank, and Bryk (1994) compared growth models of reading achievement using the grade equivalent metric and using interval-level scores based on Rasch calibration. They found that the results were very sensitive to the metrics used.

Theoretically, structural equation modeling approaches could also be used for vertical equating. However, McArdle, Grimm, Hamagami, and Ferrer-Caja (2002) noted that such efforts to date with continuous measures have typically involved untestable assumptions and have often led to estimation difficulties. At the same time, studies to date have not carefully established common pools of items (or subscales) that could be used to link the different forms of the instrument. Mehta et al. (2004) addressed vertical equating of ordinal items.

CONCLUSION

Researchers have increasingly recognized the value of longitudinal designs for the study of stability and change, for understanding developmental processes, and for establishing the direction of hypothesized causal effects. Researchers have increasingly gone beyond the minimal two-wave longitudinal design and now often include several measurement waves. These multiwave designs potentially permit the researcher to move beyond traditional analyses such as correlation, regression, and analysis of variance and use promising newer analysis approaches such as the autoregressive, latent state–trait models, and growth curve models presented in this chapter.[4] These analyses can potentially provide better answers to traditional questions in longitudinal research. They also permit researchers to raise interesting new questions that were rarely, if ever, considered within the traditional analytic frameworks. For example, latent trait–state models can provide definitive information about the role of states and traits, a classic problem in personality measurement. Growth curve models permit researchers to identify variables that explain individual differences

---

[4]Ferrer and McArdle (2003) and McArdle and Nesselroade (2003) provide a review of these and several other recently developed longitudinal models that could not be included in this chapter because of space limitations.

in growth trajectories, a question that was not raised until the development of these models.

Longitudinal researchers, like researchers in many other areas of psychology (see Aiken, West, Sechrest, & Reno, 1990) have often paid minimal attention to measurement issues. And historically, such lack of attention could be justified because the traditional measurement practices were "good enough" to provide adequate tests of the hypotheses. Answering questions within a traditional null hypothesis testing framework about the simple existence of a difference between means or of a correlation does not require sophisticated measurement. Ordinal level measurement provides sufficient information. And statistical methods like ANOVA and regression that were designed for interval-level scales have proven to be relatively robust even when applied to ordinal scales. So long as the assumptions of the procedure (residuals are independent, normally distributed, and have constant variance) are met, the traditional measures produce reasonable answers (Cliff, 1993). And researchers could compensate for the loss of statistical power associated with the use of ordinal measurement by moderate increases in sample size. However, psychologists have begun to ask more complex questions about the size and the form of relationships. What is the magnitude of the effect of treatment? How much do boys versus girls gain in proficiency in mathematics achievement from Grade 1 to 3? Does the acquisition of vocabulary in children between 12 and 24 months show a linear or exponential increase? Proper answers to such questions require more sophisticated measurement.

There is an intimate relationship between theory, methodological design, statistical analysis, and measurement. Many traditional questions about the *stability* of constructs and the relationship of one construct to another over time can be adequately answered even without achieving interval-level measurement. Some added benefits do come from interval-level measurement: More powerful statistical tests and a more definitive interpretation of exactly what construct is or is not stable (and to what degree) can be achieved. But, in contrast, as psychologists ask increasingly more sophisticated theoretical questions about *change* over time and

use more complex statistical analyses that are capable of providing answers to these questions, interval-level measurement will be required. The exemplary initial demonstrations of the newer statistical models for modeling change have deliberately used interval-level measures. To cite two examples, Cudeck (1996) reported nonlinear models of growth in physical measures (e.g., height) and number of correct responses in learning. McArdle and Nesselroade (2003) emphasized growth models using a Rasch-scaled cognitive measure (the Woodcock–Johnson measure of intelligence). As these newer statistical models of growth are applied to current measures of psychological characteristics (e.g., attitudes, traits), the limitations of many current measures will become more apparent. For example, how can researchers distinguish between linear growth and growth to an asymptote if they cannot be confident that measurements have been made on an interval scale? Evidence of measurement quality traditionally cited in reports of instrument development—adequate coefficient alpha, test–retest correlation, and correlations with external criteria—will not be sufficient for longitudinal researchers who wish to model growth using the newer statistical models that demand interval-level measurement.

In this chapter we have emphasized four features of longitudinal measurement for psychological characteristics. These features can be viewed as desiderata that can help ensure that the measurement of constructs over time is adequate for the study of growth and change. These desiderata can be achieved using Rasch or IRT approaches for dichotomous or ordered categorical items and confirmatory factor analysis procedures for continuous items.

1. Scales developed to measure the construct of interest should ideally be unidimensional. In cross-sectional studies, the use of scales with more than one underlying dimension has led to considerable complexity in the interpretation of the results of studies using these scales. Although multidimensional scales may be used in longitudinal studies, interpretation will be challenging because each of the underlying dimensions may change at different rates over time.

2. Scales should attempt to achieve an interval level of measurement. The same numerical difference at different points on the scale should indicate the same amount of change in the underlying construct.

3. Measurement invariance over time should be established to ensure that the construct has a stable meaning. Each of the items on the instrument should measure the same construct at each measurement wave. The goal is to produce measures that assess only change on the construct and not differential functioning of items as their meaning changes over time.

4. Measures should use items and response formats that are appropriate for the age or grade level of the participants. The different forms of the measure must be linked and equated onto a single common scale. This practice is commonly used in educational research where procedures for vertical equating of measures containing both different and overlapping items have been well developed. For psychological measures, this issue of externally developing age-appropriate measures will often arise in longer duration studies that cross different developmental periods.

Achieving these desiderata will provide a different degree of challenge for different areas of longitudinal research in psychology. Some existing areas such as the study of physical growth and the growth of cognitive abilities have long used measures that meet these desiderata. Emerging areas will need to ensure that they address these issues as they develop new measurement scales. And in many other existing areas researchers will need to rescale existing instruments to develop measures that more adequately meet these desiderata. But, in each case, there will be a clear payoff. Researchers will have a substantially enhanced ability to ask and properly answer interesting new questions about change in important psychological constructs.

PART IV

APPLIED MULTIMETHOD RESEARCH

CHAPTER 22

USING MULTIPLE METHODS IN PERSONALITY PSYCHOLOGY

Brent W. Roberts, Peter Harms, Jennifer L. Smith, Dustin Wood, and Michelle Webb

In many ways, Campbell and Fiske's (1959) article on multitrait–multimethod (MTMM) approaches to construct validity has stood like a Platonic ideal for personality psychologists since its publication. In the ideal study, and scientific world, our constructs should converge in a robust and coherent fashion across diverse methods. Moreover, we should all aspire to use multiple methods in both validating our measures and in investigating our ideas. Interestingly, that Platonic ideal is not realized as often as expected. If one looks closely at the empirical literature in personality psychology, the expectation that abstract constructs should converge across methods is seldom met at the level implied in the original article. This is not to argue that the Platonic ideal is not appropriate. Rather, one of the major points we would like to make in this chapter is that the ideal of the MTMM approach is often taken too literally and is sometimes misused or misinterpreted. Why speak such apostasies? In large part, because we are motivated to reiterate points made, ironically, by Fiske himself (Fiske, 1971).

What are these points? The first is that different methods, or modes as Fiske (1971) described them, are seldom innocuous. Thus, the literal assumption drawn from Campbell and Fiske (1959) that measures of similar constructs drawn from different methods should converge quite robustly is not met as often as we would like. This can lead to erroneous and nihilistic conclusions, such as the construct of interest, like depression, does not exist (e.g., Lewis, 1999). The second point is the assumption that monomethod studies are problematic, inadequate, and should be avoided at all costs. Or, conversely, we should all be doing multimethod studies. This directive fails to consider the empirical fact just mentioned, which is that measures of the same construct seldom correlate highly enough across methods to warrant averaging across methods (Fiske, 1971). What are needed, rather than mandates to perform multimethod studies, are theoretical models that successfully incorporate and explain both the overlap and lack thereof of identical constructs across methods. In our following review, we will attempt to highlight the few theories and empirical examples that have done so.

Our third point is that the focus on multiple methods has inadvertently led to a misguided boondoggle to search for the methodological holy grail—the one method that deserves our ultimate attention. Campbell and Fiske (1959) should not be saddled with full responsibility for this phenomenon beyond the fact that they made it clear that we should be pursuing multiple methods. Leave it to human nature that psychologists would take that idea and try to one up the multimethod approach by finding the ultimate method. Thus, we have had hyperbolic statements made for and against particular methods made since the 1960s. People have argued that self-reports are fundamentally flawed and indistinguishable from response styles (Hogan & Nicholson, 1988; Rorer, 1965), that observer ratings are the seat of personality psychology (Hofstee, 1994), that projective tests do not work (Dawes, 1994), and that we should prioritize online measures over all other techniques (Kahneman, 1999).

As will be seen in the following reviews, none of these positions is defensible.

As the methods used are often tied inextricably to the ideas in a field, we will first provide a working definition of the field of personality psychology that will serve as an organizing heuristic for the subsequent review. As will be seen, this is a true case of form following function, as the content categories within the field of personality are each dominated by specific methods. Then, we review recent multimethod studies within and across the content domains of personality psychology. We will end with some thoughts about particulars of multimethod approaches in personality psychology.

WHAT IS PERSONALITY PSYCHOLOGY?

Personality psychology is the study of the individual differences in traits, motives, abilities, and life stories that make each individual unique (Roberts & Wood, in press). Figure 22.1 depicts the primary units of focus in our definition of personality, which reflects what we describe as the neosocioanalytic perspective on personality. For the purposes of this chapter, we will focus on the left-hand portion of the model and forgo a discussion of social roles and culture, so as to focus on the traditional content and methods of personality psychology. As can be seen in Figure 22.1 there are four "units of analysis" or domains that make up the core of personality: traits, motives, abilities, and narratives. These four domains are intended to subsume most, if not all, of the broad categories of individual differences in personality psychology.

The first domain, traits, subsumes the enduring patterns of thoughts, feelings, and behaviors that distinguish people from one another. Or, more euphemistically speaking, traits refer to what people typically think, feel, or do. In this regard, we view traits from a neo-Allportian perspective (Funder, 1991). From this perspective, traits are real, not fictions of people's semantic memory. They are causal, not just summaries of behavior. Moreover, they are learned. Even with identical genetically determined temperaments, two individuals may manifest different traits because of their unique life experiences.

Much attention has been dedicated to finding a working taxonomy of traits, and many accept the Big Five as a minimal number of domains (Goldberg, 1993). We prefer the Big Seven (Benet-Martinez & Waller, 1997). The Big Seven adds global positive and negative evaluation to the Big Five and is a better representation of the entire trait domain. We prefer this model because, as will be seen later, one distinct characteristic of our definition of personality is the inclusion of reputation as a key element that has been underemphasized in the field. And although people may not describe themselves often with terms such as "evil" or "stunning," they do describe others in these terms.

Motivation, broadly construed, is the second domain of personality and subsumes all the things that people feel are desirable. We define the domain of motives as what people desire, need, and strive for—or perhaps more simply, what people *want* to do. This category includes values, interests, preferences, and goals (e.g., Holland, 1997), in addition to the classic notion of motives and needs (e.g., Murray, 1938). Currently, this domain is less coherent than the trait domain because there is no working taxonomy to organize the units of analysis. Nonetheless, there are striking commonalities across diverse areas, such as motives, goals, values, and interests. For example, in each of these domains of motivation, one can find superordinate themes of agency (desire for status and power) and communion (desire for acceptance and belonging). So, for example, the primary motivational units have been achievement, power (agency) and affiliation (communion; Smith, 1992). The higher-order factors that subsume most value dimensions also reflect power and affiliation (Schwarz & Bless, 1992).

The third domain reflects abilities and the hierarchical models identified in achievement literatures—that is what people *can* do (Lubinski, 2000). Specifically, intelligence is an individual's "entire repertoire of acquired skills, knowledge, learning sets, and generalization tendencies considered intellectual in nature that [is] available at any one period of time" (Humphreys, 1984, p. 243). Two models of abilities prevail. The first decomposes generalized intelligence (*g*), into constituent ele-

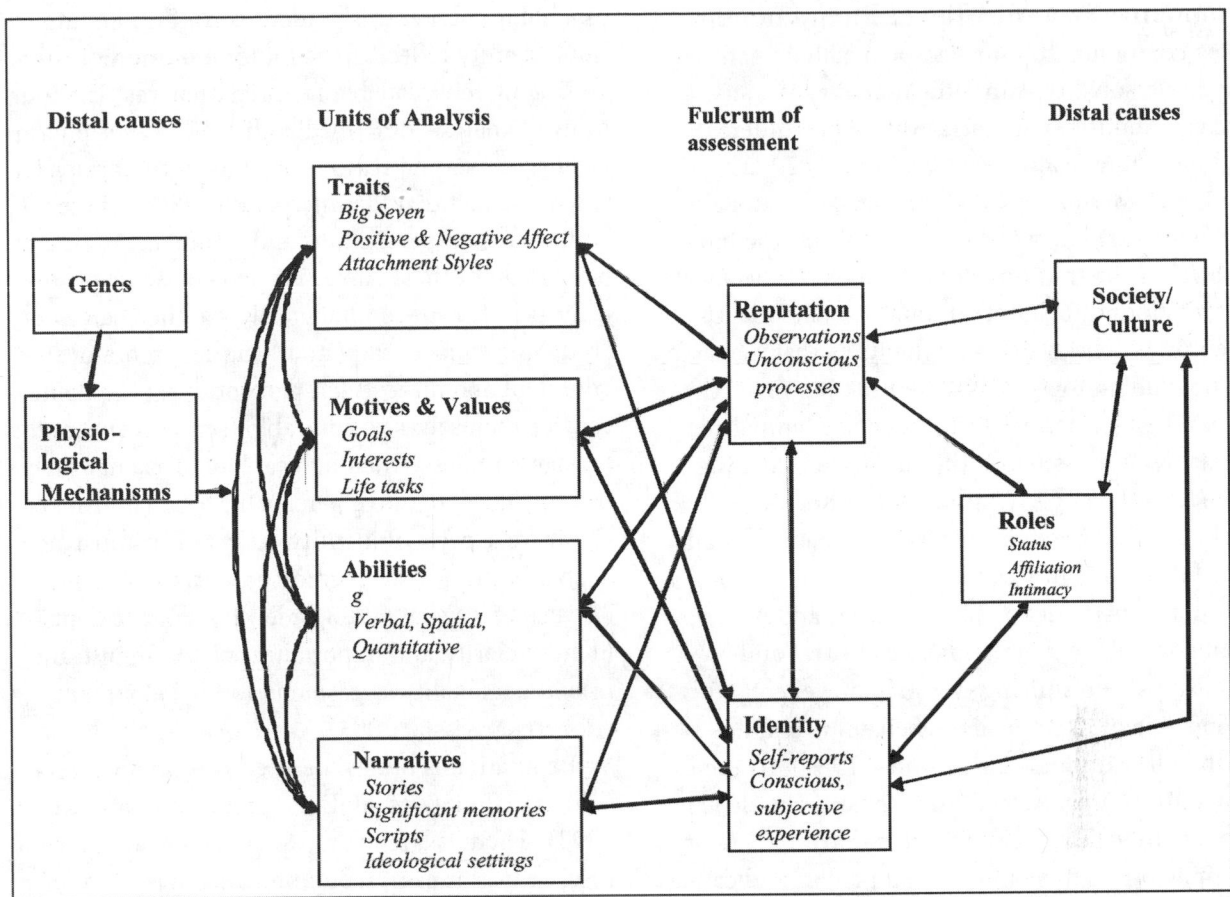

FIGURE 22.1. A neo-socioanalytic topographical model of personality psychology.

ments of verbal, quantitative, and spatial abilities. The second decomposes g into two domains of fluid and crystallized intelligence (Horn & Cattell, 1966). The most radical feature of our system is that individual differences in ability should be a primary focus of personality researchers. How people differ on abilities is clearly important from both pragmatic and theoretical perspectives, and any description of an individual life would be inadequate if it were not included.

The final domain focuses on the content of personal stories and narratives that people use to understand themselves and their environments (McAdams, 1993). A critical point to consider in any model of personality is that although individuals can be classified in terms of traits, abilities, and goals, they often (if not generally) communicate information about themselves quite differently

than a simple nomothetic classification on these characteristics, and one common strategy is the use of illustrative stories (McAdams, 1993) or scripts (de St. Aubin, 1999). People find it very easy to tell stories about themselves, others, and their environments. These narratives in turn help people create meaning and purpose in their lives and, predictability, in the events they observe and experience and provide explanations of how people have come to be in their present circumstances.

The identification of these four domains is cursory and deserves greater attention. Nonetheless, we feel that this is a sufficient start to organizing the units of analysis found within personality psychology and, more clearly than other systems, identifies what we study and, in part, the methods we use to study individuals.

Personality Is a Multilevel Phenomenon

A key component of our neosocioanalytic perspective on personality is that the domains of traits, motives, abilities, and narratives can be differentiated in hierarchical terms (see Hooker, 2002; Hooker & McAdams, 2003; Mayer, 1995; Roberts & Pomerantz, in press). For example, at the broadest level of the trait domain one finds the personality traits found in standard omnibus personality inventories. These are often the traits that make up the now ubiquitous measures of the Big Five. The midlevel of the continuum can be conceptualized by narrow traits, such as the subfacets of the Big Five (Roberts, Bogg, Walton, Chernyshenko, & Stark, 2004). These constructs are broader than discrete behaviors but less broad than traits, as they are often constrained to specific roles and interpersonal contexts (e.g., relationships, work, and friendships). Presumably, these midlevel constructs are more stable than discrete behaviors and less stable than broad traits (e.g., Conley, 1984). At the most narrow level, we find the constituent elements of traits: thoughts, feelings, and behaviors. So, for example, one can be a depressed person, indicating a broad generalizable pattern of depressed affect across time and situation, yet experience different daily moods or states that do not correspond directly to one's trait level.

The hierarchical structuring of each domain of personality adds another layer of methods on top of the methods typically identified within personality psychology (see following). So, not only can one assess personality through global ratings of personality traits, but also through daily mood ratings or frequencies of behaviors. Or, similarly, one could assess a person's motivations through broad ratings of values and interests or the relevant actions they take in their lives, such as exercising and eating well as manifestations of valuing health. The information gleaned from these different levels constitutes different methods that are partially overlapping, yet distinct in important ways.

The Methodological and Conceptual Fulcrum: Identity and Reputation

According to our conceptualization of personality, the components of personality are manifest in two psychological media: the identity and the reputation. Identity reflects the sum total of opinions that are cognitively available to a person across the four units of analysis described earlier. We use the term *identity* for several reasons. The most important reason is the fact that identity pertains to both the content of self-perceptions and the meta-cognitive perception of those same self-perceptions. Specifically, people can simultaneously see themselves as "outgoing" and a "carpenter" and feel more or less confident about those self-perceptions. Or, people can see themselves as agreeable (self-percept) and at the same time see their agreeableness as changeable or not (meta-cognitive percept). These latter meta-cognitive aspects of identity, reflected in constructs such as entity versus incremental orientation (Dweck & Leggett, 1988), identity achievement, identity clarity, and importance, play a significant role in personality assessment and development (Roberts & Caspi, 2003).

Reputation is others' perspectives about a person's traits, motives, abilities, and narratives (Craik, 1993). There is a tendency to consider observer ratings, or in this case, reputational ratings, as higher quality than self-reports (Hofstee, 1994). This position holds some merit, as a good assessment of a person's reputation entails asking the opinion of more than one person. Thus, reputational ratings, by their very nature, are often intrinsically more reliable than self-reports because self-reports only entail the opinion of one person. Reputations also guide significant decisions, such as whether to hire a person, admit them to graduate school, marry them, or simply be their friend.

From our perspective, the self-reports used to assess identity and the observer ratings used to assess reputation both afford unique, yet flawed, information about a person. Certain psychological phenomena, such as feelings of anxiety, may best be accessed through self-reports of identity. On the other hand, determining a person's true levels of agreeableness might be better assessed through the opinion of their friends and relatives who may be less defensive about another person's behavior than their own. Each perspective is potentially defective, in that neither the persons reporting on themselves nor the persons reporting on a friend or relative are

perfectly accurate. Accepting the fact that there are two flawed and distinct ways to understand a person confronts and solves several dilemmas that have plagued personality psychology for decades. For example, it automatically incorporates the fact that people can and do attempt to manage their identity to shape their reputation. People do not always tell the whole truth about themselves to employers, friends, family, and strangers. Self-presentation is a fact in human nature and must be successfully incorporated into any theory of personality and cannot be incorporated without a distinction between identity and reputation (Hogan & Roberts, 2000).

Despite the spirit of the MTMM approach spelled out by Campbell and Fiske (1959), the convergence of self-reports and observer ratings of personality and other phenomena has never been as high as one would hope. In most cases, the convergence averages between .3 and .6 (Funder, 1987). One of the clear conceptual and methodological advances in the field of personality psychology is the Realistic Accuracy Model (RAM; Funder, 1995), which provides a clear theoretical model identifying why identity and reputation are not more highly correlated. In this model, for a strong tie to exist between self-reports and observer ratings four conditions must hold. First, the person being perceived must do something relevant to the psychological dimension of interest. If one wants to judge whether a person is conscientious or not, then it is imperative that they act in a conscientious fashion. Second, the behavior, thought, or feeling must be displayed in a way that it is made available to the observer. Like the proverbial tree falling in an empty forest, private actions do little to influence one's reputation, unless of course they are made public. Third, the observer must detect the behavior. If the person watching does not perceive the behavior, then it might as well not have occurred. Finally, the observed act must be used in an appropriate way. For example, to some people, being clean may be a sign of conscientiousness, whereas to others it may be an indication of neuroticism (e.g., obsessiveness). The extent to which these four conditions hold determines the level of correspondence between self and observers across psychological domains.

The RAM model has implications beyond the relationship between observer/reputation and self-reports/identity. It also applies to the accuracy of self-reports themselves, in the absence of any observer data. For example, we often ask young people to rate themselves on a variety of personality dimensions without ever asking ourselves whether these individuals make good judges of their own personality. For example, a young person may be more than willing to say that they are a good leader, based not on experience but on the hope that someday they will become one (relevance). Or, quite possibly, a person may do something relevant to a trait but not notice it (detection). That is to say, people may not be aware of the importance or relevance of the diagnostic nature of their own behavior. Finally, people may use self-relevant information in idiosyncratic ways that might not conform to how scientists define or understand a nomothetically derived construct. With the exception of the availability stage of the RAM model, it seems that the remaining mechanisms for accuracy can be applied to a number of issues across psychology and personality psychology in particular.

Measures of identity and reputation also do not correlate as high as expected because they are assessed through distinct methods that afford different types of information (see Meyer et al., 2001). Clearly, identity-related assessments permit greater access to internal states and experiences that do not happen or are not visible in the company of others. Reputations, on the other hand, may be less tarnished with self-enhancement tendencies and provide a more objective profile of the information that is publicly available to people or experts (Hofstee, 1994). Reputational information may not be ideal because its validity is undermined by the fact that observers do not have complete access to a person's thoughts, feelings, and behaviors (Spain, Eaton, & Funder, 2000), although conversely, individuals may be unaware of some of their own behavioral tendencies that impact their reputations. Using both identity and reputational information and understanding their relationship is paramount for the science of personality. We will find that the distinction

between identity and reputation runs through each of the domains of personality psychology and often acts as a fulcrum for understanding multimethod studies in personality psychology.

The methods found within the categories of identity and reputation can be further divided into the set of methods that have historically dominated the field of personality psychology. Broadly speaking, methods of assessment in personality psychology can be organized around the acronym "LOTS" (Block, 1993). L stands for life data, or the narrative content of a person's life. O stands for observer data, which can come from peers as well as trained professionals. T stands for test data and typically reflects objective performance measures. And finally, S stands for self-reports, or the subjective inferences we have about ourselves. Typically, S and L data are acquired through self-report techniques of ratings or interviews. T and O data are acquired through observer reports because the tests typically have to be scored by computer or person, and observer ratings clearly must be acquired through peers, family members, or interviewers. These four approaches to assessment subsume the majority of the methodological efforts in personality psychology.

MULTIPLE METHODS WITHIN THE NEOSOCIOANALYTIC FRAMEWORK OF PERSONALITY

A more complete conceptualization of personality psychology points to many ways in which multiple methods can be brought to bear on the study of personality. First, within each domain of traits, motives, abilities, and narratives there are rich methodological traditions and differences. So, for example, traits have often been assessed using self-reports of typical behaviors. Similarly, motives and goals have been assessed from the perspective of the person (e.g., S data) and the psychologist who interprets a projective test such as the TAT (e.g., O data). Cognitive ability has been traditionally assessed through tests of maximal performance (e.g., T data), but can also be assessed via self-reports. In contrast, the narrative approach focuses on open-ended interviews, written responses, or biographical documents to understand individual differences (e.g., L data).

The field of personality typically utilizes diverse methods in an attempt to understand how individuals differ from one another. This also makes studies that combine assessments from each of these disparate domains intrinsically multimethod studies. We highlight examples of these types of studies from each domain.

There are more traditional multimethod approaches within each domain of personality. For example, within the domain of personality traits, evaluating the efficacy of self-reports and observer ratings has been a constant struggle for several decades. Within the motives domain a long-standing controversy has been whether to assess motives using implicit or explicit techniques. We will highlight studies within each domain that have endeavored to use more than one method within domain.

Multiple Methods and Personality Traits

As we noted, one of the persistent disputes in personality psychology is between those who believe that self-reports or observer methods should hold priority in the field. The programmatic efforts of David Funder and his colleagues demonstrate that multiple methods bring multiple perspectives to our efforts to understand the behavioral manifestation of personality traits. For example, people judging the behaviors of others perceive different cues as more relevant to personality than the individuals themselves (Funder & Sneed, 1993).

In other studies, the usefulness of self- and observer ratings of personality have been tested across a variety of domains, including predicting behavior, emotions, and personal negativity. The key to testing the utility of different methods is separating the perspectives of self and observer from the criterion of interest. To do this, Kolar, Funder, and Colvin (1996) set up a study in which the participants provided self-report personality ratings, close acquaintances provided an additional set of personality ratings, and the behavior of participants was coded from videotaped interactions. Thus, the two sets of predictors and criteria did not suffer from methodological overlap. For behavior in a typical social setting, such as meeting a stranger or having a discussion, observer ratings tended to predict behavior better than self-reports (Kolar, Fun-

der, & Colvin, 1996). For example, the correlation between self-reported tendency to initiate humor and actual behavior of initiating humor was .09. In contrast, a composite of the rating of the participants' tendency to initiate humor of two close acquaintances correlated .23 (*p* <.05) with actual behavior. Clearly, what we believe to be a joke is not perceived by others to be funny, which might explain why more people don't laugh at our jokes.

Spain et al. (2000) used a similar design to both replicate Kolar et al. (1996) and extend the design to see if self-reports might be superior in specific settings, such as when one is predicting emotion rather than behavior. Consistent with expectations, self-reported personality ratings were more strongly related to experience sampling assessments of emotion than observer ratings of personality traits. This presumably derives from the fact that emotions are internal events that are not always shared with others as overt, visible behaviors. Their private nature makes them a natural target for self-reports rather than observer ratings. Interestingly, self-reported personality ratings did better than observer ratings of personality in predicting social interactions. For example, self-reported extraversion was correlated with demonstrating social skills, as judged by a set of trained raters, whereas a composite of acquaintance ratings was essentially uncorrelated with the same behavior. In fact, for extraversion, self-reports were twice as good as observer ratings of extraversion in predicting behaviors.

Clearly, based on this research alone, we cannot make any strong generalizations about the superiority of self-reports and observer ratings of personality. This is itself important, as it undermines claims that any given perspective is superior. Studies that actually use multiple methods arrive at more equivocal conclusions. This point is driven home conceptually in a review of the utility of psychological assessment (Meyer et al., 2001). In describing the importance of using multiple methods of personality assessment in clinical settings, Meyer et al. (2001) argued that each method affords a clinician, and by default a researcher, information that may not be strongly overlapping, yet still quite valid. That is to say that asking parents about a child's depression may not result in high agreement with

the child's assessment (e.g., Lewis, 1999). Rather than seeing this as an indictment of either perspective or the construct of interest, we should use both of these perspectives and more (e.g., teachers, peers, siblings) to gauge the nature and progress of the phenomenon. For example, a child may have effectively hidden depression from his or her parents, but not hidden the same phenomena from his or her peers. The discrepancy itself may be both interesting and relevant to the experience of depression, as it might reflect alienation and disengagement from parents that might be a contributing factor to the depression.

The perspective that no single method holds priority extends to arguments against the use of projective measures (Dawes, 1994). For example, in our meta-analysis of the longitudinal consistency of personality trait measures (Roberts & DelVecchio, 2000), we found that projective measures of personality traits were as consistent as observer and self-report methods of personality assessment. Moreover, in particular cases, projective measures outperform other methods, such as in the assessment of dependency (Bornstein, 1999). This does not to provide a ringing endorsement for projective tests, as it is clear that specific projective tests and particular measures derived from projective tests do not demonstrate adequate reliability and validity (Lilienfeld, Wood, & Garb, 2000). Nonetheless, blanket statements that they should not be used are not warranted given the evidence.

The idea that perspectives that differ in terms of their hierarchical relationship to personality provide different, yet equally valid information was demonstrated nicely by a recent study of satisfaction with one's vacation (Wirtz, Kruger, Napa-Scollon, & Diener, 2003). In this study, participants rated how satisfied they thought they would be with an upcoming vacation. In addition, they completed an online assessment of their emotional experiences during the vacation using experience-sampling methods. A week later, they rated how satisfied they were with their vacation. Interestingly, anticipated and retrospective ratings of satisfaction were much higher than online ratings of satisfaction, indicating a slight disjoint between actual experience and higher-order evaluations of that same experience. Moreover, the

different methods yielded different information. The online experiences were strong predictors of the retrospective ratings of satisfaction, which were in turn the most important predictor of wanting to go on a similar vacation in the future. The effect of actual experience on the desire to go on a similar vacation was entirely mediated by the higher-order generalizations about satisfaction, which indicates that the different methods yielded complementary information rather than redundant information. This study counters the argument that online assessments should be prioritized over broader, sometimes retrospective reports of personality (e.g., Kahneman, 1999), as it was the global self-reports that predicted long-term intentions rather than direct, behavioral measures of experience.

Within the trait domain, we find many of the classic arguments about multiple methods, such as the utility of self-reports versus other ratings and newer perspectives manifest in assessing personality across multiple levels of breadth or across different contexts. Consistent with the neosocioanalytic framework that a differentiated conceptualization of personality leads to a multimethod approach, each of these different methods revealed complementary and useful information. What we still lack, of course, are theoretical systems to account for the complementary rather than overlapping nature of the information gleaned from different methods. Systems like the RAM model are a step in the right direction, but more conceptual and theoretical work is needed.

Motives and Goals

Research in the domain of motives has had two major methodological and theoretical schools, which address the study of this broader question in quite different ways. The first school, the need approach to motivation, begins with the assumption that people are often unaware of the fundamental forces that motivate their behavior. The second major school, the goal approach, attempts to understand explicit motives and interests as the means to reach a deeper, underlying understanding of motivation. Need theorists believe that motivation is not accessible through conscious processes and that it should be interpreted through expert analysis of

material generated by a person without their knowledge of what is being assessed. In contrast, goal theorists have no qualms about assessing goals using conscious processing.

The need approach to motivation is clearly connected historically to the use of the Thematic Apperception Test (TAT), which was initially developed by Murray (1938). Following the belief that individuals are unaware of their motives and unable to report accurately on them, the TAT was designed as a projective technique under the belief that "when a person interprets an ambiguous social situation he is apt to expose his own personality as much as the phenomenon to which he is attending" (p. 531). These observations together form the theoretical basis of the TAT, where participants are asked to take the part of story-writers and create stories on the basis of ambiguous pictures. Although the traditional TAT paradigm is the one most commonly associated with the assessment of Murray's needs, several alternative routes to the assessment of Murray's needs have been developed. For instance, Schmalt (1999) developed a "semiprojective" grid technique in which individuals are asked to rate what characters in TAT-like pictures are thinking or feeling from a fixed set of options.

The second school of thought within the domain of motivation is that of the goal approach, which begins by asking individuals what they are typically trying to do in their everyday lives. Whereas theorists working within the need approach to motivation state that behavior is determined largely by discrepancies between actual states and unconscious motives, goal theorists believe behavior is largely influenced by discrepancies that are consciously accessible (Emmons, 1986, 1989). Further, whereas needs are conceptualized as broad, decontextualized, and fundamental constructs (Winter, John, Stewart, Klohnen, & Duncan, 1998), goals are assumed to vary hierarchically in their level of abstraction, ranging from specific and short-term goals such as "what I'm currently concerned with doing" (Klinger, 1975; Little, 1983), to more-enduring midlevel constructs such as personal strivings that reflect "what I'm typically trying to do" (Emmons, 1986) and finally to more broad and long-term life goals such as establishing a career or finding a relationship partner

(Roberts & Robins, 2000). Each of these levels is associated with a slightly different method, although generally these methods are idiographic, allowing respondents to give open-ended responses to the instructions and rely on conscious acknowledgement of one's aspirations.

Consistent with Fiske's (1971) argument that method can have a profound effect on construct validity, one of the long-standing controversies within the field of motivation is whether implicit or explicit methods of assessing motivations assess the same constructs. McClelland, Koestner, and Weinberger (1989) argued that measures such as the TAT and questionnaire measures such as the Jackson PRF are measures of distinct constructs, labeled *implicit needs* and *self-attributed needs*, respectively. Presumably, implicit measures should predict *operant* behaviors that are relatively uncontrolled by the environmental, such as job level attained in organizations and behavior occurring under natural conditions (McClelland, 1980). Self-attributed motives should be more predictive of respondent behaviors, such as school grades, personality, and intelligence tests, where the behavior is elicited and constrained by environmental stimuli.

In a meta-analysis of the literature on achievement motivation comparing the utility of self-attributed ratings of motives to implicit measures of motives, Spangler (1992) found support for this hypothesis. Implicit measures were more predictive of outcomes when attaining the outcomes involved challenges or incentives that were intrinsic to the task, such as moderate risk and time pressures, whereas self-attributed measures were more predictive of performance in tasks that involved social incentives, such as challenging goals set up by the experimenter or norms that encouraged achievement. Interestingly, implicit motives were also found to decrease in their relation to task performance when the number of social incentives involved with the task was high. Consistent with the interpretation of implicit needs as somewhat akin to intrinsic motivation, Spangler suggested that social incentives may conflict or otherwise suppress the effect of implicit needs on performance.

Recently, research has attempted to form a more complete picture of the associations between motive measures by looking simultaneously at the measures used by need and goal theorists. Emmons and McAdams (1991) examined the relations between the Jackson PRF, personal strivings, and TAT measures for the assessment of the achievement, affiliation, intimacy, and power motivations. The authors found modest relations between matching TAT and striving categories for achievement, intimacy, and power motives, indicating that, to some extent, these methods may be measuring the same underlying construct. On the other hand, the self-reported PRF was related to matching dimensions of personal strivings for power and achievement measures, but was irregularly related to the TAT motives. For instance, self-reported dominance was related positively to TAT achievement, but was unrelated to TAT power. The authors concluded that personal strivings may lie somewhere between self-attributed motives and implicit motives in that strivings appeared to relate to the TAT and PRF better than these scales relate to each other.

However, a second study looking at motives for power, affiliation, and achievement (King, 1995) failed to replicate Emmons and McAdams' (1991) findings. King (1995) failed to find direct relationships between the TAT and a battery of other motive measures, including the PRF as well as strivings, reported wishes, and early memories coded using Winter's (1991) running text system. This study also failed to find relationships between the PRF and strivings measures of power or affiliation motives. The lack of relationship between the PRF and TAT motives conformed well to Spangler's (1992) finding of an average correlation between TAT and self-attributed motives of $r = .09$ across 36 studies, which suggests that implicit and self-attributed motives are not independent, but are very nearly so. Although clearly more research needs to be done, it seems reasonable to conclude from these studies that the degree of commonality between implicit and explicit methods of assessing motives is not high.

The controversy over implicit and self-attributed needs has fostered an environment in which very few researchers have combined motive measures with personality measures from the other three domains of personality (i.e., trait, ability, or narra-

tive). In their attempt to integrate the domains of traits and motives, Winter et al. (1998) suggested that implicit motives and personality traits generally interact in their prediction of life outcomes. More specifically, they hypothesized that motives represent a person's fundamental goals and desires, whereas traits channel the expression of these motives toward specific paths. In looking at extraversion in combination with affiliation and power motivation in two samples of women, the authors found extraverts preferred volunteer work, combined family and work roles more frequently, and had more stable romantic relationships—but only if they were also high in affiliation motivation. Similarly, extraverts rated work relationships as more important than introverts, but only if they also were high in power motivation. In some cases, crossover interactions were found, where extraverts had more satisfying relationships than introverts when both were high in affiliation motivation, but the reverse was true when both were low on the motive. Winter and his colleagues had hypothesized this last interaction by considering the introverted, low-affiliation individuals as most effective at working alone and unconcerned about the opinions of others, whereas introverted high-affiliation individuals desired friendship and affection but were ineffective at maintaining it because of their awkwardness in interpersonal situations. It is interesting to note that for all of the life outcomes the authors investigated, main effects between traits and motives were rare, and the importance of the constructs would be missed if considered separately.

Although some studies exist examining the relationship between different motive measures, we found surprisingly few studies that have looked at the simultaneous interplay of motive and other personality constructs in the prediction of other outcomes. We suggest that not examining motives in combination with other domains results in a failure to fully understand the importance of motives, or worse, it may lead to erroneous conclusions about what motives are and do. For instance, early research on achievement motivation was stymied for decades by the empirical finding of negative relationships between the motive and variables such as popularity (Boyatzis, 1973). Given the current

theorizing concerning trait–motive relationships, this can now be understood as a by-product of an achievement–extraversion interaction, which explains how extraverts and introverts differentially handle their level of achievement motivation (Winter et al., 1998).

The domain of motives, much like the domain of traits, is marked by the use of distinct methods that do not converge as highly as one would like. In part, this divergence is consistent with the theoretical underpinnings of the two approaches. Researchers who adopt the implicit motive approach are skeptical of cognitive appraisals of needs. In contrast, researchers who use the self-attributed approach find this less problematic. It is clear from the studies using these two approaches that they both bring independent complementary predictive variance to the research endeavor. Furthermore, when combined with methods and constructs from the trait domain, we find clear predictions of important life outcomes (Winter et al., 1998).

Abilities

Assessing intelligence has traditionally focused on multiple forms of test data (T data). Standard measures of intelligence typically attempt to gather information on a wide variety of traits considered to be at the core of general mental ability. However, numerous efforts have been made to move beyond traditional assessment approaches. These have included measures of specific cognitive abilities, intellectual interests, and self-report measures of intelligence.

Testing cognitive abilities has traditionally included a variety of measurements and techniques, such as problem-solving tasks, assessments of school performance, information acquisition tasks, as well as matrix problems that require highly abstract conditional discriminations. The reason for the success in tapping general cognitive abilities using a variety of techniques largely has to do with the degree to which general mental ability permeates all learning, reasoning, and problem-solving abilities. Further, aggregations of measures of spatial skills, verbal reasoning, and quantitative abilities measure general mental ability more efficiently

than aggregations of information items because the reasoning problems used in these measures typically capture a greater degree of common-factor variance associated with *g* (Gustafsson, 2002). Consequently, the most popular measures of general mental ability include a variety of assessments designed to tap several broad domains highly related to general mental ability, such as verbal, quantitative, reasoning, and visuospatial skills.

The search for alternative methods of measuring general mental ability more purely has often led to the use of elementary cognitive tasks (ECTs) that measure processing speed and working memory (Jensen, 1998). These tasks highlight the hierarchical nature of intelligence and our earlier point that assessments across different levels of abstraction typically constitute related but different methods. ECTs have proved to be a popular alternative methodology for measuring general mental ability because such tasks avoid the bias that may be introduced in measurement by prior training and experience. It also is argued that basic cognitive mechanisms underlie all thinking, reasoning, and decision-making processes, and therefore such mechanisms would be substantially related to general mental ability (Kyllonen & Christal, 1990).

Interestingly, Carroll's (1993) analysis of the structure of general mental ability showed that tasks measuring reaction time, inspection time, and discrimination ability were only weakly related to general mental ability. Indeed, early skepticism regarding the efficacy of using such measures to measure general mental ability was the result of such measures being used in isolation. However, it has been demonstrated that scores on such experimental tasks can be aggregated to form a reasonable representation of general mental ability if enough experiments are carried out across a variety of cognitive task domains (Green, 1978). It has been noted that correlations between combined reaction time scores from a number of ECTs and general mental ability approach the size typically seen with psychometric power tests (Jensen, 1998). Further, the combined scores from a number of ECTs can be used to predict upward of 70% of the heritable part of the variance in general mental ability. For the purposes of experimentation, it should be noted

that aggregations of ECTs form two general factors, perceptual speed and working memory (Ackerman, Beier, & Boyle, 2002). These factors are, as a result of aggregation, both highly related to general mental ability, with working memory being the more highly related to *g* of the two (Ackerman et al., 2002).

Another approach to measuring general mental ability has been to use self-reports of intelligence or intellectual engagement (Paulhus & Harms, 2004). This approach has been much maligned by intelligence theorists because of the fact that self-report intelligence measures rarely exceed validities of .50 with typical tests of maximal performance of cognitive ability (Paulhus, Lysy, & Yik, 1998). Nonetheless, the search for better self-report measures has persisted because of the interest in finding a non-stressful and easily administered technique for obtaining performance information.

One of the more comprehensive and successful self-report measures of intelligence has been the Typical Intellectual Engagement (TIE) scale developed by Goff and Ackerman (1992). The premise behind this scale is that knowledge is accumulated over time through effort and motivated engagement in learning. It is therefore believed that this measure will better reflect daily behavior because it constitutes a test of typical intellectual performance. This is distinguished from a test of maximal intellectual performance, such as an SAT test, where it can be assumed that the individual is bringing their full cognitive resources to bear to succeed and attain a better outcome.

The TIE scale has been instrumental in integrating measures of the components of Ackerman's PPIK theory, a multimethod approach to understanding intellectual functioning that integrates intelligence-as-*process*, *personality*, *interest*, and intelligence-as-*knowledge* (Rolfhus & Ackerman, 1999). By assessing each of these domains, Rolfhus and Ackerman attempted to get a better approximation of the contribution of each to scores on knowledge and intelligence tests. Participants' general mental ability was assessed using a composite of verbal, mathematical, and spatial abilities. Their personalities and interests were assessed using standard measures of the Big Five personality traits, interests, and typical intellectual engagement. Sub-

jects also completed a battery of tests measuring their knowledge in a wide variety of domains including humanities, sciences, civics, and mechanics. This study demonstrated that a substantial higher-order Knowledge factor emerges from factor analysis of the knowledge domains that accounts for approximately 50% of the variance in domain knowledge. Further analyses showed that this general factor was significantly correlated with crystallized intelligence, which was represented by a composite of verbal ability tests. This suggests that the general knowledge factor is highly related, but not identical, to crystallized intelligence. These findings also suggest that a substantial part of the variance in knowledge test performance remains to be predicted by more domain-specific influences, such as interests and personality. For instance, Extraversion was shown to be negatively related to all but one of the domain knowledge tests, with Openness to Experience and Typical Intellectual Engagement also demonstrating significant, positive relationships across the knowledge domains. Measures of interests also proved to be related to domain knowledge scores, but were more specific with regard to matching content domains. Realistic interests were related to mechanical knowledge domains, Investigative interests were mostly related to science domains, and Artistic interests were most highly related to knowledge domains that reflected the humanities.

Like the domain of motives, one finds that combining tests of cognitive ability with measures taken from other domains, and thus other methods, maximizes our ability to predict important outcomes. One of the best multimethod studies that integrated multiple measures of intelligence, knowledge, interests, and personality measures to real-world performance outcomes was Project A (Campbell, 1985). Borman, White, Pulakos, and Oppler (1991) analyzed data from 4,362 first-term soldiers in nine U.S. Army jobs. Subjects were assessed for cognitive ability using the ASVAB, as well as job knowledge, dependability, and achievement orientation measures that were developed for the study. To assess performance, hands-on proficiency measures and supervisory ratings were taken, and the number of disciplinary actions and awards received were recorded. Path modeling demonstrated that although achievement orientation and dependability made independent, although small, contributions to supervisory ratings, the impact of general mental ability on supervisory ratings of job performance was completely mediated by job knowledge, which in turn was mediated by task proficiency. Further, dependability was positively related to job knowledge and negatively related to disciplinary actions. Achievement orientation was positively related to the number of awards a soldier received. The model demonstrated by this analysis shows that although general mental ability has a huge impact on job knowledge, and job knowledge is substantially related to task proficiency, it is by no means the largest of the contributors to job performance ratings by supervisors. Personality factors and outcomes associated with personality factors also make significant direct contributions to supervisory ratings.

There are many different approaches to the study and measurement of general mental ability. The most successful approaches, and consequently the most widely used, have used measures from across content domains to gain a fuller representation of the cognitive functioning required in reasoning, decision making, and other thought processes. Alternative approaches such as information processing techniques using elementary cognitive tasks have proved to be successful as indicators of general mental ability, but only when they are assessed and aggregated across modalities, content domains, and tasks. Other alternatives, such as self-report measures of intelligence and intellectual interest, have shown promise as indicators of general mental ability, but may be best suited to offering a more integrated picture of how basic brain processes, working memory, and personality may be related to real-world outcomes in intellectual functioning.

Life Story Narrative as a Means of Investigating Personality

Like the first three domains of personality, the use of narrative methods in multimethod research is a novel occurrence, yet has thus far been informative to the understanding of individual differences. Qualitative assessments of personality begin at the

most basic level with the case study and progress to rigorously assessed structured interviews (McAdams, 1996, 1999). Qualitative data is frequently gathered in the form of open-ended questions concerning a topic of interest to the researcher. Consistent with the perspective that each domain of personality is arranged hierarchically, qualitative data can be examined at both the micro- and macrolevels. Microlevel assessment is concerned with specific linguistic patterns within the narrative such as pronoun usage or specific word type frequencies (e.g., Pennebaker & Francis, 1996). In contrast, macrolevel assessment focuses on the broad themes throughout a narrative, such as redemption sequences (McAdams, Reynolds, Lewis, Patten, & Bowman, 2001). Such thematic coding is often developed by the researchers after listening to interviews or reading written narratives. Trained coders can then rate each qualitative datum on the varying themes of interest. Topics that are open to narrative methods are limited only by the creativity and ambition of the researcher, and the richness of the data can afford multiple opportunities to better understand the personality of an individual. For example, McAdams' life story interview (McAdams, 1996, 1999) asks people to describe low points, turning points, and religious beliefs among other experiences. Each of these stories can be examined individually for specific types of experiences (e.g., questioning of parents' religious beliefs, difficult times) to broad life-span themes, such as agency and communion. Qualitative data can thus be converted into data that is quantitatively assessable without losing the nuances of the qualitative form. Additionally, excerpts from qualitative data may be used to reiterate a theoretical point. Examples from three studies will help to illuminate these methodologies. A substantial amount of narrative research concerns the reaction of an individual to difficult life events in his or her life. Theoretically, the manner in which an individual responds to traumatic experiences that threaten his or her view of self and the surrounding world is critical for understanding the identity of that individual. If an individual is able to construct a coherent self from a difficult life event, he or she is considered to have a healthy identity.

A recent multimethod study provides a clear example of the utility of the narrative approach. Parents of children with Down syndrome were contacted through a support group mailing list as well as through area hospitals (King, Scollon, Ramsey, & Williams, 2000). The parents were initially asked self-report questions concerning well-being, administered a projective test of ego development, and asked to write a story about when they were first told that their child had Down syndrome. Two years after the initial assessment, parents again responded to self-report measures of well-being and a projective measure of ego development. The narratives were assessed by three independent raters for themes of accommodation (exploration, shifts in perspective, activity) and closed (denial, negative affect). Parents who were low in ego development at Time 1 who wrote in an accommodative manner demonstrated increased ego development 2 years later. Parents who wrote narratives in both an accommodative and closure style had higher feelings of stress-related growth at the 2-year follow-up. This research provides an example of how healthy processing (i.e., exploring the impact of the event on the self and discovering a positive resolution about this experience) of difficult events on an individual level allows for healthier, more mature functioning later in life (King et al., 2000).

Helson (1992) examined more general identity threatening events in the writing of women's difficult life experiences in an ongoing, multimethod longitudinal study. Information was gathered about the age at which women experienced difficult, identity-changing life events and various personality factors that influenced the onset of such experiences. In addition, information about identity status (achieved, moratorium, foreclosed, and diffuse) was used to understand the meaning and effect of difficult times. Women who had a diffuse identity presented more themes related to negative evaluations of themselves. Foreclosed women wrote mainly about having bad partners or overload. Achieved/moratorium women wrote primarily about becoming psychologically independent and its consequences. Additionally, as women's vulnerability began to decrease and confidence began to increase on personality measures around 30 years of

age, an increase in identity themes occurs. This research suggests that the rewriting of the life story occurs in middle age for women, and that this is associated with an increased importance of independence, which is in turn related to healthy identity functioning.

Pals (2005) combined the narratives of the women in the Mills study with themes parallel to those of King et al. (2000) to illustrate not only the correlation between personality on the trait level and narrative level, but also the dynamic interactive processes of trait and narrative conceptualizations of personality. Narratives from women who had participated in the longitudinal study described earlier (Helson, 1992) were coded for themes of resolution (overall resolution, positive ending, low negative ending, low lasting wounds, coherent ending) and impact on self (open response, narrative complexity, low self-distancing, acknowledged wounds, positive self-transformation, and active approach). These two dimensions were then used in conjunction with age 21 and age 52 responses to personality measures of open versus defensive coping (a combination of tolerance of ambiguity and reverse scored repression) and ego-resiliency to predict physical and psychological health outcomes at age 61. Findings demonstrated that whereas coping openness at age 21 was related to clinician-rated maturity at age 61, this relation was mediated by the extent to which women composed a narrative that was open to expressing the impact of the negative events on the self. Further, whereas a resolved narrative was related to subjective well-being at age 61, this effect was mediated by ego resiliency at ages 21 and 52, suggesting a dynamic interaction of trait and narrative personality in relation to healthy functioning.

Qualitative research provides the researcher with an ability to not only examine the individual, but also the world in which the individual exists and the events that precipitate change in the individual, thus providing a complex and invaluable source of data for understanding the person as a whole. Used in combination with other methods, it is clear that narrative data can not only add a deeper, more complex understanding of basic psychological phenomena, but also account for important variance in addition to standard methods, such as self-reported personality traits.

CONCLUSION

It is clear from our review that the field of personality psychology is intrinsically a multimethod field. Within and across each domain of personality, methods as diverse as self-reports, observer ratings, projective tests, test of maximal performance, and qualitative interpretations of narratives are brought to bear on understanding individual differences in thoughts, feelings, and behaviors. Consistent with our neosocioanalytic framework, many of the methods correlate quite strongly with content. Self-reports and observer ratings tend to be used more often in the assessment of personality traits, and the complement of hierarchically related constructs such as affect and behavior. The use of projective tests bridges domains, but is primarily located in the assessment of motives. Tests of maximal performance have the potential to bridge domains, but are similarly found almost entirely in the content domain of abilities. Finally, one's story is almost exclusively the domain of methods that focus on life data. Moreover, within each domain researchers are beginning to use multiple methods to assess the hierarchically related constructs within a content category, such as when broad trait measures are combined with the assessment of daily mood or behavior (e.g., Wirtz et al., 2003).

Despite the impressive methodological plurality across and within domains in personality psychology, there remains a tremendous unrealized potential to bring multiple methods to bear on relevant topics. For example, the use of test data in domains other than abilities remains untapped, despite provocative studies pointing to the potential to assess personality traits in ways other than asking someone to rate themselves on a personality inventory. Experimental tests, such as the "go, no-go" task in which people are told to inhibit a response to a cue when a stop signal tone is emitted have systematic relationships to personality traits such as impulse control (Logan, Schachar, & Tannock, 1997) and related forms of psychopathology, such as delinquency (Mezzacappa, Kindlon, & Earls, 2001). The interesting question

that is as yet untested is whether tests like these can be aggregated into a reliable index of individual differences in personality traits, just as the elementary cognitive tasks have been aggregated to tap into cognitive ability.

Despite the examples cited earlier, it remains anomalous for researchers to use more than one method to investigate almost any phenomena in personality psychology. Too much time and effort have gone into reifying one or another technique as the gold standard method for assessing construct such as traits (e.g., Hofstee, 1994) or motives (McClelland et al., 1989). Also, there is a tendency to approach method variance as if it is uninteresting and an expectation that it should not play a role in the type of information gleaned from an assessment (cf. Ozer, 1986). This somewhat disrespectful approach to multiple methods quite possibly

derives from the article that inspired this book (e.g., Cronbach & Gleser, 1953), in which the construct of interest is supposed to supersede the method and therefore converge in a robust fashion across diverse techniques of assessment. In contrast, more realistic appraisals of the information taken from multiple methods point to a more sobering conclusion that the information acquired from multiple methods may in fact be more independent than previously expected (Fiske, 1971; Meyer et al., 2001; Ozer, 1986). Therefore, different methods of assessment provide complementary information rather than perfectly overlapping information. This only reinforces the point that researchers should use multiple methods in personality psychology by default to arrive at a more complete understanding of their research interests, whether it is traits, motives, abilities, or life narratives.

CHAPTER 23

MEASURING EMOTIONS: IMPLICATIONS OF A MULTIMETHOD PERSPECTIVE

Randy J. Larsen and Zvjezdana Prizmic-Larsen

Other chapters of this book address various conceptual concerns about multiple methods, about convergent and divergent validity, and about the distinction between method and error variance. The construct of "emotion" provides special challenges for assessment, thus bringing these abstract conceptual issues into sharp relief. We therefore begin our chapter on emotion measurement with a few deliberations concerning these special challenges. We then present three broad categories of measures of emotion—language, behavior, and physiology—and discuss strengths and problems and describe several examples of each. Understanding the relationships between different facets of emotion measures will be a theoretical as well as methodological achievement. Modeling multiple methods within a consensual or method-invariant space will be an important contribution to this area as well as to provide researchers with a parsimonious system for organizing multiple methods. Until then, researchers should always consider using multiple methods in emotion research because doing so will almost always lead to gains measurement precision.

EMOTION FROM A SYSTEMS PERSPECTIVE

Before something can be measured it must be defined. Is there an adequate definition of emotion? Although emotion researchers do not fully agree on a single, consensual definition (cf. Ekman & Davidson, 1994), researchers have long debated its facets

and components. A consideration of these components provides a working definition of emotion useful in planning measurement strategies. Moreover, a working definition is appropriate because it may be refined and extended over time as new findings about the nature of emotion emerge.

A useful working definition can be gleaned from a systems perspective on emotions (e.g., Bradley & Lang, 2000), which holds that emotion is a multifaceted construct inferred from multiple indicators. The multiple facets of emotions are manifest in multiple response systems. According to Lang's bioinformational theory (1979), the systems of primary importance are the behavioral system, the language system, and the physiological system. Each of these systems, in turn, consists of multiple subsystems. For example, the language system contains evaluative self-reports of emotion as well as vocal and paravocal features of speech associated with emotions. The physiological system contains subsystems such as the central nervous system (brain), the peripheral nervous system (sympathetic, parasympathetic), and the hormonal system. Each of these subsystems can be thought of as a channel that carries potential information about the emotional state of the person.

To make measurement matters more complicated, the multiple channels themselves are not tightly connected to each other, thereby not offering well-calibrated or interchangeable indicators. To paraphrase Venables's (1984) statement about

Preparation of this manuscript was supported by grant RO1-MH63732 from the National Institute of Mental Health.

arousal, the multiple response systems involved in the manifestation of emotion are themselves loosely and imperfectly coupled, plus the response systems complexly interact with, and mutually influence, each other. For example, facial expressions appear to amplify subjective feelings (e.g., Larsen, Kasimatis, & Frey, 1992). Emotion generates loosely organized and temporally cascading changes across a wide array of psychological and physiological domains, including subjective experience, facial actions, central and peripheral nervous system activation, cognitive appraisals, information processing changes, and behavioral action tendencies.

In the optimal case, assessing emotions would involve measurement across many of these multiple components simultaneously. Streams of data obtained from multiple response systems may converge on the underlying construct of emotion and increase the relative confidence that we can place in the composite indicator. However, given the loosely coupled and complexly interacting nature of emotional response systems, researchers should not expect perfect or even substantial convergence across multiple indicators.

Examples of response discordance between different measures of the "same" emotion are not difficult to find. For example, Nesse et al. (1985) used nine different measures of distress obtained when subjects were in the presence of a phobic object and found only modest convergence across methods. Bradley and Lang (2000) concluded that covariation between measures of different response systems, supposedly indicating the same latent construct, "seldom accounts for more than 10–15% of the variance" (p. 244). Even when using multiple, synchronized measures, the underlying psychological construct of "emotion" still remains some inferential distance from (i.e., is only probabilistically related to) the composite of observable indicators.

The situation just described implies that the use of multimethod assessment, although not an absolute solution, is nevertheless acutely necessary in the emotion domain. Researchers should be particularly on guard against the false virtue of reductionistic interpretations or "operational definitions" of emotion in monomethod terms. Emotion is not a

self-report of emotion, nor is it a P300 response to stimulus, or a potentiated startle reflex, nor is it an appraisal of some event. Emotion must be conceived in a postpositivistic fashion, as a theoretical construct to be inferred from multiple observables. As a scientific term, *emotion* carries surplus meaning beyond any single measure and thus is best represented by a multimethod composite. Although this is generally good advice for any theoretical construct, it is especially appropriate for emotion because of the multiple channels involved in the creation and manifestation of emotion.

Emotions as Dimensions Versus Discrete Categories

Another thorny issue researchers need to consider before making measurement decisions concerns whether emotions are discrete and/or dimensional constructs. The issue concerns whether emotions can best be conceptualized as two or three broad dimensions (e.g., Larsen & Diener, 1992) or as two (Meehl, 1975; Mower, 1960) or four (Gray, 1982) or five (Oatley & Johnson-Laird, 1987) or six (Frijda, 1993) or eight (Plutchik, 1980; Tomkins, 1984) or nine (Ekman, 1992; Izard, 1977) separate and distinct categories of experience. This issue goes back more than 100 years (Darwin, 1872/1965; Spencer, 1890; Wundt, 1897) and continues to be debated (cf. Diener, 1999). The most consensually agreed-upon dimensional view of emotion is represented by the circumplex model (Russell, 1980; Watson & Tellegen, 1985), which posits that emotions conform to a circular or radex arrangement with the coordinates of the circular space representing combinations of valence and arousal. The measurement implications of the circumplex model, including the need for multimethod measurement of emotion dimensions, are discussed in Larsen and Diener (1992) as well as Larsen and Fredrickson (1999).

Proponents of the discrete emotion viewpoint argue that the dimensional view often blurs meaningful distinctions between emotions (e.g., fear and anger and disgust are all similarly high-arousal unpleasant emotions). The main measurement issue implicit within this exchange of ideas concerns specificity: Measures that fit the discrete emotion view can be transformed to a dimensional arrange-

ment post hoc, but the converse is not always possible. For this reason, researchers should consider a priori whether distinctions between specific negative or between specific positive emotions are likely to be part of the theoretical or empirical agenda. If there is the slightest possibility for this need to discriminate basic emotions, then researchers should pursue emotion specificity rather than dimensional assessment.

Temporal Duration: Emotions as States, Emotions as Traits

Emotions are dynamic processes that take place over time—often rapidly, but sometimes gradually— involving a cascade of different response systems, such as those mentioned earlier. Each response system has its own dynamic and duration. For example, the central nervous system is very fast (with negative stimuli producing changes at around milliseconds; Smith, Cacioppo, Larsen, & Chartrand, 2003), the cardiac system somewhat slower (with changes taking place on a beat-by-beat basis), the skin conductance system somewhat slower still (at least 2 seconds poststimulus before a response can occur), and the hormone system is even slower. One critical measurement issue involves isolating the targeted response system within this temporal cascade. When does the response begin and when does it end? Structuring observation of these response systems within the right temporal window will greatly increase the chances of observing emotion-related changes. Imprecision at this stage can dilute the targeted emotional episode within a wash of emotion-irrelevant moments (see Levenson, 1988).

Another issue concerns making sure that the measure has sufficient temporal resolution to properly assess the chosen response system. Some indicators of emotion—for example, an increase in cardiac output—might last less than 6 seconds (e.g., Witvliet & Vrana, 2000). The cardiovascular system is exquisitely controlled, and so this response system typically returns to preemotion levels relatively quickly. The experience of emotion, however, could last much longer, or even be assessed later, using recall measures. Cardiac measures cannot be recalled, nor can output be averaged over long time periods because a transient emotion

signal can be lost in the average. Self-report measures aggregated over that same time span, however, should accurately reflect the experiential component of emotion.

The discussion so far assumes that the researcher is interested in assessing emotions as states. To conceptualize emotions as states is to emphasize the short-lived (typically), intense (relatively), and situation-caused (mostly) changes in response systems responsible for emotional experience and for supporting resultant behaviors. Because the state conception identifies emotions as quickly changing, measures should be temporally fine-grained, with a temporal resolution that is smaller (ideally much smaller to provide reliable aggregate measures) than the expected duration of the transient emotion-related change.

A third issue about assessing emotion states concerns the temporal proximity of emotion measures to the emotion state itself. Researchers should consider obtaining measures during an emotion experience. This is certainly feasible for measures of the expressive system, such as those obtained from video records or through physiological recording devices, but perhaps this is less feasible for measures obtained via self-report or through a cognitive assessment or through emotion-sensitive tasks, which typically interrupt the ongoing emotion state. Also, emotion measures can be obtained on more than one occasion so as to assess change. When pre- and postmeasures are not feasible or practical, measures that minimize the delay between emotion experience and emotion measurement should be sought.

Although emotions are typically thought of as states, these states nevertheless fluctuate around some mean or average level for each person. Persons differ reliably from each other in their average level of various emotions (Larsen, 2000). As such, emotions can also be conceptualized as having enduring traitlike components, that these emotion traits relate to causes "inside" the person (e.g., personality), thereby exhibiting some degree of consistency and stability (Diener & Larsen, 1984). The concept of an emotion trait refers to the set point or expected value for a person on a particular emotion, other things being equal (George, 1996).

Emotions are thus hybrid phenomena, consisting of both trait and state components, allowing the researcher to focus on one or the other component in addressing various questions (Watson & Tellegen, 2002).

Why is the distinction between state and trait emotion important to the researcher? First, researchers should be aware that people bring emotional dispositions to the assessment setting; not everyone shows up in the same emotional state. To the extent that emotion dispositions refer to the "expected value" of emotion for an individual, people are likely to have predictable emotional levels. This level may work according to the law of initial values to influence subsequent reactivity. Understanding how emotion traits work, and the causes and consequences of specific emotional dispositions, will help psychologists predict and explain specific emotional reactions. Lastly, states and traits can easily be confused, the variance components that are due to each can become blended, and so researchers need to be aware of this distinction. It is not difficult to find papers in the emotion literature where a correlation is computed between some measured emotion (say positive affect) and some other variable (say helping), and the authors interpret this as a state relationship, as in "people are more likely to help when in a positive mood." However, when measuring emotions in people "off the street," researchers are as likely to be tapping emotion traits as states. Consequently, it may really be that the kind of person who is most likely to be in a positive state (high trait PA) is also the most likely kind of person to be helpful. To infer state effects when emotion traits have been measured is to confound the two sources of variability in emotion measures. To infer state effects researchers should use experimental designs where a manipulation of emotion serves as the independent variable, an emotion measure is included as a manipulation check, and some other theoretical construct serves as the dependent variable.

Emotion traits are receiving a good deal of attention from personality researchers, as well as from psychologists interested in motivation and the biological bases of behavior. When it comes to trait emotion, the dimensional perspective may be the

most useful, whereas for the state approach the categorical view of emotion measurement may be most useful. Zelenski and Larsen (2002) presented data showing that structural conclusions about the emotion domain are related to whether the researcher is analyzing between- or within-subject correlations. That is, because emotions are states, they vary within subjects over time. Such variability is inherently different from between-subject variability. Within-subject analyses (of each subject across 60 measurement occasions in the Zelenski & Larsen, 2002 data) yielded structural support for multiple categories of emotion, whereas between-subject analyses (of each subjects' average emotion scores aggregated over the 60 observations) yielded support for the dimensional structure, with the factors being positive and negative emotionality. Positive affect and negative affect exhibit different structural relationships depending on whether they are assessed as states or traits (Schmukle, Egloff, & Burns, 2002).

Emotion: Special Concerns About Reliability and Validity

Measurement reliability is often thought of as a high test–retest correlation, which is not an accurate conceptualization. Reliability, as an aspect of measurement, refers to the degree to which observed scores reflect the "true" amount of the construct being measured. We never have access to "true" scores, so we must estimate reliability. A test–retest correlation is an appropriate estimate of reliability for between-subjects constructs (i.e., for trait constructs), where the variability of interest is between participants. With trait constructs we assume little or no meaningful within-participant variance. Intelligence is a good example of a between-subject, or strictly trait, construct, where we assume that, for any single individual, intelligence is stable and not easily changed, at least not over a few weeks or months. As such, reliable measures of intelligence will demonstrate high test–retest correlations, and test–retest results are adequate reliability estimates.

Emotion, on the other hand, is often typically conceptualized as a within-subject construct (i.e., as a state construct), and we therefore assume that

it may change frequently within any single individual. To make matters more complicated, as already noted, emotion can be *both* a between-subjects construct as well as a within-subject construct, where there is meaningful variance within people over time (i.e., reactivity) as well as meaningful variance between individuals (i.e., individual differences in set-point or expected value). Because emotions are hybrid state–trait constructs, we cannot use simple test–retest correlations as estimates of measurement reliability.

Another estimate of reliability is through internal consistency indicators, such as coefficient alpha, or odd-even item-composite correlations. These are actually measures of item homogeneity, assessing the degree to which items measure the same underlying construct. Because many self-report emotion measures are factor analytically constructed, such item homogeneity is built in during the scale construction process. Internal consistency analysis is thus one way to estimate reliability, and it works equally well for both state and trait measures. However, internal consistency estimates of reliability work only for multi-item scales. Single-item measures, whether they are self-reports, observer ratings, or an experimental task, simply cannot be examined in terms of internal consistency. One could, however, estimate the consistency across multiple indicators, but such an analysis is verging more on construct validity than on the classical concern of measurement reliability of the single measures themselves.

Researchers using single measures of emotion are really left in the dark about measurement reliability. One might choose to ignore reliability concerns altogether and focus instead on concerns about validity. This appears reasonable because measurement reliability sets the upper bound on validity correlations. In other words, a measure cannot correlate with external criteria higher than it can correlate with itself. As such, valid measures are de facto reliable. However, a researcher who passes up reliability concerns proceeds at some risk of being unable to make credible conclusions, particularly if some hypothesized validity relationship is not found. However, strong evidence for validity, with multiple converging methods and replicated patterns of association, can add credibility to the claim that a particular measure is reliable.

Measurement reliability is most crucial when it comes to interpreting failures to refute the null hypothesis. For example, if a study was conducted, and the predicted relationships were not found, three obvious reasons must be entertained: Either the theory was wrong, the measures used were not reliable, or some auxiliary conditions of the study were not met (cf. Meehl, 1978, for more detailed discussion). When a study fails to find the predicted results, and the researcher is confident that the measures used are reliable, then the set of reasons is narrowed to questioning the theory or looking for something that might have gone wrong with the procedure or data. It is precisely in such circumstances that reliability evidence is crucial. In the absence of evidence for reliability, conclusions cannot be made about whether the theory was adequately tested. However, because there are typically several different measures of the same facet of emotion (e.g., multiple observational ratings, or ratings from several raters), the facets measures can be modeled for reliability.

As for validity concerns, the construct of emotion also poses several unique challenges to researchers. Emotion is a theoretical construct that is only probabilistically linked to observable indicators. Even though it may be represented by many different measures, emotion is not equivalent, nor can it be reduced to, any single measure. This underscores the importance of construct validity, especially multimethod construct validity, in understanding the scientific meaning of emotion terms.

In construct validity (Cronbach & Meehl, 1955), meaning is given to a scientific term (e.g., emotion) by the nomological network of assertions in which that term appears. Our theories and measurement models guide us in proposing a network of associations around the construct. The proposed links in this network then become hypotheses to be tested in empirical research. In construct validation, theory testing and measurement development proceed in tandem. Each link in the network helps add to the scientific meaning of the term as well as providing evidence on the validity of the measure.

Some links in the network refer to positive associations (convergent validity), and some refer to negative or null associations (discriminant validity). In addition, some links specify the conditions under which emotions are likely to be evoked (predictive validity).

The total collection of relationships—links in the nomological network—built up around the construct of "emotion," or around specific emotions, creates a mosaic of research findings (Messick, 1980). When enough pieces of the network are in place, we "get the picture." That is, when enough empirical results are available about what something is, what it isn't, and what it predicts, we begin to have the feeling that we "understand" it and can measure it. Moreover, the credibility of our scientific understanding of the meaning of a construct grows with the diversity of the methods that go into establishing the nomological links. That is, the greater the methodological distance between two nodes in a nomological network (e.g., a physiological measure correlating with an evaluative self-report), then greater credibility is given to claims regarding the scientific meaning of the construct. This is not to say that our understanding of a construct is complete at this point; construct validity is always unfinished, and things are always "true until further notice." Nevertheless, there comes a point where we reach some consensual agreement about the scientific meaning of a construct, such as emotion, as well as the utility of the different measures that are used as indicators of that construct.

Because emotions implicate multiple response systems (e.g., facial action, autonomic activity, subjective experience, action tendencies), the issue arises about whether we should expect strong convergence among indicators of these different response systems. This validity question is particularly vexing in emotion research because of the nature of the multiple response systems (i.e., loosely coupled and complexly interacting systems). Moreover, the various response systems have functions beyond serving as indicators of emotion. For instance, in addition to reacting to emotions, the autonomic nervous system functions to regulate to metabolic input and output and to maintain homeostasis. The facial muscles, in addition to producing outward expressions of feelings, are used for vocalizing and eating. The cardiovascular system, in addition to speeding up during emotion, functions mainly to circulate blood to all organs of the body. These so-called emotional response systems have more to do that just respond to emotions, and this should make any researcher question the validity of any single measure of "emotion," such as heart rate. Perhaps the strongest evidence for validity is when a theory about a particular emotion can be used to generate predictions about the conditions under which that emotion will be evoked, or the type of persons for whom that emotion will be most easily evoked. Couple this with measurement theory and a knowledge of multiple measures of emotion, and very specific predictions may be generated and tested.

Because the various components of emotion will never correlate substantially with each other, because of the concerns described, they pose special challenges to those researchers interested in using some of the statistical models described elsewhere in this handbook. That is, emotion measures may not cohere well enough to be modeled by the standard techniques. More advanced methods, especially those that can accommodate multiple but weakly correlated measures, will be needed in the areas of emotion.

Emotion researchers need to keep clearly in mind that constructs are never purely measured. Rather, all measures are construct-method composites. For example, the measurement of anxiety is not the same across different methodological contexts. Instead, we should consider using terms that specify the method and the construct together, such as self-reported anxiety or cardiovascular anxiety or observer-rated anxiety. This acknowledges the fact that the theoretical meaning of a construct is given, in part, by the methods used to measure it. We turn now to a consideration of specific methods of measurement commonly used in the emotion domain.

METHODS FOR MEASURING EMOTION

As mentioned earlier, the components of emotion can be conveniently categorized into three broad, only somewhat overlapping, output systems (after Lang, 1979): (a) *language*, which includes evalua-

tive self-reports of experience, modifications of speech patterns by emotions, and expressive communications; (b) *behavior*, which includes overt acts and functional behavior sequences, such as flight or fight, approach, and threat behavior, as well as the modulation of other behaviors by emotion; and (c) *physiology*, which includes central and peripheral nervous system changes that support emotional behavior or prepare the person for responding, as well as somatic expressive changes and hormonal changes that coordinate the discharge and replacement of energy stores. As presented by Bradley and Lang (2000), these three output systems provide a three-dimensional framework for considering measures of emotion. We present this framework in the form of a data box (Cattell, 1988; Larsen, 1989).

Emotions can be thought of as events that produce variability along these three main dimensions. Each dimension of this framework refers to a category of variables that have been theoretically and empirically related to emotion. A theoretical challenge in the emotion area is to sort out this response diversity by explaining when response patterns across the three dimensions will be integrated and when they will be discordant. Until then, researchers would be well advised to include, at the least, measures from each of the three dimensions.

We turn now to a brief review of various measures that make up each of the three dimensions. Our intent is to provide a sampling of the major methods that have been developed in the three broad areas of emotion output. We will not provide an exhaustive review of what is known about each measure, nor is our review intended to be exhaustive within each type of measurement method. Rather, our intent is to provide examples of specific methods, describe a few strengths and weakness of each, and provide references for interested readers to pursue for further details.

Emotion Assessed Through Language

Self-report evaluations of emotion. Self-report measures, where participants provide an evaluation of their emotional experience, form the most diverse yet most widely used set of assessment tools for measuring emotion (Larsen & Fredrickson, 1999). Measures range from rating scales and adjective checklists, to analog scales and real-time rating dials. Proponents of self-report measures (e.g., Baldwin, 2000) assume that participants are in a privileged position to monitor, assess, and integrate information about their own emotions, and therefore self-report measures should not be thought of as second-rate proxies for better measures. Critics of self-report measures (e.g., Schaeffer, 2000), on the other hand, argue that there are so many biases, distortions, and methodological limitations that self-reports of anything, even one's home address, are fraught with error and misinformation. Self-report measures are nevertheless the most widely used assessment tools in emotion research.

Although there are a great many self-report instruments, considerable similarities can be found among them. Here we present a few exemplars and highlight themes and issues common to self-report measures. Reviews of specific self-report instruments can be found in Larsen and Fredrickson (1999), MacKay (1980), and Stone (1995; Stone, Turkkan, Bachrach, Jobe, Kurtzman, & Cain, 2000).

An assessment strategy with a good deal of face validity is simply to ask participants to rate how they are or were feeling on a single emotion dimension. That dimension might be a global affective evaluation (e.g., How unpleasant are you feeling?) or a specific emotion (How angry do you feel?). And the response scale might be unipolar (not at all angry to extremely angry) or bipolar (unpleasant to pleasant), with response options that are Likert-type scales (e.g., 5-, 7-, or 9-point formats). Or the response might be in a checklist format, where the respondent indicates whether or not a specific emotion was experienced. Such measures are simple to construct, easily understood by participants, and brief to administer. Virtually any emotion term can anchor a scale or be put onto a checklist, making self-report indispensable for researchers targeting specific, discrete emotions, as well as those researchers using multiple items to reflect global dimensions of emotion.

A variation on self-report is the experience sampling method, where participants make frequent reports over an extended time period. Although this

method allows researchers to ask unique theoretical questions about emotion (e.g., Larsen, 1987), the measurement concerns remain mainly those associated with simple self-report. See Bolger, Davis, and Rafaeli (2003) for a review of this method.

A variation on rating scales makes the response a visual analog that presents the participant with a horizontal line separating two opposing adjectives, which lessens stereotyped responding. A related technique is to make the question itself an analog of the emotion being assessed. For example, the participant might be presented with a series of five cartoon faces, going from a neutral expression on one face to an extreme frown on another. This has the advantages of being useful with participants for whom adjectives might not be meaningful, such as very young children or participants from different language groups.

Another useful strategy in self-report is to have the participants indicate, in real time, how they are feeling by turning a dial, moving a mouse, adjusting a computer display, or in some way modifying an analog display of the emotion on which they are reporting. The general strategy across these techniques is to collect self-reports of subjective experience on a moment-by-moment basis, either online as the emotion is experienced, or retrospectively as the original episode is "replayed."

Conceptually, the most basic real-time self-report measure can be viewed as a single-item measure with a temporal dimension added. Using some mechanical input device (e.g., a mouse or joystick), respondents adjust a computer display as often as necessary so that it always reflects how they are feeling each moment throughout an extended episode (e.g., Schuldberg & Gottlieb, 2002, used such a device to obtain 1,400 affect readings over 2.5 minutes for each subject). Several researchers have described continuous "rating dials" of this sort (Bradley & Lang, 2000; Bunce, Larsen, & Cruz, 1993; Fredrickson & Kahneman, 1993; Gottman & Levenson, 1985). Like rating scales more generally, rating dials may use either bipolar (very negative to very positive) or unipolar verbal anchors (no sadness at all to extreme sadness) and either Likert-type or visual analog scales.

Advantages to these procedures include automating self-report data collection, the ability to calibrate self-reports with other emotion measures (e.g., physiology, facial expressions) in the temporal stream, and the ability to use the technique "off line" to have participants continuously, though retrospectively, report on the emotions they were experiencing (e.g., Gottman & Levenson, 1985; Levenson & Gottman, 1983). The major disadvantage is the need for specialized equipment and the fact that the participant's attention is partially focused on the rating device. Moreover, it seems likely that continuously monitoring one's emotions may lead to a form of fatigue or may be so intrusive that it actually alters the respondent's emotions. Another drawback of this assessment strategy is that the techniques are limited to the self-report of just one or two dimensions. Although it is technically feasible, for example, to create a whole bank of rating dials (e.g., anger, fear, sadness, disgust, attraction, enjoyment, contentment), a limiting factor would be the respondent's ability to track the ebb and flow of multiple discrete emotions simultaneously.

Another category of self-report measures consists of the many standardized multi-item emotion inventories. Some of these inventories are checklists, whereas others are rating scales. These instruments are essentially variations on the self-report themes mentioned earlier, with differences having to do primarily with response scales, the number and nature of the emotion adjectives, the scoring and scale names, and the instructions that accompany the self-report tasks. The advantages of these inventories include their theory- or statistically guided development, empirical refinement and standardization, the development of norms (which allow cross-study comparisons and even meta-analysis; e.g., Larsen & Sinnett, 1991), and the accrual of research findings on specific measures and specific constructs-measure units.

One of the first self-report emotion inventories formally constructed was the 130-item Mood Adjective Checklist (MACL; Nowlis & Green, 1957). Not literally a checklist, the instructions ask the participant to rate how they feel on a Likert scale. Scoring results in 12 factor scores: aggression, anxiety,

urgency, elation, concentration, fatigue, social affection, sadness, skepticism, egotism, vigor, and nonchalance. Other researchers have proposed a simpler positive–negative valence scoring scheme (Stone, 1981). The MACL has not become widely used, most likely because it was never formally published (the original version appeared in an unpublished Naval Technical Report, Nowlis & Green, 1957).

A self-report emotion measure that eclipsed the MACL is Zuckerman and Lubin's (1965) Multiple Affect Adjective Checklist (MAACL). It is very similar to the MACL in length, with the MAACL having 132 items. The majority of the items overlap between the two inventories. The MAACL has become the most widely used self-report emotion assessment instrument in the psychological literature (Larsen & Sinnett, 1991). The MAACL's success is likely due to the fact that it is distributed by a professional test publisher and comes with a user manual, annotated references, developmental history, and psychometric properties, along with scoring keys and answer sheets. Other reasons for its popularity might be the checklist format, which makes administering the MAACL much faster than the MACL. And finally, the MAACL has only 3 subscales (depression, anxiety, and hostility), compared to 12 on the MACL. In 1985 Zuckerman and Lubin published a revised version of the Multiple Affect Adjective Checklist (MAACL–R). The revision mainly concerns the scoring format, which now allows for several pleasant emotion scores as well as global positive and negative affect and sensation seeking.

This is a good point to mention the issue of response formats. The MAACL and its revision are in the form of checklists, in which the subject merely indicates the presence or absence of a particular emotion by checking a box. Some researchers have argued that checklists are particularly susceptible to response styles and other forms of nonrandom error. Bentler (1969) argued against using checklists in psychometric assessment. Green, Goldman, and Salovey (1993) demonstrated that checklist emotion assessments contain significant nonrandom error, and they advised caution when analyzing or interpreting checklist data. However,

more recently, Schimmack, Böckenholt, and Reisenzein (2002) demonstrated that checklist and Likert-scale affect self-reports yield very similar covariance structures. The question of the impact of response format on affect ratings remains open.

Although several rating scales are available (see Stone, 1995), one of the more recent introductions is the Positive Affect Negative Affect Schedule (PANAS; Watson, Clark, & Tellegen, 1988). The PANAS is based on a dimensional model of emotion, in particular the circumplex model (Russell, 1980; Watson & Tellegen, 1985). Of the eight potential scores derivable from the circumplex model (Larsen & Diener, 1992), the PANAS focuses on two of these: Positive Affect (PA; high arousal pleasant), and Negative Affect (NA; high arousal unpleasant). The PANAS contains 10 items on each of the two scales. The items are mood adjectives and are rated on a 5-point scale, labeled as "not at all or slight," "a little," "moderately," "quite a bit," and "very much." The PA and NA scales were constructed to be uncorrelated, and they generally are (though see Zautra, Berkhof, & Nicolson, 2002, for exceptions).

Like most self-report measures, research on the validity of the PANAS has been primarily correlational. For example, extraversion correlates with frequent reports of PA, and neuroticism correlates with frequent reports of NA. In one of the first experimental studies of the PANAS, Larsen and Ketelaar (1991) induced emotions in the laboratory using guided imagery. They found that the positive induction increased PA but did not lower NA, and the negative induction increased NA but did not lower PA. Similar experimental findings on the independence of PA and NA under different inductions, using naturalistic success and failure feedback on exam performance in college students, were found by Goldstein and Strube (1994). This differential sensitivity to positive and negative emotion inductions supports the construct validity of the PANAS. Nevertheless, researchers should be very clear that the PANAS does not measure discrete emotions, which other scales do. The PANAS has its greatest utility in the assessment of the broad emotion dimensions of PA and NA.

Evaluation of self-report methods. Self-report methods are perhaps the most efficient techniques for measuring emotions. Nevertheless, they rely on assumptions that research participants are both able and willing to observe and report on their own emotions. Some issues concern a person's ability to self-report their emotions. Self-report requires memory, either working memory or longer-term memory, and so a variety of memory distortions may compromise a report (Feldman Barrett, 1997). Self-report also requires the perception of something on which to report. It is possible that a person may "have" an emotion in a nonverbal channel (e.g., autonomic activation or action tendency) yet never label that experience and hence not perceive it as an emotion at all (Tranel & Damasio, 1985). Moreover, some persons may repress emotional experiences, particularly negative or inappropriate emotional experiences, resulting in biased or incomplete report of emotions (Cutler, Bunce, & Larsen, 1996). Certain populations, for various reasons, may have meager or inaccurate comprehension of verbal information. For example, cultural psychologists have argued that some cultures have emotions, or emotion terms, that are not identifiable in other cultures (e.g., Mesquita & Frijda, 1992).

Regarding the second assumption—that participants must be willing to report on their emotions—the issue here is mainly one of response sets, where responses to items might be based, not on the emotion content of the items, but on some other factor, such as their social desirability. Here the participant is responding to the items in a manner that creates a positive impression. A different response set is extreme responding, where a participant may be motivated to use scale endpoints or large numbers in describing their emotions, a response set that can greatly distort the covariance structure of a set of ratings (Bentler, 1969).

Another potential problem with self-report is measurement reactivity, where the actual process of measurement alters the psychological construct being measured. Administering an emotion self-report may, in fact, influence the emotional state of interest. Another issue arises when researchers want to assess emotion two or more times, as in within-subject experimental designs or in experience sampling studies of emotion. One potential effect of repeated emotion measurement is stereotypic responding (Stone, 1995), where participants settle into a response profile that does not change much across the assessment occasions.

Self-report emotion measures require that subjects engage in a number of psychological processes to arrive at a rating. Understanding these processes has both theoretical as well as measurement implications. For instance, providing a global self-report implicates memory processes, as respondents recall the targeted episode, as well as aggregation processes, as respondents in some manner integrate their multiple and often varied momentary experiences into an overall rating. Both of these mental processes may obscure or misrepresent dynamic changes in emotion as experienced over time. For instance, Kahneman and his colleagues have documented that people's global reports of pain episodes draw highly from the momentary affect experienced at the most intense point during the episode, as well as the final moments of the episode, with the duration of the emotional experience largely neglected in the global self-report (Fredrickson & Kahneman, 1993; Kahneman, 1999; Kahneman, Fredrickson, Schrieber, & Redelmeier, 1993; see also Thomas & Diener, 1990 for related issues).

Other language parameters related to emotion. Another language-related channel with potential as a measure of emotion is the voice. Vocalization may be sensitive to emotion-related changes in the body (e.g., muscle tension, respiration rate, and blood pressure). Vocal analysis for emotion has traditionally followed one of two possible strategies. The simplest strategy is to have humans listen to audiotaped speech and evaluate the speaker's affective state. A more technologically advanced strategy is to have audiotapes digitized and analyzed by computer.

The ability of untrained listeners to correctly recognize or infer speakers' emotional states has been evaluated in several studies (e.g., Scherer, 1986; Scherer, Banse, Wallbott, & Goldbeck, 1991; van Bezooijen, 1984). In these studies actors are used to produce sentences in a way that imparts a specific emotional tone (e.g., anger, fear, disgust, joy, sadness). The speech samples are then stripped

of vocal content and are then played for naïve listeners who judge which emotion they perceive in the vocalization. Correct selection rates across these studies average around 55%, a rate four to five times what would be expected by chance (Pittam & Scherer, 1993). Some emotions are more easily recognized by naïve raters than others: Sadness and anger are best recognized, whereas disgust, contempt, and joy are least recognized in vocalization samples (Pittam & Scherer, 1993; van Bozooijen, Otto, & Heenan, 1983).

Studies also suggest that arousal level may be better transmitted by vocal cues than is specific hedonic content (i.e., Apple & Hecht, 1982; van Bozooijen et al., 1983). Reviews of recent research suggest that although perceivers are more accurate in judging nonspecific arousal from vocal parameters, they are nevertheless well above chance in judging pleasantness and specific emotions from speech samples that have had the verbal content removed (Bachorowski, 1999). A particularly impressive set of results is reported by Scherer, Banse, and Wallbott (2001). These researchers used professional German actors to produce vocal samples spoken in fear, anger, sadness, joy, and neutral vocal tones. The actual verbal content was then stripped away, leaving only vocalization. The samples were then taken to nine different countries in North America, Asia, and Europe, where participants from different language groups listened to the vocalizations and rated the likely emotions. Overall accuracy averaged 66%, a figure well above chance.

Researchers studying digital voice analysis are still searching for the parameters that best reflect emotion. Parameters typically assessed are (a) fundamental frequency, perceived as overall voice pitch; (b) small perturbations in the fundamental frequency; (c) intensity, indexed in decibels; and (d) speech rate or tempo (Scherer, 1986). Whereas acoustical analysis of speech most accurately reflects the nonspecific arousal of the speaker (Bachorowski & Owren, 1995), it falls far short of identifying specific emotions. For example, positive and negative emotional states are often not reliably distinguished with acoustical parameter (Scherer, 1986; see also Pittam & Scherer, 1993). Because untrained listeners can distinguish specific emo-

tions from voice samples, there must be some acoustical cues for affect. However, at this time, researchers are still searching for those cues. See Russell, Bachorowski, and Fernandez-Dols (2003) for a recent review of vocal measures of emotion.

Emotion Assessed Through Behavior

Behaviors that are linked to emotions range from the very simple, such as defensive reflex actions, to the complex, such as sequences of action tendencies. Emotions likely evolved to produce adaptive actions, such as to approach desired objects or to withdraw from dangerous objects, as well as to support more flexible action tendencies associated with survival. Researchers may take advantage of these behavioral outputs to estimate emotions.

Behavior action tendencies. One behavioral manifestation of emotion concerns the action tendencies that become more or less likely during emotion. Tasks that inquire about various actions or intentions may be linked to emotion states. One task is to ask participants how much they would like to engage in various behaviors, such as talk with a good friend, engage in some exercise, or have a pleasant meal. Teasdale and colleagues (Teasdale, Taylor, & Fogarty, 1980) reported that this task is sensitive to depressed mood or sadness, which has the action tendency of social withdrawal. When sad, people often lose interest in activities that formerly gave them pleasure. Sadness is also thought to be associated with depressed psychomotor function. Writing speed, for example, is negatively correlated with sadness and depression (see Velten, 1968, who used this task as one criterion measure in the validation study of the mood induction that bears his name). Other psychomotor tasks that have been used in emotion research include letter cancellation and smooth pursuit motor tracking tasks. Performance speed is most sensitive to sadness or depressed emotional states. Pleasant emotions, however, do not appear to increase psychomotor speed.

A variety of other behavioral tasks have been shown to be sensitive to affective states (Mayer, 1986; Mayer & Bremer, 1985; Mayer, Mamberg, & Volanth, 1988). One category of emotion-sensitive tasks consists of judgment tasks. One assessment

strategy is to have participants make probability estimates of the likelihood of various good and bad events. For example, participants may be asked the probability of being killed in an airplane crash, dying in a car accident, or contracting cancer in their lifetime. It has been shown that persons in generalized unpleasant emotional states overestimate the probability of such bad events (Johnson & Tversky, 1983). The converse—increased probability estimates of good events while in positive emotional states—also appears true (Zelenski & Larsen, 2002). Results also apply to specific emotions; for example, fearful people make pessimistic judgments of future events (Lerner & Keltner, 2000). General appraisals of events also show emotion-specific patterns (Herrald & Tomaka, 2002; Siemer, 2001).

Another emotion-sensitive behavioral task is to ask participants to generate associations to positive, neutral, and negative stimuli. For example, have participants write down as many words as come to mind in 60 seconds when they hear each of the following stimulus words: happy, disappointed, generous, destroy, peace, or pain. Mayer and Bremer (1985) showed that performance on this task correlated with naturally occurring mood. Seidlitz and Diener (1993) used a variation wherein participants recalled as many happy experiences from their own life as they could in a given time period. Participants higher on trait-positive affect recalled more pleasant experiences, in the same time period, than participants lower on trait happiness. Teasdale and colleagues (Teasdale & Fogarty, 1979; Teasdale & Russell, 1983) have also demonstrated that emotion inductions influence recall of pleasant and unpleasant events in predictable (i.e., hedonically consistent) ways.

Another behavioral strategy for assessing emotion involves various information processing parameters. Reaction times in lexical decision tasks, for example, have been shown to be sensitive to affective states (Challis & Krane, 1988). For example, the participant's task might be to judge whether a string of letters represents a word or a nonword. On each trial the letters represent either: a nonword, an emotion word (e.g., anger), or a neutral word (e.g., house). Participants in positive affective states are quicker and sometimes more accurate at judging positive words compared to participants in neutral states, and vice versa for unpleasant moods (Niedenthal & Setterlund, 1994).

A related assessment task is to present participants with incomplete word stems and ask them to add letters to complete the word. Word stems are selected so that they can be completed as an emotion term or as a neutral term. For example, ANG_ _ could be completed as ANGER or as ANGLE or ANGEL or as ANGLO; JO_ could be completed as JOY or as JOB (e.g., Rusting & Larsen, 1998). A related technique is the use of homophones (words that sound alike but have different meanings). With this technique, the subject hears the word (die or dye, for example) and is asked to write that word. Participants in an unpleasant mood are more likely to write or complete the word stems in a manner congruent with their mood (Halberstadt, Niedenthal, & Kushner, 1995).

Behaviors that are enhanced or disrupted by emotion. So far we have discussed how certain behaviors directly follow from emotional states, and how specific emotion-related tasks may be influenced by the emotional state of the participant. However, other categories of behaviors, such as the defensive reflex or perception or attentional control, may be enhanced or disrupted by emotion, and thus might be used as an indicator or measure of emotion (Compton, 2000). One such emotion-sensitive task relies on a very simple behavior—the startle reflex. The startle reflex involves a rapid shutting of the eyes (blink), pulling the chin down, and a rapid inhalation. The startle reflex is easy to elicit through the application of a sudden and loud acoustic stimulus. Startle potentiation refers to an increase in the startle response (measured as a faster or stronger eye blink) when the person is startled while they are in an unpleasant emotional state (Vrana, Spence, & Lang, 1988). The researcher most responsible for developing this technique in humans is Peter Lang (e.g., Lang, Bradley, & Cuthbert, 1990). Lang and colleagues, as well as others (Skolnick & Davidson, 2002), have demonstrated

startle potentiation for unpleasant emotions compared to neutral states. The converse—slower and weaker startle when in positive emotional states—is rarely found.

A final behavioral paradigm with potential for measurement concerns the effects emotion has on cognitive parameters such as attention (Buodo, Sarlo, & Palomba, 2002). One effect is the automatic vigilance effect (Cothran, Zelenski, Prizmic, & Larsen, 2003; Pratto & John, 1991), which refers to the "grabbing" of attention by aversive or threatening information. The so-called emotional Stroop paradigm is one example of the automatic vigilance effect, where, in naming the colors of various words, people are generally slower to name the color if the word is threat-related. Presumably, threatening stimuli are processed more carefully, especially if one is already in an aversive emotional state, resulting in slowing on the primary, nonemotional task (color naming). Another behavioral paradigm, where cognitive parameters are influenced by both the emotional state of the participant, as well as the emotional content of the stimuli, concerns emotional priming (Wentura & Rothermund, 2003), as well as other irrelevant feature tasks, such as the Affective Simon task (De Houwer, 2003), where the participant in supposed to ignore the emotional content of a stimulus while responding to some other relevant feature.

Emotion Assessed Through Physiology

Emotion output that can be assessed with physiological methods can be divided into two categories: the somatic changes and changes reflecting autonomic or central nervous system activity. The somatic changes most useful to emotion researchers concern muscle movements associated with emotional expression, particularly those somatic changes on the face.

Measures of somatic change. One useful measurement strategy is to have an observer rate how much emotion a target participant appears to be feeling, based on expressive cues. The observers might be "experts" on the target person's emotional experiences (e.g., a spouse or a therapist). One limitation

is that observer reports are based on social attributions of a target's emotional state, and such attributions will be limited by the information available, biased by a target's impression management strategies, or even influenced by the raters' own level of emotion being rated (Marcus & Miller, 1999). As such, observer ratings of emotion are probably best used in combination with other measures. One way to limit attributions is to use trained observers. A standardized training system for observers is the Specific Affect Coding System (SPAFF; Coan & Gottman, in press; Gottman & Krokoff, 1989; Gottman & Levenson, 1992; for a brief review, see Gottman, 1993). This system separates expressed emotion into specific categories of positive and negative categories (e.g., interest, affection, humor, validation, excitement/joy, anger, belligerence, domineering, contempt, disgust, tension, sadness, whining, and defensiveness). SPAFF training involves recognizing and attending to important facial, gestural, and vocal markers of emotion. Significant benefits of observer ratings are that they can be unobtrusive, can be used in naturalistic settings, are inexpensive and fast, and can provide emotion measures from a few visible cues.

Some somatic coding systems are based on specific observable changes in facial muscles. One such system for coding emotion in the face is the Facial Action Coding System (FACS; Ekman & Friesen, 1975, 1978). The FACS consists of 46 anatomically based "action units" (or AUs), which refer to a specific observable change in the face. For example, AU 1 raises the inner brows, AU 9 wrinkles the nose, and AU 12 raises the outer lip corners. The system requires extensive training and certification for reliable use (cf. Ekman & Friesen, 1975, 1978). A drawback of FACS is the extensive amount of time needed to code expressions. FACS scoring requires about 1 hour of coding for each minute of videotape (depending on the density of facial action). Researchers are developing computer vision to undertake the tiresome task of facial action coding. One of the more advanced systems is that being developed at Carnegie Mellon University under the guidance of Jeffry Cohn (see Cohn, Zlochower, Lien, & Kanade, 1999), which is able to accurately

code approximately half of the FACS action units in real time. Alternatively, Ekman and others have developed more global coding systems, which are based on fewer AUs, for coding facial action (e.g., EMFACS by Ekman & Friesen, see Fridland, Ekman, & Oster, 1986; MAX by Izard, 1979).

Somatic facial assessments may also be obtained using physiological measures of muscle contractions. The neural activation of the muscles produces action potentials that can be directly measured on the surface of the skin using electromyography (EMG) using two electrodes placed over the muscle of interest. The amount of electrical activity detected is directly proportional to the magnitude of contraction. Detailed descriptions of facial electromyographic technique may be found in Cacioppo, Petty, Losch, and Kim (1986). EMG is able to assess muscular contractions that are too small to produce visible changes (i.e., not FACS codable; Cacioppo et al., 1986). Such sensitivity has a disadvantage, however, in that electrical signals from sites other than the muscle of interest may also be detected during EMG assessments. Researchers interested in measuring emotions with facial EMG should have training in electrophysiological technique or collaborate with someone with such expertise.

Physiological measures of nervous system activity associated with emotion. Emotions are closely tied to tendencies to act in specific ways, and changes in the nervous system occur primarily to support these actions (Frijda, 1986; Lazarus, 1991). In terms of the autonomic nervous system (ANS), a few researchers hold the view that distinct emotions are associated with distinct ANS activity (e.g., Levenson, Ekman, & Friesen, 1990). Empirical support for specific autonomic patterns being associated with specific emotions has been obtained in several studies. However, the cumulative data on specific emotional "signatures" are mixed and therefore remain inconclusive (for reviews, see Cacioppo & Gardner, 1999; Cacioppo, Klein, Berntson, & Hatfield, 1993; Levenson, 1992; Zajonc & McIntosh, 1992).

Diverse autonomic measures have been used to assess emotion, some more fruitfully than others. We will mention here only a couple of the more promising measures and advise the interested reader to consult Cacioppo, Tassinary, and Berntson (2000); Stern, Davis, and Ray (1992); or Hugdahl (1996) for more details. Electrodermal activity, especially skin conductance, is a widely accepted and reliable measure used in emotion research. Another category of measures is based on respiratory activity. Perhaps the largest category of measures is those based on cardiovascular activity. This last set includes measures such as heart rate, diastolic and systolic blood pressure, cardiac output, stroke volume, and total peripheral resistance. Readers interested in cardiac measures should consult Sherwood (1993) and Sherwood et al. (1990) for details on impedance cardiography. Other researchers assess the link between respiratory and cardiovascular activity (e.g., respiratory sinus arrhythmia or heart rate variability), which appears related to emotion state (Grossman, van Beek, & Wientjes, 1990; Porges, 1995). It should be noted that professional polygraphers typically employ a multimethod approach, using measures of skin conductance, respiration, and heart rate to infer the emotion of guilt.

Researchers have recently begun to refine central nervous system measures of emotion. Scalp-recorded brain electrical activity, or electroencephalogram (EEG), has been used successfully to distinguish pleasant and unpleasant emotion states (e.g., Schmidt & Trainor, 2001), as well as individual differences in affective style (for a review, see Davidson, 1993). Other more localized imaging measures of emotion-related changes in the brain are on the horizon as well, including functional MRI (for an overview, see Berthoz, Blair, Le Clec'h, & Martinot, 2002). The versatility of functional imaging methods for studying mechanisms of emotion is significant, given its superior spatial resolution (Mayberg & McGinnis, 2000). The temporal resolution is not as good as EEG measures, however.

Many practical issues emerge when contemplating the use of physiological measures. First, these measures are typically invasive. Some measures (e.g., being inserted into a large MRI magnet) might elicit emotions (e.g., panic) themselves. Less-invasive measures are pulse rate and skin conductance. Impedance cardiography uses metal bands that cir-

cle a participant's neck and chest in several locations. Attaching these requires participants to partially disrobe. Blood pressure assessment typically uses pressurized cuffs that, when inflated, draw attention and sometimes even cause pain. Physiological measures also usually restrict participants' mobility because of wires that connect them to amplifiers and recording devices. Bodily movement can also create artifacts in measurement. In general, the use of physiological assessments requires special efforts on the part of both the researcher and the participants, but may potentially pay off with a unique methodological perspective or window on the emotional state under investigation.

SUMMARY AND CONCLUSIONS

In this chapter we presented three broad categories of measures of emotion, including language, behavior, and physiology. We argued that the construct of emotion presents several challenges for assessment, the largest of which is the fact that emotions are reflected in multiple response systems, which are themselves loosely coupled and complexly interacting. Moreover, emotions can be thought of and measured as states or traits, as broad dimensions, or as unique specific emotions and as points along a temporal cascade of change. These challenges make issues of measurement reliability and validity especially complex.

Emotion constructs have multiple indicators, and each indicator reflects varying degrees of the intended construct, as well as more than the intended construct. Consequently, researchers cannot proceed with a monomethod approach or assume that one indicator is as good as any other indicator. Multimethod approaches are especially necessary in emotion research, though clearly such an approach will require a good deal of technical expertise and skillful collaborators. Nevertheless, multimethod assessment in emotion is starting to have important theoretical payoffs. Examples can be found in the work of Vrana, who has used multiple methods to differentiate negative emotions (1993, 1995) as well as locating multiple emotion assessment methods within the dimensional space defined by valance and arousal (Vrana & Rollock, 2002; Witvliet & Vrana, 1995, 2000). Modeling multiple methods within a consensual or method-invariant space will be an important contribution to this area as well as provide researchers with a parsimonious system for organizing multiple methods. Until then, researchers should always consider using multiple methods in emotion research because doing so will almost always lead to gains in our knowledge of emotion.

CHAPTER 24

MULTIMETHOD APPROACHES TO THE STUDY OF COGNITION: THE EVOLUTION OF CONCEPTS IN RESEARCH ON HUMAN MEMORY

Aaron S. Benjamin

Similar to many scientific pursuits within psychology, the study of human cognition is an exercise that is equal parts imagination, deduction, and salesmanship. Theoretical claims are bootstrapped onto the elaborate but typically freewheeling artifices constructed by fellow psychologists who maintain equally fragile footing. Despite the blustery nature of cognitive theorizing, a central question remains unresolved: What constitutes necessary and sufficient evidence for the existence of a psychological mechanism?

Even the earliest theorists encountered situations in which multiple measures of nominally equivalent cognitive processes had different psychometric properties and showed differential effects of a common manipulation. Ebbinghaus (1885) noted, for example, that measures of relearning were much more sensitive to distant prior experience than measures of recall. Much of the history of cognitive psychology can be interpreted in the context of debates about how to reconcile such differences. The purpose of this chapter is to provide an illustration of how modern cognitive psychology deals with the divergences and convergences made apparent by the use of multiple measures and, in doing so, how those effects can be used profitably in the development of theory and the postulation of mental systems.

I will not attempt to address well-developed statistical tools that are the focus of chapters 18 to 21 and others in this volume. Rather, I will concentrate on model-based interpretations of multiple measures and how the application of such techniques

has advanced theoretical development in cognitive psychology. In doing so, I will review four topics related to the specific problems addressed by and applications of multimethod approaches to understanding cognition. In the first and largest section, I will examine several modern examples of how measurements that combine systematically related dependent variables can yield functions that are more reliable and more informative than ones that can be derived from single measures. The second section will focus on the evaluation of the theories of cognition, most specifically on the question of how formal models can be tested in such a way that emphasizes their ability to account for extant data patterns without being so powerful that they predict other invalid data sets. Third, we will address the question of how traditional behavioral measurements in cognitive psychology can be meaningfully integrated with brain-based measures assessing electromagnetic properties of cellular material in the brain or hemodynamic properties of blood flow to the brain. Finally, we will examine one domain in which prominent theorists have tried to establish guidelines for what kind of and how much evidence is necessary for the postulation of a mental system.

To tie these sections together, the accompanying examples in each section will draw on current and historical developments in research on memory, with the objective of illustrating to the reader how the judicious combination of different measures has motivated important theoretical developments in that field.

COMBINING MEASUREMENTS TO YIELD GENERALIZABLE PSYCHOLOGICAL FUNCTIONS

Often we wish to measure cognitive performance in a domain in which behavior is strongly and systematically related to some individual difference variable that we are not concerned with. This fact poses two problems from a measurement perspective. First, it adds a source of variability to our sampling distributions. This problem can be annoying and may force us into increasing the sample size of our experiment, but it is hardly fatal. A second, more dangerous, effect is that individual differences may relegate our measurements to a region of parameter space that does not reflect a meaningful or complete range of the behavior in question.

Three general strategies exist to counter the negative effects of individual differences limiting the range of our measurements. First, the researcher can use established theoretical principles in a domain to interpolate or extrapolate to portions of the function that are sparsely occupied by data. Second, the missing data can be inferred statistically by fitting a parsimonious function to the data, such as the lowest order polynomial that accounts for some predetermined proportion of the data. Third, researchers can use a data-collection strategy that ensures sampling across the range of the measurement in question. This can be done by strategically varying the conditions or instructions of an experiment in such a way so as to induce variability along the individual-difference dimension. By doing so, the function relating that dimension to the performance measure can be estimated for each subject. Here I lay out two examples of how this technique is commonly used in memory research. In both of these cases, the solution to the problem of confounding individual differences lies in the elicitation of measures across multiple strategically varied conditions.

Speed–Accuracy Trade-Offs in Recognition Memory

Consider an experiment in which subjects are asked to make a recognition judgment—that is, to decide for each in a list of stimuli whether they believe to have seen that item in a particular earlier study episode. One subject might not care much about the advancement of science, want to get out and get to lunch, and thus zip his way through our task as quickly as humanly possible, making each decision after only the least amount of deliberation. Another subject might feel as though the experimenter will treat her score as a measure of intelligence, character, or trustworthiness and thus pore over each test stimulus to extract every available mote of information from memory before making a recognition decision. Such individual differences are commonplace in decision tasks like this one. Even if we use some between-subject manipulation of learning, for example, we have faith that random assignment will wash away such strategic differences over our sample.

But what if our entire sample was like the first hypothetical subject described earlier? This scenario is not entirely unlikely at many major American universities. Our laboratory might be aesthetically unappealing, or our experimenters might have bad breath; such factors can also influence strategy selection in our subjects.

Hypothetical group means are shown in the top panel of Figure 24.1 and indicate no effect of our learning manipulation. It would be useful to know if there is a restriction placed on our data by an inadequate range of decision speeds. In this case, all subjects performed the task quickly, but we have no way of assessing that fact. Even if we measured decision response time (RT), we would be ill equipped to make any such judgments without a sense of what the "full" parameter range of response speeds should be. The solution to this problem is to create a within-subjects variable along which we manipulate the decision placement along the speed–accuracy trade-off spectrum. We might, for example, use payoffs for different combinations of correct or speedy decisions. We might simply instruct the subjects to make decisions quickly or to take their time. Perhaps most effectively, we can force subjects to withhold their response until a delimited amount of time has elapsed and then force them to make their response within a given time window (Reed, 1973). If we use such a strategy, we ensure the collection of performance data across a reasonable range of decision speeds. We

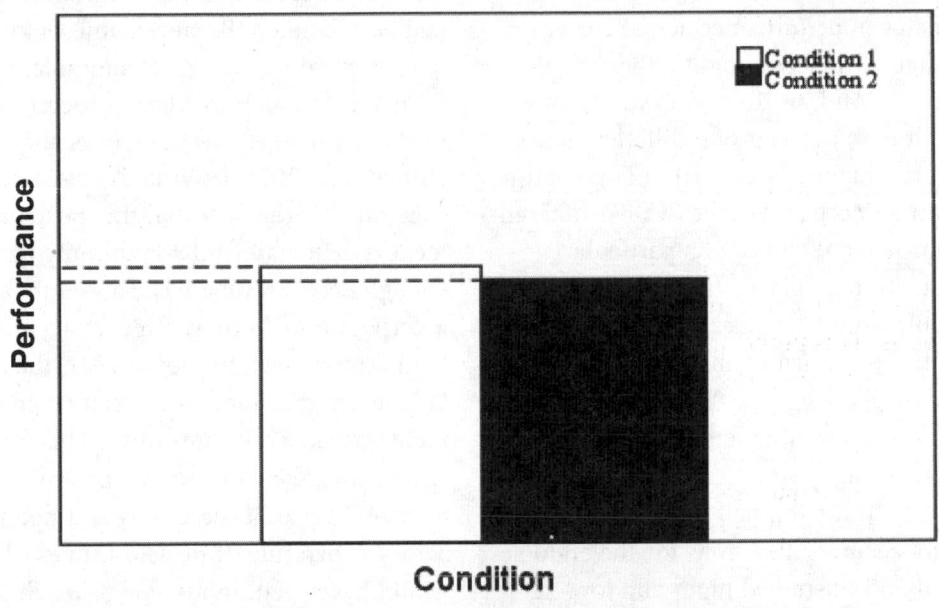

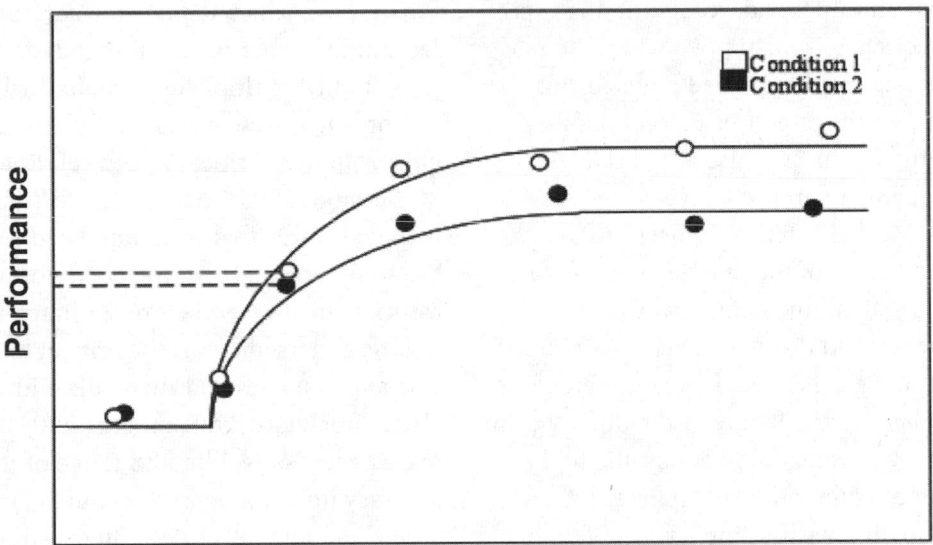

Manipulated Lag + Mean Response Time

FIGURE 24.1. Group means *(top panel)* and speed–accuracy trade-off functions *(bottom panel)* for two hypothetical conditions.

can also clearly detect those subjects that ignore our manipulation and treat them and their data appropriately.

The data in the bottom half of Figure 24.1 show what such figures look like. The data here have been fit with a shifted exponential function,

$$P = A\left(1 - e^{-R(t-I)}\right) \; for \; t \geq I \qquad (1)$$

in which A represents asymptotic accuracy, R the rate of approach to the asymptote, I the point at which performance first rises above the floor of chance performance on the task, and t the time point after the onset of the stimulus. One important aspect of such a function is that is can be used to describe behavior for each subject. Whereas an individual mean provides only a scalar value that is some unknown combination of performance and

individual-difference characteristics, this function provides estimates of performance across the entire meaningful range of the confounding individual-difference variable. And, by doing so, we can now see that our failure to detect group differences in the top part of the Figure 24.1 owed in large part to the fact that our subjects, by virtue of their inherent laziness and consequent choice of a particularly speedy decision strategy, placed themselves in a range in which it would have been quite difficult to detect an effect of our learning manipulation.

Figure 24.2 displays some actual results that demonstrate how this technique has proven useful in evaluating important theoretical questions in human cognition. In the top half of Figure 24.2 are empirical speed–accuracy functions for the endorsement of studied and unstudied high- and low-frequency words (Hintzman, Caulton, & Curran, 1994). As is commonly found, recognition is superior for low-frequency words in two ways: the rate of correct endorsement for studied items, or hit rate, is higher, and the rate of incorrect endorsement of unstudied items, or false-alarm rate, is lower, thus yielding a *mirror effect* (Glanzer & Adams, 1990). Most theoretical stances are in agreement about the nature of the difference in hit rate: The presentation of an uncommon word constitutes a distinctive event, and distinctive events are more memorable. However, there are several different extant proposals as to the nature of the difference in false-alarm rate. One suggestion is that the higher false-alarm rate to common words reflects the fact such words enjoy higher baseline levels of familiarity because of the greater number and frequency of exposures to such words, by definition (e.g., Glanzer & Adams, 1985; Hintzman, 1988).

Another suggestion is that recognition decisions are made after two sources of evidence are assessed. First, the word is matched against memory, yielding an overall assessment of mnemonic familiarity. Second, the word is evaluated as to its likely memorability, and recognition standards are set that are commensurate with that assessment (e.g., Benjamin, Bjork, & Hirshman, 1998; Brown, Lewis, & Monk, 1977). That is, after determining how familiar a word is, the subject makes a metamnemonic

assessment of how familiar it *would* be, if the word had been studied. Because subjects know high-frequency words to be less memorable, they set lower standards for such words and therefore endorse unstudied high-frequency words at a higher rate (Benjamin, 2003; cf. Wixted, 1992). Central to this suggestion is the idea that this postretrieval assessment is deliberate and should only be evident if enough decision time has elapsed for the subject to incorporate such knowledge.

As can be seen in Figure 24.2, the difference in false-alarm rate appears in each response period, including the very short ones. This result is inconsistent with the concept of a postretrieval assessment. However, if these data had not been collected across a spectrum of decision times, this conclusion would have been impossible to reach.

Now consider the display in the bottom half of Figure 24.2, which depicts results from a different recognition experiment. In that experiment, subjects studied multiple lists, each of which consisted of words that were semantically associated to a single, unstudied "critical" word (cf. Roediger & McDermott, 1995). At test, the distractor set included words that were unrelated to the themes of the study lists and also the critical unstudied high associate mentioned before. An interesting pattern of false endorsement of the critical foils is evident: The rate first rises and then falls with decision time (Heit, Brockdorff, & Lamberts, 2004). Notably, if one assessed only a limited range of the speed–accuracy function here, one could conclude that false-alarm rate to "critical" items either increases or decreases along that range, depending on where one found oneself on that function (Benjamin, 2001).

This method thus has three major advantages. First, we minimize the risk of individual difference variables colluding in such a way so as to restrict our measurements to a range in which effects are not easily detected. Second, when we reparameterize our accuracy data as the terms of the function that we fit them to, we hopefully increase the reliability and validity of our data. I say "hopefully" because such an outcome depends critically on the correctness of the function that we choose to summarize our data. The question of how to evaluate

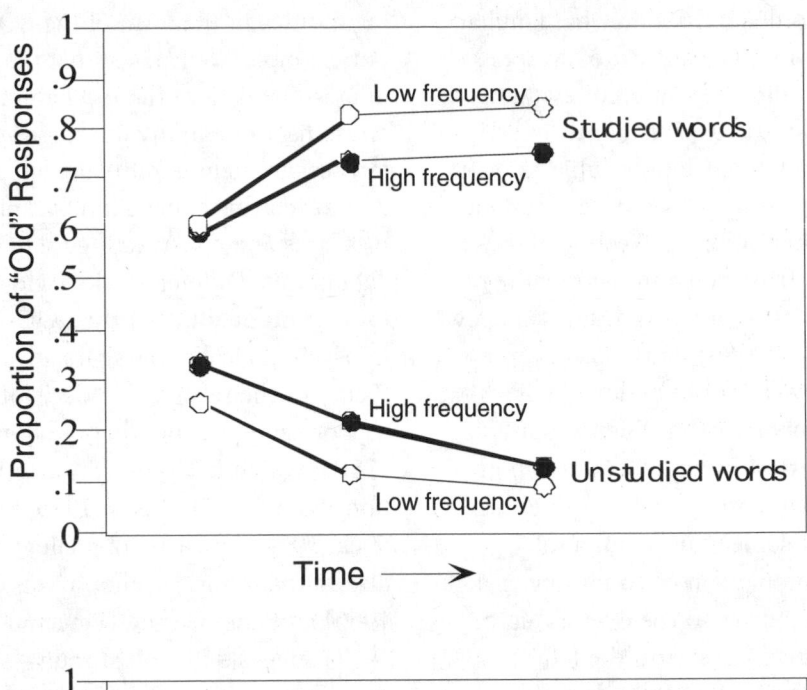

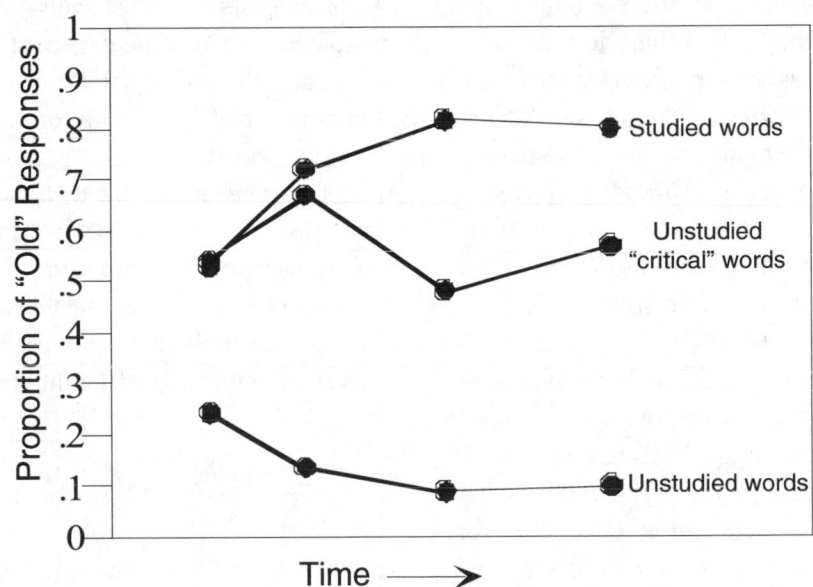

FIGURE 24.2. *Top panel:* Proportion of endorsements to old and new high- and low-frequency words across a range of decision times. *Bottom panel:* Proportion of endorsements to old, new, and new "critical" words across a range of decision times.

the correctness of a model is addressed in the next major section of this chapter. A final advantage is that the derived functions allow us to evaluate hypotheses that would be unaddressable were we to deal with single data points, for example, questions about the rate of information accrual.

Response Bias in Recognition Memory

In the previous example, I portrayed decision time as a potential individual-difference variable influencing recognition performance. Similarly, individuals can differ in the amount of evidence they demand before making a positive recognition

response. If a test word is only somewhat familiar, how is that uncertainty translated into a response? Clearly, different people bring different evidential standards to the table, and aspects of our experimental situation also influence how subjects make their decisions. Subjects might want, for example, to maximize the proportion of correct responses to old items—thinking that such a measure more validly reflects memory ability—and thus set a low recognition criterion: If a test item looks even vaguely familiar, they choose to endorse it. This somewhat arbitrary choice can influence our results: In the top part of Figure 24.3 are hypothetical group means, again corresponding to performance as a function of some manipulation of learning. Here the comparison of conditions is complicated by large differences in the overall "agreeability" of our subjects: Subjects in the left condition say "yes" more often than does the other group—to both old *and* new items. This fact reveals that our manipulation affected the decision strategies associated with recognition, but it is unclear whether it also influences memorability. To answer this question, we need to implement an experimental strategy similar to the one discussed earlier and gain experimental control over response criterion placement.

The lower part of Figure 24.3 shows performance across a wide range of response biases, plotted on axes corresponding to hit rate and false-alarm rate, yielding a receiver-operating characteristic (ROC). Such data can be elicited by, for example, having subjects complete multiple recognition tests under different payoff conditions. More commonly, subjects are asked to indicate a degree of subjective confidence along with the recognition decision; performance is then plotted as a cumulative function of the hit rate and false-alarm rate at a given confidence level and below. This technique allows for the construction of a ROC from two related but fundamentally different measures: the yes/no recognition response and subjective confidence.

In such a display, differences between subjects or between conditions that reflect differences in criterion setting for the decision component of the recognition judgment are virtually eliminated, and

regularities in the form of the ROC are evident. In our example, we can see that the dots, corresponding to the data in the top half of the figure, lie on an isodiscriminability curve. In other words, no differences in memorability are apparent. Yet we could only reach this conclusion by uniting multiple measures and constructing an ROC that fits the data points. Different tasks yield different functional forms, and qualities of the ROC can be directly tied to psychological parameters, given a well-specified theory of the recognition decision.

For example, the Theory of Signal Detection (TSD), which has evolved into a theory of recognition (Banks, 1970; Egan, 1975; Lockhart & Murdock, 1970) by virtue of analogy with problems of discrimination in psychophysics (Green & Swets, 1966) and engineering (Peterson, Birdsall, & Fox, 1954) suggests that all stimuli—studied and unstudied—elicit some degree of mnemonic evidence, and the task for the subject is to set a decision criterion at some point on the spectrum of potential evidence values.

Certain versions of this theory posit that the probability distributions for evidence are Gaussian in form. This theory has implications for the form of the ROC. Specifically, underlying Gaussian probability distributions imply that a plot of the ROC on binormal axes should yield a straight line. More formally,

$$Z(HR) = \frac{1}{\delta_S} Z(FAR) + \frac{\mu_S}{\delta_S} \qquad (2)$$

in which δ_S represents the variability of the evidence distribution for studied items, and μ_S represents its mean. This function is superimposed on the two conditions in Figure 24.3 (on probability axes).

Distributions of equal variance thus imply that that line should have unit slope. Figure 24.4 shows actual ROC and zROC functions from a representative experiment on recognition memory. The similarities among the Z-transformed functions are striking: they do indeed appear to be linear and have a slope of ~0.8 (Ratcliff, Sheu, & Gronlund, 1992). These functions thus reveal that the underlying probability distributions may well be normal, but they are apparently not of equal variance. This particular result suggests that the variance of the

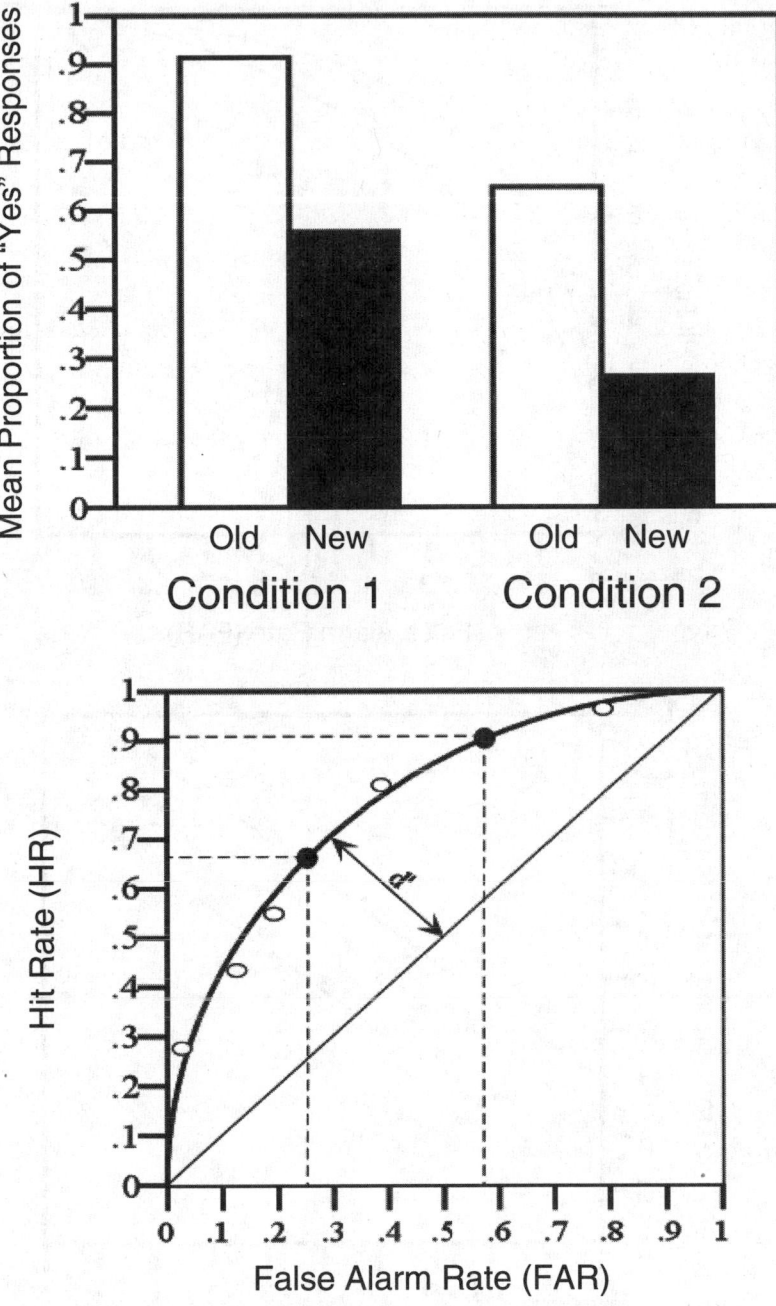

FIGURE 24.3. Hit rates and false alarm rates from two hypothetical conditions (*top panel*); hit rates and false alarm rates coplotted across a range of response criteria, as a receiver-operating characteristic (ROC; *bottom panel*). d′ indicates the discriminability of studied and unstudied stimuli.

distribution of evidence for studied items is approximately 1.25 times larger than for the distribution for unstudied items.

The form of ROC curves has also been brought to bear on the question that we introduced earlier, namely, what processes underlie the mirror effect in recognition? Consider the relationship between word frequency and recognition, as discussed in the previous section. The evidence from speed–accuracy trade-off functions was equivocal as to the question of whether a slow-acting deliberative process combines with general memory familiarity to produce

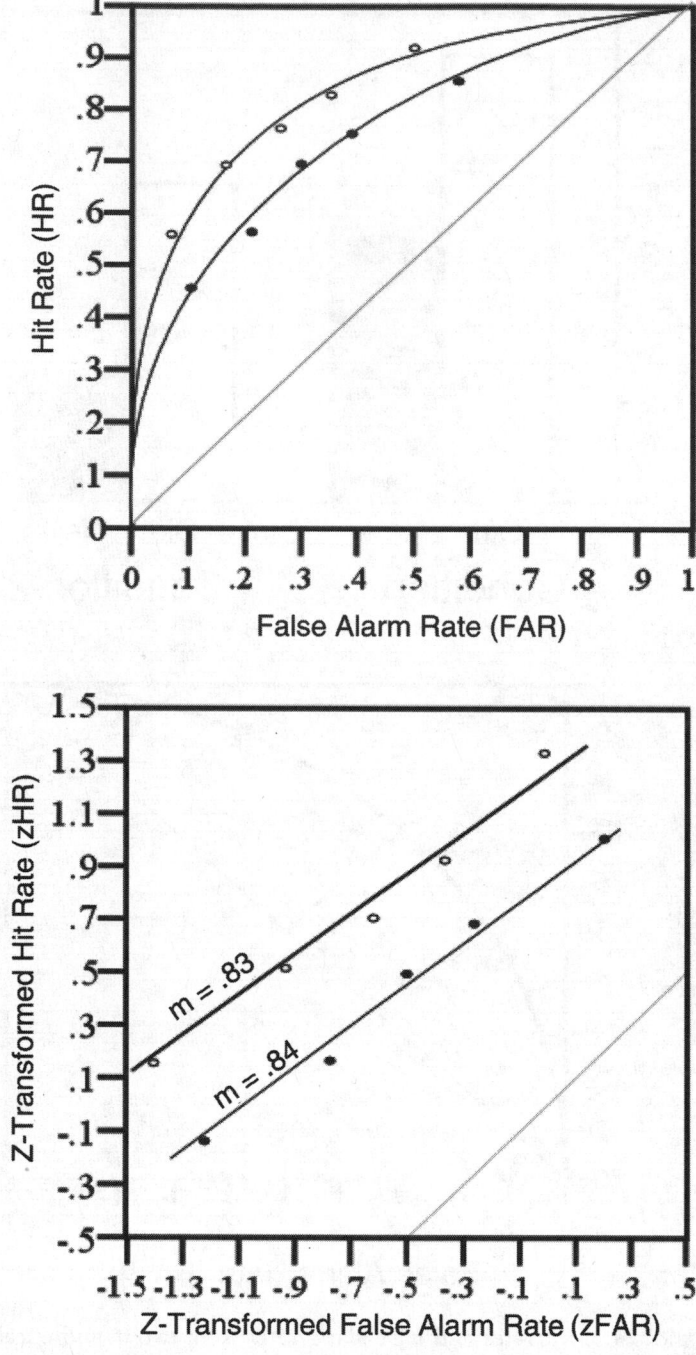

FIGURE 24.4. ROC and normalized ROC (zROC) functions from an experiment on recognition memory. The slope of the line is indicated by *m*.

the empirical dissociation seen between hit rate and false-alarm rate as a function of word frequency. In the preceding case, the argument concerned whether subjects made a postmnemonic assessment of the normative familiarity of the stimulus, thereby deriving a value against which to compare the actual experienced familiarity of the word.

Another argument is that two different processes can contribute to the endorsement of an item on a recognition test. The first is the same as that por-

trayed in the earlier argument: Stimuli enjoy some temporary boost in familiarity as a function of exposure, and this familiarity value provides some evidence of the recency or probability of past encounters with this word. Notably, however, the familiarity itself conveys nothing about the specific nature of the previous experience, so it can lead to spurious false alarms to other recently exposed but contraindicated stimuli (Jacoby, 1999) or even to unstudied stimuli that are systematically related to studied materials (Roediger & McDermott, 1995).

Familiarity is hypothesized to be augmented by an additional process, often called *recollection*, that serves to retrieve specific aspects of the prior encounter with the stimulus. One might recollect that a word was presented in italic typeface, or that a recommendation regarding life insurance came from a particularly disreputable agent, or that an author's name is familiar only because of a well-publicized tawdry scandal. Obviously, the details of a recollective experience can alter the way in which we engage a stimulus: We might choose to interact differently with a well-respected member of our field than with a convicted felon. With respect to word frequency, it has been suggested that the advantage that studied low-frequency words enjoy owes to a greater rate of recollection for such words, and that the lower false-alarm rate for unstudied low-frequency items reflects lower baseline familiarity (Reder et al., 2000).

Whereas familiarity is presumed to reflect a continuum of mnemonic evidence, recollection is typically thought to be a finite-state process. That is, recollected evidence directly implicates a specific prior experience as the locus of familiarity for an item, and that evidence specifies conclusively the status of the stimulus in question: It was experienced in the appropriate, sought-after context, or it was not. This process is finite-state in the sense that the evidence either promotes or discourages a response, with no degrees in intervening uncertainty. Finite-state models imply psychological thresholds: There is a point (or multiple points) at which there is an abrupt transition from "no evidence" to "evidence." This stands in contrast to the evidence continuum that familiarity provides, in which no amount of familiarity perfectly implicates

prior study; similarly, a complete absence of familiarity does not unequivocally imply the lack of prior exposure.

Unlike the ROC functions described for Gaussian-based evidence distributions, thresholds do not imply ROCs that intersect the origin and the point (1, 1) in probability space, nor are they necessarily linear in binormal space throughout the function. Thus, departures from linearity in the form of the zROC can be taken as evidence for the contribution of threshold-based evidence to the recognition decision.

To use this logic to address the question of how familiarity and recollection contribute to recognition, and how they can be related to the word-frequency mirror effect, Arndt and Reder (2002) estimated ROCs for the recognition of low- and high-frequency words under special conditions designed to promote the use of recollection-based recognition. Under these conditions, subjects were asked to discriminate between studied items and the plurality-reversed complements of previously studied items. Researchers have presumed that a plurality-reversed distractor should elicit approximately equal familiarity to that of the original studied item, thus leaving recollection as the only basis for correct discrimination (Hintzman & Curran, 1994; Hintzman, Curran, & Oppy, 1992). In contrast to the standard ROCs elicited by recognition, as described earlier, ROCs elicited from this task are nonlinear in Gaussian coordinates (Rotello, Macmillan, & Van Tassel, 2000) as are ROCs from other tasks thought to emphasize the contribution of recollection (Yonelinas, 1997, 1999).

In comparing these functions for high- and low-frequency words, Arndt and Reder (2002) reported nonlinear zROCs for plurality-reversed recognition and linear zROCs for standard recognition, thus replicating prior findings. More importantly, the low-frequency zROC was more convex than the high-frequency zROC, a result that suggested that a threshold recollection process played a larger role in low-frequency item recognition then in high-frequency item recognition, consistent with the interpretation of Reder et al. (2000).

More generally, it is important to note that ROC functions can be derived from theories that cannot predict raw hit rates or false-alarm rates. Thus,

only by combining the two and generalizing across different levels of decision bias can such functions be derived. I hope to have shown here that the evaluation and comparison of such functions is central to progress in understanding recognition memory.

Memory Inclusion and Exclusion

For our final example of how the combination of multiple measures can inspire theoretical advances that would otherwise be purely speculative, consider the general problem of how to purify a measure of memory so that our assessment is minimally confounded by factors that look like remembering, but are in fact simply nondeliberative influences of memory. For example, consider a memory experiment in which subjects learn semantically or associatively related pairs of words such as *bread–butter* or *wishing–well*. If we test later memory by presenting the first term of each pair and attempting to elicit the second (*bread–?*), it is an impossible task to discern whether a response of *butter* reveals mnemonic retrieval of the previous study episode or simply temporary enhanced access to that word by virtue of automatic effects and influences of memory. Even more dastardly, the response might indicate nothing more than the prelearned nature of the association—through a lapse in attention or perhaps strategic yawning, the subject may have never even seen the study pair. How can we tease out the deliberative recollective aspect of memory in such a data set?

Jacoby (1991) provided a clever solution to this problem that involves the use of multiple measures. In his experiments, subjects provided their responses under two different conditions. The first replicated the typical memory experiment, in which they were told simply to remember the target word if possible and report it. In the other condition, subjects were told explicitly to produce any word *except* the target word. The combination of these conditions allowed Jacoby (1991) to specify a theory of how deliberate and automatic influences of memory interact to produce responses in this type of cued recall paradigm. He claimed that, in the standard (henceforth, *inclusion*) condition, a response that

matched the prior study item could reflect either form of memory and assumed that their contributions were independent of one another:

$$p(target|inclusion) = R + A - RA. \qquad (3)$$

Here R indicates the probability of correct recollection of the study episode, and A indicates the probability of automatic nonrecollective influences leading to a correct response. In the condition in which subjects are told not to produce the previously studied pair word, the sources combine differently:

$$p(target|exclusion) = (1 - R)A. \qquad (4)$$

That is, if the target word were to be recollected, it would not be produced. Thus, a target response in this condition indicates a lack of such recollection. Under such conditions, the target might nonetheless be produced if automatic influences of memory lead that word to be particularly accessible. The difference between performance in these two conditions is thus equal to R and provides a model-based estimate of the recollective memory contribution to performance in the task. Given this estimate, it is easy to derive the estimate for the parameter A, which reflects the automatic nonrecollective memory influence on the task.

In one striking example of how the combination of inclusion and exclusion memory tasks yields results that would otherwise be unobtainable, consider an experiment reported by Jacoby, Toth, and Yonelinas (1993). Subjects were exposed to two lists of words, the first of which subjects were told to remember and was presented aurally. The second list was presented visually, and subjects were told to read the words aloud. During this second list, some subjects performed an additional attention-dividing task and others did not. The final recall test consisted of presenting word stems (e.g., mer—) and, in the inclusion condition, asking subjects to recall a word from either list that completed that cue; in the exclusion condition, they were instructed to specifically avoid completing the cue with a word that had been presented in either earlier study list. Table 24.1 shows the raw data for the inclusion and

TABLE 24.1

Raw Performance and Model Estimates for Previously Read Words on Tests of Recall Inclusion and Recall Exclusion as a Function of Attentional Condition

	Raw performance		Model estimates	
Attention	Inclusion	Exclusion	*R*	*A*
Full	0.61	0.36	0.25	0.47
Divided	0.46	0.46	0.00	0.46

Note. R is an estimate of the contribution of recollection to performance and *A* is an estimate of the automatic contribution of memory to performance.

exclusion of words that were presented in the visually presented (second) list as a function of the attention manipulation. It also shows the values of *R* and *A*, as reparameterized by Equations (3) and (4). Evident in those parameters is a very clear effect of attention on *R* but not *A*. It is from such results that we can conclude that the automatic effects of memory are relatively impervious to manipulations of attention, but that the deliberative, conscious contribution of recollection is not.

To once again sound the drum that is the theme of this volume, certain conclusions are made possible only by the theoretically motivated combination of multiple measures. Multimethod psychology refers to more than convergent and divergent validity; in each of the examples outlined here, studying individuals under different conditions or in different situations afforded a rich, multifaceted view of their behavior. Just as psychologists include multiple subjects in experiments to be able to generalize across individual differences and to examine effects owing to those differences, multiple methods or experimental circumstances allow the researcher to tease out effects that underlie differences between conditions (as in the final example given earlier) and additionally reduce the risk of being led astray by single oddball conditions that don't generalize

well to the naturalistic circumstances that they are intended to simulate.

ASSESSING THE ADEQUACY OF FORMAL MODELS OF COGNITION

In each of the examples outlined in the previous section, I have attempted to illustrate how the theoretical gain obtained from the combination of multiple measures was greater than the sum of the parts (the individual measures). Lurking within this apparently free lunch is a cost, however. In each case, we needed to specify a theory about the relationships among our measures before we could combine them. The cost of combining measures is measured in the assumptions that we make in specifying that theory. In particular, if our theory is wrong, the parameters that we derive from its application may be meaningless or even misleading.

In addition, more accurate theories are often derived from a careful evaluation of the specific points at which prior attempts fell short. Thus, it is critically important to subject such theories to evaluation and cull the herd appropriately. This section briefly reviews recent advances in and discussions of our understanding of how such evaluations can be conducted.

Probably the most common application of model testing involves the logic of goodness-of-fit statistical tests. Such tests assess the extent to which a specified model can handle a particular set of data. One familiar application of such a procedure involves the comparison of obtained frequencies of events to a set of predicted frequencies. The predictions come from a model that can make any number of assumptions about the relationships between the event types to one another (often, that they are independent). The sum of squared differences between the expected and obtained frequencies is the building block for a test statistic that can be compared to an appropriate chi-square distribution.

A more complex model's ability to account for a pattern of data can be summarized with a similar measure, such as Root Mean Squared Error or Percent Variance Accounted For. Such measures provide a good basis for ruling out a model: If no

combination of parameters within a model can allow it to predict a result that is commonly obtained, then something about that model is clearly wrong. To draw on an earlier discussion, if z-transformed ROC functions for recognition memory were typically curvilinear, then we would want to reconsider the assumption that the evidence distributions are Gaussian in form.

Unfortunately, unlike theories in physics, psychological theories are typically quite flexible—so much so, in fact, that there is probably a greater utility in using tools that rule out models not on what they fail to predict, but rather how much they can predict for which there is no evidence (Roberts & Pashler, 2000). If our theory of the form of the zROC was so general that it could not rule out any functional structure, we should be considerably less impressed by its ability to account for the correct linear form. Thus, more appropriate model-testing mechanisms emphasize not only the ability of the model to account for a pattern of data, but also its ability to do so simply, efficiently, and without undue flexibility. These mechanisms deal with such concerns by incorporating factors such as the number of free parameters (Akaike Information Criterion [Akaike, 1973]; Bayesian Information Criterion [Schwartz, 1978]) or even the number of free parameters and the range of function forms that the model can take (Bayesian Model Selection [Kass & Raftery, 1995]; Minimum Description Length [Hansen & Yu, 2001]). These approaches have clear advantages over simple goodness-of-fit tests, on which more complex models have an inherent fitting advantage simply by virtue of their ability to overfit data that in psychological experiments typically include a large amount of sampling error (Pitt & Myung, 2002).

What Makes Theory Useful?

So far, this discussion has emphasized accuracy and flexibility as the principal bases for model evaluation. We want our theories to predict events that happen and not to predict things that don't; if our theory does so with a reasonable degree of success, then we covet it and attempt to defend it against outside claims of inadequacy.

I want to propose a slight amendment to such a system, however. I believe that models can also be tremendously useful when they fail to provide an account for certain data. Models—particularly well-specified mathematical ones—are useful in part because they are putative isomorphisms for the system under investigation. Consider, for example, the question of how to compare the weights of objects. Masses of objects can only be directly compared with an accurate balance. Yet if I want to know whether this APA-produced tome outweighs other recent books in this domain, I don't need to truck my library over to a chemistry lab to use their balancing scales. Rather, the mass of each object is represented as a real number, and I know that the set of ordinal operators in mathematics (including > and <) correspond to "weighing more than" and "weighing less than." To return from this tortured analogy back to the original diatribe, models are useful in part because they provide a different representational system with which to talk about the components of the theory. As discussed early in this chapter, cognitive components are notably vague; grounding a theory in a more formal representational system, such as mathematics, allows us to use the sophistication of that system to derive relationships beyond what our intuitions would have provided us with—even when that formal system is not a fully accurate representation.

One excellent example of how model accuracy and model utility occasionally diverge is provided by the Rescorla-Wagner model of learning (e.g., Rescorla & Wagner, 1972). That theory was itself an attempt to address shortcomings of previous views of associative learning that postulated that contingency of events in time and space was a sufficient (and necessary) precondition for the learning of an association between the events (e.g., Bush & Mosteller, 1951). A number of important results were obtained in the late 1960s that demonstrated the inadequacy of this view by demonstrating conditions in which animals apparently did not learn an association between two stimuli despite highly contingent presentations of the stimuli. One illustrative and fundamental phenomenon is that of *blocking*, in which an organism first learns that A predicts B and later that the compound AC also

predicts B. Blocking is revealed by the fact that the organism does not engage in typical behaviors preparatory for the onset of B when exposed to C alone (Kamin, 1969). The Rescorla-Wagner model explains this result by assuming that an organism learns about the relationships between events only to the degree that outcomes are unpredictable: When an event is expected on the basis of alternative cues (e.g., A predicts B), then nothing is learned about the relationship between additional cues and that outcome (e.g., C and B). Formally, the model can be stated in a reduced form as

$$\Delta A_i = \beta(\lambda - \sum A_i) \qquad (5)$$

in which ΔA_i represents the change in the strength of the learned association between two stimuli on Trial i, β represents a learning parameter related to the intensity and associability of the two stimuli, λ represents an asymptotic learning parameter related to the outcome event, and most importantly, ΣA_i represents the summed associative strength between all available stimuli and the outcome event in question. When this value is close to λ, the term inside the parentheses approaches 0; thus learning is weak or nil.

It would be no exaggeration to state that this model has been the single most influential theory of learning since its publication. It has been imported into (or coevolved with) many other domains, including human contingency learning and causality judgments (e.g., Chapman & Robbins, 1990; cf. Cheng, 1997) and artificial learning in neural networks (as the influential delta rule; Rumelhart, Hinton, & Williams, 1986; Widrow & Hoff, 1960). It can account for a huge number of basic phenomena in associative learning (Dickenson & Macintosh, 1978; Miller, Barnet, & Grahame, 1995; Walkenbach & Haddid, 1980) and consequently has been the primary vehicle for the discussion of phenomena in animal learning in introductory textbooks.

These successes notwithstanding, there are numerous examples of how the model fails to account for behavior in the very paradigms it was designed for. To draw again on the example of blocking, as described earlier, remember that the model explains blocking as a deficit in learning—the animal fails to respond to the blocked stimulus

because nothing was learned about the relationship of that stimulus to the outcome. Certain phenomena indicate that this assumption is almost certainly false. For example, additional training following the traditional blocking procedure that presents the blocking stimulus (A, in the preceding example) paired with the *absence* of the outcome stimulus (C) can lead to *retroactive unblocking*, in which responding increases to the B stimulus, even though there were no additional presentations of that B stimulus (Arcediano, Escobar, & Matute, 2001; Blaisdell, Gunther, & Miller, 1999).

From a model-evaluation perspective, such data should lead us to cast out the Rescorla-Wagner Model as outdated and unsatisfactory. However, this approach ignores critical aspects of the scientific process; namely, the discovery of phenomena like retroactive unblocking was motivated in large part by the strong (and ultimately incorrect) predictions of the model. In other words, widespread understanding of the model led researchers to devise paradigms that tested its limits. In addition, certain generalities among the phenomena that contradict the model are only apparent in context of how the model deals with them inadequately (Miller et al., 1995). Thus we see that models serve not only as isomorphisms for the systems we study, but also as motivating and organizational tools that enhance our progress toward understanding the mechanisms they purport to represent—even when they do so incorrectly. This approach to model-based psychological science is well reflected in the quip that models should be your friends, not your lovers (Dell, 2004). You maintain them because of what they offer you, but you keep many of them and don't demand too much of any single one.

INTEGRATING COGNITION AND COGNITIVE NEUROSCIENCE

So far we have limited our discussion to (a) how the field of human memory has evolved because of the integration of multiple behavioral measurements, and (b) how the models that serve that function should be evaluated. Here I briefly confront the question of how to integrate behavioral measures with the types of data provided by

research in cognitive neuroscience. Let me warn the excitable reader that I offer no good answers to this question. I am not alone in that regard, but I do offer a few suggestions that might help guide future advances on this front.

In particular, advances in medical imaging have brought to the forefront questions about the integration of physiological data into cognitive theorizing. The issues themselves are quite old, in fact; researchers have used the electroencephalogram (EEG) and galvanic skin response (GSR) to address cognitive-like issues for about a century (Berger, 1929; Féré, 1888; Tarchanoff, 1890). The advances alluded to refer primarily to measures that allow greater spatial precision in viewing the morphological structure of the brain, as well as the transient electrical, chemical, and hemodynamic events that occur during brain function. These techniques—both the new and the old—allow the construction of spatial and temporal maps of activity during the performance of different cognitive tasks. One tack to integrating cognition and neuroscience is a primarily *exploratory* approach. Using cognitive theory to compare tasks that differ in a single putative cognitive component, either parametrically or otherwise, allows the inspired cognitive neuroscientist to compare maps of brain activity and postulate a brain region or regions that are related to the manipulated cognitive component.

Hidden within this approach is the notion that the brain is likely to have divvied up cognitive functions in the same manner as experimental psychologists have. I fear that we have not had that kind of insight, but the approach is valuable nonetheless, for it allows for the evolution of cognitive neuroscience into a second, more mature phase of theoretical development. Using a *hypothesis-testing* approach, specific neural signatures known to accompany cognitive events are sought in paradigms in which there is theoretical debate about the contribution of those cognitive components to the behavior in question. For example, changes in blood flow are apparent in areas in Broca's area 17 during mental imagery (Le Bihan et al., 1993). In addition, "small" mental images elicit greater activation in posterior visual cortex, corresponding to foveal input, whereas "large" mental images elicited greater activation in anterior visual cortex, an area that represents input from the periphery of the eye (Kosslyn et al., 1993). In each of these cases, the researchers used established knowledge about brain function—in this case, that regions of occipital cortex code visual input from the eye—to address the question of whether visual imagery is spatial or propositional in format (Finke, 1980). The evidence revealed that imagery engaged visual areas of the brain and is thus likely spatial in representation. Other recent research has used this approach to address whether people learned an association between visual and auditory stimuli by examining blood flow in visual cortex following presentation of an auditory stimulus that had previously been paired with a visual stimulus (McIntosh, Cabeza, & Lobaugh, 1998). Many other examples exist in the domains of perception, attention, memory, and language.

As results from exploratory cognitive neuroscience increase the number (and validity) of known relationships between neural signatures and cognitive components, the more scientists interested in cognitive phenomena will be able to exploit that knowledge for the purpose of furthering cognitive theory. The back-and-forth between exploratory and hypothesis-testing approaches illustrates one way by which to integrate measures from the two domains. But it is worth noting that the distinction between brain-based and behavioral measures is at least partly artificial. If we measure a button press or a verbal output from a subject, we consider that measure behavioral. Yet at multiple physiological levels, events occur during that press or vocalization that are unique to that output. Muscular events in the arm or larynx, as well as neuronal events in motor cortex, control those very actions that we measure behaviorally. Other neural events combine to derive that pattern of efferent control given the input from sensory organs. No matter what the task, a continuum of events guides the physical input (in the form of light or sound waves, for example) into physical representations in the brain into physical output (in the form of muscular contractions). Whether we

measure those behavioral endpoints or the physical events that precede and determine them—inside or outside the brain—the logic for the combination of multiple measurements remains the same.

The endpoints of this continuum will always be critical measures, however, no matter how precise our measurements of the intervening processes become. Just as it would be impossible to draw any meaningful conclusions about psychology without knowing anything about the physical stimulation to the subject, it is also quite difficult to do so without actually examining behavior. Many behavioral measurements carry with them an inherent dimension of performance quality that other intervening measures do not. If a manipulation enhances the speed or accuracy with which subjects perform a task, we are licensed to attribute to that manipulation an interpretation of quality—that it improves learning, or problem-solving speed, or attentional focus, for example. There is nothing inherently "better" from a cognitive perspective about more blood flow to a particular brain region, greater skin conductance, or higher levels of chemical uptake, even though such effects may well accompany behavioral effects that do allow such an interpretation.

On the other hand, experimental tasks often suffer from a failure to approximate real-world circumstances that elucidate the contribution of the cognitive capacity under study. In part, this may be because of the contrived nature of the chosen behavioral measure. Researchers interested in language comprehension, for example, often measure the rapidity with which subjects can identify probe stimuli as words or nonwords as an index of the degree to which previously read sentences or heard utterances (related to those words) have been comprehended. Clearly, this artificial task makes the laboratory study of language comprehension quite unlike naturalistic language comprehension. Cognitive neuroscience methods provide an opportunity to reduce the reliance on such tasks by allowing measurements in the absence of an overt behavioral task. For any given experimental situation, the choice between behavioral and brain-based measures involves trade-offs, and as the astute reader

might suspect, the combination of multiple types of measures across and within single studies often proves the most fruitful approach.

EMPIRICAL EVIDENCE AND THE POSTULATION OF MENTAL SYSTEMS

Recall that we began this chapter with a series of pithy comments about the ways in which cognitive psychologists derive evidence for theoretical entities. That task begins with an analysis of empirical data and proceeds to a theoretical interpretation only through the lens of a particular model. Although we have not emphasized it here, it is important to remember that any comparison of conditions or measures assumes some underlying model, and that those comparisons that are simple do not necessarily reflect simplicity in that underlying model.

Through our short tales in the first section, we discussed the theoretical interpretations of model-based analysis only as necessary. In this section, I outline rules that other researchers have used to guide the relation between theoretical parameters and theoretical entities. Consider the final example from the first section, in which performance from multiple recall tasks was combined to yield estimates of the contribution of deliberative recollection (R) and automatic memory retrieval (A) to cued recall (Table 24.1). The manipulation of attention had opposite effects on inclusion and exclusion probability, which made the raw data difficult to interpret. However, the model parameters told a very clear story: Attention affects recollection, but not automatic memory. This dissociation provides a first step toward the postulation that these two bases for responding actually represent different memory systems or different memory processes. What else is necessary?

The primary basis for such postulation is the existence of converging multiple dissociations (Schacter & Tulving, 1994). The evidence that aging, for example, selectively impairs recollective but not automatic memory strengthens the case that the two are separate entities (e.g., Benjamin & Craik, 2001; Jacoby, 1999). In the context of animal

learning, Lorenz (1970) argued that imprinting was a fundamentally different process than that of normal learning and pointed to various dissociations between the two, such as the presence of a critical period for the former, but not the latter (cf. Shettleworth, 1993).

Tulving (1984) argued that memory systems should be distinguished in large part on the basis of the information they store and the operations they perform on that information. Thus, *procedural memory*, which governs the executions of actions and skilled performance, can be distinguished from *declarative memory*, which contains verbalizable knowledge. Procedural memory contains information about the rapid coordination of limb movements and thus maintains a unique information store. Declarative memory maintains information in sufficiently flexible form to allow inferential processes to act on propositions in memory and thus allows unique operations unavailable to procedural memory. These differences do indeed play out as a number of dissociations in both animals and humans (Squire, 1992).

In addition, Tulving (1984) suggested that memory systems be defined in part by their neural substrates. This is an important point, given the renaissance of cognitive neuroscience briefly remarked on earlier, and I wish to offer an alternative viewpoint as a final remark. The denouement of the argument is that there is no reason why brain systems and cognitive systems should be one and the same.

But do not all the functions of cognition lie in the brain, and therefore shouldn't the structure of the brain be a reasonable playground for the construction of cognitive theories? The answer is no, for the same reason that neither protein strings, nor molecules, nor atoms, nor quarks should be the building blocks of a cognitive theory. Theoretical entities in cognitive psychology are only useful insofar as they allow a handy categorization of experimental results. Thus, despite the fact that habituation in the eye and in the ear take place in different brain regions, we nonetheless recognize a unifying concept that unites the two forms of learning.

A trickier question, however, is whether we are justified in postulating multiple cognitive components that exist in a single brain region. Consider the granddaddy of all distinctions in human memory, that between episodic and semantic memory (Tulving, 1983). Episodic memory stores events from an autobiographical perspective; semantic memory stores facts and knowledge and contains no information about specific past episodes. This distinction has been among the most useful in modern memory research and makes sense out of a huge number of empirical phenomena. Yet, numerous influential theories propose that the information underlying these two memory "systems" is one and the same. For example, Hintzman (1986) showed that a memory system that stored nothing more than specific individual events—in other words, its memory was exclusively episodic—could yield behaviors that were hallmarks for the postulation of semantic memory. Does such a demonstration imply that the distinction is no longer useful? Of course not. Although it may well turn out the brain does not honor this distinction, there is no reason why a cognitive theory should not. Similarly, we can build a reasonable model out of integers and logic components of the way in which our desktop computer performs some computational task, despite the fact that the computer's own representation is binary, and its logic components are nothing more than the arrangements of binary operators. There is no doubt that knowledge about the structure and function of brain regions can and should inform cognitive notions about memory, but there is a danger is failing to recognize additional appropriate levels of abstraction beyond the physical substrate and inappropriately besmirching theories that have desirable qualities.

SUMMARY

In this chapter, I have provided several examples of how measurements can be combined via models to yield results that are more informative and reliable than the original measurements themselves. This technique must always be accompanied by rigorous model evaluation, lest the interpretation of the parameters be misled by incorrect assumptions about their relation to one another. These same techniques apply to measurements obtained from physiological properties of the brain; doing so will

allow the burgeoning field of cognitive neuroscience to accommodate more readily to the theories of cognitive psychology. Finally, model-based interpretations provide a particularly useful way of seeking dissociations that are the fundamental building blocks of cognitive systems. A dissociation may only become evident when the correct model is imposed on the data. These dissociations should not be taken to imply dissociations at the level of the brain, nor should different brain systems necessarily influence cognitive theorizing.

CHAPTER 25

APPLYING A MULTIMETHOD PERSPECTIVE TO THE STUDY OF DEVELOPMENTAL PSYCHOLOGY

Amanda Sheffield Morris, Lara R. Robinson, and
Nancy Eisenberg

Methodological approaches to the study of developmental psychology vary as much as the processes that developmental scientists choose to research. There are strengths and weaknesses of each methodological approach, and like the measurement of many constructs in the discipline more broadly, multiple methods of assessment provide the most complete information. There are four primary ways in which researchers measure most constructs in developmental psychology: self-report, other informants (parent, teacher, or peer), observational methods, and physiological–biological measures. Experimental laboratory studies also are used to study development, particularly cognitive development, but they are less commonly used to study socioemotional development. Because of limited space, our expertise in socioemotional development, and the fact that experimental procedures are discussed in the chapter on social psychology (see Smith & Harris, chap. 26, this volume), we choose to focus on social and emotional development in this chapter and provide only a brief discussion of experimental methods (for examples of experimental methods in cognitive development, see Damon, Kuhn, & Siegler, 1998).

In addition to different methodologies used to study developmental psychology, developmental science requires the use of a variety of designs to adequately study development across the life span, influences on growth and development, and change over time. Developmental psychologists use longitudinal designs to examine the same individual over time, cross-sectional designs to examine the same construct at one point in time using a sample with predefined age groups or cohorts, and sequential designs (also called an accelerated longitudinal design) in which a combination of a longitudinal and cross-sectional design is used, following several age groups over a shorter period of time.

This chapter is structured around a discussion of each of these methods and designs. For each approach we discuss strengths and weaknesses and reliability and validity issues. We also illustrate how each method and design can be used by describing research conducted using that method with a particular construct often studied in socioemotional development. In addition, we discuss the use of different statistical techniques when particularly appropriate to a design or method. In the final section of the chapter, we provide examples of research using a multimethod approach and briefly discuss ideas for planning a multimethod study.

METHODS

In this section we will discuss several of the most commonly used research methods in developmental psychology. These include self-report, informant reports, observational methods, physiological–biological methods, and experimental methods. Different types of research call for different methodologies, and we discuss what works best in which research settings.

Self-Report: Emotion, Mood, and Coping
Self-report methods are commonly used in developmental psychology. However, several important

issues should be noted when using self-report data. First, age is an obvious concern because most children under age 8 have difficulty completing paper-and-pencil measures. Nevertheless, as we discuss briefly in this section, methods have been constructed that appear to successfully elicit young children's reports of some constructs. Second, the validity of self-report data sometimes is a concern because when self-report data are compared to other informants' reports, correlations among reporters often are variable (e.g., Achenbach, 1991). This calls into question what reports should be relied on most and how or if the data from multiple reporters should be used in combination. Third, many factors such as socioeconomic status, ethnicity, and social desirability have been found to affect responses to written measures (Knight & Hill, 1998). In response to potential cultural biases, Knight and Hill (1998) and others have begun working toward cross-cultural validation of some self-report measures (e.g., comparisons between internal consistency scores for Anglo Americans and Latino Americans on scales such as the Child's Depression Inventory; Kovacs, 1981).

One clear advantage of using self-report methods to study developmental psychology centers around the idea that the subjective experience of an individual has important implications for development. As Bronfenbrenner (1979) wrote, "the aspects of the environment that are most powerful in shaping the course of psychological growth are overwhelmingly those that have meaning to the person in a given situation" (p. 22). Certainly both objective and subjective reports provide important information; however, it may be the individual's personal subjective interpretation that is most influential in shaping development (Morris, Silk, et al., 2002).

Self-report measures are not always as objective as other methods and sometimes have low correlations with other methods. Additionally, self-report measures may not be able to assess concepts that are not always salient to the reporter (e.g., emotional reactivity). Nonetheless, self-reports often correlate with the reports of other people or observational measures. In those cases, structural equation modeling (SEM), discussed further in the longitudinal section, is a statistical technique that can be used to incorporate data from multiple informants (if they are related to some degree; e.g., Zhou et al., 2002).

Most child research before the late 1990s relied on reports and observations by trained observers or parents (Sessa, Avenevoli, Steinberg, & Morris, 2001), largely because of concerns about young children's ability to provide reliable and valid reports of their experiences. However, more recent reviewers and researchers have questioned the assumption that children cannot report important information (Miller & Aloise, 1989; Ridgeway, Waters, & Kuczaj, 1985). It is likely that developmental researchers have historically underestimated younger children's social cognitive competencies and their ability to report on their own experiences, primarily because of the methods used to assess children's beliefs and social understanding (Hart & Damon, 1986; Miller & Aloise, 1989). For example, most early researchers examining young children's person perception used open-ended interview techniques, which required extensive verbal production and expressive skills. Because young children's verbal comprehension skills are better than their verbal expressive skills (Kuczaj, 1986), observed age-related differences in children's use of dispositional terms in their descriptions of others likely reflected linguistic immaturity (Furman & Bierman, 1983). In addition, the demand characteristics of the standard interview research situation (i.e., being questioned by an unfamiliar adult) probably inhibited young children's ability to provide psychologically meaningful information in many studies. When children have been interviewed by more "benign" interviewers, such as puppets, children as young as 3½ years old have been able to provide general descriptions of their own and others' internal states and emotions with adequate stability (e.g., Denham, 1986; Eder, Gerlach, & Perlmutter, 1987). Indeed, there has been a recent surge in research attempting to assess young children's perceptions of constructs like self-concept (e.g., Eder et al., 1987), parent–child relations (Morris, Silk, et al., 2002; Morris, Steinberg, et al., 2002; Sessa et al., 2001), sympathy and empathy (e.g., Miller, Eisenberg, Fabes, & Shell, 1996), and school engagement (Measelle, Ablow, Cowan, & Cowan, 1998). Obviously, infants

and toddlers cannot provide self-report data, but this recent research with preschool and elementary-school-age children is promising.

To illustrate some of the issues involved in using self-report data in developmental research, we have chosen to highlight individuals' self-reports of mood/emotionality and coping. The advantages of using self-report for these types of constructs stem from the fact that many emotion-related processes and coping strategies are unobservable to others and, as a result, are difficult to measure. Self-report assessments tap individuals' own experience of emotion and coping, which is beneficial in understanding how self-construction and awareness affect developmental outcomes. However, self-report measures of this sort also have disadvantages; for example, some individuals may not be aware of the coping strategies that they use or may provide biased or self-serving reports of emotion or coping behavior (Eisenberg & Morris, 2002; Eisenberg, Morris, & Spinrad, 2005; Lennon, Eisenberg, & Carroll, 1983).

Researchers studying coping have identified a long list of strategies for managing stress (e.g., problem solving, cognitive restructuring, catastrophizing, emotional ventilation, physical activities, acceptance, distraction, avoidance, wishful thinking, humor, social withdrawal, alcohol or drug use, and seeking social support; Compas, Connor, Saltzman, Thomsen, & Wadsworth, 2001). Some of these coping strategies likely assess emotionality (e.g., emotional ventilation) or outcomes of coping. Thus, investigators need to carefully consider what specific measures of coping assess and how they relate to measures such as emotionality. Moreover, researchers studying children and adolescents' coping often use self-report measures that assess coping responses to hypothetical vignettes involving emotion and emotion management strategies (e.g., Band & Weisz, 1988; Saarni, 1997). These vignettes involve having children or adolescents read about a stressful situation or problem (or an experimenter reading to them the vignette) and then answer questions about how they would cope with the problem. This type of method usually is an attempt to present real-life stressful situations that occur in everyday life; however, when using hypothetical

vignettes, investigators should consider that children may report the socially desirable response and not the response he or she would enact in real life. For example, Underwood, Coie, and Herbsman (1992) found that children nominated as aggressive by their peers did not differ from children classified as nonaggressive in their reactions to videotaped vignettes designed to elicit aggression-related emotions. Moreover, Lennon et al. (1983) found that children reported more empathy when interviewed by same-sex than other-sex adult interviewers.

Children's self-reported coping strategies have also been measured in a number of recent studies with survey measures such as the Children's Coping Strategies Checklist (CCSC; Ayers, Sandler, West, & Roosa, 1996). With this measure, children rate how often they used particular coping behaviors when they had a problem in the last month. This measure has produced four factors (Active Strategies, Avoidant Strategies, Distraction Strategies, and Support Seeking Strategies). There is also a parent-report version of this questionnaire. One advantage to this type of measure is that it calls for the participant to draw on actual events that occurred and to report their coping strategies. Nevertheless, individuals may be biased in how they remember events and their own coping behaviors in these situations.

A method for collecting self-report data on mood/emotion that is becoming more popular is the experience sampling methodology (ESM; also called Ecological Momentary Assessment; EMA). ESM is designed to assess the subjective experience of individuals in their typical environment (Stone & Litcher-Kelly, chap. 5, this volume). With this methodology, participants are signaled (e.g., by a beeper or cell phone) based on a sampling schedule designed to obtain a representative sample of a person's everyday experiences (Hormuth, 1986). When signaled, participants report on predetermined emotions, activities, or thoughts (whatever is the focus of the study). This methodology constitutes an "experience-near" approach to the study of affective phenomenon, rather than the "experience-distant" approach typically used in laboratory and questionnaire research (Silk, Steinberg, & Morris, 2003). For example, Silk et al. (2003) had adolescents report on anger, sadness, and anxiety and their

emotion regulation strategies using ESM. Participants were "beeped" randomly throughout the course of a week during designated times (8:00 A.M. to 9:30 P.M. during the week and 8:00 A.M. to 11:00 P.M. on the weekend). During the target hours of each day, using a table of random numbers, one signal was programmed for every 90- to 150-minute block with the provision that no signals would occur within 60 minutes of one another. On average, participants were signaled 42 to 48 times. At each signal, adolescents completed a short checklist that assessed their anger, sadness, and anxiety. Specifically, adolescents reported how mad, sad, and nervous they were on a 5-point scale, at the current time of reporting and during their most negative experience in the past hour. Like other studies, the degree of variation in mood, or lability, was measured as the standard deviation of the individual's score across sampling points. Emotion regulation was indicated by a decrease in emotional intensity from the most negative event to the current reported mood.

One advantage to the immediate reporting of emotions/moods with ESM is that it circumvents potential memory distortions and allows for an assessment of emotional behavior in a natural context (Larson, 1987). Some disadvantages of this method involve participants *not* completing the measure at the time they are signaled, which is difficult to monitor, and the time involved for participants—individuals are typically signaled multiple times a day for a week. Hierarchical Linear Modeling (HLM) is a statistical technique that is often used to analyze these data because each time point of data collection can be used in this type of model (and not all participants have equal numbers of data points). See Drasgow and Chuah (chap. 7, this volume) for an illustration of this use of HLM.

Other Informants: Child and Infant Temperament

Probably one of the most common forms of assessment in developmental research is the use of questionnaires or interviews that assess some aspect of a participant's functioning from someone else's perspective, such as that of a parent, teacher, or peer (Neyer, chap. 4, this volume). Paper-and-pencil

measures are often used because of their efficiency. Many participants can be questioned at one time, so obtaining these reports is much less time consuming and less expensive than observational research.

Using other reports has some advantages over using self-report or observational data. Compared to children and adolescents, adults are more skilled in answering questions, and parents and teachers have the opportunity to observe children over time and in a variety of social situations. Although adults' reports on children probably are more objective (on average) than children's reports about themselves, adults' reports are subject to certain biases. Parents' reports may be influenced by social desirability, and there is some evidence that teachers may rate academically skilled children more positively in general (Underwood, 1997). One way often used to assess the validity of parents' and teachers' reports is to examine agreement among informants. However, results regarding rater agreement are often inconsistent. For example, Guthrie et al. (1997) reported that the relation between teachers' and parents' assessments of children's reactivity were modest at best. In contrast, Eisenberg et al. (1996) found that teachers' and parents' reports of reactivity and regulation (particularly the latter) were positively correlated. Differences between informants are not surprising, however, and may not indicate low validity of a measure because individuals' expression of behaviors likely varies across contexts. Indeed, differences between parents' and teachers' reports reinforce the value of obtaining information from adults who have observed children in different settings.

It has been widely shown in the literature that as children grow older, peers increase in importance; therefore, peers' reports may be used to measure friendship status as it relates to constructs such as emotion regulation and social competence. Sociometrics are the procedures used to measure peer relationships through a system of rating popularity. These procedures may be used with children as young as preschool through the use of pictures (e.g., a smile, frown, and neutral face; Asher, Singleton, Tinsley, & Hymel, 1979), or with older children using questionnaires to rank classmates and to

determine peer status, acceptance, and rejection. In addition, preschool children and elementary school children appear to be relatively good reporters of peers' anger and related constructs (e.g., aggression; Eisenberg, Pidada, & Liew, 2001; Maszk, Eisenberg, & Guthrie, 1999).

Even though a variety of constructs have been measured with other informants, we choose to illustrate the use of others' reports in reference to temperament. Temperament can be defined as psychological qualities and behaviors that display considerable variation among infants and young children and have a relatively stable physiological basis that derives from the individual's genetic constitution (Kagan, 1994, p. 16). Most temperament theorists view temperament and biology as intertwined and see temperament as having stable, enduring properties that can be modified to a degree by contextual factors, such as parenting (Rothbart & Bates, 1998). Adult-report measures of child/infant temperament include scales that assess many dimensions of temperament such as regulation (e.g., attention focusing, inhibitory control), various types of emotion (e.g., positive emotion, anger/frustration, fear, sadness), activity level, impulsivity, surgency/approach, and soothability (e.g., the Infant Behavior Questionnaire [IBQ], Rothbart, 1981; the Toddler Behavior Assessment Questionnaire [TABQ], Goldsmith, 1996; the Child Behavior Questionnaire [CBQ], ages 3–7, Goldsmith & Rothbart, 1991, Rothbart, Ahadi, Hershey, & Fisher, 2001; the Early Adolescent Temperament Questionnaire [EATQ], ages 9–15, Capaldi & Rothbart, 1992; the Dimensions of Temperament Survey—Revised [DOTs–R], Windle & Lerner, 1986). Some examples of items that assess various temperamental constructs include, "pays close attention when someone tells him or her how to do something," from the attention scale of the EATQ, and "sometimes interrupts others when they are speaking," from the impulsivity scale of the CBQ. Items reflect typical behaviors across a variety of situations and settings, selected to tap an underlying temperamental predisposition. The CBQ and EATQ are currently available in parent-report formats; others have adapted and used the CBQ for teachers

(e.g., Eisenberg et al., 1997; Murphy, Eisenberg, Fabes, Shepard, & Guthrie, 1999). The DOTs–R is another parent-report measure that taps into several aspects of temperament (e.g., task orientation) that also has an adolescent self-report version.

Parents are likely excellent reporters of child temperament because parents have viewed their children in a variety of settings and over a length of time (Rothbart & Bates, 1998). Additionally, parent-report measures, like other types of questionnaires, are inexpensive to create, apply, and analyze. Moreover, these types of measures have shown moderate to strong convergent validity with observational methods. For example, Mathney, Wilson, and Thoeben (1987) found laboratory scores of temperament correlated with maternal report (rs ranged from .38 to .52 over a year). Additionally, Rothbart (1986) found moderate convergent validity between dimensions of the IBQ and home observations of temperament. Intercorrelations between overall reactivity measured by the IBQ and home observations ranged from .43 to .46. Yet despite the strength of using both parent reports and observation, not all facets of temperament are observable, and observational results may not always generalize to outside the laboratory or structured settings.

As one might imagine, some researchers have questioned whether parents' reports of their children's temperament assess characteristics of the parent more than of the child (Kagan, 1998). Although parental bias can distort reports of temperament, Lemery, Biersach, Chipongnian, Greenberg, and Goldsmith (2001) found that parental characteristics (i.e., personality, depression, family expressiveness) were equally related to parental report and lab measures of infant temperament, suggesting that parental reporting bias does not account for all the relations of temperament with other variables.

Observational Methods: Parent–Child Relations

Observational methods are excellent tools for the study of the complex relationships examined in developmental psychology (Bakeman & Gnisci, chap. 10, this volume). One of the key distinctions between the approach of many developmentalists

and that of some other disciplines is the importance placed on context. Individuals do not exist in isolation; they actively construct their environment and simultaneously are influenced *by* their environment. The complexity of these interactions is often best captured through observational methods that allow the researcher to view the relationship and transactions in their entirety rather than testing very small and isolated pieces of the relationship. Moreover, an emphasis on the importance of context necessitates the investigation of variables in relation to specific contexts. Observational methods allow for the examination of contextual specificity.

Observational methods are thus a crucial element of developmental research, but along with their many advantages come some disadvantages. These methods result in extremely rich data, and this is both an advantage and a disadvantage. The data from observational studies are often able to capture "natural" phenomenon that cannot be verbalized or recognized by the participants themselves, and observations are less subject to experimenter effects and issues of social desirability bias (although individuals may act in socially desirable ways when they know that they are being filmed; Zegiob, Arnold, & Forehand, 1975). Yet these data are often difficult to codify or quantify, and frequently both extensive training and time are required to reach interrater reliability. Additionally, the complexity of observed relationships makes it difficult to test single constructs, therefore possibly lowering internal validity. Furthermore, observational methods performed in a laboratory sometimes may not generalize outside the specific situation, and because of the unfamiliar environment, they may be criticized for being artificial. Nevertheless, there is not another method presently available that is better at addressing relationships in context and interactions between individuals.

Convergent and discriminant validities of observational methods vary with the construct tested, the type of measure the observational method is tested against, and the population tested. For example, Black, Hutcheson, Dubowitz, Starr, and Benson-Howard (1996) found low to moderate convergent validity, *r*s = .01 to .49, of parent–child interaction observations from the Parent–Child

Early Relational Assessment (Clark, 1985) with maternal self-report on the Brief Symptom Index (Derogatis & Melisaratos, 1983) and The Parenting Stress Index (Albin, 1990), depending on the parental construct and the context (feeding or free play) of the observation. In another observational study of parent–child interaction, Crowell, Feldman, and Ginsberg (1988) found 93% discriminate validity for predicting infants' clinical status (i.e., placement into clinical or nonclinical groups) and attachment classification using their structured play procedure for assessing mother–infant interactional behavior.

Observational methods are analyzed through a variety of statistical techniques. Because they are more open to interpretation than many other methods, multiple raters are often used to ensure validity of results. Kappa statistics or correlations, depending on the type of scale, often are used for inter-rater reliability, which tests for the congruence between raters' observations (Nussbeck, chap. 17, this volume). Hierarchical linear modeling (HLM) can be used to create a model including multiple observations of an individual (Hox & Maas, chap. 19, this volume). In addition, statistical methods such as sequential analysis are used to relate patterns in the sequencing of observations of two behaviors emitted by one reporter or potentially interrelated behaviors of two actors (as in a mother–infant interaction). In lag sequential analysis, the occurrence of one behavior preceding or following another behavior is recorded, and behavior frequencies and conditional probabilities can be computed (Farrell, 1994). For example, Feldman, Greenbaum, and Yirmiya (1999) used lag analysis to compute mother–infant mutual synchrony, in which the infant leads affectively and the mother follows as a form of emotional validation.

The use of observational methods in developmental psychology can be illustrated through the study of the parent–infant attachment relationship. Reports of parenting are especially prone to social desirability biases, as this construct is often emotionally charged because the parental role is highly valued in society. Furthermore, parenting behaviors may be difficult to recognize by those in the relationship and require objective assessment. Attachment theorists hypothesize that children form "working

models" of self and attachment figures from their early relationships that serve as templates for future relationships and situations (Bowlby, 1969). Thus, the attachment relationship is an important construct that can be used to predict developmental trajectories when accurately measured.

A commonly used measure of the attachment relationship, Ainsworth, Blehar, Waters, and Wall's (1978) Strange Situation Procedure, frequently is used to activate the attachment system for observational purposes. From the attachment perspective, when an infant experiences distress, separation, fatigue, illness, fear, or other types of stress, the child's attachment system motivates him or her to seek security from a caregiver (Boris, Aoki, & Zeanah, 1999). An unfamiliar situation is believed to heighten such attachment reactions. In the Strange Situation, the infant participates in eight different episodes in an unfamiliar laboratory room where the parent and a stranger are present in varying combinations. The observations from the Strange Situation Procedure are later coded for type of attachment: securely attached, insecure-avoidant, insecure-resistant, and disorganized or disoriented (Main & Solomon, 1986). Impairments in the infant–parent attachment relationship as assessed with such methods are correlated with a variety of poor outcomes throughout the developmental literature, from psychopathologies (Fagot & Pears, 1996; Shaw, Owens, Vondra, & Keenan, 1996) to increased maltreatment risk (Cicchetti, Toth, & Maughan, 2000). Attachment classifications in the Strange Situation, when consistent and clearly observable, were also found to be useful for making predictions about the home caregiving environment (Gaensbauer et al., 1985). However, convergence between the Strange Situation and the Attachment Q-Sort (Waters & Deane, 1985), an observational rating system using a card piling technique, has been inconsistent across studies (Thompson, 1998), perhaps because the content of the two types of measures differs somewhat. Despite these inconsistencies, observational methods as illustrated by the Strange Situation Procedure can provide rich information about the nature of complex relationships in specific contexts.

Physiological–Biological Methods: Reactivity and Regulation

Developmental psychologists often use physiological measures to assess variables such as stress, hormones, heart rate, and skin conductance (Berntson & Cacioppo, chap. 12, this volume). Typically, these variables are measured along with observations or self-reports of a similar construct (e.g., a stress index is taken before or while cortisol levels are measured). In terms of their advantages, physiological and biological methods are extremely useful for measuring psychological processes that individuals are unable to report (e.g., emotional reactivity in young children). They also are relatively free from social desirability biases. Disadvantages of these methods include the cost of instruments and time spent editing and interpreting the data. Additionally, carryover effects may threaten internal validity because of previous stimuli responses affecting subsequent reactions and not accurately reflecting the individual's homeostatic state (Rothbart, Chew, & Gartstein, 2001). Moreover, physiological responses often can be due to a variety of factors, including movement and the temperature in the room. Nevertheless, researchers using psychophysiological methods have shown relations between measures of biological variables and behavior problems, aspects of temperament, and coping strategies (Rothbart & Bates, 1998).

To illustrate the use of physiological measures in developmental psychology, we discuss the measurement of reactivity and regulation and how these variables are typically measured. Major components of reactivity and regulation are the underlying physiological processes involved in arousal and its management, and both the experience of an emotion and its regulation are partly linked to the autonomic nervous system (Porges, Doussard-Roosevelt, & Maiti, 1994). Researchers of autonomic correlates of emotion have focused primarily on two branches of the nervous system: the sympathetic branch, which mobilizes the body to react in an emergency, and the parasympathetic branch, which conserves and maintains bodily resources. The parasympathetic branch works to regulate and decrease emotional arousal and usually counteracts the activation of the sympathetic branch, which is

responsible for arousal (Gottman, Katz, & Hooven, 1997). Researchers typically examine sympathetic activation in the following ways: through skin conductance levels (SCL), which indicate how much an individual sweats, and through measures of cardiovascular reactivity (CVR).

Research on parasympathetic activation/regulation has relied primarily on indices of cardiac activity. Respiratory sinus arrhythmia (RSA), heart-rate variability that occurs at the frequency of breathing, is believed to be controlled by the vagus nerve and is thought to provide a good estimate of parasympathetic influence (although some heart rate measures and programs believed to tap parasympathetic functioning, often called vagal tone, have not actually measured respiration). Baseline cardiac vagal tone or RSA has been associated with differences in infants' appropriate emotional reactivity (e.g., Stifter, Fox, & Porges, 1989), as well as with the ability to adapt to a new situation such as preschool (Fox & Field, 1989). Moreover, high RSA has been found to relate to infants' attentional abilities (e.g., Porges, 1991; Stifter et al., 1989).

Another physiological measure of emotion/reactivity involves the assessment of electroencephalographic (EEG) patterns (i.e., brain activity). Researchers using EEG patterns to assess the physiology of reactivity or regulation often examine activation in the frontal lobe and compare activation in the right versus left hemispheres. Individuals with right frontal asymmetry (less activation in the right hemisphere compared to the left) are more likely to exhibit negative affect in response to stress (Fox et al., 1995). In addition, effortful, voluntary regulation has been linked to prefrontal cortical responding (Casey et al., 1997). Further, initial evidence indicates that asymmetries in activation of the frontal cortical lobes are linked to approach versus withdrawal tendencies (Tomarken & Keener, 1998); thus, brain waves (EEG) may be associated with effortful and/or reactive approach or inhibition systems (Harmon-Jones & Sigelman, 2001). In summary, psychophysiological methods represent the future for research of constructs such as emotion regulation and reactivity because they are invaluable tools for linking unobservable internal feeling states and arousal, and processes involved in their modulation, to their behavioral manifestations.

Experimental Studies

Another method of research sometimes used to assess a variety of aspects of children's functioning is experimental studies (usually laboratory) in which some aspect of the situation is experimentally manipulated. For example, in studies of young children's regulation, investigators sometimes have manipulated the degree to which the mother is in the room or available to the child when the child is experiencing a potentially stressful situation (Diener & Mangelsdorf, 1999; Grolnick, Kurowski, McMenamy, Rivkin, & Bridges, 1998). In marital conflict research, studies have examined children's responses to conflict in a laboratory setting by having children view a video that portrays marital conflict or by having actors in a lab engage in varying forms of conflict in the child's presence (Cummings, Iannotti, & Zahn-Waxler, 1985; Davies, Harold, Goeke-Morey, & Cummings, 2002). The obvious advantage of such methods is the degree of control over the potential influences on the child. A disadvantage is that the situation often is artificial; moreover, it is difficult to experimentally manipulate many variables that developmentalists want to assess. For example, it is difficult to experimentally assess the effects of individual differences in parenting on children's outcomes with laboratory experimental studies. The investigator likely is interested in a parent's behavior in general and not as modified by the laboratory, and children cannot be "assigned" to parents and families. Nevertheless, interventions in which real parents' behaviors are modified in an experimental group and compared to a control group can provide some insights on the effects of parenting on children. Experimental methods of this sort are used relatively infrequently in longitudinal designs (except, perhaps, as part of an experimental intervention). However, they can be quite useful in studies assessing children's cognitive abilities (e.g., knowledge when provided with different types of information) and perceptual abilities.

Indeed, for researchers interested in cognitive development, experimental designs are often the

norm. In many studies of cognitive, language, and motor development, infants or children participate in tasks designed to examine children's abilities and knowledge using habituation/dishabituation paradigms in infancy (Baillargeon, 1994) and actual cognitive/motor tasks (Campos, Bertenthal, & Kermoian, 1992; Newcombe & Huttenlocher, 1992; Werker, 1989). For example, in work on theory of mind, researchers have used tasks such as the false belief task. In this task, children see a scene where a character, Maxi, puts chocolate in a drawer, and while Maxi is out of the room another person moves the chocolate. Children are asked where Maxi will look for the chocolate to determine at what age children can understand the difference between what they believe to be true and what others believe (Wimmer & Perner, 1983). These types of studies rarely use a multimethod approach, instead relying primarily on the experimental tasks to assess a specified cognitive ability.

DESIGNS

In this section we will discuss several types of research designs, such as longitudinal, cross-sectional, and sequential.

Longitudinal Designs

Developmental psychology is concerned with intraindividual change over time. Therefore longitudinal methods (Khoo, West, Wu, & Kwok, chap. 21, this volume), which involve assessments of the same group of people over time, are well suited to the goals of developmental psychology. Because developmental psychologists are particularly interested in pathways and trajectories, designs that are able to capture the progression of time and the course of a phenomenon are especially valuable. Longitudinal methods are most appropriate when the researcher is interested in the processes underlying a phenomenon, rather than merely the status of that phenomenon.

There are many advantages to longitudinal methods. First, longitudinal designs allow one to assess change, and the processes proceeding, cooccurring with, or following change within an individual. Second, they allow an individual to be compared to other individuals over the same period of time, so that issues of interindividual consistency over time can be examined. Third, they allow for a mapping of normative age trends, as well as alternative patterns of development that may occur for different groups of children. Fourth, longitudinal methods provide the opportunity for researchers to pinpoint the time of onset of a behavior. Additionally, longitudinal methods are extremely useful when interventions are used because they allow the researcher to view change in trajectories as a result of the intervention.

Despite the valuable information longitudinal studies provide, there are many disadvantages to this method. Disadvantages include the length of time needed to collect and analyze the data, the costs associated with the amount of data collection and analysis, and incentives for continued participation. Moreover, subject attrition is a major problem in longitudinal studies because the same subjects are needed to participate year after year, and it is often difficult to locate participants and to motivate them to continue participation. In addition, longitudinal designs pose specific threats to study validity because of cohort effects (e.g., wherein the effect is a reflection of the time period and not the experimental manipulation) and repeated exposure effects (wherein the participant *learns* how to answer questions or respond to other assessments because he or she has been exposed to them year after year). Additionally, longitudinal studies sacrifice depth for breadth, and therefore the results may only be generalizable to populations similar to those studied.

Because longitudinal methods produce data points over a period of time, certain statistical analyses are optimal—those that allow change to be observed over time. Structural equation modeling (SEM) is the term used to describe a category of multivariate statistical models used to estimate the relationship between observed variables and latent constructs, as well as relations among latent constructs. One type of SEM, latent growth curve modeling, is a particularly promising technique for the study of development (Duncan, Duncan, & Hops, 1996). Latent growth curve modeling (LGM)

includes observed variables that constitute the latent construct, estimates growth trajectories (patterns of change) across time, and can be used to assess the degree to which other variables (e.g., regulation) predict various trajectories for another variable (e.g., aggression). The latent slope and intercept on average define trajectories. Similar to LGM in its consideration of change as a function of time, the person-centered approach of individual growth modeling, such as Hierarchical Linear Modeling (HLM), represents individual change over time; this is done by determining the functional form (linear, cubic, quadratic) that best fits the data, in addition to the individual values of the trajectories. HLM can be used for assessing the rate of growth or change, the status of an individual at a given point in time, the rate of acceleration, and individual variation around the growth curve (Raudenbush & Chan, 1993). Therefore, this statistical technique allows for comparison of individual trajectories.

LGM and HLM differ in several ways. The LGM approach is multivariate; that is, growth curves for two variables can be estimated at the same time, and intercept and slope for one variable can be used as a predictor or explanatory variable for the intercept and slope of another variable. The LGM approach also can cluster trajectories that are similar. LGM has two restrictions as compared to HLM. Time, or a time-related variable such as age, on which growth is defined, has the same value for each subject at each time point (HLM allows the actual time or age for each subject if the measurements are not taken on exactly the same day.) Second, in LGM time-varying covariates have the same regression coefficient across subjects, whereas HLM allows for coefficients to vary across subjects.

Another statistical procedure that is sensitive to change over time is Repeated Measures Analysis of Variance (ANOVA). This statistic can be used to assess time-specific change and is similar to individual growth curve modeling in that it determines the functional form (e.g., linear, quadratic, cubic) that best fits the data. Unlike LGM and HLM, Repeated Measures ANOVA does not estimate individual trajectories; rather, the variability between subjects is

completely removed through blocking, and only overall trends are constructed.

We illustrate the use of a longitudinal design through the study of the construct of antisocial behavior. Many large longitudinal studies have focused on the development of antisocial behavior (Farrington, 1983; Loeber et al., 2002; Moffit, Caspi, Dickson, Silva, & Stanton, 1996). Longitudinal methods are well suited for this topic because they allow for the investigation of when delinquency starts, its longevity, and the link between juvenile and adult behaviors and provide timelines for the specific types of behaviors (Farrington, 1983). Because outcomes tend to differ as a function of the age of onset of the antisocial behaviors, longitudinal methods are especially important for understanding this aspect of social behavior.

One of the largest studies on aggression, the Pittsburgh Youth Study, is based on 1,517 inner-city boys. Assessment began when the boys were in elementary or middle school, and the investigators traced the development of antisocial behavior from childhood to adolescence (Loeber et al., 2002). Key findings included identification of types of delinquency pathways, long-term risk factors for delinquency, outcome differences by age of onset of antisocial behavior, and changes in alcohol and drug use as it relates to delinquency—as analyzed using growth curve modeling (Loeber et al., 2002). As is evident by this example, longitudinal designs are often the ideal method for studying developmental issues; however, these designs are not always feasible. For these reasons and others, cross-sectional designs are probably the most widely used design in developmental research (Lerner, 2002).

Cross-Sectional Designs

Cross-sectional designs examine different groups of individuals at one point in time, essentially representing a slice of development using a sample with predetermined age groups or cohorts. In the previous example, delinquency was assessed over a 15-year period; in a cross-sectional design delinquency would be measured at one time with groups of individuals of up to 15 different ages. In another study, Schaie, Willis, Jay, and Chipeur (1989) were able to examine, at one data point, cognitive abilities across

77 years of age using a cross-sectional design. Therefore, this design is generally quicker, less expensive, less likely to involve attrition, and samples are more representative when compared to longitudinal designs. Nevertheless, cross-sectional designs are not without flaws. This design is highly dependent on similarity between age groups, which is often difficult to achieve because of uncontrollable and extraneous variables. Consequently, changes attributed to age may be confounded with some other variable. Similar to longitudinal designs, cross-sectional studies are subject to cohort effects because individuals in the age cohorts are born in different time periods. Cross-sectional study data can be analyzed with some of the previously described statistical techniques: ANOVA and structural equation modeling. In addition, regression is often used to analyze cross-sectional data.

Sequential Designs

Another type of study design, sequential design or accelerated longitudinal design, attempts to resolve the confounding of age inherent in both cross-sectional and longitudinal designs. The confounding of age refers to the problem of differences attributed to age that are in actuality due to other variables such as the historical period in which the individual was born. In sequential studies, cross-sectional cohorts are assessed longitudinally over a fixed time period, typically a much shorter period of time than with a pure longitudinal design. Therefore, results refer to between- and within-cohort change. Data from this design can be analyzed using the same statistical techniques as longitudinal designs that assess differences in age (e.g., structural equation modeling, including growth curve analysis). Because sequential designs have the advantages of longitudinal *and* cross-sectional methods, it can be argued that this design is a good solution to many of the problems inherent in using longitudinal or cross-sectional designs alone, especially if the longitudinal component of the study is more than a short period of time. For example, Duncan et al. (1996) found no differences between accelerated longitudinal design and traditional longitudinal design in their ability to predict adolescent alcohol use, growth of alcohol use, and the current status of their alcohol use. Conse-

quently, this design may be a more efficient method for studies investigating developmental changes.

A MULTIMETHOD PROGRAM OF RESEARCH: EMOTION REGULATION

As probably is now evident, all methods of assessment have strengths and weaknesses (refer to Table 25.1 for a summary of all methods presented), and the method, design, and statistical procedures chosen by researchers should be based on the research question posed and the best ways to test proposed hypotheses. A multimethod approach to the study of development is often advisable, as it incorporates many methods and minimizes errors due to method or design flaws. For example, when examining the development of emotion regulation (the successful, socially appropriate management of negative and positive emotions), one might use adults' reports of children's regulation, behavioral assessments of children's regulation, self-reports of regulation (if the participants are adolescents), and physiological measures of regulatory processes (e.g., vagal tone). Emotional responding can be assessed with similar measures, with coding of facial reactions often being a key element. Which specific measures are selected will vary with the goals of the investigator. Moreover, it should be noted that different types of measures (facial, physiological, self-report) may tap different aspects of emotion regulation (or emotionality). Thus, researchers must provide clear descriptions of their measurement goals and procedures.

One reason measures used in developmental psychology differ so much is that investigators are interested in or choose to analyze different components and correlates of developmental constructs. For example, in regard to regulation, temperament theorists tend to use questionnaire measures that assess dispositional (relatively cross-situational) temperamental components of emotion regulation (e.g., effortful control, impulsivity, reactivity) that allow for generalizations across contexts and situations (although they also use observational measures). This is because they are interested in tapping underlying constitutionally based processes important in emotion regulation (Rothbart et al., 2001).

TABLE 25.1

Summary of Methods Presented

Method	Strengths	Weaknesses	Advanced statistical techniques	Sample studies
1. Self-report and experience sampling	Allows for the subjective experience of the individual	May be inappropriate for certain ages May be self-servingly biased May be culturally biased	HLM & SEM	Band & Weisz (1988) Eder et al. (1987) Silk et al. (2003)
2. Other informants	More objective than some other methods (e.g., self-reports) Report on behavior across social situations and time	Parental social desirability bias Disagreement between raters	SEM	Eisenberg et al. (1996) Guthrie et al. (1997) Maszk et al. (1999)
3. Observation	View relationship transactions Rich data	Coding difficulty Social desirability of participants May be assessed in an artificial laboratory setting Time cost is high	HLM & SEM Lag sequential analysis	Black et al. (1996) Crowell et al. (1988)
4. Physiological–biological methods	Measure psychological processes that individuals are unable to report Minimal social biases	Time and equipment costs are high Carryover effects may invalidate data	HLM & SEM	Casey et al. (1997) Stifter et al. (1989)
5. Experimental methods	More control over variables Increases understanding of causal processes	Random assignment not always possible Time costs and coding difficulty Ecological validity/artificial setting	MANOVA	Grolnick et al. (1998) Diener & Mangelsdorf (1999) Cummings et al. (1985)

Note. Many analytic methods can be used with any of the techniques, depending on the design of the study and the given measure.

Researchers interested in the role of cognition in emotion-related regulation are likely to assess either dispositional or situational cognitive processes (e.g., how individuals appraise specific emotion-eliciting situations and use cognitive distraction or cognitive restructuring to modify its significance (Heckhausen, 1997; Lazarus & Folkman, 1984). Further, individuals interested in attachment relationships often observe the ways in which young children deal with different stressors or emotions when the parent is nearby (e.g., self-soothing, fussing to parent, seeking comfort from the parent, problem solving; Diener & Mangelsdorf, 1999; Grolnick et al., 1998) or examine the relation of security of attachment to children's abilities to self-regulate (Contreras, Kerns, Weimer, Gentzler, & Tomich, 2000). In addition, many measures of emotion regulation essentially tap the outcome of such regulation, for example, if the child shows neutral or positive emotion rather than distress (Carter, Little, Briggs-Gowan, & Kogan, 1999) or is emotionally labile versus resilient (e.g., Shields & Cicchetti, 1997). Such measures are most common in research on the relation of emotion regulation to adjustment.

A number of researchers have successfully examined emotion-related regulation using multiple methods. For example, Kochanska, Murray, and Harlan (2000) used observational and parent-report measures to assess children's effortful control and found that the two methods converged, but primarily for data collected at the same point in time. Eisenberg and colleagues have used parents' and teachers' reports of emotion regulation in conjunction with observational tasks in multiple studies (e.g., Eisenberg, Fabes, Guthrie, & Reiser, 2000; Eisenberg, Gershoff, et al., 2001). They have found that observational measures of emotion regulation often are associated with adults' reports of the construct and, in combination, are related to both socialization and children's socioemotional development (e.g., adjustment, social competence). Moreover, Mezzacappa, Kindlon, and Earls (1999; Mezzacappa, Kindlon, Saul, & Earls, 1998) have used a variety of behavioral measures of regulation to examine different aspects of control and relate them to adjustment.

However, emotion regulation is not the only developmental construct suitable for the multi-method approach; the development of psychopathology is often studied using multiple raters and techniques. For example, Cole, Truglio, and Peeke (1997) examined depressive and anxious symptomatology in children and adolescents using a multitrait, multimethod, multigroup approach. Depressive symptoms were assessed in third and sixth graders by self-report (CDI; Kovacs, 1981), parent report (CDI-PF), peer report (Peer Nomination Index of Depression; Lefkowitz & Tesiny, 1980), and teacher report (Teacher's Rating Index of Depression; Cole, Martin, Powers, & Truglio, 1996); anxiety dimensions were examined using similar methods. Data were analyzed using confirmatory factor analysis, and findings suggest that in children (third graders), anxiety and depression may be the same construct, whereas, in adolescence (sixth graders), these dimensions are quite separate. Other recent multimethod studies applying a developmental framework have investigated parenting (e.g., Metzler, Biglan, Ary, & Li, 1998), school adjustment (e.g., Lewin, Hops, Davis, & Dishion, 1993), cognitions (e.g., Daleiden, Vassey, & Williams, 1996), and physical, cognitive, and socioemotional development (e.g., Trickett, 1993).

Multiple methods of assessment provide the most thorough assessment of developmental processes, allowing for examination across multiple contexts and domains (e.g., physiological indicators and teachers' reports). In fact, a trend in psychological research is the examination of constructs using latent variables with multiple indicators of a construct in structural equation modeling, as discussed previously. With this method, for example, measures derived from different methods or raters can (if they overlap statistically) contribute to a single measure of the construct that reflects some contribution from each actual measure.

Despite the benefits of a multimethod approach, such multimethod studies are not the norm (likely because of the difficulty in obtaining data from a variety of sources and the uncertainty in regard to correspondence among methods), and there are few data on the relation between physiological indicators of many constructs and questionnaires attempting to assess similar processes. Nonetheless, such approaches are clearly the wave of the future.

CONCLUSION AND TIPS FOR PLANNING A MULTIMETHOD STUDY

In conclusion, the multimethod approach is ideal for the study of developmental psychology because, as illustrated in this chapter, developmental constructs are often difficult to tap and require assessment in multiple contexts. Moreover, one single *perfect* method does not exist. Self-reports may be biased by social desirability and age constraints; other-report methods may not be useful for constructs that are difficult to observe; and observational methods may lack generalizability when performed in a laboratory setting. Psychophysiological methods are promising, but it is often difficult to control and interpret measurement of certain biological states. Nevertheless, each method has something unique to offer that may compensate for a weakness of another method: self-reports can tap internal states, other reports may be more objective, observational methods result in extremely rich data, and psychophysiological methods tap internal states that cannot be verbalized. Thus, when used in combination, these methods can represent the intended constructs more accurately than can any single measure and can broaden our theoretical scope.

Therefore we have chosen to end with a summary of a few practical tips for planning a multimethod study for developmental research, in addition to the tips provided throughout the chapter. First, start with a strong theoretical model and justification for the choice of certain types of methods. Second, choose measures with moderate to high convergent validity so you are relatively certain that your methods are measuring the same constructs, and use statistical techniques to examine relations among multiple measures. Third, be certain that your measures are appropriate for the age, ethnicity, and SES group you are investigating. Finally, do not try to do too much (although what is "too much" depends partly on your theory and resources). Choose only a few constructs and the design that best answers your research question in the most parsimonious way. The multimethod approach may be time consuming and expensive because of the resulting abundance of data, so planning accordingly is crucial to a successful program of research.

CHAPTER 26

MULTIMETHOD APPROACHES IN SOCIAL PSYCHOLOGY: BETWEEN- AND WITHIN-METHOD REPLICATION AND MULTI-METHOD ASSESSMENT

Richard H. Smith and Monica J. Harris

As social psychologists we pursue the goal of explaining social behavior by using the best methods we can muster. We usually admit the limitations of any one method. Even if a particular method seems unassailable, few social psychologists would feel confident about the validity of a finding unless it had been replicated, for example. Typically, such replication goes beyond merely repeating the same experiment. Rather, we choose a different type of method to operationalize our independent variable with the aim of conceptually replicating the effect. We might also choose alternative ways of measuring our dependent measure that match the original dependent measure as a construct but are distinct in measurement type. We might go further still and use a participant population that is distinctive to generalize the effect across variations in type of participant and culture. If we achieve a consistent, converging pattern of findings across all these variations in method, then we may hail our effect as reliable, valid, and uncontaminated by variance because of method. Even if we do *not* achieve consistent findings, such surprising patterns of data are a benefit, as they can actually sharpen our sense of the phenomenon at hand and generate new ideas.

The purpose of our chapter is to present a broad picture of the ways in which social psychologists use, or could use, multiple methods. Although we will largely emphasize the assessment end of research, we will do so in the context of the wider sense in which social psychologists can use multiple methods. Our conception of multimethod approaches makes rough distinctions between three basic ways that social psychologists use multiple methods, which we label (a) between-method replication, (b) within-method replication, and (c) multimethod assessment. We categorize the first two types as focused largely on the independent variable side of research. *Between-method replication* refers to using different methods of manipulating an independent variable (such as varying the way an independent variable is operationalized), whereas *within-method replication* refers to using variations of the same method (such as using stimulus sampling). The third type, *multimethod assessment*, varies the method used to tap the dependent variable. The general aim across the three types of replication is to vary some aspect of the independent or dependent variable while preserving the conceptual meaning of the construct being manipulated or assessed. Usually, we seek consistency of results across replication strategies. We will emphasize, however, that inconsistency often goes with the territory and is a potentially useful feature of any ongoing research program (Eid & Diener, chap. 1, this volume).

BETWEEN-METHOD REPLICATION

When social psychologists think of multiple methods, we are perhaps just as likely to focus on the independent variable as the dependent variable. There is clear virtue even in an exact or strict replication of a finding (e.g., Hendrick, 1990), but social psychologists prefer a conceptual replication, using a different operationalization of the independent

variable (e.g., Gerard & Mathewson, 1966; Pratkanis, Greenwald, Leippe, & Baumgardner, 1988). If alternative manipulations replicate the effect, then we have greater confidence that it is the supposed conceptual variable producing the effect.

Conceptual replication is valuable because manipulations are usually translations of an idea and thus are indirect representations of a manipulated variable. There are any number of ways of operationalizing an independent variable, and the more complex the manipulation the more one or more aspects of the manipulations may introduce an unwanted confound. Manipulations in social psychology are often more likely to introduce this sort of problem because in efforts to achieve sufficient realism and impact (Aronson, Ellsworth, Carlsmith, & Gonzales, 1990), some aspect of the manipulation can create unforeseeable effects, making interpretation unclear or baffling.

Researchers have various ways of categorizing methods of manipulating independent variables, but one broad distinction that is especially relevant for social psychologists, and that often translates into using different operationalizations, is between-field studies and laboratory studies. Social psychologists are most likely to use lab experiments to test their theories largely because of the high degree of control that lab experiment can more easily provide and the yield in terms of clear causal inferences. However, for all the virtues of the highly controlled lab experiment, there are also well-known ethical and practical drawbacks, especially for studying certain phenomena (e.g., reactions to terrorist attacks or natural disasters), that often make lab experiments unfeasible and make field studies desirable.

Field studies are useful even if ethical and practical challenges are absent in the laboratory. For one thing, much social psychological phenomena can be altered by participants' knowledge of their being in an experiment, despite the cleverest cover story. Field experiments in which participants are unaware of their participation eliminate this problem (although they introduce their own ethical problems in terms of lack of informed consent). Also, from a multiple method point of view, field and lab studies are far from unequal partners in the research process. A field study may add support to a hypothesized relationship through conceptual replication and produce unexpected associations that then receive further attention. Testing an idea in a field setting, once it has already been isolated in a lab setting, not only addresses issues of generalizability, but may also suggest moderating variables.

We should also note that experimentation itself need not be seen as the be-all and end-all as general research strategy. A weakness of experimentation, especially in laboratory settings, is that it can fail to capture the complex interaction of variables that are sometimes the major determinants of behavior. Indeed, many social psychological research traditions, such as those that focus on cross-cultural issues (e.g., Diener & Suh, 2000), use correlational methods more typically. Correlational research strategies seem to address the inherent complexities of social interactions in a more satisfying way than experimental approaches and represent a varied set of effective, alternative methodological approaches to tackling social psychological phenomena.

A commonly cited example (Aronson et al., 1990) of the interplay between the laboratory and the field in social psychology is the research done on the effects of mood and helping. Laboratory experiments using mood induction techniques ranging from reading positive or negative texts (e.g., Aderman, 1972) to remembering happy or sad experiences (e.g., Moore, Underwood, & Rosenhan, 1973) have found fairly consistent increased helping effect for positive mood. However, these studies suffer from potential experimenter demand problems, and as well as the sense the helping settings used are unnatural. But, the basic finding has been replicated in field settings (e.g., Isen & Levin, 1972; Underwood, Froming, & Moore, 1977). In a now-classic series of studies, Isen and Levin (1972) found that undergraduates who received cookies while studying in a library were more likely to volunteer in response to a student's request, and adults who found a dime left in a public telephone were more likely to pick up papers that were dropped in front of them. This research actually provided two conceptual replications, at both the independent (between-method replication) and dependent variable level (multimethod assessment). As Aronson et al. (1990) pointed out, the "conver-

gence of results across methods and across settings greatly enhances our confidence in both sets of findings" (p. 181). Field studies seem especially valuable in assessing the generality of an effect and in uncovering "new variables that must be brought under control if the research is to have widespread applicability" (p. 181).

Although there is considerable precedent for between-method replication using field and lab studies, most programs of social psychological research involve multiple laboratory methods. As an example of between-method replication in laboratory settings, commentaries on social psychological methods (e.g., Aronson et al., 1990; Hendrick, 1990) often cite Gerard and Mathewson's (1966) conceptual replication of the classic dissonance study by Aronson and Mills (1959) showing the effects of the severity of initiation on liking for a group. In the original study, Aronson and Mills operationalized severity by varying whether female participants had to recite obscene words to gain group membership. As compelling as this study was, one could easily generate alternative explanations for the finding and wonder about its generalizability. The Gerard and Mathewson study used shock instead of the reciting of obscene words and found the same core finding, therefore enhancing the generality and reliability of the effect and as well as the dissonance interpretation.

Hendrick (1990), in a thorough analysis of the virtues of different types of replications, offers a few suggestions for how to go about doing replications in a systematic manner. First, clarify what procedural aspects of the original study, together with other features of the experimental context (e.g., participant characteristics, mode of participant recruitment, historical and cultural context, physical setting, experimenter attributes, formatting of materials), would produce a "strict" replication if duplicated. Second, alter the original procedural details such that some variations should produce results similar to the original study and that other variations should produce results different from the original study (all decisions guided by the conceptual similarity or dissimilarity of the variations to the original manipulation). Third, resources permitting, further replicate the original finding by varying contextual variables of such as participant type, cultural setting, mode of participant recruitment, and so on.

Social psychologists actually use systematic replication much less than its scientific yield would call for (Aronson et al., 1990; Hendrick, 1990). Apart from the often forbidding additional resources required for doing systematic replication, the discipline of psychology provides little reward for the effort in terms of journal space and respect (Hendrick, 1990). Nonetheless, there seems no question that systematic replication, or some approximation of this approach, has great potential to establish the reliability, construct validity, and generalizability of an effect (also see Rosenthal, 1990). What is more, as researchers probe the range of the effect, new hypotheses often emerge, and new research directions beckon. Thus, social psychologists should embrace more consistently and vigorously this facet of multimethod research.

WITHIN-METHOD REPLICATION

The second general type of multiplicity in method involving the independent variable is replication within a specific method, usually within a particular experiment. This is an important consideration for much social psychological experimentation, although, as Wells and Windschitl (1999) showed in a recent review of this research strategy, it is underappreciated in its importance and underused. Stimulus sampling, in which multiple instances of a stimulus category are used in a particular experiment, is the prime example of this type of replication. Wells and Windschitl (1999) emphasized that stimulus sampling is especially needed "whenever individual instances in the category potentially vary from one another in ways that might be relevant to the dependent measure" (pp. 1115–1116). An example would be of using photographs to examine the effects of physical attractiveness on person perception (e.g., Alicke, Smith, & Klotz, 1986). Using only one instance to represent levels of attractiveness, given the huge variability in physical attributes potentially contributing to attractiveness, would be methodologically imprudent.

Stimulus sampling furthers external validity by enhancing the sense that any effect can be generalized across other similar stimuli. Wells and Windschitl (1999) also emphasized the role stimulus sampling plays in assessing construct validity. Only using a single instance of category to represent the category "can confound the unique characteristics of the selected stimulus with the category. What may be portrayed as a category effect could in fact be due to the unique characteristics of the stimulus selected to represent the category" (p. 1116).

Stimulus sampling may be a particularly important issue in social psychology because many social psychological experiments, all too often, end up involving a single individual to represent a category of people. To illustrate the problem Wells and Windschitl (1999) gave the hypothetical research example in which it is proposed that people give more personal space to males compared to females. The idea is tested by having a male or female confederate stand at a place in a mall by which many patrons must pass. Suppose the researcher finds, on average, that the male confederate is given 12 centimeters greater distance than the female confederate. This may seem to be good evidence of a "gender" effect, but, in fact, one is really comparing confederates who are very different in ways besides their gender. The researcher may appear to be manipulating gender, but a better way to capture what is happening is to label each condition with the name of each experimenter. If results show that "Stan" produces greater personal space than "Mary," then the ambiguity inherent in the manipulation is plain to see, and the need for multiple male and female confederates is obvious.

Interestingly, although most social psychologists are well aware of the need for multiple sampling of stimuli, in any one experiment the implementation of such sampling is often disregarded, even though the "use of one stimulus to represent a category can be construed as functionally equivalent to conducting an experiment with a sample size of $n = 1$" (Wells & Windschitl, 1999, p. 1123). Wells and Windschitl (1999) urged social psychologists to recognize the need for within-method replication, although they also acknowledged that practical considerations often preclude its extensive use. In addition, it is often unclear how one would best select a set of exemplars for a construct despite the best intentions. Even so, researchers benefit from appreciating the potential problems associated with neglecting within-method replication strategies, and they should use their common sense in taking steps to avoid these problems. Simply being aware of the tendency to assume incorrectly that the exemplars chosen to represent a category are in fact representative encourages a more careful selection process.

MULTIMETHOD ASSESSMENT

Because as social psychologists we often focus so much of our research energy on the laboratory experiment, we may be especially attuned to between- and within-method replications of our independent variables. However, we also accept the more typical conception of multimethod research that involves tapping into a dependent variable in multiple ways. Recognizing that any single source of measurement carries with it sources of bias and error, researchers ideally attempt to converge on the "truth" of a construct by assessing it through multiple measures, each with a different set of possible biases and error. When an independent variable produces similar effects across, say, a self-report, behavioral, and physiological measure, we can be more confident of the validity and generalizability of our conclusions than if only one dependent measure were used.

This logic has been endorsed repeatedly and enthusiastically in methodology texts in social psychology since the publication of Campbell and Fiske's (1959) seminal article (Aronson et al., 1990; Brewer, 2000; Cook, 1993; Houts, Cook, & Shadish, 1986; West, Biesanz, & Pitts, 2000). In practice, however, there is a regrettable overreliance on self-reports in social psychology (Diener & Scollon, 2002) stemming from a combination of factors, ranging from the economy and ease of use of self-report measures to inertia and satisfaction with such measures.

The poverty of dependent variable choices evident in much social psychological research is particularly unfortunate given that the majority of the measurement approaches described in this volume are well

suited for tackling social psychological hypotheses. In the section that follows, we present an overview of important methodological features of these methods as well as an assessment of their appropriateness for and typical use within social psychology.

Table 26.1 presents a critical overview of the research methods covered in this volume. We offer this table as a way for researchers to compare easily the advantages and disadvantages of a given method, in addition to pointing interested readers to examples of recent social psychological studies using a method. For each method, we offer our opinion of the primary strengths and weaknesses of the methodology and present our sense (based on up-to-date review papers where available or based on estimates taken from research laboratories prominently identified with the methodology that have provided recent psychometric data) of its typical reliability and validity.

Next, we offer our subjective assessment of three important features of each method that might affect researchers' decisions to use it: (a) the directness of the inference afforded by the method, (b) the reactivity of the method, and (c) the ease of data collection using the method. By the directness of inference, we mean essentially the tightness of the conceptual link between the dependent measure provided by a method and the hypothetical construct of interest. A direct measure is one in which there are few, if any, plausible explanations for scoring high on the measure other than the participant actually having high standing on the hypothetical construct. An indirect measure is one in which a high score can mean other things besides high standing on the construct.

All other things being equal, a method that offers a more direct inference is usually a more valid measure, but in social psychology, all other things are often not equal. One of the disadvantages of more direct methods is that the directness of inference is often inversely related to the reactivity of the measurement (Webb, Campbell, Schwartz, Sechrest, & Grove, 1981). Thus, we offer also our assessment of each method's reactivity, defined as the extent to which the methodology raises participants' awareness of the construct being assessed and consequently their ability to modify their responses. When the construct of interest involves

socially undesirable behaviors (e.g., prejudice), reactivity of measurement opens the real possibility of data distorted by response biases. In such cases, researchers might reasonably opt for a messier, less-direct form of measurement than a distorted—albeit direct—answer to their questions.

When interpreting our reactivity ratings, it is important to keep in mind that the judgment of reactivity refers to whether the dependent measure creates participants' awareness of the construct of interest *and hence enables them to modify their responses with respect to that construct.* Thus, a measure can be "reactive" in the sense of being obvious or intrusive yet still be considered "nonreactive" if the participants are unable to modify their behavioral response despite their awareness of the measurement process.

In some cases, a given method's variations are methodologically similar enough to each other that a single judgment of reactivity can be confidently offered for the method as a whole, as with global self-assessment methods (see Lucas & Baird, chap. 3, this volume). In other cases (Bakeman & Gnisci, chap. 10, this volume), though, the method category consists of a broad range of disparate measures, some of which are highly reactive but some of which may be completely nonreactive. For categories such as these, then, we are able merely to conclude somewhat lamely that the reactivity of measurement "varies."

EXAMPLES OF MULTIMETHOD ASSESSMENT: THE MEASUREMENT OF ATTITUDES

Testing the tripartite structure of attitudes. The measurement of attitudes is one area of research in which multimethod assessment has proven especially useful. A long-standing claim about attitudes is that they have a tripartite structure consisting of affective, behavioral, and cognitive components. Breckler (1984) pointed out that using a single method, such as self-reports, to distinguish the three attitude components may produce overestimated correlations between components, simply because of shared method variance. Thus, measuring the three components using just self-reports may mask the presence of a robust tripartite struc-

TABLE 26.1

Comparative Analysis of Methodologies Used in Social Psychology

Method	Primary strengths	Primary weaknesses	Typical reliabilities	Typical validities
Global self-assessment	Directness of inference; ease of administration	Vulnerability to social desirability biases	Very high	Moderate
Informant assessment	Can be more accurate than self-reports; social desirability less of a problem	Difficulty obtaining informants; missing data	May require multiple informants to achieve adequate reliability	Low to moderate
Observational methods	Often less reactive; source of rich data	Highly time consuming; can't tap into internal states	May require multiple observers to achieve adequate reliability	Low to moderate
Ability tests	Standardization and a wealth of normative data	Most are time consuming to administer	High	Moderate to high, depending on correspondence with criterion
Experience sampling	Provides naturalistic, "real-world" data	Less control over data collection; not good for low base-rate behaviors	Often low	Low to moderate
Text analysis	Can capture Ps experiences with a depth not attained in traditional self-reports	Reactivity can still be a problem; coding of text can be time consuming	Moderate to high	Generally high
Nonreactive methods	Avoids response biases	Often have less control, may be difficult to create for some constructs	Often low; depending on the measure, sometimes can't be assessed	Generally low
Implicit methods	Avoids self-report biases	Relative utility in predicting actual behavior not yet documented	Moderate when appropriate tests are used	Low to moderate, depending on criterion

Method	Directness of inference	Reactivity of method	Ease of measurement	Recent social psychological citations	Comments
Physiological methods	High	Moderate	Requires specialized equipment & software, extensive data cleaning		Identifies underlying biological processes of effects
Brain imaging	Moderate but depends on task and region of brain	Moderate to low	Expensive, Ps are constrained physically		Identifies underlying biological processes of effects
Web-based methods	Typically high	Low	Selection bias; lack of control over data collection		Inexpensive, easy way to reach geographically diverse samples
Global self-assessment	High	High	Very easy	Any issue of JPSP, PSPB, JESP, etc. (Lucas & Baird, chap. 3, this volume)	The DV of choice among social psychologists, for good reason
Informant assessment	High	High	Difficult	Gosling et al., 2002; Kurtz & Sherker, 2003; Katz & Joiner, 2002 (Neyer, chap. 4, this volume)	Should receive more use than it currently does
Observational methods	Varies	Varies	Difficult	Tiedens & Fragale, 2003; Dovidio et al., 2002; Bollmer et al., 2003 (Bakeman & Gnisci, chap. 10, this volume)	Behavior is, after all, the primary DV of interest, so should be considered the gold standard
Ability tests	High	High	Very easy	Chan et al., 1997; Kickul & Neuman, 2000 (Lubinski, chap. 8, this volume) limited	Relevance and utility to social psychology
Experience sampling	Low	Usually high	Very hard	Mehl & Pennebaker, 2003; Oishi, 2002; Brown & Ryan, 2003 (Stone & Litcher-Kelly, chap. 5, this volume)	Technological advances using beepers and PDAs have made this method even better

continued

TABLE 26.1 Continued

Method	Directness of inference	Reactivity of method	Ease of measurement	Recent social psychological citations	Comments
Text analysis	Moderate	Moderate	Moderate	Danner, Snowdon, & Friesen, 2001; King et al., 2000; Campbell & Pennebaker, 2003 (Mehl, chap. 11, this volume)	A promising variation on self-reports gaining in prominence
Nonreactive methods	Low	Very low	Usually difficult	Quist & Resendez, 2002; Kasser et al., 2002; Duryea & Nagel, 1995 (Fritsche & Linneweber, chap. 14, this volume)	They're a lot of fun, but probably can't surmount validity concerns
Implicit methods	Low	Low	Easy	Hull et al., 2002; Devine et al., 2002; Cunningham et al., 2001 (Robinson & Neighbors, chap. 9, this volume)	Appear to have great & growing potential for tapping attitudes
Physiological methods	Low	Low	Very difficult	Amodio et al., 2003; Herrald & Tomaka, 2003; C. R. Harris, 2001 (Berntson & Cacioppo, chap. 12, this volume)	Assuming greater importance in theories of emotion
Brain imaging	Low	Low	Very difficult	O'Doherty et al., 2003; Critchley et al., 2000; Farrow et al., 2001 (Zald & Curtis, chap. 13, this volume)	Applicable to a limited (albeit growing) number of theories in social psychology
Web-based methods	Usually high	High	Very easy	Srivastava et al., 2003; Williams et al., 2000; McKenna & Bargh, 1998 (Reips, chap. 6, this volume)	Good for studying specialized Internet groups, otherwise sampling problems abound

ture. Also, theoretically, there is little reason to assume that people's attitudes are only a function of processes captured by self-report. Nonverbal measures of physiological responses and overt behavior may tap other aspects of a person's attitude. Furthermore, each of the three components is a hypothetical, unobservable construct, and as such "no single measure can be assumed to capture its full nature" (p. 1193). The more the assessment of each component is achieved through multiple and maximally distinct methods, the more measurement errors will cancel out. As measurement method overlap increases, measurement error can accrue, producing a misleading picture of the attitude construct.

The two studies reported by Breckler (1984) took especially effective advantage of a multimethod approach. In both studies the attitude object was the domain of snakes. In the first study, participants completed four measures of *affect* (Thurstone Affect, Positive Affect and Negative Mood via the Mood Adjective Check List, and heart rate) while in the presence of an actual, live snake. The *behavioral* component was first measured by asking participants to engage in series of increasingly closer physical contact to the snake. They were also shown a series of slides of various snakes and asked how close they would be willing to get to each type of snake, as a behavioral intention. Finally, they completed a Thurstone scale that was adapted to tap behavioral intentions. The *cognitive* component consisted of a Thurstone cognition scale, a Semantic Differential, and a participant-coded favorable or unfavorable thought listing. Covariance structure analysis favored a tripartite model. With the exception of heart rate, all the measures loaded most highly on their respective factors. Furthermore, the three factors were correlated with each other but only moderately so. Using multiple methods to tap each component reduced the likelihood that overlapping measurement error would exaggerate the sense that three components were highly correlated. Thus, the *independence* between components was given a better chance to emerge.

Breckler took further advantage of multimethod assessment strategies in Study 2. He tested his supposition that measuring the three attitude components using only one type of measure would reduce the sense of independence between components. He reasoned that using a paper-and-pencil measure for all components would enhance the likelihood that all responses, even to behavioral questions, would actually be determined by participants' "verbal knowledge system." Participants in Study 2 were asked to imagine the presence of a live snake (rather than responding to an actual snake) and completed verbal report versions of the nonverbal measures used in Study 1 (in addition to the other verbal measures). Covariance structure analysis suggested that the three-factor model was superior to the one-factor model; however, compared to Study 1, the magnitude of this difference was small. Breckler (1984) argued that the use of the same method to measure the three components as well as an imagined stimulus "lead to an overestimate of correlations among affect, behavior, and cognition" (p. 1202). In Study 1 the average correlations among the components was .55, whereas in Study 2 it was .83.

Using an actual snake versus an imagined snake also appeared to affect participants' responses. This seemed especially evident when examining participants' responses to the negative and positive mood scales in the two studies. In Study 1, where participants reacted to an actual snake and thus were probably reporting more what they would actually feel about snakes, the correlation between positive and negative mood was only –.13 (*ns*). However, in Study 2, where participants imagined how they would react to a snake, the correlation was –.42 (*p.* < .01). It seems reasonable to suppose that the latter correlation more reflects participants' theories of how they react than how they might actually react.

Breckler's two studies show what a multimethod approach to tackling a question can yield. Study 1, using multiple types of measures for each attitude component, was able to show clearly that the measures designed to tap a particular component were more highly correlated with each other than they were with measures designed to tap the other components. And yet, each component was correlated enough with the other to suggest that each was sufficiently linked to a broader construct of a general

attitude. The importance of multiple types of measures was highlighted by the contrasting pattern of result in Study 2, which used only one type of measure, verbal self-report. The three components, using this single-method approach, seemed much less independent than what was evident in the multimethod Study 1. Interestingly, the variability in the degree of independence between the attitude components evident in comparing the two studies became a springboard for understanding more fully the nature of the attitude construct. Breckler speculated about a number of factors that might make each component associated with a distinct or similar response system beyond measurement overlap, such as degree to which a person's behavioral response toward the object is voluntary and consistent with the other components. A multimethod approach also leads naturally to the suggestion that future research should involve conceptual replication using other attitude domains besides snakes. Presumably, the tripartite model would emerge across attitude domains, but variations in intercomponent consistency would hardly be a problem if the underlying reasons for such variability could be systematically tracked or introduced. Domains in which people have a lot more experience, those that are more concrete, and those whose responses are mediated by more than one response system are possibilities, each of which could be tested using a multimethod approach.

The measurement of prejudice. Some attitudes are more subject to socially desirable responding than others, and in such cases the high reactivity of self-report measures becomes an even greater problem. Not only are people sometimes motivated to misrepresent their attitudes for self-presentational reason, but they may also be unaware of their true attitudes (Greenwald & Banaji, 1995). Prejudicial attitudes are prime examples. Thus, social psychologists have searched for methods besides self-reports to measure such attitudes more accurately (Devine, 1989; Dovidio, Kawakami, Johnson, Johnson, & Howard, 1997; Fazio, Jackson, Dunton, & Williams, 1995; Greenwald, McGhee, & Schwartz, 1998). The most recent of these techniques is the Implicit Association Test (IAT;

Greenwald et al., 1998), mentioned earlier, which aims to measure unconscious attitudes through tapping automatically evoked negative and positive associations with attitude objects. The IAT holds much promise because its procedure, which is based on reaction times, appears impervious to self-presentational motives. In addition, as the measure seems connected to a response system distinct from self-report measures, it may "reveal unique components of attitudes that lie outside conscious awareness and control" (Cunningham, Preacher, & Banaji, 2001, p. 163). The IAT, therefore, is an assessment method that promises to measure attitudes in a less-reactive way than traditional self-report measures while at the same time tapping aspects of attitudes that other measures might not be able to measure, even if these measures did not suffer from high reactivity.

Recent research using the IAT has taken advantage of multimethod approaches as researchers compare and contrast the reliability and validity of the IAT with other measures. A study by McConnell and Leibold (2001) is an interesting example. Participants completed the IAT and explicit (self-report, semantic differentials, and feeling thermometer) measures of prejudice and then later met with a White and then a Black experimenter in a structured social interaction. Videotapes of these interactions were coded for a number of specific prejudicial behaviors. In addition to these codings, each experimenter also made global ratings of the participants' prejudicial behavior.

Unlike some previous work (Greenwald et al., 1998), the IAT and the explicit measures were moderately correlated with each other ($r = .42, p < .01$) Both types of measures were correlated with prejudiced reactions, but the IAT was correlated with both experimenter global ratings and coders' ratings, whereas explicit measures were only correlated with experimenter ratings—even though coder ratings and experimenter ratings were correlated with each other.

The multimethod approach taken in this study allowed a number of important points to be made. First, the moderate correlation between the implicit and the explicit measures suggested that they measure overlapping but distinct constructs. This picture

was further reinforced by the pattern of correlations between these two measures and the multiple measures of prejudiced reactions. Both implicit and explicit measures were correlated with coder ratings, but only the implicit measure was correlated with experimenter ratings as well, suggesting that the IAT can predict prejudiced reactions in a way that explicit measures cannot. Prior research by Dovidio et al. (1997) indicates that only implicit measures of prejudice correlate with the type of nonverbal behavior similar to what was coded for in the present study. Nonverbal behaviors are under less conscious control than verbal speech (Babad, Bernieri, & Rosenthal, 1989; Ekman & Friesen, 1969), and so it makes sense that the IAT, billed as a measure more closely linked to unconscious processes, should correlate with nonverbal behaviors. Only by including both implicit and explicit measures of attitudes and including both nonverbal and global ratings of prejudicial behavior would this more complex sense of how prejudicial attitudes operate and predict behavior have had the opportunity to emerge.

The virtues of multimethod approaches are also evident in what was *not* done in the McConnell and Leibold study. Of course, any study has limitations, and McConnell and Leibold listed a number of features of their procedure that call for replicating the results in a way that rules out alterative explanations or that adds to their generalizability. The design of the study entailed that participants interact with the Black experimenter close on the heels of completing the measure of prejudicial attitudes, making the accessibility of conscious racial attitudes more likely and enhancing the likelihood of attitude-behavior consistency (e.g., Fazio, Powell, & Williams, 1989). McConnell and Leibold (2001) speculated that their procedure would make it more likely that the Black experimenter would be categorized as "Black," also making participants' racial attitudes more predictive of their behavior toward the Black experimenter (Smith, Fazio, & Cejka, 1996). Replicating the study without this proximity of attitude measurement and prejudicial reaction measure would test these possibilities. McConnell and Leibold also speculated that one reason why their study found a correlation between

the IAT and explicit measures is that their participants completed the IAT *after* completing the explicit measures. Prior work by Greenwald et al. (1998), in which no correlation emerged, placed the IAT *before* the explicit measures. The IAT probably sensitized participants to the issue of racial attitudes and thus may have heightened self-presentational motives. Examining this issue more systematically through a replication that varies the order of completing these measures is clearly a necessary step to take. We can add another multimethod suggestion. The McConnell and Leibold procedure might also have benefitted from stimulus sampling. Only one White experimenter and one Black experimenter were used, and thus it is quite possible that idiosyncratic features of either or both of the experimenters might have introduced confounds.

Examples of Multimethod Assessment: Interpersonal Conflict and Aggression

Agreeableness and conflict. William Graziano and his colleagues have conducted a program of research that also illustrates well the strengths and advantages of a multimethod approach in social psychology. We chose this particular study (Graziano, Jensen-Campbell, & Hair, 1996) to describe in some detail because it is a good example of all three forms of multimethod research: multimethod assessment of the dependent variables, between-method replication of the independent variable, and within-method replication of the independent variable. The article describes the results of two studies aimed at testing the hypothesis that individual differences in Agreeableness are related to patterns of conflict and preferences for conflict resolution strategies.

In Study 1, 263 undergraduates completed a measure of Agreeableness based on Goldberg's (1992) self-rating markers of the Five-Factor Model of personality. Participants then read a series of 10 conflict vignettes describing possible conflict situations in various sorts of relationships (family, friends, romantic partners, etc.), and they rated how effective each of 11 possible strategies was for resolving the conflict in that situation. The 11

strategies were then collapsed into the three broad categories of power assertion (e.g., physical action, threats, criticism); disengagement (e.g., submission, wait and see); and negotiation (e.g., compromise, third-party mediation). Analyses revealed that although both high and low Agreeableness individuals felt that negotiation and disengagement were superior forms of conflict resolution than was power assertion, participants low in Agreeableness viewed power assertion as a more effective choice than did high Agreeable participants (Graziano et al., 1996).

Study 2 of the Graziano et al. (1996) article was designed to address some of the limitations of the first study, namely that the vignette methodology, while providing greater control and avoiding problems with deception, could still be considered artificial and constraining of participants' natural reactions to conflict situations. To address these limitations, Graziano and his colleagues conducted their second study, which involved videotaping 62 same-sex dyads of varying combinations of Agreeableness (high/high; low/low; high/low) while they engaged in two mild conflict situations. One situation required the members of the dyad to arrive at a unanimous decision for a trial in which they had received material differing with respect to whether they should rule in favor of the plaintiff. The other situation required them to role-play individuals competing for a scarce resource; the role-play was set up so that a mutually acceptable solution was possible but could be arrived at only through discussion. Dependent measures for this study included participants' self-reports of the degree of conflict perceived during the interaction, ratings of their partner, and molar and molecular nonverbal variables coded by objective raters from the videotapes.

Analyses revealed that high-Agreeable participants perceived less conflict in the interaction, liked their partners better, and rated them more positively compared to low-Agreeable participants (Graziano et al., 1996). As predicted, low-Agreeable participants were more likely to elicit more conflict from their partners than high-Agreeable individuals. Agreeableness was also related to the nonverbal cues given off by participants; for example, low-Agreeable participants leaned away from their partners more often.

Interestingly, low-Agreeable individuals smiled more often when they were paired with another low-Agreeable person than when they were paired with a high-Agreeable person.

In sum, the Graziano et al. (1996) article encompasses an impressive array of introducing conflict and measuring reactions to this conflict. Between-method replication was achieved by varying three ways of introducing conflict: vignettes, a videotaped interaction involving an actual conflict situation, and role-playing. Within-method replication was achieved by creating different vignettes in Study 1 (i.e., 10 conflict vignettes involving different sorts of relationships). Multimethod assessment was achieved by including self-report, observer ratings, and nonverbal behaviors. That similar themes emerged from all these ways of introducing conflict and measuring reactions adds greatly to the validity of the Agreeableness construct and helps lead to conclusions that are relatively impervious to artifactual alternative explanations. But the Graziano et al. (1996) study also exemplifies some of the interpretive perils involved in multimethod research. For example, observers' ratings of participants' Agreeableness were only modestly correlated with participants' self-reported Agreeableness, $r(123) = .21$, $p < .05$. Although this correlation was statistically significant, it is on the low side of what would be considered desirable for a convergent validity coefficient. Moreover, computing the correlations separately by sex revealed further complications: Observers agreed significantly with self-reports for men but not for women. The question then becomes what to make of the lack of strong agreement: Which measurement source is "right"? It is this very ambiguity in knowing how to interpret results that are inconsistent across replications or variables that perhaps undermines researchers' motivations for including multiple measures or operationalizations. On the other hand, identifying limiting conditions, such apparent "failures" to replicate across dependent variables, may actually help advance theory.

Aggression and the Southern "culture of honor."
One of the most provocative theories of aggression introduced in recent years has been Richard Nis-

bett's program of research asserting that a "culture of honor" possessed by Southerners can account for the higher homicide rates in Southern cities (Nisbett, 1993; Nisbett & Cohen, 1996). The argument essentially is that because the South was originally settled by descendants from herding societies—societies characterized by a culture of honor that requires them to retaliate violently to perceived threats to property or reputation—Southern cities should be characterized by higher rates of homicide that are argument or conflict related. Obviously, this is a hypothesis that would be difficult to test definitively via a traditional 2 × 2 experimental design. Nisbett and his colleagues instead have built a case for their argument around a variety of between- and within-method replications using experimental and nonexperimental approaches and multimethod assessment using a variety of dependent measures.

The following list illustrates the remarkable variety of methodological approaches adopted by Nisbett and Cohen's research program:

1. Analysis of historical and ethnographic studies of herding societies,
2. Archival analysis of census and crime reports,
3. Representative random sample surveys,
4. Laboratory experiments assessing reactions of Southerners to insults,
5. Field experiments assessing potential employers' and newspaper writers' reactions to honor-related crimes, and
6. Archival analysis of Southern laws, voting records, and public policies regarding honor-related practices and crimes (e.g., capital punishment and gun control policies).

Moreover, the studies conducted *within* each of these methodological approaches are in turn characterized by an admirable attention to diversity of dependent variables. Take, for example, the three studies reported in Cohen, Nisbett, Bowdle, and Schwarz (1996). In Study 1, Southern and Northern male undergraduates at the University of Michigan were instructed to walk down a narrow hallway, necessitating the closing of a file drawer by a confederate. The participant had to return back down the hallway almost immediately, once again apparently inconveniencing the confederate, who

slammed the file drawer shut, bumped the participant with his shoulder, and called him an "asshole" under his breath. There were three categories of dependent measures: objective judges' ratings of how angry and amused the participant appeared after the bump; projective hostility measures (a word completion task, ratings of negative emotions shown in photographs, and completion of a neutral scenario); and an insult prime scenario, where participants were asked to finish a story involving one man making a pass at the first character's fiancée.

In Study 2, the same bumping/insult manipulation was used, but different dependent variables were assessed. Cortisol levels, which indicate stress, and testosterone levels, which are associated with aggression and dominance behavior, were measured before and after the confederate's insult. Participants were also asked to indicate how much electric shock they would be willing to experience in a later phase of the experiment, as a means of assessing their motivation to demonstrate toughness. Participants then completed a number of scenarios that were ambiguous as to whether an insult had occurred. In addition, objective judges rated the emotional expressions of the participant immediately following the bumping incident as was done in Study 1.

For Study 3, following the bump and insult, a different confederate walked down the narrow hall toward the participant. As there was not room for them to pass each other side by side, one person had to give way to the other. The confederate did not slow his pace, and the dependent measure was the distance at which the participant gave way (if at all). The participant was then led to a room containing a third confederate, who shook hands with the participant as they were introduced. This confederate recorded a rating of how firm the handshake was and the degree to which the participant's gaze was domineering. Participants also responded to a questionnaire asking them to rate how they think they would come across to the third confederate (who in one condition observed the insult), as a way of assessing whether insulted participants believed their reputations suffered as a result.

In sum, the three studies reported in Cohen et al. (1996) encompass a remarkable range of

dependent measures, with an emphasis on relatively nonreactive behavioral measures. Indeed, the almost total absence of traditional self-report variables is striking. Analyses revealed, for the most part, consistent results across dependent measures. Compared to Northerners, Southerners who were insulted (a) became more upset, as measured by their emotional reactions and cortisol levels; (b) were more likely to be cognitively primed to give aggressive responses, as measured by their reactions to the insult scenario; and (c) showed a greater inclination to behave aggressively or dominantly, as seen by their gains in testosterone levels, inclination not to give way to the other confederate, and handshaking/gaze behavior.

On some of the dependent variables, there were *no* regional differences obtained, but in one sense these nonsignificant results help in important ways to refine further the culture of honor perspective. For example, there were no differences between Southerners and Northerners in their reaction to either the neutral or ambiguous threat scenarios or on the shock acceptance measure. Cohen and his colleagues interpreted this pattern as demonstrating reassuring discriminant validity: "[T]he effect of the affront was limited to situations that concerned issues of honor, were emotionally involving, and had actual consequences for the participant's masculine status and reputation" (1996, p. 957). Clearly, Nisbett and Cohen's (1996) series of studies illustrate the full breadth and benefits of a multimethod approach to a research question.

Encouraging Adoption of Multimethod Approaches in Social Psychology

Most social psychologists agree that a multimethod perspective in conducting research is useful if not necessary. One reason for this agreement is that we can all quickly think of topic areas in which progress was held back initially by an inadequate application of multimethods—but in which progress was also advanced by a more effective application in the long run. Research on social facilitation (e.g., Guerin, 1986; Triplett, 1898; Zajonc, 1965) and group polarization (e.g., Myers & Lamm, 1976; Stoner, 1961) are classic, well-worn examples. In the case of the group polarization, the initial research appeared to show that group decisions tended to be riskier than individuals decisions (Stoner, 1961). However, this "risky shift" turned out to be dependent on the nature of the decision, and thus was an artifact of insufficient stimulus sampling (e.g., Burnstein & Vinoker, 1975; Myers & Lamm, 1976). Research using a representative range of decision types showed that groups actually tend to polarize decision making, hence the revised label of "group polarization." Both the social facilitation research and the group polarization research are part of any social psychologist's collective memory of instances in which oversights, failures, or glitches in our use of multimethods slowed progress more than necessary.

Recommendations for the field. If most social psychologists agree that a multimethod perspective in conducting research is useful if not necessary, the question then becomes, Why is this perspective not adopted more frequently in the studies we publish? Perhaps the most honest answer to that question is that a multimethod approach, particularly one that involves *all* the levels of multimethod analysis that we describe here, is quite simply a lot of work. Also, given the publish-or-perish pressures of the tenure track, the vague disrespect often given to mere replications, and the seemingly ever-expanding number of studies required per manuscript to get accepted at top journals, the temptation is great indeed to stick with a measure and/or manipulation that you know works.

The ultimate consequence of such pressures is that our discipline is confronted with a social trap: It is in most researchers' individual best interest to get more research done more quickly by using a small number of previously validated procedures and without bothering to replicate findings with other procedures or samples; yet when everybody does so, the knowledge base of our field suffers. To put it another way, until a multimethod approach to conducting research becomes either normative or required in our discipline, the costs of such approaches in terms of time, reduced productivity, and the risk of inconsistent results generally outweigh the perceived benefits to validity and theory that accrue. We thus pay lip service to multimethod

approaches in much the same way we do the necessity for cross-cultural replication: Sounds great, and somebody needs to do it, but just not me.

In Garrett Hardin's classic article, "The Tragedy of the Commons," he noted that appeals to better behavior rarely work to solve social traps and that instead what is needed is "mutual coercion, mutually agreed upon" (1968, p. 1247). Should our discipline arrive at the consensus that demonstrating construct validity through multimethod research is important, measures could in principle be taken to ensure that it is adopted more frequently. Precedence for such actions has been established before, as, for example, seen in the Task Force on Statistical Inference (Wilkinson, 1999). For many years, writers had been decrying the single-minded pursuit of *p* levels and neglect of effect sizes, to little or no effect (Cohen, 1994; Harris, 1991; Meehl, 1978). But after the American Psychological Association (APA) convened the Task Force and changed APA style in response to its recommendations to mandate the reporting of effect sizes to accompany each focused test of significance, such reporting of effect sizes is now routine. Although APA policy strictly speaking applies only to journals published by APA, most other psychological journals would follow suit.

A less heavy-handed solution our field could take is to institute norms for using multimethod approaches in a multitiered fashion through changes in editorial policy among the premier journals of our discipline. It would require only a small shift in editorial policy to request that follow-up studies within a manuscript show convergence across operationalizations of the independent and dependent variables. Change in policy could occur on a grassroots basis as well, if manuscript reviewers started including multimethod convergence as one of the criteria they evaluate before recommending acceptance in a top-tier journal.

A third course of action our field can take is to improve the education of our graduate students. In many PhD programs in social psychology, the only coverage of multimethod issues is the assignment of Campbell and Fiske's (1959) classic article. And in general, procedures for demonstrating validity often receive short shrift compared to the attention paid to reliability. This is probably because of the fact

that assessing reliability is a relatively cut-and-dried matter—you run your test–retest *r*s or coefficient alphas—but there is no single standard procedure for assessing validity. Although this makes teaching validity and multimethod issues fuzzier, it is not less important than reliability and should be given equal weight in our training.

Recommendations for individual researchers. We are pragmatic enough to realize that few, if any, of the preceding recommendations will ever actually be adopted within our discipline. What advice, then, can we offer to individual researchers who wish to enhance their use of multimethod approaches? First, we suggest that researchers do a better job of explicitly acknowledging the multimethod convergence of their findings when writing manuscripts. The more we acknowledge and appreciate multimethod convergence when it happens, the more we will notice it when it is not there.

Second, researchers should acquaint themselves with, and take advantage, of the wide variety of statistical approaches available for demonstrating multimethod agreement, such as simple correlational analyses, confirmatory factor analysis or structural equation modeling (e.g., Cunningham et al., 2001; Kiers, Takane, & ten-Berge, 1996; Koeltinger, 1991; Millsap, 1995a; Schmitt & Stults, 1986; see also Eid, Lischetzke, & Nussbeck, chap. 20, this volume), multilevel modeling (e.g., Livert, Rindskoph, Saxe, & Stirratt, 2001), treating stimuli as random factors (e.g., Kenny, 1995) in the case of analyzing within-method replication, and various computations available for assessing the success of between-method replications (Rosenthal, 1990). Even a simple correlation between two measures differing in sources of method variance can go a very long way in demonstrating multimethod agreement, especially if the alternative is relying on a single measure. Another simple approach to quantifying construct validity has been recently proposed by Westen and Rosenthal (2003), who introduced two straightforward metrices for gauging the extent of agreement between hypothesized and obtained patterns of intercorrelations.

Third, as mentioned earlier, researchers in their role as manuscript reviewers can encourage the use

of multimethod approaches in others' work by noting reliance on single-source measures or inadequate attention to stimulus sampling as a major limitation to a manuscript, perhaps even precluding publication, and by lauding evidence of attention to multimethod issues as a strength. In this vein, reviewers could help by not insisting on perfect consistency or significant results across all measures. Researchers will be more hesitant to try or report novel methods if they believe an inconsistent result would doom their publication chances. Also, as we have discussed earlier, failures to replicate across dependent measures, independent variable manipulations, or population type and culture can advance understanding by pointing out limiting conditions as much as replication can.

Researchers can and should also take care not to become paradigm bound. A measure or procedure that works and that all your buddies working in this area use is indeed convenient. But sooner or later you will have learned all that you can with this approach, or at the least you will miss out on what you *could* have learned with another approach. Social psychologists can benefit from being more familiar with research done by developmental psychologists, who tend to use multiple methods more frequently. Reading the work done by methodologically inventive researchers in personality and clinical psychology can also be very enlightening. Researchers working in other fields have developed techniques and measures that could, with minor fiddling, be put to good use in one's own field. The IAT is a good example of this, as it was originally designed to serve as an implicit measure of racial prejudice. However, it has quickly caught on in other areas of psychology and has been used to measure anything from clinical phobias (Teachman, Gregg, & Woody, 2001) to self-esteem (Greenwald & Farnham, 2000).

Finally, researchers should be cognizant that some forms of multimethod validation are more necessary than others, and we should design and evaluate studies accordingly. Stimulus sampling concerns will be less worrisome when the critical independent variable, say race, is manipulated as one word or phrase in two otherwise identical

stimulus paragraphs than they would be when only one black and one white confederate are used. If the black confederate just happened to have an unpleasant personality, for example, a more negative reaction to him or her could mean many other things besides racism. Similarly, relying on a single self-report dependent variable may be less troublesome if it involves a relatively clear-cut topic that is not likely to be prone to distortion as a result of social desirability. Lastly, as Mook (1983) so eloquently pointed out, there is a time and place for external invalidity. In some cases, for example, the initial stages of a program of research when one is happy simply to show that a given result is theoretically possible, demonstrating the result with a single measure or operationalization can be truly informative in and of itself.

CLOSING THOUGHTS

Although the main goal of this chapter is to show the relevance of multimethod assessment for social psychology, we have also tried to broaden the sense of what multimethod research entails in our subdiscipline. One way we have tried to achieve this broader goal is by making a general distinction between multiple methods focused mostly on the independent variable (between-method and within-method replication) and those focused mostly on the dependent variable (multimethod assessment). But these are only rough distinctions and are not meant to force a particular strategy into a Procrustean bed. In fact, the distinctions are somewhat unwieldy and only approximate the range of what could be classified as multimethod. Our main point is that social psychological research can proceed fruitfully in multimethod fashion on a number of distinctive, yet overlapping fronts. Our research may usually take less advantage of expansive multimethod approaches than it should, but most social psychologists realize the benefits derived from being oriented in this direction. We understand that we do better, more cumulative research to the extent that we plan our studies with multiple methods in full view and at least partially applied.

CHAPTER 27

CLINICAL PSYCHOLOGY: CONSTRUCT VALIDATION WITH MULTIPLE SOURCES OF INFORMATION AND MULTIPLE SETTINGS

G. Leonard Burns and Stephen N. Haynes

This chapter describes the importance of multiple sources of information from multiple settings for the construct validation of clinical psychology measures. We first describe the role of measurement for research in clinical psychology and for clinical judgments about clients. Because the quality of research findings and clinical judgments depend on the validity of measures, we provide an overview of procedures for the development of measures. We then consider in depth how confirmatory factor analysis can be used to model multitrait by multisource matrices for convergent and discriminant validation of measures. We describe the outcomes that would be supportive (i.e., measures with more trait than source variance) and unsupportive (i.e., measures with more source than trait variance) of construct validity. We then review the studies that used these procedures with clinical psychology measures. The findings indicate that many measures contained more source than trait variance. The final section of the chapter argues that the classic Campbell and Fiske multitrait by multimethod matrix can be expanded to include additional types of information (i.e., facets, modes, dimensions, settings, sources, instruments, methods, and occasions of measurement). This expanded measurement matrix is considered to provide a rich framework for the development and validation of measures.

Measurement is important in two areas of clinical psychology. Measurement is first a central component in all aspects of clinical research. Clinical research often involves the evaluation of the effectiveness of treatments, the identification of characteristics of per-

sons who are more or less likely to benefit from treatments, and the identification of variables that affect the outcome of treatments. Clinical research also involves the description of behavior problems and their associated features and variables associated with their onset, duration, intensity, or time-course (e.g., research on the characteristics and causes of eating disorders, conduct disorders, marital problems). Multimethod assessment (i.e., the measurement of clinical phenomena with various methods) is considered essential for good clinical research.

The second area of clinical psychology where measurement is important involves clinical judgments about clients during assessment and treatment. Clinical psychologists often estimate the chance that a client will harm himself or herself, provide psychiatric diagnoses for clients, and identify a client's most important behavior problems and concerns. Clinical psychologists also make judgments about the causes of a client's behavior problems, a client's behavioral, cognitive, and social environmental strengths, the most appropriate treatment goals for a client, the best treatment procedures to reach these goals, and the best way to evaluate the success of the client's treatment. A particularly important clinical judgment is the clinical case formulation—the integration of multiple judgments for the purpose of planning treatment (Haynes & O'Brien, 2000). Multimethod assessment is also considered important for good clinical judgments.

The validity of clinical research findings and clinical judgments depends on the validity of measures used in research and clinical activities.

Research findings and clinical judgments are usually drawn from measures derived from interviews, questionnaires, standardized tests, behavioral observations, self-monitoring, and electrophysiological and biomedical instruments. Invalid measures may lead us to overestimate, underestimate, or fail to identify treatment effects and causal relations in both research and clinical applications. Because the quality of the measures affects the quality of clinical research and clinical decisions about clients, specific, reliable, and valid measures are mandatory for the advancement of clinical psychology.

DEVELOPMENT OF CLINICAL PSYCHOLOGY MEASURES

Many strategies have been advanced for the development of reliable and valid measures and for the evaluation of these properties of existing measures. These strategies include content validation, exploratory and confirmatory factor analysis, item performance characteristics and item-response theory strategies, internal consistency, temporal stability, and convergent and discriminant validity, among others (e.g., Haynes & O'Brien, 2000, Table 11-1).

Inferences about the reliability, validity, and item-level performance of measures used in clinical psychology are often based on estimating the degree to which variance in the measure of interest is associated with variance in another measure (e.g., shared variance with a gold standard measure of the same construct, variance of an item with an aggregation of items measuring the same construct, variance of a measure with itself across time, settings, sources, and so on). These strategies provide information, usually in the form of correlations or estimates of shared variance, that suggest how much confidence we can have that the measure truly measures what it is supposed to measure (Messick, 1995); for example, how much confidence can we have in using the measure to make clinical judgments about the characteristics and causes of a client's problems or the effectiveness of the client's treatment?

These estimates of shared variance can be difficult to interpret, especially if the shared variance between the two measures is based on the same method of measurement. For example, if the two measures share the same method (e.g., two self-report measures of depression), the amount of shared variance reflects both construct and method variance. Here it is impossible to know if a correlation of .90 between the first and second self-report measure of depression reflects strong convergent validity, strong method effects, or some combination of both. Monomethod research does not provide very useful information on the construct validity of measures. Interpretation of shared variance between monomethod measures is particularly difficult when the measures contain semantically similar items.

MULTIMETHOD ASSESSMENT AND CONSTRUCT VALIDATION

With the publication of their 1959 article, "Convergent and Discriminant Validation by the Multitrait–Multimethod Matrix," Campbell and Fiske made clear the need to use multiple methods of measurement across multiple traits to evaluate the construct validity of measures.[1] Although Campbell and Fiske (1959) proposed several qualitative decision rules for the evaluation of multitrait by multimethod matrices, it was the application of confirmatory factor analysis (CFA) to multitrait by multimethod matrices that provided quantitative procedures to test simultaneously the convergent and discriminant validity of the latent traits as well as the discriminant validity of the latent methods. In addition, the CFA procedures provided information on the amount of trait, method, and error variance in *each* manifest measure (Eid, Lischetzke, Nussbeck, & Trierweiler, 2003; Lance, Noble, & Scullen, 2002).

The use of CFA to model multitrait by multimethod matrices provides a highly sophisticated set of procedures to determine the construct validity of measures. To exemplify the merits of these procedures, we first describe how CFA can be used to model a multitrait by multimethod matrix. For this

---

[1] Our use of the term *trait* in this chapter is similar to the meaning of the term *construct* where construct is defined as "a synthetic variable, usually composed of multiple systematically related elements, that is inferred but cannot be directly observed" (Haynes & O'Brien, 2000, p. 297).

example, we use the attention-deficit/hyperactivity disorder (ADHD)-inattention (IN), ADHD-hyperactivity/impulsivity (HI), and oppositional defiant disorder (ODD) constructs. We first discuss how the CFA procedures can estimate the convergent and discriminant validity of the individual symptom ratings on a rating scale, thereby allowing the selection of items with good convergent and discriminant validity. We then describe how the procedures can estimate the convergent and discriminant validity of the summary scores for the ADHD-IN, ADHD-HI, and ODD measures. In these examples, we outline the ideal results necessary to establish strong convergent and discriminant validity for the measures. We then outline the less-than-ideal results (i.e., strong method effects) and the complexities that such results create for judging the validity of measures.

After this discussion of CFA, we then review the studies that have used CFA to determine the construct validity of clinical psychology measures. The review of these studies provides information on how well certain constructs in clinical psychology are currently measured (e.g., the convergent and discriminant validity of measures of anxiety and depression in children).

The final section of the chapter offers an expansion of the Campbell and Fiske multitrait by multimethod matrix in terms of multiple types of information—facets (traits), modes, dimensions, instruments, methods, sources, settings, and occasions of measurement. We suggest that this expanded measurement matrix provides a rich conceptual framework to examine the construct validity of measures in clinical psychology (e.g., the determination of estimates of shared variance across the different types of information). This expanded matrix also underscores the issue that the validity of measures in clinical psychology can be conditional (e.g., a measure can be valid for decisions in one setting but not another).

Although our example focuses on ADHD-IN, ADHD-HI, and ODD, it is meant to provide a general framework for estimating the validity of measures for other behavior problems. We thus encourage the reader to substitute his or her favorite three constructs for our three constructs and to work through the example with the alternative constructs.

USE OF CFA TO MODEL A MULTITRAIT BY MULTIMETHOD MATRIX

Currently there are two main CFA approaches to model multitrait by multimethod matrices: the correlated trait-correlated method and the correlated uniqueness approaches (Lance et al., 2002). Lance et al. (2002) indicated that the correlated trait-correlated method approach is the better choice and "that the correlated uniqueness model be invoked only as a last analytic resort" (p. 241) when the correlated trait-correlated method approach fails (e.g., inadmissible solutions). We thus use the correlated trait-correlated method approach for this discussion (see also Eid et al., 2003).

For our example with ADHD-IN, ADHD-HI, and ODD, let us assume the use of multiple sources (mothers, fathers, teachers, and teachers' aides) rather than multiple methods. Later in the chapter we discuss the complexities associated with using multiple methods (e.g., interviews, rating scales, direct observations) to measure multiple traits. Let us also assume that each source completes the same ADHD-IN, ADHD-HI, and ODD rating scale. Here the mothers and fathers are instructed to rate the children's behavior in the home, while the teachers and aides are instructed to rate the children's behavior in the classroom. Because our example uses multiple sources and a single method (same rating scale), we refer to this example as a multitrait by multisource matrix to make a distinction between sources and methods, although the more common name is multitrait by multimethod (Campbell & Fiske, 1959).

Prerequisite Psychometric Conditions

The use of CFA to model a multitrait by multisource matrix requires a significant amount of psychometric work on the rating scale for each source prior to this analysis. First, the items and features of the scale (e.g., wording of items, rating interval, rating anchors, and so on) must have good content validity (i.e., the representativeness and relevance of the

items for the given construct; Haynes, Richard, & Kubany, 1995). Second, the distributional characteristics of measures from each item must be reasonable (e.g., skewness and kurtosis are within reasonable limits). Third, the ADHD-IN, ADHD-HI, and ODD measures on the scale must have good internal consistency. And finally, the scale must have demonstrated good structural validity for each source (i.e., separate CFA studies with mothers, fathers, teachers, and aides show the items on the ADHD-IN, ADHD-HI, and ODD measures to have the expected structural properties). Such outcomes represent the major prerequisite conditions for the use of CFA to model multitrait by multisource matrices.

Multitrait by Multisource Matrix

Figure 27.1 shows the model with individual symptom ratings. This model involves three latent trait factors (ADHD-IN, ADHD-HI, and ODD) and four latent source factors (mothers, fathers, teachers, and aides). The model contains 104 manifest variables. This involves 26 manifest variables (symptom

ratings) for mothers, 26 for fathers, 26 for teachers, and 26 for aides (each source rates the occurrence of the nine ADHD-IN, nine ADHD-HI, and eight ODD symptoms). Our purpose with this example is to demonstrate how CFA procedures can be used to estimate the convergent and discriminant validity of the *individual* symptom ratings.

Barbara Byrne (1994, chap. 6) provided guidelines for the use of CFA procedures to model multitrait by multisource matrices. She described how the convergent validity of the traits, the discriminant validity of the traits, and the discriminant validity of the sources can be tested at a macro (matrix) level by the comparison of a series of nested models. These macro tests are conceptually similar to an omnibus F-test where a significant result requires subsequent tests. In a similar manner, positive results from the model tests at the matrix level (e.g., general evidence for convergent validity of the traits, discriminant validity of traits, and discriminant validity of the sources) require an evaluation of the individual parameters in the

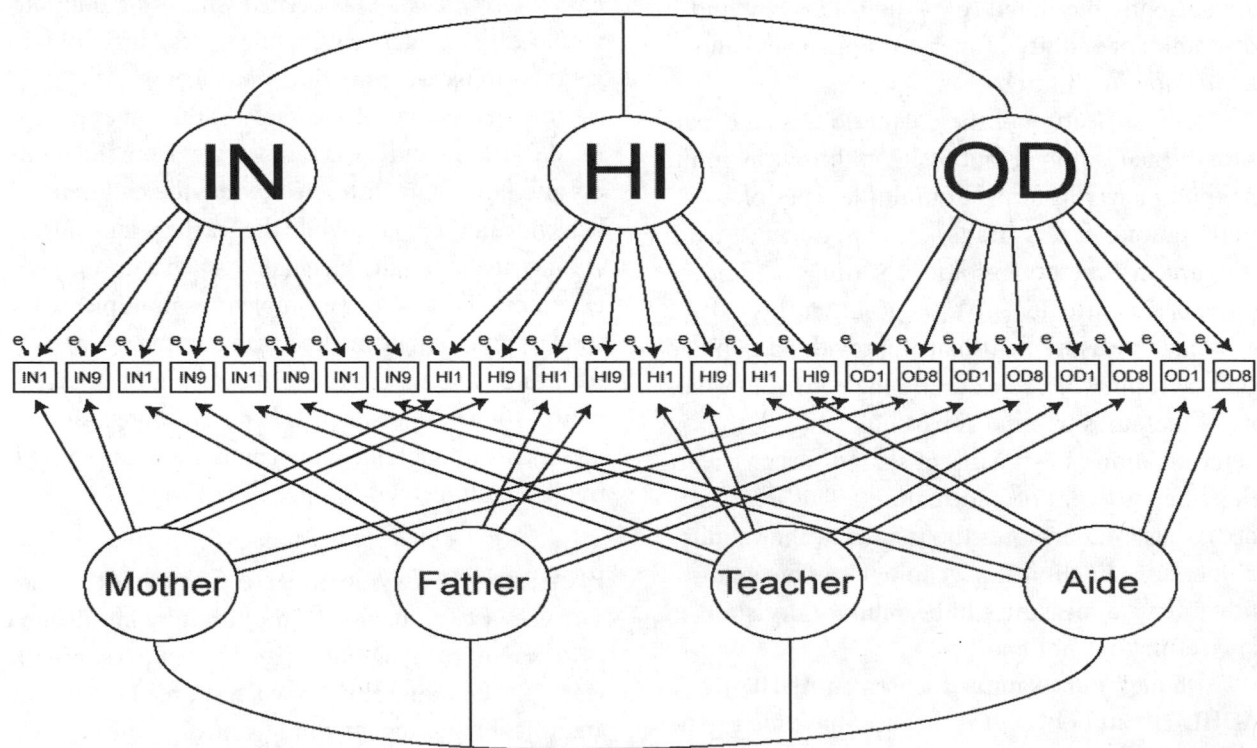

FIGURE 27.1. Heuristic representation of a multitrait by multisource model for the attention-deficit/hyperactivity disorder (ADHD)-inattention (IN), ADHD-hyperactivity/impulsivity (HI), and oppositional defiant disorder (ODD) symptom ratings (26 symptom ratings per source—nine ADHD-IN symptoms, nine ADHD-HI symptoms, and eight ODD symptoms).

model. The inspection of the individual parameters provides information on the amount of trait (construct), source, and error variance in *each* manifest variable, the magnitude of the correlations among the specific pairs of latent traits, and the magnitude of the correlations among the specific pairs of latent sources. The findings at the individual parameter level are central to the evaluation of the construct validity of each measure (manifest variable). In fact, the findings at the parameter level can significantly qualify the positive findings from the matrix levels tests (Byrne, 1994, chap. 6). Because of this, it is important to understand the meaning of trait, source, and error effects in the manifest variables.

Trait, Source, and Error Variance

Trait (construct) variance represents the systematic variance in a specific manifest variable associated with a particular latent trait, whereas source variance represents the systematic variance in a specific manifest variable associated with a particular latent source. The error variance in a specific manifest variable involves two different aspects—residual systematic variance (i.e., reliable variance not associated with trait and source factors) and nonsystematic effects (i.e., measurement error; Lance et al., 2002, p. 228). Figure 27.1 shows how the variance in each manifest variable (symptom rating) is separated into trait, source, and error effects.

Trait effects are generally considered to represent systematic variance in the manifest variables that may generalize across sources. Strong trait effects across a set of manifest variables for two or more sources are considered to indicate that the sources view the children's behavior in a similar manner (Greenbaum, Dedrick, Prange, & Friedman, 1994; Rowe & Kandel, 1997). In traditional psychometric theory, a good measure (manifest variable in this context) has a large amount of trait variance and, as will be explained later, a good measure also contains substantially more trait than source variance.

Source effects are usually considered a form of bias associated with characteristics of the rater (Fiske, 1987a). In this view, source effects are considered problematic because they distort or bias the relations among the constructs (Greenbaum et al., 1994). To determine the true relations among a set of constructs, it is considered necessary to remove the source effects from the measures. For example, to determine the unbiased relations among ADHD-IN, ADHD-HI, and ODD, the bias specific to each source must be removed from each measure so that the correlations among the three latent constructs are based on only trait variance.

Source effects can also be considered to reflect meaningful differences in the children's behavior across situations. An example of this view would be a child who shows ADHD-HI behavior in the classroom and does not show such behavior at home. Rather than bias, the mother and father provide a consensual rating for the child's ADHD-HI behavior at home, while the teacher and aide provide a consensual rating for the child's ADHD-HI behavior at school. Instead of the need to eliminate source effects to understand the true relations among ADHD-IN, ADHD-HI, and ODD, source effects can represent meaningful variance (Dishion, Burraston, & Li, 2002). We offer suggestions later in the chapter for how to distinguish between the bias and consensual views of source effects.

Although these are the typical definitions of trait and source effects, these definitions hide a significant complexity. For example, if all the ADHD-HI manifest variables for the parent and teacher sources contain approximately 70% trait variance, then a substantial amount of the variance in the ADHD-HI manifest variables generalizes across the sources, suggesting good convergent validity (as well as discriminant validity because the source effects in each manifest variable have to be less than the trait effects in this example). However, if the ADHD-HI manifest variables for the parent source contain approximately 2% trait and 84% source variance whereas the ADHD-HI manifest variables for the teacher source contain approximately 60% trait and 34% source variance (Burns, Walsh, & Gomez, 2003; Gomez, Burns, Walsh, & Moura, 2003), then the preceding definition of a trait effect runs into a conceptual dilemma (e.g., How can generalization across the parent and teacher sources occur in only one direction?). This conceptual dilemma requires a slightly different definition of trait variance at the level of a specific manifest variable.

> In a multitrait by multisource CFA, trait variance refers to the amount of systematic variance in a specific manifest vari-

able that is shared with other manifest variables (purportedly representing the same latent trait) rated by the same source assuming negligible source and method variance. If another source or sources rate the same manifest variables, their trait variance is similarly defined, but the amount of trait variance specific to the different sources for the same manifest variables may differ if the different sources impose variations in the ratings that are unique to the specific source. In the case where the amount of trait variance differs substantially between a pair of sources, as does correspondingly the amount of source variance, the accepted definition of trait variance from Campbell and Fiske, or as implied in generalizability theory, may not be appropriate. Here the large amount of source variance for one source may have a meaning and utility corresponding to the traditional definition of trait variance. (J. A. Walsh, personal communication, June 9, 2003)

This more specific definition is needed to deal with the outcome of a large discrepancy in the amount of trait variance across sources for the *same* manifest variables. We address this complexity later in the chapter. First, however, we will ignore this complexity and describe the ideal set of outcomes for construct validity from the use of CFA to model the multitrait by multisource matrix shown in Figure 27.1.

Individual Symptoms: Outcomes Required for Construct Validity

Four outcomes are required for the individual symptom ratings to have strong construct validity. First, each symptom rating in Figure 27.1 must have a substantial loading on the appropriate trait factor (i.e., each ADHD-IN symptom rating has a substantial loading on ADHD-IN trait, each ADHD-HI symptom rating has a substantial loading on the ADHD-HI trait, and each ODD symptom rating has a substantial loading on the ODD trait). Such outcomes would provide support for the convergent

validity of each symptom rating. However, even though each symptom rating has a large loading on the appropriate factor, such does not provide information on the discriminant validity of the ratings. The second outcome addresses this issue.

Second, for the symptom ratings to demonstrate discriminant validity (i.e., more trait than source variance), each symptom rating is required to have a much stronger loading on the appropriate trait factor than on its respective source factor (i.e., each ADHD-IN symptom rating has a stronger loading on the ADHD-IN trait factor than on its source factor; each ADHD-HI symptom rating has a stronger loading on the ADHD-HI trait factor than on its source factor; and each ODD symptom rating has a stronger loading on the ODD trait factor than on its source factor). If such outcomes occurred for the all the symptom ratings for each source, such outcomes would provide good support for the convergent *and* discriminant validity of the symptom ratings.

The third outcome to consider involves the correlations among the ADHD-IN, ADHD-HI, and ODD latent traits. Here there should be evidence for the discriminant validity of the three traits (i.e., the correlations among the latent traits are not too high). Discriminant validity among the traits is important because such is a prerequisite for research that attempts to identify unique attributes for each trait (e.g., unique causes, risk factors, associated features, outcomes, treatment responses and so on). For example, if the correlation between the ADHD-HI and ODD traits was higher than .90, it would be difficult to identify unique features predictive of each trait due to the small amount of unique variance in each. Such a high correlation would also suggest that ADHD-HI and ODD, as measured with these instruments and sources, did not represent separate traits.

The fourth outcome concerns the correlations among the latent source factors. Here the correlations among the mother, father, teacher, and aide source factors must also show discriminant validity (i.e., latent source correlations that are not too high). This relates to the discriminability of the sources, and very high correlations among the sources would suggest a problem of common source bias.

Of these four outcomes, outcomes 1 and 2 are the most central. If these two outcomes occur, then each symptom rating has convergent and discriminant validity. These outcomes are important because it is the amount of trait and source variance in the individual symptom ratings that determines the meaningfulness of the discriminant validity results for the latent traits and sources. For example, if the ADHD-IN, ADHD-HI, and ODD symptom ratings contained an average of 5% trait variance across the four sources, then small correlations among the three traits would not be very meaningful. In contrast, if the average amount of trait variance in the symptom ratings was 70%, small correlations among the three traits would provide good evidence for discriminant validity. The same logic applies to the interpretation of the correlations among the latent source factors.

If these outcomes occurred, then each symptom rating on this particular rating scale would have demonstrated strong convergent and discriminant validity for the four sources (i.e., the construct validity is *conditional* on this particular scale and these four sources). In addition, each of the three latent traits would have demonstrated strong convergent and discriminant validity. This evidence would therefore indicate that this particular rating scale provided a good measure of these three traits across the four sources. *To our knowledge, there is no study in clinical psychology that has used these procedures to evaluate and select the final set of items for a multisource rating scale* (e.g., out of approximately 2,000 manuscripts submitted to *Psychological Assessment* from 1998 to 2003, none used this approach).

Individual Symptoms: Problematic Outcomes

In contrast to the preceding outcomes, let us assume that each symptom rating contained more source than trait variance. In the traditional view, such a result would indicate that the symptom ratings contained mostly bias, thus indicating that the ADHD-IN, ADHD-HI, and ODD symptom ratings have no construct validity. The alternative view would argue that the strong source effects could indicate that each source has a valid, *but different,*

view of the child's behavior because the child's behavior is source specific. A third possibility is that the source effects represent a mixture of bias and validity with there being a need to determine which aspect is most important.

By having two sources in each situation (mothers and fathers for the home situation and teachers and aides for the school situation), it is possible to further investigate the reason for each symptom rating containing more source than trait variance. To do this, it is necessary to perform two separate CFAs. The first analysis would use CFA to model a multitrait (ADHD-IN, ADHD-HI, and ODD) by multisource matrix where the two sources are teachers and teachers' aides. The second analysis would use CFA to model a multitrait by multisource matrix where the two sources are mothers and fathers. If the strong source effects in the initial analysis reflect situation specific behavior, then the separate analyses for each situation should result in an increase in trait variance and a decrease in the source variance for the symptom ratings. In other words, if the teachers and aides provide similar ratings for the classroom, the mothers and fathers provide similar ratings for home, and the children's behavior is situationally specific, then the amount of trait variance should increase for each symptom rating. In contrast, if the source variance for each symptom rating was still larger than the trait variance in the separate situation analyses, then this result would favor the bias view. Additional research would then be required to determine the specific factors for the mother, father, teacher, and aide sources responsible for the bias.

Latent Trait Effects: Outcomes Required for Construct Validity

In the first example (Figure 27.1), the manifest variables were the individual symptom ratings. More typically, however, these procedures use summary scores as manifest variables (e.g., the summary score for the nine ADHD-IN, nine ADHD-HI, and eight ODD symptoms for the four sources), the focus of our second example.

Figure 27.2 shows the model for the summary scores. This model involves three latent trait factors (ADHD-IN, ADHD-HI, and ODD) and four latent

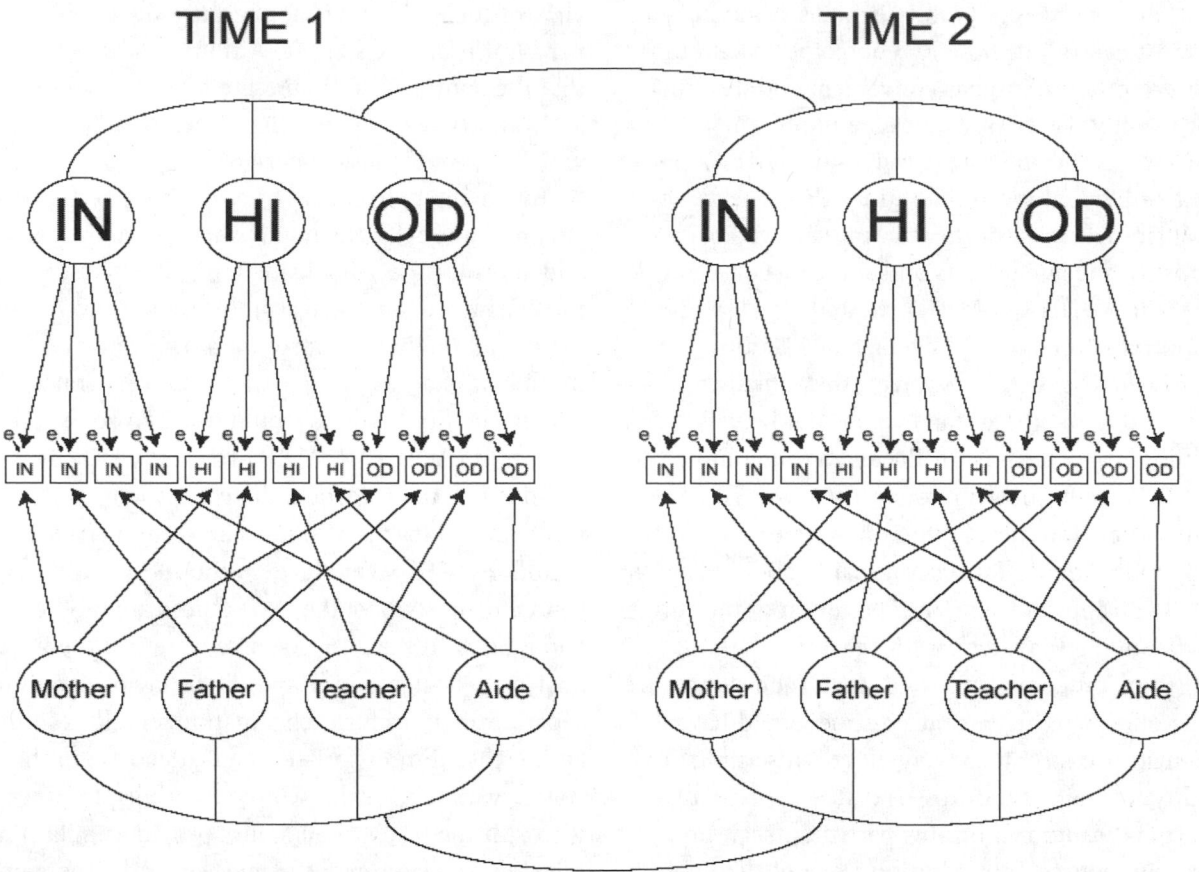

TIME 1   TIME 2

FIGURE 27.2. Heuristic representation of a multitrait by multisource model for the attention-deficit/hyperactivity disorder (ADHD)-inattention (IN), ADHD-hyperactivity/impulsivity (HI), and oppositional defiant disorder (ODD) measures across a 3-month interval.

source factors (mothers, fathers, teachers, and aides) at Time 1 with the same factors at Time 2 (3 months later). The model involves 24 manifest variables, 12 at Time 1 and 12 at Time 2. Let us also assume, given the 3-month test–retest interval, that the instructions ask the sources to rate the children's behavior for the past month. This example allows us to discuss the convergent and discriminant validity of the manifest variables at Time 1 and Time 2, the discriminant validity of the latent traits and sources *within* each assessment, and the convergent and discriminant validity of the latent traits and sources *across* time.

There are six outcomes required for the ADHD-IN, ADHD-HI, and ODD measures (manifest variables) to have strong convergent and discriminant validity. Because four of these six outcomes are conceptually the same as for the example with the individual symptom ratings, the description is briefer

here. First, each manifest variable must have a substantial loading on the appropriate trait factor. Such outcomes would provide support for the convergent validity of the ADHD-IN, ADHD-HI, and ODD measures. Second, each manifest variable is required to have a much stronger loading on its trait factor than on its source factor. These outcomes would provide support for the convergent *and* discriminant validity of each measure. Third, the ADHD-IN, ADHD-HI, and ODD latent trait factors must show convergent and discriminant validity across time (i.e., the correlation between the same trait across time is substantial, whereas the correlation between different traits across time is much smaller). Fourth, the ADHD-IN, ADHD-HI, and ODD latent trait factors are required to show discriminant validity within each assessment period (i.e., the correlations among the ADHD-IN, ADHD-HI, and ODD traits are small at Time 1 and at

Time 2). Fifth, the mother, father, teacher, and aide latent source factors must show convergent and discriminant validity across time, and sixth, the latent source factors are required to demonstrate discriminant validity at each assessment period. Of the six outcomes, outcomes 1 and 2 are again prerequisite conditions for the interpretation of the results relevant to outcomes 3 to 6.

If these six outcomes occurred, the results would indicate that the ADHD-IN, ADHD-HI, and ODD measures had strong convergent and discriminant validity (for this *specific* rating scale for these *specific* sources over this *specific* time interval, the validity thus being conditional on these parameters). Such a result (assuming good content validity) would indicate that the use of the scale by the four sources provided good measures of the three constructs.

Latent Trait Effects: Problematic Outcomes

If the source effects were greater than the trait effects for the summary score analyses, then it would be important to repeat the analyses separately for each situation. As noted earlier, if the mothers' and fathers' ratings are in agreement for the home situation and the teachers' and aides' ratings are in agreement for the school situation, then the separate analyses for each situation should result in an increase in trait variance and a decrease in the source variance for each measure. If the separate situation analyses both yielded stronger trait than source effects, then such results would support the consensual view within each situation. However, if the separate situation analyses still resulted in more source than trait variance, then the results would favor the bias view of the source effects.

Behavioral observations of ADHD-IN, ADHD-HI, and ODD symptoms in the home and classroom situations would help clarify the meaning of trait and source effects. Let us assume that the separate situation analyses yielded stronger trait than source effects for the ADHD-IN, ADHD-HI, and ODD measures. If the ADHD-IN, ADHD-HI, and ODD trait factors for the classroom analysis showed convergent and discriminant correlations with the ADHD-IN, ADHD-HI, and ODD observational

measures, and the convergent correlations of each trait with its corresponding direct observation measure were larger than the correlations of the teacher and aide source correlations with the three direct observation dimensions, then such findings would indicate that the trait effects (systematic variance across the teacher and aide sources) reflect the "reality" of the behavior observations in a specific manner. If similar results occurred for the mother and father ratings, then our understanding of the mother, father, teacher, and aide ADHD-IN, ADHD-HI, and ODD measures would be greatly increased (e.g., stronger trait than source effects within each situation with the weaker trait effects across situations being due to the situational specificity of the children's behavior). Behavioral observations within each situation could thus help to understand the meaning of trait and source effects.

COMPLEXITIES OF MULTITRAIT BY MULTIMETHOD BY MULTISOURCE ANALYSES

For our examples, we intentionally used four sources rather than multiple methods. The use of multiple methods such as interviews, rating scales, and direct observations would at first glance appear to represent an ideal multitrait (ADHD-IN, ADHD-HI, and ODD) by multimethod (interview, rating scale, and direct observations) matrix. Unfortunately, this type of matrix often contains a number of confounds that can make the interpretation of the results difficult (Burns, 1980; Cone, 1979).

One complexity concerns the time frame for each method. If the time frame for the diagnostic interview was the past 6 months, the past 1 month for the rating scale, and the past 5 school days for the observational measure, the interpretation of the findings would be problematic because of the varying time frames for each method. To eliminate this confound, it would be necessary to hold the time frame constant for each method.

A second complexity involves the source of the information across the three methods. Consider these possibilities. For the rating scale method, the source is the teacher. For the diagnostic interview method, the source represents a combination of the information provided by the parent and decisions

made about the information by the interviewer, whereas the behavioral observations during recess are made by the school counselor. Here source is confounded with method as well as situation. A possible solution would be to use the same source for each method, although this raises additional complexities.

A third complexity with multiple methods concerns the possibility that the content of the trait may be specific to the method. For example, the content of the diagnostic interview may be slightly different from the rating scale with both these methods having different content than the observational measure. Although such content differences across methods are at times appropriate because different methods have different goals (e.g., diagnosis versus treatment outcome evaluation), content differences can create problems in the use of CFA to model the matrix. Here different outcomes across the methods could be a function of the different representations of the traits in each method. To eliminate this confound, it is important that similar traits contain similar content for the different methods (e.g., the content of the ADHD-IN trait is similar for the interview, the rating scale, and the observational methods).

These complexities can make the interpretation of results from multitrait by multimethod by multisource analyses difficult. However, with careful planning, CFA can still be used to model such complex matrices and therefore provide a richer understanding of clinical psychology measures. We now turn to a review of the use of the procedures in clinical psychology.

THE AMOUNT OF TRAIT, SOURCE, AND ERROR VARIANCE IN CLINICAL PSYCHOLOGY MEASURES

An attempt was made to locate all published studies on topics in clinical psychology that used the correlated trait-correlated method CFA approach to model multitrait by multisource matrices. A search was made through PsycINFO from 1980 to the 2003 with the terms "multitrait–multimethod" and "confirmatory factor analysis." Many of the studies used the correlated uniqueness approach to separate

trait from source variance (e.g., Cole, Martin, Peeke, Henderson, & Harwell, 1998; Crystal, Ostrander, Chen, & August, 2001). In addition to the possibility that the correlated uniqueness approach artificially inflates the amount of trait variance in the measures (Lance et al., 2002), this approach also combines the source with the error variance, thus making it impossible to determine the amount of source variance in each measure (Lance et al., 2002). Given our purpose to summarize the amount of trait, source, and error variance in measures used in clinical psychology, our review covers the correlated trait-correlated method studies.

Table 27.1 summarizes the results from these studies. Two of the studies focused on the amount of trait, source, and error variance in parent and teacher ADHD rating scales (Burns et al., 2003; Gomez et al., 2003). Here the source effects were strong, being consistently larger or equal to the trait effects. The one exception was that the teacher ratings of the ADHD-HI symptoms consistently showed slightly more trait and source variance (see also Gomez, Burns, Walsh, & Hafetz, 2005). For measures of depression and anxiety in children (e.g., the Child Depression Inventory and the Revised Manifest Anxiety Scale; Cole, 1990; Cole, Truglio, & Peeke, 1997), the source effects were consistently stronger than the trait effects with there often being little trait variance in the measures of depression and anxiety.

There was only one study with two sources (mothers and fathers) in the same situation (Rowe & Kandel, 1997). Here the trait variance was greater than the source variance for measures of externalizing problems (Child Behavior Checklist aggressive and delinquent behavior scales) but not for internalizing problems (Child Behavior Checklist withdrawn, somatic complaints, and anxious/depressed scales). For teacher and mother ratings of conduct problem behaviors across 3 years (Fergusson & Horwood, 1989), the amount of source variance was slightly greater than the trait variance for mothers with the reverse occurring for teachers. In a study that used the Psychopathy Checklist—Revised, source effects were also either equal to or stronger than trait effects for interviewer and therapist ratings of personality (e.g., callous

TABLE 27.1

Trait, Source, and Error Variance in Various Clinical Psychology Measures

Source/trait	Trait	Source	Error
Gomez et al. (2003, *N* = 1,475 Australian children)[a]			
Teacher rating			
ADHD-IN symptom parcel 1	.17	.70	.13
ADHD-IN symptom parcel 2	.19	.72	.09
ADHD-HI symptom parcel 1	.45	.39	.16
ADHD-HI symptom parcel 2	.62	.37	.01
Parent rating			
ADHD-IN symptom parcel 1	.36	.46	.18
ADHD-IN symptom parcel 2	.43	.45	.12
ADHD-HI symptom parcel 1	.03	.82	.15
ADHD-HI symptom parcel 2	.03	.84	.13
Gomez et al. (2003, *N* = 285 Brazilian children)[b]			
Teacher rating			
ADHD-IN symptom parcel 1	.15	.84	.01
ADHD-IN symptom parcel 2	.13	.82	.05
ADHD-HI symptom parcel 1	.62	.33	.05
ADHD-HI symptom parcel 2	.59	.34	.07
Academic Problems	.27	.22	.51
Parent rating			
ADHD-IN symptom parcel 1	.45	.40	.14
ADHD-IN symptom parcel 2	.51	.40	.09
ADHD-HI symptom parcel 1	.02	.77	.21
ADHD-HI symptom parcel 2	.02	.91	.08
Academic Problems	.43	.06	.51
Burns, Walsh, & Gomez (2003, *N* = 360 Australian children)[c]			
First assessment (Second assessment: 3 months later)			
Teacher rating			
ADHD-IN symptom parcel 1	.18 (.18)	.68 (.71)	.14 (.11)
ADHD-IN symptom parcel 2	.25 (.18)	.65 (.74)	.10 (.07)
ADHD-HI symptom parcel 1	.54 (.56)	.36 (.37)	.10 (.08)
ADHD-HI symptom parcel 2	.57 (.50)	.33 (.39)	.10 (.11)
Parent rating			
ADHD-IN symptom parcel 1	.34 (.34)	.47 (.44)	.20 (.22)
ADHD-IN symptom parcel 2	.47 (.53)	.43 (.39)	.10 (.08)
ADHD-HI symptom parcel 1	.03 (.01)	.83 (.87)	.14 (.12)
ADHD-HI symptom parcel 2	.03 (.01)	.84 (.85)	.13 (.15)
Cole (1990, *N* = 750 fourth graders)[d]			
Self-rating			
Depression symptoms	.16	.48	.36
Social competence	.16	.35	.49
Academic competence	.09	.30	.61
Other rating			
Depression symptoms-peer	.30	.02	.68
Depression symptoms-teacher	.11	.10	.79
Social competence-peer	.79	.01	.20
Social competence-teacher	.18	.59	.23
Academic competence-peer	.69	.14	.17
Academic competence-teacher	.15	.18	.67

continued

TABLE 27.1 Continued			
Source/trait	Trait	Source	Error
Cole, Truglio, & Peeke (1997)[e] **N = 280 third graders (N = 211 sixth graders)**			
Self-rating			
Depression symptoms	.03 (.24)	.81 (.66)	.16 (.10)
Anxiety symptoms	.05 (.31)	.48 (.32)	.47 (.37)
Peer rating			
Depression symptoms	.29 (.30)	.56 (.40)	.15 (.30)
Anxiety symptoms	.06 (.03)	.67 (.92)	.27 (.05)
Teacher rating			
Depression symptoms	.04 (.21)	.69 (.58)	.27 (.21)
Anxiety symptoms	.00 (.03)	.83 (.81)	.17 (.16)
Fergusson & Horwood (1989, N = 776 children)[f]			
Mother rating			
Conduct disorder-age 7 years	.28	.44	.28
Conduct disorder-age 8 years	.36	.49	.15
Conduct disorder-age 9 years	.40	.31	.29
Teacher rating			
Conduct disorder-age 7 years	.40	.18	.42
Conduct disorder-age 8 years	.36	.29	.35
Conduct disorder-age 9 years	.41	.30	.29
Child ratings			
Conduct disorder-age 9 years	.14	—	.86
Rowe & Kandel (1997, N = 95 families)[g]			
Mother rating			
Externalizing behavior problems	.42	.26	.33
Internalizing behavior problems	.51	.45	.04
Father rating			
Externalizing behavior problems	.58	.21	.21
Internalizing behavior problems	.13	.50	.37
Windle & Dumenci (1999, N = 330 alcoholic inpatients)[h]			
Interviewer rating			
Antisocial personality attribute parcel 1	.46	.45	.09
Antisocial personality attribute parcel 2	.38	.46	.16
Antisocial behavioral attribute parcel 1	.22	.61	.17
Antisocial behavioral attribute parcel 2	.55	.27	.18
Therapist rating			
Antisocial personality attribute parcel 1	.19	.66	.15
Antisocial personality attribute parcel 2	.15	.64	.21
Antisocial behavioral attribute parcel 1	.04	.50	.46
Antisocial behavioral attribute parcel 2	.30	.28	.42
Tildesley, Hops, Ary, & Andrews (1995, N = 349 adolescents)[i]			
Parent rating			
Alcohol use	.45	.13	.42
Cigarette use	.70	.05	.25
Marijuana use	.53	.30	.16
Illicit Drugs use	.43	.17	.40
Aggression/delinquency	.26	.07	.68
Value on achievement	.57	.01	.41

Source/trait	Trait	Source	Error
Peer rating			
Alcohol use	.74	.10	.16
Cigarettes use	.84	.04	.11
Marijuana use	.76	.13	.12
Illicit drug use	.13	.43	.44
Adolescent self-rating			
Alcohol use	.65	.14	.21
Alcohol rate	.63	.10	.27
Cigarette use	.87	.05	.07
Cigarette rate	.79	.14	.07
Marijuana use	.84	.10	.06
Marijuana rate	.65	.08	.27
Illicit Drug use	.32	.39	.29
Illicit Drug rate	.27	.43	.30
Aggressive/delinquency	.21	.10	.69
Deviance	.50	.10	.40
Stacy, Widaman, Hays, & DiMatteo (1985, *N* = 194 college students)[j]			
Self-rating			
Alcohol	.62	.22	.18
Marijuana	.82	.15	.04
Cigarettes	.88	.07	.05
Self-intake			
Alcohol	.66	.22	.12
Marijuana	.81	.15	.03
Cigarettes	.83	.07	.09
Peer rating			
Alcohol	.76	.04	.20
Marijuana	.92	.00	.08
Cigarettes	.73	.16	.11
Peer intake			
Alcohol	.78	.04	.18
Marijuana	.92	.00	.09
Cigarettes	.77	.16	.08
Widaman, Stacy, & Borthwick-Duffy (1993, *N* = 157 mentally retarded adults)[k]			
Direct-care staff			
Cognitive competence	.61	.24	.15
Social competence	.37	.30	.33
Social maladaption	.56	.32	.12
Personal maladaption	.45	.29	.27
Day-shift staff			
Cognitive competence	.82	.03	.15
Social competence	.70	.01	.29
Social maladaption	.58	.28	.14
Personal maladaption	.68	.19	.13
Evening-shift staff			
Cognitive competence	.71	.13	.15
Social competence	.68	.06	.26
Social maladaption	.58	.22	.20
Personal maladaption	.59	.21	.20

Note. The trait, source, and error components sum to 1.0 within rounding error. The specific measures used in the studies can be found in the original articles.

continued

[a]Adapted from Table 7, "A Multitrait–Multisource Confirmatory Factor Analytic Approach to the Construct validity of ADHD Rating Scales," by R. Gomez, G. L. Burns, J. A. Walsh, and M. A. Moura, 2003, *Psychological Assessment, 15*, pp. 3–16. Copyright 2003 by the American Psychological Association.

[b]Adapted from Table 8, "A Multitrait–Multisource Confirmatory Factor Analytic Approach to the Construct validity of ADHD Rating Scales," by R. Gomez, G. L. Burns, J. A. Walsh, and M. A. Moura, 2003, *Psychological Assessment, 15*, pp. 3–16. Copyright 2003 by the American Psychological Association.

[c]Adapted from Table 3, "Convergent and Discriminant Validity of Trait and Source Effects in ADHD-Inattention and Hyperactivity/Impulsivity Measures Across a 3-Month Interval," by G. L. Burns, J. A. Walsh, and R. Gomez, 2003, *Journal of Abnormal Child Psychology, 31*, pp. 529–541. Copyright 2003 by Springer. Adapted with permission.

[d]Adapted from Table 3, "Relation of Social and Academic Competence to Depressive Symptoms in Childhood," by D. A. Cole, 1990, *Journal of Abnormal Psychology, 99*, pp. 422–229. Copyright 1990 by the American Psychological Association.

[e]Adapted from Table 5, "Relation Between Symptoms of Anxiety and Depression in Children: A Multitrait–Multimethod Assessment," by D. A. Cole, R. Truglio, and L. Peeke, 1997, *Journal of Consulting and Clinical Psychology, 65*, pp. 110–119. Copyright 1997 by the American Psychological Association.

[f]Adapted from Table 2, "Estimation of Method and Trait Variance in Ratings of Conduct Disorder," by D. M. Fergusson and L. J. Horwood, 1989, *Journal of Child Psychology and Psychiatry, 30*, pp. 365–378. Copyright 1989 by Blackwell. Adapted with permission.

[g]Adapted from Table 5, "In the Eye of the Beholder? Parental Ratings of Externalizing and Internalizing Symptoms," by D. C. Rowe and D. Kandel, 1997, *Journal of Abnormal Child Psychology, 25*, pp. 265–275. Copyright 1997 by Springer. Adapted with permission.

[h]Adapted from Figure 1, "The Factorial Structure and Construct Validity of the Psychopathy Checklist-Revised (PCL-R) Among Alcoholic Inpatients," by M. Windle and L. Dumenci, 1999, *Structural Equation Modeling, 6*, pp. 372–393. Copyright 1999 by Erlbaum. Adapted with permission.

[i]Adapted from Table 4, "Multitrait-Multimethod Model of Adolescent Deviance, Drug Use, Academic, and Sexual Behaviors," by E. A. Tildesley, H. Hops, D. Ary, and J. A. Andrews, 1995, *Journal of Psychopathology and Behavioral Assessment, 17*, pp. 185–215. Copyright 1995 by Springer. Adapted with permission.

[j]Adapted from Table 4, "Validity of Self-Reports of Alcohol and Other Drug Use: A Multitrait–Multimethod Assessment," by A. W. Stacy, K. F. Widaman, R. Hays, and M. R. DiMatteo, 1985, *Journal of Personality and Social Psychology, 49*, pp. 219–232. Copyright 1985 by the American Psychological Association.

[k]Adapted from Table 5, "Construct Validity of Dimensions of Adaptive Behavior: A Multitrait-Multimethod Evaluation," by K. F. Widaman, A. W. Stacy, and S. A. Borthwick-Duffy, 1993, *American Journal of Mental Retardation, 98*, pp. 219–234. Copyright 1993 by the American Association of Mental Retardation. Adapted with permission.

ness, manipulativeness, lack of empathy) and behavioral (e.g., early onset of criminal behavior, impulsivity) dimensions of antisocial personality disorder (Windle & Dumenci, 1999).

Only three studies contained measures that consistently showed more trait than source variance. Two of these studies focused on measures of alcohol, cigarette, and marijuana use (Stacy, Widaman, Hays, & DiMatteo, 1985; Tildesley, Hops, Ary, & Andrews, 1995). One possibility for this outcome may be the specificity of measures of drug use relative to the measures of anxiety, depression, conduct problems, and ADHD (e.g., the concreteness of constructs, see also Doty & Glick, 1998, pp. 380–381; Haynes & O'Brien, 2000, pp. 128–139). The third study focused on staff measures of competence in adults with a diagnosis of mental retardation (Widaman, Stacy, & Borthwick-Duffy, 1993). Part of the reason

for the large amount of trait variance in this study may be the careful attention paid to the development of the measures prior to the CFA.

An additional study appeared in a recent book chapter (Dishion et al., 2002). Here the focus was to estimate the trait, source, and error variance in measures of parenting competence (i.e., monitoring, limit setting, positive reinforcement, relationship quality, and problem solving). The three sources were parents, adolescents, and staff. Nearly all the measures contained more source than trait variance. The authors also reported that the source effects predicted authority conflict and drug use with these correlations being stronger at times than the correlations of trait effects with authority conflict and drug use. These correlations suggest that the source effects in this study contained meaningful variance rather than only bias.

With the exception of the two studies that focused on alcohol/drug use and one study where the focus was on adjustment in adults with a diagnosis of mental retardation, all the other studies indicated that source effects were stronger than trait effects. Several recommendations stem from these results. First, clinical research and clinical decisions should probably never occur on the basis of a single source because of the pervasive nature of source effects. Second, given that the amount of trait variance appears to increase when measures have a higher level of specificity (e.g., Doty & Glick, 1998), it may be possible to develop measures with larger amounts of trait variance with more careful attention to content validity (Haynes et al., 1995). Third, the use of CFA to model multitrait by multisource matrices should be mandatory in the latter stages of the validation of multisource rating scales. And, finally, research should begin to clarify the meaning of source effects. If source effects remain strong even with more careful attention to the development of more specific measures, then it becomes increasingly important to understand these effects (e.g., Dishion et al., 2002).

The development of measures in clinical psychology could also benefit from a broader framework than the traditional multitrait by multimethod matrix. In this final section, we describe how the matrix can be expanded to include additional types of information.

MULTIPLE TYPES OF INFORMATION: EXPANDING THE MULTITRAIT–MULTIMETHOD MATRIX

The types of information relevant to the development of measures in clinical psychology include facets, modes, dimensions, instruments, methods, sources, occasions, and settings (Haynes & O'Brien, 2000). Although it is not practical to use CFA to model the complete matrix in a single study, CFA can model different aspects of the matrix dependent on the specific goals and stage of measure development (e.g., a multifacet by multisource study; a multifacet by multimethod by multisource by multioccasion study). In addition, we wish to emphasize that each of these types of information represent a potentially significant cause of variability in measures of clinical phenomena and to understand clinical phenomena, the development of measures needs to examine these influences in a systematic manner.

Facets of Measurement

A facet refers to an internally consistent and clinically relevant aspect of a particular clinical phenomena. A facet can represent a general construct (trait in the terminology of Campbell & Fiske). A facet can also represent a more specific aspect of a broader construct. For example, although a general facet could represent the construct of depression, the general facet of depression could be broken down into cognitive, emotional, motivational, behavioral, and somatic subfacets. Given that the level of specificity can be increased indefinitely, both theoretical and practical considerations (e.g., what judgments will be based on the obtained measures) are important in the determination of the level of specificity appropriate for the particular research and clinical goals.

A facet contains the population of elements relevant to the construct (or subconstruct), and these elements provide the basis for the selection of interview questions, rating scale items, self-monitoring items, behavioral codes, stimuli for laboratory measures, and so on. The elements within a facet should be highly correlated with each other. Each element within a facet should also correlate higher with its own facet (convergent validity) than with other facets (discriminant validity). This aspect of discriminant validity is all too seldom considered in the development of measures (Burns & Walsh, 2002). Content validity is critical here because it ensures that the facets and elements in the measure appropriately reflect the facets and elements of the construct (Haynes et al., 1995). Without good content validity, there is a strong likelihood that the outcomes from CFA and other procedures (e.g., item response theory analyses) will be difficult to interpret.

Modes of Measurement

Response modes represent organizational schemes (taxonomies) for behavior. One example of

response modes includes motor, verbal, cognitive, emotional, and physiological response systems. Another example is the emotional–motivational, language–cognitive, and sensory–motor basic behavioral repertoires of psychological behaviorism (Staats, 1996). The measurement of multiple response modes is important because behavior problems can have multiple response modes that can be discordant and asynchronous across time and clients as well as differentially controlled by other events and differentially sensitive to treatment. For these reasons, a measure with multiple modes of measurement has the potential to provide a better understanding of clinical phenomena. Each response mode for a particular facet, however, would need to demonstrate discriminant validity with the other response modes for the facet in order to be useful.

It is important to note that facets and modes can overlap at times. For example, the facets of a particular construct, such as anxiety, might include the motor, cognitive, and physiological response modes. Here the three general response modes are functioning as facets of the anxiety construct. Within the cognitive mode, however, several different facets might represent the different types of cognitive anxiety. Thus, although there can be overlap between facets and modes, the distinction is still an important one.

Dimensions of Measurement

Clinical phenomena can be described in terms of multiple dimensions (parameters) of measurement. The more common dimensions include frequency, duration, magnitude (intensity), and time course of the particular problem behavior. For example, the oppositional defiant disorder (ODD) symptom "argues with adults" can be measured in terms of frequency (number of occurrences per unit of time), duration (length of occurrences), magnitude (intensity/severity of occurrences), and time course (pattern of occurrence across time). As was the case for response modes, clients can differ in terms of which dimension is most problematic (e.g., a high frequency and low intensity of arguments for one child versus a low frequency and high intensity for another child). In addition, the different dimensions of a behavior problem may only show moder-

ate correlations as well as be controlled by different influences. Finally, the dimensions may be impacted differentially by treatment.

Settings of Measurement

The setting refers to the location in the environment where the measurement occurs. The setting can involve various situations in the client's natural environment such as a classroom, a playground, a family room at home, or work. The setting can also involve an analogue situation where the client is exposed to hypothesized causal variables that are expected to bring about the occurrence of the clinical problem (e.g., noncompliance in a young child in response to parental commands in a clinic playroom task). Given that the occurrence of the behavior problem may be conditional on properties of situations, the measurement process should include multiple situations to obtain a more comprehensive understanding of the problem.

Sources of Measurement

The source of the information represents the person providing the information about the participant (or client). Sources can include the participant, the participant's spouse, the participant's parents, the participant's teachers, the participant's clinician, and so on. Given the strong source effects in most clinical psychology measures (Table 27.1), a better understanding of clinical phenomena occurs with the use of multiple sources.

Instruments of Measurement

Several different instruments are often offered as measures of the same construct (e.g., the many parent and teacher rating scales of ADHD and ODD). If only a single instrument is used in a multitrait by multisource study, then the construct validity results are limited to the specific instrument (e.g., the generalizability of the Child Behavior Checklist constructs across parent and teacher sources rather than the generalizability of the constructs across sources). The use of multiple instruments within the same method of measurement can begin to address this issue. However, a problem can occur when instruments are simply selected because they share the same "title" without a careful considera-

tion if the multiple measures of depression, as an example, differ in facets, modes, and dimensions of measurement. If the scales measure different facets, modes, and dimensions of depression, then it is difficult to interpret the convergent correlations among the instruments.

Methods of Measurement

The more common methods of measurement in clinical psychology include interviews, rating scales, standardized tests, self-monitoring, behavioral observation, and psychophysiological procedures. These methods can be designed to provide specific information on the facets, modes, and dimensions of the particular problem for multiple sources in multiple settings across multiple occasions. The development of interviews, rating scales, observational systems, and self-monitoring procedures with similar facets, modes, and dimensions for conceptually related constructs (e.g., anxiety and depression; ADHD and ODD) would facilitate research on such constructs. Such highly specific measures would also allow better clinical decisions about individual clients (e.g., Haynes & O'Brien, 2000, chaps. 6 and 7).

Occasions of Measurement

Occasions of measurement refer to the number of times a variable is measured across time. A single method (rating scale) with a single source (parent) at a single time point provide little information about the time course of the particular problem. The behavior could be stable, increasing, or decreasing as well as changing rapidly or slowly across time. Given the dynamic nature of behavior (i.e., the modes and dimensions of a behavior problem can change across time) and the dynamic nature of controlling conditions for the behavior, a more complete understanding of the behavior problem occurs with multiple measurements across time (time-series measurement procedures).

Summary

This measurement matrix indicates the types of information to consider in the development of clinical psychology measures. Although the application of the matrix to the development of measures of

ADHD, ODD, anxiety, depression, and other clinical phenomena is demanding, more useful measures for research and clinical decisions would occur if greater systematic attention were given to the various components in this matrix.

Consider the application of the matrix to the development of measures of ADHD-IN, ADHD-HI, and ODD. For each construct, it would be necessary to specify the facets and subfacets as well as the elements in the various facets. It would also be necessary to specify the response modes and dimensions within each facet. The next step would be the incorporation of the facets, modes, and dimensions into methods of measurement appropriate for these constructs (e.g., interviews, ratings scales, observational measures, laboratory measures). An additional step would be the specification of the sources, settings, and occasions of measurement for each method with a careful consideration of the purpose of the measurement (e.g., diagnostic decisions, evaluation of treatment effectiveness, identification of associated features of the clinical phenomena, and so on). The accomplishment of these steps with good content validity and without confounding facets, modes, dimensions, and occasions across methods would require a great deal of work. In addition, these measurement construction steps are important prerequisite conditions for the application of CFA to the measurement matrix. Although a great deal of work, this process would provide a much more specific understanding of the multiple causes of variability in measures of ADHD and ODD.

SUMMARY AND RECOMMENDATIONS

In this chapter we first described how CFA can be used to model multitrait by multisource matrices to determine the convergent and discriminant validity of measures in clinical psychology. Here we described the outcomes necessary for measures to have strong construct validity as well as the less-than-ideal outcomes for the construct validity of measures. We hope that our description of how to use CFA to model multitrait by multisource matrices results in more researchers using these procedures as part of the evaluation of clinical psychology measures.

We then reviewed the studies in clinical psychology that used CFA to model multitrait by multisource matrices. First, these procedures have seldom been used in clinical psychology. And, when these procedures are used, the studies indicate that most of the clinical psychology measures contain more source than trait variance, therefore suggesting poor construct validity for the measures. These results (Table 27.1) provide additional data for why clinical decisions should not be made on the basis of a single source. In our opinion, the field of clinical psychology should make greater use of these procedures for measurement development as well as to understand the nature of the strong source effects.

Our final suggestion concerned the need to expand the Campbell and Fiske (1959) multitrait by multimethod matrix in terms of multiple types of information (e.g., facets, modes, dimensions, instruments, methods, sources, occasions, and settings). We suggested that this expanded measurement matrix provides a richer framework for the development and the evaluation of measures. The careful use of this matrix should provide a more detailed understanding of the multiple causes of variability in clinical psychology measures and thus a better understanding of clinical phenomena.

CHAPTER 28

MULTIMETHOD APPROACHES IN HEALTH PSYCHOLOGY

Bärbel Knäuper and Rupert Klein

Health psychology is a fairly new discipline, having emerged as a formally organized subdiscipline of psychology only in the late 1970s (Division 38, Health Psychology, of the American Psychological Association was founded in 1978). As a consequence, its boundaries are still somewhat fuzzy. Matarazzo, in 1980, defined health psychology as the

> aggregate of the specific educational, scientific, and professional contributions of the discipline of psychology to the promotion and maintenance of health, the prevention and treatment of illness, the identification of etiologic and diagnostic correlates of health, illness and related dysfunction, and the improvement of the health care system and health policy formation.
> (Matarazzo, 1980, p. 815)

A more pragmatic definition holds that it is the study of the role of psychological factors in the cause, progression, and consequences of health and illness (Ogden, 1996). The psychological factors include, in particular, the behavioral and lifestyle variables that affect a person's susceptibility to physical illness, the adaptation to illness, and the preventive behaviors that people engage in (see American Psychological Association, 1976). Health psychology can be distinguished from the related field of behavioral medicine, which, according to a definition by Schwartz and Weiss (1978), is concerned with psychological phenomena only if they contribute to physical disorders as an endpoint.

There are various scientific disciplines that health psychology research questions touch on, including medicine (particularly immunology, endocrinology, behavioral medicine, cardiology, oncology, occupational health, and psychiatry), epidemiology, public health, sociology, and education. Within psychology itself, relevant areas include behavioral neuroscience, physiological psychology, psychopharmacology, social psychology, personality psychology, developmental psychology, educational psychology, and clinical psychology. Each of these areas has excelled in the development of their own methods to target their specific research questions. Health psychology, which can be viewed as applying "the accumulated knowledge from the science and profession of generic psychology to the area of health" (Matarazzo, 1987, p. 41), uses all these methods to study its specific questions and beyond that has developed its own unique arsenal of methods and approaches.

Health psychology research benefits from using multiple methods because it studies the bases of health and illness from a variety of perspectives: biological, cognitive, emotional, social, organizational, and policy making. Obviously, the methodological approaches used within these subdomains differ widely, and their coordination, integration, and interpretation pose challenges to researchers. Common methods in health psychology include strategies discussed in detail in previous chapters. These are self-report methods such as those discussed in chapter 3 (e.g., paper-pencil or computerized questionnaires, tests, surveys, observational

methods using verbal codes), but also nonreactive methods such as those discussed in chapter 9 (e.g., analyses of archives, diaries, or patients' records) and implicit methods such as those detailed in chapter 10 (e.g., reaction time measurement). Other typical methods include physiological (e.g., electrocardiography, electromyography, electroencephalography, and skin responses) and biochemical methods (e.g., cortisol analyses). On the most molecular level, health psychology uses brain imaging and other currently evolving methods in behavioral neuroscience to study its research questions.

These research methods are often used in one-shot studies such as surveys, case studies, correlational studies, or experiments. Experiments can range from natural experiments to randomized controlled trials. However, designs with several points of assessment (e.g., panel surveys, longitudinal studies), or time-series designs in which data are collected from various times per minute to various times per week over extended periods of time (e.g., experience-sampling techniques) are also commonly used. To illustrate, each of the methods and research designs just listed have been used in the past to study psychosocial, behavioral, and lifestyle determinants of cardiovascular disease and cancer, the leading causes of death in industrialized countries.

The purpose of this chapter is to describe how previous researchers have used multiple-method strategies in health psychology to discuss some of the problems with the predominance of self-report measures and to outline strategies that can be used to overcome these problems.

PREVIOUS RESULTS OF MULTIMETHOD STRATEGIES

Even though a wide variety of methods are used in health psychology research, multiple-method strategies are rarely used in the sense of Campbell and Fiske's (1959) multitrait–multimethod analysis, which requires the use of several methods to measure the same construct or phenomenon to be able to separate trait from method influences. Instead, most studies in health psychology are currently characterized by predicting health behavior or health outcomes using only one measure for each

predictor variable. Furthermore, many studies utilize solely self-report measures for assessing the various constructs (Skelton & Strohmetz, 1990). Scrutinizing the methods sections of all *Health Psychology* articles published in 2002 revealed that 60% (44 out of 73) of the reported studies rely exclusively on self-reports.

A PsycARTICLES search for the keyword "multimethod" in the journal *Health Psychology* for articles published since 1988 revealed zero results. Conducting the same search for all 40 APA journals revealed 94 results, but none of the articles deal specifically with a health psychology research question. Similarly, the search for "triangulation" led to zero results in *Health Psychology*; the search "triangulation + health" led to four results, two of them with health psychology themes. The search "physiological + self-report + health" led to the most successful outcome, with a total of 19 health psychology results when conducting the search in all APA journals. Some of these studies are described following, but it should be noted that none of these used multimethod strategies in the sense of Campbell and Fiske's (1959) multiple indicator notion. A review of the articles found suggests that studies using multiple methods in health psychology research can be organized into four categories: (a) using multiple methods to assess different predictors of an outcome variable, (b) using multiple self-report methods for construct validation purposes, (c) using a combination of self-reports and other methods for construct validation purposes (e.g., self- and proxy reports or self-report and physiological measures), and (d) using multiple methods in successive steps of research program (e.g., qualitative, then quantitative). Examples for each of the four categories are described following.

Using Multiple Methods to Assess Different Predictors of an Outcome Variable

Many classical studies in health psychology test the various health behavior models that have been proposed since the 1970s. The most prominent models include structural models such as the health belief model (Becker, 1974; Rosenstock, 1974), the theory

of reasoned action/planned behavior (Ajzen & Fishbein, 1980; Fishbein & Ajzen, 1975), and the protection motivation theory (Rogers, 1983), as well as more dynamic health behavior models that describe the processes of health behavior change such as the transtheoretical (stages of change) model (Prochaska & DiClemente, 1984). All models conceptualize health behavior as being predicted by a variety of social–cognitive factors, including risk perception or perceived susceptibility, perceived severity, outcome-expectancies, perceived self-efficacy, attitude, intention, and so on. Numerous studies have been conducted testing the various models in different areas of health behavior (smoking, exercise, safer sexual behaviors, alcohol, etc.). Most of these studies, by nature, use solely self-report measures (questionnaires or psychometric scales) for assessing the predictor variables because these are social–cognitive variables that are difficult to assess using other methodologies.

In contrast, studies predicting health outcomes, such as morbidity or mortality, usually include predictor variables at different levels: physiological, social, and psychological. A recent example is a study by Niaura and colleagues (Niaura et al., 2002), who used people's responses to a hostility questionnaire, anthropometric data, serum lipids, fasting insulin concentrations, blood pressure, and self-reported nicotine, alcohol and caloric consumption to predict the incidence of coronary heart disease in older men. Obviously, studies such as this one are not multimethod studies in the sense of Campbell and Fiske (1959), which requests establishing evidence of constructs by using multiple methods for each. In fact, the combination of multiple methods (e.g., physiological and self-report) in studies like the one just described is neither used to scrutinize construct validity nor to capitalize on the combination of multiple methods. Rather, multiple constructs are assessed to maximize the amount of explained variance in the criterion variable (in this case the incidence of coronary heart disease). The combined uses of physiological, endocrinological, and self-report methods do not serve the purpose of assessing different dimensions of the same construct.

Using Multiple Self-Report Measures for Construct Validation

It can be stated with some certainty that almost all health psychology research, whether it addresses molecular or broad research questions, involves self-reports of some kind. Reasons for this dominance of self-report measures include that objective measures (e.g., physiological or observational measures) are often not easy to obtain and that for many constructs that health psychologists are interested in, no "objective" indictors exist. For example, no objective measure of self-efficacy is available or currently even conceivable, as the degree of perceived self-efficacy is a subjective phenomenon. Similarly, no reliable objective measures for constructs such as pain or stress exist and, therefore, these constructs are also measured using self-reports or at least self-reports are used as one measure among others.

In many areas of health psychology a multitude of self-report measures has been developed for measuring one and the same construct or related constructs. Prominent examples of constructs for which a large amount of self-report measures exist are stress, self-efficacy, or quality of life. Establishing the validity of these measures or deciding which one is the "best" is made difficult by the fact that often no external criterion of validity exists. In such cases, multiple self-report measures are used for establishing validity and for gaining a better understanding of which aspect of the construct is assessed by a particular self-report measure. A typical example of such a study is Hadorn and Hays' (1991) validation of an instrument to assess health-related quality of life and an instrument for preferences of different health-related quality-of-life states. The authors used multitrait–multimethod (MTMM) analysis (Campbell & Fiske, 1959) to evaluate the construct validity (convergent and discriminant validity) of the two measures. They used two self-report measurement techniques each to assess health-related quality of life and preferences of different health-related quality-of-life states. As a procedure for implementing the MTMM strategy the authors used confirmatory factor analysis. Their analyses support the construct validity of self-reported health-related quality of life, leading the

authors to conclude that either of the two self-report instruments can be used to assess patients' perceived quality of life. On the other hand, they found substantial method variance and little valid trait variance for preferences of different health-related quality-of-life states, a finding that led the authors to replace these measures in future studies.

Another example of this approach is Goldbeck and Schmitz's (2001) study comparing three different generic quality-of-life instruments to examine measurement effects on quality-of-life results in cystic fibrosis patients. The three self-report measures differed in the type of target population for which they were originally developed, the time frame for answering the questions (from the present to the past 4 weeks), and the aspects they address (e.g., well-being and functioning, psychosocial health, physical health). Calculated were internal consistency, convergent and discriminant validity (correlation patterns, common factor analysis), and external validity (correlations with symptom and pulmonary function scores, with intensity of therapy; comparisons with healthy peers) of the three instruments. The analyses revealed comparable reliability (internal consistency) of the three self-report measures, but only partial overlap between them (comparably low interscale correlations), indicating limited convergent validity. Apparently, each questionnaire tapped a slightly different aspect of the construct "quality of life." For example, the social dimension of quality of life is poorly represented in one of the instruments whereas general life satisfaction is poorly represented in another instrument. Both these instruments emphasize more health-related aspects of quality of life. Thus, the analyses revealed in which domain the respective scales perform best. The results of studies such as those just described contribute to a better understanding of the various facets of a theoretical construct and help researchers to choose the instrument(s) that are appropriate for the specific purpose of their study. Although none of the three instruments may cover all dimensions of relevance for describing quality of life in patients with cystic fibrosis, the shortcoming of each individual instrument can be overcome by using them together (Goldbeck & Schmitz, 2001).

A third example is a study by Martin and colleagues (Martin et al., 2000), who assessed construct validity using an adaptation of Campbell and Fiske's (1959) MTMM approach, this time for assessing the convergent and discriminant validity of a migraine-specific quality-of-life questionnaire (MSQ; Jhingran, Osterhaus, Miller, Lee, & Kirchdoerfer, 1998). Specifically, the authors used three analyses to establish construct validity. First, they estimated the MTMM based on a multi-trait–monomethod correlation matrix containing interscale correlations and Cronbach's alpha (internal consistency coefficients) on the diagonal of the correlation matrix. Convergent and discriminant validity were estimated by correlating the MSQ scores with scores from two other self-report measures. The results revealed low to moderate correlations with the other self-report measures, leading the authors to the conclusion that their instrument measures a related, but distinct construct.

Altogether, these examples demonstrate that such studies can assist researchers in identifying the purposes for which a certain self-report measure is suitable. Furthermore, they help in interpreting the divergent results found in studies using different self-report methodologies to measure the same construct. Opposite results may be found if different studies used instruments that emphasize a different dimension or facet of a construct. This is of particular importance when measuring complex phenomena such as stress, where measurement instruments can differ, for example, in their degree of specificity or generality or whether they assess chronic or acute conditions (see Hurrell, Nelson, & Simmons, 1998).

Using a Combination of Self-Reports and Other Methods for Construct Validation Purposes

The most frequent examples of studies that use different methods to assess different aspects of one and the same construct are those that combine observational or physiological measures (described in Stone & Litcher-Kelly, chap. 5, this volume and Mehl, chap. 11, this volume, respectively) with self-report measures or studies that combine proxy ratings (Neyer, chap. 4, this volume) with self-ratings in assessing a construct. The assessment of physio-

logical indicators or observational data in combination with social and psychological variables may allow a researcher to overcome the limitations of self-report measures by combining it with methods that more objectively quantify the construct in question (e.g., blood pressure, heart rate, serum cholesterol, cortisol, lipids, or insulin function).

The most prominent examples for using different methodologies to assess one and the same construct can be found in the area of stress research (see Hurrell et al., 1998). In fact, they point out that this is an increasing trend, particularly in job stress studies. A typical example is a study by Carrere, Evans, Palsane, and Rivas (1991), who investigated the relationship between job strain (excess of job demands over job decision latitude) and physiological and psychological stress in urban public transit operators. Various physiological indicators of stress were assessed including blood pressure (before and after the work shift) and urinary catecholamine assays. In addition, observers recorded nonverbal indicators of stress. These include automanipulative behaviors such as scratching or repetitive play with objects such as tapping one's fingers on the steering wheel. Finally, self-reports of stressors and strains were also utilized. The results showed that enhanced job strain was related to elevated catecholamine levels, more unobtrusive behavioral indexes of stress, and higher self-reported occupational strain.

Another typical example is a study by Lundberg and colleagues (Lundberg et al., 1999), who investigated psychophysiological stress responses, muscle tension, and neck and shoulder pain among female supermarket cashiers, measuring stress using self-reports and physiological indicators (catecholamines, blood pressure, heart rate, and electromyographic [EMG] activity). Results showed that women who reported more musculoskeletal pain reported more work stress and were also found to have higher blood pressure. These physiological measures validated the self-reported stress levels of the cashiers.

Illustrative of studies using multiple methodological strategies for assessing a construct from a different area is a study by Tinsley and colleagues (Tinsley, Holtgrave, Erdley, & Reise, 1997). The authors compared self, peer, and teacher ratings of youth's risk propensity and explored the relationships of these measures to the self-reported frequency of risk behaviors in children. The analyses showed low congruence between the three types of assessments of risk propensity. Specifically, peers and teachers tended to agree more with each other than either of them agreed with the self-reports provided by the children. The authors concluded from these results that the construct of risk propensity is qualitatively assessed in different ways by the three types of raters, resulting in varying predictive utility of the measures for risk behavior. Although peer and teacher assessments were found to be valid predictors of children's self-reported risk behaviors, the children's own ratings of their risk propensity seemed to tap a somewhat different dimension of the construct.

These studies are excellent examples of how the understanding of construct relationships and the prediction of health behaviors and health outcomes can benefit from using multiple indicators for assessing a theoretical construct.

Utilizing Multiple Methods in Successive Steps of Research Programs

Multiple methods can also be used in successive steps of a research program to gain an increasingly better understanding of a construct and its relations with other constructs. Examples for this are research programs that start out with qualitative research methods and subsequently conduct studies in which more traditional, quantitative techniques are used. For example, Johnston, Corban, and Clarke (1999) used a multimethod approach for studying adherence issues in sport and exercise. Specifically, they began the data collection process using grounded theory. Grounded theory is an exploratory qualitative data collection technique that gathers data either from a single source or from a variety of sources, including interviews, field observations, and archival research. Qualitative data is continuously sampled and analyzed using coding and theoretical sampling procedures as outlined in Strauss and Corbin (1990). Following the specified coding schemes, the interpretation of data and production of theory co-evolve by feeding into and shaping one another to create a theory that (a) fits

the data well, (b) provides understanding, (c) is generalizable, and (d) clarifies the conditions under which it applies. Subsequently, the researchers used multidimensional scalogram analysis as an exploratory quantitative procedure. Finally, they conducted structural equation modeling based on the results of their earlier qualitative and quantitative analyses. Their aim was to demonstrate that the use of both methodologies together in one research program can lead to a more complete understanding of the factors relating to adherence in sport and exercise settings. By first using the exploratory qualitative and quantitative methods to develop possible models of exercise adherence for males and females, they were able to identify variables related to sport and exercise adherence and the promotion of particular adherence models. These could then be tested with structural equation modeling. The outcome was a validated adherence model that was supported by well-substantiated information obtained from the qualitative and quantitative analyses.

PROBLEMS AND ISSUES

As the preceding review demonstrates, many health psychology studies use multiple measures. But only those described under (b) through (d) truly reflect the use of multimethod strategies in the sense of Campbell and Fiske (1959). To date, only a few studies have been conducted in each of these categories. This is also apparent in the low incidence rate that has been found up to now for the topic of multimethod strategies in the major health psychology journals such as *Health Psychology*, the *British Journal of Health Psychology*, or *Psychology & Health*.

Particularly evident in health psychology is the predominance of self-report measures. Chapter 3 discusses the benefits and drawbacks of using self-report measures in psychological studies. The predominant use of these measures causes a variety of possible problems, including (a) shared response bias, (b) lack of construct validity, (c) method specificity, and (d) tainted predictor–criterion relationships (i.e., conceptual overlap between predictors and criterion). First, certain constant sources of error can bias reports to all the different self-report measures used in a study. These can be response

styles or response sets such as acquiescence, self-deception, social desirability, defensiveness, or idiosyncrasies in the use of numbers. For example, defensiveness could lead certain individuals to underreport both perceived stress and perceived symptoms, thereby falsely increasing the correlation between the two variables. If other, non-self-report measures were not simultaneously assessed in the study, the possibility arises that high correlations simply reflect common method biases (Spector, 1994). This has, for example, been brought forward by Larsen (1992), who found an association between neuroticism and inflated self-reports of the frequency and severity of gastrointestinal, respiratory, and depressive symptoms at both the time of encoding and at later recall. In other words, individuals high in neuroticism showed inflated scores on self-reports, thereby creating a common method bias in the data (Larsen, 1992). The inclusion of an objective measure such as medical records could prevent erroneous inferences drawn from self-report data.

Second, scores of self-report measures may in some circumstances not be a valid reflection of the construct that the instrument purportedly measures (e.g., hostility) but may rather reflect an individual's standing on an unrelated construct, (e.g., defensiveness). This could be the case, for example, when people respond to items in a certain way (e.g., responding defensively to a measure of hostility) but the use of this response style is not discovered by the researchers. The scores on the measure are then interpreted as measuring hostility, whereas, in fact, they reflect defensiveness. In this case, associations found between the predictor (e.g., the hostility measure) and an outcome (e.g., cardiovascular disease) may in fact reflect an independent association between defensiveness and cardiovascular disease. Indeed, such associations between, for example, defensive responding and hypertensive status (e.g., Mann & James, 1998) and between defensive responding and higher blood pressure (e.g., Shapiro, Goldstein, & Jamner, 1995) have been found. Rutledge, Linden, and Davies (2000) demonstrated the problem just outlined nicely in a study predicting cardiovascular health. They found that response styles (e.g., self-deception) in personality questionnaires in fact were themselves predic-

tive of poor cardiovascular health. Response styles were found to be important independent predictors of blood pressure changes across a 3-year interval, leading the authors to conclude that they are important personality traits that play a role in the regulation of blood pressure levels, rather than confounds in the prediction of cardiovascular health.

Third, if solely self-report measures are used to establish validity, important facets of the theoretical construct may be overlooked because the self-report measure might simply not be able to capture this particular aspect of the construct. For example, there might be aspects of quality of life or pain that individuals cannot easily express in verbal terms. The most commonly cited examples to illustrate this problem, as well as the most rigorous attempts to resolve this measurement problem, can be found in the area of stress research and therein particularly the measurement of stressors (Hurrell et al., 1998). Different types of indicators (self-report, proxy report, observational, quantitative measures of the work environment) are increasingly used in combination to address this problem. It is now commonly recognized that perceptions of the work environment are not a proxy for the objective work environment and that both objective and subjective concepts of stress deserve attention on their own and in combination (Spector, 1994).

A final problem of the sole use of self-report measures is the possibility of conceptual (i.e., item) overlap between the predictor variables and the criterion, meaning that the items might essentially be assessing the same construct, which may then be falsely interpreted as a psychologically meaningful correlational or even causal predictor–outcome relationship (Burns, 2000; Hurrell et al., 1998). Kasl (1978) referred to this problem as the "triviality trap" (p. 14). An example, again from stress research, would be if measures assessing stressors (aspects of work and work environment) and measures assessing strain (reactions to stress) have overlapping items (Hurrell et al., 1998). Furthermore, in cross-sectional studies, respondents' answers to self-report measures assessing the predictor variables can affect their responses to subsequent self-report measures assessing the criterion variable and vice versa. For instance, filling out a psychometric

scale measuring perceived self-efficacy regarding exercising can affect the exercise frequency or endurance that people report when asked in the context of the same questionnaire. Hence, the relationship between predictors and criterion variable becomes tainted, again leading to the false belief that meaningful, valid relationships between independent constructs were found when, in fact, the associations are not genuine (Hurrell et al., 1998). One measure to safeguard against tainted predictor–criterion relationships is better construct explications. If the predictor constructs and the criterion construct are each clearly defined and clearly delineated from each other and other constructs in the study, the problem of conceptual overlap is less likely to occur. If, however, items are not unique to a certain measure, this results in poor discriminant validity of the assessed constructs and their association with the criterion. In sum, more careful construct explication at the design stage (where measures are chosen) is required to secure the detection of valid associations.

A strategy for overcoming the problems that have been described in the sole use of self-report measures is triangulation, which simply means that a particular phenomenon is assessed in multiple modalities. In the area of stress research, for example, self-report measures of strain (reactions to stressful work conditions) can be backed up with more objective indicators such as physiological measures or observational data (Hurrell et al., 1998). If the multimodal assessment methods all yield the same result, one can be quite sure that the observed associations are valid. If discrepancies emerge, they will require follow-up investigations, and those may lead to further insights into the phenomenon under study. In fact, convergent validity between measures assessing the same construct using different modalities are as a rule relatively modest in health psychology, often not exceeding $r = .20$. This reflects not only that the individual measures assess different aspects in different modalities, but also the unreliability in the measures themselves.

Strong data analytic techniques may take care of some of the aforementioned problems, namely, method bias and predictor–criterion overlap. For

example, multivariate data analysis techniques involving structural equation modeling (SEM; e.g., confirmatory factor analysis, regression models, or path analysis; see Eid, Lischetzke, & Nussbeck, chap. 20, this volume) explicitly recognize measurement as difficult and potentially biased. In SEM, measurement error is explicitly modeled so that unbiased estimates for the relations between theoretical constructs, represented by latent (i.e., unmeasured) factors, can be derived. This is accomplished by requiring researchers to start by specifying and testing a measurement model before proceeding on to examining the structural relationships that their theory suggests. Convergent and discriminant validity can be assessed by estimating the goodness of fit of the measurement model (Anderson & Gerbing, 1988). SEM thus allows an estimate of how much the model is affected by the way the constructs are measured.

SEM or other powerful data analysis techniques, however, cannot take care of the basic problem that the specific measures or combinations of measures used may not capture all relevant dimensions of the predictors (e.g., Cohen, Kessler, & Gordon, 1995). In other words, SEM cannot "repair" the damage caused if measures were chosen that are not good indicators of the theoretical constructs or if the measures are unreliable. Thus, for valid theory testing, a well-thought-out choice of measures and an improvement in the (self-report) measures themselves is essential.

In addition to being aware of problems using self-report measures in research and addressing them with modern data analytical techniques, health psychology could benefit from more meta-analytic studies. Meta-analyses can provide critical information for the design of correlational or experimental studies. Specifically, meta-analysis allows an estimation of the relations among constructs much more reliably than can be done in single studies. The results of meta-analyses can thus reveal which theoretical constructs consistently show reliable relations with other constructs and can thereby help formulating a meaningful nomological network for the prediction of health behavior or health behavior change. Based on the results of meta-

analyses, theories of health behavior and health behavior change can be modified and refined, and then exposed to renewed empirical testing.

FINAL CONCLUSIONS

To summarize, in health psychology research there is a need for the use of more objective measures to replace or complement self-report measures and a need for more truly multimethod studies that incorporate measures that assess a construct with different modalities (Hurrell et al., 1998). A first step in planning a health psychology study should always be a thorough explication of the theoretical constructs involved. In the process of construct explication, all facets of the construct need to be described and distinguished from related constructs. This is a crucial step at the design stage of a study because it guides the selection of appropriate measurement instruments that avoid the problems of construct overlap and, therefore, prevents weakened validity. This is particularly important when analyzing causal relationships, such as trying to understand the mechanisms between risk conditions and disease. Obviously, to conclude that certain conditions have direct causal effects for diseases, the conditions need to be clearly defined and the causal pathways (i.e., the theoretical constructs on these pathways) need to be thoroughly explicated. In many areas of health psychology this can quickly become a very complex process because different causal mechanisms can operate at the physiological, social, psychological, cognitive, and behavioral levels.

To improve research in health psychology, more collaboration between the subdisciplines in psychology is needed as well as collaboration across disciplines. Traditionally, the different disciplines that study health psychology research questions have developed and used different methodological approaches (e.g., physiological markers vs. self-report measures). Enhanced communication between disciplines will allow researchers to approach the complexity of the research questions in a more-comprehensive, less-isolated way. To achieve this, multimethod strategies have to be

taught to new generations of researchers in more multidisciplinary oriented programs. Furthermore, and more so than at present, research questions should also transverse specific diseases or health behavior problems, thereby targeting the broader principles and mechanisms that underlie the health-related phenomena. This is critical for the advancement of knowledge in the field of health psychology.

CHAPTER 29

MULTIMETHODS IN INDUSTRIAL AND ORGANIZATIONAL PSYCHOLOGY: EXPANDING "METHODS" TO INCLUDE LONGITUDINAL DESIGNS

Andrew G. Miner and Charles L. Hulin

The general case for multiple operations in the study of constructs in psychology has been made several times (e.g., Bridgman, 1927; Campbell & Fiske, 1959; Dunnette, 1966; Garner, Hake, & Eriksen, 1956). It has been established that appropriate measurement and manipulation of psychological constructs depends fundamentally on the use of multiple independent methods, each of which imperfectly captures an underlying construct. The use of more than one operationalization of a construct is necessary to ensure that observed relationships are due to relations among constructs and not methods.

Industrial and organizational (I/O) psychology has struggled to measure constructs using more than one method for two reasons. First, researchers often lack access to experimental designs that can provide a source of alternative operationalizations; many constructs are bound to their organizational context and cannot be reasonably isolated in the lab (e.g., organizational commitment). Second, organizations are often reluctant to undertake the time, cost, and effort necessary to move beyond standard paper-and-pencil or online self-report surveys. Some research endeavors in I/O psychology have resulted in remarkable demonstrations of the application of multiple methods. However, such endeavors represent the exception to the rule that it is difficult to achieve multiple methods in organizational settings. In this chapter we describe four characteristics of most research in the field. One of these four characteristics, the discounting of dynamic process in research design, is explored in further detail. The chapter addresses some potential

benefits of using dynamic, within-person, designs more frequently.

BACKGROUND

I/O psychology is, from one viewpoint, a pragmatic psychology. Much research is devoted to the prediction of behavior in organizations. For example, what are the psychological factors that lead a group of employees to attempt to change a dissatisfying or stressful situation by unionizing? What factors go into decisions to quit one's job? What psychological traits best predict job performance across a wide range of occupations? Effort typically goes into identifying measures that accurately predict these types of outcomes because *the outcomes themselves* are important. Indeed, one popular method of selecting employees, biographical data, relies primarily on empirical keying to score individual items according to the options that best predict job success. Perhaps as a result of a tension to identify measures that predict our chosen behaviors well, we have not used the multitrait–multimethod (MTMM) approach to triangulate on theoretical constructs, preferring instead to use the measures that best predict the behaviors. There are counterexamples, a few of which we describe following, but most I/O psychologists would probably admit that at some level we are driven by pragmatic concerns of prediction (Hulin, 2001).

Some in the field have addressed these issues. Dunnette (1966), an I/O psychologist, argued points quite similar to Campbell and Fiske's (1959)

in his provocative "fads, fashions, and folderol" article. Dunnette warned against researchers whose findings or theory depended on one operation. Researchers with one method are limited; their findings are equally limited. Their research is method—rather than problem—oriented; disentangling method and construct variance may be impossible if results are based on monomethod studies. If the methods generate systematic error variance not related to the construct being assessed but correlated with other responses, the theory and its evidence may be misleading. Through demonstration that multiple methods and measures independently converge on the same conclusions, researchers can avoid ascribing errors in measurement to effects at the construct level (Campbell & Fiske, 1959).

A DESCRIPTION OF RESEARCH

Unfortunately, the main points of the original Campbell and Fiske article are distorted nearly as often as they are heeded. In I/O psychology, Campbell and Fiske's arguments are often cited in the empirical literature but frequently in contexts that are but pallid reflections of the points of the MTMM work, distorted by the twin mirrors of exigencies of field research and difficulties of developing truly *independent* methods of assessing related traits. Real-world restrictions on research designs in organizations create four characteristics that describe much I/O research:

1. Many studies rely primarily on self-reports.
2. Theory and measurement instruments are often intertwined.
3. Methods dictate and limit theory.
4. Time is either ignored or arbitrary.

These four characteristics are not meant to describe *all* research in the field, nor are they meant to describe the shortcomings of researchers working in the area. Rather, they are intended to be a description of the evolved state of much research in organizational environments.

Self-Report

Many organizational results are based on data collected from employees who complete structured, self-report, paper-and-pencil or online surveys.[1] To the extent that attitude, personality, opinion, and interest constructs are best measured using self-reports, *and they often are*, this is an acceptable method of obtaining data. However, as a field, we are limited by what appears to be an overreliance on self-reports.

In organizational studies, self-reports are a particular concern because surveys are commonly done with management's endorsement. Employees manipulate their responses not only for ordinary social desirability, but also because they are concerned about confidentiality. This can create an incentive for individuals to manipulate their responses lest they be caught reporting that their boss is an idiot or their colleagues are clueless. Unless the surveys are clearly anonymous or 100% guaranteed confidential, participants have an incentive to distort.

This creates a dilemma for researchers who attempt to diversify methodologically. Collecting data in addition to self-reports requires that participants be identifiable. One cannot give anonymous surveys if one needs to match to data collected using other methods. Therefore, researchers are in a dilemma: the best way to ensure that response manipulation is minimized is to give anonymous surveys, but this makes the possibility of matching to data collected using alternative methods impossible.

In attempts to create alternative methods, researchers occasionally word questions somewhat differently or use different response scales (e.g., using Likert, yes/?/no, or other verbal response formats). However, this does not generate different methods. The number of facets the resulting measures share with each other remains unfortunately large. Correlations among measures are artificially inflated because of the common measurement operations shared by the different response formats. The method variance contained in each measure gets treated as construct or trait variance. In addition,

---

[1]We exclude cognitive ability tests from our analyses and restrict ourselves to self-report surveys and scales that assess preference, opinion, attitude, personality, or interest constructs. Ability assessments have measurement problems that are quite different.

self-reports only tap a portion of the construct space, the verbally accessible and socially acceptable part. The remainder of the construct space is seldom measured. This is significant if the portion that is measured is not representative of the whole space. Indicators of a construct may be seriously deficient.

Confounding of Theories and Methods

Our multiple measures differ too little from one another and are drawn from a restricted universe of assessments. Indeed, some theories are supported not only by single measurement operations but also by single measures of constructs.

There is a volume of research on theories that documents correlations not among constructs, but among the *measures* that go with the theory. For example, most studies that test Hackman and Oldham's (1976, 1980) theory of work design use the scale that they published with the theory, the Job Diagnostic Survey. Without multiple scales that measure constructs proposed by the theory, it is impossible to partition observed covariance into construct-relevant and scale-relevant variance. In essence, the scale becomes the construct (see also Idaszak, Bottom, & Drasgow, 1988; Idaszak & Drasgow, 1987).

As another example, consider Herzberg's Two-Factor Theory (Herzberg, Mausner, & Snyderman, 1959). Herzberg proposed that the factors that cause job satisfaction were different than the factors that cause dissatisfaction. He derived his theory based on field studies where he asked employees to list the attributes of their jobs that made them satisfied and, separately, those that made them dissatisfied. Employees consistently listed different sources of satisfaction and dissatisfaction. Herzberg and his colleagues concluded that job satisfaction and job dissatisfaction were in fact two independent factors and not opposite poles of one dimension.

The theory received much attention in the years that followed, but many researchers had trouble replicating Herzberg's results if they used any other research method. Eventually, a research on Two-Factor Theory put the matter to rest by pointing out that Herzberg's theory could only be replicated by using his original item set (Schneider & Locke, 1971). The entire theory rested on the survey/interview method used to collect the data. Using alternative methods caused the predictions of the theory to fail.[2]

The problem seems to be structural in social science. Responsibility lies partially with researchers, but also with editors, who correctly require that published works rely on validated scales. Referees try to ensure that published results are based on prevalidated scales with demonstrated construct validity so that results are not due to idiosyncrasies of the scale used. Unfortunately, this creates a situation for researchers who, with limited time and space on questionnaires, risk not being published if they use new or alternative measurement operations without extensive validation.

The issue is not the validity of many of our basic scales. Indeed, a large number of scales can be argued to have substantial construct validity. The issue is that even our validated measures contain substantial, albeit unknown, amounts of stable method and self-presentation variance that masquerades as construct variance. When no other scales are available or acceptable or the exigencies of publishing intervene, the researcher has little choice but to use the validated ones.

The argument for multiple operationalizations for constructs is consistent with the logical positivist philosophy of science that held sway in psychology from the 1930s to the 1950s. This approach appeared to assume that measures are equivalent to the construct they assess. However, to argue that this implies acceptance of single measures and methods of operationalizing a construct distorts the logical positivism philosophy. Bridgman, one of the founders of logical positivism,

---

[2]The extensive debate among mood researchers outside I/O psychology about the "true" factor structure of mood reports also illustrates our point. Some researchers proposed that negative and positive moods are polar opposites (Russell, 1980), whereas others proposed that negative and positive moods were not opposites, but independent dimensions (Watson & Tellegen, 1985). Only because different researchers used different items to measure mood for several years was it possible to have a theoretical dispute, apparently informed by data, about something so fundamental. Once measurement error was corrected in the Positive and Negative Affect Schedule (PANAS; Watson & Tellegen, 1985), evidence for independence was diminished (Green, Goldman, & Salovey, 1993), and consensual structures begin to emerge (Tellegen, Watson, & Clark, 1999).

argued that operational definitions are without significance unless *at least two methods are known of getting to the terminus*. One could have been a dedicated positivist (e.g., Bridgman, 1927, 1945) and still not fallen into the trap of relying on single operations of a construct. Even assuming a concept is synonymous with a set of operations, any operation does not necessarily produce a concept. Defining a phenomenon by the operations that produced it has a specious precision because *it is a description of a single isolated event* (Bridgman, 1927, p. 248), not a construct.

Restriction of Theory by Existing Methods

Our long-standing love affair with copying machines and their spawn, paper-and-pencil items and scales, has also generated a related and perhaps more serious problem. When a substantially new construct is hypothesized by theory, our tendency to use the same assessment techniques used for previous theories and constructs is likely to generate empirical evidence that suggests the new construct adds but little to our pool of variance. Correlated error variance among the original variables and the new constructs may overwhelm any independent variance related to new constructs.

One example of this is the inclusion of affect in theories of attitudes and behavioral intentions (e.g., Fishbein, 1980; Triandis, 1980). When affect or emotion constructs referred to in these theories were studied in empirical research, they were assessed using paper-and-pencil items to elicit descriptions of the stimulus object in terms of such items as *nauseating, disgusting,* or *a source of pleasure*. Empirically, these scales, putatively assessing affect aroused by a stimulus object, contributed trivially to the prediction of behavioral intentions beyond that accounted for by more traditional measures of cognitive evaluations of the stimulus objects *with which they shared many assessment facets*. Emphases on affect or emotion in attitudes, including job attitudes, withered away despite our definitions of these constructs as reflecting affective reactions toward an object.

It is not at all clear that affective reactions can or should be measured independently from ongoing experience and interaction with the object of interest. Is it safe to assume that affective reactions to "cigarettes," for example, are equivalent and constant between what is reported on a questionnaire in the lab and when one is in a smoky bar at 11 P.M. on a Saturday night or when one has just finished breakfast on the third day of attempting to quit smoking? Researchers who attempted to study the role of affect in attitudes and behaviors seem, in retrospect, to have reached a "methodological stalemate" (Larson & Csikszentmihalyi, 1983) in which methods appropriate to an earlier theory or construct are applied to test all derivations from that theory and from new theories in the same general content area.

Time Is Either Ignored or Arbitrary

The fourth characteristic of general research in I/O psychology is that our data are usually cross-sectional and static. As in other areas of psychology, it is difficult to obtain longitudinal data sets. As a result, process theory about how variables should be causally related is relegated to introduction and discussion sections of papers, whereas the method and results describe cross-sectional data collection. Designs that rely on such static, between-person, variance in measures are useful for a substantial but not unlimited range of questions.

Relying on static data collections forces researchers to make three assumptions: (a) within-person variance is either uninteresting, error, or will not address our theoretical questions; (b) measurement operations used to assess static or aggregated measures are immune from influences due to respondents' current standing on constructs or this extraneous variance is small, random, and can be relegated to the error term; and (c) we know the intervals across which we should aggregate recall measures and participants can accurately aggregate.

The first point, that within-person variance is not interesting, is important. It can best be addressed with the very data that our research designs do not typically collect: within-person data. Closer examination of many theories will likely reveal that they would be more completely addressed by analyzing both within- *and* between-

person variance in their central constructs. For example, up to the early 1990s the field defined "affective reactions" to one's job as relatively static job satisfaction. Only recently has attention been focused on the idea that employees may not have stable levels of job satisfaction across time and that this dynamic variance is systematically related to important variables (Ilies & Judge, 2002; Weiss & Cropanzano, 1996).

The answer to question 2 is more difficult because even granting that dynamic variance may be random across individuals, it will not be randomly distributed across responses to the questionnaire. Suppose, for example, that commitment and job satisfaction are positively correlated *over time*. In periods when one is committed to the organization, one also has high levels of job satisfaction. If we measure both variables in only one time period and inspect only the between-persons correlation matrix, this within-persons correlation will inflate the size of the observed between-persons relationship. Brief and his colleagues demonstrated that state variables can influence responses on supposedly static instruments when they induced higher scores on a "static" job satisfaction instrument by elevating state mood with a gift of a cookie (Brief, Butcher, & Roberson, 1995).

Third, the appropriate interval across which to aggregate observations depends on an understanding of rate of change of our constructs and a well-articulated theory of organizational and individual time. Such theory would specify intervals across which stability can be expected and the relative amounts of change expected across other, longer, intervals. For example, stability of job attitudes will depend on economic, political, organizational, and psychological processes. How many times does the boss need to engage in harassment or how often does it need to occur before attitudes change? Is once enough or must it become a pattern spaced over time? How fast do people change their evaluation of their job? How general are the factors that cause change over time? What are the temporal characteristics of the feedback from behaviors onto the attitudes that precipitated the behaviors? Without theories that provide answers to such questions,

we use what seems intuitively appropriate. We are operating at the intersection of organizational and psychological time, and we have little guidance. So, we slice into an organization at one time point and ignore trajectories of variables that may alter our observations. These are issues that have received little attention in the literature beyond a few comprehensive theories (e.g., Naylor, Pritchard, & Ilgen, 1980) and recent studies that document rates of change following, for example, organizational entry (Chan & Schmitt, 2000). The result of this oversight is temporal misspecification. The time intervals across which measures are aggregated or recalled are arbitrary; they are often dictated neither by theoretical requirements nor empirical data relevant to the appropriate length of time intervals in organizations or in the lives or organizational employees. Beyond a few examples, little thought is given to how fast or slow we might expect variables of interest to change or fluctuate across time. Applications of computational modeling in which rates of change are explicitly modeled based on differing sets of assumptions about underlying states and processes provide one avenue for studying temporal questions (Ilgen & Hulin, 2000).

The arbitrariness of time frame is evident from the wording of organizational surveys themselves. Subjects are often given an arbitrary time frame over which to integrate their experience for responding to our surveys (e.g., "in general how do you rate your . . ."). We have little good evidence about how individuals construct responses to such questions. Do they accurately recall their actual experiences, or do they use beliefs, implicit theories, stereotypes, and other heuristics to generate self-reports?

Evidence addressing this latter question exists for individuals making reports about how they feel or have felt. Studies that compare retrospective reports of affect (over the past few weeks) to actual reports taken during the same time period indicate that the two do not match (Thomas & Diener, 1990). Individuals fail to recall accurately their own affect because they are overly influenced by a variety of factors, including beliefs about particular situations (Arntz, van Eyck, & Heijmans, 1990;

Levine, 1997; McFarland, Ross, & DeCourville, 1989), sex-related stereotypes about emotional experience (Eisenberg & Lennon, 1983; LaFrance & Banaji, 1992), personality (Feldman Barrett, 1997), and intensity of emotional experience (Kahneman, 1999; Robinson & Clore, 2002b). Recent work suggests that this discrepancy is due to two different emotional reporting mechanisms: recall up to about 2 weeks is based on actual experience, and longer-term recall is based on semantic beliefs about typical experiences (Robinson & Clore, 2002a, 2002b). Thus, whereas current and short-term reports of affective experience are based on actual recall of affect episodes, retrospective reports about frequency of emotions can be biased by a number of factors associated with semantic belief structures. Such evidence for other important organizational variables is lacking.

Exceptions to Our Description

We paint a slightly caricatured picture of the field to make a point. Many organizational researchers can, and do, use alternative methods to collect some of their data. For example, many studies of quitting, retirement, and absence use objective organizational reports of such behavior. Other studies of leadership and citizenship behavior, for example, use peer, subordinate, and spousal reports of such behaviors. These studies are stronger for using multisource data; however, it is still the rare study that uses more than one source of data to measure a single construct. Moreover, many key constructs would simply be poorly measured using objective or other reports. Consider job satisfaction, perceptions of organizational justice, fairness, and job withdrawal intentions. It is difficult to obtain assessments other than self-reports of these variables. Thus, when alternative methods are used, they are used sparingly and usually for constructs that lend themselves well to alternative measurement. Nonetheless there have been exceptions, to which we now turn.

Researchers at AT&T in the 1960s applied Campbell and Fiske's (1959) ideas to measure abilities of their managers in what became called the "assessment center" (Bray, 1982; Bray, Campbell, & Grant, 1974). Following on earlier work done to

select spies during World War II, these researchers developed a complex and realistic set of exercises in their attempts to assess many components of abilities and motivations that contributed to effective job performance. Each ability or motivation was assessed using multiple methods. For example, a trait was assessed using paper-and-pencil tests, in-basket exercises, ratings by observers of interactions in group discussion, and ratings by interviewers obtained from one-on-one interactions in interviews. Multiple traits of each person going through the assessment process were assessed using multiple independent methods. At least two raters rated each trait within each method. Using such comprehensive measures, it was possible for researchers to generate a true multitrait–multimethod matrix of the sample of managers.

Unfortunately, more than anything else, this study revealed just how difficult it is to assess subjective traits such as interpersonal ability using fallible human raters. The scores raters assigned were often better predicted by their ratings of other individuals than they were by ratings of the same trait by other raters or by other methods or exercises (Robertson, Gratton, & Sharpley, 1987; Sackett & Dreher, 1982; Sackett & Harris, 1988). In other words, the heterotrait–monomethod correlations were consistently stronger than the monotrait–heteromethod correlations. Scores were consistent within-method but less so across methods within-assessees.

This problem has reemerged in recent years with multirater ("360 degree") assessment systems. Multirater assessment attempts to augment traditional supervisor ratings of performance with ratings from other, operationally independent, observers such as peers, subordinates, and customers. It is a direct attempt to overcome the limitations of single-source data in performance rating. Evidence from this approach indicates small ratee effects coupled with very large rater effects and within-rater correlations (Scullen, Mount, & Goff, 2000), akin to the large method effects for assessment centers noted earlier. Who does the rating of performance matters far more than performance itself.

The assessment center studies and the multirater approach to performance ratings are noteworthy for

the problems they highlight. They are vivid examples of the difficulty of obtaining reliable and independent assessments in organizational research. They also suggest that substantially high estimates of scale reliability and "convergent" validity of our measures may be due to shared method variance as much as the consistencies of individuals' standings on constructs.

Research has continued, however, without an adequate solution to the problem of shared method variance. This implies that when our conclusions are based on single-method, single-source data, they may have substantial amounts of correlated error variance. Multimethod and multisource data are valued; they might be argued to be the gold standard in I/O field research. However, the constraints of field research and the biases of I/O researchers have limited the extent to which multiple operations of single constructs appear in the literature.

MULTIPLE OBSERVATIONS VERSUS MULTIPLE METHODS

The issues we have raised so far are not unique and are unlikely to take the field of I/O psychology by storm. Others have made similar points without lasting effects (e.g., Dunnette, 1966). Much research in organizations is simply too constrained by realities of working in the field to take full advantage of conducting research according to Campbell and Fiske's (1959) approach. Therefore, we would like to reconsider some of the field's chronic measurement problems from a slightly different angle.

To begin, let us consider the correlation between a single assessment at two different time periods:

$$r_{t_1 t_2}$$

This correlation is affected by four factors. First, the longitudinal stability of the measured construct influences the observed correlation. This is the true score in classical test theory. Second, systematic error variance between Times 1 and 2 influences the

observed correlation. Both these factors will cause the observed correlation to be high. The MTMM approach attempts to reduce artificial inflation of $r_{t_1 t_2}$ because of systematic, and correlated, error variance. Through the use of multiple methods it triangulates on true construct variance and, ideally, reduces correlated error variance to zero.

Two other factors act to reduce $r_{t_1 t_2}$: random error and dynamic construct variance. Constructs are assumed stable in classical test theory; any fluctuation is assumed to be due to random error and lumped along with dynamic construct variance into the error term.[3] This thought experiment illustrates that if constructs vary systematically and meaningfully across time, meaningful variance is being ignored. Further detail on other measurement issues is in a preceding chapter (Khoo, West, Wu, & Kwok, chap. 21, this volume).

We propose that the field of I/O needs to reduce the influences of systematic error variance, but should also concern itself with dynamic construct variance that artificially lowers observed correlations among constructs. Dynamic construct variance traditionally is combined with random error variance, but if constructs do change across time, then ignoring this variance excludes study of interesting phenomena.

For example, one of I/O psychology's most popular constructs, job satisfaction, is typically assessed at one time and correlated with variables collected at the same or different times. Researchers conclude that job satisfaction is systematically related to other variables and constructs. However, this research enterprise assumes that job satisfaction is a stable construct that does not vary appreciably across time. Evidence suggests that this is not a safe assumption. The first study that directly questioned this assumption asked whether individuals in positive moods reported higher job satisfaction than those in neutral moods. Results showed that individuals who were placed into positive moods at the time they took a job satisfaction survey scored significantly higher on it than those whose moods

---

[3]Most researchers estimate reliability using coefficient α. When reliability is computed in this way, dynamic construct variance would be assigned to true variance assuming individual items covary positively over time. To the extent that average item intercorrelation (coefficient α) is high because items covary across time rather than between persons will be the extent to which dynamic construct variance is assigned to true variance.

were not so manipulated (Brief et al., 1995). Further evidence indicates that individuals' levels of satisfaction vary widely across times of the day and days of the week when asked repeatedly in a diary design (Ilies & Judge, 2002). Both studies draw attention to the conclusion that satisfaction cannot be assumed to remain stable as events and feedback from behaviors impinge on it across time.

This does not deny that job satisfaction has a stable portion of variance, but unless this portion is large compared to its total variance, we cannot ignore dynamic fluctuations. It strains credibility to assume that construct job satisfaction does not vary across time and that any fluctuations are error variance.

The published stability coefficients for well-constructed measures of job satisfaction suggest, at first glance, that these measures are indeed stable across time. Coefficients vary across measures, studies, and time intervals, but stability coefficients ranging from .70 to .85 have been obtained (e.g., Smith, Kendall, & Hulin, 1969). These indicate acceptable levels of stability for traitlike measures and suggest the statelike fluctuations are minor. However, it is likely that much of the variance in job attitude scores that is treated as stable is actually systematic response variance associated with personality, concerns about the confidentiality of attitude scale responses, and other stable response artifacts. All forms of stable variance are lumped into construct variance and may significantly inflate the stability estimates of these measures.

One might argue that job satisfaction is a poor example compared to something more traitlike and stable, such as personality. However, evidence suggests that all the Big 5 personality dimensions vary as much across time as they do across individuals (Fleeson, 2001). These estimates of the within-versus between-person variance are at odds with the T_1, T_2 reliabilities of .80 to .85. Thus, not even "traits" such as personality are safe from the assumptions about stability.

This is not a trivial consideration. Our past theories about what was important to study and our past methods were, more or less, in alignment. We had theories about assumed static constructs, and we used methods best suited to studying static variables and constructs. It is not clear which came

first; reciprocal influences are likely. However, it appears clear from both theoretical and empirical perspectives that although we have learned much about individuals in organizations, there is much that our methods have relegated to the trash bin of error variance that deserves to be resurrected and analyzed for lawful and consistent antecedents and consequences.

IMPLICATIONS

Theories of organizational behavior posit dynamic processes. Inherent in the generation of predictions is how variables operate and interact over time. For example, the observation that conscientiousness should relate to job performance inherently posits that conscientious individuals engage in behaviors that enhance their job performance to a greater extent than nonconscientious individuals. This hypothesis is typically tested across individuals by relating trait conscientiousness to some level of aggregated performance. It is likely that there is a set of behaviors that mediate the relationship between conscientiousness and job performance. Such behaviors consist in part of ensuring that assigned tasks are done, infrequently missing meetings, following up with others more often, arranging work in a logical fashion, setting goals and subgoals to be accomplished during a workday (Ryan, 1970), and coping with personal problems during nonwork times. Studies that address variance over time are crucial to understanding the processes behind well-documented relationships.

Mediating behaviors are likely to influence some, but not all, aspects of an employee's job performance. One can hypothesize that these mediating behaviors occur more frequently in conscientious employees but still not assume they are static and completely regularly occurring aspects of how conscientious employees organize their workdays. Nor do we need to assume that trait conscientiousness is a fixed characteristic of individuals. It is likely that state conscientiousness may fluctuate across time and situations, although it should be higher in individuals with high degrees of trait conscientiousness. The degree of stability will likely depend in part on the consistency and impact of feedback from behav-

iors that typify conscientiousness. Episodic mediating behaviors are more likely to occur when state conscientiousness is high. These mediating behaviors are likely to be related to performance effectiveness during those times.

The picture this presents is a dynamic, within-person, instantiation of the much-studied between-person correlation between trait conscientiousness and aggregated overall performance (Barrick & Mount, 1991). We can assume that between-person observations will generalize to some within-person processes without also taking the step of assuming fixed, static traits and behaviors. As we move away from a pragmatic field concerned with documenting relationships to a more theoretically oriented one, dynamic processing understanding will become crucial.

For example, we might think of organizational commitment as a relatively more stable variable than is mood. However, even organizational commitment varies about its long-term mean over time. Some weeks we are very committed to our organizations, others, not so because of, for example, a press story that the CEO of our organization and his captive finance committee recently awarded him a 20-year increase in his years with the organization to increase his retirement benefits; no such additions to rank-and-file employees' years of service were made. These deviations are regarded as random minor fluctuations or measurement errors in the current application of classical measurement theory. As a consequence of this, they are ignored in our studies of the constructs; within-person, across-time variances in the assessments of the construct are neither studied nor analyzed for possible relations with antecedents or behavioral consequences. We do not investigate the potential antecedents and consequences of fluctuations of these variables because we assume these fluctuations to be random error.

For example, some have suggested that understanding of how personality influences outcomes may be achieved by examination of such intrapersonal variability (e.g., Block, 1995; Pervin, 1994). Personality does not express itself in a vacuum. Individuals constantly choose and react to situations in their environment. That is, personality processes might be better understood by examining how they predict momentary behavior, affect, and cognition. In response, researchers (Moskowitz & Cote, 1995; Cote & Moskowitz, 1998) developed the behavioral concordance model building on prior work that examined situational concordance (Diener, Larson, & Emmons, 1984; Emmons, Diener, & Larsen, 1986). A few recent studies have documented the utility of such models for understanding several dimensions of personality (Cote & Moskowitz, 1998; Gable, Reis, & Elliot, 2000; Moskowitz & Cote, 1995). Applied to I/O endeavors such an approach could, for example, help researchers understand how personality interacts with job characteristics to influence job performance across time and across people with different personality profiles. Key is the idea that we need to get data about how personality operates across situations to get a better understanding about how it operates in work settings.

In summary, we believe that increasing attention to dynamic construct variance is important for two reasons. First, it is important to address a potential misestimation of error terms. If researchers sweep meaningful variance in constructs into their error terms inappropriately, they commit errors potentially as large as artificially inflating correlations by using common methods. Second, we see potential for the expansion of theory to process rather than documentation of correlations by increasing access and attention to temporal ordering. We recognize such a focus will make most organizational research more difficult, just as Dunnette (1966) argued decades ago. Managers will undoubtedly resist efforts to extend data collection beyond familiar survey instruments administered at one arbitrary time and the occasional supervisory evaluations of performance. Researchers will also object to attempts to partition temporal variance into true and error components rather than simply assuming that temporal variance is all error. However, the alternative is to continue the status quo and to ignore what seem to be serious problems with theory/data interfaces.

SOME ALTERNATIVE METRICS

In an ideal world of construct validity, we would collect data whose assessment methods share a minimum of facets (e.g., structured vs. semistruc-

tured vs. unstructured, paper-and-pencil vs. observations by others, verbal vs. behavioral, accessible vs. inferred by observers, transparent vs. masked) with other assessments of these constructs. As this book details, other areas of psychology have developed metrics that could and should be applied to I/O research. These other assessments could include such measures as behavioral traces (Fritsche & Linneweber, chap. 14, this volume; Webb, Campbell, Schwartz, & Sechrest, 1966), direct observational reports (Neyer, chap. 4, this volume), semistructured techniques (Hulin & Maher, 1959), peer reports, self-reports that minimize verbal content (Kunin, 1955), event or signal sampling (Stone & Litcher-Kelly, chap. 5, this volume), response times to attitude items (Fazio & Olson, 2003; Fazio & Williams, 1986; Robinson & Neighbors, chap. 9, this volume), and objective metrics. Explorations of theory/data interfaces using alternative research disciplines such as computational modeling (Glomb & Miner, 2002; Ilgen & Hulin, 2000; Seitz, Hulin, & Hanisch, 2000; Seitz & Miner, 2002) should also be included in our research techniques.

One area we would like to highlight is reaction time measures. Such measures allow inferences about cognitive processes that are inaccessible with verbal self-reports. Use of such metrics opened up new areas of conceptual development about many constructs and popularized new areas of study. For example, the use of reaction time metrics permitted scientists to study the organization of material in memory (Schneider & Shiffrin, 1985) and the categorization of objects in perception and memory (Benjamin, chap. 24, this volume). In social psychology, such measurement operations have permitted theory to extend to such areas as "implicit attitudes," or attitudes that are not readily verbally accessible and reportable or reportable (Greenwald & Banaji, 1995; Greenwald, McGhee, & Schwartz, 1998), or attitude accessibility (Fazio & Williams, 1986).

Research indicates that chronically accessible attitudes are better predictors of some behaviors than are attitudes less chronically accessible. For example, Fazio and Williams (1986) showed that attitude accessibility was a predictor of behavior

after controlling for attitude strength in a study of voting intentions in the months preceding the 1984 presidential election. Individuals with chronically accessible attitudes toward the candidates voted how they said they would more often than did those with less-accessible attitudes, even though both groups rated the candidates identically.

Even though many of our most popular constructs are attitudes (e.g., job satisfaction, organizational commitment, justice), little work has been done on accessibility within the field of I/O. When a participant in a study answers "Yes" to the query, "Are your coworkers boring?" we do not know whether they constantly evaluate their coworkers as boring and avoid them as much as possible, or whether they just escaped from a long and boring conversation with colleagues. Of course, on average, we'd expect people with more negative overall evaluations to respond affirmatively more often. However, the modest relations between attitudes and relevant behaviors suggest attention paid to accessibility of attitudes might pay substantial dividends in the strength and generality of relations between job attitudes and behaviors. It is also possible that less-accessible attitudes represent an independent pool of variance that is reliably related to different outcomes than chronically accessible attitudes.

The issue of chronic accessibility is broader than responses to structured questionnaire items. It deals with a characteristic of our theories. We assume the constructs we measure influence outcomes consistently across time. In the case of weak, or nonchronically accessible, or attitudes whose accessibility varies depending on affective factors, this may not be a safe assumption. Worse, it is unlikely that this assumption causes only random error in prediction. If only the subset of people with chronically accessible attitudes drives our results, we may be generalizing inappropriately.

Chronic accessibility might matter little for I/O psychology. The case could be made (e.g., Hulin, 2001) that work represents such an important part of most people's lives, that attitudes about work will always be chronically accessible. This may be why job attitude/job behavior relations are typically stronger than more elusive social attitude/social

behavior relations (Hulin & Judge, 2003); it should be investigated. The point is that without using reaction time measures or alternate metrics to complement verbal self-reports, I/O researchers will fail to investigate this potentially important component of an immensely popular topic within the field.

CONCLUSION

Overreliance on self-report data potentially biases our results and may overestimate the construct validity of our measures. Although a construct such as organizational commitment may be efficiently and accurately measured by asking a series of questions about how committed one is to their organization, sole reliance on such measures restricts our ability to ensure we have captured the underlying construct. Further, we compound this reliance on a narrow range of assessments by using analyses that cannot distinguish between construct, trait, or true variance with systematic error variance due to methods. We tend to lump all nonrandom error into construct variance when it comes to estimating stability or reliability of our measures.

Decades ago there were calls to use multiple methods to achieve construct validity in psychological research. I/O psychology struggles with these calls because much research is done in the field, where it is difficult to gain access to employees to assess their characteristics and responses even once; forget about multiple ways. As a consequence, we argue that the field has evolved its theories to study only those variables and constructs that are measurable using self-report data gathered in surveys.

The efforts to expand measurement beyond single methods have met resistance; it is difficult to obtain low monomethod–heterotrait correlations. We suggest that this problem of achieving low monomethod–heterotrait correlations is somewhat intractable as long as human raters are involved, and they will be for I/O research for the near future.

Given this situation, what can we expect about the nature of I/O research? We only account for a portion of the total variance in our constructs, but the amount of *covariance* that we do account for may be an overestimate of the true state of affairs because while we are assessing manifestations of a portion of the total construct space, we are using methods that potentially share much correlated method variance. This tends to generate strong correlations among the few multiple measures of a construct.

It seems clear there are direct and mutual influences between theory and methods. Theories that cannot be tested with available methods are given little credence and are not studied. Our methods do a very good job assessing static traits or aggregating observations over arbitrary temporal intervals. This leads us to focus our theoretical/conceptual efforts on theories that address static questions and static analyses. A consideration of these issues may suggest we need to modify both our theories and our methods. Methods that allow us to address such variation in our theories should generate hypotheses about dynamic states, episodic behaviors, and fluctuations in patterns of individuals' responses.

As a potential solution we propose that researchers expand their use of longitudinal designs, in particular short-term longitudinal designs that tap dynamic constructs. We also urge that within-person variance in important constructs should be analyzed to determine possible implications for our theories. Our recommendations are not panaceas, but they do open possibilities for better understanding of change in constructs across time. We argue that it is only through studying and understanding change that our field can be freed from the confines of static research that is adept at documenting relationships, but relegates process theory to the introduction and discussion sections. Without methods that directly address process, it is difficult to parse the many possible process explanations for any given observed static relationship.

CHAPTER 30

A MULTIMETHOD PERSPECTIVE ON SELF-CONCEPT RESEARCH IN EDUCATIONAL PSYCHOLOGY: A CONSTRUCT VALIDITY APPROACH

Herbert W. Marsh, Andrew J. Martin, and Kit-Tai Hau

In this chapter we begin with a brief overview of the construct validity approach that underpins our multimethod perspective to self-concept research. After briefly reviewing the theoretical basis for our self-concept research, we provide an overview of the different multimethod approaches used in this research program. We have, somewhat arbitrarily, divided this into four sections. First we focus on a wide variety of applications of the multitrait–multimethod (MTMM) design, the traditional multimethod approach. Second, we briefly review some of our cross-cultural research where results from multiple countries are compared to evaluate the cross-cultural generalizability of our research. Third we describe some additional analytic approaches that fit within our broader perspective of the multimethod approach. Finally, we explore some broader perspectives on the multimethod approach.

CONSTRUCT VALIDATION: A MULTIPLE PERSPECTIVE APPROACH

Psychology focuses on hypothetical constructs—unobservable, theoretical abstractions—inferred indirectly on the basis of observable indicators of the construct. A critical issue is how well the observable indicators represent the hypothetical construct—the extent to which the theoretical construct is well represented by the test scores; well

defined, related to variables and conditions to which it is theoretically and logically connected, and unrelated to variables and conditions to which it is not theoretically and logically connected. Hence, evidence used to evaluate construct validity includes the content of measures, response processes by participants, internal structure in terms of consistency and factor structure, convergent and discriminant relations with other constructs, criterion-related validity, and validity generalization to relevant and similar situations or populations. To the extent that there are multiple indicators of each construct it is typically possible to: evaluate each indicator; discard or replace ineffective ones and assign appropriate weights to the others; evaluate and correct for measurement error; evaluate the internal structure of the indicators; and test for systematic, nonrandom sources of bias (e.g., method effects).

In psychological research it is advisable to consider multiple outcome measures to test the construct validity of the outcome construct, rival hypotheses, and competing theories. For example, an intervention designed to enhance academic self-concept should have a stronger effect on academic self-concept than on physical self-concept. This provides a possible test of potential biases such as the Hawthorne effect, Halo effects, or postgroup euphoria effects. Multiple outcome measures allow for

We would like to dedicate this chapter to D. Campbell and D. Fiske, who pioneered the multimethod approach with their development of multitrait–multimethod methodology that has been so central in our research. Our respect for their work and its influence on our research is shown in that Herbert W. Marsh is the person who has cited their classic work the most. We would also like to thank our many colleagues who have contributed to our self-concept research program. K.-T. Hau pursued this research, in part, while a Visiting Scholar at the SELF Research Centre (University of Western Sydney). The research was funded in part by grants from the Australian Research Council.

tests of unintended outcomes (positive and negative). For example, interventions that enhance skills but lead to more negative self-concepts are likely to have very different implications to a program that increases both skill levels and the corresponding area of self-concept (see Marsh & Peart, 1988).

Particularly in nonexperimental research with variables that are not or cannot be experimentally manipulated, it is often desirable to have multiple indicators of the independent or mediating variables. Even in experimental and quasi-experimental studies, it is advisable to have multiple operationalizations of the experimentally manipulated variable. Thus, for example, Marsh and Peart (1988) compared competitive and cooperative interventions designed to enhance physical fitness. Although both interventions enhanced fitness, the cooperative intervention also enhanced physical self-concept, whereas the competitive intervention led to the reduction in physical self-concept relative both to pretest scores and to scores for a randomly assigned no-treatment control group. They argued that the short-term gains in physical fitness were likely to be undermined by declines in physical self-concept associated with the competitive intervention. Hence, construct validation is relevant to experimental as well as nonexperimental research.

It is also valuable to test the same hypothesis with different research methodologies. For example, the limitations and threats to the validity of interpretations are quite different in experimental, correlational, survey, action research, interview, and case study approaches. To the extent that there is a convergence in results from different research methodologies and samples, the construct validity of the interpretations is enhanced. Rather than argue about the relative merits of alternative methodologies, it makes more sense to recognize that no one methodological approach is inherently superior.

In conclusion, the critical ingredient underlying this cursory discussion of construct validity is the emphasis on *multiple* perspectives based on *multiple* methods. Good research involves the use of: *multiple* indicators of each construct, *multiple* constructs and tests of their a priori relations, *multiple* outcome measures, *multiple* independent/manipulated variables, *multiple* methodological approaches, and *multiple* researchers with different methodological perspectives. In each case, the multiple perspectives provide a foundation for evaluating construct validity based on appropriate patterns of convergence and divergence and for refining measurement instruments, hypotheses, theory, and research agendas.

THEORETICAL SELF-CONCEPT MODEL: CONSTRUCT VALIDATION FROM A MULTIMETHOD PERSPECTIVE

In their classic review of self-concept research, theory, and measurement, Shavelson, Hubner, and Stanton (1976) developed an influential multidimensional, hierarchical model of self-concept. Rather than emphasizing the shortcomings of existing self-concept research, Shavelson et al. contended that "our approach is constructive in that we (a) develop a definition of self-concept from existing definitions, (b) review some steps in validating a construct interpretation of a test score, and (c) apply these steps in examining five popularly used self-concept instruments" (p. 470). An ideal construct definition, they emphasized, should consist of the nomological network containing within-network and between-network components. The within-network portion pertains to specific features of the construct—its components, structure, and attributes and theoretical statements relating these features. Within-network studies test, for example, the dimensionality of self-concept to show that the construct has consistent, distinct multidimensional components (e.g., physical, social, and academic self-concept) using empirical techniques such as factor analysis or MTMM analysis. The between-network portion of the definition locates the construct in a broader conceptual space, establishing a logical, theoretically consistent pattern of relations between measures of self-concept and other constructs. Hence, as early as 1976, self-concept was developed along lines demanding multimethod approaches to support its validity.

Factor analysis played a contentious role in early self-concept research. Historically, most evaluations of the dimensionality self-concept measures were exploratory factor analyses (e.g., see Marsh & Richards, 1988; also see Shavelson et al., 1976;

Wylie, 1989) intended to "discover" the underlying factors based on responses to large pools of items that were not derived from an explicit theoretical model. Because of a combination of poorly designed instruments and reliance on exploratory factor analyses, items typically loaded on multiple factors and observed factors were ambiguous in relation to a priori factors and not replicable in subsequent studies. Marsh and Hocevar (1985) provided one of the early applications of confirmatory factor analysis (CFA) to evaluate first- and higher-order factor self-concept structures in relation to responses to an instrument specifically constructed to test theoretical predictions from the Shavelson et al. (1976) model. The use of multiple indicators to measure a latent construct through the application of CFA and other appropriate statistical analyses is a standard starting point in a multimethod approach to construct validation.

Consistent with this construct validity perspective, Marsh (1993a; Marsh, Craven, & Debus, 1998) argued that theory, measurement, and empirical research are inexorably intertwined so that the neglect of one will undermine the others. From this perspective, Shavelson et al. (1976) provided a theoretical blueprint for constructing self-concept instruments, designing within-network studies of the proposed structure of self-concept, testing between-network hypotheses about relations with other constructs, and eventually rejecting and revising the original theory (Marsh & Hattie, 1996). This chapter examines a number of methods that have been pivotal to our evolving self-concept research program specifically and to the development of this construct as one of the most important constructs in educational psychology. We show— through presentation of multimethods in self-concept research—that multimethod research offers enormous advantages to the researcher that has the potential to substantially enhance the validity of findings within any research program.

Particularly in the last decade, there have been substantial advances in the methodological sophistication of self-concept research that have been stimulated in part by the development of stronger, multidimensional self-concept instruments. Here we briefly summarize some of the methodological approaches that have been particularly effective in answering some of the "big" questions emanating from our research program. Although presented in the context of self-concept research, the issues, challenges, and multimethod solutions should have broad applicability. We also emphasize that new and possibly more appropriate methodological approaches to many of these substantive issues are still evolving as is made clear from the wealth of material included in this book.

MULTITRAIT–MULTIMETHOD (MTMM) DESIGNS AND ANALYSES: EVALUATION OF CONVERGENT AND DIVERGENT VALIDITY

The MTMM design is the essence of multimethod research. It has been used widely in self-concept research to provide evidence of convergent and discriminant validity and is one of the criteria on which self-concept instruments are routinely evaluated (e.g., Byrne, 1996; Marsh & Hattie, 1996; Wylie, 1989). In the development of the MTMM approach, Campbell and Fiske (1959) advocated the assessment of construct validity by measuring multiple traits (T1, T2, etc.) with multiple methods (M1, M2, etc.). In self-concept research, the multiple traits typically represent multiple dimensions of self-concept. The term *multiple methods* was used very broadly by Campbell and Fiske to refer to multiple tests or instruments, multiple methods of assessment, multiple raters, or multiple occasions. Whereas the analytic procedures for evaluating MTMM data are appropriate for different types of multiple methods, the substantive interpretations differ depending on the nature of the multiple methods. Campbell and Fiske's paradigm is, perhaps, the most widely used construct validation design. Although their original guidelines are still widely used to evaluate MTMM data, important problems with their guidelines are well known (see reviews by Marsh, 1989, 1993b; Marsh & Grayson, 1995). More recently, researchers have used CFA approaches to evaluate MTMM data in relation to a prescribed taxonomy of MTMM models specifically designed to evaluate different aspects of convergent and discriminant validity (Marsh, 1989; Marsh & Grayson, 1995; Widaman, 1985). In this section,

we begin with an overview of the CFA approach to MTMM data, describe some traditional applications of MTMM studies in self-concept research, and then explore some extensions to the logic of MTMM design and analyses to demonstrate its flexibility.

CFA Approaches to MTMM Data

Using CFA approaches to MTMM data, researchers can define models that posit a priori trait and method factors and test the ability of such models to fit the data. In the general MTMM model (Marsh, 1989; Marsh & Grayson, 1995; Widaman, 1985); (a) there are at least three traits ($T = 3$) and three methods ($M = 3$); (b) $T \times M$ measured variables are used to infer $T + M$ a priori factors; (c) each measured variable loads on one trait factor and one method factor but is constrained so as not to load on any other factors; (d) correlations among trait factors and among method factors are freely estimated, but correlations between trait and method factors are fixed to be zero; and (e) the uniqueness of each scale is freely estimated but assumed to be uncorrelated with the uniquenesses of other scales. This general model with correlated traits and correlated methods (CFA-CTCM), provides apparently unambiguous interpretation of convergent validity, discriminant validity, and method effects: large trait factor loadings indicate support for convergent validity, large method factor loadings indicate the existence of method effects, and large trait correlations—particularly those approaching 1.0—indicate a lack of discriminant validity.

A taxonomy of models (Marsh, 1989, 1993b; Widaman, 1985) was proposed to evaluate MTMM data that systematically varied the way that traits and methods were represented. Particularly important was the correlated uniqueness model (CFA-CTCU) in which method effects are inferred from correlated uniquenesses among measured variables based on the same method instead of method factors. Correlated uniquenesses reflect the covariation between two measured variables that are measured with the same method after taking into account the effects of the trait factors. The rationale is that correlations among all measures should be explained in terms of the correlated traits so that any residual

covariation between two variables measured with the same method reflects method effects. To the extent that these correlated uniquenesses are consistently large, statistically significant, and interpretable, there is support for method effects in addition to the effects of the traits. From a practical perspective, the CFA-CTCU model almost always results in proper solutions, whereas the traditional CFA-CTCM model typically results in improper solutions. For example, Marsh and Bailey (1991), using 435 MTMM matrices based on real and simulated data, showed that the CFA-CTCM model typically resulted in improper solutions (77% of the time), whereas the CFA-CTCU model nearly always (98% of the time) resulted in proper solutions. Improper solutions for particularly the CFA-CTCM models were more likely when the MTMM design was small (i.e., 3 Trait × 3 Method vs. 5 Trait × 5 Method), when the sample size was small, and when the assumption of unidimensional method effects was violated. From this practical perspective, the complications in comparing the different MTMM models may be of limited relevance because in many applications only the CFA-CTCU model results in a proper solution. Because of the inherent instability of CFA-MTMM models, Marsh and Grayson (1995) recommended that studies should contain at least four traits, at least three methods, and a sample size of at least 250.

CFA Approach to MTMM Studies of Different Self-Concept Instruments

What is the relation between scales based on responses from new and existing self-concept instruments? Historically, self-concept research was plagued by a surfeit of idiosyncratic instruments that hindered communication among researchers and research syntheses. This situation invited the Jingle-Jangle Fallacy (Marsh, 1994) whereby researchers mistakenly assumed that two scales with the same label measured the same construct or that two scales with different labels measured different constructs. The MTMM design in which the multiple methods are the different instruments has been highly effective in addressing this critical issue, as illustrated by two studies summarized in this section.

Examining three academic self-concept traits. In a classic example of this MTMM approach, Marsh (1989, 1993b) examined the relations between three academic self-concept traits (math, verbal, and general school) measured by three different instruments. The 9 scores representing all combinations of the 3 traits and 3 methods were based on multi-item scales, and the three instruments had strong psychometric properties. Consistent with theory and considerable prior research, math and verbal self-concepts were nearly uncorrelated with each other and were substantially correlated with school self-concept. In the CFA MTMM analysis, the trait factor loadings were consistently large (convergent validity), the trait factor correlations were small or moderate (discriminant validity), and the correlated uniqueness (method effects) were small to moderate. Method effects were smaller for the first instrument than the second and particularly the third instrument, whereas trait effects were smaller for the third instrument. Hence the results supported the convergent and discriminant validity of the self-concept responses and provided useful diagnostic information about each of the three instruments.

Examining preadolescent responses to three self-concept instruments. Marsh (1990b) demonstrated the CFA approach to MTMM data based on preadolescent responses to three widely used self-concept instruments. He demonstrated two interesting variations on the typical MTMM design in that not all traits were assessed by all the different measures. First, two instruments contained self-esteem scales, whereas the third did not. Hence, the general self-trait factor was represented by two indicators instead of three. Second, one instrument contained two separate physical scales representing physical appearance and physical ability; one instrument contained only one physical scale apparently representing physical ability; one instrument contained only one physical scale apparently representing physical appearance. An evaluation of alternative MTMM models demonstrated the need to separate physical ability and physical appearance trait factors. The MTMM analyses provided support for convergent validity for all three instruments and for the divergent validity for two of the instruments, but also contributed to understanding the multidimensional structure of self-concept and particularly the physical facet of self-concept.

In summary, the MTMM design in which the multiple methods are different instruments is very useful in the construct validation of new and existing measures. Importantly, this multimethod approach also provides clear tests of jingle-jangle fallacies based on clusters of seemingly similar constructs based on different instruments, different theoretical perspectives, and results from different research teams.

CFA Approach to MTMM Studies of Self–Other Agreement

How well do self-report self-concept ratings by self agree with inferred self-concept ratings based on responses by significant others (e.g., teacher, family member, friend)? This long-standing debate in self-concept research has important theoretical, substantive, and practical implications. Following Shavelson et al. (1976), Marsh (e.g., Marsh, 1990c, 1993a; Marsh & Craven, 1997) stressed that inferred self-concept is a separate construct and should not be confused with self-concept ratings that are necessarily based on some form of self-report. Thus, for example, even if young children have inflated self-perceptions of their competence in relation to perceptions by significant others and objective measures, their self-reports are a valid representation of their self-concept, and inferred self-concepts by significant others that disagree with the self-reports are not. Inferred self-concepts are, however, useful to (a) determine how accurately self-concept can be inferred by external observers, (b) validate interpretations of responses to self-concept instruments, and (c) test theoretical hypotheses. The MTMM design in which the multiple methods are different respondents has been highly effective in addressing this critical issue, as illustrated by the three studies summarized in this section.

A study using teacher and student responses. When multiple dimensions of self-concept are represented by both self-ratings and inferred-ratings,

MTMM analysis provides an important analytical tool for testing the construct validity of the responses (Marsh, 1990b). Summarizing results from 8 MTMM studies, Marsh reported significant agreement between multiple self-concepts inferred by primary school teachers and student responses. Across 7 self-concept scales and 8 studies, the mean convergent validity (self–other agreement on matching scales) was .30. Student–teacher agreement was strongest where the teachers could most easily make relevant observations (math, .37; reading, .37; school, .33; physical ability, .38; and, perhaps, peer relations, .29). Student–teacher agreement was reasonably specific to each area of self-concept. These studies demonstrated that external observers can infer self-concepts in many areas with modest accuracy and support the construct validity of self-concept responses.

A study using teachers and parent responses about student self-concepts. Marsh and Craven (1991) extended this research in a comparison of the abilities of elementary school teachers, mothers, and fathers to infer multiple self-concepts of preadolescent children. Responses by mothers and by fathers were slightly more accurate than those by teachers, but the relative accuracy of teachers, mothers, and fathers in assessing different components of self-concept did not vary much with the specific component of self. All three groups were more accurate in their inferences about physical ability, reading, mathematics, and general school self-concepts than other specific scales or self-esteem self-concept. Self–other agreement in this study tended to be better than had been found in other research, but this was apparently because children and significant others all completed the complete SDQI instrument, whereas earlier studies typically relied on single-item ratings by teachers to represent each self-concept scale.

A study with responses from university students and their significant others. Much stronger results were found in MTMM studies of SDQIII responses in a small Australian study (N = 151; Marsh & O'Niell, 1984) and in a large Canadian study (N = 941; Marsh & Byrne, 1993). In both

studies, university students completed the SDQIII and asked the "person in the world who knew them best" to complete the SDQIII as if they were that person (significant others typically were family members, boy/girlfriends). Self–other agreement was very high (mean r = .57), and four of the scales had self–other correlations over .75. Both the traditional Campbell–Fiske guidelines and CFA models of MTMM data provided strong support for the convergent and discriminant validity of the ratings. Both the size of self–other correlations and the pattern of results across the 13 SDQIII scales were remarkably similar in the two studies. Apparently, self–other agreement was so good in both studies because the participants were older and thus knew themselves better and based their self-responses on more objective, observable criteria; both participants and significant others made their responses on the same well-developed instrument; self–other agreement was for specific characteristics rather than for broad, ambiguous characteristics or an overall self-concept; responses to these specific characteristics were based on multi-item scales rather than single-item responses used in many studies; and the significant others in these studies knew the participants better and in a wider range of contexts than the observers in most research. These results imply that external observers are best able to infer self-concepts when participants are older and responses are based on psychometrically strong instruments designed to measure multiple dimensions of self-concept.

MTMM Extensions: Relations Among Multidimensional Profiles for Different Constructs

How well do profiles of achievements in different school subjects agree with corresponding profiles of academic self-concept? To what extent can self-concept/achievement relations be explained in terms of higher-order constructs (e.g., general achievement and general self-concept)? Marsh (1992) explored these issues in a study of relations between academic self-concept and achievement in 8 school subjects. He adapted the traditional MTMM methodology so that the multiple traits were the eight different school subjects and the multiple

methods referred to the two different constructs (academic achievement and self-concept). Whereas the study obviously had a two-facet design (8 school subjects × 2 constructs), neither of the facets was really a "method" facet. Nevertheless, the logic underlying MTMM provided useful insights. Correlations between matching areas of achievement and self-concept (convergent validities) were substantial for all 8 school subjects (.45 to .70; mean r = .57), whereas correlations between achievement and self-concept in nonmatching subjects were systematically lower (.17 to .54; mean r = .33). These results support convergent and discriminant validity of the self-concept responses and the content specificity of relations between academic self-concept and achievements.

Marsh (1992) then tested alternative CFA models of the 64 correlations between the 8 achievement and 8 self-concept scores. In Model 1 only relations between the 8 matching achievement and self-concept scores were freely estimated; the remaining 56 relations were fixed to be zero. The paths leading from each achievement score to the matching self-concept scale were all substantial (.45 to .70; mean = .57), and the model provided a very good fit to the data (TLI = .96). In Model 2, one higher-order achievement factor and one higher-order self-concept factor was posited, and the relations between the 8 achievement scores and the 8 self-concept scores were represented in terms of the correlation between the pair of higher-order factors. Although the correlation between the higher-order factors was very high (r = .83), the goodness of fit of the model was poor (TLI = .719). In summary, the results provided strong support for the construct (convergent) validity of multiple dimensions of academic self-concept in relation to academic achievement and the content specificity (discriminant validity) of the relations. The findings also demonstrated that the relations between specific (lower-order) self-concept and achievement factors were not represented adequately by higher-order factors.

In an interesting follow-up of this research, Marsh and Yeung (1997) showed that academic self-concepts in each school subject were more predictive of subsequent coursework selection in different school subjects than the corresponding

school grades. Both self-concept and achievement were substantially related to each other and to coursework selection. However, when both self-concept and grades were used to predict coursework selection, self-concept contributed substantially beyond the effect of grades, whereas grades made no significant contribution beyond the contribution of self-concept.

MTMM Extensions: The Multifaceted Nature of Measurement Error

Psychological measurement studies traditionally focus only on internal consistency measures of reliability—the extent of agreement among multiple items designed to infer the same construct. Although items are an important facet of measurement error, there are other sources of measurement error such as time (as in test–retest stability approaches to reliability). Thus, studies that ignore other sources of unreliability provide inflated reliability estimates. Can multiple facets of measurement error be modeled simultaneously within the same study?

Marsh and Grayson (1994a) extended the logic of MTMM analyses to address this issue for responses to 6 self-esteem items collected on 4 occasions (a 6 item × 4 occasion design). This is an interesting extension of the traditional MTMM design in that both facets (items and time) represent what are typically considered to be method facets, and there were no multiple trait factors. Starting with the classical measurement theory and extending the logic of MTMM analyses, Marsh and Grayson (1994a) developed SEM models to partition variance into common factor, time-specific, item-specific, and residual components. They emphasized items and time as sources of measurement error used to assess reliability, but outlined how their approach could easily be expanded to include additional facets (e.g., the use of multiple markers when evaluating essays so that there would be time-specific, item-specific, marker-specific, and residual components of error). Although they considered only a single self-concept factor, their approach could also be extended to include multiple traits like those traditionally emphasized in self-concept research. Whereas Marsh and Grayson

447

developed their models from the perspective of SEM, analogous developments have been incorporated into generalizability theory and its focus on validity generalizability (see Schmidt & Hunter, 1996; Shavelson & Webb, 1991).

MTMM Extensions: The Multiple-Indicator Approach

The Campbell–Fiske guidelines are frequently criticized for being based on correlations among observed variables rather than among latent constructs. Ironically, in the typical CFA MTMM approach, a single scale score—often an average of multiple items—is used to represent each trait-method combination. Marsh (1993b; Marsh & Hocevar, 1988), however, argued that it is stronger to incorporate the multiple indicators explicitly into the MTMM design. When multiple indicators are used to represent each scale, CFAs at the item level result in a MTMM matrix of latent correlations, thereby eliminating many of the objections to the Campbell–Fiske guidelines. Furthermore, CFA MTMM models can be applied to the latent MTMM matrix in much the same way as they are applied to correlations among measured variables. For example, when a first-order factor is defined by multiple indicators of each trait–method combination, trait and method factors can be represented as second-order factors. This multiple indicator approach also provides a rigorous test of the a priori factor structure used to construct scale scores that is typically untested in the traditional MTMM approaches. With this approach, researchers can separate measurement error that is due to lack of agreement among multiple items from residual variance that is unexplained by trait and method effects. Marsh (1993b) demonstrated this multiple indicator approach for 4 self-concept scales measured on each of four occasions (a 4 scale × 4 time MTMM design) using multiple indicators of each of the 16 (4 × 4) trait–method combinations.

Marsh, Richards, Johnson, Roche, and Tremayne (1994) demonstrated an interesting variation of this MTMM approach and the importance of attending to the item level in a study of one new and two existing physical self-concept instruments. They began with a content analysis of items and classified scales from the three instruments as matching, partially matching, or nonmatching. Treating the extent of "matchingness" as having at least three categories was an important concession in that existing measures typically do not consist of parallel scales as is implicit in the traditional MTMM application. They initially conducted a large CFA based on multiple indicators to represent the 11, 5, and 7 a priori factors from the three instruments. They then applied the traditional Campbell–Fiske criteria to their latent MTMM (23 × 23 correlation) matrix resulting from their CFA, emphasizing that inferences were based on latent correlations based on their measurement model relating multiple indicators and latent factors. Based on the a priori predictions derived from their content analysis, the 167 correlations between the 23 latent constructs representing different instruments were classified into 3 a priori categories: 9 convergent validities in which the scales were most closely matched (.79 to .90; median $r = .84$), 6 convergent validities in which the scales were less closely matched (.61 to .73; median $r = .68$), and the remaining 152 correlations among nonmatching constructs (.02 to .74; median $r = .44$). In support of construct validity—and the usefulness of the two categories of matchingness—correlations in the first category were systematically larger than those in the second category. There was also good support for discriminant validity in that the remaining 152 correlations were smaller than convergent validities.

Summary of MTMM Studies

Following from Campbell and Fiske (1959), the MTMM design is the most widely applied paradigm to study the effects of multiple methods and has been particularly important in self-concept research. Here we have illustrated classic examples of the MTMM design (methods as multiple instruments or multiple raters), but also demonstrated its flexibility with a variety of applications that do not fit the standard MTMM paradigm. These include applications in which there are two trait facets (parallel achievement test scores and self-concept factors) but no method facets, where there are two or more

facets of measurement error (time, items) but no multiple trait factors, and analyses that begin with multiple indicators of each trait–method combination. Taken together, these applications demonstrate why the logic underlying the MTMM design is central to the multimethod approach.

CROSS-CULTURAL GENERALIZABILITY: NATIONALITIES AS THE MULTIPLE METHODS

To what extent do psychometric properties of self-concept responses and theoretical predictions from self-concept theory generalize across different cultures and nationalities? Cross-cultural comparisons provide researchers with a valuable, heuristic basis to test the external validity and generalizability of their measures, theories, and models. In their influential overview of cross-cultural research, Segall, Lonner, and Berry (1998) stated that cross-cultural research's three complementary goals were "to transport and test our current psychological knowledge and perspectives by using them in other cultures; to explore and discover new aspects of the phenomenon being studied in local cultural terms; and to integrate what has been learned from these first two approaches in order to generate more nearly universal psychology, one that has pan-human validity" (p. 1102) From this perspective cross-cultural research is clearly an important application of multimethod research in which different cultures and nationalities constitute the multiple methods. Here we illustrate two applications of this cross-cultural approach from our self-concept research, although we also present other applications later in the chapter.

Cross-Cultural Evaluations of Self-Concept Instruments

Strong tests of the cross-cultural generalizability of responses to self-concept instruments are possible when responses to the same instrument are collected in different cultures or countries. Critical design features are the translation of items from the original language into a different language and ensuring that the samples from different countries are appropriately comparable. When parallel data from multiple countries are available, Byrne (2003) described the application of multigroup CFA tests of factorial invariance that can be used to evaluate the cross-cultural generalizability of self-concept instruments. In an application of this approach, Marsh, Tomás-Marco, and Asci (2003) demonstrated the appropriateness of the Physical Self Description Questionnaire (PSDQ) for Spanish and Turkish students, as well as the Australian students for whom it was originally developed.

Extending this approach, Tomás-Marco, González-Romá, and Marsh (2003) expanded this multisample CFA approach to incorporate covariance and mean structure in a comparison of matched responses (in terms of gender and age) by Spanish and Australian high school students. With the inclusion of the mean structure, they showed how this approach was largely analogous to but, perhaps, more flexible than traditional item response theory approaches to this problem. The model of strict factor invariance—invariance of item factor loadings, intercepts, and uniquenesses—was supported. Because the PSDQ items did not show differential item functioning across the Spanish and Australian versions, the observed average scale scores and scale variances could be meaningfully compared across groups. A failure of this model, however, would have suggested that items had different meaning in each country and, perhaps, would have invalidated these inference-based comparisons based on latent factors or scale scores (also see discussion by Marsh & Grayson, 1994b, about invariance responses by the same group over time, rather than different groups).

Cross-Cultural Evaluations of Theoretical Models: The Internal–External Frame of Reference

The internal–external frame of reference model describes a seemingly paradoxical pattern of relations between math and verbal self-concepts and corresponding measures of achievement (see Marsh, 1986, 1990c, 1993a; Marsh, Byrne, & Shavelson, 1988; Marsh & Hau, 2003; Marsh, Kong, & Hau, 2001) and why math and verbal self-concepts are

almost uncorrelated, even though corresponding areas of academic achievement are substantially correlated (typically .5 to .8, depending on how achievement is measured). According to this model, academic self-concept in a particular school subject is formed in relation to two comparison processes or frames of reference. The first is the *external* (normative) reference in which students compare their self-perceived performances in a particular school subject with the perceived performances of other students in the same school subject. It predicts, not surprisingly, that good math skills lead to higher math self-concepts and that good verbal skills lead to higher verbal self-concepts. The second is an *internal* (ipsative-like) reference in which students compare their own performance in one particular school subject with their own performances in other school subjects. According to this process, good math skills should lead to *lower* verbal self-concepts (once the positive effects of good verbal skills are controlled) and good verbal skills should lead to lower math self-concept.

In a particularly strong test of the cross-cultural generalizability of predictions from this model, Marsh and Hau (2004) evaluated responses from nationally representative samples of 15-year-old students from 26 countries who completed common achievement tests and self-concept surveys. In support of a priori predictions, (a) math and verbal achievements were highly correlated, whereas math and verbal self-concepts were nearly uncorrelated; and (b) math and verbal achievements each had positive effects on the matching self-concept domain, but negative effects on nonmatching domains (e.g., verbal achievement had a positive effect on verbal self-concept but a negative effect on math self-concept). Very demanding tests of invariance that required all four path coefficients relating the two achievement test scores to the corresponding self-concept measures to be the same in each of the 26 countries provided a good fit to the data. Because there was such good support for predictions based on the internal–external frame of reference model and such good support for the generalizability of these results across the 26 countries, the results clearly supported the construct validity of the model and its cross-cultural generalizability.

OTHER APPROACHES USED IN A MULTIMETHOD PERSPECTIVE TO SELF-CONCEPT RESEARCH

Multicohort–Multioccasion Designs to Cross-Validate Developmental Trends

Marsh (1998; also see Baltes & Nesselroade, 1979) argued that multicohort–multioccasion designs provide a stronger basis for assessing developmental self-concept differences than a typical cross-sectional methodology (comparisons of different age cohorts collected on a single occasion) or a true longitudinal methodology (comparisons of responses by a single age cohort collected on multiple occasions). In particular, the juxtaposition of the age effects based on the (cross-sectional) age cohort and the true longitudinal comparisons based on multiple occasions within each age cohort provide an important multimethod approach to cross-validating interpretations based on these two alternative methods of evaluating developmental trends. Marsh, Craven, and Debus (1998) used a multicohort–multioccasion design with two waves of data collected 1 year apart with the same children in each of three age cohorts. The contrast between cross-sectional and true longitudinal comparisons provided a much stronger basis for evaluating age-related differences in reliability, stability over time, dimensionality, and gender differences.

In another application of this approach, Marsh (1998) evaluated age and gender effects in 10 physical self-concept scales for elite athletes and nonathletes, based on responses from four high-school-age cohorts who each completed the same instrument four times during a 2-year period. Across all 10 physical self-concepts there were substantial differences because of group (athletes > nonathletes), gender (males > females), and gender × group interactions (gender differences smaller for athletes than nonathletes). There were no significant effects of age cohort (year in school) and only very small effects of occasions. Thus longitudinal and cross-sectional comparisons were in agreement showing that mean levels of physical self-concept were stable over this potentially volatile adolescent period and that this stability generalized over gender, age, and the athlete groups. Wen, Marsh, and Hau (2003)

extended the analysis of this data to incorporate a growth modeling approach that provided many advantages in assessing individual patterns of growth as well as mean differences averaged across all individuals within a cohort (e.g., age cohorts) or groups (e.g., gender or athletic groups).

Anticipating subsequent emphases on latent growth modeling and the analysis of mean structures, Marsh and Grayson (1994b) developed procedures to evaluate invariance of mean structures at the item level over time. Based on five waves of data collected over an 8-year period, they showed that their approach was more flexible than the traditional repeated measures approach. They also found, however, a potential lack of invariance at the item intercept level over time, suggesting that the meaning of some items may have changed over this early-adolescent to late-adolescent period and posing a threat to the interpretation of self-concept latent means over time. Based on these results they proposed a hierarchy of invariances and what substantive interpretations were justified at different levels of invariance. Although their focus was on longitudinal data, it could easily be extended to a multicohort–multioccasion design that combined cross-sectional and longitudinal approaches. This combined approach could address, for example, the issue of whether noninvariance in item intercepts reflected a developmental shift in the interpretations of the items or cohort differences in the way adolescents interpret item wording.

Studies summarized in this section demonstrate the usefulness of the multicohort–multioccasion design for cross-validating interpretations based on cross-sectional and longitudinal methodologies. It is important to emphasize, however, that this type of multimethod data opens up rich possibilities for evaluating a wide range of substantive developmental issues using a variety of analytic techniques (e.g., Bijleveld & van der Kamp, 1998; Little, Schnabel, & Baumert, 2000).

Reciprocal Effects Model: Causal Ordering of Academic Self-Concept and Achievement

A critical question in self-concept research is the causal ordering of academic self-concept and achievement. Self-concept researchers (e.g., Byrne, 1996; Marsh, 1990c, 1993a; Marsh, Byrne, & Yeung, 1999) have attempted to resolve the theoretical "chicken–egg" debate about whether academic self-concept "causes" academic achievement or achievement "causes" academic self-concept. Byrne (1996) noted that much of the interest in the self-concept–achievement relation stemmed from the belief that academic self-concept has motivational properties that affect subsequent academic achievement. Calsyn and Kenny (1977) contrasted self-enhancement (self-concept causes–achievement) and skill development (achievement causes self-concept) models of the self-concept–achievement relation. Largely because of limitations in statistical techniques used prior to the 1980s to test causal models, researchers typically argued for "either–or" conclusions. In critiques of this research, Marsh (1990a, 1990c, 1993a; also see Marsh et al., 1999) argued that much of this research was methodologically unsound and inconsistent with the academic self-concept theory. He emphasized that it was widely accepted that prior academic achievement was one determinant of academic self-concept so that the critical question was whether there also existed a causal link from prior academic self-concept to subsequent achievement. The statistical significance and size of this path was of critical importance whether or not it was larger than the path from prior academic achievement to subsequent academic self-concept. Marsh further argued that a more realistic compromise between the self-enhancement and skill-development models was a "reciprocal effects model" in which prior self-concept affects subsequent achievement and prior achievement affects subsequent self-concept.

Marsh (1990a) tested the causal ordering of academic self-concept and academic achievement with four waves of data (last 3 years of high school and 1 year after high school graduation) based on standardized test scores, school grades, and academic self-concept. He found support for reciprocal effects in which the largest paths were from prior academic self-concept to subsequent school grades. In a recent review of research in this area, Marsh et al. (1999) summarized clear support for a reciprocal effects model from a range of different studies.

Recent research demonstrated that this support for the reciprocal effects model generalized to different cultural–national settings in a large nationally representative sample of Hong Kong students (Marsh, Hau, & Kong, 2002) and large samples of East and West German students at the time of the fall of the Berlin Wall (Marsh, Köller, & Baumert, 2001).

Marsh et al. (1999) concluded that there was insufficient research evaluating developmental trends in causal modeling research. To address this issue, Guay, Marsh, and Boivin (2003) extended this research to evaluate developmental trends in a multicohort–multioccasion design for responses by students in Grades 2, 3, and 4 (i.e., three age cohorts, each with three measurement occasions— see discussion of multicohort–multioccasion designs). The structural equation model for the total sample supported a reciprocal effects model for the first two waves of data (paths leading from prior self-concept to subsequent achievement and from prior achievement to subsequent self-concept) and a self-enhancement effect (paths leading from prior self-concept to subsequent achievement) between the second and the third waves. This pattern was replicated in tests of the invariance of the structural equation model across the three age cohorts, demonstrating support for the generalizability of the reciprocal effects models across these preadolescent ages. In addition to critical substantive implications, this research demonstrated the strength of a multimethod approach in disentangling the reciprocal effects of different constructs.

Multilevel Analysis to Evaluate Cross-Level Relations in the Big-Fish-Little-Pond Effect (BFLPE)

Does attending schools with exceptionally bright students increase or decrease academic self-concept? Do the effects of these academically selective schools vary for students differing in academic ability? In this section we describe multilevel modeling approaches to evaluate these issues. In most studies conducted in school settings, individual student characteristics and those associated with groups (day-care centers, classrooms, schools, etc.) are confounded because groups are typically not established according to random

assignment. Students within the same group are typically more similar to other students in the same group than they are to students in other groups. Even when students are initially assigned at random, they tend to become more similar to each other over time. Furthermore, the apparently same variable may have a very different meaning when measured at different levels. For example, Marsh's (1987, 1991; Marsh, Chessor, Craven, & Roche, 1995; Marsh & Parker, 1984) research into the BFLPE research suggests that a measure of ability at the student level provides an indicator of a student attribute, whereas school-average ability at the school level becomes a proxy measure of a school's normative environment. Thus, the average ability of a school has an effect on student self-concept above and beyond the effect of the individual student's ability. Multilevel modeling is designed to resolve the confounding of these two effects by facilitating a decomposition of any observed relationship among variables, such as self-concept and ability, into separate within-school and between-school components (see Goldstein, 1995; Raudenbush & Bryk, 2002; Snijders & Bosker, 1999).

In the theoretical model underlying the BFLPE (Marsh & Parker, 1984), it is hypothesized that students compare their own academic ability with the academic abilities of their peers and use this social comparison impression as one basis for forming their own academic self-concept. A negative BFLPE occurs when equally able students have lower academic self-concepts when they compare themselves to more-able classmates, and higher academic self-concepts when they compare themselves with less-able classmates. In support of this theoretical model, Marsh and Craven (2003) summarized results from a diverse range of studies using different samples and methodological approaches showing that (a) educationally disadvantaged students have higher academic self-concepts in special education classes than in regular mixed-ability (mainstreamed) classes, whereas (b) academically gifted students have higher academic self-concepts in regular, mixed-ability classes than in specialized education settings for gifted students. Hence, academic achievement measured at the individual child level has a positive effect on academic self-concept (i.e.,

one's own high levels of individual achievement lead to high self-concept), whereas the academic achievement measured at the group level has a negative effect (i.e., high average school achievement leads to low self-concept).

Marsh, Köller, and Baumert (2001) evaluated predictions from the BFLPE for East and West German students at the time of the fall of the Berlin Wall. Multilevel longitudinal data (2,778 students, 161 classes) from large cohorts of seventh-grade East and West German students were collected at the start of the reunification of the school systems. Multilevel modeling demonstrated a negative BFLPE; attending classes where class-average achievement was higher led to lower academic self-concepts. West German students had attended schools that were highly stratified in relation to ability before and after the reunification, whereas East German students first attended selective schools after the reunification. Consistent with theoretical predictions based on this difference, the negative BFLPE—the negative effect of class-average achievement—was more negative in West German schools at the start of the reunification. This difference, however, was smaller by the middle of the year and had disappeared by the end of the first postreunification school year. Whereas East and West German results both supported the negative BFLPE, their differences supported theoretical predictions, extended theory, and demonstrated how changes in school policy influence the formation of academic self-concept.

Marsh, Kong, and Hau (2000) conducted longitudinal multilevel path models (7,997 students, 44 high schools, 4 years) to evaluate the effects of school-average achievement and perceived school status on academic self-concept in Hong Kong. Consistent with a priori predictions based on the BFLPE, higher school-average achievements led to lower academic self-concepts (contrast effects) and to higher perceived school status that had a counterbalancing positive effect on self-concept (reflected glory, assimilation effects). Hence, attending a school where school-average achievement was high simultaneously resulted in a more demanding basis of comparison for one's own accomplishments (the stronger, negative contrast effect) and a source of pride (the

weaker, positive reflected glory effect). In support of the typically negative effect of school-average ability, the net effect of these two counterbalancing processes (a larger negative contrast effect and a smaller positive assimilation effect) was negative.

Marsh and Hau (2003) conducted the most comprehensive cross-cultural study of the BFLPE, based on nationally representative samples of approximately 4,000, 15-year-olds from each of 26 countries (103,558 students, 3,848 schools, 26 countries), who completed the same self-concept instrument and achievement tests. Consistent with the BFLPE, the effects of school-average achievement were negative in all 26 countries ($M = -.20$, $SD = .08$). Results of their three-level multilevel model (Level 1 = students, Level 2 = schools, Level 3 = country) indicated that the effects of individual achievement were positive (linear term = .384, quadratic term = .069), whereas the effects of school-average achievement—the BFLPE—were negative (−.206). The interaction between individual student achievement and school-average achievement was not significant, indicating that the negative effect of school-average achievement was consistent across the range of student achievement levels. Variation in the school-average achievement effect (.007) was small, but highly significant— indicating that there was statistically significant variation from country to country in the size of the BFLPE. In separate analyses of each of the 26 countries, the BFLPE was significantly negative in 24 of 26 countries (−.02 to −.36). In each of the 26 countries, the effect of individual achievement on academic self-concept was significantly positive (.14 to .63; $M = .38$, $SD = .11$). The averages across results from the separate two-level models for each of the 26 countries agreed closely with those from the three-level analyses for the total group. Support for the generalizability of the BFLPE across countries suggested that the social comparison processes leading to the BFLPE may approach what Segall et al. (1998, p. 1102) refer to as a "nearly universal psychology, one that has pan-human validity"—one goal of cross-cultural research.

Multilevel modeling demonstrated here is important because the juxtaposition between the

effects of individual achievement and class- or school-average achievement is inherently a multilevel problem so that any attempt to model the data at a single level is likely to cause problems. Whereas multilevel modeling is clearly relevant for BFLPE studies, it is also relevant in nearly all research in which individuals are clustered into classes (or other groups). Indeed, it can be argued that nearly all educational psychology research and psychological research more generally could benefit by taking a multilevel perspective, recognizing that social phenomena mostly occur in groups that are not formed randomly and that group members tend to become more similar as they interact with each other. By simultaneously considering data from multiple levels, the researcher opens up new substantive issues related to group-level variables and their interaction with individual-level variables that are typically ignored in studies of individuals.

SOME BROADER PERSPECTIVES OF THE MULTIMETHOD APPROACH

In this final section we discuss three more expansive views of the multimethod approach: Complementary qualitative methods, multiple research teams, and meta-analysis. These broader perspectives point to ways to move beyond the use of multiple quantitative approaches discussed in this volume to other ways of designing multimethod research.

Complementary Qualitative Methods

Thus far we have described diverse quantitative methods that have been highly effective in addressing key issues relevant to the self-concept and which have been critical to the conduct of our overall research program. However, we have not yet addressed the potentially illuminating role of qualitative methods in combination with quantitative research. We argue that qualitative methods provide complementary, nonoverlapping advantages beyond those that quantitative methods can provide (and vice versa). Tracey, Marsh, and Craven (2003) demonstrate this complementarity in illuminating, conceptualizing, extending, and clarifying quantita-

tive findings in research into inclusion and segregation of students with mild intellectual disabilities. Moreover, through follow-up qualitative work it was possible to refine existing theory and inform current practices relevant to student intellectual disabilities.

Tracey et al. (2003) contrasted two competing perspectives—labeling theory and the BFLPE based on social comparison theory—on the impacts of separation from or inclusion in regular classes. Labeling theory suggests that placing these students in special classes with other students with disabilities will lead to lower self-concepts, whereas the BFLPE (see earlier discussion) predicts that this same placement will enhance the self-concepts of students with disabilities. Tracey et al. (2003) evaluated the impact of educational placement in regular classes and special education classes on the self-concepts, using a combination of cross-sectional and longitudinal studies based on both quantitative and qualitative data. Their path models showed that students with mild intellectual disability placed in a special class reported significantly higher peer relationships, reading, mathematics, general school, and general self-concept factors than students with mild intellectual disability placed in regular classes. Whereas the negative effect of inclusion into regular classes was predicted a priori for the academic and self-esteem self-concept scales, the negative effect on peer self-concepts was, perhaps, unexpected. Taken together, these findings supported the BFLPE and contradicted labeling theory (and current policy practice in many countries).

In the qualitative component of this research, interviews were conducted with students from both regular and special classes who had a mild intellectual disability. The aim of the qualitative phase was to determine key themes that underpinned the quantitative findings and to explore how, through children's eyes, the BFLPE was "played out" in their lives. Whereas the quantitative findings showed *that* BFLPEs were relevant to students with mild intellectual disabilities, the aim of the qualitative data was to show *how* BFLPEs were manifested. Through a process of "pattern coding" (Miles & Huberman,

1994), four broad themes or constructs emerged. Particularly relevant was the theme of *peer relationships*. Interestingly, students in regular and special classes both experienced negative peer relationships, but the sources of those difficulties were different. Students in regular classes reported negative social interactions with students within their own class as well as those from other classes, whereas students in special classes reported negative interactions with students from other classes. These data suggested that students with mild intellectual disability in special classes had their own class as a safe haven, whereas students with mild intellectual disability in regular classes did not feel acceptance in any context.

These qualitative findings supported quantitative findings, but the qualitative data provided insights not gained through the quantitative phase. In particular, the qualitative results offered an explanation of why placement in regular classes (inclusion) had negative effects on peer self-concept and informed the nature of stigmatization in regular and special-class settings. More generally, the study demonstrates how multimethod research in the form of qualitative–quantitative synergies can contribute insights to interpretation that might not be possible through the application of either research methodology in isolation.

Multiple Research Teams as Multiple Methods

Particularly in the heyday of all-encompassing learning theories, it was common for competing research teams to challenge each other's work. Studies by one team would be critiqued, reanalyzed, replicated, or extended by another research team to evaluate predictions based on competing theoretical perspectives. This multimethod approach has also been evident in our self-concept research, in which colleagues have challenged our conclusions or we challenged the conclusions of others: Marsh and Yeung's (2001) reanalysis of Bong's earlier research challenged her interpretation of the internal–external frame of reference model; Marsh, Byrne, and Shavelson's (1988) reanalysis of Byrne and Shavelson's research clarified the multidimensional nature of self-concept; Marsh, Walker, and Debus

(1991) demonstrated how frame of reference has different effects on self-concept and self-efficacy in response to Skaalvik's failure to replicate the internal–external frame of reference effect; Marsh, Roche, Pajares, and Miller (1997) clarified methodological issues in Pajares' self-efficacy research; Marsh, Plucker, and Stocking's (2001) reanalysis of Plucker's earlier research demonstrated that the SDQII worked well with gifted students; Marsh and Craven (1998) pointed out methodological problems and logical inconsistencies in Gross's rebuttal of the BFLPE for gifted students; Marsh (1993c) began an ongoing debate and dialogue with Pelham about the role of importance, certainty, and ideals in moderating or mediating relations between specific components of self-concept and global measures of self-esteem; Marsh and Rowe's (1996) reanalysis of Rowe's earlier research clarified the effects of single-sex versus coeducational math classes; and Marsh, Byrne, and Yeung's (1999) reanalysis of Byrne's classic causal-ordering study established new criteria for this research paradigm. Interestingly, most of these reanalyses, critiques, extensions, and ongoing dialogues involved such constructive interaction between research teams that initial differences were substantially resolved in subsequent publications, frequently co-authored by the so-called competing researchers. Although apparently less common, constructive dialogues and even rebuttals between different researchers are a potentially important application of the multimethod perspective in which the multiple methods are the researchers themselves.

Using Meta-Analysis to Compare and Integrate Multimethod Research

A critical challenge in the systematic evaluation of multimethod research is how to compare and integrate results from multiple studies that use different outcome measures, different research designs, different samples, different methodologies, and different statistical analyses. An important limitation to the multimethod approach is that an individual study or even a research program is typically too narrow in focus to take full advantage of the multimethod approach. Hence, the potential value of the

multimethod approach may require the researchers to compare and integrate the results from a large number of different studies. Although not traditionally viewed as a multimethod analysis, meta-analysis provides a framework for this task. Whereas the focus of meta-analysis historically has been on the synthesis of research, more recent research has focused on the identification of different methodological aspects of research that have a substantial influence on the results. Thus, for example, there is often an overly simplistic attempt to reduce the findings to a single outcome variable per study. Although greatly simplifying the statistical analyses, this approach ignores potentially important differences associated with specific outcomes. Becker (2000) reviewed different approaches to this problem (e.g., treating each outcome as independent, combining outcomes into a single score, creating independent data sets), but recommended new approaches that require researchers to model the dependency of multiple outcomes using multivariate statistical techniques such as the multilevel modeling approach outlined by Raudenbush and Bryk (2002). In summary, meta-analysis offers the multimethod analyst access to a wide variety of different studies that span an entire research literature rather than the limited number of multiple methods that can be incorporated into a single study.

CONCLUSION

Multimethod research is a systematic, natural extension of the construct validity approach that has been an explicit basis of our self-concept research program and is implicit in most psychological research. Much of the logic from this multimethod perspective is derived from Campbell and Fiske's heuristic development of MTMM analyses and the many advances in this approach to construct validation. The essence of the construct validity approach is to look for areas of convergence and nonconvergence in measures of the same construct across multiple methods. At the microlevel, the multiple "methods" might be different items used to infer the same latent construct. At an intermediate level of abstraction, the multiple methods might be different instruments designed to measure parallel or overlapping constructs or responses from different types of informants making self-ratings about themselves or ratings of others. At a higher level of abstraction the multiple methods might be different constructs that are posited to be related or fundamentally different research methodologies (e.g., qualitative and quantitative studies). In our research we have expanded this notion of multiple perspectives to include multilevel modeling to evaluate the extent of generalizability, for example, across different schools and across whole countries. We have also viewed cross-cultural research as another application of multimethod research in which the multiple nationalities or cultures are seen as multiple methods to test the generalizability of our measures, empirical results, and theoretical predictions. Whereas this diversity of multimethod applications is not easily encapsulated into a neat multimethod taxonomy, the essence of the approach is to interrogate psychological research findings from multiple perspectives—multiple indicators, multiple outcomes, multiple independent variables, multiple methodologies, multiple analytical approaches, and multiple settings. The extent to which these multiple perspectives are incorporated into research designs impacts substantially on the construct validity of the results and the confidence with which conclusions can be generalized.

CHAPTER 31

THE FINALE: TAKE-HOME MESSAGES FROM THE EDITORS

Ed Diener and Michael Eid

The chapters in this volume have exceeded our expectations—we have learned much and hope that readers have, too. The chapters on specific domains of psychology are excellent, and the chapters on specific methods are superb. Further, the articles devoted to new statistical approaches for measurement are cutting edge and can help most researchers catch up with the field. In what follows, we outline several of the major points we take from this volume.

MULTIPLE OPERATIONS SHOULD REIGN

A message in several chapters of this volume is that investigators often have become discouraged with using multiple methods because such measures often do not converge, with measures of the same constructs correlating at low levels with each other and varying in different patterns with external variables. Burns and Haynes (chap. 27, this volume) found that many measures contain more source than trait variance. Indeed, Roberts et al. (chap. 22, this volume) find the lack of convergence between measures to be so discouraging that they suggest that multiple measures have been oversold, and that perhaps we do not need to use them. If one examines the multimeasure studies that exist in the literature, it is clear that measures of the same constructs based on different methods often correlate at disappointing levels. Only when measures depend on the same method do they sometimes correlate at moderate to strong levels. Why, then, do we persist in our insistence that multiple measures are crucial for scientific advances?

One reason, discussed later, for the centrality of multiple measures in our thinking is that every measurement method, even the best ones, possesses substantial shortcomings and limitations. Thus, by using different methods with different limitations, researchers can eliminate specific artifacts from their conclusions because the artifacts are unlikely to influence all the diverse measures they use. Another reason to use multiple measures is that one can better estimate the underlying construct by using several measures, each of which is influenced by that construct but also by other factors as well. For example, if we measure altruism by asking people to donate their plasma to the blood drive, we have a measure that is influenced by altruism, but also influenced by curiosity and interest in medicine, by having a hemophiliac in one's family, and by one's past medical experiences. If, however, we obtain several additional and different measures of altruism, such as helping a person who has dropped her books, donating money to a child welfare fund, and volunteering to work on a Walkathon to collect money for AIDS research, we hope that this aggregate of measures represents the latent construct of altruism. Ahadi and Diener (1989) made this point over a decade ago—that no single behavior ever represents the influence of a single construct—and Schmitt (chap. 2, this volume) forcefully makes this point again.

But what of the fear that our measures will not converge and may even show different patterns with external variables? Our answer is that this can be discouraging at first, but it can be an excellent aid to scientific insight. In this situation we will

realize that our concept might be overly simple, or that our measures might be contaminated. Lack of convergence can be disheartening at first, but can represent a wonderful opportunity for scientific progress. Let us examine several examples. Imagine that we measure well-being through people's global reports of their happiness, as well as through the reports of friends, and with an experience-sampling measure in which people report their moods at random moments over 2 weeks. Imagine, too, that we want to determine whether our respondents are happier if they obtain more physical exercise. The outcomes of this study might discourage the investigator because the three types of measures correlate with each other only .30, and only the experience-sampling measure shows a correlation with exercise. At this point the researcher is likely to wish that two of the measures would just disappear. But what we have here is an opportunity to understand something about the well-being measures, as well as the way in which exercise might influence well-being. For example, perhaps exercise influences mood in the short term, but not long term, and the informant and global reports are not sensitive enough to pick up this effect. However, the informant reports might correlate more highly with job performance than the other two measures because they represent how happy the person appears to others. Finally, the global reports of happiness might represent a person's self-concept to a greater degree than the other two measures, and therefore be able to best predict certain long-term choices the person makes. It might take the investigator several more studies to understand this pattern, but think what has been gained—the realization and understanding that happiness is not a monolithic concept, and that different measures capture specific aspects of it.

Let us examine yet another example, this one on heritability. Imagine a researcher who locates a large number of young adult twins who were separated at birth, with both monozygotic and dizygotic twins in the sample. Also suppose that the researcher would like to estimate the heritability of extraversion and does so by administering to all twins a self-report extraversion questionnaire. However, if a heritability of .45 is found for the trait, based on

the relative size of correlations for the two types of twins, what does the coefficient mean? It could be that extraversion is heritable at .45, but this coefficient could be contaminated by the heritability of response predispositions such as conformity, number-use tendencies such as avoiding extreme answers, or inherited dispositions related to memory recall. Without other types of extraversion measures, it is impossible to conclude much about the heritability of extraversion per se. Adding other measurement methods such as informant reports of extraversion (Eid, Riemann, Angleitner, & Borkenau, 2003) can help the researcher—either by converging with the self-report measures, and thus giving strength to the conclusions, or by diverging and thereby showing that the measures reflect influences in addition to extraversion per se. If researchers begin to take a longer-term perspective on their research beyond the findings of single studies, it is evident that the use of multiple measures is likely to enormously aid scientific understanding.

As Cronbach (1995, p. 145) stressed, method variance is not "the serpent in the psychologist's Eden" but a topic of constructive and theory-driven research. The explanation of method effects can enhance validity by suppressing method-specific variance and by detecting moderator variables that might at least guarantee the validity of the scale for a subgroup of individuals. Eid, Schneider, and Schwenkmezger (1999) have shown how the knowledge of the causes of method effects can be used to pinpoint suppressor variables in a multi-method study to enhance validity. They repeatedly assessed mood states and the perceived deviation of mood states from the habitual mood level (Do you feel better or worse than you generally feel?) after the same lecture. Moreover, they asked individuals to judge their general mood level. They found a high but imperfect correlation between two methods measuring the general mood level (mean of repeatedly mood states versus judgments of one's general mood). One possible explanation of this imperfect association was the hypothesis that the situation after a lecture was not representative for one's life, and that therefore the aggregated states were composed of two parts—one being representative for one's life in general and one indicating a

systematic deviation of one's mood after the lecture from one's general mood level. Indeed, there was stability in the deviation scores, showing that individuals had a tendency to generally feel better or worse after the same lecture. This general deviation variable was uncorrelated with the global trait assessment but highly correlated with the aggregated states. This indicates that the general mood deviation score can be used as a suppressor variable to suppress the variance in the aggregated state scores that was atypical for one's life in general and only typical for the lecture situation. Consequently, using this suppressor variable significantly increased the convergent validity coefficient for the two methods measuring a mood trait (aggregated states versus a global judgment). Hence, suppressing method-specific variance can help to establish higher convergent validity.

A deeper understanding of method effects can also result in the conclusion that there might be convergent validity for some subgroups but not for others (differential convergent validity). Miller and Cardy (2000), for example, found higher convergence of self- and other reported performance appraisals for low self-monitors than for high self-monitors. Again, theoretical predictions from theories of self-monitoring could enhance our understanding of method effects and could be used to detect differential validity.

RESEARCHERS NEED TO LEARN ABOUT THE NEW METHODS

In this volume a number of relatively new methods are described, such as computer-based testing and the experience-sampling method. Other methodologies such as the implicit reaction time method of assessing memory network relationships and the use of the Web to collect data are promising as well. We would like to encourage researchers to continue to scan the horizon for new methods that they can use in their studies. It is not that we should adopt new methods uncritically, or that new methods are necessarily superior. However, researchers do run a danger when they get locked into the use of a single method and use it repeatedly over years of study. The findings become restricted to a single paradigm and type of measure, and often researchers cannot see the broader picture. Thus, examining and trying new methods goes along with the point we made earlier—it is important to use more than one measurement method—and sometimes it is worth trying novel methods.

ALL MEASURES HAVE SHORTCOMINGS

Part of the motivation to use multiple methods comes when a researcher realizes that his or her measures are imperfect. At times researchers do not think about their measures, but simply take them on faith in an unquestioning way because they have face validity and other researchers use the same methods. At other times scientists use only one method because they adopt an ideology that asserts that a particular methodology is superior to all the others. Both are shortsighted beliefs because they fail to recognize that each and every type of measure has limitations.

Certain ideologies claim that measures within their tradition are superior to other types of measures, which are flawed. For example, many behaviorists claimed that behavioral observation was the only method for understanding psychological phenomena, and other types of measures such as self-reports, biological assays, or projective techniques were badly flawed. Similarly, some researchers with a reductionistic worldview claim that biological measures, for example brain imaging and measures of hormones, are the only measures that are likely to advance science. These views are dangerous for several reasons. First, they fail to recognize that the biological and behavioral methods, although they might be more objective in some ways, have limitations and shortcomings. Measures of hormones, for example, can be influenced by extraneous factors such as time of day and the medications a participant is ingesting, and often the hormones do not map directly onto psychological constructs. Furthermore, the biological measures are given meaning in reference to other measures, such as self-reports or behavioral observations. When one delves into any biological measure, it becomes evident that the meaning of the measure can be complex and can be confounded by a host of artifacts.

Some scientists believe that only observable physical behavior should be studied. But behavioral observations can be contaminated by reactivity and by the perceptions of the coders. Furthermore, the behavior being coded will represent only one example of the construct in question and is likely to be influenced by factors other than the underlying construct. Thus, even though biological and behavioral observation measures can be valuable in our understanding, and certainly ought to be included in more investigations, these measures have flaws just as do self-reports, informant reports, and other "softer" measures.

SELF-REPORT METHODS NEED TO BE SUPPLEMENTED WITH OTHER METHODS

Some fields in the behavioral sciences rely almost exclusively on global self-report surveys of respondents. Skeptics point to instances where self-report instruments have gone wrong and decry the numerous studies in which a bevy of self-report scales are merely correlated with one another. The proponents of the self-report technique cite the validity of self-report measures in some studies, as well as the virtue that people themselves often know information that cannot be obtained by other methods. Both views are correct—the measures are flawed and also have utility—meaning that self-report measures should be used in many studies, but must be supplemented with other types of measures.

An example of self-reports of grades, weight, and height, from a study conducted in Ed Diener's laboratory by Frank Fujita and Heidi Smith, is illustrative of the strengths and weaknesses of the method. We asked a group of 222 undergraduate respondents for their height in inches, their weight in pounds, and their grade-point averages at the university. They did not know that we would also acquire external objective measures of these variables—from a measuring tape, a balance scale, and their college transcripts—and correlate the two types of measures. How accurate were people? Respondents overestimated their height by 1.36 inches on average and their grades by .58 points on a 4.0 scale and underestimated their weight by 6.5 pounds. The correlations between the self-reported score and the objective indicators were extremely high for height, $r = .96$, and weight, $r = .94$, and moderate for grades, $r = .41$. Note that although the weight correlation is extremely high, most people underestimated their weight. Furthermore, the self-reported weight, despite its accuracy at the level of the cross-person correlation, was far off the mark for some subjects. Eight respondents out of the 146 for whom we had objective weight data underestimated their weight by more than 20 pounds! One respondent overestimated his height by 7 inches, and there were 11 individuals out of 197 who overestimated their grade-point average by 1.5 points or more, over a third of the full range of the grade scale going from 0 to 4.0! Two subjects misreported their grades by more than 2 points, equivalent to reporting an A average when one's grades are really Cs. Thus, the degree of accuracy appears to be relatively high when examining the correlations, but not so high when examining absolute accuracy or the accuracy of specific individuals.

Another interesting finding is that the underestimations and overestimations across the three domains were not correlated significantly with one another—the Pearson correlations ranged from .05 to .11 between the three misreporting scores. In addition, none of the three misreporting scores came even close to correlating significantly with scales of social desirability such as the Crowne-Marlowe, the Balanced Inventory of Desirable Responding scales, or the Edwards Social Desirability Scale (see Paulhus, 1991, for a review of these scales), with correlations ranging from −.02 to .13. Because the different misreporting scores did not correlate with each other, it is not surprising that they did not correlate with the social desirability scales either, suggesting that misreporting might be particular to the domain and situation rather than a general characteristic. The best predictor of the accuracy of grade estimation was having a high GPA, $r = .67$. In other words, people with high grades misreported their grades less than did people with low grades.

The lessons from Fujita's study are manifold. First, whether self-reports are considered accurate or inaccurate will depend on the self-report content (height was more accurately reported than grades), on the purposes of the study (e.g., whether one needs a precise measure or only a general estimate),

and on whether one needs an absolute measure or a relative measure. Another clear lesson is that just because there are high correlations between self-report and objective measures, even in the .90s, does not mean that the score is necessarily accurate for all purposes or for all individuals. Because the weight of college students shows large variations between individuals (from 99 to 233 pounds in our sample), even misestimates of 20 pounds might not result in a low correlation between the self-report and the objective measure, because the correlation is influenced by the variability of scores between individuals. Furthermore, a consistent tendency toward underestimation might leave a large correlation between the two scores intact. Nonetheless, underestimations of weight by over 25 pounds could be extremely important in many situations (think of the wedding dress that is 25 pounds too small). Furthermore, people's degree of exaggeration is inconsistent from one domain to another and is not necessarily predicted by scales of social desirability. We can take from this study that self-reports can be accurate or inaccurate, depending on the researcher's domain and purpose, and that much can be learned from augmenting self-reports with other types of data.

We extensively use self-report data in our own research and yet warn readers that additional forms of measurement are almost always desirable when it is possible to obtain them. Of course the validity of self-report is not an either–or question, because the validity is likely to vary across domains and across the question of "Validity for what?" We know from the work of Schwarz and Strack (1999) and others that self-report is not a simple process in which respondents generate a simple answer to a unitary question; rather, self-report involves complex inferences and mental processes. The point we will make later is that self-report responses, like the responses to all measures, need to be embedded in the theory so that it includes predictions of how the self-reports are generated.

THERE ARE DRAMATIC ADVANCES IN THE STATISTICS OF MEASUREMENT

Most researchers were exposed to classical test theory during their training and so understand meas-

ures in terms of ideas related to reliability and validity. Oftentimes they have memorized some types of reliability and several types of validity. This simple approach to measurement can aid an investigator to proceed with his or her work, but is woefully inadequate compared to the psychometric sophistication we now possess. Some investigators have also been exposed to generalizability theory, and a few understand the triangles in Campbell and Fiske's (1959) multitrait–multimethod matrix. Our hope is that this volume has exposed readers to a deeper understanding of measurement that they can apply in their own research. A reader of this volume might no longer ask whether a test is valid, but will ask whether it is valid for certain purposes, and how a measure triangulates with other measures of the same supposed construct.

The statistics for analyzing the psychometric properties of our measures have gone beyond simple zero-order correlations coefficients. Modern statistical approaches can be used to model method-specific influences that correspond to theoretical assumptions about method effects. Data-analytic approaches such as loglinear modeling, item response theory, multilevel modeling, and models of generalizability theory, as well as structural equation modeling, enable researches to test hypotheses about the sources and generalizability of method effects in an appropriate way. Moreover, latent variable approaches allow us to separate unsystematic measurement error from systematic method-specific effects and to measure latent variables that can be related to other variables to explain trait and method effects.

MULTIPLE METHODS, NOT JUST MEASURES

Several authors in this volume argue that the need for multiple methods can be extended in new directions. Although some are despairing of multiple methods of measurement because of their frequent lack of convergence, others call for more applications of the basic idea of multiple methods. Miner and Hulin, in their chapter (chap. 29, this volume) on organizational research, call for a longitudinal dimension, with sampling over time, as a type of

multimethod, and Marsh, Martin, and Hau (chap. 30, this volume) make a similar argument for cross-cultural measurement as a type of multiple method. Burns and Haynes (chap. 27, this volume) extend multiple method measurement to include more dimensions, including not only the method of measurement, but also including dimensions, facets, settings, modes, and occasions. In addition, multiple methods can be extended to experimentation, where multiple treatments and control groups can allow researchers to gain greater insight into the causal mechanisms in any given area (Smith & Harris, chap. 26, this volume). We welcome these extensions of multiple operations and yet want to remind readers that many of the same issues will apply to them as apply to multiple measures.

When using multiple occasions, experimental manipulations, organizations, cultures, and so forth, researchers need to be prepared for the fact that there might only be modest convergence between them. Just as with multiple measures, it is a relief when other types of multiple methods produce similar conclusions. But one should not despair if this is not the case—as long as one is patient and understands that scientific progress takes time. Much can be learned when different cultural patterns are pursued in further research, when a pattern is sought in longitudinal differences, or when experimental manipulations of supposedly the same construct lead to different outcomes. Indeed, we would argue that it is in these circumstances, just when researchers sometimes give up in despair, that the conditions are right for important advances in science. If the researcher persists, he or she is likely to discover interesting points in nature, where a construct is really two distinct concepts or where the effects of a variable depend on the context. Thus, multiple methods are likely to lead to a more complex and sophisticated science.

THEORIES SHOULD INCLUDE MEASUREMENT AS A CORE ELEMENT

Because measures often converge only at modest levels unless they are very similar instruments using the same method, many researchers have despaired of multimethod measurement. Rather than despair, we counsel that researchers must begin to integrate measurement into their theories. Different methods of measuring the same supposed underlying construct, in fact, often measure somewhat different phenomena, different aspects of a construct. For example, fear is a general concept, but biological measures, labeling of the emotion, and behavior are likely to be only loosely coupled, as Larsen and Prizmic-Larsen (chap. 23, this volume) indicate. These authors concede that different methods often converge only modestly and point to studies such as Nesse et al.'s (1985), which found that nine measures of distress correlated at relatively low levels with each other. However, Schmitt (chap. 2, this volume) as well as Larsen and Prizmic-Larsen suggest that different methods may in fact be measuring different concepts, which are in turn related at a higher-order level in more abstract constructs. For this reason, researchers need to be very clear how various types of measures fit together theoretically and not simply correlate them or derive latent variables from them. Because different methods very often measure somewhat different concepts rather than the same underlying construct, the idea that there are multiple methods measuring the same concept is likely in most instances to be faulty. The way out of this impasse is to integrate measurement into our theories. The search for the perfect multitrait–multimethod matrix has been elusive because of the mistaken assumption that different methods of a concept will necessarily be measuring the same underlying entity. We believe that they often measure different entities or aspects of a phenomenon, and that theory is needed to explain how these different components fit into a higher-order more abstract construct.

Theory is also needed to determine whether a researcher has more than one method. For example, are informant reports by family members versus by friends one method or two? Are the reports of the mother and father one method or two? One approach to methods has been to envision them as being on a continuum of similarity, going from very dissimilar (e.g., a life satisfaction report versus a

measure of the hormone cortisol) or very similar (e.g., a self-report on a 5-point versus 7-point scale). This approach is a starting point, but begs the question of similar in what way, and another question, similar along several dimensions or one? Clearly the question of whether one has distinct methods or not cannot be answered in an either–or way, but we maintain that it can only be adequately answered in reference to a theory of how the measures are produced and what aspects of the construct they represent.

An example of how measures must be theory-defined concepts comes from the work on happiness of Ed Diener. In this arena many researchers have used global questions about happiness, basically asking people to rate how happy they have been during the past year on a scale ranging from 1 to 10, or similar questions. Other researchers ask respondents globally how satisfied they are, or how satisfied they are with particular domains such as marriage or work. In contrast, Kahneman (1999) called for a focus on online measures in which people's affective experience is sampled over time. In our own studies, we find that these two types of measures converge only moderately. People are only modestly accurate at remembering their emotions in global recall measures; yet we have argued that the global measures are also important because they may reflect what choices people will make in the future. Furthermore, the global measures can be used much more easily in large surveys and represent an overall assessment people make of their lives. In other words, there are two types of measures of happiness that correlate at moderate levels, and different scientists have argued for the priority of each measurement method. If one takes a simple multimethod approach, we should use both methods and consider the overlap between the two types of measures to be true happiness. If one accepts the

advice offered by Roberts and his colleagues (chap. 22, this volume), a researcher might focus his or her work on one type of measure and be content with understanding it. We, however, take a third approach—that understanding the two types of measures, and when and how they relate, is crucial to scientific understanding. Measure methods are not theoretical nonentities; they are themselves theoretically important. Furthermore, measurement is not a "mere" technical pursuit, but is inherently theoretical in nature. If we truly know how to measure a thing, then we understand it. Thus, advances in the behavioral sciences will be intimately tied to our success in measuring our constructs.

Campbell and Fiske's (1959) classic work on multimethod measurement was brilliant in alerting us to the importance of using multiple methods to assess our constructs. Over the years, however, many researchers became disheartened with the approach because the convergence between measures based on different methods was often modest. Our book is a call for renewed interest in multiple measures and methods. We view both the convergences and divergences between measures to be invaluable sources of information for scientists and an opportunity to integrate theory and measurement. The divergence between methods should not be discouraging; it is one of the best levers we have for understanding our phenomena. In addition, every method has its peculiar shortcomings, and the use of multiple methods with different limitations can greatly aid in controlling measurement artifacts. Furthermore, we believe that the use of multiple methods is the major way to understand and assess method variance. Our hope is that this handbook serves to stimulate a new wave of research that fully embraces multiple methods, and that a revolution in sophisticated scientific knowledge will ensue.

REFERENCES

Achenbach, T. M. (1991). *Manual for the Child Behavior Checklist and 1991 Profile*. Burlington: University of Vermont, Department of Psychiatry.

Achenbach, T. M., & Edelbrock, C. (1987). *Manual for the Youth Self-Report and Profile*. Burlington: University of Vermont, Department of Psychiatry.

Achenbach, T. M., McConaughy, S. H., & Howell, C. T. (1987). Child/adolescent behavioral and emotional problems: Implications of cross-informant correlations for situational specificity. *Psychological Bulletin, 101,* 213–232.

Ackerman, P. L., Beier, M. E., & Boyle, M. O. (2002). Individual differences in working memory within a nomological network of cognitive and perceptual speed abilities. *Journal of Experimental Psychology: General, 131,* 567–589.

Ackerman, T. A., Evans, J., Park, K.-S., Tamassia, C., & Turner, R. (1999). Computer assessment using visual stimuli: A test of dermatological skin disorders. In F. Drasgow & J. B. Olson-Buchanan (Eds.), *Innovations in computerized assessment* (pp. 137–150). Mahwah, NJ: Lawrence Erlbaum Associates.

Adams, R. J., Wilson, M., & Wang, W. (1997). The multidimensional random coefficients multinomial logit model. *Applied Psychological Measurement, 21,* 1–23.

Adams, R. J., Wilson, M., & Wu, M. L. (1997). Multilevel item response models: An approach to errors in variables regression. *Journal of Educational and Behavioral Statistics, 22,* 47–76.

Adamson, L. B., Bakeman, R., & Deckner, D. F. (2004). The development of symbol-infused joint engagement. *Child Development, 75,* 1171–1187.

Aderman, D. (1972). Elation, depression, and helping behavior. *Journal of Personality and Social Psychology, 24,* 91–101.

Affleck, G., Tennen, H., Urrows, S., & Higgins, P. (1991). Individual differences in the day-to-day experience of chronic pain: A prospective daily study of rheumatoid arthritis patients. *Health Psychology, 10,* 419–426.

Affleck, G., Tennen, H., Urrows, S., & Higgins, P. (1992). Neuroticism and the pain-mood relation in rheumatoid arthritis: Insights from a prospective daily study. *Journal of Clinical and Consulting Psychology, 60,* 119–126.

Affleck, G., Zautra, A., Tennen, H., & Armeli, S. (1999). Multilevel daily process designs for consulting and clinical psychology: A preface for the perplexed. *Journal of Consulting and Clinical Psychology, 67,* 746–754.

Agresti, A. (1990). *Categorical data analysis*. New York: John Wiley & Sons.

Agresti, A. (1992). Modeling patterns of agreement and disagreement. *Statistical Methods in Medical Research, 1,* 201–218.

Agresti, A., & Lang, J. B. (1993). Quasi-symmetric latent class models with applications to rater agreement. *Biometrics, 49,* 131–139.

Aguirre, G. K., & D'Esposito, M. (1999). Experimental design for brain fMRI. In C. Moonen & P. A. Bandettini (Eds.), *Functional MRI* (pp. 369–380). Berlin, Germany: Springer-Verlag.

Aguirre, G. K., Zarahn, E., & D'Esposito, M. (1998). The variability of human, BOLD hemodynamic responses. *Neuroimage, 8,* 360–369.

Ahadi, S., & Diener, E. (1989). Multiple determinants and effect size. *Journal of Personality and Social Psychology, 56,* 398–406.

Aiken, L. R. (1999). *Personality assessment. Methods and practices*. Seattle, WA: Hogrefe & Huber.

Aiken, L. S., West, S. G., Sechrest, L., & Reno, R. R. (1990). Graduate training in statistics, methodology, and measurement in psychology: A survey of Ph.D. programs in North America. *American Psychologist, 45,* 721–734.

Ainsworth, M. D. S., Blehar, M., Waters, E., & Wall, S. (1978). *Patterns of attachment*. Hillsdale, NJ: Lawrence Erlbaum Associates.

Ajzen, I., & Fishbein, M. (1980). *Understanding attitudes and predicting behavior*. Englewood Cliffs, NJ: Prentice Hall.

Akaike, H. (1973). Information theory and an extension of the maximum likelihood principle. In B. N. Petrox & F. Caski (Eds.), *Second International Symposium on Information Theory* (pp. 267–281). Budapest, Hungary: Akademiai Kiado.

Akaike, H. (1987). Factor analysis and AIC. *Psychometrika, 52,* 317–332.

Albert, S. (1977). Temporal comparison theory. *Psychological Review, 84*, 485–503.

Albin, R. R. (1990). *Parenting stress index manual.* Charlottesville, VA: Pediatric Psychology Press.

Albright, L., Kenny, D. A., & Malloy, T. E. (1988). Consensus in personality judgments at zero acquaintance. *Journal of Personality and Social Psychology, 55*, 387–395.

Alicke, M. A., Smith, R. H., & Klotz, M. L. (1986). Judgments of physical attractiveness: The role of faces and bodies. *Personality and Social Psychology Bulletin, 12*, 381–389.

Allport, G. W. (1937). *Personality, a psychological interpretation.* New York: Henry Holt.

Allport, G. W. (1961). *Pattern of growth in personality.* New York: Henry Holt.

Altmann, J. (1974). Observational study of behaviour: Sampling methods. *Behaviour, 49*, 227–267.

Altmann, S. A. (1965). Sociobiology of rhesus monkeys. II. Stochastics of social communication. *Journal of Theoretical Biology, 8*, 490–522.

Alwin, D. F., Cohen R. L., & Newcomb, T. M. (1991). *Political attitudes over the life span: The Bennington women after fifty years.* Madison: University of Wisconsin Press.

Ambady, N., Hallahan, M., & Rosenthal, R. (1995). On judging and being judged accurately in zero-acquaintance situations. *Journal of Personality and Social Psychology, 69*, 518–529.

Ambady, N., & Rosenthal, R. (1992). Thin slices of expressive behavior as predictors of interpersonal consequences: A meta-analysis. *Psychological Bulletin, 111*, 256–274.

American Psychological Association (APA), Task Force on Health Research. (1976). Contributions of psychology to health research: Patterns, problems, and potentials. *American Psychologist, 31*, 263–274.

American Psychological Association. (2002). Ethical principles of psychologists and code of conduct. *American Psychologist, 57*, 1060–1073.

Amodio, D. M., Harmon-Jones, E., & Devine, P. G. (2003). Individual differences in the activation and control of affective race bias as assessed by startle eyeblink response and self-report. *Journal of Personality and Social Psychology, 84*, 738–753.

Analog. (2003). Retrieved May 2, 2003, from http://www.analog.cx

Anastasi, A. (1988). *Psychological testing* (6th ed.). New York: Macmillan.

Anderson, C. A., & Bushman, B. J. (2002). Human aggression. *Annual Review of Psychology, 53*, 27–51.

Anderson, J. C., & Gerbing, D. W. (1988). Structural equation modeling in practice: A review and recommended two-step approach. *Psychological Bulletin, 3*, 411–423.

Anderson, J. R. (1982). Acquisition of cognitive skill. *Psychological Review, 89*, 369–406.

Anderson, J. R. (1983). *The architecture of cognition.* Cambridge, MA: Harvard University Press.

Anderson, S. M. (1984). Self-knowledge and social inference. The diagnosticity of cognitive/affective and behavioral data. *Journal of Personality and Social Psychology, 46*, 294–307.

Andrich, D. (1978). A rating formulation for ordered response categories. *Psychometrika, 43*, 561–573.

Andrich, D. (1988). *Rasch models for measurement.* London: Sage.

Aneshensel, C. S., Frerichs, R. R., & Huba, G. J. (1984). Depression and physical illness—a multiwave, nonrecursive causal model. *Journal of Health and Social Behavior, 24*, 340–371.

Antonak, R. F., & Livneh, H. (1995). Randomized response technique: A review and proposed extension to disability attitude research. *Genetic, Social, and General Psychology Monographs, 1*, 97–145.

Apple, W., & Hecht, K. (1982). Speaking emotionally: The relation between verbal and vocal communication of affect. *Journal of Personality and Social Psychology, 42*, 864–875.

Arcediano, F., Escobar, M., & Matute, H. (2001). Reversal from blocking in humans as a result of posttraining extinction of the blocking stimulus. *Animal Learning and Behavior, 29*, 354–366.

Ariely, D., Kahneman, D., & Loewenstein, G. (2000). Joint comment on "When does duration matter in judgment and decision making?" *Journal of Experimental Psychology: General, 129*, 524–529.

Arndt, J., & Reder, L. M. (2002). Word frequency and receiver-operating characteristic curves in recognition memory: Evidence for a dual-process interpretation. *Journal of Experimental Psychology: Learning, Memory, and Cognition, 28*, 830–842.

Arntz, A., van Eck, M., & Heijmans, M. (1990). Predictions of denial pain: The fear of any expected evil is worse that the evil itself. *Behaviour Research and Therapy, 28*, 29–42.

Aronson, E., Ellsworth, P. C., Carlsmith, J. M., & Gonzales, M. H. (1990). *Methods of research in social psychology.* New York: McGraw-Hill.

Aronson, E., & Mills, J. (1959). The effect of severity of initiation on liking for a group. *Journal of Abnormal and Social Psychology, 59*, 177–181.

Ary, D., & Suen, H. K. (1985). Statistical significance of percent interobserver agreement reliability. *Midwestern Educational Researcher, 6*, 31–33.

Asendorpf, J. B. (1991). *Die differenzielle Sichtweise in der Psychologie* [The individual difference perspective in psychology]. Göttingen, Germany: Hogrefe.

Asendorpf, J. B., & Ostendorf, F. (1998). Is self-enhancement healthy? Conceptual, psychometric, and empirical analysis. *Journal of Personality and Social Psychology, 74*, 955–966.

Asher, S. B., Singleton, L. C., Tinsley, L. C., & Hymel, B. R. (1979). A reliable sociometric measure for preschool children. *Developmental Psychology, 15*, 443–444.

Ayers, T. S., Sandler, I. N., West, S. G., & Roosa, M. W. (1996). A dispositional and situational assessment of children's coping: Testing alternative models of coping. *Journal of Personality, 64*, 923–958.

Baba, S., Ozawa, H., Nakamoto, Y., Ueshima, H., & Omae, T. (1990). Enhanced blood pressure to regular daily stress in urban hypertensive men. *Journal of Hypertension, 8,* 647–655.

Babad, E., Bernieri, F. J., & Rosenthal, R. (1989). Nonverbal communication and leakage in the behavior of biased and unbiased teachers. *Journal of Personality and Social Psychology, 56,* 89–94.

Bachorowski, J. (1999). Vocal expression and perception of emotion. *Current Directions in Psychological Science, 8,* 53–57.

Bachorowski, J., & Owren, M. J. (1995). Vocal expression of emotion: Acoustic properties of speech are associated with emotional intensity and context. *Psychological Science, 6,* 219–224.

Baer, D. M. (1977). Reviewer's comment: Just because it's reliable doesn't mean that you can use it. *Journal of Applied Behavior Analysis, 10,* 117–119.

Bagby, R. M., Rector, N. A., Bindseil, K., Dickens, S. E., Levitan, R. D., & Kennedy, S. H. (1998). Self-report ratings and informants' ratings of personalities of depressed outpatients. *American Journal of Psychiatry, 155,* 437–443.

Bagozzi, R. P. (1993). Assessing construct validity in personality research: Applications to measures of self-esteem. *Journal of Research in Personality, 27,* 49–87.

Baillargeon, R. (1994). How do infants learn about the physical world? *Current Directions, 3,* 133–140.

Bakeman, R. (2000). Behavioral observations and coding. In H. T. Reis & C. K. Judd (Eds.), *Handbook of research methods in social psychology* (pp. 138–159). New York: Cambridge University Press.

Bakeman, R., & Adamson, L. B. (1984). Coordinating attention to people and objects in mother–infant interaction. *Child Development, 55,* 1278–1289.

Bakeman, R., & Brownlee, J. R. (1980). The strategic use of parallel play: A sequential analysis. *Child Development, 51,* 873–878.

Bakeman, R., & Brownlee, J. R. (1982). Social rules governing object conflicts in toddlers and preschoolers. In K. H. Rubin & H. S. Ross (Eds.), *Peer relationships and social skills in childhood* (pp. 99–111). New York: Springer-Verlag.

Bakeman, R., Deckner, D. F., & Quera, V. (2004). Analysis of behavioral streams. In D. M. Teti (Ed.), *Handbook of research methods in developmental psychology* (pp. 394–420). Oxford, England: Blackwell Publishers.

Bakeman, R., & Gottman, J. M. (1997). *Observing interaction: An introduction to sequential analysis* (2nd ed.). New York: Cambridge University Press.

Bakeman, R., & Quera, V. (1995). *Analyzing interaction: Sequential analysis with SDIS and GSEQ.* New York: Cambridge University Press.

Bakeman, R., & Quera, V. (2000). OTS: A program for converting Noldus observer data files to SDIS files. *Behavior Research Methods, Instruments, and Computers, 32,* 207–212.

Baker, F. (1992). *Item response theory. Parameter estimation techniques.* New York: Marcel Dekker.

Baker-Brown, G., Ballard, E. J., Bluck, S., De Vries, B., Suedfeld, P., & Tetlock, P. E. (1992). The conceptual/integrative complexity scoring manual. In C. P. Smith (Ed.), *Motivation and personality: Handbook of thematic content analysis* (pp. 401–418). New York: Cambridge University Press.

Baldwin, W. (2000). Information no one else knows: The value of self-report. In A. A. Stone, J. S. Turkkan, et al. (Eds.), *The science of self-report: Implications for research and practice* (pp. 3–7). Mahwah, NJ: Lawrence Erlbaum Associates.

Ball, S., Fox, P. T., Herscovitch, P., & Raichle, M. E. (1988). Control state stability for PET brain imaging: "eyes-closed rest," same day versus separate day. *Neurology 38* (Suppl. 1), 363.

Ball, S. A., Rounsaville, B. J., Tennen, H., & Kranzler, H. R. (2001). Reliability of personality disorder symptoms and personality traits in substance-dependence inpatients. *Journal of Abnormal Psychology, 110,* 341–352.

Baltes, P. B., & Nesselroade, J. R. (Eds.). (1979). *Longitudinal research in the study of behavior and development.* New York: Academic Press.

Baltes, P. B., Reese, H. W., & Lipsitt, L. P. (1980). Life-span developmental psychology. *Annual Review of Psychology, 31,* 65–110.

Banaji, M. R. (2001). Implicit attitudes can be measured. In H. L. Roediger, J. S. Nairne, I. Neath, & A. Suprenant (Eds.), *The nature of reasoning: Essays in honor of Robert G. Crowder* (pp. 117–150). Washington, DC: American Psychological Association.

Band, E., & Weisz, J. R. (1988). How to feel better when it feels bad: Children's perspectives on coping with everyday stress. *Developmental Psychology, 24,* 247–253.

Bandettini, P. A., Wong, E. C., Hinks, R. S., Tikofsky, R. S., & Hyde, J. S. (1992). Time course EPI of human brain function during task activation. *Magnetic Resonance in Medicine, 25,* 390–397.

Banks, W. P. (1970). Signal detection theory and human memory. *Psychological Bulletin, 74,* 81–99.

Barker, R. G. (1978). *Habitats, environments and human behavior: Studies in the ecological psychology and ecobehavioral science of the Midwest Psychological Field Station: 1947–1972.* San Francisco: Jossey-Bass.

Barker, R. G. (1968). *Ecological psychology.* Stanford, CA: Stanford University Press.

Baron, N. S. (1998). Letters by phone or speech by other means: The linguistics of e-mail. *Language & Communication, 18,* 133–170.

Barrick, M. B., & Mount, M. K. (1991). The big five personality dimensions and job performance: A meta-analysis. *Personnel Psychology, 44,* 1–26.

Bartholomew, D. J. (1987). *Latent variable models and factor analysis.* Oxford, England: Oxford University Press.

Bassili, J. N. (1996). Meta-judgmental versus operative indexes of psychological attributes: The case of measures of attitude strength. *Journal of Personality and Social Psychology, 71,* 637–653.

Batchelder, W. H. (1998). Multinomial processing tree

models and psychological assessment. *Psychological Assessment, 10*, 331–344.

Batchelder, W. H., & Riefer, D. M. (1990). Multinomial processing models of source monitoring. *Psychological Review, 97*, 548–564.

Batchelder, W. H., & Riefer, D. M. (1999). Theoretical and empirical review of multinomial process tree modeling. *Psychonomic Bulletin & Review, 6*, 57–86.

Bauer, D. J., & Curran, P. J. (2004). The integration of continuous and discrete latent variable models: Potential problems and promising opportunities. *Psychological Methods, 9*, 3–29.

Baxter, J. C. (1970). Interpersonal spacing in natural settings. *Sociometry, 33*(4), 444–456.

Bayen, U. J., Murnane, K., & Erdfelder, E. (1996). Source discrimination, item detection, and multinomial models of source monitoring. *Journal of Experimental Psychology: Learning, Memory, and Cognition, 22*, 197–215.

Bechtel, R. B. (1967). Hodometer research in museums. *Museum News, 45*, 23–26.

Becker, B. J. (2000). Multivariate meta-analysis. In H. E. A. Tinsley & S. D. Brown (Eds.), *Handbook of applied multivariate statistical and mathematical modeling* (pp. 499–526). San Diego, CA: Academic Press.

Becker, M. H. (1974). The health belief model and personal health behavior. *Health Education Monographs, 2*, 324–508.

Becker, M., Buder, E., Bakeman, R., Price, M., & Ward, J. (2003). Infant response to mother call patterns in *Otolemur garnettii*. *Folia Primatologica, 74*, 301–311.

Becker, P. M., & Agresti, A. (1992). Log-linear modeling of pairwise interobserver agreement on a categorical scale. *Statistics in Medicine, 11*, 101–114.

Becker, P. M., & Clogg, C. C. (1989). Analysis of sets of two-way contingency tables using association models. *Journal of the American Statistical Association, 84*, 142–151.

Bejar, I. I., & Braun, H. I. (1999). *Architectural simulations: From research to implementation*. (Research Memorandum 99-2). Princeton, NJ: Educational Testing Service.

Benbow, C. P., & Stanley, J. C. (1996). Inequity in equity: How "equity" can lead to inequity for high-potential students. *Psychology, Public Policy, and Law, 2*, 249–292.

Benet-Martinez, V., & Waller, N. G. (1997). Further evidence for the cross-cultural generality of the Big Seven Factor model: Indigenous and imported Spanish personality constructs. *Journal of Personality, 65*, 567–598.

Benjamin, A. S. (2001). On the dual effects of repetition on false recognition. *Journal of Experimental Psychology: Learning, Memory, and Cognition, 27*, 941–947.

Benjamin, A. S. (2003). Predicting and postdicting the effects of word frequency on memory. *Memory & Cognition, 31*, 297–305.

Benjamin, A. S., Bjork, R. A., & Hirshman, E. (1998). Predicting the future and reconstructing the past: A Bayesian characterization of the utility of subjective fluency. *Acta Psychologica, 98*, 267–290.

Benjamin, A. S., & Craik, F. I. M. (2001). Parallel effects of aging and time pressure on memory for source: Evidence from the spacing effect. *Memory & Cognition, 29*, 691–697.

Bennett, R. E., Morley, M., & Quardt, D. (2000). Three response types for broadening the conception of mathematical problem solving in computerized tests. *Applied Psychological Measurement, 24*, 294–309.

Bennett, R. E., Steffen, M., Singley, M. K., Morley, M., & Jacquemin, D. (1997). Evaluating an automatically scorable, open-ended response type for measuring mathematical reasoning in computer-adaptive tests. *Journal of Educational Measurement, 34*, 162–176.

Ben-Shakhar, G., & Dolev, K. (1996). Psychophysiological detection through the guilty knowledge technique: Effects of mental countermeasures. *Journal of Applied Psychology, 81*, 273–281.

Ben-Shakhar, G., & Furedy, J. J. (1990). *Theories and applications in the detection of deception*. New York: Springer-Verlag.

Bentler, P. M. (1969). Semantic space is (approximately) bipolar. *Journal of Psychology, 71*, 33–40.

Bentler, P. M., & Bonett, D. G. (1980). Significance tests and goodness-of-fit in the analysis of covariance structures. *Psychological Bulletin, 88*, 588–606.

Berendt, B. (2002). Using site semantics to analyze, visualize, and support navigation. *Data Mining & Knowledge Discovery, 6*, 37–59.

Berendt, B., & Brenstein, E. (2001). Visualizing individual differences in Web navigation: STRATDYN, a tool for analyzing navigation patterns. *Behavior Research Methods, Instruments, & Computers, 33*, 243–257.

Berger, H. (1929). Über das Elektrenkephalogramm des Menschen. *Archiv für Psychiatrie und Nervenkrankheiten, 87*, 527–570.

Bergman, M. E., Donovan, M. A., & Drasgow, F. (2001). *Situational judgment, personality, and cognitive ability: Are we really measuring different constructs?* Paper presented at the 16th Annual Conference of the Society for Industrial and Organizational Psychology, San Diego, CA.

Berk, R. A. (1979). Generalizability of behavioral observations: A clarification of interobserver agreement and interobserver reliability. *American Journal of Mental Deficiency, 83*, 460–472.

Berker, T. (2002). World Wide Web use at a German University—Computers, sex and imported names. Results of logfile analysis. In B. Batinic, U.-D. Reips, & M. Bosnjak (Eds.), *Online Social Science*. Seattle, WA: Hogrefe & Huber.

Berkowitz, L. (1989). Frustration–aggression hypothesis: Examination and reformulation. *Psychological Bulletin, 106*, 59–73.

Berkowitz, L., & Daniels, L. R. (1964). Affecting the salience of the social responsibility norm: Effects of past help on the response to dependency relationships. *Journal of Abnormal and Social Psychology, 68*, 275–281.

Bernardin, H. J., Cooke, D. K., & Villanova, P. (2000). Conscientiousness and agreeableness as predictors of rating leniency. *Journal of Applied Psychology, 85*, 232–234.

Bernieri, F. J., Gillis, J. S., Davis, J. M., & Grahe, J. E. (1996). Dyadic rapport and the accuracy of its judgments across situations: A lens model analysis. *Journal of Personality and Social Psychology, 71,* 110–129.

Bernieri, F. J., Zuckerman, M., Koestner, R., & Rosenthal, R. (1994). Measuring person perception accuracy: Another look at self–other agreement. *Personality and Social Psychology Bulletin, 20,* 367–378.

Berntson, G. G., Bigger, J. T., Eckberg, D. L., Grossman, P., Kaufmann, P. G., Malik, M., et al. (1997). Heart rate variability: Origins, methods, and interpretive caveats. *Psychophysiology, 34,* 623–648.

Berntson, G. G., & Cacioppo, J. T. (2000). From homeostasis to allodynamic regulation. In J. T. Cacioppo, L. G. Tassinary, & G. G. Berntson (Eds.), *Handbook of psychophysiology* (pp. 459–481). Cambridge, England: Cambridge University Press.

Berntson, G. G., & Cacioppo, J. T. (2004). Heart rate variability: Stress and psychiatric conditions. In M. Malik & A. J. Camm (Eds.), *Dynamic electrocardiography* (pp. 56–63). New York: Futura.

Berntson, G. G., Cacioppo, J. T., Binkley, P. F., Uchino, B. N., Quigley, K. S., & Fieldstone, A. (1994). Autonomic cardiac control: III. Psychological stress and cardiac response in autonomic space as revealed by pharmacological blockades. *Psychophysiology, 31,* 599–608.

Berntson, G. G., Cacioppo, J. T., & Quigley, K. S. (1991). Autonomic determinism: The modes of autonomic control, the doctrine of autonomic space, and the laws of autonomic constraint. *Psychological Review, 98,* 459–487.

Berntson, G. G., Cacioppo, J. T., & Quigley, K. S. (1993). Respiratory sinus arrhythmia: Autonomic origins, physiological mechanisms, and psychophysiological implications. *Psychophysiology, 30,* 183–196.

Berntson, G. G., Cacioppo, J. T., & Quigley, K. S. (1994). Autonomic cardiac control. I. Estimation and validation from pharmacological blockades. *Psychophysiology, 31,* 572–585.

Berntson, G. G., Sarter, M., & Cacioppo, J. T. (1998). Anxiety and cardiovascular reactivity: The basal forebrain cholinergic link. *Behavioral Brain Research, 94,* 225–248.

Berry, K. J., & Mielke, P. W. (1988). A generalization of Cohen's kappa agreement measure to interval measurement and multiple raters. *Educational and Psychological Measurement, 48,* 921–933.

Berthoz, S., Blair, R. J. R., Le Clec'h, G., & Martinot, J. L. (2002). Title: Emotions: From neuropsychology to functional imaging. *International Journal of Psychology, 37,* 193–203.

Bestgen, Y. (1994). Can emotional valence in stories be determined from words? *Cognition & Emotion, 8,* 21–36.

Biber, D. (1988). *Variation across speech and writing.* Cambridge, England: Cambridge University Press.

Bierhoff, H.-W., Klein, R., & Kramp, P. (1991). Evidence for the altruistic personality from data on accident research. *Journal of Personality, 59,* 263–280.

Biesanz, J. C., West, S. G., & Kwok, O.-M. (2003). Personality over time: Methodological approaches to the study of short-term and long-term development and change. *Journal of Personality, 71,* 905–942.

Biesanz, J. C., West, S. G., & Millevoi, A. (2004). What do you learn about someone over time? Acquaintanceship and the development of person- and trait-centered agreement in judgments of personality. Manuscript submitted for publication.

Bijleveld, C. C. J. H., & van der Kamp, L. J. T. (1998). *Longitudinal data analysis. Designs, models and methods.* London: Sage.

Birkimer, J. C., & Brown, J. H. (1979). Back to basics: Percentage agreement measures are adequate, but there are easier ways. *Journal of Applied Behavior Analysis, 12*(4), 535–543.

Birnbaum, M. H. (1992). Issues in utility measurement. *Organizational Behavior & Human Decision Processes, 52,* 319–330.

Birnbaum, M. H. (2000). SurveyWiz and FactorWiz: JavaScript Web pages that make HTML forms for research on the Internet. *Behavior Research Methods, Instruments, and Computers, 32*(2), 339–346.

Birnbaum, M. H. (2001). A Web-based program of research on decision making. In U.-D. Reips & M. Bosnjak (Eds.), *Dimensions of internet science* (pp. 23–55). Lengerich, Germany: Pabst.

Birnbaum, M. H. (2004). Human research and data collection via the Internet. *Annual Review of Psychology, 55,* 803–832.

Birnbaum, M. H., & Reips, U.-D. (2005). Behavioral research and data collection via the Internet. In R. W. Proctor & K.-P. L. Vu (Eds.), *The handbook of human factors in Web design* (pp. 471–492). Mahwah, NJ: Lawrence Erlbaum Associates.

Bishop, Y. M. M., Fienberg, S. E., & Holland, P. W. (1975). *Discrete multivariate analysis: Theory and practice.* Cambridge, MA: MIT Press.

Black, M. M., Hutcheson, J. J., Dubowitz, H., Starr, R. H., & Berenson-Howard, J. (1996). The roots of competence: Mother–child interaction among low income, urban, African American families. *Journal of Applied Developmental Psychology, 17,* 367–391.

Blackman, M. C., & Funder, D. C. (1998). The effect of information on consensus and accuracy in personality judgment. *Journal of Experimental Social Psychology, 34,* 164–181.

Blair, E., & Burton, S. (1987). Cognitive processes used by survey respondents to answer behavioral frequency questions. *Journal of Consumer Research, 14,* 280–288.

Blaisdell, A. P., Gunther, L. M., & Miller, R. R. (1999). Recovery from blocking achieved by extinguishing the blocking CS. *Animal Learning and Behavior, 27,* 63–76.

Blampied, N. M. (2000). Single-case research designs: A neglected alternative. *American Psychologist, 55,* 960.

Blascovich, J., Loomis, J., Beall, A., Swinth, K., Hoyt, C., & Bailenson, J. (2002). Immersive virtual environment technology as a methodological tool for social psychology. *Psychological Inquiry, 13,* 103–124.

Block, J. (1965). *The challenge of response sets*. New York: Appleton-Century-Crofts.

Block, J. (1977). Advancing the science of personality: Pragmatic shift or improving the quality of research. In D. Magnusson & N. S. Endler (Eds.), *Psychology at the crossroads: Current issues in interactional psychology* (pp. 37–73). Hillsdale, NJ: Lawrence Erlbaum Associates.

Block, J. (1993). Studying personality the long way. In D. C. Funder & R. D. Parke (Eds.), *Studying lives through time: Personality and development* (pp. 9–41). Washington, DC: APA science volumes.

Block, J. (1995). A contrarian view of the five-factor approach to personality description. *Psychological Bulletin, 117*, 187–215.

Block, J. (2002). *Personality as an affect processing system: Toward an integrative theory*. Hillsdale, NJ: Lawrence Erlbaum Associates.

Bloom, B. S. (1964). *Stability and change in human characteristics*. New York: John Wiley & Sons.

Bloom, M., & Fischer, J. (1982). Reactivity and the use of unobtrusive measures. In M. Bloom & J. Fischer (Eds.), *Evaluating practice: Guidelines for the accountable professional* (pp. 200–217). Englewood Cliffs, NJ: Prentice Hall.

Bochner, S. (1979). Designing unobtrusive field experiments in social psychology. In L. Sechrest (Ed.), *Unobtrusive measurement today* (pp. 33–45). San Francisco: Jossey-Bass.

Bock, R. D., & Aitkin, M. (1981). Marginal maximum likelihood estimation of item parameters: Application of the EM algorithm. *Psychometrika, 46*, 443–459.

Bohner, G., Danner, U. N., Siebler, F., & Samson, G. B. (2002). Rape myth acceptance and judgments of vulnerability to sexual assault: An Internet experiment. *Experimental Psychology, 49*, 257–269.

Bolger, N., Davis, A., & Rafaeli, E. (2003). Dairy methods: Capturing life as it is lived. *Annual Review of Psychology, 54*, 579–616.

Bolger, N., DeLongis, A., Kessler, R. C., & Schilling, E. A. (1989). Effects of daily stress on negative mood. *Journal of Personality and Social Psychology, 57*, 808–818.

Bolger, N., & Eckenrode, J. (1987, August). *Coping with a major stressful event: A prospective daily diary study*. Paper Presented at the Annual Convention of the American Psychological Association, New York.

Bollmer, J. M., Harris, M. J., Milich, R., & Georgesen, J. C. (2003). Taking offense: Effects of personality and teasing history on behavioral and emotional reactions to teasing. *Journal of Personality, 71*, 557–603.

Bordia, P. (1996). Studying verbal interaction on the internet: The case of rumor transmission research. *Behavior Research Methods, Instruments, and Computers, 28*(2), 149–151.

Borg, I. (1994). Evolving notions of facet theory. In I. Borg & P. P. Mohler (Eds.), *Trends and perspectives in empirical social research* (pp. 178–200). Berlin, Germany and New York: De Gruyter.

Borg, I., & Shye, S. (1995). *Facet theory: Form and content*. Newbury Park, CA: Sage.

Boring, E. G. (1950). *A history of experimental psychology* (2nd ed.). Englewood Cliffs, NJ: Prentice Hall.

Boris, N. W., Aoki, Y., & Zeanah, C. H. (1999). The development of infant–parent attachment: Considerations for assessment. *Infants and Young Children, 11*, 1–10.

Borkenau, P. (1990). Traits as ideal-based and goal-derived social categories. *Journal of Personality and Social Psychology, 58*, 381–396.

Borkenau, P., & Liebler, A. (1992). Trait inferences: Sources of validity at zero acquaintance. *Journal of Personality and Social Psychology, 62*, 645–657.

Borkenau, P., & Liebler, A. (1993). Convergence of stranger ratings of personality and intelligence with self-ratings, partner ratings, and measured intelligence. *Journal of Personality and Social Psychology, 65*, 546–553.

Borkenau, P., Mauer, N., Riemann, R., Spinath, F. M., & Angleitner, A. (2004). Thin slices of behavior as cues for personality and intelligence. *Journal of Personality and Social Psychology, 58*, 419–428.

Borkenau, P., Riemann, R., Angleitner, A., & Spinath, F. M. (2001). Genetic and environmental influences on observed personality: Evidence from the German Observational Study of Adult Twins. *Journal of Personality and Social Psychology, 80*, 655–668.

Borman, W., White, L., Pulakos, E., & Oppler, S. (1991). Models of supervisory performance ratings. *Journal of Applied Psychology, 76*, 863–872.

Bornstein, R. F. (1999). Criterion validity of objective and projective dependency tests: A meta-analytic assessment of behavioral prediction. *Psychological Assessment, 11*, 48–57.

Bosnjak, M. (2001). Participation in non-restricted Web surveys: A typology and explanatory model for item non-response. In U.-D. Reips & M. Bosnjak (Eds.), *Dimensions of Internet science* (pp. 193–208). Lengerich, Germany: Pabst.

Bosson, J. K., Swann, W. B., & Pennebaker, J. W. (2000). Stalking the perfect measure of implicit self-esteem: The blind men and the elephant revisited? *Journal of Personality and Social Psychology, 79*, 631–643.

Bower, G. H. (1981). Mood and memory. *American Psychologist, 36*, 103–128.

Bowlby, J. (1969). Attachment and loss. *Attachment Volume 1*. New York: Basic Books.

Boyatzis, R. E. (1973). Affiliation motivation. In D. C. McClelland & R. S. Steele (Eds.), *Human motivation: A book of readings* (pp. 252–275). Morristown, NJ: General Learning Press.

Boyce, T. E., & Geller, E. S. (2002). An instrumented vehicle assessment of problem behavior and driving style: Do younger males really take more risks? *Accident Analysis and Prevention, 34*, 51–64.

Bozdogan, H. (1987). Model selection and Akaike's information criterion (AIC): The general theory and its analytical extensions. *Psychometrika, 52*, 345–370.

Bradburn, N. M., Rips, L. J., & Shevell, S. K. (1987). Answering autobiographical questions: The impact of memory and inference on surveys. *Science, 236*, 157–161.

Bradley, M. M., & Lang, P. J. (2000). Measuring emotion: Behavior, feeling, and physiology. In R. D. Lane & L. Nadel (Eds.), *Cognitive neuroscience of emotion* (pp. 242–276). New York: Oxford University Press.

Branje, S. J. T., van Aken, M. A. G., van Lieshout, C. F. M., & Mathijssen, J. J. J. P. (2003). Personality judgments in adolescents' families: The perceiver, the target, the relationship, and the family. *Journal of Personality, 71,* 49–81.

Bray, D. W. (1982). The assessment center and the study of lives. *American Psychologist, 37,* 180–189.

Bray, D. W., Campbell, R. J., & Grant, D. L. (1974). *Formative years in business: A long-term study of managerial lives.* New York: John Wiley & Sons.

Breckler, S. J. (1984). Empirical validation of affect, behavior, and cognition as distinct components of attitude. *Journal of Personality and Social Psychology, 47,* 1191–1205.

Bredenkamp, J. (2001). Laboratory experiment: methodology. In: N. J. Smelser & P. B. Baltes (Eds.), *International encyclopedia of the social & behavioral sciences* (pp. 8226–8232). Oxford, England: Elsevier/Pergamon.

Brenner, V. (2002). Generalizability issues in Internet-based survey research: Implications for the Internet addiction controversy. In B. Batinic, U.-D. Reips, & M. Bosnjak (Eds.), *Online social sciences* (pp. 93–114). Seattle, WA: Hogrefe & Huber.

Brett, M., Johnsrude, I. S., & Owen, A. M. (2002). The problem of functional localization in the human brain. *Nature Review Neuroscience, 3,* 243–249.

Breuner, C. W., & Orchinik, M. (2002). Plasma binding proteins as mediators of corticosteroid action in vertebrates. *Journal of Endocrinology, 175,* 99–112.

Brewer, M. B. (2000). Research design and issues of validity. In H. T. Reis & C. M. Judd (Eds.), *Handbook of research methods in social and personality psychology* (pp. 3–16). Cambridge, England: Cambridge University Press.

Bridgman, P. W. (1927). *The logic of modern physics.* New York: Macmillan.

Bridgman, P. W. (1945). Some general principles of operational analysis. *Psychological Review, 52,* 246–249.

Brief, A. P., Butcher, A. H., & Roberson, L. (1995). Cookies, disposition, and job attitudes: The effects of positive mood-inducing events and negative affectivity on job satisfaction in a field experiment. *Organizational Behavior and Human Decision Processes, 62,* 55–62.

Briggs, S. R., & Cheek, J. M. (1986). On the nature of self-monitoring: Problems with assessment, problems with validity. *Journal of Personality and Social Psychology, 54,* 663–678.

Bringmann, W. G., Lück, H. E., Miller, R., & Early, C. E. (Eds.). (1997). *A pictorial history of psychology.* Chicago: Quintessence.

Brizer, D. A., Crowner, M. L., Convit, A., & Volavka, J. (1988). Videotape recording of inpatient assaults: A pilot study. *American Journal of Psychiatry, 145,* 751–752.

Broderick, J., Schwartz, J., Shiffman, S., Hufford, M., & Stone, A. (2003). Signaling does not insure diary compliance. *Annals of Behavioral Medicine, 26,* 295–305.

Brody, N. (1992). *Intelligence* (2nd ed.). New York: Academic Press.

Brody, N. (1994). Psychometric theories of intelligence. In R. J. Sternberg (Ed.), *Encyclopedia of human intelligence* (pp. 868–875). New York: Macmillan.

Brody, N. (2003). Construct validation of the Sternberg Triarchic Abilities Test (STAT): Comment and reanalysis. *Intelligence, 31,* 319–329.

Bronfenbrenner, U. (1979). *The ecology of human development.* Cambridge, MA: Harvard University Press.

Brown, G. W., & Harris, T. (1978). *Social origins of depression: A study of psychiatric disorder in women.* New York: John Wiley & Sons.

Brown, J., Lewis, V. J., & Monk, A. F. (1977). Memorability, word frequency, and negative recognition. *Quarterly Journal of Experimental Psychology, 29,* 461–473.

Brown, J. D., & Dutton, K. A. (1995). Truth and consequences: The costs and benefits of accurate self-knowledge. *Personality and Social Psychology Bulletin, 21,* 1288–1296.

Brown, K. W., & Ryan, R. (2003). The benefits of being present: Mindfulness and its role in psychological well-being. *Journal of Personality and Social Psychology, 84,* 822–848.

Brown, W. (1910). Some experimental results in the correlation of mental abilities. *British Journal of Psychology, 3,* 296–322.

Browne, M. W. (1984). The decomposition of multitrait-multimethod matrices. *British Journal of Mathematical and Statistical Psychology, 37,* 1–21.

Browne, M. W., & Zhang, G. (in press). Developments in the factor analysis of individual time series. In R. Cudeck & R. MacCallum (Eds.), *Factor analysis at 100: Historical developments and future directions.* Mahwah, NJ: Erlbaum.

Bruner, J. S. (1957). On perceptual readiness. *Psychological Review, 64,* 123–152.

Brunswik, E. (1934). *Wahrnehmung und Gegenstandswelt* [Perception and the world of objects]. Wien, Germany: Deuticke.

Brunswik, E. (1947). Systematic and representative design of psychological experiments. Berkeley: University of California Press.

Brunswik, E. (1949). *Systematic and representative design of psychological experiments.* Berkeley and Los Angeles: University of California Press.

Brunswik, E. (1956). *Perception and the representative design of psychological experiments.* Berkeley: University of California Press.

Bryk, A. S., & Raudenbush, S. W. (1992). *Hierarchical linear models for social and behavioral research: Applications and data analysis methods.* Newbury Park, CA: Sage.

Buchanan, T. (2001). Online personality assessment. In U.-D. Reips & M. Bosnjak (Eds.), *Dimensions of Internet science* (pp. 57–74). Lengerich, Germany: Pabst.

Buchanan, T., Ali, T., Heffernan, T. M., Ling, J., Parrott, A. C., Rodgers, J., & Scholey, A. B. (in press). Non-equivalence of online and paper-and-pencil psychological tests: The case of the Prospective Memory Questionnaire. *Behavior Research Methods*.

Buchanan, T., Johnson, J. A., & Goldberg, L. R. (2005). Implementing a five-factor personality inventory for use on the Internet. *European Journal of Psychological Assessment, 21*, 115–127.

Buchanan, T., & Reips, U.-D. (2001, October 10). Platform-dependent biases in online research: Do Mac users really think different? In K. J. Jonas, P. Breuer, B. Schauenburg, & M. Boos (Eds.), *Perspectives on Internet research: Concepts and methods*. Retrieved December 27, 2001, from http://server3.uni-psych.gwdg.de/gor/contrib/buchanan-tom.

Buchanan, T., & Smith, J. L. (1999). Using the Internet for psychological research: Personality testing on the World-Wide Web. *British Journal of Psychology, 90*, 125–144.

Buchheim, A., & Mergenthaler, E. (2000). The relationship among attachment representation, emotion-abstraction patterns, and narrative style: A computer-based text analysis of the Adult Attachment Interview. *Psychotherapy Research, 10*, 390–407.

Buchner, A., Erdfelder, E., Steffens, M. C., & Martensen, H. (1997). The nature of memory processes underlying recognition judgments in the process dissociation procedure. *Memory & Cognition, 25*, 508–517.

Buchner, A., Erdfelder, E., & Vaterrodt-Plünnecke, B. (1995). Toward unbiased measurement of conscious and unconscious memory processes within the process dissociation framework. *Journal of Experimental Psychology: General, 124*, 137–160.

Buchner, A., & Wippich, W. (2000). On the reliability of implicit and explicit memory measures. *Cognitive Psychology, 40*, 227–259.

Buckner, R. L. (1998). Event-related fMRI and the hemodynamic response. *Human Brain Mapping, 6*, 373–377.

Buckner, R. L., Bandettini, P. A., O'Craven, K. M., Savoy, R. L., Petersen, S. E., Raichle, M. E., & Rosen, B. R. (1996). Detection of cortical activation during averaged single trials of a cognitive task using functional magnetic resonance imaging. *Proceedings of the National Academy of Sciences of the United States of America, 93*, 14878–14883.

Bunce, S. C., Larsen, R. J., & Cruz, M. (1993). Individual differences in the excitation transfer effect. *Personality and Individual Differences, 15*, 507–514.

Bungard, W. (Ed.). (1980). *Die gute Versuchsperson denkt nicht: Artefakte in der Sozialpsychologie* [The good subject does not think: Artifacts in social psychology]. München, Germany: Urban und Schwarzenberg.

Bungard, W., & Lück, H. E. (1997). Nichtreaktive Meßverfahren. [Nonreactive measures]. In J. L. Patry (Ed.), *Feldforschung: Methoden und Probleme sozialwissenschaftlicher Forschung unter natürlichen Bedingungen* [Field research: Methods and problems of social scientific research under natural conditions]. Bonn, Germany: Verlag Hans Huber.

Buodo, G., Sarlo, M., & Palomba, D. (2002). Attentional resources measured by reaction times highlight differences within pleasant and unpleasant, high arousing stimuli. *Motivation & Emotion, 26*, 123–138.

Burns, G. L. (1980). Indirect measurement and behavioral assessment: A case for social behaviorism psychometrics. *Behavioral Assessment, 2*, 197–206.

Burns, G. L. (2000). Problem of item overlap between the Psychopathy Screening Device and attention deficit hyperactivity disorder, oppositional defiant disorder, and conduct disorder rating scales. *Psychological Assessment, 12*, 447–450.

Burns, G. L., & Walsh, J. A. (2002). The influence of ADHD-Hyperactivity/Impulsivity symptoms on the development of oppositional defiant disorder symptoms in a two year longitudinal study. *Journal of Abnormal Child Psychology, 30*, 245–256.

Burns, G. L., Walsh, J. A., & Gomez, R. (2003). Convergent and discriminant validity of trait and source effects in ADHD-Inattention and hyperactivity/impulsivity measures across a 3-month interval. *Journal of Abnormal Child Psychology, 31*, 529–541.

Burnstein, E., & Vinokur, A. (1975). Persuasive argumentation and social comparison as determinants of attitude polarization. *Journal of Experimental Social Psychology, 13*, 315–332.

Bush, R. R., & Mosteller, F. (1951). A mathematical model for simple learning. *Psychological Review, 58*, 313–323.

Buss, D. M. (1999). Human nature and individual differences: The evolution of the human personality. In L. Pervin & O. P. John (Eds.), *Handbook of personality* (2nd ed., pp. 31–56). New York: Guilford Press.

Buss, D. M., & Craik, K. H. (1983). The act frequency approach to personality. *Psychological Review, 90*, 105–126.

Buxton, R. B. (2002). *Introduction to functional magnetic resonance imaging: Principles and techniques*. Cambridge, England: Cambridge University Press.

Byrne, B. M. (1994). *Structural equation modeling with EQS and EQS/Windows*. Thousand Oaks, CA: Sage.

Byrne, B. M. (1996). *Measuring self-concept across the life span: Issues and instrumentation*. Washington, DC: American Psychological Association.

Byrne, B. M. (2003). Testing for equivalent self-concept measurement across culture: Issues, caveats, and application. In H. W. Marsh, R. G. Craven, & D. M. McInerney (Eds.), *International advances in self research* (Vol. 1, pp. 291–314). Greenwich, CT: Information Age.

Cacioppo, J. T. (1994). Social neuroscience: Autonomic, neuroendocrine, and immune responses to stress. *Psychophysiology, 31*, 113–28.

Cacioppo, J. T., & Berntson, G. G. (1992). Social psychological contributions to the decade of the brain: Doctrine of multilevel analysis. *American Psychologist, 47*, 1019–1028.

Cacioppo, J. T., Berntson, G. G., Binkley, P. F., Quigley, K. S., Uchino, B. N., & Fieldstone, A. (1994). Autonomic cardiac control. II. Basal response, noninvasive

indices, and autonomic space as revealed by autonomic blockades. *Psychophysiology, 31,* 586–598.

Cacioppo, J. T., Berntson, G. G., Lorig, T. S., Norris, C. J., Rickett, E., & Nusbaum, H. (2003). Just because you're imaging the brain doesn't mean you can stop using your head: A primer and set of first principles. *Journal of Personality and Social Psychology, 85,* 650–661.

Cacioppo, J. T., Berntson, G. G., Sheridan, J. F., & McClintock, M. K. (2000). Multi-level integrative analyses of human behavior: The complementing nature of social and biological approaches. *Psychological Bulletin, 126,* 829–843.

Cacioppo, J. T., & Gardner, W. L. (1999). Emotions. *Annual Review of Psychology, 50,* 191–214.

Cacioppo, J. T., Hawkley, L. C., & Berntson, G. G. (2003). The anatomy of loneliness. *Current Directions in Psychological Science, 12,* 71–74.

Cacioppo, J. T., Hawkley, L. C., Crawford, L. E., Ernst, J. M., Burleson, M. H., Kowalski, R. B., et al. (2002). Loneliness and health: Potential mechanisms. *Psychosomatic Medicine, 64,* 407–417.

Cacioppo, J. T., Klein, D. J., Berntson, G. G., & Hatfield, E. (1993). The psychophysiology of emotion. In M. Lewis & J. M. Haviland (Eds.), *Handbook of emotions* (pp. 119–142). New York: Guilford Press.

Cacioppo, J. T., Petty, R. E., Losch, M. E., & Kim, H. S. (1986). Electromyographic activity over facial muscle regions can differentiate the valence and intensity of affective reactions. *Journal of Personality and Social Psychology, 50,* 260–268.

Cacioppo, J. T., Tassinary, L. G., & Berntson, G. G. (2000). *Handbook of psychophysiology* (2nd ed.). New York: Cambridge University Press.

Calfee, R. C. (1985). *Experimental methods in psychology.* New York: Holt, Rinehart & Winston.

Calsyn, R., & Kenny, D. A. (1977). Self-concept of ability and perceived evaluations by others: Cause or effect of academic achievement? *Journal of Educational Psychology, 69,* 136–145.

Campbell, D. T. (1957). Factors relevant to the validity of experiments in social settings. *Psychological Bulletin, 54,* 297–312.

Campbell, D. T., & Fiske, D. W. (1959). Convergent and discriminant validation by the multitrait–multimethod matrix. *Psychological Bulletin, 56,* 81–105.

Campbell, D. T., & O'Connell, E. J. (1967). Method factors in multitrait-multimethod matrices: Multiplicative rather than additive? *Multivariate Behavioral Research, 2,* 409–426.

Campbell, D. T., & Stanley, J. C. (1963). *Experimental and quasi-experimental designs for research.* Boston: Houghton Mifflin.

Campbell, J. P. (1985). *Improving the selection, classification, and utilization of Army enlisted personnel: Annual report, 1985 fiscal year* (Tech. Rep. No. 746). Alexandria, VA: U.S. Army Research Institute for the Behavioral and Social Sciences.

Campbell, J. P. (1990). Modeling the performance prediction problem in industrial and organizational psychology. In M. D. Dunnette & L. M. Hough (Eds.), *Handbook of industrial and organizational psychology* (2nd ed., Vol. 1, pp. 687–732). Palo Alto, CA: Consulting Psychologists Press.

Campbell, J. P. (1996). Group differences and personnel decisions: Validity, fairness, and affirmative action. *Journal of Vocational Behavior, 49,* 122–158.

Campbell, R. S., & Pennebaker, J. W. (2003). The secret life of pronouns: Flexibility in writing style and physical health. *Psychological Science, 14,* 60–65.

Campos, J. J., Bertenthal, B. I., & Kermoian, R. (1992). Early experience and emotional development: The emergence of wariness of heights. *Psychological Science, 3,* 61–64.

Canli, T., Sivers, H., Whitfield, S. L., Gotlib, I. H., & Gabrieli, J. D. (2002). Amygdala response to happy faces as a function of extraversion. *Science, 296,* 2191.

Capaldi, D. M., & Rothbart, M. K. (1992). Development and validation of an early adolescent temperament measure. *Journal of Early Adolescence, 12,* 153–173.

Carr, H. A., & Kingsbury, F. A. (1938). The concept of traits. *Psychological Review, 45,* 495–524.

Carrere, S., Evans, G. W., Palsane, M. N., & Rivas, M. (1991). Job strain and occupational stress among urban public transit operators. *Journal of Occupational Psychology, 64,* 305–316.

Carroll, J. B. (1993). *Human cognitive abilities: A survey of factor-analytic studies.* Cambridge, England: Cambridge University Press.

Carroll, J. B. (1997). Psychometrics, intelligence, and public perception. *Intelligence, 24,* 25–52.

Carstensen, C., & Rost, J. (1998). *MULTIRA* [Computer program]. Kiel: IPN – Leibniz-Institute for Science Education. Available from http://www.multira.de

Carter, A. S., Little, C., Briggs-Gowan, M. J., & Kogan, N. (1999). The infant-toddler social and emotional assessment (ITSEA): Comparing parent ratings to laboratory observations of task mastery, emotion regulation, coping behaviors, and attachment status. *Infant Mental Health Journal, 20,* 375–392.

Carver, C. S. (1989). How should multifaceted personality constructs be tested? Issues illustrated by self-monitoring, attributional style, and hardiness. *Journal of Personality and Social Psychology, 56,* 577–585.

Carver, C. S., & Scheier, M. F. (1981). The self-attention-induced feedback loop and social facilitation. *Journal of Experimental Social Psychology, 17,* 545–568.

Casey, B. J., Trainor, R., Giedd, J., Vauss, Y., Vaituzis, C. K., Hanburger, S., et al. (1997). The role of the anterior cingulate in automatic and controlled processes: A developmental neuroanatomical study. *Developmental Psychobiology, 30,* 61–69.

Caspi, A., Sugden, K., Moffitt, T. E., Taylor, A., Craig, I. W., Harrington, H., et al. (2003). Influence of life stress on depression: Moderation by a polymorphism in the 5-HTT gene. *Science, 301,* 386–389.

Castelli, L., Zogmaister, C., & Arcuri, L. (2001). Exemplar activation and interpersonal behavior. *Current Research in Social Psychology, 6,* 33–45.

Catledge, L., & Pitkow, J. (1995). *Characterizing browsing strategies in the World-Wide-Web.* Paper presented

at the Third International World-Wide-Web Conference. Retrieved March 6, 2003, from http://www.igd.fhg.de/archive/1995_www95/papers/80/userpatterns/UserPatterns.Paper4.formatted.html

Cattell, R. B. (1957). *Personality and motivation structure and measurement.* New York: World Book Company.

Cattell, R. B. (1966). The data box: Its ordering of total resources in terms of possible relational systems. In R. B. Cattell (Ed.), *Handbook of multivariate experimental psychology* (pp. 67–128). Chicago: Rand McNally.

Cattell, R. B. (1971). *Abilities: Their structure and growth.* Boston: Houghton Mifflin.

Cattell, R. B. (1988). The data box: Its ordering of total resources in terms of possible relational systems. In J. R. Nesselroade & R. B. Cattell (Eds.), *Handbook of multivariate experimental psychology* (2nd ed., pp. 69–130). New York: Plenum Press.

Cattell, R. B., Cattell, A. K., & Rhymer, R. M. (1947). P-technique demonstrated in determining psychophysiological source traits in a normal individual. *Psychometrika, 12,* 267–288.

Ceci, S. J. (1996). [Guest Editor] IQ in society. *Psychology, Public Policy, and Law, 2,* 403–645.

Cervone, D., & Shoda, Y. (1999). Beyond traits in the study of personality coherence. *Current Directions in Psychological Science, 8,* 27–32.

Challis, B. H., & Krane, R. V. (1988). Mood induction and the priming of semantic memory in a lexical decision task: Asymmetric effects of elation and depression. *Bulletin of the Psychonomic Society, 26,* 309–312.

Chan, D., & Schmitt, N. (1997). Video-based versus paper-and-pencil method of assessment in situational judgment tests: Subgroup differences in test performance and face validity perceptions. *Journal of Applied Psychology, 82,* 143–159.

Chan, D., & Schmitt, N. (2000). Interindividual differences in intraindividual changes in proactivity during organizational entry: A latent growth modeling approach to understanding newcomer adaptation. *Journal of Applied Psychology, 85,* 190–210.

Chan, D., Schmitt, N., DeShon, R. P., Clause, C. S., et al. (1997). Reactions to cognitive ability tests: The relationships between race, test performance, face validity perceptions, and test-taking motivation. *Journal of Applied Psychology, 82,* 300–310.

Chaplin, W. F., John, O. P., & Goldberg, L. R. (1988). Conceptions of states and traits: Dimensional attributes with ideals as prototypes. *Journal of Personality and Social Psychology, 54,* 541–557.

Chaplin, W. F., Phillips, J. B., Brown, J. D., Clanton, N. R., & Stein, J. L. (2000). Handshaking, gender, personality, and first impressions. *Journal of Personality and Social Psychology, 79,* 110–117.

Chapman, G. B., & Robbins, S. J. (1990). Cue interaction in human contingency judgment. *Memory & Cognition, 18,* 537–545.

Chappel, E. (1970). *Culture and the biological man: Explanations in behavioral anthropology.* New York: Holt, Rinehart & Winston.

Chaudhuri, A., & Mukerjee, R. (1988). *Randomized response: Theory and techniques.* New York: Marcel Dekker.

Cheek, J. M. (1982). Aggregation, moderator variables, and the validity of personality tests. *Journal of Personality and Social Psychology, 43,* 1254–1269.

Cheng, P. W. (1997). From covariation to causation: A causal power theory. *Psychological Review, 104,* 367–405.

Chernyshenko, O. S., Stark, S., Chan, K.-Y., Drasgow, F., & Williams, B. (2001). Fitting item response theory models to two personality inventories: Issues and insights. *Multivariate Behavioral Research, 36,* 523–562.

Cherulnik, P. D. (1975). An independent validation of the lost-letter technique. *Journal of Social Psychology, 96,* 299–300.

Christensen, R. (1997). *Loglinear models and logistic regression* (2nd ed.). New York: Springer.

Christensen, T. C., Wood, J. V., & Barrett, L. F. (2003). Remembering everyday experience through the prism of self-esteem. *Personality and Social Psychology Bulletin, 29,* 51–62.

Cialdini, R. B., & Baumann, D. J. (1981). Littering: A new unobtrusive measure of attitude. *Social Psychology Quarterly, 44,* 254–259.

Cicchetti, D. V., & Feinstein, A. R. (1990). High agreement but low kappa: II. Resolving the paradoxes. *Journal of Clinical Epidemiology, 43,* 551–558.

Cicchetti, D. V., Toth, S. L., & Maughan, A. (2000). An ecological transactional model of child maltreatment. In A. J. Sameroff, M. Lewis, & S. M. Miller (Eds.), *Handbook of developmental psychopathology.* New York: Kluwer.

Clark, H., & Shober, M. (1992). Asking questions and influencing answers. In J. Tanur (Ed.), *Questions about questions: Inquiries into the cognitive bases of surveys* (pp. 15–48). New York: Russell Sage Foundation.

Clark, R. (1985). *The Parent-Child Early Relational Scale.* Unpublished manuscript.

Clark, S. J., & Desharnais, R. A. (1998). Honest answers to embarrassing questions: Detecting cheating in the randomized response model. *Psychological Methods, 3,* 160–168.

Cleary, T. A., Humphreys, L. G., Kendrick, S. A., & Wesman, A. (1975). Educational uses of tests with disadvantaged students. *American Psychologist, 30,* 15–41.

Cliff, N. (1993). What is and isn't measurement. In G. Keren & C. Lewis (Eds.), *A handbook for data analysis in the behavioral sciences: Methodological issues* (pp. 59–63). Hillsdale, NJ: Lawrence Erlbaum Associates.

Clogg, C. C. (1982). Some models for the analysis of association in multiway cross-classifications having ordered categories. *Journal of the American Statistical Association, 77,* 803–815.

Clogg, C. C. (1995). Latent class models. In G. Arminger, C. C. Clogg, & M. E. Sobel (Eds.), *Handbook of statistical modeling for the social and behavioral sciences* (pp. 311–359). New York: Plenum.

Clogg, C. C., & Eliason, S. R. (1987). Some common problems in log-linear analysis. *Sociological Methods and Research, 16,* 18–44.

Clyman, S. G., Melnick, D. E., & Clauser, B. E. (1999). Computer-based case simulations from medicine: Assessing skills in patient management. In A. Tekian, C. H. McGuire, & W. C. McGahie (Eds.), *Innovative simulations for assessing professional competence* (pp. 29–41). Chicago: University of Illinois, Department of Medical Education.

Coan, J. A., & Gottman, J. M. (in press). The specific affect (SPAFF) coding system. In J. A. Coan & J. J. B. Allen (Eds.), *The handbook of emotion elicitation and assessment.* New York: Oxford University Press.

Coan, R. W. (1964). Facts, factors, and artifacts: The quest for psychological meaning. *Psychological Review, 71,* 123–140.

Cohen, D., Nisbett, R. E., Bowdle, B. F., & Schwarz, N. (1996). Insult, aggression and the Southern culture of honor: An "experimental ethnography." *Journal of Personality and Social Psychology, 70,* 945–960.

Cohen, J. A. (1994). The earth is round (*p* < .05). *American Psychologist, 49,* 997–1003.

Cohen, J. A. (1960). A coefficient of agreement for nominal scales. *Educational and Psychological Measurement, 20,* 37–46.

Cohen, J. A. (1968). Weighted kappa: Nominal scale agreement with provision for scaled disagreement or partial credit. *Psychological Bulletin, 70,* 213–220.

Cohen, S., Kessler, R. C., & Gordon, L. U. (1995). Strategies for measuring stress in studies of psychiatric and physical disorders. In S. Cohen, R. C. Kessler, & L. U. Gordon (Eds.), *Measuring stress: A guide for health and social scientists* (pp. 3–28). New York: Oxford University Press.

Cohn, J. F., Zlochower, A. J., Lien, J., & Kanade, T. (1999). Automated face analysis by feature point tracking has high concurrent validity with manual FACS coding. *Psychophysiology, 36,* 35–43.

Cohn, M. A., Mehl, M. R., & Pennebaker, J. W. (in press). Linguistic indicators of psychological change after September 11, 2001. *Psychological Science.*

Coie, J. D., Cillessen, A. H. N., Dodge, K. A., Hubbard, J. A., Schwartz, D., Lemerise, E. A., & Bateman, H. (1999). It takes two to fight: A test of relational factors and a method for assessing aggressive dyads. *Developmental Psychology, 35,* 1179–1188.

Cole, D. A. (1990). Relation of social and academic competence to depressive symptoms in childhood. *Journal of Abnormal Psychology, 99,* 422–429.

Cole, D. A., Martin, J. M., Peeke, L., Henderson, A., & Harwell, J. (1998). Validation of depression and anxiety measures in white and black youths: Multitrait–multimethod analyses. *Psychological Assessment, 3,* 261–276.

Cole, D. A., Martin, J. M., Powers, B., & Truglio, R. (1996). Modeling casual relations between academic and social competence and depression: A multitrait–multimethod longitudinal study of children. *Journal of Abnormal Psychology, 105,* 258–270.

Cole, D. A., Truglio, R., & Peeke, L. (1997). Relation between symptoms of anxiety and depression in children: A multitrait–multimethod–multigroup assessment. *Journal of Consulting and Clinical Psychology, 65,* 110–119.

Collins, L. M., & Sayer, A. G. (Eds.). (2001). *New methods for the analysis of change.* Washington, DC: American Psychological Association.

Colvin, C. R. (1993a). Childhood antecedents of young-adult judgability. *Journal of Personality, 61,* 611–635.

Colvin, C. R. (1993b). "Judgable" people: Personality, behavior, and competing explanations. *Journal of Personality and Social Psychology, 64,* 861–873.

Colvin, C. R., Block, J., & Funder, D. C. (1995). Overly positive self-evaluations and personality: Negative implications for mental health. *Journal of Personality and Social Psychology, 68,* 1152–1162.

Colvin, C. R., & Bundick, M. J. (2001). In search of the good judge of personality: Some methodological and theoretical consideration. In J. A. Hall & F. J. Bernieri (Eds.), *Interpersonal sensitivity: Theory and measurement* (pp. 47–65). Mahwah, NJ: Lawrence Erlbaum Associates.

Colvin, C. R., & Funder, D. C. (1991). Predicting personality and behavior. *Journal of Personality and Social Psychology, 60,* 884–894.

Committee on Population. (2001). *Cells and surveys: Should biological measures be included in social science research?* Washington, DC: National Academy Press.

Committee to Review the Scientific Evidence on the Polygraph. (2003). *The polygraph and lie detection.* Washington, DC: National Academies Press.

Compas, B. E., Connor, J. K., Saltzman, H., Thomsen, A. H., & Wadsworth, M. E. (2001). Coping with stress during childhood and adolescence: Problems, progress, and potential in theory and research. *Psychological Bulletin, 127,* 87–127.

Compton, R. (2000). Ability to disengage attention predicts negative affect. *Cognition & Emotion, 14,* 401–415.

Computerization Implementation Committee. (2001). *Computerizing the Uniform CPA examination issues, strategies, and policies: An update* (Briefing Paper #2). Jersey City, NJ: American Institute of Certified Public Accountants.

Cone, J. D. (1979). Confounded comparisons in triple response mode assessment research. *Behavioral Assessment, 11,* 85–95.

Conger, A. (1980). Integration and generalization of kappas for multiple raters. *Psychological Bulletin, 2,* 322–328.

Conley, J. J. (1984). The hierarchy of consistency: A review and model of longitudinal findings on adult individual differences in intelligence, personality, and self-opinion. *Personality and Individual Differences, 5,* 11–26.

Contreras, J., Kerns, K. A., Weimer, B. L., Gentzler, A. L., & Tomich, P. L. (2000). Emotion regulation as a mediator of associations between mother–child

attachment and peer relationships in middle childhood. *Journal of Family Psychology, 14,* 111–124.

Cook, T. D. (1985). Postpositivist critical multiplism. In L. Shotland & M. M. Mark (Eds.), *Social science and social policy* (pp. 21–62). Newbury Park, CA: Sage.

Cook, T. D. (1993). A quasi-sampling theory of the generalization of causal relationships. In L. B. Sechrest & A. G. Scott (Eds.), *New directions for program evaluation* (pp. 39–81). San Francisco: Jossey-Bass.

Cook, T. D., & Campbell, D. T. (1979). *Quasi-experimentation: Design and analysis issues for field studies.* Chicago: Rand McNally.

Coomber, R. (1997, June 30). Using the Internet for survey research. *Sociological Research Online, 2.* Retrieved June 16, 2002, from http://www.socresonline.org.uk/2/2/2.html

Coren, S., & Suedfeld, P. (1990). A power test of conceptual complexity: Textual correlates. *Journal of Applied Social Psychology, 20,* 357–367.

Corno, L., Cronbach, L. J., et al. (Eds.). (2002). *Remaking the concept of aptitude: Extending the legacy of Richard E. Snow.* Mahwah, NJ: Lawrence Erlbaum Associates.

Cortina, J. M. (1993). What is coefficient alpha? An examination of theory and application. *Journal of Applied Psychology, 78,* 98–104.

Costa, P. T., & McCrae, R. R. (1980). Still stable after all these years: Personality as a key to some issues in adulthood and old age. In P. B. Baltes & O. G. Brim (Eds.), *Life-span development and behavior* (pp. 66–102). New York: Academic Press.

Costa, P. T., & McCrae, R. R. (1988). Personality in adulthood: A six-year longitudinal study of self-reports and spouse ratings on the NEP Personality Inventory. *Journal of Personality and Social Psychology, 54,* 853–863.

Costello, A. J. (1973). The reliability of direct observations. *Bulletin of the British Psychological Society, 26,* 105–108.

Cote, S., & Moskowitz, D. S. (1998). On the dynamic covariation between interpersonal behavior and affect: Prediction from neuroticism, extraversion, and agreeableness. *Journal of Personality and Social Psychology, 75,* 1032–1046.

Cothran, D. L., Zelenski, J. M., Prizmic, Z., & Larsen, R. J. (2003). *Do emotion words interfere with naming emotion faces, and vice versa? Stroop-like interference versus automatic vigilance for negative information.* Manuscript submitted for publication.

Couto, R. A. (1987). Participatory research: Methodology and critique. *Clinical Sociology Review, 5,* 83–90.

Craik, F. I. M., & Tulving, E. (1975). Depth of processing and the retention of words in episodic memory. *Journal of Experimental Psychology: General, 104,* 268–294.

Craik, K. H. (1993). Accentuated, revealed, and quotidian personalities. *Psychological Inquiry, 4,* 278–281.

Critchfield, T. S., Tucker, J. A., & Vuchinich, R. E. (1998). Self-report methods. In K. A. Lattal & M. Perone (Eds.), *Handbook of research methods in human operant behavior* (pp. 435–470). New York: Plenum Press.

Critchley, H., Daly, E., Phillips, M., Brammer, M., Bullmore, E., Williams, S., et al. (2000). Explicit and implicit neural mechanisms for processing of social information from facial expressions: A functional magnetic resonance imaging study. *Human Brain Mapping, 9,* 93–105.

Crocker, L., & Algina, J. (1986). *Introduction to classical and modern test theory.* Fort Worth, TX: Harcourt, Brace, Jovanovich.

Cronbach, L. J. (1951). Coefficient alpha and the internal structure of psychological tests. *Psychometrika, 16,* 297–334.

Cronbach, L. J. (1955). Processes affecting scores on "understanding of others" and "assumed similarity." *Psychological Bulletin, 52,* 177–193.

Cronbach, L. J. (1957). The two disciplines of psychology. *American Psychologist, 12,* 671–684.

Cronbach, L. J. (1960). *Essentials of psychological testing.* New York: Harper & Row.

Cronbach, L. J. (1970). *Essentials of psychological testing* (3rd ed.). New York: Harper & Row.

Cronbach, L. J. (1975). Five decades of public controversy over mental testing. *American Psychologist, 30,* 1–14.

Cronbach, L. J. (1976). Measured mental abilities: Lingering questions and loose ends. In B. D. Davis & P. Flaherty (Eds.), *Human diversity: Its causes and social significance* (pp. 207–222). Cambridge, MA: Ballinger.

Cronbach, L. J. (1989). Construct validity after thirty years. In R. L. Linn (Ed.), *Intelligence: Measurement, theory, and public policy* (pp. 147–171). Urbana: University of Illinois Press.

Cronbach, L. J. (1995). Giving method variance its due. In P. E. Shrout & S. T. Fiske (Eds.), *Personality research, methods, and theory. A Festschrift honoring Donald W. Fiske* (pp. 145–157). Hillsdale, NJ: Lawrence Erlbaum Associates.

Cronbach, L. J., & Gleser, G. C. (1953). Assessing similarity between profiles. *Psychological Bulletin, 50,* 456–473.

Cronbach, L. J., Gleser, G. C., Nanda, H., & Rajaratnam, N. (1972). *The dependability of behavioral measurements: Theory of generalizability of scores and profiles.* New York: John Wiley & Sons.

Cronbach, L. J., & Meehl, P. E. (1955). Construct validity in psychological tests. *Psychological Bulletin, 52,* 281–302.

Cronbach, L. J., Rajaratnam, N., & Gleser, G. C. (1963). Theory of generalizability: A liberalization of reliability theory. *The British Journal of Statistical Psychology, 16,* 137–163.

Cronbach, L. J., & Snow, R. E. (1977). *Aptitudes and instructional methods: A handbook for research on interactions.* New York: Irvington.

Crowell, J. A., Feldman, S. S., & Ginsberg, N. (1988). Assessment of mother–child interaction in preschoolers with behavior problems. *Journal of the American Academy of Child and Adolescent Psychiatry, 27,* 303–311.

Crowne, D. P., & Marlowe, D. (1964). *The approval motive: Studies in evaluative dependence.* New York: John Wiley & Sons.

Cruise, C., Porter, L., Broderick, J., Kaell, A., & Stone, A. (1996). Reactive effects of diary self-assessment in chronic pain patients. *Pain, 67*, 253–258.

Crystal, D. S., Ostrander, R., Chen, R. S., & August, G. J. (2001). Multimethod assessment of psychopathology among DSM-IV subtypes of children with attention-deficit/ hyperactivity disorder: Self-, parent, and teacher reports. *Journal of Abnormal Child Psychology, 29*, 189–206.

Csikszentmihalyi, M. (1994). *Flow: The psychology of optimal experience.* New York: Harper Collins.

Csikszentmihalyi, M., & Larson, R. (1987). Validity and reliability of the experience–sampling method. *Journal of Nervous & Mental Disease, 175*, 526–536.

Cudeck, R. (1988). Multiplicative models and MTMM matrices. *Journal of Educational Statistics, 13*, 131–147.

Cudeck, R. (1989). Analysis of correlation matrices using covariance structure models. *Psychological Bulletin, 105*, 317–327.

Cudeck, R. (1996). Mixed-effects models in the study of individual differences with repeated measures data. *Multivariate Behavioral Research, 31*, 371–403.

Cullen, M. J., Hardison, C. M., & Sackett, P. R. (2004). Using SAT-grade and ability-job performance relationships to test predictions derived from stereotypic treat theory. *Journal of Applied Psychology, 89*, 220–230.

Cummings, E. M., Iannotti, R. J., & Zahn-Waxler, C. (1985). Influence of conflict between adults on the emotions and aggression of young children. *Developmental Psychology, 21*, 495–507.

Cunningham, W. A., Preacher, K. J., & Banaji, M. R. (2001). Implicit attitude measures: Consistency, stability, and convergent validity. *Psychological Science, 12*, 163–170.

Curran, P. J., & Bollen, K. A. (2001). The best of both worlds: Combining autoregressive and latent curve models. In L. M. Collins & A. G. Sayer (Eds.), *New methods for the analysis of change* (pp. 105–136). Washington, DC: American Psychological Association.

Cutler, S. E., Bunce, S. C., & Larsen, R. J. (1996). Repressive coping style and its relation to daily emotional experience and remembered emotional experience. *Journal of Personality, 64*, 379–405.

Daleiden, E. L., Vassey, M. W., & Williams, L. L. (1996). Assessing children's states of mind: A multitrait, multimethod study. *Psychological Assessment, 8*, 125–134.

Damon, W., Kuhn, K., & Siegler, R. S. (Eds.). (1998). *Handbook of child psychology, Vol. 2, cognition, perception, and language.* New York: John Wiley & Sons.

Danner, D. D., Snowdon, D. A., & Friesen, W. V. (2001). Positive emotions in early life and longevity: Findings from the nun study. *Journal of Personality and Social Psychology, 80*, 804–813.

Darroch, J. N., & McCloud, P. I. (1986). Category distinguishability and observer agreement. *Australian Journal of Statistics, 28*, 371–388.

Darwin, C. (1965). *The expression of emotions in man and animals.* Chicago: University of Chicago Press. (Original work published 1872)

Davidson, R. J. (1993). The neuropsychology of emotion and affective style. In M. Lewis & J. M. Haviland (Eds.), *Handbook of emotions* (pp. 143–154). New York: Guilford Press.

Davidson, R. J., Goldsmith, H. H., & Scherer, K. R. (Eds.). (2003). *Handbook of affective sciences.* New York: Oxford University Press.

Davier, M. von (2001). *WINMIRA* [Computer program]. Kiel: IPN—Leibniz-Institute for Science Education. Available from http://www.winmira.de.

Davies, M., Stankov, L., & Roberts, R. D. (1998). Emotional intelligence: In search of an elusive construct. *Journal of Personality and Social Psychology, 75*, 989–1015.

Davies, P. T., Harold, G. T., Goeke-Morey, M. C., & Cummings, E. M. (2002). *Child emotional security and interparental conflict* (Monographs of the Society for Research in Child Development, Serial No. 270, Vol. 67). Boston: Blackwell.

Davis, A. (1995). The experimental method in psychology. In G. M. Breakwell, S. Hammond, & C. Fife-Schaw (Eds.), *Research methods in psychology* (pp. 50–68). London: Sage.

Davis, M. H., & Kraus, L. A. (1997). Personality and empathic accuracy. In W. Ickes (Ed.), *Empathic accuracy* (pp. 144–168). New York: Guilford Press.

Davis, T. R. (1984). The influence of the physical environment in offices. *Academy of Management Review, 9*, 271–283.

Dawes, R. M. (1994). *House of cards: Psychology and psychotherapy built on myth.* New York: The Free Press.

Dawis, R. V. (1992). The individual differences tradition in counseling psychology. *Journal of Counseling Psychology, 39*, 7–19.

De Houwer, J. (2003). A structural analysis of indirect measures of attitudes. In J. Musch & C. Klauer (Eds.), *The psychology of evaluation: Affective processes in cognition and emotion* (pp. 219–244). Mahwah, NJ: Lawrence Erlbaum Associates.

de St. Aubin, E. (1999). Personal ideology: The intersection of personality and religious beliefs. *Journal of Personality, 67*, 1105–1139.

Deary, I. J. (2000). *Looking down on human intelligence: From psychometrics to the brain.* New York: Oxford University Press.

Deary, I. J., Whalley, L. J., Lemmon, H., Crawford, J. R., & Starr, J. M. (2000). The stability of individual differences in mental ability from childhood to old age: Follow-up of the 1932 Scottish Mental Survey. *Intelligence, 28*, 49–55.

DeCharms, R. (1968). *Personal causation.* New York: Academic Press.

Deckner, D. F., Adamson, L. B., & Bakeman, R. (2003). Rhythm in mother-infant interactions. *Infancy, 4*, 201–217.

DeGrado, T. R., Turkington, T. G., Williams, J. J., Stearns, C. W., Hoffman, J. M., & Coleman, R. E. (1994). Performance characteristics of a whole-body PET scanner. *Journal of Nuclear Medicine, 35*, 1398–1406.

Delespaul, P. (1995). *Assessing schizophrenia in daily life—The Experience Sampling Method.* Maastricht, the Netherlands: Maastricht University Press.

Dell, G. S. (2004). Connectionism and cognitive neuropsychology: Comments on Harley's reflections. *Cognitive Neuropsychology, 21,* 27–30.

Denham, S. A. (1986). Social cognition, prosocial behavior, and emotion in preschoolers: Contextual validation. *Child Development, 57,* 194–201.

DePaulo, B. M., Lindsay, J. J., Malone, B. E., Muhlenbruck, L., Charlton, K., & Cooper, H. (2003). Cues to deception. *Psychological Bulletin, 129,* 74–122.

Derogatis, L. R., & Melisaratos, N. (1983). The Brief Symptom Inventory: An introductory report. *Psychological Medicine, 13,* 595–605.

D'Esposito, M., Ballard, D., Aguirre, G. K., & Zarahn, E. (1998). Human prefrontal cortex is not specific for working memory: a functional MRI study. *Neuroimage, 8,* 274–282.

D'Esposito, M., Zarahn, E., & Aguirre, G. K. (1999). Event-related functional MRI: Implications for cognitive psychology. *Psychological Bulletin, 125,* 155–164.

Devine, P. G. (1989). Stereotypes and prejudice: Their automatic and controlled components. *Journal of Personality and Social Personality, 56,* 5–18.

Devine, P. G., Plant, E. A., Amodio, D. M., Harmon-Jones, E., & Vance, S. L. (2002). The regulation of explicit and implicit race bias: The role of motivations to respond without prejudice. *Journal of Personality and Social Psychology, 82,* 835–848.

DeVries, M. (1992). *The experience of psychopathology.* Cambridge, England: Cambridge University Press.

Dickenson, A., & Mackintosh, N. J. (1978). Classical conditioning in animals. In M. R. Rosensweig & L. W. Porter (Eds.), *Annual Review of Psychology* (Vol. 29, pp. 587–612). Palo Alto, CA: Annual Reviews.

Diener, E. (1999). Introduction to the special section on the structure of emotion. *Journal of Personality and Social Psychology, 76,* 803–804.

Diener, E., & Larsen, R. J. (1984). Temporal stability and cross-situational consistency of affective, cognitive, and behavioral responses. *Journal of Personality and Social Psychology, 47,* 871–883.

Diener, E., Larsen, R. J., & Emmons, R. A. (1984). Person X situation interactions: Choice of situations and congruence response models. *Journal of Personality and Social Psychology, 47,* 580–592.

Diener, E., & Scollon, C. N. (2002). Our desired future for personality psychology. *Journal of Research in Personality, 36,* 629–637.

Diener, E., & Suh, E. M. (Eds.). (2000). *Culture and subjective well-being.* Cambridge, MA: MIT Press.

Diener, M. L., & Mangelsdorf, S. C. (1999). Behavioral strategies for emotion regulation in toddlers: Associations with maternal involvement and emotional expressions. *Infant Behavior and Development, 22,* 369–383.

Dillman, D. A. (2000). *Mail and Internet surveys: The tailored design method* (2nd ed.). New York: John Wiley & Sons.

Dillman, D. A., & Bowker, D. K. (2001). The Web questionnaire challenge to survey methodologists. In U.-D. Reips & M. Bosnjak (Eds.), *Dimensions of Internet science* (pp. 159–178). Lengerich, Germany: Pabst.

Dillman, D. A., Tortora, R. D., & Bowker, D. K. (1998). Principles for constructing Web surveys. *SESRC Technical Report 98–50.* Pullman, WA.

Dillon, W. R., & Mullani, R. (1984). A probabilistic latent class model for assessing inter-judge reliability. *Multivariate Behavioral Research, 19,* 438–458.

Dimock, P. H., & Cormier, P. (1991). The effects of format differences and computer experience on performance and anxiety on a computer-administered test. *Measurement and Evaluation in Counseling and Development, 24,* 119–126.

Dishion, T. J., Burraston, B., & Li, F. (2002). Family management practices: Research design and measurement issues. In Z. Sloboda & W. J. Bukoski (Eds.), *Handbook for drug abuse prevention: Theory, science, and practice* (pp. 587–607). New York: Plenum Press.

Dixon, N. F. (1981). *Preconscious processing.* London: John Wiley & Sons.

Dodson, C. S., Holland, P. W., & Shimamura, A. P. (1998). On the recollection of specific- and partial-source information. *Journal of Experimental Psychology: Learning, Memory, and Cognition, 24,* 1121–1136.

Donovan, M. A., Drasgow, F., & Probst, T. (2000). Does computerizing paper-and-pencil job attitude scales make a difference? New IRT analysis offers insight. *Journal of Applied Psychology, 85,* 305–313.

Doty, D. H., & Glick, W. H. (1998). Common methods bias: Does common methods variance really bias results? *Organizational Research Methods, 1,* 374–406.

Doucette-Gates, A., Brooks-Gunn, J., & Chase-Lansdale, P. (1998). The role of bias and equivalence in the study of race, class, and ethnicity. In V. C. McLoyd & L. Steinberg (Eds.), *Studying minority adolescents: Conceptual, methodological, and theoretical issues* (pp. 211–236). Mahwah, NJ: Lawrence Erlbaum Associates.

Dovidio, J. F., Kawakami, K., & Gaertner, S. L. (2002). Implicit and explicit prejudice and interracial interaction. *Journal of Personality and Social Psychology, 82,* 62–68.

Dovidio, J. F., Kawakami, K., Johnson, C., Johnson, B., & Howard, A. (1997). On the nature of prejudice: Automatic and controlled processes. *Journal of Experimental Social Psychology, 33,* 510–540.

Dudgeon, P. (1994). A reparameterization of the Restricted Factor Analysis model for multitrait–multimethod matrices. *British Journal of Mathematical and Statistical Psychology, 49,* 283–308.

Dumenci, L. (2000). Multitrait–multimethod analysis. In H. E. A. Tinsley & S. D. Brown (Eds.), *Handbook of applied multivariate statistics and mathematical modeling* (pp. 583–611). San Diego, CA: Academic Press.

Duncan, J., & Owen, A. M. (2000). Common regions of the human frontal lobe recruited by diverse cognitive demands. *Trends in Neurosciences, 23,* 475–483.

Duncan, S. C., Duncan, T. E., & Hops, H. (1996). Analysis of longitudinal data within accelerated longitudinal designs. *Psychological Methods, 1,* 236–248.

Dunnette, M. D. (1966). Fads, fashion, and folderol in psychology. *American Psychologist, 21,* 343–352.

Duryea, E., & Nagel, L. (1995). Behavior assessment and cross-validation by surrogate measures in drug prevention research. *Journal of Drug Education, 25,* 335–342.

Dweck, C. S., & Leggett, E. L. (1988). A social-cognitive approach to motivation and personality. *Psychological Review, 95,* 256–273.

Dwyer, J. H. (1983). *Statistical models for the social and behavioral sciences.* New York: Oxford.

Ebbinghaus, H. (1885). *Über das Gedächtnis.* Leipzig, Germany: Duncker and Humblot.

Eckenrode, J., & Bolger, N. (1995). Daily and within-day event measurement. In S. Cohen, R. Kessler, & L. Gordon (Eds.), *Measuring stress: A guide for health and social scientists* (pp. 80–101). Oxford, England: Oxford University Press.

Eckes, T. (2004). Beurteilerübereinstimmungen und Beurteilerstrenge: Eine Multifacetten-Rasch-Analyse von Leistungsbeurteilungen im "Test Deutsch als Fremdsprache" (TestDaF) [Interrater agreement und interrater strictness: A multifacet Rasch analysis of judgments of achievements in "Test Deutsch als Fremdsprache" (TestDaF)]. *Diagnostica, 50,* 65–77.

Eder, R. A., Gerlach, S. G., & Perlmutter, M. (1987). In search of children's selves: Development of the specific and general components of the self-concept. *Child Development, 58,* 1044–1050.

Edwards, A. L. (1953). The relationship between the judged desirability of a trait and the probability that the trait will be endorsed. *Journal of Applied Psychology, 49,* 342–344.

Edwards, A. L. (1957). *The social desirability variable in personality assessment and research.* Ft. Worth, TX: Dryden Press.

Egan, J. P. (1975). *Signal detection theory and ROC analysis.* New York: Academic Press.

Eichstaedt, J. (2001). Reaction time measurement by JAVA-applets implementing Internet-based experiments. *Behavior Research Methods, Instruments, & Computers, 33,* 179–186.

Eid, M. (1996). Longitudinal confirmatory factor analysis for polytomous item responses: Model definition and model selection on the basis of stochastic measurement theory. *Methods of Psychological Research—Online, 1,* 65–85.

Eid, M. (2000). A multitrait–multimethod model with minimal assumptions. *Psychometrika, 65,* 241–261.

Eid, M., & Diener, E. (1999). Intraindividual variability in affect: Reliability, validity, and personality correlates. *Journal of Personality and Social Psychology, 76,* 662–676.

Eid, M., & Diener, E. (2001). Norms for experiencing emotions in different cultures. *Journal of Personality and Social Psychology, 81,* 869–885.

Eid, M., & Diener, E. (2004). Global judgments of subjective well-being: Situational variability and long-term stability. *Social Indicators Research, 65,* 245–277.

Eid, M., & Langeheine, R. (1999). The measurement of consistency and occasion specificity with latent class models: A new model and its application to the measurement of affect. *Psychological Methods, 4,* 100–116.

Eid, M., & Langeheine, R. (2003). Separating stable from variable individuals in longitudinal studies by mixture distribution models. *Measurement, 1,* 179–206.

Eid, M., Lischetzke, T., Nussbeck, F., & Geiser, C. (2004). *Die Multitrait–Multimethod–Analyse: Entwicklung neuer Modelle und ihre Anwendung in der Differentiellen und Diagnostischen Psychologie* [Multitrait–multimethod analysis: Development of new models and their applications in personality psychology and psychological assessment]. Geneva, Switzerland: University of Geneva, Report for the German Research Foundation.

Eid, M., Lischetzke, T., Nussbeck, F. W., & Trierweiler, L. I. (2003). Separating trait effects from method-specific method effects in multitrait–multimethod models: A multiple indicator CTC(M-1) model. *Psychological Methods, 8,* 38–60.

Eid, M., Notz, P., Steyer, R., & Schwenkmezger, P. (1993). Validating scales for the assessment of mood level and mood variability by latent state-trait analyses. *Personality and Individual Differences, 16,* 63–76.

Eid, M., Riemann, R., Angleitner, A., & Borkenau, P. (2003). Sociability and positive emotionality: Genetic and environmental contributions to the covariation between different facets of extraversion. *Journal of Personality, 7,* 319–346.

Eid, M., Schneider, C., & Schwenkmezger, P. (1999). Do you feel better or worse? On the validity of perceived deviations of mood states from mood traits. *European Journal of Personality, 13,* 283–306.

Eisenberg, N., Fabes, R. A., Guthrie, I. K., Murphy, B. C., Maszk, P., Holmgren, R., & Suh, K. (1996). The relations of regulation and emotionality to problem behavior in elementary school children. *Development and Psychopathology, 8,* 141–162.

Eisenberg, N., Fabes, R. A., Guthrie, I. K., & Reiser, M. (2000). Dispositional emotionality and regulation: Their role in predicting quality of social functioning. *Journal of Personality and Social Psychology, 78,* 136–157.

Eisenberg, N., Fabes, R. A., Shepard, S. A., Murphy, B. C., Guthrie, I. K., Jones, S., et al. (1997). Contemporaneous and longitudinal prediction of children's social functioning from regulation and emotionality. *Child Development, 68,* 642–664.

Eisenberg, N., Gershoff, E. T., Fabes, R. A., Shepard, S. A., Cumberland, A. J., Lososya, S. H., et al. (2001). Mothers' emotional expressivity and children's behavior problems and social competence: Mediation through children's regulation. *Developmental Psychology, 37,* 475–490.

Eisenberg, N., & Lennon, R. (1983). Sex differences in empathy and related constructs. *Psychological Bulletin, 94,* 100–131.

Eisenberg, N., & Morris, A. S. (2002). Children's emotion-related regulation. In H. Reese & R. Kail (Eds.), *Advances in child development and behavior, 30,* 189–229.

Eisenberg, N., Morris, A. S., & Spinrad, T. L. (2005). Emotion-related regulation: The construct and its measurement. In D. M. Teti (Ed.), *Handbook of research methods in developmental psychology* (pp. 423–442). Oxford, England: Blackwell Publishers.

Eisenberg, N., Pidada, S., & Liew, J. (2001). The relations of regulation and negative emotionality to Indonesian children's social functioning. *Child Development, 72,* 1747–1763.

Ekman, P. (1992). An argument for basic emotions. *Cognition and Emotion, 6,* 169–200.

Ekman, P., & Davidson, R. (Eds.). (1994). *The nature of emotion: Fundamental questions.* New York: Oxford University Press.

Ekman, P., & Friesen, W. V. (1969). Nonverbal leakage and clues to deception. *Psychiatry, 32,* 88–106.

Ekman, P., & Friesen, W. V. (1975). *Unmasking the face.* Englewood Cliffs, NJ: Prentice-Hall.

Ekman, P., & Friesen, W. V. (1978). *Facial action coding system.* Palo Alto, CA: Consulting Psychologists Press.

Elaad, E. (1990). Detection of guilty knowledge in real-life criminal applications. *Journal of Applied Psychology, 75,* 521–529.

Elaad, E., Ginton, A., & Jungman, N. (1992). Detection measures in real-life criminal guilty knowledge tests. *Journal of Applied Psychology, 77,* 757–767.

Ellingson, J. E., Sackett, P. R., & Hough, L. M. (1999). Social desirability concerns in personality measurement: Issues of applicant comparison and construct validity. *Journal of Applied Psychology, 84,* 155–166.

Ellingson, J. E., Smith, D. B., & Sackett, P. R. (2001). Investigating the influence of social desirability on personality factor structure. *Journal of Applied Psychology, 86,* 122–133.

Embretson, S. E., & Reise, S. P. (2000). *Item response theory for psychologists.* Mahwah, NJ: Lawrence Erlbaum Associates.

Emmons, R. A. (1986). Personal strivings: An approach to personality and subjective well-being. *Journal of Personality and Social Psychology, 51,* 1058–1068.

Emmons, R. A. (1989). The personal striving approach to personality. In L. A. Pervin (Ed.), *Goal concepts in personality and social psychology* (pp. 87–126). Hillsdale, NJ: Lawrence Erlbaum Associates.

Emmons, R. A., Diener, E., & Larsen, R. J. (1986). Choice and avoidance of everyday situations: Two models of reciprocal interactionism. *Journal of Personality and Social Psychology, 51,* 815–826.

Emmons, R. A., & McAdams, D. P. (1991). Personal strivings and motive dispositions: Exploring the links. *Personality and Social Psychology Bulletin, 17,* 648–654.

Epstein, S. (1983). Aggregation and beyond: Some basic issues on the prediction of behavior. *Journal of Personality, 51,* 360–392.

Epstein, S. (1986). Does aggregation produce spuriously high estimates of behavior stability? *Journal of Personality and Social Psychology, 50,* 1199–1210.

Erdfelder, E., & Buchner, A. (1998a). Decomposing the hindsight bias: A multinomial processing tree model for separating recollection and reconstruction in hindsight. *Journal of Experimental Psychology: Learning, Memory, and Cognition, 24,* 387–414.

Erdfelder, E., & Buchner, A. (1998b). Process dissociation measurement models: Threshold theory or detection theory? *Journal of Experimental Psychology: General, 127,* 83–96.

Erdfelder, E., Faul, F., & Buchner, A. (1996). G*Power: A general power analysis program. *Behavior Research Methods, Instruments, and Computers, 28,* 1–11.

Ernst, J. M., & Cacioppo, J. T. (1999). Lonely hearts: Psychological perspectives on loneliness. *Applied and Preventive Psychology, 8,* 1–22.

Eysenck, H. J. (1983). Cicero and the state-trait theory of anxiety: Another case of delayed recognition. *American Psychologist, 38,* 114–115.

Fagot, B. I., & Pears, U. C. (1996). Changes in attachment during the third year: Consequences and predictions. *Development and Psychopathology, 8,* 325–341.

Faigman, D. L., Kaye, D. H., Saks, M. J., & Sanders, J. (1997). *Modern scientific evidence: The law and science of expert testimony.* St. Paul, MN: West Publishing.

Farrell, A. D. (1994). Structural equation modeling with longitudinal data strategies for examining group differences and reciprocal relationships. *Journal of Consulting and Clinical Psychology, 62,* 477–487.

Farrington, D. P. (1983). Offending from 10 to 25 years of age. *Prospective Studies of Crime and Delinquency.* Hingham, MA: Kluwer.

Farrow, T. F. D., Zheng, Y., Wilkinson, I. D., Spence, S. A., Deakin, J. F. W., Tarrier, N., et al. (2001). Investigating the functional anatomy of empathy and forgiveness. *Neuroreport: For rapid communication of neuroscience research, 12,* 2433–2438.

Farzaneh, F., Riederer, S. J., & Pelc, N. J. (1990). Analysis of T2 limitations and off-resonance effects on spatial resolution and artifacts in echo-planar imaging. *Magnetic Resonance in Medicine, 14,* 123–139.

Fazio, R. H. (1989). On the power and functionality of attitudes: The role of attitude accessibility. In A. Pratkanis, S. Breckler, & A. Greenwald (Eds.), *Attitude structure and function* (pp. 153–179). Hillsdale, NJ: Lawrence Erlbaum Associates.

Fazio, R. H. (1995). Attitudes as object-evaluation associations: Determinants, consequences, and correlates of attitude accessibility. In R. E. Petty & J. A. Krosnick (Eds.), *Attitude strength: Antecedents and consequences* (pp. 247–282). Hillsdale, NJ: Lawrence Erlbaum Associates.

Fazio, R. H., Jackson, J. R., Dunton, B. C., & Williams, C. J. (1995). Variability in automatic activation as an unobtrusive measure of racial stereotypes: A bona fide pipeline? *Journal of Personality and Social Psychology, 69,* 1013–1027.

Fazio, R. H., & Olson, M. A. (2003). Implicit measures in social cognition research: Their meaning and uses. *Annual Review of Psychology, 54,* 297–327.

Fazio, R. H., Powell, M. C., & Williams, C. J. (1989). The role of attitude accessibility in the attitude-to-behavior process. *Journal of Consumer Research, 16,* 280–288.

Fazio, R. H., & Williams, C. J. (1986). Attitude accessibility as a moderator of the attitude-perception and attitude-behavior relations: An investigation of the 1984 presidential election. *Journal of Personality and Social Psychology, 51,* 505–514.

Feinstein, A. R., & Cicchetti, D. V. (1990). High agreement but low kappa: I. The problems of two paradoxes. *Journal of Clinical Epidemiology, 43,* 543–549.

Feldman, R., Greenbaum, C. W., & Yirmiya, N. (1999). Mother–infant affect synchrony as an antecedent of the emergence of self-control. *Developmental Psychology, 35,* 223–231.

Feldman Barrett, L. (1997). The relationships among momentary emotion experiences, personality descriptions, and retrospective ratings of emotion. *Personality and Social Psychology Bulletin, 23,* 1100–1110.

Feldt, L. S., & Brennan, R. L. (1989). Reliability. In R. L. Linn (Ed.), *Educational measurement* (3rd ed., pp. 105–146). New York: Macmillan.

Féré, C. (1888). Note on changes in electrical resistance under the effect of sensory stimulation and emotion. *Comptes Rendus des Seances de la Societe de Biologie (Ser. 9), 5,* 217–219.

Fergusson, D. M., & Horwood, L. J. (1989). Estimation of method and trait variance in ratings of conduct disorder. *Journal of Child Psychology and Psychiatry, 30,* 365–378.

Fernandez, G., Specht, K., Weis, S., Tendolkar, I., Reuber, M., Fell, J., et al. (2003). Intrasubject reproducibility of presurgical language lateralization and mapping using fMRI. *Neurology, 60,* 969–975.

Ferrer, E., & McArdle, J. J. (2003). Alternative structural models for multivariate longitudinal data analysis. *Structural equation modeling, 10,* 493–504.

Festinger, L. (1954). A theory of social comparison processes. *Human Relations, 7,* 117–140.

Fiedler, K., Schmid, J., & Stahl, T. (2002). What is the current truth about polygraph lie detection? *Basic and Applied Social Psychology, 24,* 313–324.

Fienberg, S. E. (1980). *The analysis of cross-classified categorical data.* Cambridge, MA: MIT Press.

Finch, J. F. (1998). Social undermining, support satisfaction, and affect: A domain-specific lagged effects model. *Journal of Personality, 66,* 315–334.

Finch, J. F., & West, S. G. (1997). The investigation of personality structure: Statistical models. *Journal of Research in Personality, 31,* 439–485.

Finke, R. A. (1980). Levels of equivalence in imagery and perception. *Psychological Review, 87,* 113–132.

Fischer, G. H. (1973). The linear logistic test model as an instrument in educational research. *Acta Psychologica, 37,* 359–374.

Fischer, G. H. (1995a). Derivations of the Rasch model. In G. H. Fisher & I. W. Molenaar (Eds.), *Rasch models. Foundations, recent developments, and applications* (pp. 15–38). Berlin, Germany: Springer.

Fischer, G. H. (1995b). The linear logistic test model. In G. H. Fisher & I. W. Molenaar (Eds.), *Rasch models. Foundations, recent developments, and applications* (pp. 131–156). Berlin, Germany: Springer.

Fischer, G. H., & Formann, A. K. (1982). Some applications of logistic latent trait models with linear constraints on the parameters. *Applied Psychological Measurement, 6,* 397–416.

Fishbein, M. (1980). A theory of reasoned action: Some applications and implications. In H. Howe & M. M. Page (Eds.), *Nebraska Symposium on Motivation: Beliefs, attitudes, and values* (pp. 65–116). Lincoln: University of Nebraska Press.

Fishbein, M., & Ajzen, I. (1975). *Belief, attitude, intention, and behavior: An introduction to theory and research.* Reading, MA: Addison-Wesley.

Fiske, D. W. (1971). *Measuring the concepts of personality.* Chicago: Aldine-Atherton.

Fiske, D. W. (1987a). Construct invalidity comes from method effects. *Educational and Psychological Measurement, 47,* 285–336.

Fiske, D. W. (1987b). On understanding our methods and their effects. *Diagnostica, 33,* 188–194.

Fleeson, W. (2001). Toward a structure- and process-integrated view of personality: Traits as density distributions of states. *Journal of Personality and Social Psychology, 80,* 1011–1027.

Fleiss, J. L. (1971). Measuring nominal scale agreement between many raters. *Psychological Bulletin, 76,* 378–382.

Fleiss, J. L. (1975). Measuring agreement between two judges on the presence and absence of a trait. *Biometrics, 31,* 651–659.

Fleiss, J. L. (1981). *Statistical methods for rates and proportions.* New York: John Wiley & Sons.

Fleiss, J. L., & Cohen, J. (1973). The equivalence of weighted Kappa and the intraclass correlation coefficient as measures of reliability. *Educational and Psychological Measurement, 33,* 613–619.

Fodor, J. A. (1983). *The modularity of mind.* Cambridge, MA: MIT Press.

Folger, R., & Belew, J. (1985). Nonreactive measurement: A focus for research on absenteeism and occupational stress. *Research in Organizational Behavior, 7,* 129–170.

Foltz, P. W., Kintsch, W., & Landauer, T. K. (1998). The measurement of textual coherence with latent semantic analysis. *Discourse Processes, 25,* 285–307.

Forman, A. K. (1992). Linear logistic latent class analysis for polytomous data. *Journal of the American Statistical Association, 87,* 476–486.

Forman, R. F., & McCauley, C. (1986). Validity of the positive control test using the field practice model. *Journal of Applied Psychology, 71,* 691–698.

Fowler, J. S., Ding, Y. S., & Volkow, N. D. (2003). Radiotracers for positron emission tomography imaging. *Seminars in Nuclear Medicine, 33,* 14–27.

Fowler, J. S., Volkow, N. D., Ding, Y. S., Wang, G. J., Dewey, S., Fischman, M. W., et al. (1999). Positron emission tomography studies of dopamine-enhancing drugs. *Journal of Clinical Pharmacology* (Suppl.), 13S–16S.

Fox, J. A., & Tracy, P. E. (1986). *Randomized response: A method for sensitive surveys.* Beverly Hills, CA: Sage.

Fox, N. A., & Field, T. M. (1989). Individual differences in young children's adjustment to preschool. *Journal of Applied Developmental Psychology, 10,* 527–540.

Fox, N. A., Rubin, K. H., Calkins, S. D., Marshall, T. R., Coplan, R. J., Porges, S. W., et al. (1995). Frontal activation asymmetry and social competence at four years of age. *Child Development, 66,* 1771–1784.

Fox, P. T., & Raichle, M. E. (1986). Focal physiological uncoupling of cerebral blood flow and oxidative metabolism during somatosensory stimulation in human subjects. *Proceedings of the National Academy of Sciences of the United States of America, 83,* 1140–1144.

Fox, P. T., Raichle, M. E., Mintun, M. A., & Dence, C. (1988). Nonoxidative glucose consumption during focal physiologic neural activity. *Science, 241,* 462–464.

Fredrickson, B. L., & Kahneman, D. (1993). Duration neglect in retrospective evaluations of affective episodes. *Journal of Personality and Social Psychology, 65,* 45–55.

Frick, A., Bächtiger, M. T., & Reips, U.-D. (2001). Financial incentives, personal information, and dropout in online studies. In U.-D. Reips & M. Bosnjak (Eds.), *Dimensions of Internet science* (pp. 209–219). Lengerich, Germany: Pabst.

Fridland, A. J., Ekman, P., & Oster, H. (1986). Facial expressions of emotion: Review of literature, 1970–1983. In A. Siegman & S. Feldstein (Eds.), *Nonverbal behavior and communication* (pp. 143–223). Hillsdale, NJ: Erlbaum.

Friedmann, M. P., & Wilson, R. W. (1975). Application of unobtrusive measures to the study of textbook usage by college students. *Journal of Applied Psychology, 60,* 659–662.

Frijda, N. H. (1986). *The emotions.* Cambridge, MA: Cambridge University Press.

Frijda, N. H. (1993). The place of appraisal in emotion. *Cognition & Emotion Special Issue: Appraisal and beyond: The issue of cognitive determinants of emotion, 7,* 357–387.

Friston, K. J., Frith, C. D., Liddle, P. F., & Frackowiak, R. S. (1993). Functional connectivity: the principal-component analysis of large (PET) data sets. *Journal of Cerebra Blood Flow and Metabolism, 13,* 5–14.

Friston, K. J., Holmes, A. P., Poline, J. B., Grasby, P. J., Williams, S. C., Frackowiak, R. S., & Turner, R. (1995). Analysis of fMRI time-series revisited. *Neuroimage, 2,* 45–53.

Friston, K. J., Holmes, A. P., Worsley, K. J., Poline, J. B., Frith, C. D., & Frackowiak, R. J. (1994). Statistical parametric maps in functional imaging: A general linear approach. *Human Brain Mapping, 2,* 89–90.

Friston, K. J., Price, C. J., Fletcher, P., Moore, C., Frackowiak, R. S., & Dolan, R. J. (1996). The trouble with cognitive subtraction. *Neuroimage, 4,* 97–104.

Fritsche, I. (2003). *Entschuldigen, rechtfertigen und die verletzung sozialer normen* [Excusing, justifying, and the violation of social norms]. Weinheim, Germany: Beltz/PVU.

Funder, D. C. (1987). Errors and mistakes: Evaluating the accuracy of social judgment. *Psychological Bulletin, 101,* 75–90.

Funder, D. C. (1991). Global traits: A neo-Allportian approach to personality. *Psychological Science, 2,* 31–39.

Funder, D. C. (1995). On the accuracy of personality judgment: A realistic approach. *Psychological Review, 102,* 652–670.

Funder, D. C. (1999). *Personality judgment. A realistic approach to person perception.* San Diego, CA: Academic Press.

Funder, D. C. (2004). *The Personality Puzzle* (3rd ed.). New York: W. W. Norton.

Funder, D. C., & Colvin, C. R. (1988). Friends and strangers. Acquaintanceship, agreement, and the accuracy of personality judgment. *Journal of Personality and Social Psychology, 55,* 149–158.

Funder, D. C., & Colvin, C. R. (1991). Explorations in behavioral consistency: Properties of persons, situations, and behaviors. *Journal of Personality and Social Psychology, 60,* 773–794.

Funder, D. C., & Dobroth, K. M. (1987). Differences between traits: Properties associated with interjudge agreement. *Journal of Personality and Social Psychology, 52,* 409–418.

Funder, D. C., Kolar, D. W., & Blackman, M. C. (1995). Agreement among judges of personality: Interpersonal relations, similarity, and acquaintanceship. *Journal of Personality and Social Psychology, 69,* 656–672.

Funder, D. C., & Sneed, C. D. (1993). Behavioral manifestations of personality: An ecological approach to judgmental accuracy. *Journal of Personality and Social Psychology, 64,* 479–490.

Furman, W., & Bierman, K. L. (1983). Developmental changes in young children's conceptions of friendship. *Child Development, 54,* 549–556.

Gable, S. L., Reis, H. T., & Elliot, A. J. (2000). Behavioral activation and inhibition in everyday life. *Journal of Personality and Social Psychology, 78,* 1135–1149.

Gaensbauer, T. J., Harmon, R. J., Culp, A. M., Schultz, L. A., Van Doorninck, W. J., & Dawson, P. (1985). Relationships between attachment behavior in the laboratory and the caretaking environment. *Infant Behavior and Development, 8,* 355–369.

Gage, N. L., & Cronbach, L. J. (1955). Conceptual and methodological problems in interpersonal perception. *Psychological Review, 62,* 411–422.

Gangestad, S. W., Simpson, J. A., DiGeronimo, K., & Biek, M. (1992). Differential accuracy in person perception across traits: Examination of a functional hypothesis. *Journal of Personality and Social Psychology, 62,* 688–698.

Ganz, P. A., Lee, J. J., & Siau, J. (1990). Quality of life assessment: An independent prognostic variable for survival in lung cancer. *Cancer, 67*, 3131–3135.

Gardner, H. (1983). *Frames of mind.* New York: Basic Books.

Gardner, H. (1993). *Multiple intelligences: The theory in practice.* New York: Basic Books.

Garner, W. G., Hake, H. W., & Eriksen, C. W. (1956). Operationism and the concept of perception. *Psychological Review, 63*, 149–159.

Gelfland, D. M., & Hartmann, D. P. (1975). *Child behavior analysis and therapy.* New York: Pergamon.

George, J. M. (1996). Trait and state affect. In K. R. Murphy (Ed.), *Individual differences and behavior in organizations* (pp. 145–171). San Francisco: Jossey-Bass.

Gerard, H. B., & Mathewson, G. C. (1966). The effects of severity of initiation on liking for a group: A replication. *Journal of Experimental Social Psychology, 2*, 278–287.

Gerber, L., Schwartz, J., & Pickering, T. (1998). Does the relationship of ambulatory blood pressure to position and location vary by age, sex, race/ethnicity, or body mass index? *American Journal of Human Biology, 10*, 459–470.

Gifford, R. (1991). Mapping nonverbal behavior on the interpersonal circle. *Journal of Personality and Social Psychology, 61*, 279–288.

Gifford, R. (1994). A lens-mapping framework for understanding the encoding and decoding of interpersonal dispositions in nonverbal behavior. *Journal of Personality and Social Psychology, 66*, 398–412.

Gigerenzer, G., & Selten, R. (Eds.). (2001). *Bounded rationality: The adaptive toolbox.* Cambridge, MA: The MIT Press.

Gillespie, D. F., & Perry, R. W. (1973). Research strategies for studying the acceptance of artistic creativity. *Sociology and Social Research, 58*, 48–55.

Gilliland, S. W. (1994). Effects of procedural and distributive justice on reactions to a selection system. *Journal of Applied Psychology, 79*, 691–701.

Glanzer, M., & Adams, J. K. (1985). The mirror effect in recognition memory. *Memory & Cognition, 13*, 8–20.

Glanzer, M., & Adams, J. K. (1990). The mirror effect in recognition memory: Data and theory. *Journal of Experimental Psychology: Learning, Memory, & Cognition, 16*, 5–16.

Gleser, G. C., Cronbach, L. J., & Rajaratnam, N. (1965). Generalizability of scores influenced by multiple sources of variance. *Psychometrika, 30*, 395–418.

Gleser, G. C., Gottschalk, L. A., & Watkins, J. (1959). The relationship of sex and intelligence to choice of words: A normative study of verbal behavior. *Journal of Clinical Psychology, 15*, 183–191.

Glomb, T. M., & Miner, A. G. (2002). Exploring patterns of aggressive behaviors in organizations: Assessing model-data fit. In J. M. Brett & F. D. Drasgow (Eds.), *Psychology of work: Theoretically based empirical research.* Mahwah, NJ: Lawrence Erlbaum Associates.

Gnisci, A., & Bakeman, R. (2000). *L'osservazione e l'analisi sequenziale dell'interazione.* Milan, Italy: L.E.D.

Gockenbach, S., Bosnjak, M., & Göritz, A. (2003, March 30). *Untersuchung stereotyper Beantwortungsmuster bei Matrixfragen in Web-Surveys* [Investigation on stereotypic response patterns within matrix questions in Web surveys]. Paper presented at the German Online Research Conference, Duisburg, Germany.

Goff, M., & Ackerman, P. L. (1992). Personality-intelligence relations: Assessment of typical intellectual engagement. *Journal of Educational Psychology, 84*, 537–552.

Goldbeck, L., & Schmitz, T. G. (2001). Comparison of three generic questionnaires measuring quality of life in adolescents and adults with cystic fibrosis: The 36-item short form health survey, the quality of life profile for chronic diseases, and the questions on life satisfaction. *Quality of Life Research, 10*, 23–36.

Goldberg, L. R. (1992). The developing of markers for the Big-Five factor structure. *Psychological Assessment, 4*, 26–42.

Goldberg, L. R. (1993). The structure of phenotypic personality traits. *American Psychologist, 48*, 26–34.

Goldman, B. A., & Saunders, J. L. (1974). *Directory of unpublished experimental mental measures, Volume 1.* New York: Behavioral Publications.

Goldsmith, H. H. (1996). Studying temperament via construction of the Toddler Behavior Assessment Questionnaire. *Child Development, 67*, 218–235.

Goldsmith, H. H., & Rothbart, M. K. (1991). Contemporary instruments for assessing early temperament by questionnaire and in the laboratory. In A. Angleitner & J. Strelau (Eds.), *Explorations in temperament* (pp. 249–272). New York: Plenum Press.

Goldstein, H. (1995). *Multilevel statistical models.* London: Arnold and New York: Halsted.

Goldstein, M. D., & Strube, M. J. (1994). Independence revisited: The relation between positive and negative affect in a naturalistic setting. *Personality & Social Psychology Bulletin, 20*, 57–64.

Gomez, R., Burns, G. L., Walsh, J. A., & Hafetz, N. (2005). A multitrait–multisource confirmatory factor analytic approach to the construct validity of ADHD and ODD rating scales with Malaysian children. *Journal of Abnormal Child Psychology, 33*, 241–254.

Gomez, R., Burns, G. L., Walsh, J. A., & Moura, M. A. (2003). A multitrait–multisource confirmatory factor analytic approach to the construct validity of ADHD rating scales. *Psychological Assessment, 15*, 3–16.

Goodman, L. A. (1973). The analysis of multidimensional contingency tables when some variables are posterior to others: A modified path analysis approach. *Biometrika, 60*, 179–192.

Goodman, L. A. (1974). Exploratory latent structure analysis using both identifiable and unidentifiable models. *Biometrika, 61*, 215–231.

Goodman, L. A. (1978). *Analyzing qualitative/categorical data. Loglinear models and latent structure analysis.* London: Addison-Wesley Publishing Company.

Gordon, R. A. (1997). Everyday life as an intelligence test. *Intelligence, 24,* 203–320.

Gore, A. C., & Roberts, J. L. (2003). Neuroendocrine systems. In L. R. Squire, F. E. Bloom, S. K. McConnell, J. L. Roberts, N. C. Spitzer, & M. J. Zigmond (Eds.), *Fundamental neuroscience* (2nd ed., pp. 1031–1065). New York: Academic Press.

Gorin, A. A., & Stone, A. A. (2001). Recall biases and cognitive errors in retrospective self-reports: A call for momentary assessments. In A. Baum, T. Revenson, & J. Singer (Eds.), *Handbook of health psychology* (pp. 405–413). Mahwah, NJ: Lawrence Erlbaum Associates.

Göritz, A., Reinhold, N., & Batinic, B. (2002). Online panels. In B. Batinic, U.-D. Reips, & M. Bosnjak (Eds.), *Online social sciences* (pp. 27–47). Göttingen, Germany: Hogrefe & Huber.

Gosling, S. D., John, O. P., Craik, K. H., & Robins, R. W. (1998). Do people know how they behave? Self-reported act frequencies compared with on-line codings by observers. *Journal of Personality and Social Psychology, 74,* 1337–1349.

Gosling, S. D., Ko, S. J., Mannarelli, T., & Morris, M. E. (2002). A room with a cue: Personality judgments based on offices and bedrooms. *Journal of Personality and Social Psychology, 82,* 379–398.

Gottfredson, L. S. (1997). Intelligence and social policy (special issue). *Intelligence, 24*(1).

Gottfredson, L. S. (2002). *g:* Highly general and highly practical. In R. J. Sternberg & E. L. Grigorenko (Eds.), *The general intelligence factor: How general is it?* (pp. 331–380). Mahwah, NJ: Lawrence Erlbaum Associates.

Gottfredson, L. S. (2003a). The challenge and promise of cognitive career assessment. *Journal of Career Assessment, 11,* 115–135.

Gottfredson, L. S. (2003b). Dissecting practical intelligence theory: Its claims and evidence. *Intelligence, 31,* 343–397.

Gottfredson, L. S. (2004). Intelligence: Is it the epidemiologists' elusive "fundamental cause" of social class inequalities in health? *Journal of Personality & Social Psychology, 86,* 174–199.

Gottman, J. M. (1979). *Marital interaction: Experimental investigations.* New York: Academic Press.

Gottman, J. M. (1993). Studying emotion in social interaction. In M. Lewis & J. M. Haviland (Eds.), *Handbook of emotions* (pp. 475–487). New York: Guilford.

Gottman, J. M., Katz, L. F., & Hooven, C. (1997). *Meta-emotion.* Mahwah, NJ: Lawrence Erlbaum Associates.

Gottman, J. M., & Krokoff, L. (1989). Marital interaction and marital satisfaction: A longitudinal view. *Journal of Consulting and Clinical Psychology, 57,* 47–52.

Gottman, J. M., & Levenson, R. W. (1985). A valid measure for obtaining self-report of affect. *Journal of Consulting and Clinical Psychology, 53,* 151–160.

Gottman, J. M., & Levenson, R. W. (1992). Marital processes predictive of later dissolution: Behavior, physiology and health. *Journal of Personality and Social Psychology, 63,* 221–233.

Gottschalk, L. A. (1995). *Content analysis of verbal behavior: New findings and clinical applications.* Hillsdale, NJ: Lawrence Erlbaum Associates.

Gottschalk, L. A., & Bechtel, R. J. (1989). Artificial intelligence and the computerization of the content analysis of natural language. *Artificial Intelligence in Medicine, 1,* 131–137.

Gottschalk, L. A., & Bechtel, R. J. (1995). Computerized measurement of the content analysis of natural language for use in biochemical and neuropsychiatric research. *Computer Methods and Programs in Biomedicine, 47,* 123–130.

Gottschalk, L. A., Stein, M., & Shapiro, D. (1997). The application of computerized content analysis of speech to the diagnostic process in a psychiatric outpatient clinic. *Journal of Clinical Psychology, 53,* 427–441.

Gough, G. (1985). Reasons for slimming and weight loss. In D. Canter (Ed.), *Facet theory* (pp. 245–259). New York: Springer.

Graesser, A., Wiemer-Hastings, K., Wiemer-Hastings, P., Kreuz, R., & the Tutoring Research Group. (1999). AutoTutor: A simulation of a human tutor. *Journal of Cognitive Systems Research, 1,* 35–51.

Graham, F. K. (1984). An affair of the heart. In M. G. H. Coles, J. R. Jennings, & J. A. Stern (Eds.), *Psychophysiological perspectives: Festschrift for Beatrice and John Lacey* (pp. 171–187). New York: Van Nostrand Reinhold.

Graves, R. E. (1991). The use of experimental techniques in clinical trials. In E. Mohr & P. Brouwers (Eds.), *Handbook of clinical trials: The neurobehavioral approach* (pp. 121–130). Amsterdam: Swets & Zeitlinger.

Gray, J. A. (1982). *The neuropsychology of anxiety.* Oxford, England: Oxford University Press.

Grayson, D., & Marsh, H. W. (1994). Identification with deficient rank loading matrices in confirmatory factor analysis: Multitrait–multimethod models. *Psychometrika, 59,* 121–134.

Graziano, W. G., Jensen-Campbell, L. A., & Hair, E. C. (1996). Perceiving interpersonal conflict and reacting to it: The case for Agreeableness. *Journal of Personality and Social Psychology, 70,* 820–835.

Green, B. F. (1978). In defense of measurement. *American Psychologist, 33,* 664–670.

Green, B. F., Bock, R. D., Humphreys, L. G., Linn, R. L., & Reckase, M. D. (1984). Technical guidelines for assessing computerized adaptive tests. *Journal of Educational Measurement, 21,* 347–360.

Green, D. M., & Swets, J. W. (1966). *Signal detection theory and psychophysics.* New York: John Wiley & Sons.

Green, D. P., Goldman, S. L., & Salovey, P. (1993). Measurement error masks bipolarity in affect ratings. *Journal of Personality and Social Psychology, 64,* 1029–1041.

Green, S. B. (2003). A coefficient alpha for test-retest data. *Psychological Methods, 8,* 88–101.

Greenbaum, P. E., Dedrick, R., Prange, M., & Friedman, R. (1994). Parent, teacher, and child ratings of prob-

lem behaviors of youngsters with serious emotional disturbances. *Psychological Assessment, 6,* 141–148.

Greenberg, B. G., Abdul-Ela, A., Simmons, W. R., & Horvitz, D. G. (1969). The unrelated question randomized response model: Theoretical framework. *Journal of the American Statistical Association, 64,* 520–539.

Greenwald, A. G., & Banaji, M. R. (1995). Implicit social cognition: Attitudes, self-esteem, and stereotypes. *Psychological Review, 102,* 4–27.

Greenwald, A. G., Banaji, M. R., Rudman, L. A., Farnham, S. D., Nosek, B. A., & Mellott, D. (2002). A unified theory of implicit attitudes, stereotypes, self-esteem, and self-concept. *Psychological Review, 109,* 3–25.

Greenwald, A. G., & Farnham, S. D. (2000). Using the Implicit Association Test to measure self-esteem and self-concept. *Journal of Personality and Social Psychology, 79,* 1022–1038.

Greenwald, A. G., McGhee, D. E., & Schwartz, J. L. K. (1998). Measuring individual differences in implicit cognition: The implicit association test. *Journal of Personality and Social Psychology, 74,* 1464–1480.

Grice, H. P. (1975). Logic and conversation. In P. Cole & T. Morgan (Eds.), *Syntax and semantics: Vol. 3, Speech acts* (pp. 41–58). New York: Seminar Press.

Grice, H. P. (1989). *Studies in the way of words.* Cambridge, MA: Harvard University Press.

Grolnick, W. S., Kurowski, C. O., McMenamy, J. M., Rivkin, I., & Bridges, L. J. (1998). Mothers' strategies for regulating their toddlers' distress. *Infant Behavior and Development, 21,* 437–450.

Groom, C. J., & Pennebaker, J. W. (2002). Words. *Journal of Research in Personality, 36,* 615–621.

Groom, C. J., Stone, L. D., Newman, M. L., & Pennebaker, J. W. (2004). *Sex differences in language use: An analysis of text samples from 70 studies.* Manuscript submitted for publication.

Grossman, P., van Beek, J., & Wietjes, C. (1990). A comparison of three quantification methods for estimation of respiratory sinus arrhythmia. *Psychophysiology, 27,* 702–714.

Guay, F., Marsh, H. W., & Boivin, M. (2003). Academic self-concept and academic achievement: Development perspectives on their causal ordering. *Journal of Educational Psychology, 95,* 124–136.

Guerin, B. (1986). Mere presence effects in humans: A review. *Journal of Personality and Social Psychology, 22,* 38–77.

Guilford, J. P. (1954). *Psychometric methods.* New York: McGraw-Hill.

Guilford, J. P. (1967). *The nature of human intelligence.* New York: McGraw-Hill.

Gusnard, D. A., Ollinger, J. M., Shulman, G. L., Cloninger, C. R., Price, J. L., Van Essen, D. C., et al. (2003). Persistence and brain circuitry. *Proceedings of the National Academy of Sciences of the United States of America, 100,* 3479–3484.

Gustafsson, J. E. (2002). Measurement from a hierarchical point of view. In H. L. Braun, D. G. Jackson, & D. E. Wiley (Eds.), *The role of constructs in psychological and educational measurement* (pp. 73–95). Mahwah, NJ: Lawrence Erlbaum Associates.

Gustafsson, J. E., & Snow, R. E. (1997). Ability profiles. In R. F. Dillon (Ed.), *Handbook on testing* (pp. 107–135). Westport, CT: Greenwood Press.

Guthrie, I. K., Eisenberg, N., Fabes, R. A., Murphy, B. C., Holmgren, R., Maszk, P., & Suh, K. (1997). The relations of regulation and emotionality to children's situational empathy-related responding. *Motivation and Emotion, 21,* 87–108.

Guttman, L. (1954). An outline of some new methodology for social research. *Public Opinion Quarterly, 18,* 395–404.

Haacke, E. M., Brown, R. W., Thompson, M. R., & Venkatesan, R. (1999). *Magnetic resonance imaging: Physical principles and sequence design.* New York: John Wiley & Sons.

Haberman, S. J. (1978). *Analysis of qualitative data. Vol. 1. Introductory topics.* New York: Academic Press.

Haberman, S. J. (1979). *Analysis of qualitative data. Vol. 2. New developments.* New York: Academic Press.

Hackman, J. R., & Oldham, G. R. (1976). Motivation through the design of work: Test of a theory. *Organizational Behavior and Human Performance, 60,* 159–170.

Hackman, J. R., & Oldham, G. R. (1980). *Work redesign.* Reading, MA: Addison-Wesley.

Hadorn, D. C., & Hays, R. D. (1991). Multitrait–multimethod analysis of health-related quality-of-life measures. *Medical Care, 28,* 829–840.

Hagenaars, J. A. (1990). *Categorical longitudinal data: Loglinear panel, trend, and cohort analysis.* Newbury Park, CA: Sage.

Hagenaars, J. A. (1993). *Loglinear models with latent variables.* Newbury Park, CA: Sage.

Halberstadt, J. B., Niedenthal, P. M., & Kushner, J. (1995). Resolution of lexical ambiguity by emotional state. *Psychological Science, 6,* 278–282.

Hambleton, R. K., & Swaminathan, H. (1989). *Item response theory. Principles and applications.* Boston: Kluwer-Nijhoff.

Hammond, K. R. (1996). *Human judgment and social policy.* New York: Oxford University Press.

Hansen, M. H., & Yu, B. (2001). Model selection and the principle of minimum description length. *Journal of the American Statistical Association, 96,* 746–774.

Hardin, G. (1968). The tragedy of the commons. *Science, 162,* 1243–1248.

Harkness, A. R., Tellegen, A., & Waller, N. G. (1995). Differential convergence of self-report and informant data for multidimensional personality questionnaire traits: Implications for the construct of negative emotionality. *Journal of Personality Assessment, 64,* 185–204.

Harmon-Jones, E., & Sigelman, J. (2001). State anger and prefrontal brain activity: Evidence that insult-related relative left-prefrontal activation is associated with experienced anger and aggression. *Journal of Personality and Social-Psychology, 80,* 797–803.

Harrell, T. H., & Lombardo, T. A. (1985). Validation of an automated 16PF administration procedure. *Journal of Personality Assessment, 48,* 638–642.

Harris, C. R. (2001). Cardiovascular responses of embarrassment and effects of emotional suppression in a social setting. *Journal of Personality and Social Psychology, 81,* 886–897.

Harris, M. J. (1991). Significance tests are not enough: The role of effect-size estimation in theory corroboration. *Theory and Psychology, 1,* 375–382.

Harrison, D. A., & McLaughlin, M. E. (1996). Structural properties and psychometric qualities of organizational self-reports: Field tests of connections predicted by cognitive theory. *Journal of Management, 22,* 313–338.

Hart, D., & Damon, W. (1986). Developmental trends in self-understanding. *Social Cognition, 4,* 388–407.

Hart, R. P. (1984). *Verbal style and the presidency: A computer-based analysis.* New York: Academic Press.

Hart, R. P. (2000). *Campaign talk: Why elections are good for us.* Princeton, NJ: Princeton University Press.

Hart, R. P. (2001). Redeveloping DICTION: Theoretical considerations. In M. West (Ed.), *Theory, method, and practice in computer content analysis* (pp. 43–60). New York: Ablex.

Hartigan, J. A., & Wigdor, A. K. (1989). *Fairness in employment testing: Validity generalization, minority issues, and the General Aptitude Test Battery.* Washington, DC: National Academy Press.

Hartmann, D. P. (1977). Considerations in the choice of interobserver reliability estimates. *Journal of Applied Behavior Analysis, 10,* 103–116.

Hartmann, D. P., & Gardner, W. (1979). On the not so recent invention of interobserver reliability statistics: A commentary on two articles by Birkimer and Brown. *Journal of Applied Behavior Analysis, 12,* 559–560.

Hartmann, D. P., & Wood, D. D. (1982). Observational methods. In A. S. Bellack, M. Hersen, & A. E. Kazdin (Eds.), *International handbook of behavior modification and therapy* (pp. 109–138). New York: Plenum.

Hattie, J. (1985). Methodology review: Assessing unidimensionality of tests and items. *Applied Psychological Measurement, 9,* 139–164.

Hawkins, R. P., & Dotson, V. A. (1975). Reliability scores that delude: An Alice in Wonderland trip through the misleading characteristics of interobserver agreement scores in interval recording. In E. Ramp & G. Semb (Eds.), *Behavior analysis: Areas of research and application* (pp. 359–376). Englewood Cliffs, NJ: Prentice Hall.

Hawkley, L. C., Burleson, M. H., Berntson, G. G., & Cacioppo, J. T. (2003). Loneliness in everyday life: Cardiovascular activity, psychosocial context, and health behaviors. *Journal of Personality and Social Psychology, 85,* 105–120.

Hayes, A. F., & Dunning, D. (1997). Construal processes and trait ambiguity: Implication for self-peer agreement in personality judgment. *Journal of Personality and Social Psychology, 72,* 664–677.

Haynes, S. N., & O'Brien, W. H. (2000). *Principles and practice of behavioral assessment.* New York: Kluwer Academic/Plenum.

Haynes, S. N., Richard, D. C. S., & Kubany, E. S. (1995). Content validity in psychological assessment: A functional approach to concepts and methods. *Psychological Assessment, 7,* 238–247.

Hays, W. L. (1994). *Statistics.* London: Harcourt Brace.

Heckhausen, J. (1997). Developmental regulation across adulthood: Primary and secondary control of age-related challenges. *Developmental Psychology, 33,* 176–187.

Heeger, D. J., & Ress, D. (2002). What does fMRI tell us about neuronal activity? *Nature Reviews Neuroscience, 3,* 142–151.

Heit, E., Brockdorff, N., & Lamberts, K. (2004). Strategic processes in false recognition memory. *Psychonomic Bulletin & Review, 11,* 380–386.

Helson, R. (1992). Women's difficult times and the rewriting of the life story. *Psychology of Women Quarterly, 16,* 331–347.

Hempel, C. G., & Oppenheim, P. (1948). Studies in the logic of explanation. *Philosophy of Science, 15,* 135–175.

Hendrick, C. (1990). Replications, strict replication, and conceptual replications: Are they important? In J. W. Neuliep (Ed.), *Handbook of replication research in the behavioural and social sciences* (Special Issue). *Journal of Social Behavior and Personality, 5,* 41–49.

Henker, B., Whalen, C., & Jamner, L. D. (2002). Anxiety, affect, and activity in teenagers: Monitoring daily life with electronic diaries. *Journal of the American Academy of Child and Adolescent Psychiatry, 41,* 660–670.

Herrald, M. M., & Tomaka, J. (2002). Patterns of emotion-specific appraisal, coping, and cardiovascular reactivity during an ongoing emotional episode. *Journal of Personality & Social Psychology, 83,* 434–450.

Herrnstein, R. J., & Murray, C. (1994). *The bell curve: Intelligence and class structure in American life.* New York: Free Press.

Herscovitch, P., Markham, J., & Raichle, M. E. (1983). Brain blood flow measured with intravenous H215O. I. Theory and error analysis. *Journal of Nuclear Medicine, 24,* 782–789.

Herzberg, F., Mausner, B., & Snyderman, B. (1959). *The motivation to work.* New York: John Wiley & Sons.

Higgins, E. T. (1996). Knowledge activation: Accessibility, applicability, and salience. In E. T. Higgins & A. W. Kruglanski (Eds.), *Social psychology: Handbook of basic principles* (pp. 133–168). New York: Guilford.

Hintzman, D. L. (1986). "Schema abstraction" in a multiple-trace memory model. *Psychological Review, 93,* 411–428.

Hintzman, D. L. (1988). Judgments of frequency and recognition memory in a multiple-trace memory model. *Psychological Review, 95,* 528–551.

Hintzman, D. L., Caulton, D. A., & Curran, T. (1994). Retrieval constraints and the mirror effect. *Journal of Experimental Psychology: Learning, Memory, and Cognition, 20,* 275–289.

Hintzman, D. L., & Curran, T. (1994). Retrieval dynamics of recognition and frequency judgments: Evidence for separate processes of familiarity and recall. *Journal of Memory & Language, 33,* 1–18.

Hintzman, D. L., Curran, T., & Oppy, B. (1992). Effects of similarity and repetition on memory: Registration without learning? *Journal of Experimental Psychology: Learning, Memory, and Cognition, 18,* 667–680.

Hiskey, S., & Troop, N. A. (2002). Online longitudinal survey research: Viability and participation. *Social Science Computer Review, 20,* 250–259.

Hofstee, W. K. B. (1994). Who should own the definition of personality? *European Journal of Personality, 8,* 149–162.

Hogan, R. T., & Nicholson, R. A. (1988). The meaning of personality test scores. *American Psychologist, 43,* 621–626.

Hogan, R. T., & Roberts, B. W. (2000). A socioanalytic perspective on person/environment interaction. In W. B. Walsh, K. H. Craik, & R. H. Price (Eds.), *New directions in person-environment psychology* (pp. 1–24). Mahwah, NJ: Lawrence Erlbaum Associates.

Hogenraad, R. (2003). The words that predict the outbreak of wars. *Empirical Studies of Arts, 21,* 5–20.

Hogenraad, R., McKenzie, D. P., Morval, J., & Ducharme, F. A. (1995). Paper trails of psychology: The words that made applied behavioral sciences. *Journal of Social Behavior and Personality, 10,* 491–516.

Holland, J. L. (1997). *Making vocational choices: A theory of vocational personalities and work environments* (3rd ed.). Lutz, FL: Psychological Assessment Resources.

Honts, C. R. (1996). Criterion development and validity of the CQT in field application. *Journal of General Psychology, 123,* 309–324.

Honts, C. R., Devitt, M. K., Winbush, M., & Kircher, J. C. (1996). Mental and physical countermeasures reduce the accuracy of the concealed knowledge test. *Psychophysiology, 33,* 84–92.

Hooker, K. (2002). New directions for research in personality and aging: A comprehensive model for linking level, structures, and processes. *Journal of Research in Personality, 36,* 318–334.

Hooker, K., & McAdams, D. P. (2003). New directions in aging research: Personality reconsidered. *The Journal of Gerontology: Psychological Sciences, 58,* P296–P304.

Hopkins, B. L., & Hermann, J. A. (1977). Evaluating interobserver reliability of interval data. *Journal of Applied Behavior Analysis, 10,* 121–126.

Hormuth, S. E. (1986). The sampling of experiences in situ. *Journal of Personality, 54,* 262–293.

Horn, J. L., & Cattell, R. B. (1966). Refinement and test of the theory of fluid and crystallized general intelligences. *Journal of Educational Psychology, 57,* 253–270.

Horswill, M. S., & Coster, M. E. (2001). User-controlled photographic animations, photograph-based questions, and questionnaires: Three instruments for measuring drivers' risk-taking behavior on the Internet. *Behavior Research Methods, Instruments, and Computers, 33,* 46–58.

House, A. E., House, B. J., & Campbell, M. B. (1981). Measures of interobserver agreement: Calculation formulas and distribution effects. *Journal of Behavioral Assessment, 3,* 37–57.

Houts, A. C., Cook, T. D., & Shadish, W. R. (1986). The person-situation debate: A critical multiplist perspective. *Journal of Personality, 54,* 52–105.

Hox, J. J. (2002). *Multilevel analysis. Techniques and applications.* Mahwah, NJ: Lawrence Erlbaum Associates.

Hoyle, R. H., Harris, M. J., & Judd, C. M. (2002). *Research methods in social relations.* Belmont, CA: Thomson Learning.

Hoyt, W. T. (2000). Rater bias in psychological research: When is it a problem and what can we do about it? *Psychological Methods, 5,* 64–86.

Hu, X., Le, T. H., Parrish, T., & Erhard, P. (1995). Retrospective estimation and correction of physiological fluctuation in functional MRI. *Magnetic Resonance in Medicine, 34,* 201–212.

Hufford, M., & Shields, A. (2002). Electronic diaries: Applications and what works in the field. *Applied Clinical Trials, 46–59.*

Hufford, M., Stone, A., Shiffman, S., Schwartz, J., & Broderick, J. (2002). Paper vs. electronic diaries: Compliance and subject evaluations. *Applied Clinical Trials, 38–43.*

Hugdahl, K. (1996). *Psychophysiology: The mind–body perspective.* Boston: Harvard University Press.

Hui, S. L., & Zhou, X. H. (1998). Evaluation of diagnostic tests without gold standards. *Statistical Methods in Medical Research, 7,* 354–370.

Hulin, C. L. (2001). Applied psychology and science: Differences between research and practice. *Applied Psychology: An International Review, 50,* 225–234.

Hulin, C. L., Drasgow, F., & Parsons, C. K. (1983). *Item response theory: Application to psychological measurement.* Homewood, IL: Dow Jones–Irwin.

Hulin, C. L., & Humphreys, L. G. (1980). Foundations of test theory. In *Construct validity in psychological measurement* (pp. 5–12). Proceedings of a colloquia on theory and application in education and employment. Princeton, NJ: Educational Testing Service.

Hulin, C. L., & Judge, T. R. (2003). Job attitudes: A theoretical and empirical review. In W. C. Borman, D. R. Ilgen, & R. J. Klimoski (Eds.), *Handbook of psychology, Volume 12: Industrial and organizational psychology* (pp. 255–276). New York: John Wiley & Sons.

Hulin, C. L., & Maher, B. A. (1959). Changes in attitudes toward law and justice concomitant with imprisonment. *Journal of Criminal Law, 50,* 245–248.

Hulin, C. L., Miner, A. G., & Seitz, S. T. (2001). Computational modeling in organizational sciences: Contributions of a third research discipline. In F. D. Drasgow & N. Schmitt (Eds.), *Measuring and analyzing behavior in organizations.* San Francisco: Jossey-Bass.

Hull, J. G., Slone, L. B., Meteyer, K. B., & Matthews, A. R. (2002). The nonconsciousness of self-consciousness. *Journal of Personality and Social Psychology, 83,* 406–424.

Humphreys, L. G. (1962). The organization of human abilities. *American Psychologist, 17,* 475–483.

Humphreys, L. G. (1976). A factor model for research on intelligence and problem solving. In L. Resnick (Ed.),

The nature of intelligence (pp. 329–340). New York: John Wiley & Sons.

Humphreys, L. G. (1984). General intelligence. In C. R. Reynolds & R. T. Brown (Eds.), *Perspectives on bias in mental testing*. New York: Plenum.

Humphreys, L. G. (1990). View of a supportive empiricist. *Psychological Inquiry, 1,* 153–155.

Humphreys, L. G., Lubinski, D., & Yao, G. (1993). Utility of predicting group membership and the role of spatial visualization in becoming an engineer, physical scientist, or artist. *Journal of Applied Psychology, 78,* 250–261.

Hunt, E. B. (1999). Multiple views of multiple intelligence. *Contemporary Psychology, 46,* 5–7.

Hurrell, J. J., Nelson, D. L., & Simmons, B. L. (1998). Measuring job stressors and strains: Where we have been, where we are, and where we need to go. *Journal of Occupational Health Psychology, 3,* 368–389.

Iacono, W. G. (2000). The detection of deception. In J. T. Cacioppo, L. G. Tassinary, & G. G. Berntson (Eds.), *Handbook of psychophysiology* (2nd ed., pp. 772–793). New York: Cambridge University Press.

Iacono, W. G., & Patrick, C. J. (1999). Polygraph ("lie detector") testing: The state of the art. In A. K. Hess & I. B. Weiner (Eds.), *The handbook of forensic psychology* (2nd ed., pp. 440–473). New York: John Wiley & Sons.

Ickes, W. (1993). Empathic accuracy. *Journal of Personality, 61,* 587–610.

Idaszak, J. R., Bottom, W. P., & Drasgow, F. (1988). A test of the measurement equivalence of the revised Job Diagnostic Survey: Past problems and current solutions. *Journal of Applied Psychology, 73,* 647–656.

Idaszak, J. R., & Drasgow, F. (1987). A revision of the Job Diagnostic Survey: Elimination of a measurement artifact. *Journal of Applied Psychology, 72,* 69–74.

Ilgen, D. R., & Hulin, C. L. (2000). *Computational modeling of behavioral processes in organizations: The third scientific discipline in behavioral research.* Washington, DC: American Psychological Association.

Ilies, R., & Judge, T. A. (2002). Understanding the dynamic relationships among personality, mood and job satisfaction: A field experience sampling study. *Organizational Behavior & Human Decision Processes, 89,* 1119–1139.

Isen, A. M., & Levin, P. F. (1972). The effect of feeling good on helping: Cookies and kindness. *Journal of Personality and Social Psychology, 21,* 384–388.

Isen, A. M., Shalker, T. E., Clark, M. S., & Karp, L. (1978). Affect, accessibility of material in memory, and behavior: A cognitive loop? *Journal of Personality and Social Psychology, 36,* 1–12.

Izard, C. E. (1977). *Human emotions.* New York: Plenum Press.

Izard, C. E. (1979). *The maximally discriminative facial movement coding system* (MAX). Newark: Instructional Resources Center, University of Delaware.

Jackson, D. N., & Messick, S. (1958). Content and style in personality assessment. *Psychological Bulletin, 55,* 243–252.

Jacoby, L. L. (1991). A process dissociation framework: Separating automatic from intentional uses of memory. *Journal of Memory and Language, 30,* 513–541.

Jacoby, L. L. (1998). Invariance in automatic influences of memory: Toward a user's guide for the process dissociation procedure. *Journal of Experimental Psychology: Learning, Memory, and Cognition, 24,* 1–36.

Jacoby, L. L. (1999). Ironic effects of repetition: Measuring age-related differences in memory. *Journal of Experimental Psychology: Learning, Memory, and Cognition, 25,* 3–22.

Jacoby, L. L., & Kelley, C. M. (1987). Unconscious influences of memory for a prior event. *Personality and Social Psychology Bulletin, 13,* 314–336.

Jacoby, L. L., Toth, J. P., & Yonelinas, A. P. (1993). Separating conscious and unconscious influences of memory: Measuring recollection. *Journal of Experimental Psychology: General, 122,* 139–154.

James, W. (1890). *Principles of psychology.* New York: Holt.

Jamison, R., Gracely, R., Raymond, S., Levine, J., Marino, B., Herrmann, T., et al. (2002). Comparative study of electronic vs. paper VAS ratings: A randomized, crossover trial using healthy volunteers. *Pain, 99,* 341–347.

Janetzko, D. (2003). Statistical applications via internet—Collecting, analyzing, and presenting data in network environments. The technical side. Retrieved March 7, 2003, from http://cogweb.iig.uni-freiburg.de/SAI/TECHNICS/

Jaroura, D., & Brennan, R. L. (1983). Multivariate generalizability models for tests developed from tables of specifications. In L. J. Fyans (Ed.), *Generalizability theory: Inferences and applications* (pp. 83–101). San Francisco: Jossey-Bass.

Jedidi, K., Jagpal, H. S., & de Sarbo, W. S. (1997). STEMM: A general finite structural equation modeling. *Journal of Classification, 14,* 23–50.

Jensen, A. R. (1980). *Bias in mental testing.* New York: Free Press.

Jensen, A. R. (1998). *The g factor.* Westport, CT: Praeger.

Jensen, A. R. (2005). Mental chronometry and the unification of differential psychology. In R. J. Sternberg & J. Pretz (Eds.), *Cognition and intelligence* (pp. 26–50). Cambridge, England: Cambridge University Press.

Jezzard, P., Matthews, P. M., & Smith, S. M. (Eds.). (2001). *Functional MRI: an Introduction to methods.* Oxford, England: Oxford University Press.

Jhingran, P., Osterhaus, J. T., Miller, D. W., Lee, J. T., & Kirchdoerfer, L. (1998). Development and validation of the Migraine-Specific Quality of Life Questionnaire. *Headache, 38,* 295–302.

Jodoin, M. G. (2003). Measurement efficiency of innovative item formats in computer-based testing. *Journal of Educational Measurement, 40,* 1–15.

John, O. P., Angleitner, A., & Ostendorf, F. (1988). The lexical approach to personality: A historical review of trait taxonomic research. *European Journal of Personality, 2,* 171–203.

John, O. P., & Robins, R. W. (1993). Determinants of interjudge agreement on personality traits: The Big Five domains, observability, evaluativeness, and the unique perspective of the self. *Journal of Personality, 61,* 521–551.

John, O. P., & Robins, R. W. (1994). Accuracy and bias in self-perception: Individual differences in self-enhancement and narcissism. *Journal of Personality and Social Psychology, 66,* 206–219.

Johnson, E. J., & Tversky, A. (1983). Affect, generalization, and the perception of risk. *Journal of Personality and Social Psychology, 45,* 21–31.

Johnson, L. C., & Bolstad, O. D. (1973). Methodological issues in naturalistic observation: Some problems and solutions for field research. In L. A. Hamerlynck, L. C. Hardy, & E. J. Mash (Eds.), *Behavior change: Methodology, concepts, and practice* (pp. 7–67). Champaign, IL: Research Press.

Johnson, M. K., Hashtroudi, S., & Lindsay, D. S. (1993). Source monitoring. *Psychological Bulletin, 114,* 3–28.

Johnston, L. H., Corban, R. M., & Clarke, P. (1999). Multi-method approaches to the investigation of adherence issues within sport and exercise: Qualitative and quantitative techniques. In S. J. Bull (Ed.), *Adherence issues in sport and exercise* (pp. 263–288). Chichester, England: John Wiley & Sons.

Joinson, A., & Reips, U.-D. (in press). Personalized salutation, power of sender and response rates to Web-based surveys. *Computers in Human Behavior.*

Jones, E. E., & Sigall, H. (1971). The bogus pipeline: A new paradigm for measuring affect and attitude. *Psychological Bulletin, 76,* 349–364.

Jöreskog, K. G. (1969). A general approach to confirmatory factor analysis. *Psychometrika, 34,* 183–202.

Jöreskog, K. G. (1979). Statistical methods and methods for the analysis of longitudinal data. In K. G. Jöreskog & D. Sörbom (Eds.), *Advances in factor analysis and structural equation models* (pp. 129–169). Cambridge, MA: Abt Books.

Judge, T. A., Erez, A., Bono, J. E., & Thoresen, C. J. (2002). Are measures of self-esteem, neuroticism, locus of control, and generalized self-efficacy indicators of a common core construct? *Journal of Personality and Social Psychology, 83,* 693–710.

Kaasinen, V., & Rinne, J. O. (2002). Functional imaging studies of dopamine system and cognition in normal aging and Parkinson's disease. *Neuroscience and Biobehavioral Reviews, 26,* 785–793.

Kagan, J. (1994). On the nature of emotion. In N. A. Fox (Ed.), *Monographs of the Society for Research in Child Development,* 59 (Serial No. 240), 7–24.

Kagan, J. (1998). Biology and the child. In W. Damon (Series Ed.) & N. Eisenberg (Vol. Ed.), *Handbook of child psychology: Vol. 3. Social, emotional and personality development* (pp. 25–100). New York: John Wiley & Sons.

Kahneman, D. (1999). Objective happiness. In D. Kahneman & E. Diener (Eds.), *Well-being: The foundations of hedonic psychology* (pp. 3–25). New York: Russell Sage Foundation.

Kahneman, D., Diener, E., & Schwarz, N. (Eds.). (1999). *Well-being: The foundations of hedonic psychology.* New York: Russell Sage Foundation.

Kahneman, D., Fredrickson, B. L., Schreiber, C. A., & Redelmeier, D. A. (1993). When more pain is preferred to less: Adding to a better end. *Psychological Science, 4,* 401–405.

Kamata, A. (2001). Item analysis by the hierarchical generalized linear model. *Journal of Educational Measurement, 38,* 79–93.

Kamin, L. J. (1969). Selective association and conditioning. In N. J. Mackintosh & W. K. Honig (Eds.), *Fundamental issues in associative learning* (pp. 42–64). Halifax, Canada: Dalhousie University Press.

Kanwisher, N., McDermott, J., & Chun, M. M. (1997). The fusiform face area: a module in human extrastriate cortex specialized for face perception. *Journal of Neuroscience, 17,* 4302–4311.

Kasl, S. V. (1978). Epidemiological contributions to the study of work stress. In C. L. Cooper & R. L. Payne (Eds.), *Stress as work* (pp. 3–38). New York: John Wiley & Sons.

Kass, R. E., & Raftery, A. E. (1995). Bayes factors. *Journal of the American Statistical Association, 90,* 773–793.

Kasser, T., Koestner, R., & Lekes, N. (2002). Early family experiences and adult values: A 26-year, prospective longitudinal study. *Personality and Social Psychology Bulletin, 28,* 826–835.

Kates, N., & Adams, J. (1982). Behavioral mapping in an office setting: Where employees choose to work. *EDRA: Environmental Design Research Association* (13), 397–405.

Katz, J., & Joiner, T. E. (2002). Being known, intimate, and valued: Global self-verification and dyadic adjustment in couples and roommates. *Journal of Personality, 70,* 33–58.

Kazdin, A. E. (1979). Unobtrusive measures in behavioral assessment. *Journal of Applied Behavior Analysis, 12,* 713–724.

Kelley, H. H. (1973). The process of causal attribution. *American Psychologist, 28,* 107–128.

Kelley, T. L. (1927). *Interpretation of educational measurements.* New York: World Book.

Kelley, T. L. (1928). *Crossroads in the mind of man: A study of differential abilities.* Stanford, CA: Stanford University Press.

Kelley, T. L. (1939). Psychological factors of no importance. *Journal of Educational Psychology, 30,* 139–143.

Kelly, G. A. (1963). *A theory of personality: The psychology of personal constructs.* New York: Norton.

Kelly, M. B. (1977). A review of the observational data collection and reliability procedures reported in the Journal of Applied Behavior Analysis. *Journal of Applied Behavior Analysis, 10,* 97–101.

Kemeny, M. E. (2003). The psychobiology of stress. *Current Directions in Psychological Science, 12,* 124–129.

Kennan, R. P. (1999). Gradient echo and spin echo methods for functional MRI. In C. Moonen & P. A. Bandettini (Eds.), *Functional MRI* (pp. 127–136). Berlin, Germany: Springer.

Kennedy, J. J. (1983). *Analyzing qualitative behavior. Introductory log-linear analysis for behavioral research.* New York: Praeger Publishers.

Kenny, D. A. (1976). An empirical application of confirmatory factor analysis to the multitrait–multimethod matrix. *Journal of Experimental Social Psychology, 12,* 247–252.

Kenny, D. A. (1979). *Correlation and causality.* New York: John Wiley & Sons.

Kenny, D. A. (1985). Quantitative methods for social psychology. In G. Lindzey & E. Aronson (Eds.), *Handbook of social psychology* (Vol. 1, pp. 487–508). New York: Random House.

Kenny, D. A. (1991). A general model of consensus and accuracy in interpersonal perception. *Psychological Review, 92,* 155–163.

Kenny, D. A. (1993). A coming of age for research on interpersonal perception. *Journal of Personality, 61,* 789–807.

Kenny, D. A. (1994). *Interpersonal perception. A social relations analysis.* New York: Guilford Press.

Kenny, D. A. (1995). The multitrait–multimethod matrix: Design, analysis, and conceptual issues. In P. E. Shrout & S. T. Fiske (Eds.), *Personality research, methods, and theory. A festschrift honoring D. W. Fiske* (pp. 111–124). Hillsdale, NJ: Lawrence Erlbaum Associates.

Kenny, D. A., & Acitelli, L. (1994). Measuring similarity in couples. *Journal of Family Psychology, 8,* 417–431.

Kenny, D. A., & Acitelli, L. K. (2001). Accuracy and bias in the perception of the partner in a close relationship. *Journal of Personality and Social Psychology, 80,* 439–448.

Kenny, D. A., & Albright, L. (1987). Accuracy in interpersonal perception: A social relations analysis. *Psychological Bulletin, 102,* 390–402.

Kenny, D. A., Albright, L., Malloy, T. E., & Kashy, D. A. (1994). Consensus in interpersonal perception: Acquaintanceship and the big five. *Psychological Bulletin, 116,* 245–258.

Kenny, D. A., & Kashy, D. A. (1992). The analysis of the multitrait–multimethod matrix by confirmatory factor analysis. *Psychological Bulletin, 112,* 165–172.

Kenny, D. A., & Zautra, A. J. (2001). Trait-state models for longitudinal data. In L. M. Collins & A. G. Sayer (Eds.), *New methods for the analysis of change* (pp. 243–263). Washington, DC: American Psychological Association.

Kenrick, D. T., & Stringfield, D. O. (1980). Personality traits and the eye of the beholder: Crossing some traditional philosophical boundaries in the search of consistency in all of the people. *Psychological Review, 87,* 88–104.

Kerlinger, F. N. (1973). *Foundations of behavioral research.* New York: Holt, Rinehart & Winston.

Khoo, S. T., Butner, J., & Ialongo, N. (2004). *Latent curve modeling of a multidimensional construct.* Unpublished manuscript, Psychology Department, Arizona State University.

Kickul, J., & Neuman, G. (2000). Emergent leadership behaviors: The function of personality and cognitive ability in determining teamwork performance and KSAS. *Journal of Business and Psychology, 15,* 27–51.

Kiehl, K. A., & Liddle, P. F. (2003). Reproducibility of the hemodynamic response to auditory oddball stimuli: A six-week test-retest study. *Human Brain Mapping, 18,* 42–52.

Kiers, H., Takane, Y., & ten-Berge, J. (1996). The analysis of multitrait–multimethod matrices via constrained components analysis. *Psychometrika, 61,* 601–628.

Kiesler, S., Siegel, J., & McGuire, T. W. (1984). Social psychological aspects of computer-mediated communication. *American Psychologist, 39*(10), 1123–1134.

Kihlstrom, J. F. (1987). The cognitive unconscious. *Science, 237,* 1445–1452.

Kindt, M., & Brosschot, J. F. (1998). Stability of cognitive bias for threat cues in phobia. *Journal of Psychopathology & Behavioral Assessment, 20,* 351–367.

King, L. A. (1995). Wishes, motives, goals, and personal memories: Relations of measures of human motivation. *Journal of Personality, 63,* 985–1007.

King, L. A., Scollon, C. K., Ramsey, C., & Williams, T. (2000). Stories of life transition: Subjective well-being and ego development in parents of children with Down syndrome. *Journal of Research in Personality, 34,* 509–536.

Kingsbury, G. G., & Zara, A. R. (1991). Procedures for selecting items for computerized adaptive tests. *Applied Measurement in Education, 2,* 359–375.

Kirk, R. E. (1995). *Experimental design: Procedures for the behavioral sciences.* Pacific Grove, CA: Brooks/Cole.

Kirsch, I. S., Jungeblut, A., Jenkins, L., & Kolstad, A. (1993). *Adult literacy in America: A first look at the results of the National Adult Literacy Survey.* Princeton, NJ: ETS.

Kirschner, N. M. (1976). Effect of need for approval and situational variables on the viewing of erotic material. *Journal of Consulting and Clinical Psychology, 44,* 869.

Klauer, K. C., & Wegener, I. (1998). Unraveling social categorization in the "Who Said What?" paradigm. *Journal of Personality and Social Psychology, 75,* 1155–1178.

Klein, S. B., Loftus, J., & Kihlstrom, J. F. (1996). Self-knowledge of an amnesic patient: Toward a neuropsychology of personality and social psychology. *Journal of Experimental Psychology: General, 125,* 250–260.

Kleitman, N. (1963). *Sleep and wakefulness* (2nd ed.). Chicago: University of Chicago Press.

Klinger, E. (1975). Consequences of commitment to and disengagement from incentives. *Psychological Review, 82,* 223–231.

Knight, G. P., & Hill, N. (1998). Measurement equivalence involving minority youth. In V. McLeod & L. Steinberg (Eds.), *Studying minority adolescents: Conceptual, methodological, and theoretical issues.* Mahwah, NJ: Lawrence Erlbaum Associates.

Knoke, D., & Burke, P. J. (1980). *Loglinear models.* Sage University Paper series on Quantitative Applications in the Social Sciences. Beverly Hills, CA: Sage.

Kochanska, G., Murray, K., & Harlan, E. T. (2000). Effortful control in early childhood: Continuity and

change, antecedents, and implications for social development. *Developmental Psychology, 36,* 220–232.

Koeltinger, R. (1991). Analysis of multitrait multimethod matrices. In W. E. Saris & A. van Meurs (Eds.), *Evaluation of measurement instruments by meta-analysis of multitrait multimethod studies* (pp. 81–92). Oxford, England: North-Holland.

Koepp, M. J., Gunn, R. N., Lawrence, A. D., Cunningham, V. J., Dagher, A., Jones, T., et al. (1998). Evidence for striatal dopamine release during a video game. *Nature, 393,* 266–268.

Kolar, D. W., Funder, D. C., & Colvin C. R. (1996). Comparing the accuracy of personality judgments by the self and knowledgeable other. *Journal of Personality, 64,* 311–337.

Kolen, M. J., & Brennan, R. L. (1995). *Test equating.* New York: Springer.

Kosslyn, S. M., Alpert, N. M., Thompson, W. L., Maljkovic, V., Weise, S., Chabris, C. F., et al. (1993). Visual mental imagery activates topographically organized visual cortex: PET investigations. *Journal of Cognitive Neuroscience, 5,* 263–287.

Kovacs, M. (1981). Rating scales to assess depression in school-aged children. *Acta Paedospychiatrica, 46,* 301–315.

Kraemer, H. C. (1984). Item selection for profiles: A reanalysis of international profile of schizophrenia. *Psychological Bulletin, 96,* 297–309.

Krahé, B. (1986). Similar perceptions, similar reactions: An ideographic approach to cross-situational coherence. *Journal of Research in Personality, 20,* 349–361.

Krantz, J. H., Ballard, J., & Scher, J. (1997). Comparing the results of laboratory and World Wide Web samples on the determinants of female attractiveness. *Behavior Research Methods, Instruments, & Computers, 29,* 264–269.

Krantz, J. H., & Dalal, R. (2000). Validity of web-based psychological research. In M. H. Birnbaum (Ed.), *Psychological experiments on the Internet* (pp. 35–60). San Diego, CA: Academic Press.

Kratochwill, T. R., & Wetzel, R. J. (1977). Observer agreement, credibility, and judgment: Some considerations in presenting observer agreement data. *Journal of Applied Behavior Analysis, 10,* 133–139.

Kremen, A. M., & Block, J. (1998). The roots of ego-control in young adulthood: Links with parenting in early childhood. *Journal of Personality and Social Psychology, 75,* 1062–1075.

Kretschmer, E. (1928). Experimentelle Typenpsychologie. Sinnes- und denkpsychologische Resultate [Experimental psychology of types. Results in the psychology of sensation and thought]. *Zeitschrift für die Gesamte Neurologie und Psychiatrie, 113,* 776–796.

Krippendorff, K. (1980). *Content analysis: An introduction to its methodology.* Beverly Hills, CA: Sage.

Krosnick, J. A., & Fabrigar, L. R. (in press). *Designing great questionnaires: Insights from psychology.* New York: Oxford University Press.

Krüger, M. (1994). *Sekseverschillen in schoolleiderschap* [Gender differences in school leadership]. Alphen a/d Rijn, the Netherlands: Samson.

Kruglanski, A. W. (1989a). *Lay epistemics and human knowledge: Cognitive and motivational bases.* New York: Plenum.

Kruglanski, A. W. (1989b). The psychology of being "right": The problem of accuracy in social perception and cognition. *Psychological Bulletin, 106,* 395–409.

Kuczaj, S. A. (1986). Thoughts on the intentional basis of early object word extension: Evidence from comprehension and production. In S. A. Kuczaj & M. D. Barrett (Eds.), *The development of work meaning: Progress in cognitive development research* (pp. 99–120). New York: Springer-Verlag.

Kulikowich, J. M., & Young, M. F. (2001). Locating an ecological psychology methodology for situated action. *Journal of the Learning Sciences, 10,* 165–202.

Kuncel, N. R., Hezlett, S. A., & Ones, D. S. (2001). A comprehensive meta-analysis of the predictive validity of the Graduate Record Examinations: Implications for graduate student selection and performance. *Psychological Bulletin, 127,* 162–181.

Kunin, T. (1955). The construction of a new type of attitude measure. *Personnel Psychology, 8,* 65–77.

Kurtz, J. E., & Sherker, J. L. (2003). Relationship quality, trait similarity, and self-other agreement on personality ratings in college roommates. *Journal of Personality, 71,* 21–48.

Kwong, K. K., Belliveau, J. W., Chesler, D. A., Goldberg, I. E., Weisskoff, R. M., Poncelet, B. P., et al. (1992). Dynamic magnetic resonance imaging of human brain activity during primary sensory stimulation. *Proceedings of the National Academy of Sciences of the United States of America, 89,* 5675–5679.

Kyllonen, P. C., & Christal, R. E. (1990). Reasoning ability is (little more than) working memory capacity?! *Intelligence, 14,* 389–433.

LaBrie, J. W., & Earleywine, M. E. (2000). Sexual risk behavior and alcohol: Higher base rates revealed using the unmatched count technique. *The Journal of Sex Research, 37,* 321–326.

Lacey, J. I., & Lacey, B. C. (1980). The specific role of heart rate in sensorimotor integration. In R. F. Thompson, L. H. Hicks, & V. B. Svyrkov (Eds.), *Neural mechanisms of goal-directed behavior and learning* (pp. 405–509). New York: Academic Press.

LaFrance, M., & Banaji, M. R. (1992). Towards a reconsideration of the gender-emotion relationship. In M. S. Clark (Ed.), *Review of personality and social psychology* (Vol. 14, pp. 178–201). Newbury Park, CA: Sage.

Lai, S., Hopkins, A. L., Haacke, E. M., Li, D., Wasserman, B. A., Buckley, P., et al. (1993). Identification of vascular structures as a major source of signal contrast in high resolution 2D and 3D functional activation imaging of the motor cortex at 1.5 preliminary results. *Magnetic Resonance in Medicine, 30,* 387–392.

Laird, N. M., & Ware, H. (1982). Random-effects models for longitudinal data. *Biometrics, 38,* 963–974.

Lance, C. E., Noble, C. L., & Scullen, S. E. (2002). A critique of the correlated trait-correlated method and correlated uniqueness models for multitrait–multimethod data. *Psychological Methods, 7*, 228–244.

Landauer, T. K., & Dumais, S. T. (1997). A solution to Plato's problem: The latent semantic analysis theory of the acquisition, induction, and representation of knowledge. *Psychological Review, 104*, 211–240.

Landauer, T. K., Foltz, P. W., & Laham, D. (1998). An introduction to latent semantic analysis. *Discourse Processes, 25*, 259–284.

Landis, J. R., & Koch, G. G. (1975a). A review of statistical methods in the analysis data arising from observer reliability studies (Part I). *Statistica Neerlandica, 29*, 101–123.

Landis, J. R., & Koch, G. G. (1975b). A review of statistical methods in the analysis data arising from observer reliability studies (Part II). *Statistica Neerlandica, 29*, 151–161.

Landis, J. R., & Koch, G. G. (1977). The measurement of observer agreement for categorical data. *Biometrics, 33*, 159–174.

Lang, P. J. (1979). A bio-informational theory of emotion. *Psychophysiology, 16*, 495–512.

Lang, P. J., Bradley, M. M., & Cuthbert, B. N. (1990). Emotion, attention, and the startle reflex. *Psychological Review, 97*, 377–395.

Lange, N. (1999). Statistical procedures for functional MRI. In C. Moonen & P. A. Bandettini (Eds.), *Functional MRI* (pp. 301–335). Berlin, Germany: Springer.

Langeheine, R. (1994). Latent variables Markov models. In A. von Eye & C. C. Clogg (Eds.), *Latent variables analysis: Applications for developmental research* (pp. 373–395). Thousand Oaks, CA: Sage.

Langeheine, R., & Rost, J. (Eds.). (1988). *Latent trait and latent class models*. New York: Plenum.

Lanza, S. T., Flaherty, B. P., & Collins, L. M. (2003). Latent class and latent transition analysis. In J. A. Schinka & W. F. Velicer (Eds.), *Handbook of psychology: Vol. 2. Research methods in psychology* (pp. 663–685). New York: John Wiley & Sons.

Larsen, R. J. (1987). The stability of mood variability: A spectral analytic approach to daily mood assessments. *Journal of Personality & Social Psychology, 52*, 1195–1204.

Larsen, R. J. (1989). A process approach to personality: Utilizing time as a facet of data. In D. Buss & N. Cantor (Eds.), *Personality psychology: Recent trends and emerging directions* (pp. 177–193). New York: Springer-Verlag.

Larsen, R. J. (1992). Neuroticism and selective encoding and recall of symptoms: Evidence from a combined concurrent-retrospective study. *Journal of Personality and Social Psychology, 62*, 480–488.

Larsen, R. J. (2000). Emotion and personality: Introduction to the special symposium. *Personality and Social Psychology Bulletin, 26*, 651–654.

Larsen, R. J. (2003). Variations *on the irrelevant feature paradigm: Utility of studying emotion with Stroop-like,* Simon-like, and priming tasks. Unpublished manuscript, Washington University, St. Louis, MO.

Larsen, R. J., & Diener, E. (1992). Problems and promises with the circumplex model of emotion. *Review of Personality and Social Psychology, 13*, 25–59.

Larsen, R. J., & Fredrickson, B. L. (1999). Measurement issues in emotion research. In D. Kahneman, E. Diener, & N. Schwarz (Eds.), *Well-being: The foundations of hedonic psychology* (pp. 40–60). New York: Russell Sage Foundation.

Larsen, R. J., Kasimatis, M., & Frey, K. (1992). Facilitating the furrowed brow: An unobtrusive test of the facial feedback hypothesis applied to unpleasant affect. *Cognition and Emotion, 6*, 321–338.

Larsen, R. J., & Ketelaar, T. (1991). Personality and susceptibility to positive and negative emotional states. *Journal of Personality and Social Psychology, 61*, 132–140.

Larsen, R. J., & Sinnett, L. (1991). Meta-analysis of manipulation validity: Factors affecting the Velten mood induction procedure. *Personality and Social Psychology Bulletin, 17*, 323–334.

Larson, R. (1987). On the independence of positive and negative affect within hour-to-hour experience. *Motivation and Emotion, 11*, 145–156.

Larson, R., & Csikszentmihalyi, M. (1983). The experience sampling method. In H. T. Reis (Ed.), *Naturalistic approaches to studying social interaction*. San Francisco: Jossey-Bass.

Laruelle, M., & Huang, Y. (2001). Vulnerability of positron emission tomography radiotracers to endogenous competition. New insights. *The Quarterly Journal of Nuclear Medicine, 45*, 124–138.

Laucken, U., Mees, U., & Chassein, J. (1988). Logographie der Gegenwehr. ["Logography" of resistance.] *Zeitschrift fuer Sozialpsychologie, 19*, 264–274.

Laugwitz, B. (2001). A Web experiment on color harmony principles applied to computer user interface design. In U.-D. Reips & M. Bosnjak (Eds.), *Dimensions of Internet science* (pp. 131–145). Lengerich, Germany: Pabst.

Lazarsfeld, P. F., & Henry, N. W. (1968). *Latent structure analysis*. Boston: Houghton Mifflin.

Lazarus, R. S. (1991). *Emotion and adaptation*. New York: Oxford University Press.

Lazarus, R. S., & Folkman, S. (1984). *Stress, appraisal, and coping*. New York: Springer.

Le Bihan, D., Turner, R., Zeffiro, T. A., Cuenod, C. A., Jezzard, P., & Bonnerot, V. (1993). Activation of human primary visual cortex during visual recall: A magnetic resonance imaging study. *Proceedings of the National Academy of Sciences, 90*, 11802–11805.

Lecky, P. (1945). *Self-consistency: A theory of personality*. New York: Long Island Press.

Lee, F., & Peterson, C. (1997). Content analysis of archival data. *Journal of Consulting and Clinical Psychology, 65*, 959–969.

Lefkowitz, M. M., & Tesiny, E. P. (1980). Assessment of childhood depression. *Journal of Consulting and Clinical Psychology, 53*, 647–656.

Lehrer, P., Isenberg, S., & Hochron, S. (1993). Asthma and emotion: A review. *Journal of Asthma, 30,* 5–21.

Lemery, K. S., Biersach, P., Chipongian, L., Greenberg, D., & Goldsmith, H. H. (2001, April). *Parental characteristics are related to both parent report and lab-based measures of infant temperament.* Paper presented at the 64th meeting of the Society for Research in Child Development, Minneapolis, MN.

Lennon, R., Eisenberg, N., & Carroll, J. (1983). The assessment of empathy in early childhood. *Journal of Applied Developmental Psychology, 4,* 295–302.

Lerner, J. S., & Keltner, D. (2000). Beyond valence: Toward a model of emotion-specific influences on judgement and choice. *Cognition & Emotion Special Issue: Emotion, Cognition, and Decision Making, 14,* 473–493.

Lerner, R. M. (2002). Methodological issues in the study of development. In R. M. Lerner (Ed.), *Concepts and theories of human development.* Mahwah, NJ: Lawrence Erlbaum Associates.

Lestienne, R. (2001). Spike timing, synchronization and information processing on the sensory side of the central nervous system. *Progress in Neurobiology, 65,* 545–591.

Levenson, R. W. (1988). Emotion and the autonomic nervous system: A prospectus for research on autonomic specificity. In H. L. Wagner (Ed.), *Social psychophysiology and emotion: Theory and clinical applications* (pp. 17–42). Chichester, England: John Wiley & Sons.

Levenson, R. W. (1992). Autonomic nervous system patterning in emotion. *Psychological Science, 3,* 23–27.

Levenson, R. W., Ekman, P., & Friesen, W. V. (1990). Voluntary facial action generates emotion-specific autonomic nervous system activity. *Psychophysiology, 27,* 363–384.

Levenson, R. W., & Gottman, J. M. (1983). Marital interaction: Physiological linkage and affective exchange. *Journal of Personality and Social Psychology, 45,* 587–597.

Levesque, M. J., & Kenny, D. A. (1993). Accuracy of behavioral predictions at zero acquaintance: A social relation analysis. *Journal of Personality and Social Psychology, 65,* 1178–1187.

Levin, J. M., Frederick, B. B., Ross, M. H., Fox, J. F., von Rosenberg, H. L., Kaufman, M. J., et al. (2001). Influence of baseline hematocrit and hemodilution on BOLD fMRI activation. *Magnetic Resonance Imaging, 19,* 1055–1062.

Levine, L. J. (1997). Reconstructing memory for emotions. *Journal of Experimental Psychology: General, 126,* 165–177.

Lewin, L. M., Hops, H., Davis, B., & Dishion, T. J. (1993). Multimethod comparison of similarity in school adjustment of siblings and unrelated children. *Developmental Psychology, 29,* 963–969.

Lewis, M. (1999). On the development of personality. In L. A. Pervin & O. P. John (Eds.), *Handbook of personality theory and research* (2nd ed., pp. 327–346). New York: The Guilford Press.

Liebetrau, A. M. (1983). *Measures of association.* Beverly Hills, CA: Sage Publications.

Lilienfeld, S. O., Wood, J. M., & Garb, H. N. (2000). The scientific status of projective techniques. *Psychological Science in the Public Interest, 1,* 27–66.

Linacre, J. M. (1989). *Many-faceted Rasch-measurement.* Chicago: MESA Press.

Lindsay, P. H., & Norman, D. A. (1972). *Human information processing.* New York: Academic Press.

Linneweber, V. (1993). Wer sind die Experten? "User needs analysis" (UNA), "post occupancy evaluation" (POE) und Städtebau aus sozial- und umweltpsychologischer Perspektive. [Who are the experts? "User needs analysis" (UNA), "post occupancy evaluation" (POE) and urban development from the perspective of social and environmental psychology]. In H. Harloff (Ed.), *Psychologie des Wohnungs- und Siedlungsbaus: Psychologie im Dienste von Architektur und Stadtplanung* [Psychology of house building: Psychology at the service of architecture and town planning] (pp. 75–85). Göttingen, Germany: Verlag für Angewandte Psychologie.

Linneweber, V. (2000). *Sexualisierte Gewalt an Kindern und Jugendlichen: Ansätze präventiver Arbeit* (2nd ed.). [Sexualized violence against children and youth: Approaches of preventive work]. Magdeburg, Germany: Kultusministerium des Landes Sachsen-Anhalt.

Little, B. R. (1983). Personal projects: A rationale and method for investigation. *Environment and Behavior, 15,* 273–309.

Little, T. D., Schnabel, K. U., & Baumert, J. (Eds.). (2000). *Modeling longitudinal and multilevel data.* Mahwah, NJ: Lawrence Erlbaum Associates.

Liu, T. T., Frank, L. R., Wong, E. C., & Buxton, R. B. (2001). Detection power, estimation efficiency, and predictability in event-related fMRI. *Neuroimage, 13,* 759–773.

Livert, D., Rindskopf, D., Saxe, L., & Stirratt, M. (2001). Using multilevel modeling in the evaluation of community-based treatment programs, *Multivariate Behavioral Research, 36,* 155–183.

Llabre, M. M., Clements, N. E., Fitzhugh, K. B., Lancelotta, G., Mazzagatti, R. D., & Quinones, N. (1987). The effect of computer-administered testing on test anxiety and performance. *Journal of Educational Computing Research, 3,* 429–433.

Locander, W., Sudman, S., & Bradburn, N. M. (1976). An investigation of interview method, threat and response distortion. *Journal of the American Statistical Association, 71,* 269–275.

Lockhart, R. S., & Murdock, B. B. (1970). Memory and the theory of signal detection. *Psychological Bulletin, 74,* 100–109.

Loeber, R., Stouthamer-Loeber, M., Farrington, D. P., Lahey, B. B, Keenan, K., & White, H. (2002). Editorial introduction, Three longitudinal studies in Pittsburgh: The Developmental Trends Study, the Pittsburgh Youth Study, and the Pittsburgh Girls Study. *Criminal Behavior, 12,* 1–23.

Loevinger, J. (1954). Effect of distortion on item selection. *Educational and Psychological Measurement, 14,* 441–448.

Loftus, E. F., Smith, K. D., Klinger, M. R., & Fiedler, J. (1992). Memory and mismemory for health events. In J. M. Tanur (Ed.), *Questions about questions: Inquiries into the cognitive bases of surveys* (pp.102–137). New York: Russell Sage Foundation.

Logan, G. D., Schachar, R. J., & Tannock, R. (1997). Impulsivity and inhibitory control. *Psychological Science, 8,* 60–64.

Logothetis, N. K. (2002). The neural basis of the blood-oxygen-level-dependent functional magnetic resonance imaging signal. *Philosophical Transactions of the Royal Society of London. Series B: Biological Sciences, 357,* 1003–1037.

Logothetis, N. K., Pauls, J., Augath, M., Trinath, T., & Oeltermann, A. (2001). Neurophysiological investigation of the basis of the fMRI signal. *Nature, 412,* 150–157.

Lohman, D. F. (2000). Complex information processing and intelligence. In R. J. Sternberg (Ed.), *Handbook of human intelligence* (2nd ed., pp. 285–340). Cambridge, MA: Cambridge University Press.

Lord, F. M. (1980a). *Applications of item response theory to practical testing problems.* Hillsdale, NJ: Lawrence Erlbaum Associates.

Lord, F. M. (1980b). Small N justifies Rasch methods. In D. J. Weiss (Ed.), *Proceedings of the 1979 Adaptive testing conference.* Minneapolis: University of Minnesota.

Lord, F. M., & Novick, M. R. (1968). *Statistical theories of mental test scores.* Reading, MA: Addison-Wesley.

Lorenz, K. (1970). Notes. In R. Martin (Ed.), *Studies in animal and human behavior* (Vol. 1, pp. 101–258), London: Methuen. (Originally published 1935)

Lovallo, W. R., & Thomas, T. L. (2000). Stress hormones in psychophysiological research: Emotional, behavioral, and cognitive implications. In J. T. Cacioppo, L. G. Tassinary, & G. G. Berntson (Eds.), *Handbook of psychophysiology* (pp. 342–367). Cambridge, England: Cambridge University Press.

Lubart, T. I. (2003). In search of creative intelligence. In R. J. Sternberg, J. Lautrey, & T. L. Lubart (Eds.), *Models of intelligence: International perspectives* (pp. 279–292). Washington, DC: American Psychological Association.

Lubinski, D. (2000). Assessing individual differences in human behavior: "Sinking shafts at a few critical points." *Annual Review of Psychology, 51,* 405–444.

Lubinski, D. (2004). Cognitive abilities: 100 years after Spearman's (1904) "'General intelligence,' objectively determined and measured." *Journal of Personality and Social Psychology, 86,* 96–111.

Lubinski, D., & Benbow, C. P. (1995). An opportunity for empiricism: Review of Howard Gardner's *Multiple intelligences: The theory in practice. Contemporary Psychology, 40,* 935–938.

Lubinski, D., & Dawis, R. V. (1992). Aptitudes, skills, and proficiencies. In M. D. Dunnette & L. M. Hough (Eds.), *Handbook of industrial/organizational psychol-ogy* (2nd ed., Vol. 3, pp. 1–59). Palo Alto, CA: Consulting Psychology Press.

Lubinski, D., & Humphreys, L. G. (1997). Incorporating general intelligence into epidemiology and the social sciences. *Intelligence, 24,* 159–201.

Lubinski, D., Tellegen, A., & Butcher, J. N. (1983). Masculinity, femininity, and androgyny: Viewed and assessed as distinct concepts. *Journal of Personality and Social Psychology, 44,* 428–439.

Lubinski, D., Webb, R. M., Morelock, M. J., & Benbow, C. P. (2001). Top 1 in 10,000: A 10-year follow-up of the profoundly gifted. *Journal of Applied Psychology, 86,* 718–729.

Luborsky, L. B. (1953). Intraindividual repetitive measurements (P-technique) in understanding psychotherapeutic change. In O. H. Mowrer (Ed.), *Psychotherapy: Theory and research* (pp. 389–413). New York: Ronald Press.

Lucas, R. E., Diener, E., & Suh, E. M. (1996). Discriminant validity of subjective well-being measures. *Journal of Personality and Social Psychology, 71,* 616–628.

Luecht, R. M., & Nungester, R. J. (1998). Some practical examples of computer-adaptive sequential testing. *Journal of Educational Measurement, 35,* 229–249.

Lundberg, U., Dohns, I. E., Melin, B., Sandsjö, L., Palmerud, G., Kadefors, R., et al. (1999). Psychophysiological stress responses, muscle tension, and neck and shoulder pain among supermarket cashiers. *Journal of Occupational Health Psychology, 4,* 245–255.

Lundy, A. (1988). Instructional set and thematic apperception test validity. *Journal of Personality Assessment, 52,* 309–320.

Luo, D., Thompson, L. A., & Detterman, D. K. (2003). The causal factor underlying the correlation between psychometric *g* and scholastic performance. *Intelligence, 31,* 67–83.

Luo, D., Thompson, L. A., & Detterman, D. K. (2005). The criterion validity of tasks of basic cognitive processes. *Intelligence, 33.*

Lupien, S. J., & McEwen, B. S. (1997). The acute effects of corticosteroids on cognition: integration of animal and human model studies. *Brain Research Reviews, 24,* 1–27.

Lykken, D. T. (1959). The GSR in the detection of guilt. *Journal of Applied Psychology, 43,* 385–388.

Lykken, D. T. (1960). The validity of the guilty knowledge technique: The effects of faking. *Journal of Applied Psychology, 44,* 258–262.

Lykken, D. T. (1968). Statistical significance in psychological research. *Psychological Bulletin, 70,* 151–159.

Lykken, D. T. (1974). Psychology and the lie detection industry. *American Psychologist, 29,* 725–739.

Lykken, D. T. (1998). *A tremor in the blood: Uses and abuses of the lie detector* (2nd ed.). Reading, MA: Perseus Books.

Macefield, V. G., Elam, M., & Wallin, B. G. (2002). Firing properties of single postganglionic sympathetic neurons recorded in awake human subjects. *Autonomic Neuroscience, 10,* 146–159.

MacKay, C. J. (1980). The measurement of mood and psychophysiological activity using self-report techniques. In I. Martin & P. Venables (Eds.), *Techniques in psychophysiology* (pp. 501–562). New York: John Wiley & Sons.

MacLaren, V. V. (2001). A quantitative review of the guilty knowledge test. *Journal of Applied Psychology, 86,* 674–683.

MacLeod, C. (1993). Cognition in clinical psychology: Measures, methods, or models? *Behaviour Change, 10,* 169–195.

MacLeod, C. (1999). Anxiety and anxiety disorders. In T. Dalgleish & M. J. Power (Eds.), *Handbook of cognition and emotion* (pp. 447–477). New York: John Wiley & Sons.

MacLeod, C., & Hagan, R. (1992). Individual differences in the selective processing of threatening information, and emotional responses to a stressful life event. *Behaviour Research and Therapy, 30,* 151–161.

MacLeod, C., Rutherford, E., Campbell, L., Ebsworthy, G., & Holker, L. (2002). Selective attention and emotional vulnerability: Assessing the causal basis of their association through the experimental manipulation of attentional bias. *Journal of Abnormal Psychology, 111,* 107–123.

Magnusson, D., & Ekehammar, B. (1978). Similar situations–similar behaviors? A study of the intraindividual congruence between situation perception and situation reactions. *Journal of Research in Personality, 12,* 41–48.

Main, M., & Solomon, J. (1986). Procedures for identifying as disorganized/disoriented during the Ainsworth Strange Situation. In M. T. Greenberg, D. Cicchetti, & E. M. Cummings (Eds.), *Attachment in the preschool years* (pp. 121–160). Chicago: University of Chicago Press.

Maitra, R., Roys, S. R., & Gullapalli, R. P. (2002). Test-retest reliability estimation of functional MRI data. *Magnetic Resonance in Medicine, 48,* 62–70.

Malloy, T. E., & Albright, L. (1990). Interpersonal perception in a social context. *Journal of Personality and Social Psychology, 58,* 419–428.

Mann, S. J., & James, G. D. (1998). Defensiveness and essential hypertension. *Journal of Psychosomatic Research, 45,* 139–148.

Marangoni, C., Garcia, S., Ickes, W., & Teng, G. (1995). Empathic accuracy in a clinically relevant setting. *Journal of Personality and Social Psychology, 68,* 854–869.

Marco, C., & Suls, J. (1993). Daily stress and the trajectory of mood: Spillover, response assimilation, contrast and chronic negative affectivity. *Journal of Personality and Social Psychology, 64,* 1053–1063.

Marcoulides, G. A. (1996). Estimating variance components in generalizability theory: The covariance structure analysis approach. *Structural Equation Modeling, 3,* 290–299.

Marcus, D. K., & Miller, R. S. (1999). The perception of "live" embarrassment: A social relations analysis of class presentations. *Cognition & Emotion, 13,* 105–117.

Marsh, H. W. (1986). Verbal and math self-concepts: An internal/external frame of reference model. *American Educational Research Journal, 23,* 129–149.

Marsh, H. W. (1987). The big-fish-little-pond effect on academic self-concept. *Journal of Educational Psychology, 79,* 280–295.

Marsh, H. W. (1989). Confirmatory factor analysis of the multitrait–multimethod data: many problems and a few solutions. *Applied Psychological Measurement, 13,* 335–361.

Marsh, H. W. (1990a). The causal ordering of academic self-concept and academic achievement: A multiwave, longitudinal panel analysis. *Journal of Educational Psychology, 82,* 646–656.

Marsh, H. W. (1990b). Confirmatory factor analysis of multitrait–multimethod data: The construct validation of multidimensional self-concept responses. *Journal of Personality, 58,* 661–692.

Marsh, H. W. (1990c). A multidimensional, hierarchical model of self-concept: Theoretical and empirical justification. *Educational Psychology Review, 2,* 77–172.

Marsh, H. W. (1991). The failure of high ability high schools to deliver academic benefits: The importance of academic self-concept and educational aspirations. *American Educational Research Journal, 28,* 445–480.

Marsh, H. W. (1992). The content specificity of relations between academic achievement and academic self-concept. *Journal of Educational Psychology, 84,* 35–42.

Marsh, H. W. (1993a). Academic self-concept: Theory measurement and research. In J. Suls (Ed.), *Psychological perspectives on the self* (Vol. 4, pp. 59–98). Hillsdale, NJ: Lawrence Erlbaum Associates.

Marsh, H. W. (1993b). Multitrait–multimethod analyses: Inferring each trait/method combination with multiple indicators. *Applied Measurement in Education, 6,* 49–81.

Marsh, H. W. (1993c). Relations between global and specific domains of self: The importance of individual importance, certainty, and ideals. *Journal of Personality and Social Psychology, 65,* 975–992.

Marsh, H. W. (1994). Sport motivation orientations: Beware of the jingle-jangle fallacies. *Journal of Sport and Exercise Psychology, 16,* 365–380.

Marsh, H. W. (1998). Age and gender effects in physical self-concepts for adolescent elite-athletes and non-athletes: A multi-cohort-multi-occasion design. *Journal of Sport & Exercise Psychology, 20,* 237–259.

Marsh, H. W., & Bailey, M. (1991). Confirmatory factor analysis of multitrait–multimethod data: A comparison of the behavior of alternative models. *Applied Psychological Measurement, 15,* 47–70.

Marsh, H. W., & Byrne, B. M. (1993). Do we see ourselves as others infer: A comparison of self-other agreement on multiple dimensions of self-concept from two continents. *Australian Journal of Psychology, 45,* 49–58.

Marsh, H. W., Byrne, B. M., & Shavelson, R. J. (1988). A multifaceted academic self-concept: Its hierarchical structure and its relation to academic achievement. *Journal of Educational Psychology, 80,* 366–380.

Marsh, H. W., Byrne, B. M., & Yeung, A. S. (1999). Causal ordering of academic self-concept and achievement: Reanalysis of a pioneering study and revised recommendations. *Educational Psychologist, 34,* 155–167.

Marsh, H. W., Chessor, D., Craven, R. G., & Roche, L. (1995). The effects of gifted and talented programs on academic self-concept: The big fish strikes again. *American Educational Research Journal, 32,* 285–319.

Marsh, H. W., & Craven, R. G. (1991). Self-other agreement on multiple dimensions of preadolescent self-concept: The accuracy of inferences by teachers, mothers, and fathers. *Journal of Educational Psychology, 83,* 393–404.

Marsh, H. W., & Craven, R. G. (1997). Academic self-concept: Beyond the dustbowl. In G. Phye (Ed.), *Handbook of classroom assessment: Learning, achievement and adjustment* (pp. 131–198). San Diego, CA: Academic Press.

Marsh, H. W., & Craven, R. G. (1998). The big fish little pond effect, optical illusions, and misinterpretations: A response to gross (1997). *Australasian Journal of Gifted Education, 7,* 6–15.

Marsh, H. W., & Craven, R. G. (2003). The pivotal role of frames of reference in academic self-concept formation: The big fish little pond effect. In F. Pajares & T. Urdan (Eds.), *Adolescence and education* (Volume II). Greenwich, CT: Information Age.

Marsh, H. W., Craven, R. G., & Debus, R. L. (1998). Structure, stability, and development of young children's self-concepts: A multicohort-multioccasion study. *Child Development, 69,* 1030–1053.

Marsh, H. W., & Grayson, D. (1994a). Longitudinal confirmatory factor analysis: Common, trait-specific, item-specific, and residual-error components of variance. *Structural Equation Modeling, 1,* 116–145.

Marsh, H. W., & Grayson, D. (1994b). Longitudinal stability of latent means and individual differences: A unified approach. *Structural Equation Modeling, 1,* 317–359.

Marsh, H. W., & Grayson, D. (1995). Latent variable models of multitrait–multimethod data. In R. H. Hoyle (Ed.), *Structural equation modeling. Concepts, issues, and applications* (pp. 177–198). Thousand Oaks, CA: Sage.

Marsh, H. W., & Hattie, J. (1996). Theoretical perspectives on the structure of self-concept. In B. A. Bracken (Ed.), *Handbook of self-concept* (pp. 38–90). New York: John Wiley & Sons.

Marsh, H. W., & Hau, K. T. (2003). Big fish little pond effect on academic self-concept: A crosscultural (26 country) test of the negative effects of academically selective schools. *American Psychologist, 58,* 1–13.

Marsh, H. W., & Hau, K. T. (2004). Explaining paradoxical relations between academic self-concepts and achievements: Cross-cultural generalizability of the internal-external frame of reference predictions across 26 countries. *Journal of Educational Psychology, 96,* 56–67.

Marsh, H. W., Hau, K. T., & Kong, C. K. (2002). Multilevel causal ordering of academic self-concept and achievement: Influence of language of instruction (English vs. Chinese) for Hong Kong students. *American Educational Research Journal, 39,* 727–763.

Marsh, H. W., & Hocevar, D. (1985). The application of confirmatory factor analysis to the study of self-concept: First and higher order factor structures and their invariance across age groups. *Psychological Bulletin, 97,* 562–582.

Marsh, H. W., & Hocevar, D. (1988). A new, more powerful approach to multitrait–multimethod analyses: Application of second-order confirmatory factor analysis. *Journal of Applied Psychology, 73,* 107–117.

Marsh, H. W., Köller, O., & Baumert, J. (2001). Reunification of East and West German school systems: Longitudinal multilevel modeling study of the big fish little pond effect on academic self-concept. *American Educational Research Journal, 38,* 321–350.

Marsh, H. W., Kong, C. K., & Hau, K. T. (2000). Longitudinal multilevel modeling of the big fish little pond effect on academic self-concept: Counterbalancing social comparison and reflected glory effects in Hong Kong high schools. *Journal of Personality and Social Psychology, 78,* 337–349.

Marsh, H. W., Kong, K. W., & Hau, K. T. (2001). Extension of the internal/external frame of reference model of self-concept formation: Importance of native and non-native languages for Chinese students. *Journal of Educational Psychology, 93,* 543–553.

Marsh, H. W., & O'Niell, R. (1984). Self description questionnaire III: The construct validity of multidimensional self-concept ratings by late adolescents. *Journal of Educational Measurement, 21,* 153–174.

Marsh, H. W., & Parker, J. W. (1984). Determinants of student self-concept: Is it better to be a relatively large fish in a small pond even if you don't learn to swim as well? *Journal of Personality and Social Psychology, 47,* 213–231.

Marsh, H. W., & Peart, N. (1988). Competitive and cooperative physical fitness training programs for girls: Effects on physical fitness and on multidimensional self-concepts. *Journal of Sport and Exercise Psychology, 10,* 390–407.

Marsh, H. W., Plucker, J. A., & Stocking, V. B. (2001). The Self-Description Questionnaire II and gifted students: Another look at Plucker, Taylor, Callahan & Tomchin's (1997) "Mirror, Mirror on the Wall." *Educational and Psychological Measurement, 93,* 87–102.

Marsh, H. W., & Richards, G. E. (1988). The Tennessee Self Concept Scales: Reliability, internal structure, and construct validity. *Journal of Personality and Social Psychology, 55,* 612–624.

Marsh, H. W., Richards, G. E., Johnson, S., Roche, L. A., & Tremayne, P. (1994). Physical Self-Description Questionnaire: Psychometric properties and a multitrait–multimethod analysis of relations to existing instruments. *Journal of Sport and Exercise Psychology, 16,* 270–305.

Marsh, H. W., Roche, L. A., Pajares, F., & Miller, D. (1997). Item-specific efficacy judgments in mathematical problem solving: The downside of standing

too close to trees in a forest. *Contemporary Educational Psychology, 22,* 363–377.

Marsh, H. W., & Rowe, K. J (1996). The effects of single-sex and mixed-sex mathematics classes within a coeducational school: A reanalysis and comment on Rowe (1988; Rowe, Nix & Tepper, 1986). *Australian Journal of Education, 40,* 147–161.

Marsh, H. W., Tomás-Marco, I., & Asci, F. H. (2003). Cross-cultural validity of the physical self description questionnaire: Comparison of factor structures in Australia, Spain, and Turkey. *Research Quarterly for Exercise and Sport, 73,* 257–270.

Marsh, H. W., Walker, R., & Debus, R. (1991). Subject-specific components of academic self-concept and self-efficacy. *Contemporary Educational Psychology, 16,* 331–345.

Marsh, H. W., & Yeung, A. S. (1997). Coursework selection: The effects of academic self-concept and achievement. *American Educational Research Journal, 34,* 691–720.

Marsh, H. W., & Yeung, A. S. (2001). An extension of the internal/external frame of reference model: A response to Bong (1998). *Multivariate Behavioral Research, 36,* 389–420.

Marshalek, B., Lohman, D. F., & Snow, R. E. (1983). The complexity continuum in the radix and hierarchical models of intelligence. *Intelligence, 7,* 107–128.

Martin, B., Pathak, D., Sharfman, M., Adelman, J., Taylor, F., Kwong, W., & Jhingran, P. (2000). Validity and reliability of the Migraine-Specific Quality of Life Questionnaire (MSQ V. 2.1). *Headache, 40,* 204–215.

Martindale, C. (1990). *The clockwork muse: The predictability of artistic change.* New York: Basic Books.

Mason, J. W. (1968). Organization of psychoendocrine mechanisms. *Psychosomatic Medicine, 30,* 791–808.

Mason, J. W. (1975). A historical view of the stress field. *Journal of Human Stress, 1,* 6–12.

Masters, G. N. (1982). A Rasch model for partial credit scoring. *Psychometrika, 60,* 523–547.

Maszk, P., Eisenberg, N., & Guthrie, I. K. (1999). Relations of children's social status to their emotionality and regulation: A short-term longitudinal study. *Merrill-Palmer Quarterly, 45,* 468–492.

Matarazzo, J. D. (1980). Behavioral health and behavioral medicine: Frontiers for a new health psychology. *American Psychologist, 35,* 807–817.

Matarazzo, J. D. (1987). Relationships of health psychology to other segments of psychology. In G. C. Stone, S. M. Weiss, J. D. Matarazzo, N. E. Miller, J. Rodin, C. D. Belar, et al. (Eds.), *Health psychology: A discipline and a profession* (pp. 41–59). Chicago: University of Chicago Press.

Mathews, A., & MacLeod, C. (1994). Cognitive approaches to emotion and emotional disorders. *Annual Review of Psychology, 45,* 25–50.

Mathney, A. P., Wilson, R. S., & Thoeben, A. S. (1987). Home and mother: Relations with infant temperament. *Developmental Psychology, 21,* 486–494.

Mayberg, H. S., & McGinnis, S. (2000). Brain mapping: The applications. In A. W. Toga & J. C. Mazziotta (Eds.), *Brain mapping: The systems* (pp. 491–522). San Diego, CA: Academic Press.

Mayer, J. D. (1986). How mood influences cognition. In N. E. Sharkey (Ed.), *Advances in cognitive science* (pp. 290–314). Chichester, England: Ellis Horwood.

Mayer, J. D. (1995). A framework for the classification of personality components. *Journal of Personality, 63,* 819–877.

Mayer, J. D., & Bremer, D. (1985). Assessing mood with affect-sensitive tasks. *Journal of Personality Assessment, 49,* 95–99.

Mayer, J. D., Mamberg, M. M., & Volanth, A. J. (1988). Cognitive domains of the mood system. *Journal of Personality, 56,* 453–486.

McAdams, D. P. (1993). *The stories we live by: Personal myths and the making of the self.* New York: William Morrow.

McAdams, D. P. (1996). Personality, modernity, and the storied self: A contemporary framework for studying persons. *Psychological Inquiry, 7,* 295–321.

McAdams, D. P. (1999). The psychology of life stories. *Review of General Psychology, 5,* 100–122.

McAdams, D. P., Reynolds, J., Lewis, M., Patten, A., & Bowman, P. (2001). When bad things turn good and good things turn bad: Sequences of redemption and contamination in life narratives and their relation to psychosocial adaptation in midlife adults and in students. *Personality and Social Psychology Bulletin, 27,* 474–485.

McArdle, J. J. (2001). A latent difference score approach to longitudinal dynamic structural analyses. In R. Cudeck, S. du Toit, & D. Sörbom (Eds.), *Structural equation modeling: Present and future* (pp. 342–380). Lincolnwood, IL: Scientific Software International.

McArdle, J. J., Grimm, K., Hamagami, F., & Ferrer-Caja, E. (2002, October). *Modeling latent growth curves using longitudinal data with non-repeated measurements.* Paper presented at the meeting of the Society for Multivariate Experimental Psychology, Charlottesville, VA.

McArdle, J. J., & Nesselroade, J. R. (2003). Growth curve analysis in contemporary psychological research. In J. A. Schinka & W. F. Velicer (Eds.), *Handbook of psychology: Vol. 2. Research methods in psychology* (pp. 447–480). New York: John Wiley & Sons.

McClellan, W. M., Anson, C., Birkeli, K., & Tuttle, E. (1991). Functional status and quality of life: Predictors of early mortality among patients entering treatment for end stage renal disease. *Journal of Clinical Epidemiology, 44,* 83–89.

McClelland, D. C. (1980). Motive dispositions: The merits of operant versus respondent measures. In L. Wheeler (Ed.), *Review of personality and social psychology* (Vol. 1, pp. 11–41). Beverly Hills, CA: Sage.

McClelland, D. C. (1987). *Human motivation.* New York: Cambridge University Press.

McClelland, D. C., & Atkinson, J. W. (1948). The projective expression of needs, I: The effect of different intensities of the hunger drive on perception. *Journal of Psychology, 25,* 205–222.

McClelland, D. C., Koestner, R., & Weinberger, J. (1989). How do self-attributed and implicit motives differ? *Psychological Review, 96,* 690–702.

McConnell, A. R., & Leibold, J. M. (2001). Relations among the Implicit Association Test, discriminatory behavior, and explicit measures of racial attitudes. *Journal of Experimental Social Psychology, 37,* 435–442.

McCrae, R. R. (1994). The counterpoint of personality assessment: Self-reports and observer ratings. *Assessment, 1,* 159–172.

McCrae, R. R., & Costa, P. T. (1983). Social desirability scales: More substance than style. *Journal of Consulting and Clinical Psychology, 51,* 882–888.

McCrae, R. R., & Costa, P. T. (1994). The stability of personality: Observations and evaluations. *Current Directions in Psychological Science, 3,* 173–175.

McCutcheon, A. C. (1987). *Latent class analysis.* Beverly Hills, CA: Sage.

McDonald, R. P. (1999). *Test theory.* Mahwah, NJ: Lawrence Erlbaum Associates.

McEwen, B. S. (2000). The neurobiology of stress: from serendipity to clinical evidence. *Brain Research, 886,* 172–189.

McFarland, C., Ross, M., & DeCourville, N. (1989). Women's theories of menstruation and biases in the recall of menstrual symptoms. *Journal of Personality and Social Psychology, 57,* 522–531.

McGraw, K. O., Tew, M. D., & Williams, J. E. (2000). PsychExps: An on-line psychology laboratory. In M. H. Birnbaum (Ed.), *Psychological experiments on the Internet* (pp. 219–233). San Diego, CA: Academic Press.

McIntosh, A. R. (1999). Mapping cognition to the brain through neural interactions. *Memory, 7,* 523–548.

McIntosh, A. R., Cabeza, R. E., & Lobaugh, N. J. (1998). Analysis of neural interactions explains the activation of occipital cortex by an auditory stimulus. *Journal of Neurophysiology, 80,* 2790–2796.

McKenna, K. Y. A., & Bargh, J. A. (1998). Coming out in the age of the Internet: Identity "demarginalization" through virtual group participation. *Journal of Personality and Social Psychology, 75,* 681–694.

McKenzie, C. R. M., & Nelson, J. D. (2003). What a speaker's choice of frame reveals: Reference points, frame selection, and framing effects. *Psychonomic Bulletin and Review, 10,* 596–602.

McNatt, D. B. (2000). Ancient Pygmalion joins contemporary management: A meta-analysis of the result. *Journal of Applied Psychology, 85,* 314–322.

McNemar, Q. (1964). Lost: Our intelligence? Why? *American Psychologist, 19,* 871–882.

Mead, A. D., & Drasgow, F. (1993). Equivalence of computerized and paper-and-pencil cognitive ability tests: A meta-analysis. *Psychological Bulletin, 114,* 449–458.

Meaney, M. J. (2001). Maternal care, gene expression, and the transmission of individual differences in stress reactivity across generations. *Annual Review of Neuroscience, 24,* 1161–92.

Measelle, J., Ablow, J. C., Cowan, P. A., & Cowan, C. P. (1998). Assessing young children's views of their academic, social, and emotional lives: An evaluation of the self-perception scales of the Berkeley Puppet Interview. *Child Development, 69*(6), 1556–1576.

Meehl, P. E. (1945). An investigation of a general normality or control factor in personality testing. *Psychological Monographs, 59*(4, Whole No. 274).

Meehl, P. E. (1975). Hedonic capacity: Some conjectures. *Bulletin of the Menninger Clinic, 39,* 295–307.

Meehl, P. E. (1978). Theoretical risks and tabular asterisks: Sir Karl, Sir Ronald, and the slow progress of soft psychology. *Journal of Consulting and Clinical Psychology, 46,* 806–834.

Meehl, P. E. (1990). Appraising and amending theories: The strategy of Lakatosian defense and two principles that warrant it. *Psychological Inquiry, 1,* 108–141.

Mehl, M. R., & Pennebaker, J. W. (2003). The sounds of social life: A psychometric analysis of students' daily social environments and natural conversations. *Journal of Personality and Social Psychology, 84,* 857–870.

Mehta, P. D., Neale, M. C., & Flay, B. R. (2004). Squeezing interval change from ordinal panel data: Latent growth curves with ordinal outcomes. *Psychological Methods, 9,* 301–333.

Mehta, P. D., & West, S. G. (2000). Putting the individual back in individual growth curves. *Psychological Methods, 5,* 23–43.

Meier, B. P., & Robinson, M. D. (2004). Does quick to blame mean quick to anger?: The role of agreeableness in dissociating blame and anger. *Personality and Social Psychology Bulletin, 30,* 1472–1484.

Meiser, T., & Bröder, A. (2002). Memory for multidimensional source information. *Journal of Experimental Psychology: Learning, Memory, and Cognition, 28,* 116–137.

Mellenbergh, G. J., Kelderman, H., Stijlen, J. G., & Zondag, E. (1979). Linear models for the analysis and construction of instruments in a facet design. *Psychological Bulletin, 86,* 766–776.

Menon, G., & Yorkston, E. (2000). The use of memory and contextual cues in the formation of behavioral frequency judgements. In A. Stone, J. Turkkan, C. Bachrach, J. Jobe, H. Kurtzman, & V. Cain (Eds.), *The science of self-report: Implications for research and practice* (pp. 63–79). Mahwah, NJ: Lawrence Erlbaum Associates.

Meredith, W. (1993). Measurement invariance, factor analysis and factorial invariance. *Psychometrika, 58,* 525–543.

Meredith, W., & Horn, J. L. (2001). The role of factorial invariance in modeling growth and change. In L. M. Collins & A. G. Sayer (Eds.), *New methods for the analysis of change* (pp. 203–240). Washington, DC: American Psychological Association.

Mergenthaler, E. (1996). Emotion-abstraction patterns in verbatim protocols: A new way of describing psychotherapeutic processes. *Journal of Consulting and Clinical Psychology, 64,* 1306–1315.

Mergenthaler, E., & Bucci, W. (1999). Linking verbal and non-verbal representations: Computer-analysis of referential activity. *British Journal of Medical Psychology, 72,* 339–354.

Mesquita, B., & Frijda, N. H. (1992). Cultural variations in emotions: A review. *Psychological Bulletin, 112,* 179–204.

Messick, S. (1960). Dimensions of social desirability. *Journal of Consulting Psychology, 24,* 279–287.

Messick, S. (1980). Test validity and the ethics of assessment. *American Psychologist, 35,* 1012–1027.

Messick, S. (1989). Validity. In R. L. Linn (Ed.), *Educational measurement* (pp. 13–103). New York: Macmillan.

Messick, S. (1991). Psychology and methodology of response styles. In R. E. Snow & D. E. Wiley (Eds.), *Improving inquiry in social science: A volume in honor of Lee J. Cronbach* (pp. 161–200). Hillsdale, NJ: Lawrence Erlbaum Associates.

Messick, S. (1992). Multiple intelligences or multilevel intelligence? Selective emphasis on distinctive properties of hierarchy: On Gardner's *Frames of Mind* and *Sternberg's Beyond IQ* in the context of theory and research on the structure of human abilities. *Psychological Inquiry, 3,* 365–384.

Messick, S. (1995). Validity of psychological assessment. *American Psychologist, 50,* 741–749.

Mesulam, M. M. (1990). Large-scale neurocognitive networks and distributed processing for attention, language, and memory. *Annals of Neurology, 28,* 597–613.

Metzler, C. W., Biglan, A., Ary, D. V., & Li, F. (1998). The stability and validity of early adolescents' reports of parenting constructs. *Journal of Family Psychology, 12,* 600–619.

Meyer, A.-E., Stuhr, U., Wirth, U., & Ruester, P. (1988). 12-year follow-up study of the Hamburg short psychotherapy experiment: An overview. *Psychotherapy & Psychosomatics, 50,* 192–200.

Meyer, G. J., Finn, S. E., Eyde, L. D., Kay, G. G., Moreland, K. L., Dies, R. R., et al. (2001). Psychological testing and psychological assessment. *American Psychologist, 56,* 128–165.

Mezzacappa, E., Kindlon, D., & Earls, F. (1999). Relations of age to cognitive and motivational elements of impulse control in boys with and without externalizing behavior problems. *Journal of Abnormal Child Psychology, 27,* 473–483.

Mezzacappa, E., Kindlon, D., & Earls, F. (2001). Child abuse and performance task assessments of executive functions in boys. *Journal of Child Psychology & Psychiatry & Allied Disciplines, 42,* 1041–1048.

Mezzacappa, E., Kindlon, D., Saul, J. P., & Earls, F. (1998). Executive and motivational control of performance task behavior, and autonomic heart-rate regulation in children: Physiological validation of two-factor solution inhibitory control. *Journal of Child Psychology and Psychiatry, 39,* 525–531.

Micko, H.-C. (1970). Eine Verallgemeinerung des Meßmodells von Rasch mit einer Anwendung auf die Psychophysik der Reaktionen [A generalization of the Rasch measurement model with application to the psychophysics of responses]. *Psychologische Beiträge, 12,* 4–22.

Miles, M. B., & Huberman, A. M. (1994). *Qualitative data analysis: A expanded sourcebook* (2nd ed.). Thousand Oaks, CA: Sage.

Milgram, S., Mann, L., & Harter, S. (1965). The lost-letter technique: A tool of social science research. *Public Opinion Quarterly, 29,* 437–438.

Miller, G. (1995). *The science of words.* New York: Scientific American Library.

Miller, J. D. (1984). *A new survey technique for studying deviant behavior.* Unpublished Ph.D. dissertation, George Washington University, Department of Sociology.

Miller, J. S., & Cardy, R. L. (2000). Self-monitoring and performance appraisal: Rating outcomes in project teams. *Journal of Organizational Behavior, 21,* 609–629.

Miller, P. A., Eisenberg, N., Fabes, R. A., & Shell, R. (1996). Relations of moral reasoning and vicarious emotion to young children's prosocial behavior toward peers and adults. *Developmental Psychology, 32,* 210–219.

Miller, P. H., & Aloise, P. A. (1989). Young children's understanding of the psychological causes of behavior: A review. *Child Development, 60,* 257–285.

Miller, R. R., Barnet, R. C., & Grahame, N. J. (1995). Assessment of the Rescorla-Wagner model. *Psychological Bulletin, 117,* 363–386.

Millsap, R. E. (1995a). Measurement invariance, predictive invariance, and the duality paradox. *Multivariate Behavioral Research, 30,* 577–605.

Millsap, R. E. (1995b). The statistical analysis of method effects in multitrait–multimethod data: A review. In P. E. Shrout & S. T. Fiske (Eds.), *Personality research, methods, and theory. A festschrift honoring D. W. Fiske* (pp. 93–109). Hillsdale, NJ: Lawrence Erlbaum Associates.

Millsap, R. E., & Tein, J.-Y. (in press). Assessing factorial invariance in ordered-categorical measures. *Multivariate Behavioral Research.*

Mislevy, R. J. (1984). Estimating latent distributions. *Psychometrika, 49,* 359–381.

Mislevy, R. J., Beaton, A. E., Kaplan, B., & Sheehan, K. M. (1992). Estimating population characteristics from sparse matrix samples of item responses. *Journal of Educational Measurement, 29,* 133–161.

Mitchell, S. K. (1979). Interobserver agreement, reliability, and generalizability of data collected in observational studies. *Psychological Bulletin, 86,* 376–390.

Moffit, T. E., Caspi, A., Dickson, N., Silva, P., & Stanton, W. (1996). Childhood-onset versus adolescent-onset antisocial conduct problems in males: Natural history from ages 3 to 18 years. *Development and Psychopathology, 8,* 399–424.

Mogg, K., & Bradley, B. P. (1998). A cognitive-motivational analysis of anxiety. *Behaviour Research and Therapy, 36,* 809–848.

Mogg, K., Bradley, B. P., Dixon, C., Fisher, S., Twelftree, H., & McWilliams, A. (2000). Trait anxiety, defensiveness and selective processing of threat: An investigation using two measures of attentional bias. *Personality and Individual Differences, 28,* 1063–1077.

Molenaar, I. (1995). Estimation of item parameters. In G. H. Fischer & I. W. Molenaar (Eds.), *Rasch models. Foundations, recent developments, and applications* (pp. 39–52). Berlin, Germany: Springer.

Monroe, R., & Monroe, R. (1971). Household density and infant care in an East African society. *Journal of Social Psychology, 83,* 9–13.

Montada, L., & Bierhoff, H.-W. (Eds.). (1990). *Altruism in social systems.* Toronto, Ontario, Canada: Hogrefe.

Mook, D. G. (1983). In defense of external invalidity. *American Psychologist, 38,* 379–387.

Moonen, C., & Bandettini, P. A. (Eds.). (1999). *Functional MRI.* Berlin, Germany: Springer-Verlag.

Moore, B. S., Underwood, B., & Rosenhan, D. (1973). Affect and altruism. *Developmental Psychology, 8,* 99–104.

Moore, G. E. (1965). Cramming more components on to integrated circuits, *Electronics, 38,* 114–117.

Morris, A. S., Silk, J. S., Steinberg, L., Sessa, F. M., Avenevoli, S., & Essex, M. J. (2002). Temperamental vulnerability and negative parenting as interacting predictors of child adjustment. *Journal of Marriage and Family, 64,* 461–471.

Morris, A. S., Steinberg, L., Sessa, F. M., Avenevoli, S., Silk, J. S., & Essex, M. J. (2002). Measuring children's perceptions of psychological control: Developmental and conceptual considerations. In B. K. Barber (Ed.), *Intrusive parenting: How psychological control affects children and adolescents* (pp. 125–159). Washington, DC: American Psychological Association.

Moskowitz, D. S. (1986). Comparison of self-reports, reports by knowledgeable informants, and behavioral observation data. *Journal of Personality, 54,* 294–317.

Moskowitz, D. S., & Cote, S. (1995). Do interpersonal traits predict affect? A comparison of three models. *Journal of Personality and Social Psychology, 69,* 915–624.

Moskowitz, D. S., & Schwarz, J. C. (1982). Validity comparison of behavior counts and ratings by knowledgeable informants. *Journal of Personality and Social Psychology, 42,* 518–528.

Mossey, J. M., & Shapiro, E. (1982). Self-rated health: A predictor of mortality among the elderly. *American Journal of Public Health, 72,* 800–808.

Motowidlo, S., & Burnett, J. (1995). Aural and visual sources of validity in structured employment interviews. *Organizational Behavior and Human Decision Processes, 61,* 239–249.

Mower, O. H. (1960). *Learning theory and behavior.* New York: John Wiley & Sons.

Mulligan, N. W., & Hirshman, E. (1997). Measuring the bases of recognition memory: An investigation of the process dissociation framework. *Journal of Experimental Psychology: Learning, Memory, and Cognition, 23,* 280–304.

Muraki, E. (1990). Fitting a polytomous item response model to Likert-type data. *Applied Psychological Measurement, 14,* 59–71.

Murphy, B. C., Eisenberg, N., Fabes, R. A., Shepard, S., & Guthrie, I. K. (1999). Consistency and change in children's emotionality and regulation: A longitudinal study. *Merrill-Palmer Quarterly, 46,* 413–444.

Murray, C. (1998). *Income, inequality, and IQ.* Washington, DC: American Enterprise Institute.

Murray, H. A. (1938). *Explorations in personality.* New York: Oxford University Press.

Musch, J., Bröder, A., & Klauer, K. C. (2001). Improving survey research on the World Wide Web using the randomized response technique. In U.-D. Reips & M. Bosnjak (Eds.), *Dimensions of Internet science* (pp. 179–192). Lengerich, Germany: Pabst.

Musch, J., & Reips, U.-D. (2000). A brief history of Web experimenting. In M. H. Birnbaum (Ed.), *Psychological experiments on the Internet* (pp. 61–88). San Diego, CA: Academic Press.

Muthén, B. O. (1984). A general structural equation model with dichotomous, ordered categorical, and continuous latent variable indicators. *Psychometrika, 49,* 115–132.

Muthén, B. O. (1994). Multilevel covariance structure analysis. *Sociological Methods & Research, 22,* 376–398.

Muthén, B. O. (1996). Growth modeling with binary responses. In A. von Eye & C. Clogg (Eds.), *Categorical variables in developmental research: Methods of analysis* (pp. 37–54). San Diego, CA: Academic.

Muthén, B. O. (2002). Beyond SEM: General latent variable modeling. *Behaviormetrika, 29,* 81–117.

Muthén, B. O. (in press). Latent variable analysis: Growth mixture modeling and related techniques for longitudinal data. In D. Kaplan (Ed.), *Handbook of quantitative methodology for the social sciences.* Thousand Oaks, CA: Sage.

Muthén, B. O., & Khoo, S. T. (1998). Longitudinal studies of achievement growth using latent variable modeling. *Learning and Individual Differences, 10,* 73–101.

Muthén, L. K., & Muthén, B. O. (2004). *Mplus User's guide.* Los Angeles: Muthén & Muthén.

Myers, D. G., & Lamm, H. (1976). The group polarization phenomenon. *Psychological Bulletin, 83,* 602–627.

National Work Group on Literacy and Health. (1998). Communicating with patents who have limited literary skills. *The Journal of Family Practice, 46,* 168–176.

Nay, W. (1979). *Multimethod clinical assessment.* New York: Gardner Press.

Naylor, J. C., Pritchard, R. D., & Ilgen, D. (1980). *A theory of behavior in organizations.* New York: Academic Press.

Nederhof, A. J. (1985). Methods of coping with social desirability bias: A review. *European Journal of Social Psychology, 15,* 263–280.

Neisser, U., Boodoo, G., Bouchard, T. J., Jr., Boykin, A. W., Brody, N., Ceci, S. J., et al. (1996). Intelligence: Knowns and unknowns. *American Psychologist, 51,* 77–101.

Nelson, E., Conger, B., Douglass, R., Gephart, D., Kirk, J., Page, R., et al. (1983). Functional health status levels of primary care patients. *Journal of the American Medical Association, 249,* 3331–3338.

Nesse, R. M., Curtis, G. C., Thyer, B. A., McCann, D. S., Huber-Smith, M., & Knopf, R. F. (1985). Endocrine and cardiovascular responses during phobic anxiety. *Psychosomatic medicine, 47,* 320–332.

Nesselroade, J. R., & Bartsch, T. W. (1977). Multivariate perspectives on the construct validity of the trait-state distinction. In R. B. Cattell & R. M. Dreger (Eds.), *Handbook of modern personality theory* (pp. 221–238). Baton Rouge, LA: Hemisphere Publications.

Neuberg, S. L., Judice, T. N., & West, S. G. (1997). What the need for closure scale measures and what it does not: Toward conceptually and operationally differentiating among related epistemic motives. *Journal of Personality and Social Psychology, 72,* 1396–1412.

Neuendorf, K. A. (2002). *The content analysis guidebook.* Thousand Oaks, CA: Sage.

Neuenschwander, S., Castelo-Branco, M., Baron, J., & Singer, W. (2002). Feed-forward synchronization: propagation of temporal patterns along the retinothalamocortical pathway. *Philosophical Transactions of the Royal Society of London. Series B: Biological Sciences, 357,* 1869–1876.

Newcombe, N., & Huttenlocher, J. (1992). Children's early ability to solve perspective-taking problems. *Developmental Psychology, 28,* 635–643.

Neyer, F. J., Banse, R., & Asendorpf, J. B. (1999). The role of projection and empathic accuracy in dyadic perception between older twins. *Journal of Social and Personal Relationships, 16,* 419–442.

Niaura, R., Todaro, J. F., Stroud, L., Spiro, A., Ward, K. D., & Weiss, S. (2002). Hostility, the metabolic syndrome, and incident coronary heart disease. *Health Psychology, 21,* 588–593.

Nicholson, R. A., & Hogan, R. T. (1990). The construct validity of social desirability. *American Psychologist, 45,* 290–291.

Nicolson, N. A. (1991). Stress, coping, and cortisol dynamics in daily life. In M. deVries (Ed.), *The experience of psychopathology* (pp. 21–42). Cambridge, England: Cambridge University Press.

Niedenthal, P. M., & Setterlund, M. B. (1994). Emotion congruence in perception. *Personality and Social Psychology Bulletin, 20,* 401–411.

Nisbett, R. E. (1993). Violence and U.S. regional culture. *American Psychologist, 48,* 441–449.

Nisbett, R. E., & Cohen, D. (1996). *Culture of honor: The psychology of violence in the south.* Boulder, CO: Westview Press.

Noll, D. C., Cohen, J. D., Meyer, C. H., & Schneider, W. (1995). Spiral K-space MR imaging of cortical activation. *Journal of Magnetic Resonance Imaging, 5,* 49–56.

Noll, D. C., Stenger, V. A., Vazquez, A. L., & Peltier, S. J. (1999). Spiral scanning in MRI. In C. Moonen & P. A. Bandettini (Eds.), *Functional MRI* (pp. 149–160). Berlin, Germany: Springer.

Norem, J. K. (1998). Why should we lower our defenses about defense mechanisms? *Journal of Personality, 66,* 895–917.

Nowlis, V., & Green, R. (1957). The experimental analysis of mood. *Technical Report, Office of Naval Research,* Contract No. Nonr-668(12).

Nunnally, J. C., & Bernstein, I. H. (1994). *Psychometric theory.* New York: McGraw-Hill.

Nussbeck, F. W., Eid. M., & Lischetzke, T. (in press). Analysing multitrait–multimethod data with structural equation models for ordinal variates applying the WLSMV estimator: What sample size is needed for valid results? *British Journal of Mathematical and Statistical Psychology.*

Nyberg, S., Farde, L., & Halldin, C. (1996). Test-retest reliability of central [11C]raclopride binding at high D2 receptor occupancy. A PET study in haloperidol-treated patients. *Psychiatry Research, 67,* 163–171.

Oatley, K., & Johnson-Laird, P. N. (1987). Towards a cognitive theory of emotions. *Cognition & Emotion, 1,* 29–50.

Obrist, P. A. (1981). *Cardiovascular psychophysiology: A perspective.* New York: Plenum.

O'Doherty, J., Winston, J., Critchley, H., Perrett, D., Burt, D. M., & Dolan, R. J. (2003). Beauty in a smile: The role of medial orbitofrontal cortex in facial attractiveness. *Neuropsychologia, 41,* 147–155.

Ogawa, S., Lee, T. M., Kay, A. R., & Tank, D. W. (1990). Brain magnetic resonance imaging with contrast dependent on blood oxygenation. *Proceedings of the National Academy of Sciences of the United States of America, 87,* 9868–9872.

Ogawa, S., Tank, D. W., Menon, R., Ellermann, J. M., Kim, S. G., Merkle, H., et al. (1992). Intrinsic signal changes accompanying sensory stimulation: Functional brain mapping with magnetic resonance imaging. *Proceedings of the National Academy of Sciences of the United States of America, 89,* 5951–5955.

Ogden, J. (1996). *Health psychology: A textbook.* Buckingham, England: Open University Press.

Oishi, S. (2002). The experiencing and remembering of well-being: A cross-cultural analysis. *Personality and Social Psychology Bulletin, 28,* 1398–1406.

Olson-Buchanan, J. B., Drasgow, F., Moberg, P. J., Mead, A. D., Keenan, P. A., & Donovan, M. A. (1998). Interactive video assessment of conflict resolution skills. *Personnel Psychology, 51,* 1–24.

Orne, M. T. (1962). On the social psychology of the psychological experiment: With particular reference to demand characteristics and their implications. *American Psychologist, 17,* 776–783.

Ozer, D. J. (1986). *Consistency in personality.* Berlin, Germany: Springer Publishing Company.

Ozer, D. J. (1989). Construct validity in personality assessment. In D. M. Buss & N. Cantor (Eds.), *Personality psychology: Recent trends and current directions* (pp. 224–234). New York: Springer Publishing Company.

Ozer, D. J., & Reise, S. P. (1994). Personality assessment. *Annual Review of Psychology, 45,* 357–388.

Padgett, D. A., Sheridan, J. F., Dorne, J., Berntson, G. G., Candelora, J., & Glaser, R. (1998). Social stress and the reactivation of latent herpes simplex virus-type 1. *Proceedings of the National Academy of Sciences, 95,* 7231–7235.

Page, S. (2000). Community research: The lost art of unobtrusive methods. *Journal of Applied Social Psychology, 30,* 2126–2136.

Pals, J. L. (2005). *Transforming the self: A two-dimensional process model of identity construction within narratives of difficult life events*. Manuscript in preparation.

Park, B., & Judd, C. M. (1989). Agreement on initial impressions: Differences due to perceivers, trait dimensions, and target behaviors. *Journal of Personality and Social Psychology, 56,* 493–505.

Parker, K. J., Schatzberg, A. F., & Lyons, D. M. (2003). Neuroendocrine aspects of hypercortisolism in major depression. *Hormones and Behavior, 43,* 60–66.

Parshall, C. G., Spray, J. A., Kalohn, J. C., & Davey, T. (2002). *Practical considerations in computer-based testing*. New York: Springer-Verlag.

Parten, M. B. (1932). Social participation among preschool children. *Journal of Abnormal and Social Psychology, 27,* 243–369.

Paterson, L. (1998). Multilevel multivariate regression: An illustration concerning school teachers' perception of their pupils. *Educational Research and Evaluation, 4,* 126–142.

Patrick, C. J., & Iacono, W. G. (1991). The validity of the control question polygraph test: The problem of sampling bias. *Journal of Applied Psychology, 76,* 229–238.

Patterson, G. R. (1995). Orderly change in a stable world: The antisocial trait as a Chimera. In J. M. Gottman (Ed.), *The analysis of change*. Mahwah, NJ: Lawrence Erlbaum Associates.

Paulhus, D. L. (1981). Control of social desirability in personality inventories: Principal-factor deletion. *Journal of Research in Personality, 15,* 383–388.

Paulhus, D. L. (1984). Two-component models of socially desirable responding. *Journal of Personality and Social Psychology, 46,* 598–609.

Paulhus, D. L. (1991). Measurement and control of response bias. In J. P. Robinson, P. R. Shaver, et al. (Eds.), *Measures of personality and social psychological attitudes. Measures of social psychological attitudes* (Vol. 1., pp. 17–59). San Diego, CA: Academic Press.

Paulhus, D. L., & Bruce, M. N. (1992). The effect of acquaintanceship on the validity of personality impressions. *Journal of Personality and Social Psychology, 63,* 816–824.

Paulhus, D. L., & Harms, P. D. (2004). Measuring cognitive ability with the overclaiming technique. *Intelligence, 32,* 297–314.

Paulhus, D. L., & John, O. P. (1998). Egoistic and moralistic biases in self-perception: The interplay of self-deceptive styles with basic traits and motives. *Journal of Personality, 66,* 1025–1060.

Paulhus, D. L., Lysy, D., & Yik, M. S M. (1998). Self-report measures of intelligence: Are they useful as proxy measures of IQ? *Journal of Personality, 66,* 525–554.

Paunonen, S. V. (1989). Consensus in personality judgments: Moderating effects of target-rater acquaintanceship and behavior observability. *Journal of Personality and Social Psychology, 56,* 823–833.

Paunonen, S. V., & Jackson, D. N. (1987). Accuracy of interviewers and students in identifying the personality characteristics of personnel managers and computer programmers. *Journal of Vocational Behavior, 31,* 26–36.

Pavot, W. G., Diener, E., Colvin, C. R., & Sandvik, E. (1991). Further validation of the Satisfaction With Life Scale: Evidence for the cross-method convergence of well-being measures. *Journal of Personality Assessment, 57,* 149–161.

Peak, H., & Boring, E. G. (1926). The factor of speed in intelligence. *Journal of Experimental Psychology, 9,* 71–94.

Pearson, R. W., Ross, M. A., & Dawes, R. M. (1992). Personal recall and the limits of retrospective questions in surveys. In J. M. Tanur (Ed.), *Questions about questions: Inquiries into the cognitive bases of surveys* (pp. 65–94). New York: Russell Sage Foundation.

Pedhazur, E. J., & Schmelkin, L. (1991). *Measurement, design, and analysis: An integrated approach*. Mahwah, NJ: Lawrence Erlbaum Associates.

Pennebaker, J. W., & Francis, M. E. (1996). Cognitive, emotional, and language processes in disclosure. *Cognition and Emotion, 10,* 601–626.

Pennebaker, J. W., Francis, M. E., & Booth, R. J. (2001). *Linguistic inquiry and word count (LIWC): LIWC 2001*. Mahwah, NJ: Lawrence Erlbaum Associates.

Pennebaker, J. W., & King, L. A. (1999). Linguistic styles: Language use as an individual difference. *Journal of Personality and Social Psychology, 77,* 1296–1312.

Pennebaker, J. W., Mayne, T. J., & Francis, M. E. (1997). Linguistic predictors of adaptive bereavement. *Journal of Personality and Social Psychology, 72,* 863–871.

Pennebaker, J. W., Mehl, M. R., & Niederhoffer, K. G. (2003). Psychological aspects of natural language use: Our words, our selves. *Annual Review of Psychology, 54,* 547–577.

Pennebaker, J. W., & Stone, L. D. (2003). Words of wisdom: Language use over the life-span. *Journal of Personality and Social Psychology, 85,* 291–301.

Perfetti, C. A. (1998). The limits of co-occurrence: Tools and theories in language research. *Discourse Processes, 25,* 363–377.

Pervin, L. A. (1994). A critical analysis of current trait theory. *Psychological Inquiry, 5,* 103–113.

Peters, M., Sorbi, M., Kruise, D., Kerssens, J., Verhaak, P., & Bensing, J. (2000). Electronic diary assessment of pain disability and psychological adaptation in patients differing in duration of pain. *Pain, 84,* 181–192.

Peterson, C. (1992). Explanatory style. In C. P. Smith (Ed.), *Motivation and personality: Handbook of thematic content analysis* (pp. 376–382). New York: Cambridge University Press.

Peterson, C., Schulman, P., Castellon, C., & Seligman, M. E. P. (1992). The explanatory style scoring manual. In C. P. Smith (Ed.), *Motivation and personality: Handbook of thematic content analysis* (pp. 383–392). New York: Cambridge University Press.

Peterson, W. W., Birdsall, T. G., & Fox, W. C. (1954). The theory of signal detectability. *Transactions of the IRE Professional Group on Information Theory, 4,* 171–212.

Petrella, J. R., Coleman, R. E., & Doraiswamy, P. M. (2003). Neuroimaging and early diagnosis of Alzheimer disease: A look to the future. *Radiology, 226,* 315–336.

Petrill, S. A., & Brody, N. (2002). Personality and individual differences. In H. Pashler & J. Wixted (Eds.), *Stevens handbook of experimental psychology: Volume 4. Methodology in experimental psychology* (pp. 563–600). New York: John Wiley & Sons.

Piliavin, J. A., Dovidio, J. F., Gaertner, S. L., & Clark, R. D. (1981). *Emergency intervention.* New York: Academic Press.

Pitt, M. A., Kim, W., & Myung, I. J. (2003). Flexibility versus generalizability in model selection. *Psychonomic Bulletin & Review, 10,* 29–44.

Pitt, M. A., & Myung, I. J. (2002). When a good fit can be bad. *Trends in Cognitive Science, 6,* 421–425.

Pitt, M. A., Myung, I. J., & Zhang, S. (2002). Toward a method of selecting among computational models of cognition. *Psychological Review, 109,* 472–491.

Pittam, J., & Scherer, K. R. (1993). Vocal expression and communication of emotion. In M. Lewis & J. M. Haviland (Eds.), *Handbook of emotions* (pp. 185–197). New York: Guilford Press.

Plutchik, R. (1980). *Emotion, a psychoevolutionary synthesis.* New York: Harper & Row.

Podlesny, J. A. (1993). Is the guilty knowledge polygraph technique applicable in criminal investigations? A review of FBI case records. *Crime Laboratory Digest, 20,* 57–61.

Poline, J. B., & Mazoyer, B. M. (1994). Enhanced detection in brain activation maps using a multifiltering approach. *Journal of Cerebral Blood Flow and Metabolism, 14,* 639–642.

Popping, R. (2000). *Computer-assisted text analysis.* London: Sage Publications.

Porges, S. W. (1991). Vagal tone: An autonomic mediator of affect. In J. Garber & K. A. Dodge (Eds.), *The development of emotional regulation and dysregulation* (pp. 111–128). Cambridge, England: Cambridge University Press.

Porges, S. W., Doussard-Roosevelt, J. A., & Maiti, A. K. (1994). Vagal tone and the physiological regulation of emotion. In N. A. Fox (Ed.), *Emotion regulation: Behavioral and biological considerations,* 59, (Serial No. 240). *Monograph of the Society for Research in Child Development,* pp. 167–186.

Porges, S. W. (1995). Cardiac vagal tone: A physiological index of stress. *Neuroscience and Biobehavioral Reviews, 19,* 225–233.

Posner, M. I., Boies, S. J., Eichelman, W. H., & Taylor, R. L. (1969). Retention of visual and name order of single letters. *Journal of Experimental Psychology, 79,* 1–16.

Posner, M. I., Petersen, S. E., Fox, P. T., & Raichle, M. E. (1988). Localization of cognitive operations in the human brain. *Science, 240,* 1627–1631.

Posner, M. I., & Raichle, M. E. (1996). *Images of mind.* New York: Scientific American Library.

Powers, D. E., Burstein, J. C., Chodorow, M., Fowles, M. E., & Kukich, K. (2002). Stumping *e-rater*: Challenging the validity of automated essay scoring. *Computers in Human Behavior, 18,* 103–134.

Pratkanis, A. R., Greenwald, A. G., Leippe, M. R., & Baumgardner, M. H. (1988). In search of reliable persuasion effects. III. the sleeper effect is dead. Long live the sleeper effect. *Journal of Personality and Social Psychology, 54,* 203–218.

Pratto, F., & John, O. P. (1991). Automatic vigilance: The attention-grabbing power of negative social information. *Journal of Personality and Social Psychology, 61,* 380–391.

Preckel, F., & Thiemann, H. (2003). Online versus paper-pencil-version of a high potential intelligence test. *Swiss Journal of Psychology, 62,* 131–138.

Price, C. J., & Friston, K. J. (1997). Cognitive conjunction: a new approach to brain activation experiments. *Neuroimage, 5,* 261–270.

Prochaska, J. O., & DiClemente, C. C. (1984). *The transtheoretical approach: Crossing the traditional boundaries of therapy.* Malabar, FL: Krieger.

Quan, N., Avitsurn, R., Starkn, J. L., He, L., Lai, W., Dhabhar, F., & Sheridan, J. F. (2003). Molecular mechanisms of glucocorticoid resistance in splenocytes of socially stressed male mice. *Journal of Neuroimmunology, 137,* 51–58.

Quist, R. M., & Resendez, M. G. (2002). Social dominance threat: Examining social dominance theory's explanation of prejudice as legitimizing myths. *Basic and Applied Social Psychology, 24,* 287–293.

Raichle, M. E. (1983). Positron emission tomography. *Annual Review of Neuroscience, 6,* 249–267.

Raichle, M. E. (1988). Circulatory and metabolic correlates of brain function in normal humans. In V. B. Mountcastle & F. Plum (Eds.), *Handbook of physiology of the nervous system V* (pp. 643–673). Bethesda, MD: American Physiological Society.

Rand, K., Hoon, E., Massey, J., & Johnson, J. (1990). Daily stress and recurrence of genital herpes simplex. *Archives of Internal Medicine, 150,* 1889–1893.

Rasch, G. (1960). *Probabilistic models for some intelligence and attainment tests.* Copenhagen, Denmark: Nielsen & Lydiche.

Rasch, G. (1980). *Probabilistic models for some intelligence and attainment tests. Expanded edition.* Chicago: University of Chicago Press.

Ratcliff, R., Sheu, C.-F., & Gronlund, S. D. (1992). Testing global memory models using ROC curves. *Psychological Review, 99,* 518–535.

Rathje, W. L. (1984). The garbage decade. *American Behavioral Scientist, 28,* 9–29.

Raudenbush, S. W., & Bryk, A. S. (2002). *Hierarchical linear models.* Thousand Oaks, CA: Sage.

Raudenbush, S. W., Bryk, A. S., Cheong, Y. F., & Congdon, R. (2000). *HLM 5. Hierarchical linear and nonlinear modeling.* Chicago: Scientific Software International.

Raudenbush, S. W., & Chan, W. S. (1993). Application of a hierarchical linear model to the study of adolescent deviance in an overlapping cohort design. *Journal of Consulting and Clinical Psychology, 61,* 941–951.

Raudenbush, S. W., Rowan, B., & Kang, S. J. (1991). A multilevel, multivariate model for studying school climate with estimation via the EM algorithm and application to U.S. high-school data. *Journal of Educational Statistics, 16, 4,* 295–330.

Raudenbush, S. W., & Sampson, R. (1999). Assessing direct and indirect associations in multilevel designs with latent variables. *Sociological Methods and Research, 28,* 123–153.

Raykov, T. (1997). Estimation of composite reliability for congeneric measures. *Applied Psychological Measurement, 22,* 173–184.

Read, T. R., & Cressie, N. A. (1988). *Goodness-of-fit statistics for discrete multivariate data.* New York: Springer Verlag.

Redelmeier, D. A., & Kahneman, D. (1996). Patients' memories of painful medical treatments: Real-time and retrospective evaluations of two minimally invasive procedures. *Pain, 66,* 3–8.

Redelmeier, D. A., Katz, J., & Kahneman, D. (2003). Memories of colonoscopy: A randomized trial. *Pain, 104,* 187–194.

Reder, L. M., Nhouyvanisong, A., Schunn, C. D., Ayers, M. S., Angstadt, P., & Hikari, K. (2000). A mechanistic account of the mirror effect for word frequency: A computational model of remember/know judgments in a continuous recognition paradigm. *Journal of Experimental Psychology: Learning, Memory, & Cognition, 26,* 294–320.

Reder, S. (1998). Dimensionality and construct validity of the NALS assessment. In M. C. Smith (Ed.), *Literacy for the twenty first century* (pp. 37–57). Westport, CT: Praeger.

Reed, A. (1973). Speed-accuracy trade-off in recognition memory. *Science, 181,* 574–576.

Reilly, M. D. (1984). Household refuse analysis and market research. *American Behavioral Scientist, 28*(1), 115–128.

Reips, U.-D. (1995). The *Web experiment method.* Retrieved January 6, 2002, from http://www.genpsy.unizh.ch/Ulf/Lab/WWWExpMethod.html

Reips, U.-D. (1997). Das psychologische Experimentieren im Internet [Psychological experimenting on the Internet]. In B. Batinic (Ed.), *Internet für Psychologen* (pp. 245–265). Göttingen, Germany: Hogrefe.

Reips, U.-D. (2000). The Web experiment method: Advantages, disadvantages, and solutions. In M. H. Birnbaum (Ed.), *Psychological experiments on the Internet* (pp. 89–114). San Diego, CA: Academic Press.

Reips, U.-D. (2001). The Web Experimental Psychology Lab: Five years of data collection on the Internet. *Behavior Research Methods, Instruments, and Computers, 33,* 201–211.

Reips, U.-D. (2002a). Context effects in Web surveys. In B. Batinic, U.-D. Reips, & M. Bosnjak (Eds.), *Online social sciences* (pp. 69–79). Seattle, WA: Hogrefe & Huber.

Reips, U.-D. (2002b). Internet-based psychological experimenting: Five do's and five don'ts. *Social Science Computer Review, 20,* 241–249.

Reips, U.-D. (2002c). Standards for Internet-based experimenting. *Experimental Psychology, 49,* 243–256.

Reips, U.-D. (2002d). Theory and techniques of Web experimenting. In B. Batinic, U.-D. Reips, & M. Bosnjak (Eds.), *Online social sciences.* Seattle, WA: Hogrefe & Huber.

Reips, U.-D. (2003, August 25–27). *Seamless from concepts to results: Experimental Internet science.* Paper presented at the symposium "Decision Making and the Web," 19th biannual conference on Subjective Probability, Utility, and Decision Making (SPUDM), Swiss Federal Institute of Technology (ETH), Zurich, Switzerland.

Reips, U.-D., & Bosnjak, M. (2001). *Dimensions of internet science.* Lengerich, Germany: Pabst.

Reips, U.-D., & Lengler, R. (2005). The "web experiment list": A Web service for the recruitment of participants and archiving of Internet-based experiments. *Behavior Research Methods, 37,* 287–292.

Reips, U.-D., Morger, V., & Meier, B. (2001). *"Fünfe gerade sein lassen": Listenkontexteffekte beim Kategorisieren* ["Letting five be equal": List context effects in categorization]. Unpublished manuscript, available at http://www.psychologie.unizh.ch/sowi/reips/papers/re_mo_me2001.pdf

Reips, U.-D., & Mürner, B. (2004). *Stroop Invaders: A Web site to create arcade game-style Internet-based experiments in the Stroop paradigm.* Manuscript in preparation.

Reips, U.-D., & Mürner, B. (2005). *Stroop Invaders: A Web tool for creating Internet-based Stroop experiments in game format.* Manuscript submitted for publication.

Reips, U.-D., & Musch, J. (1999, November 18). *Using the randomized response technique on the WWW.* Paper presented at the 29th Society for Computers in Psychology (SCiP) Conference, Los Angeles, CA.

Reips, U.-D., & Neuhaus, C. (2002). WEXTOR: A Web-based tool for generating and visualizing experimental designs and procedures. *Behavior Research Methods, Instruments, and Computers, 34,* 234–240.

Reips, U.-D., & Stieger, S. (2004). Scientific LogAnalyzer: A Web-based tool for analyses of server log files in psychological research. *Behavior Research Methods, Instruments, and Computers, 36,* 304–311.

Reis, H. T., & Gable, S. L. (2000). Event-sampling and other methods for studying everyday experience. In H. Reis & C. Judd (Eds.), *Handbook of research methods in social and personality psychology* (pp. 190–223). Cambridge, England: Cambridge University Press.

Reise, S. P., & Waller, N. G. (1990). Fitting the two-parameter model to personality data: The parameterization of the Multidimensional Personality Questionnaire. *Applied Psychological Measurement, 14,* 45–58.

Reise, S. P., & Waller, N. G. (1993). Traitedness and the assessment of response pattern scalability. *Journal of Personality and Social Psychology, 65,* 143–151.

Reise, S. P., & Waller, N. G. (2002). Item response theory for dichotomous assessment data. In F. Drasgow & N. Schmitt (Eds.), *Measuring and analyzing behavior in organizations* (pp. 88–122). San Francisco: Jossey-Bass.

Repp, A. C., Deitz, D. E. D., Boles, S. M., Deitz, S. M., & Repp, C. F. (1976). Differences among common methods for calculating interobserver agreement. *Journal of Applied Behavior Analysis, 9,* 109–113.

Rescorla, R. A., & Wagner, A. R. (1972). A theory of Pavlovian conditioning: Variations in the effectiveness of reinforcement and nonreinforcement. In A. H. Black & W. F. Prokasy (Eds.), *Classical conditioning II: Current research and theory* (pp. 64–99). New York: Appleton-Century-Crofts.

Reynolds, H. T. (1977a). *Analysis of nominal data.* Beverly Hills, CA: Sage Publications

Reynolds, H. T. (1977b). *The analysis of cross-classifications.* New York: Free Press.

Richman, W. L., Kiesler, S., Weisband, S., & Drasgow, F. (1999). A meta-analytic study of social desirability distortion in computer-administered questionnaires, traditional questionnaires, and interviews. *Journal of Applied Psychology, 84,* 754–775.

Richter, T., Naumann, J., & Noller, S. (2003). LOGPAT: A semi-automatic way to analyze hypertext navigation behavior. *Swiss Journal of Psychology, 62,* 113–120.

Ridgeway, D., Waters, E., & Kuczaj, S. A. (1985). The acquisition of emotion descriptive language: Receptive and productive vocabulary norms for ages 18 months to 6 years. *Developmental Psychology, 21,* 901–908.

Riefer, D. M., Hu, X., & Batchelder, W. H. (1994). Response strategies in source monitoring. *Journal of Experimental Psychology: Learning, Memory, & Cognition, 20,* 680–693.

Riefer, D. M., Knapp, B. R., Batchelder, W. H., Bamber, D., & Manifold, V. (2002). Cognitive psychometrics: Assessing storage and retrieval deficits in special populations with multinomial processing tree models. *Psychological Assessment, 14,* 184–201.

Riessman, C. K. (1993). *Narrative analysis.* Newbury Park, CA: Sage.

Rijmen, F., Tuerlincks, F., deBoeck, P., & Kuppens, P. (2003). A nonlinear mixed model framework for item response theory. *Psychological Methods, 8,* 185–205.

Rindskopf, D. (1990). Nonstandard log-linear models. *Psychological Bulletin, 108,* 150–162.

Rinella, S., Ferguson, L., & Sager, E. (1970). Personality-impression formation as a function of visual cues and set. *Perceptual & Motor Skills, 31,* 427–430.

Roberts, B. W., Bogg, T., Walton, K., Chernyshenko, O. S., & Stark, S. (2004). A lexical approach to identifying the lower-order structure of conscientiousness. *Journal of Research in Personality, 38,* 164–178.

Roberts, B. W., & Caspi, A. (2003). The cumulative continuity model of personality development: Striking a balance between continuity and change in personality traits across the life course. R. M. Staudinger & U. Lindenberger (Eds.), *Understanding human development: Lifespan psychology in exchange with other disciplines* (pp. 183–214). Dordrecht, the Netherlands: Kluwer Academic Publishers.

Roberts, B. W., & DelVecchio, W. F. (2000). The rank-order consistency of personality traits from childhood to old age: A quantitative review of longitudinal studies. *Psychological Bulletin, 126,* 3–25.

Roberts, B. W., & Pomerantz, E. M. (in press). On traits, situations, and their integration: A developmental perspective. *Personality and Social Psychology Review.*

Roberts, B. W., & Robins, R. W. (2000). Broad dispositions, broad aspirations: The intersection of personality traits and major life goals. *Personality and Social Psychology Bulletin, 26,* 1284–1296.

Roberts, B. W., & Wood, D. (in press). Personality development in the context of the neo-socioanalytic model of personality. In D. Mroczek & T. Little (Eds.), *Handbook of personality development.* Mahwah, NJ: Lawrence Erlbaum Associates.

Roberts, C. W. (1997). *Text analysis for the social sciences: Methods for drawing statistical inferences from texts and transcripts.* Mahwah, NJ: Lawrence Erlbaum Associates.

Roberts, S., & Pashler, H. (2000). How persuasive is a good fit? A comment on theory testing. *Psychological Review, 107,* 358–367.

Robertson, I., Gratton, L., & Sharpley, D. (1987). The psychometric properties and design of managerial assessment centres: Dimensions into exercises won't go. *Journal of Occupational Psychology, 60,* 187–195.

Robinson, B. F., & Bakeman, R. (1998). ComKappa: A Windows 95 program for calculating kappa and related statistics. *Behavior Research Methods, Instruments, and Computers, 30,* 731–732.

Robinson, M. D. (2004). Personality as performance: Categorization tendencies and their correlates. *Current Directions in Psychological Science, 13,* 127–129.

Robinson, M. D., & Clore, G. L. (2002a). Belief and feeling: Evidence for an accessibility model of emotional self-report. *Psychological Bulletin, 128,* 934–960.

Robinson, M. D., & Clore, G. L. (2002b). Episodic and semantic knowledge in emotional self-report: Evidence for two judgment processes. *Journal of Personality and Social Psychology, 83,* 198–215.

Robinson, M. D., Johnson, J. T., & Shields, S. A. (1998). The gender heuristic and the database: Factors affecting the perception of gender-related differences in the experience and display of emotions. *Basic and Applied Social Psychology, 20,* 206–219.

Robinson, M. D., & Kirkeby, B. S. (in press). Happiness as a belief system: Individual differences and priming in emotion judgments. *Personality and Social Psychology Bulletin.*

Robinson, M. D., Solberg, E. C., Vargas, P. T., & Tamir, M. (2003). Trait as default: Extraversion, subjective well-being, and the distinction between neutral and positive events. *Journal of Personality and Social Psychology, 85,* 517–527.

Robinson, M. D., Vargas, P. T., & Crawford, E. G. (2003). Putting process into personality, appraisal, and emotion: Evaluative processing as a missing link. In J. Musch & C. Klauer (Eds.), *The psychology of evaluation: Affective processes in cognition and emotion* (pp. 275–306). Mahwah, NJ: Lawrence Erlbaum Associates.

Robinson, M. D., Vargas, P. T., Tamir, M., & Solberg, E. C. (2004). Using and being used by categories: The case of negative evaluations and daily well-being. *Psychological Science, 15,* 521–526.

Rodgers, J., Buchanan, T., Scholey, A. B., Heffernan, T. M., Ling, J., & Parrott, A. (2001). Differential effects of Ecstasy and cannabis on self-reports of memory ability:

A web-based study. *Human Psychopharmacology: Clinical and Experimental, 16,* 619–625.

Roediger, H. L., & McDermott, K. B. (1995). Creating false memories: Remembering words not presented in lists. *Journal of Experimental Psychology: Learning, Memory, & Cognition, 21,* 803–814.

Roese, N. J., & Jamieson, D. W. (1993). Twenty years of bogus pipeline research: A critical review and meta-analysis. *Psychological Bulletin, 114,* 363–376.

Rogers, R. W. (1983). Cognitive and psychological processes in fear appeals and attitude change: A revised theory of protection motivation. In J. T. Cacioppo & R. E. Petty (Eds.), *Social psychophysiology* (pp. 153–176). New York: Guilford Press.

Roghmann, K., & Haggerty, R. (1973). Daily stress, illness, and use of health services in young families. *Pediatric Research, 7,* 520–526.

Rojas, R. (Ed.). (2001). *Encyclopedia of computers and computer history.* Chicago: Fitzroy Dearborn.

Rolfhus, E., & Ackerman, P. L. (1999). Assessing individual differences in knowledge: Knowledge, intelligence, and related traits. *Journal of Education Psychology, 91,* 511–526.

Rorer, L. G. (1965). The great response-style myth. *Psychological Bulletin, 63,* 129–156.

Rosen, L. D., & Maguire, P. (1990). Myths and realities of computer phobia: A meta-analysis. *Anxiety Research, 3,* 175–191.

Rosenberg, S. D., Blatt, S., Oxman, T. E., McHugo, G., & Ford, R. (1994). Assessment of object relatedness through lexical content analysis of the TAT. *Journal of Personality Assessment, 63,* 345–362.

Rosenstock, I. M. (1974). Historical origins of the health belief model. *Health Education Monographs, 2,* 1–8.

Rosenthal, R. (1976). *Experimenter effects in behavioral research.* New York: Irvington.

Rosenthal, R. (1990). Replication in behavioral research. Handbook of replication research in the behavioral and social sciences. [Special Issue] *Journal of Social Behavior and Personality, 5,* 1–30.

Roskam, E. E. (1990). Formalized theory and the explanation of empirical phenomena. In J. J. Hox & J. de Jong-Gierveld (Eds.), *Operationalization and research strategy* (pp. 179–198). Amsterdam: Swets & Zeitlinger.

Ross, M. A. (1989). The relation of implicit theories to the construction of personal histories. *Psychological Review, 96,* 341–357.

Rost, J. (1990). Rasch models in latent classes: An integration of two approaches to item analysis. *Applied Psychological Measurement, 14,* 271–282.

Rost, J. (1991). A logistic mixture distribution model for polytomous item responses. *The British Journal of Mathematical and Statistical Psychology, 44,* 75–92.

Rost, J. (1996). *Testtheorie testkonstruktion* [Test theory, test construction]. Bern, Switzerland: Huber.

Rost, J. (2001). The growing family of Rasch models. In A. Boomsma, M. A. J. van Duijn, & T. A. B. Snijders (Eds.), *Essays on item response theory* (pp. 26–42). New York: Springer.

Rost, J. (2003). Latent class analysis. In R. Fernández-Ballasteros (Ed.), *Encyclopedia of psychological assessment* (Vol. 1, pp. 539–543). Thousand Oaks, CA: Sage.

Rost, J., & Carstensen, C. (2002). Multidimensional Rasch measurement via item component models and faceted designs. *Applied Psychological Measurement, 26,* 42–56.

Rost, J., & Spada, H. (1983). Die Quantifizierung von Lerneffekten anhand von Testdaten [Quantification of learning effects by test data]. *Zeitschrift für Differentielle und Diagnostische Psychologie, 4,* 29–49.

Rotello, C. M., Macmillan, N. A., & Van Tassel, G. (2000). Recall-to-reject in recognition: Evidence from ROC curves. *Journal of Memory & Language, 43,* 67–88.

Rothbart, M. K. (1981). Measurement of temperament in infancy. *Child Development, 52,* 569–578.

Rothbart, M. K. (1986). Longitudinal observation of infant temperament. *Developmental Psychology, 22,* 356–365.

Rothbart, M. K., Ahadi, S. A., Hershey, K. L., & Fisher, P. (2001). Investigations of temperament at three to seven years: The Children's Behavior Questionnaire. *Child Development, 72,* 1394–1408.

Rothbart, M. K., & Bates, J. E. (1998). Temperament. In W. Damon (Series Ed.) and N. Eisenberg (Vol. Ed.), *Handbook of child psychology: Vol. 3. Social, emotional, personality development* (pp. 105–176). New York: John Wiley & Sons.

Rothbart, M. K., Chew, K. H., & Garstein, M. A. (2001). Assessment of temperament in early development. In L. T. Singer & P. S. Zeskind (Eds.), *Biobehavioral assessment of the infant.* New York: Guilford.

Rowe, D. C., & Kandel, D. (1997). In the eye of the beholder? Parental ratings of externalizing and internalizing symptoms. *Journal of Abnormal Child Psychology, 25,* 265–275.

Roznowski, M. (1987). Use of tests manifesting sex differences as measures of intelligence: Implications for measurement bias. *Journal of Applied Psychology, 72,* 480–483.

Rubenstein, R., Paradis, A., & Munro, L. (1993). A comparative study of a traveling exhibition at four public settings in Canada. *Environment and Behavior, 25,* 801–820.

Rumelhart, D. E., Hinton, G. E., & Williams, R. J. (1986). Learning internal representations by error propagation. In D. E. Rumelhart & J. L. McClelland (Eds.), *Parallel Distributed Processing: Explorations in the Microstructure of Cognition* (Vol. 1, pp. 318–362). Cambridge, MA: MIT Press.

Rumsfeld, J. S., MaWhinney, S., McCarthy, M., Jr., Shroyer, A. L. W., VillaNueva, C. B., O'Brien, M., et al. (1999). Health-related quality of life as a predictor of mortality following coronary artery bypass graft surgery. *JAMA: Journal of the American Medical Association, 281,* 1298–1303.

Ruppertsberg, A. I., Givaty, G., Van Veen, H. A. H. C., & Bülthoff, H. (2001). Games as research tools for visual perception over the Internet. In U.-D. Reips & M. Bosnjak (Eds.), *Dimensions of Internet science* (pp. 147–158). Lengerich, Germany: Pabst.

Rushton, J. P., Brainerd, C. J., & Pressley, M. (1983). Behavioral development and construct validity: The principle of aggregation. *Psychological Bulletin, 94,* 18–38.

Russell, J. A. (1980). A circumplex model of affect. *Journal of Personality and Social Psychology, 39,* 1161–1178.

Russell, J. A., Bachorowski, J., & Fernandez-Dols, J. (2003). Facial and vocal expressions of emotion. *Annual Review of Psychology, 54,* 329–349.

Rusting, C. L., & Larsen, R. J. (1998). Personality and cognitive processing of affective information. *Personality & Social Psychology Bulletin, 24,* 200–213.

Rutledge, T., Linden, W., & Davies, R. F. (2000). Psychological response styles and cardiovascular health: Confound or independent risk factor? *Health Psychology, 19,* 441–451.

Rutten, G. J., Ramsey, N. F., van Rijen, P. C., & van Veelen, C. W. (2002). Reproducibility of fMRI-determined language lateralization in individual subjects. *Brain and Language, 80,* 421–437.

Ryan, T. A. (1970). *Intentional behavior.* New York: Ronald Press.

Saarni, C. (1997). Coping with aversive feelings. *Motivation and Emotion, 21,* 45–63.

Sackett, G. P. (1979). The lag sequential analysis of contingency and cyclicity in behavioral interaction research. In J. D. Osofsky (Ed.), *Handbook of infant development* (pp. 623–649). New York: John Wiley & Sons.

Sackett, P. R., & Dreher, G. F. (1982). Constructs and assessment center dimensions: Some troubling empirical findings. *Journal of Applied Psychology, 67,* 401–410.

Sackett, P. R., Hardison, C. M., & Cullen, M. J. (2004). On interpreting stereotypic threat as accounting for African American–White differences on cognitive tests. *American Psychologist, 59,* 7–13.

Sackett, P. R., & Harris, M. M. (1988). A further examination of the constructs underlying assessment center ratings. *Journal of Business & Psychology, 3,* 214–229.

Sackett, P. R., Schmitt, N., Kabin, M. B., & Ellingson, J. E. (2001). High-stakes testing in employment, credentialing, and higher education. *American Psychologist, 56,* 302–318.

Samejima, F. (1969). Estimation of latent ability using a response pattern of graded scores. *Psychometrika Monograph, 17.*

Sampson, R., Raudenbush, S. W., & Earls, T. (1997). Neighborhoods and violent crime: A multilevel study of collective efficacy. *Science, 227,* 918–924.

Sanders, C. E., Lubinski, D., & Benbow, C. P. (1995). Does the Defining Issues Test measure psychological phenomena distinct from verbal ability?: An examination of Lykken's query. *Journal of Personality and Social Psychology, 69,* 498–504.

Sands, W. A., Waters, B. K., & McBride, J. R. (Eds.). (1997). *Computerized adaptive testing: From inquiry to operation.* Washington, DC: American Psychological Association.

Saris, W. E., & van Meurs, A. (1991). Evaluation of measurement instruments using a structural modeling approach. In P. P. Biemer, R. M. Groves, L. E. Lyberg, N. A. Mathiowetz, & S. Sudman (Eds.), *Measurement errors in surveys* (pp. 575–597). New York: John Wiley & Sons.

Sarter, M., Berntson, G. G., & Cacioppo, J. T. (1996). Brain imaging and cognitive neuroscience. Toward strong inference in attributing function to structure. *The American Psychologist, 51,* 13–21.

SAS Institute. (2000). *SAS procedures.* Cary, NC: SAS Publishing.

Saucier, G., & Ostendorf, F. (1999). Hierarchical subcomponents of the Big Five personality factors: A cross-language replication. *Journal of Personality and Social Psychology, 76,* 613–627.

Savoy, R. L., Ravicz, M. E., & Gollub, R. (1999). The psychophysical laboratory in the magnet:stimulus delivery, response recording and safety. In C. Moonen & P. A. Bandettini (Eds.), *Functional MRI* (pp. 347–365). Berlin, Germany: Springer.

Schacter, D. L., & Tulving, E. (1994). *Memory systems 1994.* Cambridge, MA: MIT Press.

Schaeffer, N. C. (2000). Asking questions about threatening topics: A selective overview. In A. A. Stone, J. S. Turkkan, et al. (Eds.), *The science of self-report: Implications for research and practice* (pp. 105–121). Mahwah, NJ: Lawrence Erlbaum Associates.

Schafer, J. L. (1997). *Analysis of incomplete multivariate data.* London: Chapman & Hall.

Schaible-Rapp, A., & Kugelmann, W. (1982). Büroraum, Raumnutzung und Arbeitsverhalten bei komplexen kognitiven Tätigkeiten. [Office space, spatial and working behavior in cognitively complex occupations]. *Psychologische Beiträge, 24,* 370–387.

Schaie, K. W., Willis, S. L., Jay, G., & Chipeur, H. (1989). Structural invariance of cognitive abilities across the adult life span: A cross-sectional study. *Developmental Psychology, 25,* 652–662.

Scheers, N. J. (1992). Methods, plainly speaking: A review of randomized response techniques. *Measurement and Evaluation in Counseling and Development, 25,* 27–41.

Schell, T. L., Klein, S. B., & Babey, S. H. (1996). Testing a hierarchical model of self-knowledge. *Psychological Science, 7,* 170–173.

Scherer, K. R. (1978). Personality inference from voice quality. *European Journal of Social Psychology, 8,* 467–487.

Scherer, K. R. (1986). Vocal affect expression: A review and a model for future research. *Psychological Bulletin, 99,* 143–165.

Scherer, K. R., Banse, R., & Wallbott, H. G. (2001). Emotion inferences from vocal expression correlate across languages and cultures. *Journal of Cross-Cultural Psychology, 32,* 76–92.

Scherer, K. R., Banse, R., Wallbott, H. G., & Goldbeck, T. (1991). Vocal cues in emotion encoding and decoding. *Motivation and Emotion, 15,* 123–148.

Schimmack, U., Böckenholt, U., & Reisenzein, R. (2002). Response styles in affect ratings: Making a mountain

out of a molehill. *Journal of Personality Assessment, 78,* 461–483.

Schimmack, U., Diener, E., & Oishi, S. (2002). Life-satisfaction is a momentary judgment and a stable personality characteristic: The use of chronically accessible and stable sources. *Journal of Personality, 70,* 345–384.

Schimmer, B. P., & Parker, K. L. (1996). Adrenocorticotropic hormone: Adrenocortical steroids and their synthetic analogs; inhibitors of the synthesis and actions of adrenocortical hormones. In J. G. Hardman, L. E. Limbird, P. B. Molinoff, R. W. Ruddon, & A. G. Gilman (Eds.), *Goodman & Gilamn's: The pharmacological basis of therapeutics* (9th ed., pp. 1459–1485). New York: McGraw-Hill.

Schmalt, H. (1999). Assessing the achievement motive using the grid technique. *Journal of Research in Personality, 33,* 109–130.

Schmidt, D. B., Lubinski, D., & Benbow, C. P. (1998). Validity of assessing educational-vocational preference dimensions among intellectually talented 13-year olds. *Journal of Counseling Psychology, 45,* 436–453.

Schmidt, F. L., & Hunter, J. E. (1996). Measurement error in psychological research: Lessons from 26 research scenarios. *Psychological Methods, 1,* 199–223.

Schmidt, F. L., & Hunter, J. E. (1998). The validity and utility of selection methods in personnel psychology: Practical and theoretical implications of 85 years of research findings. *Psychological Bulletin, 124,* 262–274.

Schmidt, L. A., & Trainor, L. J. (2001). Frontal brain electrical activity (EEG) distinguishes valence and intensity of musical emotions. *Cognition & Emotion, 15,* 487–500.

Schmidt, M. E., Ernst, M., Matochik, J. A., Maisog, J. M., Pan, B. S., Zametkin, A. J., et al. (1996). Cerebral glucose metabolism during pharmacologic studies: Test-retest under placebo conditions. *Journal of Nuclear Medicine, 37,* 1142–1149.

Schmidt, W. C. (1997). World Wide Web survey research: Benefits, potential problems, and solutions. *Behavior Research Methods, Instruments, and Computers, 29,* 274–279.

Schmidt, W. C. (2001). Presentation accuracy of Web animation methods. *Behavior Research Methods, Instruments and Computers, 33,* 187–200.

Schmidt-Reinwald, A., Pruessner, J. C., Hellhammer, D. H., Federenko, I., Rohleder, N., Schurmeyer, T. H., & Kirschbaum, C. (1999). The cortisol response to awakening in relation to different challenge tests and a 12-hour cortisol rhythm. *Life Sciences, 64,* 1563–1660.

Schmitt, M., & Borkenau, P. (1992). The consistency of personality. In G.-V. Caprara & G. L. Van Heck (Eds.), *Modern personality psychology. Critical reviews and new directions* (pp. 29–55). New York: Harvester-Wheatsheaf.

Schmitt, M., & Steyer, R. (1993). A latent state-trait model (not only) for social desirability. *Personality and Individual Differences, 14,* 519–529.

Schmitt, N. (1996). Uses and abuses of coefficient alpha. *Psychological Assessment, 8,* 350–353.

Schmitt, N., & Stults, D. M. (1986). Methodological review: Analysis of multitrait–multimethod matrices. *Applied Psychological Measurement, 10,* 1–22.

Schmukle, S. C., Egloff, B., & Burns, L. R. (2002). The relationship between positive and negative affect in the Positive and Negative Affect Schedule. *Journal of Research in Personality, 36,* 463–475.

Schneider, J., & Locke, E. A. (1971). A critique of Hertzberg's incident classification system and a suggested revision. *Organizational Behavior and Human Performance, 23,* 441–457.

Schneider, W., & Shiffrin, R. M. (1985). Categorization (restructuring) and automatization: Two separable factors. *Psychological Review, 92,* 424–428.

Schnurr, P. P., Rosenberg, S. D., & Oxman, T. E. (1986). A methodological note on content analysis: Estimates of reliability. *Journal of Personality Assessment, 50,* 601–609.

Schuldberg, D., & Gottlieb, J. (2002). Dynamics and correlates of microscopic changes in affect. *Nonlinear Dynamics, Psychology, and Life Sciences, 6,* 231–257.

Schultheiss, O. C., & Brunstein, J. C. (2001). Assessment of implicit motives with a research version of the TAT: Picture profiles, gender differences, and relations to other personality measures. *Journal of Personality Assessment, 77,* 71–86.

Schuster, C. (2001). Kappa as a parameter of a symmetry model for rater agreement. *Journal of Educational and Behavioral Statistics, 26,* 331–342.

Schütz, A., & Machilek, F. (2003). Who owns a personal home page? A discussion of sampling problems and a strategy based on a search engine. *Swiss Journal of Psychology, 62,* 121–129.

Schwartz, G. (1978). Estimating the dimension of a model. *The Annals of Statistics, 6,* 461–464.

Schwartz, G. E., & Weiss, S. M. (1978). Yale conference on behavioral medicine: A proposed definition and statement of goals. *Journal of Behavioral Medicine, 1,* 3–12.

Schwartz, J., & Stone, A. (1998). Data analysis for EMA studies. *Health Psychology, 17,* 6–16.

Schwartz, J., & Stone, A. (2005). Analysis of real-time data. In A. Stone, S. Shiffman, & A. Atienza (Eds.), *The science of real-time data capture.* New York: Oxford University Press.

Schwartz, S. H. (1977). Normative influences on altruism. In L. Berkowitz (Ed.), *Advances in experimental social psychology* (Vol. 10, pp. 221–279). New York: Academic Press.

Schwartz, S. H. (1992). Universals in the content and structure of values: Theoretical advances and empirical tests in 20 countries. In M. P. Zanna (Ed.), *Advances in experimental social psychology* (Vol. 25, pp. 1–66). San Diego, CA: Academic Press.

Schwarz, N. (1996). *Cognition and communication: Judgmental biases, research methods, and the logic of conversation.* Mahwah, NJ: Lawrence Erlbaum Associates.

Schwarz, N. (1999). Self-reports: How the questions shape the answers. *American Psychologist, 54,* 93–105.

Schwarz, N., & Bless, H. (1992). Constructing reality and its alternatives: Assimilation and contrast effects in social judgment. In L. L. Martin & A. Tesser (Eds.), *The construction of social judgments* (pp. 217–245). Hillsdale, NJ: Lawrence Erlbaum Associates.

Schwarz, N., Bless, H., Strack, F., Klumpp, G., Rittenauer-Schatka, H., & Simons, A. (1991). Ease of retrieval as information: Another look at the availability heuristic. *Journal of Personality and Social Psychology, 61,* 195–202.

Schwarz, N., & Clore, G. L. (1983). Mood, misattribution, and judgments of well-being: Informative and directive functions of affective states. *Journal of Personality and Social Psychology, 45,* 513–523.

Schwarz, N., & Clore, G. L. (1996). Feelings and phenomenal experiences. In E. T. Higgins & A. W. Kruglanski (Eds.), *Social psychology: Handbook of basic principles* (pp.433–465). New York: Guilford Press.

Schwarz, N., Groves, R. M., & Schuman, H. (1998). Survey methods. In D. T. Gilbert & S. T. Fiske (Eds.), *The handbook of social psychology* (Vol. 1, pp. 143–179). New York: McGraw-Hill.

Schwarz, N., Hippler, H. J., Deutsch, B., & Strack, F. (1985). Response scales: Effects of category range on reported behavior and comparative judgments. *Public Opinion Quarterly, 49,* 388–395.

Schwarz, N., Knäuper, B., Hippler, H. J., Noelle-Neumann, E., & Clark, F. (1991). Rating scales: Numeric values may change the meaning of scale labels. *Public Opinion Quarterly, 55,* 570–582.

Schwarz, N., & Strack, F. (1999). Reports of subjective well-being: Judgmental processes and their methodological implications. In D. Kahneman & E. Diener (Eds.), *Well-being: The foundations of hedonic psychology* (pp. 61–84). New York: Russell Sage Foundation.

Schwarz, N., Strack, F., & Mai, H. P. (1991). Assimilation and contrast effects in part/whole question sequences: A conversational logic analysis. *Public Opinion Quarterly, 55,* 3–23.

Schwarz, N., & Sudman, S. (Eds.). (1996). *Answering questions: Methodology for determining cognitive and communicative processes in survey research.* San Francisco: Jossey-Bass.

Schwarz, N., Wänke, M., & Bless, H. (1994). Subjective assessments and evaluations of change: Some lessons learned from social cognitive research. *European Review of Social Psychology, 5,* 181–210.

Schwarz, S., & Reips, U.-D. (2001). CGI versus JavaScript: A Web experiment on the reversed hindsight bias. In U.-D. Reips & M. Bosnjak (Eds.), *Dimensions of Internet science* (pp. 75–90). Lengerich, Germany: Pabst.

Schweigert, W. A. (1998). Physical trades and archival data: Two nonreactive measurement techniques. In W. A. Schweigert (Ed.), *Research methods in psychology: A handbook* (pp. 174–182). Pacific Grove, CA: Brooks/Cole.

Scissons, E. H. (1976). Computer administration of the California Psychological Inventory. *Measurement and Evaluation in Guidance, 9,* 22–25.

Sclove, S. L. (1987). Application of model-selection criteria to some problems in multivariate analysis. *Psychometrika, 52,* 333–343.

Scullen, S. E., Mount, M. K., & Goff, M. (2000). Understanding the latent structure of job performance ratings. *Journal of Applied Psychology, 85,* 956–970.

Sechrest, L. (1963). Incremental validity: A recommendation. *Educational and Psychological Measurement, 23,* 153–158.

Sechrest, L. (Ed.). (1979). *Unobtrusive measurement today.* San Francisco: Jossey-Bass.

Secord, P. F., & Greenwood, J. D. (1995). Self-knowledge of psychological states: The status of subjects' accounts. In P. E. Shrout & S. T. Fiske (Eds.), *Personality research, methods, and theory: A festschrift honoring Donald W. Fiske* (pp. 201–219). Hillsdale, NJ: Lawrence Erlbaum Associates.

Seeman, T. E. (2000). Health promoting effects of friends and family on health outcomes in older adults. *American Journal of Health Promotion, 14,* 362–370.

Segal, Z. V. (1988). Appraisal of the self-schema construct in cognitive models of depression. *Psychological Bulletin, 103,* 147–162.

Segal, Z. V., & Ingram, R. E. (1994). Mood priming and construct activation in tests of cognitive vulnerability to unipolar depression. *Clinical Psychology Review, 14,* 663–695.

Segall, M. H., Lonner, W. J., & Berry, J. W. (1998). Cross-cultural psychology as a scholarly discipline: On the flowering of culture in behavioral research. *American Psychologist, 53,* 1101–1110.

Seidlitz, L., & Diener, E. (1993). Memory for positive versus negative life events: Theories for the difference between happy and unhappy persons. *Journal of Personality and Social Psychology, 64,* 654–663.

Seitz, S. T., Hulin, C. L., & Hanisch, K. A. (2000). Simulating withdrawal behaviors in work organizations: An example of a virtual society. *Nonlinear Dynamics, Psychology, & Life Sciences, 4,* 33–65.

Seitz, S. T., & Miner, A. G. (2002). Integration of catastrophe theory with models of employee withdrawal: Computational models. In J. M. Brett & F. D. Drasgow (Eds.), *Psychology of work: Theoretically based empirical research.* Mahwah, NJ: Lawrence Erlbaum Associates.

Seltzer, M. H., Frank, K. A., & Bryk, A. (1994). The metric matters: The sensitivity of conclusions about growth in student achievement to choice of metric. *Educational Evaluation and Policy analysis, 16,* 41–49.

Selye, H. (1956). *The stress of life.* New York: McGraw-Hill.

Semin, G. R., & Fiedler, K. (1988). The cognitive functions of linguistic categories in describing persons: Social cognition and language. *Journal of Personality and Social Psychology, 54,* 558–568.

Semin, G. R., & Fiedler, K. (1991). The linguistic category model, its bases, applications, and range. In W.

Stroebe & M. Hewstone (Eds.), *European Review of Social Psychology, 2,* 1–30.

Sessa, F. M., Avenevoli, S., Steinberg, L., & Morris, A. S. (2001). Correspondence among informants on parenting: Preschool children, mothers, and observers. *Journal of Family Psychology, 15,* 53–68.

Shadish, W. R. (1995). The logic of generalization: Five principles common to experiments and ethnographies. *American Journal of Community Psychology, 23,* 419–428.

Shadish, W. R., Cook, T. D., & Campbell, D. T. (2002). *Experimental and quasi-experimental designs for generalized causal inference.* Boston: Houghton Mifflin.

Shannon, C., & Weaver, W. (1949). *The mathematical theory of communication.* Urbana: University of Illinois Press.

Shapiro, D., Goldstein, I. B., & Jamner, L. D. (1995). Effects of anger/hostility, defensiveness, gender, and family history of hypertension on cardiovascular reactivity. *Psychophysiology, 32,* 425–435.

Shapiro, G. (1997). The future of coders: Human judgments in a world of sophisticated software. In C. W. Roberts (Ed.), *Text analysis for the social sciences: Methods for drawing statistical inferences from texts and transcripts* (pp. 225–238). Mahwah, NJ: Lawrence Erlbaum Associates.

Shapiro, G., & Markoff, J. (1997). A matter of definition. In C. W. Roberts (Ed.), *Text analysis for the social sciences: Methods for drawing statistical inferences from texts and transcripts* (pp. 8–31). Mahwah, NJ: Lawrence Erlbaum Associates.

Sharp, S. E. (1898–1899). Individual psychology: a study in psychological method. *American Journal of Psychology, 10,* 329–391.

Shaughnessy, J. J., & Zechmeister, E. B. (1990). Unobtrusive measures of behavior. In J. J. Shaughnessy & E. B. Zechmeister (Eds.), *Research methods in psychology* (4th ed., pp. 159–186). New York: McGraw-Hill.

Shavelson, R. J., Hubner, J. J., & Stanton, G. C. (1976). Self-concept: Validation of construct interpretations. *Review of Educational Research, 46,* 407–441.

Shavelson, R. J., & Webb, N. M. (1991). *Generalizability theory: A primer.* Thousand Oaks, CA: Sage.

Shavelson, R. J., Webb, N. M., & Rowley, G. L. (1989). Generalizability theory. *American Psychologist, 44,* 922–932.

Shaw, D. S., Owens, E. B., Vondra, J. I., & Keenan, K. (1996). Early risk factors and pathways in the development of early disruptive behavior problems, *Development and Psychopathology, 8,* 679–699.

Shea, D. L., Lubinski, D., & Benbow, C. P. (2001). Importance of assessing spatial ability in intellectually talented young adolescents: A 20-year longitudinal study. *Journal of Educational Psychology, 93,* 604–614.

Shedler, J., Mayman, M., & Manis, M. (1993). The illusion of mental health. *American Psychologist, 48,* 1117–1131.

Shepard, R. N., & Metzler, J. (1971). Mental rotation of three-dimensional objects. *Science, 191,* 701–703.

Sheridan, J. F., Stark, J. L., Avitsur, R., & Padgett, D. A. (2000). Social disruption, immunity, and susceptibility to viral infection. Role of glucocorticoid insensitivity and NGF. *Annals of the New York Academy of Sciences, 917,* 894–905.

Shermis, M. D., & Lombard, D. (1998). Effects of computer-based test administrations on test anxiety and performance. *Computers in Human Behavior, 14,* 111–123.

Sherwood, A. (1993). Using impedance cardiography in cardiovascular reactivity research. In J. Blascovich & E. S. Katkin (Eds.), *Cardiovascular reactivity to psychological stress and disease* (pp. 157–199). Washington, DC: American Psychological Association.

Sherwood, A., Allen, M. T., Fahrenberg, J., Kelsey, R. M., Lovallo, W. R., & van Doornen, L. J. P. (1990). Committee Report: Methodological guidelines for impedance cardiography. *Psychophysiology, 27,* 1–23.

Shettleworth, S. J. (1993). Varieties of learning and memory in animals. *Journal of Experimental Psychology: Animal Behavior Processes, 19,* 5–14.

Shields, A., & Cicchetti, D. V. (1997). Emotion regulation among school-age children: The development and validation of a new criterion q-sort scale. *Developmental Psychology, 33,* 906–916.

Shiffman, S., Gwaltney, C., Balabanis, M., Liu, K., Paty, J., Kassel, J., et al. (2002). Immediate antecedents of cigarette smoking: An analysis from ecological momentary assessment. *Journal of Abnormal Psychology, 111,* 531–545.

Shiffman, S., Hufford, M., Hickcox, M., Paty, J., Gnys, M., & Kassel, J. (1997). Remember that? A comparison of real-time versus retrospective recall of smoking lapses. *Journal of Consulting and Clinical Psychology, 65,* 292–300.

Shiffrin, D. (1994). *Approaches to discourse.* Cambridge, MA: Blackwell.

Shrout, P. E., & Fiske, S. T. (Eds.). (1995). *Personality research, methods, and theory: A festschrift honoring Donald W. Fiske.* Hillsdale, NJ: Lawrence Erlbaum Associates.

Shrout, P. E., & Fleiss, J. L. (1979). Intraclass correlations: Uses in assessing rater reliability. *Psychological Bulletin, 86,* 420–428.

Siemer, M. (2001). Mood-specific effects on appraisal and emotion judgements. *Cognition & Emotion, 15,* 453–485.

Silbersweig, D., Stern, E., Frith, C., Cahill, C., Schnorr, L., & Grootoonk, S. (1993). Detection of thirty-second cognitive activations in single subjects with positron emission tomography: A new low-dose H215O Regional Cerebral blood flow three-dimensional imaging technique. *Journal of Cerebral Blood Flow and Metabolism, 13,* 617–629.

Silk, J. S., Steinberg, L., & Morris, A. S. (2003). Adolescents' emotion regulation in daily life: Links to depressive symptoms and problem behavior. *Child Development, 74,* 1869–1880.

Simmons, M., Nides, M., Rand, C., Wise, R., & Tashkin, D. (2000). Unpredictability of deception in compli-

ance with physician prescribed bronchodilator inhaler use in a clinical trial. *Chest, 118,* 290–295.

Simonton, D. K. (2003). Qualitative and quantitative analyses of historical data. *Annual Review of Psychology, 54,* 617–640.

Simpson, J. A., Ickes, W., & Blackstone, J. (1995). When the head protects the heart: Empathic accuracy in dating relationships. *Journal of Personality and Social Psychology, 69,* 629–641.

Singer, J. D., & Willett, J. B. (2002). *Applied longitudinal data analysis: Modeling change and event occurrence.* New York: Oxford University Press.

Skelton, J. A., & Strohmetz, D. B. (1990). Priming symptom reports with health-related cognitive activity. *Personality and Social Psychology Bulletin, 16,* 449–464.

Skolnick, A., & Davidson, R. J. (2002). Affective modulation of eyeblink startle with reward and threat. *Psychophysiology, 39,* 835–850.

Smith, C. P. (Ed.). (1992). *Motivation and personality: Handbook of thematic content analysis.* Cambridge, MA: Cambridge University Press.

Smith, C. P. (2000). Content analysis and narrative analysis. In H. T. Reis & C. M. Judd (Eds.), *Handbook of research methods in social and personality psychology* (pp. 313–335). Cambridge, MA: Cambridge University Press.

Smith, D. B., & Ellingson, J. E. (2002). Substance versus style: A new look at social desirability in motivating contexts. *Journal of Applied Psychology, 87,* 211–219.

Smith, E. R., Fazio, R. H., & Cejka, M. A. (1996). Accessible attitudes influence categorization of multiple categorizable objects. *Journal of Personality and Social Psychology, 71,* 888–898.

Smith, N. K., Cacioppo, J. T., Larsen, J. T., & Chartrand, T. L. (2003). May I have your attention, please: Electrocortical responses to positive and negative stimuli. *Neuropsychologia, Special Issue: The cognitive neuroscience of social behavior, 41,* 171–183.

Smith, P. C., Kendall, L., & Hulin, C. L. (1969). *The measurement of satisfaction in work and retirement.* Chicago: Rand McNally.

Smither, J. W., Reilly, R. R., Millsap, R. E., Pearlman, K., & Stoffey, R. W. (1993). Applicant reactions to selection procedures. *Personnel Psychology, 46,* 49–76.

Smyth, J., Okenfels, M., Porter, L., Kirschbaum, C., Hellhammer, D., Stone, A., et al. (1997). Stressors and mood measured on a momentary basis are associated with salivary cortisol secretion. *Psychoneuroendocrinology, 23,* 353–370.

Snijders, T. A. B., & Bosker, R. (1999). *Multilevel analysis. An introduction to basic and advanced multilevel modeling.* Thousand Oaks, CA: Sage.

Snow, R. E. (1986). On intelligence. In R. J. Sternberg & D. K. Detterman (Eds.), *What is intelligence?* (pp. 133–139). Norwood, NJ: Ablex.

Snow, R. E., Kyllonen, P. L., & Marchalek, B. (1984). The topography of ability and learning correlations. In R. J. Sternberg (Ed.), *Advances in the psychology of human intelligence* (Vol. II, pp. 47–104). Hillsdale, NJ: Lawrence Erlbaum Associates.

Snow, R. E., & Lohman, D. F. (1989). Implications of cognitive psychology for educational measurement. In R. L. Linn (Eds.), *Educational measurement* (3rd ed., pp. 263–331). New York: Collier.

Snyderman, M., & Rothman, S. (1987). Survey of expert opinion on intelligence and aptitude testing. *American Psychologist, 42,* 137–144.

Sobel, M. E. (1995). The analysis of contingency tables. In G. Arminger, C. C. Clogg, & M. E. Sobel (Eds.), *Handbook of statistical modeling for the social and behavioral sciences* (pp. 251–310). New York: Plenum.

Sommer, R. (1983). Social design. Creating buildings with people in mind. Englewood Cliffs, NJ: Prentice Hall.

Sorrentino, R. M., Roney, C. J. R., & Hanna, S. E. (1992). Uncertainty orientation. In C. P. Smith (Ed.), *Motivation and personality: Handbook of thematic content analysis* (pp. 419–427). New York: Cambridge University Press.

Spain, J. S., Eaton, L. G., & Funder, D. C. (2000). Perspective on personality: The relative accuracy of self versus others for the prediction of emotion and behavior. *Journal of Personality, 68,* 837–867.

Spangler, W. D. (1992). Validity of questionnaire and TAT measures of need for achievement: Two meta-analyses. *Psychological Bulletin, 112,* 140–154.

Spath-Schwalbe, E., Uthgenannt, D., Voget, G., Kern, W., Born, J., & Fehm, H. L. (1993). Corticotropin-releasing hormone-induced adrenocorticotropin and cortisol secretion depends on sleep and wakefulness. *Journal of Clinical Endocrinology and Metabolism, 77,* 1170–1173.

Spearman, C. (1904). "General intelligence," objectively determined and measured. *American Journal of Psychology, 15,* 201–292.

Spearman, C. (1910). Correlation calculated from faulty data. *British Journal of Psychology, 3,* 271–295.

Spearman, C. (1927). *The abilities of man: Their nature and measurement.* New York: Macmillan.

Specht, K., Willmes, K., Shah, N. J., & Jancke, L. (2003). Assessment of reliability in functional imaging studies. *Journal of Magnetic Resonance Imaging, 17,* 463–471.

Spector, P. E. (1994). Using self-report questionnaires in OB research: A comment on the use of a controversial method. *Journal of Organizational Behavior, 15,* 385–392.

Spencer, H. (1890). *The principles of psychology.* New York: D. Appleton.

Spiel, C. (1994). Latent trait models for measuring change. In A. von Eye & C. C. Clogg (Eds.), *Latent variables analysis: Applications for developmental research* (pp. 274–293). London: Sage.

Spinks, T. J., Jones, T., Bloomfield, P., Bailey, D., Miller, M., Hogg, D., et al. (2000). Physical characteristics of the ECAT EXACT3D positron tomograph. *Physics in Medicine and Biology, 45,* 2601–2618.

Squire, L. R. (1992). Memory and the hippocampus: A synthesis from findings with rats, monkeys, and humans. *Psychological Review, 99,* 195–231.

Srivastava, S., John, O. P., Gosling, S. D., & Potter, J. (2003). Development of personality in early and mid-

dle adulthood: Set like plaster or persistent change? *Journal of Personality and Social Psychology, 84,* 1041–1053.

Staats, A. W. (1996). *Behavior and personality: Psychological behaviorism.* New York: Springer.

Stacy, A. W., Widaman, K. F., Hays, R. D., & DiMatteo, M. R. (1985). Validity of self-reports of alcohol and other drug use: A multitrait–multimethod assessment. *Journal of Personality and Social Psychology, 49,* 219–232.

Stanger, C., & Lewis, M. (1993). Agreement among parents, teachers, and children on internalizing and externalizing behavior problems. *Journal of Clinical Child Psychology, 22,* 107–115.

Steffens, M. C., Buchner, A., Martensen, H., & Erdfelder, E. (2000). Further evidence on the similarity of memory processes in the process dissociation procedure and in source monitoring. *Memory & Cognition, 28,* 1152–1164.

Stegbauer, C., & Rausch, A. (2002). Lurkers in mailing lists. In B. Batinic, U.-D. Reips, & M. Bosnjak (Eds.), *Online social sciences* (pp. 263–274). Seattle, WA: Hogrefe & Huber.

Steiger, J. H. (2002). When constraints interact: A caution about reference variables, identification constraints and scale dependencies in structural equation modeling. *Psychological Methods, 7,* 210–227.

Stern, R. M., Davis, C. M., & Ray, W. J. (1992). *Psychophysiological recording* (2nd ed.). New York: Oxford University Press.

Sternberg, R. J. (1992). Psychological Bulletin's top 10 "Hit Parade." *Psychological Bulletin, 112,* 387–388.

Sternberg, R. J. (Ed.). (1994). *Encyclopedia of human intelligence* (two volumes). New York: Macmillan.

Stevens, S. S. (1946). On the theory of scales of measurement. *Science, 103,* 677–680.

Stevens, S. S. (1951). Mathematics, measurement, and psychophysics. In S. S. Stevens (Ed.), *Handbook of experimental psychology* (pp. 1–49). New York: John Wiley & Sons.

Steyer, R. (1989). Models of classical psychometric test theory as stochastic measurement models: Representation, uniqueness, meaningfulness, identifiability, and testability. *Methodika, 3,* 25–60.

Steyer, R., Ferring, D., & Schmitt, M. (1992). States and traits in psychological assessment. *European Journal of Psychological Assessment, 2,* 79–98.

Steyer, R., Gabler, S., & Rucai, A. A. (1996). Individual causal effects, average causal effects, and unconfoundedness in regression models. In F. Faulbaum & W. Bandilla (Eds.), *Softstat '95. Advances in statistical software 5* (pp. 203–210). Stuttgart, Germany: Lucius & Lucius.

Steyer, R., & Schmitt, M. (1990). The effects of aggregation across and within occasions on consistency, specificity, and reliability. *Methodika, 4,* 58–94.

Steyer, R., Schmitt, M., & Eid, M. (1999). Latent state-trait theory and research in personality and individual differences. *European Journal of Personality, 13,* 389–408.

Sticht, T. (1975). *Reading for working: A functional literacy anthology.* Alexandria, VA: Human Resources Research Organization.

Stifter, C. A., Fox, N. A., & Porges, S. W. (1989). Facial expressivity and vagal tone in 5-month and 10-month old infants, *Infant Behavior and Development, 12,* 127–137.

Stinson, L., & Ickes, W. (1992). Empathic accuracy in interactions of male friends vs. male strangers. *Journal of Personality and Social Psychology, 62,* 787–797.

Stocking, M. L., & Lewis, C. (2000). Methods of controlling the exposure of items in CAT. In W. van der Linden & C. Glas (Eds.), *Computerized adaptive testing: Theory and practice* (pp. 163–182). Boston: Kluwer.

Stocking, M. L., & Swanson, L. (1993). A method for severely constrained item selection in adaptive testing. *Applied Psychological Measurement, 17,* 277–292.

Stone, A. (1981). The association between perceptions of daily experiences and self- and spouse-rated mood. *Journal of Research in Personality, 15,* 510–522.

Stone, A. (1987). Event content in a daily survey is differentially associated with concurrent mood. *Journal of Personality and Social Psychology, 52,* 56–58.

Stone, A. (1995). Measures of affective response. In S. Cohen, R. Kessler, & L. Gordon (Eds.), *Measuring stress: A guide for health and social scientists* (pp. 148–171). New York: Cambridge.

Stone, A., Broderick, J., Schwartz, J., Shiffman, S., Litcher-Kelly, L., & Calvanese, P. (2003). Intensive momentary reporting of pain with an electronic diary: Reactivity, compliance, and patient satisfaction. *Pain, 104,* 343–351.

Stone, A., Hedges, S. M., Neale, J. M., & Satin, M. S. (1985). Prospective and cross-sectional mood reports after no evidence of a "Blue Monday" phenomenon. *Journal of Personality and Social Psychology, 49,* 129–134.

Stone, A., Kessler, R. C., & Haythornthwaite, J. (1991). Measuring daily events and experiences: Decisions for the researcher. *Journal of Personality, 59,* 575–607.

Stone, A., Neale, J., Cox, D., Napoli, A., Valdimarsdottir, H., & Kennedy-Moore, E. (1994). Daily events are associated with a secretory response to an oral antigen in humans. *Health Psychology, 13,* 440–446.

Stone, A., Shiffman, S., & Atienza, A. (in press). *The science of real-time data capture.*

Stone, A., Shiffman, S., & DeVries, M. (1998). Rethinking our self-report assessment methodologies: An argument for collecting ecological valid, momentary measurements. In D. Kahneman, E. Diener, & N. Schwarz (Eds.), *Foundations of hedonic psychology: Scientific perspectives on enjoyment and suffering* (pp. 26–39). New York: Russell Sage Foundation.

Stone, A., Shiffman, S., Schwartz, J., Broderick, J., & Hufford, M. (2002). Patient non-compliance with paper diaries. *British Medical Journal, 324,* 1193–1194.

Stone, A., Turkkan, J. S., Bachrach, C. A., Jobe, J. B., Kurtzman, H. S., & Cain, V. S. (2000). *The science of self-report: Implications for research and practice.* Mahwah, NJ: Lawrence Erlbaum Associates.

Stone, L. D., & Pennebaker, J. W. (2002). Trauma in real time: Talking and avoiding online conversations

about the death of Princess Diana. *Basic and Applied Social Psychology, 24,* 173–184.

Stone, P. J., Dunphy, D. C., Smith, M. S., & Ogilvie, D. M. (1966). *The General Inquirer: A computer approach to content analysis.* Cambridge, MA: MIT Press.

Stoner, J. A. F. (1961). *A comparison of individual and group decisions involving risk.* Unpublished master's thesis, Massachusetts Institute of Technology, 1961. Cited by D. G. Marquis in Individual responsibility and group decisions involving risk. *Industrial Management Review, 3,* 8–23.

Strack, F., & Martin, L. L. (1987). Thinking, judging, and communicating: A process account of context effects in attitude surveys. In H. Hippler, N. Schwarz, & S. Sudman (Eds.), *Social information processing and survey methodology* (pp. 123–148). New York: Springer-Verlag.

Strack, F., Martin, L. L., & Schwarz, N. (1988). Priming and communication: Social determinants of information use in judgments of life satisfaction. *European Journal of Social Psychology, 18,* 429–442.

Strack, F., Schwarz, N., Chassein, B., Kern, D., & Wagner, D. (1990). Salience of comparison standards and the activation of social norms: Consequences for judgments of happiness and their communication. *British Journal of Social Psychology, 29,* 303–314.

Strack, F., Schwarz, N., & Gschneidinger, E. (1985). Happiness and reminiscing: The role of time perspective, affect, and mode of thinking. *Journal of Personality and Social Psychology, 49,* 1460–1469.

Strack, F., Schwarz, N., & Wänke, M. (1991). Semantic and pragmatic aspects of context effects in social and psychological research. *Social Cognition, 9,* 111–125.

Straka, R., Fish, J., Benson, S., & Suh, J. (1997). Patient self-reporting of compliance does not correspond with electronic monitoring: An evaluation using Isosorbide Dinitrate as a model drug. *Pharmacotherapy, 17,* 126–132.

Strauss, A. L., & Corbin, J. (1990). *Basics of qualitative research: Grounded theory procedures and techniques.* Newbury Park, CA: Sage.

Stricker, L. J., & Bejar, I. I. (2004). Test difficulty and stereotypic treat on the GRE general test. *Journal of Applied Social Psychology, 34,* 563–597.

Stricker, L. J., & Ward, W. C. (2004). Stereotypic treat, inquiring about test takers' ethnicity and sex, and standardized test performance. *Journal of Applied Social Psychology, 34,* 665–693.

Strome, E. M., Wheler, G. H., Higley, J. D., Loriaux, D. L., Suomi, S. J., & Doudet, D. J. (2002). Intracerebroventricular corticotropin-releasing factor increases limbic glucose metabolism and has social context-dependent behavioral effects in nonhuman primates. *Proceedings of the National Academy of Sciences, 99,* 15749–15754.

Strube, G. (1987). Answering survey questions: The role of memory. In H. J. Hippler, N. Schwarz, & S. Sudman (Eds.), *Social information processing and survey methodology* (pp. 86–101). New York: Springer.

Sudman, S., & Bradburn, N. M. (1973). Effects of time and memory factors on response in surveys. *Journal of the American Statistical Association, 68,* 805–815.

Sudman, S., Bradburn, N. M., & Schwarz, N. (1996). *Thinking about answers: The application of cognitive processes to survey methodology.* San Francisco: Jossey-Bass.

Suedfeld, P., Tetlock, P. E., & Streufert, S. (1992). Conceptual/integrative complexity. In C. P. Smith (Ed.), *Motivation and personality: Handbook of thematic content analysis* (pp. 393–400). New York: Cambridge University Press.

Suen, H. K., & Ary, D. (1989). *Analyzing quantitative behavioral observation data.* Hillsdale, NJ: Lawrence Erlbaum Associates.

Suen, H. K., Ary, D., & Ary, R. (1986). A note on the relationship among eight indices of interobserver agreement. *Behavioral Assessment, 8,* 301–303.

Suen, H. K., & Lee, P. S. (1985). Effects of the use of percentage agreement on behavioral observation reliabilities. *Journal of Pathology and Behavioral Assessment, 7,* 221–234.

Suls, J., Wan, C., & Blanchard, E. (1994). A multilevel data-analytic approach for evaluation of relationships between daily life stressors and symptomatology: Patients with irritable bowel syndrome. *Health Psychology, 13,* 103–113.

Suppes, P., & Zinnes, J. L. (1963). Basic measurement theory. In R. D. Luce, R. R. Bush, & E. Galanter (Eds.), *Handbook of mathematical psychology* (pp. 1–76). New York: John Wiley & Sons.

Swain, A. J. (1975). *Analysis of parametric structures for variance matrices.* Unpublished doctoral dissertation, University of Adelaide, Australia.

Swann, W. B. (1984). Quest for accuracy in person perception: A matter of pragmatics. *Psychological Review, 91,* 457–477.

Sympson, J. B., & Hetter, R. D. (1985, October). Controlling item-exposure rates in computerized adaptive testing. *Proceedings of the 27th annual meeting of the Military Testing Association* (pp. 973–977). San Diego, CA: Navy Personnel Research and Development Center.

Szalai, A. (1966). The multinational comparative time budget research project: A venture in international research cooperation. *American Behavioral Scientist, 10,* 30.

Taft, R. (1955). The ability to judge people. *Psychological Bulletin, 52,* 1–23.

Takane, Y., & de Leeuw, J. (1987). On the relationship between item response theory and factor analysis of discretized variables. *Psychometrika, 52,* 393–408.

Tamir, M., & Robinson, M. D. (2004). *The happy spotlight: Emotional experience and selective attention.* Manuscript submitted for publication.

Tanner, M. A., & Young, M. A. (1985). Modeling agreement among raters. *Journal of the American Statistical Association, 80,* 175–180.

Tarchanoff, J. (1890). Galvanic phenomena in the human skin during stimulation of the sensory organs and during various forms of mental activity. *Pflugers*

Archiv für die gesammte Physiologie des Menschen und der Tiere, 46, 46–55.

Teachman, B. A., Gregg, A. P., & Woody, S. R. (2001). Implicit processing of fear-related stimuli among individuals with snake and spider fears. *Journal of Abnormal Psychology, 110,* 226–235.

Teasdale, J. D., & Fogarty, S. J. (1979). Differential effects of induced mood on retrieval of pleasant and unpleasant events from episodic memory. *Journal of Abnormal Psychology, 88,* 248–257.

Teasdale, J. D., & Russell, M. L. (1983). Differential effects of induced mood on the recall of positive, negative and neutral words. *British Journal of Clinical Psychology, 22,* 163–171.

Teasdale, J. D., Taylor, R., & Fogarty, S. J. (1980). Effects of induced elation-depression of the accessibility of memories of happy and unhappy experiences. *Behavior Research and Therapy, 18,* 339–346.

Tellegen, A. (1993). Folk concepts and psychological concepts in personality and personality disorder. *Psychological Inquiry, 4,* 122–130.

Tellegen, A., Watson, D., & Clark, L. A. (1999). On the dimensional and heirarcical structure of affect. *Psychological Science, 10,* 297–303.

Tennen, H., & Affleck, G. (2002). The challenge of capturing daily processes at the interface of social and clinical psychology. *Journal of Social and Clinical Psychology, 21,* 610–627.

Thomas, D. L., & Diener, E. (1990). Memory accuracy in the recall of emotions. *Journal of Personality and Social Psychology, 59,* 291–297.

Thompson, R. S. (1998). Early sociopersonality development. In W. Damon & N. Eisenberg (Eds.), *Handbook of child psychology: Social, emotional, and personality development.* New York: John Wiley & Sons.

Thompson, W. D., & Walter, S. D. (1988a). A reappraisal of the kappa coefficient. *Journal of Clinical Epidemiology, 41,* 949–958.

Thompson, W. D., & Walter, S. D. (1988b). Kappa and the concept of independent errors. *Journal of Clinical Epidemiology, 41,* 969–970.

Thorndike, R. L., & Stein, S. (1937). An evaluation of the attempts to measure social intelligence. *Psychological Bulletin, 34,* 275–285.

Thorndike, R. M., & Lohman, D. F. (1990). *A century of ability testing.* Chicago: Riverside.

Thornton, G. C., & Zorich, S. (1980). Training to improve observer accuracy. *Journal of Abnormal Psychology, 65,* 351–354.

Thurstone, L. L. (1937). *The reliability and validity of tests.* Ann Arbor, MI: Edwards.

Thurstone, L. L. (1938). *Primary mental abilities.* Chicago: University of Chicago Press.

Tiedens, L. Z., & Fragale, A. R. (2003). Power moves: Complementarity in dominant and submissive nonverbal behavior. *Journal of Personality and Social Psychology, 84,* 558–568.

Tildesley, E. A., Hops, H., Ary, D., & Andrews, J. A. (1995). Multitrait–multimethod model of adolescent deviance, drug use, academic, and sexual behaviors.

Journal of Psychopathology and Behavioral Assessment, 17, 185–215.

Tinsley, B. J., Holtgrave, D. R., Erdley, C. A., & Reise, S. P. (1997). A multimethod analysis of risk perceptions and health behaviors in children. *Educational and Psychological Measurement, 57,* 197–209.

Tinsley, H. E. A., & Weiss, D. J. (2000). Interrater reliability and agreement. In H. Tinsley & S. D. Brown (Eds.), *Handbook of applied multivariate statistics and mathematical modeling* (pp. 96–124). San Diego, CA: Academic Press.

Tisak, J., & Tisak, M. S. (2002). Permanency and ephemerality of psychological measures with application to organizational commitment. *Psychological Methods, 5,* 175–198.

Tolman, E. C. (1932). *Purposive behavior in animals and men.* New York: Appleton-Century.

Tomarken, A. J., & Keener, A. D. (1998). Frontal brain asymmetry and depression: A self-regulatory perspective. *Cognition and Emotion, 12,* 387–420.

Tomás-Marco, I., González-Romá, V., & Marsh, H. W. (2003). *Testing for item and factor parameter invariance on a Spanish version of the Physical Self-Description Questionnaire: An application of Mean and Covariance Structure Analysis.* Manuscript submitted for publication.

Tomkins, S. P. (1984). *The origins of mankind.* Cambridge, MA: Cambridge University Press.

Tonidandel, S., & Quinones, M. A. (2000). Psychological reactions to adaptive testing. *International Journal of Selection and Assessment, 8,* 7–15.

Tourangeau, R. (1999). Context effects on answers to attitude questions. In M. G. Sirken, D. J. Hermann, S. Schechter, N. Schwarz, J. M. Tanur, & R. Tourangeau (Eds.), *Cognition and survey research* (pp. 111–131). New York: John Wiley & Sons.

Tourangeau, R., Rips, L. R., & Rasinski, K. (2000). *The psychology of survey response.* Cambridge, MA: Cambridge University Press.

Tourangeau, R., Singer, E., & Presser, S. (2003). Context effects in attitude surveys: Effects on remote items and impact on predictive validity. *Sociological Methods and Research, 31,* 486–513.

Tracey, D. K., Marsh, H. W., & Craven, R. G. (2003). Self-concepts of preadolescents with mild intellectual disabilities: Issues of measurement and educational placement. In H. W. Marsh, R. G. Craven, & D. M. McInerney (Eds.), *International advances in self research* (Vol. 1, pp. 203–230). Greenwich, CT: Information Age.

Tranel, D., & Damasio, A. R. (1985). Knowledge without awareness: An autonomic index of facial recognition by prosopagnosics. *Science, 228,* 1453–1454.

Trepagnier, C. (2002). Tracking gaze of patients with visuospatial neglect. *Topics in Stroke Rehabilitation, 8,* 79–88.

Triandis, H. C. (1980). Values, attitudes, and interpersonal behavior. In H. E. Howe & M. M. Page (Eds.), *Nebraska Symposium on Motivation 1979* (Vol. 27, pp. 195–259). Lincoln: University of Nebraska Press.

Trickett, P. K. (1993). Maladaptive development of school-aged, physically abused children: Relationships with the child-rearing context. *Journal of Family, 7*(1), 134–147.

Trierweiler, L. I., Eid, M., & Lischetzke, T. (2002). The structure of emotional expressivity: Each emotion counts. *Journal of Personality and Social Psychology, 82*, 1023–1040.

Triplett, N. (1898). The dynamogen factors in pacemaking and competition. *American Journal of Psychology, 9*, 507–533.

Tronick, E., Als, H., Adamson, L. B., Wise, S., & Brazelton, T. B. (1978). The infant's response to entrapment between contradictory messages in face-to-face interaction. *Journal of the American Academy of Child Psychiatry, 17*, 1–13.

Tuerlinckx, F., De Boeck, P., & Lens, W. (2002). Measuring needs with the Thematic Apperception Test: A psychometric study. *Journal of Personality and Social Psychology, 82*, 448–461.

Tulving, E. (1983). *Elements of episodic memory.* New York: Oxford University Press.

Tulving, E. (1984). Multiple learning and memory systems. In K. M. J. Lagerspetz & P. Niemi (Eds.), *Psychology in the 1990's* (pp. 163–184). Amsterdam, Holland: Elsevier.

Tunn, S., Mollmann, H., Barth, J., Derendorf, H., & Krieg, M. (1992). Simultaneous measurement of cortisol in serum and saliva after different forms of cortisol administration. *Clinical Chemistry, 38*, 1491–1494.

Uebersax, J. S. (1987). Diversity of decision-making models and the measurement of interrater agreement. *Psychological Bulletin, 101*, 140–146.

Uebersax, J. S. (1992). Modeling approaches for the analysis of observer agreement. *Investigative Radiology, 27*, 738–743.

Uebersax, J. S. (2003, May 10). *Latent class analysis.* Retrieved June 2, 2003, from http://ourworld.compuserve.com/homepages/jsuebersax/index.htm.

Uebersax, J. S., & Grove, W. M. (1990). Latent class analysis of diagnostic agreement. *Statistics in Medicine, 9*, 559–572.

Ugurbil, K., Hu, X., Chen, W., Zhu, X. H., Kim, S. G., & Georgopoulos, A. (1999). Functional mapping in the human brain using high magnetic fields. *Philosophical Transactions of the Royal Society of London. Series B: Biological Sciences, 354*, 1195–1213.

Underwood, B., Froming, W. J., & Moore, B. S., (1977). Mood, attention, and altruism: A search for mediating variables. *Developmental Psychology, 13*, 541–542.

Underwood, M. K. (1997). Top ten pressing questions about the development of emotion regulation. *Motivation and Emotion, 21*, 127–146.

Underwood, M. K., Coie, J. D., & Herbsman, C. R. (1992). Display rules for anger and aggression in school-aged children. *Child Development, 63*, 366–380.

Vaes, J., Paladino, M. P., Castelli, L., Leyens, J.-P., & Giovanazzi, A. (2002). The lost e-mail: Prosocial reactions induced by uniquely human emotions. *Journal of Personality and Social Psychology, 41*, 521–534.

van Bezooijen, R. (1984). *The characteristics and recognizability of vocal expression of emotions.* Dordrecht, the Netherlands: Foris.

van Bezooijen, R., Otto, S. A., & Heenan, T. A. (1983). Recognition of vocal expressions of emotion: A three-nation study to identify universal characteristics. *Journal of Cross-Cultural Studies, 14*, 387–406. 23

van der Linden, W. J. (2000). Constrained adaptive testing with shadow tests. In W. J. van der Linden & C. A. W. Glas (Eds.), *Computerized adaptive testing: Theory and practice* (pp. 27–52). Boston: Kluwer.

van der Linden, W. J., & Glas, C. A. W. (Eds.). (2000). *Computerized adaptive testing: Theory and practice.* Boston: Kluwer.

van Egeren, L., & Madarasmi, S. (1992). Blood pressure and behavior: Mood, activity, and blood pressure in daily life. In M. DeVries (Ed.), *The experience of psychopathology: Investigating mental disorders in their natural settings* (pp. 240–252). Cambridge, MA: Cambridge University Press.

van Oyen Witvliet, C., & Vrana, S. R. (2000). Emotional imagery, the visual startle, and covariation bias: An affective matching account. *Biological Psychology, 52*, 187–204.

van Zandt, T. (2000). ROC curves and confidence judgments in recognition memory. *Journal of Experimental Psychology: Learning, Memory, and Cognition, 26*, 582–600.

Varey, C. A., & Kahneman, D. (1992). Experiences extended across time: Evaluation of moments and episodes. *Journal of Behavioral Decision Making, 5*, 169–185.

Veldhuis, J. D., Iranmanesh, A., Naftolowitz, D., Tatham, N., Cassidy, F., & Carroll, B. J. (2001). Corticotropin secretory dynamics in humans under low glucocorticoid feedback. *Journal of Clinical Endocrinology and Metabolism, 86*, 5554–5563.

Velten, E. (1968). A laboratory task for the induction of mood states. *Behavior Research and Therapy, 6*, 473–482.

Venables, P. H. (1984). Arousal: An examination of its status as a concept. In M. G. H. Coles, J. R. Jennings, & J. A. Stern (Eds.), *Psychophysiological perspectives* (pp. 134–142). New York: Van Nostrand Reinhold.

Vermunt, J. K. (1997a). *Loglinear models for event histories. Advanced Quantitative Techniques in the Social Sciences.* Thousand Oaks, CA: Sage Publications.

Vermunt, J. K. (1997b). *LEM: A general program for the analysis of categorical data.* Retrieved from http://www.kub.nl/faculteiten/fsw/organisatie/departementen/mto/software2.html

Vermunt, J. K. (2003). Multilevel latent class models. In R. M. Stolzenberg (Ed.), *Sociological methodology 2003* (pp. 213–239). Washington, DC: ASA.

Vernon, P. E. (1933). Some characteristics of the good judge of personality. *Journal of Social Psychology, 4*, 42–58.

Vispoel, W. P. (1987). Improving the measurement of musical ability through adaptive testing. In G. Hayes

(Ed.), *Proceedings of the 29th International ADCIS Conference* (pp. 221–228). Bellingham, WA: ADCIS.

Vispoel, W. P. (1999). Creating computerized adaptive tests of music aptitude: Problems, solutions, and future directions. In F. Dragow & J. B. Olson-Buchanan (Eds.), *Innovations in computerized assessment* (pp. 151–176). Mahwah, NJ: Lawrence Erlbaum Associates.

Viswesvaran, C., & Ones, D. S. (2002). The role of general mental ability in industrial, work, and organizational psychology. [Special Issue] *Human performance, 15,* 1–231.

Voracek, M., Stieger, S., & Gindl, A. (2001). Online replication of evolutionary psychology evidence: Sex differences in sexual jealousy in imagined scenarios of mate's sexual versus emotional infidelity. In U.-D. Reips & M. Bosnjak (Eds.), *Dimensions of Internet science* (pp. 91–112). Lengerich, Germany: Pabst.

Vrana, S. R. (1993). The psychophysiology of disgust: Differentiating negative emotional contexts with facial EMG. *Psychophysiology, 30,* 279–286.

Vrana, S. R. (1995). Emotional modulation of skin conductance and eyeblink responses to a startle probe. *Psychophysiology, 32,* 351–357.

Vrana, S. R., & Rollock, D. (2002). The role of ethnicity, gender, emotional content, and contextual differences in physiological, expressive, and self-reported emotional responses to imagery. *Cognition and Emotion, 16,* 165–192.

Vrana, S. R., Spence, E. L., & Lang, P. J. (1988). The startle probe response. A new measure of emotion? *Journal of Abnormal Psychology, 97,* 487–491.

Wainer, H., Bradlow, E. T., & Du, Z. (2000). Testlet response theory: An analog for the 3PL model useful in testlet-based adaptive testing. In W. J. van der Linden & C. A. W. Glas (Eds.), *Computerized adaptive testing: Theory and practice* (pp. 245–269). Boston: Kluwer.

Wainer, H., & Kiely, G. (1987). Item clusters and computerized adaptive testing: A case for testlets. *Journal of Educational Measurement, 24,* 185–202.

Walkenbach, J., & Haddid, N. F. (1980). The Rescorla-Wagner theory of conditioning: A review of the literature. *The Psychological Record, 30,* 497–509.

Walker, L., & Sorrells, S. (2002). Brief report: Assessment of children's gastrointestinal symptoms for clinical trials. *Journal of Pediatric Psychology, 27,* 303–307.

Warm, T. A. (1989). Weighted likelihood estimation of ability in item response theory. *Psychometrika, 54,* 427–450.

Warner, S. L. (1965). Randomized response: A survey technique for eliminating evasive answer bias. *Journal of the American Statistical Association, 60,* 63–69.

Waters, E., & Deane, K. E. (1985). Defining and assessing individual differences in attachment relationships: Q-methodology and the organization of behavior in infancy and early childhood. In I. Bretherton & E. Waters (Eds.), *Growing points of attachment theory and research. Monographs of the Society for Research in Child Development, 50* (1/2, serial No. 209), 41–65.

Watson, D. (1989). Strangers' ratings of the five robust personality factors: Evidence of a surprising convergence with self-report. *Journal of Personality and Social Psychology, 57,* 120–128.

Watson, D., & Clark, L. A. (1991). Self versus peer ratings of specific emotional traits: Evidence of convergent and discriminant validity. *Journal of Personality and Social Psychology, 60,* 927–940.

Watson, D., Clark, L. A., & Tellegen, A. (1988). Development and validation of brief measures of positive and negative affect: The PANAS Scales. *Journal of Personality and Social Psychology, 54,* 1063–1070.

Watson, D., Hubbard, B., & Wiese, D. (2000). Self-other agreement in personality and affectivity: The role acquaintanceship, trait visibility, and assumed similarity. *Journal of Personality and Social Psychology, 78,* 546–558.

Watson, D., & Tellegen, A. (1985). Toward a consensual structure of mood. *Psychological Bulletin, 98,* 219–235.

Watson, D., & Tellegen, A. (2002). Aggregation, acquiescence, and the assessment of trait affectivity. *Journal of Research in Personality, 36,* 589–597.

Webb, E. J., Campbell, D. T., Schwartz, R. D., & Sechrest, L. (1966). *Unobtrusive measures: Nonreactive research in the social sciences.* Chicago: Rand McNally.

Webb, E. J., Campbell, D. T., Schwartz, R. D., Sechrest, L., & Grove, J. B. (1981). *Nonreactive measures in the social sciences.* Boston: Houghton Mifflin.

Weber, R. P. (1990). *Basic content analysis.* Newbury Park, CA: Sage.

Weintraub, W. (1981).*Verbal behavior: Adaptation and psychopathology.* New York: Springer.

Weintraub, W. (1989). *Verbal behavior in everyday life.* New York: Springer.

Weiss, H. M., & Cropanzano, R. (1996). Affective events theory: A theoretical discussion of the structure, causes and consequences of affective experiences at work. In B. M. Staw & L. L. Cummings (Eds.), *Research in organizational behavior* (Vol. 19, pp. 1–74). Greenwich, CT: JAI Press.

Weiss, R., Buchanan, W., Altstatt, L., & Lombardo, J. (1971). Altruism is rewarding. *Science, 171,* 1262–1263.

Wells, G. L., & Windschitl, P. D. (1999). Stimulus sampling and social psychological experimentation. *Personality and Social Psychology Bulletin, 25,* 1115–1124.

Wen, Z. L., Marsh, H. W., & Hau, K. T. (2003, April). *Analyses of latent growth: Comparison between models based on items and scales.* Paper presented at the AERA Annual Meeting, Chicago.

Wentura, D., & Rothermund, K. (2003). The "meddling-in" of affective information: A general model of automatic evaluation. In J. Musch & K. C. Klauer (Eds.), *The psychology of evaluation: Affective processes in cognition and emotion* (pp. 51–86). Mahwah, NJ: Lawrence Erlbaum Associates.

Werker, J. F. (1989). Becoming a native listener. *American Scientist, 77,* 54–59.

Werner, A. (2002). Contact measurement in the WWW. In B. Batinic, U.-D. Reips, & M. Bosnjak (Eds.), *Online social science*. Seattle, WA: Hogrefe & Huber Publishers.

West, M. D. (Ed.). (2001). *Theory, method, and practice in computer content analysis*. New York: Ablex.

West, S. G., Biesanz, J. C., & Pitts, S. C. (2000). Causal inference and generalization in field settings: Experimental and quasi-experimental designs. In H. T. Reis & C. M. Judd (Eds.), *Handbook of research methods in social and personality psychology* (pp. 40–84). Cambridge, MA: Cambridge University Press.

West, S. G., & Finch, J. F. (1997). Personality measurement: Reliability and validity. In R. Hogan, J. Johnson, & S. Briggs (Eds.), *Handbook of personality psychology* (pp. 143–164). San Diego, CA: Academic.

West, S. G., & Hepworth, J. T. (1991). Data analytic strategies for temporal data and daily events. *Journal of Personality, 59,* 609–662.

Westen, D., & Rosenthal, R. (2003). Quantifying construct validity: Two simple measures. *Journal of Personality and Social Psychology, 84,* 608–618.

Westmeyer, H. (1972). *Logik der Diagnostik. Grundlagen einer normativen Diagnostik (Logic of psychological assessment. Foundations of a normative theory of assessment)*. Stuttgart, Germany: Kohlhammer.

Wheeler, L., & Reis, H. (1991). Self-recording of everyday life events: Origins, types, and uses. *Journal of Personality, 59,* 339–354.

Wickens, T. D. (1989). *Multiway contingency tables analysis for the social sciences*. Hillsdale, NJ: Lawrence Erlbaum Associates.

Wickens, T. D. (1993). Analysis of contingency tables with between-subjects variability. *Psychological Bulletin, 113,* 191–204.

Wicklund, R. A., & Gollwitzer, P. M. (1981). Symbolic self-completion, attempted influence, and self-deprecation. *Basic and Applied Social Psychology, 2,* 89–114.

Widaman, K. F. (1985). Hierarchically nested covariance structure models for multitrait–multimethod data. *Applied Psychological Measurement, 9,* 1–26.

Widaman, K. F., & Reise, S. P. (1997). Exploring the measurement invariance of psychological instruments: Applications in the substance use domain. In K. J. Bryant, M. Windle, & S. G. West (Ed.), *The science of prevention: Methodological advances from alcohol and substance abuse research*. Washington, DC: American Psychological Association.

Widaman, K. F., Stacy, A. W., & Borthwick-Duffy, S. A. (1993). Construct validity of dimensions of adaptive behavior: A multitrait–multimethod evaluation. *American Journal of Mental Retardation, 98,* 219–234.

Widrow, B., & Hoff, M. (1960). Adaptive switching circuits. *1960 WESCON Convention Record,* pp. 96–104.

Wiedmann, K.-P., & Buxel, H. (2001). Using non-reactive observation methods in online research. *Planung & Analyse, Special English Edition,* 38–42.

Wigdor, A. K., & Garner, W. R. (Eds.). (1982). *Ability testing: Uses, consequences, and controversies,* Part I.

Report of the Committee, Part 2: *Documentation section.* Washington, DC: National Academy Press.

Wigdor, A. K., & Green, B. F. (1991). *Performance assessment for the work place*. Washington, DC: National Academy Press.

Wiggins, J. S. (1964). Convergences among stylistic response measures from objective personality tests. *Educational and Psychological Measurement, 24,* 551–562.

Wiggins, J. S. (1973). *Personality and prediction: Principles of personality assessment*. Reading, MA: Addison-Wesley.

Wilhelm, O., & McKnight, P. E. (2002). Ability and achievement testing on the World Wide Web. In B. Batinic, U.-D. Reips, & M. Bosnjak (Eds.), *Online social sciences* (pp. 151–180). Seattle, WA: Hogrefe & Huber.

Wilk, S. L., Desmarais, L. B., & Sackett, P. R. (1995). Gravitation to jobs commensurate with ability: Longitudinal and cross-sectional tests. *Journal of Applied Psychology, 80,* 79–85.

Wilk, S. L., & Sackett, P. R. (1996). Longitudinal analysis of ability-job complexity fit and job change. *Personnel Psychology, 49,* 937–967.

Wilkinson, L. (1999). Statistical methods in psychology journals: Guidelines and explanation. *American Psychologist, 54,* 594–604.

Willems, E. P., & Raush, H. L. (Eds.). (1969). *Naturalistic viewpoints in psychological research*. New York: Holt, Rinehart & Winston.

Willett, J. B. (1988). Questions and answers in the measurement of change. In E. Z. Rothkopf (Ed.), *Review of research in education* (Vol. 15, pp. 345–422). Washington, DC: American Educational Research Association.

Willett, J. B., & Sayer, A. G. (1994). Using covariance structure analysis to detect correlates and predictors of change. *Psychological Bulletin, 116,* 363–381.

Williams, J. M. G., Mathews, A., & MacLeod, C. (1996). The emotional Stroop task and psychopathology. *Psychological Bulletin, 120,* 3–24.

Williams, K. D., Cheung, C. K. T., & Choi, W. (2000). Cyberostracism: Effects of being ignored over the Internet. *Journal of Personality and Social Psychology, 79,* 748–762.

Williams, W. M. (2000). Perspectives on intelligence testing, affirmative action, and educational policy. *Psychology, Public Policy, and Law, 6*(1) 5–19.

Willoughby, R. R. (1935). The concept of reliability. *Psychological Review, 42,* 153–165.

Wimbush, J. C., & Dalton, D. R. (1997). Base rate for employee theft: Convergence of multiple methods. *Journal of Applied Psychology, 82,* 756–763.

Wimmer, H., & Perner, J. (1983). Beliefs about beliefs: Representation and constraining function of wrong beliefs in young children's understanding of deception. *Cognition, 13,* 103–128.

Windle, M., & Dumenci, L. (1999). The factorial structure and construct validity of the Psychopathy Checklist-Revised (PCL-R) among alcoholic inpatients. *Structural Equation Modeling, 6,* 372–393.

Windle, M., & Lerner, R. M. (1986). Reassessing the dimensions of temperamental individuality across the life span: The revised dimensions of temperament survey (DOTS-R). *Journal of Adolescent Research, 1*, 213–230.

Winkielman, P., Knäuper, B., & Schwarz, N. (1998). Looking back at anger: Reference periods change the interpretation of emotion frequency questions. *Journal of Personality and Social Psychology, 75*, 719–728.

Winter, D. G. (1991). Measuring personality at a distance: Development and validation of an integrated system for scoring motives in running text. In A. J. Stewart, J. M. Healy Jr., & D. J. Ozer (Eds.), *Perspectives in personality: Approaches to understanding lives* (Vol. 3, pp. 59–89). London: Jessica Kingsley Publishers.

Winter, D. G. (1992). Content analysis of archival materials, personal documents, and everyday verbal productions. In C. P. Smith (Ed.), *Motivation and personality: Handbook of thematic content analysis* (pp. 110–125). New York: Cambridge University Press.

Winter, D. G. (1994). *Manual for scoring motive imagery in running text* (4th ed.). Unpublished manuscript, University of Michigan.

Winter, D. G., John, O. P., Stewart, A. J., Klohnen, E. C., & Duncan, L. E. (1998). Traits and motives: Toward an integration of two traditions in personality research. *Psychological Review, 105*, 230–250.

Winter, D. G., & Stewart, A. J. (1977). Power motive reliability as a function of retest instruction. *Journal of Consulting and Clinical Psychology, 45*, 436–440.

Wirtz, D., Kruger, J., Napa-Scollon, C., Diener, E. (2003). What to do on spring break? The role of predicted, on-line, and remembered experience in future choice. *Psychological Science, 14*, 520–524.

Wissler, C. (1901). The correlation between mental and physical tests. *Psychological Review*, Monograph No. 3.

Wittmann, W. W. (1988). Multivariate reliability theory: Principles of symmetry and successful validation strategies. In J. R. Nesselroade & R. B. Cattell (Eds.), *Handbook of multivariate experimental psychology* (pp. 505–560). New York: Plenum Press.

Witvliet, C. V. O., & Vrana, S. R. (1995). Psychophysiological responses as indices of affective dimensions. *Psychophysiology, 32*, 436–443.

Witvliet, C. V. O., & Vrana, S. R. (2000). Emotional imagery, the visual startle, and covariation bias: An affective matching account. *Biological Psychology, 52*, 187–204.

Wixted, J. T. (1992). Subjective memorability and the mirror effect. *Journal of Experimental Psychology: Learning, Memory, & Cognition, 18*, 681–690.

Woodrow, H. (1921). Intelligence and its measurement. *Journal of Educational Psychology, 12*, 207–210.

Woodruffe, C. (1984). The consistency of presented personality: Additional evidence from aggregation. *Journal of Personality, 52*, 307–317.

Worsley, K. J., Marrett, S., Neelin, P., Vandal, A., Friston, K., & Evans, A. (1996). A unified statistical approach for determining significant signals in images of cerebral activation. *Human Brain Mapping, 4*, 58–73.

Wothke, W. (1995). Covariance components analysis of the multitrait–multimethod matrix. In P. E. Shrout & S. T. Fiske (Eds.), *Personality research, methods, and theory. A festschrift honoring D. W. Fiske* (pp. 125–144). Hillsdale, NJ: Lawrence Erlbaum Associates.

Wothke, W. (1996). Models for multitrait–multimethod matrix analysis. In G. A. Marcoulides & R. E. Schumacker (Eds.), *Advanced structural equation modeling. Issues and techniques* (pp. 7–56). Mahwah, NJ: Lawrence Erlbaum Associates.

Wothke, W., & Browne, W. W. (1990). The direct product model for the MTMM matrix parameterized as a second order factor analysis model. *Psychometrika, 55*, 255–262.

Wright, B. D., & Masters, G. N. (1982). *Rating scale analysis*. Chicago: Mesa Press.

Wright, B. D., & Stone, M. H. (1979). *Best test design*. Chicago: Mesa Press.

Wu, M. L., Adams, R. J., & Wilson, M. (1997). *ConQuest—Generalised item response modelling software, draft release 2*. Camberwell: Australian Council for Educational Research.

Wundt, W. (1897). *Outlines of psychology* (C. H. Judd, Trans.). New York: G. E. Stechert.

Wylie, R. C. (1989). *Measures of self-concept*. Lincoln: University of Nebraska Press.

Yacoub, E., & Hu, X. (2001). Detection of the early decrease in fMRI signal in the motor area. *Magnetic Resonance in Medicine, 45*, 184–190.

Yonelinas, A. P. (1997). Recognition memory ROCs for item and associative information: The contribution of recollection and familiarity. *Memory & Cognition, 25*, 747–763.

Yonelinas, A. P. (1999). The contribution of recollection and familiarity to recognition and source-memory judgments: A formal dual-process model and an analysis of receiver operating characteristics. *Journal of Experimental Psychology: Learning, Memory, and Cognition, 26*, 1415–1434.

Yonelinas, A. P., & Jacoby, L. L. (1996). Response bias and the process dissociation procedure. *Journal of Experimental Psychology: General, 125*, 422–434.

Yu, J., & Bellezza, F. S. (2000). Process dissociation as source monitoring. *Journal of Experimental Psychology: Learning, Memory, & Cognition, 26*, 1518–1533.

Yule, P., & Cooper, R. P. (2003). Express: A Web-based technology to support human and computational experimentation. *Behavior Research Methods, Instruments, and Computers, 35*, 605–613.

Zajonc, R. B. (1965). Social facilitation. *Science, 149*, 269–274.

Zajonc, R. B., & McIntosh, D. N. (1992). Emotions research: Some promising questions and some questionable promises. *Psychological Science, 3*, 70–74.

Zald, D. H. (2003). The human amygdala and the emotional evaluation of sensory stimuli. *Brain Research Reviews, 41*, 88–123.

Zald, D. H., Boileau, I., El Deredy, W., Gunn, R., McGlone, F., Dichter, G., & Dagher, A. (2004). Dopamine transmission in the human striatum dur-

ing monetary reward tasks. *Journal of Neuroscience, 24,* 4105–4112.

Zald, D. H., Donndelinger, M. J., & Pardo, J. V. (1998). Elucidating dynamic brain interactions with across-subjects correlational analyses of PET data: The functional connectivity of the amygdala and orbitofrontal cortex during olfactory tasks. *Journal of Cerebral Blood Flow and Metabolism, 18,* 896–905.

Zarahn, E., Aguirre, G. K., & D'Esposito, M. (1999). Temporal isolation of the neural correlates of spatial mnemonic processing with fMRI. *Brain Research Cognitive Brain Research, 7*(3), 255–268.

Zautra, A. J., Berkhof, J., & Nicolson, N. A. (2002). Changes in affect interrelations as a function of stressful events. *Cognition & Emotion, 16,* 309–318.

Zegiob, L. E., Arnold, S., & Forehand, R. (1975). An examination of observer effects in parent–child interactions. *Child Development, 46,* 509–512.

Zeldow, P. B., & McAdams, D. P. (1993). On the comparison of TAT and free speech techniques in personality assessment. *Journal of Personality Assessment, 60,* 181–185.

Zelenski, J. M., & Larsen, R. J. (2002). Predicting the future: How affect-related personality traits influence likelihood judgments of future events. *Personality and Social Psychology Bulletin, 28,* 1000–1010.

Zelli, A., & Dodge, K. A. (1999). Personality from the bottom up. In D. Cervone & Y. Shoda (Eds.), *The coherence of personality: Social-cognitive bases of consistency, variability, and organization* (pp. 94–126). New York: Guilford Press.

Zenisky, A. L., & Sireci, S. G. (2002). Technological innovations in large-scale assessment. *Applied Measurement in Education, 15,* 337–362.

Zhou, Q., Eisenberg, N., Losoya, S., Fabes, R. A., Reiser, M., Guthrie, I. K., et al. (2002). The relations of parental warmth and positive expressiveness to children's empathy-related responding and social functioning: A longitudinal study. *Child Development, 73,* 893–915.

Zubieta, J. K., Smith, Y. R., Bueller, J. A., Xu, Y., Kilbourn, M. R., Jewett, D. M., et al. (2001). Regional mu opioid receptor regulation of sensory and affective dimensions of pain. *Science, 293,* 311–315.

Zucker, M., Morris, M. K., Ingram, S. M., Morris, R. D., & Bakeman, R. (2002). Concordance of self- and informant ratings of adults' current and childhood attention-deficit/hyperactivity disorders symptoms. *Psychological Assessment, 14,* 379–389.

Zuckerman, M., & Lubin, B. (1965). *The multiple affect adjective check list.* San Diego, CA: Educational and Industrial Testing Service.

Zuckerman, M., & Lubin, B. (1985). *Manual for the Multiple Affect Adjective Checklist–Revised.* San Diego, CA: Educational and Industrial Testing Service.

Author Index

Subject Index

ABOUT THE EDITORS

Michael Eid, PhD, is professor of psychology at the University of Geneva (Switzerland). He received his doctorate from the University of Trier (Germany) in 1994, and he has been professor and visiting professor at several German universities. He has been editor of *Methods of Psychology Research–Online* and *Diagnostica* and is currently editor of *Methodology–European Journal of Research Methods in the Social and Behavioral Sciences*. His main research interests concern the analysis of multitrait–multimethod data, longitudinal data analysis, structural equation modeling, and item-response theory. His more applied research focuses on subjective well-being and health psychology.

Ed Diener, PhD, is Alumni Distinguished Professor of Psychology at the University of Illinois at Urbana–Champaign. He received his doctorate at the University of Washington in 1974 and has been a faculty member at the University of Illinois ever since. Dr. Diener is past president of both the International Society of Quality-of-Life Studies and the Society of Personality and Social Psychology. He was the editor of the *Journal of Personality and Social Psychology* from 1998 to 2003 and is currently the editor of the *Journal of Happiness Studies*; he is also the founding editor of *Perspectives on Psychological Science*, which will first appear in 2006. Dr. Diener is a fellow of five professional societies and is listed as one of the highly cited psychologists by the Institute of Scientific Information, with over 9,000 citations to his credit. He won the 2000 Distinguished Researcher Award from the International Society of Quality-of-Life Studies. Dr. Diener has won several teaching awards, including the Oakley Kundee Award for Undergraduate Teaching at the University of Illinois.

Professor Diener's research is focused on the measurement of well-being, temperament and personality influences on well-being, theories of well-being, income and well-being, and cultural influences on well-being. He has edited three recent books: *Well-Being: The Foundations of Hedonic Psychology* (with Daniel Kahneman and Norbert Schwarz), *Advances in Quality of Life Studies* (with Don Rahtz), and *Culture and Subjective Well-Being* (with Eunkook Suh). Dr. Diener's most recent large project is creating a set of national indicators of well-being, working under the auspices of the positive psychology movement.